FAMILY LAW

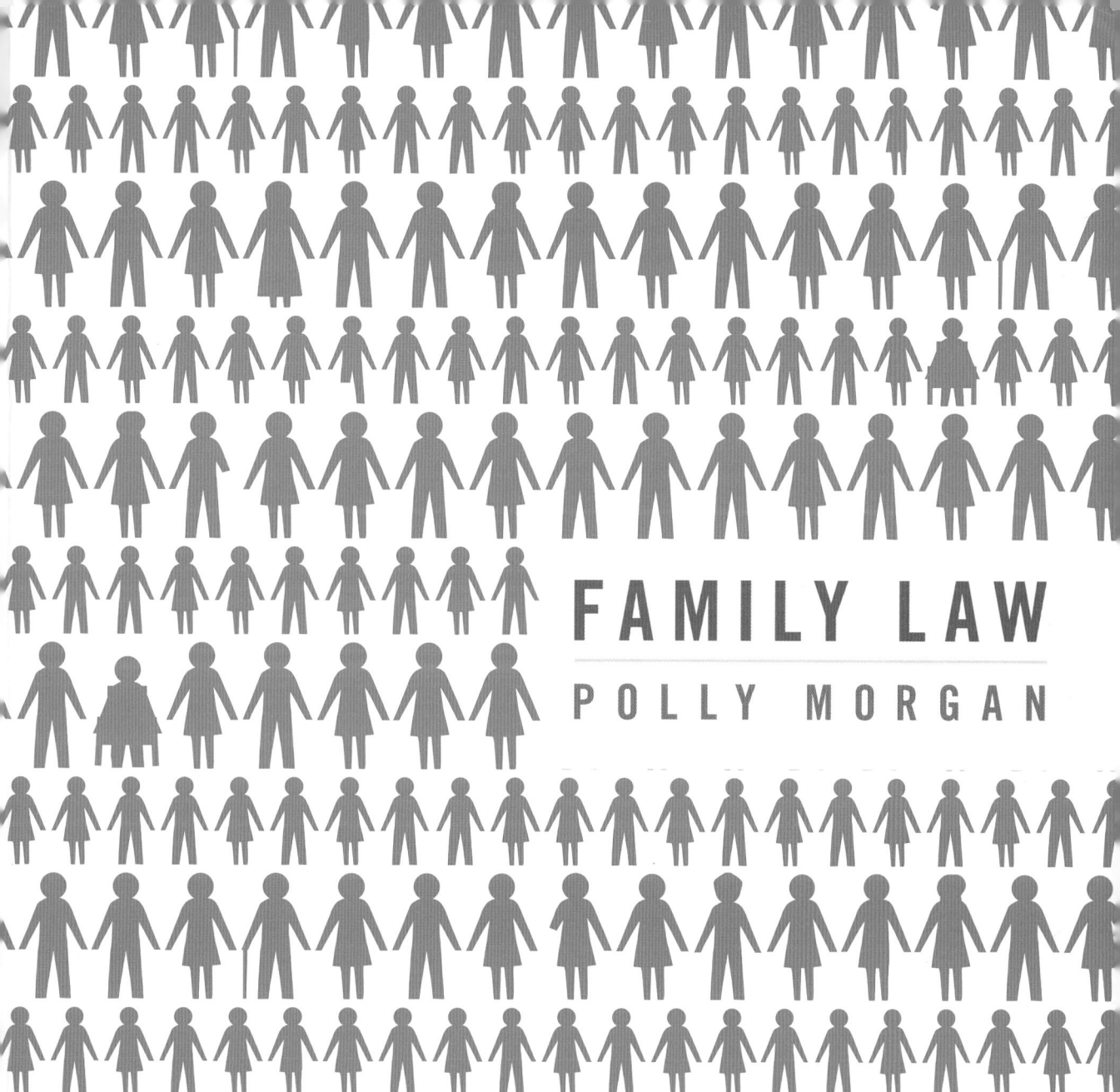

FAMILY LAW

POLLY MORGAN

OXFORD

UNIVERSITY PRESS

OXFORD
UNIVERSITY PRESS

Great Clarendon Street, Oxford, OX2 6DP,
United Kingdom

Oxford University Press is a department of the University of Oxford.
It furthers the University's objective of excellence in research, scholarship,
and education by publishing worldwide. Oxford is a registered trade mark of
Oxford University Press in the UK and in certain other countries

First Edition 2021
Impression: 1

Public sector information reproduced under Open Government Licence v3.0
(http://www.nationalarchives.gov.uk/doc/open-government-licence/open-government-licence.htm)

Published in the United States of America by Oxford University Press
198 Madison Avenue, New York, NY 10016, United States of America

British Library Cataloguing in Publication Data
Data available

Library of Congress Control Number: 2021933934

ISBN 978–0–19– 883424–3

Printed in Great Britain by
Bell & Bain Ltd., Glasgow

This book is dedicated to Rosalie Grace Mailey, with love

Preface

When Oxford University Press first approached me to write a textbook, I was at once excited and apprehensive. A textbook is a significant endeavour and so this has proven to be, consuming several years and encompassing several periods of legislative reform. I would like to thank my development editor, Stephanie Southall, for her sustained good cheer and good advice through the project. She has borne the brunt of chivvying me along. I would also like to thank my family, friends, and colleagues who have laughed at the seeming endlessness of the project. My lovely colleague Selina Watts even took on more marking to enable me to finish the last chapter and, as all academics will know, marking is the worst part of the job. I have been useless around the house for quite some time, and left my mother undefended against my cat's demands. I should like to thank the anonymous reviewers for their helpful comments and suggestions which have helped shape the book. I do not underestimate the time commitment involved in reviewing work, and I am grateful to you. Any mistakes are my own.

For the students among you, a word of advice: do not let the size of this book intimidate you. I have used my own students' feedback, as well as the feedback provided by student and lecturer reviewers of the drafts, to produce a text that I hope you find friendly and clear, with simple explanations and diagrams of the relevant legal processes, and which reflects the diverse reality of family life in England and Wales, which is the jurisdiction covered by this book. There are reading lists designed to give you a good starting point for your own research. There are realistic scenarios to show you how to apply the principles, and the focus boxes—there are two kinds, 'think critically', and 'know-how'—are for those points where you might go 'hold on a minute—what's that about?' They delve deeper into particular issues (as do the videos where I discuss challenging topics), and emphasise the importance of academic research, policy documents, and legal history in understanding the law and its development.

My experience as a practising solicitor has helped me to think about how an issue may arise in practice, and where practice differs from law, as it often does. Only by understanding this can you analyse whether the law is successful in meeting its aims, or needs to be reformed—or indeed, whether the law's aims should be different. That kind of learning hits the higher levels of Bloom's taxonomy of learning—that you should not merely be able to explain what the law is, but also to be able to analyse it, apply it, and create your own proposals.

The law is as stated to December 2020, with a couple of small revisions in March 2021.

Polly Morgan
March 2021

Acknowledgements

The author and publisher would like to thank Lucy Yeatman, Director of the Liverpool Law Clinic at the University of Liverpool, for her exceptional contribution to the online resources. Her determination and dedication to write excellent material for the student self-assessment was sincerely appreciated.

The author and publisher would also like to thank all the academics and students who reviewed material throughout the writing process. Your feedback was helpful and informative, and we hope you find the material to be an incredibly useful resource for your teaching and learning.

Grateful acknowledgement is made to all the authors and publishers of copyright material which appears in this book, and in particular to the following for permission to reprint material from the sources indicated:

European Court of Human Rights: extract from *Opuz v Turkey* App no. 33401/02 (ECHR, 9 June 2009), http://hudoc.echr.coe.int/eng?i=001-92945.

Hart Publishing: extract from © R George, 2012, *Ideas and Debates in Family Law*, Hart Publishing, and Imprint of Bloomsbury Publishing Plc., p75, fn 2.

LM Fox Harding: extracts from LM Fox Harding, 'The Children Act 1989 in Context: Four Perspectives in Child Care Law and Policy' Part I: (1991) 13 JSWFL (3), 179; LM Fox Harding, 'The Children Act 1989 in Context: Four Perspectives in Child Care Law and Policy' Part II: (1991) 13 JSWFL (4), 285.

Incorporated Council of Law Reporting: [1991] 1 AC 107, [1990] 2 WLR 867, [1985] 3 WLR 830, [1986] AC 112.

Oxford University Press: extract from C. Chambers, *Against Marriage: An Egalitarian Defence of the Marriage-Free State* (OUP 2017) 147.

Crown copyright material and public section information is reproduced under the terms of the Open Government Licence v3.0 (http://www.nationalarchives.gov.uk/doc/open-government-licence/): figures 2.1, 2.2, 2.3, 4.2, 5.2, 5.3, 11.2, 12.1, and tables 2.1, 3.1, 5.2, 6.1, 6.2, 7.1, 7.2, 7.3, 7.4 ,7.6, 8.2, 8.3, 10.1, 11.1, 11.3, 12.1, 12.3.

Every effort has been made to trace and contact copyright holders prior to going to press but this has not been possible in every case. If notified, the publisher will undertake to rectify any errors or omissions at the earliest opportunity.

Guide to Using this Book

ELEVATE YOUR LEARNING WITH *FAMILY LAW*

Fresh, engaging, and thought-provoking, *Family Law* uses captivating scenarios and critical discussion to bring the law to life!

 You can find all of the multimedia elements described here in the **online resources**: www.oup.com/he/morgan1e

OUTLINE what you will be learning

A **Learning Checklist** opens each chapter to indicate which topics are covered, and how you can expect to measure your understanding.

UNDERSTAND the law

Key Cases are outlined in detail and include key judgments as well as author explanation. This helps you to recognise the important elements of each Key Case and appreciate its contribution to the development of family law, and encourages you to analyse a new scenario in a way that still considers legal precedent, but also factors in new cases, subtle but divergent details, and changes to the law.

APPLY the law to new real-world scenarios

Inspired by the author's experience as a family solicitor, the **Scenarios** at the start of each chapter present examples of real-world situations encountered in family law. Scenarios are also revisited throughout the chapter in the **Scenario Illustrations**, giving you the chance to reinforce your learning of the law applied within the socio-legal context.

ANALYSE AND CRITICALLY EXAMINE the law

Focus boxes are designed for those moments when you find yourself thinking 'hold on a minute, what's that about?' Elaborating on topics that are mentioned in the chapters, **Focus: Know-How** boxes provide background information or context on how something works, while **Focus: Think Critically** boxes provide socio-legal context and explore points of debate and controversy.

WATCH, LISTEN, AND LEARN

In 12 **author videos** (transcripts available), Polly Morgan discusses the most challenging topics in each chapter to support the chapter discussion, such as new developments in the law and instances where cultural sensitivities might interact with domestic family law.

CHECK YOUR UNDERSTANDING

Self-test opportunities, including multiple-choice, true or false, and multi-response questions, all with instant feedback, **test your understanding** of each chapter topic.
Scenario questions are provided for each chapter, also with instant feedback, enabling you to practise applying the legal principles from the chapter to new scenarios.

Bullet point lists of **key points** end each chapter to summarise important information covered in the chapter. They help to check your understanding and double as a handy revision tool.

GO FURTHER WITH YOUR LEARNING

Further Reading: Some starting points are carefully cultivated reading lists designed to support you in the challenge of undertaking quality research. Annotations accompany each recommended resource to inform you of the focus of each resource, and act as a platform to guide your further independent reading and research around the chapter topic. **Online** you can also read an additional chapter on **Elderly Care**, to broaden your learning.

RESOURCES FOR LECTURERS

www.oup.com/he/morgan1e

Family Law offers a selection of **online resources** to support your teaching of family law. Adopting lecturers can access the following:

- Mini-guides, which are organised thematically and provide topics and ideas for class debate and discussion;
- Downloadable versions of every figure and table included in the book;

Brief Contents

Detailed Contents

4 Financial Provision on Divorce   161

5 Cohabitants and Remedies Not Dependent on Marriage

6 Financial Support for Children   350

9 Children's Rights and Welfare

523

12   Child Protection: Care, Supervision, and Adoption   770

Table of Cases

International Cases

European Court of Human Rights

Table of Legislation

Regulations and Other Statutory Instruments (England and Wales)

Table of Treaties and International Instruments

Introduction

1.1 An introduction to the themes of this book

Most people do not know a great deal about family law. It is only when a problem arises that they become aware of concepts and terms such as parental responsibility, constructive trusts, voidable marriages, or section 47 investigations. When the matter has concluded, it is not unusual for them to say to their lawyer, 'thank you for your help and no offence but I hope I never have to see you again'. Rather than being associated in people's minds with happy family events, family lawyers are often associated with relationship breakdown, childcare disputes, financial problems, or children being taken into care or adopted. When people hear about these things from friends or neighbours, or read about a person's divorce in the gossip columns, they may end up with an inaccurate view of what the law is. They may expect others' experiences to be typical. But in family law there is no such thing as a typical case.

Yet, as you read this book, a number of different issues and themes will arise time and again. Who does family law protect and, conversely, who does it fail to protect? What human rights affect family law? When and how should the state intervene when someone is at risk of harm within their family, whether adult or child? What rules should there be about how people conduct their intimate relationships, or the quality of parenting they provide? To what extent should people be able to regulate the terms of their own relationships or the consequences of breakdown? What responsibilities do people have to their children, and how does the law recognise the status of being a parent?

The Office for National Statistics defines a family as 'a married, civil partnered or cohabiting couple with or without children, or a lone parent with at least one child, who live at the same address'.[1] On this basis it calculates that there are 19,153,000 families in the UK. In this book, we have tried to emphasise the diversity of family forms. These statistics hide considerable differences in how parents wish to raise their children and in the economic and social positions of families as well as their race, culture, and sexuality. It ignores caring relationships, multiple-generational relationships, and families of choice. On the cover to this book you may at first notice a series of little male and female figures. If you look more closely, you will see that there are non-binary figures, figures with physical disabilities,

---

[1] Office for National Statistics, *Families and Households Dataset* (2019).

elderly people, and those wearing religious clothing. Family law applies to all of these people, of course, but it can have a different effect on some of them compared to others. Some relationships are ignored by the law altogether.

Of the 19 million families in the UK recognised by the Office for National Statistics' definition, 12,740,000 are headed by married couples and there are an additional 46,000 couples in civil partnerships. This means that marriage is still the most common family form within the UK. In *Chapter 2* we ask what accounts for the continued popularity of marriage. What are the legal consequences? Is being married a privileged social status? Is there a human right to marry? Does marriage have one meaning or many? Is civil partnership equal to marriage? How can a valid marriage be formed, and what happens if you get the formalities of marriage wrong or a person is forced to marry? What does marriage mean to gay couples who for so long were excluded from this most significant recognition of family relationships?

But, over a 20-year period, 42 per cent of marriages will end in divorce. The state regulates the exit from marriage just as it does entry to marriage and the consequences of marriage. Those seeking a divorce are often surprised that the law does not currently allow people to divorce simply because they want to, but requires either that their spouse be at fault or a period of separation. At the time of writing (November 2020) a new divorce law has been passed but is not yet in force. This introduces no-fault divorce after a few months of separation. Will the removal of fault and blame from the law change our expectations of behaviour within marriage?

Many people think that getting their divorce decree terminates the financial responsibilities and rights of marriage, but this is not the case. In *Chapter 4* we look at financial provision on divorce or dissolution and the extent to which parties can reach their own agreements. We consider the principles underlying our financial remedy law and what they tell us about the role of the state and the values of paternalism, autonomy, and equality.

Although at 3,515,000 the number of couples who live together without being married is small compared to the number of married couples, it is cohabitation that is increasing. In *Chapter 5* we consider the legal protections for cohabiting couples and discover that they are very limited compared to those available to couples who are or were married, and ask whether we should introduce a scheme of divorce-style rights for cohabitants, or whether there should be areas of family life that are free of state regulation. This is an argument about whether it is the role of the state to protect the vulnerable at the expense of individual choice. It is not only in reform of cohabitation law that this is an issue: it is also an argument against permitting married couples to enter into binding nuptial agreements. Just as the state regulates the entry and exit to marriage, so too does it place parameters on the financial outcomes of a divorce which may be surprising to those of you familiar with freedom of contract. Although individual autonomy is respected, it is curtailed: only if an agreement is objectively fair will a judge make it enforceable.

Yet, at the same time, successive governments have encouraged private ordering: couples making their own decisions. To encourage the use of non-court resolution, those wishing to make an application to court relating to the upbringing of their children or financial provision on divorce must first attend a mediation information and assessment meeting. Non-dispute resolution is actively promoted as a way of resolving inheritance disputes, disputes with doctors around the medical treatment of children, trusts of land claims, and claims under Schedule One Children Act 1989 for the financial support of children. The Child Maintenance Service levies a charge for using its services and actively encourages parents to make their own arrangements. While non-court resolution has many advantages including speed, the number of mediations actually fell after the passing of the Legal Aid, Sentencing and Punishment of Offenders Act 2012 (LASPO): fewer people saw lawyers and lawyers were the principal source of referrals to family mediation. Before the cuts to legal aid imposed by LASPO, 80 per cent of legally aided MIAMs were referred by solicitors. After LASPO, the figure was 10 per cent, as people involved in a dispute had no guidance about the options available to them. Alongside this fall came a very significant rise in the number of court applications. Some of those applications—we do not know how many—will be from people who have entirely meritorious cases which, if resolved, will have a significant impact on their own or their children's lives. One of the key themes that run throughout this book, therefore, is the balance to be struck between individual autonomy and private ordering, on the one hand, and the protective role of the state and judicial discretion on the other.

We see similar arguments about the role of the state in other aspects of family law too. Of the 19 million families in the UK, over 8 million of them have dependent children living with them and a further 2.8 million of them previously had children who were dependent on them. There are 2,452,000 families headed by a single parent mother and 400,000 by a single-parent father. Parents are encouraged to reach their own agreements about child maintenance, and as we see in *Chapter 6* the Child Maintenance Service levies a charge for arranging child maintenance itself, even though there are significant social benefits to children being financially supported. This is part of an ideology of personal responsibility. In *Chapter 8* we discuss the concept of parental responsibility under the Children Act 1989 and successive government attempts to legislate for good parents.

Beyond ideology, there are practical reasons for the emphasis on private ordering. Significant budget cuts and court closures, a shortage of judges, and (currently) the backlog of work caused by closures during the COVID-19 pandemic have all contributed. It is

FOCUS Know-How

Non-court dispute resolution

There are various forms of non-court dispute resolution:

- Negotiations between the parties or through their legal representatives, if they have them
- Mediation, where the parties reach agreement and can ask a court to turn their agreement into an order. In the family law mediation model, unlike commercial mediation, the parties' lawyers are not usually present, and whether the parties are in the same or separate rooms depends upon their preferences
- Collaborative law, introduced from the United States, in which the parties and specially trained lawyers commit to resolving issues amicably at a series of meetings, without contested proceedings
- Arbitration, in which a qualified arbitrator (often a barrister or retired judge) hears the case as a judge would and makes a decision on the outcome. This can avoid court delay and enables the parties to appoint a specialist in the area in dispute. Arbitration is rare in family law, but growing.

true, too, that non-court resolution has many advantages. It enables the parties to reach an outcome that is tailored to them, it avoids court costs, delays, and litigation risk, and (where children are concerned) may make a future coparenting relationship easier. Many cases before the family courts relate to agreements that have broken down, and the most common reason is that the parties simply cannot work together.[2] But non-court resolution is not a panacea, and not all cases are suitable. A significant number of children cases, for example, involve allegations of domestic abuse or other risks to children. We explore this topic in *Chapter 10* and domestic abuse more broadly in *Chapter 7*.

There is one area of family life where state intervention has increased and that is in the area of child protection. In *Chapter 11* we look at the rising numbers of children subject to child protection interventions and potential reasons for this. There is no more fundamental interference with family life than removing a person's child from them to be adopted by someone else. As Sonia Harris-Short has written, through adoption, the state is 'uniquely engaged in the process of creating and destroying family life'.[3] An *extra chapter*, on elder law, can be found online. While not currently taught by many institutions, it is an interesting area of law and one likely to become increasingly important as people live longer lives.

It is here that we come to one of the most significant elements of family law, the influence of the *European Convention on Human Rights* both before and after its incorporation into our domestic law. Its importance is a seam running through this book, from our discussion of whether there is a human right to marry in *Chapter 2*, to the positive duties on the state to protect victims of domestic abuse in *Chapter 7*, to the ascription of parentage and parental responsibility in *Chapter 8*, to asking whether there is a right to contact with one's children or parents in *Chapter 10*, to the difficult role that the state has in supporting children to be raised within their families whilst ensuring that they are not harmed (*Chapters 11 and 12*). In *Chapter 9* we ask whether children can be said to have human rights and, if so, what rights, and what a child's autonomy rights—the right to make his own decision—means for our domestic laws based on children's welfare.

It is possible that in the near future the Human Rights Act 1998 will be repealed. Whilst this would not be the result of the UK leaving the European Union (because, while they have signatory member states in common, the ECHR is not an instrument of the European Union but rather of a separate organisation called the Council of Europe), a number of members of Parliament have called for its repeal and replacement. This presents an area of uncertainty, as does *Brexit* itself. At the time of writing, the UK has committed to leaving the European Union but the transition period has not yet reached its end. A great many questions remain unanswered. Which of the rights and responsibilities given to us by EU laws will remain in, or be incorporated into, our domestic laws? To what extent will the UK go its own way whilst the remaining states of the EU move towards harmonisation in matters of family law? What effect will this have upon families that comprise people of different nationalities living and working in the UK or travelling between the UK and other states and issues such as child abduction, child contact, and the reciprocal recognition of orders between states?

---

[2] L Trinder, J Hunt, A Macleod, J Pearce, and H Woodward, *Enforcing Contact Orders: Problem-Solving or Punishment?* (University of Exeter/Nuffield Foundation 2013).
[3] S Harris-Short, 'Making and Breaking Family Life: Adoption, the State, and Human Rights' (2008) 35(1) *Journal of Law and Society* 28, 28.

1.2 **Some issues with access to justice**

Family lawyers are used to uncertainty. We operate within an area of law in which judicial discretion is widespread. In financial proceedings on divorce, for example, judges are simply required to reach an outcome that is fair. In matters pertaining to a child's upbringing, judges must do what is best for the child. A system which leaves considerable discretion to judges is one that enables its outcomes to be tailored precisely to a particular family situation, so that justice can be done in an individual case. More prescriptive formulae or guidance would result in outcomes that were unfair in some cases. But discretion comes at a price, both financial and ideological. Systems which are highly discretionary encourage litigation because the outcomes are unpredictable. Prejudices can be hidden within the scope of discretion. Litigants in person may struggle to find and apply the law.

The accessibility or otherwise of the law is particularly important because of the loss of legal aid in the majority of family law cases as a result of the Legal Aid, Sentencing and Punishment of Offenders Act 2012 (LASPO). Legal aid is now only available for certain case types which are shown in Table 1.1. Note that in many cases, legal aid is only available where there is evidence that the applicant is a victim of domestic abuse or that there are certain types of harm to a child.

Even if the type of case is within the scope of legal aid, the parties may have to pass the means test and the merits test. The means test concerns the financial resources of the person applying for legal aid. In many cases, a person will earn too much to be eligible for legal aid even though they may struggle to afford a solicitor. This is because the eligibility criteria are very stringent.[4]

The merits test involves consideration by the Legal Aid Agency of the applicant's prospects of success, whether the costs are proportionate or reasonable compared to the benefits gained by winning the case, and whether a hypothetical reasonable person would use their own money to pursue the case or not consider the expenditure worth it. In cases involving protection from domestic abuse, this is not usually a problem. Note that a person can lose legal aid if the case begins to go against them. This can happen in children cases if a report by Cafcass, the Child and Family Court Advisory and Support Service, is unfavourable to the legally aided person.

If a party recovers or preserves money or property as a result of a case for which they are legally aided, they may have to repay their legal aid. This is called the 'statutory charge'. The Legal Aid Agency may register unpaid debt to them as a charge on the applicant's home and charge interest at a not insignificant 8 per cent per annum until the debt is repaid.

LASPO has led to a sharp rise in the number of people representing themselves at court (known as litigants in person or self-representing litigants). In 2019, of 111,606 parties in private law disputes about children of the kind discussed in Chapter 10, 65 per cent—some 72,869 people (41,183 respondents and 31,686 applicants)—had no recorded legal representative. In 2011, pre-LASPO, the figure was 39 per cent.[5]

Although there have been a number of efforts to simplify procedures and forms so that they can be better used by people representing themselves, family law is particularly difficult

---

[4] You can find them here: https://www.gov.uk/guidance/civil-legal-aid-means-testing#eligibility-limits.
[5] Ministry of Justice, *Family Court Statistics Quarterly April to June 2020* (2020) at Table 11.

TABLE 1.1 Types of case where legal aid is available

Type of case	Eligibility
Divorce, civil partnership dissolution, and judicial separation proceedings and related financial remedy cases	Domestic abuse victims only, and subject to means and merits test.
Applications under the Children Act cases (private law) concerning arrangements for a child or for decisions about their upbringing (prohibited steps and specific issues applications)	Domestic abuse victims only, and subject to means and merits test
Applications under Schedule 1 to the Children Act 1989	Domestic abuse victims only, and subject to means and merits test
Applications for a forced marriage protection order	Means and merits tested
Applications for a female genital mutilation protection order	Means and merits tested
Applications for a non-molestation order or occupation order under the Family Law Act 1996 or an order under the Protection from Harassment Act 1997	Means and merits tested
Proceedings brought by a local authority for a care or supervision order, or for a child assessment or emergency protection order	Available irrespective of means to parents and those with parental responsibility. Child represented by legal aided lawyer appointed by guardian
Child abduction cases (legal proceedings to recover a child taken abroad or prevent them being abducted)	Available irrespective of means if the Hague Convention or Brussels II Revised Regulation applies; otherwise subject to means and merits test
Mediation	There is legal aid for mediation for both child and divorce and related finance matters. The first meeting is free for both parties if one of them is legally aided, but for subsequent meetings only the person eligible on means-testing for legal aid will get it.
Applications relating to children[6]	Children who are parties will be legally aided (either to instruct their own solicitor or for the guardian to instruct a solicitor) If the child who is the subject of the application is at risk of abuse from another person, and the case is to protect the child from that other person, then legal aid is available to the adult bringing the application

---

[6] In theory, an application for contact with your former child who has been adopted by another family is a category of cases that since 2015 has been eligible for legal aid, but Andrew Pack has explained how this is theory rather than practice at https://suesspiciousminds.com/tag/can-i-get-legal-aid-to-apply-for-post-adoption-contact/ accessed 23 November 2020.

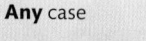 **Any** case	Exceptional case funding is available for those cases which would not otherwise be eligible if there is evidence that failure to fund the case would breach a party's rights under the ECHR/ Human Rights Act 1998 or under EU law; and the unrepresented litigant would not otherwise be able to present their case effectively and without obvious unfairness. (*Gudaviciene and Others v Director of Legal Aid Casework and Anor*).[7] This involves consideration of the complexity of the legal and factual issues; the procedural complexity of the case; the importance of the case; and the applicant's ability to represent themselves (including their physical and mental health, language abilities, and educational level). It has been said that 'if a litigant in person is able to complete [the exceptional funding application] form, they are almost able to show that they are able to represent themselves, so it is self-defeating'.[8]

for litigants in person for a number of reasons. Firstly, the law is not easy to locate. It is heavily discretionary, as we have said, and guidance on the principles to be applied are found within cases which a person new to the law may not be able to find. The outcome in one case may wildly differ from an outcome in a different case even though on the surface they both seem to be about the same thing. Second, family law involves issues that are important to us: the right to see our child, our financial independence, or personal safety, or ability to become or to remain a parent. Emotions can often run high in family courts. For family lawyers, that is part of the excitement, but we have the privilege of not being personally involved.

Of course, some of the law that you read about in this book may have shaped your lived experience. If you have picked this book up at university, there may well be students in your class who were subjected to domestic abuse, or taken into care, or whose relationship with one parent has been shaped by relationship breakdown or child arrangements proceedings. Most students will marry or cohabit at some point. Some may seek to change legal gender, or enter into arranged marriages, disagree with their parents over medical treatment, or face homelessness. Some people choose to study family law precisely because it helps them to make sense of their experiences. Some parts of this book may be distressing even to those whose lives have been far away from some of the cases we discuss.

As you read this book, consider how you might experience the law coming to it as a lay person rather than as a scholar guided by a lecturer. How would you have located this law if not for its neat packaging as a book or e-book? How might you have applied the law to your own divorce or child dispute? How could you, as a lawyer, help others with family law difficulties?

 Visit the **online resources** to watch a video of Polly Morgan discussing this chapter topic, and to check your understanding of this chapter with self-test questions and scenario questions.

---

[7] [2014] EWCA Civ 1622.

[8] Evidence given by Resolution member David Emmerson to the Justice Select Committee on 2 September 2014. Resolution is an organisation for family lawyers. See House of Commons Justice Committee, *Impact of Changes to Civil Legal Aid under Part 1 of the Legal Aid, Sentencing and Punishment of Offenders Act 2012* (HC 2014-15, HC 311) para 43.

Marriage and Civil Partnership

LEARNING CHECKLIST

By the end of this chapter, you should be able to:

- *Explain* the legal requirements for the formation of a valid marriage and what factors a court may consider when determining the validity of a marriage
- *Discuss* the basis on which a marriage may be void, voidable, or a non-marriage, and the implications of each, and *evaluate* the continuing need for a law of nullity
- *Explain* the different legal steps that can be taken to prevent or end a forced marriage and *evaluate* the success of these
- *Identify* the ways in which the state regulates marriage, and *critically discuss* what state interests are involved
- *Describe* the rules surrounding recognition of marriages entered into abroad
- *Explain* the mechanism whereby an individual can change their legal gender and the range of perspectives on the legal consequences of this for existing marriages and civil partnerships
- *Critically evaluate* the differences between different-sex marriage, same-sex marriage, and civil partnership and use a range of perspectives to *evaluate* the extent to which these differences are legally and socially important
- *Evaluate* to what extent it can be said that there is a human right to marry.

SCENARIO 1

Helen and Ned

Helen and Ned are a different-sex couple who have recently become engaged and are planning their wedding. They are looking into different venues to hire for the ceremony and reception, and what paperwork they need to do before they can marry. They currently live together and are wondering what effect getting married has on their legal position.

SCENARIO 2

Mark and Jamal

Mark and Jamal are a same-sex couple who are looking to formalise their relationship by getting married. Their preference is to marry in the garden of a local hotel, where they can also hold the reception. They are unsure about who should marry them, but are thinking about asking a humanist celebrant.

SCENARIO 3

Raheem and Fatima

Raheem and Fatima are a different-sex couple married in accordance with the Islamic faith. Their marriage was arranged by their respective parents and the wedding was held at the mosque they attend. Fatima saw a documentary about Islamic marriages and has become concerned about whether her marriage to Raheem is legal or not. She is also concerned because Raheem is refusing to have sexual relations with her.

SCENARIO 4

Mabel and Karen

Marie is a solicitor. She has been contacted by Mabel. Mabel married David in 1986. A couple of years ago, David told Mabel that he wanted to transition to female and is now known as Karen. Mabel is presently very unsure about whether she should remain in a relationship with Karen, and she has come to see Marie for advice about the legal implications for the marriage.

2.1 Introduction

Most adults in the United Kingdom are married.[1] It is, therefore, appropriate that we start this book as you will probably start your family law course: by considering marriage and asking 'just what is so special about it?' To what extent can marriage still be considered an event of cultural, social, and legal significance?

To begin our discussion, we are first going to consider how one gets married, tracing the historical evolution and popularity of marriage to the present day. We consider how valid marriages may be formed, and the risks of invalidity particularly associated with religious marriage ceremonies. We will consider the grounds on which a marriage can be annulled, rather than ended by divorce, and what relevance these grounds have in the present day.

We then turn to evaluating the social and legal significance of marriage. What would happen if we abolished all the legal consequences of marriage, so it became a symbolic ceremony only? Would marriage still retain the desirability that it has in many people's eyes? In section 2.12.5, we consider why couples marry today, and we discover that social expectation and tradition are still influential motivators. We will look at how the state encourages people to marry and why it does so—as well as what the legal and social privileging of marriage meant for same-sex couples who were for so long denied entry to this institution.

Marriage is not the only option now available to couples wanting to formalise their relationships. There are two different regimes in England and Wales.

1. *Marriage.* From 29 March 2014, as a result of the Marriage (Same-Sex Couples) Act 2013 coming into force, marriage became available to same-sex couples.

---

[1] Office of National Statistics, *Population Estimates by Marital Status and Living Arrangements, England and Wales: 2019* (2020).

2. *Civil partnership.* Introduced by the Civil Partnership Act 2004, it has virtually all the legal consequences of marriage but until 2019 was open to same-sex couples only. It was introduced to meet demand for the legal recognition and protection of gay and lesbian couples at a time when same-sex marriage did not have popular support.

In this chapter we consider to what extent civil partnerships are equal to marriage, both legally and in terms of public perception. Recently, there has been a further important change, as in 2019 civil partnerships were opened up to different-sex couples after a campaign that positioned civil partnership as a desirable and more modern alternative to marriage. Is the future of marriage not marriage at all?

2.2 Historical context

Initially, marriage was a purely religious institution and not the concern of the state. As early as the twelfth century, the Church legislated for public and formal marriage ceremonies.[2] A promise to marry someone was binding and the parties could be compelled to go through with the marriage, which took place before a priest.[3] If a question arose as to its validity, the ecclesiastical (church) courts would resolve the matter according to church law. Divorce did not exist: if a party wished to leave a marriage they could only do so (short of death) by annulling the marriage.[4] Following the Reformation—the period from 1532 in which King Henry VIII disestablished the Catholic Church and established the Church of England—we begin to see some of the traditions and requirements of marriages that we still have today. These include the requirement to call the banns in a church to announce a forthcoming wedding, or the need to obtain a marriage licence,[5] and regulation of the times and places at which marriages could take place. While the state may have left it to the Church of England to regulate marriages, the reality is that post-Reformation the fortunes of the Church were closely tied to the interests of the state.

The move to explicit state regulation of marriage came about as a result of the execution of Charles I in 1649 and the subsequent Interregnum led by Oliver Cromwell. As Bailey argues, 'Marriage mattered in much the same ways as it matters today. Governments attempted to control it, the church tried to retain some hold on it, pundits bemoaned its state, and most proclaimed it the key to social order.'[6] The Marriage Act 1653 broke the control of the Church, banning church weddings and providing that parties could be married only by magistrate. Although this requirement was repealed in 1660 with the Restoration of Charles II to the throne, by this time people no longer saw marriage as a purely ecclesiastical matter, but an issue regulated by both the Church and Parliament.

---

[2] R Probert, 'The Misunderstood Contract Per Verba De Praesenti', in (author) *Marriage Law and Practice in the Long Eighteenth Century* (Cambridge University Press 2009).

[3] The binding nature of an engagement was ended by the 1753 Act.

[4] Divorce is discussed at length in Chapter 3.

[5] The banns are a verbal announcement of an upcoming marriage, repeated over several weeks. They are still read in advance of Church of England weddings today, and enable any person with reason to object to the marriage the opportunity to do so. These were required from 1604.

[6] J Bailey, *Unquiet Lives: Marriage and Marriage Breakdown in England, 1660–1800* (Cambridge University Press 2003) 2.

However, in practice regulation was largely ineffective. People could desert a spouse, relocate, and remarry bigamously with no one the wiser. Marriages were not necessarily conducted by legitimate priests but also by defrocked priests or itinerant priests, or conducted outside the parties' parish or outside the hours within which weddings were meant to be conducted. Marriages conducted in this way are known as 'clandestine marriages'.[7] To those who had land and property, the lack of consensus 'about how a legally binding marriage should be carried out'[8] meant uncertainty about whether a marriage was valid, with consequences for the inheritance of land and titles. In 1695, the Marriage Duty Act imposed a tax on marriage as a way of raising funds for war with France, and at the same time sought to end clandestine marriages by imposing severe penalties on clergymen who married couples without prior reading of the banns or a valid licence.[9] The inadvertent consequence of the 1695 Act and its successors was a significant rise in weddings taking place in areas outside Church control, such as prisons and the immediate area surrounding them, so as to marry in a way that avoided the legislative restrictions.[10] One of the most popular places was Fleet Prison in London, which at one point accounted for half of all London weddings.[11] The consequences of over-regulation, therefore, and of financially penalising marriages, were deliberate attempts to avoid both.

In 1753, A Bill for the Better Preventing of Clandestine Marriage, better known as Lord Hardwicke's Marriage Act, was passed in a further attempt to regulate marriage. It provided that all weddings had to take place before a priest in a church and according to certain formalities which are not dissimilar to those we have today, including the presence of two witnesses, and the reading of the banns on three successive Sundays or the obtaining of a licence. Importantly, proper records had to be kept and the priest could not marry those under 21 if their parents objected.[12] The churches in question were those of the Church of England as the established church, and it was not possible for other religious groups to marry in their own religious buildings or according to their own rite, nor was a secular wedding possible. There were some exceptions. Jewish ceremonies could be conducted and to this day form an exception to the legal formalities required of other religious groups. There is some uncertainty over the position of Quakers (Members of the Society of Friends). It seems that the fact that Quaker ceremonies do not involve a presiding officiant may have been fatal to recognition of them. However, along with Jewish weddings, since 1773 Quakers have always been able to marry according to their own rites.[13] When we consider the current law surrounding the formation of marriage at section 2.4.3, we see that these two groups continue to be in a privileged position as far as conducting their own ceremonies are concerned.

---

[7] See L Stone, *Uncertain Unions: Marriage in England 1660–1753* (Oxford University Press 1992) for examples of such marriages.

[8] L Stone, *Uncertain Unions: Marriage in England 1660–1753* (Oxford University Press 1992) 31.

[9] RB Outhwaite, *Clandestine Marriage in England 1500–1850* (The Hambledon Press 1995) 14.

[10] L Stone, *Road to Divorce: England 1530–1987* (Oxford University Press, 1992) 96–115.

[11] RB Outhwaite, *Clandestine Marriage in England 1500–1850* (The Hambledon Press 1995) 31.

[12] An Act for the Better Preventing of Clandestine Marriage 1753 ss 14 and 3. You can find this Act at http://statutes.org.uk/site/the-statutes/eighteenth-century/1753-26-geo-2-c-33-prevention-of-clandestine-marriages/ accessed 17 August 2018.

[13] HSQ Henriques, 'Jewish Marriages and the English Law' (1908) 20(3) *The Jewish Quarterly Review* 391, 409, citing Haggard's Consistorial Reports vol. II, p40.

Although the 1753 Act can be seen as part of a wider move from custom and common law to regulation in the 18th century, it was not uncontentious. There was concern that the formalisation of marriage would lead to women being abandoned when previously even a clandestine marriage would have given them some legal protection. This is because, for women, marriage had certain important legal consequences, namely the loss of her as a legal person. 'By marriage', wrote Blackstone in 1765,

> the husband and wife are one person in law: that is, the very being or legal existence of the woman is suspended during the marriage, or at least is incorporated and consolidated into that of the husband: under whose wing, protection, and cover, she performs every thing; . . . and her condition during her marriage is called her coverture.[14]

A woman's property became her husband's upon marriage.[15] If they separated, a husband would be able to refuse his wife permission to see their children;[16] he would be entitled to her earnings (if any); and he could beat her, imprison her,[17] and rape her[18] without committing any crime. Bacon asserts that 'The husband hath by law power and dominion over his wife.'[19] Under such conditions, some women may have been very glad to be abandoned, but it often meant relentless destitution.[20] In Chapter 4, we can see the legacy of coverture in modern laws on financial provision on divorce.

The requirement that marriages be formed through religious ceremonies was brought to an end in 1836 with the introduction of a civil (i.e. non-religious, or secular) marriage process (not to be confused with civil partnership, which is a separate regime to marriage). This enabled people to marry in a register office after first giving notice and then obtaining a superintendent registrar's licence, as is the case today. As we shall see, although the number of religious bodies whose religious ceremonies are recognised as lawful have increased, there remains a difference in approach between ceremonies conducted by the Church of England, Quakers, and according to Jewish rites, when compared to other groups.[21] Indeed, although there have been a number of subsequent Acts, the formalities of entering into a marriage remain similar to the position as in 1836.

2.3 Marriage today

Marriage has continued to be the dominant family form throughout the twentieth century and into the twenty-first.

> In the 1950s and 1960s it was the only way you could respectably have sex, live with the man you loved, have children—or even, for many women, leave home. 'Living in sin' was not done, illegitimacy was stigmatised, unmarried mothers were considered an unspeakable

---

[14] Blackstone, *Commentaries on the Laws of England* (1765–1769).
[15] Until the Married Woman's Property Act 1882.
[16] Until the Custody of Infants Act 1839.
[17] Until *R v Jackson* [1891] 1 QB 67.
[18] Until *R v R* [1991] UKHL 12; yes, that is 1991.
[19] Bacon's *Abridgement of the Law* (1768).
[20] In 1675, Grace Allenson, reflecting on her unhappy marriage, told her servant "that if she might have but bread and water to live on she were happy if she could but be quiet with it". Joanne Bailey, quoting the deposition of the servant in the cruelty separation case *Allenson v Allenson*, 1675: *Unquiet Lives: Marriage and Marriage Breakdown in England, 1660–1800* (Cambridge University Press 2003) 1.
[21] RB Outhwaite, *Clandestine Marriage in England 1500–1850* (The Hambledon Press 1995).

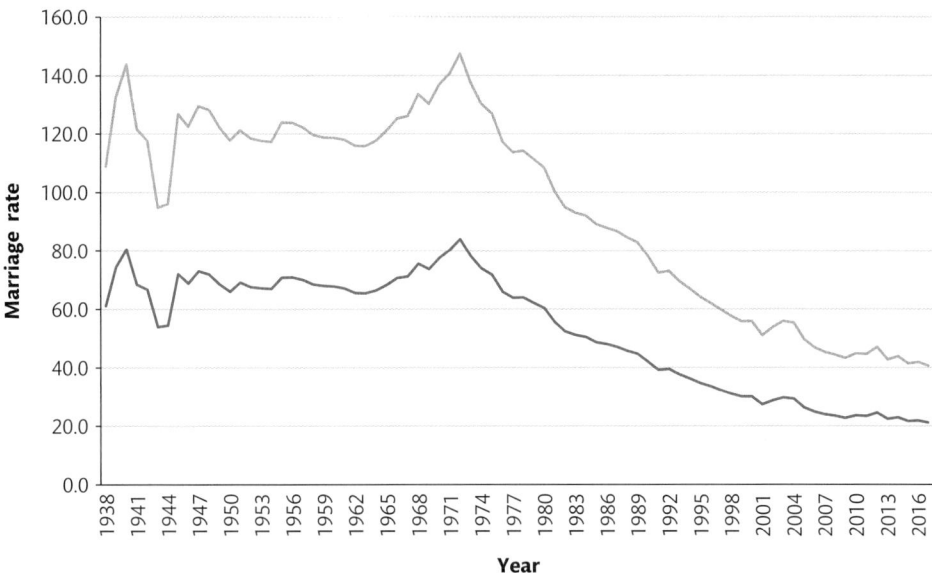

FIGURE 2.1 Number of marriages per 1,000 unmarried men (top line) and women (bottom line) aged 16 or over—the marriage rate—for different-sex couples between 1937 and 2017

Source: Adapted from data provided by Office of National Statistics. Office of National Statistics, *Marriages in England and Wales: 2017* (2020).

disgrace and treated with appalling brutality . . . . Marriage was attractive to those women who, before anti-discrimination laws, had little chance of acquiring a home of their own or a comparable standard of living by their own efforts.[22]

With an increase in the population, more equal numbers of men and women than had been the case following the two world wars, and sufficient economic prosperity to enable young couples to set up home, marriage reached a peak in 1972.[23] Since then, the marriage rate has fallen steadily, and is now at its lowest since records began, with around 240,000 couples marrying each year.[24] Figure 2.1 shows this decline. Increasingly, people are co-habiting.[25] Those who are marrying do so at a later age than previously, and the divorce rate is around about 42 per cent.

Nevertheless, despite the dramatic decrease in the marriage rate, people are still marrying. Married couples remain the prevailing family form in the UK and most young people indicate that, if they met the right person, they would want to marry them.[26]

---

[22] R Auchmuty, 'Law and the Power of Feminism: How Marriage Lost Its Power to Oppress Women' (2012) 20 *Feminist Legal Studies* 71, 73.

[23] See L Fox Harding, *Family, State and Social Policy* (Macmillan 1996) 48–9. For the marriage rate, see Office of National Statistics, *Statistical Bulletin: Marriages in England and Wales 2015* (ONS 2018).

[24] Office of National Statistics, *Marriages in England and Wales: 2017* (2020).

[25] Office of National Statistics, *Population Estimates by Marital Status and Living Arrangements, England and Wales: 2002 to 2017* (2018).

[26] W Wang and K Parker, *Public Views on Marriage* (Pew Research Centre 2014). Available at http://www.pewsocialtrends.org/2014/09/24/chapter-1-public-views-on-marriage/ accessed 29 September 2019.

To a modern reader, this brief historical account of marriage makes for uncomfortable reading. But is marriage any different now to its patriarchal past? A number of feminist scholars would argue that it is not. Fineman, for example, has argued that marriage 'has not been a neutral social, cultural, or legal institution. It has shaped the aspirations and experiences of women and men in ways that have historically disadvantaged women.'[27] The YBA Wife ('why be a wife?') campaigns of the 1970s highlighted legal inequalities between the sexes and the prevalence of gendered roles with the man as breadwinner and the woman as homemaker. 'Marriage was a powerful means whereby property (and with property, power) was concentrated in the male domain, and it was therefore the most significant means by which the inequality of the sexes was both institutionalised and perpetuated.'[28] For Katherine O'Donovan, marriage involves 'the sacrifice of personal autonomy, but not on equal terms for the parties'.[29] Despite the continued existence of gendered roles within the family, it is doubtful whether many couples today believe that the institution of marriage is inherently contrary to gender equality. Gone now is the concept that the wife lost her legal identity on marriage. She can now own her own property, has the right to care for her children,[30] and her body is her own. To hit her or rape her is a criminal offence. She can get divorced and when she does so she is entitled to share in the assets of the marriage. People may take the view, as Lady Hale does, that '[a] desire to reject legal patriarchy is no longer a rational reason to reject marriage'.[31] Far from being a manifestation of coverture with her as legal object being passed from one man to another, the bride's father giving her away to the groom is seen simply as a nice tradition.

2.4 The requirements for a valid marriage

As we shall see in section 2.12.1, marriage has particular legal consequences. It is clearly important for state institutions such as government departments to know who is married and who is not, and thus which people have obtained the legal rights and responsibilities that come with marriage. Some regulation of the entry and exit to marriage is therefore necessary. The law does this by prescribing particular rules surrounding the ceremony itself, and what the parties must do before the ceremony and afterwards. In this section, we look at how people can form a valid marriage when their marriage takes place in England and Wales. The Marriage Act 1949 sets out these requirements, and the Matrimonial Causes Act 1973 then deals with the consequences of non-compliance, which may include the marriage being invalid. Unfortunately, as we shall see, the law is not very clear and the risks of not complying are exacerbated by the increasing number of locations at which it is possible to marry and the different treatment of certain religious groups.

Many of these requirements also apply to those entering into civil partnerships. The requirements for a valid civil partnership are further discussed in section 2.14.1 and in Table 2.3.

---

[27] MA Fineman, 'Why Marriage?' (2001) 9(1) *Virginia Journal of Social Policy and the Law* 239.

[28] K McK Norrie, 'Marriage Is for Heterosexuals – May the Rest of Us Be Saved from It' (2000) 12(4) *Child and Family Law Quarterly* 363.

[29] K O'Donovan, 'Marriage: A Sacred or Profane Love Machine?' (1993) 1(1) *Feminist Legal Studies* 75, 75.

[30] Subject to a court deciding that this is not in the children's interests.

[31] *Re P (Adoption: Unmarried Couple)* [2008] UKHL 38 at [109].

2.4.1 Marriage of a minor

In order to form a valid marriage, the parties must have capacity to marry. A marriage or civil partnership to someone aged *under* 16 is void under s2 Marriage Act 1949. A person aged 16 or 17 (who has not married before) can only marry with either the consent of all those with parental responsibility for them, a decision by the Registrar General to dispense with that consent, or a court order.[32] However, where there is a 'live with' order in force, only the permission of the person with whom the child lives is required.[33] The failure to obtain such consent does not render the marriage automatically void: if all other requirements for a lawful marriage are met, the marriage will still be valid.[34] For a civil partnership, however, the situation is different. Failure to get consent does appear to render the partnership void.[35]

The number of 16- and 17-year-olds marrying with parental consent is lower currently than in recent years. Table 2.1 shows the latest available figures, which are for 2017. Note that the number of girls marrying before they are adults is higher than the number of boys; this gender difference implies that these young women were principally marrying adult men. However, these figures are for registered marriages in England and Wales and therefore exclude the potentially much higher number of marriages taking place for British teenagers taken abroad or those 'married' in ceremonies that do not comply with marriage law, something more common in certain faith groups. Some of these marriages, both in this jurisdiction, and abroad, will be forced marriages, which we discuss at 2.9 of this chapter.

In October 2020, Pauline Latham MP introduced a private member's bill, the Marriage and Civil Partnership (Minimum Age) Bill, which would remove the ability of 16- and 17-year-olds to marry with parental consent and criminalise child marriage in England and Wales. At the time of writing, it is not known whether this bill will be given legislative time by the government, which is the only chance of it succeeding.

2.4.2 Before the wedding

Marriages can be formed through a secular (meaning non-religious) civil ceremony or through a religious ceremony. The terms 'civil' and 'religious' simply describe the type of ceremony that has created a valid marriage. There is no difference in legal effect.

TABLE 2.1 Number of 16- and 17-year-olds marrying with parental consent in 2017

	Men	Women	
Aged 16	9	56	
Aged 17	34	84	
Total			183

Source: Office of National Statistics, *Marriages in England and Wales 2017 Dataset* (2020).

---

[32] A full list of those whose consent is necessary is set out in s3 Marriage Act 1949. The Registrar General can dispense with consent where a parent is inaccessible or absent, or lacks the legal capacity to consent (for example because they are seriously disabled).
[33] Marriage Act 1949, s3.
[34] It is not within the void elements set out in the Matrimonial Causes Act 1973.
[35] See ss4 and 49 Civil Partnership Act 2004.

Unless they are marrying under the Church of England or Church in Wales, it is necessary for the parties to first notify the register office of their intention to marry. This is the case whether the parties intend to have their ceremony in a secular location such as a hotel or the register office itself, or in a religious location such as a mosque, synagogue, or Catholic church. The registrar records the parties' intention to marry in the marriage notice book, alongside the parties' details and their declaration that there are no lawful impediments to the marriage. After 28 days, the statutory notice period, the parties will receive a superintendent registrar's certificate. This enables them to marry within three months of the date they gave notice. The purpose of this notice period is to enable objections to be made, including, for example, objections on the basis of immigration fraud, the reason why the notice period was increased in 2015 from 15 days to 28.[36]

The situation is different to those who want to marry according to the rites of the Church of England or Church in Wales. Here, it is not necessary to notify the register office or obtain a superintendent's certificate. Instead, notice of the marriage will usually be given by the reading of the banns for three successive Sundays in the church where the ceremony is to be held, and in the parties' parish church(es) if different.[37] Alternatively, the parties may obtain a common licence from a bishop or a special licence from the Archbishop of Canterbury. A common licence is used where the parties cannot fulfil the residence requirements, such as because they do not live in England or Wales, or because their home address is likely to change during the time when banns are read out. Special licences can be obtained where the parties need to marry elsewhere than a church, such as in a hospital, hospice, their home (for example, for medical/disability reasons), or in a privately-owned chapel.

There is an exception to the freedom to marry under the Church of England or Church in Wales without a superintendent's certificate. Under the Immigration Act 2014, foreign nationals from outside the European Economic Area can only marry in the Church if they have either a certificate or a special licence. This was part of a package of measures designed to address so-called 'sham marriages': those conducted purely for immigration purposes.

2.4.3 The wedding ceremony

At present, all wedding ceremonies must take place in a permanent structure such as a building, not in a garden, marquee, or other outdoor or impermanent space. Beyond that, the requirements differ according to the nature of the ceremony selected by the parties, as set out in Table 2.2.

Civil (secular) ceremonies

Approximately three quarters of couples choose to have a non-religious wedding.[38] This is known as a civil marriage and is not to be confused with civil partnership. Civil ceremonies can be conducted in a register office (11 per cent of civil weddings; the current

---

[36] Immigration Act 2014, amending the Marriage Act 1949 s31(1).
[37] Marriage Act 1949 s48(1)(b).
[38] Office of National Statistics, *Statistical Bulletin: Marriages in England and Wales 2015* (2018).

fee is £46 plus £4 for a copy of the marriage certificate) or in a range of different approved premises (89 per cent).[39] Such ceremonies must not contain any religious element but must be purely secular, although the parties can have a religious aspect to the day—just not the ceremony itself. The Marriage Act 1949 s45(2) states that 'no religious service shall be used at any marriage solemnised in the office of the superintendent registrar'. The Marriages and Civil Partnerships (Approved Premises) Regulations 2005 states that the ceremony cannot include extracts from an authorised religious marriage service or from sacred religious texts; be led by a minister of religion or other religious leader; involve a religious ritual or series of rituals; include hymns or other religious chants; or include any form of worship.[40]

Although there is flexibility in the format and content of the service, the marriage is formed by the making of certain verbal declarations: the parties must declare than they do not know of any lawful impediment to the marriage and that they take their partner to be their lawfully wedded wife or husband. The marriage is conducted by a registrar, who is an officer of the local authority, in the presence of two witnesses.[41] The marriage is then recorded in the marriage register.

Religious ceremonies: Church of England

The Church of England and Church in Wales may conduct marriages according to their own rites. These require that the marriage is solemnised by a clerk in Holy Orders in the presence of two witnesses. The marriage is then recorded in the marriage register kept by the church in question, with older copies of the marriage registers usually being sent to the local register office for retention.

Religious ceremonies: Quaker and Jewish

The situation is slightly different for Quakers (properly known as members of the Society of Friends) and Jewish people. While anyone wishing to marry according these faiths must first notify the register office and obtain a superintendent registrar's certificate, they have been able to conduct ceremonies according to their own rites since Lord Hardwicke's Marriage Act 1753. This means that the venue does not need to be one licensed by the local authority (and can be outside), the ceremony does not need to be conducted by a registrar or person authorised by the local authority (indeed, Quaker weddings do not involve an officiant), and they do not need to use the form of wording required of civil ceremonies. They must, however, register the marriage.

Table 2.2 outlines the requirements for a marriage ceremony by type.

Religious ceremonies: All other religions

The position differs yet again for other faith groups. As you can see from Table 2.2, they must first notify the register office and obtain a superintendent registrar's certificate. They must also ensure that their venue is a certified place of worship that is registered for the solemnisation of marriages and that the person conducting the wedding is legally autho-rised to do so at that location. This means that if the religious figure who is present is not

---

[39] Office of National Statistics, *Statistical Bulletin: Marriages in England and Wales 2015* (2018).
[40] SI 2005/3168.
[41] Religious leaders are not eligible to become registrars of different-sex marriages.

TABLE 2.2 Requirements for a marriage ceremony by type

	Preliminaries	Rites	Venue	Celebrant
Secular civil ceremony	Notify register office.	Prescribed form of words.	Must take place in approved premises which 'cannot be used solely or mainly for religious purposes, or have been so used and have not subsequently been used solely or mainly for other purposes'.[42] Common venues are a register office, stately home, or hotel.	Registrar (an official appointed by the local authority).
Church of England and Church in Wales	Reading of banns or Bishop's common licence or Archbishop's special licence.[43]	Own rites.	Does not need licensing by local authority.	Clerk in holy orders such as a vicar.
Jewish	Notify register office.	Own rites.	No restrictions as to place are specified in legislation.	Rabbi (does not need separate authorisation), or under Rabbi's authority.
Quaker (Society of Friends)	Notify register office.	Own rites.	No restrictions as to place are specified in legislation.	None, but the marriage will be registered by the local Registering Officer.
All other religious groups	Notify register office.	Prescribed form of words.	A certified place of worship which is also registered for the solemnisation of marriages.[44]	A registrar or someone authorised to conduct weddings at that location (who may be a religious leader).

authorised, a local authority registrar or other authorised person will also need to be there. Finally, they must ensure that a prescribed form of words is used, have two witnesses, and register the marriage. It is here that problems have arisen, with some couples finding later that their marriage is not valid because they have not complied with certain of these requirements.[45] This can have serious consequences. In some cases, parties have not known

---

[42] This is the Civil Partnership Act 2004 s6 definition of 'religious premises'; the Marriages and Civil Partnerships (Approved Premises) Regulations 2005 says authorised premises cannot be 'religious premises'.

[43] See http://www.facultyoffice.org.uk/special-licences/obtaining-a-special-marriage-licence/ accessed 17 August 2018.

[44] The list can be found at https://www.gov.uk/government/collections/places-of-religious-worship-and-the-solemnisation-of-marriages accessed 19 November 2018. Registration is made through the Superintendent Registrar for the local district.

[45] At section 2.6.4 we discuss which of these formalities is significant enough that it will cause the wedding to be invalid.

for decades that they were not legally married: to them, the religious ceremony was all that they needed, when in fact it was legally deficient in a number of ways.

Note that under the Gender Recognition Act 2004, no clergyman of the Church of England or clerk in holy orders of the Church in Wales is obliged to solemnise the marriage of a person who has changed their legal gender.[46] These two groups are specifically mentioned because the Marriage Act 1949 imposes a legal obligation on them to marry anyone residing in their parish or who meet other criteria. There is no such legal obligation on the part of leaders of other faiths, so there is no legislation addressing the point. Individual faiths will decide their own position.

SCENARIO 1

Illustration 1: Helen and Ned

The steps that Helen and Ned will need to take prior to their wedding will depend upon their choice of ceremony. If the wish to marry within the Church of England, they do not need to notify the register office, but the banns must be read for three successive Sundays in the church where they intend to marry, unless they have a common or special licence dispensing with this requirement.

If they are Catholic, however, and wish to marry in a Catholic church, they will need to notify the register office beforehand and obtain a superintendent registrar's certificate. They will also need to ensure that the church in question is registered for the solemnisation of marriages and that someone who is authorised to conduct weddings is present during the ceremony. That may be the priest, or it may be another member of the diocese. If these two issues cannot be resolved, they will need to arrange for a separate register office ceremony to avoid their marriage being void.

Even if they appreciate that Church of England and Catholic churches have different rites for weddings, Ned and Helen will almost certainly have not appreciated that the state imposes different requirements on marriages in the Church of England to those in the Catholic Church, and be unable to discern why this is.

Prisoners

It is possible to marry while in prison, whether that is in a space designated for worship or otherwise, subject to certain eligibility criteria and the obtaining of a superintendent registrar's certificate.[47] It is also possible for a prisoner to obtain temporary release in order to marry outside the prison, but again this depends upon certain criteria being met.[48]

SCENARIO 2

Illustration 1: Mark and Jamal

Mark and Jamal's plan to marry in the garden of a hotel is flawed. Gardens are not authorised as places where marriages can be conducted. Therefore, the ceremony itself will need to take place in a building, even if they want to then hold the reception outside.

---

[46] Marriage Act 1949 s5B, as amended by the Gender Recognition Act 2004.
[47] Marriage Act 1983, amending the Marriage Act 1949.
[48] National Offender Management Service, *Marriage of Prisoners and Civil Partnership Registration* (PSI 14/2016) (Ministry of Justice 2016).

They also want to ask a humanist celebrant, but this is not currently possible. Humanism is not a religion so such a ceremony would not be covered by the law on religious ceremonies. If Jamal and Mark had a religious faith, they may be able to have a religious service, but this depends on whether the religion has opted in to conducting same-sex marriage. Mark and Jamal will instead need to use a registrar, an official appointed by the local authority. They could have a civil ceremony in a hotel or register office for the legal consequences, and follow it with a humanist blessing in the garden that aligns with their own personal beliefs.

SCENARIO 3

Illustration 1: Raheem and Fatima

As Raheem and Fatima are Muslim, they do not fall under the procedures for the Church of England or Church in Wales, or those who are Quaker or Jewish. To have formed a valid marriage, they must therefore have notified the register office, waited the statutory period, and then obtained the superintendent registrar's certificate.

Fatima will also need to determine whether the ceremony in a mosque included the prescribed words and that the mosque was registered for marriages, and that an authorised person (or registrar) was present. Only a small proportion of mosques are registered buildings; a far fewer proportion than for other religious buildings of other faiths. The fact that some mosques are and some are not may cause additional confusion: Fatima may have a valid marriage but her friend, married in a neighbouring mosque, may not.

2.5 Introduction to nullity

The term 'nullity' refers to marriages which are not valid. Nullity has a very long history. Until 1858, the validity of marriages was solely within the realm of the ecclesiastical courts. Nowadays, the validity of a marriage is determined by the state through its own courts.

There are three main categories of nullity.

- A void marriage is a marriage that, due to some defect that was present at the time of the ceremony, has never been valid. It has been void *ab initio*—void from the start. The parties have therefore never been married.

- A non-marriage is an 'event with marital qualities' or 'non-qualifying ceremony'[49] that is not sufficiently close to resembling a valid marriage to count even as void.[50] Actors who are playing a wedding scene in a film are taking part in a non-marriage. However, sometimes parties who wanted to marry have deviated from the requirements of marriage law in a way that renders the marriage neither valid nor meets one of the grounds on which a marriage is stated to be void.

---

[49] *Attorney General v Akhter and Khan* [2020] EWCA Civ 122 (Key Case 2.2).
[50] *Hudson v Leigh* [2009] EWHC 1306 (Fam) [4] (Body J).

- A voidable marriage is a marriage that exists until one of the parties has obtained a decree of nullity. If they never do that, the marriage remains valid. The grounds of voidability tend to relate more closely to the characteristics of the parties than the grounds on which a marriage is automatically void from the start.

The situations that give rise to a void or voidable marriage are listed in the Matrimonial Causes Act 1973. Non-marriages created via non-qualifying ceremonies are a recently recognised category and not mentioned in statute.

It is important to understand the distinction between the three categories in order to be able to ascertain whether the marriage exists and what legal steps to take to recognise the position. Table 2.3 outlines the key features of each type. One key difference relates to the ability to apply for a financial settlement at the end of the marriage, which applies to valid, void, and voidable marriages, but not to non-marriages.

TABLE 2.3 The differences between void, voidable, and non-marriages

	Formation	Ending	Financial settlement on end?
Valid marriage or civil partnership	A ceremony which complies with the formalities and where the parties have capacity to marry. A civil partnership is an alternative to marriage and also requires capacity.	The normal divorce procedure (called dissolution for civil partners).	A claim for financial provision can be made on divorce or dissolution. For marriages including same-sex marriages, this is under Matrimonial Causes Act 1973. For civil partners it is under the Civil Partnership Act 2004.
Void marriage	A ceremony which either: 1. does not comply with the formalities and the consequence of that failure is listed in the 1973 Act as creating a void marriage; or 2. where the parties have not got the legal capacity to marry because they are within the prohibited degrees of relationship (s11(a) MCA 1973); one or both parties is aged under 16 (s11(a) MCA 1973); or one or both parties is already lawfully married (s11(b) MCA 1973). Any person can seek a declaration as to the status of the marriage.	There is no need to annul the marriage because there was no marriage—it was void *ab inito* (from the start). However, a declaration confirming this would be a good idea in case either party wanted to remarry or as evidence re tax, inheritance, etc.	Yes, but conduct by a party is one of the issues that courts can take into account when determining an appropriate financial settlement (see Chapter 4). A deliberate bigamist would get nothing, or much less than the innocent party.

Non-marriage	An event with marital qualities but which does not give rise to a valid marriage or a void one. Includes both non-qualifying ceremonies and situations where there was no intention to marry, such as acting a wedding scene in a play.	There is no need to annul the marriage because there was no marriage. However, a declaration confirming this would be a good idea.	No. There is nothing to hang a claim on.
Voidable marriage or civil partnership	A marriage which exists and is valid unless and until one of the parties seeks to annul it by virtue of 1. Non-consummation (wilful or incapable) (does not apply to same-sex couples) 2. Lack of consent—duress, mistake, lack of capacity 3. Mental disorder 4. Venereal disease (does not apply to same-sex couples) 5. Pregnancy by someone else 6. Transitioning legal gender	Seek a decree of nullity.	Yes.

In the next sections, we consider each of these categories in turn, identifying the differences between them.

2.6 Void marriages

A void marriage is one that, 'owing to the presence of an impediment at the time of the ceremony, will be regarded . . . as never having taken place'. The marriage is invalid from the start ('ab initio') because of a condition existing at the time of the ceremony.

STATUTORY EXTRACT *s11 Matrimonial Causes Act 1973*

Grounds on which a marriage is void:

A marriage celebrated after 31st July 1971, other than a marriage to which section 12A applies, shall be void on the following grounds only, that is to say—

(a) that it is not a valid marriage under the provisions of the Marriage Acts 1949 to 1986 (that is to say where—
  (i)   the parties are within the prohibited degrees of relationship;
  (ii) either party is under the age of sixteen; or
  (iii) the parties have intermarried in disregard of certain requirements as to the formation of marriage);
(b) that at the time of the marriage either party was already lawfully married or a civil partner . . .
(d) in the case of a polygamous marriage entered into outside England and Wales, that either party was at the time of the marriage domiciled in England and Wales.

For the purposes of paragraph (d) of this subsection a marriage is not polygamous if at its inception neither party has any spouse additional to the other.

While the requirements for a valid marriage are set out in the Marriage Act 1949, it is only those impediments set out in s11 Matrimonial Causes Act 1973 that cause a marriage to be void.

A further category, that the parties must be respectively male and female (s11(c) Matrimonial Causes Act 1973), was removed by the Marriage (Same-Sex Couples) Act 2013. The nullity grounds for civil partners and same-sex married couples are discussed at 2.14.1 and 2.15.1 respectively.

2.6.1 Prohibited degrees

If the parties are within the prohibited degrees of relationship, it means that they have a close blood relationship with one another ('consanguinity') or are related by marriage ('affinity'). Not all such relationships are prohibited, but a marriage to someone in specified categories is void.[51] The close blood relationships which are not permitted are those listed in Schedule 1 to the Marriage Act 1949: you cannot marry your parent or child, your sibling[52] or their child, your grandparent or grandchild, or a parent's sibling. Such limitations are easy to justify because of the risk of genetic defects in the couple's children as a result of their high degree of shared genetic material, although as Deech has pointed out, these also exist in cousin marriages, which are common among some ethnic and religious communities in England and entirely lawful.[53] You are also prohibited from marrying your adoptive parent or adoptive child, including those formerly in this category, notwithstanding the usual lack of a genetic tie. This implies a general moral queasiness about the conversion of a parenting relationship into a sexual one.

More distant still from genetic considerations are prohibitions on marrying someone who is related to you by marriage but with whom you share no blood tie. The origin of this lies with the ecclesiastic courts and their belief that marriage made a couple 'one flesh', something that the law reflected for centuries through the doctrine of coverture. It was therefore incestuous to have sexual relations with someone to whom you were related by marriage.[54] Gradually, such prohibitions have been removed, with the Deceased Wife's Sister's Marriage Act 1907 and the Deceased Brother's Widow's Marriage Act 1921 enabling one to marry the titular relation.[55] More recently, the European Court of Human Rights ruled that the prohibition on marrying one's parent-in-law breached Article 12, leading to the legalisation of such marriages.[56] The government had unsuccessfully sought

---

[51] Matrimonial Causes Act 1973 s11(a)(i) and ss3 and 49 Civil Partnership Act 2004.

[52] Sibling means brother, sister, half-brother or half-sister. Marriage Act 1949 Sch 1, Part 1, para 1(2).

[53] R Deech, 'Cousin Marriage' (2010) 40(June) *Family Law* 619. A number of countries prohibit cousin marriage; England and Wales do not.

[54] An example is *Wing v Taylor (Falsely calling herself Wing)* (1861) 2 Swabey & Tristram 278, in which the marriage was void because the groom's sexual relationship with the bride's mother prior to the marriage brought them within the degrees of affinity that applied at the time.

[55] The timing of the Deceased Brother's Widow's Marriage Act 1921 reflects the high number of widows after the First World War.

[56] The Marriage Act 1949 (Remedial) Order 2007 was passed in response to *B and L v UK* 36536/02; [2006] 1 FLR 35. Ms L was the former wife of Mr B's son. Schäfer notes that a personal Act of Parliament could already be used to circumvent this rule, and it was already alright if both former spouses had died and the parties were aged over 21. See Lawrence Schäfer, 'Marrying an In-Law? The Future of Prohibited Degrees of Affinity and Consanguinity in English Law', (2008) 20(2) *Child and Family Law Quarterly* 219.

to justify the prohibition on the basis that it prevented sexual rivalry within the family and protected children for whom the situation might be confusing.[57]

At the present time, there is only one affinity-based absolute prohibition remaining and that is marrying or entering into a civil partnership with a former stepchild or step-grandchild unless both parties are aged over 21 and the child/grandchild was never a 'child of the family', i.e., a child who lived in the same household and was treated as a child or grandchild of the person they are intending to marry.[58] It is therefore possible to marry a stepchild as long as you did not live with or parent them when they were a minor.

Remember that these are limitations on *marrying*. There are no legal limitations on cohabiting outside of marriage with someone within the prohibited degrees unless any sexual relations would also constitute criminal incest.

2.6.2 Aged under 16

While a marriage to a young person aged 16 or 17 is valid but requires certain consents (see section 2.4.1), a marriage by or to a child under 16 is void in England and Wales.[59] For the recognition of child marriages legally constituted abroad, see section 2.10.

2.6.3 Bigamy

It is not currently possible in England and Wales for a person to be married or civilly partnered to more than one other person at the same time. Any purported marriage that takes place in England or Wales when a party is already married or civilly partnered will therefore be void.[60] A party may also be liable to conviction for the criminal offences of making a false declaration about a marriage[61] or bigamy.[62]

However, it is possible for a polygamous marriage to be *recognised* in England and Wales, provided that the wedding was conducted in a country that permits polygamy and the parties to the marriage were domiciled[63] there at the time. It is therefore not possible for parties domiciled in England or Wales to go abroad to enter into a polygamous marriage; such a marriage would not be recognised in this country because they will not satisfy the domicile requirement.[64] This is discussed further at section 2.10.1.

Annulments on the basis of bigamy are rare these days, even among nullity cases. A survey of the few bigamy cases reported in recent years shows the particular risks associated with religious ceremonies, and/or weddings abroad, because of issues with the availability of records or difficulties in ascertaining whether a ceremony conducted abroad resulted in a valid marriage. *AAM v KG* involved a man with a wife and child in Bangladesh, although

---

[57] JM Scherpe, 'Should There Be Degrees of Prohibited Degrees?' (2006) 65(1) *Cambridge Law Journal* 32. The parties could still confuse the children by simply cohabiting without marrying.
[58] Marriage Act 1949 as amended by the Marriage (Prohibited Degrees of Relationship) Act 1986.
[59] Matrimonial Causes Act 1973 s11(a)(ii), Marriage Act 1949 s2, and Civil Partnership Act 2004 ss3 and 49.
[60] Matrimonial Causes Act 1973 s11(b) and Civil Partnership Act 2004 ss3 and 49.
[61] Contrary to Perjury Act 1911 s3.
[62] Offences against the Person Act 1961 s57.
[63] See section 2.10 for an explanation of domicile.
[64] Matrimonial Causes Act 1973 s11(d).

the evidence as to whether or not there was a marriage was very unclear. Nevertheless, the court found that he was already married at the time that he entered into a religious marriage in Wales.[65] *K v K (Nullity: Bigamous Marriage)* concerns a man who, while legally married, entered into a religious ceremony with another woman who did not know of the existing marriage. This second marriage was void.[66] Not all bigamy cases involve deliberate deception, however: the bigamist may well genuinely believe that a first marriage did not exist, as in *Fereshteh Azizi v Gholam Reza Aghaty.*[67]

2.6.4 Errors in the formalities

As we have seen, certain failures to comply with the law will render a marriage void even if they are 'innocent' breaches: marriage to someone aged under 16; bigamous/polygamous marriages; marriages within the prohibited degrees. One or both parties lack capacity to marry in these circumstances. However, sometimes, the parties make mistakes in the way that they have formed the marriage itself, such as by not holding the wedding in a building, or not obtaining a superintendent registrar's licence when this is needed. They have married 'in disregard of certain requirements as to the formation of marriage' set out in the Marriage Act 1949.[68] Failing to comply these formalities can also mean the marriage is void—but it depends on the type of mistake. Section 11 Matrimonial Causes Act says that a marriage will be void if it is not valid under the 1949 Act, but legislation does not define which requirements are 'certain requirements'.

Some breaches of marriage law will render a marriage void if both parties were aware of the defect at the time of the ceremony and thus 'knowingly and wilfully' breached the requirements. For example, a same-sex marriage will be void if the couple have 'knowingly and wilfully' had a religious ceremony without the relevant religious governing body approving the conduct of same-sex marriages.[69] If the parties marry under the Church of England, voiding breaches include knowingly and wilfully marrying without the banns being correctly read or a licence, or where the marriage is solemnised by someone not in Holy Orders.[70] Probert suggested that 'It remains an open question as to whether the parties must know that they have not complied with certain formalities, or whether they must also be aware that those formalities were necessary to a valid marriage'.[71] (Note that the requirement of 'knowingly and wilfully' is in the statute—the Court of Appeal decision in Key Case *Attorney General v Akhter and Khan* (see section 2.7) suggests that the parties' state of knowledge is, apart from this, irrelevant to the status of their marriage.)

Not all types of breach affect the validity of a marriage, even if the breach was 'knowing and wilful'. For example, the Marriage Act 1949 specifically states that the court will

---

[65] [2018] EWHC 283 (Fam).
[66] [2016] EWHC 3380 (Fam).
[67] [2016] EWHC 110 (Fam).
[68] Matrimonial Causes Act 1973 s11.
[69] Marriage Act 1949 s49A.
[70] Marriage Act 1949 s25.
[71] R Probert, 'When Are We Married? Void, Voidable, and Non-Existent Marriages' (2002) 22 *Legal Studies* 398, 400.

not hear evidence (and thus the marriage cannot be invalidated upon) the parties' failure to reside in the registration district, or them marrying in a place that was not a party's usual place of worship or which was not a certified place of worship at all, or lack of the necessary consent in the case of a person aged 16 or 17.[72] Such marriages will therefore be valid despite the breach. There are also some types of breaches that the legislation does not address, such as what happens if you do not have two witnesses or if the marriage is not registered. It appears that these will not affect the validity of the marriage.[73]

In some cases where the parties have made multiple mistakes of different types, a court has to untangle whether the 'marital event' has resulted in a valid marriage, a void marriage, or even, if the parties have really gone wrong, a non-qualifying ceremony that has resulted in a 'non-marriage'. The Civil Partnership Act is much clearer about this, as we see at 2.14.1.

2.6.5 Recognising the void status

Because the Matrimonial Causes Act 1973 says that marriages subject to any of these five impediments are void from the beginning, it is not necessary to take steps to annul them—there is nothing to annul. However, there are obvious practical reasons why one should obtain formal legal recognition of the void status, called a Declaration of Marital Status. One cannot, for example, seek to marry someone else and simply tell the registrar that the first marriage did not count. Outsiders will naturally assume that a wedding resulted in a marriage. It is therefore strongly advisable to obtain a declaration that the marriage was void at its inception. Such a declaration can be made by the court on an application by anyone who has sufficient interest in the matter, not merely one of the parties.[74]

2.7 Non-marriages and non-qualifying ceremonies

We saw in section 2.6.4 that even though the parties may have breached the formalities of a marriage, it is not in every case that the marriage will be void: some will nevertheless still be valid. However, there is yet another category. The law sets out the circumstances in which a marriage is valid, and the circumstances in which a marriage is void, but there are many ways in which a ceremony can be conducted which falls between these two categories and cannot be classified as either. This has led to the recognition by courts of a category (not mentioned in statute) of 'event[s] with marital qualities'[75] that do not form marriages at all, not even void ones. These are known as 'non-marriages' because they fall outside the requirements of a valid marriage set out in the Marriage Act 1949. 'It is clear from the logic—or lack of logic—of the Marriage Act 1949 that a concept of non-marriage

---

[72] The full list is contained in Marriage Act 1949 s48. Note however that this does not include Church of England: a same-sex marriage purporting to be according to the rites of the Church of England would be void. Note also that a civil partnership requires parental consent if aged 16 or 17 but failure to get this appears to render the marriage void, unlike in the case of a marriage. See ss4 and 49 Civil Partnership Act 2004.

[73] *Wing v Taylor (Falsely calling herself Wing)* (1861) 2 Swabey & Tristram 278.

[74] Cf a voidable marriage which requires an application by one of the parties.

[75] *Hudson v Leigh* [2009] EWHC 1306 (Fam) [4] (Body J).

is necessary, since a marriage conducted outside the framework of the Act can be neither void nor valid.'[76]

As Hughes J said in *A-M v A-M*:

> Plainly it is not every event to which somebody seeks to apply for 'marriage' which is within the section . . . A clear example of what would be outside it might be a staged dramatic marriage 'ceremony' conducted in a play or in the course of a television soap opera. Another might be the exchange of promises between small children. The same would apply, as it seems to me, to 'alternative marriage' rights consciously and deliberately conducted altogether outside the Marriage Acts and never intended or believed to create any recognisable marriage.[77]

While the classic example of a non-marriage is two actors acting out a wedding on stage, there many cases, usually but not always involving religious minority groups, who have taken part in a marriage-like event that is neither void nor valid. In *Attorney General v Akhter and Khan*, the courts preferred the term 'non qualifying ceremony' to describe these situations, considering that the term non-marriage is a 'negative and potentially insulting term' for an event that presumably had meaning to the parties.[78]

Accepting, as many judges have done, that a category of non-marriages exists, the harder issue is distinguishing between non-marriages and void marriages. What does each look like? This is particularly difficult because of the structure of the Marriage Act 1949 and the myriad ways in which parties may fall outside of it. 'Such is the ingenuity of human beings that we will always be able to come up with some sort of ritual or happening which one party claims created a marriage, but which the other says fell short of doing so.'[79] One judge has remarked that the distinction between the two categories 'may seem artificial and elusive to the uninitiated'.[80] Moreover, it can be hard to reconcile the reasoning in some cases with the reasoning in others.[81] We can see this by comparing two cases.

- *Gereis v Yagoub*[82] is a case in which the parties had 'married' in a Coptic Orthodox Christian church. They had not notified the register office and therefore had no licence, the church was not registered for the solemnisation of marriages, and the priest was not an authorised celebrant. The priest testified that he had advised the parties to have a civil ceremony as well (which would have created a valid marriage) but there were difficulties with their booking at the register office and they did not end up doing so. The parties had 'knowingly and wilfully' intermarried without complying with the relevant requirements, so there was no valid marriage: the issue was whether there was a void marriage or whether there was a non-marriage. The judge held that the

---

[76] R Probert, 'When Are We Married? Void, Voidable, and Non-Existent Marriages' (2002) 22 *Legal Studies* 398, 402.

[77] [2001] 2 FLR 6 [55].

[78] [2018] EWFC 54 at [8] (Williams J), that statement approved by the Court of Appeal [2020] EWCA Civ 122 at [7] (Sir Terence Etherton MR, King and Moylan LJJ).

[79] *Hudson v Leigh* [2009] EWHC 1306 (Fam) [70] (Body J).

[80] *Gandhi v Patel* [2001] All ER (D) 436 (Park J).

[81] See V Le Grice QC, 'A Critique of Non-Marriage' [2013, October] *Family Law* 1278.

[82] [1997] 1 FLR 854.

ceremony had 'the hallmarks of an ordinary Christian marriage and that both parties treated it as such, at least to the extent that they cohabited after it, whereas they
had not before, that they had sexual intercourse, which they had not before, and that
the respondent had claimed married man's tax allowance, which he had not before.
[Moreover], those who attended the ceremony clearly assumed that they were attending an ordinary Christian marriage, . . . and that what happened gave all the appearance of and had the hallmarks of a marriage that would be recognized as a marriage
but for the requirements of the Marriage Act.' Accordingly, it was a void marriage, not
a non-marriage.

- In *Gandhi v Patel*, the husband and wife held a Hindu marriage ceremony in an Indian
restaurant in England.[83] The ceremony was conducted by a Brahmin priest, and was
conducted according to the religious requirements of Hinduism but did not comply
with the Marriage Act 1949 in relation to location, celebrant, or registration, and the
judge was sceptical of the wife's claims not to know that some formalities were required for a valid marriage to be created. Moreover, the husband was already married
to someone else, and that marriage had not been dissolved. This was a non-marriage.

In each case there was no licence, no registered venue, and no authorised celebrant, and
both cases involved parties who 'knowingly and wilfully' married in breach of the formalities. However, one was held to be void and the other a non-marriage. Is the difference in
treatment the result of the degree to which the event resembled, on the surface, a wedding,

KEY CASE *Hudson v Leigh* [2009] EWHC 1306 (Fam)

Miss Hudson was a devout Christian and Mr Leigh described himself as an 'atheist Jew'. She would
not consider herself married without a church wedding and he would not consider himself married
without a register office wedding. While living in South Africa, the parties (who were English) asked
the minister of Miss Hudson's church to conduct a religious ceremony on the roof terrace of Mr
Leigh's Cape Town home (avoiding a church). Although the ceremony included multiple references
to 'marriage' and the parties took one another as 'husband' and 'wife', by agreement, the minister
had omitted the words 'no lawful impediment', 'your lawful wife', 'your lawful husband', and 'have
been lawfully married' from the ceremony. They had also, in Miss Hudson's words, 'consciously
failed to comply with certain formalities which are usually required for a marriage to take place'
under South African law and intended to have a register office ceremony once they were back in
England. Unfortunately, the parties separated before the intended English register office wedding
could take place, leaving open the issue of whether the rooftop ceremony was a valid marriage (Miss
Hudson's initial but optimistic position), a void marriage (Miss Hudson's alternative position), or a
non-marriage (Mr Leigh's position).

Body J reviewed the previous case law, including *Gereis v Yagoub* and *Gandhi v Patel*, and suggested that 'questionable ceremonies should . . . be addressed on a case by case basis', taking
account of:

- whether the ceremony or event set out or purported to be a lawful marriage;
- whether it bore all or enough of the hallmarks of marriage;

[83] [2001] All ER (D) 436.

- whether the three key participants (most especially the officiating official) believed, intended and understood the ceremony as giving rise to the status of lawful marriage; and
- the reasonable perceptions, understandings and beliefs of those in attendance. In most if not all reasonably foreseeable situations, a review of these and similar considerations should enable a decision to be satisfactorily reached.[84]

Accordingly, he held that in this case there was a non-marriage, and a declaration that the ceremony did not create the status of marriage between the parties was made.

with one in a church and the other a restaurant? Was the fact that one was Christian and one not influential (it should not be)? Or was it about the way in which the parties had treated the event—their intentions? In *Hudson v Leigh*, the judge had to reconcile the different approaches that had been taken to date and came up with a list of four factors that, although not exhaustive, would assist a judge in identifying whether the event was a non-marriage or a void one.

It appeared following *Hudson v Leigh* that whether the parties have a void marriage or a non-marriage was a combination of intention and appearance. The less firm the intentions of the parties and their celebrant and the fewer the hallmarks of a marriage ceremony, the more likely it was that there was a non-marriage rather than a void marriage.

But what was the position if the parties intended to conduct a valid marriage but did not succeed? Given the recognition of intention in *Hudson v Leigh*, was intention alone enough to bring the marriage into the category of void, rather than non-marriage? *El Gamal v Al-Maktoum*, heard after *Hudson* by the same judge, held that it was not. While 'intention is relevant to the status achieved or not achieved by a questionable ceremony', if the ceremony makes no attempt to comply with the Marriage Act then their intentions are not sufficient to bring the marriage within the Marriage Act and thereby render it void rather than a non-marriage.[85]

However, this line of cases focused on intention was brought to an abrupt reversal by the Court of Appeal in our next Key Case, *Attorney General v Akhter and Khan*.

KEY CASE *Attorney General v Akhter and Khan* [2020] EWCA Civ 122, *known at first instance as* NA v MSK [2018] EWFC 54

Nasreen Akhter and Mohammed Khan underwent an Islamic marriage ceremony at a restaurant in London in 1998. They were both aware at the time that this did not create a valid English marriage, because the imam had told them. Williams J, the judge at first instance, found that they had intended to have a register office ceremony at a later time and that Ms Akhter repeatedly raised the need for this over a number of years with Mr Khan and he refused to do so. The parties had four children and separated in 2016. The husband argued that there was a non-marriage because s11 Matrimonial Causes Act sets out the circumstances in which a marriage will be void (see 2.6) and this situation did not meet those criteria. The wife argued that the marriage should be treated as void on the ground

---

[84] *Hudson v Leigh* [2009] EWHC 1306 [79] (Fam).
[85] *El Gamal v Al-Maktoum* [2012] 2 FLR 387, 394, 395 (Bodey J).

that it was a marriage entered into in disregard of certain requirements as to the formation of marriage, and that to hold that it was a non-marriage would infringe her human rights.

The first instance judgment

Williams J considered the factors mentioned in *Hudson v Leigh*. He found that the parties had been 'embarking on a process which was intended to include a civil ceremony in which the marriage would be registered', and that the ceremony 'bore all the hallmarks of a marriage in that it was held in public, witnessed, officiated by an imam, involved the making of promises and confirmation that both the husband and wife were eligible to marry'.

While rejecting most of the rights arguments, he nevertheless considered that 'in respect of those who sought to effect or intended to effect a legal marriage . . . Article 8 supports an approach to interpretation and application which the finding of a decree of a void marriage rather than a wholly invalid marriage'. Describing his approach as 'a slightly more flexible interpretation . . . informed by fundamental rights arguments', he therefore held that the marriage was void, rather than a non-marriage.[86] It is, however, hard to reconcile this decision with its predecessors given that the imam, the parties, and their families were aware that the ceremony would not create a lawful marriage.

The appeal judgment

The Attorney General[87] appealed. The Court of Appeal (Sir Terence Etherton MR, King and Moylan LJJ) held that the ceremony had not created a void marriage because it was a 'non-qualifying ceremony'. Accordingly, no decree of nullity could be granted.

The ceremony was defective in a number of ways—it took place in a building not registered for marriages, there had been no notice given at the register office and there was no superintendent registrar's certificate, and no authorised person was present. Whether a ceremony created a valid or void marriage was to be determined at the time, and could not fluctuate depending on factors such as whether the parties had children. To adopt the approach taken by Williams J would 'fundamentally undermine the need for the parties and the state to know, as from the date of the ceremony, whether the parties are or are not validly married'.

The fact that the parties intended to marry and intended to undertake a civil ceremony later had no effect on the status of the ceremony actually undertaken. 'The parties' intentions cannot change what would otherwise be a non-qualifying ceremony into one which is within the scope of the 1949 Act. Their intentions provide no legal justification for changing the effect of the only ceremony which in fact took place.'

The effect of the Court of Appeal's decision is that any ceremony that does not create a valid marriage but which does not fulfil the criteria to be void as set down in the 1973 Act will be non-qualifying and give rise to a non-marriage. The degree to which it resembles a marriage and the parties' intentions cannot turn it into a void marriage, let alone a valid one.

2.7.1 Consequences of the difference between void and non-marriages

You may wonder why the parties to these Key Cases are arguing about the distinction between a void marriage and a non-marriage, particularly when they both accept that the marriage is certainly not valid. The reason is financial: parties to a void marriage can still

---

[86] [2018] EWFC 54 [80] (Williams J).
[87] The Chief Legal Adviser to the Crown, who is a member of Parliament.

make financial remedy claims against one another, whereas the parties to a non-marriage cannot. A financial remedy claim is a claim for financial provision—a share of the parties' assets. This incentivises the financially weaker party to claim that there is a void marriage and the wealthier to claim that there is a non-marriage. This means that Ms Akhter and others in her position can avail herself of no financial remedies on the end of the relationship other than those available to cohabitants or those who are co-parents (which are very much less generous) and (for groups that use dowries) perhaps a claim for breach of contract for return of dowry.[88] Had the marriage been void, she would have the same rights as on divorce.

It may seem odd that a party is entitled to make a financial remedy claim for a marriage that was void from the start. As Ruth Deech has pointed out, however, even in the case of a void marriage 'expectations have been created on the part of the "spouses" and before the world: they have elected to take on themselves as far as possible the legal consequences of marriage even though they may not in fact have been free to marry'.[89] Moreover, some parties to void marriages will be entirely innocent of wrongdoing. Jerry Hall and Mick Jagger apparently did not realise that their marriage, around a campfire in Bali, was not valid under Balinese law until they sought legal advice twenty years and four children later; she received a substantial settlement.

In other cases, however, there may be wrongdoing. A knowing bigamist, for example, is likely to find their settlement reduced or refused entirely. This is because under s25(2)(g) Matrimonial Causes Act 1973, the court can take serious misconduct into account in making a financial remedy order.[90] There is also a public policy argument that a person should not benefit from their own crimes. In *Whiston v Whiston* the Court of Appeal stated that 'since bigamy was a crime which undermined fundamental notions of monogamous marriage, the court would not as a matter of public policy entertain an application for financial relief'.[91] This does not apply to innocent parties to the marriage or someone who did not know they were already married.

SCENARIO 3

Illustration 2: Raheem and Fatima

We can now see the consequences for Raheem and Fatima of their marriage potentially being invalid, which is that the marriage would be either void or a non-marriage. If they split up, the financially weaker of them—statistically the woman, especially if they have children—will be in a precarious position as the court will not be able to make a financial remedy order, i.e., share the other person's assets. They will be in a position no different to that of cohabitants.

---

[88] For a discussion of cohabitants' remedies, see Chapter 5 and for financial support for children, see Chapter 6.
[89] R Deech, 'The Case against Legal Recognition of Cohabitation' (1980) 29(2/3) *The International and Comparative Law Quarterly* 480, 484.
[90] See Chapter 4.
[91] [1995] Fam 198.

FOCUS Think Critically

The disproportionate effect on Islamic marriages

You may have noticed that these cases involve parties from minority religious groups. The problems surrounding the invalidity of marriages that fail to meet the formalities disproportionately affect minority groups. In particular, a significant proportion of ceremonies that have been held to be non-qualifying, i.e., giving rise to non-marriages (as opposed to void marriages) involve Muslims, perhaps because it can be common for Muslims to marry in hotels or their homes rather than at mosques, and perhaps because only a few mosques have been licensed for marriage.[92] In *Attorney General v Akhter and Khan*, Williams J felt that there were:

> cases where the application of the term 'non-marriage' seems inapt and indeed pejorative. The parties may have undergone a public marriage ceremony conducted by an official, witnessed by others, in which they confirmed there was no impediment to them marrying, that they consented and that they committed themselves to each other which they, their family and communities accepted led to them being married. They may have lived a married life and been accepted as married by their communities and the state. They may have had children. To all intents and purposes, they have been married. To characterise all of that as a non-marriage in law feels instinctively uncomfortable in 2018 and might rightly be regarded as insulting by many (although not all) of the participants.[93]

The Court of Appeal in fact agreed with this part of his judgment, which is why they adopted the phrase 'non-qualifying ceremony' even as they stripped Ms Akhter's financial security from her.

Like Ms Akhter, some participants in non-qualifying ceremonies are aware that the ceremonies do not form a lawful marriage. Academic Rajnaara Akhtar has found that while a number of Muslim couples intended to follow their religious ceremony with one that was legally valid, they simply had not got around to it.[94] Others thought that a legally valid ceremony was not needed, although the study does not say whether this was because they thought they had equivalent rights, or whether they did not seek those rights. There is also a risk that one party to a non-qualifying ceremony will have intended that the other obtain no legal rights, unbeknownst to their purported spouse, or as in *Akhter*, refuse to progress to a civil ceremony as a form of leverage. The Muslim Marriages Working Group thought that young Muslims were less likely to register their marriages than previous generations and may consider religious marriages to be 'an experimental union of partners not ready for [legally binding] commitment . . . as testing out the relationship'.[95] This implies that some people are entering into religious marriages that they actually intend to be legally invalid. Indeed, Akhtar argues that this reflects a 'process of transition from one set of cultural norms to another . . . towards the widely accepted cultural norm of cohabitation'.[96]

The lack of financial remedies available at the end of a non-marriage other than those usually available to cohabitants affects the economically weaker member of the couple more seriously, and that is usually the woman. Le Grice, who was Ms Akhter's barrister, argues that '[t]here is no reason why the woman should suffer because she, as a matter of personal autonomy, elected to marry in a

---

[92] F Read, 'Non-Recognition of Islamic Marriages in England and Wales' [2012, November] *International Family Law* 452, 452.

[93] [2018] EWFC 54 [8] (Williams J).

[94] RC Akhtar, 'Unregistered Muslim Marriages: An Emerging Culture of Celebrating Rites and Conceding Rights' in J Miles, P Mody, and R Probert, *Marriage Rites and Rights* (Bloomsbury 2015).

[95] Muslim Marriages Working Group, *Submission and Final Report* (2012) 4.

[96] RC Akhtar, 'Modern Traditions in Muslim Marriage Practices, Exploring English Narratives' (2018) *Oxford Journal of Law and Religion* 1.

manner which reflected the belief system of herself and the man to whom she, as a matter of personal autonomy, considered herself to be married'.[97] For him, the current interpretation of the law breaches the human rights of the parties.[98] He argues that the failure of the law to treat all religions and denominations equally is a form of religious discrimination that could be avoided by reforming the requirements of a valid marriage, or even, as the Siddiqui Review suggested, launching a publicity campaign emphasising the need for a parallel secular ceremony, or making the celebrant legally responsible for ensuring validity.[99] Increased criminal sanctions have even been suggested.[100] *Akhter* demonstrates a need for legislative reform.[101]

2.7.2 Reforming the formalities

You may well have formed the view that the current law is not particularly clear. Even in 1973 the Law Commission thought that the law fell 'woefully short. . . particularly perhaps as regards simplicity and intelligibility',[102] but felt that the Church would oppose the simplest solution, which was to require everyone to marry through a civil ceremony.[103] From 1994, the locations at which marriages could take place was widened so that the parties could hold a civil ceremony in approved premises and not merely in a register office.[104] In 2002, the government put forward proposals to remove the remaining restrictions on the location of a wedding, but these proposals were abandoned.[105] Nevertheless, parties can now marry in a wide range of places, by different types of celebrant. The piecemeal nature of the reforms since 1949 and the different treatment of different religious groups has increased the potential for confusion. As Rebecca Probert has argued, 'Given the diversity of routes to a valid marriage that now exist, it can no longer be assumed that there is sufficient knowledge of the legal requirements for the formation of a valid marriage for those in attendance to be able to distinguish between marriages that comply with the law and those that do not.'[106] In our more diverse society there is 'much more scope for genuine misunderstanding'.[107] A purported marriage could be void or voidable or a non-marriage

---

[97] V Le Grice QC, 'A Critique of Non-Marriage' [2013, October] *Family Law* 1278, 1285. Le Grice acted in a number of these cases, including *Akhter*.

[98] See Le Grice's submissions in *Akhter*, where he references Articles 6, 8, 12, and 14, European Convention on Human Rights, Art 1 of Protocol 1 to the ECHR, Article 3 UN Convention on the Rights of the Child, and Article 16 UN Convention on the Elimination of all Forms of Discrimination Against Women.

[99] M Siddiqui, *The Independent Review into the Application of Sharia Law in England and Wales* (Cm 9560, 2018).

[100] See R Probert, 'Criminalising Non-Compliance with Marriage Formalities?' [2018] *Family Law* 702 for a discussion of the limited existing sanctions.

[101] R Sandberg, 'Farewell, "Flexible" Fudge". The position of unregistered religious marriages returns to square one' (Law and Religion blog 25 February 2020). Available at https://www.lawandreligionuk.com/2020/02/25/farewell-flexible-fudge-the-position-of-unregistered-religious-marriages-returns-to-square-one/ accessed 30 August 2020.

[102] S Cretney, *Family Law in the Twentieth Century: A History* (OUP 2003) 26.

[103] J Eekelaar, 'Marriage: A Modest Proposal' [2013, January] *Family Law* 83.

[104] Marriage Act 1994, which was introduced by Giles Brandreth MP as a private member's bill.

[105] HM Government, *Civil Registration: Vital Change: Birth, Marriage and Death Registration in the 21st Century* (Cm 5355, 2002).

[106] R Probert, '*Hayatleh v Modfy*: Presuming the Validity of a Known Ceremony of Marriage' [2018] *Child and Family Law Quarterly* 61, 69.

[107] R Probert, 'The Evolving Concept of "Non-Marriage"' (2013) 25(3) *Child and Family Law Quarterly* 314, 316.

or even, despite the breach, valid: the Marriage Act 1949 lays down what should happen, but the Matrimonial Causes Act 1979 gives us the consequences of only certain breaches. Despite evidence that a failure to comply with the formalities can be deliberate in some cases in order to avoid the consequences of marriage, we cannot assume that all parties enter into such arrangements with their eyes open.

'The most direct way in which the civil recognition of Muslim [and other religious minority] marriages could be better ensured would undoubtedly involve reform of the Marriage Act.'[108] In 2014, the government asked the Law Commission to identify the issues that needed to be addressed in order to reform marriage law. Unfortunately, despite having asked for this work to be done, the government's response to the Law Commission's scoping report was to indicate that other types of family law reform were a higher legislative priority.[109]

Nevertheless, in September 2019, the Law Commission released a consultation paper containing a set of proposals to reform wedding ceremonies.[110] The outcome of this consultation is yet to be established at the time of writing, but the paper makes a number of suggestions as to what reform could look like. The most important reforms relate to the location of weddings, those who can conduct lawful ceremonies, and the effects of non-compliance.

The scheme is based upon the regulation of the person officiating the wedding, rather than, as now, a mix of officiant, venue, and content. Couples who wanted to marry would need to lodge notice and wait a statutory period, as they do now, and at the end of this would receive a schedule (like a marriage licence) which authorises them to marry within a specific period.

All ceremonies would need to take place in the presence of one authorised officiant. That could be, as now, a local authority registrar or a religious leader, but it would be widened to include officiants of 'non-religious belief organisations' such as humanism, and trained independent celebrants. The officiant would not need to conduct the ceremony but has to ensure compliance with the requirement of two witnesses, consent to the marriage, and the signing of the schedule. The officiant would need to uphold the dignity and solemnity of the marriage, but the ceremony could otherwise take whatever form the parties wanted (or their religious faith, if any, required). Religious content could be included in otherwise secular ceremonies.

During the ceremony each party would be required to express their consent to the marriage and the marriage would be formed when the parties expressed this consent (compare this to the current requirements for civil partnerships, which are formed on the signing of the register). Marriages would still need to be registered for record-keeping purposes.

Tighter regulation of officiants would mean that the location of the ceremony within England or Wales would not matter. People would be able to marry in gardens, on beaches, and in other outside spaces, and venues would not need to be authorised and could even include private homes and cruise ships that have their home port in England or Wales.

---

[108] K O'Sullivan and L Jackson, 'Muslim Marriage (Non) Recognition: Implications and Possible Solutions (2017) 39(1) *Journal of Social Welfare and Family Law* 22, 32.

[109] For the scoping paper and government response, see https://www.lawcom.gov.uk/project/marriage-law/ accessed 11 August 2018.

[110] Law Commission, *Getting Married: A Consultation on Wedding Law* (Consultation Paper 247, 3 September 2020). Available at https://www.lawcom.gov.uk/project/weddings/ accessed 28 September 2020.

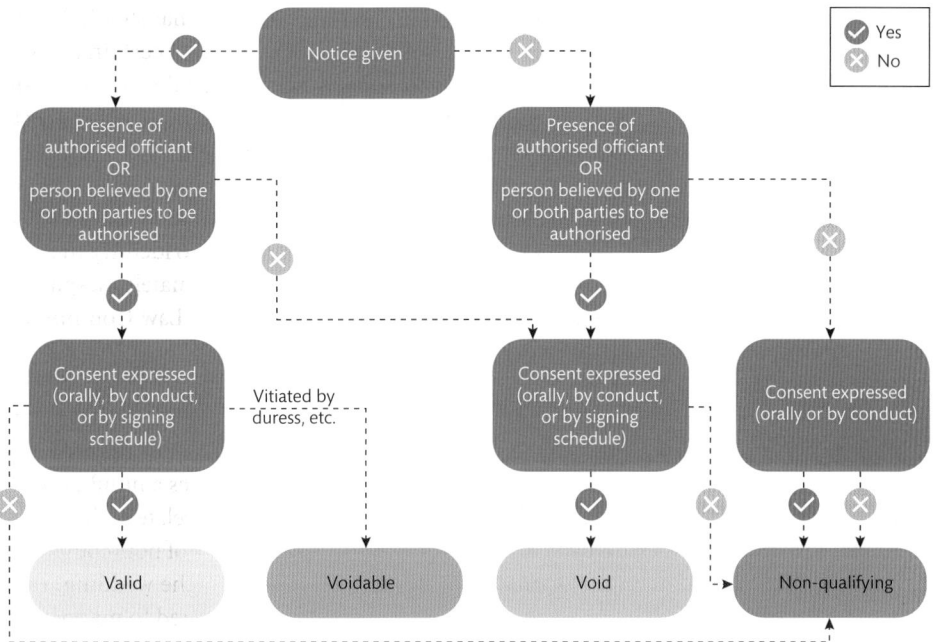

FIGURE 2.2 **Effect of (non)compliance on validity of marriage**

Source: Appendix 6 to Law Commission, *Getting Married: A Consultation on Wedding Law* (Consultation Paper 247, 3 September 2020).

A breach by the officiant of their obligations simply results in the officiant being sanctioned. Only a small number of breaches would affect the validity of the marriage, and these are set out in Figure 2.2, which is taken from the Law Commission's proposal document. These would be the requirement to give notice and obtain a schedule; and that the parties consent (this still being fundamental to a marriage). A marriage would be valid if the couple gave notice and consented to be married in the presence of an officiant or a person who at least one of them believed to be an officiant. The marriage would be void (rather than non-qualifying) if the couple did not give notice, even if they still consented to be married.

These proposals, if accepted, would harmonise almost all weddings irrespective of religion or belief status. As such, there would be much less scope for people to find themselves in non-qualifying ceremonies, although the Law Commission points out that reform of the law relating to cohabitation would enable those currently caught in non-qualifying ceremonies to be protected too.

2.8 **Voidable marriages**

A voidable marriage is one that is valid until it is annulled on specific grounds provided by s12 Matrimonial Causes Act 1973. The court will issue a decree of nullity.

A voidable marriage is therefore different from a void marriage or a non-marriage, in that voidable marriages exist unless and until they are annulled whereas void marriages and non-marriages never existed.[111] The distinction can be important. In *Ward v Secretary of State*, the widow of an army officer remarried and as a result stopped receiving the survivor's benefit of the officer's pension.[112] Even though her subsequent marriage was annulled, she was unable to resume receipt of the pension because the second marriage was voidable not void and thus had existed up to the point of annulment. In *Wiggins v Wiggins*, the wife entered into a second marriage while awaiting the annulment of her first. As the first marriage was voidable and not void *ab initio*, it existed at the point she entered into her second marriage. She had therefore committed bigamy.[113]

The grounds on which a marriage is voidable under s12 Matrimonial Causes Act tend to relate either to physical or mental capacity to marry or some other fundamental issue which is more personal to the parties than those that render a marriage void.

STATUTORY EXTRACT *ss12 and 12A Matrimonial Causes Act 1973*

12 Grounds on which a marriage is voidable

(1) A marriage celebrated after 31st July 1971, other than a marriage to which section 12A applies, shall be voidable on the following grounds only, that is to say—
  (a) that the marriage has not been consummated owing to the incapacity of either party to consummate it;
  (b) that the marriage has not been consummated owing to the wilful refusal of the respondent to consummate it;
  (c) that either party to the marriage did not validly consent to it, whether in consequence of duress, mistake, unsoundness of mind, or otherwise;
  (d) that at the time of the marriage either party, though capable of giving a valid consent, was suffering (whether continuously or intermittently) from mental disorder within the meaning of the Mental Health Act 1983 of such a kind or to such an extent as to be unfitted for marriage;
  (e) that at the time of the marriage the respondent was suffering from venereal disease in a communicable form;
  (f) that at the time of the marriage the respondent was pregnant by some person other than the petitioner;
  (g) that an interim gender recognition certificate under the Gender Recognition Act 2004 has, after the time of the marriage, been issued to either party to the marriage;
  (h) that the respondent is a person whose gender at the time of the marriage had become the acquired gender under the Gender Recognition Act 2004.
(2) Paragraphs (a) and (b) of subsection (1) do not apply to the marriage of a same sex couple.

12A Grounds on which a marriage converted from a civil partnership is void or voidable

(1) This section applies to a marriage which has been converted, or is purported to have been converted, from a civil partnership under section 9 of the [Marriage (Same Sex Couples) Act 2013] and regulations made under that section.
(2) A marriage which results from the purported conversion of a void civil partnership is void.

---

[111] In the case of marriages conducted after 31 July 1971 (the Matrimonial Causes Act 1973 consolidated and re-enacted the relevant sections from the Nullity of Marriage Act 1971).
[112] [1990] 1 FLR 119.
[113] [1958] 1 WLR 1013.

> (3) A marriage which results from the conversion of a civil partnership is voidable if any of paragraphs (c) to (h) of section 12(1) applied at the date from which the marriage is treated as having subsisted in accordance with section 9(6) of the 2013 Act.

An application for annulment has to be made by one of the parties to the marriage, unlike a void marriage where the application can be made by any interested party. This reflects the fact that voidable grounds are more closely related to the personal interests of the parties than social or public policy reasons. It also means that the marriage cannot be annulled after the death of the parties.

2.8.1 Inability to consummate

The first occasion of intercourse within a marriage is called 'consummating the marriage'. It is possible for one party to seek to annul the marriage because the other party is not able to have sexual intercourse with them. The first ground of nullity, therefore, is that the marriage has not been consummated owing to the incapacity of either party to consummate it.[114] Consummation refers to penetrative sexual intercourse, requiring a penis and a vagina, and thus is not a ground available to same-sex couples.[115]

In the days when many people would be virgins on marriage, the capacity of a person to have sex would not be known until after marriage. In order to count as consummation, the intercourse must be 'ordinary and complete', not 'partial and imperfect':[116] this requires full penetration but not necessarily ejaculation.[117] It is irrelevant whether the parties had sex before they married, or whether they engage or engaged in other forms of sexual activity. What matters is whether there has been at least one occasion of 'complete' intercourse after the parties were married, even if it never occurs again and irrespective of whether the parties used a condom[118] or are capable of conceiving children.[119] Indeed, as Herring has pointed out, 'the act is described entirely in physical terms with no response required from the wife. It privileges heterosexual relations and a particular form of heterosexual activity'.[120]

Where one or both parties is incapable of 'ordinary and complete' intercourse, the marriage can be annulled on an application by either of them. A justification for annulment on the ground of non-consummation is given by Dr Lushington, the judge in the ecclesiastical case *D-E v A-G* (1844):

> I apprehend that we are all agreed that, in order to constitute the marriage bond between young persons, there must be the power, present or to come, of sexual intercourse. Without

---

[114] s12 (1)(a) Matrimonial Causes Act 1973.

[115] Although same-sex married couples and civil partners cannot meet the definition of consummation, the Civil Partnership Act 2004 does not mention consummation as a ground of nullity anyway. The Marriage (Same-Sex Couples) Act 2013 specifically says that consummation (wilful or incapable) does not apply: see Sch 4 Pt 3.

[116] *D-E v A-G* also known as *D v A* (1844) 163 ER 1039, 1045 (Dr Lushington).

[117] *Cackett v Cackett* [1950] P 253, in which the husband, contrary to the wishes of the wife, used the withdrawal method.

[118] *Baxter v Baxter* [1948] AC 274 (HL).

[119] *D-E v A-G* also known as *D v A* (1844) 163 ER 1039, 1045 (Dr Lushington).

[120] J Herring, 'Why Marriage Needs to Be Less Sexy', in J Miles, P Mody, and R Probert (eds), *Marriage Rites and Rights* (Bloomsbury 2015) 280.

that power neither of two principal ends of matrimony can be attained, namely, a lawful indulgence of the passions to prevent licentiousness, and the procreation of children, according to the evident design of Divine Providence.[121]

The Matrimonial Causes Act 1937 put this ground on a statutory footing.[122] It is now found in s12(1)(a) Matrimonial Causes Act 1973. The Law Commission report on nullity that preceded this Act recommended the retention of non-consummation as a ground of nullity, on the basis that to the Church impotence vitiated consent to the marriage because consent to marriage was taken to include consent to sex with one's spouse.[123] It is questionable whether such a view would, or should, prevail today, centring as it does the heterosexual penetrative act within the marriage.

Consummation is not a ground for annulling a same-sex marriage or civil partnership. It is unclear whether a trans woman in a different-sex relationship is capable in law of consummating a marriage if she has a surgically constructed vagina, or, conversely, whether a trans man is capable of consummation with a surgically constructed penis. In *SY v SY* the wife, who was not transgender, could consummate the marriage only because her vaginal canal had been enlarged through surgery; this was, nonetheless, consummation.[124] Had she refused to undertake that surgery, there would have been an inability to consummate (rather than a wilful refusal).[125] However, in *Corbett v Corbett*, which concerned a trans woman, Ormrod J referred to intercourse with a surgically constructed vagina as 'the reverse of ordinary, and in no sense natural',[126] thus taking it outside the definition of 'ordinary and complete' from *D-E v A-G*.[127] This suggests that courts may distinguish between natural vaginal canals which have an uncommon formation and those constructed entirely through surgery. Given recent legal reforms such as the Gender Recognition Act 2004, however, it may be that a court today would rule that consummation with a trans individual had occurred where penetration had. However, there have been no more recent cases which could demonstrate a change in attitude, possibly reflecting the general decline in the number of nullity suits.

2.8.2 Refusal to consummate

While physically capable, a party may not wish to have sexual intercourse with their spouse. Prior to 1937, this was not a basis on which a marriage could be annulled, whether under ecclesiastical or secular law, although it was a defence to a petition for restitution of conjugal rights and could form evidence of incapacity.[128] However, since then, it has

---

[121] *D-E v A-G* also known as *D v A* (1844) 163 ER 1039, 1045 (Dr Lushington).

[122] J Jackson, 'Consent of the Parties to Their Marriage', (1951) 14(1) *Modern Law Review* 1, 17.

[123] Law Commission, *Family Law: Report on Nullity of Marriage* (Law Com No 33 1970) para 24. While capacity to marry does include capacity for sexual relations, consent to marriage is no longer considered consent to sex: see *R v R* [1991] UKHL 12.

[124] [1963] P 37.

[125] *S v S* [1956] P 1.

[126] *Corbett v Corbett (otherwise Ashley)* [1971] P 83, 105. Ormrod J thought that the judge's comments in *SY* should be considered obiter.

[127] See R Probert, 'How would *Corbett v Corbett* be decided today?' (2005) 35 *Family Law* 382 and A Sharpe, *Transgender Jurisprudence: Dysphoric Bodies of Law* (Routledge 2002).

[128] A Borkowski, 'Wilful Refusal to Consummate: "Just Excuse"', [1994] *Family Law* 684, 684.

been possible to annul a marriage on the ground that the respondent (the other party) has wilfully refused to consummate the marriage.[129] This ground applies to different-sex marriages only—but it does depend on the circumstances surrounding the refusal, and not all refusals will justify an annulment. In *Horton v Horton* the House of Lords held that wilful 'connoted a settled and definite decision arrived at without just excuse'.[130] It therefore follows that if the refusing party has a 'just excuse' for refusing intercourse the ground is not made out. Such a situation arose in *Jodla v Jodla*, where the wife would not consummate the marriage unless and until their register office ceremony was, as the husband had promised, followed by a Catholic ceremony.[131] 'By his refusal to proceed with the church ceremony, the necessity for which as a pre-condition to matrimonial cohabitation was understood by both, the husband in the particular circumstances of this case, made it impossible for the wife, with a good conscience, to live with him as husband and wife, and this refusal, or this failure to proceed with the church ceremony, was, in this case, a just excuse for her to refuse sexual intercourse.'[132]

In determining whether there has been a settled and definite decision, the judge should have regard to the whole history of the marriage. This includes whether the request for intercourse was made with 'such tact persuasion and encouragement as an ordinary [spouse] would use in the circumstances': 'He must show that he himself has acted as a reasonable man would have acted with a view to overcoming his wife's reluctance before he can successfully assert wilful refusal by her.'[133]

SCENARIO 3

Illustration 3: Raheem and Fatima

Fatima is concerned because Raheem will not have sexual relations with her. In fact, all the law is concerned with is one type of sexual relation—penetrative intercourse. Fatima and Raheem could engage in a number of different sexual acts and not affect the validity of the marriage. If, however, Raheem refuses intercourse then Fatima could seek to annul the marriage on the ground of wilful non-consummation. For Fatima, being able to annul the marriage may be preferable to a divorce, which may be frowned upon in her community. However, this requires the court to consider, in detail, their sexual relations (including why Raheem does not want them), which would be very distressing for them both.

2.8.3 Lack of consent

The parties must consent to the marriage. 'There cannot be a valid marriage in the absence of consent. That rule is absolute and unqualified.'[134]

---

[129] Section 12(1)(b) Matrimonial Causes Act 1973.
[130] [1947] 2 All ER 871, 874A-B (HL) (Lord Jowitt).
[131] *Jodla v Jodla* [1960] 1 WLR 236. For similar facts, see *Kaur v Singh* [1972] 1 All ER 292 (CA).
[132] *Jodla v Jodla* [1960] 1 WLR 236, 239 (Hewson J).
[133] *Baxter v Baxter* [1947] 1 All ER 387, 388G-H (CA) (Lord Greene). This also applies, of course, if it is the wife seeking to persuade the husband to engage in intercourse.
[134] *Sheffield City Council v E and S* [2004] EWHC 2808 (Fam) [101] (Munby P).

There are two aspects to this. First, they must be capable of giving a consent that is valid in law. This means that they must be able to understand not only that they are taking part in a marriage ceremony but the 'responsibilities normally attaching to marriage' so as to understand the 'nature of the contract'.[135] A person who lacks the ability to understand this cannot form a lawful marriage.[136] Second, they must actually consent to the proposed marriage. A person who enters into a marriage under duress does not consent validly to the marriage. Indeed, there are specific civil and criminal laws which are designed to protect those who may be forced into marriage and to punish those responsible. Similarly, a person who enters into a marriage by mistake does not consent to the marriage.

Sections s12(1)(c) Matrimonial Causes Act 1973 and s50(1)(a) Civil Partnership Act 2004 enable either party to seek to annul the marriage or partnership because they or their spouse 'did not validly consent to it, whether in consequence of duress, mistake, unsoundness of mind or otherwise'. It is therefore different to some of the other grounds of nullity, which require the 'innocent party' to bring the case. Given that consent can be seen as fundamental to the formation of a marriage, one might have expected to see lack of it as rendering the marriage automatically void *ab initio*, rather than merely voidable. In fact, that appears to have been the position for many centuries. However, now it is simply a ground on which a marriage is voidable, meaning that only the parties to the marriage (or someone acting on their behalf if they lack mental capacity) can seek to annul the marriage.[137] The rather dated rationale given for this by the Law Commission in its review of nullity in 1970 is that it would enable courts to take each situation on a case-by-case basis.[138] A court must be satisfied that the pressure or threats are sufficient to vitiate consent.

Duress

A marriage can be annulled by one of the parties on the grounds that they entered into the marriage or partnership as a result of duress. Even if they said 'I do', if they were subjected to such pressure that their will was overborne, that is not valid consent. Whatever form the duress takes—threats, coercion, physical violence, imprisonment—it 'is a coercion of the will so as to vitiate consent'.[139]

It is no longer necessary for the threats to be so extreme as to create an immediate threat to life, limb, or liberty, as was the situation in the extraordinary case of *Szechter v Szechter*, which involved a marriage to free a seriously ill political prisoner whose continued imprisonment would have resulted in her death.[140] However, on the other end of the scale, it

---

[135] *In the Estate of Park (Deceased)* [1954] P 112, 127 (Singleton LJ). This test was adopted by Munby LJ in *Sheffield City Council v E* [2004] EWHC 2808 (Fam).

[136] *Fulwood's Case* (1683) Cro. Car. 482, in which Mr Fulwood 'violently, and with force, and against the will of (one) Sarah, took and carried the said Sarah to St Saviour's, and there married her'.

[137] A Litigation Friend will act for parties who lack capacity to litigate. This is usually a relation of the person but the Official Solicitor acts as a Litigation Friend where no one else is suitable.

[138] Law Commission, *Family Law: Report on Nullity of Marriage* (Law Com No 33 1970) para 65.

[139] *Pao On v Lau Yiu Long* [1980] AC 614, 635 (PC) (Lord Scarman).

[140] [1971] P 286. Mr Szechter, an opponent of the Polish government that they were keen to exile, agreed to leave Poland only if he could marry and take the political prisoner with him. Prior to her imprisonment, she had been like a daughter to him and to the wife he divorced in order to marry her.

is not duress if a party has entered into a marriage 'in order to escape from a disagreeable situation, such as penury or social degradation'.[141] What matters is whether the applicant's will was overborne sufficiently that they did not truly consent to the marriage. This is a subjective test: it considers the effect of the duress on the applicant him or herself, and not whether 'a person of ordinary courage and resolution' would have been more resilient in the same situation.[142] In *Hirani v Hirani*, the Court of Appeal held that threats by 19-year-old Ms Hirani's parents to throw her out of their home if she did not marry a man she had not previously met was sufficient to overbear Ms Hirani's will, given that she was entirely dependent upon her parents and had nowhere else to go nor access to any money.[143] A different person experiencing the same threats as Ms Hirani but who was older and/or more financially independent or emotionally resilient may not have been experiencing duress.

Duress is an aspect of forced marriage, which we discuss more fully in section 2.9.

Mistake

There are two kinds of mistake that can form the basis of an annulment. First, a marriage is voidable if at the time of the celebration one or both of the parties was mistaken as to the nature of the ceremony. One example of this is *Mehta v Mehta*, in which an Englishwoman in India thought that the ceremony being undertaken was to convert her to the Hindu faith and did not realise that it was in fact a marriage ceremony.[144] More recently, in *Alfonso-Brown v Milwood*, the husband alleged that a celebration conducted in Ghana in the Ga language was an engagement ceremony, not, as the wife alleged, a wedding ceremony. The court held that it was not a wedding ceremony, but that even if it had been the husband had not consented to being married then and there, only to becoming engaged.[145]

Second, a person may have been mistaken about the identity of the person they married: for example, the groom intended to marry Ursula, but Isabella had taken her place in disguise.[146] A variation on this scenario can be found in the recent bizarre case of *Islam v Islam*, in which the wife married someone at a London register office, and then fraudulently claimed that person was the respondent, the man she actually wanted to marry.[147] Had she genuinely believed she was marrying the respondent, that would have been a case of mistake. As it was, she was very much involved in the fraud and, because she intended to marry the person at the register office with her and only pretended that was the respondent, she found herself married—to her co-conspirator.

Mistake is therefore an aspect of consent: in neither situation can a party be said to have consented to the marriage that took place. As you may expect, annulments obtained on the basis of mistake are few and far between.

Mistakes of the kind that enable a marriage to be voided do not include mistakes as to the personality or character of your spouse *even if* you would not have married them if

---

[141] [1971] P 286.
[142] [1886–90] All ER Rep 363.
[143] (1983) 4 FLR 232.
[144] [1945] 2 All ER 690.
[145] [2006] EWHC 642 (Fam).
[146] Paraphrasing Ayliff, *Parergon Juris Canonici*, quoted by Joseph Jackson, 'Consent of the Parties to Their Marriage', (1951) 14(1) *Modern Law Review* 1, 18.
[147] [2003] EWHC 1298 (Fam).

you had known the reality. If you thought you were marrying someone nice but instead you marry an abuser, your remedy is divorce not nullity. This is the case even if they had lied to you about their real name, age, occupation, wealth, etc., as if a party consents to the marriage it does not matter if that consent was the result of fraud or misrepresentation provided the consent was genuine, i.e., not the result of duress. 'If he is capable of consent, and has consented, the law does not ask how the consent has been induced.'[148]

We can see this best through a case from New Zealand, *C v C*, which almost certainly also represents the correct position under the law of England and Wales.[149]

> **KEY CASE** *C v C* [1942] NZLR 356
>
> A widow met a man who claimed to be the successful Australian boxer Michael Miller, a person who did exist. She married him three days later and then discovered that he was not the successful Australian boxer Michael Miller: in fact, he was not called Michael Miller at all, nor was he an Australian, nor a boxer, nor wealthy.
>
> The New Zealand Supreme Court adopted the principles described in the line of English cases set out above, and held that this was 'a case of real consent although induced by fraud, and not a case of no consent or absence of consent. The petitioner truly intended to marry the human being to whom she was married. . . This lady's ambition was not to be the wife of that human being who is Michael Miller. The point was that she was willing to marry this man whom she believed to be able to support her, and the identity of Michael Miller in the matter was merely accidental.'[150] As this did not constitute a mistake as to identity, the marriage could not be annulled on that basis.

This outcome seems quite harsh: surely the fact that he was a well-known person may have had something to do with why she married him so quickly? But that was not the approach taken by the court. The Supreme Court found that she consented to marry the man she married, and that while the fact that he had lied to her may have induced her consent, *she still consented*.

A mistake as to identity that would render the marriage voidable is therefore 'limited to such fraud as procures the appearance without the reality of consent'.[151]

It may be that when a party realises the mistake they nevertheless choose to continue with the marriage, and such a marriage would entirely valid. From a contract law perspective, this is a ratification of the marriage contract.[152]

---

[148] *Sullivan v Sullivan* (1818) 161 ER 728, 732.
[149] [1942] NZLR 356. But see *Militante v Ogunwomoju* [1994] Fam Law 17, in which a marriage was annulled when the petitioner married a man using a false name. *C v C* was not cited and the correctness of *Militante* is doubted. The case note by G Douglas at [1994] *Family Law* 17 notes that it was not possible to tell 'whether the petitioner was arguing that she thought she was marrying a different man, or simply that she thought the man had a different name'.
[150] At 358–9 (Callan J).
[151] *Moss v Moss* [1897] P 263.
[152] *Valier v Valier* (1925) 133 LT 830.

Unsoundness of mind or otherwise

A marriage can be annulled if, at the time of the ceremony, one or both of the parties was suffering from an 'unsoundness of mind' such that they did not validly consent to the marriage. This could be the result of a temporary illness or a permanent disability such as a learning disability. In *Sheffield City Council v E and S*, Munby P set out the factors necessary to determining whether a person had capacity to marry, identifying that this involved the answer to two questions:

1. Do they understand the nature of the marriage contract?
2. Do they understand the duties and responsibilities that normally attach to marriage?

It is not about whether or not the decision to marry is a sensible one. 'It is not the business of [the local authority] or even the court to adjudicate on the wisdom of contracts to marry. If a woman . . . has the capacity to marry a "suitable" partner then she has the capacity to marry anybody, and that is her business and nobody else's.'

KEY CASE *Sheffield City Council v E and S* [2004] EWHC 2808 (Fam)

The local authority brought proceedings under the inherent jurisdiction[153] in relation to the planned marriage between a 21-year-old disabled woman with the mental age of a 13-year-old ('E') and a 37-year-old convicted child sex offender ('S').[154] The court had to decide whether E had the mental capacity to marry. Whether a person has capacity depends upon the context. More complex decisions require greater capacity. It is therefore possible to have capacity to make simple decisions but not to make other, more complex ones.

Munby P held that:

> It is not enough that someone appreciates that he or she is taking part in a marriage ceremony or understands its words. He or she must understand the nature of the marriage contract. This means that he or she must be mentally capable of understanding the duties and responsibilities that normally attach to marriage. That said, the contract of marriage is in essence a simple one, which does not require a high degree of intelligence to comprehend. The contract of marriage can readily be understood by anyone of normal intelligence.

The judge then went on to identify what the 'duties and responsibilities that normally attach to marriage' were:

> In my judgment the matter can be summarised as follows: marriage, whether civil or religious, is a contract, formally entered into. It confers on the parties the status of husband and wife, the essence of the contract being an agreement between a man and a woman to live together, and to love one another as husband and wife, to the exclusion of all others. It creates a relationship of mutual and reciprocal obligations, typically involving the sharing of a common home and a common domestic life and the right to enjoy each other's society, comfort and assistance.

---

[153] For an explanation of the inherent jurisdiction, see the focus box in Chapter 9.
[154] [2004] EWHC 2808 (Fam).

He also cautioned that:

> There are many people in our society who may be of limited or borderline capacity but whose lives are immensely enriched by marriage. We must be careful not to set the test of capacity to marry too high, lest it operate as an unfair, unnecessary and indeed discriminatory bar against the mentally disabled. Equally, we must be careful not to impose so stringent a test of capacity to marry that it becomes too easy to challenge the validity of what appear on the surface to be regular and seemingly valid marriages.

Note also that 'Generally speaking, capacity to marry must include the capacity to consent to sexual relations . . . [which] must for this purpose be the same in its essentials as that required by the criminal law.'[155] In *Mundell v Name 1*, Mostyn J held that it was also necessary for the person to understand that at the end of a marriage a person may bring a financial claim, but that this did not require them to understand financial remedy law.[156]

Capacity to marry is not, therefore, a high hurdle—it does not require special or even normal levels of intelligence. Those who are disabled do not lose their human rights, and the right to marry—at least the right of a man with a woman, as we shall see—is contained in Article 12 European Convention on Human Rights (ECHR). In *Mundell* Mostyn J also said that 'If one was to draw up a hierarchy of human rights, one would have the right to enter into a marriage and found a family as being near the top of the list because the right to form a marriage has been in play in our society since the very dawn of time.' If the hurdle was set higher, we would deny entry to marriage to those entitled to acknowledgment and recognition of their love of another person, as well as access to the legal protections that being married brings.

So far, we have considered capacity as something that may be affected by illness or disability. But a party may also be unable to consent as a result of a self-inflicted incapacity such as drunkenness, or being high on drugs during the ceremony. It appears from *Sullivan v Sullivan*[157] that the same approach would be taken to self-inflicted incapacities as to any other kind. That is what Jackson, writing in 1951, assumes, but there are no recent cases on this.[158]

2.8.4 Mental disorder

It is a ground to annul the marriage that 'at the time of the marriage either party, though capable of giving valid consent, was suffering (whether continuously or intermittently) from a mental disorder within the meaning of the Mental Health Act 1983, of such kind or to such an extent as to be unfitted for marriage'. There are several aspects to this provision, which is found in s12(1)(d) Matrimonial Causes Act 1973 and 50(1)(b) Civil Partnership

---

[155] *X City Council v MB and others* [2006] EWHC 168 (Fam.) (Munby J). But see *NB v MI* [2021] EWHC 224 (Fam) for a contrary view. Mental capacity to consent means the ability to do so; it is a separate issue whether or not the person would ever choose to exercise that consent.
[156] [2019] EWCOP 50.
[157] *Sullivan v Sullivan* (1818) 161 ER 728.
[158] J Jackson, 'Consent of the Parties to Their Marriage' (1951) 14(1) *Modern Law Review* 1, 6.

Act 2004.[159] First, the mental disorder must exist at the time of the ceremony; if it arises later it is not a basis to annul the marriage although it may be possible to divorce.[160] Second, the provision adopts the broad meaning of 'mental disorder' that is used by the 1983 Act, namely 'any disorder or disability of the mind'. Third, it is not enough to have a disorder—the disorder has to render the person 'unfitted for marriage'. In *Bennett v Bennett*, Ormrod J thought that 'this must really mean something very much like the test of unsoundness of mind although perhaps not quite the same; it really must mean something in the nature of "Is this person capable of living in a married state and of carrying out the ordinary duties and obligations of marriage?"'[161] For those duties and obligations of marriage, we can draw a parallel with the requirements set down in the Key Case *Sheffield City Council v E* for entry into marriage.

2.8.5 Venereal disease

It is possible to annul a marriage if at the time of the marriage the respondent was suffering from a venereal disease (a sexually transmitted infection) in a communicable form. This ground, now s12(1)(e) Matrimonial Causes Act 1973, was introduced by the Matrimonial Causes Act 1937 but does not define what a venereal disease is and therefore what conditions are covered. During discussion of the clause in Parliament, the government noted that it 'originally wanted to insert a definition of the term "venereal disease" in the bill, but it was found difficult and on the whole unnecessary to do so. The words "in a communicable form" are sufficient to serve as a definition and to indicate the purpose of the Clause.'[162]

Despite the confidence of former legislators, it is not known whether a marriage can be annulled if the venereal disease is easily cured. A literal approach to interpreting the statute implies that you should be able to annul the marriage: all that matters is whether the respondent was suffering from a communicable venereal disease at the time of the wedding, not whether it was subsequently cured. A purposive approach, however, might look to the fact that the centuries-old origins of this ground is to do with fertility and the spread of diseases, which implies that a court should not annul the marriage where the illness is easily curable with no long-term effects on fertility. The quote from *Hansard* that 'the words "in a communicable form" are sufficient to serve as a definition and to indicate the purpose of the Clause' give some support to this.

This ground is not found in the Civil Partnership Act 2004, but does apply to those in same-sex marriages. It is unclear whether the omission from the Civil Partnership Act was an attempt to modernise the law or was for some other reason.

---

[159] Section 50(1)(b) Civil Partnership Act 2004 states that 'at the time of its formation either of them, though capable of giving a valid consent, was suffering (whether continuously or intermittently) from a mental disorder of such a kind or to such an extent as to be unfitted for civil partnership'. The definition of mental disorder is that of the 1983 Act at s50(2). The wording is therefore different but the effect identical.

[160] As we see in Chapter 3, prior to the introduction of purely no-fault divorce, a divorce was permitted on the basis of a party's behaviour including behaviour arising as a result of mental illness. The behaviour must have been such that it would be unreasonable to require the petitioner to live with it. This did not require the respondent to be at fault.

[161] *Bennett v Bennett* [1969] 1 WLR 430, 434.

[162] HC Deb 23 July 1937 vol 326, col 2627.

2.8.6 Pregnancy by another

This provision[163] enables a marriage to be annulled by a spouse on the basis that his (or her) wife was pregnant by someone else at the time of the ceremony. The applicant must not have known about the pregnancy at the time. There is no mirror provision enabling a wife to seek annulment on the ground that her husband has impregnated another woman; historically, sexual chastity and fidelity by women has been taken much more seriously than that of men, and any child born to a married woman is presumed to be that of her husband.[164] The provision is therefore designed to help ensure that any children born in wedlock are in fact the children of both parties.

The Civil Partnership Act also enables annulment on the ground that 'the respondent was pregnant by some person other than the applicant': s50(1)(c). Of course, a gay male couple cannot satisfy this provision, but a lesbian couple could do so (using donated sperm), as could a transgender man who retains female reproductive organs.

2.8.7 Transitioning gender

Since the Gender Recognition Act 2004, it has been possible for a person to change their legal sex from male to female or vice versa by obtaining a gender recognition certificate (see Focus: Know-How: The Gender Recognition Act 2004). There are two grounds relating to gender transition on which a marriage or civil partnership can be annulled:

1. If one of the spouses/partners obtains an interim gender recognition certificate during the marriage or partnership, either party can seek an annulment.

2. A person who marries or civilly partners someone who has a gender recognition certificate can seek an annulment if they did not know that at the time of the wedding.

We will consider these in turn.

Section 12(1)(g) Matrimonial Causes Act allows either party—the transitioning party or their spouse—to annul the marriage on the ground that an interim gender recognition certificate under the Gender Recognition Act 2004 has, after the time of marriage, been issued to either party of the marriage. An annulment can therefore be sought against the wishes of the other party.[165]

If a married person in a different-sex relationship was to change gender, henceforth their marriage would be between two people of the same sex. This understandably caused a legal problem prior to the introduction of laws permitting same-sex marriage. The controversial solution was to require such couples to divorce or (under this provision)

---

[163] Matrimonial Causes Act 1973 s12(1)(f), but originating in the Matrimonial Causes Act 1937.

[164] See Chapter 8.

[165] It would also be possible to divorce. Now, there is a no-fault ground (see Chapter 3). Prior to exclusively no-fault divorce, it was presumably possible to divorce on the basis of that the other party had behaved in such a way that the petitioner cannot reasonably be expected to live with them, whether that behaviour was the respondent changing legal gender or refusing to continue with a marriage to a person changing their gender. There appear to be no authorities on the point, but such behaviour does not have to be unreasonable or faulty: the unreasonableness applies to the continuation of cohabitation in such circumstances.

to annul their marriage before a gender recognition certificate would be granted. In the meantime, the spouse who wished to change legal gender could only obtain an interim certificate valid for six months. Once the divorce or annulment was completed, the parties could, if they wanted, enter into civil partnership but, because they were now same-sex, could not remarry.

The *Pink Paper* reports that 'around 30 couples were forced to annul their marriages in this way. They have described it as like having their marriages "stolen".'[166] The European Court of Human Rights rejected a claim by a devout Christian couple that the choice between remaining married and gaining legal recognition of one spouse's gender was a breach of their human rights, specifically Articles 8, 9, 12, 13, 14 and Article 1 of Protocol 1, on the basis that they could enter into a civil partnership instead.[167]

However, in *MB v Secretary of State for Work and Pensions*, a similar issue arose in respect of an applicant who was a married transgender woman without a gender recognition certificate. As the law therefore saw her as legally male, she was unable to receive her state pension at the lower age applicable (at that time) to women. Only by divorcing her wife, which she did not want to do for religious reasons, could she obtain a full gender recognition certificate and thereby her pension at the lower age. The Supreme Court asked the Court of Justice of the European Union—remember, not the same institution as the European Court of Human Rights—to determine as a preliminary issue whether there was a breach of European Union law. Since the holder of an interim gender recognition certificate must have satisfied the physical and psychological criteria for gender recognition, the question was whether imposition of a further condition [annulment] for obtaining a full certificate only constituted unlawful discrimination contrary to the Equal Treatment Directive, because it applied to married applicants only.[168] The ECJ held that it would be a breach.[169] For the position now that same-sex marriage has been introduced, see 2.15.

It is also possible to annul a civil partnership on the ground that either civil partner has been issued an interim certificate: s50(1)(d) Civil Partnership Act 2004. Since the introduction of different-sex civil partnerships as a result of the case of the Key Case *R (on the application of Steinfeld and Keidan)* it is no longer necessary for civil partners seeking to change their legal gender to first annul their partnership.

SCENARIO 4

Illustration 1: Mabel and Karen

Mabel has sought solicitor Marie's advice about her marriage to Karen (formerly David), who is transitioning legal gender. As Mabel and Karen are married, in the days before the Marriage (Same-Sex

---

[166] N Payton, 'What Is the Trans "Spousal Veto" and Why Does It Matter?' (*The Pink Paper*, 7 August 2015).

[167] *Parry v UK* (2006) 42971/05, [2006] ECHR 1157. Legally irrelevant but possible motivation for you: the applicants were represented by a student law clinic.

[168] [2016] UKSC 53.

[169] *MB v Secretary of State for Work and Pensions*, Advocate General's Opinion, Court of Justice of the European Communities Case C-451/16, and Grand Chamber Judgment of 26 June 2018.

Couples) Act 2013 they would have had to divorce in order for Karen to obtain a full gender recognition certificate. If Mabel wanted to cause difficulties, she could have significantly held up or refused a divorce and therefore kept Karen from obtaining the certificate. Moreover, if they wanted to continue their relationship, they could not remarry but only enter into a civil partnership.

Marie advises Mabel that now that same-sex marriage exists, if they want to continue the marriage they can. What Mabel will need to do is discussed at Scenario 4 Illustration 4.

The second provision allows one party to the marriage or partnership to seek an annulment if the other party, the respondent to the application, 'is a person whose gender at the time of the marriage had become the acquired gender under the Gender Recognition Act 2004'. This provision therefore permits a marriage to be annulled if the applicant has married a person who has a gender recognition certificate, provided that the applicant did not know that at the time of the ceremony.[170] The provision does not apply if the applicant has married someone who has transitioned but who has not obtained legal recognition of that through a gender recognition certificate, which was the situation of the applicant in *MB v Secretary of State for Work and Pensions*.

FOCUS Know-How

The Gender Recognition Act 2004

For most people, the sex[171] they are assigned at birth—male or female—matches the way they see themselves. You may have seen this referred to as 'cisgendered'. That is not the case for everyone. Although statistics vary, the government 'tentatively estimates' that around 200,000–500,000 people in the UK have a medical condition called gender dysphoria, which means that their apparent biological sex, as assigned at birth, is not the same as the gender with which they identify, causing them distress.[172] Although we do not know what causes gender dysphoria, it is not to be confused with being gay[173] or being a cross-dresser.

As Lord Nicholls said in *Bellinger v Bellinger*, 'Gender dysphoria seems always to have existed. But before the advent of gender reassignment treatment a claim by a transsexual person to be recognised in his or her self-perceived gender would have been hopeless. The anatomy of his or her body of itself would have refuted the claim.'[174] Medical knowledge was not such that a person could change sexual characteristics. Even when medical knowledge enabled gender confirmation surgery, the law did not recognise this by enabling a person to change their legal gender from that set out in their birth certificate.

This was the case until the Gender Recognition Act 2004. The Act now enables a person to change their legal gender by acquiring a gender recognition certificate. The individual must first be diagnosed with gender dysphoria and live in their 'acquired'[175] gender for at least two years. It is not

---

[170] Matrimonial Causes Act 1973 s12(1)(h).

[171] Although this is rather simplistic, the term 'sex' is understood to refer to an individual's physical characteristics, whereas 'gender' refers to the individual's self-identity and the social or cultural expectations imposed on that person. However, the terms are used interchangeably by many institutions.

[172] Government Equalities Office, *Trans People in the UK* (2018).

[173] Approximately one-third of trans people identify as lesbian, gay, or bisexual (which is higher than the general population), about one-third identify as heterosexual, and one-third identify as asexual.

[174] *Bellinger v Bellinger* [2003] UKHL 21, [29] (Lord Nicholls).

[175] 'Acquired' is in inverted commas because it is not acquired by the person: that is how they always have been. It is that they have acquired legal recognition of that fact.

necessary for them to have gender confirmation surgery, but they do have to demonstrate in their application to a gender recognition panel that they have gender dysphoria and wish to live in their 'acquired' gender permanently, and surgery helps evidence that. The effect of the certificate is that the person is now recognised for all purposes as being their 'acquired' gender and they are entitled to a new birth certificate.[176] In the event that an application is refused, appeal can be made to the Family Division of the High Court.[177]

Possession of a gender recognition certificate therefore allows a person to marry in their acquired gender. However, it has no retrospective effect. In *P v P (Transgender Applicant for Declaration of Valid Marriage)*, the applicant had transitioned from female to male and had undergone gender confirmation surgery, but he had not obtained a certificate and did not realise he needed to do so. His marriage in 2009 was void because he was legally female and had married a woman at a time when the Matrimonial Causes Act declared same-sex marriages to be void *ab initio*.[178] The fact that same-sex marriages subsequently became lawful or that he may go on to obtain a certificate did not retrospectively make that marriage lawful.

A child's sex at birth, and thus their gender, is classified according to their genitalia, but the reality is that there are many intersex conditions or differences of sex development wherein a person has both male and female sexual characteristics, whether primary, secondary, hormonal, or chromosomal. Although it is possible for someone to apply to court for a declaration as to their sex before they marry, it is not always clear what is the correct designation. Does one consider, for example, only the genitalia? What if the person's chromosomes do not match their genitalia, or if they have underdeveloped genitalia or both male and female internal or external sexual organs? What about their hormones? What weight should be given to the way the individual sees themselves? Should that be determinative? In *Corbett v Corbett*, the court determined sex on the basis of three factors, gonadal (presence of testicles or ovaries), chromosomes, and genitalia: the fact that Mrs Corbett identified as female did not mean that the court considered her female.[179] In *W v W (Nullity: Gender)*,[180] these three factors did not provide a conclusive answer to the sex of the respondent, who had male chromosomes and was likely to have male gonads,[181] but who was genitally intersex and psychologically female, and who had androgen insensitivity syndrome, a condition that affects those who are chromosomally male but causes some feminisation of the sexual organs and meant she had breasts.[182] Although the respondent had been assigned male sex at birth, Charles J held that she was female. As Herring and Chau point out, however, the fact that the court considered more factors than the three identified in *Corbett* was simply because those factors were inconclusive.[183] It was not because the law had moved on since *Corbett*'s rather reductive stance.[184]

The present law on gender recognition does not help all intersex individuals, because it requires them to be diagnosed with gender dysphoria when they may not have any form of dysphoria. Instead, the issue may be that because they had inconclusive sexual characteristics, when they were born, their parents or doctors assigned them what turns out in retrospect to have been the wrong gender.

---

[176] However, they still retain their original status as father or mother of a child. See Chapter 8.

[177] As in *Jay v Secretary of State for Justice* [2018] EWHC 2620 (Fam).

[178] [2019] EWHC 3105 (Fam), a very interesting read. P could have entered into a civil partnership rather than married his partner and that would have been lawful.

[179] *Corbett v Corbett (otherwise Ashley)* [1971] P 83.

[180] [2001] 1 FLR 324.

[181] Testicles and/or ovaries.

[182] Consider how violating this case must have been for the respondent.

[183] J Herring and P-L Chau, 'Assigning Sex and Intersexuals' [2001] *Family Law* 762.

[184] For a critique of *Corbett*, see A Sharpe, 'English Transgender Law Reform and the Spectre of Corbett' (2002) 10 *Feminist Legal Studies* 65 and H Brooke, *Conjugal Rites: Marriage and Marriage-Like Relationships before the Law* (Palgrave 2007) among many others.

Indeed, it was not unusual in the past for surgery to be conducted on young babies' genitalia with a view to making them look the chosen gender.[185]

Under the present legal regime, there is a choice between two legal options, male or female. There is presently no legal recognition that a person may feel agendered (without a gender) or not fully any gender (non-binary). Although some countries now legally recognise a third gender or a non-binary category, this is not presently the case in England and Wales. A judicial review brought by an agendered person into the government's refusal to issue passports with a third gender category, X, failed, although the Supreme Court will hear the case soon.[186] Our law 'is based on the assumption that gender is, and should be, binary and ideally static rather than manifold and fluid.'[187]

SCENARIO 4

Illustration 2: Mabel and Karen

Mabel has sought solicitor Marie's advice about her marriage to Karen (formerly David), who is transitioning legal gender. They married before Karen announced her transition. Marie advises that if Mabel therefore objects to remaining married, she has two options. She can divorce Karen, or she can wait until Karen has obtained an interim gender recognition certificate, and then seek an annulment on that basis. If Karen does not seek a gender recognition certificate, or if this process is not quick enough for Mabel, then Mabel's only option is divorce.

Let us change the scenario a little. What if Karen had transitioned earlier? That would be a valid same-sex marriage only if Karen had obtained a gender recognition certificate. Even if Karen presented as female and even if she had undergone gender confirmation surgery, the law would see her as male until she has a gender recognition certificate. If she does not have one, then it would be a valid different-sex marriage. The legal consequences are the same.

If Mabel had been unaware of Karen's change of legal gender at the time of the wedding ceremony, she can seek to annul the marriage on that basis. However, if Karen had simply presented as female and undergone surgery but not obtained a gender recognition certificate, the marriage could not be annulled, because the grounds relate only to those with certificates.

2.8.8 Statutory bars for voidable marriages

As a void marriage is void *ab initio*, there are no legal obstacles to someone bringing an application for a court declaration as to the status of the purported marriage. However, there are bars in the case of voidable marriages, which are found in s13 Matrimonial Causes Act 1973. These reflect the more personal character of the voidable grounds compared to those that render a marriage automatically void. The 'innocent party' will waive their right to

[185] See C Quinn, 'Medically Necessary Or "Cruel"? Inside the Battle over Surgery on Intersex Babies' (WGBH, 24 October 2019), available at https://www.wgbh.org/news/science-and-technology/2019/10/24/medically-necessary-or-cruel-inside-the-battle-over-surgery-on-intersex-babies and S Daniani, 'Are hasty operations on intersex children becoming a thing of the past?' (*The Guardian*, 14 July 2020), available at https://www.theguardian.com/lifeandstyle/2020/jul/14/intersex-children-hasty-operations accessed 25 August 2020.

[186] *R (On the Application of Christie Elan-Cane) v Secretary of State for the Home Department* [2018] EWHC 1530 (Admin).

[187] F Renz, 'Consenting to Gender? Trans Spouses after Same Sex Marriage', in D Monk and N Barker (eds), *From Civil Partnership to Same Sex Marriage 2004–2014: Interdisciplinary Reflections* (Routledge 2015).

have the marriage annulled by continuing with the marriage beyond a certain period, by behaving so as to imply that they would not annul it, or by marrying notwithstanding the ground. The grounds of voidability are waivable breaches of the marital contract.

There are three types:

- Conduct by the petitioner
- Time delay
- Knowing about the issue

We will discuss each in turn.

Conduct by the petitioner

If a petitioner knew that he or she had grounds to seek an annulment but acted in such a way that the respondent reasonably believed they would not do so, the court can refuse to annul the marriage if it would also be unjust to the respondent to do so.

In *D v D*, the wife was unable to consummate the marriage without having minor surgery.[188] When the husband sought annulment on the ground of non-consummation, the court held that by adopting two children with the wife he had acted in such a way that the latter reasonably believed he would not do so. However, in order to block the annulment, it also had to be unjust to annul the marriage. While there would have been a time when annulling the marriage in this way would have had adverse consequences for the wife in terms of financial position or care of the children, at the time this case was decided, as now, she had the same rights after annulment as she would if the husband simply divorced her. This meant that the annulment would not cause her injustice.

Time delay

There are time limits for bringing an application. This is six months in the case of receipt of an interim gender recognition certificate[189] but three years in relation to all other grounds. There is some flexibility as to time limits where the petitioner has at some time during the three years suffered from mental disorder within the meaning of the Mental Health Act 1983, and in all the circumstances of the case it would be just to grant leave for the institution of proceedings after three years have elapsed.[190] For a discussion of how this statutory bar affects victims of forced marriage, and judicial creativity in resolving that problem, please see section 2.9.4.

Knowing about the issue

If the petitioner wishes to bring a nullity suit based on the respondent having a communicable venereal disease, being pregnant by another at the time of the wedding, or having changed legal gender, the court must be satisfied that the petitioner was ignorant of this at the time of the marriage.

It is always open to the parties to divorce rather than seek to annul the marriage. This avoids the specific bars in nullity cases.

---

[188] [1979] Fam 70.
[189] Ground 12(1)(g) not (h).
[190] Matrimonial Causes Act 1973 s13(4).

SCENARIO 4

Illustration 3: Mabel and Karen

We established at illustration 2 that if Karen had a gender recognition certificate legally changing her gender from male to female, and she obtained this prior to their marriage, Mabel could bring nullity proceedings against her on that basis. We now know that there is a three-year time limit for her doing so. (The six-month deadline applies to those who, during the marriage, obtain an interim gender recognition certificate, not this provision which relates to having a gender recognition certificate at the time of the wedding.) After this time, she is deemed to have waived her right to consider this a 'deal breaker'.

2.9 Forced marriage

In many cultures, it is common for parents to take a leading role in selecting a spouse for their son or daughter. In the vast majority of such arranged marriages, the (adult) child will have a free choice as to whether to marry the person selected for them by their family; they are entirely consensual marriages. However, a small proportion of these marriages will not be the result of free choice but involve one or both parties being forced to marry when they do not consent to that, or when they lack the capacity to consent as a result of their age or a disability. In between, as we discuss in Scenario 3 Illustration 4, there is not always a clear dividing line between arranged and forced marriages because of the complex interrelationship of familial, cultural, and social pressure experienced by the intended spouses. Gangoli et al. note that some parents who force their children into marriage believe that in doing so they are 'upholding the cultural practices of their country of origin, [when] in reality practices and traditions there had 'moved on'. It may therefore be 'a product of the diasporic experience and not a "traditional practice"'.[191]

Forced marriages serve a number of different purposes including a wish to control women's sexuality and autonomy. In *Hirani v Hirani*, discussed in section 2.8.3, Ms Hirani was Hindu and her parents coerced her into marriage to another Hindu man in order to prevent her from associating with a Muslim man. But forced marriage can also have practical purposes, as Idriss identifies, such as assisting in immigration, strengthening family links, and fulfilling long-term commitments.[192] In such situations, withdrawing from the commitment is perceived as dishonouring the family. They can also, ironically, be intended to serve a protective purpose. Forced marriages often involve those with physical or mental disabilities whose marriages are designed to provide them with spousal caregivers.

2.9.1 The harm of forced marriage

Where there is a lack of capacity due to disability, it may be that coercion and threats are simply not required. In most cases, however, forced marriage involves coercion, threats, and even violence being used to overbear the will of the victim. This 'embraces a range of

---

[191] G Gangoli, A Razak, and M McCarry, *Forced Marriage and Domestic Violence among South Asian Communities in North East England* (University of Bristol and Northern Rock Foundation 2006).

[192] MM Idriss, 'Forced Marriages – The Need for Criminalisation?' [2015] 9 *Criminal Law Review* 687.

behaviour, encompassing low-level attrition and emotional blackmail at one extreme and the full spectrum of domestic violence at the other, culminating in murder in a tiny number of horrific cases.'[193] It is therefore closely linked to so-called 'honour-based' violence.

Specific harms associated with forced marriage include:

- distress caused by the acts to force the victim into marriage, for instance threats of social isolation or threats of violence against the victim or the victim's family;

- rearing a child produced from the forced marriage, including children from forced pregnancies;

- binding the victim for life to a person who has committed grave crimes, such as rape during the course of the marriage;

- depriving the victim of the opportunity for consensual marriage as a fundamental human right and the corresponding psychological injury to the victim;

- fear of being ostracised from the victim's community if the victim refused to enter a forced marriage or left a forced marriage.[194]

A number of crimes may be implicated in forced marriages, including harassment, abduction, kidnapping, assault, threats to kill, rape and other forms of sexual assault, as well as conspiracy to commit these offences. There are also possible immigration offences and potential torts including false imprisonment and trespass to the person. Forced marriage is therefore a significant abuse of human rights. Indeed, the 'the UN recognises [it] as a form of contemporary slavery, trafficking and sexual exploitation'.[195] The COVID-19 pandemic has reportedly increased the risk of child marriage in some South Asian and Sub-Saharan African countries as children are forced out of school to work or marry.[196] Article 16(2) of the Universal Declaration of Human Rights provides that marriages should be entered into 'only with the free and full consent of the intending spouses'. Article 12 ECHR, the right to marry, has been taken to include a right not to marry. As Choudhry writes, 'the effects of forced marriage will often be sufficiently intense to engage Article 3' and therefore the positive obligations on the state to protect an individual from infringement.[197]

The majority of forced marriage cases dealt with in the UK have an international element—they involve the threat of a forced marriage overseas. Some victims are taken abroad, perhaps on a pretext, and when they are abroad their passport and any money is taken from them and they are told that they have no alternative but to marry. An example of this can be found in *NS v MI*.[198] The victim of the forced marriage, P, was 16 years old when her parents took her from the UK, where she had always lived, to Pakistan, saying that this was for a holiday. When they arrived, P's passport was taken away from her and

[193] N Khanum, *Forced Marriage, Family Cohesion, and Community Engagement: National Learning through a Case Study of Luton* (Equality in Diversity 2008) 11.
[194] Taken from C Proudman, 'The Criminalisation of Forced Marriage', [2012, April] *Family Law* 460.
[195] UN Working Group on Contemporary Forms of Slavery, 28th Session, Geneva (June 2003).
[196] 'Coronavirus risks "greatest surge in child marriages in 25 years"' (*BBC News* 1 October 2020); S Cousins, '2.5 million more child marriages due to COVID-19 pandemic', (2020) 396(10257) *The Lancet* 1059.
[197] S Choudhry, 'Forced Marriage: The European Convention on Human Rights and the Human Rights Act 1998', Chapter 3 in A Gill and S Anitha (eds), *Forced Marriage: Introducing a Social Justice and Human Rights Perspective* (Zed Books 2011).
[198] [2006] EWHC 1646 (Fam).

she was told that she had to marry her cousin. If she did not do so, her parents told her that they would kill themselves and that she would never be able to return to the UK. She was subjected to unrelenting pressure and moral blackmail over the course of several months before she underwent the marriage ceremony. On her marriage she was permitted to return to the UK and the marriage was annulled for duress. She declined to make a criminal complaint about her parents, and reconciled with them.

The government's Forced Marriage Unit, which assists victims, helps between 1,200 and 1,400 people each year. The government has estimated that there are in the region of 5-8,000 forced marriages reported per annum, but there will be many that go unreported.[199] It has dealt with cases involving over 90 countries, of which the most common are Pakistan (by a significant margin), Bangladesh, India, and Afghanistan. However, about 5 per cent of cases involve forced marriages that are to take place within the UK.[200] Forced marriage cases do exist among white Western families, members of the travelling and Gypsy communities, and among Hispanic communities.[201] It is a form of violence that transcends cultural and religious practice. What were the 'shotgun weddings' that would follow an unintended pregnancy if not a form of forced marriage?

Most victims are female, but about 19 per cent of those assisted by the Unit are male, and while the vast majority of marriages will involve children and young people, that is not always the case—the oldest victim the Unit helped in 2017 was 100 years old. People who are lesbian, gay, bisexual, transgender, or who are disabled are particularly at risk because marriage can be seen as a way of 'correcting' sexuality or providing a long-term carer for seriously disabled people.[202] A list of warning signs of a potential or current forced marriage is at Figure 2.3.

Education	Health	Employment	Home life	Police involvement
• Frequent absence • Not returning from visits abroad • Fear of upcoming holidays • Decline in behaviour and assessment results • Being removed from school	• Being unable to see a health worker unaccompanied • Self-harm, suicide attempts, depression, eating disorders • Unwanted pregnancy • Female genital mutilation	• Poor performance • Frequent absences • Unable to attend business trips or events • No control over own earnings • Cannot work flexible hours	• Early marriage of siblings • Death of a parent • Unreasonable restrictions on leaving home • Suicide or self-harm of siblings • Close scrutiny by relations when at school/work	• Running away from home • Acid attacks and other serious offences against the person • Going missing • Reports of domestic abuse and disputes in the family

FIGURE 2.3 Warning signs of risk of future/existing forced marriage

Source: Adapted from HM Government, *Multi-Agency Practice Guidelines: Handling Cases of Forced Marriage* (2014) Open Government Licence v.2. to re-use this information.

---

[199] Department for Children, Schools and Families, *Forced Marriage–Prevalence and Service Response*, Research Briefing 128 (2009).

[200] Forced Marriage Unit, *Forced Marriage Unit Statistics 2019* (Home Office and Ministry of Justice 2020).

[201] MM Idriss, 'Forced Marriages – The Need for Criminalisation?' [2015] 9 *Criminal Law Review* 687.

[202] See HM Government, *Multi-Agency Practice Guidelines—Handling Cases of Forced Marriage* (2013).

Prior to 2007, there were no powers specifically designed to address forced marriages or—given that 'in this kind of case one needs to bear in mind that prevention is better than cure'[203]—to provide a coherent power aimed at preventing harm in the first place. A number of existing laws and processes were being utilised instead, with varying degrees of success. For example, the existing criminal law covers many of the crimes often committed when forcing someone to marry, such as kidnap, rape, and threats. The inherent jurisdiction and wardship were being used to protect potential victims who, through reason of age or disability, lacked mental capacity, as were applications to the Court of Protection for a declaration about whether or not an individual had the capacity to enter into a marriage. Where the alleged victim was a child, care proceedings could be brought or an emergency protection order made.[204] Where a victim was shown to lack capacity, an application could be brought on their behalf for a declaration of nullity (lack of consent being a voidable ground, and thus restricted to applications by or on behalf of a party). As such, most reports were made not by victims, but by legal, educational, or healthcare professionals, and local authorities.

The first legal deterrence specifically addressing forced marriage came in 2007 with the introduction of forced marriage protection orders. In 2014, a criminal offence of forcing someone to marry was introduced.

SCENARIO 3

Illustration 4: Raheem and Fatima

The fact that Fatima and Raheem had an arranged marriage does not make theirs a forced marriage. A forced marriage involves a lack of consent: a normal arranged marriage requires the parties to consent, even if the bride or groom is chosen or approved by parents or other family members. Only if the bride or groom is incapable of giving consent or does not give consent freely will the marriage be forced.

However, the issue of whether or not a person's will has been overborne is subjective. This means that it is not always clear whether a marriage has been forced or not. In fact, there is no clear line between encouragement to enter into a marriage; the effect of cultural, social, and familial expectations and pressures; and when those pressures become sufficient to overbear a person's free will. Women in particular experience a range of pressures to marry,

> including issues related to poverty, pregnancy and sexuality, as well as social norms and expectations underpinned by patriarchal structures and institutions. . . . respect for parents and religion is not a spontaneous feeling that arises within the subject. It is a gendered, socially and culturally constructed mode of behaviour, which in particular communities is enforced through a range of related concepts [such as honour and shame]. This preoccupation with free will ignores the fact that consent is constructed in the context of power imbalances and gendered norms and, crucially, often in the absence of explicit threats.[205]

---

[203] *X City Council v MB and others* [2006] EWHC 168 (Fam.) (Munby J).

[204] *Re B; RB v FB* [2008] EWHC 1436 (Fam.) Care proceedings are s31 Children Act 1989 and emergency protection s44. For wardship and the inherent jurisdiction, see Chapter 9.

[205] S Anitha and A Gill, 'Reconceptualising Consent and Coercion within an Intersectional Understanding of Forced Marriage', Chapter 2 in A Gill and S Anitha (eds), *Forced Marriage : Introducing a Social Justice and Human Rights Perspective* (Zed Books 2011).

When does reluctant consent become no consent? Some cases will be clear-cut, but many will be less so. A number of different interviews undertaken by Gangoli et al. with members of the South Asian community in North East England show this, with a proportion of those in what they describe as arranged marriages identifying an element of force or coercion but not defining themselves as being in a forced marriage.[206] This helps explain the relatively low levels of victim reporting as well as the difficulties that the law has faced in addressing forced marriages.

2.9.2 Forced marriage protection orders

Forced marriage protection orders are injunctions created by the Forced Marriage (Civil Protection) Act 2007. Although they are a type of civil injunction, breach of one is a criminal offence and the police can therefore arrest a person who breaches the order without the order having to specifically include a power of arrest.[207] The breach is punishable by up to five years in prison. In s63A(6) of the Family Law Act 1996 force is defined as 'coercing by threats or other psychological means'.

Applications for an order can be made by the victim themselves, or a relevant third party authorised by the Lord Chancellor (currently only local authorities fall within this designation).[208] Other third parties such as the police, family members, or the Official Solicitor can apply with the leave of the court. In deciding whether to grant leave, the court must have regard to all the circumstances including the applicant's connection with the person to be protected; the applicant's knowledge of the circumstances of the person to be protected; and the wishes and feelings of the person to be protected so far as they are reasonably ascertainable.[209] This means that the wishes and feelings of the person to be protected are not necessarily determinative. The court can also make an order of its own volition. Ruth Gaffney-Rhys notes that reprisals may be less likely if the victim has not made the application themselves (assuming they are able to do so).[210] An application can be made ex parte (without notice to the respondent).

In 2019, there were 352 applications made, comprising:

- 24 made by the potential victims
- 192 made by local authorities
- 131 made by third parties
- 5 made by others, presumably a court of its own volition.[211]

---

[206] G Gangoli, A Razak, and M McCarry, *Forced Marriage and Domestic Violence among South Asian Communities in North East England* (University of Bristol and Northern Rock Foundation 2006).

[207] The Forced Marriage (Civil Protection) Act 2007 inserts 63CA in the Family Law Act 1996. Initially breach was a contempt of court punishable by up to two years in prison; the criminalisation of a breach and the sentence were changed by the Anti-Social Behaviour, Crime and Policing Act 2014 and now align with the penalties for breach of a non-molestation order.

[208] Section 1 Forced Marriage (Civil Protection) Act 2007, amending Family Law Act 1996.

[209] Section 1 Forced Marriage (Civil Protection) Act 2007 inserting s63C(4) Family Law Act 1996.

[210] R Gaffney-Rhys, 'Developments in the Field of Forced Marriage' [2008] *International Family Law* 26.

[211] Ministry of Justice, *Family Court Statistics Quarterly October to December 2019* (2020) (table 2).

As you can see, the most common applicant is the local authority, who may become aware of a potential forced marriage through child protection work, schools and colleges, health or police referrals, or housing related enquiries.[212] Of those victims whose age was known, 262 were aged 17 and under. Rather unhelpfully, the statistics do not differentiate between those aged under 16 (for whom a marriage would have been automatically void due to their age) and those aged 16 or 17 (for whom the marriage is voidable for lack of consent).[213]

The order can contain 'such prohibitions, restrictions or requirements . . . as the court considers appropriate' to prevent a victim from being forced into a marriage without their 'free and full consent', or protect them if they have already been married.[214] Common terms include prohibiting someone from taking the victim out of the jurisdiction, requiring them to surrender the victim's passport, and/or prohibiting someone from contacting the victim, forbidding someone from taking any steps to cause or permit the victim from undergoing any ceremony or purported ceremony or betrothal of marriage inside or outside the UK, or requiring the victim to be brought to the British High Commission or embassy if they have been taken abroad.[215]

The Act has been praised for enabling 'potential victims to attain swift and effective legal recourse to prevent a forced marriage from taking place'[216] and for being 'a significant improvement on the collage of [prior] laws'.[217] The civil, rather than criminal, nature of the order may also incentivise potential victims to seek help: many victims do not want their family members to get into serious legal trouble, and may well be living with those against whom the order is made or entirely dependent upon them. However, the fact that the orders are not criminal (save for the fact that breach is a criminal offence) has also been criticised. Forced marriage, Proudman argues, 'forms a distinct inhumane act of sufficient gravity that it should be considered as a separate crime distinct from existing criminal offences which can be prosecuted separately'.[218] A civil remedy does not 'speak to the harm caused by the offence: it does not properly demonstrate why the criminal justice system should be interested in regulating or punishing forced marriage'.[219] Moreover, the lack of monitoring of victims' situations after they have been protected by an order, means that we do not know whether they are successful. Many victims will remain living with their families, the very people from whom they are being protected.[220] Certainly, in 2011 Parliament's Home Affairs Select Committee concluded that the orders had not reduced the numbers of forced marriages.[221]

---

[212] See HM Government, *Multi-Agency Practice Guidelines: Handling Cases of Forced Marriage* (2014).

[213] For statistics on those marrying at 16 or 17, see 2.4.1.

[214] Section 63B Family Law Act 1996.

[215] See H Patel and R Langdale QC, 'Forced Marriage: The Concept and Law' [2009] *Family Law* 726.

[216] Southall Black Sisters, *Forced Marriage Consultation: Response to the Civil Protection Bill* (2006).

[217] R Gaffney-Rhys, 'Developments in the Field of Forced Marriage' [2008] *International Family Law* 26.

[218] C Proudman, 'The Criminalisation of Forced Marriage', [2012, April] *Family Law* 460.

[219] A Gill and S Anitha, 'The Illusion of Protection? An Analysis of Forced Marriage Legislation and Policy in the UK' (2009) 31(3) *Journal of Social Welfare and Family Law* 257, 262.

[220] This was an issue that was raised in evidence to the Home Affairs Select Committee. See House of Commons Home Affairs Committee, *Forced Marriage, Eighth Report of Session 2010–12* (2011).

[221] House of Commons Home Affairs Committee, *Forced Marriage, Eighth Report of Session 2010–12* (2011).

2.9.3 Criminalisation of forced marriage

In light of the criticisms of forced marriage protection orders, in 2012 the government consulted on whether it should create a specific criminal offence relating to forced marriage. Responses were split: some saw advantages in terms of deterring people from forcing others to marry, while others thought that criminalisation would make victims less likely to report in case their family members were gaoled, and/or they faced repercussions within their community. There was also concern that children might be taken abroad for marriages at a younger age so as to reduce the chance of them seeking help. While acknowledging the latter view, the government ultimately chose to introduce a new criminal offence.[222]

In 2014, the Anti-Social Behaviour, Crime and Policing Act therefore made it a specific criminal offence to force someone to marry. The penalty is imprisonment for up to seven years.

STATUTORY EXTRACT *s121 Anti-Social Behaviour, Crime and Policing Act 2014*

121 Offence of forced marriage: England and Wales:

(1) A person commits an offence under the law of England and Wales if he or she
   (a) uses violence, threats or any other form of coercion for the purpose of causing another person to enter into a marriage, and
   (b) believes, or ought reasonably to believe, that the conduct may cause the other person to enter into the marriage without free and full consent.
(2) In relation to a victim who lacks capacity to consent to marriage, the offence under subsection (1) is capable of being committed by any conduct carried out for the purpose of causing the victim to enter into a marriage (whether or not the conduct amounts to violence, threats or any other form coercion).
(3) A person commits an offence under the law of England and Wales if he or she
   (a) practises any form of deception with the intention of causing another person to leave the United Kingdom, and
   (b) intends the other person to be subjected to conduct outside the United Kingdom that is an offence under subsection (1) or would be an offence under that subsection if the victim were in England or Wales.

There have been relatively few prosecutions under the new offence. As we have seen, there is a grey area between arranged marriages and forced marriages, and the law needs clear evidence of the latter to be able to act. It is therefore no surprise that prosecuted cases tended to involve the most serious aspects of forced marriage, including being abandoned abroad, physical violence, rape of a child, and threats to kill.[223] In about half of

---

[222] Home Office, *Forced Marriage: A Consultation. Summary of Responses* (Home Office 2012).
[223] See 'Forced marriage jail first as Cardiff man sentenced' (*BBC News* 10 June 2015) available at https://www.bbc.co.uk/news/uk-wales-33076323; H Summers, 'Birmingham woman guilty of duping daughter into forced marriage' (*The Guardian*, 22 May 2018) available at https://www.theguardian.com/uk-news/2018/may/22/birmingham-woman-guilty-of-duping-daughter-into-forced-marriage; and 'Forced marriage: Parents guilty of luring daughter to Bangladesh' (*BBC News* 29 May 2018) all accessed 30 August 2020.

unsuccessful or discontinued prosecutions the victim did not support the prosecution or retracted the complaint.[224] This suggests that those who anticipated that many victims would be reluctant to invoke the criminal law were correct. Gill and Anitha argue the Act's 'focus on matters of law comes at the expense of recognising the subtleties of the socio-cultural practices and gendered experiences of coercion that underpin forced marriage'.[225] Only when we address these issues can an effective solution be found.

2.9.4 Nullity and forced marriage

As we know from section 2.8.3, a marriage without consent is voidable under s12 Matrimonial Causes Act 1973. It is also possible to divorce. However, within the communities affected by forced marriage, divorce is often met with serious disapproval. For these reasons, nullity is often preferred by victims of forced marriage, in order to 'as far as possible remove any stigma that would otherwise attach to the fact that a person in the petitioner's situation has been married'.[226]

As we also saw, however, under s13 a statutory bar applies: the application for annulment must be brought within three years of the marriage. This assumes that the victim is able to seek legal help in that time. In reality, once married, 'women [who are the majority of victims] are often unable to exit forced marriages because of continued gender surveillance after marriage, social norms against divorce in some communities, and immigration control in the case of immigrant women'.[227] In *B v I (Forced Marriage)*, for example, the wife was not able to seek help in the first three years of the marriage, and when she 'was finally able to make contact with someone via the internet and, with their help, . . . leave the family home . . . her actions put her at risk of serious injury and loss of life, for bringing shame upon her family, [and] she had to assume a secret identity.' Recognising that divorce was not an option for the applicant—'she would be doomed, if that be the right word, to a scenario where members of her own community regarded her as in some way unacceptable because of her divorce'—Baron J used the inherent jurisdiction to 'get around' the time limit and instead of nullifying the marriage declared that there was never a marriage capable of being recognised in the English jurisdiction.[228] In other words, there was a non-marriage, and there is no time bar for those. As Gaffney-Rhys points out, while on the facts the resulting inability to apply for a financial remedy order was of no consequence for B, this will not be the case for all victims in the same position.[229]

---

[224] Crown Prosecution Service, *CPS Forced Marriage Key Reasons for Unsuccessful Prosecutions 2010–2015* [dataset]. Available at https://www.cps.gov.uk/underlying-data/cps-forced-marriage-key-reasons-unsuccessful-prosecutions-2010-2015 accessed 30 August 2020.
[225] AK Gill and S Anitha, 'Forced Marriage Legislation in the UK: A Critique', in authors (eds), *Forced Marriage: Introducing a Social Justice and Human Rights Perspective* (Zed Books 2011) 143.
[226] *P v R (Forced Marriage: Annulment Procedure)* [2003] 1 FLR 661 [17] (Coleridge J).
[227] G Gangoli, K Chantler, M Hester, and A Singleton, 'Understanding Forced Marriage', in AK Gill and S Anitha (eds), *Forced Marriage: Introducing a Social Justice and Human Rights Perspective* (Zed Books 2011) 27.
[228] *B v I (Forced Marriage)* [2010] 1 FLR 1721.
[229] R Gaffney-Rhys, 'The Legal Status of Forced Marriages: Void, Voidable, or Non-Existent?' [2010] *International Family Law* 336.

FOCUS Think Critically

Is there a need for nullity?

In 2018, the last year in which separate statistics for the number of annulments are available, there were 269 annulments between different-sex couples.[230] Compared to the 90,000 divorces, this is a tiny proportion of those wishing to end a relationship. It is therefore necessary to consider whether there is a continuing use for the grounds of voidability: non-consummation, consent, mental disorder, venereal disease, pregnancy, or gender transition.

It is clearly desirable that marriages that involve a lack of consent should be dissolvable. Such marriages could of course be terminated by divorce, but, as discussed above, continued availability of nullity helps members of certain minority ethnicities to avoid the stigma presently associated with divorce. It may be that in the future there is less stigma. However, consent is a fundamental element of marriage: if you do not intend to marry, why should you have to divorce? The problem is that a nullity suit is no less onerous than a divorce; indeed many nullity suits are more expensive because they end up in the High Court.

It is certainly the case that the grounds on which a marriage is voidable demonstrates the historical importance of sex and procreation to marriage, or, rather, sex and procreation *within* marriage, so that one's heirs were legitimate. Consummation, venereal disease, and pregnancy by another all justified dissolving the marriage. Violence and rape, on the other hand, did not do so for many centuries. Consummation made sense when there was an enforceable duty to live with one's spouse and when it was lawful for a man to force sex on his wife. But this is not the case today. It is a ground which makes a certain kind of sexual relationship (heterosexual, penetrative) into a central aspect of the marriage so that an inability or refusal to have sex after marriage can justify the annulment of the whole marriage, a marriage which may have involved mutual love, support, and companionship. Ironically, if you were to write a contract with a partner for the provision of sexual services, that would be void as a matter of public policy, as we see in Chapter 5, and compliance may even involve the commission of criminal offences relating to prostitution. The argument that procreation is central to marriage is challenged by the fact that infertility has never been a ground of annulment in this jurisdiction.[231] A party wishing to dissolve a marriage in order to have children with a fertile partner would need to divorce. But all that is required of marriage is a single act of consummation, not a continuing sexual relationship. In any case 'given the sensitivity of the matter and the attendant embarrassment'[232] of detailing attempts at intercourse, who would want to bring a petition on the basis of non-consummation? Far better to simply divorce on a no-fault basis.

Similar criticisms can be made in respect of the grounds of mental illness or change of gender. The introduction of no-fault divorce has further removed the need for annulment. With previous no-fault divorces only available after a wait of two or five years from the end of the marriage, couples could have used annulment instead of fault-based divorce in relation to these two issues which are not issues of poor marital behaviour but circumstances outside the parties' control. A further ground is having a communicable venereal disease. In the past, many venereal diseases that would have affected fertility, or perhaps even been fatal. Modern medicine has provided a cure for many of these, or provided a means to reduce the effects or transmission risk. When we consider recent cases on nullity, venereal disease is not pleaded. Instead, the most recent cases of the last few years have been about lack of consent (forced marriage) and bigamy (a void ground rather than a voidable one) caused or contributed to by marriages across different jurisdictions.

It is therefore necessary to ask whether some or all of the grounds of voidability should be dispensed with, perhaps retaining only consent, the most fundamentally important of the voidable grounds.

---

[230] Office for National Statistics, NOMIS dataset to *Divorces in England and Wales: 2018* (2019) (access these via the 'Explorable datasets for divorces in England and Wales' link on the ONS website).

[231] For the American context and a discussion of the state interest in sex in marriage, see LD Borten, 'Sex, Procreation, and the State Interest in Marriage' (2002) 102(4) *Columbia Law Review* 1089.

[232] A Borkowski, 'Wilful Refusal to Consummate: "Just Excuse"' [1994] *Family Law* 684, 685.

2.10 **Foreign marriages**

When a couple marries abroad, provided they meet the requirements of that country as to capacity and formalities, they will be legally married there. But will their marriage be recognised in England or Wales, and therefore attract all the legal consequences of marriage here?

A marriage which is entered into outside England and Wales will be recognised here if three conditions are satisfied:

- Each party had capacity to marry according to the law of their country of domicile (this is known as 'essential validity'). For example, a marriage formed abroad by someone aged under 16 who is domiciled in England[233] would not be recognised in England, as English law does not permit the marriage to someone aged under 16.[234] A person's country of domicile can be their 'domicile of origin': the country in which their father was domiciled at the time the person is born (or their mother's domicile in the case of a child born to an unmarried couple or married parents who live apart).[235] It is possible to lose one's domicile of origin, but this is not achieved simply by becoming habitually resident in another country. Instead, a person must live in that country and intend to make it their permanent home, thereby creating a 'domicile of choice'. Each person to a marriage may therefore have a separate country of domicile.

- The formalities required by the law of the country in which the marriage took place were complied with (this is known as 'formal validity'). There are special rules governing the marriages of members of the armed forces who are posted abroad.

- The marriage is not manifestly unjust or contrary to public policy. On rare occasions, a marriage which meets the first two criteria will nevertheless not be recognised in England and Wales for reasons of justice or public policy. John Murphy has criticised public policy in this context as being 'nebulous', 'ill defined' 'left unarticulated' in judgments, and potentially 'susceptible to accusations of cultural imperialism'.[236] One recent example of the public policy objection is *City of Westminster* v *C*,[237] in which the marriage was performed over the telephone between a woman domiciled in Bangladesh and a man domiciled in England. Although the court considered issues of capacity to marry (the man had very severe learning difficulties) and which country's law should apply, it ultimately decided that the marriage would not be recognised under English law in any event, on the grounds of public policy.

2.10.1 **Polygamous marriages**

As we see at section 2.6.3, a marriage between more than two people is void if that marriage was entered into in England and Wales. But the position may be different if the parties live abroad. There are three situations than may arise.

---

[233] Or by someone domiciled in England to someone aged 16 who was domiciled abroad in a country where the age of marriage is lower: *Pugh v Pugh* [1951] P 482.

[234] Matrimonial Causes Act 1973 s11.

[235] Domicile and Matrimonial Proceedings Act 1973 s3.

[236] J Murphy, 'Rationality and Cultural Pluralism in the Non-Recognition of Foreign Marriages' (2000) 49 *International and Comparative Law Quarterly* 643.

[237] [2008] 2 FCR 146.

- *The parties were domiciled in England or Wales, but were married in a country that permits polygamy:* A person who is domiciled in England or Wales (or, indeed, in any other country that does not permit polygamous marriage) who already has a spouse cannot travel to a country that permits polygamous marriage and whilst there marry someone else. Under English law, that person does not have capacity enter into that second marriage because they are already married. However, the fact that a country permits polygamy does not affect the validity of a monogamous marriage entered into in that country.[238] It is only subsequent marriages that are invalid.

  In rare situations, instead of looking at the parties' domicile, validity can be determined by the laws of the country of their intended matrimonial home.

- *The parties were domiciled in a country that permits polygamy but married in England/ Wales:* A polygamous marriage entered into in England by a person domiciled in a country that permits polygamy will not be recognised as valid in England: the marriage took place in England (or Wales) but it does not comply with the formalities laid down by English/Welsh law. It is unlikely that the country of domicile will recognise the purported marriage as valid because it was not valid where it was formed.

- *The parties were both domiciled and married in a country that permits polygamy:* Polygamous marriages between persons who are domiciled in a country that permits polygamous marriages and who married there satisfy the first two criteria above. Their marriage will thus be recognised if the parties move to England and Wales, although there are immigration restrictions and, in the case of child brides or grooms, child protection issues[239] and a risk that the marriage will not be recognised for public policy reasons.[240] In 2008, the government estimated that there were fewer than 1,000 legally recognised polygamous marriages in the UK as a whole.[241] There is, however, some evidence that unregistered (i.e. unlawful) polygamous marriages 'are more commonplace than might be expected' among minority communities.[242]

2.10.2 Presumed marriages

In centuries past, as we have seen, there was often a lack of written marriage records, and even where evidence did exist it could be of doubtful truth. If a question arose over the status of a relationship, '[t]he fact that the couple had lived together and been reputed to be married might be the only available evidence that there had been an actual ceremony of marriage at some point'.[243] These days, a lack of evidence is rare, but could arise where

---

[238] Private International Law (Miscellaneous Provisions) Act 1995 Part II.

[239] See Written Answer by Lord Nash to the Bishop of St Albans, 16 December 2014, available at https://www.parliament.uk/business/publications/written-questions-answers-statements/written-question/Lords/2014-12-09/HL3558 accessed 11 August 2018. See also the resulting *Daily Mirror* article: https://www.mirror.co.uk/news/uk-news/home-office-powerless-legal-loophole-4846514 accessed 11 August 2018.

[240] *Alhaji Mohamed v Knott* [1969] 1 QB 1. Although that child marriage was recognised, the judge indicated that may not always be the case. Perhaps much depends upon public mores of the time.

[241] Barbara Follett MP, Minister for Women and Equalities, HC Deb 21 January 2008 vol 470, col 1510W.

[242] L Casey, *The Casey Review: A Review into Opportunity and* (Department for Communities and Local Government 2016) para 8.45.

[243] R Probert, 'The Presumptions in Favour of Marriage' (2018) 77(2) *Cambridge Law Journal* 375, 378.

the court was concerned with a decades-old marriage conducted abroad in a place lacking reliable records or where records had been destroyed by natural disaster or warfare.

In certain circumstances, it is possible to presume that a valid marriage has taken place notwithstanding a lack of formal documentary proof. This gives us a starting point that the parties are validly married. The presumption operates in situations where the existence or non-existence of a valid marriage *cannot be proved either way*, but where there was a purported wedding ceremony or event that was in theory capable of resulting in a marriage that was valid in the place it was undertaken.[244] Logically, this must be a requirement: it cannot be possible for a party to allege a marriage, provide no evidence, and rely on the presumption, unless there is something for that presumption to hang on—i.e., a ceremony of some kind. Otherwise, we could all assert the presumption to allege that we are married to our favourite celebrity, lack of evidence notwithstanding.

While the presumption gives us a starting point that the ceremony did indeed result in a valid marriage,[245] the presumption is rebuttable by evidence to the contrary. The person asserting that the marriage is not valid has the burden of proving that.

It is important to note that the presumption does not make a void marriage or a non-marriage into a valid marriage. The presumption operates where there is no proof either way. If there is proof on the balance of probabilities that the marriage was not validly created, this rebuts the presumption.[246] In her article 'The Presumptions in Favour of Marriage', Probert explains that as '[t]he presumption is that the ceremony was regular, . . . as a matter of logic it cannot arise at all where the ceremony is known to be irregular'.[247] An example of this is Key Case *Attorney General v Akhter and Khan*, where 'the evidence given by both the wife and the husband clearly established that the ceremony was not one which could create a valid English marriage and [this] positive evidence of the parties rebutted any presumption'.[248] Citing Probert's article, Williams J notes that 'the presumption based on cohabitation and reputation arose from problems created by an evidential void or deficiency. It is difficult to see why as a matter of policy or justice it should be wheeled into action where the evidence is clear and complete.'[249]

Some courts have held that the presumption only applies where the parties have cohabited for a long period after the purported ceremony.[250] Probert—an acknowledged expert in this area—argues compellingly that this is a misreading of earlier case law and that a marriage does not become valid through lapse of time.[251] It is perhaps more correct to treat judges' references to long-term cohabitation as evidence of their reluctance to hold that a marriage is not a marriage without compelling evidence that it is not, especially given the

---

[244] R Probert, '*Hayatleh v Modfy*: Presuming the Validity of a Known Ceremony of Marriage' [2018] *Child and Family Law Quarterly* 61.

[245] Or that later registration created a valid marriage, where registration is a requirement for validity (which is not the case in England and Wales).

[246] Probert suggests that *Adjudication Officer v Bath* [2000] 1 FLR 8 was wrong in using the presumption to remedy defects in the ceremony: see '*Hayatleh v Modfy*: Presuming the Validity of a Known Ceremony of Marriage' [2018] *Child and Family Law Quarterly* 61.

[247] R Probert, 'The Presumptions in Favour of Marriage' (2018) 77(2) *Cambridge Law Journal* 375, 396.

[248] [2018] EWFC 54 [14] (Williams J).

[249] [2018] EWFC 54 [40] (Williams J).

[250] See *Adjudication Officer v Bath* [2000] 1 FLR 8 and the line of subsequent cases.

[251] R Probert, 'The Presumptions in Favour of Marriage' (2018) 77(2) *Cambridge Law Journal* 375, 392.

serious implications of holding that a couple are not married. We can contrast this with the stricter approach taken where there is evidence, and that evidence is that there was insufficient compliance with the formalities.[252]

SCENARIO 2

Illustration 5: Raheem and Fatima

The law of presumed marriage does not assist Raheem and Fatima. We know that their marriage was held at the mosque they attend. If that marriage is shown to have been invalid as a result of non-compliance with the formalities, they cannot use the presumption of marriage to rescue them: it does not apply where we know that a marriage was invalid. It will only help if we are unable to determine whether the marriage was valid or not. Given the availability of marriage records and other evidence in England and Wales, a court should never be in a position of not being able to make a determination, and having to rely on the presumption, where the marriage was conducted here.

2.11 The myth of common law marriage

As we see at 2.4, there are specific requirements in order to form a valid marriage. Yet many people believe that if you live with someone for a period of time that person will acquire 'divorce style' rights as a 'common law spouse' even though there has not been a marriage ceremony. Such rights may include the right to a financial settlement at the end of the relationship or the death of a partner. Various periods of time have been suggested as giving rise to these entitlements: six months, 12 months, or five years are commonly mentioned.

But there is no such thing as common law marriage. If we think of a common law marriage as one that arises by custom, the closest we get to it in English law are the unregulated marriages that took place before Lord Hardwicke's Marriage Act 1753 but those were purported marriages formed improperly, not marriages formed through common law. Probert argues that 'the concept of "common-law marriage" is in fact a nineteenth-century American invention, based on a misinterpretation of English authorities'.[253] The reality is that parties who live together without being married never acquired the same rights and responsibilities as a married couple and, as we shall see in Chapter 5, are even now in a significantly weaker legal position. Moreover, if parties mistakenly believe that the law will protect them when it does not, they may not take essential steps to protect themselves.

Yet this myth is pervasive. In 2001, the British Social Attitudes Survey found that 56 per cent of those surveyed believed that the legal effects of marriage and cohabitation were the same.[254] Apart from minor differences, this belief transcended age, social class,

---

[252] See, e.g., *Hudson v Leigh.*
[253] R Probert, 'Cohabitation: Current Legal Solutions' (2009) 62(1) *Current Legal Problems* 316, 319.
[254] A Barlow, S Duncan, G James, and A Park, 'Just a Piece of Paper? Marriage and Cohabitation', in Alison Park and National Centre for Social Research (eds), *British Social Attitudes: Public Policy, Social Ties: The 18th Report* (Sage 2001).

geographical region, and religious belief.[255] Quite why it is a common misbelief is harder to pin down. James et al. found that 'what an individual believes about common law marriage seems to depend largely upon the knowledge in their particular social network, rather than more formal sources of information'.[256]

But the responsibility cannot be laid merely at the hands of friends and relations. A number of James' interviewees suggested that their legal views 'were influenced by information from government institutions and official forms and documentation'.[257] The government, for example, often treats married and cohabiting couples the same for the purpose of determining eligibility for means-tested social security benefits. Some insurance price comparison sites still give a relationship option that includes 'common law married' when they appear to mean cohabiting. Much of the confusion stems from the habit, from the 1960s and onwards, of newspapers referring to parties' cohabitants as their common law spouses.[258] Both marriage and cohabitation increased in the 1960s and it is possible that these references were an attempt to add an appearance of respectability to informal relationships. James et al. believe that the prevalence of the marriage myth may in part be attributable to the fact that the concept reflects people's lived experience and their belief that the law will recognise and be fair to their particular situation: 'belief—or non-belief—in common law marriage rests upon notions of social logic, fairness and morality. Beliefs about what the law does are conflated with beliefs about what the law ought to do.'[259]

2.12 The importance of marriage

Now that we have seen how people marry, and the implications of getting that wrong, we need to assess what effect marriage has upon the parties' rights and responsibilities and what meanings marriage has to the parties and to the state itself. In light of this, we can then assess whether there is, or should be, a human right to marry.

2.12.1 The legal consequences of marriage

Usually, when we enter into an important contract, we make sure that the terms of the contract are embodied in writing. Although some terms and conditions can be complex and go unread, that information is there if you choose to look. That is not the case with marriage. It has been said that marriage is the only contract you sign where you do not know the terms in advance (and perhaps not until you consult a divorce lawyer if it breaks down).

---

[255] G James, A Park, and A Barlow, *Cohabitation, Marriage and the Law: Social Change and Legal Reform in the 21st Century* (1st edn, Hart 2005).
[256] G James, A Park, and A Barlow, *Cohabitation, Marriage and the Law: Social Change and Legal Reform in the 21st Century* (1st edn, Hart 2005) 43.
[257] G James, A Park, and A Barlow, *Cohabitation, Marriage and the Law: Social Change and Legal Reform in the 21st Century* (1st edn, Hart 2005) 44.
[258] R Probert, 'The Evolution of the Common-Law Marriage Myth' (2011, March) *Family Law* 283, 284.
[259] G James, A Park, and A Barlow, *Cohabitation, Marriage and the Law: Social Change and Legal Reform in the 21st Century* (1st edn, Hart 2005) 45.

As with many aspects of family law, the law has developed incrementally and is found in a number of different places and requires a familiarity with legal methods to understand. The legal consequences of marriage are the same whether the parties are in a different-sex marriage or a same-sex marriage. However, there are significant differences between married couples and those who live together, or have children together, but who have not married. Table 5.1 in Chapter 5 compares their respective positions and discusses domestic partnership regimes that exist or are proposed around the world as an alternative to marriage.

In this section, we highlight the main legal consequences of marriage.

Property and finances

Marriage does not affect the ability of the spouses to hold property of all kinds individually. This can be contrasted with the position in some other countries which make a distinction between sole and community property, and with the position prior to 1882, when a woman's property was transferred to her husband upon marriage. This separate property regime is counterbalanced by broad legal powers to redistribute property at the end of the marriage irrespective of the source of the asset. During the marriage itself, the parties have a legal obligation to provide 'reasonable maintenance' to the other.[260] Spouses also have 'home rights'—the right to occupy a matrimonial home even if the property is in the sole name of their spouse. Such rights end on divorce or dissolution or as a result of a court order regulating occupation under Part IV Family Law Act 1996.[261]

In addition to these property rights, there are also some tax advantages tied to being married or civilly partnered. These include the ability to reduce tax using the Married Couple's Allowance, the ability to transfer investments between them without being taxed (and therefore take advantage of any unused capital gains tax allowance of their spouse and reduce the circumstances in which inheritance tax is charged). Married couples are also considered lower risk than unmarried couples by insurers, leading to cheaper car insurance. According to price comparison site Compare the Market, 'single drivers are at twice the risk of having an accident behind the wheel compared to people who are living in matrimonial bliss'.[262]

On death

A spouse is in a better position than an unmarried partner in a number of ways. First, their status as next of kin will be respected. They will be able to make arrangements for the funeral. While that may seem obvious, this was something that was denied to a number of gay men and lesbians who were until recently unable to marry and thus to protect their relationship in this way. They will not have to pay inheritance tax on any assets that are left to them by their late spouse. If there is a Will that does not provide sufficiently for them, they have a more valuable claim to financial provision under the Inheritance (Provision

---

[260] Domestic Proceedings and Magistrates' Courts Act 1978 s1, Matrimonial Causes Act 1973 s27, and Civil Partnership Act 2004 Sch 5 and 6. The former common law duty on husbands to maintain wives was abolished by the Equality Act 2010 s198 although that section is not yet in force. For a rare case on s27, see *H v H* [2015] EWHC B24 (Fam).

[261] See Chapter 7.

[262] https://www.comparethemarket.com/car-insurance/content/getting-married/ accessed 4 August 2018.

for Family and Dependants) Act 1975 than does an unmarried partner or dependant.[263] If their spouse has died intestate (that is, without leaving a valid Will), they will nevertheless inherit some or all of the estate.[264] There are various state benefits arising from widowhood to which they may also be entitled, such as a bereavement payment, bereavement allowance, bereavement support payment, or widowed parents' allowance. They will be eligible to receive the survivor's benefits under their late spouse's pension, which can be extremely valuable. They can succeed to a secured tenancy in their late spouse's name. They can also make a claim under the Fatal Accidents Act 1976 if their spouse was killed in that way; the survivor of an unmarried couple can only make such a claim if they have cohabited with the deceased for at least two years.

Parentage and parental responsibility

A father who is married to the mother of his children will obtain automatic parental responsibility for the children. There is also a legal presumption that any children born to his wife are legitimate, i.e., that he is the father of them. These aspects are discussed in more detail in Chapter 8.

Immigration

Whether or not a person is married or in an unmarried relationship, they may experience difficulties in entering the UK to be with their partner. It is possible to obtain a visa to enter the UK if your spouse or fiancé(e) is a British citizen, or has 'indefinite leave to remain' or proof of permanent residence in the UK, or has refugee status or humanitarian protection in the UK. However, this is subject to the person already in the UK having a minimum income—even if they are a refugee—with which to support their spouse/fiancé(e). In 2015, a report for the Children's Commissioner for England and Wales estimated that 15,000 children were separated from a parent due to such immigration rules.[265]

Unmarried couples who do not intend to marry will also need to show that they have been living together in a relationship for at least two years in order to demonstrate that the relationship is 'genuine and subsisting'.

Criminal cases

Historically, a consequence of the doctrine of unity—that 'by marriage, the husband and wife are one person in law'[266]—was that one spouse could not testify against the other in criminal proceedings. This is not now the case: a person can testify against their spouse or civil partner and can be compelled to do so provided that they themselves are not also being prosecuted. However, they can be compelled only where the offences involve specified sexual offences against a person aged under 16; an assault on, or injury or threat of injury to the testifying spouse themselves; or attempting or conspiring to commit, aiding,

---

[263] See Chapter 5.
[264] See Chapter 5.
[265] Middlesex University and the Joint Council for the Welfare of Immigrants, *Family Friendly? The impact on children of the Family Migration Rules: A review of the financial requirements* (Children's Commissioner for England 2015).
[266] Blackstone, *Commentaries on the Laws of England* (1765–1769).

abetting, counselling, procuring or inciting the commission of one of these offences.[267] The fact that a person can be compelled to testify does not, of course, mean that the prosecution would want to adduce testimony if the witness is hostile to the prosecution's case.

In *R (on the application of the Crown Prosecution Service) v Registrar General of Births, Deaths and Marriages* an accused murderer on remand sought to marry his partner, who was due to be called as a prosecution witness. The Crown Prosecution Service sought to persuade the prison governor not to permit the marriage before the trial, because once married she would not be a compellable witness to a charge of murder. The Court of Appeal said that there was no public policy objection to the marriage despite this consequence.[268]

Surnames

While it is still common to adopt the husband's surname on marriage, this is not legally necessary. People can use any surname they want, provided that they do not hold themselves out as having a title when they do not, seek to use an obscene name, or use a particular name to defraud people.

SCENARIO 1

Illustration 2: Helen and Ned

Helen and Ned have been living together and their decision to marry has been taken on the basis of their wish to express their commitment to one another (we discuss why people marry in section 2.12.5). It is likely that they will not be aware of many of the legal differences between being married and continuing to live together without being married. We discuss the differences between marriage and cohabitation in Chapter 5, and it is only by reading that that you will be able to understand the considerable differences in position. Upon marriage, Helen and Ned will acquire a number of rights and responsibilities that they would not otherwise have, such as a claim to the other's property if their relationship breaks down (cohabitants would only be able to make a claim if they could fit themselves within trusts law, or if they have children); a right to be maintained by the other person during the marriage; preferential treatment of the survivor on death; and automatic acquisition of parental responsibility by Ned over any children born to Helen during the marriage. Most of these consequences will only become apparent when the relationship breaks down, one of them dies, or there is an issue with their health or their children. If they had not married, their relatively weak position is likely also to only become apparent when the worst happens.

2.12.2 Marriage as a contract or status

Marriage involves the parties entering into a contract with one another, but also gives them a status: they are married, with all the legal consequences of that. Those consequences are mandatory: the parties cannot select from a menu only those rights and responsibilities they want: 'marriage law is table d'hôte, rather than à la carte'.[269] It is, as Lady Hale

---

[267] Police and Criminal Evidence Act 1984, s80.
[268] [2003] 1 All ER 540, 549.
[269] M Hibbs, C Barton, and J Beswick, 'Why Marry? Perceptions of the Affianced' [2001] *Family Law* 197, 202.

said in the nuptial agreements case *Radmacher v Granatino*, a 'package which the law of the land lays down'.[270] Society has decided what the content of the package should be, and this overrides the personal preferences of the parties. As the feminist academic Katharine O'Donovan has written, marriage 'is only open to certain persons under specified conditions according to law. Termination of marriage can only occur as denoted by law, and not by the partners . . . Law regulates entry into marriage, the ceremony, the consummation and validity. In that sense law constitutes the marriage'.[271]

It is therefore the case that marriage does not follow the normal rules of contract law. As we can see, the law of nullity reflects some common contract vitiating factors, such as duress or mistake, but does not mirror these exactly. Moreover, despite the serious implications, the bar for capacity to marry is set fairly low: marriage is considered a relatively simple contract compared to certain contracts in other areas of life. There is little regulation outside the criminal law of how the parties behave to one another during the marriage. Importantly, however, the end of the marriage is tightly regulated. Indeed, Bettle and Herring have argued that 'a marriage only attracts significant legal consequences when a party seeks to exit from it'[272] and this may be the first point at which these consequences become apparent to the parties.

It is because the state controls formation and dissolution of marriage that marriage is often referred to as a status, rather than a contract. In fact, it contains elements of both. Hafen has argued in the North American context that in recent years 'individual interests have taken on such an overpowering significance that it is difficult for the contemporary mind to see any interests other than individual ones'.[273] In this jurisdiction, the parties can live together or not, arrange their finances how they want, have children or not. As in the United States, the trend in recent years has been to permit ever-greater private ordering. Nevertheless, the parties do not have absolute freedom of contract in all areas.[274] They are subject to what Lady Hale has termed 'an irreducible minimum' obligation, such as to provide financial support to one another and their children.[275]

Why does the state impose these terms on the married? The answer is that marriage is important to the state.

2.12.3 Why the state likes marriage

Legal marriage 'is a public institution, created by law to promote public policy and to further social interests'.[276] These are some of the interests that have been asserted.

---

[270] *Radmacher v Granatino* [2010] UKSC 42 [132].

[271] K O'Donovan, 'Marriage: A Sacred or Profane Love Machine?' (1993) 1(1) *Feminist Legal Studies* 75, 75.

[272] J Bettle and J Herring, '"With This Diode I Thee Wed": Marrying Robots and What This Tells Us about 21st Century Marriage' (*Family Law Week*, 25 March 2014).

[273] BC Hafen, 'The Constitutional Status of Marriage, Kinship, and Sexual Privacy—Balancing the Individual and Social Interests' (1983) 81 *Michigan Law Review* 463, 469. Hafen was talking about the American context, but the trend is the same within the UK.

[274] J Halley, 'Behind the Law of Marriage (I): From Status/Contract to the Marriage System' (2010) 6 *Unbound* 1.

[275] *Radmacher v Granatino* [2010] UKSC 42 [132].

[276] L Wardle, 'Is Marriage Obsolete?' (2003) 10(1) *Michigan Journal of Gender and Law* 189.

Orderly transmission of property

As we see in section 2.2, for many centuries the state did not regulate marriage. When it did intervene, it was out of self-interest because of the consequences of inappropriate marriages and the effect on legitimacy and succession to property. Economic concerns remain a key aspect of marriage regulation today. Marriage assists the orderly transfer of property on death or when the relationship breaks down. However, the economic differences between marriage and cohabitation are not natural consequences but reflect state decisions to give remedies and obligations to those who are married and not to those who are unmarried. Laws on intestacy (see Chapter 5) and on child support (Chapter 6) demonstrate how it is possible to implement a regime that transfers property without the necessity of marriage.

State convenience

Dewar has argued that 'Marriage is a convenient conceptual device for making families visible in law, provided that most family life is conducted within marriage.'[277] It is easier to regulate the behaviours of definable units. For example, where a couple is married, the state knows what legal responsibilities each party has towards the other. This is unclear in the case of unmarried cohabitants, who virtually always do not have such responsibilities unless they individually contract to do so. There are therefore administrative reasons why marriage is useful to the state.

To say that someone is married is a useful shorthand for a range of different factors. The economist Robert Rowthorn argues that 'knowing whether or not a couple is married convey[s] a valuable information to outsiders about the likely stability of their relationship, their capacity as parents, and other personal attributes such as health or reliability', albeit that this is not the case for every married couple.[278] (There is some evidence that married people, particularly men, live longer and are healthier than those who are unmarried.[279])

Response to public demand

Part of the state's role is to provide a service to its citizens. As people want to marry, the state should 'do what it can to provide that institution, educate the public about it, and make access to it easy'.[280] We know that most, if not all societies have established a form of marital-style commitment—a way for two or more people to be perceived externally by their relationship to one another. Within the couple, as we see at section 2.12.5, marriage can provide 'an orderly framework' for parties to express their commitment to one another.[281]

---

[277] J Dewar, 'Family Law and Its Discontents', (2000) 14 *International Journal of Law, Policy, and the Family* 59, 62.

[278] R Rowthorn, 'Marriage as a Signal', in AW Dnes and R Rowthorn (eds), *The Law and Economics of Marriage and Divorce* (Cambridge University Press 2010).

[279] See The Harvard Health Blog: 'The Health Advantages of Marriage' (2016) available at https://www.health.harvard.edu/blog/the-health-advantages-of-marriage-2016113010667 and Harvard Men's Health Watch, 'Marriage and Men's Health' (2010). Available at https://www.health.harvard.edu/newsletter_article/marriage-and-mens-health accessed 12 August 2018. See also LJ Waite and M Gallagher, *The Case for Marriage; Why Married People Are Happier, Healthier, and Better Off Financially* (Doubleday 2000).

[280] BH Bix, 'State Interest and Marriage – The Theoretical Perspective' (2003) 32 *Hofstra Law Review* 93.

[281] Law Commission of Canada, *Beyond Conjugality: Recognizing and Supporting Close Personal Adult Relationships* (2001).

The argument that the state is responding to public demand applies to many functions of the state: voters respond to political parties that respond to voters' personal needs and ideologies. It applies to divorce law, too. That does not mean that the law always meets current needs or reflects current views. As this chapter may have made you realise, some aspects of the law are greatly in need of reform in order to respond to today's family life. The state, through Parliament, may have different priorities—such as the other considerations discussed here—or may be slow to move, or our Parliamentarians may not truly reflect the wishes of the majority; or conversely may reflect the wishes of the majority but overlook those of minority groups.

Containing sexuality/sexual desire

Gallagher has argued that 'marriage is the way in which every society attempts to channel the erotic energies of men and women into a relatively narrow but highly fruitful channel—to give every child the father his or her heart desires. . . . By socially defining and supporting a particular kind of sexual union, the society defines for its young what the preferred relationship is and what purposes it serves.'[282] In so doing, however, it disadvantages and stigmatises other forms of relationship (historically, same-sex relationships; and interracial relationships in some US states), which may also serve the same state and personal purposes and over which the participants may have no control: the lack of gay marriage did not result in people converting to heterosexuality, it just excluded them from protection. Moreover, in Chapter 2 when we consider fault-based divorce laws, we conclude that the power of the law to make people within the preferred relationships behave in a certain way is relatively weak. As sexual behaviour outside marriage has become common in our culture, the power of marriage as a mechanism to control or direct sexual desire has been reduced.

Encouragement of mutual dependence

On divorce, the parties have obligations to one another that to some extent compensates them for decisions made in the marriage (see Chapter 4), such as one person giving up work to care for the children. There is also a state interest here: mutual responsibilities reduce the need for the state to offer financial and practical support to a family. If the parties have moral and legal obligations to one another, this alleviates the state of this burden. For example, if a person becomes ill or disabled, the cost to the state of caring for them is significantly reduced if they can be cared for by their family instead. Research has estimated that the work done by family carers saves the state around £119 billion per year.[283] Marriage is 'its own little security system' . . . '[t]he more the private family can look after its own, the less the state will have to do so.'[284]

As a better way to raise children

If marriage is seen as having a primary purpose in procreation, then children's interests are seen as justifying a state interest in marriage. The apparent benefit for children is a

---

[282] M Gallagher, 'What Is Marriage For? The Public Purposes of Marriage Law' (2002) 62 *Louisiana Law Review* 773.

[283] Carers UK and L Buckner, *Valuing Carers* (University of Leeds 2011).

[284] Lady Hale, 'Equality and Autonomy in Family Law' (2011) 33(1) *Journal of Social Welfare and Family Law* 3, 4.

much-cited argument in favour of marriage, because there is evidence that children born to married couples fare better than those of unmarried or single parents on a range of different criteria, from educational attainment to wealth to criminality. The right-wing think tank Centre for Social Justice cites a reduction in risk of violence and abuse, improved child and adult mental health, better job prospects, and reduced drug and alcohol dependency.[285] 'The first essential public purpose of marriage', the conservative pro-marriage campaigner Gallagher argues, 'is to encourage the people who make the baby to stick together and take care of each other and the baby together as a family unit.'[286] However, when the parties' relationship is acrimonious, research shows that it is better for children if the parties divorce than remain together in conflict.[287] The benefits to children arise from stability and happiness, not marriage per se.

Evaluation

Let us consider these benefits of marriage. Are they limited to marriage? Are they causally linked to marriage or simply correlations? The better outcomes for children could be linked not to the fact that the parents are married but rather to the fact that married parents tend to be better off financially than those of unmarried parents, in part because of the financial consequences that we have chosen to grant to married couples during and on breakdown of the marriage. The health benefits of marriage could be linked to the availability of personal care from another family member. Those in married relationships are less likely to experience domestic abuse than those in cohabiting relationships, but this does not mean that marriage is less violent *because* people are married. It could simply be that we are less likely to go on to marry those who are abusive. The careful selection of a marital partner may account 'for most—if not all—of marriage's seeming benefits'.[288] These benefits are not innate characteristics of marriage: they are characteristics of stability and commitment, things that are present in many non-married relationships too.

We therefore have to ask ourselves whether we could achieve the same outcomes for people not through marriage, but by giving additional rights and responsibilities to unmarried couples. This is a controversial issue and is discussed at greater length in Chapter 5. Some people say that making cohabitation more like marriage will help people who do not know that married couples have more rights and therefore do not marry. Others say that the state should not intervene to regulate all relationships and that rights and responsibilities should not apply to everyone, but only those who choose to marry.

But there is another possibility. What if, instead of increasing cohabitants' rights and responsibilities to make them more similar to those of married couples, we instead abolished marriage as giving any rights and responsibilities at all?

---

[285] Centre for Social Justice, *Why Is the Government Anti-Marriage? Family Policy Derived from Strong Evidence Would Lead to Policies Which Supported Marriage* (2009) Available at https://www.centreforsocialjustice.org.uk/library/government-anti-marriage-family-policy-derived-strong-evidence-lead-policies-supported-marriage accessed 21 November 2018.

[286] M Gallagher, 'What Is Marriage For? The Public Purposes of Marriage Law' (2002) 62 *Louisiana Law Review* 773.

[287] See the Chapter 3 focus box 'How does divorce affect children?'

[288] FF Furstenberg, 'Should Government Promote Marriage?' (2007) 26(4) *Journal of Policy Analysis and Management* 956.

2.12.4 What if we abolished marriage?

Writing in 1984, well before the introduction of same-sex marriage, Carol Smart argued that:

> The aim of the contemporary feminist critique of marriage is to provide for the possibility of eradicating this oppressive context and allowing for a much wider range of potential relationships. A primary goal must be to jettison the privileged status of the heterosexual married couple, . . . The aim is not to extend the legal and social definition of marriage to cover cohabitees or even homosexual couples, it is to abandon the status of marriage altogether and to devise a system of rights, duties or obligations which are not dependent on any form of 'coupledom' or marriage or quasi-marriage.[289]

There are two principal ways in which this abolition of marriage as a rights-giving institution could take effect. One option is to provide a civil registration scheme that provides a holistic package of rights and responsibilities. This may look very much like marriage, but, crucially, would not be limited to romantic two-person relationships. The second option is that rights and responsibilities should be available on a piecemeal basis with no single package deal available.

In 2001, the Canadian Law Commission proposed the abolition of marriage as a rights-giving institution and its replacement with a civil registration scheme—the first of the two options outlined above. It said that if the parties wanted a wedding, they could have a wedding, but that no legal consequences would flow from that. Instead, any two people, whether in a romantic relationship or not, could register to attain rights and responsibilities in respect of one another. Many countries already require a separate civil marriage in order for there to be legal effect; what made *Beyond Conjugality* different was that it suggested that people should be free to register non-conjugal relationships (i.e., non-sexual/romantic) such as siblings or carer–caree, as well as conjugal relationships. The legal privileging of romantic relationships would end. The Commission argued that marriage was 'no longer a sufficient model to respond to the variety of relationships that exist' and that other types of relationships than just marriage were 'also characterized by emotional and economic interdependence, mutual care and concern and the expectation of some duration'. If the aim was to provide a regime that promoted stability and certainty, there was no need to limit legal recognition to only certain types of adult relationship.[290] This idea proved far too controversial for the government of Canada and was not taken any further.

Martha Fineman favours the second option: 'the abolition of marriage as a legal category and, with it, the demise of the entire set of special rules attached to it, doing away with the laws of marriage and divorce as well as altering those areas in which "spouse" is a consequential category such as tax law or probate and estate rules.'[291] The state would be neutral about different relationship forms and would not favour some forms more than others by giving those forms greater protections. This would mean that there was no single

---

[289] C Smart, *The Ties That Bind: Law and the Reproduction of Patriarchal Relations* (Routledge 1984) 144.
[290] Law Commission of Canada, *Beyond Conjugality: Recognizing and Supporting Close Personal Adult Relationships* (2001).
[291] MA Fineman, 'Why Marriage?' (2001) 9(1) *Virginia Journal of Social Policy and the Law* 239.

status that would provide rights and responsibilities and parties who wanted to acquire them would need to do so through other legal mechanisms, such as contract or tort law. For example, unjust enrichment could form the basis of property redistribution at the end of a relationship, assuming the parties had not privately contracted what should happen. 'A tort for intentional infliction of emotional or psychological harm might emerge, for example. Norms that prohibit harassment (including stalking), verbal assault, and emotional abuse among strangers would be applied in defining appropriate conduct between sexual intimates.'[292] The remedies available would be piecemeal not, like marriage, a single holistic set. Thus, Clare Chambers has proposed that:

> Sex is regulated by laws requiring consent and, perhaps, limiting what can be consented to (for example, laws prohibiting extreme BDSM[293]). Emotional interdependence is largely unregulated in liberal societies, although the UK Serious Crime Act 2015 created a new offence of coercive control in intimate and family relationships. Care may be regulated by state provision of payments or respite for those with caring responsibilities. . . . In the marriage-free state, regulations pertaining to each of these relationship practices would stand separately, recognizing that individuals form relationships with different people for different functions. Piecemeal regulation thus starts by working out what justice requires in any given area of human life, and secures that requirement for everyone.[294]

Ultimately, therefore 'it is not necessary or inevitable that the state be involved in marriage at all'.[295] The state's role could be limited to the provision of regulations applicable to everyone across a wide range of contexts, rather than simply the conjugal two-person model we have in the UK.

If you consider this an undesirable approach and that we should retain marriage, think about this: is marriage, to you, about these rights and responsibilities, or is there something more to it?

2.12.5 Why do people marry?

The much quoted definition of marriage from the English 1866 case of *Hyde v Hyde* is that 'marriage, as understood in Christendom, may for this purpose be defined as the voluntary union for life of one man and one woman, to the exclusion of all others'.[296] Given the availability of divorce, the introduction of same-sex marriage, and the recognition of polygamous marriages validly conducted abroad, one might legitimately wonder whether any part of this statement remains remotely true, albeit that 'that is what people still hope and contract for when they marry'.[297] Marriage has different meanings to different people. It can, as Fineman says, be:

> a legal tie, a symbol of commitment, a privileged sexual affiliation, a relationship of hierarchy and subordination, a means of self-fulfilment, a societal construct, a cultural

---

[292] MA Fineman, 'Why Marriage?' (2001) 9(1) *Virginia Journal of Social Policy and the Law* 239.

[293] Bondage, domination, sadism, and masochism; or bondage, discipline, submission, and masochism.

[294] C Chambers, *Against Marriage: An Egalitarian Defence of the Marriage-Free State* (OUP 2017) 147.

[295] B Bix, 'State Interest and Marriage: The Theoretical Perspective' (2003) 32 *Hofstra Law Review* 93, 94.

[296] *Hyde v Hyde and Woodmansee* [1866] LR 1 P & D 130.

[297] Lady Hale, 'The Future of Marriage', in N Lowe and G Douglas (eds), *The Continuing Evolution of Family Law* (Family Law 2009) 188.

phenomenon, a religious mandate, an economic relationship, a preferred reproductive unit, a way to ensure against poverty and dependency, a romantic ideal, a natural or divined connection, a stand-in for morality, a status, or a contractual relationship.[298]

In the Mandi tribe of rural Bangladesh, men marry both a woman and her (previously widowed) mother. 'Widows who wish to remarry, reported *The Guardian*, must choose a man from the same clan as their dead husband to preserve the clan alliance. The only available single men, however, are often much younger men in their late teens. So the custom evolved: a widow would offer one of her daughters as a second bride to take over her marital duties—including sex and child-bearing—when the girl came of age.'[299] In other cultures, including the dominant culture in England and Wales, 'whereas marriage used to be a socially prescribed context for the exercise of long-term sexual relationships and, in particular, the raising of a family, the strength of that social prescription has declined, for many, to vanishing point'.[300] (We can look to the grounds of nullity for some ideas of what marriage used to be about.) For many people in British society, marriage is now individualistic and companionate: people marry for love and because it is 'the done thing': a cultural norm. The state, of course, cannot compel love: no amount of legal regulation can do that. However, it could be that some form of recognised commitment to another person meets a psychological need to belong.

A study by the Oxford Centre for Family Law and Policy[301] of those who married in the 1980s found that there were five main reasons why people marry, but compliance with convention was the most common reason:

1. (Most popular.) To comply with convention as a result of a religious, social or cultural practice or 'a desire to follow the wishes of parents'. This was particularly the case for those belonging to an ethnic minority.[302]

2. 'As a proclamation to the outside world of an attitude which each, internally, had towards each other.' The marriage itself had no significance for the couple themselves.

3. Symbolically important in confirming the parties' internal commitment to one another.

4. Marriage was not the end of a process but the established 'a framework within which a process of deepening commitment would take place. Typically, the event which was seen to complete the process was the arrival of children.'

5. (Least popular.) To achieve pragmatic objectives, such as immigration or tax benefits.

---

[298] MA Fineman, 'Why Marriage?' (2001) 9(1) *Virginia Journal of Social Policy and the Law* 239.

[299] A Haworth, '"My Mother and I Are Married to the Same Man": Matrilineal Marriage in Bangladesh' (*The Guardian*, 2 June 2013).

[300] J Eekelaar, 'Why People Marry: The Many Faces of an Institution' (2007) *Family Law Quarterly* 413.

[301] J Eekelaar, 'Why People Marry: The Many Faces of an Institution' (2007) *Family Law Quarterly* 413.

[302] For a discussion of the differences between minority ethnic and white British respondents in the Oxford study, see M Maclean and J Eekelaar, 'The Significance of Marriage: Contrasts between White British and Ethnic Minority Groups in England' (2005) 27 *Law & Policy* 379.

In a larger study, Hibbs, Barton, and Beswick found that:

> No one claimed, or admitted to, financial reasons for marriage. Love was the single highest-ranking reason given for marriage. The 'other' category included such answers as 'about time', 'felt right', 'recognition', 'social norm', 'let's do it', 'wanted a party', 'just graduated', 'spur of the moment', 'like each other's company', 'conventional thing to do', 'fiancée wanted to', 'what a funny question' and 'family bereavement' (causing a re-evaluation of priorities). One woman cited religion. Two respondents when asked 'why?' answered 'why not?' Only one person, a woman, said 'for legal reasons'. Four women said that they did not know why they were marrying. . .[303]

However, the lack of financial reasons for marrying has to be seen in light of the knowledge, or lack thereof, of the study's participants. Forty-one per cent 'thought marriage would not change the legal nature of their relationship with their partner, and 37% thought it would not have legal consequences for them with regard to their present or future children'.[304] This is, of course, not the case. Moreover, while financial/pragmatic reasons are the least popular, they are not unimportant to those who are all too aware of their precarious legal position. Consider the situation of an elderly gay man in the period prior to the Civil Partnership Act 2004. He would have no ability to protect his partner from inheritance tax on his death, his partner would not be entitled to a widower's pension, and nor could he ensure that his partner was recognised as his next-of-kin and thus able to make medical and/or burial decisions. The introduction of civil partnerships provided enormous practical protection to such couples.

It also provided them with social recognition. In a study by Shipman and Smart, civil partnerships were seen as giving couples recognition and respect from both their wider family and the general public.[305]

2.13 Is there a human right to marry?

Marriage laws have long been used to exclude or devalue certain communities. For centuries, marriage was permitted in England only according to the rites of the established Church, excluding those who practised other religions or Christian denominations unless they wished to pretend to be Anglican. The Nazis prohibited marriage between Jewish and non-Jewish people. Laws preventing mixed-race marriages—indeed criminalising the parties to them—existed throughout many southern US states well into the twentieth century.[306] 'Systematic exclusion of any group of people from the institution of marriage has been (and continues to be) a powerful way of oppressing that group in terms both of concrete rights and responsibilities and – more crucially still – in terms of the symbolic message that the group so discriminated against is unworthy of equality, and is less than human.'[307] As Probert says, 'couples may articulate their decision to marry in terms of

---

[303] M Hibbs, C Barton, and J Beswick, 'Why Marry? Perceptions of the Affianced' [2001] *Family Law* 197, 200–1.

[304] M Hibbs, C Barton, and J Beswick, 'Why Marry? Perceptions of the Affianced' [2001] *Family Law* 197, 201.

[305] B Shipman and C Smart, 'It's Made a Huge Difference': Recognition, Rights and the Personal Significance of Civil Partnership' (2007) 12(1) *Sociological Research Online*. Available at doi:10.5153/sro.1340 accessed 16 August 2018.

[306] Until struck down by the US Supreme Court in the landmark case *Loving v. Virginia* 388 US 1 (1967).

[307] C Kitzinger and S Wilkinson, 'The Re-Branding of Marriage: Why We Got Married Instead of Registering a Civil Partnership' (2004) 14(1) *Feminism and Psychology* 127, 132.

commitment and security rather than legal ties and financial provision, but it is the latter rules that give meaning to the former.'[308] State-recognised marriage provides affirmation of the relationship as well as a privileged legal status.

Marriage is a right contained in both the European Convention on Human Rights and the UN's International Covenant on Civil and Political Rights. In this section, we consider some of the key cases applying to same-sex marriage and domestic partnership regimes, as well as whether there is a right to marry someone with whom you are in a blood or affinity relationship.

2.13.1 Is gay marriage a human right?

Art 12 ECHR states that:

> Men and women of marriageable age have the right to marry and to found a family, according to the national laws governing the exercise of this right.

Art 23 of the Covenant says that:

1. The family is the natural and fundamental group unit of society and is entitled to protection by society and the State.

2. The right of men and women of marriageable age to marry and to found a family shall be recognized.

3. No marriage shall be entered into without the free and full consent of the intending spouses.

4. States Parties to the present Covenant shall take appropriate steps to ensure equality of rights and responsibilities of spouses as to marriage, during marriage and at its dissolution. In the case of dissolution, provision shall be made for the necessary protection of any children.

It is important to note that neither definition is absolute. In each case the right is constrained by references to 'men and women', which is a different word choice to saying 'all persons' or 'everyone'. In the case of the Covenant, the UN Human Rights Committee found in *Joslin v New Zealand* that refusal to allow same-sex marriage did not breach Art 23 because the term 'men and women', rather than 'everyone' or 'all persons', 'has been consistently and uniformly understood as indicating that the treaty obligation . . . is to recognize as marriage only the union between a man and a woman wishing to marry each other.'[309] In a similar vein, in *Rees v UK*, the European Court of Human Rights found that 'the right to marry guaranteed by Art 12 refers to the traditional marriage between persons of opposite biological sex. This appears also from the wording of the Article which makes it clear that Art 12 is mainly concerned to protect marriage as the basis of the family.'[310] All other Articles refer to 'everyone' or 'no one', so the different phrasing in Art 12 must be deliberate. Same-sex marriage therefore falls outside the protection of Art 12, at least at present.

---

[308] R Probert, 'Cohabitation: Current Legal Solutions' (2009) 62(1) *Current Legal Problems* 316.
[309] *Juliet Joslin et al. v New Zealand*, Communication No 902/1999, UN Doc. A/57/40 (2002) para 8.2.
[310] *Rees v UK* (Application no. 9532/81) (1986) [49].

The right to marry is closely linked to the (wider) Art 8 ECHR right to private and family life. In *Karner v Austria*, the applicant alleged a breach of Art 8 taken in conjunction with Art 14 when he was refused the right to succeed to his deceased partner's tenancy because they were in a gay relationship.[311] This difference in treatment compared to a different-sex couple is discrimination under Art 14 unless it pursues a legitimate state aim and the measure is reasonably proportionate to the aim.[312] The Court held that protection of the family 'in the traditional [i.e., heterosexual] sense' may be a legitimate aim of the state that justifies discrimination, but that states have a narrow margin of appreciation.[313] As Helen Fenwick has pointed out, in relation to social issues where there is a diversity of views among the different states, the court tries to identify common ground among the majority of states and concedes only a narrow margin of appreciation to states that fall outside that. In cases where there is no consensus, the margin is wider.[314] Here, there was no legitimate state aim that justified the discrimination.

In 2010, in *Schalk and Kopf v Austria*, the Court, noting that 'a considerable number of member States have afforded legal recognition to same-sex couples', accepted that same-sex relationship constituted family life under Art 8—a development from the previous position of recognising same-sex relationships only as an aspect of Art 8's 'private life'.[315] However, it also noted as regards Art 12 that 'there is not yet a majority of states providing for legal recognition of same-sex couples. The area in question must therefore still be regarded as one of evolving rights with no established consensus, where states must also enjoy a margin of appreciation in the timing of the introduction of legislative changes.'[316] This consensus-identifying approach means that 'the Court generally tends to follow, rather than lead. Once a consensus emerges, it will probably impose it on the recalcitrant members of its interpretative community . . . But until that happens, it will leave the democratic processes in diverse European societies to come up with their own solutions'.[317]

Although Schalk and Kopf lost their case, the Court's statement indicates an acceptance that the then wide margin of appreciation would narrow as an increasing number of states accepted same-sex marriage, and that in due course, therefore, 'recalcitrant members' would find themselves in breach, even if they were not presently. At the time, England and Wales had civil partnerships—a separate regime of rights for same-sex couples—but did not yet have same-sex marriage.

In *Valliantos and others v Greece*, the Court again had to consider Art 8 in light of the Greek state's opening of marriage and a separate domestic partnership scheme to

---

[311] Art 14 prohibits discrimination on the basis of sex; this has been interpreted as including sexual orientation: *Sutherland v United Kingdom* Application No 25186/94 (1997); *Salgueiro Da Silva Mouta v Portugal* Application No 33290/96 (1999). See D McGoldrick, 'The Development and Status of Sexual Orientation Discrimination under International Human Rights Law' (2016) 16(4) *Human Rights Law Review* 613.

[312] For an explanation of legitimate aims and proportionality, see Chapter 9 at 9.4.1.

[313] *Karner v Austria* (Application no. 40016/98) (2003) para 40.

[314] H Fenwick, 'An ECHR Right to Access a Registered Partnership?' in JM Scherpe and A Hayward (eds), *The Future of Registered Partnerships* (Intersentia 2017) 471, 473.

[315] *Schalk and Kopf v Austria* (Application no. 30141/04) (2010) para 93.

[316] Para 105.

[317] Dr Marko Milanovic, 'No Right to Same-Sex Marriage under the ECHR' (*EJIL Talk*, 24 June 2010). Available at https://www.ejiltalk.org/no-right-to-same-sex-marriage-under-the-echr/ accessed 17 August 2018.

different-sex couples only.[318] The Court held that this was a breach of Art 8 coupled with Art 14 in that while Greece's justification, the protection of the traditional family including children of couples who did not want to marry, was a legitimate aim the restriction of the domestic partnership scheme to different-sex couples was not necessary to achieve this aim.

Valliantos was followed by *Oliari and Others v Italy* (2015). Here, building on *Valliantos*, the Court recognised that a failure to provide any framework of rights for same-sex couples, even short of marriage, meant that Italy had 'overstepped their margin of appreciation' and was in breach of Art 8.[319] As Hayward has written, 'Italy had . . . failed to identify a community interest that could be balanced against the "momentous" interests of the applicants'.[320] However, despite finding that the trend towards legal recognition 'has continued to develop rapidly in Europe since the Court's judgment in *Shalk and Kopf*', the Court drew back from holding that Art 12 was breached.[321] Jens Scherpe has observed that this is 'perfectly in line with the cautious approach the court takes in socially and culturally sensitive areas, and particularly family law'.[322]

The present position, therefore, is that states may offer same-sex couples a scheme of legal protections such as a domestic partnership scheme but (at this time, as there is no consensus) not necessarily marriage, and not necessarily something with the same or equivalent rights and responsibilities to marriage. Whether they *must* do so, or whether *Oliari* is fact specific[323] is yet to be tested. This is part of Art 8, not Art 12. It represents a step towards equality, but is not yet equality.

2.13.2 Other limitations on marriage

So far, we have considered the right to marry in the context of sexuality, but there are of course other limitations on marrying, such as age or prohibited degrees. One of the concerns expressed in some discussions about the introduction of civil partnership and same-sex marriage respectively was that these would create a slippery slope to requiring recognition of other relationships such as those which are incestuous. The actor Jeremy Irons, for example, queried whether same-sex marriage could lead to fathers being entitled to marry their sons. Perhaps anticipating arguments about the purpose of consanguinity restrictions, he reportedly said, 'It's not incest between men. Incest [law] is there to protect us from inbreeding, but men don't breed.'[324]

---

[318] Applications nos. 29381/09 and 32684/09 (2013).

[319] *Oliari and Others v Italy* (Applications nos. 18766/11 and 36030/11) (2015) paras 178 and 185.

[320] A Hayward, 'Same-Sex Registered Partnerships: A Right to Be Recognised?' (2016) 75 *Cambridge Law Journal* 27, 29.

[321] *Oliari and Others v Italy* (Applications nos. 18766/11 and 36030/11) (2015) para 192.

[322] JM Scherpe, 'The Legal Recognition of Same-Sex Couples in Europe and the Role of the European Court of Human Rights' (2013) 10 *The Equal Rights Review* 83, 90.

[323] Because of the discordance between Italian popular and judicial support for a same-sex regime and the government's failure to implement a scheme. See Helen Fenwick, 'An ECHR Right to Access a Registered Partnership?' in JM Scherpe and A Hayward (eds), *The Future of Registered Partnerships* (Intersentia 2017) 471, 492.

[324] V Ward, 'Jeremy Irons Claims Gay Marriage Laws Could Lead to a Father Marrying His Son' (*The Telegraph*, 4 April 2013).

It is important to remember that society defines what laws shape marriage. 'Marriage, as an institution, is not a natural phenomenon but is rather a legal structure', writes McK Norrie,

> and as such it is one that is defined artificially by the law. So the law has the choice of how to define marriage and how to limit access to it. . . . Removing one limitation to marriage, the requirement that it be between an opposite-sex couple, does not mean that we have to remove all limitations. What it does, of course, mean is that it is legitimate to question every limitation in order to ensure that it continues to serve some justifiable purpose in today's society. But there is nothing unusual about that.[325]

While it is sensible to question the purpose of certain restrictions on marriage, as long as those restrictions serve a legitimate social aim there is no slippery slope, and a legitimate state interest is much easier to show in relation to these kinds of limitations than when seeking to justify the denial of legal protections for same-sex couples. The state clearly has a legitimate interest in protecting children from underage marriages, for example.

Similarly, although the scope of consanguinity prohibited degrees varies by country, it is a legitimate aim is to limit the physical and emotional harm that can be caused to children of a couple who are closely related. However, there is also a moral dimension. In *Stübing v Germany*, a man convicted of multiple counts of incest with his sister (whom he had first met when he was an adult) claimed this was a breach of Art 8. While acknowledging that there was an interference with his right to private and family life, the European Court of Human Rights held that it was justified by reference to Art 8(2) for the protection of morals and the rights and interests of others. The Court held that 'where . . . there is no consensus within the [states], either as to the relative importance of the interest at stake or as to the best means of protecting it, particularly where the case raises sensitive moral or ethical issues, the states' margin of appreciation will be wider'.[326] It therefore follows that if a majority of states decriminalised certain types of incest (which is not the case now), the margin would narrow. As we see at 2.6.1, affinity restrictions are less likely to fulfil a legitimate state aim than those based on consanguinity.[327]

2.14 Civil partnerships

Civil partnership is a domestic partnership regime similar to marriage in function. Until 2019, it was open to same-sex couples only.

Civil partnerships were introduced by the Civil Partnership Act 2004, with the earliest ceremonies taking place in December 2005. The genesis of the Act was a private member's bill by Lord Lester of Herne Hill QC, a barrister who practised in the area of human rights. In its original incarnation, the bill was not limited to same-sex couples only, but entitled any two people, whether in a romantic relationship or not, to register after living together for more than six months, and thereby acquire certain legal rights. The Labour government then put forward its own bill, which received support from the Liberal Democrats,

---

[325] K McK Norrie, 'Marriage Is for Heterosexuals – May the Rest of Us Be Saved from It' (2000) 12(4) *Child and Family Law Quarterly* 363.
[326] *Stübing v Germany* (Application no. 43547/08) (2012) para 60.
[327] *B and L v UK* 36536/02; [2006] 1 FLR 35.

Plaid Cymru, the Scottish National Party, and most, but by no means all, Conservative MPs. Despite cross-party support, 'few activists and commentators were confident that the bill would succeed in the House of Lords'[328] and the Labour government sought to assure reluctant peers that the bill did not create gay marriage by another name.[329]

The Act limited civil partnerships to same-sex couples only. It therefore represented, at that time, the only method by which such couples could obtain marriage-like protections. Although it has always been open to same-sex couples to enter into contracts regulating certain aspects of their relationship, such as property, they had no power to require institutions or laws to provide them with equivalent protections. The protections given by civil partnerships were therefore immensely important, although whether civil partnership is an equivalent status to marriage is something we discuss at 2.14.2.

In 2006, nearly 15,000 civil partnerships were formed, an expected peak as people rushed to take advantage of this new legal recognition and protection. Over subsequent years, the number of partnerships stabilised at around 5,000 to 6,000 per year, which was higher than government predictions, However, the number fell sharply with the introduction of same-sex marriage in spring 2014 and in 2016 only 890 civil partnerships were formed. Given the availability of same-sex marriage since March 2014 (as a result of the Marriage Same-Sex Couples Act 2013), those same-sex couples still entering into civil partnerships are making a positive choice of them over same-sex marriage.[330] In 2019, the latest available statistics, there were 994 civil partnerships.[331] About two-thirds of these were between male couples.

As a result of the Key Case *R (on the application of Steinfeld and Keidan)*, civil partnerships were opened up to different-sex couples from 31 December 2019.[332] The number of different-sex couples entering into civil partnerships in preference to marriage is currently unknown, although 165 different-sex couples entered into a civil partnership on the first day they were lawful.

2.14.1 The legal consequences of civil partnership

Civil partnerships provide almost all the same legal consequences as marriage—those set out in section 2.12.1. This was achieved by complex and lengthy provisions in the Civil Partnership Act 2004, which amended other statues that we have considered in this chapter or simply provided mirror provisions within the Civil Partnership Act itself.

Before we go onto consider the social differences between marriage and civil partnership, let us first consider the legal differences.

Formation of a civil partnership and nullity

A civil partnership is formed by the signing of the register, not (as with marriage) by the form of words spoken at the ceremony. As with marriage, there are rules surrounding

---

[328] C Smart, '"Can I Be Bridesmaid?" Combining the Personal and Political in Same-Sex Weddings' (2008) 11(6) *Sexualities* 761, 762.

[329] See M White, 'Partners Bill "Is Not Law for Gay Marriage"' (*The Guardian*, 13 October 2004).

[330] Office of National Statistics, *Statistical Bulletin: Civil Partnerships in England and Wales: 2016* (2017).

[331] Office of National Statistics, *Statistical Bulletin: Civil Partnerships in England and Wales: 2019* (2020).

[332] On the coming into force of the Civil Partnership (Opposite-Sex Couples) Regulations 2019 (SI 1458/2019).

prior notice of intended marriage, the obtaining of a licence or superintendent registrar's certificate, location of the ceremony, witnesses, and the presence of a civil partnership registrar, who may be a minister of religion.[333] This is different from the position regarding marriages: ministers of religion are allowed to become civil partnership registrars working for the local authority, but cannot apply to become marriage registrars. This is because the Registration of Births, Deaths and Marriages Regulations 1968 disqualifies ministers from acting as marriage registrars but the same restriction was not included in the Civil Partnership Act 2004. Where a minister does become a registrar of civil partnerships, they must ensure that the secular nature of their role as registrar is maintained.[334]

Since the Equality Act 2010, civil partnerships can take place in approved religious premises although the part of the ceremony dealing with signing of the register must be secular.[335] Before this legislative change, civil partnerships could only be formed at a purely secular event. This reflects the considerable opposition of religious groups who responded to the government's civil partnership proposals.[336]

The Act is prescriptive as to when a civil partnership will be void for lack of compliance with the formalities. Where a person is aged under 16, already married or civilly partnered, or within the prohibited degrees, the partnership will be void *ab initio*. Moreover, while parental consent is required for those aged 16 or 17, any subsequent partnership in the absence of consent is void, which is not the case with marriage (see section 2.4.1 above). This could simply reflect a desire for legal clarity given the confusion we have seen as to when a marriage is void.

The voidable grounds for a civil partnership are the same as for marriage except that it is not possible to obtain an annulment on the ground of inability to consummate, wilful refusal to consummate, or that the respondent was suffering from a venereal disease at the time of the ceremony. The government stated that by not amending the definition of consummation to encompass forms of sexual activity available to same-sex couples they were 'not altering the legal position unnecessarily', an explanation that Herring says 'hardly deserves the name'.[337] This difference between civil partnership and marriage remains notwithstanding the opening of partnerships to different-sex couples.

---

[333] This is different to the position regarding marriage. See General Register Office, *Civil Partnerships on Religious Premises: Further Information* (December 2019). Available at https://www.gov.uk/government/publications/civil-partnerships-on-religious-premises-further-information/civil-partnerships-on-religious-premises-further-information accessed 25 August 2020.

[334] See General Register Office, *Civil Partnerships on Religious Premises: Further Information* (December 2019). Available at https://www.gov.uk/government/publications/civil-partnerships-on-religious-premises-further-information/civil-partnerships-on-religious-premises-further-information accessed 25 August 2020.

[335] Section 202.

[336] See discussion in P Johnson and RM Vanderbeck, 'Sacred Spaces, Sacred Words: Religion and Same-Sex Marriage in England and Wales' (2017) 44(2) *Journal of Law and Society* 228.

[337] J Herring, Why Marriage Needs to Be Less Sexy', in J Miles, P Mody, and R Probert (eds), *Marriage Rites and Rights* (Bloomsbury 2015) 227, quoting HM Government, *Equal Marriage: The Government's Response* (The Stationery Office 2012).

SCENARIO 2

Illustration 2: Mark and Jamal

Instead of marrying, Mark and Jamal could have a civil partnership. They have a choice between the two legal regimes. As described above, there are differences in the ceremony itself. Note two consequences of the civil (secular) nature of a civil partnership:

(1) Even if they have a religious ceremony, the actual partnership is formed by the signing of the register and this part of the ceremony must be secular.

(2) A religious leader can become a civil partnership registrar, although religions are not required to conduct civil partnership ceremonies.[338]

We can compare this to same-sex marriage, where:

(3) The marriage is formed by prescribed words and can be religious provided the religious organisation has opted in to conducting same-sex marriages.

(4) The marriage must be conducted by someone authorised to conduct marriages in that venue, who can be a religious leader, so would not conduct the wedding in the capacity of a registrar.

Dissolution of a civil partnership

Dissolution is the civil partnership equivalent to divorce, and is exactly the same, save that the relevant provisions are contained in the Civil Partnerships Act 2004. Prior to the introduction of no-fault divorce, it was not, however, possible to dissolve a civil partnership on the fact of adultery. Adultery requires intercourse with someone of the opposite sex, but even if one's civil partner had intercourse with someone of the opposite sex, adultery was simply not mentioned in the Civil Partnership Act as a basis on which a marriage can be ended, although it could be classed as a form of behaviour. This is discussed further in Chapter 3.

While all types of financial remedies available to divorcing married couples are also available to civil partners—the Civil Partnership Act contains provisions that mirror those in the Matrimonial Causes Act 1973—there has been inbuilt discrimination with respect to pensions. When a pension holder dies, their spouse will receive a survivor's pension, which is less than the pension holder's pension but can still be valuable. Pension schemes were allowed to offer the widow(er)s of civil partners a survivor's pension that only took account of the pension rights that had accrued since the Civil Partnership Act came into force on 5 December 2005. This was a much smaller amount than if it was based on the value of a pension for its whole existence, as would be the case for a married couple: in the case of *Walker v Innospec*, this meant that Mr Walker's civil partner would receive £1,000 per year on Mr Walker's death compared to £45,700 if Mr Walker had been in a heterosexual marriage. Moreover, this discrimination also applied to same-sex married couples, using the same date of 5 December 2005 even though same-sex marriage was introduced later. It therefore created inequality not only between civil partners and married couples

---

[338] Section 10 of the Civil Partnership (Opposite-sex Couples) Regulations 2019 (SI 1458/2019).

but between different-sex and same-sex married couples. In 2017, this discrimination was declared unlawful by the Supreme Court on Mr Walker's application.[339] Subsequently, the Government decided that benefits for survivors of civil partnerships or same-sex marriages would generally be aligned with those for widows of opposite-sex marriages for *public service pension schemes*, 'but not to make further retrospective changes (i.e. not to fully equalise survivors benefits for widowers of opposite-sex marriage with those of widows)'.[340] For private sector pension schemes, compliance with the judgment is a matter for them, and if they do not eliminate the discrimination because of the cost, it will be necessary to bring a separate legal challenge. There are approximately 27 million people in the UK as a whole employed in the private sector.

Table 2.4 sets out the differences between civil partnership and marriage and highlights also that although marriage and same-sex marriage are the same institution, there are some differences which relate to (a) a refusal to redefine consummation to incorporate same-sex sexual acts; and (b) a refusal to equalise the pension provision. We discuss same-sex marriage in section 2.15.

TABLE 2.4 Differences between marital regimes

	Marriage	Same-sex marriage	Civil Partnerships
Open to whom?	Different-sex couples	Same-sex couples from 2013	Same-sex couples; and from 2019 different-sex couples
Nature of wedding ceremony	Civil or religious	Civil or (since the Equality Act 2010) religious if religion has opted in	Civil, but can have religious element if kept separate
Formation of marriage	Formed by saying prescribed form of words	Formed by saying prescribed form of words	Formed by signing CP Register
Ending	Marriage is ended by divorce	Marriage is ended by divorce	Divorce is called 'Dissolution'
Nullity grounds	Consummation or venereal disease grounds of nullity	Venereal disease is a ground of nullity but lack of consummation is not	No consummation or venereal disease ground to annul CP
Pensions	Occupational pension schemes—schemes will take account of all rights accrued to a surviving spouse.	Schemes will take into account of only the rights accrued since the Civil Partnership Act came into force on 5 December 2005 so on death the survivor will get less than a heterosexual survivor. This is the case even though the parties are married not partnered.	Schemes will take into account of only the rights accrued since the Civil Partnership Act came into force on 5 December 2005 so on death the survivor will get less than the survivor of a different-sex marriage.

---

[339] *Walker* v *Innospec Limited and others* [2017] UKSC 47 [5] (Lord Kerr).
[340] House of Commons Library, Briefing Paper CBP 03035: *Pensions: Civil Partnerships and Same Sex Marriages* (17 July 2019).

2.14.2 Are civil partnerships equal to marriage?

Whether you believe that civil partnerships are equal to marriage depends upon your perspective both on these legal differences and on whether or not there is a social or symbolic difference between marriage and civil partnerships. Consider the case of *Wilkinson v Kitzinger*, decided before the introduction of same-sex marriage.

KEY CASE *Wilkinson v Kitzinger and others* [2006] EWHC 2022 (Fam)

Wilkinson and Kitzinger are two British academics in a long-term relationship. When Professor Wilkinson went to work in Canada in 2003, she and Professor Kitzinger married under Canadian law, which permitted same-sex marriage. At the time, neither civil partnership nor same-sex marriage existed in England and Wales. 'Getting married provided a ten-minute solution to what would otherwise have taken weeks of our lives: for the cost of a marriage licence ($100) and a marriage commissioner ($75) we gained, with a few signatures, around 120 rights and responsibilities in Canadian law that would otherwise have had to use lawyers to assemble piecemeal.' 'Everything changed,' Wilkinson said. 'I hadn't realised what it was like to be treated as normal.'[341]

Although civil partnership was in the meantime introduced in England and Wales, at the time ss212–218 Civil Partnership Act 2004 provided that same-sex marriages conducted abroad were to be recognised as civil partnerships in England and Wales. On returning together to England, Wilkinson's and Kitzinger's Canadian marriage was therefore recognised as a civil partnership, not as a marriage. Had they been respectively male and female, their marriage would of course have been recognised as a marriage. As civil partners, Wilkinson and Kitzinger had all the rights, responsibilities and privileges of marriage, with the exception of those outlined in Table 2.4. But they did not have the name. In their eyes, 'the status of marriage had been taken from them'.[342] Wilkinson therefore sought a declaration as to her marital status, arguing that their marriage should be recognised as such under s5 Family Law Act 1986, and that ss212–218 Civil Partnership Act, and s11(c) Matrimonial Causes Act, which said that marriage was only between a man and a woman, breached Articles 8, 12, and 14 ECHR. Art 8 is the (qualified) right to private and family life, Art 12 is the right to marry, and Art 14 is the right to non-discrimination in the exercise of another right.[343]

The judge, Sir Mark Potter, held that denying same-sex couples the right to marry did not breach Art 8 because Art 8 'does not impose a positive obligation to establish for unmarried couples a status analogous to that of married couples'[344] but is rather concerned with 'measures by the state which interfere with the respect to the private sphere (for example by criminalising or condemning consensual sexual conduct between two adults)'.[345] Moreover, civil partnership accords 'the benefits of marriage in all but name'.[346]

The judge did hold that same-sex couples were treated differently to different-sex couples as far as Article 12 was concerned, recognising (as the European Court of Human Rights has not) that the right to marry applied to same-sex couples. (See section 2.13.1). However, this difference in treatment did not breach Art 14, because it had a legitimate aim, which was 'preserving and supporting the concept and institution of marriage as a union between persons of opposite sex or gender', and

---

[341] S Jeffreys, 'Mrs and Mrs' (*The Guardian*, 10 June 2006). Quoted by R Auchmuty, 'What's So Special about Marriage?' The Impact of *Wilkinson v Kitzinger*' (2008) 20(4) *Child and Family Law Quarterly* 475, 478.

[342] R Auchmuty, 'What's So Special about Marriage?' The Impact of *Wilkinson v Kitzinger*' (2008) 20(4) *Child and Family Law Quarterly* 475, 478.

[343] These provisions were removed by the Marriage (Same-Sex Couples) Act 2013.

[344] *Wilkinson v Kitzinger and others* [2006] EWHC 2022 (Fam) [86] (Sir Mark Potter P).

[345] *Wilkinson v Kitzinger and others* [2006] EWHC 2022 (Fam) [85] (Sir Mark Potter P).

[346] *Wilkinson v Kitzinger and others* [2006] EWHC 2022 (Fam) [88] (Sir Mark Potter P).

was a proportionate way of achieving that aim.[347] Moreover, Parliament had taken steps to minimise the effects of the discrimination by creating civil partnerships.

The judge held that same-sex relationships were, 'as a matter of objective fact and common understanding',[348] different from marriage, which was 'a means not only of encouraging monogamy but also the procreation of children and their development and nurture in a family unit (or "nuclear family") in which both maternal and paternal influences are available in respect of their nurture and upbringing. . . . [T]o accord a same-sex relationship the title and status of marriage would be to fly in the face of the Convention as well as to fail to recognise physical reality.'[349]

The judgment appeals to a narrow conception of marriage, and in her discussion of this case, Rosemary Auchmuty has criticised the judge's statement about the purpose of marriage as 'contentious in almost every respect'.[350] She points to the states that permit same-sex marriage, the ways in which marriage and particularly the role of fathers have changed through the centuries, the high divorce rate, and the number of children being raised by same-sex couples—some 18,000 same-sex couples in the UK have dependent children.[351] Nevertheless, the label 'marriage' was important to Wilkinson and Kitzinger. Their claim was one of formal equality: they wanted the same status as a different-sex couple who had also married in Canada.[352] The fact that they had virtually the same rights and responsibilities as a married couple did not compensate for this. They saw recognition of their marriage as a civil partnership as a 'consolation prize' and thus 'offensive and demeaning'.[353] 'I want to be able to refer to Celia as my wife and have that immediately and unproblematically understood as meaning that she is my life-partner with all the connotations and social consequences that using the term "wife" or "husband" has', Sue Wilkinson told the court.[354] After all, if civil partnership was equivalent to marriage, why recognise their marriage as a civil partnership? Is having a separate regime for same-sex persons inherently discriminatory even if it gives, as the judge said, the benefits of marriage in all but name'?[355]

Rob George puts this best:

It might be said that the existence of a separate legal regime for same-sex couples implies that one of two things is happening. One possibility is that there is a legal difference between marriage and civil partnership, in which case one group (almost undoubtedly same-sex couples, rather than opposite-sex couples) is being discriminated against in law. While there are small differences they may be sufficiently small to dismiss this option. The more

---

[347] *Wilkinson v Kitzinger and others* [2006] EWHC 2022 (Fam) [122] (Sir Mark Potter P).

[348] *Wilkinson v Kitzinger and others* [2006] EWHC 2022 (Fam) [121] (Sir Mark Potter P).

[349] *Wilkinson v Kitzinger and others* [2006] EWHC 2022 (Fam) [118, 120] (Sir Mark Potter P).

[350] R Auchmuty, '"What's So Special about Marriage?" The Impact of *Wilkinson v Kitzinger*' (2008) 20(4) *Child and Family Law Quarterly* 475, 480.

[351] A dependent child is one aged under 16 or 16–18 in full-time education. Office of National Statistics, *Statistical Bulletin: Families and Households 2017* (2017).

[352] R Auchmuty, '"What's So Special about Marriage?" The Impact of *Wilkinson v Kitzinger*' (2008) 20(4) *Child and Family Law Quarterly* 475, 483.

[353] *Wilkinson v Kitzinger and others* [2006] EWHC 2022 (Fam), [5].

[354] *Wilkinson v Kitzinger and others* [2006] EWHC 2022 (Fam), [21]. Quote from her affidavit in the proceedings.

[355] *Wilkinson v Kitzinger and others* [2006] EWHC 2022 (Fam), [88].

likely possibility is that the only difference is in the name, and that two different but equal systems are in operation. But this too is discrimination: cf the US Supreme Court's reasoning in *Brown v Board of Education of Topeka*, saying clearly that two institutions which perform the same function but which are separate from one another cannot, by definition, be equal and are, consequently, discriminatory.[356]

This view is not, however, one shared by all gay and lesbian couples. Clarke, Burgoyne, and Burns found that while some same-sex couples saw civil partnership as a 'second class version of marriage', this was not a view shared by everyone and even the name 'civil partnership' was significant for some and but not at all important to others. Moreover, even if they thought it was not equal to marriage:

> many participants held multiple positions on legal recognition and felt it possible both to oppose civil partnership on ideological grounds and support (and indeed enter into a) civil partnership on pragmatic grounds. For those participants, the day-to-day realities of life meant that civil partnership represented the best option for protecting their finances and/or their families.[357]

The views of gay men and lesbians towards civil partnership and, later, marriage, reflect the diversity of the same-sex couples, socially, economically, and politically.

FOCUS Think Critically

Perspectives on civil partnership

(1) Civil partnership is similar to marriage
- This is a good thing. 'If we preach that the values inherent in marriage—love, mutual commitment and responsibility—strengthen and enrich society, how can we claim that the replication of such values for gay couples will cause damage?'[358] 'There is no justification for maintaining the current distinctions between same-sex and heterosexual conjugal unions in light of current understandings of the state's interests in marriage.'[359]
- This is a bad thing. This is 'counterfeit marriage' that 'dismantles' traditional marriage. 'Circulating fake money cheats those who receive it and can damage the economy. In the same way giving same-sex couples and temporary relationships the same status as marriage devalues the currency of marriage.'[360]
- This is a bad thing. 'Government recognition also involves state regulation and control . . . we were free, before marriage, to "pick and choose" what rights we wanted in relation to each other and to change these as our relationship altered over the years.'[361]

---

[356] R George, *Ideas and Debates in Family Law* (Hart 2012), p75, fn 2. The *Brown* case is a seminal American case that led to the racial desegregation of schools. The US Supreme Court held that the fact that black children and white children were in separate schools created discrimination, even if the academic provision was equal, because of the sense of inferiority segregation created.

[357] V Clarke, C Burgoyne, and M Burns, 'Just a Piece of Paper? A Qualitative Exploration of Same-Sex Couples' Multiple Conceptions of Civil Partnership and Marriage' (2006) 7(2) *Lesbian and Gay Psychology Review* 141, 156.

[358] Alan Duncan MP, *Hansard* HC Deb 12 October 2004 vol 425, col 184.

[359] Law Commission of Canada, *Beyond Conjugality: Recognizing and Supporting Close Personal Adult Relationships* (2001).

[360] Christian Institute, *Counterfeit Marriage: How 'Civil Partnerships' Devalue the Currency of Marriage* (2002). Available at https://www.christian.org.uk/wp-content/uploads/counterfeit-marriage.pdf accessed 16 August 2018.

[361] C Kitzinger and S Wilkinson, 'The Re-Branding of Marriage: Why We Got Married Instead of Registering a Civil Partnership' (2004) 14(1) *Feminism and Psychology* 127, 141–2.

- This is no threat to marriage. 'The traditional family is not protected by granting it a benefit which is denied to people who cannot or will not become a traditional family.'[362] 'True, the two institutions [marriage and civil partnership] are designed on similar lines, but they are designed on parallel lines; and parallel lines, as we all know, never meet.'[363]
- This constitutes an assimilation into the heterosexist norm: 'equality is granted, but only on heterosexual terms'. Real equality would 'come about by the law recognising the legitimacy of a variety of forms of domestic relationship'.[364] 'The liberal agenda may, indeed, grant us rights to hitherto heterosexual privileges. But unless we are careful, it will do so in its terms, naturally assuming that heterosexual values are the norm, if not the best.'[365] We should 'abandon the status of marriage altogether and to devise a system of rights, duties or obligations which are not dependent on any form of 'coupledom' or marriage or quasi-marriage.[366] 'Marriage as an institution and as a model for love is not the best we could do—and certainly does not reflect the best we are doing.'[367]

(2) Civil partnership is not similar to marriage

- This is a good thing. 'For us, a civil partnership best reflects who we are, how we see our relationship and our role as parents—a partnership of equals.'[368]
- This is a good thing. 'Entry into marriage. . . is a means to de-radicalise and normalise queer or non-conventional relationships which operate with different values and codes to those found in heterosexual relationships.'[369]
- This is a bad thing. 'Genuine equality would involve exactly the same legal opportunities being available to homosexuals and heterosexuals. . . . Could this be the lingering odour of homophobia?'[370]
- This is temporary. Civil partnership is a necessary stepping stone to full marriage equality. 'To go for anything more, at this stage, would I fear result in a major backlash.'[371] 'A change in the law will change people's understanding of . . . umm . . . same sex couples and it . . . it will lead to less prejudice I think and I hope and more social acceptance but at the same time it does. . . it says you're "B" list I think.'[372]

(3) Does a comparison matter?

- It does not matter. 'It is likely that whatever the name attached to the formal legal vehicle which creates the status, over time the institutions will merge in social consciousness and practice, and their futures will be bound up with each other.'[373]
- It did matter. Despite their benefits, 'civil partnerships were, in part, introduced to avoid having to concede the demand for same-sex marriage. They created a segregated, mutually-exclusive two-tier system of relationship law.'[374]

---

[362] *Ghaidan v Godin-Mendoza* [2004] UKHL 30 [143] (Lady Hale).

[363] Alan Duncan MP, *Hansard* HC Deb 12 October 2004 vol 425, col 184.

[364] KMcK Norrie, 'Marriage Is for Heterosexuals – May the Rest of Us Be Saved from It' (2000) 12(4) *Child and Family Law Quarterly* 363. He was writing before civil partnerships were introduced.

[365] R Auchmuty, 'Same-Sex Marriage Revived: Feminist Critique and Legal Strategy' (2004) 14(1) *Feminism and Psychology* 101, 124.

[366] C Smart, *The Ties That Bind: Law and the Reproduction of Patriarchal Relations* (Routledge 1984) 144.

[367] C Donovan, 'Why Reach for the Moon? Because the Stars Aren't Enough' (2004) 14(1) *Feminism and Psychology* 25, 28.

[368] From the couple's website, Equal Civil Partnerships <http://equalcivilpartnerships.org.uk/> accessed 2 July 2018.

[369] C Smart, 'Same-Sex Couples and Marriage: Negotiating Relational Landscapes with Families and Friends' (2007) 55 (4) *The Sociological Review* 671, 671.

[370] L Crompton, 'The Civil Partnership Bill 2004: The Illusion of Equality' [2–4] Family Law 888, 889.

[371] M Bowley QC, 'A Too Fragile Social Fabric?' (1995) 145 *New Law Journal* 1883.

[372] Interview with 'Katie', in A Rolfe and E Peele, '"It's a Double-Edged Thing": The Paradox of Civil Partnership and Why Some Couples Are Choosing Not to Have One' (2011) 21(3) *Feminism and Psychology* 317, 323.

[373] J Eekelaar, 'Why People Marry: The Many Faces of an Institution' (2007) *Family Law Quarterly* 413.

[374] P Tatchell, 'Civil Partnerships: An Important Advance But Flawed' (*Blog, Peter Tatchell Foundation*, 18 December 2015).

- It does matter even now. Whether or not civil partnerships were equal to marriage then, the introduction of same-sex marriage in 2013 created a hierarchy in which civil partnerships are now seen as lesser than marriage.[375]

2.14.3 Different-sex civil partnerships

When same-sex marriage was introduced, the government consulted on what should happen about civil partnerships.[376] Options included abolishing them but letting existing civil partners remain civil partners; abolishing them and forcibly converting all existing civil partnerships into marriages; or expanding civil partnerships to different-sex couples. The consultation revealed no consensus about what should happen, so the government decided not to make any changes for the time being, although it appears that when Justine Greening was Minister for Women and Equalities she did draw up proposals for Parliament to open up civil partnership to different-sex couples.[377] However, this never progressed.

The asymmetry resulting from same-sex couples having access to two legal regimes, civil partnership and marriage, but different-sex couples having access to one only, was the subject of a legal challenge in England and Wales. Civil partnership, once seen as a stepping stone to full marriage equality for gay and lesbian couples, was seen by some straight couples as a desirable alternative to marriage. This was the view of the applicants in our next Key Case, *Steinfeld and Keidan* (2018), in which the Supreme Court held that the Civil Partnership Act's limitation to same-sex couples only was incompatible with the human rights of the applicants, a different-sex couple.

KEY CASE *R (on the application of Steinfeld and Keidan) v Secretary of State for International Development (in substitution for the Home Secretary and the Education Secretary)* [2018] UKSC 32

Rebecca Steinfeld and Charles Keidan are a different-sex couple who wanted a civil partnership, not a marriage. They view marriage as incompatible with their values because it has 'patriarchal baggage'. They state on their website:

Personally, we wish to form a civil partnership because that captures the essence of our relationship and values. For us, a civil partnership best reflects who we are, how we see our relationship and our role as parents—a partnership of equals. We want a civil partnership to cement our commitment and strengthen the security of our family unit.[378]

---

[375] This was the view of some participants in a study of same-sex couples: A Jowett and E Peel, 'A Question of equality and Choice: Same-Sex Couples' Attitudes towards Civil Partnership after the Introduction of Same-Sex marriage' (2017) 8(1) *Psychology and Sexuality* 69.

[376] Department for Culture, Media, and Sport, *Consultation on the Future of Civil Partnership in England and Wales* (2014).

[377] Department for Culture, Media, and Sport, *Civil Partnership Review (England and Wales): Report on Conclusions* (2014). See O Boycott, 'Plan to Extend Civil Partnerships Revealed in Government Report' (*The Guardian*, 13 May 2018).

[378] From the couple's website, Equal Civil Partnerships <http://equalcivilpartnerships.org.uk/> accessed 2 July 2018.

> As a different-sex couple, they were, though, ineligible to enter into a civil partnership. They therefore brought an application for judicial review of the government's refusal to allow them a civil partnership, arguing that this breached their Article 8 right to private and family life and did so in a way that discriminated against them on the basis of their sexuality (Article 14). The government did in fact accept that there was inequality but said it wanted more time to consider what to do.
>
> Despite losing in the High Court and Court of Appeal, Steinfeld and Keidan won their case in the Supreme Court, which made a declaration that the Civil Partnership Act's limitation to same-sex couples only was incompatible with the applicants' human rights. The Supreme Court said that the government's position of wanting to wait and consider what to do was not acceptable as it meant that the unlawful discrimination would continue for the duration of that consideration period.

The Supreme Court's declaration of incompatibility with human rights did not mean that Parliament had to change the law, although that is usually the outcome of such declarations. The obligation on the government was to remove the discrimination that gave same-sex couples a choice of marriage or civil partnership and different-sex couples just marriage. The government had two options to achieve this. One was to open civil partnership up to different-sex couples. Many countries do have domestic partnership schemes that exist as an alternative to marriage for different-sex couples. However, an alternative open to the government was to abolish civil partnerships, because that would also remove the discrimination by treating all couples the same—they would all only be able to get married. If the government abolished civil partnerships then not only would Steinfeld and Keidan not be able to have one, but neither would any couple, straight or gay. Such a move may have been accompanied by a forceful conversion of existing partnerships to marriage as had been previously proposed. Statistics show that although the number of civil partnerships plunged after the introduction of same-sex marriage, some gay couples are still choosing to enter into or remain in partnerships in preference to marriage, a trend particularly marked in those aged over 50.[379] For these couples, and for those such as Steinfeld and Keidan for whom marriage carries patriarchal and/or religious baggage, the end of civil partnerships would be a 'pyrrhic' victory: a victory that came at such cost it might as well have been a defeat. A number of European countries phased out separate schemes for same-sex couples when they introduced same-sex marriage, so the precedent for this route certainly existed.[380]

In October 2018 the government announced that it would open up civil partnerships to opposite-sex couples, which happened through the passing of the Civil Partnership (Opposite-sex Couples) Regulations 2019, which came into force on 31 December 2019.[381] The outcome of the case was that both different-sex and same-sex couples can now choose between civil partnership and marriage. Civil partnerships have not been altered in order to eliminate the difference between them and marriage, so that couples choosing to enter into a partnership are in a different position to those who are married on those issues outlined in Table 2.4.

---

[379] Office of National Statistics, *Statistical Bulletin: Civil Partnerships in England and Wales 2017* (2018).
[380] See H Fenwick and A Hayward, 'Rejecting Asymmetry of Access to Formal Relationship Statuses for Same and Different-Sex Couples at Strasbourg and Domestically' (2017) *European Human Rights Law Review* 544, 546.
[381] SI 1458/2019.

Reaction to Steinfeld and Keidan's action has been mixed. The outcome of opening up civil partnerships to different-sex couples enables equality of choice between same and different-sex couples and the freedom to choose between different regimes which attract different statuses. In doing so, they may change the way that civil partnerships are perceived; after all, they themselves did not perceive them as lesser but as better. However, a key criticism that can be made of Steinfeld and Keidan's actions is that they risked the status of gay couples' existing civil partnerships, a form legal protection that was extremely hard won. They were coming from a privileged position. They had never had to fight for respect or recognition of a heterosexual relationship. For them, civil partnerships simply represented a more modern alternative to marriage.[382] Certainly, from a feminist standpoint marriage is tainted by its patriarchal origins. But there is irony in a different-sex couple wanting to enter into an institution which was designed as an *alternative to equality*: Wilkinson and Kitzinger's 'consolation prize'. Those who see civil partnerships as lesser than marriage will consider that it is a privilege to be able to choose to have slightly fewer rights and arguably less respect, rather than to have no choice in that.

SCENARIO 1

Illustration 3: Helen and Ned

Helen and Ned have the choice of marrying or entering into a civil partnership. The legal differences are relating to nullity and to pensions. Prior to no-fault divorce, there would also have been differences relating to the adultery fact on which a divorce can be obtained. These differences may not appear very important to Helen and Ned, although if they were sensible they would speak to their pension providers about their compliance with the *Walker* judgment. It is more likely that their decision between marriage and civil partnership will be based on their subjective perceptions of the meaning and importance of each.

2.15 Same-sex marriage

In 2013, civil partnerships were restricted to same-sex couples and marriage was still restricted to different-sex couples only. The introduction of same-sex marriage in that year ultimately reflects an acceptance that civil partnership was not perceived as equal to marriage and that gay and lesbian couples still sought entry to the institution of marriage, as well perhaps as an acceptance that arguments against same-sex marriage had largely been undermined by the fact that civil partnerships had not 'devalued the currency of marriage' as predicted by campaign group the Christian Institute.[383] The government itself acknowledged the former argument when it introduced the Marriage (Same-Sex Couples) Bill:

---

[382] Similar comments were made by those different-sex couples who had civil partnerships immediately that they became open to them. See 'Civil Partnerships: First Mixed-Sex Unions Take Place' (*BBC News* 31 December 2019). Available at https://www.bbc.co.uk/news/uk-50953410 accessed 31 August 2020.
[383] Christian Institute, *Counterfeit Marriage: How 'Civil Partnerships' Devalue the Currency of Marriage* (2002). Available at https://www.christian.org.uk/wp-content/uploads/counterfeit-marriage.pdf accessed 16 August 2018.

To those who argue that civil partnerships exist and contain very similar rights, that marriage is 'just a word' and that this Bill is unnecessary, I say that that is not right. A legal partnership is not perceived in the same way and does not have the same promises of responsibility and commitment as marriage. All couples who enter a lifelong commitment together should be able to call it marriage.[384]

After the controversy surrounding the introduction of civil partnerships, the introduction of same-sex marriage was relatively uncontroversial, with MPs voting 400 to 175 in favour of the bill becoming law, along the same party lines as the Civil Partnership Act eight years earlier. Nevertheless, there was concern that religious institutions might be required to conduct same-sex marriages that went against their beliefs. For this reason, there are a number of provisions in the Act which cover this area.

2.15.1 The legal consequences of same-sex marriage

The Marriage (Same-Sex Couples) Act 2013 is nowhere near as complex a piece of drafting as the Civil Partnership Act. It simply provides for same-sex marriages to be lawful (s1) and lets the consequences flow naturally from that with relatively few adjustments.

Formation of a same-sex marriage and nullity

For civil (i.e., secular) ceremonies, the process is the same for different-sex and same-sex couples, so ceremonies can be conducted in register offices and in registered buildings such as hotels and stately homes.

Religious organisations can also conduct same-sex marriages, but each organisation must first opt in to doing so by providing written consent.[385] Those that have opted in include the Unitarian Church (the largest group), Spiritualist Church, and United Reformed Church.[386] For some organisations, this is centrally determined, but in other organisations, such as the Baptist Church, each branch is a 'relevant governing authority' within the meaning of the Act and thus free to make its own decision.[387] However, not all religious organisations wish to conduct same-sex marriages, and the Act specifically states that no organisation can be compelled to opt-in or conduct a religious same-sex marriage and, even if the organisation opts in, no individual within that organisation can be compelled to conduct a same-sex marriage.[388] This means that a religious marriage ceremony of a same-sex couple would only be valid if the governing body of the religious organisation has opted in; a minister is willing to conduct a same-sex marriage; and any place of worship at which the marriage is to take place has been registered for the marriage of same-sex couples.

---

[384] Maria Miller MP, HC Deb 5 February 2013 vol 558, col 127 (second reading of the bill).

[385] The process is laid down in the Marriage Act 1949 although the relevant provisions were inserted by the Marriage (Same-Sex Couples) Act 2013.

[386] P Johnson, RM Vanderbeck, and S Falcetta, *Religious Marriage of Same-Sex couples: A Report on Places of Worship in England and Wales Registered for the Solemnization of Same-Sex Marriage* (University of York and University of Leeds 2017).

[387] Marriage Act 1949, s26A(3). See P Johnson, RM Vanderbeck, and S Falcetta, *Religious Marriage of Same-Sex couples: A Report on Places of Worship in England and Wales Registered for the Solemnization of Same-Sex Marriage* (University of York and University of Leeds 2017).

[388] Section 2.

As with different-sex marriage there are some organisations which are treated different-ly. Quakers and Jewish people can simply conduct same-sex marriages according to their own rites (as they can with different-sex couples). In relation to the Church of England there is a 'quadruple lock' which prevents the Church from opting in to conducting same-sex marriages without primary legislation being passed. For the Church in Wales, the Lord Chancellor can, on the application of the Church's governing body, make secondary legislation enabling same-sex marriages.

Conversion of a civil partnership

Civil partners are able to convert to same-sex marriage through a simple administrative procedure.[389] Note that it is not possible to convert a marriage to a partnership. The effect of conversion is that the date of marriage is backdated to the date of formation of their civil partnership.[390]

SCENARIO 2

Illustration 3: Mark and Jamal

Mark and Jamal could enter into a civil partnership and then, if they wanted, convert to a marriage at a later point in time. They could not, however, do it the other way around: a same-sex marriage cannot be converted to a civil partnership.

Nullity

A same-sex marriage can be annulled on all of the same grounds as the marriage of a different-sex couple with the exception of wilful or incapable consummation which is not available as a ground.[391] Unlike civil partnerships, a same-sex marriage *can* be annulled due to the presence of a communicable venereal disease, including in circumstances when the marriage is formed by conversion from a civil partnership.[392]

Changing legal gender

The introduction of same-sex marriage eased the legal problems surrounding the recogni-tion of marriages in which one spouse changed legal gender. Previously, as we see at 2.8.7, the parties would have needed to annul their marriage and then, if they wished, refor-malise their relationship as a civil partnership. Since same-sex marriage, the parties have been able to remain married through one partner's legal change of gender.[393] However, the spouse who is not changing legal gender must provide a statutory declaration to the gender recognition panel that they consent to the marriage continuing after the issue of a full gender recognition certificate.[394] This was controversial. It can be seen as making

---

[389] Marriage (Same-Sex Couples) Act 2013, s9.
[390] Section 9(6)(b). See also Marriage of Same Sex Couples (Conversion of Civil Partnership) Regulations 2014/3181.
[391] Marriage (Same-Sex Couples) Act 2013, Schedule 4 Part 3.
[392] Matrimonial Causes Act 1973 s12A (3).
[393] Gender Recognition Act 2004 s11A, as amended by the Marriage (Same-Sex Couples) Act 2013.
[394] Gender Recognition Act 2004 s3(6B), as amended by the Marriage (Same-Sex Couples) Act 2013.

a person's gender dependent on the permission of someone else, notwithstanding that changing gender is considered a (qualified) human right.[395] 'The trans community's views are almost universal in their condemnation of the legislation; which disempowers an already underprotected minority group in favour of reinforcing the idea that gay marriages are something straight people need protection from finding themselves a part of', reported one response to the government.[396] *The Pink Paper* has argued that 'the main intention of the spousal veto was to give greater importance to the feelings of cis people, over the legal rights and protections of trans people'.[397]

The alternative view 'is not that the spouse consents to their partner's gender recognition, but is rather a requirement that the spouse acknowledge the change in the nature of their marriage promises. By their consent the spouse is updating those promises.'[398] If the spouse does not consent to the marriage continuing, it will need to be annulled in order for the trans person to proceed from an interim to a full gender recognition certificate.

SCENARIO 4

Illustration 4: Mabel and Karen

On our original version of this scenario, Mabel has sought Marie's advice after her husband David has indicated a wish to change legal gender to female and be known as Karen. If Mabel and Karen decide to continue with their marriage, and if Karen wishes to obtain a gender recognition certificate, Mabel will need to provide a statutory declaration to the gender recognition panel that she consents to the marriage continuing after the issue of a full gender recognition certificate to Karen (the so-called 'spousal veto'). If she does not do that, the parties will have to annul their marriage or divorce before Karen can get her full certificate.

Many transgender people do not seek gender recognition certificates. There is nothing to prevent David from living as Karen without a certificate. There may well be practical difficulties with this, but many transgender people live this way, in part because the process of obtaining a certificate is presently quite difficult.

2.16 Conclusion

You may have found, as you read this chapter, that what you thought you knew about getting married, or the consequences of marriage, was frequently incorrect. Marriage laws are complex and their rationale at times baffling or of questionable modern application. Incorrect information is widespread (common law marriage!) and unexpected differences between religions can leave the unwary without legal protections, something they only find out when it is too late. Marriage law has a legacy of discrimination: by gender, by religion,

---

[395] In *Christine Goodwin v the United Kingdom* (1996) 22 EHRR 123 the Court finally accepted that state failure to permit a route to change legal gender was a breach of Article 8.

[396] Z Kirk-Robinson, *Report to the Consultation on the Spousal Veto* (Conservative Party LGBTory Group, n.d.)

[397] N Payton, 'What Is the Trans "Spousal Veto" and Why Does It Matter?' (*The Pink Paper*, 7 August 2015).

[398] S Whittle, 'Sex, Love & Consent; Gender Recognition in the Marriage (Same Sex Couples) Act 2013' (3 November 2013). Available at http://whittlings.blogspot.com/2013/11/sex-love-consent-gender-recognition-in.html accessed 8 August 2018.

by race and ethnicity, and by sexuality. It has been used to privilege some relationships at the expense of others. For some, this history has caused them to reject marriage and to turn to civil partnership as a more modern and equal alternative. But civil partnership was conceived precisely to avoid marriage equality, and there is still no recognised human right to marry a person of the same-sex. Couples are free to choose between two regimes, but there are no consistent views on the meaning and importance of either.

The fact that most young people want to marry suggests that despite the issues that we have outlined, marriage retains its lure. It serves a need for commitment and companionship that for most people is not met long-term by simply living together. But nearly half of all marriages fail. What this says about marriage is something that we consider in our next chapter.

 KEY POINTS

- The marriage rate is now at its lowest since records began, with around 240,000 couples marrying each year. Nevertheless, married couples remain the prevailing family form in England and Wales.

- The Marriage Act 1949 sets out the requirements of a valid marriage. Marriages can be formed through a secular (meaning non-religious) civil ceremony or through a religious ceremony. The requirements for forming a valid marriage vary depending on whether the wedding is to be secular or religious, and which religion. Confusion over the requirements for certain religious groups has meant that some people who had a religious ceremony may have unwittingly (or deliberately) not entered into a marriage that is recognised by the state.

- A void marriage is a marriage that, due to some defect that was present at the time of the ceremony, has never been valid. Only those impediments set out in s11 Matrimonial Causes Act 1973 cause a marriage to be void. A non-marriage is an 'event with marital qualities' or 'non-qualifying ceremony' that is not sufficiently close to resembling a valid marriage to count even as void. A voidable marriage is a marriage that exists until one of the parties has obtained a decree of nullity. If they never do that, the marriage remains valid. The grounds of voidability tend to relate more closely to the characteristics of the parties than the for automatically void marriages.

- A forced marriage is a marriage in which one or both of the parties lacks the mental capacity to consent or is marrying against their will. A forced marriage is voidable under s12 Matrimonial Causes Act 1973 for lack of consent and it is also possible to divorce. Forced marriage protection orders are a civil injunction prohibiting the marriage of a person named in the order, and breach is a criminal offence. There is also a separate criminal offence of forcing someone to marry.

- Marriage has a number of legal consequences relating to mutual financial support, parental responsibility and inheritance. It is because the state controls formation and dissolution of marriage that marriage is often referred to as a status, rather than a contract. While parties have some freedom of contact, there are some rights and responsibilities from which they cannot opt out. This reflects the state's multiple interests in marriage. There is no such thing as common law marriage. People who live together without being married never acquired the same rights and responsibilities as a married couple.

- Marriage laws have long been used to exclude or devalue certain communities. The European Court of Human Rights does not currently recognise a human right to marry someone of the same sex, because of the wording of Article 12 ECHR. However, it does recognise same-sex relationships as falling within the protections of Article 8. Transgender individuals can change their legal gender by obtaining a gender recognition certificate. They can then marry or enter into a civil partnership in their acquired gender.

- Civil partnerships were introduced by the Civil Partnership Act 2004 as an alternative to providing same-sex couples with marriage. Civil partnerships provide almost all the same legal consequences as marriages but there is a question over whether they offer an equivalent status to marriage. The Marriage (Same-Sex Couples) Act 2013 amended the law to allow for same-sex marriage, and in 2019 civil partnerships were opened to different-sex couples.

 # FURTHER READING: SOME STARTING POINTS

- A look at the statistics will help you to evaluate the relative popularity of marriage and civil partnership. As always, your first ports of call should be the Office of National Statistics' population estimates releases and statistical bulletins. For nullity statistics, you can look at the underlying NOMIS datasets given with each statistical bulletin.

- For the rules surrounding the formation of valid marriages and civil partnerships, look at the Marriage Act 1949, the Matrimonial Causes Act 1973, and the Civil Partnership Act 2004. Ensure you read versions that are up to date with amendments. Good information can also be found on the General Register office website.

- For an overview of nullity, see R Probert, 'When Are We Married? Void, Voidable, and Non-Existent Marriages' (2002) 22 *Legal Studies* 398 and 'The Evolving Concept of "Non-Marriage"' (2013) 25(3) *Child and Family Law Quarterly* 314. It is the Court of Appeal decision in *Akhter Attorney General v Akhter and Khan* [2020] EWCA Civ 122 which represents the current state of the law. For research on forced marriage, look first at A Gill and S Anitha (eds), *Forced Marriage : Introducing a Social Justice and Human Rights Perspective* (Zed Books, 2011). For the other grounds of nullity, there are various good articles footnoted.

- Rajnaara Akhtar has written about the reasons for unregistered marriages in two interesting pieces: 'Unregistered Muslim Marriages: An Emerging Culture of Celebrating Rites and Conceding Rights' in J Miles, P Mody, and R Probert, *Marriage Rites and Rights* (Bloomsbury 2015) and 'Modern Traditions in Muslim Marriage Practices, Exploring English Narratives' (2018) *Oxford Journal of Law and Religion* 1.

- For an evaluation of the importance and purposes of marriage, see MA Fineman, 'Why Marriage?' (2001) 9(1) *Virginia Journal of Social Policy and the Law* 239 and K O'Donovan, 'Marriage: A Sacred or Profane Love Machine?' (1993) 1(1) *Feminist Legal Studies* 75 for feminist perspectives; and for conservative perspectives L Wardle, 'Is Marriage Obsolete?' (2003) 10(1) *Michigan Journal of Gender and Law* 189 and M Gallagher, 'What Is Marriage For? The Public Purposes of Marriage Law' (2002) 62 *Louisiana Law Review* 773. A radical reimagining of marriage is the Law Commission of Canada's report *Beyond Conjugality: Recognizing and Supporting Close Personal Adult Relationships* (2001), which is online. BH Bix, 'State Interest and Marriage – The Theoretical Perspective' (2003) 32 *Hofstra Law Review* 93 is very readable.

- For the human right to marriage there are good commentaries by Helen Fenwick and Andy Hayward: H Fenwick, 'An ECHR Right to Access a Registered Partnership?' in JM Scherpe and A Hayward (eds), *The Future of Registered Partnerships* (Intersentia 2017) 471; A Hayward, 'Same-Sex Registered Partnerships: A Right to Be Recognised?' (2016) 75 *Cambridge Law Journal* 27; and both together in 'Rejecting Asymmetry of Access to Formal Relationship Statuses for Same and Different-Sex Couples at Strasbourg and Domestically' (2017) *European Human Rights Law Review* 544.

- For the ways in which same-sex marriage and civil partnerships are perceived, see the thought-provoking 'Marriage Is for Heterosexuals – May the Rest of Us Be Saved from It' (2000) 12(4) *Child and Family Law Quarterly* 363 by K McK Norrie; R Auchmuty, 'What's So Special about Marriage?' The Impact of *Wilkinson v Kitzinger* (2008) 20(4) *Child and Family Law Quarterly* 475; and the case itself at [2006] EWHC 2022 (Fam).

 Visit the **online resources** to watch a video of Polly Morgan discussing this chapter topic, and to check your understanding of this chapter with self-test questions and scenario questions.

Ending a Marriage or Civil Partnership

3

LEARNING CHECKLIST

By the end of this chapter, you should be able to:

* *Identify* elements of the current law that have their origins in previous centuries, and *explain* how the current law came about

* *Explain* the current legal requirements for a divorce including the legal meaning of each of the five facts and *critically discuss* the practical and tactical advantages of using one fact over another fact, or one jurisdiction over another, where there is a choice

* *Identify* the procedural and legal differences between the current law and the new law

* *Evaluate* the strengths and weaknesses of the current law by reference to academic commentary and research

* *Critically discuss* arguments for and against the removal of fault-based divorce by reference to different policy objectives and the ways in which research and prior experience shows people may behave

* *Critically discuss* the outcomes of research on the effect of divorce on children

* *Formulate* alternatives to the present law.

SCENARIO 1

Clare Newton's marriage to her husband Robert has come to an end. They were happy for the first few years. Then in January 2006, Robert met another woman, Sarah, and had a sexual relationship with her. He broke this off when Clare discovered the affair in November 2006. The parties went to Relate and were able to continue their marriage but they did not spend much time together thereafter. In May 2020, Robert discovered that Clare had been spending a lot of time with a neighbour, Mr Montgomery, although Clare says that they are simply friends. Clare and Robert have not shared the same bedroom since May 2018, nor had sex. Their solicitor asked about whether they spend time together and she said that they did, albeit rather miserably, eat and watch television together until July 2018, when, after a works' night out, a drunken Robert crashed on the sofa of Suky Jones, a receptionist at his office. Clare said that ever since this event her relationship with Robert has been 'fractious'.

They separated on 12 December 2018, when Robert moved into his own accommodation, leaving Clare in the matrimonial home, Larchwood. Clare wants to issue divorce proceedings on the basis of Robert's adultery with Suky. Although he has not admitted the adultery, it seems that Suky has moved in with Robert.

Robert has now told Clare that he wants to divorce her on the basis of her behaviour. His lawyer has written to Clare and enclosed a draft divorce petition for her to consider. The petition states that since July Clare has repeatedly verbally harangued Robert, has destroyed his prized collection of antique watches during an argument, has repeatedly rung up Robert's employer to tell them that he is 'an utter, utter, bastard', and has posted insulting messages about Robert and Suky on Facebook.

3.1 Introduction

In 2019, 107,599 people divorced their spouse. Over a 20-year period, about 42 per cent of marriages will end this way.[1] While the likelihood of divorce decreases significantly after the first ten years of marriage, the divorce rate is nevertheless increasing among the retired.[2] Divorce is a common part of life.

In this chapter we consider the current law of divorce, its historical origins and strengths and weaknesses, before turning to the new law of divorce which will come into effect in autumn 2021. We consider why reform was needed and the role in which divorce plays in our society, including what it says about marriage itself. We do so through the lens of Clare and Robert Newton, the couple in our scenario.

3.2 A brief history of divorce

The history of divorce is the history of social norms and expectations, and of the clash between idealism and reality. We can see in our present law the traces of the earliest divorces and, indeed, the situation prior to the first divorces.

3.2.1 Before divorce

Prior to the seventeenth century, marriages could be brought to an end only by the death of one of the parties or by an annulment granted by the ecclesiastical Consistory courts. As discussed in Chapter 2, there are specific grounds for nullity and these do not include the fact that the parties are no longer in love or one party is behaving badly or has committed adultery. Those who wished to separate but who did not have the grounds for annulment could separate informally, or seek a separation *a mensa et thoro* (from bed

---

[1] Office for National Statistics, *Divorces in England and Wales: 2019* (2020). This figure includes civil partnerships. The rate of civil partnership dissolution has fallen from a 2016 high, but numbers are so small it is impossible to do a comparison with the divorce rate. The Office for National Statistics have suggested that the rate for 2019 is significantly higher than 2018 when there were 90,871 because the courts have cleared a 2018 backlog; over the two years the number of divorces averages around 100,000 per annum.

[2] The proportion of the population aged 65 and over increased by 20% between 2004 and 2014, but their divorce rate by 46%. Office of National Statistics, 'Marriage and Divorce on the Rise at 65 and Over', 18 July 2017. Available at https://visual.ons.gov.uk/marriage-and-divorce-on-the-rise-at-65-and-over/ accessed 15 October 2020.

and board) from the ecclesiastical courts. Informal separation was a risky business.[3] Such agreements were of doubtful enforceability if the husband later petitioned for restitution of his conjugal rights or the Church got involved.[4] Some bishops were particularly keen on enforcing the obligation on spouses to live together and a refusal to reconcile could lead to excommunication.[5]

The purpose of a formal separation *a mensa et thoro* through the ecclesiastical courts was to enable the parties to live separately without religious penalty and to require the husband to pay maintenance to the wife. There were two grounds: that the other party was life-threateningly cruel or adulterous. However, a separation did not dissolve the marriage and so the parties were unable to marry another person.[6] As Waller writes, 'for many centuries, marriage was the single most important vehicle for the transmission of land in England', and thus of crucial importance to the landed classes who populated the Lords.[7] If a man could not remarry, any further children he had would be illegitimate and ineligible to inherit his estate.[8] It was this that prompted the introduction of divorce.

3.2.2 The first divorces: 1600–1857

The first divorce is usually considered to be that of Lord Roos and his wife Anne Pierrepont in the seventeenth century.[9] Anne had given birth to two children while not engaging in a sexual relationship with him. Without the grounds for an annulment, in 1663 Lord Roos obtained a separation *a mensa et thoro* because of Anne's adultery. As this did not enable him to remarry, in 1667 a sympathetic House of Lords passed an Act for Illegitimating the Children of the Lady Anne Roos to disinherit her sons,[10] followed in 1670 by An Act for Lord Roos to Marry Again.[11]

This established a precedent that an Act of Parliament could enable lawful remarriage. Thereafter, others also sought divorce by private Act of Parliament. However, this was a lengthy and expensive process and therefore restricted to those with a great deal of money and time. The first step was still to obtain a separation *a mensa et thoro* from the

---

[3] SM Butler, *Divorce in Medieval England: From One to Two Persons in Law* (Routledge 2013) 61.

[4] See R Probert, *Divorced, Bigamist, Bereaved?* (Takeaway Books 2015) 85. A claim for restitution of conjugal rights was to enforce the duty to live with your spouse. It is now abolished.

[5] R Phillips, *Putting Asunder: A History of Divorce in Western Society* (Cambridge University Press 1988) 284.

[6] *Rye v Fuliambe* (1602) 72 ER 838, deciding that William, Marquess of Northampton's ecclesiastical separation did not dissolve his marriage to Anne Bowrgshe.

[7] M Waller, *The English Marriage* (John Murray 2010) 3.

[8] There is an interesting discussion of whether a church separation a mensa et thoro had been taken by some as enabling remarriage and whether this was actually permitted: see K Kesselring, 'Licensed or Licentious? Divorce with Remarriage in Reformation England', *Legal History Miscellany* (23 October 2016) available at https://legal-historymiscellany.com/2016/10/23/divorce-with-remarriage-in-reformation-england/ accessed 11 October 2020.

[9] Henry VIII's *divorces a vincula matrimonii* ('from the bonds of marriage'), while often called divorces, were actually annulments.

[10] Members of the House of Commons appear to have been bribed by a good dinner at the Dog Tavern at Westminster, following which Lord Roos' lawyer 'carried them all to the House of Commons and they passed the bill, as the committee, without any amendments, and ordered it to be reported the next day': Eveline Cruickshanks, 'MANNERS, John, Lord Roos (1638–1711), of Belvoir Castle, Leics', in BD Henning (ed), *The History of Parliament: The House of Commons 1660–1690* (Secker & Warburg 1983).

[11] A transcript of the Act can be found in *The Law Review and Quarterly Journal of British and Foreign Jurisprudence Vol 1: November 1844–February 1845* (Owen Richards Law Publisher 1845) 363 fn1.

ecclesiastical courts. From 1798 it also became necessary for the husband to successfully sue his wife's lover for criminal conversation (that is the taking of the wife's affections away from her husband) and for assault and trespass—presumably onto his wife's body, his property. Then, the House of Lords would examine the evidence (even though this had been heard by both the ecclesiastical and civil courts already), approve the bill, and send it to the House of Commons, and then for Royal Assent. Divorce at this time was therefore well out of the reach of all but the wealthiest.

Given that Parliamentary divorces were so difficult to obtain, it is perhaps unsurprising that some people killed their spouse, or simply left and either formed new unmarried relationships or remarried bigamously, notwithstanding that bigamy was, from 1604, a criminal offence. Frost has found that some people treated their own bigamy trials as akin to divorce proceedings and asked the judge if this meant they could 'remarry after serving their time' (they could not).[12] Some drew up their own divorce papers in the erroneous belief that they would be valid. Another, albeit rarer, way, was to sell one's wife at the local market or inn, usually to a lover lined up ready to purchase.[13] A commission would be paid to the clerk of the market just as with the sale of cattle, and while some women sold for a significant amount, others sold for only a leg of mutton. In an era when wives pledged their husband's credit to buy goods, and thus her debts were his responsibility (see Chapter 4), this served a useful purpose: it alerted locals publicly that another man was now financially responsible for her. Overall, the number of reported wife sales is roughly equivalent to the number of Parliamentary divorces—and that is just those that made their way into the newspapers.[14] Nevertheless, wife sale has important symbolic value: wives were property, and the sale price, Phillips writes, was 'the poor man's equivalent of damages for criminal conversation'.[15]

Although a husband could seek a Parliamentary divorce on the grounds of his wife's adultery alone, Parliament took a more restrictive view of a wife's petition. Many women did not, in any event, have sufficient funds to bring suit unless her husband was required to pay: until 1882, a woman's property transferred to her husband on marriage. Thus, 'in 186 years of Parliamentary divorce' and 193 divorces granted to men, 'only four women successfully braved the legal and social obstacles of English society to find permanent relief by legislation',[16] the first being in 1801.[17] In each of the four successful cases (out of eight brought by women[18]), the husband's adultery was 'compounded by either incest or bigamy'.[19] It appears that cruelty, however severe, was insufficient: Ann Dawson's husband engaged in 'beastly drunkenness', whipped and kicked her, threw hot coffee at her face, set up house with a mistress, and threw her down the stairs. Yet not only did her petition, initiated

---

[12] GS Frost, *Living in Sin: Cohabiting as Husband and Wife in Nineteenth-Century England* (Manchester University Press 2008) 86.

[13] Examples of wives selling men are either non-existent or 'very rare', depending on the source.

[14] R Phillips, *Putting Asunder: A History of Divorce in Western Society* (Cambridge University Press 1988) 289.

[15] R Phillips, *Putting Asunder: A History of Divorce in Western Society* (Cambridge University Press 1988) 293.

[16] A Horstman, *Victorian Divorce* (Croom Helm 1985) 24.

[17] S Wolfram, 'Divorce in England 1700–1857' (1985) 5(2) *Oxford Journal of Legal Studies* 155, 162.

[18] CS Gibson, *Dissolving Wedlock* (Routledge 1994) 40.

[19] CS Gibson, *Dissolving Wedlock* (Routledge 1994) 41. For a description of each case, see S Wolfram, 'Divorce in England 1700–1857' (1985) 5(2) *Oxford Journal of Legal Studies* 155, 174–5. Incest at this time included incest by affinity as well as consanguinity (blood relationship), so it was incestuous to sleep with someone related to you by marriage. Affinity and consanguinity are discussed in Chapter 2.

in 1848, fail five times, but in Parliament Lord Campbell said that her bill did not show anything which 'would prevent the parties once more living together as good Christians'.[20]

SCENARIO 1

Illustration 1

Let's pause here and consider the position of Clare and Robert had they lived in this era. The facts do not enable Clare to divorce Robert—he has not committed incest or bigamy on top of his adultery. Robert might have more success in divorcing Clare: being seen in the company of a man other than her husband might well be taken as evidence of her adultery. As we see in Chapter 4, the financial consequences of such a finding would be awful for Clare, and if they had any children she would lose custody of them to Robert, to see them again only with his agreement. Depending on who wins the criminal conversation suit, either Robert or Mr Montgomery might be financially ruined and end up in debtors' prison. Certainly, even if Robert is successful, the procedure will have taken years and cost him a great deal of money.

However, their remedies, if any, would depend upon their wealth. Could Robert afford a separation *a mensa et thoro* followed by a lawsuit against Mr Montgomery for criminal conversation, and then an Act of Parliament? Or would he resort to self-help, drafting his own (invalid) petition, taking her to market, or forming a bigamous marriage to Suky? The options are pretty bleak for all involved.

3.2.3 Judicial divorces: 1857–1910

In 1857, Parliament dramatically reformed the law, passing the Matrimonial Causes Act 1857. The Act is an example of what Lawrence Stone has called 'a growing acceptance of secular control over all aspects of life'.[21] It removed the jurisdiction of the ecclesiastic courts in respect of separations *a mensa et thoro*, nullity, restitution of conjugal rights, and suits of jactitation of marriage.[22] Separations were replaced with secular 'judicial separations', although these functioned along the same lines, in that they did not terminate the marriage and permitted separation on more lenient grounds than could be used for divorce (either adultery *or* desertion *or* cruelty). Importantly, the Act also established secular divorce courts and a divorce process. For the first time, a marriage could be legally dissolved without its own Act.

Nevertheless, the grounds for men and women to seek divorce were different. A man could divorce for his wife's adultery alone. He no longer had to bring a case in the ecclesiastic courts and sue his wife's lover for criminal conversation first: he could, however, cite the lover as a co-respondent in the divorce. A wife needed to show that

> her Husband has been guilty of incestuous Adultery,[23] or of Bigamy with Adultery, or of Rape, or of Sodomy[24] or Bestiality, or of Adultery coupled with such Cruelty as without

---

[20] 'Appeals' (*The Times*, 22 April 1848). *The Times Digital Archive*.

[21] L Stone, *Road to Divorce: England 1530–1987* (Oxford University Press 1990) 353–4.

[22] A false claim that one is married to a particular individual.

[23] Incestuous adultery was defined as adultery 'committed by a Husband with a Woman with whom if his Wife were dead, he could not lawfully contract Marriage by reason of her being within the prohibited Degrees of Consanguinity or Affinity', thus being wider than adultery with a blood relation.

[24] Sodomy is anal intercourse. The term is now considered offensive. See A Milner, 'Sodomy as a Ground for Divorce' (1960) 23(1) *Modern Law Review* 43.

Adultery would have entitled her to a Divorce *a Mensa et Thoro*, or of Adultery coupled with Desertion, without reasonable Excuse, for Two Years or upwards. . .[25]

Why this double standard between male and female petitioners? Horstman explains that it was because of the risk of the wife committing adultery and thereby giving birth to children who had to be maintained by the husband, and stood to inherit, but who were not in fact his—the Lord Roos situation. In contrast, if the husband committed adultery, any resulting child was illegitimate, and he would not have to maintain it.[26] This double standard, established by an all-male Parliament, did not meet universal approval even at the time, as an 1857 *Bristol Mercury* editorial noted that 'opinion is growing that the husband is unduly favoured'.[27] Probert argues that it is nevertheless 'surprising that the opposition to an idea which is now accepted as self-evidently unjust should be so muted'.[28]

In its first year of operation, 1858, the court heard 253 petitions for divorce, of which 97 were brought by wives. That there were so many petitions by women was, Phillips points out, 'phenomenal' in view of the added hurdle.[29] It was also unexpected: legislators had wrongly assumed women would prefer judicial separation, yet 'women who might have been expected to take this option clearly chose not to do so'.[30] The Act led to a significant increase in the number of divorces, from around 3.3 per year before 1857 to 150 per year after it. By current standards this is tiny but, in the context of the time, nonetheless a 'watershed'. [31]

The process of obtaining a divorce may have become more accessible to the new middle classes, but it was nonetheless expensive and humiliating. A full hearing, sometimes before a jury, was required. Public galleries were full, and newspapers reported the proceedings in considerable detail.[32] There was little nuance: 'To the Victorian public, the successful petitioner was innocent, blameless and good; the convicted respondent was guilty, depraved and bad.'[33] This view was reinforced by the law. The Act was based on the idea of matrimonial offences—breaches of the marriage contract, such as adultery, desertion, cruelty, and incest, that justified an innocent party seeking a divorce. Mutual guilt, condoning the wrongdoing, or the parties colluding in getting a divorce were all fatal to a petition because there was no innocent party deserving of relief. These concepts were 'lifted straight out of' ecclesiastical law.[34] Our current law is based on these facts too: adultery, desertion and behaviour (albeit not at the level of cruelty or incest) are all facts on which a divorce can, in present day England or Wales, be obtained.

---

[25] Matrimonial Causes Act 1857 s27.

[26] A Horstman, *Victorian Divorce* (Croom Helm 1985) 20 and 82.

[27] *Bristol Mercury*, 7 March 1857.

[28] R Probert, 'The Double Standard of Morality in the Divorce and Matrimonial Causes Act 1857' (1999) 28 *Anglo-American Law Review* 73.

[29] R Phillips, *Putting Asunder: A History of Divorce in Western Society* (Cambridge University Press 1988) 412.

[30] GL Savage, 'The Operation of the 1857 Divorce Act, 1860–1910: A Research Note' (1983) 16(4) *Journal of Social History* 103, 105.

[31] S Wolfram, 'Divorce in England 1700–1857' (1985) 5(2) *Oxford Journal of Legal Studies* 155, 156.

[32] For an example, see *Burroughs v Burroughs* (*The Times* 3 February 1862) 11.

[33] CS Gibson, *Dissolving Wedlock* (Routledge 1994) 61.

[34] *Putting Asunder: A Divorce Law for Contemporary Society: Report of a Group appointed by the Archbishop of Canterbury in January 1964* (SPCK 1966) 26–7.

SCENARIO 1

Illustration 2

It would appear that as a result of the 1857 Act Robert is in a better position to gain a divorce than would have been the case previously. The cost of proceedings has decreased, and he can still rely on Clare's adultery, which is likely to be inferred from simply being seen in Mr Montgomery's company, perhaps coupled with the testimony of some household staff. Robert no longer has to seek separation *a mensa et thoro* first, and the suits for criminal conversation have been abolished (although he can cite Mr Montgomery as a co-respondent).

In order for Clare to petition against Robert, she would need to show adultery coupled with incest, bigamy, cruelty, two years' desertion, sodomy, bestiality, or that Robert had raped another woman (it is, in this era, no crime to rape one's own wife). She might therefore have grounds if she can prove adultery with Suky after he has deserted her for two years. Yet she must herself be blameless. Her liaison, with Mr Montgomery, however innocent by today's standards, might mean that she is denied a divorce.

3.2.4 Divorce on the rise 1910–1966

The divorce rate rose steadily throughout the following decades, with a particular rise between 1910 (581 decrees of divorce or nullity) and 1920 (3,090 decrees), perhaps influenced by the 'hasty marriages and prolonged separations' associated with the first world war.[35] Attempts to expand the grounds of divorce in 1920 and 1921 failed, but demand was such that, in 1922, 26 divorce registries were established outside London. The Matrimonial Causes Act 1923 abolished the 'illogical and unsatisfactory'[36] difference between the facts available to both men and women, enabling each to divorce on the ground of the other's adultery alone, in addition to the existing facts.[37] Thereafter, the proportion of petitions filed by women increased significantly, from 41 per cent of petitions in 1921 to 62 per cent in 1924, a figure which is not dissimilar to that of today.[38]

Most divorce suits were, by this time, undefended adultery petitions, but the judge still had to be satisfied that adultery had occurred. Where a husband and wife both wished to divorce, they had every incentive to collude (work together) in producing witness evidence of adultery that would satisfy a judge. One common way of proving adultery was for the husband to stay in a hotel overnight with a woman who was not his wife and was, perhaps, hired for the purpose: adultery was not expected to take place, merely the appearance of such to the hotel staff, who could then testify as about it.[39] However, they could not

---

[35] GL Savage, 'The Operation of the 1857 Divorce Act, 1860–1910: A Research Note' (1983) 16(4) *Journal of Social History* 103, 108.

[36] R Probert, 'The Double Standard of Morality in the Divorce and Matrimonial Causes Act 1857' (1999) 28 *Anglo-American Law Review* 73.

[37] Matrimonial Causes Act 1923 s1.

[38] CS Gibson, *Dissolving Wedlock* (Routledge 1994) 85.

[39] The barrister John Mortimer recounts his efforts to have hotel staff remember him and his lover Penelope, so that her husband could procure a divorce—even setting fire to hotel bed sheets proved unsuccessful. See J Mortimer, *Clinging to the Wreckage* (Penguin Books 1982/1995) 94.

be seen to be colluding, or they would be refused a divorce and even and be imprisoned for conspiring to manufacture false evidence.[40] Cretney argues that the 1923 reforms, by satisfying many people just enough, stalled greater attempts to improve the divorce process.[41] The law still required one party to have committed a matrimonial offence and the other to be innocent of wrongdoing, even if that did not reflect reality.

Thus, as the Archdeacon of Coventry put it, 'those who wish to bring an end to marriage are forced to take one of two alternatives—either one must commit adultery or one must commit perjury'.[42] It was the implications of this situation which resulted in a further legal change—the Matrimonial Causes Act 1937. The Act enabled both men and women to divorce on the basis of the other's adultery, cruelty, desertion for three years, or because the other party was incurably of unsound mind. No divorces were permitted in the first three years of marriage except with court permission for exceptional reasons, and the standard of proof of adultery was beyond a reasonable doubt—the criminal, rather than the usual civil standard. This was designed to allay the Church of England's fears about collusion and thereby procure Church support for the Act.[43]

As with the increases that had followed previous reforms of divorce law, the number of petitions rose, doubling between 1937 and 1939. Adultery remained the most used ground, followed by desertion (about a third of petitions) and then cruelty. Collusion through 'hotel divorces' remained common and even desertion could be falsified by the writing of a goodbye letter—perhaps backdated three years—to make it appear as though one party had deserted the other without justification.[44] Despite this, many people who wished to do so were still unable to divorce. First, the process remained expensive. Although the government had introduced a poor persons' procedure in 1914—an early form of legal aid—it was distinctly ungenerous in both the help it gave and who was eligible for it.[45] It was not until 1949 that a new and better scheme of legal aid was introduced. Second, the standard of evidence required was very high.

3.2.5 The origins of our current law

By the early 1950s, the law was (once again) 'seen as thoroughly hypocritical and the stance of the Church . . . as harsh and unyielding. Increasingly the position of the state was seen itself as immoral . . . and those who sought to force people to stay together in miserable marriages . . . were seen as the ones without compassion and understanding.'[46] Stephen Cretney observed a three day public trial in 1953, at the end of which the husband was found not to have committed adultery beyond reasonable doubt, despite practically admitting it, and on the husband's counter-petition, the wife's conduct was dismissed as simply the 'ordinary

---

[40] See CS Gibson, *Dissolving Wedlock* (Routledge 1994) 97.

[41] S Cretney, *Family Law in the Twentieth Century: A History* (Oxford 2003) 222.

[42] Quoted by CS Gibson, *Dissolving Wedlock* (Routledge 1994) 97, himself quoting AP Herbert MP, HC Deb 1937, vol 317, col 2082.

[43] S Redmayne, 'The Matrimonial Causes Act 1937: A Lesson in the Art of Compromise' (1993) 13(2) *Oxford Journal of Legal Studies* 183.

[44] S Cretney, *Family Law in the Twentieth Century: A History* (Oxford 2003) 259.

[45] For a discussion of this, see CS Gibson, *Dissolving Wedlock* (Routledge 1994) 86ff.

[46] C Smart, 'Divorce in England 1950–2000: A Moral Tale?' in SN Katz, J Eekelaar, and M Maclean (eds), *Cross Currents: Family Law and Policy in the United States and England* (Oxford University Press 2000) 370.

wear and tear of conjugal life' rather than cruelty. This unhappy couple, each keen to be free of the other, were destined to remain married. 'Those whom the law had made one flesh were thus to remain legally yoked together; and the public interest in upholding the institution of marriage had . . . been triumphantly asserted', writes Cretney.[47]

Accordingly, by the early 1950s there was concerted pressure for reform, notably gathered behind a private member's bill introduced by Eirene White MP in 1951. This sought to introduce a further ground of divorce, unilateral divorce on the basis of seven years' separation. This suggested for the first time that marriages should be dissolved not because of matrimonial offences, but simply because they had broken down.[48] Yet Mrs White withdrew her bill when a Royal Commission on Marriage and Divorce was established. Unfortunately, despite producing a 405-page report, the Commission was unable to agree on what should be done.[49]

It took until 1969 for Parliament to pass the Divorce Reform Act, a significant, modernising piece of legislation that, subsequently consolidated into the Matrimonial Causes Act 1973, forms the basis of our current law. This Act was influenced by two important reports. The first of these was 1966's *Putting Asunder*, a report commissioned by the Archbishop of Canterbury.[50] The authors 'emphatically' rejected divorce by mutual consent but argued that there should be a single ground of divorce, familiar from Mrs White's bill: the irretrievable breakdown of the marriage.[51] The judge's role was to determine whether a marriage had irretrievably broken down by conducting a sort of inquest into the marriage. Specific facts such as adultery 'would no longer have to be regarded as an independent and self-sufficient reason for dissolving a marriage', but would simply be evidence of irretrievable breakdown.[52]

Putting Asunder met with generally positive approval and the Law Commission was tasked with considering whether and how its proposals could be implemented. It published its report *Reform of the Grounds of Divorce: The Field of Choice* only a few months later.[53] It set out its views on the purposes of divorce:

> A good divorce law should seek to achieve the following objectives: (i) To buttress, rather than to undermine, the stability of marriage; and (ii) When, regrettably, a marriage has irretrievably broken down, to enable the empty legal shell to be destroyed with the maximum fairness, and the minimum bitterness, distress and humiliation. . . .

> In addition to these two main objectives, another important requirement is that the divorce law should be understandable and respected. . . . If it is thought to be hypocritical or otherwise unworthy of respect, it will not only fail to achieve those objectives but may bring the whole of the administration of justice into disrespect.[54]

---

[47] S Cretney, 'Divorce Reform in England – Humbug and Hypocrisy, or a Smooth Transition?' in M Freeman (ed), *Divorce—Where Next?* (Dartmouth 1996) 39–40.

[48] Discussed in S Cretney, *Family Law in the Twentieth Century: A History* (Oxford 2003) 324–6.

[49] Cmd 9678, 1956.

[50] The Archbishop's dismay at the content of the report he commissioned is discussed in S Cretney, *Family Law in the Twentieth Century: A History* (Oxford 2003) 365 fn 298.

[51] *Putting Asunder: A Divorce Law for Contemporary Society: Report of a Group appointed by the Archbishop of Canterbury in January 1964* (SPCK 1966) 34.

[52] *Putting Asunder: A Divorce Law for Contemporary Society: Report of a Group appointed by the Archbishop of Canterbury in January 1964* (SPCK 1966) 65.

[53] Law Commission, *Reform of the Grounds of Divorce: The Field of Choice* (Cmnd 3123, 1966).

[54] Law Commission, *Reform of the Grounds of Divorce: The Field of Choice* (Cmnd 3123, 1966) paras 15 and 18.

The Commissioners felt that the *Putting Asunder* idea of a trial or inquest into whether the marriage had irretrievably broken down was too 'elaborate, time-consuming and expensive'[55] to be practical, and, moreover, 'might be humiliating and distressing and not achieve the second of the two objectives of a reformed divorce law set out [above]'.[56] They also felt that it was unnecessary: unless the marriage had broken down the parties would not be before the court in the first place.[57] The Commission recommended instead that there should be either divorce with six months' separation as proof of irretrievable breakdown—it felt that a longer period might create hardship—or, if that short a period was not acceptable to Parliament, a longer period of separation could be added as a ground of divorce in addition to the existing grounds based on matrimonial offences. This was in direct conflict to the views of *Putting Asunder*, which cautioned against a combined system of offences plus breakdown, viewing the two as inherently incompatible.

What ultimately resulted was a compromise including elements of both schemes. Irretrievable breakdown was made the sole ground of divorce, yet the court would infer such breakdown if one or more of five facts existed, three of which were based on matrimonial offences, and two on a period of separation:

(a) that the respondent has committed adultery and the petitioner finds it intolerable to live with the respondent;

(b) that the respondent has behaved in such a way that the petitioner cannot reasonably be expected to live with the respondent;

(c) that the respondent has deserted the petitioner for a continuous period of at least two years immediately preceding the presentation of the petition;

(d) that the parties to the marriage have lived apart for a continuous period of at least two years immediately preceding the presentation of the petition and the respondent consents to a decree being granted; or

(e) that the parties to the marriage have lived apart for a continuous period of at least five years immediately preceding the presentation of the petition.

In order to address specific concerns, the Act also preserved the 1937 Act's requirement that the parties not commence proceedings in the first three years of marriage unless they could show exceptional circumstances; and, in order to encourage reconciliation where possible, it permitted the parties to reconcile for up to six months without having to abandon the petition. In view of concern that wives would be abandoned, impoverished, by this 'Casanova's charter',[58] it also created a specific hardship defence to divorces brought on the basis of separation.

The effect of the Act, which came into force in 1971, was considerable. As Lord Denning put it:

> Parliament has decreed: 'If the marriage has broken down irretrievably, let there be a divorce.' It carries no stigma, but only sympathy. It is a misfortune which befalls both.

---

[55] Law Commission, *Reform of the Grounds of Divorce: The Field of Choice* (Cmnd 3123, 1966) para 71.
[56] Law Commission, *Reform of the Grounds of Divorce: The Field of Choice* (Cmnd 3123, 1966) para 59.
[57] Law Commission, *Reform of the Grounds of Divorce: The Field of Choice* (Cmnd 3123, 1966) para 71.
[58] This phrase was coined by Lady Summerskill in a speech and thereafter much repeated.

No longer is one guilty and the other innocent. No longer are there long contested divorce suits. Nearly every case goes uncontested. The parties come to an agreement, if they can, on the things that matter so much to them. . . . If they cannot agree, the matters are referred to a judge in chambers.[59]

The number of petitions rose by nearly 45,000 in one year.[60] Ruth Deech has noted that 'each successive attempt in the twentieth century to bring the statute law into line with "reality" has resulted in an increase in the divorce rate'. The law is liberalised in response to public demand, and because the current law is manipulated by those who would wish it to be different; once reformed, the rate rises and the cycle starts again: 'The pressure on the divorce system leads to a relaxation of practice and procedure in divorce, then to a call for a change in the law to bring it into line with reality, and then to yet another increase in divorce.'[61] But as we shall see, this does not necessarily mean that more liberal divorce laws are causing this rise in divorce. Over a fifth of the petitions issued during this rise were on the fact of five years' separation, and many were older couples previously unable to honestly divorce by the requirement to prove fault.[62] The 1970s represent not the high point of divorce—we have since surpassed its record—but the high point of marriage. In the same year that the number of petitions rose so sharply, 426,000 marriages were conducted: the highest number ever recorded.[63]

We will consider each of these five facts in further detail, as the Divorce Reform Act is almost identical to our current law. In 1973, Parliament passed the Matrimonial Causes Act. This consolidated the Divorce Reform Act with a separate 1970 Act that dealt with the financial consequences of divorce, but left its provisions intact. Thus, while the current law is contained in the Matrimonial Causes Act 1973, it is the same as the Divorce Reform Act 1969 with two exceptions. In 1973, in recognition of spiralling numbers of divorces, the government introduced the so-called 'special procedure' for undefended divorces, which meant that a hearing was no longer necessary and the matter considered on paper,[64] and in 1984, as a result of the significant number of people applying for the three year time bar for divorce to be truncated on the grounds of exceptional circumstances, the time bar was reduced to one year.[65] Apart from these two changes, the law of divorce has not changed for some fifty years. Some aspects of the current law can be traced back far longer, to centuries past and the social and moral concerns that occupied our ancestors.

As you read the next section, on the current law, consider: Does the law as it is today reflect the society we live in now? And, if not, should it do so, or should it be a moral bulwark against the tides of change?

---

[59] *Wachtel v Wachtel* [1973] Fam 72, 89.

[60] Office of National Statistics, *Statistical Bulletin: Divorce in England and Wales 2018* (ONS 2019) gives the historical figures.

[61] R Deech, 'Divorce – A Disaster', [2009] *Family Law* 1048, 1053.

[62] See CS Gibson, *Dissolving Wedlock* (Routledge 1994) 108.

[63] Office of National Statistics, *Statistical Bulletin: Divorce in England and Wales 2018* (ONS 2019).

[64] This was an administrative change, not contained in any Act. It also enabled the government to remove legal aid from undefended divorces.

[65] Matrimonial and Family Proceedings Act 1984.

3.3 **The current law**

As we have seen, the current law on divorce is contained in the Matrimonial Causes Act 1973, and this is a combination of a system based on Matrimonial offences (fault) and a system based on separation for a period of time without the need to show fault.

All those wishing to obtain a divorce have to show that, on the balance of probabilities, their marriage has broken down irretrievably: s1(1). This is the sole ground of divorce in England and Wales. (If you thought it was 'irreconcilable differences', you've been watching too much American television.)

In order to demonstrate that the marriage has irretrievably broken down, the person seeking the divorce—the petitioner[66]—must show that one or more of five facts set out in ss 1(2)(a)-(e) applies.

For civil partners, the relevant law is set out in s44 Civil Partnership Act 2004. Once more, the sole ground is irretrievable breakdown, and the facts are the same as those in the Matrimonial Causes Act, with one exception: as discussed at 3.3.1.1, there is no adultery fact.

STATUTORY EXTRACT *Matrimonial Causes Act 1973*

s1 Divorce on breakdown of marriage

(1) Subject to section 3 below, a petition for divorce may be presented to the court by either party to a marriage on the ground that the marriage has broken down irretrievably.

(2) The court hearing a petition for divorce shall not hold the marriage to have broken down irretrievably unless the petitioner satisfies the court of one or more of the following facts, that is to say—

    (a) that the respondent has committed adultery and the petitioner finds it intolerable to live with the respondent;

    (b) that the respondent has behaved in such a way that the petitioner cannot reasonably be expected to live with the respondent;

    (c) that the respondent has deserted the petitioner for a continuous period of at least two years immediately preceding the presentation of the petition;

    (d) that the parties to the marriage have lived apart for a continuous period of at least two years immediately preceding the presentation of the petition (hereafter in this Act referred to as 'two years' separation') and the respondent consents to a decree being granted;

    (e) that the parties to the marriage have lived apart for a continuous period of at least five years immediately preceding the presentation of the petition (hereafter in this Act referred to as 'five years' separation').

(3) On a petition for divorce it shall be the duty of the court to inquire, so far as it reasonably can, into the facts alleged by the petitioner and into any facts alleged by the respondent.

(4) If the court is satisfied on the evidence of any such fact as is mentioned in subsection (2) above, then, unless it is satisfied on all the evidence that the marriage has not broken down irretrievably, it shall, subject to section 5 below, grant a decree of divorce.

Note: For civil partners, the facts are mirrored in s44 Civil Partnership Act 2004 with the exception of adultery.

---

[66] The court forms use both the word 'petitioner' and the word 'applicant' for the person who files the divorce petition.

All divorces or civil partnership dissolutions are started by the filing of a petition which will state that the marriage has broken down, indicate which one or more of the facts the petitioner is relying upon (while more than one fact can be pleaded, most people rely on just one), and explain why that fact is applicable. While the petitioner must satisfy the court that on the balance of probabilities the fact stated in his or her petition is true, the petitioner does not actually have to show that the fact s/he uses is the *reason* why the marriage broke down.[67] A causal link is not required. In any case, that may be impossible to know: there may be multiple events which could have fatally fractured a marriage before it finally ends. It is not possible to file for divorce unless the marriage or civil partnership has existed for one year, not counting the day of marriage, even though a couple may have separated well before this.[68]

Section 1(4) says that the court 'shall' grant a divorce. The court can only refuse to do this if either no fact is found to exist, or where it thinks that the marriage has not irretrievably broken down. There is one further exception which is where a petition is based on five years' separation, where the court can also refuse a divorce where it would cause 'grave hardship' to the respondent.[69]

We will now explore in more detail the five facts that parties can rely on to prove that their marriage has irretrievably broken down, before we look at the court process.

3.3.1 The five facts: Adultery

There are three elements to be satisfied for a successful adultery petition: (1) the respondent has committed adultery; (2) the petitioner must find it intolerable to live with the respondent; and (3) the parties must have separated within six months of the petitioner finding out about the adultery.

Adultery has a specific legal definition. It is a voluntary[70] act of sexual intercourse between someone who is married and a person of the opposite sex who is not their spouse.[71] There must at least be partial penetration of the female by the male—trying but failing is insufficient.[72] Other forms of sexual activity do not constitute adultery even though people may consider them just as much of a betrayal.[73] Sexual activity with someone of the same sex does not constitute adultery either. This is discussed at 3.3.1.

It is extremely difficult to prove adultery if the respondent denies it. The most sensible step is to write to the proposed respondent before filing an adultery petition to ask if they admit the adultery and are prepared to make a written statement to that effect. While it is possible to ask the court to infer that there has been adultery from the circumstances, on

---

[67] *Stevens v Stevens* [1979] 1 WLR 885.

[68] Matrimonial Causes Act 1973 s3(1), inserted by the Matrimonial and Family Proceedings Act 1984; Civil Partnership Act 2004 s41.

[69] Matrimonial Causes Act 1973 s5. As discussed at 3.2.5 of this chapter, we can trace this exception back to the debates about whether the Matrimonial Causes Act 1973 would operate as a 'Casanova's Charter' with feckless men divorcing innocent women using the five years' separation fact and leaving them in poverty.

[70] It is therefore impossible for the victim of rape to be considered to have committed adultery.

[71] Matrimonial Causes Act 1973 s1(6).

[72] *Dennis v Dennis (Spillet Cited)* [1955] P 153.

[73] They could form part of a behaviour petition, however.

the basis that there has been inclination and opportunity,[74] such as moving in together, if the respondent does not admit adultery it is often more sensible to switch to a different fact to avoid evidential difficulties should the respondent defend the petition. The respondent might be prepared to accept that he or she has had what we might euphemistically call an inappropriately close relationship with another, which could found the basis of a behaviour petition, even if they are not willing to admit to (or perhaps have not committed) adultery itself.[75]

SCENARIO 1

Illustration 3

Unless Robert admits to adultery with Suky, Clare would have to invite the court to infer adultery from the fact that Robert and Suky are now living together. It does not matter that the adultery was not the cause of the marriage ending. The fact that Robert and Clare are separated does not prevent it from being adultery: they are still married, so any intercourse between Robert and Suky is adulterous.

You cannot get divorced on the basis of your own adultery; it has to be adultery by the other party, your spouse. It is only the 'wronged' party who can choose to end the marriage for this reason. This reflects adultery's origins as a matrimonial offence with the parties seen as wrongdoer and wronged person respectively.

Most adultery petitions will say something along the lines of 'The respondent has committed adultery with a [woman/man] whom the petitioner chooses not to name. The adultery took place at various times in London. The petitioner finds it intolerable to live with the respondent.' It is possible in an adultery petition to name the co-respondent—the person with whom your spouse has committed adultery—rather than simply call them 'a woman' or 'a man'. The petitioner can also ask the court to order that they pay some or all of the petitioner's costs. As the term 'co-respondent' suggests, doing this makes them a party to the divorce suit. While essential in past centuries, naming a co-respondent is now considered undesirable both for practical reasons (it means you have to serve the papers on them and prove service if they do not cooperate, and they tend not to cooperate) and because it is likely to increase the acrimony in the divorce very considerably for no advantage other than revenge—and revenge does not come cheap. The solicitor Vanessa Lloyd Platt has argued that 'In a modern world—where divorce has become a familiar fact of life—citing third parties in divorce cases has a whiff of the Victorian age.'[76]

---

[74] *Farnham v Farnham* (1925) 153 LT 320. John Mortimer, whose father was, like him, a barrister specialising in divorce, said that his father 'would say, "Wonderful day in court, John. Managed to prove adultery by evidence of opportunity and inclination. But really, the only evidence I had was footprints upside down on the dashboard of an Austin 7 motor car parked in Hampstead Garden Suburb."' John Mortimer, 'Sleeping Juries and My Life in the Law' *The Independent* (London, 5 June 2001).

[75] *Wachtel v Wachtel* [1973] Fam 72.

[76] V Lloyd Platt, 'Should a Packed Lunch Be Grounds for a Divorce?' (*The Times* 28 March 2012) section T2 p4.

In addition to showing on the balance of probabilities that adultery has occurred, the petitioner *must* also show that s/he finds it intolerable to live with the respondent. However, per Lord Denning MR in *Cleary v Cleary*, this does not need to be *because of* the adultery:

> I think the two facts [adultery and intolerability] are independent and should be so treated. Take this very case. The husband proves that the wife committed adultery and that he forgave her and took her back. That is one fact. He then proves that, after she comes back, she behaves in a way that makes it quite intolerable to live with her. She corresponds with the other man and goes out at night and finally leaves her husband, taking the children with her. That is another fact. It is in consequence of that second fact that he finds it intolerable—not in consequence of the previous adultery. On that evidence, it is quite plain that the marriage has broken down irretrievably.[77]

This approach also recognises that adultery may be a symptom of a marriage that has already irretrievably broken down for other reasons, rather than the cause of the breakdown. However, the court must still be satisfied that it is actually intolerable, rather than just unpleasant, to live with the respondent. This is subjective—does *this* petitioner find it intolerable to live with *this* respondent? What is intolerable for one may not be intolerable to another.

If the parties lived together in the same household for a period exceeding, or periods together exceeding, six months after it became known to the petitioner that the respondent had committed adultery, then that adultery cannot be the basis of a divorce petition.[78] The reason that there is a six-month grace period is to give time for the parties to assess whether the marriage has indeed irretrievably broken down or can be saved. If they are still together after this, the law treats the adultery as having been 'condoned' (legally forgiven) by the petitioner, although if the respondent cheats again then the fact the petitioner condoned adultery in the past does not mean they have to do so in the future.[79] The parties must therefore separate within six months of knowledge of adultery, even if they do not get divorced immediately.

SCENARIO 1

Illustration 4

Clare found out about Robert's affair with Sarah too long ago for it to form the basis of a petition. She is deemed to have condoned it, as they stayed together for more than a decade afterwards. The fact that it may have caused a significant fracture in their relationship is neither here nor there, on an adultery petition.

  If Clare were to use adultery with Sarah as the fact on which she relies, she would have needed to have separated from Robert by the end of six months of finding out about it. This does not necessarily mean them living in separate houses as long as they are in separate households within the house.

---

[77] *Goodrich v Goodrich* [1971] 1 WLR 1142 (HC) and *Cleary v Cleary* [1974] 1 WLR 73 (CA).
[78] Matrimonial Causes Act 1978 s2(1).
[79] *Carr v Carr* [1974] 1 WLR 1534 (CA).

FOCUS Know-How

What is separation?

While separation usually involves one party moving out, in some cases the parties cannot actually afford to live in separate properties and are therefore forced by circumstances to live together until their financial settlement is agreed. This does not mean that they are not separated. The legislation says that the parties are to be 'treated as living apart unless they are living with each other in the same household'. '[I]t does not use the word "house", which relates to something physical, but "household", which has an abstract meaning . . . a word which essentially refers to people held together by a particular kind of tie, even if temporarily separated.'[80] In *Hopes v Hopes*, Lord Denning noted that:

> The husband who shuts himself up in one or two rooms of his house, and ceases to have any-thing to do with his wife, is living separately and apart from her as effectively as if they were separated by the outer door of a flat. They may meet on the stairs or in the passageway, but so they might if they each had separate flats in one building. . . . [Separation] is reached when they cease to be one household and become two households.[81]

In order to determine whether the parties are in the same household or merely in the same house, the petitioner will need to explain, in their statement in support of petition, what the domestic ar-rangements have been since the date of alleged separation, the date when the petitioner knew of the adultery, or the last example of behaviour (as the case may be). It is not necessary to build a wall down the middle of the house as one couple we know of did, but the court will need to be satisfied that the domestic arrangements—cooking, eating, sleeping, and chores—are separate. In *Mouncer v Mouncer*[82] the parties occupied separate bedrooms, but shared the use and cleaning of all of the other rooms, and they ate together with the wife cooking for them both. 'The fact that they did this from the wholly admirable motive of caring properly for their children cannot change the result of what they did', which was to remain a household and thus not be separated.

In addition to not living in the same household, at least one party must also have an intention to separate. While noting that '[t]here is something unattractive in the idea that in effect time . . . can begin to run against a spouse without his or her knowledge, the Court of Appeal held in *Santos v Santos* that it is not necessary to have communicated that intention'.[83] This means that deciding on a precise date of separation is extremely difficult in some cases.

Note that in the cases of adultery, behaviour, and desertion, there is a six-month grace period in which the parties can stay in the same household without it affecting the petition. This is to encour-age reconciliation and discourage hasty decision-making. Apart from this, if they have to remain in the same home, they will need to separate their domestic arrangement and thereby show that they are in separate households.

Same-sex couples and adultery

As you can see, the definition of adultery is gendered: it depends on one person being legally male and one person being legally female.[84] A man who cheats on his wife (or husband) with another man cannot be divorced on the fact of his adultery, for he has

---

[80] *Santos v Santos* [1972] Fam 247, 262 (CA) (Sachs LJ).

[81] *Hopes v Hopes* [1949] P 227.

[82] [1972] 1 WLR 321 (Wrangham J).

[83] [1972] Fam 247, 260.

[84] It was a great deal more complicated prior to a legal mechanism to change gender, which was the Gender Rec-ognition Act 2004.

not committed adultery. A lesbian who cheats on her wife or civil partner with another woman does not commit adultery either. And following gender confirmation surgery, a person who has cheated on their spouse or civil partner would not have committed adultery even if one had a penis and one a vagina, provided that they were both legally female.[85]

For civil partners, adultery is not a basis for divorce at all, whoever it is with. It is simply not mentioned in the Civil Partnership Act. When writing the Act, the government declined to amend the definition of adultery to encompass same-sex acts, saying that 'it would not be possible nor desirable' to do this.[86] Some commentators have pointed out that this sends a message that same-sex relationships are not expected to be sexually monogamous; or that it is a 'denial of lesbian and gay sexuality' that has 'heterosexist connotations in that the "real" sex act enshrined in the law remains a heterosexual, penetrative one'.[87] Certainly, lesbian participants in Rosemary Auchmuty's study of civil partnership dissolutions were 'astonished' by its omission.[88] Even though civil partnerships are now available to different-sex couples, adultery remains excluded.

Eekelaar takes the view that 'its absence from the [Act] cannot imply any less commitment for same-sex spouses than opposite-sex ones [because] any manifestation of infidelity could entitle divorce as "unreasonable behaviour".'[89] Indeed, the inclusion of sexual misconduct within the parameters of the behaviour fact was confirmed by the government at the time the bill was before Parliament.[90] There are two objections to this. First, it is possible that calling something adultery gives it a moral significance in the eyes of the petitioner that behaviour does not encompass. Second, under the adultery fact the petitioner has to find it intolerable to live with the respondent, which is a subjective determination. Under the behaviour fact, the assessment includes an objective element—whether the petitioner can reasonably be expected to live with the respondent (see 3.3.2).[91]

Unlike civil partners, however, a same-sex married person *can* commit adultery. The Marriage (Same-Sex Couples) Act 2013 achieved same-sex marriage through the simple removal of the requirement in s11 Matrimonial Causes Act 1973 that the parties to a marriage be respectively male and female. The adultery provisions in the Matrimonial Causes Act remained intact and therefore apply equally to same-sex couples—right down to the definition of adultery as requiring opposite-sex penetrative intercourse. Thus, to commit adultery in a same-sex marriage, the respondent must have had penetrative sexual intercourse with someone of the opposite legal sex, which may be unlikely.

---

[85] One can have gender confirmation surgery without seeking a legal change of gender, and vice versa. However, when seeking a legal change of gender, medical reports need to be provided which ask what surgery you have and if you have not had it, the reason why.

[86] Women and Equality Unit, *Responses to Civil Partnership: A Framework for Legal Recognition of Same-Sex Couples* (Department of Trade and Industry 2003) 36.

[87] N Barker, *Not the Marrying Kind: A Feminist Critique of Same-Sex Marriage* (Palgrave 2013) 186.

[88] R Auchmuty, 'The Experience of Civil Partnership Dissolution: Not "Just Like a Divorce"' (2016) 38(2) *Journal of Social Welfare and Family Law* 152, 161.

[89] J Eekelaar, 'Perceptions of Equality: The Road to Same-Sex Marriage in England and Wales' (2014) 28(1) *International Journal of Law, Policy and the Family* 1, 16.

[90] Baroness Scotland, *Hansard* (House of Lords) 10 May 2004, and Women and Equality Unit, *Responses to Civil Partnership: A Framework for Legal Recognition of Same-Sex Couples* (Department of Trade and Industry 2003) 36.

[91] There is a fascinating discussion of the difference between the subjective test for adultery and the test for behaviour in the debates on the Divorce Reform Act 1969: HL Deb 10 July 1969, vol 303, col 1206ff.

3.3.2 The five facts: Behaviour

When the Divorce Law Reform Act 1969 (the predecessor of the Matrimonial Causes Act 1973) was debated in Parliament, the clear expectation among MPs was that people would wait to use the two years' separation fact and avoid the fault-based facts. Yet behaviour has always been the most common fact relied on, used in about half of all petitions for reasons discussed at 3.4.1.3. To bring a successful application, the petitioner must prove, on the balance of probabilities:

a) behaviour by the respondent

b) that means it would be unreasonable for the petitioner to have to continue to live with the respondent, and

c) that the marriage has irretrievably broken down.

The behaviour complained of could be deliberate or it could be unintentional. While this is often thought of as a fault-based fact of divorce, it could be behaviour that is entirely out of the control of the respondent and for which he or she cannot be blamed at all, such as behaviour caused by a mental or physical illness, as in Key Case *Thurlow v Thurlow*. However, behaviour of some sort is necessary, whether that is doing something or not doing something, positive or negative.[92] The Law Commission considered this a 'significantly different and more flexible concept' than if the behaviour had to be in itself unreasonable.[93]

> **KEY CASE** *Thurlow v Thurlow* [1975] 2 All ER 979
>
> The wife suffered from epilepsy and a neurological disorder. As her health deteriorated, she became unable to stand or walk, feed herself, or dress herself, and became incontinent. She burned soft furnishings by throwing them on the heater and would wander in the streets. Ultimately, she had to be hospitalised for the rest of her life. The husband visited her for several hours each day after work. In granting the husband a divorce, Rees J held that:
>
> > If the behaviour stems from misfortune such as the onset of mental illness or from disease of the body, or from accidental physical injury, the court will take full account of all the obligations of the married state. These will include the normal duty to accept and to share the burdens imposed on the family as a result of the mental or physical ill-health of one member. It will also consider the capacity of the petitioner to withstand the stresses imposed by the behaviour, the steps taken to cope with it, the length of time during which the petitioner has been called on to bear it and the actual or potential effect on his or her health. The court will then be required to make a judgment as to whether the petitioner can fairly be required to live with the respondent. The granting of the decree to the petitioner does not necessarily involve any blameworthiness on the part of the respondent . . . .[94]
>
> It is therefore technically wrong to call this fact 'unreasonable' behaviour: it's not the behaviour that has to be unreasonable. What is unreasonable is to require the respondent to continue to have to live with the petitioner. In Mr Thurlow's case he had no prospect of ever being able to have a domestic life with his wife, and that was nobody's fault.

---

[92] *Thurlow v Thurlow* [1975] 2 All ER 979.
[93] Law Commission, *Family Law: The Ground for Divorce* (Law Com No 191, 1990) para 2.10.
[94] [1975] 2 All ER 979, 987.

The court also has to determine whether or not the behaviour is of a type or level that makes it unreasonable to expect the petitioner to live with the respondent. The fact that the petitioner may him or herself find the situation unbearable is not determinative.[95] In *Lang v Lang*, the Privy Council noted that 'A husband's irritating habits may so get on the wife's nerves that she leaves him as a direct consequences of them, but she would not be justified in doing so. Such irritating idiosyncrasies are parts of the lottery in which every spouse engages on marrying, and taking the partners of the marriage "for better, for worse".'[96] The test to be applied, per Dunn J in *Livingstone-Stallard v Livingstone-Stallard*, is 'would any right-thinking person come to the conclusion that this husband has behaved in such a way that this wife cannot reasonably be expected to live with him, taking into account the whole of the circumstances and the characters and personalities of the parties?'[97] When considering what a right-thinking person may conclude, we look not at 'the man or woman on the Routemaster clutching their paper bus ticket on the day in October 1969 when the 1969 Act received the Royal Assent, but the man or woman on the Boris Bus with their Oyster Card in [the present day]'.[98]

There is therefore an objective element ('would any right-thinking person') and a subjective element that enables the court to consider the cumulative effect on the petitioner ('this wife'; or, as in our scenario, 'this husband'). 'A judge does, and must, try to read the minds of the parties in order to evaluate their conduct. In matrimonial cases we are not concerned with the reasonable man as we are in cases of negligence. We are dealing with this man and this woman and the fewer a priori assumptions we make about them the better.'[99] Moreover, '[w]hat may be regarded as trivial disagreements in a happy marriage could be salt in the wound in an unhappy marriage.'[100] It is therefore important to state how the behaviour has affected the petitioner, as in the particulars of behaviour contained in the wife's petition in Key Case *Owens v Owens*.

Section 2(3) MCA 1973 requires the courts to ignore any cohabitation by the parties in the same household after the final incident of behaviour cited, as long as that period does not exceed six months. If the behaviour is continuing, then the six months will run from the date of the petition. It can hardly be unreasonable to live with the respondent if the petitioner has continued to do so for more than six months after the final act. As with the other facts, the requirement is separate households but not necessarily separate houses.

The leading cases on behaviour tend to be decades old and indicate a somewhat harsh approach to married life. In *Buchler*, for example, the court said that the behaviour 'must exceed in gravity such behaviour, vexatious and trying though it may be, as every spouse bargains to endure when accepting the other "for better, for worse". The ordinary wear and tear of conjugal life does not in itself suffice.'[101] In *Ash v Ash*, Bagnall J thought that 'a violent petitioner can reasonably be expected to live with a violent respondent; a petitioner who is addicted to drink can reasonably be expected to live with a respondent who

---

[95] *Pheasant v Pheasant* [1972] Fam 202.

[96] *Lang v Lang* [1955] AC 402, 418 (Privy Council). Privy Council cases are influential because the Privy Council comprises the same judges as our Supreme Court, but are not binding on our domestic courts.

[97] [1974] 2 All ER 766, 771.

[98] *Owens v Owens* [2017] EWCA Civ 182, [41] (Munby P).

[99] *Gollins v Gollins* [1964] AC 644, 660 (Lord Reid).

[100] Munby P in *Owens v Owens* [2017] EWCA Civ 182 at [32], referring to Hallett LJ's comments during argument.

[101] [1947] P. 25, 46. This is a pre-Matrimonial Causes Act case.

is similarly addicted . . . if each is equally bad, at any rate in similar respects, each can reasonably be expected to live with the other.'[102]

Over time, this approach has become more lenient. In particular, judges saw the Matrimonial Causes Act 1973 as a reforming statute that allowed them to sweep aside even older and harsher case law. In *Livingstone-Stallard*, mentioned above, the judge found that the 'young wife was subjected to a constant atmosphere of criticism, disapproval and boorish behaviour on the part of her husband', who had 'formed the opinion that she was worthy of criticism, because she was a person who potentially did things well and by his criticism would be able to do things even better'. This was sufficient for a divorce on the facts.

More recently, it has been considered best practice to include only the minimum level of particulars necessary to get a divorce, both so the legal process does not add to the acrimony and distress that often accompanies a divorce and so that the respondent has less incentive to defend the divorce. 'The challenge for the divorce lawyer is therefore to draft an anodyne petition, carefully navigating the narrow waters between Scylla and Charybdis to minimise the risks that if the petition is too anodyne it may be rejected by the court whereas if it is not anodyne enough the respondent may refuse to cooperate. Since the former risk is probably very low in practice (and if it materialises) the remedy is simply an amendment sufficiently "beefing up" the petition as to satisfy the court. . . many petitions are anodyne in the extreme.'[103] Typically, therefore, a behaviour petition will include maybe four or five examples of such mild or 'anodyne'[104] behaviour. The particulars given by the wife in Key Case *Owens v Owens* are a good example of this and similar in style and content to many behaviour petitions filed each day. The state of the marriage is reduced to five short paragraphs; there is potentially much to be read between the lines although it is not the court's role to look behind what is expressly stated. Of course, one serious allegation is sufficient—you would not need four or five things if you were alleging (for example) violence unless there was a possibility that one would need to be withdrawn.

This is all very well if the petition is not defended, or where the particulars have been the subject of judicial determination previously, as for example a petition on the basis of a criminal conviction for downloading child pornography or domestic violence. But where the allegations are mild because the reality is mild, there will be difficulty if the petition is defended. The reason that we know about the *Owens* particulars is because their divorce *was* defended, and the courts applied the early case law set out in this section, in all its severity.

KEY CASE *Owens v Owens* [2018] UKSC 41

Mr and Mrs Owens married in 1978 and separated in 2015. She petitioned for divorce on the fact of her husband's behaviour. Her petition gave the following particulars:

1. The Respondent prioritised his work over home life and was often inflexible in making time available for the family, often missing family holidays and family events. This has caused the Petitioner much unhappiness and made her feel unloved.

---

[102] [1972] Fam 135, 140.
[103] *Owens v Owens* [2017] EWCA Civ 182 [93] (Munby P).
[104] *Hadjimilitis v Tsavliris* [2003] 1 FLR 81 [15] (Alison Ball QC).

2. During the latter years of the marriage the Respondent has not provided the Petitioner with love, attention, or affection and was not supporting of her role as a homemaker and mother which has made the Petitioner feel unappreciated.

3. The Respondent suffers from mood swings which caused frequent arguments between the parties which were very distressing and hurtful for the Petitioner who has concluded that she can no longer continue to live with the Respondent.

4. The Respondent has been unpleasant and disparaging about the Petitioner both to her and to their family and friends. He speaks to her and about her in an unfortunate and critical and undermining manner. The Petitioner has felt upset and/or embarrassed by the Respondent's behaviour towards her as well as in front of family and friends.

5. As a result of the Respondent's behaviour towards her, the Petitioner and the Respondent have until recently lived separate lives under the same roof for many years and have not shared a bedroom for several years. On 10 February 2015, the Petitioner moved into rented accommodation and the parties have been living separate and apart since that date.[105]

The language used this petition is very typical of behaviour petitions. It sets out the behaviour and the effect that it had on the petitioner, so as to prove both the existence of the fact and that it rendered it unreasonable for Mrs Owens to have to live with her husband.

Mr Owens defended the petition, denying both that the relationship had irretrievably broken down and that he had behaved in such a way that Mrs Owens should not reasonably be expected to live with him. Mrs Owens then amended the particulars stated above to include 27 allegations in the same vein. As with all defended cases that are not dropped, the application went to a full trial at which the parties gave evidence.

The judge at first instance, HHJ Tolson QC, held that Mrs Owen's petition was 'flimsy'[106] and 'exaggerated' and that it was *not* unreasonable for her to continue to live with the husband. This meant that she was not entitled to a divorce. While the marriage had broken down in reality, it was not deemed to have broken down legally.

'With no enthusiasm whatsoever',[107] the Court of Appeal upheld the decision, noting that 'Parliament has decreed that it is not a ground for divorce that you find yourself in a wretchedly unhappy marriage, though some people may say it should be. Such is the law which it is our duty to apply.'[108]

Mrs Owens appealed to the Supreme Court. She argued that:

- The judge had not made findings about 23 of the 27 allegations and had treated the rest as minor or isolated, so that he did not consider the cumulative effect of Mr Owens' behaviour on her.

- He had interpreted s1(2)(b) wrongly by saying that the behaviour had to be the cause of the marital breakdown when no causal link is required. the Supreme Court simply noted that this had not been argued in the Court of Appeal and Mrs Owens' lawyers must have been of the view that the judge's misstatements 'represented too weak a foundation for a conclusion that he had fallen into elementary error'. It therefore dismissed this point.

- He had implied that the conduct itself needed to be unreasonable, which again is not required. The Supreme Court 'deferred to the "unrivalled authority" of the Court of Appeal, which had rejected an appeal on that point' notwithstanding its correctness in law.[109]

The case therefore turned on the first of the three points above—the behaviour issue.

---

[105] Recorded in the CA judgment at [2017] EWCA Civ 182 [4].
[106] Recorded in the CA judgment at [2017] EWCA Civ 182 [46].
[107] *Owens v Owens* [2017] EWCA Civ 182 [99] (Hallett LJ).
[108] *Owens v Owens* [2017] EWCA Civ 182 [84]–[85] (Munby P).
[109] P Morgan, 'The Public Tragedy of the Owens' Divorce' (2019) 41(1) *Journal of Social Welfare and Family Law* 100.

The Court rejected arguments by Mrs Owens and by the family lawyers' organisation, Resolution, which had intervened in the case, that the focus should be on the petitioner's subjective response to the behaviour, so that if she genuinely feels she cannot live with the respondent that should determine the case. But this would mean that no other fact would be needed—all a petitioner would need to do was say they did not want to live with the respondent. The Supreme Court said that *Pheasant v Pheasant*[110] which had already rejected this argument back in 1972 was a correct statement of the law.

The Court held that whether it was unreasonable for the petitioner to live with the respondent 'obviously requires to be informed by changing social norms'.[111] The statement in *Ash v Ash* that 'a violent petitioner can reasonably be expected to live with a violent respondent' was 'almost comical'.[112] However, even applying current social norms it could not be said that HHJ Tolson was wrong to find that Mrs Owens could be expected to live with Mr Owens (it was irrelevant that she had moved out).

This meant that Mrs Owens' appeal was dismissed, although just as had happened in the Court of Appeal, several judges said that they had 'an uneasy feeling' or that the case was 'troubling' because the way the trial was run (no witnesses other than the parties, and a particular focus on only a few of the allegations due to shortness of time). Lady Hale, in particular, noted that the trial 'was not set up or conducted in a way which would enable the full flavour of [the husband's] conduct to be properly evaluated' despite the potential cumulative effect that his may have had on Mrs Owens over the course of a great many years.[113]

Lord Wilson, with whom Lord Hodge and Lady Black agreed, noted that 'Parliament may wish to consider whether to replace a law which denies to Mrs Owens any present entitlement to a divorce in the above circumstances'.[114] By the standards of judicial language, that was a serious criticism of the law.

Owens therefore reiterates that although the key case law on behaviour is decades old, it still applies, albeit that when not defended a mild petition will almost always be successful. Given the ways in which divorce petitions had been drafted mildly and 'nodded through' courts without much of a problem, the denial of divorce in this case came as a tremendous shock to the public. In particular, there was considerable sympathy for Mrs Owens. Such was the reaction, that it was instrumental in triggering reform of the law of divorce, something we discuss at 3.4.5 of this chapter.

3.3.3 The five facts: Desertion

Desertion involves the respondent leaving the petitioner, without justification, for at least two years immediately preceding the presentation of the petition. There are two aspects to the separation. First, the respondent must have actually separated from the petitioner and, second, he or she must have intended to bring cohabitation to an end. One without the other is insufficient.[115] However, despite a tendency to think of desertion as abandonment or going AWOL and joining the Foreign Legion, this is not necessary. As with the other facts here, separation can include being in the same home provided that the parties can show that they are two households in one home. Moreover, the spouse who leaves is

---

[110] [1972] Fam 202.
[111] Paras [32] (Lord Wilson, with whom Lord Hodges and Lady Black agreed) and [47] (Lady Hale).
[112] Para [33] (Lord Wilson).
[113] Para [50].
[114] Paragraph [45].
[115] *Buchler v Buchler* [1947] P 25.

not necessarily the person who doing the deserting—it may be the person who has compelled them to leave who is the deserter, forcing that on the other party through their behaviour.[116] He or she is deemed to have intended to cause the marriage to end even if they did not anticipate or want that consequence.[117] This is called constructive desertion.

It is very easy to get muddled about what this fact requites. It is not desertion if:

- the petitioner agreed to the separation
- the parties reconcile for one or more periods exceeding six months in all, as this causes desertion to comes to an end. (They can reconcile for periods totalling up to six months, which would not count towards the two years.[118])
- the desertion is justified. In *Quoraishi v Quoraishi*, the husband petitioned for divorce on the wife's desertion as she had left him. The court held that she was justified in doing so because the husband had taken a second wife in Islamic law when he knew that she would not accept that.[119]

Desertion is rarely used these days, accounting for only 351 decrees in 2018, compared to 41,843 for behaviour.[120] Most family lawyers prefer to use the same facts as evidence for a behaviour petition, as this does not require a two-year wait, but there has been an increase in desertion petitions lodged by self-represented litigants.[121] Alternatively, if two years has elapsed, then a lawyer may negotiate the respondent's consent to a decree based on two years' separation rather than (the more blameworthy) desertion for two years. Either way, desertion petitions are usually unnecessary. For this reason, when it designed civil partnerships the government considered not including desertion albeit that in the end it did so, concluding that it 'will assist in some circumstances and will also help some partners who have to apply for maintenance [during the course of the marriage]'.[122]

3.3.4 The five facts: Two years' separation and the respondent's consent

Whereas the three facts we have looked at so far are all based on the old idea of matrimonial offences, for this fact irretrievable breakdown is demonstrated by the fact of separation for at least two years coupled with the respondent's consent to the divorce proceedings. The separation must be continuous and immediately preceding the petition although under s2(5) the parties can reconcile for up to six months without affecting this. Moreover, as with other facts, separation can occur while the parties are living in the same house.

---

[116] *Hopes v Hopes* [1949] P 227.
[117] *Lang v Lang* [1955] AC 402 (Privy Council).
[118] Section 2(5) Matrimonial Causes Act 1973.
[119] (1983) 4 FLR 706 (Butler-Sloss J); upheld on appeal: [1985] FLR 780 (CA).
[120] Office of National Statistics, *Divorce Dataset 2018* (ONS 2019). There were two desertion decrees for same-sex married couples. There are no available statistics on the facts on which civil partnership dissolutions are based.
[121] F Gibb, 'Confusing Legal Lingo puts DIY Divorces on the Rocks' (*The Times* 9 October 2017) 17. This is not an entirely accurate headline, as the figures stated are increases in *successful* desertion petitions, not those that are rejected. The number of desertion petitions rejected is unknown.
[122] Women and Equality Unit, *Responses to Civil Partnership: A Framework for Legal Recognition of Same-Sex Couples* (Department of Trade and Industry 2003) 36.

As part of the divorce process, the respondent will complete a box indicating his or her consent to the divorce in the acknowledgment of service form. Ignoring the proceedings or not opposing them is insufficient: there needs to be active consent. This consent can, however, be withdrawn up to the point at which decree nisi is pronounced and any attempt between the parties to have a binding contract not to withdraw consent appears to be unenforceable.[123] After decree nisi, the respondent can only withdraw consent with the permission of the court on the basis that he or she has been misled about any matter that he or she took into account when deciding to give consent.[124]

3.3.5 The five facts: Five years' separation

This is the fact to use where no other fact applies and where the respondent will not consent to a divorce based on two years' separation. It is unilateral divorce: it enables the petitioner to divorce the respondent based on the length of their separation irrespective of whether the respondent wants the divorce. However, unlike the other grounds, there is a defence of undue hardship, which we explore at 3.3.6.2.

3.3.6 Additional considerations for separation petitions

There are two additional considerations for two- and five-year separation petitions. The first is that the respondent is able to apply to court to have their financial position after divorce considered, and the grant of decree absolute can thus be conditional upon certain financial acts by the respondent. The second is that for five years' separation petitions only, there is also an absolute defence to divorce: that it would cause 'grave hardship'. This may not merely hold up the decree but can prevent it altogether.

Consideration of financial position after divorce

The respondent to a two or five years' separation petition can apply to court to have their financial position after divorce considered.[125] Such an application must be made before decree absolute and cannot be made where there is any fact pleaded other than two or five years' separation. In order to make the decree absolute, the court must be satisfied either that the petitioner does not have to make financial provision for the respondent or that such financial provision 'is reasonable and fair or the best that can be made in the circumstances'.[126]

Given that in most cases financial remedy proceedings or negotiations will be running in parallel to the divorce proceedings, this clause is primarily leverage to bring a keen-to-be-divorced but financially shy person to the negotiating table. Note that the court can issue decree absolute anyway, either on the basis that it is desirable or where the respondent has undertaken to make such financial provision for the respondent as the court may approve.

---

[123] *Sutton v Sutton* [1984] FLR 579. Cf to enforceability of conditional consent, e.g. not to pursue a costs order.
[124] Matrimonial Causes Act 1973 s10(1).
[125] Matrimonial Causes Act 1973 s10(2)–(4).
[126] Matrimonial Causes Act 1973 s10(3).

This provision is most useful when the petitioner has a valuable pension and the spouse's benefits under that pension would be lost on decree absolute. While courts now have powers to make pension sharing orders, those benefits—which can be immensely valuable—would be lost if the petitioner died in the period between decree absolute and the making of a pension sharing order. While it may seem unlikely that a party would die in this relatively small window, it does happen and the financial consequences can be catastrophic. For that reason, the parties usually agree to pause the divorce at decree nisi until a financial remedy order is made. If the petitioner will not agree, then this provision is the respondent's remedy, albeit only where the petition is based on separation.

Defence on the basis of grave hardship

As you can see in Table 3.1, both men and women use five-year petitions in roughly the same numbers. Nevertheless, this was not anticipated when the law was drafted and there was Parliamentary concern that permitting unilateral divorce would be a 'Casanova's charter' enabling a husband to ditch an older wife in favour of a younger one. For that reason, Parliament created a specific defence to five-year separation petitions: the court can refuse a decree if the dissolution of the marriage itself *will* cause—not *might* cause—grave financial or other hardship to the respondent *and* that it would in all the circumstances be wrong to dissolve the marriage.[127] The hardship must result from the legal ending of the marriage not separation.

Such a case may be where the wife is reliant on the husband's pension and would lose that on decree absolute, as in *Le Marchant v Le Marchant*, where the court threatened to dismiss the husband's divorce petition unless he put forward 'a proposal which is acceptable to the court as reasonable in all the circumstances, which is sufficient to remove the element of grave financial hardship'.[128] This defence is unlikely to cause the dismissal of a petition these days because of the court's wide powers to distribute the parties' financial assets on divorce, including pensions. However, it may be reason to adjourn a decree pending financial settlement.

3.3.7 Dissolving a same-sex marriage or civil partnership

As we have seen, dissolving a same-sex marriage is no different to dissolving an opposite-sex marriage, right down to the definition of adultery as being with someone of the opposite sex. For civil partnerships, the law on dissolution is also the same as for divorce, except that adultery is not a fact at all but would rather be classed as behaviour. When the Civil Partnership Act 2004 was introduced, however, the government took the opportunity to modernise the language. Thus the legislation refers to the applicant and respondent rather than petitioner and respondent, a decree nisi is a conditional order and a decree absolute a final order, and, just to take the romance out of it, an engagement to marry is a 'civil partnership agreement'.[129]

---

[127] Matrimonial Causes Act 1973 s5.
[128] [1977] 1 WLR 559, 563 (Ormrod LJ).
[129] Civil Partnership Act 2004 s73.

The fact that the law is virtually the same does not necessarily mean, however, that the experiences of same-sex couples is the same as those of divorcing opposite-sex couples. Rosemary Auchmuty interviewed a number of gay men and lesbians who were in the process of dissolving civil partnerships. There were, and remain, relatively few same-sex marriage and civil partnership dissolutions and therefore 'there was no common understanding about what dissolution might entail or how it would feel, such as there is about divorce'.[130] As the number of same-sex divorces and dissolutions increases, we will know better whether the divorce facts used between same-sex and different-sex couples are different, and whether the experience of different-sex couples dissolving civil partnerships will be different to the experience of dissolving a marriage.

3.3.8 Judicial separations

Some couples wish to separate physically and financially but not divorce. Rather than simply effect an informal separation, they could seek a decree of judicial separation (known as separation orders in the case of civil partners). This is the modern equivalent of the separation a *mensa et thoro*, in that it does not end the marriage and the parties cannot therefore remarry.

While in centuries past, a judicial or Church separation brought an end to the enforceable obligation to cohabit with one's spouse, that obligation that no longer exists. These days, judicial separation is most useful for those couples who are opposed to divorce for religious reasons or where a divorce would cause an important benefit to be lost, such as the pension benefits available to a widow or widower on their spouse's death.

The advantages over informal separation are:

- you do not need to wait one year from the date of the marriage before you file, which is a requirement of divorce;
- the status of being judicially separated is recognised;
- separation removes the spouse from the line of inheritance if one of the parties has died without making a valid Will (see Chapter 5);
- the court can make a financial remedy order (see Chapter 4) providing the parties with a financial settlement. (It cannot make a pension sharing order, although the widow(er) of a pension holder receives benefits by virtue of being a spouse anyway)

Note that being judicially separated does not prevent you from deciding later to get divorced.

To obtain a judicial separation, the petitioner is required to prove one of the usual five facts[131] but, unlike divorce, there is no need to prove irretrievable breakdown. The process is much the same as for a divorce and uses the same petition form, except that you can file within the first year of the marriage and there is no decree absolute at the end of it, only a decree of separation. The Divorce, Dissolution, and Separation Act 2020 reforms

---

[130] R Auchmuty, 'The Experience of Civil Partnership Dissolution: Not "Just Like a Divorce"' (2016) 38(2) *Journal of Social Welfare and Family Law* 152, 171.

[131] Four in the case of civil partners, as adultery is excluded as in divorce.

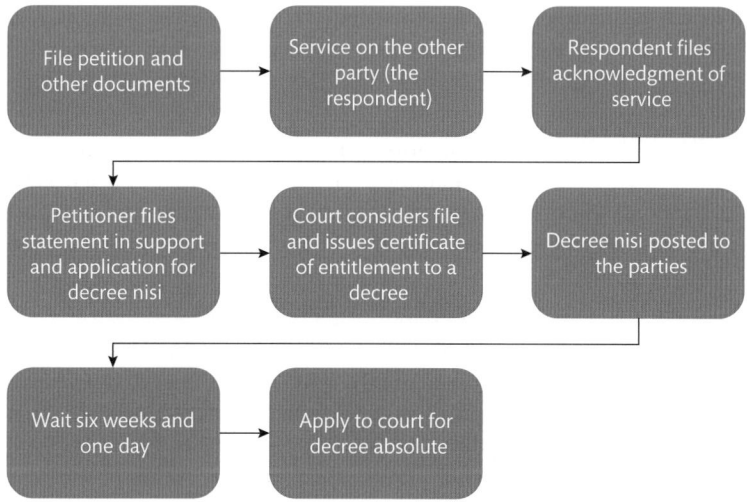

FIGURE 3.1 The procedure for an undefended divorce

the requirements for judicial separations to replace proof of the five facts with a simple statement by the applicant that they wish for a judicial separation. This is discussed in more detail at 3.5.2.

Judicial separation is little used. In 2019, there were 260 applications, and 148 decrees.[132]

3.3.9 The procedure for an undefended divorce or dissolution

There is no such thing as a 'quickie divorce' as all undefended divorces or dissolutions have to follow the same procedure. That said, the process is relatively straightforward and, unless there is a problem, the parties should not have to attend court at all. Matters are addressed through the post under what is called the 'undefended' or 'special' procedure.[133] This process is shown in Figure 3.1.

Filing the petition

The petition is a form that asks for details of the parties and their marriage ceremony; what is being sought (a divorce, a dissolution of a civil partnership, or a judicial separation); and the reason for that, i.e., that the marriage has irretrievably broken down; and which fact is relied upon. The petitioner will need to provide a brief supporting explanation of why the marriages has broken down, known as 'the particulars'. He or she files the divorce petition, statement of reconciliation, marriage certificate (if lost, the register office or church will be able to provide a duplicate), and court fee, either by posting these to their regional divorce processing centre or by using an online portal.

Where the petitioner is represented by a lawyer, the lawyer must also complete a Statement of Reconciliation, which is a very short form in which the lawyer confirms whether or not he or she has discussed the possibility of reconciliation with the petitioner

---

[132] Ministry of Justice, *Family Court Tables: England and Wales: October to December 2019* (table 12).
[133] Family Procedure Rules 7.19 and 7.20.

and provided information about 'persons qualified to help effect a reconciliation', such as Relate.[134] There does not seem to be any consequences to saying 'no' to both.[135] Petitioners without legal representation do not have to file the statement.

Acknowledgment of service

The court issues the petition and posts it to the respondent (and, in the case of adultery, any co-respondent). He or she then has seven days to complete and file (post back to the court) the acknowledgment of service form.[136] This short document requires the respondent to confirm are indeed the named respondent; the date and location at which they received the petition; and that they concede the court has jurisdiction. The respondent will also need to state whether or not they consent to the divorce (and, in the case of adultery, whether they admit the adultery); and whether they have any objection to the court ordering them to pay the costs of the proceedings if the petitioner has asked for that.

If the petitioner is concerned that the respondent is going to ignore the petition, then he or she can either ask the court bailiff to serve the papers in person or hire a process server to do that. The process server will file an affidavit at court confirming that they served the petition, so if the respondent does *not* acknowledge service the petitioner can proceed with the case. If the respondent cannot be found it is possible to apply to proceed without that.

Statement in support

The petitioner then completes and files a statement in support of divorce.[137] This says that they stand by the petition and still want a divorce. If the parties are still living in the same house, the statement will set out why they are nevertheless in separate households or six

FOCUS Know-How

Can you ignore proceedings?

While the respondent is free to ignore proceedings, this is never a sensible tactic. It might slow down the divorce slightly as the petitioner either has to instruct a bailiff or process server to effect service, although if the petitioner is asking the court to order the respondent to pay the petitioner's costs all the respondent is doing is adding to a bill they will have to pay. If the respondent cannot be found at all, the petitioner can make an application asking the court to dispense with the need to serve the petition on the respondent. In such a case the divorce will proceed with no input from the respondent, because he or she has not actively defended the case. Ignoring the proceedings does not prevent a divorce going through unless the divorce is on the basis of two years' separation where the respondent's consent is a requirement. If a party wants to be troublesome, it is better to actively defend the proceedings than ignore them.

---

[134] Family Procedure Rules, Practice Direction 5A.

[135] A judge could as a result ask for more information on which to determine that the marriage has irretrievably broken down. However, some practitioners say 'no' to both routinely, with no effect. Failure to file a statement at all would be a breach of the Family Procedure Rules.

[136] Family Procedure Rule 7.12.

[137] Family Procedure Rule 7.19.

months have not elapsed. The court will use this information to determine whether the parties are separated. This form is then sent to court along with an application for decree nisi.

Certificate of entitlement

This is the stage that in the past would have involved a trial. These days, for an undefended divorce, the judge or court officer simply reads the papers. If satisfied that the marriage has irretrievably broken down and the fact pleaded applies, the court will then issue a certificate of entitlement to a decree and list the date on which decree nisi is to be pronounced. If costs are claimed, the judge/officer will also certify that the petitioner is entitled to his or her costs.[138] If not satisfied with the paperwork, they may ask for more information (for example about the living arrangements) or list a case management hearing.

Decree nisi

On the scheduled date, decree nisi is pronounced and the decree posted to the parties. This is a conditional divorce decree (and is known as a 'conditional order' in the case of civil partners). Six weeks and one day after decree nisi, the petitioner can apply for the court to make the decree absolute (final). This six week window exists to allow a government solicitor known as the Queen's Proctor time to intervene in the proceedings and give a good reason why the decree should not be made absolute.[139] This is rare, and happens if the petition is fraudulent, as was the case for 180 petitions discussed in *Rapisarda v Colladon (Irregular Divorces)*.[140] Procedural error or outright fraud can void a decree, including the decree absolute, with the effect that any subsequent remarriage is invalid for bigamy.

Decrees nisi are pronounced in open court. This is usually achieved by the court usher announcing 'Smith v Smith, Jones v Jones, decrees nisi' to a waiting room of baffled people there for an entirely different kind of case. There is no hearing unless the petitioner has asked for costs against the respondent and the respondent has indicated his opposition to that in his acknowledgment of service, in which case the judge will need to hear from each of them and make a decision.

Many people pause the divorce at decree nisi and do not proceed to decree absolute until they have reached agreement on the terms of a financial remedy order. Remaining married while this is resolved can be very sensible, especially if there are valuable pensions, as a spouse is in a much stronger position than an ex-spouse if one of the parties dies before a financial order is made. This means that, rather than the time between nisi and absolute being the statutory minimum of six weeks and one day, the average is actually 25 weeks. Thus, most divorces take about a year altogether.

Decree absolute

Six weeks and one day from decree nisi, the petitioner can apply for decree absolute (no hearing needed). The court will issue the decree absolute a few days later and post it to them. This means that when the parties receive the decree, they will find out that they have, unbeknownst to them, been divorced for a few days already. The effect of the decree absolute is to end the marriage. The parties are no longer next of kin and each is free to

---

[138] Family Procedure Rule 7.20(2)(a).

[139] Matrimonial Causes Act 1973 s8; Civil Partnership Act 2004 s39. The Queen's Proctor is also the Treasury Solicitor, head of the government legal department.

[140] [2014] EWFC 35.

remarry. Any financial remedy orders that have been made will come into effect. Any home rights of occupation (see Chapter 7) will be terminated unless there is an order under the Family Law Act that specifically extends these. Any legacy to their former spouse in a Will becomes void, as does any appointment of the former spouse as trustee or executor—unless the Will explicitly states that it is to survive divorce. The parties should both be advised to make new Wills.

If the petitioner does not apply for decree absolute, it is open to the respondent to apply to court him or herself. However, there would be a hearing in this situation, at which a judge would decide whether or not to grant the decree.

Costs of divorce

It is possible for a petitioner to ask in the petition that the respondent pay some or all of the expenses he or she will incur in pursuing the divorce, such as lawyers' fees and court fees. The respondent might agree to pay it all, or to pay a certain amount, or object altogether to paying costs. It is common to negotiate on this issue. If the respondent will allow a divorce to proceed undefended only if costs are not being sought by the petitioner, such agreement is binding on the parties.[141] The Resolution *Guide to Good Practice* recommends that 'If the claim would not be pursued if the petition proceeds on an undefended basis, make that clear in the petition or at least explain to the spouse in advance so as to avoid it being construed as a hostile act. . . .Try to achieve consensus before issuing any application.'[142]

Costs orders will not usually be made for five-year separation petitions unless the parties agree to split the costs; they are also rare for two-year separation petitions.[143] In the case of an adultery petition, a costs order is almost inevitable and not generally worth arguing about unless the costs are excessive.[144] If a co-respondent has been cited in the adultery petition, he or she can be ordered to pay costs too.

SCENARIO 1

Illustration 5

Robert Newton's lawyer has followed best practice in writing to Clare and enclosing a draft divorce petition, rather than sending the petition straight to court.[145] This has given Clare the opportunity to take the petition to a solicitor for advice, the result of which is that Clare has agreed to cooperate with the petition and the process can then proceed smoothly and constructively. After all, she wants a divorce too, so even if she disagrees with the petition, provided it makes no serious allegations against her, it is not in her interests to try to defend proceedings or hold them up. Michael Horton takes the view that when the parties agree that the particulars are toned down as a condition of not defending the petition such agreements are binding on the parties.[146]

---

[141] M Horton, *Compromise in Family Law: Law and Practice* (Lexis Nexis 2017) para 3.39.

[142] Resolution, *Guide to Good Practice: Working With Litigants In Person* (Resolution 2016) 5.

[143] Allum, Hodson, and Clark agree: M Allum and D Hodson with S Clark, 'Imminent Changes to Divorce/Dissolution Petitions and to the Family Procedure Rules' in *Lexis Nexis Jordans Family Law*, 19 July 2017.

[144] Note that this does not include costs relating to financial settlement, which are usually much greater.

[145] Law Society, *Family Law Protocol* (Law Society 2010) para 1.11.1 and Resolution *Guide to Good Practice: Drafting Documents* (Resolution 2017) 5.

[146] M Horton, *Compromise in Family Law: Law and Practice* (Lexis Nexis 2017) para 3.34.

In our scenario, Clare's agreement to the divorce is also conditional on Robert not claiming costs from her. That is fair enough considering that she also has grounds to divorce him. Robert is likely to agree to this: he wants a divorce and, in any case, divorce costs are likely to be subsumed within the overall division of assets on divorce.

While advance notice is suitable for most cases, there are some where it is best to file without prior notice. For example, if there is a dispute about the appropriate jurisdiction then it will be important to file a petition in your chosen jurisdiction before the other party files in their favoured jurisdiction. Jurisdiction races are discussed further at 3.6.1 in the focus box *Know-How: Forum shopping*.

Cross-petitions, where each files their own petition against the other, are possible (as in *McCartney v Mills McCartney*[147]) but they are usually a demonstration of obstinacy over simplicity. If, as we see at 3.4.1, the fact stated is seen as a means to an end rather than an accurate explanation of the reasons the marriage has broken down, then there is no reason to cross-petition.

3.3.10 Religious considerations

While a divorce may be perfectly valid in law, different religions and denominations may have different tenets about divorce. Those who are of religious faith may therefore need to take further steps in order to be divorced in the eyes of their religion.

Where both parties were married according to Jewish rites, they may, in addition to their civil divorce, need to obtain a 'Get' to effect a religious divorce. Only the most liberal synagogues do not require this. Judaism allows mutual consent divorce, so there is no need to show unreasonable behaviour, separation, or adultery as will be necessary in their legal divorce. However, the granting of a Get is in the gift of the husband: he has to provide it to the wife, and she has to accept it.

Wives who refuse to receive a Get account for only 2 per cent of cases where there is a dispute. In the vast majority of cases, it is the husband who is refusing to provide the wife with a Get, and the consequences for her are much more serious than the consequences upon a husband. She becomes a so-called 'chained wife', unable to remarry in her religion and unable to enter into a relationship with another man without being considered adulterous. The consequence of this is that any children of that new relationship will be considered 'mamzer' in Jewish law, a status that has serious and permanent religious consequences for them and their descendants.[148]

Recognising the serious consequences of refusal of a Get on women, some Beth Din (Jewish rabbinical courts) seek to put social and financial pressure on a husband who is refusing a Get by encouraging the local community to 'consider whether it is appropriate for them to have social or business contacts with him until the Get is given'.[149] Some (secular) courts have also been willing to refuse decree absolute until the husband provides the wife with a Get, using both the inherent jurisdiction and the broadly drafted power in s9

---

[147] [2008] EWHC 401 (Fam).

[148] In contrast, further children of the husband would not be mamzer and there is a procedure, *heter meah rabbanim*, for a husband to be considered divorced without the wife's consent.

[149] S Rocker, '"Shun" Husband Refusing to Grant His Wife a Get, Beth Din Tells Shuls' *The Jewish Chronicle* (London, 6 November 2015).

STATUTORY EXTRACT *s10A Matrimonial Causes Act 1973*

Proceedings after decree nisi: religious marriage

(1) This section applies if a decree of divorce has been granted but not made absolute and the parties to the marriage concerned
  (a) were married in accordance with—
    (i) the usages of the Jews, or
    (ii) any other prescribed religious usages; and
  (b) must cooperate if the marriage is to be dissolved in accordance with those usages.
(2) On the application of either party, the court may order that a decree of divorce is not to be made absolute until a declaration made by both parties that they have taken such steps as are required to dissolve the marriage in accordance with those usages is produced to the court.
(3) An order under subsection (2)—
  (a) may be made only if the court is satisfied that in all the circumstances of the case it is just and reasonable to do so; and
  (b) may be revoked at any time.

Matrimonial Causes Act 1973 to 'deal with the case as it thinks fit'.[150] To avoid any doubt, this power was explicitly put on a statutory footing by the Divorce (Religious Marriages) Act 2002, which inserts a S10A into the 1973 Act.[151]

This enables courts to order that a decree of divorce is not to be made absolute until the parties declare that they have taken such steps as are required to dissolve the marriage in accordance with the requirements of either the Usages of the Jews or another 'prescribed religion'. This will help in those cases where the husband wants a civil divorce either immediately or, later, to remarry, but will not assist in those cases where he does not want the marriage to end, or where the decree absolute has already been granted.

Currently, the only 'prescribed religion' is Judaism, but other religions can opt into such regulation. None have yet done so, although Proudman notes that some judges and lawyers have mistakenly assumed that the Act applies to Islamic divorce.[152] In Islam, as in Judaism, a wife cannot remarry in the religion unless her divorce is also religiously recognised. The absence of Islam from the 2002 Act meant that Baron J had to find another way of exerting leverage over a Muslim husband in *A v T (Ancillary Relief: Cultural Factors)*.[153] The parties were Iranian and the wife was reliant on the husband agreeing to a divorce in order for it to be recognised in Iran, as she did not have sufficient grounds under Iranian law to divorce him. Baron J ordered that the husband pay an additional lump sum to the wife, representing the whole of her 'marriage portion' (dowry), if he did not provide her with a Talaq recognised in Iranian law.

Indeed, courts have long used their financial remedy powers to exert financial leverage even though this is outside the Act, which concerns only the granting of a divorce decree.

---

[150] *O v O (Jurisdiction: Jewish Divorce)* [2000] 2 FLR 147.
[151] This inserted s10A into the Matrimonial Causes Act 1973.
[152] C Proudman, 'Religious Marriages: Staying a Decree Absolute in Order to Increase the Chances of Obtaining a Religious Divorce' (*Family Law Week*, 17 January 2013).
[153] [2004] EWHC 471 (Fam).

In *Moher v Moher*, the Court of Appeal ordered the husband to pay periodical payments to the wife until he had sought a Get, holding that the courts' powers of leverage were not restricted to the contents of s10A.[154] After all, the inability of a woman to remarry without the Get deprives her of the financial security that remarriage could bring. At the time of writing, the government has given Parliament assurances that it will issue guidance on whether refusal of a Get constitutes domestic abuse within the meaning of the new Domestic Abuse Act 2021 (see Chapter 7).

3.3.11 Defending a divorce

In the event that the divorce is defended, the undefended 'special' procedure does not apply. The respondent can defend divorce proceedings by indicating this in the acknowledgment of service and then filing an Answer which denies that the marriage has irretrievably broken down and/or the fact pleaded. The petitioner is very likely to need to bolster her petition with further or more detailed allegations, and there will need to be a case management hearing, witness statements, and other evidence in support before a full contested trial.

Where the respondent is arguing that the marriage has not irretrievably broken down, it is not enough to simply say that. He or she will need to advance a positive case as to why it can be saved.[155] There are no reported examples of such a claim being made successfully.[156] A judge is not likely to think that a marriage can be saved by one person asserting that it can, while across the courtroom their spouse says it has broken down, and has filed a divorce petition on the strength of it.

A more successful tactic is to deny the fact alleged. Thus, if the petition is on the fact of behaviour, the respondent may deny the behaviour alleged and/or that it is unreasonable for the petitioner to have to reside with him. If it is on adultery, the respondent may deny the adultery or show evidence that it is not intolerable for the petitioner to live with him—perhaps the adultery was more than six months ago. If it is desertion, the respondent could argue that there was no separation, or there was, but it was with the petitioner's consent, which would be fatal to such a petition, or that the period is not yet two years. If it is two years' separation, the respondent simply withhold his consent. For five years' separation, the respondent has a statutory defence of hardship, discussed above, or can argue that five years have not elapsed.

Why are there so few defended divorces?

'The majority of divorces, ostensibly based on fault, are really divorces by consent since they are undefended.'[157] Even if the respondent threatens to defend the divorce or perhaps even starts down the road of a defence, they do not usually proceed to defend the petition.

Munby P noted in his decision in *Owens* that:

> In the year to January 2017, there were 113,996 petitions for divorce. The details are not published, but I understand that, over the same period, notice of intention to defend was given in some 2,600 acknowledgements of service (some 2.28% of all petitions) while actual

---

[154] [2019] EWCA Civ 1482, following a precedent set in 1969 in the case of *Brett v Brett* [1969] 1 WLR 487.

[155] *Kisala v Kisala* (1973) 117 Solicitors' Journal 664 (Bagnall J).

[156] S Cretney, *Family Law in the Twentieth Century: A History* (Oxford 2003) 222.

[157] A Bainham, 'Men and Women Behaving Badly: Is Fault Dead in English Family Law?' (2001) 21(2) *Oxford Journal of Legal Studies* 219, 222.

answers filed were about 760 (some 0.67% of all petitions). There are no available statistics, but one can safely assume that the number of petitions which proceed to a final contested hearing is minute, probably little more than a handful. So, the attritional effect of the process itself reduces from an initial 2.28% of respondents who are minded to oppose the petition to an utterly trivial, let us say something of the order of magnitude of 0.015%, of respondents who actually carry their opposition through to a contested hearing.[158]

About 37 per cent of respondents do not formally defend the proceedings by filing an Answer. Instead, they write on the acknowledgment that they do not agree with the particulars and/or the divorce but go no further. Such statements have no effect on the divorce. They are just ignored.[159]

There are several possible reasons for the lack of defended divorces:

1.   If one party believes, sufficiently to file divorce proceedings, that the marriage is over, that is a strong indication that the marriage is over. The chances are that this decision was not made lightly or quickly. It is therefore very unlikely that the respondent will be able to save the marriage at this very late stage if the petitioner does not want that. In every reported case the judge has found the marriage to be irretrievably broken at the end of a contested hearing (although there are cases where the fact is not found proven).

2.   In order for the court to determine whether the fact is proved and the marriage has irretrievably broken down, it will need to hold a full hearing into the state of the marriage, which is very intrusive. It is likely to include witness evidence from friends and others who have observed the marriage or specific incidents within it.

3.   Such hearings are generally open to the public[160] and media. In *Savva v Savva*, the parties found themselves held up for ridicule in the *Daily Mail*, under the headline 'Husband battling to save his marriage tells judge his wife should be denied divorce because she "must be mad to leave me"'.[161] Photographs of Mr and Mrs Owens appeared in all the newspapers, and public sympathy lay with Mrs Owens at the expense of Mr Owens' reputation. Perhaps you are unsympathetic to him, trying to cling onto his marriage against his wife's will. But should either of them suffer this public indignity?[162]

4.   This is also a good illustration of a further point: the hearing is very, very unlikely to help a fragile marriage. The respondent who claims that the marriage has not broken down but is capable of continuing must walk a very difficult, perhaps impossible, line between refuting the truth of what the petitioner is saying and yet not alienating the petitioner further. In *Hadjimilitis v Tsavliris*, the husband appears not to have taken this on board. The manner of his defence meant that any prospect of

---

[158] *Owens v Owens* [2017] EWCA Civ 182 [98] (Munby P).

[159] L Trinder, D Braybrook, C Bryson, L Coleman, C Houlston, and M Sefton, *Finding Fault? Divorce Law and Practice in England and Wales* (Nuffield Foundation 2017) 13.

[160] FPR 2010, 7.16 (1).

[161] *Daily Mail* (London, 9 May 2012).

[162] See also V Lloyd Platt, 'Should a Packed Lunch Be Grounds for a Divorce?' (*The Times* 28 March 2012) section T2 p4.

reconciliation was well and truly shot—he said that the wife 'was not supportive to him either emotionally or practically, was a bad mother, was neither a proper home-maker nor childcarer, was moody and irritable, temperamental and erratic, had an indifferent relationship with her stepchildren and was more interested in herself and her own pleasures than the family and was a drug taker and adulteress'[163]—while also claiming that the marriage had not broken down and could be mended through therapy.

5.   The petitioner, on the other hand, will, once faced with a defended petition, want to amend his or her petition to provide stronger and more detailed particulars. He or she will not only be seeking to prove the truth of the petition but also casting doubt on the respondent's motivations for defending the petition. The solicitor Alison Hayes suggests, for example, that defended divorces can be about a wish to control the petitioner, avoid or delay financial proceedings, cost the petitioner money, or to see them worn down and humiliated.[164] Thus the parties will become more and more entrenched and more hostile in their positions.

6.   The costs of the proceedings are high because of the legal work involved in drafting the pleadings and in conducting hearings. It is likely that the loser will be ordered to pay the 'winner's' legal costs. Legal aid is not available except to victims of domestic violence and a case in which a victim wished to defend a divorce will naturally be rare.

7.   Proceedings take sufficiently long that if the parties agree that the marriage has irretrievably broken down, a two years' separation petition may be possible.

8.   In some situations, a solicitor may very well recommend that the respondent should defend any allegations of illegal acts or any allegations that might affect arrangements for the children, or at least should not admit the truth of them without legal advice. Apart from this, however, the allegations within the petition are unlikely to have any wider implications. For example, only behaviour which is 'obvious and gross'—a very high standard—or which constitutes financial misconduct affect the distribution of the assets at the end of the marriage.

Thus, defending such allegations 'requires, time, money, and emotional energy far beyond the resources of most respondents'.[165]

And at the end of it all:

9.   It is unlikely that a defence would succeed.

For these reasons, you may think that a respondent who does not want a divorce, or who wants a divorce but does not like what is said in the petition, may understandably feel that the law has not given him a fair and accessible opportunity to defend himself. An alternative view, however, is that it should be impossible to force one's spouse to remain married against their will. In the next section, we discuss these and other perspectives the current law.

---

[163] [2003] 1 FLR 81, 93.
[164] A Hayes, 'Fighting for a Lost Cause' (2003) 3 (Nov) *Family Law Journal* (Legalease) 11.
[165] Law Commission, *Family Law: The Ground for Divorce* (Law Com No 192, 1990) para 2.11.

3.4 Why reform the law?

As we have seen, the legislation providing for divorce is nearly 50 years old. Much of the case law interpreting these statutes dates from the same period and reflects an attitude to divorce that is arguably out of step with the modern era. In this section, we look at criticisms that have been made of the current law, and some previous reform attempts.

3.4.1 Criticisms of the current law

It has been the subject of repeated and stringent criticisms by judges, lawyers, academics, and those who have used the process to get divorced. These criticisms were made with some force by the Law Commission in a 1990 report, *Family Law: The Ground for Divorce*. In that report, the Commissioners said that the law is confusing and misleading; discriminatory and unjust; distorts the parties' bargaining positions; provokes unnecessarily hostility and bitterness; does nothing to save the marriage; and can make things worse for children.

Let's take a look at these and other criticisms of the law. As you have read through the chapter so far, many of these are likely to have become apparent to you already.

It is illogical

Although, as we have seen, it is considerably less restrictive than the laws that preceded it, the parties cannot simply divorce on the basis that their marriage has broken down. They have to prove irretrievable breakdown, certainly, but that is not enough: they also have to demonstrate one of the five facts. That, said the Law Commission, is confusing and misleading.[166] Why have both elements? (Answer: as we see at 3.2.5, it was a historical compromise.)

Of course, the fact chosen does not need to have any connection to the reality of why the marriage broke down. As a matter of law, no causal link is necessary. The Law Commission thought this gap between practice and theory 'can only lead to confusion and lack of respect for the law'.[167] In any event, it may be impossible to determine who is to blame—perhaps no one is, or both are. Relationships peter out, people feel neglected or have separate interests, life gets in the way of romance and communication. Suddenly, a life apart seems to have more potential or interest. This is the rather prosaic reality of many divorces, the kind of complex and nuanced reality that the law struggles to fit into the box on the petition form. But it is not for the parties to determine that their marriage has irretrievably broken down; the petitioner must persuade a judge that it has. Whatever she says—and even if the respondent agrees with the divorce—a judge may take a different view.

Lack of scrutiny

The fact that judge, rather than the parties, determines whether the fact is proved and the marriage broken down is somewhat surprising given that, these days, court officers spend an average of four minutes on the petition, acknowledgment, statement in support

---

[166] Law Commission, *Family Law: The Ground for Divorce* (Law Com No 192, 1990) para 2.8.
[167] Law Commission, *Family Law: The Ground for Divorce* (Law Com No 192, 1990) para 2.8.

TABLE 3.1 Facts of divorce used in 2019 in England and Wales, by petitioner gender

Fact	Petitioner is husband	Petitioner is wife	
Adultery	3,651	6,476	
Behaviour	14,125	32,929	
Desertion	136	257	
2 years' separation	13,273	16,709	
5 years' separation	9,226	10,231	
Adultery combined with behaviour (two facts pleaded)	77	212	
Total	**40,488**	**66,814**	**107,302**

Source: Office of National Statistics, *Divorce Tables 2019* (table 5). Different-sex couples only.

and other documents in total.[168] The court's role is to 'enquire, so far as it reasonably can, into the facts alleged'; in other words, to consider the paperwork and see if there appears to be, on the face of it, irretrievable breakdown and one of the five facts.[169] If so, there is no need to inquire further. Petitions are still rejected, but the usual reason for rejection is improper completion of the forms rather than something substantive, so they simply need amending and refiling. The process has become so administrative and requires such little substantive legal knowledge that it is a 'waste' of an experienced judge's time.[170]

It encourages acrimony

As you can see from Table 3.1, behaviour remains the most popular fact for divorce, as it has been since the current law was introduced. There are two main reasons for this. First, unlike adultery, about which there is an objective truth (it happened, or it did not happen), behaviour encompasses a wider range of events and a much higher degree of subjectivity, in that it takes into account the characters and personalities of the parties (see 3.3.2). To put it bluntly, lawyers generally have no difficulty finding unreasonable behaviour in any marriage. As one solicitor told a researcher, 'Basically it's a farce, because you're just saying "All we have to do is get a form of words. As long as you're not telling any lies, we'll get it through" . . . You cobble up some words which will do the business.'[171] It is only when defended that a judge might hold that the behaviour was insufficiently strong to render it unreasonable for the petitioner to continue to live with the respondent. But, most petitions are not defended. Second, if there is no adultery then it is the only other option that does not involve at least a two-year wait to divorce. As such, couples wanting to divorce immediately are pushed towards making allegations in order to get an earlier divorce. Other countries which have a mixed fault and no-fault system, as we do, do not use fault to such

[168] L Trinder, D Braybrook, C Bryson, L Coleman, C Houlston, and M Sefton, *Finding Fault? Divorce Law and Practice in England and Wales* (Nuffield Foundation 2017) 13.
[169] Matrimonial Causes Act 1973 s1(3).
[170] D Norgrove, *Family Justice Review Final Report* (Ministry of Justice 2011) para 4.166.
[171] L Trinder, D Braybrook, C Bryson, L Coleman, C Houlston, and M Sefton, *Finding Fault? Divorce Law and Practice in England and Wales* (Nuffield Foundation 2017) 12, quoting a lawyer in a lawyers' focus group.

a great extent.[172] Unless we believe people are inherently worse behaved in England, there must be something about the process or our expectations of marriage that differentiate us.

If the parties use the no-fault facts of two or five years' separation, it is not necessary for them to be in separate houses as long as they are in separate households. To show this 'inevitably requires the parties to cooperate in a most unnatural and artificial lifestyle'[173] and separate shared chores, meals, and socialising. Where they do not do so, they may be held not to be separated. This was the situation in *Mouncer v Mouncer*,[174] discussed at 3.3.1 in the focus box *Know-How: What Is Separation?*, where the couple's attempt at normalising the divorce for their children meant that they were held to be in the same household and thus not separated. Yet it is surely a good thing if parties forced to live together by circumstances are cooperative and civil to one another. This is especially the case if there are children, as this can significantly mitigate the effect of divorce on children (see 3.4.1 at focus box *Think Critically: How Does Divorce Affect Children?*). Any system that requires parties who are trying to get through a divorce without unnecessary hurt and upset to add to that upset is not a good system.

FOCUS Think Critically

The gender of petitioners

As you can see from Table 3.1, about 60 per cent of petitions are filed by women, and the fact most frequently relied upon is the respondent's unreasonable behaviour.

Does the fact that men are less likely than women to file for divorce mean that men are more committed to the marriage? Or, given the predominance of behaviour and adultery petitions by female petitioners, that men behave worse than women?

Possibly—but not necessarily. Davis and Murch certainly found that 'In general . . . not only were women the initiators of divorce, they were correspondingly less likely to regret the ending of the marital relationship.' Men, on the other hand, were more likely to regret the marriage ending and, if they remarried, to wish that they were still married to their former spouse. This is all the sadder for the fact that Davis and Murch also found that 'whilst the husband had not wanted a divorce, he had not wanted much of a marriage either—and it was this which had promoted his wife to issue proceedings . . . It also appeared in a few instances that the wife's filing of the divorce petition was a kind of desperate last throw for the husband's affections.'[175] Leaving aside the issues of whether men behave more badly, or women are more likely to call it quits, there is a possible practical reason for women's reliance on behaviour petitions. In most opposite-sex households, the man is still the primary breadwinner.[176] When the parties separate, the wife may not have the luxury of waiting to divorce on two years' separation, but need a financial order quickly. A two- or five-year delay 'is difficult to achieve without substantial resources of one's own or the co-operation of the other spouse'.[177]

---

172 See, for example, Scotland, which has a mixed system and has always used fault in fewer petitions.

173 Law Commission, *Family Law: The Ground for Divorce* (Law Com No 191, 1990) para 2.12.

174 *Mouncer v Mouncer* [1972] 1 WLR 321 (Wrangham J).

175 G Davis and M Murch, *Grounds for Divorce* (Clarendon Press 1988) 33–5.

176 S Connolly, M Aldrich, M O'Brien, S Speight, and E Poole, 'Britain's Slow Movement to a Gender Egalitarian Equilibrium: Parents and Employment in the UK 2001–13' (2016) *Work, Employment and Society* 1.

177 Law Commission, *Family Law: The Ground for Divorce* (Law Com No 191, 1990).

An alternative explanation, therefore, could be that women are more likely than men to file using behaviour or adultery because those immediately give the court jurisdiction to make a financial remedy order, including an interim order. This may be particularly true of divorces among those of low or moderate wealth. The Law Commission felt that it was 'unjust and discriminatory of the law to provide for a civilised "no-fault" ground for divorce which, in practice, is denied to a large section of the population' for financial reasons.[178] Moreover, this additional financial consideration means that the parties' respective bargaining positions may become distorted by who wants a divorce, who can afford a divorce, and who can afford to delay. If the petitioner is desperate for a divorce for financial reasons, for example, the respondent can use that desperation to extract a price, in financial or other terms. Thus we move farther and farther away from the idea that the law is accurately apportioning responsibility for the breakdown of the marriage.

It encourages falsification and exaggeration

The undefended procedure means that petitions which are untrue, or only partially true, are seldom spotted, especially if both parties wish to divorce and the respondent thus has no incentive to challenge the petition. In a survey for the family law solicitors' organisation Resolution, 27 per cent of admitted their particulars of behaviour were not true but that a behaviour petition was the easiest way forward.[179] More likely than complete falsification of the particulars is that they are a subjective or a somewhat exaggerated version of the truth, converted by the petitioner's solicitor into language that will satisfy the court and not cause the respondent to object. 'The bogus adultery cases of the past may have all but disappeared but their modern equivalents are the flimsy behaviour petition or the pretence that the parties have been living apart for the full two years.'[180] Indeed, the degree of collaboration that marks the present law would have put paid to any divorces in past centuries. As Munby P has said, the 'law which the judges have to apply and the procedures which they have to follow are based on hypocrisy and lack of intellectual honesty. The simple fact is that we have, and have for many years had, divorce by consent, not merely in accordance with section 1(2)(d) of the 1969 Act but, for those unwilling or unable to wait for two years, by means of a consensual, collusive, manipulation of section 1(2)(b). It is ironic that collusion, which until the doctrine was abolished by section 9 of the 1969 Act was a bar to a decree, is now the very foundation of countless petitions and decrees.'[181]

In many cases the petition is the subject of some negotiation that has resulted in an agreed form of wording. Even the Resolution *Guide to Good Practice on Correspondence 2016* includes a suggested letter that acknowledges that 'neither of you is solely responsible for your marriage breaking down' and then invites the respondent to cooperate with a behaviour petition that is 'as mild and uncontentious as possible' 'in order to obtain a divorce sooner' than two years.[182] Thus 'In practice . . . divorce petitions are best viewed

[178] Law Commission, *Family Law: The Ground for Divorce* (Law Com No 191, 1990).
[179] Resolution News Release, 'MPs Need to Get behind No-Fault Divorce if They're Serious about Reducing Family Conflict', 3 December 2015.
[180] Law Commission, *Family Law: The Ground for Divorce* (Law Com No 191, 1990) para 2.11.
[181] *Owens v Owens* [2017] EWCA Civ 182.
[182] Resolution, *Guide to Good Practice on Correspondence* (Resolution 2016). Available at http://www.resolution.org.uk/site_content_files/files/good_practice_guide_correspondence.pdf accessed 23 July 2017.

as a narrative produced to secure a legal divorce. They are not—as a lay person might suppose they should be—an accurate reflection of why the marriage broke down and who was "to blame".'[183]

FOCUS Think Critically

How does divorce affect children?

In 2013, the last year for which there are available statistics about children, 114,720 couples got divorced.[184] These couples between them had 94,864 children aged under 16 and 41,204 children aged over 16.[185]

There have been multiple studies about children's experiences of parental separation and the effect upon them. Of course, these findings do not dictate how any individual child may respond, but instead give us propensities and trends. Some of the studies are also quite old, and it is possible that as divorce has become more common the effect on an individual child may be mitigated by the fact that it is normal and accepted within their social group. If we go back a few decades, divorce was much more stigmatised and children of divorce seen as coming from 'broken homes'.[186]

Amato and Keith's metastudy—which collated the data used by 92 previous studies, together involving over 13,000 children—found 'children of divorce experience a lower level of wellbeing than do children living in continuously intact families'.[187] Multiple studies have shown that people whose parents divorced when they were children are more likely to have lower educational attainment and lower income than children from intact families; and are more likely to access state benefits. They are more likely to get divorced themselves, have children younger, and become single parents.[188] They are more likely to experience anxiety and depression, low self-esteem, and dissatisfaction with friendships. These outcomes are consistent across social classes and across different race and ethnic groups.[189]

It is, however, difficult to separate cause from effect. Are such outcomes caused by divorce, or are they because divorce is more likely in families that are dysfunctional in the first place? We know that 'families in which divorce occurs are different in a variety of important ways from families that remain intact'.[190] We know, for example, that there are higher levels of conflict, parental mental illness, and/or economic difficulties in families that break down. However, such outcomes are not necessarily *caused by* divorce. Rather, as Cherlin et al. suggest, it could be 'the conditions that existed

---

[183] L Trinder, D Braybrook, C Bryson, L Coleman, C Houlston, and M Sefton, *Finding Fault? Divorce Law and Practice in England and Wales* (Nuffield Foundation 2017) 12.

[184] Office of National Statistics, *Divorces in England and Wales: Children of Divorced Couples: Historical Data* (2015).

[185] These are 'children of the family', that is children of both parties or those who are treated by them as though they were their own children: Matrimonial Causes Act 1973 s52.

[186] C Brown, 'Ameliorating the Effects of Divorce on Children' (2009) 22 *Journal of the American Academy of Academic Lawyers* 461.

[187] PR Amato and B Keith, 'Parental Divorce and the Well-Being of Children: A Meta-Analysis' (1991) 110(1) *Psychological Bulletin* 26, 30.

[188] FF Furstenberg and KE Kiernan, 'Delayed Parental Divorce: How Much Do Children Benefit?' (2001) 63 *Journal of Marriage and Family* 446, 455.

[189] TS Hanson, 'Does Parental Conflict Explain Why Divorce Is Negatively Associated with Child Welfare?', (1999) 77(4) *Social Forces* 1283.

[190] FF Furstenberg and KE Kiernan, 'Delayed Parental Divorce: How Much Do Children Benefit?' (2001) 63 *Journal of Marriage and Family* 446, 454.

well before the separation occurred' that predict children's well-being post-divorce.[191] We know that children of families experiencing high conflict, parental mental illness, or economic difficulties have worse outcomes after divorce than other children of divorced parents.[192]

Would children be better off if their parents stayed together? Morrison and Coiro thought not, if the parents are in conflict. They found that children experienced greater behavioural problems if their parents remained married but argued frequently than if the parents separated. While separation was harmful to children, 'the adverse effects of frequent marital quarrels is larger than the deleterious effect of separation and divorce'.[193] Indeed, on a range of factors, children whose parents divorce do as well as or better than children whose parents stay in high-conflict marriages.[194] Marital conflict can mean that children learn poor conflict resolution strategies from their parents, experience inconsistent or harsh discipline through lack of parental cooperation, and have their attachment bonds with their parents disrupted.[195] 'Disruption in these primary bonds interferes with the child's developmental progress and presents both cognitive and emotional problems that may persist long after adjustments have been made in the routines of daily life.'[196] However, if the marriage deteriorates suddenly, or the end of the marriage is not preceded by open conflict, children's well-being will be reduced, not improved, by divorce.[197]

Girls and boys may react differently the stress of divorce. On the face of it, girls seem less affected than boys by divorce, but it could be the nature of their reactions: they are more likely to become withdrawn, anxious, and well-behaved (pro-social) than boys. Boys are more likely to act out antisocially through aggression and noncompliance; this may distract the parents from their own conflict.[198] Each is a different way of attempting to defuse interparental conflict. Each could also be the effect of witnessing their parents' coping strategies, as we know that children model behaviour on that of their same-gender parent: if a mother's conflict response is emotional and physical withdrawal, her daughter may respond the same way, for example.[199]

Parents' views about the effects of divorce on children depends on whether they themselves are married or divorced, whether they instigated the divorce, and even whether their own parents were divorced. Their perceptions are coloured by their own experiences and choices.[200] Thus married parents 'evaluated the impact of divorce on children more negatively than did divorced fathers and

---

[191] AJ Cherlin, FF Furstenberg, PL Chase-Lansdale, KE Kiernan, PK Robins, DR Morrison, and JO Teitler, 'Longitudinal Studies of Effects of Divorce on Children in Great Britain and the United States' (1991) 252(5011) *Science* 1386, 1388.

[192] AJ Cherlin, FF Furstenberg, PL Chase-Lansdale, KE Kiernan, PK Robins, DR Morrison, and JO Teitler, 'Longitudinal Studies of Effects of Divorce on Children in Great Britain and the United States' (1991) 252(5011) *Science* 1386.

[193] DR Morrison and MJ Coiro, 'Parental Conflict and Marital Disruption: Do Children Benefit When High-Conflict Marriages Are Dissolved?' (1999) 61(3) *Journal of Marriage and Family* 626, 635.

[194] TS Hanson, 'Does Parental Conflict Explain Why Divorce Is Negatively Associated with Child Welfare?' (1999) 77(4) *Social Forces* 1283.

[195] RE Emery, 'Interparental Conflict and the Children of Discord and Divorce' (1982) 92(2) *Psychological Bulletin* 310, 324.

[196] RD Hess and KA Camara, 'Post Divorce Family Relationships as Mediating Factors in the Consequences of Divorce for Children' (1979) 35(4) *Journal of Social Issues* 79, 94.

[197] PR Amato, L Spencer Loomis, and A Booth, 'Parental Divorce, Marital Conflict, and Offspring Well-Being during Early Adulthood' (1995) 73(3) *Social Forces* 895.

[198] RE Emery, 'Interparental Conflict and the Children of Discord and Divorce' (1982) 92(2) *Psychological Bulletin* 310, 323.

[199] SM Jekielek, 'Parental Conflict, Marital Disruption and Children's Emotional Well-Being' (1998) 76 *Social Forces* 905.

[200] M Moon, 'The Effects of Divorce on Children: Married and Divorced Parents' Perspectives' (2011) 52(5) *Journal of Divorce and Remarriage* 344, 347.

mothers', and those who initiated the divorce reported fewer negative effects on children than did those who did not initiate the divorce. This may mean that parents who are considering whether to get divorced may overestimate the harm to their children, while perhaps underestimating the harm of staying in a high-conflict situation.

Few studies have asked children how they felt about divorce. For some children, divorce feels as though a parent is rejecting them or that they are losing a parent. Only about 10 per cent of 4-year-olds believe that their parent continues to be their parent when they are no longer living in the same house as the child.[201] However, feelings of loss cannot solely account for the deterioration in children's well-being following divorce. If that was the case, then we would see the same effect on children who have a parent who dies. However, Amato and Keith found that bereaved children generally have greater well-being, at least in the long term, than those whose parents have divorced.[202] While parental death understandably has an effect on children, this effect tends not to result in problems that persist into adulthood. Divorce, on the other hand, has a long-lasting effect on educational attainment, socio-economic disadvantage when grown up, and mental illness.

While these studies sound alarming, Amato emphasises that the differences in well-being between divorced and intact families are not, in fact, statistically large.[203] Moreover, if the key risk factor is 'interparental conflict occurring prior, during, and after the legal processes of divorce',[204] then the effects of divorce on children can be mitigated by reducing conflict behaviours (including in litigation, perhaps by turning to mediation or collaborative family law), communicating with children about what is happening, being sensitive to children's feelings, and enabling them to have contact with both parents, or, at least, information about them.[205] Some jurisdictions now have mandatory parenting classes for those who are divorcing. In England and Wales, many voluntary organisations run 'parenting after parting' or 'parenting in partnership' sessions which aim to help separated couples parent cooperatively.

It does nothing to save the marriage

We can see throughout the history of divorce law reform that Parliamentarians and others have been concerned that people decide to get divorced without much thought. During Parliamentary debates about the Divorce Reform Act 1969, an example was given of 'the sort of [adultery] case which may arise': 'the case of a wife whose pride is hurt but who thinks it is much more hurt than it really is, and having consulted a solicitor about it and having launched a petition, is rather sorry about it.'[206] More recently, the Law Commission worried that commencing the divorce process may create an unstoppable 'juggernaut effect'.[207] There are, therefore, various procedural requirements that encourage reconciliation and the saving of saveable marriages: the six-month windows for the parties to

---

[201] H McGurk and M Glachan, 'Children's Conceptions of the Continuity of Parenthood Following Divorce' 28(3) *Journal of Child Psychology and Psychiatry* 427.

[202] PR Amato and B Keith, 'Parental Divorce and the Well-Being of Children: A Meta-Analysis' (1991) 110(1) *Psychological Bulletin* 26.

[203] PR Amato, 'Children's Adjustment to Divorce: Theories, Hypotheses, and Empirical Support' (1993) 55(1) *Journal of Marriage and Family* 23.

[204] C Brown, 'Ameliorating the Effects of Divorce on Children' (2009) 22 *Journal of the American Academy of Academic Lawyers* 461, 462.

[205] Y Walczak and S Burns, *Divorce: The Child's Point of View* (Harper & Row 1984).

[206] Baroness Birk in the House of Lords debates on the Divorce Reform Act 1969: HL Deb 10 July 1969, vol 303, col 1234.

[207] Law Commission, *Facing the Future—A Discussion Paper on the Ground for Divorce* (Law Com No 170, 1988) para 3.49.

explore the future of their marriage in cases of adultery or behaviour; the fact that any so-licitor acting for the petitioner must file a Statement of Reconciliation confirming whether or not they have discussed the prospect of reconciliation with their client; and the two- or five-year delays when there is no fault. Trinder's study found little evidence that these had any effect, but even if they did, the unintentional practical advantages of using fault-based grounds undermines all of these.[208] Indeed, it goes further than simply doing nothing to save the marriage, but actually hinders reconciliation. 'The necessity of making allega-tions "draws the battle lines" at the outset . . . and destroys any chance of reconciliation.'[209] Even if the parties both want a divorce, and even if they are cooperating in that process, there is nothing guaranteed to cause distress like a divorce petition through the door that says the marriage has broken down because *you* have behaved unreasonably. Even some-thing that you might see as a means to an end can hurt.[210]

3.4.2 Alternatives to the present system

The system that we have in England and Wales is just one of many different models around the world. Here are some of the most common:

- A purely fault-based system that permits divorce only when the other party has breached some form of marital obligation, commonly fidelity.

- Mutual consent divorce permits a divorce when both parties agree. This does not usu-ally involve any allegations of fault, and there may or may not be a requirement to separate for a period first.

- Unilateral divorce that enables one party to divorce the other whether or not that other party agrees. This does not usually involve any allegations of fault on the part of the respondent, simply that one party wishes to end the marriage. There may or may not be a requirement to separate for a period first. All no-fault systems require some mechanism for the parties to divorce unilaterally, i.e., when one party wants a divorce but the other does not. This protects those seeking to exit abusive relationships.

The system that we have in England and Wales is a mixture of all of these. Desertion, behaviour, and adultery are all fault-based facts (although as we noted at 3.3.2, the re-spondent does not have to be culpable for their behaviour); two years' separation with the respondent's consent is a mutual consent fact; and the five years' separation fact is unilateral divorce because it does not require the respondent's consent. Other countries have different variations:

- In Sweden, the parties can divorce by mutual agreement or unilaterally. It has not been necessary to show fault since 1973. There is a mandatory reconsideration period of six to 12 months in certain circumstances, such as if there are children under 16,

---

[208] L Trinder, D Braybrook, C Bryson, L Coleman, C Houlston, and M Sefton, *Finding Fault? Divorce Law and Practice in England and Wales* (Nuffield Foundation 2017) 16.
[209] Law Commission, *Facing the Future—A Discussion Paper on the Ground for Divorce* (Law Com No 170, 1988) para 3.48.
[210] This is borne out by respondents to Liz Trinder's study: L Trinder, D Braybrook, C Bryson, L Coleman, C Houl-ston, and M Sefton, *Finding Fault? Divorce Law and Practice in England and Wales* (Nuffield Foundation 2017) 15.

because one party requests it, or because the respondent does not agree to the divorce. At the end of this period, the divorce is granted.

- In Australia, it is necessary to show irretrievable breakdown and to have been separated for at least 12 months—it is not necessary to show fault. Most divorces are applied for by the parties together rather than one person unilaterally seeking a divorce. As with our law, it is possible to be held to be separated while the parties remain in the same home, although they are more lenient about sharing household tasks. However, the court cannot grant a divorce if there is a reasonable likelihood of cohabitation being resumed.[211] Those who file for divorce without having been married for at least two years must attend counselling to discuss reconciliation, although there are exceptions such as in cases of violence.

- In Denmark, the rules depend on whether the parties mutually agree to a divorce. If they do, then they can divorce immediately or following a formal period of separation. It is not necessary to show fault. If the other party does not want a divorce, then they must be formally separated for at least six months before a divorce can be obtained unilaterally. The formal separation is granted by the state administration and it is not a judicial process. No separation period is required if there has been adultery, violence, bigamy, abduction of a mutual child, or if the parties have been informally living apart for at least two years because of a history of 'disagreements'.

- In the US, different states have different laws, but no-fault divorce is possible in all states, either as the sole ground of divorce or as one of several. In New York—the last state to introduce no-fault divorce—there are seven possible grounds: irretrievable breakdown (no-fault); cruel and inhuman treatment; abandonment (i.e., desertion); imprisonment of the spouse for at least three consecutive years; and adultery with third party evidence (fault-based grounds); and divorce either after one year's formal separation or a judgment of separation.[212]

In addition to these legal differences, there are also procedural differences. In many countries, such as Denmark, divorce is an administrative procedure overseen by a state agency, rather than (as in New York) a judicial procedure. Here in England, we are moving further away from a judicial process towards one that is administrative because the process does not require the expertise of judges.

However, the movement away from fault is not universal and has resulted, particularly in America, in so-called pro-marriage movements which seek to reduce the incidence of divorce by encouraging and supporting the institution of marriage. In three southern US states, Arkansas, Louisiana, and Arizona, couples have the option of entering into a 'covenant marriage', which restricts the grounds of divorce available to them if the marriage breaks down and requires both premarital and pre-divorce counselling. Based on a Christian belief in the lifelong nature of marriage, covenant marriage can be seen as a backlash against the prevalence of no-fault divorce regimes. As Nock, Sanchez, and Wright observe:

> The no-fault divorce concept rested on an assumption that the misery of poor marriages and the costs of prolonged, difficult divorces could be lessened by access to easier, less-punitive grounds and procedures for divorce. The assumption behind covenant marriage is

---

[211] Family Law Act 1975 ss 48–49.
[212] Domestic Relations Law § 170.

that the miseries of marital dissolution can be lessened or avoided altogether by helping couples better understand the implications of getting married, encouraging them to take their marriage vows more seriously, and by making divorce more difficult to obtain.[213]

The underlying fear of the 'growing marriage revitalization movement'[214] is that no-fault divorce has made divorces easier and caused a rise in the number of divorces, with consequential impacts on personal, social, and economic well-being. Divorce—and, indeed, the breakdown of any committed relationship—has significant social costs. These include higher rates of criminality and poverty, greater reliance on state benefits, poorer educational attainment for children and higher rates of mental illness. Overall, the cost of relationship breakdown (married and unmarried relationships) has been estimated at up to £48 billion per year, although there are considerable causative and methodological flaws in such estimates.[215]

States therefore try to use divorce laws to try to reduce the incidence of family breakdown, to influence the parties on how to behave during and after divorce, and to require certain (usually financial) responsibilities of those who divorce, and thereby mitigate the effects of marital breakdown on the family involved and wider society. As Wardle has noted, 'People are vulnerable in marriages, and when marriages fail, society must pick up the pieces'.[216]

3.4.3 Should the law recognise fault?

If, as Mary Welstead argues, 'Most partners will be able to find at least one of the facts, even if it may require a little imagination, some ingenuity, a significant expenditure of emotional energy, and, in some cases, money,' what is the purpose of requiring parties to do so? If the scrutiny of petitions is so little, and the allegations in uncontested petitions so dubious, that 'conceptually and procedurally, it is far more difficult to terminate those other pillars of a stable life, employment and a tenancy, than marriage,'[217] what purpose does it serve to make parties undergo 'an often painful, and sometimes destructive, legal ritual with no obvious benefits for the parties or the state'?[218] Why not simply do what many other countries do, and allow marriages to be dissolved after a period of separation, or immediately at the request of one or both parties?

Whether or not you think that law should recognise fault depends on what you think the aim of divorce law should be, and this is closely linked to how you see marriage. There are certainly a number of arguments in favour of retaining fault-based facts of divorce— but there are also strong counter-arguments. Let us explore some of these.

---

[213] SL Nock, LA Sanchez, and JD Wright, *Covenant Marriage: The Movement to Reclaim Tradition in America* (Rutgers University Press 2008) 11.

[214] L Wardle, 'Is Marriage Obsolete?' 10 *Michigan Journal of Gender and Law* 189, 204.

[215] See the Relationships Foundation's Costs of Family Failure Index http://www.relationshipsfoundation.org/family-policy/cost-of-family-failure-index/, and also see the single parent group Gingerbread's response to this, 'Challenging the Costs of Relationship Breakdown' (2015) at https://gingerbread.org.uk/uploads/media/17/9425.pdf accessed 15 October 2020.

[216] L Wardle, 'The Attack on Marriage as the Union of a Man and a Woman' (2007) 83 *North Dakota Law Review* 1365, 1369–70. Be warned that you may find the content of this article to be pretty offensive.

[217] R Deech, 'Divorce – A Disaster' [2009] *Family Law* 1048, 1050.

[218] L Trinder, D Braybrook, C Bryson, L Coleman, C Houlston, and M Sefton, *Finding Fault? Divorce Law and Practice in England and Wales* (Nuffield Foundation 2017) 169.

Sometimes one party really is at fault

Fault-based facts may reflect reality: marriages can and do fail because one person, solely or predominantly, is at fault. When the law permits divorce on a fault-based fact, it recognises this.

One problem with this is that it assumes that we can identify why the marriage broke down. The present procedure for an undefended divorce does not allow for anything other than a face-value consideration of the petition and acknowledgment. If all petitions had to undergo greater scrutiny involving an actual trial, as with a defended divorce, the whole court system would collapse under the weight of divorce work. Moreover, such an exercise would be extremely difficult even for experienced judges. Liz Trinder's research found that 29 per cent of respondents to a fault divorce said the fact used had very closely matched the reason for the separation; twice as many petitioners thought so.[219] Truth is therefore in the eye of the beholder. More than that: only two thirds of petitioners agreed that their own petition closely matched the reason for the separation. Life is more complex than the statutory categories.

It vindicates the innocent party

The Law Commission of 1998 felt that fault enabled the 'innocent party' to feel validated in seeking a divorce. For the petitioning party, 'the notion of fault, of attributing blame to one party and exonerating the other, is what the legal system should be about, it is what ensures that justice is not only done but seen to be done.'[220] Or, as Baroness Young put it, no-fault divorce 'creates injustice for anyone who believes in guilt and innocence'.[221]

There are three objections to this argument. One is that while many people come to law expecting that the law will vindicate their feelings, they are likely to be disappointed in this. While the certificate of entitlement to a decree and decree nisi will each state that the petitioner is entitled to a divorce on their specified fact, at no stage is there a big pronouncement that the petitioner has been wronged. The vindication is the divorce itself; but no-fault divorce would achieve that same end.

Second, we must bear in mind that the behaviour ground, while commonly called unreasonable behaviour, encompasses within it behaviour which is out of the control of the respondent, such as that resulting from physical or mental illness. It is therefore wrong and unfair to assume that just because one party has divorced the other on the ground of behaviour, the respondent is in any way culpable.

The main objection to the vindication argument is that in many situations the law may not be able to identify the blameworthy at all. In Liz Trinder's study, 71 per cent of people wanted to retain fault yet 61 per cent thought it unfair to blame only one party which is, of course, what the petition does.[222] Should the law vindicate the feelings of a petitioner

---

[219] L Trinder, D Braybrook, C Bryson, L Coleman, C Houlston, and M Sefton, *Finding Fault? Divorce Law and Practice in England and Wales* (Nuffield Foundation 2017) 12.

[220] S Day Sclater and C Piper, *Undercurrents of Divorce* (Ashgate 1999) 6.

[221] Baroness Young, HL Deb 29 February 1996, vol 569, col 1638.

[222] L Trinder, D Braybrook, C Bryson, L Coleman, C Houlston, and M Sefton, *Finding Fault? Divorce Law and Practice in England and Wales* (Nuffield Foundation 2017) 137.

who is herself responsible in some way for the breakdown of the marriage? What if both are at fault equally? Of both at fault only to the extent that they each could have put more effort into the marriage, communicated better, and got through their difficulties before they became fatal? What if a wife commits adultery because she feels no affection from her husband? But what if he has not been affectionate because she has been dismissive of him and critical? Consider Clare and Robert Newton in our scenario. Which of the events of their marriage caused the fatal blow? Do the parties themselves even know? If the law cannot accurately apportion blame, then it risks causing injustice. And, as Ellman asks, even if the law can sometimes accurately apportion blame, would this 'cause more harm to more divorcing parties than the no-fault alternative?'[223]

It provides an emotional outlet

Ruth Deech argues that the petitioner's ability to cite adultery, behaviour, or desertion by the respondent provides an essential outlet for the petitioner's feelings, thereby enabling them to psychologically 'move on'. If there is no such outlet, the argument goes, the hostility and bitterness a party feels may be redirected and 'make for more resentment in the separate but parallel proceedings for maintenance and property and maybe in making arrangements for the children'.[224]

It is difficult to support the incorporation of acrimony as a deliberate feature of the law's design as opposed to an inadvertent consequence. In any case, the argument that fault acts as an outlet for emotions is not supported by research. In 1988, the Law Commission found that the presentation of a petition created or exacerbated hostility; it was not simply that behaviour or adultery petitions occurred in already-bitter cases.[225] Whether the respondent was collaborating with the petition, had not thought anything was wrong and received it out of the blue, or had 'been guilty of violence or other serious misconduct', the petition sowed the 'seeds of post-divorce ill feeling' in the respondent—and in the petitioner, too, for having to focus on what was bad in the marriage.[226] More than thirty years after the Law Commission's research, Trinder et al. found the same thing, as in their study '62% of petitioners and 78% of respondents said using fault had made the process more bitter, 21% of fault-respondents said fault had made it harder to sort out arrangements for children, and 31% of fault-respondents thought fault made sorting out finances harder'.[227]

No-fault divorce will cause more divorces

Some studies have shown that the introduction of a no-fault divorce process (such as divorce through a period of separation or mutual agreement) goes hand in hand with a

---

[223] IM Ellman, 'The Misguided Movement to Revive Fault Divorce, and Why Reformers Should Look Instead to the American Law Institute' (1997) 11 *International Journal of Law, Policy and the Family* 216, 217.

[224] R Deech, 'Divorce – A Disaster', [2009] *Family Law* 1048.

[225] Law Commission, *Facing the Future—A Discussion Paper on the Ground for Divorce* (Law Com No 170, 1988) para 3.26.

[226] Law Commission, *Facing the Future—A Discussion Paper on the Ground for Divorce* (Law Com No 170, 1988) para 3.27.

[227] L Trinder, D Braybrook, C Bryson, L Coleman, C Houlston, and M Sefton, *Finding Fault? Divorce Law and Practice in England and Wales* (Nuffield Foundation 2017) 15.

rise in the divorce rate.[228] It therefore follows that if the state wishes to limit the number of divorces, it should not dispense with fault-based laws.

Certainly, some studies show that immediately after the introduction of a no-fault process, there is a temporary increase in the divorce rate. This, it is argued, is caused by the fact that those who were unable to divorce have, as a result of the introduction of a no-fault process, become able to divorce, and so they do so in the years immediately following the change in the law. Thus, the rise is 'a temporary phenomenon caused by a backlog of unmet demand'.[229] After the backlog is cleared, the rate of divorce stabilises. In fact, in every reform of the law we discussed when we looked at the history of divorce at 3.2, liberalisation of the law has resulted in an increase in the number of divorces, and until 1969 we had a purely fault-based system.

While a number of studies of no-fault divorce have shown a permanent increase in the divorce rate, many have been attacked as 'subject to serious methodological criticism'.[230] Most recent research has tended to disprove any long-term causal link. For example, a study of unilateral divorce laws in the US found that while reforms led to a spike in the divorce rate, this 'dissipates over time. After a decade, no effect can be discerned.'[231] While the divorce rate has undoubtedly risen overall in recent decades, these studies attribute this not to no-fault divorce but 'almost entirely to other factors, such as new employment prospects for women, welfare benefits and changing social attitudes'.[232] Our expectations of marriage have changed, so that there is greater emphasis on individual self-fulfilment, and therefore so have our ideas about when to end a marriage and what constitutes a good reason for doing so.

The argument that fault should be retained in order to act as a brake on divorce rates also assumes that people who do not or cannot divorce stay together. Is a marriage saved simply because divorce is too difficult? Those who divorce immediately after a liberalisation of the law—the people in the temporary spike—are not necessarily people who woke up one day and decided to call their marriage quits when they were recently happy. It is more likely that those people's marriages were 'legally intact but factually dead', and they were already separated or contemplating separation and the new law has simply provided them with the opportunity to divorce.[233] In other words, making divorce difficult does not necessarily mean that people stay together. They may separate anyway and, without being

---

[228] See, for example, MF Brinig and FH Buckley, 'No-Fault Law and At-Fault People' (1998) 18 *International Review of Law and Economics* 325; L Gonzáles and TK Viitanen, 'The Effect of Divorce Laws on Divorce Rates in Europe' (2006) Institute for the Study of Labor Discussion Paper 2023; and PA Nakonezny, RD Shull, and JL Rodgers, 'The Effect of No-Fault Divorce Law on the Divorce Rates across the 50 States and Its Relation to Income, Education, and Religiosity' (1995) 57(2) *Journal of Marriage and the Family* 477.

[229] R Rowthorn, 'Marriage and Trust: Some Lessons from Economics' (1999) 23 *Cambridge Journal of Economics* 661, 676.

[230] L Trinder, 'In Anticipation of a Temporary Blip: Would a Change in the Divorce law Increase the Divorce Rate?' Part of the Finding Fault Project. Available at https://www.familylaw.co.uk/news_and_comment/in-anticipation-of-a-temporary-blip-would-a-change-in-the-divorce-law-increase-the-divorce-rate accessed 15 October 2020.

[231] J Wolfers, 'Did Unilateral Divorce Raise Divorce Rates? A Reconciliation and New Results' (2003) NBER Working Paper 10014, 13.

[232] R Rowthorn, 'Marriage and Trust: Some Lessons from Economics' (1999) 23 *Cambridge Journal of Economics* 661, 676.

[233] IM Ellman, 'The Misguided Movement to Revive Fault Divorce, and Why Reformers Should Look Instead to the American Law Institute' (1997) 11 *International Journal of Law, Policy and the Family* 216, 225.

able to divorce, any new relationship they enter into will be outside remarriage. Thus, 'while legal barriers can affect the rate of formal divorce, it is far less clear they can affect the rate of actual marital demise.'[234] The quality of a relationship is surely unaffected by the availability of divorce.

It sends a moral message from society

As Eekelaar says, divorce law 'reflects a particular vision of the moral foundations of marriage'.[235] To proponents of fault, grounds such as adultery, desertion, or behaviour reflect what Schneider describes as 'an ideal of marital relations [that] included duties of life-long mutual responsibility and fidelity', breach of which justify the ending of a marriage.[236] In doing so, society's disapproval is communicated as a warning and disincentive to those who are contemplating behaving similarly. In contrast, no-fault divorce laws, Schneider argues,

> represent a deliberate decision that the morality of each divorce is too delicate and complex for public, impersonal, and adversarial discussion; represent a decision that the moral standard of life-long fidelity ought no longer be publicly enforced; and represent a decision to diminish the extent of mutual spousal responsibility that will be governmentally required.[237]

When Ruth Deech says that we now 'live in a society where there are no constraints on private morality, no judgmentalism, no finger wagging or name calling, only acceptance of anything that anyone does, short of the criminal law, in the name of the pursuit, if not of individual happiness, then at least individual choice', she is not being complimentary.[238] She is suggesting that divorce laws ought to send a message about what is socially acceptable behaviour.

There are several issues here. The first is whether that should be a role for divorce law. As we will see when we consider the Family Law Act 1996, attempts to use laws to influence divorcing behaviour have not been successful; and at 3.2 when we looked at the history of divorce laws, we saw that legislators' expectations about how people would use the laws were often wrong. A second issue is whether, if laws should send a message, they are capable of doing so. Does a finding of fault on divorce send a moral message to the parties and/or the wider world? It is certainly arguable that the fact on which a divorce is obtained has no effect whatsoever in our present system because it cannot correctly ascribe fault in many cases, and because the process does not provide the vindication that pro-fault advocates seek, and because of the high levels of exaggeration and falsification.

Another consideration for legal reform is that our understanding of what is morally correct behaviour changes over time. As we see at 3.2, for centuries only adultery by the wife was considered a transgression serious enough to end a marriage, the husband's

---

[234] IM Ellman, 'The Misguided Movement to Revive Fault Divorce, and Why Reformers Should Look Instead to the American Law Institute' (1997) 11 *International Journal of Law, Policy and the Family* 216, 219.

[235] J Eekelaar, *Regulating Divorce* (Clarendon Press 1991) 15.

[236] CE Schneider, 'Moral Discourse and the Transformation of American Family Law' (1085) 83 *Michigan Law Review* 1803, 1809.

[237] CE Schneider, 'Moral Discourse and the Transformation of American Family Law' (1085) 83 *Michigan Law Review* 1803, 1809.

[238] R Deech, 'Divorce – A Disaster' [2009] Family Law 1048, 1049.

adultery being irrelevant. Even then that was less about morality—if it was, why the gender difference?—and more about the practicalities of knowing one's offspring were legitimate. Consider the example of Ann Dawson, discussed at 3.2.2, whose drunken husband whipped and kicked her, threw hot coffee at her face, set up house with a mistress, and threw her down the stairs: giving her a divorce was more morally objectionable to the Parliamentarians of the time than making her suffer such appalling violence.

One perspective on no-fault systems is that they reflect a different kind of moral good, one which prioritises individual happiness. Ellman has described the introduction of no-fault divorce as being 'accompanied by cultural changes that . . . focus on individual fulfilment more than mutual commitment, that emphasize marriage's potential for happiness and de-emphasize its obligations, and that value individual independence and disparage mutual interdependence'.[239] If the marriage is not working, the individual is justified in seeking individual happiness elsewhere. If, indeed, in Eekelaar's words, 'the pursuit of individual fulfilment has now replaced subservience to duty as the hallmark of marriage',[240] one consequence is that this may reduce the harms associated with staying in a bad relationship. It enables each spouse to 'draw his or her own line as to the degree of harm he or she is prepared to receive from the other'.[241] In an interesting article about divorce in Hollywood films, Thomas Deegan identifies that instead of being judgmental, films in the no-fault era portrayed an errant spouse 'as having the courage to opt out of a failed marriage which was suffocating both partners', thereby influencing audiences to 'support the shift in cultural values from permanence in marriage to love in marriage'. 'The old notions of "right" and "wrong" have shifted', he concludes.[242]

No-fault divorce encourages opportunism

Let us take the argument that no-fault divorce encourages self-fulfilment at the expense of family duties one step further. Economists argue that without fault there is 'no incentive other than a moral obligation or a feeling of affection to prevent either party from engaging in post-contractual opportunism,' such as prioritising one's own interests over those others in the family unit or the family unit itself.[243] No-fault reduces the security offered by marriage and increases risk or uncertainty.[244] In contrast, where divorces are more difficult to obtain, people will 'have the confidence to make long-term investments in their relationship',[245] such as by raising children, looking after the home, or earning money. This 'lifetime stream of spousal services' (as Cohen terms it) also means that alternative opportunities are foregone.[246] Such contributions may take years to come to fruition, such

---

[239] IM Ellman, 'The Misguided Movement to Revive Fault Divorce, and Why Reformers Should Look Instead to the American Law Institute' (1997) 11 *International Journal of Law, Policy and the Family* 216, 229.

[240] J Eekelaar, *Regulating Divorce* (Oxford University Press 1991) 15–16.

[241] J Eekelaar, *Regulating Divorce* (Oxford University Press 1991) 40.

[242] T Deegan, 'Hollywood's Changing Morality' (1986) 15(2) *Cinéaste* 24, 24.

[243] MF Brinig and SM Crafton, 'Marriage and Opportunism' (1994) 23 *Journal of Legal Studies* 869, 879.

[244] MF Brinig and SM Crafton, 'Marriage and Opportunism' (1994) 23 *Journal of Legal Studies* 869, 892.

[245] R Rowthorn, 'Marriage and Trust: Some Lessons from Economics' (1999) 23 *Cambridge Journal of Economics* 661, 661.

[246] L Cohen, 'Marriage, Divorce, and Quasi Rents; or, I Gave Him the Best Years of My Life' (1987) 16 *Journal of Legal Studies* 267, 267.

as when career success is reached, or children grown, and as Brinig and Crafton point out 'may be worthless of the relationship does not endure'.[247] This means that on divorce a party may suffer opportunity or financial losses because the role they undertook in the marriage. In particular, the division of labour in a marriage in accordance with gender may cause significant losses to those women who have taken on a 'traditional' wifely role.[248] As Dnes writes:

> In a traditional marriage, many of the domestic services provided by the wife occur early in the marriage [and, if children, will potentially outlast the marriage], whereas the support offered by the male will grow in value over the longer term . . . the husband might be tempted to take the wife's early services and dump her to enjoy his later income without her and she will tend to be worth less on the remarriage market than a male of similar age.[249]

On this argument, therefore, the end of a marriage causes losses that 'should be allocated to the blameworthy.'[250]

However, there appears to be little evidence that the availability of fault-based grounds affects people's behaviour either before or within marriage, or actually inhibits people from leaving the marriage. As the Law Commission has written,

> If one is 'guilty' but divorce is what he wants, then it is scarcely acting as a restraint . . . Allowing the innocent party to punish the guilty by refusing the divorce is unlikely in today's society to change that behaviour. If divorce is not what the guilty party wants, then the important sanction is not so much the public marking of his or her guilt but the break-down of the marriage itself.[251]

If we really wanted to disincentivise bad behaviour, then a financial sanction beyond divorce itself is necessary, such as allocating the at-fault person less of the matrimonial assets. We do not have that in England, and it would be unworkable for the reasons already discussed. Moreover, as Ellman says, 'fans of fault often make the mistake of thinking that fault laws protect the innocent. They do not. They protect the person who does not care about delaying the divorce, at the expense of the person who does—and who may have very good reasons for wanting out. . . . no matter how we design [a fault-based process] it is inevitable that in many cases they will give bargaining leverage to the wrong spouse.'[252]

---

[247] MF Brinig and SM Crafton, 'Marriage and Opportunism' (1994) 23 *Journal of Legal Studies* 869, 871.
[248] L Cohen, 'Marriage, Divorce, and Quasi Rents; or, I Gave Him the Best Years of My Life' (1987) 16 *Journal of Legal Studies* 267, 267.
[249] AW Dnes 'Marriage Contracts', pp864–86 in B Bouckaert and G De Geest (eds), *Encyclopedia of Law and Economics, Volume III, The Regulation of Contracts* (Edward Elgar 2000).
[250] IM Ellman, 'The Misguided Movement to Revive Fault Divorce, and Why Reformers Should Look Instead to the American Law Institute' (1997) 11 *International Journal of Law, Policy and the Family* 216, 217. This idea, that the division of labour within a marriage causes differential loss at the end of it, is discussed at greater length in Chapter 4 in the context of financial provision on divorce.
[251] Law Commission, *Family Law: The Ground for Divorce* (Law Com No 192, 1990) para 3.7.
[252] IM Ellman, 'The Misguided Movement to Revive Fault Divorce, and Why Reformers Should Look Instead to the American Law Institute' (1997) 11 *International Journal of Law, Policy and the Family* 216, 224.

3.4.4 Previous attempts to reform the law

In 1996, Parliament sought to reform the law of divorce to eliminate fault and there-fore eliminate many of the problems highlighted in this chapter and in the Law Commission's 1990 report *The Ground for Divorce*.[253] It did this by introducing, in the Family Law Act 1996, a no-fault system that provided for divorce over a period of time. The actual result, however, was some way from the process envisaged by the Commission. Ultimately, the relevant parts of the Act never became law, although they were piloted in a number of areas.

Under the Family Law Act, anyone wanting a divorce had to first attend an information meeting at which they would be provided with information about the divorce process, the availability of mediation and legal advice; legal aid; the well-being of children; the financial issues that may arise; and how to seek protection against violence. The govern-ment said this would make them 'aware of the enormous emotional, social and economic upheaval involved in divorce'.[254] 'A system which encourages an acrimonious legal battle makes it less likely that such relationships can be maintained in the years ahead and serves rather to increase the trauma for the children', argued the government.[255] Unfortunately for them, rather than discouraging people from divorcing, it actually had the opposite effect. It 'tended to tip those who were uncertain about their marriage into divorce mode', probably by providing a visible pathway.[256] It also made them more likely to instruct a law-yer: 'All the evidence from the pre-implementation pilot studies was that . . . the more peo-ple knew about the divorce process, the more they wanted a lawyer to help them through it.'[257] The take-up of mediation was a scant 7 per cent. Roger Kay suggests that participants' dislike of 'being shepherded away from professional legal advice . . . is a symptom of the feeling among divorcing parties that they are in some way powerless', and they therefore rebelled against it.[258] The fact that they were provided with the same 'structured, imper-sonal and routine'[259] information and that there was no personalised advice may have also encouraged them to seek legal advice.

A further, linked role for the meetings was to encourage reconciliation by direct-ing the parties to marriage guidance counselling. As Walker points out, the Exeter Family Study, showing harm to children caused by divorce, had just been published.[260] McCarthy et al. note that 'MPs considered even 5% fewer divorces to be worthwhile in terms of the benefits which would accrue to families, to society and to the public purse'.[261] 'The Green Paper returns to the theme of reconciliation again and again', noted Andrew Bainham at the time. 'This is not so much a leitmotif as the grating

---

[253] Law Commission, *Family Law: The Ground for Divorce* (Law Com No 192, 1990).

[254] Quoted by J Walker, 'Information Meetings Revisited' (2000) 30(5) *Family Law* 303.

[255] *Marriage and the Family Law Act: The New Legislation Explained* (Lord Chancellor's Department 1996), quoted by J Eekelaar, M Maclean, and S Beinart, in *Family Lawyers: The Divorce Work of Solicitors* (Hart 2000) 2.

[256] P McCarthy, J Walker, and D Hooper, 'Saving Marriage – A Role for Divorce Law?' (2000) 30(6) *Family Law* 385.

[257] J Dewar, 'Family Law and Its Discontents' (2000) 14(1) *International Journal of Law, Policy and the Family* 59, 79.

[258] R Kay, 'Whose Divorce Is it Anyway – the Human Rights Aspect' (2004) 34(12) *Family Law* 853.

[259] J Walker, *Information Meetings and Associated Provisions within the Family Law Act 1996* (Lord Chancellor's Department, 2001), Summary, 7.

[260] J Walker, 'Radiating Messages: An International Perspective' (2003) 52 *Family Relations* 406, 409.

[261] P McCarthy, J Walker, and D Hooper, 'Saving Marriage – A Role for Divorce Law?' (2000) 30(6) *Family Law* 385.

repetitiveness of a broken record.'[262] However, about 21 per cent people at the information meetings had already tried marriage counselling in the previous year and more than half had already separated. Of those who did go to counselling after the meeting, fewer than half went for help saving the marriage; most went for help ending it.[263]

The next step after an information meeting was to wait at least three months, following which one or both parties could file a statement of marital breakdown. While irretrievable breakdown was thus retained as the sole ground of divorce, the five facts were abolished, creating a no-fault system. After the statement, the parties would then wait a further nine months before the petitioner could apply for an order of divorce. If there were children under 16 or one party requested an extension, this would be extended to 15 months. The Law Commission had believed that these waiting periods would provide 'convincing proof that the marital relationship is indeed irreparable' and would 'give the parties a realistic time within which to resolve the practical questions and to decide whether or not they wish to be reconciled'.[264] 'We believe that it is necessary to intervene strongly to create a pathway to reconciliation', said one MP.[265] Unfortunately, although designed to allow people to reflect and negotiate, the waiting periods also gave divorcing couples the opportunity to prolong one another's agony, and a specific exception had to be created to prevent domestic violence perpetrators from seeking the 15 months' extension.

In light of the results from the pilots, the government took the decision not to bring the divorce provisions in the Act into force, calling them 'unworkable'. Parliament had 'tried to set out general aspirations on how to divorce well: adults should be reasonable, self-denying, conciliatory, and fully conscious of the implications of their actions for themselves and for others.' [266] It found, in reality, that it just was not possible 'to coerce people into being reasonable and co-operative'.[267] The relevant provisions of the Act were finally abolished by the Children and Families Act 2014.

Yet the 1996 Act's flaw was not no-fault divorce per se, but the underlying attempts to change people's behaviour. 'The government agreed to a range of amendments designed to save marriages, thereby adding to the complexity of the legislation and contributing to its eventual demise.'[268] They introduced mediation to save money and (as they thought) reduce hostility. They promoted reconciliation in the erroneous belief that people were not thinking divorce through. They failed to realise that prolonging divorce is all very well if the parties *will* reconcile given enough time, but is more commonly a route to prolonged hurt. They failed to anticipate how people getting divorced might behave. The experience is an indication that 'family law legislation that seeks to impose a specific ideology of proper divorcing behaviour will not work'.[269]

---

[262] A Bainham, 'Divorce and the Lord Chancellor: Looking to the Future or Getting Back to Basics?' (1994) 53(2) *Cambridge Law Journal* 253, 255.

[263] P McCarthy, J Walker, and D Hooper, 'Saving Marriage – A Role for Divorce Law?' (2000) 30(6) *Family Law* 385.

[264] Law Commission, *Family Law: The Ground for Divorce* (Law Com No 192, 1990) para 5.25.

[265] Paul Boateng MP, Labour spokesman on the Bill, *Hansard*, HC Standing Committee E, col 12, 7 May 1996, quoted by P McCarthy, J Walker, and D Hooper, 'Saving Marriage – A Role for Divorce Law?' (2000) 30(6) *Family Law* 385.

[266] J Dewar, 'The Normal Chaos of Family Law' (1998) 61(4) *The Modern Law Review* 467, 483.

[267] J Dewar, 'Family Law and Its Discontents' (2000) 14 *International Journal of Law, Policy and the Family* 59, 79.

[268] J Walker, 'Radiating Messages: An International Perspective' (2003) 52 *Family Relations* 406, 409.

[269] J Dewar, 'Family Law and Its Discontents' (2000) 14 *International Journal of Law, Policy and the Family* 59.

Since the Act's demise, governments steered clear of divorce reform for a number of years, despite repeated calls for the introduction of a (workable) no-fault system by the President of the Supreme Court (Baroness Hale), two Presidents of the Family Division (James Munby and Nicholas Wall), a persistent campaign by the solicitors' group Resolution, and, in 2015, one no-fault private member's bill by Richard Bacon MP. Bacon's bill did not in fact abolish fault, but enabled a sixth fact, divorce on the basis of mutual consent without a waiting period.[270] The Labour Party Manifesto 2017 also included a commitment to introduce no-fault divorce.

3.4.5 Impetus for reform

It took two developments for the government to finally agree to present a divorce reform bill to Parliament.

The first of these was the publication, while *Owens* was between appeals, of the results of a large research project, *Finding Fault*. This looked at how divorces operated, by reading court files, and by interviewing judges, lawyers, and people going through a divorce. The researchers also conducted a survey of public attitudes to divorce. We have already drawn on some of their findings in section 3.4.1. Their main findings were that:

- '62% of petitioners and 78% of respondents said using fault had made the process more bitter, 21% of fault-respondents said fault had made it harder to sort out arrangements for children, and 31% of fault respondents thought fault made sorting out finances harder.'

- 'The substantive law is so complicated that some unrepresented people are simply unable to get a divorce within a reasonable timeframe.'

- 14 per cent of petitions were returned as incorrectly completed.

- There was no evidence that fault reduces divorce. 'Our evidence pointed the other way: fault enables a quick exit from a marriage. . . . The lack of evidence that fault can protect marriage is not surprising given evidence of gaps in public understanding of the grounds for divorce and the ease and rapidity with which a fault divorce can be obtained, especially with legal advice.'

- 71 per cent thought that fault should remain part of the law.

- 'In none of the 592 cases in our file or observation samples did the court raise questions about whether the petition was true.'

- 'Only 29% of respondents to a fault divorce said the fact used had very closely matched the reason for the separation.'[271]

Either side of the release of this report, in October 2017, were the Court of Appeal and Supreme Court decisions in the Key Case of *Owens v Owens*. The outcome of the case was headline news—a very unfortunate state for the parties. The Ministry of Justice responded

---

[270] No-Fault Divorce Bill 2015–16. Available at https://services.parliament.uk/bills/2015-16/nofaultdivorce.html accessed 15 October 2020.

[271] L Trinder, D Braybrook, C Bryson, L Coleman, C Houlston, and M Sefton, *Finding Fault? Divorce Law and Practice in England and Wales* (Nuffield Foundation 2017).

to the judgment by noting that 'the current system of divorce creates unnecessary antagonism in an already difficult situation. We are already looking closely at possible reforms'.[272] That the government felt it necessary to respond to a couple's divorce proceedings demonstrates the level of public consternation, as people realised, first, that divorce was not a private matter between the parties, and second, that unhappiness was insufficient to procure a divorce. As such, public sympathy lay mainly with Mrs Owens. In *The Guardian*, Suzanne Moore asked 'She's gone all the way to the Supreme Court to prove she wants out of the marriage. So why not set her free?'[273] *The New Statesman* smelled a 'whiff of sexism' in the first instance decision.[274] A number of commentators on Twitter used the fact that Mr Owens defended the divorce as evidence that he had a controlling nature. While the case served an important purpose in highlighting the need for reform, the parties did not deserve their marriage to be dissected in this damaging way, either in court or in the media.

In the next section, we look at the contents of the new law, the Divorce, Dissolution and Separation Act 2020, and its passage through Parliament.

3.5 The new law

The Divorce, Dissolution and Separation Act 2020 introduces a purely no-fault divorce system to England and Wales, and is due to come into force in autumn 2021. The Act applies equally to the dissolution of civil partnerships and also reforms the facts relevant to judicial separation. The relevant sections of the new Act are given below, but they operate by amending the Matrimonial Causes Act 1973 and the Civil Partnership Act 2004 so when the Act comes into force it is those statutes in their amended form that you will need to consult.

3.5.1 Reform of divorce and dissolution

The Act retains 'irretrievable breakdown' of the marriage as the sole ground for divorce and civil partnership dissolution (s1(1)). This is proven by the applicant—previously the 'petitioner'—filing a statement saying that the marriage has broken down (s1(2)). Accordingly, when the Act comes into force, the existing five facts—adultery, behaviour, desertion, or two or five years' separation—will cease to exist. This means that there will be no differences between marriages and civil partnership in the facts available, as there will be no facts for either.

Courts are required by s3 of the Act to treat the statement as 'conclusive evidence that the marriage has broken down irretrievably'. They do not need to enquire into the circumstances. Unlike under the current law, and as seen in *Owens v Owens*, it will not be possible for a party to allege that the fact is not true (because there will be no facts) and/or that the marriage has not irretrievably broken down. There will be no defence of grave hardship as there is now for five-year separation petitions, although the respondent will be

[272] F Gibb, 'Ministers Are Ready to Support Reform of Archaic Divorce Laws' (*The Times*, 28 July 2018).
[273] S Moore, The Courts Can't Make Tini Owens Love Her Husband (*The Guardian*, 25 July 2018).
[274] K Daly, The Unhappy Marriage of Tini Owens Shows Why We Need to Reform Outdated Divorce Laws (*New Statesman*, 25 July 2018).

able to apply for the court to consider their financial position after divorce in exactly the way that this operates now (see 3.3.6.2 of this chapter). Apart from this, which is more of a temporary delay, it will be impossible to defend a divorce other than by raising issues of fraud, lack of jurisdiction, or another procedural irregularity. It is therefore a system of unilateral divorce on demand.

Under the current law, it is not possible for the parties to file jointly (the nearest equivalent is cross-applications where they each file separate petitions against the other). Under the new Act the parties could choose to file a joint application if their divorce was something they both wanted. If one party later changed their mind, the application by the other spouse will still proceed.

The Act creates a 20-week period between the filing of the statement with the court (*not* service on the other party) and the conditional order (formerly known as the decree nisi) (s1(5)). In addition, the six-week period between nisi stage and decree absolute (now known as the 'final order') will be retained (s1(4) for marriages, s4 for civil partnerships), giving an overall waiting period of 26 weeks, which is six months. As is the case now, the court can reduce this period in any particular case—this sometimes happens where one of the parties is terminally ill. However, it will remain impossible for a party to file for divorce or dissolution within the first year of the marriage or civil partnership (Sch 1 para 3).

SCENARIO 1

Illustration 6

Let us now consider what would happened if the Newtons had divorced under the 2020 Act. If they both agreed that the marriage was over, they could file their application and statement of marital breakdown jointly. Alternatively, either one of them could have filed the application. They would then wait 20 weeks, confirm they still wanted a divorce, and then receive the conditional order, wait a further six weeks, and then obtain the final order.

Would this process have felt differently to them than a divorce under the current law? Would the fact that Clare had no mechanism to raise Robert's adultery or name Suky mean that the law did not vindicate her, or provide her with an outlet for her hurt? Or would her hurt be less if Robert petitioned on a no-fault basis rather than saying that Clare has behaved unreasonably, when he has committed adultery? How about the interests of society? Have they been lost, or has society altered its views on the purpose of divorce laws?

In addition to these provisions, there are a number of consequential amendments which simply replace the words 'decree nisi' and 'decree absolute' with the words 'conditional order' and 'final order' in the Matrimonial Causes Act, the Civil Partnership Act and various other pieces of legislation. This process is outlined in Figure 3.2.

3.5.2 Reform of judicial separation

Under the current law, a party wishing to obtain a judicial separation needs to prove that one of the five facts exists, but not that the marriage has irretrievably broken down (s17 Matrimonial Causes Act 1973; see 3.3.8 of this chapter). The 2020 Act amends this

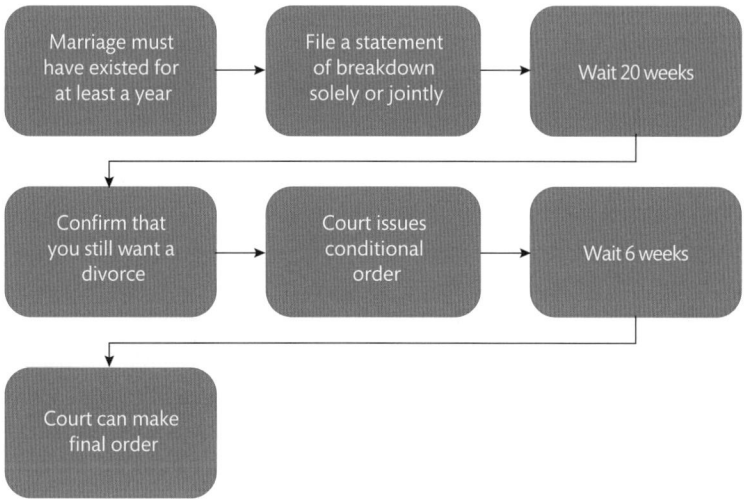

FIGURE 3.2 Process for a divorce or dissolution under the 2020 Act

requirement so that a person who wishes to be judicially separated will simply make a statement that they want a judicial separation (s5). As with divorce, it will be possible for one of the parties to file or for the parties to file a joint application.

3.5.3 The passage of the Act

Despite the *Finding Fault* research and *Owens*, it is nevertheless surprising that the government proposed a wholly no-fault system, given the experience of the Family Law Act 1996. It could have chosen from a number of alternatives, such as reducing the five-year unilateral divorce period to encourage no-fault divorces while retaining the option of fault. Perhaps Parliament had learned its lesson about attempting to influence divorcing behaviour, for the Act retained its coherence and integrity during its passage through Parliament and was passed by a large majority in both Houses (231 for, 16 against in the Commons). Such opposition as there was focused on some of the familiar arguments that we addressed in section 3.4.3 of this chapter. Fiona Bruce MP, for example, said that:

> The removal of fault sends out the signal that marriage can be unilaterally exited with no available recourse for the party who has been left . . . Making divorce easier and quicker will inevitably change the nature of the commitment that is made when marrying, because those doing so will recognise that it is something that can be exited easily and quickly, without having to prove that the relationship has broken down. Commitment within marriage will become unreliable. People will marry less due to the low expectation of permanence in marriage, and they will cohabit more as the distinction between the two is eroded and what marriage really means becomes confused. No longer 'till death us do part', but 'until I give you six months' notice to quit,' with no reason given.[275]

---

[275] HC Deb, 17 June 2020, c849. You can read this speech in full at https://www.theyworkforyou.com/debates/?id=2020-06-17e.849.0 as well as in *Hansard*, accessed 15 October 2020.

There were a number of amendments proposed by a small number of legislators. Although they were voted down, they give a flavour of the nature of opposition to no-fault divorce and the six-month timetable. The proposed amendments included:

- increasing the six-month period to one year;
- providing additional funding for marriage counselling;
- prohibiting either party from making a financial remedy claim within the first twenty weeks of the divorce process, i.e., until conditional order stage, which would have been harmful to the financially weaker party or victims of financial abuse; and
- providing parties with information about marriage counselling.

Professor Liz Trinder and colleagues, whose *Finding Fault* research has been utilised by the government to support their case for reform, also responded to the each of the proposed amendments by explaining why they were inadvisable and reiterating that some similar measures in the Family Law Act 1996, such as the emphasis on marriage counselling, been deeply unsuccessful.[276]

3.6 International divorces

In order for a divorce to proceed, the court must have jurisdiction—the legal power or authority to hear the case. While this is not an issue for people who have lived in England or Wales for a long time, it can be problematic in cases where one or both parties lives or has lived overseas. Similar issues apply when a person obtains a divorce in another jurisdiction, as specific rules apply to whether that divorce will be recognised in this jurisdiction.

3.6.1 Jurisdiction to grant divorce

Section 5 of the Domicile and Matrimonial Proceedings Act 1973 (as amended) gives the courts of England and Wales jurisdiction to hear divorce cases where one or more of the following is true:

- The parties are both habitually resident in England and Wales. This is the most commonly used ground. There is a significant jurisprudence on what is meant by habitual residence. For the purposes of divorce, the Court of Appeal in *Tan v Choy* held that a person is habitually resident somewhere if there is 'permanence or stability' to their living there and that place must be 'the centre of the person's interests'.[277] One can only have one habitual residence at a time.[278] Whether or not someone is habitually resident in a place is a question of fact.

---

[276] You can find these at https://www.nuffieldfoundation.org/project/finding-fault-divorce-law-in-practice-in-england-and-wales accessed 15 October 2020.
[277] [2014] EWCA Civ 251 [31].
[278] *Marinos v Marinos* [2007] EWHC 2047 (Fam).

- The petitioner and respondent were last habitually resident in England and Wales and one of them still resides there. 'What are required are two things: (i) habitual residence on a particular day and (ii) residence, though not necessarily habitual residence, during the relevant immediately preceding period.'[279]

- The respondent is habitually resident in England and Wales.

- The petitioner is habitually resident in England and Wales and has resided there for at least a year immediately prior to the presentation of the petition. This is to prevent the petitioner from moving to England or Wales in order to immediately file proceedings here.

- The petitioner is both domiciled and habitually resident in England and Wales and has resided there for at least six months immediately prior to the petition. Domicile involves a higher degree of permanence than habitual residence, in that most people retain their domicile of origin—the country in which they were born.

- The petitioner and respondent are both domiciled in England and Wales or one of them is.

For same-sex couples, jurisdiction is set out in the Marriage (Same Sex Couples) (Jurisdiction and Recognition of Judgments) Regulations 2014 and the Domicile and Matrimonial Proceedings Act 1973. For civil partners, whether same or different-sex, the jurisdiction is in the Civil Partnership (Jurisdiction and Recognition of Judgments) Regulations 2005. The grounds contained in these Regulations mirror above, save that there is no sole domicile ground.

Where none of the above applies, the court may still have jurisdiction:

- In the case of civil partners, because they entered into the civil partnership in England and Wales.

- In the case of a same-sex married couple, because they married each other under the law of England and Wales and it would be in the interests of justice for the court to assume jurisdiction in their case.

FOCUS Know-How

Forum shopping

Where the parties have close connections to more than one country, they may have the ability to pursue a divorce in one of several different jurisdictions. This is increasingly common, as people move internationally more than ever before. Yet the law on divorce differs considerably across

---

[279] See *Marinos v Marinos* [2007] EWHC 2047 (Fam). Note, however, that there are conflicting, albeit obiter comments in another High Court decision, *Munro v Munro* [2007] EWHC 3315 (Fam). The wording on the petition has been criticised as being 'made without reference to settled law': M Allum and D Hodson with S Clark, 'Imminent Changes to Divorce/Dissolution Petitions and to the Family Procedure Rules', *Lexis Nexis Jordans Family Law*, 19 July 2017. The *Marinos'* interpretation was preferred in *V v V* [2011] EWHC 1190 (Fam); see J Viney, 'Habitual Residence – Habitual Problems' (*Family Law Week* 2014). Available at http://www.familylawweek.co.uk/site.aspx?i=ed128552 accessed 15 October 2020.

different countries, from unilateral divorce on demand, to fault-based divorce, to divorce after a period of separation, or a combination of these. Moreover, the financial consequences of the divorce, or the way in which child disputes are addressed, may be significantly different in one country compared to another. Consequently, it is common for wealthy parties to go 'forum shopping': they look at which countries have jurisdiction to hear their case and file in the jurisdiction that is most favourable to them. London has been called the divorce capital of the world because our financial provision laws are, compared to many jurisdictions, very generous to the economically weaker party in a couple/a homemaker/primary carer and we therefore attract a lot of petitions filed by women. The parties may find themselves in a 'petition race' to file in their different preferred jurisdictions first. Rather than do what solicitors should do in an ideal world, which is try to negotiate the contents of the petition before it is filed, it may be necessary to file first and negotiate amendments later.

Where the other potential jurisdiction is outside the EU, the court will look at which of the two jurisdictions is the best placed to hear the case and which is the more inconvenient—the principle of *forum non conveniens*.

Within the EU, the European Court of Justice has held that the petitioner can choose the jurisdiction he or she prefers.[280] Where there are rival petitions, Art 19 of the Brussels II Revised Regulation requires the later of them to be stayed (put on hold) 'until such time as the jurisdiction of the court first seised is established', i.e., the first court accepts or declines jurisdiction. This is the principle of *lis pendens*. Now that the UK is not part of the EU, this does not apply, but its effect is shown by our next case, which was decided when the UK was within the Union and the Regulation therefore applied.

In *Villiers v Villiers*,[281] Mrs Villiers, who was living in England, made a claim for spousal maintenance in England under s27 Matrimonial Causes Act 1973, following divorce proceedings in Scotland.[282] Mr Villiers argued that this was forum shopping, designed to avoid the much more restrictive rules around spousal maintenance under Scottish law. He was doubtless right in this—but the EU Maintenance Regulation[283] permitted her to apply in the EU jurisdiction she preferred. The Supreme Court held that s27 was freestanding: it was a separate cause of action to the divorce proceedings, so that *lis pendens* did not apply. The fact that the Scottish courts might have been better placed to hear the application was irrelevant, as the principle of *forum non conveniens* was disapplied by the Maintenance Regulation. The Regulation was specifically designed to give applicants 'an unfettered choice' of jurisdiction, including the freedom to choose the jurisdiction that would be best for them.[284] The outcome of this case, however, is—per Lord Wilson's dissent—that a spouse will have 'untrammelled licence' to go forum shopping in a similar situation within the EU.[285]

Mutual recognition across jurisdictions

Where someone has been divorced abroad, they may need to know whether or not the law of England and Wales will recognise that divorce, for example so they can remarry, or make

---

[280] Case C-168/08 *Laszlo Hadadi v Csilla Marta Mesko* [2009] ECR I-06871.
[281] [2020] UKSC 30.
[282] Scotland has its own divorce and financial remedy laws. For the purposes of the maintenance Regulation, Scotland is considered a different jurisdiction even though the UK as a whole is one state for the purposes of EU membership.
[283] The full name of the Maintenance Regulation is Council Regulation (EC) No 4/2009 on jurisdiction, applicable law, recognition and enforcement of decisions and cooperation in matters relating to maintenance obligations.
[284] Para [41] (Lord Sales).
[285] Para [180]. We wrote about *Villiers* for two blog posts for the Transparency Project, which explain this complex case simply: 'State of the Union: Scotland, England, and the Villiers Divorce Case' (16 December 2019) and 'A Triad of Judgments from the Supreme Court' (1 July 2020), both available at http://www.transparencyproject.org.uk/?s=villiers accessed 16 October 2020.

a financial claim under the Matrimonial and Family Proceedings Act 1984 (see Chapter 4). Conversely, where someone has divorced in England and Wales, they may want that divorce to be recognised in another country.

A divorce which takes place in one member state of the EU will be recognised in another EU member state under the provisions of the Brussels II Revised Regulation, sometimes called Brussels II *bis*.[286] Courts have a discretion not to recognise other countries' divorces if manifestly contrary to public policy, or if insufficient or no notice of the divorce was given to the respondent spouse, or if recognition would be irreconcilable with an earlier judgment.[287]

The Jurisdiction and Judgments (Family) (Amendment etc) (EU Exit) Regulations 2019 and the Civil Partnership and Marriage (Same Sex Couples) (Jurisdiction and Judgments) (Amendment etc.) (EU Exit) Regulations 2019 withdrew England and Wales from Brussels II, except for cases which were ongoing on withdrawal day.[288] In the case of petitions, this means that the petition will need to have been initiated[289] on or before 31 December 2020 to be automatically recognised in EU countries, even if the actual decrees are after this date. If a petition was initiated in 2020 in England/Wales and then in 2021 in an EU country (or vice versa), the later petition must be stayed, just as it would be now.

Now that the UK has left the EU and the mutual recognitions provisions in Brussels II do not apply, courts in the UK will treat EU divorces in the same way as third-party countries' divorces were already treated. This means that recognition in this country of a divorce started overseas depends on a number of factors set out in the Family Law Act 1986, which implemented the Hague Divorce Recognition Convention of 1970. The Act states that an overseas divorce that has been obtained through 'judicial or other proceedings' will be recognised if (a) it is effective under the law of the country in which it was obtained, and (b) at the date when those proceedings were begun, either party was either habitually resident or domiciled in that country or was a national of that country. Judicial or other proceedings means either a court or a formal body authorised by the state to dissolve marriages. If, however, the divorce was not obtained in proceedings—a Talaq divorce, for example—then it will only be recognised in England if (a) it is effective under the law of the country in which it was obtained, and (b) at the date when those proceedings were begun, either both parties were domiciled in that country or one was domiciled in that country and the other was domiciled in a country that recognised that divorce, and (c) neither party had been habitually resident in the UK throughout the period of one year

---

[286] Regulation 2201/2003 concerning jurisdiction and the recognition and enforcement of judgments in matrimonial matters and the matters of parental responsibility.

[287] Brussels II Revised.

[288] See House of Commons Library, *Getting Divorced If There Is No Deal Brexit* (Briefing paper 08671, 9 October 2019).

[289] David Hodson discusses the uncertainty about the definition of initiation and whether the petition would need to be lodged or issued to satisfy this requirement in 'Family Law Leaves the EU: Still Relying on EU Laws after All Those Years' at https://www.iflg.uk.com/blog/family-law-leaves-eu-still-relying-eu-laws-after-all-those-years accessed 11 October 2020.

immediately preceding that date. The courts have a discretion not to recognise the divorce is if manifestly contrary to public policy, there has been a breach of natural justice, if recognition would be contrary to public policy in England and Wales, or if recognition would be irreconcilable with an earlier judgment. Whether a divorce that took place in England or Wales will be recognised in another country depends on that country's own laws and whether they are party to the Hague Divorce Recognition Convention.

3.7 Conclusion

In this chapter, we have traced the development of the law, from the era before divorce through to the first Parliamentary divorces and the development of a secular, judicial system. We have seen that each time the law has been reformed since the first secular divorces, the number of divorces has risen; but we have also seen that this is not necessarily because liberal divorce laws cause relationship breakdown. At the time of writing, the Divorce, Dissolution, and Separation Act 2020 has been passed, but is not yet in force. We can expect its introduction to be accompanied by a temporary increase in the number of divorces. What we do not yet know is whether the Act will successfully alleviate the problems of the current law.

Consider these competing aims: Divorce should be relatively painless, enabling people to come out if it with a decent relationship with their former spouse and a clear vision of their future life, but if we make it too hard it is bad for the children. Divorce should be hard so that people have the security of marriage to behave in marriage in a certain way, such as giving up work to have children, but it should not be so easy that people divorce on a whim and incur the social and economic disadvantages of divorce. Divorce should be easy so that people do not have to stay in harmful marriages, but not so difficult that people choose to live apart without divorce. Divorce should be quick, so that the legal system does not prolong hurt, but it should give not be so quick that there is insufficient time for reflection and consideration. Divorce laws should encourage reconciliation but should also treat participants as adults who know what they want, and not tie together those who should, in the interests of themselves and their children, be safely apart. Divorces happen inevitably and therefore should be as dignified as possible, but divorces should also emphasise morality and provide justice and vindication. Reconciling these aims is impossible; the problem is that it has not stopped people from trying.

 KEY POINTS

- The only ground of divorce in England and Wales is that the marriage has irretrievably broken down, which is evidenced by one or more of five facts: adultery by the other party; behaviour by the other party; desertion by the other party for two years; two years' separation with mutual consent; or five years' separation. In the case of civil partners, there are four facts, adultery being omitted.

- Adultery, behaviour, and desertion are commonly known as fault-based facts, even though behaviour may be out of the control of the respondent (such as that caused by a mental illness). Absent fault, the petitioner can seek a divorce on the basis that the parties have been separated for at least two years, provided that the respondent consents to a divorce. Without the respondent's consent, the petitioner would need to wait five years.

- There are several reasons why most petitions are not defended, including the cost and distress of defending divorce proceedings.

- There have been many and serious criticisms of the present divorce law, including lack of scrutiny and logic; encouragement of acrimony, falsification, and exaggeration; and its failure to do anything to save the marriage. Alternatives to the present system include pure no-fault divorce, whether unilateral or by mutual consent, or a return to a pure fault-based process. In 2017, the combined effect of the Supreme Court decision in Key Case *Owens v Owens* and the Finding Fault research turned public and legislative attention to the reform of divorce law.

- The Divorce, Dissolution and Separation Act 2020, which is due to enter into force in autumn 2021, introduces a purely no-fault system in which one or both parties to a marriage or a civil partnership files a statement of marital breakdown and after six months is entitled to a divorce.

 # FURTHER READING: SOME STARTING POINTS

- For the history of divorce law, see Stephen Cretney's *Family Law in the Twentieth Century* (Oxford University Press 2003), Lawrence Stone's *Road to Divorce: England 1530–1987* (Oxford University Press 1990), Roderick Phillips, *Putting Asunder: A History of Divorce in Western Society* (Cambridge University Press 1988), and Colin Gibson, *Dissolving Wedlock* (Routledge 1994). Although not an 'academic' tome, Rebecca Probert's *Divorced, Bigamist, Bereaved?* (Takeaway Books 2015) is a good guide to how divorce laws have changed over time, from an acknowledged expert.

- The various reports that have reformed family law in the twentieth and twenty-first centuries are *Putting Asunder: A Divorce Law for Contemporary Society: Report of a Group appointed by the Archbishop of Canterbury in January 1964* (SPCK 1966) and the Law Commission report that follows it, *Reform of the Grounds of Divorce: The Field of Choice* (Cmnd 3123, 1966); and *Family Law: The Ground for Divorce* (Law Com No 192, 1990). For essential reading on problems with the current law, see Trinder et al., *Finding Fault? Divorce Law and Practice in England and Wales* (Nuffield Foundation 2017). This has a number of related documents including responses to the various amendments as the Divorce, Dissolution and Separation Bill progressed through Parliament: see https://www.nuffieldfoundation.org/project/finding-fault-divorce-law-in-practice-in-england-and-wales.

- For other critiques of the existing law, and arguments about the fault and no-fault processes, see Andrew Bainham, 'Men and Women Behaving Badly: Is Fault Dead in English Family Law?' (2001) 21(2) *Oxford Journal of Legal Studies* 219; Ruth Deech, 'Divorce – A Disaster' [2009] *Family Law* 1048; John Eekelaar, *Regulating Divorce* (Oxford University Press 1991) and Ira Mark Ellman, 'The Misguided Movement to Revive Fault Divorce, and Why Reformers Should Look Instead to the American Law Institute' (1997) 11 *International Journal of Law, Policy and the Family* 216.

- For the economic/opportunist arguments, see Margaret F Brinig and FH Buckley, 'No-Fault Law and At-Fault People' (1998) 18 *International Review of Law and Economics* 325; Margaret F Brinig and Steven M Crafton, 'Marriage and Opportunism' (1994) 23 *Journal of Legal Studies* 869; Lloyd Cohen, 'Marriage, Divorce, and Quasi Rents' (1987) 16 *Journal of Legal Studies* 267; and Robert Rowthorn, 'Marriage and Trust: Some Lessons from Economics' (1999) 23 *Cambridge Journal of Economics* 661.

- There are a number of precedent-setting cases discussed in this chapter, especially in relation to the behaviour ground, but the most important case, which includes a detailed discussion of the previous case law, is *Owens v Owens*. We recommend you read Court of Appeal report at [2017] EWCA Civ 182 as well as the Supreme Court at [2018] UKSC 41; the former is particularly illuminating. We have written about the Supreme Court stage at P Morgan, 'The Public Tragedy of the Owens' Divorce' (2019) 41(1) *Journal of Social Welfare and Family Law* 100.

- Statistics on divorce are available from both the Ministry of Justice and the Office of National Statistics. Look at the latter's annual statistical bulletins *Divorce in England and Wales*. The Ministry of Justice publishes *Family Court Statistics Quarterly, England and Wales*, and the underlying datasets which provide much more detail, at https://www.gov.uk/government/collections/family-court-statistics-quarterly.

 Visit the **online resources** to watch a video of Polly Morgan discussing this chapter topic, and to check your understanding of this chapter with self-test questions and scenario questions.

4 Financial Provision on Divorce

LEARNING CHECKLIST

By the end of this chapter, you should be able to:

- *Identify* how financial settlements are reached and the courts' powers in relation to financial provision on divorce
- *Identify* the statutory factors relevant to a settlement, *describe* what each means, and *apply* these to fictional scenarios
- *Explain* the principles of needs, compensation, and sharing, and *explain* how they relate to the s25 factors
- *Critically evaluate* the principles of needs, compensation, and sharing using others' arguments to support your own
- *Identify* how the state regulates financial provision on divorce, and *critically discuss* why the parties do not have absolute freedom of contract and whether they should
- *Apply* the principles set out in *Radmacher v Granatino* to a fictional scenario involving a nuptial agreement
- *Critically evaluate* the respective benefits and disadvantages of a more certain, less discretionary system.

SCENARIO 1

Dora and Brian

Dora (75) and Brian (73) have been married for 54 years and are now retired, Brian from being a bus driver and Dora from raising their three (now middle-aged) children. Divorcing at their age is not unusual: so-called 'silver divorces' are on the rise in England and Wales. Their assets are a house worth £450,000 with no mortgage, a car worth £5,000, savings £29,000 and antiques worth £18,000. Dora receives a state pension. Brian receives a state pension and an occupational pension.

SCENARIO 2

Jan and Ahmed

Jan (25) and Ahmed (23) are a young couple who have been married for three years and have two young children (3 and 5). They have a house worth £180,000 with a mortgage of £91,000. That gives net equity of £89,000. The house was bought with the assistance of Ahmed's parents, who contributed £50,000 to the purchase price.

Ahmed works as a teacher earning £26,000 per year. After tax and national insurance, this gives him £1,768 per month. He does not currently contribute to a pension because he cannot afford it. Given the age of their youngest child, Jan does not currently work outside the home. They receive child benefit of £148.95 per month and universal credit of £210.73 per month.

They have savings of £300. They have a joint credit card that Jan uses for food shopping, and that has a balance of £2,000 to be repaid.

SCENARIO 3

Mary and Steve

Mary (aged 55) and Steve (aged 62) have reluctantly decided that their 15-year marriage is at an end and have each instructed solicitors. Their assets are in the region of £20 million.

Steve is a retired member of a once-popular rock band, which had a number of hits in the 1980s. He is currently interested in environmental issues and has started a small organic gardening business. Mary is a PR manager for a music company. They have one child, Betty, aged 12, who is in private school. Steve lives on the income from his £10 million investments and royalties from his albums, which together give him about £400,000 per year after tax. Mary earns £80,000 after tax and national insurance. They both contribute to their living expenses and the school fees come from a joint account.

They have two houses, the former matrimonial home, which is valued at £5 million and is in Steve's sole name, and a holiday home valued at £350,000 after capital gains tax. Both were bought by Steve from his savings. They have a valuable art collection worth in excess of £4 million, cash savings of £400,000 and some high-performance cars. They have no pensions other than state pensions.

4.1 Introduction

When a marriage or civil partnership comes to an end, the parties will need to consider what financial consequences their divorce, dissolution, or judicial separation will bring.[1] The parties will need to think about where to live and what money to live on in the future. They will need to value their present assets and think about how to divide them. If they can agree this themselves then they can ask the court to turn their agreement into an order. Sometimes the parties cannot agree what to do, and turn to the court for a judicial decision. While the parties may think that their financial situation is a private matter between them, even if they agree what should happen the court must approve their proposals as fair in order for them to be enforceable. It is therefore important for the parties to understand the principles that the courts apply, and the practical implications. This includes the fact that in England and Wales the courts have very wide powers to redistribute assets, including income, between the parties irrespective of which party is the legal owner. As Lord Denning said:

> The family court takes the rights and obligations of the parties all together and puts the pieces into a mixed bag. Such pieces are the right to occupy the matrimonial home or have

---

[1] This chapter is adapted from one we wrote for *Family Law* (1st edn, OUP 2018) edited by Ruth Lamont. We are very grateful for Dr Lamont's kind agreement to our adopting that as the basis for this chapter.

a share in it, the obligation to maintain the wife and children, and so forth. The court then takes out the pieces and hands them to the two parties – some to one party and some to the other – so that each can provide for the future with the pieces allotted to him or to her. The court hands them out without paying any too nice a regard to their legal or equitable rights but simply according to what is the fairest provision for the future.[2]

In deciding how to exercise its powers, the courts will apply broad principles, derived mostly from case law, which tell us what fairness can look like and what rights and responsibilities should stem from married life. Yet fairness is a subjective concept, and it will become evident that both Parliament and the judiciary have struggled to provide a coherent set of legal principles that can be applied to the wide range of family situations that come before the courts. For example, should obligations to financially support your spouse continue post-divorce? How should the law recognise the value of child-raising compared to earning money? To what extent should a couple be able to reach their own agreement even if it leaves one party on benefits and the other comfortably off? These are all aspects of one issue: what exactly does fairness look like?

This chapter looks at the courts' powers, the legal principles, the practical implications, and the problems that may arise in financial remedy practice. To illustrate these, we will consider a number of different scenarios involving couples of varying ages, with different degrees of wealth, and with and without children, and with various other considerations such as the nature and source of the assets thrown into the mix. This will enable us to see how these principles are applied to try to give a fair outcome despite the unique situation of each family.

It is worth acknowledging that although we will use the terminology 'husband' and 'wife', the same law—the Matrimonial Causes Act 1973 and all its case law—applies (with a few exceptions) to same-sex married couples and unless otherwise stated, all statutory references are to the Matrimonial Causes Act 1973, in its most current amended form. For civil partners, the law is set out in the Civil Partnership Act 2004, which mirrors the financial provisions of the Matrimonial Causes Act 1973. Accordingly, the case law principles from marriage are equally applicable to civil partnerships.[3] However, the law described in this chapter applies only to couples who have been married or civilly partnered to one another. As discussed in Chapter 5, there are no equivalent protections in England and Wales (our jurisdiction) for unmarried couples. (You can find a comparison between married and unmarried couples at the end of a relationship in Table 5.1 in Chapter 5).

4.2 **Key financial issues to be resolved on divorce**

Each of the couples in our scenarios need somewhere to live post-divorce and sufficient money to live on. The level of their assets will obviously affect their standard of living post-divorce, but there are other relevant considerations that we will discuss as the chapter progresses, such as what they need based on their personal circumstances and the importance of the general principle of sharing the matrimonial assets. There are also practical issues relating to house price costs, childcare costs, health, mortgage borrowing capacity,

---

[2] *Hanlon v The Law Society* [1980] 1 All ER 763 (CA), 770 [g]–[h].
[3] *Lawrence v Gallagher* [2012] EWCA Civ 394.

etc., all of which need to be resolved. The principles and processes that apply are the same for each of these couples, but the effect on them will be very different.

For now, let us start by considering when and how they may reach a financial settlement linked to their divorce.

4.2.1 When do they start resolving financial matters?

The parties usually seek to agree how to divide their property while the divorce itself is happening in the background. The first step, for both parties, is to gather together information about their financial position. While the divorce process itself is usually straightforward, exchanging financial information, obtaining any necessary valuations, and negotiating a settlement all take place in parallel with the divorce process and can take more time and be more costly. Indeed, most of the work of divorce lawyers is on financial settlements rather than the divorces themselves. Although the average financial remedy case takes 25 weeks, some will take considerably longer and this is often why couples complain that their divorces take years.[4]

While this is going on, the parties will in parallel be going through the different steps of the divorce process: it does not matter which gets ahead except (a) the court has no jurisdiction to deal with financial matters prior to issue of divorce proceedings; (b) the court cannot make a financial remedy order until decree nisi although the parties may reach agreement before then; and (c) a financial remedy order (as opposed to an interim order) will not take effect until decree absolute.

It is common to pause the divorce at decree nisi stage until such time as agreement is reached. This is because if a party was to die this would enable the surviving spouse to obtain the widow/widower's benefit under the deceased's pension, something lost on decree absolute. Once the financial remedy order is made, decree absolute is then obtained, and as we describe in 4.10, the parties then comply with the terms of the order.

4.2.2 How do the parties resolve financial matters?

Hitchings, Miles, and Woodward found that the most common way in which parties reach agreement is through negotiation by their solicitors, usually through an exchange of written offers and counter-offers of settlement.[5] However, they may alternatively reach agreement through discussions between themselves, mediation, or other forms of non-court dispute resolution.

Most lawyers will attempt to negotiate a settlement without issuing court proceedings. If the parties do reach agreement—about 72 per cent do—they can write to the court asking the court to turn that agreement into a *consent order*.[6] They will supply the court with a summary of their respective financial positions as well as key facts about themselves such as their ages, the length of the marriage, and whether there are any children. This will

---

[4] Ministry of Justice, *Family Court Statistics Quarterly England and Wales January—March 2020.* Some will take less time and some more. This information is in the underlying dataset.
[5] E Hitchings, J Miles, and H Woodward, 'Assembling the Jigsaw Puzzle: Understanding Financial Settlement on Divorce' [2014] *Family Law* 209, 310.
[6] Ministry of Justice, *Family Court Statistics Quarterly England and Wales January—March 2020.*

enable a judge to determine whether the proposal is *objectively fair* to each party. The court will only make an order in terms that are objectively fair, and in determining whether the proposal is objectively fair the fact that the parties presumably think it fair is not determinative, although it is influential. As we shall see in section 4.8 on nuptial agreements, the parties to a marriage do not have absolute freedom of contract.[7]

If the parties are unable to reach agreement, then one of them can make an application to court to start the financial remedy process, meaning that the court will issues orders requiring the parties to produce financial documentation and attend hearings.[8] Divorce proceedings must have first been issued, as the financial remedy process is ancillary to the main suit of divorce (this is why you may see it referred to by its former name of 'ancillary relief'). Even where an application is made, which happens in about 28 per cent of cases, settlement during the process is still common. Only 10 per cent get as far as a final hearing.[9]

Research by the Competition and Markets Authority and the Legal Services Board has shown that the average cost of a divorce where there is some dispute over the assets is somewhere between £2,000 and £4,000 with regional variations. These figures must be taken with a pinch of salt, because cases vary significantly in complexity, the parties' attitudes are to some extent reflected in their costs, and it appears—although is rather unclear—that these figures do not include VAT, court fees, or other disbursements. The research found a relationship between higher service quality and higher prices.[10]

We know from research that in determining whether to settle a case and on what terms, or whether to proceed to a final hearing, the parties are influenced by a number of factors, both legal and non-legal. Robert Mnookin and Lewis Kornhouser have argued that people 'do not bargain over the division of family wealth . . . in a vacuum; they bargain in the shadow of the law'.[11] When parties negotiate, they will weigh up their prospects doing better at court than through negotiation outside court, and the costs (financial, temporal, and emotional) of going to court. At the same time, each will need to consider matters from the other's perspective: what is his or her attitude to risk and prospects of success, and how much cost can they bear? Hitchings et al. have that the parties' emotional readiness to reach a settlement is also important.[12] Even if both want the divorce (which is not always the case) they may be at very different stages in their acceptance of the process. If they have begun to adjust to the divorce, it may be on the basis of an anticipated future

---

[7] For what happens if a party changes their mind after reaching an agreement but before the order is made, see section 4.8 on nuptial agreements.

[8] Other reasons for making an application are where the other party is reluctant to disclose financial information or set out their position, or where the prospects of agreement are slim because one party is being unreasonable. Sometimes it is necessary to make an application without prior attempts at out-of-court settlement, such as when one party suspects the other of hiding or dissipating assets, or there is a risk of one party becoming bankrupt.

[9] Ministry of Justice, *Family Court Statistics Quarterly England and Wales January—March 2020*. This 10 per cent statistic has stayed the same for several years.

[10] Competition and Markets Authority and the Legal Services Board, *Prices of Individual Consumer Legal Services in England and Wales 2020* (2020).

[11] RN Mnookin and L Kornhauser, 'Bargaining in the Shadow of the Law: The Case of Divorce' (1979) 88 *Yale Law Journal* 950. For a discussion of law's shadows in financial remedy cases, see E Hitchings 'Official, operative and Outsider Justice: The Ties That (May Not) Bind in Family Financial Disputes' (2017) 29(4) *Child and Family Law Quarterly* 359.

[12] E Hitchings, J Miles, and H Woodward, 'Assembling the Jigsaw Puzzle: Understanding Financial Settlement on Divorce' [2014] *Family Law* 209, 313.

lifestyle which is simply unrealistic. For example, they may believe that there is always a 50–50 split, or, as Dowding suggests, that a party who leaves forfeits the assets not taken with them.[13] They may expect the same outcome as their friend had and resist advice to the contrary. They may believe that the law has not recognised the harm being done to them by an unwanted marital breakdown, and seek to use the legal process to vindicate their position. There may be significant issues of trust, including about financial disclosure.[14] Some parties may refuse to engage with the process: perhaps they do not like the advice they are receiving or have had no advice, or mistakenly believe that nothing can happen without their consent. All of these issues can inhibit settlement.

4.2.3 What is a fair outcome?

Later in this chapter, we are going to look at the key cases that help us to determine what is fair. However, it is crucially important to remember that there is never only one fair outcome. Instead, there is a range of objectively fair settlements, and in order for the court to approve the settlement it must fall into this range, as shown in Figure 4.1. That means that a settlement may still be adjudged fair even if a party could have negotiated to get more, or would perhaps have been awarded more had they had a better lawyer (or any lawyer) or framed an argument in a more persuasive way. It may be fair even if the parties themselves both think—for different reasons—that the outcome is deeply unfair.

Given the number of considerations, approaches, principles, and practicalities, the high level of discretion that the courts have, and the different views the parties may have on the desirability of certain outcomes, any attempt to find the single fair outcome is doomed to failure: such a thing does not exist.

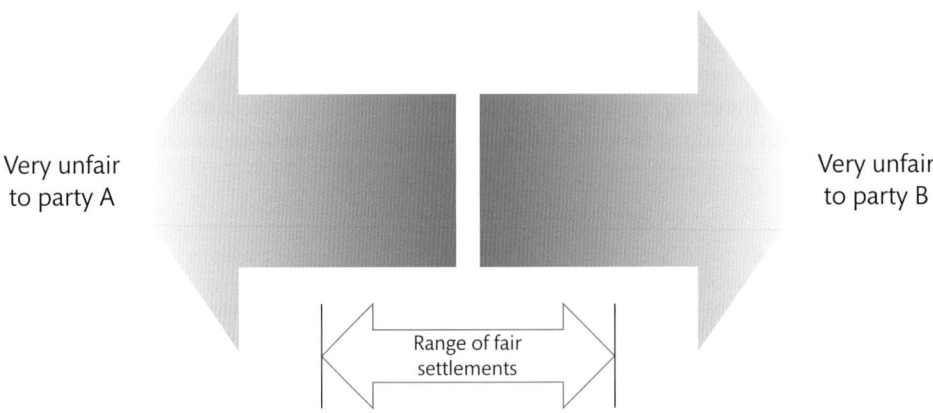

Very unfair
to party A

Very unfair
to party B

Range of fair
settlements

FIGURE 4.1 A range of fair settlements

---

[13] See S Dowding, 'Self-Determination of Judicial Imposition? Translating the Theory into Practice', in J Miles and R Probert (eds), *Sharing Lives, Dividing Assets* (Hart 2009).
[14] E Hitchings, J Miles, and H Woodward, 'Assembling the Jigsaw Puzzle: Understanding Financial Settlement on Divorce' [2014] *Family Law* 209, 314.

4.2.4 The importance of a court order

Whether the parties reach agreement and send a draft consent order to the court, or they have to use the contested court process, the ultimate outcome should be to have a financial remedy order. The claims that each party has against the other on divorce are not terminated by decree absolute, but only by so-called 'clean break' provisions in a financial remedy order (see section 4.5.2).

If there is no order, it is quite possible to be long divorced and for a former spouse to come back years later and seek financial support—even if the parties had informally agreed at the time who was to have what asset and had put that into effect. As it is the embodiment of the arrangements in a court order which renders them enforceable, *not* the agreement between the parties itself, there is nothing to stop an application being made.[15]

While the decades-long gap in *Wyatt* may be extreme, as Barton and Bissett-Johnson point out, there have for many years been more divorces granted than financial remedy orders made, whether on a consensual or contested basis, and each of these is a potential future claim that could have a serious effect upon the financial functioning of a client's new family unit or planned retirement. A lack of knowledge of the implications, a lack of assets at the time of the divorce, and (more recently) the loss of legal aid may all have contributed to this.[16]

KEY CASE *Wyatt v Vince* [2015] UKSC 14

At the time of their divorce, the parties had two children and no money. They had lived a 'profoundly unsettled' life as new-age travellers in converted camper vans, reliant on state benefits and surviving 'hand to mouth'. This meant there were no assets to split.

Following their divorce, Mr Vince set up a green energy company, Ecotricity, as a result of which he became a multi-millionaire. He provided no regular or significant financial support to Ms Wyatt or the children until their son approached adulthood.

In 2011, nearly twenty years after decree absolute and thirty years after separation, Ms Wyatt applied for a financial remedy order. At the time, she was living on a combination of state benefits, and earnings interrupted by periods of ill-health. The Court of Appeal dismissed her claim, calling it an abuse of process.

The Supreme Court upheld her appeal, holding that 'consistently with the potentially life-long obligations which attend a marriage, there is no time-limit for seeking orders for financial provision.'[17]

It cautioned that Ms Wyatt's claim may have had little value in the circumstances, which were that the money was earned after the divorce so their matrimonial assets were few, and she had delayed substantially in making an application even after Mr Vince had become wealthy. However, this had to be balanced against the fact that she had made a significant contribution to the marriage by raising their children alone (see 4.5), and that may justify an order for a relatively modest sum.

---

[15] *de Lasala v de Lasala* [1980] AC 546.

[16] See C Barton and A Bissett-Johnson, 'The Declining Number of Ancillary Relief Financial Orders' [2000] *Family Law* 94.

[17] At [32] (Lord Wilson).

4.3 **The contested financial remedy process**

Although the assets may differ considerably, the financial remedy process itself is one-size-fits-all irrespective of whether the parties are billionaires or arguing about who should bear the burden of their debts. As shown in Figure 4.2, this involves a number of court hearings, the disclosure of financial information to the other party, and—ultimately—a judge making a decision and imposing that upon the parties.[18] The judge must reach an outcome that objectively fair and this may result in an outcome that neither party has sought.

Before this, there are two stages which are designed to encourage settlement. First, a person wishing to make an application to court must attend a mediation information and assessment meeting (MIAM) unless one of the exceptions applies.[19] There is, however, no requirement that the parties mediate if one or both does not wish to do so. Second, part of the contested process is a hearing known as a Financial Dispute Resolution Appointment which is designed to obtain a judge's 'off-the-record' advice about the parameters of a fair settlement. At this hearing, the judge will help the parties to understand if one of them is being unrealistic in what they are seeking or is unlikely to succeed with a particular argument. Hitchings' research has shown that many parties reach agreement at or just after this hearing.[20]

Occasionally a party believes that if they do not comply with the directions or do not attend court then the court will not be able to make a final order. That is not the case. The court simply will not have the benefit of the recalcitrant party's arguments and thus when the court makes an order it is likely to be at the harsher end of fairness to that party—and accompanied by an order that the recalcitrant party pay the litigation costs. Moreover, breach of a court order is a contempt of court and if the court attaches a penal notice to a directions order the outcome of a breach may well be imprisonment.

While wealthy parties may incur more costs than the average because of the valuations and specialist expertise required, the fact that the process is one-size-fits-all means that going to court involves a certain level of expense that may be disproportionate in lower asset cases. It is also unlikely that a party will be able to recoup their costs from their spouse. The usual order, whether this is by consent or following a contested hearing, is 'no order as to costs', i.e. that each party pays his or her own costs only.[21] The rationale behind this was explained by Parker H in *T v T*: it is that 'each party has an interest in determining how the matrimonial assets should be divided or allocated, and each is usually in a position to meet costs out of his/her allotted share.'[22] However, the court can make a costs order against one party 'where it considers it appropriate to do so because of the conduct of a party in relation to the proceedings'.[23] For example, if disclosure is not full and frank, a party may be at risk of costs, or, indeed, of the final order being overturned.[24]

---

[18] You can find forms A and E on the Ministry of Justice website at https://www.gov.uk/government/collections/divorce-and-civil-partnership-dissolution-forms.

[19] FPR r3.8: exceptions include evidenced domestic abuse, bankruptcy, lack of mediator availability, and urgency because of a risk of loss of evidence.

[20] E Hitchings, J Miles, and Hy Woodward, 'Assembling the Jigsaw Puzzle: Understanding Financial Settlement on Divorce' [2014] *Family Law* 209, 314.

[21] FPR 28.3(5). Cf Civil Procedure Rules. However, on an appeal a costs order where the loser pays the winner's costs is very likely.

[22] *T v T* [2013] EWHC B3 (Parker J).

[23] FPR 28.3(6).

[24] *Sharland v Sharland* [2015] UKSC 60; *Gohil v Gohil* [2015] UKSC 61.

Costs

Mediation Information and Assessment Meeting
- A MIAM (mediation information and assessment meeting) is compulsory for the person wanting to apply to court unless one of the exceptions applies. The mediator will sign a form to enable the party to proceed to court if the case is not suitable for mediaton or either party does not wish to mediate.

Application for financial remedy issued
- The application is made in Form A. The court will issue the application and make a directions order with a standard timetable. The court will list the final hearing at least 12 weeks away.

Court issues directions
- The court's directions order will require the parties to provide each other and the court with information about their financial positions in a prescribed form (Form E) along with documentary proof. Once each party has had the opportunity to consider the other party's financial information, they prepare a Questionnaire of any questions they have about the other party's financial position, a Statement of Issues that need to be resolved, a Chronology of the key dates in the marriage/assets, a schedule of the costs incurred so far, and an indication of whether they are ready to proceed straight to the FDR.

First Directions Appointment
- This is a short case management hearing where the judge and parties consider whether any further evidence is needed before the case can proceed further. For example, they may need a single joint expert valuation of an asset such as a house or company.
- If a Questionnaire has been served then replies to that will need to be timetabled. The parties will also need to prepare a Statement of Orders Sought and updated costs schedule for the next hearing.

Financial Dispute Resolution Appointment
- The FDR is a hearing aimed at encouraging settlement. The parties reveal their 'without prejudice' negotiating positions to the judge, i.e., what they would really settle for, rather than what they intend to seek if the case proceeds to a final hearing (their open position). The judge gives an indication of the parameters of a fair settlement in the circumstances of the case, which helps identify whether one or both parties is being unrealistic.
- Many cases settle at this stage, but if they do not then the case is listed for a final hearing. In very complex cases, a further interim case management hearing may be required.

Final hearing
- A full hearing at which the judge hears evidence and makes an order. The judge cannot be the same judge who conducted the FDR, and will have no access to the parties' without prejudice positions.
- Each party usually bears their own costs.
- Approximately 10% of cases reach this stage.

FIGURE 4.2 The financial remedy court process

Although lawyer-led processes still account for the vast majority of financial settlements, the loss of legal aid, and perhaps a distrust of lawyers and courts, has led to an increasing number of people acting for themselves (known as litigants-in-person or self-represented litigants). It is a complex process to navigate without legal advice—and that is before we come to the relevant legal provisions and principles.

4.4 The court's powers

Whether the judge is making the order on a joint application by parties who have reached agreement or is rendering a decision following a contested hearing, the court can only order something if it has the power to do so under Part II Matrimonial Causes Act 1973, namely:

- Order a party to pay the other a lump sum or sums.
- Order a party to make periodical payments to the other party (spousal maintenance).
- Order a party to make periodical payments for the benefit of a child (child maintenance—limited powers here because of the existence of a separate child maintenance scheme).
- Order the transfer of ownership of property, known as a 'property adjustment order'. Property in this context means any type of asset, not merely 'real property' (houses).
- Order the sale of property and decide how the proceeds should be shared out.
- Order that property be held on trust for use by the other party or a child.
- Order a pension provider to share a party's pension fund or to send a proportion of the pension income, when it is in payment, to the other party.
- Vary a prenuptial or postnuptial agreement.

We will now look at each of these in turn, starting with lump sums and periodical payments for spouses and children. The courts' powers to make these orders is found in s23 Matrimonial Causes Act 1973, and there are mirror provisions in the Civil Partnership Act 2004.

Statutory Extract *s23 Matrimonial Causes Act 1973*

Financial provision orders in connection with divorce proceedings etc.

(1) On granting a decree of divorce, a decree of nullity of marriage or a decree of judicial separation or at any time thereafter (whether, in the case of a decree of divorce or of nullity of marriage, before or after the decree is made absolute), the court may make any one or more of the following orders, that is to say:

    (a) an order that either party to the marriage shall make to the other such periodical payments, for such term, as may be specified in the order;

    (b) an order that either party to the marriage shall secure to the other to the satisfaction of the court such periodical payments, for such term, as may be so specified;

    (c) an order that either party to the marriage shall pay to the other such lump sum or sums as may be so specified; . . .

4.4.1 Lump sums

A lump sum order under s23(1)(c) requires one party to pay the other a lump sum or sums within a specified time or on the occurrence of certain events. If one party retains the former matrimonial home, for example, they may pay the other party a lump sum by way of compensation, for example. Note the phrasing of the provision: it is 'an order' for the payment of a sum or sums, and multiple separate orders cannot therefore be made. Under s31(1) the court has power to vary or discharge an order for the payment of a lump sum by instalments 'or to suspend any provision thereof temporarily', however, and could do so by stretching payment over a very long period.

4.4.2 Periodical payments

Periodical payments for spouses are commonly known as spousal maintenance, as distinct from child maintenance. Under s23(1)(a) Matrimonial Causes Act 1973, the court can order one party to make regular (usually monthly) payments to the other party post-divorce.[25] Where there is sufficient capital meet a party's housing and income needs, it may not be necessary to have periodical payments but they can be useful where one party cannot survive on their own income. The amount that may be ordered will depend on the claimant's budgetary needs and whether the amount identified 'represents a fair proportion of the respondent's available income'.[26]

One of the more controversial aspects of periodical payments is the fact that they are a potentially open-ended liability. While an order can be a specified term, this term can be extended by further order unless there is a s28(1A) provision saying that the term is non-extendable. In some cases, the order is that the maintenance will be payable for as long as both parties are alive. This is known as a joint lives order.[27] When considering whether to make a joint-lives or term order, with or without a s28(1A) bar, the Family Justice Council guidance distributed to judges recommends considering a wide range of factors about the recipient's earning capacity, childcare obligations, age, and health, as well as the payer's ability to pay.[28] 'It is almost impossible to be 'scientific'; thus there is considerable judicial discretion.'[29] It is also possible for either party to apply for the amount of the periodical payments to be varied up or down as their circumstances change.[30] The maintenance can even be set at a nominal amount, such as one pence per year, the purpose of which is simply to keep the claim for maintenance open in case the recipient needs to apply to vary it up to a 'real' amount. It must, however, end if the recipient remarries or enters into a civil partnership, and the payer may well make an application for the payments

---

[25] Orders can be made after decree nisi but will not take effect until decree absolute: Matrimonial Causes Act 1973 ss 23(1) and (5).

[26] *NS v SS (Spousal Maintenance)* [2014] EWHC 4183 (Fam) [46] (Mostyn J).

[27] Indeed, because the recipient has been maintained by the payer within the meaning of the Inheritance (Provision for Family and Dependants) Act 1975, if the payer dies while paying maintenance, the recipient has a claim against their estate.

[28] The full list is at Family Justice Council, *Guidance on 'Financial Needs' on Divorce* (Ministry of Justice 2016) para 68.

[29] *Parlour v Parlour/McFarlane v McFarlane* [2004] EWCA Civ 872 [60] (Bennett J).

[30] Section 31.

to reduce or end upon the recipient's cohabitation, although such an application may not be successful.[31] Under s23(1)(b) the order can be secured against assets of the payer (usually a house) if there is a risk of non-payment, but this is not common.

If there is enough capital to do it, the payer could give the recipient a lump sum instead of ongoing periodical payments, and this would give the parties a clean break. This is called 'capitalisation' and can happen at any stage. Where the maintenance is lifetime, the parties may refer to the *Duxbury* tables to work out how big a sum is needed.[32] These are actuarial tables that take into account average life expectancy, state pension drawdown, tax rates, interest rates, and inflation to come to a guesstimated capital sum that, if invested, could yield the income required and be entirely used up at the end of the recipient's *actuarial* life expectancy.

4.4.3 Financial support for children

Section 23 allows not only for financial provision for spouses, but also for children of the family. This includes the power to order a lump sum, periodical payments, and/or transfers of property for children. However, the Child Support Act 1991 created a scheme for the payment of child maintenance. Consequently, judges retain only limited powers to make orders under the Matrimonial Causes Act 1973, either by agreement or where the child support scheme does not apply.[33] Financial provision for children and the interrelationship of the Child Support Act scheme and the Matrimonial Causes Act are discussed in Chapter 6.

4.4.4 Property adjustment orders

> **Statutory Extract** *Section 24 Property adjustment orders in connection with divorce proceedings etc.*
>
> (1) (1) On granting a decree of divorce, a decree of nullity of marriage or a decree of judicial separation or at any time thereafter (whether, in the case of a decree of divorce or of nullity of marriage, before or after the decree is made absolute), the court may make any one or more of the following orders, that is to say:
>
>   (a) an order that a party to the marriage shall transfer to the other party, to any child of the family or to such person as may be specified in the order for the benefit of such a child such property as may be so specified, being property to which the first-mentioned party is entitled, either in possession or reversion;
>
>   (b) an order that a settlement of such property as may be so specified, being property to which a party to the marriage is so entitled, be made to the satisfaction of the court for the benefit of the other party to the marriage and of the children of the family or either or any of them;
>
>   (c) an order varying for the benefit of the parties to the marriage and of the children of the family or either or any of them any ante-nuptial or postnuptial settlement . . .

---

[31] Section 28(1).

[32] Named for *Duxbury v Duxbury* [1992] Fam 62 and located in the Family Law Bar Association's annual *At a Glance* guide. Payments are not prevented from being commuted into a lump sum by later order even though lump sums must usually be in a single order.

[33] Child Support Act 1991 s8.

Section 24A Orders for sale of property
(1) Where the court makes . . . a secured periodical payments order, an order for the payment of a lump sum or a property adjustment order, then, on making that order or at any time thereafter, the court may make a further order for the sale of such property as may be specified in the order, being property in which or in the proceeds of sale of which either or both of the parties to the marriage has or have a beneficial interest, either in possession or reversion.

A property adjustment order is an order changing the parties' interests in property of any kind (e.g. house, savings/investments, cars, furniture) whether owned in possession or reversion. It is the type of order you would use to transfer any assets between the spouses.

There are two types.

The first type is a property transfer order under s24(1)(a). This provides that a party transfer specified property into the name of the other spouse, a child of the family, or any other person specified in the order. This may be in exchange for a lump sum from the other party—e.g., 'you can have the house if you take out a bigger mortgage to give me £75,000'. Where A needed the house now and could not downsize or raise a lump sum, but it is fair for B to have some money from it in the future, transfer could be made subject to a charge, i.e., the matrimonial home is transferred to A subject to a charge in favour of B for £20,000 plus interest or—if you preferred to draft it this way—10 per cent of the equity in the house. The charge would need to be redeemed on the happening of certain trigger events.

The second type is a settlement order under s24(1)(b). This provides that property be held on trust for the parties. For example, you could settle the house on trust for the parties as equitable tenants in common in the unequal shares of (for example) 90 per cent to A and 10 per cent to B, but B cannot realise his 10 per cent until the happening of certain trigger events. It is for the parties to negotiate the triggers they want, or the court to decide them. Common triggers for both types are: the youngest child turning 18 (known as a *Mesher* order[34]); the death, remarriage or cohabitation of the occupying party (if these do not happen, the occupier potentially therefore has the use of the property for life (a *Martin* order[35])); or a combination of both, as in *Sawden v Sawden*.[36] On trigger, the house will need to be sold or A will need to find some other way of raising the money to pay B. Such orders have fallen out of favour because of concerns that at the trigger event the occupying party may still not be able to rehouse themselves. It is also unfair on the party who cannot extricate his or her money from the property for some years.

Hitchings and Miles' survey of a sample of court files has shown that Mesher and Martin orders are used very rarely. Much more commonly, the house is sold or transferred outright to one of the parties (with or without a lump sum by way of compensation).[37]

Although not a property adjustment order, under the Family Law Act 1996 the court can transfer some types of 'dwelling house' tenancies between spouses or civil partners. The Act contains a list of factors to take into account in deciding whether to do this.[38]

---

[34] Named for *Mesher v Mesher and Hall* [1980] 1 All ER 126 (heard 1973).
[35] Named for *Martin v Martin* [1978] Fam 12.
[36] [2004] EWCA Civ 339.
[37] E Hitchings and J Miles, *Financial Remedies on Divorce: The Need for Evidence-Based Reform* (Nuffield Foundation 2018).
[38] Sch 7 para 5.

4.4.5 Property sale orders

Under s24A Matrimonial Causes Act 1973, the court has the power to order the sale of property when, in the same order or a previous order, it has ordered secured periodical payments, lump sum, or property adjustment. Property sale can be a useful back-up plan: for example, default sale of the matrimonial home can be triggered when a party fails to raise the funds to 'buy out' the other's interest. Often the financial remedy order will specify that one party can have the house transferred into their sole name on condition that they pay a lump sum to the other (and if they can release them from any joint mortgage), and if that does not happen within a specified period the house is to be put on the market.

FOCUS Know-How

A quick guide to residential mortgages

Students are often confused about how mortgages work, so this is a quick basic guide. A mortgage involves the home-owner (the 'mortgagor') borrowing money from a lender (the 'mortgagee'). In exchange, the debt is secured against the house as a *legal charge*. This means that if the mortgagor fails to pay back the debt the mortgagee will seek a court order to repossess the house and sell it in order to get its money back.

Mortgagees comprises the standard high street lenders (banks and building societies), as well as a number of more specialist or second tier lenders for those with bad credit (you might have heard of 'sub-prime mortgages').

The mortgagor will repay the loan in monthly instalments. They might repay the loan and the interest (a repayment mortgage) or just the interest (an interest-only mortgage). If it is the latter, they will still have the whole initial amount (the 'principal') to pay at the end of the mortgage term.

The *mortgage term* is how long they borrow the money for. Most mortgages run until the retirement age of the borrower, although some run up to age 75. Terms of 25, 30, 35 years are common. The longer the term, the lower the monthly repayments. However, the mortgagor will be repaying more overall because the interest has more time to accumulate.

The *equity* in a property is its value after the mortgage is repaid. For example, if a house is worth £150,000 and the mortgagor borrowed £120,000 of that, the equity is £30,000. In a recession, some houses will be in *negative equity*. This is where the mortgagor owes the lender more money than the house is worth because the house has fallen in value since the mortgage was taken out.

The amount a person wants to borrow as a proportion of the total value of the house is the *loan to value ratio* (LTV). If a person wanted to buy a house for £300,000 and needed to borrow £200,000 of that, then the loan to value ratio is 60 per cent: they are borrowing 60 per cent of the value of the property. The higher the loan as a proportion of the house value, the more risk there is for the lender if house prices fall. They usually reflect this risk with higher interest rates for higher LTVs.

Remortgaging is the act of taking out a mortgage (with the existing lender or another lender) and using the money to pay off the previous mortgage. There are two reasons to do this. First, a better interest rate might be available from a different lender. Second, it enables the mortgagor to increase the amount they borrow, assuming that there is a mortgagee willing to lend more. On divorce, if one spouse wants to stay in the matrimonial home, they may need to raise a lump sum to compensate their husband or wife for that. They could do this by remortgaging for an increased amount, being the amount of the existing mortgage (to pay that off) plus the lump sum needed to pay to the other party.

If the bank will not remortgage for a higher amount, then the borrower could take out a *second mortgage* with a second lender. Their security is postponed behind the first lender, the first lender is paid off before the second lender and anything left is equity. Because it is more risky to be a second lender, interest rates are much higher.

> **Statutory Extract** *Section 24B Pension sharing orders in connection with divorce proceedings etc.*
>
> (1) On granting a decree of divorce or a decree of nullity of marriage or at any time thereafter (whether before or after the decree is made absolute), the court may, on an application made under this section, make one or more pension sharing orders in relation to the marriage.
> (4) . . . the order may require the person responsible for the pension arrangement in question, if at any time any payment in respect of any benefits under the arrangement becomes due to the party with pension rights, to make a payment for the benefit of the other party.

4.4.6 Pension orders

It is never sensible to overlook pensions on divorce, even if retirement is some time away, as this is a potentially valuable resource. The court can make two kinds of orders, a pension sharing order or an attachment order. Alternatively, it is possible to offset one party's entitlement to a pension share by giving that person more of the other assets instead.

A pension sharing order (s24B) requires the trustees of one party's pension fund to transfer a percentage of his or her pension fund to a fund in the other party's name. The two funds will thereafter operate entirely separately, so it is a type of clean break order. This means that the recipient cannot draw their new pension before their own retirement date, even if their former spouse can draw it sooner. It also means that the pension stays in existence if the former spouse dies or if the recipient remarries. A pension sharing order cannot be made if the divorce petition was issued before 1 December 2000, the date on which pension sharing came into existence,[39] nor is it possible to share a basic state pension. It is, however, possible to share pensions that are already in payment. There are pension sharing compensation orders (s24E) to share compensation received from the Pension Protection Fund in relation to an insolvent scheme.

The value that is being shared is the 'cash equivalent transfer value' at the date the pension provider implements the pension share. Accordingly, the order must be expressed as a percentage rather than a fixed sum because of the way that pension funds change in value slightly from day to day; this also means that the chosen percentage will, at the time of implementation of the share, be worth slightly more or less than anticipated by the parties.

There are two common ways to approach what proportion of the pension should be shared. These are to seek to share a percentage that will give each party the same income in retirement (although this may not be fair if needs dictate a different division), or to equalise the cash equivalent transfer value itself.[40] These are not the same thing and as the case *W v H* makes clear, there is no hard and fast rule about which is more appropriate.[41] Moreover, the parties may want to only share the proportions of their pensions that relate to the marriage when they may have had the pensions for years previously. To complicate matters further, the cash equivalent value may not be an accurate reflection of the true

---

[39] With the coming into force of the Welfare Reform and Pensions Act 1999.
[40] H Woodward, *A Guide to the Treatment of Pensions on Divorce: The Report of the Pension Advisory Group* (2019).
[41] *W v H (Divorce: Financial Remedies)* [2020] EWFC B10.

value of the pension. This is usually the case with final salary pension schemes. That means that even if each party has the same pension transfer value, the benefits they will get from each of those pensions can be dramatically different.[42] Expert advice is needed here.

It is for this reason that parties often turn to offsetting or ignore pensions altogether. Woodward found that pension orders were made in only 13.8 per cent of cases in her study of court records, and that in most cases where a pension order was made the parties were in their early 50s, in contrast to non-pension order cases where on average they were about ten years younger.[43] This difference obviously reflects proximity to retirement but suggests other reasons why the pension share may not have been made for 40-somethings: they are more likely to have dependent children meaning that the primary carer has a greater need for rehousing capital and may forsake a pension order for that capital, and the duration of the marriage may be shorter, meaning that the share may be smaller and more capable of being fairly offset.

An attachment order (ss25B(4)) directs the pension scheme trustees to give *x* per cent of each payment (or any lump sum) to the pensioner's ex-spouse from whenever the pension starts to be drawn. The beneficiary of the order will only receive payments once the pension holder draws the pension, and only for as long as the pension holder is alive and the recipient has not remarried (s28)—all things that do not affect a pension *share*. It thus leaves women, as the more likely recipients, vulnerable to the shorter life expectancy of their former husbands. Pension sharing was introduced because of these disadvantages of attachment orders.

Instead of sharing or attaching, the parties might agree to offset the difference in their pension values by giving extra capital to the party with the less valuable pensions. This can help that party meet their immediate needs, but they may be glad to have had a pension when they get older. The other party may prefer to keep his or her pension unshared even if it means giving up capital now, but this may leave them less protected against the ups and downs of pre-retirement life, such as redundancy or supporting a second family. Judges have taken various different approaches to calculating an appropriate offsetting amount, but a discount will often be applied to the cash alternative because of the potentially long period before retirement and the flexibility of capital.[44]

The basic state pension cannot be shared. However, the additional state pension (aka SERPS or the second state pension) can be shared, but this pension only exists for people who retired before 6 April 2016. A competent lawyer should always get a statement for this, as, while most SEPRS pensions are not valuable, a minority are extremely valuable because of additional contributions made by the holder.

4.4.7 Variation of a nuptial agreement

We discuss nuptial agreements at section 4.8.

---

[42] See page 37 of H Woodward, *A Guide to the Treatment of Pensions on Divorce: The Report of the Pension Advisory Group* (2019) for an illustration of this.
[43] H Woodward, 'Everyday Financial Remedy Orders: Do They Achieve Fair Pension Provision on Divorce?' [2015] *Child and Family Law Quarterly* 151. This is an interesting article.
[44] See R Taylor and H Woodward, 'Apples or Pears? Pension Offsetting on Divorce' [2015] *Family Law* 1485.

4.4.8 Undertakings and agreements

In the event that the parties want to do something that is not within the court's powers to order, that party may give an undertaking—put simply, make a solemn promise to the court—or otherwise record their agreement on that particular issue. These would appear on the order as a recital rather than in the body of the order which is limited to those aspects of the settlement that it is in the court's powers to order. Although a party cannot be forced to give an undertaking or record an agreement, a recital or undertaking is just as enforceable.[45]

4.4.9 Debts

While courts can redistribute assets owned by the parties, they cannot transfer debts because they have no powers in respect of non-parties and creditors are non-parties. This means that courts cannot order a creditor to release one spouse from a joint liability such as a mortgage or loan. The creditor may be approached and asked to do so, but it is not in their interests to reduce the number of debtors they could pursue for payment. If there is not sufficient money to pay off the debt at the time of the divorce, the order may make one party pay the debt over time and indemnify the other if the creditor pursues them.

SCENARIO 2

Illustration 1: Jan and Ahmed

Jan has a credit card which has a balance of £2,000. We are told that she uses this for food shopping. This means that she applies it for the benefit of the family, so it is a debt that should be met by both of them. However, the court has no power to order the credit card company to give Ahmed a credit card and transfer half the balance to him. It will deal with the credit card by ensuring that Jan has sufficient money to pay it. This might mean giving her more money in the overall settlement. If the card had been used for her own purposes, such as gambling, the court may take a different view and treat the debt as Jan's problem to solve from her own assets.

Although this credit card is for a relatively modest amount of debt, the same approach will apply to debts of many millions. If they are debts incurred for the benefit of the family then the court will take that debt into account when it shares the parties' assets.

4.4.10 Disposing of assets to defeat claims on divorce

It is not uncommon for a party to try to hide or dispose of assets in order to prevent the other party acquiring them on divorce. Success largely depends on the degree of prior planning involved: the required information that the parties must provide to one another includes 12 months' bank statements, so the mysterious disappearance of some savings will generally be noticed. It is possible to get to the bottom of transactions by obtaining

---

[45] See *BSA v NVT* [2020] EWHC 2906 (Fam), in which the judge rejects an argument that a recital recording a party's agreement to do something was not enforceable because it was only a recital.

orders permitting oral examination of the party, production of documents appointments, or orders preventing a party from leaving the jurisdiction. Where a party has disposed of an asset, the court can set aside (undo) that disposal. It is also possible to obtain a freezing injunction to prevent dealings with certain assets.[46]

4.4.11 Interim orders

The court also has the power to make some interim orders (not merely case management directions) while proceedings are ongoing. For example, the court can order interim spousal maintenance previously known as 'maintenance pending suit' (s22) and/or order that one party provides the other with money for lawyers' fees (s22ZA). In *Rattan v Kuwad*, the Court of Appeal explained that s22 provided the court with:

> an extremely valuable power because it enables the court to make an order to meet the income needs of a spouse and the children at a time when they might be in real need of financial support following the parties' separation and the commencement of proceedings. It is intended to provide the court with the ability to act expeditiously and to make an order which meets that need at an early stage of the proceedings when the evidential picture might be far from clear. It is a very broad statutory power which extends to the court making such order as the judge 'thinks reasonable'.

The provision may, for example, be used to order the respondent to pay the mortgage on the family home if they have stopped making payments and the applicant cannot afford the payment by themselves.[47]

4.5 Deciding what order to make: The statutory guidance

We have considered what orders a court could make, but not *why* the court may make an order in particular terms. Sections 25 and 25A Matrimonial Causes Act 1973 (or, for civil partners, within the Civil Partnership Act 2004, which contains mirror provisions) provides guidance to the courts. This guidance will also be borne in mind by parties seeking to negotiate their own settlement, as a court will need to approve that as being fair by reference to this guidance.

4.5.1 The general approach

Section 25(1) tells us that in deciding what it should do, the court should consider 'all the circumstances of the case'.

In doing this, the court has to give 'first consideration' to the welfare of any child of the family[48] aged under 18. 'This is a clear recognition of the reality that, although the couple

---

[46] See s37 Matrimonial Causes Act 1973, the inherent jurisdiction of the High Court under s37 Senior Courts Act 1983, and FPR 20.2.

[47] [2021] EWCA Civ 1 (Moylan LJ).

[48] A child of the family is defined at s52.

> **Statutory Extract** *s25 Matrimonial Causes Act 1973*
>
> (1) It shall be the duty of the court in deciding whether to exercise its powers under section 23, 24, 24A, 24B or 24E above and, if so, in what manner, to have regard to all the circumstances of the case, first consideration being given to the welfare while a minor of any child of the family who has not attained the age of eighteen.

may seek to go their separate ways, they are still jointly responsible for the welfare of their children.'[49] In practice, first consideration is 'invariably' interpreted as ensuring children are properly housed, but it can also affect whether or not the court should expect a primary carer to work, and, if so, for how many hours. '[T]he security and stability of children depends in large part upon the security and stability of their primary carers.'[50] Note, however, the decision in *Suter v Suter and Jones* that the wording is 'first consideration' so they are not, as with child arrangements orders, the paramount consideration; the welfare of the children is not overriding.[51] The objective is fairness between the spouses.

4.5.2 Encouragement of a clean break

After making whatever arrangements it thinks fair, such as transfer or sale of property or pension sharing, it is usual that the financial remedy order will include a clause that permanently terminates any further claims so that one of them cannot return to court for more money later. An order containing this type of clause is a *clean break order*. Where there are periodical payments, there is no clean break, at least of the recipient's claims against the payer's income, but you could have an order terminating the recipient's other claims (lump sum orders, property adjustment orders, pension sharing orders and pension attachment orders) and all the claims of the payer. Note that it is not possible to clean break an obligation to support children, only claims between the parties themselves.[52]

There are two relevant clauses. First, under s25A(1) the court has a duty to consider 'whether it would be appropriate' to exercise its powers so that 'the financial obligations of each party towards the other [i.e. periodical payments] will be terminated as soon after the grant of the decree as the court considers just and reasonable'. Second, where a court decides to make a periodical payments order anyway, s25A(2) requires the court to consider 'whether it would be appropriate to require those payments to be made or secured only for such term as would in the opinion of the court be sufficient to enable the [recipient] to adjust without undue hardship to the termination of his or her financial dependence on the other party'. Thus the court can impose a limited term on a maintenance order and include a clause that it is not possible to extend this.

In Key Case *Miller/McFarlane*, Lady Hale described these provisions as a 'a powerful encouragement' to consider using capital and property to reach a clean break settlement,

---

[49] *Miller v Miller/McFarlane v McFarlane* [2006] UKHL 24 [128] (Lady Hale).
[50] *Miller v Miller/McFarlane v McFarlane* [2006] UKHL 24 [128] (Lady Hale).
[51] *Suter v Suter and Jones* [1987] 2 FLR 232 (CA).
[52] *Crozier v Crozier* [1994] Fam 114.

rather than having ongoing periodical payments. However, they do not operate as pre-sumptions (starting points) in favour of a clean break. There may well be cases where a clean break will never be just and reasonable, and it 'is not to be achieved at the expense of a fair result'.[53] Periodical payments can be a valuable safety net. If one had a clean break and then fell into financial difficulties—perhaps as a result of illness or redundancy—there is no ability to return to court. The court should therefore be quite certain that independence can be achieved: 'Hope, without pious exhortations to end dependency, is not enough.'[54] There are also situations where litigation misconduct such as the hiding of assets means that the court refuses to implement a clean break so as to enable the party left without resources to potentially obtain money in the future.[55]

Both the requirement to give first consideration to the children, and the requirement to consider a clean break were introduced into the 1973 Act by the Matrimonial and Family Proceedings Act 1984. There are good reasons for it:

1. As Lord Scarman noted in *Minton v Minton*, '[a]n object of the modern law is to encourage each to put the past behind them and to begin a new life which is not over-shadowed by the relationship which has broken down.'[56] A clean break recog-nises that the marriage is at an end, and so are the mutual rights and responsibilities that existed with it.

2. Continuing obligations (by way of periodical payments) can cause bad feeling be-tween the parties. The recipient may be financially dependent on those payments to live, but a vindictive (or disorganised) ex-spouse can leave the recipient on tenter-hooks every month for receipt.

3. The payer may feel that the recipient is not taking responsibility for their own finan-cial independence but relying on the payer's hard work. He or she may feel also that the recipient is deliberately avoiding remarriage so as to keep receiving money.

4. Planning for the future is difficult: the payer has indeterminable commitment: if his or her income increases, or the recipient falls into financial difficulties, s/he may face an application for increased payments. While an application to terminate can be made on the basis of the recipient's cohabitation (so the payer has reason to look over the recipient's shoulder to see how often the new partner is staying over) courts are reluctant to equate cohabitation with marriage.[57] This can seem very unfair, though, where the payer observes the recipient in a new relationship that is effec-tively marriage in all but name.

5. Many people want a clean break.[58]

---

[53] *Miller v Miller/McFarlane v McFarlane* [2006] UKHL 24 [133–4] (Lady Hale).

[54] *C v C (Financial Provision: Short Marriage)* [1997] 2 FLR 26, 46 (Ward LJ).

[55] *Quan v Bray & Others* [2018] EWHC 3558 (Fam); *Joy v Joy-Marancho and Others (No 3)* [2015] EWHC 2507 (Fam), and *AW v AH, BB, and C Limited* [2020] EWFC 22.

[56] [1979] AC 593, 608.

[57] Cohabiting relationships have a higher breakdown rate, and do not have the legal signifier of commitment that is the marriage certificate. See *Kimber v Kimber* [2000] 1 FLR 383; *Grey v Grey* [2010] 1 FLR 1764 (CA).

[58] E Hitchings and J Miles, *Financial Remedies on Divorce: The Need for Evidence-Based Reform* (Nuffield Foun-dation 2018).

However, while the legal structures for formal equality may exist, there remains substantive inequality between men and women, and financial outcomes post-divorce are worse for women. While there is a gender pay gap, these outcomes also reflect the allocation of roles in the marriage. This means that the consequences of a decision made within the marriage may outlast the marriage itself.

Take, for example, the situation of a woman who becomes pregnant, takes maternity leave, and thereafter returns to work part-time. The average cost of putting a child in nursery for 25 hours per week is £6,000 per year,[59] so although the most common working pattern where there are children is for the mother to work part time,[60] financially it may not be worthwhile. Some parents may also feel social pressure not to put their children in nursery full-time.[61] As the House of Lords has recognised, '[t]he career break which results from concentrating on motherhood and the family in the middle years of their lives comes at a price which in most cases is irrecoverable.'[62] Heather Joshi found that a mother of two will lose over 40 per cent of her lifetime earnings compared to a woman without children.[63]

A few years later, let us assume that our fictional mother and her husband divorce. It is probable that the children will have their main home with her: 86 per cent of single parents are women.[64] She will thus continue to contribute to the marriage by parenting post-divorce. Until the children are of sufficient age for her working hours (and thus her mortgage capacity) to increase, she may well need both a majority of the available capital and regular future income from the husband. Even if she could work full-time, 'the welfare of children may not be best served by their custodial parent's self-sufficiency'.[65] It may be better for the children for a primary carer to work part-time, even if that means spousal maintenance is needed. As Connolly et al. argue, 'British societal infrastructure still tends to promote and support a full-time breadwinner plus part-time carer model.'[66]

During the marriage and afterwards, the husband has much greater scope to build a career. This is where spousal maintenance comes in: it mitigates the effect of the decisions made during the marriage to divide roles in this way.[67]

---

[59] J Rutter, *Childcare Costs Survey* (Family and Childcare Trust 2015).http://www.familyandchildcaretrust.org/sites/default/files/files/Childcare_cost_survey_2015_Final.pdf accessed 15 November 2016.

[60] A Park, C Bryson, E Clery, J Curtice, and M Phillips (eds) *British Social Attitudes: The 30th Report* (NatCen Social Research 2013). https://www.bsa.natcen.ac.uk/media/38723/bsa30_full_report_final.pdf accessed 13 September 2020.

[61] There are conflicting studies on the effects of nursery on children, but as examples of the kinds of pressures that may impact upon parents, see S Doughty, 'Working Mothers Risk Damaging their Child's Prospects', (*Daily Mail*, 14 March 2001) http://www.dailymail.co.uk/news/article-30342/Working-mothers-risk-damaging-childs-prospects.html and J Carvel, 'Working Mothers "Bad for Children"', *The Guardian* (London, 14 November 2003) https://www.theguardian.com/money/2003/nov/14/workandcareers accessed 16 November 2016.

[62] *Miller v Miller/McFarlane v McFarlane* [2006] UKHL 24 [118] (Lord Hope).

[63] H Joshi, 'The Cash Opportunity Costs of Childbearing: An Approach to Estimation Using British Data' (1990) 44(1) *Population Studies* 41.

[64] Office of National Statistics, *Statistical Bulletin, Families and Households in the UK 2019* (ONS 2019).

[65] E Jackson, F Wasoff, M Maclean, and R Emerson Dobash, 'Financial Support on Divorce: The Right Mixture of Rules and Discretion?' (1993) 7 *International Journal of Law and the Family* 230, 238.

[66] See also S Connolly, M Aldrich, M O'Brien, S Speight, and E Poole, 'Britain's Slow Movement to a Gender Egalitarian Equilibrium: Parents and Employment in the UK 2001–13' (2016) *Work, Employment and Society* 1, 16.

[67] Of course, if the parties had swapped traditional roles, so the husband was primary carer, then he could claim maintenance: the law is facially neutral.

You may wish to consider, however, to what extent it is appropriate to 'place that burden on the ex-spouse when it stems from the broader societal inequality of women [or parents] as much, if not more than, the couple's own financial decision-making'.[68] A society in which childcare and social care was free or much cheaper, where the pay gap was closed, and where there was a more equal division of parenting tasks may would have fewer inequalities to remedy—but this would come at cost to the state, i.e., the taxpayer.

SCENARIO 2

Illustration 2: Jan and Ahmed

Jan and Ahmed are in a difficult predicament. Raising their two children will be costly. If, as is statistically likely, the children live with Jan after divorce and have contact with Ahmed, then Ahmed will—unless he has the children exactly half of the time—need to pay child maintenance (see Chapter 6). They will need to think about how the money can be stretched to rehouse themselves. A clean break may be attractive to Ahmed, because Jan's earnings will be much reduced by the need to fit around the children's daycare (which is expensive) and schooling, and he will not want the uncertainty of her being able to apply to increase the amount of (spousal) periodical payments that he makes. He will want to know what money he has, and be able to build it unimpeded. There is not much incentive for Jan to agree to a clean break, though, unless she has a high proportion of the capital, and even then it may be insufficient compensation for the risk.

4.5.3 The section 25(2) factors

We have considered what orders a court could make, but not *why* the court may make an order in particular terms. It is all very well to say that the order should be fair, but what does a fair order look like? How do the negotiating parties or the court decide on an appropriate outcome in any given situation?

The answer is that there is statutory guidance in ss 25 and 25A the Matrimonial Causes Act 1973 (or, for civil partners, within the Civil Partnership Act 2004, which contains mirror provisions). Section 25 provides a non-exhaustive list of factors that 'the court shall in particular have regard to' when considering 'all the circumstances of the case', with the aim of guiding the court towards a fair outcome. The list applies whether the judge is making a decision at a contested final hearing or considering a joint consent application. It applies to families at all points on the economic spectrum too, from multi-billion-pound cases to those involving parties who are impoverished. However, as the factors 'are not listed in any hierarchical order or order of importance',[69] the weight to be accorded to each one will vary depending on the circumstances of each case.[70] Some may not be relevant at all to a particular case, but where a factor is relevant, *Robson v Robson* tells us that it 'must be placed in the scales and given its due weight'.[71]

[68] G Douglas, 'Simple Quarrels? Autonomy v Vulnerability' in R Probert and C Barton (eds), *Fifty Years in Family Law: Essays for Stephen Cretney* (Intersentia 2012) 217, 219.
[69] *Robson v Robson* [2010] EWCA Civ 1171 [43] (Ward LJ).
[70] *Piglowska v Piglowski* [1999] UKHL 27.
[71] *Robson v Robson* [2010] EWCA Civ 1171 [43] (Ward LJ).

Statutory Extract *Section 25 Matrimonial Causes Act 1973*

(2) In deciding whether to exercise its powers the court shall in particular have regard to the following matters—

(a) the income, earning capacity, property and other financial resources which each of the parties to the marriage has or is likely to have in the foreseeable future, including in the case of earning capacity any increase in that capacity which it would in the opinion of the court be reasonable to expect a party to the marriage to take steps to acquire;

(b) the financial needs, obligations and responsibilities which each of the parties to the marriage has or is likely to have in the foreseeable future;

(c) the standard of living enjoyed by the family before the breakdown of the marriage;

(d) the age of each party to the marriage and the duration of the marriage;

(e) any physical or mental disability of either of the parties to the marriage;

(f) the contributions which each of the parties has made or is likely in the foreseeable future to make to the welfare of the family, including any contribution by looking after the home or caring for the family;

(g) the conduct of each of the parties, if that conduct is such that it would in the opinion of the court be inequitable to disregard it;

(h) in the case of proceedings for divorce or nullity of marriage, the value to each of the parties to the marriage of any benefit . . . which, by reason of the dissolution or annulment of the marriage, that party will lose the chance of acquiring.

Please note that when considering orders in respect of financial provision for children, as opposed to financial provision for a spouse (which will affect the children indirectly), there is a list of extra factors to consider at s25(3). These are discussed in Chapter 6.

The parties' financial resources (s25(2)(a))

The court must take into account the financial position of the parties. Sometimes this is relatively straightforward, but in other cases the parties may have complex financial arrangements, such as offshore trusts or values that are contingent on certain events, such as stock market flotation.[72] As well as legal interests, the court can take into account assets to which the parties are beneficially entitled, such as under discretionary trusts, although this does depend on the powers and practice of the trustees in distributing funds to the party.

It is important to consider the future, as well as current, position of the parties. Is one on a career track? Is there a known prospect of redundancy? Could a party undertake training to increase their earning potential? Could they work more hours? Note that the earning capacity mentioned in s25(2)(a) includes capacity which is currently unused—for example, it is open to you to argue that your spouse may only work 16 hours per week now, but could work 30, and agree a settlement that takes account of that. Is a party likely to inherit money imminently? One has to be careful of taking into account future inheritances other than those which are imminent, as people change their Wills or live longer than expected. Nevertheless, inheritances can be a useful source of funds.

---

[72] See, e.g., *Charman v Charman (No 4)* [2007] EWCA Civ 503 (trust); *Sharland v Sharland* [2015] UKSC 60 (flotation).

In theory, therefore, any asset is 'up for grabs' by the other party. This is why full disclosure is so important. However, it is important to explain to the parties that just because the court *could* make an order over a particular asset, it does not mean that it will. There may be very good reasons, considered in this chapter, not to do so.

Finally, the type of asset may be relevant to what the parties wish to do with it. One party may be willing to take risker assets, but more of them. For example, an asset that is less likely to fall in value (a 'copper-bottomed' asset) such as a house may be more sought-after than shares in a new business which are riskier. For an example of this gone horribly wrong, *Myerson v Myerson (No. 2)*, where the husband took risker assets than the wife and their value crashed after the order was made.[73] Similarly, a pension share that can only be drawn on retirement may be less desirable to a party than a smaller amount of cash now, because cash can be used to meet immediate needs.

Needs, standard of living, and disability (ss25(2)(b, c, e))

A consideration of the financial needs of the parties is likely to occupy most of the attention of those advising divorcing parties. As we see in section 4.7.1, need can encompass a wide range of different aspects. Specifically, need can be related to the standard of living enjoyed during the marriage and any disabilities of the parties. In *C v C (Financial Provision: Personal Damages)*, for example, the husband was seriously disabled as the result of a car accident, and his housing needs absorbed nearly all the available funds. Indeed, it was not sensible to provide the wife with any capital as this would reduce her eligibility for state benefits that were more valuable than any available lump sum from the husband.[74]

Section 25 also directs the court to look at the parties' financial obligations and responsibilities, which could include, for example, school fees or financial support for a new family, or, as in one unreported case, the need to remain in the matrimonial home because it was next door to a party's elderly parents. More commonly, financial obligations include debts that have to be repaid, such as credit cards, loans, hire-purchase agreements, and mortgages or rent. For the court's powers regarding debts, see 4.4.8.

Age, duration of marriage, and contributions (ss25(2)(d, f))

The duration of the marriage is relevant to the three rationales for dividing property—needs, compensation, and sharing—set out in Key Case *Miller/McFarlane*. The needs arising from a short marriage are generally likely to be less than the needs arising from a long marriage, unless there are children. Similarly, relationship-generated disadvantage is less likely, and there is a weaker case for sharing the marital fruits: '[t]his reflects the instinctive feeling that parties will generally have less call upon each other on the breakdown of a short marriage.'[75] When calculating the length of the marriage, most courts include a period of prior cohabitation if it moved seamlessly into marriage.[76]

When considering the duration of the marriage, it is common to take into account pre-marital cohabitation that has moved seamlessly to marriage. It is not always easy to determine when cohabitation commenced: there is no clear marker such as that provided

---

[73] *Myerson v Myerson (No 2)* [2009] EWCA Civ 282.
[74] [1995] 2 FLR 171.
[75] *Miller v Miller/McFarlane v McFarlane* [2006] UKHL 24 [24] (Lord Nicholls).
[76] *GW v RW* [2003] EWHC 611 (Fam) [33] (Mostyn J).

by a marriage certificate. However, the court will look for 'an accumulation of markers of marriage which eventually will take the relationship over the threshold into a quasi-marital relationship which may then either be added to the marriage to establish a longer marriage or which becomes a weightier factor as one of the circumstances of the case'.[77]

The parties' ages also reflect their needs. A younger party may have the potential to earn better than someone older who has not been in the job market recently. An older party may have specific personal care needs that a younger person does not.

Contribution is to the *welfare* of the family and consequently can be financial or non-financial. It is common to distinguish between contributions from outside the marriage and contributions made within the marriage.

A contribution from outside the marriage is often financial as this is what is most easily measurable. Such a contribution could be pre-owned assets such as savings or property. It could be a gift from a parent or an inheritance. Contributions such as these will *be non-matrimonial* in nature (see 4.7.3) unless they later become mingled with matrimonial assets. As such, they are a contribution that is unmatched by the other party.[78] As a s25 factor this kind of contribution is a reason to depart from the starting point of equal division of the assets. This is discussed further in 4.7.3.

Contributions from within the marriage are different. In Key Case *White v White*, the House of Lords held that '[i]f, in their different spheres, each contributed equally to the family, then in principle it matters not which of them earned the money and built up the assets. There should be no bias in favour of the money-earner and against the home-maker and the child-carer.'[79] Each party has made an equal contribution in cash or in kind. The likelihood, therefore, is that the parties' contributions with the marriage are to be treated as equal.

Following *White v White*, some husbands began to argue that they had made a contribution of *matrimonial assets* that was so significant that it should be given considerable weight as a s25 factor and justify them receiving the bulk of the assets after needs had been met: in other words, that their contribution went above and beyond the kind of equal-but-different contributions that the House of Lords spoke of in *White*. These are known as 'stellar' or 'special' contribution arguments. They are almost always made (a) by husbands and (b) in relation to *financial* contribution.

Arguments that a person has made a stellar contribution to the marriage are not usually successful.[80] There appear to have been only 3 successful claimants in reported cases: the husbands in *Sorrell v Sorrell*,[81] in which the husband was the founder of the world's largest advertising agency and was described as 'one of the most exceptional and talented businessmen'; *Cowan v Cowan*,[82] where it was his 'genius to perceive the potential of bin liners

---

[77] *IX v IY* [2018] EWHC 3053 [68] (Williams J). See also *Kimber v Kimber* [2000] 1 FLR 383 for the markers, and *M v M* [2004] EWHC 668 (Fam).

[78] If each brought the same into a marriage, then their contributions from outside the marriage would cancel one another out.

[79] [2001] 1 AC 596, 605[D]–[E] (Lord Nicholls).

[80] For examples of unsuccessful cases, see *H v H* [2010] EWHC 158 (Fam) and *Evans v Evans* [2013] EWHC 506 (Fam).

[81] [2005] EWHC 1717 (Fam).

[82] [2001] EWCA Civ 679.

which would revolutionise the collection and disposal of household waste' and—the word 'genius' appearing again—*Cooper-Hohn v Hohn*,[83] where the husband, an investor, had accrued assets of between $1.35 and $1.6 billion and established a charitable foundation with assets of $4.5 billion. In *Work v Gray*, Holman J noted that:

> the fact that judges have used the word 'genius' in this context does tend to underline how exceptional, individual and special the quality has to be. . . . [H]ard work alone is not enough. Many people work extremely hard at every level of society and employment. . . . It is clear also that a successful claim to a special contribution requires some exceptional and individual quality in the spouse concerned. Being in the right place at the right time, or benefiting from a period of boom is not enough.[84]

What courts are looking for are those 'characteristics or circumstances . . . of a wholly exceptional nature, such that it would very obviously be inconsistent with the objective of achieving fairness for them to be ignored'.[85] In Key Case *Miller/McFarlane*, Lord Nicholls said that 'parties should not seek to promote a case of "special contribution" unless the contribution is so marked that to disregard it would be inequitable. A good reason for departing from equality is not to be found in the minutiae of married life.'[86] Lady Hale thought that 'the question of contributions should be approached in the much the same way as conduct': 'Only if there is such a disparity in their respective contributions to the welfare of the family that it would be inequitable to disregard it should this be taken into account in determining their shares.'[87] In *XW v XH*, the wife, who cared for the parties' seriously disabled child, was held to have made an 'incalculable' contribution equal to that of the husband, whose contribution was to the marital wealth of nearly £300 million. His was not a stellar contribution because it lacked the 'necessary disparity' to hers.[88]

Even where an argument is successfully advanced, it is unlikely to give rise to percentages of division of matrimonial property further from equality than 66.6%–33.3%.[89] Courts have kept such awards in 'narrow bounds'[90] because of the 'inherent gender discrimination'[91] of such arguments. A good example of this is *Cooper-Hohn* in which the wife had worked, often from the early hours to after midnight, for the charitable foundation, which 'demanded of her the skills and qualities which would have been needed in any CEO' and was the primary carer of four children.[92] Mrs Cooper-Hohn argued that if this was not itself also a stellar contribution, what more could she do? While theoretically possible, it would be tremendously difficult to show stellar contribution other than by making (large amounts of) money.

Stellar contribution arguments do not reflect a partnership view of marriage, because they expressly argue that one party has done more for the marriage than the other. Of

---

[83] [2014] EWHC 4122 (Fam) [282]–[283] (Roberts J).
[84] *Work v Gray* [2015] EWHC 834 (Fam) [142]–[144].
[85] *Lambert v Lambert* [2002] EWCA Civ 1685 [70] (Bodey J).
[86] *Miller v Miller/McFarlane v McFarlane* [2006] UKHL 24 [67].
[87] *Miller v Miller/McFarlane v McFarlane* [2006] UKHL 24 [146] (Lady Hale).
[88] *XW v XH* [2019] EWCA Civ 2262.
[89] *Charman v Charman (No 4)* [2007] EWCA Civ 503 [90] (Sir Mark Potter P).
[90] *Charman v Charman (No 4)* [2007] EWCA Civ 503 [88] (Sir Mark Potter P).
[91] *Charman v Charman (No 4)* [2007] EWCA Civ 503 [80] (Sir Mark Potter P).
[92] [2014] EWHC 4122 (Fam) [273] (Roberts J).

course, the counter argument is that some marriages are not equal partnerships in reality. One party may have done the daily grind of a marriage (whether outside the home, at home, or both) while the other party has not pulled their weight. Indeed, that may be a reason for the divorce. Morally, therefore, there could be an argument for this to be reflected in the financial settlement to a greater extent that is currently recognised.

SCENARIO 1

Illustration 1: Dora and Brian

Dora and Brian are our older couple, with a marriage that has lasted 54 years. The length of the marriage is a s25 factor in its own right. However, it also has implications for some of the other s25 factors. After a very long marriage such as this, it is very likely that the couple will have mingled their assets so that there is very little non-matrimonial property. It is also relevant to their needs. As an older couple, they are likely to need accessible accommodation which may increase the expense of rehousing them. That is a capital need. They may need carers, or even to go into a care home—and care homes are extremely expensive. This is an income need, but perhaps we can top up the pension income by using up some of their capital.

Their financial needs may be short-term (based on a limited life expectancy, although it could still be a decade or more), but those needs may be high while they exist. A competent solicitor will consider what those needs are, cost them, and think carefully about how to structure a settlement to maximise the availability of state aid so that they are eligible for certain state benefits and can maximise the state's contribution to care costs.

Conduct (s25(2)(g))

Conduct and contribution are 'opposite sides of a coin'.[93] Both financial and non-financial misconduct can affect the appropriate financial settlement. However, we have moved away from a situation in which adultery, for example, would determine the financial outcome: 'the court should not reduce its order for financial provision merely because of what was formerly regarded as guilt or blame. To do so would be to impose a fine for supposed misbehaviour in the course of an unhappy married life' (and, of course, take up huge amounts of court time).[94] For conduct to be taken into account it has to be 'such that it would in the opinion of the court be inequitable to disregard it', and in *Wachtel v Wachtel* Ormrod J interpreted this as conduct that was 'obvious and gross'.[95] As Lady Hale said in Key Case *Miller/McFarlane*, 'it is simply not possible for any outsider to pick over the events of a marriage and decide who was the more to blame for what went wrong, save in the most obvious and gross cases.'[96] In *S v S* Burton J refers to conduct as needing to have the 'gasp'

---

93 *Miller v Miller/McFarlane v McFarlane* [2006] UKHL 24 [164] (Lord Mance).
94 *Wachtel v Wachtel* [1972] Fam 72 (CA), 90 (Lord Denning MR).
95 *Wachtel v Wachtel* [1972] Fam 72 (CA), 80.
96 [2006] UKHL 24.

factor (the facts of that case—a hair-raising catalogue of events in which neither persons nor ornaments were safe—merely caused a 'gulp').[97]

Most cases that do reach this 'gasp factor' standard—helpfully reviewed by Burton J—involve very serious physical attacks on the spouse, as in *H v H (Financial Relief: Attempted Murder as Conduct)*, in which the husband was serving 12 years for attempted murder, having stabbed the wife repeatedly in front of their children. The court held that:

> The conduct was not merely a backdrop to the s25 exercise; it had had direct consequences for the wife which had to be taken into account: it had seriously affected her mental health; it had imposed a move away from home; it had almost destroyed her earning capacity, in particular her police career; it was likely to have an impact upon the children in later years, which the wife would have to cope with; it had deprived the wife of any prospect of financial or parenting support from the husband for many years to come; and it could have an impact on her established relationship with a man. It was necessary that the wife be made as secure as possible, free from financial worry or pressure.

The court held that this was not merely conduct which it would be inequitable to disregard: it was conduct at the very top of the scale. The court:

> should not be punitive or confiscatory for its own sake; . . . the proper way to have regard to the conduct is as a potentially magnifying factor when considering the wife's position under the other subsections and criteria . . . it places her needs . . . as a much higher priority to those of the husband because the situation in which the wife now finds herself in is, in a very real way, his fault.[98]

The court awarded her all of their jointly owned house, all of its contents, bank accounts, and insurance policies, totalling about £180,000, leaving the husband with £30,000 plus his pension and £50,000 of his sole assets. In another case, also called *H v H*, the husband attempted to rape the wife and seriously assaulted her. The judge referred to 'the extremity and horror of the violence to which the wife was subjected'.[99] The husband went to prison, and the wife got all the assets including the jointly owned matrimonial home, with the husband keeping his pension. In each of these cases, all or virtually all of the joint assets have gone to the victim, leaving the husband with his pension and any solely owned assets. Had the wives' needs not been met by the assets they were awarded, it is easy to imagine the court dipping into the husband's solely owned assets too.

While litigation misconduct such as failing to comply with a court direction or hiding assets will usually be penalised by making a costs order against that party rather than giving them fewer of the assets,[100] there are exceptions. In *F v F (Ancillary Relief: Substantial Assets)* the husband's conduct of the litigation was so bad that it became conduct that it was inequitable to disregard under s25(2)(g).[101] In *B v B (Financial Provision: Welfare of Child and Conduct)*, the husband's misconduct was financial (in transferring assets out of the jurisdiction) and criminal (child abduction). He went to prison, with the result

---

[97] [2006] EWHC 2793 (Fam) [57], citing *W v W* [1976] Fam 107, 110[D] (Sir George Baker P).
[98] [2005] EWHC 2911 (Fam) [44] (Charles J).
[99] [1994] 2 FCR 1031.
[100] Even when this means they end up below the level of their assessed needs: *MB v EB (No 2)* [2019] EWHC 3676 (Fam).
[101] [1995] 2 FLR 45.

that the financial and practical burden of raising the child would be borne by the wife alone. Conduct and contribution were closely linked and provided a reason to depart from equality.[102]

However, the courts can also assume that a party has assets which it has not disclosed and make an order on that basis, if that party has failed to give full and frank disclosure; and/or undo transactions that are intended to defeat the court, such as transferring assets to third parties so they are not available to be awarded to the other spouse; and/or act as though dissipated assets still exist and are available to the dissipater. For example, if the court was going to award the wife £100,000, but considered that she had dissipated £30,000 unreasonably, then the court would award her the balance of £70,000. In *McCartney v Mills McCartney*, the celebrity divorce of former Beatle Paul McCartney and Heather Mills, Bennett J added £500,000 back into the wife's assets to represent her 'completely unreasonable expenditure'.[103]

Loss of benefit (s25(2)(h))

Although this factor seems to be infrequently directly pleaded, it would be relevant to the loss of pension rights that a party would have received on this or her spouse's death had they been married at the time.

SCENARIO 2

Illustration 3: Jan and Ahmed

In designing an appropriate settlement for them, note that there are two young children whose welfare is the first consideration. We must consider also 'all the circumstances of the case'. The following s25 factors are relevant. First, this is a short marriage. Ahmed's parents have contributed towards the purchase price of the house. This is not unusual. We need to ascertain whether the parents have protected their investments by way of a declaration of trust giving them a beneficial interest in the property (see Chapter 5). If so, then that investment of £50,000 by the parents is not a marital asset to be distributed. However, if the parents did not protect it in this way, then, while it is a contribution on the side of Ahmed, its use as a matrimonial home makes it a matrimonial asset (see 4.7.3). There are no conduct issues and no compensation issues.

4.6 Introduction to the principles

So far, we have discussed what powers the court has and certain issues that may be pertinent to the outcome. However, s25 has not provided us with any information about why certain things are relevant. For example, it says we should consider the ages of the parties, but nowhere does it state how being older or younger should affect the outcome nor how much weight we should give to age compared to any other s25 factor, such as need or contribution. In fact, nowhere in the Matrimonial Causes Act 1973 is there any guidance on

---

[102] [2002] 1 FLR 555.
[103] [2008] EWHC 401 (Fam) [179].

how each factor should affect the outcome of the proceedings. It is axiomatic that the outcome should be fair, but it has fallen onto courts to explain why and how the assets should be divided between the parties. Unfortunately, most of the reported cases involve high net worth couples because they are the only parties who can afford the costs of bringing an appeal. This means that practitioners have to interpret how they may be applicable to middle and low asset couples. Patrick Parkinson has compared the judge to:

> a bus driver who is given a large number of instructions about how to drive the bus, and the authority to do various actions such as turning left or right. There is also the occasional advice or correction offered by three senior drivers [the Court of Appeal]. The one piece of information which he or she is not given is where to take the bus. All he or she is told is that the driver is required to drive to a reasonable destination.[104]

We will therefore attempt to illustrate the principles through our scenarios, so that you can see how the different s25 factors come into play, and how practical considerations can moderate the principles.

First, it is necessary to consider several crucially important cases that have given lower courts guidance on the principles to apply. The most important of all such cases is *White v White*. More recently, the House of Lords *Miller/McFarlane* provided us with three rationales for dividing the assets. These are two of the Key Cases discussed in this chapter. To understand how important these decisions were, we need to go back to the situation before *White v White*.

4.6.1 A brief history of marital property law

Until 1882, a married woman could not legally own property, and coverture,[105] the legal doctrine that a married woman's legal identity was subsumed into that of her husband, meant that she could not enter into contracts other than to prevent her starvation, and instead would have to pledge her husband's credit for the purchase of necessities.[106] In return, the husband was obliged by common law and ecclesiastical law to support her during the marriage.

What happened if the marriage broke down depended on the relative wealth of the parties. Cretney explains that from 1667 to 1857, the period in which an individual private Act of Parliament was required for each divorce, 'a functionary called the Ladies' Friend took care to ensure that legally enforceable provision was made for the wife before the Bill was allowed to pass'; the adulterous wife, however, would almost certainly receive nothing.[107] For those unable to afford an Act—only about 325 such Acts were passed[108]—it was possible to obtain

---

[104] P Parkinson, 'The Diminishing Significance of Initial Contributions to Property' (1999) 13 *Australian Journal of Family Law* 52, 53.

[105] Blackstone wrote in his *Commentaries on the Laws of England* (1765–1769) that 'By marriage, the husband and wife are one person in law: that is, the very being or legal existence of the woman is suspended during the marriage, or at least is incorporated and consolidated into that of the husband: under whose wing, protection, and cover, she performs every thing; . . . and her condition during her marriage is called her coverture.'

[106] *James v Warren* (1706) 90 ER 956.

[107] S Cretney, *Family Law in the Twentieth Century: A History* (OUP 2003), Chapter 10 fn3.

[108] S Wolfram, 'Divorce in England 1700–1857' (1985) 5(2) *Oxford Journal of Legal Studies* 155, 156. Only four of these were granted to women. Most were granted to (male) members of the aristocracy.

a separation through the ecclesiastical courts. While not ending the marriage, it allowed the parties to live separately and could require the husband to pay 'alimony' to the wife.[109] A less expensive option was for the parties to informally separate, in which case the wife's male relations might negotiate financial provision on her behalf. In such negotiations the wife had little leverage, and Probert suggests that such agreements were of doubtful enforceability if the husband later petitioned for restitution of his conjugal rights.[110]

About one quarter of working women were married,[111] but their wages belonged to their husbands. As the middle class developed in the mid-nineteenth century, so did an ideology built around the 'angel in the house'[112] and her breadwinner husband. If the marriage broke down, the wife's position was very precarious, unless her family had been sufficiently wealthy and savvy to ensure prior to the marriage that some property was held on trust for her use, so as to 'protect a woman's property from the ravages to which her marriage exposed it'.[113] Even then, it was primarily about protecting family assets for the benefit of future generations: 'A marriage settlement is never made for the benefit and protection of the wife alone'.[114]

The Matrimonial Causes Act 1857 marked a considerable change, dispensing with the need for an Act, establishing secular divorce courts, and enabling a woman to petition for divorce, albeit on more stringent grounds than those available to her husband. The Act gave the new divorce courts the power to require the husband to financially support the wife by securing for her a fund from which she could draw. The husband was therefore not liable to make payments from income (although this changed with the Matrimonial Causes Act 1866), nor was there any power to order the transfer of assets to the wife.[115] However, the existence of a statutory power to award any 'alimony' *after* divorce (as opposed to the common law and ecclesiastical duties that lasted only *during* marriage, or a concession in an individual divorce Act of Parliament), was 'entirely novel'.[116] In *Hyman v Hyman*, the House of Lords described this power as 'granted partly in the public interest to . . . prevent the wife from being thrown up the public for support'.[117]

In assessing the wife's entitlement, her conduct was of considerable importance. Nicholas Mostyn, speaking extra-judicially, has noted that this is 'logical for as long as the power was based on what has been called the contractual analogy, which reasoned that had she remained married, she would have been entitled to her husband's support and that, since she had lost that entitlement only as a result of his misconduct, he should compensate her. Thus an innocent wife would be awarded alimony; a guilty

---

[109] The term 'alimony' is still used in the United States for spousal maintenance.

[110] See R Probert, *Divorced, Bigamist, Bereaved?* (Takeaway Books 2015), p85. A claim for restitution of conjugal rights was to enforce the duty to live with your spouse.

[111] See J Pahl, *Money and Marriage* (Macmillan 1989) p19.

[112] As coined by Coventry Patmore in the frankly nauseating poem 'The Angel in the House' from 1854.

[113] M Finer and O McGregor, 'History of the Obligation to Maintain', appendix to the *Report of the Committee on One Parent Families* (the Finer Report) (Cmnd 5629, 1974) 97.

[114] The Attorney-General speaking in the House of Lords 10 June 1868, as reported in *The Times* the following day.

[115] S Cretney, *Family Law in the Twentieth Century: A History* (OUP 2003), pp395–8.

[116] N Mostyn J, 'Spousal Maintenance: Where Did It Come From, Where Is it Now, and Where Is it Going?' Address by Mr Justice Mostyn to the Devon and Somerset Law Society 16 October 2018. Available at https://www.judiciary.uk/announcements/speech-by-mr-justice-mostyn-at-the-devon-and-somerset-law-society/ accessed 29 July 2019.

[117] *Hyman v Hyman* [1929] AC 601, 629 (Lord Atkin).

wife would not.'[118] He goes on to note that there *were* cases in which adulterous wives were awarded a modest 'compassionate allowance' so that she was, in the words of one judge of the time, 'made to feel that her livelihood depends on her leading a chaste life in the future . . . the strongest pressure ought to be put upon her not to lapse again into sin'.[119]

It was in 1882 that the fundamentally important Married Women's Property Act enabled a married woman to hold property (including any earnings) separately to her husband— 'a system of separation of property coupled with the husband's duty to maintain his wife'.[120] The Parliamentary debates record a recognition of the economic importance of women's work.[121] Nevertheless, even when it became more common for married women to work outside the home, any financial contributions made by the wife to the household, including the mortgage, were treated as gifts, rather than giving rise to any entitlement to a share in the property on divorce. Pahl has suggested that the Act 'did little to alter the financial dependency of wives on their husbands'.[122] After the Second World War, a line of cases held that she was entitled to a share of the value of the matrimonial home proportionate to her financial contribution. However, if she had given up work to have children, and consequently made no financial contribution, then the law did not protect her.[123] She would be awarded spousal maintenance, but courts lacked the power to order the provision of capital until the Matrimonial Causes Act 1963. The level of maintenance was based on what the husband could afford and the degree to which she was morally blameless, rather than an assessment of what she needed.[124] Too bad also if the husband was in financial need, rather than the wife: the court had no power to order her to maintain him unless he was insane.[125] Indeed, the common law duty of a husband to maintain his wife—finally abolished by the Equality Act 2010—was never matched by a reciprocal obligation, even once women routinely went out to work.

In 1970, the Matrimonial Proceedings and Property Act (later consolidated into the Matrimonial Causes Act 1973) gave courts, for the first time, a statutory objective: 'to place the parties, so far as it is practicable and, having regard to their conduct, just to do so, in the financial position in which they would have been if the marriage had not broken down and each had properly discharged his or her financial obligations and responsibilities towards the other' (s5(1)).[126] It also gave courts, in addition to maintenance and lump sums, the power to order property adjustment. As Lady Hale has written:

> The law became sex-neutral, in that the same remedies and principles were applied both to husbands and to wives. . . . The law also became much kinder to homemakers

---

[118] N Mostyn J, 'Spousal Maintenance: Where Did It Come From, Where Is it Now, and Where Is it Going?' Address by Mr Justice Mostyn to the Devon and Somerset Law Society 16 October 2018. Available at https://www.judiciary. uk/announcements/speech-by-mr-justice-mostyn-at-the-devon-and-somerset-law-society/ accessed 29 July 2019.

[119] *Squire v Squire and O'Callaghan* [1905] P 4 (Sir Francis Jenue P).

[120] Lady Hale, 'Equality and Autonomy in Family Law' (2011) 33(1) *Journal of Social Welfare and Family Law* 3, 8.

[121] See the *Hansard* debates at http://hansard.millbanksystems.com/lords/1870/jul/18/no-125-committee

[122] J Pahl, *Money and Marriage* (Macmillan 1989) p22.

[123] See discussion by Lord Denning in *Wachtel v Wachtel* [1973] Fam. 72 (CA), 92ff.

[124] C Smart, *The Ties that Bind: Law, Marriage and the Reproduction of Patriarchal Relations* (Routledge & Kegan Paul 1984), p89.

[125] Matrimonial Causes Act 1937, s10(2), discussed in the *Report of the Committee on One-Parent Families* (the Finer Report) (Cmnd 5629, 1974) at [4.44].

[126] The 1970 objective of putting the parties in the financial position in which they would have been if the marriage had not broken down—'equality of misery'—ultimately proved impossible to achieve, and in 1984, the Matrimonial and Family Proceedings Act abolished it.

and care-givers. All the actual and foreseeable resources of either party—property and income—could be shared out in whatever way the court thought just, depending on the facts and circumstances of the individual case.[127]

The 1970 Act explicitly provided that the court consider the 'contributions made by each of the parties to the welfare of the family, including any contributions made by looking after the home or caring for the family'.[128] As Lord Denning put it in the 'landmark'[129] case *Wachtel v Wachtel*, as far as the matrimonial home was concerned, '[j]ust as the wife who makes substantial money contributions usually gets a share, so should the wife who looks after the home and cares for the family for 20 years or more.'[130] There were many such women—in 1975 the husband was still the primary breadwinner in 95 per cent of marriages.[131] The court had new powers to transfer the matrimonial home to the wife, at least temporarily, for example under a *Mesher* order.[132] However, this happened in only a minority of cases. In *Wachtel* itself, for example, the wife was awarded maintenance at one third of her husband's income and a lump sum equivalent to one third of the value of the matrimonial home, plus child maintenance. Why one third? While acknowledging that it was 'much criticised', Lord Denning found it a useful starting point because, absent the wife, the husband will have greater expense. Whereas the wife will 'do most of the housework herself' or 'remarry, in which case her new husband will provide for her', the apparently undomesticated husband 'must get some woman to look after the house—either a wife, if he remarries, or a housekeeper, if he does not. He will also have to provide maintenance for the children'.[133]

In noting that the husband needed the domestic services of 'some woman', Lord Denning was, in his chauvinistic way,[134] at least accepting that the wife's contribution had an economic value; and this case is also extremely important because it held that conduct was only relevant to maintenance insofar as it was 'obvious and gross' rather than run-of-the-mill. However, in *Trippas v Trippas* he held that the husband was entitled to more because he earned it. The wife did not work in the husband's business and thus was not entitled to a share of its value, as 'all she did was what a good wife does. She gave moral support to her husband by looking after the home.'[135] This valuing of financial contribution over a contribution in kind—a good wife is not an equal wife—led ultimately in the 1980s and 1990s to awards based on the *reasonable requirements* of the poorer spouse, i.e., her needs, objectively judged by close reference to her budget, even if there was a large surplus in excess of that. As Lady Hale explains, this meant that 'vast sums in lawyers' fees

---

[127] Lady Hale, 'Equality and Autonomy in Family Law' (2011) 33(1) *Journal of Social Welfare and Family Law* 3, 8.
[128] This is now contained in the consolidating Matrimonial Causes Act 1973 as one of the s25 factors (s25(2)(f). Section 25's wording is slightly different: it directs the court to consider also contributions 'likely in the foreseeable future'.
[129] Lady Hale, 'Equality and Autonomy in Family Law' (2011) 33(1) *Journal of Social Welfare and Family Law* 3, 8.
[130] [1973] Fam. 72, 94.
[131] K O'Donovan, *Sexual Divisions in Law* (Weidenfeld & Nicolson 1985) 151.
[132] See J Eekelaar, 'Post-Divorce Financial Obligations', in SN Katz, J Eekelaar, and M Maclean, *Cross Currents: Family Law and Policy in the US and England* (OUP 2000) 408, 409–13.
[133] *Wachtel v Wachtel* [1972] Fam 72 (CA), 94.
[134] A more charitable view is given by Mostyn J, who refers to these comments as 'reflect[ing] the world-view of a man born in 1899': *SS v NS* [2014] EWHC 4183 [40].
[135] [1973] Fam 134, 141.

were devoted to poring over the wife's budget and deciding how many times she needed to go to the hairdresser and how much she needed to spend upon food. The idea that a wife might have a little extra to save for a rainy day or to leave to her family if she died was seen as going beyond what she reasonably required.'[136]

The term *reasonable requirements* was coined in *O'D v O'D*[137] but it is in *Dart v Dart*[138] that we see the logical endpoint of this approach: the wife was awarded £4 million of total marital wealth of £400 million. Her reasonable requirements were being treated as determinative of her award, irrespective of the fact that the s25 factors are in no particular order of importance, and irrespective of any view of marriage as a partnership in which each contributes equally in cash or in kind.

As Lord Nicholls has stated, '[t]he glass ceiling thus put in place was shattered by the decision of your Lordships' House in the *White* case.'

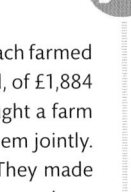

KEY CASE *White v White* [2001] 1 AC 596

The Whites were husband and wife farmers descended from farming families. They had each farmed before they married in 1961. Mrs White brought into the marriage assets, in cash or kind, of £1,884 and Mr White £1,135, and together they set up a farming partnership. In 1962, they bought a farm for £32,000 with the help of a mortgage and £14,000 which Mr White's father gave to them jointly. Over the subsequent years, they acquired more land and their partnership expanded. They made pension provision. They had children. In 1993, Mr White also inherited a neighbouring farm whose land he and Mrs White had already been farming for some years. By the time of the first instance decision, their total assets were £4.6 million of which £1.52 million was Mrs White's half share of their partnership and her pensions. Mr White had his half share of their partnership, his pensions, and also the neighbouring farm.

At first instance, Holman J awarded Mrs White £980,000 (21 per cent of the assets). The judge found that this was all that Mrs White required to meet her reasonable needs for housing and income. The eventual House of Lords decision records Holman J's thinking as follows:

> Mrs White's wish to have enough money to enable her to buy a farm of her own was not a reasonable requirement. It was unwise and unjustifiable to break up the existing, established farming enterprise so that she could embark, much more speculatively, on another. This provision for Mrs White would leave Mr White with an amount exceeding his reasonable requirements simply in terms of a home and income. But, additionally, he reasonably required to be able to continue farming in a worthwhile way. The financial contributions from his family made this reasonable.[139]

Mr White, of course, may have resented the fact that Mrs White would no longer need to work for a living but Mrs White did want to farm and thus she appealed to the Court of Appeal, which increased her award to £1.5 million. Even if the value of the inherited farm was excluded, this still equated to only about 40 per cent of the total assets. Both parties appealed to the House of Lords,

136 Lady Hale, 'Equality and Autonomy in Family Law' (2011) 33(1) *Journal of Social Welfare and Family Law* 3, 8.
137 [1976] Fam. 83.
138 [1996] 2 FLR 286.
139 Holman J's view as summarised by Lord Nicholls at [2001] 1 AC 596, 601[F]–602[A].

which upheld the quantum of the Court of Appeal decision, if not its reasoning. Lord Nicholls, with whom the other Lords agree, held that:

- 'The statutory provisions lend no support to the idea that a claimant's financial needs, even interpreted generously and called reasonable requirements, are to be regarded as determinative . . . the end product of this assessment of financial needs should be seen, and treated by the court, for what it is: only one of the several factors to which the court is to have particular regard'.[140]

- 'In seeking to achieve a fair outcome, there is no place for discrimination between husband and wife and their respective roles. . . . If, in their different spheres, each contributed equally to the family, then in principle it matters not which of them earned the money and built up the assets. There should be no bias in favour of the money-earner and against the home-maker and the child-carer.'[141]

- Before reaching a firm conclusion and making an order along those lines, a judge would always be 'well advised to check his tentative views against the *yardstick of equality* of division. As a general guide, equality should be departed from only if, and to the extent that, there is good reason for doing so'.[142] This is not to introduce a presumption or a starting point of equal division.[143]

- Assets inherited by or gifted to a party to a marriage represent a contribution made by that party, which is a relevant s25 factor. 'The judge should . . . decide how important it is in the particular case. The nature and value of the property, and the time when and circumstances in which the property was acquired, are among the relevant matters to be considered. However, in the ordinary course, this factor can be expected to carry little weight, if any, in a case where the claimant's financial needs cannot be met without recourse to this property. . . . The initial cash contribution made by Mr White's father in the early days cannot carry much weight 33 years later.'[144]

- And, per Lord Cooke: 'Bearing in mind that it was a marriage of more than 30 years, that there were three children and that the wife was an active partner in the farming business as well as meeting the responsibilities of wife and mother, the only plausible reason for departing from equality can be the financial help given by the husband's father. . . . the significance of this is diminished . . . over a long marriage . . . My only doubt is whether the help from the husband's father should be seen as justifying a difference of the order of 20% in the overall shares of the parties. I think that £1.5m was probably about the minimum that could have been awarded to Mrs White without exposing the award to further increase on further appeal.'[145]

4.6.2 After *White*

In its clear focus on equality and non-discrimination, *White* moved courts away from what Diduck has called 'the "traditional" family values of provider/dependant' and into a rights-based discourse that proved fatal to the concept of reasonable requirements.[146]

---

[140] [2001] 1 AC 596, 608C–D; 609A.
[141] [2001] 1 AC 596, 605B–E.
[142] [2001] 1 AC 596, 605F–G.
[143] [2001] 1 AC 596, 606B–F.
[144] [2001] 1 AC 596, 610F–G; 611B.
[145] [2001] 1 AC 596, 615F–G; 616A.
[146] A Diduck, 'What Is Family Law For?' (2011) 64 *Current Legal Problems* 287, 299.

'The "yardstick of equality of division" [instead] filled the vacuum which resulted.'[147] Notwithstanding Lord Nicholls' rejection of either a starting point or legal presumption of equal division, it did become more common thereafter for parties to share capital, if not income, equally. For this reason, and for its respect for equality as between gender roles, *White* is of fundamental importance to the position of women in society.

Of course, while the Lords tried to provide general guidance, *White* was a long marriage in which the parties had each fully contributed. But what of a short marriage in which the contributions of one were significantly greater than the other, or a long marriage in which the separation of breadwinner and homemaker roles meant the homemaker would be in a significantly worse position than the breadwinner post-divorce? The yardstick of equality did not seem to provide a fair approach to such situations. A few years after *White*, in two cases that were joined on appeal, *Miller v Miller* and *McFarlane v McFarlane*, the Lords had once more to provide guidance on the requirements of fairness.

KEY CASE *Miller v Miller and McFarlane v McFarlane* [2006] UKHL 24

Mr and Mrs Miller had been married for two years and nine months, with no prior cohabitation and no children. He was 39 and she 33. When they married, Mr Miller's assets were £16.7 million; in October 2004 (post-separation) they stood at about £17.5 million, plus whatever value should be attributed to his 200,000 shares in New Star, an asset management fund that he ran. Estimates for the shares, which had increased in value during their marriage, ranged from £12–18 million. Mrs Miller's assets were £100,000 but she had debts of £300,000. She had given up a job earning £85,000 once she married. The issue was how much Mrs Miller should be awarded when the assets were generated by the husband before and during the short marriage.

Mr and Mrs McFarlane had been married for 16 years with two years' prior cohabitation. Both were 46 years old. They had three children, aged 16, 15, and 9. Until 1990, when Mr McFarlane was promoted, the parties earned the same amount; indeed, Mrs McFarlane, a solicitor at a leading city law firm, at times earned more. In 1991, before the birth of their second child, the parties agreed the wife should abandon her career and bring up the children. Mr McFarlane continued in his accountancy career, becoming a partner at Deloitte. The capital in the marriage was worth around £3 million, which they agreed to split equally. However, Mr McFarlane earned £750,000 per year net, and the wife nothing, and only potentially £30,000 if she retrained. It was inevitable that he should pay spousal maintenance, and it was also agreed that this should be for their joint lives or further order. The issue was how much maintenance.

The two leading judgments in *Miller* and *McFarlane* are those of Lord Nicholls, whose judgment in *White* was so important, and Lady Hale.

- Per Lord Nicholls: 'In the search for a fair outcome it is pertinent to have in mind that fairness generates obligations as well as rights. The financial provision made on divorce by one party for the other, still typically the wife, is not in the nature of largesse. It is not a case of "taking away" from one party and "giving" to the other property which "belongs" to the former. The claimant is not a supplicant. Each party to a marriage is entitled to a fair share of the available property. The search is always for what are the requirements of fairness in the particular case.'
- 'What then, in principle, are these requirements? The statute provides that first consideration shall be given to the welfare of the children of the marriage. . . .Beyond this several elements, or strands, are readily discernible': needs, compensation, and equal sharing.' (In *Charman*, Sir

---

[147] *Charman v Charman (No 4)* [2007] EWCA Civ 503, [64] (Sir Mark Potter P).

Mark Potter noted that the three rationales identified in *Miller/McFarlane*—needs, compensation, and sharing—each derive from s25 and can be linked back to s25.[148])

- 'The most common rationale for departing from equal division is that the relationship has generated needs which it is right that the other party should meet.' 'Mutual dependence begets mutual obligations of support.'
- Compensation is 'aimed at redressing any significant prospective economic disparity between the parties arising from the way they conducted their marriage.' Compensation will not be a factor in every marriage.
- 'The equal sharing principle derives from the basic concept of equality permeating a marriage as understood today. . . . When their partnership ends each is entitled to an equal share of the assets of the partnership, unless there is a good reason to the contrary. In considering equal sharing, the Lords distinguished between matrimonial property and non-matrimonial property. Matrimonial property should be shared equally unless there is good reason not to do so. The contribution of non-matrimonial property is part of 'all the circumstances of the case' and potentially gives a reason to depart from equality in favour of the contributor.
- 'In general, it can be assumed that the marital partnership does not stay alive for the purpose of sharing future resources unless this is justified by need or compensation. The ultimate objective is to give each party an equal start on the road to independent living.'

Applying these principles to Mr and Mrs Miller's situation:

- Mrs Miller's needs were 'comparatively small' and she would be able to return to work as she had not been out of the employment market for long. She should be entitled to 'a gentle transition' from the standard of living during the marriage 'to the standard she could expect as a self-sufficient woman'.[149] 'The judge was also entitled to regard the high standard of living enjoyed by the parties during the marriage.'[150]
- She had no claim to compensation for relationship-generated disadvantage.
- The husband brought substantial wealth into the marriage at its outset. That was non-matrimonial property. 'That was a major contribution he made to the marriage'[151] that justified a departure from equality.
- However, the wife was entitled to share in the matrimonial assets. 'Although the marriage was short, the matrimonial property was of great value'.[152] It included their two homes and 'the considerable increase of the husband's wealth during the marriage'.[153]

The court awarded Mrs Miller £5 million. This represented less than one-third of the value of the New Star shares, 'reflecting the amount of work done by the husband on this business project before the marriage', and was about one-sixth of the husband's assets.[154]

And for Mr and Mrs McFarlane:

- The parties' contributions 'were of different but equal value', as reflected in the equal division of the capital.[155]

[148] Sir Mark Potter at *Charman* [69]: each derive from s25(1) and (2) 'although two of them are not expressly mentioned' , each of the three distributive principles can be collected from s25(2), or at any rate from s25(1) and (2), of the Act and that each of the matters set out in (b) to (h) of s25(2) can conveniently be assigned to one or another of the three of them'.
[149] Lady Hale at [157]–[158].
[150] Lord Nicholls at [72].
[151] Lord Nicholls at [69].
[152] Lord Nicholls at [71].
[153] Lady Hale at [158].
[154] Lord Nicholls at [73].
[155] Lord Nicholls at [84].

- The husband's earnings 'were the result of the parties' joint endeavours at the early stages of his professional career'. He would continue to benefit from that, not just during the marriage but also afterwards. Conversely, 'as primary carer of the three children, the wife continued to be at economic disadvantage and continued to make a contribution from which the children and, indirectly, the husband benefited. He was relieved of the day-to-day responsibility for their children.' She had foregone a career 'as successful and highly paid as the husband's'.[156]
- 'It would be manifestly unfair if her income award were confined to her needs. This is a paradigm case for an award of compensation in respect of the future economic disparity sustained by the wife, arising from the way the parties conducted their marriage.'[157]
- The husband's income was considerably in excess of the parties' needs and the wife was entitled to 'generous income provision' and to 'a share in the very large surplus, on the principles both of sharing the fruits of the matrimonial partnership and of compensation for the comparable position she would have been in had she not compromised her own career for the sake of them all'.[158]

Mrs McFarlane therefore received half of the capital plus spousal maintenance of £250,000 per year from Mr McFarlane for the duration of their joint lives. Mr McFarlane also paid her child maintenance of £60,000 per year and paid the children's school fees.

4.7 The principles of need, compensation, and sharing

Since *Miller/McFarlane*, courts have applied the three strands, or rationales, of needs, compensation, and sharing to a wide range of cases. Each of these principles is discussed in more detail below.

4.7.1 Needs

Fairness almost always requires each party's needs to be met on divorce, subject to there being sufficient money to do so. As Hynes points out, need is undefined by statute and what it encompasses is situation specific.[159] It generally involves the parties having somewhere to live— 'there is nothing more awful than homelessness'[160]—and sufficient money to live on. But need 'is a very broad concept',[161] capable of encompassing a wide range of types of expenditure. In the majority of cases, the outcome is determined not by principle (in which needs should be generously interpreted per *Miller/McFarlane*)[162] but by what is actually possible with the assets available.

---

[156] Lord Nicholls at [90]–[92].
[157] Lord Nicholls at [93].
[158] Lady Hale at [154].
[159] T Hynes, 'Limited Assets: Meeting Reasonable Needs – Is there Enough to Go Around?' [2020, May] *Family Law* 618.
[160] *Cordle v Cordle* [2001] EWCA Civ 1791 [33] (Thorpe LJ).
[161] Law Commission, *Matrimonial Property, Needs and Agreements* (Law Com No 343, 2014) glossary.
[162] See Lady Hale at [144].

Most needs 'will have been generated by the marriage',[163] but some needs, such as those caused by age or disability (both s25 factors) will not be, and it appears these must still be met, as in *Miller/McFarlane* Lord Nicholls seems not to make a distinction between needs generated by the relationship and those external to the relationship.[164] Lady Hale similarly notes that the 'most common source of need is the presence of children, whose welfare is always the first consideration, *or of other dependent relatives, such as elderly parents*' (emphasis added).

For her, however, the key is that such needs are 'linked to the parties' relationship, either causally or temporally, and not to extrinsic, unrelated factors, such as a disability arising after the marriage has ended'.[165]

Heenan has suggested four types of causal and temporal connection to a marriage:

1. Causal and temporal, e.g., where both parties agree that one should give up work during the marriage to care for the children

2. Causal but not temporal, such as where a child becomes very ill following the end of the marriage, and one parent gives up work to care for them

3. Temporal but not causal, for example where a party gives up work during the marriage for a reason not related to the marriage, such as to care for elderly parents

4. Neither temporal or causal, e.g., where a spouse suffers a disability after the end of the marriage. Needs under this fourth category would not have to be met.[166]

The approach taken in *Miller/McFarlane* was affirmed by Lord Wilson in another Key Case, *Wyatt v Vince*, which considered how needs may function when the financial remedy order was brought several decades post-divorce.[167]

In *MB v EB* the wife argued that the husband's needs did not flow from the marriage 'but from his own psychological make-up and his inability or unwillingness to make something of his life'.[168] Nevertheless, she was required to meet his needs, albeit that these were nowhere near the level that he sought, because she had known of these difficulties, and they had been exacerbated by a head injury occurring on their honeymoon.[169] There was, in this unusual-fact case, a causal connection, but a very limited one.

Mostyn J has suggested that where needs are *not* causally connected to the marriage any periodical payments should be aimed only at alleviating hardship because the sole justification for them in that situation would be 'macro-utilitarian' based on the theory that 'it is better that the ex-husband picks up the cost of the ex-wife's support rather than the hard-pressed taxpayer. This . . . is a matter of social policy'.[170]

[163] *Miller v Miller/McFarlane v McFarlane* [2006] UKHL 24 [11] (Lord Nicholls).
[164] *Miller v Miller/McFarlane v McFarlane* [2006] UKHL 24 [11] (Lord Nicholls).
[165] *Miller v Miller/McFarlane v McFarlane* [2006] UKHL 24 [137]–[138] (Lady Hale).
[166] A Heenan, 'Causal and Temporal Connections in Financial Remedy Cases: The Meaning of Marriage' (2018) 30(1) *Child and Family Law Quarterly* 75.
[167] *Wyatt v Vince* [2015] UKSC 14 [33]. For a discussion of needs in this case, see L Ferguson, '*Wyatt v Vince*: The Reality of Individualised Justice – Financial Orders, Forensic Delay, and Access to Justice' (2015) 27(2) *Child and Family Law Quarterly* 195.
[168] The court had to determine a number of preliminary issues, reported at [2019] EWHC 1649 (Fam).
[169] *MB v EB (No 2)* [2019] EWHC 3676 (Fam). In the event, the husband's award was completely wiped out by the costs that he had to pay when the court found he had run the case unreasonably.
[170] *SS v NS* [2014] EWHC 4183 [31] and [46].

While both parties' needs must be met, they are specific to the individual—based on such s25 factors as the standard of living during the marriage, the ages of the parties (an elderly party may have modest needs as a result of short life expectancy, for example, but conversely they may require a large proportion in order to meet the costs of a nursing home or carer), earning capacity, the duration of the marriage, the existence of any disability, the presence of children, and the responsibilities that each party has. Thus there is ample scope for disagreement: the parties may agree that each should be housed, for example, but not the size of house or whether a party should buy or rent. They must obviously also have enough money to meet their necessary outgoings but may disagree over what standard of living is appropriate. In *Ipekci*, the Court called the assessment of needs 'a pure exercise of discretion, one of the few remaining exercises in the field of family law that can be properly described as truly discretionary as opposed to the formation of a qualitative decision. The width of the discretion is not limitless, but it is wide.'[171]

In low asset cases, the court's role is to 'stretch modest finite resources so far as possible to meet the parties' needs'.[172] Of course, even in cases where the assets are modest—one house, a few savings, probably a few credit card debts—meeting needs uses up all of the assets, so the other principles, compensation and sharing, simply do not come into play. The requirement to give first consideration to the welfare of any children means that the primary carer is more likely have his or her needs met in priority:

> The invariable practice in English law is to try to maintain a stable home for the children after their parents' divorce . . . Giving priority to the children's welfare should also involve ensuring that their primary carer is properly provided for, because it is well known that the security and stability of children depends in large part upon the security and stability of their primary carers.[173]

This means, in practice, that a home for the children is a priority:

> The most pressing need of the parties is housing. For their security, and consistent with their status as home-owners during their lives together, purchased accommodation should surely be striven for. They, and their minor daughter who is the court's first consideration, need no less if it can be achieved.[174]

Where it is possible to rehouse both parents in purchased properties, that should be the aim, even if it requires the parties to financially stretch themselves or borrow. Per the Court of Appeal in *M v B (Ancillary Proceedings: Lump Sum)*:

> In all these cases it is one of the paramount considerations, in applying the section 25 criteria, to endeavour to stretch what is available to cover the need of each for a home, particularly where there are young children involved. Obviously the primary carer needs whatever is available to make the main home for the children, but it is of importance, albeit it is of lesser importance, that the other parent should have a home of his own where the children can enjoy their contact time with him. Of course, there are cases where there is not enough

---

[171] *Ipekci v McConnell* [2019] EWFC 19, [29] (Mostyn J).
[172] *Miller v Miller/McFarlane v McFarlane* [2006] UKHL 24 [12] (Lord Nicholls). For an extremely low asset case, see *Delaney v Delaney* [1990] 2 FLR 457. Such cases are rarely appealed because of the cost.
[173] *Miller v Miller/McFarlane v McFarlane* [2006] UKHL 24 [128] (Lady Hale).
[174] *RM v TM* [2020] EWFC 41.

to provide a home for either. Of course, there are cases where there is only enough to provide one. But in any case, where there is, by stretch and a degree of risk-taking, the possibility of a division to enable both to rehouse themselves, that is an exceptionally important
consideration and one which will almost invariably have a decisive impact on outcome.[175]

If it is not possible for both parties to buy, then the children's needs will prevail and this
is why in low asset cases the primary carer will receive the bulk of the available assets.[176]

SCENARIO 2

Illustration 4: Jan and Ahmed

This is a tricky case. There are not very many resources, which is often the case with a young couple
and small children. It is unlikely that there will be any resources left after we have met their needs.
We need to stretch this money as far as it will go to ensure everyone's needs are met. This is a short
marriage, but there are children and giving first consideration to the welfare of the children may
mean that the primary carer is (in the short term at least) better off.

The difficulty here is that Jan does not work and would not be expected to do so until the children are older. Some mortgage companies will take benefits into account but they are few and far
between. No bank will lend her enough money to buy a house, even if we gave her all the equity.
The welfare of the children is likely to be best served by the security of owner-occupied property
where at all possible. We could leave Jan in the house under a *Mesher* order (see 4.4.4). But she will
not be able to persuade a mortgage company to give her a mortgage, so Ahmed will continue to be
liable on that mortgage. Even if we make Jan pay the mortgage instalments, the mortgage company
will come after him if Jan defaults on payment. And, even if Ahmed was to get together enough
money to buy his own house, he will not be able to buy with a mortgage as long as he is stuck on
another mortgage: he does not earn enough for two mortgages. He will have to rent, and this too
will be difficult because renting is often more expensive than paying a mortgage. If the children live
with Jan, he will also have to pay child maintenance (see Chapter 6).

Leaving Jan in the house in this way is very risky for Ahmed, and it means he has no capital now.
But it would be on the basis of a clean break—after all, Jan cannot fairly have all the capital and periodical payments too. Of course, Ahmed is free to concentrate on his career but this is surely cold
comfort—this outcome is very bad for him in the short term. But in the long term, a clean break,
especially when Jan's earnings will be limited for years and years by the presence of children, is very
advantageous.

A second option would be to sell the house and divide up the capital. Ahmed may be able to
buy a small flat, depending on house prices where he lives, by putting down a deposit and getting a
mortgage (which he can do, as the mortgage on the matrimonial home will have been paid off when
it was sold). Jan would definitely need to rent.

So which is the fairest outcome—a *Mesher* order, with Jan staying in the house and Ahmed renting,
or both having a lump sum to put towards rent with a possibility that Ahmed could buy? This may
depend on which party you are acting for. Both proposals are fair, but each is very far from ideal, and
each party and their children will live in financially poorer circumstances. As we noted, fairness may
mean equal misery. This is by far the most difficult of our scenarios.

---

[175] *M v B (Ancillary Proceedings: Lump Sum)* [1998] 1 FLR 53, 60 (Thorpe LJ).
[176] T Hynes, 'Limited Assets: Meeting Reasonable Needs – Is there Enough to Go Around?' [2020, May] *Family Law* 618.

There is no entitlement to be able to buy a property,[177] however, and depending on the situation one or both parties may need to rent either in the private sector or through a council or housing association. If there are competing needs, then it may be equal misery, or it may be that the court determines that one party's needs are more pressing than those of the other party. Fairness will determine the outcome.[178]

For moderate asset cases, an assessment of need usually starts with consideration of the standard of living during the marriage.[179] For most people, it is simply impossible to continue to live to the same standard once the assets are divided between two households. If, however, there are sufficient assets, then the needs will not be the fundamentals of life, but a more generous quantification. The need may be for a four-bedroom detached house rather than a two-bed terrace, and a new car rather than a second-hand one. In high-asset cases the standard of living experienced during the marriage means that court will cater to needs that a less wealthy person would view as luxury: in *McCartney v Mills McCartney*, Heather Mills received £25 million, including funds for a house in London, a housekeeper, a wine cellar, and a holiday home, and this was based entirely on her claims under the need principle.[180] In *Robson v Robson*, needs included property sufficient to continue to stable and exercise horses.[181] Mrs Juffali received £62 million based on her needs, but this is not the highest award on a needs-only basis, for the wife in *AAZ v BBZ* received £224 million for her needs, including for £67 million for houses and lifetime maintenance equivalent to £5 million per year. If you think this is greedy, note that the husband had assessed his income needs at an eye-watering £25 million per year.[182] Thus, '"needs" does not mean needs. It is a term of art. Obviously, no one actually needs 25m, or 62m, or 224m, for accommodation and sustenance.'[183]

It has been said that 'the inclusion in the section 25 factors of the marital standard of living is a statutory recognition of the relative elasticity of the concept of needs.'[184] While 'the lifestyle enjoyed during the marriage sets a level or benchmark that is relevant to the assessment of the level of the independent lifestyles to be enjoyed by the parties',[185] it is not, however, quite true to say, as Ruth Deech has, that '[i]f you marry a captain of industry, you become one yourself for all time, at least as far as the standard of living is concerned.'[186] In *BD v FD*, Moylan J said that '[t]he use of the standard of living as the benchmark emphatically does not mean that . . . in every case needs are to be met at that level either at all or for more than a defined period (of less than life).' Particularly after a short marriage, where the standard of living has been experienced for a shorter time, or in cases where the party in need has future earning potential, the court may well use the standard of living simply

---

[177] Lord Hoffman's view in *Piglowska v Piglowski* [1999] UKHL 27 was that *M v B* is not authority for a right to purchased accommodation but simply a useful guideline.
[178] See section 4.5.2 for discussion of the outcomes of divorce for men and women.
[179] Section 25(2)(c); *SS v NS* [2014] EWHC 4183.
[180] All needs of Heather Mills McCartney identified in [2008] EWHC 401 (Fam). Compensation did not apply on the facts; and the husband's wealth was almost wholly pre-marital (he was, of course, one of the Beatles).
[181] [2010] EWCA Civ 1171.
[182] *Juffali v Juffali* [2016] EWHC 1684 (Fam); *AAZ v BBZ* [2016] EWHC 3234 (Fam).
[183] *FF v KF* [2017] EWHC 1093 at [18] (Mostyn J).
[184] *Juffali v Juffali* [2016] EWHC 1684 (Fam) [145] (Roberts J).
[185] *G v G* [2012] EWHC 167 (Fam) [136] (Charles J).
[186] R Deech, 'What's a Woman Worth?' [2009] *Family Law* 1140, 1140.

as a benchmark of *short-term* needs with a subsequent tapering to enable 'a gentle transition from that standard to the standard that [he or] she could expect as a self-sufficient [person]'.[187] This reflects the fact that 'the objective of financial orders made to meet needs should be to enable a transition to independence, to the extent that it is possible'[188] and that 'the ultimate objective is to give each party an equal start on the road to independent living'.[189] Thus the court may provide more generously in the early years post-divorce or for the duration of children's minority, with a reduction sometime later. It could do so by providing a lump sum that will be used up, or periodical payments with an end-date or a taper, or a house from which a party will need to downsize in the future in order to free up money to live on. A transition to independence may, of course, not be possible in some cases or at least not without interfering with the overall objective of fairness. This is particularly likely where there has been a long marriage where one party has been out of the employment market for decades. In such cases, an order would cater to lifetime needs.

SCENARIO 3

Illustration 1: Mary and Steve

Mary and Steve are our high net worth couple—the former musician and his PR manager wife. One of the issues in the case is what level of lifestyle Mary would be entitled to maintain after divorce, when virtually all of their money predates their relationship. Mary earns £80,000 per year. We need to know whether she can meet her needs, generously interpreted, within this figure, and the parties may well argue about that. If she cannot, her needs will have to be met from Steve's savings and these are mostly non-matrimonial (see 4.7.3.1). We need to consider both of their needs, but it is Mary who would be the recipient of money as the lesser earner.

Let us apply some principles:

- Their daughter, whose welfare is the first consideration, is entitled to a lifestyle commensurate with that of her parents—it would not be in her interests for her to see very disparate lifestyles between her parents.
- We first need to put a figure on Mary's needs. Does her income of £80,000 per year meet her needs? Her current lifestyle provides a benchmark for her needs going forward. However, that does not mean she is always entitled to that level of lifestyle. Her age, earning capacity, and the length of the marriage all help us to determine how long she should be able to live that lifestyle for.
- This is a mid-to-long marriage. Mary has maintained a wealthy lifestyle for 15 years. There is a stronger argument for her being able to carry that lifestyle on than there would be in the case of a short marriage.
- She is aged 55. She has about 10 to 12 years of working life ahead of her and as there are no pensions she will need to use capital to supplement her state pension. In the case of a medium to long marriage with a party near(ish) to retirement, the court will almost certainly meet those needs generously, but may consider it reasonable for her needs to slowly reduce. It may be helpful to look at her lifestyle over two periods: before retirement, and after retirement, perhaps with a reduction in lifestyle on retirement.

---

[187] *Miller v Miller/McFarlane v McFarlane* [2006] UKHL 24 [158] (Lady Hale).
[188] Law Commission, *Matrimonial Property, Needs and Agreements* (Law Com No 343, 2014) para 3.67.
[189] *Miller v Miller/McFarlane v McFarlane* [2006] UKHL 24 [144] (Lady Hale).

4.7.2 Compensation

Although not mentioned explicitly in the Matrimonial Causes Act, compensation is another of the rationales for the redistribution of assets identified in the judgments of Lord Nicholls and Lady Hale in *Miller/McFarlane*. Its purpose is to redress 'any significant prospective economic disparity between the parties arising from the way they conducted their marriage'. This is not as simple as one giving up work to take care of children. Even where both work, there may not be 'completely equal opportunity for both.'[190] There are many kinds of decisions that could affect the parties:

> The couple may move from the city to the country; they may move to another country; they may adopt a completely different life-style; one of them may give up a well-paid job that she hates for the sake of a less lucrative job that she loves; one may give up a dead-end job to embark upon a new course of study. These sorts of things happen all the time in a relationship.[191]

Compensation therefore reflects 'the differential risk between the parties'[192] of the way in which they have ordered their lives, and their shared responsibility for the consequences. As Mostyn J noted in *SS v NS*, 'for many women the marriage is the defining economic event of their whole lives and the decisions made in it may well reverberate for many years after its ending'.[193]

In some cases, compensation will not arise at all. In *Mills-McCartney*, for example, the wife's compensation claim was rejected as, if anything, marriage to Paul McCartney had enhanced the wife's career prospects.[194] In *Radmacher v Granatino* the majority held that 'the husband's decision to abandon his lucrative career in the city for the fields of academia was not motivated by the demands of his family, but reflected his own preference.'[195] In each case, the award was instead based on the applicant's need. In most cases, needs will, as we have considered, absorb all the assets, so there will be nothing to meet any compensation claim. Compensation, therefore, is only really relevant in cases where the other party, 'who has been the beneficiary of the choices made during the marriage, is a high earner with a substantial surplus over what is required to meet needs'.[196]

Mr and Mrs McFarlane are a paradigmatic example. Mrs McFarlane gave up work to be a full-time parent; her husband continued his career. They arranged their affairs

> . . . in a way that has greatly advantaged the husband in terms of his earning capacity but left the wife severely handicapped so far as her own earing capacity is concerned. Then the wife suffers a double loss: a diminution in her earning capacity and the loss of a share in her husband's enhanced income.[197]

---

[190] *Miller v Miller/McFarlane v McFarlane* [2006] UKHL 24 [138] (Lady Hale).
[191] *Radmacher v Granatino* [2010] UKSC 42 [188] (Lady Hale).
[192] J Eekelaar, 'Property and Financial Settlement on Divorce – Sharing and Compensating' [2006] *Family Law* 754, 756.
[193] *SS v NS* [2014] EWHC 4183 [30].
[194] [2008] EWHC 401 (Fam) [84].
[195] *Radmacher v Granatino* [2010] UKSC 42 [121] (Lord Philips P).
[196] *Miller v Miller/McFarlane v McFarlane* [2006] UKHL 24 [140] (Lady Hale).
[197] *Miller v Miller/McFarlane v McFarlane* [2006] UKHL 24 [13] (Lord Nicholls).

When providing sufficient to meet a party's needs, you are to some extent also compensating them for the fact they cannot meet those needs themselves as a result of decisions made in the relationship. So one needs to be careful of double-counting. But in *Miller/McFarlane*, Lady Hale thought that 'the economic disadvantage generated by the relationship may go beyond need, however generously interpreted'[198] and 'in some cases, compensation could justify a greater award than needs and equal sharing'. For Mrs McFarlane, for example, an award limited to her needs, even generously assessed, would leave her significantly worse than that of her former husband. She assessed her needs as carer for three children as £128,000 per year, of which her earning capacity was about £30,000. The husband assessed his needs as £60,000–80,000. His net income was £750,000. If she was awarded only the extra £100,000 she required (significant though this is by 'ordinary' standards), she would be £650,000 worse off than her former husband *per year* as a result of the choice they made that she would give up work to care for their children. Even if we interpreted her needs more generously, a purely needs based approach will not meet the requirements of fairness.

Despite this, in a series of cases, lower court judges have treated compensation as falling simply within a generous assessment of needs—see *VB v JP* ('any element of compensation is best dealt with by a generous assessment of her continuing needs'),[199] *McFarlane (No. 2)*,[200] *B v S*,[201] and, most notably, *SA v PA*. In the latter case, Mostyn J thought that:

- It will only be in a very rare and exceptional case where the principle will be capable of being successfully invoked.

- Such a case will be one where the court can say without any speculation, i.e., with almost near certainty, that the claimant gave up a very high earning career which had it not been foregone would have led to earnings at least equivalent to that presently enjoyed by the respondent.

- Such a high earning career will have been practised by the claimant over an appreciable period during the marriage. Proof of this track-record is key.

- Once these findings have been made compensation will be reflected by fixing . . . the award . . . towards the top end of the discretionary bracket applicable for a needs assessment on the facts of the case. Compensation ought not be reflected by a premium or additional element on top of the needs-based award.[202]

Thus, where compensation is a relevant factor, the line of cases leading to *SA v PA* indicates that it will be assessed not as a separate head of claim or premium on top of a needs-based award, but instead within generously assessed need. While this approach seems to have attracted the most judicial favour, it is not a universal view: within a month of Mostyn J's judgment, Coleridge J in *H v H* awarded an additional element for compensation on top of the wife's needs on the basis that 'there remains a very small number of cases where it stares the court in the face and to ignore it and simply approach the case on the basis of the more

---

[198] *Miller v Miller/McFarlane v McFarlane* [2006] UKHL 24 [140] (Lady Hale).
[199] [2008] EWHC 112 (Fam) [59] (Sir Mark Potter P).
[200] [2009] EWHC 891 (Fam) (Charles J). This was the wife's application to vary the maintenance payments for herself and the parties' children following the original House of Lords decision.
[201] [2012] EWHC 265 (Fam) (Mostyn J).
[202] [2014] EWHC 392 (Fam) [36]–[37].

simplistic "needs" argument does not do full justice'.[203] In Key Case *Wyatt v Vince*, Lord Wilson described the applicant's case for compensation as much more powerful than her claim for needs, in the context of a case in which she had solely borne the financial burden of raising the parties' children but considerable time had elapsed since the end of the marriage.[204] Wyatt represents, therefore, the Supreme Court reiterating its initial conception of compensation as not limited to those situations involving the loss of a high flying career.

The academic Jo Miles suggests that 'an award should only contain an element of compensation, as distinct from need, to the extent that the relevant losses exceed the applicant's needs'.[205] This seems to reflect much better what was intended by the House of Lords in *Miller/McFarlane*, as Lady Hale spoke of 'a premium above needs'.[206] But it is very much the minority approach.

FOCUS Think Critically

Attacks on Compensation

Of the three rationales identified in *Miller/McFarlane*, it is compensation that has been subjected to the most sustained judicial and academic attacks. There are a number of reasons why it has been so contentious, and these go both to the theoretical basis of compensation and to its practical implementation. (For convenience, and to reflect statistical likelihood, we will refer to the applicant for compensation as the wife.)

1. Lady Hale's statement that compensation is 'for the comparable position which she might have been in',[207] if taken at face value, requires the court to assess what position the wife would have been in if the parties had made different decisions during the marriage. This is extremely difficult. One cannot safely assume that the wife would have had a continuous high-earning career.[208] A great many situations could have intervened, such as redundancy, ill health, changes of career, house moves, or changes in the job market, and affected the wife's career and thus the quantification of her loss. There must also 'be a high possibility that, had the [wife] not had a relationship with the [husband] . . . she will have had one with another person'.[209] Thus her loss is based on the fact that *this* marriage failed, and the risks inherent in the decision were therefore realised. 'The most direct measure of her financial loss would compare her situation at divorce to the hypothetical situation had she married a different man.'[210] And who knows what the situation would be then? 'It is simply not possible (and highly undesirable and costly) to conduct . . . a speculative "what if. . .?" exercise to reconstruct the parties' marriage on a different basis.'[211]

2. In most other areas of law in which compensation arises, such as employment law or personal injury, the recipient of the compensation is an innocent victim of a tort or breach of contract. Yet, in

[203] *H v H* [2014] EWHC 760 (Fam). It is interesting to note that Coleridge J and Mostyn J have each given speeches about divorce law which seems to indicate very different views about marriage itself. Both speak, of course, from a position of privilege.

[204] [2015] UKSC 14.

[205] J Miles, '*Charman v Charman*: Making Sense of Need, Compensation and Equal Sharing after *Miller/McFarlane*' [2008] *Child and Family Law Quarterly* 378, 389.

[206] *Miller v Miller/McFarlane v McFarlane* [2006] UKHL 24 [140] (Lady Hale).

[207] *Miller v Miller/McFarlane v McFarlane* [2006] UKHL 24 [154] (Lady Hale).

[208] *SA v PA* [2014] EWHC 392 (Fam) [30] (Mostyn J).

[209] J Eekelaar, 'Property and Financial Settlement on Divorce – Sharing and Compensating' [2006] *Family Law* 754, 756.

[210] American Law Institute, *Principles of Family Dissolution: Analysis and Recommendations* para 5.05 comment e (ALI 2002). Cited by J Eekelaar in his useful discussion (n 167).

[211] *RP v RP* [2006] EWHC 3409 (Fam) [64] (Coleridge J).

a financial remedy context, the wife may well have been a willing participant in the decisions that have given rise to the compensation claim. As Ferguson has said, 'If each decision were part of a joint life plan, why should we presume that the now-impoverished spouse did not make those decisions for her benefit? . . . The character of the self-sacrificing wife is attributed to her retrospectively.'[212]

3. The parties may well be entirely happy with their respective roles. The husband may prefer his role as a breadwinner. The wife may have been happy to give up or reduce her work—perhaps she hated her job. However, Lady Hale thought '[t]he fact that she might have wanted to do this is neither here nor there. Most breadwinners want to go on breadwinning. The fact that they enjoy their work does not disentitle them to a proper share in the fruits of their labours.'[213]

4. It is unrealistic to take the view that each individual party to a marriage is free to make a decision in a vacuum in which they only have their own self-interests to worry about—and would we want family life to be like that? Making sacrifices or compromises is a normal part of marriage. It does not follow from that that we should therefore ignore the different consequences of such decisions. Indeed, if such decisions are made as a result of a view of marriage as a joint endeavour, there is a strong moral case for recognition.

5. 'It is not only in [the child's] interests but in the community's interests that parents, whether mothers or fathers and spouses, whether husbands or wives, should have a real choice between concentrating on breadwinning and concentrating on home-making and child-rearing, and do not feel forced, for fear of what might happen should their marriage break down much late in life, to abandon looking after the home and the family to other people for the sake of maintaining a career.'[214]

6. There appears to be no particular justification for limiting the claims to those who have lost a high-flying career. There are all sorts of other sacrifices or compromises people make that have financial consequences post-divorce.

For the most part, compensation survives, barely, as a pale imitation of its creators' apparent intention. The general judicial trend was summed up rather bluntly by Valentine Le Grice QC in his response to the Law Commission's consultation on needs: 'Compensation is a useless concept in assessing spousal support. . . . Since the concept was introduced by the House of Lords it has been politely and rightly ignored by Judges at first instance.'[215] This does not mean that the courts do not take account of the aspects of marital life that give rise to compensation. It means that they treat these as part of need. The question is whether in doing so they are giving sufficient weight to this issue.

In most cases, a spouse will be—in purely financial terms—better off being the breadwinner than the recipient of compensation. Although they will have to meet the other's needs post-divorce, those needs, even generously interpreted, will not be as much as the breadwinner will retain. As we see above, even Mrs McFarlane—held up as the paradigm of someone who has given up a high-flying career and is entitled to compensation for it—will not retain as much through maintenance as she would have obtained had she continued on her career, given that she was at one stage earning more than Mr McFarlane and was on a similar career track. (But here's the rub: what if she had been impeded in her career by a non-child related issue? And does it matter that she presumably wanted to have children, and presumably agreed to give up her career for them? Many of the commentators disagree with Lady Hale's views on these points.)

But even in a case where the assets are lower, it is usually still better *in the longer term* to be the breadwinner. We noted in section 4.7.1 that the requirement to give first consideration to the welfare

---

[212] L Ferguson, 'Family, Social Inequalities, and the Persuasive Force of Interpersonal Obligation' (2008) 22 *International Journal of Law, Policy and the Family* 61, 75.

[213] *Miller v Miller/McFarlane v McFarlane* [2006] UKHL 24 [154] (Lady Hale).

[214] *SRJ v DWJ (Financial Provision)* [1999] 2 FLR 179, 182 (Hale J).

[215] Law Commission, *Matrimonial Property, Needs and Agreements* (Law Com No 343, 2014) para 3.27.

of the child may mean the primary carer takes the bulk of the capital. Despite this, women usually have much worse outcomes in the long term than men both if they are primary carers of children and *even if they do not have children*. Fisher and Low, using data from the British Household Panel Survey, found that following divorce, women's average household income falls by 31 per cent, after controlling for household size (such as whether they have children with them), and only returns to its pre-divorce average some nine years later.[216] For women, benefits income is important, especially in the early years. Some 23 per cent of wives move from non-receipt of benefits to receipt after separation compared to 7 per cent of husbands.[217] The Fawcett Society found that 'women who have divorced have a higher level of debt than their male counterparts, which goes against the general trend of men having higher levels of debt than women.'[218] Westaway and McKay found that women have fewer savings too—68 per cent of divorced women have less than £1,500 in savings, compared to 51 per cent of divorced men.[219]

However, women's financial recovery is not due to their earnings, which do not change these prospects significantly, even with retraining. (In fact, where there are children, retraining 'is associated with income growth being 53% lower', which 'may indicate that retraining is undertaken to accommodate childcare responsibilities'[220] and thus more about convenient working patterns than economic advantage.) Instead, Westaway and McKay found that the return to pre-divorce average is most commonly due to the inclusion in the household finances of a new partner's income: within four years, 43 per cent of women are remarried or cohabiting.[221] Older women, those in poor health, and those with children have lesser prospects of financial recovery, perhaps due to a lesser chance of repartnering.[222] Five years from separation, men have an income that is 25 per cent higher on average than their pre-separation income (compared to 9 per cent lower for women).[223] Many men do repartner—about 51 per cent remarry or cohabit within four years—but Fisher and Low suggest that 'men repartner with women whose personal income is cancelled out by the extra costs to the household', so, for men, repartnering often has a neutral financial effect.[224]

4.7.3 Sharing

The third of the rationales from *Miller/McFarlane* is sharing 'the fruits of the matrimonial partnership'.[225] Lord Nicholls refers to 'equal sharing' and the 'sharing entitlement'. In *Charman*, the Court of Appeal thought 'those phrases describe more than a yardstick for

[216] H Fisher and H Low, 'Who Wins, Who Loses and Who Recovers from Divorce?' in J Miles and R Probert (eds), *Sharing Lives, Dividing Assets: An Inter-Disciplinary Study* (Hart 2009) 228. See also H Fisher and H Low, 'Finances after Divorce in the Short and Long Term' [2018] *Family Law* 1533; and 'Recovery from Divorce: Comparing High and Low Income Couples' (2016) 30 *International Journal of Law, Policy, and the Family* 338.

[217] S Jarvis and SP Jenkins, 'Marital Splits and Income Changes: Evidence from the British Household Panel Survey' 53(2) *Population Studies* 237, 251–2.

[218] J Westaway and S McKay, *Women's Financial Assets and Debts* (Fawcett Society 2007) 25.

[219] J Westaway and S McKay, *Women's Financial Assets and Debts* (Fawcett Society 2007) 36.

[220] J Westaway and S McKay, *Women's Financial Assets and Debts* (Fawcett Society 2007) 242.

[221] J Westaway and S McKay, *Women's Financial Assets and Debts* (Fawcett Society 2007) 239.

[222] J Westaway and S McKay, *Women's Financial Assets and Debts* (Fawcett Society 2007) 244.

[223] SP Jenkins, 'Marital Splits and Income Changes over the Longer Term' (2008) Institute for Social and Economic Research Working Paper https://www.iser.essex.ac.uk/files/iser_working_papers/2008-07.pdf accessed 9 September 2016.

[224] H Fisher and H Low, 'Who Wins, Who Loses and Who Recovers from Divorce?', in J Miles and R Probert (eds), *Sharing Lives, Dividing Assets: An Inter-Disciplinary Study* (Hart 2009) 240.

[225] *Miller v Miller/McFarlane v McFarlane* [2006] UKHL 24 [207] (Lady Hale).

use as a check' and took it 'to mean that property should be shared in equal proportions unless there is a good reason to depart from such proportions'.[226] But what property—and what constitutes 'good' reasons?

Matrimonial and non-matrimonial property

When discussing the sharing principle, Lord Nicholls and Lady Hale distinguished between matrimonial property—sometimes known as 'marital acquest' or 'family assets'—and non-matrimonial property. Although the sharing principle applies to both matrimonial and non-matrimonial assets, 'to the extent that . . . property is non-matrimonial, there is likely to be better reason for departure from equality'.[227]

Lord Nicholls' definition of matrimonial property:[228]

- Assets 'acquired during the marriage otherwise than by inheritance or gift'.
- The 'financial product of the parties' common endeavour'. (This might involve money that was received after separation, but which was the product of work done during the marriage.)
- 'Even if this was brought into the marriage at the outset by one of the parties, [the parties' matrimonial home] usually has a central place in any marriage. So it should normally be treated as matrimonial property for this purpose.'

Lady Hale's definitions:[229]

- Family assets of a capital nature such as the family home and its contents.
- Other assets which 'were obviously acquired for the use and benefit of the whole family, such as holiday homes, caravans, furniture, insurance policies, and other family savings.'
- 'Family businesses or joint ventures in which they both work.'

Under both Lady Hale's and Lord Nicholls' formulations, the matrimonial home is normally a matrimonial asset.[230]

In other ways, these definitions are slightly different. Whereas Lord Nicholls defines non-matrimonial property as that which the parties 'bring with them into the marriage or acquire by inheritance or gift during the marriage' (a narrow definition of non-marital property), Lady Hale takes the view that 'in a matrimonial property regime which still starts with the premise of separate property, there is still some scope for one party to acquire and retain separate property which is not automatically to be shared equally between them'.[231] It is this latter view that seemed more favoured by the other Lords and was

---

[226] *Charman v Charman (No 4)* [2007] EWCA Civ 503 [65] (Sir Mark Potter P).

[227] *Charman v Charman (No 4)* [2007] EWCA Civ 503 [66] (Sir Mark Potter P).

[228] *Miller v Miller/McFarlane v McFarlane* [2006] UKHL 24 [21]–[22].

[229] *Miller v Miller/McFarlane v McFarlane* [2006] UKHL 24 [149].

[230] It is conceivable that there may be a rare case which involves an extremely pricey house brought into an extremely short marriage in which needs can be met without recourse to the house, where fairness would justify it not being treated as matrimonial, so it is probably not correct to say it will *always* be a matrimonial asset. *Sharp v Sharp* [2017] EWCA Civ 408 gives comfort to this view.

[231] *Miller v Miller/McFarlane v McFarlane* [2006] UKHL 24 [153].

subsequently described in *Charman* as 'perhaps the more pragmatic'.[232] In *Sharp v Sharp*,[233] the Court of Appeal cited this view when considering the status of Mrs Sharp's bonuses, which she had largely kept separate. It held that 'where both spouses have largely been in full-time employment and where only some of their finances have been pooled, . . . fairness may well require a reduction from a full 50% share or the exclusion of some property from the 50% calculation'. The Court excluded Mrs Sharp's bonuses from the matrimonial assets but, crucially, this was a short, childless marriage in which these were not required to meet the husband's needs. In *XW v XH*, a differently-constituted Court of Appeal held that this was key to the decision and that *Sharp* was not of wider application.[234]

The increase in value of an asset during the marriage can also be matrimonial even if the base value at the start of the marriage is not. Some practitioners make a further distinction between the active and passive growth of such assets: active growth is a matrimonial asset because it involved endeavour during the marriage; passive growth is non-matrimonial.[235]

Application of sharing to matrimonial and non-matrimonial property

Matrimonial property should be shared equally unless there is good reason not to do so. A good reason may be found in section 25 and the principles set out in *Miller/McFarlane*: need (most commonly); compensation; conduct if inequitable to disregard; and contribution, but only if it is stellar (see 4.5.3.3). We know from *Charman* that a successful stellar contribution argument justifies a departure from equal sharing of matrimonial property because it is a special contribution to *matrimonial* property, not a special contribution of *non*-matrimonial property; and that 'fair allowance for special contribution within the sharing principle would be most unlikely to give rise to percentages of division of matrimonial property further from equality than 66.6%–33.3%.'

To these reasons for departing from equal sharing of matrimonial property, we can add three practical reasons linked to the nature of the assets: (1) a party taking 'copper-bottomed assets'—those that are safe from significant fluctuations in value—may receive less than someone who is taking the risker assets such as shares, to reflect the level of risk;[236] (2) in order to achieve a clean break, one party may take more capital instead of ongoing periodical payments from the other, higher earning, party; and (3) instead of a pension share.

Non-matrimonial property is a contribution to the marriage by one party and its source is usually outside the marriage. In *Hart v Hart*, the Court of Appeal noted that non-matrimonial property can 'be broadly defined in the negative, namely as being assets (or that part of the value of an asset) which are not the financial product of or generated by the parties' endeavours during the marriage. Examples usually given are assets owned by one spouse before the marriage and assets which have been inherited or otherwise given to a spouse from, typically, a relative of theirs during the marriage.'[237] The presence of

---

[232] *Charman v Charman (No 4)* [2007] EWCA Civ 503 [85] (Sir Mark Potter P).
[233] *Sharp v Sharp* [2017] EWCA Civ 408.
[234] *XW v XH* [2019] EWCA Civ 2262.
[235] For a discussion, see *JL v SL (No 2)* [2015] EWHC 360 (Fam).
[236] As in *Wells v Wells* [2002] EWCA Civ 476 and *Myerson v Myerson (No 2)* [2009] EWCA Civ 282.
[237] *Hart v Hart* [2018] Fam. 93, [2] (Moylan LJ).

non-matrimonial assets *potentially* gives a reason to depart from equality in favour of the contributor. Whether the court actually does this depends on the following:

- First, even if there are non-matrimonial assets, we must still meet needs and if we cannot do that from just the matrimonial assets we will need to utilise the non-matrimonial assets too. As Lord Nicholls said in *White*, the contribution of non-matrimonial assets 'can be expected to carry little weight, if any, in a case where the claimant's financial needs cannot be met without recourse to this property'.[238] This means that in reality we are only concerned about the distinction between matrimonial and non-matrimonial property where there is a surplus above needs to argue over.

- Some non-matrimonial assets may have become mingled with the matrimonial property 'in circumstances in which the contributor may be said to have accepted that it should be treated as matrimonial property'; or because it has been used as, or to buy, a matrimonial home.[239] Thus, the non-matrimonial assets may have become matrimonial.

- Some assets may be partly matrimonial ('partly the product, or reflective, of marital endeavour') and partly non-matrimonial ('partly the product, or reflective, of a source external to the marriage'[240]). An example is the farm in *White v White*: although initially some of the investment was non-matrimonial by the husband's father, the parties developed and worked the farm jointly for thirty years and it was therefore reflective both of a source external to the marriage and the product of the parties' joint endeavour. A pension is another good example: some part of its value may predate the marriage (non-matrimonial) and some accrued during the marriage (matrimonial). A party may seek to share only the part of the value attributable to the marriage, although this is not always very easy to calculate and arguments over valuation can become expensive.

- It may be unfair to give much weight to a contribution of non-matrimonial property in the case of a long marriage. This is particularly the case if 'over time matrimonial property of such value has been acquired as to diminish the significance of the initial contribution by one spouse of non-matrimonial property'.[241] Consider that in *White* the court approached the inheritance of a second farm by the husband as justifying a division in the husband's favour, but the House of Lords took the view that it was less important a contribution than the Court of Appeal had thought.

The court has considerable discretion to consider, in light of the above, whether to reflect non-matrimonial assets in the outcome of the case at all, and, if so, how. There are two main approaches, which Bethany Hardwick has labelled *scientific* and *artistic*. The scientific approach decides first to whether the alleged non-matrimonial property should, bearing in mind mingling and the duration of the marriage, be reflected at all in the outcome. Second, if it decides it should be reflected, it then ring-fences such

---

[238] *White v White* [2001] 1 AC 596, 610[G].
[239] *K v L* (n 217) [18] (Wilson LJ). Contrast with *Robson v Robson*.
[240] *Hart v Hart* [2018] Fam. 93, [2] (Moylan LJ).
[241] *K v L* [2011] EWCA Civ 550 [18] (Wilson LJ).

assets for the contributing party, and applies the sharing principle to the remainder of the assets subject to a cross-check of fairness. This is not always easy: indeed in *Hart v Hart* the judge found a scientific or 'formulaic' calculation of non-matrimonial assets impossible due to the length of the marriage and the husband's lack of cooperation with providing information.[242] The artistic approach simply involves adjusting away from equal division of all the matrimonial and non-matrimonial assets to take account of the fact that non matrimonial assets are within the pool, although as in *Hart* some attempt to place a rough figure on those will need to be made. This is a more broad-brush approach.

There are advantages and disadvantages to both methods.[243] Whichever method is used, it seems that 'there is no ground for sharing the non-matrimonial assets other than 100% to the contributor and 0% to the other'[244] under the *sharing* principle itself. There appear to be no reported cases in which the sharing principle has been applied to *purely* non-matrimonial assets, although there are cases where they have been included for other reasons, such as need, or shared because they are no longer purely non-matrimonial but have become co-mingled over time. In *JL v SL*, Mostyn J said that 'Given that a claim to *share* non-matrimonial property (as opposed to having a sum awarded from it to meet needs) would have no moral or principled foundation it is hard to envisage a case where such an award would be made. If you like, such a case would be as rare as a white leopard.'[245]

Perhaps the final comment should go to Wilson LJ in *Jones v Jones*: 'Application of the sharing principle is inherently arbitrary; such is, I suggest, a fact which we should accept and by which we should cease to be disconcerted.'[246]

SCENARIO 2

Illustration 5: Jan and Ahmed

Jan and Ahmed own a house which they bought with the help of Ahmed's parents. Let us assume that this financial help was a gift rather than a loan or an interest that the parents protected under a declaration of trust. We will treat it as money available to them. Is it a matrimonial asset? It was gifted to Ahmed—it is a non-matrimonial contribution on his side. But it was put into a matrimonial home, and that is a matrimonial asset, so it has been merged with a matrimonial asset. In the circumstances of the case, we are not that concerned by the distinction, because although this is a short marriage in which contribution is important, the parties have children who are our first consideration. We now know that this means that we need to look first at housing them. Even if the gift was entirely non-matrimonial, it will be utilised if necessary to meet the parties' needs, and it is very much necessary in this case.

---

[242]　HJ Wildblood QC, as discussed in the Court of Appeal at [2018] Fam. 93.

[243]　For a discussion of the case law and the advantages and disadvantages, see B Hardwick, 'What's Mine Is (*Not) Yours – the Treatment of Non-Matrimonial Property: No Longer a Lawless Science?' http://www.familylaw.co.uk/news_and_comment/what-s-mine-is-not-yours-the-treatment-of-non-matrimonial-property-no-longer-a-lawless-science accessed 23 November 2016.

[244]　*Jones v Jones* [2011] EWCA Civ 41 [33] (Wilson LJ).

[245]　[2015] EWHC 360 (Fam) [22].

[246]　*Jones v Jones* [2011] EWCA Civ 41 [35].

SCENARIO 3

Illustration 2: Mary and Steve

Steve's assets and income mainly derive from his former career as a rock star, and this predates their relationship. We therefore need to consider to what extent there is matrimonial property here. The former matrimonial home, valued at £5 million net, is in Steve's sole name and was bought by him from his savings. However, under both Lady Hale's and Lord Nicholls' formulation, this is a matrimonial asset and is subject to the sharing principle. They also have a holiday home. Again, under both formulations this is a matrimonial asset.

Their art collection is something to which they have both contributed. It may be possible on an artwork-by-artwork basis to divide this up according to who purchased what (the scientific method!), but there is an argument for it to be considered as a matrimonial asset. Although Steve may have utilised a non-matrimonial asset to purchase the artworks (his savings from his career), it has become mingled with Mary's contribution.

The rest of Steve's savings and investments could be matrimonial or non-matrimonial. They derive from a non-matrimonial source (his earnings pre-marriage) and although royalties are still coming in, that again derives from work done before the marriage. Consider the passive/active growth distinction discussed at 4.7.3.

Remember that we are talking here about the sharing principle: irrespective of whether these are matrimonial or non-matrimonial, if required to meet needs we will use them. We only need to make this distinction in this case because there is a surplus above needs to argue over.

4.7.4 The three principles and periodical payments

In *Miller/McFarlane*, Lady Hale rejected the application of the sharing principle to future income: 'the marital partnership does not stay alive for the purpose of sharing future resources unless this is justified by need or compensation'.[247] As Thorpe LJ thought when considering *McFarlane* in the Court of Appeal:

> The cross-check of equality is not appropriate for a number of reasons. First in many cases the division of income is not just between the parties, since there will be children with a priority claim for the costs of education and upbringing. Second Lord Nicholls [in *White*] suggested the use of the cross-check in dividing the accumulated fruits of past shared endeavours. In assessing periodical payments the court considers the division of the fruits of the breadwinner's future work in a context where he may have left the child-carer in the former matrimonial home, where he may have to meet alternative housing costs and where he may have in fact or in contemplation a second wife and a further child.[248]

To this, one could add that it has never been thought advisable to disincentive a person from working and retaining the majority of what they earn for their own ends.

In *Waggott v Waggott*, an excellent summary of the law on this point, Moylan LJ explicitly addressed whether an earning capacity was capable of being a matrimonial asset to which the sharing principle applied, concluded that

> there are a number of reasons why the clear answer is that it is not . . . any extension of the sharing principle to post-separation earnings would fundamentally undermine the court's

---

[247] *Miller v Miller/McFarlane v McFarlane* [2006] UKHL 24 [144].
[248] *Parlour v Parlour/McFarlane v McFarlane* [2004] EWCA Civ 872 [106].

ability to effect a clean break. . . . it would apply to every case in which one party had earnings which were greater than the other's, regardless of need. This could well be a very significant number of cases. . . . in my view *Miller* . . . [does] not support the extension of the sharing principle to an earning capacity.[249]

This approach was subsequently followed in *O'Dwyer v O'Dwyer*, in which Francis J noted:

> that it is now settled law that income cannot be shared. An award of periodical payments (absent rare compensation cases) must be based on properly analysed arithmetic reflecting need, albeit that the judge is still left with a significant margin of discretion as to how generously the concept of need should be interpreted.[250]

Given the subsequent attacks on compensation, we are left with the view expressed by Mostyn J in *SS v NS*: that an award of periodical payments 'should only be made by reference to needs, save in a most exceptional case where it can be said that the sharing or compensation principle applies'.[251]

4.7.5 Needs, compensation, and sharing: How do they fit together?

You would be forgiven for being confused about how these three rationales come together.

In *Miller/McFarlane*, Lady Hale thought that 'there cannot be a hard and fast rule about whether one starts with equal sharing and departs if need or compensation supply a reason to do so, or whether one starts with need and compensation and shares the balance.'[252] Lord Nicholls thought that '[t]here can be no invariable rule on this.'[253] This is not at all helpful to the practitioner: the two approaches do lead to different outcomes, as Jo Miles has illustrated:

> Suppose an asset pool of 200 units. Suppose party A has needs of 30 units and party B of 70 units. On a 'meet needs and then share surplus equally' approach, A would receive 80 units and B 120. On the 'equal sharing and then modify if needs require' approach, A and B would each receive 100 units.[254]

On the first option, meet needs (and compensation) and then share surplus, A and B have the same surplus above their needs to meet a lifestyle. On the second option, B's greater needs are met within B's equal share of the assets: B will have less discretionary spending but 'the need principle does not evidently justify depriving A of any more than is required to meet B's needs, and if B's needs can be amply met by an equal share, what justification (in terms of either of these two principles) is there for doing more?'[255]

---

[249] [2018] EWCA Civ 727, [122]–[128].
[250] [2019] EWHC 1838 (Fam), [22].
[251] [2014] EWHC 4183 at [46]. See also his comments in *B v S* [2012] EWHC 265 (Fam) [79].
[252] *Miller v Miller/McFarlane v McFarlane* [2006] UKHL 24 [144].
[253] *Miller v Miller/McFarlane v McFarlane* [2006] UKHL 24 [29].
[254] J Miles, '*Charman v Charman*: Making Sense of Need, Compensation and Equal Sharing after *Miller/McFarlane*' [2008] *Child and Family Law Quarterly* 378, 389. For further discussion: R George, *Ideas and Debates in Family Law* (Hart 2012) 96–9.
[255] J Miles, '*Charman v Charman*: Making Sense of Need, Compensation and Equal Sharing after *Miller/McFarlane*' [2008] *Child and Family Law Quarterly* 378, 389.

In *Charman* the court 'appears to favour a starting point of equal sharing modified by need, rather than meeting need and then sharing any surplus'.[256] Indeed, in purely practical terms, it is very much easier to start with an equal division of the capital (sharing) and then consider whether there is any reason to depart from that. Such an approach also sends a message: 'there may be something intangible (and, more concretely, an enhancement of bargaining position) to be gained from the idea that each party is prima facie *entitled* to an equal share of the capital and that a non-owner applicant is not merely a "needy supplicant".'[257]

If we take equal sharing as a starting point, we should then ask ourselves whether there are reasons, found in s25, for departing from that and giving one party more of the assets. In *Scatliffe v Scatliffe*, Lord Wilson concluded that:

> in an ordinary case the proper approach is to apply the sharing principle to the matrimonial property and then ask whether, in the light of all the matters specified (in the statute), the result of so doing represents an appropriate overall disposal. In particular it should ask whether the principles of need and/or of compensation, best explained in the speech of Baroness Hale in the *McFarlane* case . . . require additional adjustment in the form of transfer to one party of further property, even of non-matrimonial property, held by the other.[258]

In the majority of cases, there is indeed likely to be a reason to depart from equal sharing, which could be:

- To meet needs (see section 4.7.1)
- To reflect (mis)conduct, if inequitable to disregard (see 4.5.3)
- Because one party has made a stellar contribution to matrimonial assets, within the limits outlined in *Charman* (see 4.5.3)
- To reflect the presence of non-matrimonial assets (this could be achieved by removing these assets from the pot before sharing the rest, or by including them in the pot and then splitting the pot unequally, i.e., the scientific or artistic methods) (4.7.3)
- To provide a party with compensation for relationship generated disadvantage (see 4.7.2)
- To capitalise a periodical payments claim to enable a clean break (see 4.4.2 and 4.5.2)
- To provide an offsetting lump sum instead of a pension share (see 4.4.6)
- Because one party has taken riskier assets than the other (see 4.5.3)
- Because of the presence of a prenuptial agreement (see 4.7.3)

Need is likely to be the most common. However, if by sharing the assets equally we have also succeeded in meeting each party's needs, then great: 'While need is often a sound

---

[256] J Miles, '*Charman v Charman*: Making Sense of Need, Compensation and Equal Sharing after *Miller/McFarlane*' [2008] *Child and Family Law Quarterly* 378, 389.

[257] J Miles, '*Charman v Charman*: Making Sense of Need, Compensation and Equal Sharing after *Miller/McFarlane*' [2008] *Child and Family Law Quarterly* 378, 389.

[258] [2017] AC 93, [25].

rationale, it should not be seen as a limiting principle if other rationales apply.'[259] Referring to the *Miller/McFarlane* decision, the Court of Appeal in *Charman* noted that:

> It is clear that, when the result suggested by the needs principle is an award of property greater than the result suggested by the sharing principle, the former result should in principle prevail: per Baroness Hale in *Miller* at [paragraphs] 142 and 144. . . . It is also clear that, when the result suggested by the needs principle is an award of property less than the result suggested by the sharing principle, the latter result should in principle prevail: per Lord Nicholls in *Miller* at 28 and 29 and Baroness Hale at 139.[260]

Thus, if equal sharing gives you more than meets your needs, you should get equal sharing. If needs gives you more, you get needs. Compensation, following *SA v PA*, is usually treated as within a generous assessment of need, so there is an overlap there and a risk of double-counting.

Therefore, these three strands or rationales should not be treated as separate heads of claim as they would in a personal injury case, for example, by adding one to the other.[261] 'The outcome of ancillary relief cases depends upon the exercise of a singularly broad judgment that obviates the need for the investigation of minute detail and equally the need to make findings on minor issues in dispute.' Courts should instead 'paint their canvas with a broad brush rather than a fine sable', and the judge should conclude his or her consideration by assessing whether, in light of all elements of the case, the outcome is fair.[262]

SCENARIO 2

Illustration 6: Jan and Ahmed

So far, we have considered the relevant s25 factors, and realised that there is insufficient money to each buy a house, so one or both of them will need to rent.

This is a situation in which we have to depart from equal sharing to meet needs. What of income? If the parties divide their capital equally, then Jan has a good case for periodical payments. The level of these will depend on her need and what Ahmed can afford (see 4.4.2). She will also receive child maintenance. If Jan retains the matrimonial home, her claim for periodical payments is weak—a clean break should be the price of Ahmed sacrificing his capital until the children are older. But there is one more complicating factor: the effect of our outcomes on state benefits. After divorce, Jan will be eligible for universal credit of (at the time of writing) around £800 per month. If she remains in the house she may also get some money to help pay her mortgage interest too. If she acquires lots of cash savings, this affects her eligibility for those.

---

[259] *Miller v Miller/McFarlane v McFarlane* [2006] UKHL 24 (Lady Hale).
[260] See *Charman v Charman (No 4)* [2007] EWCA Civ 503 [73].
[261] *RP v RP* [2006] EWHC 3409 (Fam).
[262] *Parra v Parra* [2002] EWCA Civ 1886 [22] (Thorpe LJ).

SCENARIO 3

Illustration 3: Mary and Steve

Remember that 'the ultimate objective is to give each party an equal start on the road to independent living': *Miller/McFarlane* at para 144 (Lady Hale). Here, we have a lot of capital but some of it is non-matrimonial. We need to decide what assets should be subject to the sharing principle and which should not. We do not divide up the non-matrimonial assets unless justified by need or compensation. There is no compensation claim, so the issue is whether we can meet their needs from the matrimonial assets only.

We have already noted that the two houses would be matrimonial. The artwork and cash savings are also likely to be matrimonial. You can see from the artwork that working out what is matrimonial and what is not can be difficult. A judge could try to place a figure on the non-matrimonial assets and give them to Steve before sharing the matrimonial assets. This would be the scientific approach. Alternatively, he or she could take a broader approach (the artistic method) and simply divide all the assets unequally to allow for the fact that some are non-matrimonial.

It would appear that unless Mary has unusually high needs, she is likely to have her *capital* needs met by a half share of the capital assets. We then need to turn to income. The fact that she earns a large amount does not mean she is not entitled to periodical payments: it depends on whether those earnings meet her needs. She has no entitlement to his future earnings under the sharing principle and there is no compensation claim. If Steve does have to supplement Mary's earnings through periodical payments, we should be mindful that the court is under a duty to consider a clean break. That means Steve may want to give her extra capital instead of ongoing periodical payments. A note of caution, though, related to the practicalities of the structure of the settlement: Steve's income is partly from interest on his investments which means that if we reduce his capital he gets less interest and thus less income.

Finally, do a cross-check of fairness. In light of the above, does the outcome you are proposing fall within a range of fair settlements?

4.7.6 Certainty versus discretion

As we have seen, lawyers advising couples on financial settlement have to take into account a huge number of factors before giving their opinion—all the circumstances of the case, filtered through the prism of the s25 factors, the three principles from *Miller/McFarlane*, the encouragement of independence, and what is actually possible with the assets one has. This is a highly discretionary system, a 'luxury discretion',[263] in which no single factor is always weighted more heavily, no mathematical formula is applied, and judges make comments like this:

- 'The quantification of periodical payments is more an art that a science. The parameters of s25 are so wide that it might be said that it is almost impossible to be "scientific"... no family judge in exercising this jurisdiction can achieve perfection given the width of s25. He or she can only do his best to get as near to it as is possible in the circumstances of any particular case.'[264]

---

[263] E Cooke, '*Miller/McFarlane*: Law in Search of Discrimination' (2007) *Child and Family Law Quarterly* 98.
[264] *Parlour v Parlour/McFarlane v McFarlane* [2004] EWCA Civ 872.

- 'Application of the sharing principle is inherently arbitrary; such is, I suggest, a fact which we should accept and by which we should cease to be disconcerted.'[265]

- 'There can be no invariable rule on this. . . . Needless to say, it all depends upon the circumstances.'[266]

- 'In reading and re-reading all the now familiar authorities, attempting to expose and explain the underlying principles, one is reminded of a frenzied butterfly hunter in a tropical jungle trying to entrap a rare and elusive butterfly using a net full of holes. As soon as it appears to have been caught it escapes again and the pursuit continues.'[267]

- 'So far as the "needs" principle is concerned, there is an almost unbounded discretion . . . Like equity in the old days, the result seems to depend on the length of the judge's foot.'[268]

Given both the legal uncertainty and the wide range of potentially fair case outcomes, research by Davis et al. found that it was impossible to tell from the case files what the outcome of a financial remedy case was to be.[269] Indeed, it has been suggested that the extent of the discretion may be so wide as to 'enable a judge to elect between outcomes'. 'In such cases . . . it is not necessarily healthy to pretend that the conclusion has been inexorably determined by prior principle.'[270]

At 4.2.2, we noted that people bargain in the shadow of law; that is, they consider what would happen if they went to court when considering whether to settle and on what terms. A more certain outcome, whether through clearer rules or even a mathematical formula, could also help ensure that like cases were treated alike. If the law is unpredictable, then parties may be more likely to litigate, as there is everything to 'play for'. Discretionary systems are expensive, for the parties and the court system. At a time when legal aid is mostly unavailable and people are attempting to represent themselves, it is even more important that they should be able to identify, understand, and apply the relevant legal principles.

But the price of predictability is fairness in some cases. A one-size-fits-all approach would mean some parties had 'harsh or unfair' outcomes that should not exist if the parties' exact circumstances are taken into account. The 'flexibility and sensitivity' our legal system provides enables a judge or practitioner to consider each couple's unique situation and tailor an outcome that is fair for them.[271] While like situations should be treated alike, our discretionary system understands that every case is unique and consequently that there is no such thing as a truly 'like' case.

In recent years, there has been a general trend away from discretion and towards rule-based outcomes in a number of legal systems.[272] In England, successive governments have

---

[265] *Jones v Jones* [2011] EWCA Civ 41.

[266] *Miller v Miller/McFarlane v McFarlane* [2006] UKHL 24 [29] (Lord Nicholls).

[267] *Charman v Charman* [2006] EWHC 1879 (Fam) (Coleridge J).

[268] *FF v KF* [2017] EWHC 1093 (Fam) [18] (Mostyn J).

[269] G Davis, J Pearce, R Bird, H Woodward, and C Wallace, 'Ancillary Relief Outcomes' [2000] *Child and Family Law Quarterly* 43.

[270] S Cretney, 'The Family and the Law – Status or Contract?' [2003] *Child and Family Law Quarterly* 403, 416.

[271] *Miller v Miller/McFarlane v McFarlane* [2006] UKHL 24 [122] (Lady Hale).

[272] E Jackson, F Wasoff, M Maclean, and R Emerson Dobash, 'Financial Support on Divorce: The Right Mixture of Rules and Discretion?' (1993) 7 *International Journal of Law and the Family* 230.

sought to limit judicial discretion by providing more certainty of outcome.[273] One example is the introduction of a statutory child maintenance scheme with a mathematical formula to calculate the appropriate level of child maintenance. In 1998 the government consultation document *Supporting Families* proposed that there should be a hierarchy of principles that could be applied on divorce; the same document also proposed that prenuptial agreements be recognised subject to a number of safeguards.[274] However, these proposals were never actioned and indeed the Lord Chancellor's Ancillary Relief Advisory Group rejected the idea, although it was in favour of the codifying case law principles.[275]

Since then, the Law Commission has also considered whether the law should be reformed to be more certain. They considered mathematical formulae for periodical payments and binding nuptial agreements.[276] Most academic and judicial respondents to their consultation favoured limiting discretion by providing guidelines but not dispensing entirely with judicial discretion. As a result, the Family Justice Council has developed guidelines for judges and members of the public in an attempt to encourage consistency in decision-making and make the law more accessible to the public, but these do not have the status of law.

In 2017, Baroness Ruth Deech has introduced a private member's bill into Parliament which seeks to amend the Matrimonial Causes Act 1973 by reducing discretion in the way courts dealt with periodical payments, non-matrimonial property, and nuptial agreements.[277] Lord Wilson has suggested that the bill's supporters:

> believe too readily what they see in the papers and . . . regard the exceptional cases as the norm. . . . This leads them to exaggerate the difficulties of our current system and to ignore the virtue of principles which have a sufficient degree of elasticity to enable a reasonable result to be fitted to each case. Some of the rigid provisions which the group have included in their proposed reform bill . . . would have had grotesque consequences if they were to have been applied to a number of the cases in which I have participated.[278]

FOCUS Know-How

Summary of the principles and practicalities

1. Consider 'all the circumstances of the case': s25(1).
2. Give 'first consideration' to the welfare of any child of the family aged under 18: s25(1).
3. Which factors in s25(2)(a)–(h), are relevant to your client's case, and what effect will they have? (Note that this is not an exhaustive list.)
   a. the income, earning capacity, property and other financial resources which each of the parties to the marriage has or is likely to have in the foreseeable future, including in the case of earning capacity any increase in that capacity which it would in the opinion of the court be reasonable to expect a party to the marriage to take steps to acquire (s25(2)(a))

---

[273] See G Douglas and A Perry, 'How Parents Cope Financially on Separation and Divorce – Implications for the Future of Ancillary Relief' (2001) *Child and Family Law Quarterly* 67.

[274] Home Office, *Supporting Families* (The Stationery Office 1998).

[275] Ancillary Relief Advisory Group, *Possible Reforms to the Substantive Law on Ancillary Relief* (Lord Chancellor's Department 1998).

[276] Law Commission, *Matrimonial Property, Needs and Agreements* (Law Com No 343, 2014) para 3.129.

[277] Divorce (Financial Provision) Bill 310 of 2017–19 [HL].

[278] Lord Wilson, 'Changes over the Centuries in the Financial Consequences of Divorce'. Address to the University of Bristol Law Club, 20 March 2017. Available at https://www.supremecourt.uk/docs/speech-170320.pdf accessed 21 March 2017.

b. the financial needs, obligations and responsibilities which each of the parties to the marriage has or is likely to have in the foreseeable future (s25(2)(b))

c. the standard of living enjoyed by the family before the breakdown of the marriage (s25(2)(c)
    This is relevant to quantum of periodical payments, for example, and the assessment of housing needs.

d. the age of each party to the marriage and the duration of the marriage (s25(2)(d))
    This goes to needs, compensation, and sharing, as the longer the marriage the stronger the justification for each principle. For example, older parties are likely to have specific needs, fewer (if any) working years ahead, and may have adopted traditional breadwinner/homemaker roles.

e. any physical or mental disability of either of the parties to the marriage (s25(2)(e))
    This goes to needs, but should be causally or temporally connected to the marriage: Miller/McFarlane (see 4.7.1).

f. the contributions which each of the parties has made or is likely in the foreseeable future to make to the welfare of the family, including any contribution by looking after the home or caring for the family
    White v White: no discrimination between homemaker and breadwinner in their matrimonial contributions unless can show stellar contribution to matrimonial assets.
    Non-matrimonial assets are a contribution in one party's favour. Will you deal with these through the artistic method—adjusting away from equal division of all the assets to reflect the fact that some are non-matrimonial—or through the scientific method—calculating the amount of non-matrimonial assets and then giving them to the contributor before sharing the rest?

g. the conduct of each of the parties, if that conduct is such that it would in the opinion of the court be inequitable to disregard it
    Described in Wachtel v Wachtel as 'obvious and gross'. Litigation misconduct such as failure to disclose assets usually dealt with through a costs order although in rare cases can be 'obvious and gross' and thus full under s25 and justify innocent party getting greater share of the assets. (See 4.5.3.)

h. the case of proceedings for divorce or nullity of marriage, the value to each of the parties to the marriage of any benefit . . . which, by reason of the dissolution or annulment of the marriage, that party will lose the chance of acquiring.

    Also: Nuptial agreements, not falling explicitly under any part of s25(2), are still considered 'part of all the circumstances of the case'; also implied within conduct.

4. Remember that 'the ultimate objective is to give each party an equal start on the road to independent living': *Miller/McFarlane* at para 144 (Lady Hale).

5. Now you've identified which factors are relevant, apply the three principles.
    There is no hard and fast rule about whether you start with sharing or with needs. However, starting with sharing has symbolic merit (see 4.7.5).
    We suggest you start with sharing. What does a 50/50 split of the assets look like?

6. Are there principled reasons to adjust away (deviate from) equal sharing of capital?
    Are each party's needs met by equal sharing? If not, an adjustment away from equal sharing will be necessary, and it may be necessary to dip into any non-matrimonial assets.
    To provide a party with compensation for relationship generated disadvantage? Case law trend is to include this as part of a generous assessment of need (see 4.7.2).
    To reflect (mis)conduct, if inequitable to disregard (see 4.5.3)?
    Because one party has made a stellar contribution to matrimonial assets, within the limits outlined in Charman v Charman (No 4) (see 4.5.3)? Unlikely to justify more than a slight deviation from equal sharing: Charman at para 90.
    To reflect the presence of non-matrimonial assets (if using artistic method and have not under scientific method already removed these) (see section 4.7.3).

Because of the presence of a prenuptial agreement, which is capable to affecting what is fair (See 4.8)? Remember not to treat needs, compensation, and sharing as different heads of award, one added to the other: RP v RP (see 4.7.2).

7. Are there practical reasons to adjust away (deviate from) equal sharing of capital?

   One party may give the other extra capital instead of periodical payments, to enable a clean break. This is called 'capitalising'.

   Similarly, one may give the other extra capital—and offsetting lump sum—instead of a pension share (see 4.4.6).

   Be careful not to capitalise everything because it is no help at all to have a clean break and intact pension if you have nowhere to live.

   You could have an unequal split because one party has taken riskier assets than the other and to compensate for this has taken more of them (see 4.7.4).

8. Remember that you get the higher amount of sharing, needs, and compensation.

   Per the Court in Charman: 'It is clear that, when the result suggested by the needs principle is an award of property greater than the result suggested by the sharing principle, the former result should in principle prevail: per Baroness Hale in Miller at [paragraphs] 142 and 144. . . . It is also clear that, when the result suggested by the needs principle is an award of property less than the result suggested by the sharing principle, the latter result should in principle prevail: per Lord Nicholls in Miller at 28 and 29 and Baroness Hale at 139.'

9. Remember that there is no principle of equal sharing of incomes post-divorce (see 4.7.4) but that you can use pension share or capital to meet needs.

10. Think about the practicalities of the settlement structure as well as the quantum:

    Consider capital: has your client got enough money to rehouse themselves and meet their capital needs?

    Consider income: has your client got enough money to live on? If not, consider a periodical payments order or, if there is enough money, consider capitalising this for a clean break.

    Consider pensions: Do not forget these. Do not treat these as capital available now, but just because they are not accessible until pensionable age does not mean they are not important.

    Is there a plan for the future? Consider future resources including pensions, and whether your client will have to downsize to free up capital in the event of a future drop in income.

11. If considering periodical payments:

    Consider terminating claims 'as soon after the grant of the decree as the court considers just and reasonable': s25A(1).

    Consider terminating any periodical payments once recipient can 'adjust without undue hardship': s25A(2).

    'The marital standard of living is relevant to the quantum of spousal maintenance but is not decisive. That standard should be carefully weighed against the desired objective of eventual independence': SS v NS.

    Where needs are not causally connected to the marriage any periodical payments should be aimed only at alleviating hardship: SS v NS.

    Do not forget that child maintenance will be paid according to the statutory formula (see Chapter 6) unless they exceed the income cap.

12. Do a cross-check of fairness. In light of the above, does the outcome you are proposing fall within a range of fair settlements?

Now that we have summarised all of the relevant considerations, and structured them into some kind of order, let us apply them to one of our scenarios—that of our older couple, Dora and Brian.

SCENARIO 1

Illustration 2: Dora and Brian

Which factors in s25(2)(a)–(h), are relevant to their case? This is a long marriage and it is likely that most of the assets have accrued during that marriage and thus would be matrimonial. In any case, the significance of any non-matrimonial asset brought into the early days of the marriage is likely to be very little (see *White*). As both are retired, they have no capacity to increase their incomes except by using capital to top up their pensions. They have no mortgage borrowing capacities, or very tiny ones. We need to consider what financial needs each has—this will be linked to 'any physical or mental disability of either of the parties to the marriage'. Do they need carers or a care home? Do they need ground-floor accommodation? These needs, given the length of the marriage, are likely to be temporally or causally linked to the marriage. We should be mindful that they had traditional breadwinner/homemaker roles and that under *White* if each contributed equally in their own sphere then each has made an equal contribution. The fact that Brian earned the money is irrelevant. Neither of them meets the parameters for having made a stellar contribution. There are no conduct issues here. Dora only has a state pension, whereas Brian has a state and an occupational pension. On divorce, she will lose the widow's benefit that she would get from Brian's pension if he were to die while they were still married.

They have total assets of £502,000. A starting point of equal division would give them £251,000 each. Are there *principled* reasons to adjust away (deviate from) equal sharing of capital? We need to ensure that their needs are met by equal sharing. This will depend upon house prices in the area in which they live. If they cannot afford to buy properties, one or both of them may have to rent. They will have other needs, for example for a car (or to keep the car they have). This is not a case for compensation as neither has given up a high-flying career for the sake of the family. There are no non-matrimonial assets, but if there were we are likely to need to use them anyway. £502,000 divided between two of them is not a lot.

Are there *practical* reasons to adjust away (deviate from) equal sharing of capital? Assuming both of their needs are met by an equal sharing of capital, we have one possible justification for deviating from this, and that is related to the difference in their pension incomes. Their state pensions cannot be shared. However, Brian's occupational pension could be shared. He may want to give Dora more capital instead of a pension share.

We need to ensure that they have enough money to live on through a combination of their pension incomes, and any state benefits for which one or both is eligible. Because virtually all their capital will need to be used to rehouse them, it is unlikely that they will be able to invest money to yield another source of income. (Remember that any time we use capital that money is not available to be invested.) Although there is no starting point of *equal sharing* of future income, there is a strong justification for a needs-based division of income. This is a long marriage and Brian's pension was built up during the marriage and comprises marital income—it is not the product of work that post-dates the marriage. As their incomes are pensions, we could look at a pension share. An earmarking order is also possible but less desirable as it depends on Brian being alive. A periodical payments order would have the same effect as earmarking, in that it shares a proportion of his income with Dora, but again is less secure than a pension share.

Now we turn to think about the practicalities of the settlement structure as well as the quantum. Does a pension share and equal division of capital give them sufficient money to live on? If not, can you vary the order to ensure both parties' needs are met, even though that may result in an unequal division of either capital or pension income? Do a cross-check of fairness. In light of the above, does the outcome you are proposing fall within a range of fair settlements?

4.8 **Nuptial agreements**

In this section, we are going to look at a form of private ordering, nuptial agreements. A nuptial agreement is an agreement that governs how the parties will divide their assets on divorce. There are four types of nuptial agreement, but they are best thought of as being on the same continuum.

1. Prior to getting married, the parties may wish to agree what financial arrangements may apply if they were to divorce. They may therefore draw up a *prenuptial agreement*.

2. If they intended to do so, but did not get around to it before the wedding, they could draw up a *postnuptial agreement*, which is one made during the marriage but before the marriage has irretrievably broken down. Alternatively, the couple may hit a rocky patch in their marriage and reach a postnuptial agreement in case their marriage was to break up in the future.

3. If the marriage has broken down, the parties may reach agreement only at the point of divorce, and that is what we have assumed throughout this chapter so far. We will call this an *agreement to compromise or settle their respective financial claims*. This will be embodied in a draft order, a consent order, and forwarded to a judge for approval, as described in 4.2.4.

4. Sometimes, however, the parties may be separated for a period prior to the divorce yet still want to resolve financial matters. In this situation, they may choose to enter into a *separation agreement*. When they do eventually divorce, they can draw the terms of that agreement up into a draft order for the court's consent.

You can see these different types of agreement in Figure 4.3. Keep this continuum in your mind, as the time that lapses between when the agreement is entered into and when it is to be enforced can be important to the court's decision about whether to follow the agreement.

Historically, prenuptial and postnuptial agreements were not upheld for public policy reasons: by anticipating the breakdown of a marriage it was thought that they encouraged or incentivised breakdown and thus were contrary to society's interests. The same concerns were not relevant to separation agreements or agreements for the compromise of claims on divorce, as the marriage has already broken down when these are drawn up, and consequently these have been common (separation agreements more so in the years prior to widely available divorce) and lawful.

If the parties are in agreement with the terms they want, and are asking the court to turn that agreement into a consent order, a judge nevertheless has to approve it as objectively fair by reference to the factors listed in s25 Matrimonial Causes Act 1973 and the principles expounded in Key Cases *White v White* and *Miller/McFarlane*. An agreement between the parties, whether made prior to the marriage or following its breakdown is a s25 factor. Although not mentioned expressly, it is part of all the circumstances of the case and it can be considered conduct that it is inequitable to disregard. The judge has to consider what importance/weight this factor has against the other s25 factors. The fact of agreement does

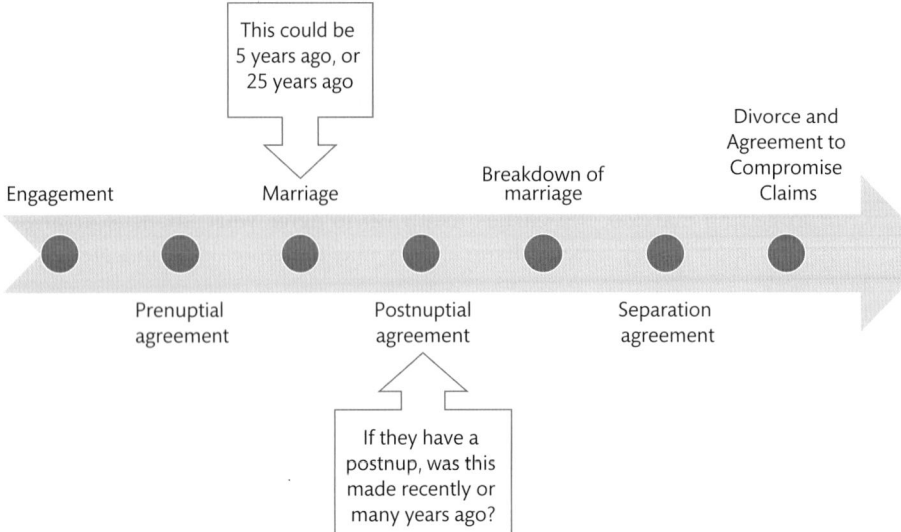

FIGURE 4.3 Nuptial agreements on a continuum

not obviate the need for the court to undertake its own assessment of whether the proposal is fair. If the judge will not approve the order, the parties will need to renegotiate or make a financial remedy application and ask a judge to decide the sharing of the assets.

A more difficult situation arises when one party seeks to resile from (back out of) an agreement and the other party wishes to hold them to it and get the court to turn the terms into a court order. This could happen to any kind of nuptial agreement, whether made the previous day or years previously. In this situation, the response of the other side may well be 'tough – we have a concluded agreement and you're stuck with it'. But things are a little more complicated than that. As stated in *Xydhias v Xydhias*:

> an agreement for the compromise of an ancillary relief application does not give rise to a contract enforceable in law. The parties seeking to uphold a concluded agreement for the compromise of such an application cannot sue for specific performance. The only way of rendering the bargain enforceable, whether to ensure that the applicant obtains the agreed transfers and payments, or whether to protect the respondent from future claims, is to convert the concluded agreement into an order of the court.[279]

In other words, and rather confusingly, the position even if the agreement is valid in the sense that no standard contract vitiating factors are present—mistake, duress, incapacity, undue influence, etc.—and the parties are thus bound by it, the agreement cannot be enforced unless approved by a court. At that point, its authority stems from the court order itself not the prior agreement: *de Lasala v de Lasala*.[280] Thus in the event of a dispute about the agreement (or if one party is claiming there is no agreement at all), one party— probably the one seeking to uphold the agreement—should apply to court. Any clause that

---

[279] [1999] 2 All ER 386.
[280] *de Lasala v de Lasala* [1980] AC 546. Cf civil litigation where an agreed settlement derives its authority from the contract made between the parties: *Purcell v FC Trigell Ltd* [1971] 1 QB 358.

seeks to prevent this is ineffective for public policy reasons, a long-standing principle deriving from *Hyman v Hyman*[281] and now found in s34(1) Matrimonial Causes Act 1973.[282]
There are two potential court routes:

1. The easiest and most common way is to apply to court and make the resiling party 'show cause' why an agreement reached should not be converted into an order. This places the burden onto whoever is seeking to get out of the agreement to justify why they should not be held to it (perhaps they say there was never an agreement at all).

2. Alternatively, if it is a written agreement, then it may be valid under s34 Matrimonial Causes Act 1973 as a 'maintenance agreement': an agreement *between parties to a marriage*, in *writing*, which contains *financial arrangements*, whether made during marriage or after the dissolution or annulment of the marriage. (Note therefore that this does not mean 'maintenance' in the sense of periodical payments. It means financial settlement generally.) The court has the power to vary a maintenance agreement.

Whichever route is used, the court cannot shirk its statutory obligation to consider all of the s25 factors. 'The determination of an application by a court which has failed to have regard to them is unlawful'.[283] The fact of a prior agreement is a s25 factor (conduct) as well as being part of all the circumstances of the case. So how important is it as a s25 factor? The case of *Edgar v Edgar* tells us that:

> in deciding the weight to be given [to the prior agreement], regard must be had to the conduct of both parties leading up to the prior agreement, and to their subsequent conduct in consequence of it. It is not necessary in this connection to think in formal legal terms, such as misrepresentation or estoppel; *all* the circumstances as they affect each of two human beings must be considered in the complex relationship of marriage. So the circumstances surrounding the making of the agreement are relevant. Undue pressure by one side, exploitation of a dominant position to secure an unreasonable advantage, inadequate knowledge, possibly bad legal advice, an important change of circumstances, unforeseen or overlooked at the time of the making of the agreement, are all relevant to the question of justice between the parties.[284]

These factors help us to consider whether the agreement was properly and fairly arrived at. If it was, as Ormrod LJ also said (and this is much quoted in subsequent cases):

> Important too is the general proposition that formal agreements properly and fairly arrived at with competent legal advice should not be displaced unless there are good and substantial grounds for concluding that an injustice will be done by holding the parties to the terms of their agreement. There may well be other considerations which affect the justice of this case; the above list is not intended to be an exhaustive catalogue.

Thus, the existence of an agreement is potentially a very weighty s25 factor, or even of 'magnetic importance'[285]: 'clearly when people make an agreement like this it is a very

---

[281] [1929] AC 601 (HL).

[282] The rest of the agreement is unaffected. This inability to oust the jurisdiction of the court would affect an arbitration clause although one assumes that given the circumstances of an arbitration any decision reached by the arbitrator would be likely upheld.

[283] Lord Wilson delivering the Supreme Court's single judgment in Key Case *Wyatt v Vince*, citing as authority Lord Brandon of Oakbrook in *Livesey (formerly Jenkins) v Livesey* [1985] AC 424, *437*.

[284] [1980] 1 WLR 1410 (CA) (Ormrod LJ).

[285] *Crossley v Crossley* [2007] EWCA Civ 1491 [15] (Thorpe LJ).

important factor in considering what is the just outcome of the proceedings . . . what they themselves felt to be fair.'[286]

In order to determine whether the resiling party is stuck with the agreement they made, we therefore need to consider the status of the agreement, its substantive content, and the process that gave rise to it. The court will want to have 'good and substantial' grounds for not holding the parties to that agreement, namely a change in the parties' circumstances since the agreement was made that renders it unfair (it is not enough to show that you made a bad bargain);[287] and/or that the agreement does not make proper provision for any child of the family;[288] and/or it casts 'onto the public purse an obligation which ought properly to be shouldered within the family', which is contrary to public policy.[289]

Given that prenuptial and postnuptial agreements were traditionally contrary to public policy and thus invalid, the *Edgar* approach was never applied to such agreements. However, in *Macleod v Macleod* the Privy Council, considering a postnuptial agreement, rejected such policy reasons as outmoded.[290] Once they were out of the way, the Board then had to consider how to treat such an agreement. It held that the *Edgar* approach should be applied to postnuptial agreements in the same way as separation agreements and agreements for the compromise of financial remedy proceedings. It did not extend this approach to prenuptial agreements, however, taking the view that they were 'very different from' postnuptial agreements. It may well, of course, have been that the Board preferred that Parliament legislate if it wanted to change the status of prenuptial agreements. However, given that Parliament failed to do so, the Supreme Court had to address the issue of prenuptial agreements subsequently, in *Radmacher v Granatino*. In doing so, it provided guidance on the current approach to all four types of agreement, and held that the approach taken in *Macleod* was wrong.

KEY CASE *Radmacher v Granatino* [2010] UKSC 42

Prior to the wedding of wealthy German heiress Katrin Radmacher to French investment banker Nicolas Granatino, the former's family notary drew up a prenuptial agreement that provided that in the event of a divorce neither party would make a financial claim against the other. Mr Granatino was given a draft of the agreement around 24 July 1998, although it was in German which was a language he did not speak. He did not have the document translated, nor did he obtain independent legal advice, and the document did not include details of the parties' assets. It did not mention the prospect of children and thus made no provision for them (although it is possible that the parties thought that post-divorce any children would live with Ms Radmacher who had more than enough money to raise them). On 1 August 1998, the notary verbally translated the document to Mr Granatino, and he then immediately signed it. The parties married in the November in England, where they lived.

By the time the parties divorced eight years later, a number of aspects of their lives had changed. The parties had two daughters who were to divide their time between their parents. Instead of

---

[286] *Brockwell v Brockwell* [1975] CAT 468 (CA) (Ormrod LJ).
[287] Derived from *Edgar* and ss34–5 Matrimonial Causes Act 1973.
[288] Derived from *Edgar* and ss34–5 MCA.
[289] *Macleod v Macleod* [2008] UKPC 64 (Lady Hale). By public purse, Lady Hale means social housing and social security benefits. See also *Hyman v Hyman* [1929] AC 601 (HL).
[290] [2008] UKPC 64. The Privy Council is the highest court of the Isle of Man. The Manx legislation under discussion in the case mirrored that of England and Wales. The Board of the Council is made up of Supreme Court judges. This means their decision, while not directly binding, is highly influential.

continuing to earn $US 470,000 in banking, the husband had retrained as a biochemist earning £30,000. The wife's father, on the other hand, had gifted her additional monies during the marriage, bringing her annual income to £2.6 million and her total wealth to £100 million. Mr Granatino argued that the prenuptial agreement—which of course provided that he should retain only his own assets—should be disregarded and that he should receive his needs, which (bearing in mind that needs do bear some relevance to the marital lifestyle) he put at £6.9 million.

At first instance,[291] Baron J had to consider what weight the prenuptial agreement should have as a section 25 factor, specifically one of the circumstances of the case. She held that the award to Mr Granatino 'should be circumscribed to a degree' to reflect the existence of the agreement, but that it was necessary for the agreement to be varied in order to meet Mr Granatio's needs. Baron J's reasons for departing from the agreement were based on a comparison of the agreement with good practice, against which the agreement was deficient in a number of ways: lack of financial disclosure, lack of independent legal advice, lack of provision for the children, and a failure to meet Mr Granatino's needs. Nevertheless, its existence acted as a 'discounting factor' pointing her to 'the lower end of the bracket' when meeting Mr Granatino's needs.[292] She awarded him £2.5 million to buy a house; £700,000 to pay his debts; £25,000 for a car; and £2.34 million being capitalised maintenance of £100,000 per year for life. In respect of provision for the children, she ordered Ms Radmacher to purchase a further house in Germany that Mr Granatino could stay in while he visited the children there, and to pay child maintenance of £35,000 per annum per child to cover the time when children were with him. (The court had jurisdiction regarding child maintenance because Ms Radmacher's income exceeds the statutory child maintenance scheme cap: see Chapter 6.)

The Court of Appeal upheld Ms Radmacher's appeal on the basis that Baron J had made only a 'negligible' discount to reflect the agreement whereas the appeal judges saw the existence of the agreement as of considerable weight as a s25 factor. That being the case, they held that 'the major funds (housing and income for the husband) should be provided for him in his role as father rather than as former husband . . . this approach is necessary to give proper weight to the ante-nuptial contract.'[293] Thus his chosen house should revert to Ms Radmacher when the children left home, and the element of the lump sum that was in lieu of spousal maintenance should be sufficient only to last Mr Granatino until the youngest child was 22.

Mr Granatino then appealed to the Supreme Court.

While it did not alter the quantum of the Court of Appeal decision, the majority of the Lords held that 'there should be respect for individual autonomy. The court should accord respect to the decision of a married couple as to the manner in which their financial affairs should be regulated. It would be paternalistic and patronising to override their agreement simply on the basis that the court knows best'.[294] Thus:

> the court should give effect to a nuptial agreement that is freely entered into by each party with a full appreciation of its implications unless in the circumstances prevailing it would not be fair to hold the parties to their agreement.[295]

Lady Hale dissented, preferring a more neutral formulation that avoided a starting point that the agreement would be followed. This was 'Did each party freely enter into an agreement, intending it to have legal effect and with a full appreciation of its implications? If so, in the circumstances as they now are, would it be fair to hold them to their agreement?' The reasons for her dissent are considered in the Focus box *Think Critically: Should parties be able to decide for themselves?*

---

[291] Reported as *NG v KR (Pre-Nuptial Contract)* [2008] EWHC 1532.

[292] *NG v KR (Pre-Nuptial Contract)* [2008] EWHC 1532 [93].

[293] *Radmacher v Granatino* [2009] EWCA Civ 649 [50]–[51] (Thorpe LJ).

[294] *Radmacher v Granatino* [2010] UKSC 42 [78].

[295] *Radmacher v Granatino* [2010] UKSC 42 [75] (Lord Philips for the majority).

4.8.1 The *Radmacher* guidance

As we have seen, the starting point provided by *Radmacher* is that the court should give effect to a nuptial agreement that is freely entered into by each party with a full appreciation of its implications unless in the circumstances prevailing it would not be fair to hold the parties to their agreement.[296]

What does this test mean in practice? Let us break it down.

The procedural aspect

The circumstances surrounding the drawing up of the agreement is a key element of the *Radmacher* test. Was the agreement freely entered into by each party with a full appreciation of its implications? There are a number of aspects to this.

- Did the parties intend to create legal relations?

This is an essential element of any contract so if there was no intention then the agreement is void. Post-*Radmacher* 'it will be natural to infer that parties who enter into an ante-nuptial agreement [or, any other kind of nuptial agreement] to which English law is likely to be applied intend that effect should be given to it'[297] because (in theory) they will know that *Radmacher* creates a starting point that such agreements are valid.

Linked to this, we can consider that if the parties have a connection to a jurisdiction in which prenuptial agreements are the norm or where the parties elect a statutory property regime prior to the marriage, then the parties may well expect even an agreement under English/Welsh law to be binding on them. Where the agreement itself was drawn up in a foreign jurisdiction, following which the parties moved to England or Wales, then 'in order to have influence here' (as a s25 factor) the court must find that 'the parties intended the agreement to have effect wherever they might be divorced [rather than in just their home country] *and most particularly* were they to be divorced in a jurisdiction that operated a system of discretionary equitable distribution.' Moreover, it 'would be wholly unjust to attribute weight to the agreement when under the law that the parties elected it would be afforded no weight.'[298]

- Were any of the standard elements that vitiate any contract present, e.g. duress or fraud, or was a party induced to enter into the agreement because of a misrepresentation?

Radmacher says that 'even if the agreement does not have contractual force, those factors will negate any effect the agreement might otherwise have. But unconscionable conduct such as undue pressure[299] (falling short of duress) will also be likely to eliminate the weight to be attached to the agreement, and other unworthy conduct, such as exploitation of a dominant position to secure an unfair advantage, would reduce or eliminate it.'[300]

---

[296] *Radmacher v Granatino* [2010] UKSC 42 [75] (Lord Philips for the majority).
[297] *Radmacher v Granatino* [2010] UKSC 42 [70] (Lord Philips for the majority).
[298] *Ipekci v McConnell* [2019] EWFC 19 (Mostyn J).
[299] As in *NA v MA* [2006] EWHC 2900 (Fam) when, after a seven-year marriage, the wife signed—in a state of distress—a postnuptial agreement when the husband gave her an ultimatum: sign it today or the marriage is over and you cannot return home.
[300] *Radmacher v Granatino* [2010] UKSC 42 [71] (Lord Philips for the majority).

It would appear that pressure that is not caused by the other party is also sufficient.[301]

In considering any such pressures, the court 'may take into account a party's emotional state' as well as factors such as the parties' age and maturity, and whether either or both had been married or been in long-term relationships before. 'For such couples their experience of previous relationships may explain the terms of the agreement, and may also show what they foresaw when they entered into the agreement. What may not be easily foreseeable for less mature couples may well be in contemplation of more mature couples.'[302]

- In the case of a prenuptial agreement, 'another important factor may be whether the marriage would have gone ahead without an agreement, or without the terms which had been agreed'.

As Lord Phillips notes, 'this may cut either way.'[303] For the wealthier party, a prenuptial agreement may be a condition of them marrying; thus without it the poorer spouse would have no marital claims at all because there would be no marriage. Why should the poorer spouse be able to resile from an agreement that was a prerequisite for marrying? Yet the flip side is that, for the poorer spouse, the fact that the prenuptial agreement is a condition to marrying may cause them to feel pressure to sign an unfair agreement. Such pressure may be greater the closer to the wedding date the negotiations take place. (In practice, one always receives enquiries from clients wanting a prenup for their wedding later that week. Such agreements would be very open to attack on the 'pressure' ground. A postnuptial agreement would be more likely to be upheld but after the wedding the wealthier party lacks leverage to require that.)

- Did each party have independent legal advice?

Independent legal advice is 'obviously desirable' because it will make it harder for a party to try to resile from the agreement by claiming that they were pressured into the agreement or did not understand it. However, lack of it is not fatal to the agreement, as we can see in *Radmacher* itself. Nevertheless, it is good practice. Indeed, it may be sensible for the wealthier party to pay for the poorer to receive independent legal advice to give the agreement a greater chance of being upheld.

In *Ipekci v McConnell*, the husband received legal advice, but the lawyer concerned had previously acted for the wife and this could not be said to be independent. The judge cited this 'apparent bias' as one of several justifications that were cumulatively sufficient for him not to give the agreement any weight at all as a 25 factor.[304]

- Was there disclosure of all *material* financial information?

Not every case will require full financial disclosure: 'if it is clear that a party is fully aware of the implications of an ante-nuptial agreement and indifferent to detailed particulars of the other party's assets, there is no need to accord the agreement reduced weight because

[301] *Z v Z (No2)* [2011] EWHC 2878 (Fam) [60] (Moor J).
[302] *Radmacher* at para [72] (Lord Phillips). For an example of a more mature and life-experienced couple, see *Crossley v Crossley* [2007] EWCA Civ 1491.
[303] *Radmacher v Granatino* [2010] UKSC 42 [72] (Lord Philips for the majority).
[304] *Ipekci v McConnell* [2019] EWFC 19 (Mostyn J).

he or she is unaware of those particulars. What is important is that each party should have all the information that is material to his or her decision to enter into an agreement on those terms'.[305] Mr Granatino knew that Ms Radmacher was fabulously wealthy and that was sufficient in that case. It may be that where the asset base is modest or low full financial disclosure is required because every penny may be material to the decision.

The key theme in the above criteria is whether the parties knew what they were doing and made their decision freely. Some of these elements will cause the agreement to be wholly disregarded by the court. Some of them will simply reduce the weight the court gives to the agreement as a s25 factor (part of 'all the circumstances of the case'). That would then enable other s25 factors to attain more prominence in the assessment of fairness. An absolute rule about the effect of non-disclosure or lack of independent legal advice is not necessary because agreements are not automatically binding.[306]

The substantive aspect

The second part of the *Radmacher* test is whether in the prevailing circumstances it would be unfair to hold the parties to their agreement. The prevailing circumstances mean the circumstances at the time that the court is asked to follow or not follow the terms of the nuptial agreement.

- 'If the terms of the agreement are unfair from the start, this will reduce its weight, although this question will be subsumed in practice in the question of whether the agreement operates unfairly having regard to the circumstances prevailing at the time of the breakdown of the marriage.' Thus one should consider the content of the agreement against the current reality (the prevailing circumstances): the assets, the needs, the children, any disabilities or illnesses—all those elements that affect the parties' future financial position.

- Would the agreement, if followed, leave a party in 'a predicament of real need' while the other enjoys a sufficiency or more?

Lord Phillips again: 'The parties are unlikely to have intended that their ante-nuptial agreement should result, in the event of the marriage breaking up, in one partner being left in a predicament of real need, while the other enjoys a sufficiency or more, and such a result is likely to render it unfair to hold the parties to their agreement.'[307] Thus an agreement should be departed from to the extent required to meet these real needs. However, 'Where each party is in a position to meet his or her needs, fairness may well not require a departure from their agreement.'

The position, therefore, is that an agreement that leaves a party in real needs should be modified so as to meet those needs. What, however, are 'real needs'? When Lord Phillips used this phrase in *Radmacher*, did he mean this to be different from the usual generously assessed needs? As we see elsewhere in this chapter, the combination of the judges' broad-brush approaches (see section 4.7.6) and the influence of the other s25 factors give judges tremendously wide discretion in the assessment of needs. However, we suggest that for the public

---

[305] *Radmacher* at para [69] (Lord Phillips).
[306] *Radmacher* at para [69] (Lord Phillips).
[307] *Radmacher* at para [82] (Lord Phillips).

policy reasons articulated in *Macleod*, an agreement that left one party with recourse to benefits is unlikely to be held to meet their real needs if the other party has retained a surplus.

In *Kremen v Agrest*, Mostyn J interpreted the phrase as implying that it meant only 'that minimum amount required to keep a spouse from destitution' when he gave an example of a spouse having become incapacitated. This implies that it could be very much lower than the usual assessment of needs. However, later in the same judgment Mostyn J ultimately rejected the agreement, because, among other reasons, it failed to address the wife's 'reasonable needs', saying that there needed to be 'clear evidence of significant economic capacity on the part of the claimant spouse before the assessment of needs was suppressed to that minimal level imposed on Mr Granatino'.[308] In *Ipekci v McConnell*, the same judge noted that he did 'not take the language used by the Supreme Court, namely "predicament of real need" as signifying that needs when assessed in circumstances where there is a valid prenuptial agreement in play should be markedly less than needs assessed in ordinary circumstances. If you have reasonable needs which you cannot meet from your own resources, then you are in a predicament. Those needs are real needs.'[309]

While sympathetic to Mostyn's reasoning, the fact that the Supreme Court chose to use the phrase 'real needs' in preference to the more widely used 'reasonable needs' or 'needs generously interpreted' surely implies that there is a difference, that 'real needs' are not as generous as 'reasonable needs' or 'needs generously interpreted'. Miles has suggested that it is a 'narrower concept'.[310] That is not to imply that near destitution is the appropriate standard either. In *WW v HW (Prenuptial Agreement: Needs: Conduct)* Nicholas Cusworth QC, sitting as a deputy High Court Judge, declined to provide the husband with the minimum required to keep him from destitution, holding that

> even where there is an agreement, fairness will not necessarily equate to near destitution. The level at which a party's needs should be assessed, if they are not met by an agreement which might otherwise be binding upon them, must surely depend upon all of the circumstances of the case, amongst which the fact of the agreement may feature prominently as a depressing factor. But each case will be different. . . . In *Radmacher* itself, [the award] could hardly be equated to 'destitution'.[311]

As we see in 4.7.1, the parties' lifestyle forms the starting point for an assessment of needs and for the wealthy this can be very generous. It appears that the current position is that an agreement between the parties that provides less generously would be followed as long as it meets those lesser reasonable needs.

- Does it discriminate against a homemaker?

Radmacher tells us that 'if the devotion of one partner to looking after the family and the home has left the other free to accumulate wealth, it is likely to be unfair to hold the parties

---

[308] *Kremen v Agrest (No.11) (Financial Remedy: Non-Disclosure: Post-Nuptial Agreement)* [2012] EWHC 45 (Fam) [73] (Mostyn J).

[309] [2019] EWFC 19 [27]. For a useful comment on this case, see B Sloan, 'Departing from Prenuptial Agreements to Meet Needs in England and Wales', in C Declerck and W Pintens (eds), *Patrimonium 2019* (die Keure 2019).

[310] J Miles, 'Marital Agreements and Private Autonomy in England and Wales', in JM Scherpe (ed.), *Marital Agreements and Private Autonomy in Comparative Perspective* (Hart 2012).

[311] [2015] EWHC 1844 (Fam).

to an agreement that entitles the latter to retain all that he or she has earned.'[312] That does not mean that the agreement cannot discriminate: discrimination is the very raison d'etre of many agreements that often protect the earner at the expense of a primary carer. Rather, it means that the terms cannot be entirely one-sided when the parties have undertaken the traditional gender roles of homemaker and breadwinner during the marriage, given that *White* gives these equal value. If they are, then the terms could be varied by the court.

- Does the agreement provide adequately for any children of the family?

'A nuptial agreement cannot be allowed to prejudice the reasonable requirements of any children of the family.'[313] If it does, the agreement will be varied to the extent necessary to provide for the children. Do not forget that statutory child maintenance will be payable in any event (assuming the parties live in England and Wales) but, depending on the case, that may not be sufficient to meet their reasonable requirements.

- Finally, although not explicitly discussed in *Radmacher*, we should add one further criterion, which is how the parties have managed their money since the agreement was drawn up.

If, for example, the agreement provided that each party should retain their own income and assets without co-mingling, and they have done so, that is a strong reason for the agreement being followed by the court. King LJ thought in *Versteegh v Versteegh* that '"Fairness" does not, in my judgment, require a court to ignore the precept upon which the parties have governed their affairs for over 20 years.'[314] This is because the ways in which the parties have governed their affairs is an indication of what they themselves considered fair, and this should influence the courts' assessment of fairness in their case.

Note that the presence of one of these substantive aspects does not mean the agreement will not be upheld in part. Where the parties have agreed the terms and are simply asking that they be embodied in a consent order, the court is likely to write to them explaining the judge's reservations, so they can negotiate some changes and resubmit the order. Where the parties are not in agreement, because one is seeking to back out of the agreement, they will be in court on a contested basis.

Either way, the most likely outcome is that the agreement will be changed only insofar as is necessary to remedy the unfairness. It may still be very favourable to one party. As Holman J said in *Luckwell v Limata*, the 'over-arching criterion remains the search for "fairness", in accordance with section 25 as explained by the House of Lords in *Miller/ McFarlane* (i.e. needs, sharing and compensation), but an agreement is capable of altering what is fair, including in relation to "need"'.[315] Unless a vitiating element is present, the court is not applying the principles derived from *White* and *Miller/McFarlane* as though the agreement had never existed. The agreement's existence 'is capable of affecting the

---

[312] *Radmacher* at para [81] (Lord Phillips). Note that the majority took the view that there was no compensation factor in this case. 'The husband's decision to abandon his lucrative career in the city for the fields of academia was not motivated by the demands of his family, but reflected his own preference' [121]. Lady Hale viewed this differently [194].
[313] *Radmacher* at para [77] (Lord Phillips).
[314] [2018] EWCA Civ 1050.
[315] [2014] EWHC 502 (Fam) at [130].

overall balance of what is fair as one of the factors or rationales to be taken into account in the application of the statutory discretion', so that a fair outcome where there is a nuptial agreement may be less generous than a fair outcome where there was no agreement at all.[316] We can see this from *Radmacher* itself, in which the Court of Appeal varied the terms slightly to give the husband use of a house and a lump sum, neither of which was provided for in the nuptial agreement itself, but did not give the husband anywhere near the amount he would have received had there been no nuptial agreement. (Although this would not have been half the assets anyway, given their source as the wife's family wealth i.e. non-matrimonial.)

As Lord Wilson has pointed out, 'clearly a contract which makes less provision for a party than he or she would have secured under the ordinary law does not, on that account, generate an unfair outcome; any contrary conclusion would make the prenuptial contract not worth the paper on which it was written.'[317] This goes back to the purpose of a nuptial agreement, which is to opt out of the 'provision to which [the poorer spouse] . . . would otherwise be entitled' at the end of the marriage, i.e., what would otherwise be considered a fair settlement based on the principles of needs, compensation, and sharing.[318]

However, there are limits to this. Consider the language used in *Radmacher*. Needs must still be met. To some extent any compensation claim must also still be met, but the phrase used in *Radmacher*—'[I]f the devotion of one partner to looking after the family and the home has left the other free to accumulate wealth, it is likely to be unfair to hold the parties to an agreement that entitles the latter to retain all that he or she has earned'— is not an unqualified assertion that in such circumstances the agreement would be ignored: it would be more likely to be varied to address that particular deficiency. Thus, even though 'of the three strands identified in *White v White* and *Miller v Miller*, it is the first two, needs and compensation, which can most readily render it unfair to hold the parties to an ante-nuptial agreement',[319] the assessment of those strands may be significantly less generous than would otherwise be the case. '[I]t is in relation to the third strand, sharing, that the court will be most likely to make an order in the terms of the nuptial agreement in place of the order that it would otherwise have made.'[320]

Thus the agreement can make 'provisions that conflict with what the court would otherwise consider to be the requirements of fairness'.[321] That is, after all, the purpose of a nuptial agreement—if you would get the same outcome going to court, why enter into one?

The Key Case *KA v MA* shows us how the Radmacher guidance and subsequent case law interpretation may be applied.

---

[316] *V v V (Pre-Nuptial Agreement)* [2012] 1 FLR 1315, 1329 (Charles J). See also *Radmacher* at [75].

[317] Lord Wilson, 'Changes over the Centuries in the Financial Consequences of Divorce'. Address to the University of Bristol Law Club, 20 March 2017. Available at https://www.supremecourt.uk/docs/speech-170320.pdf accessed 21 March 2017.

[318] *Radmacher* at [137] (Lady Hale).

[319] J Miles, 'Marriage and Divorce in the Supreme Court and the Law Commission: For Love or Money?' (2011) 74(3) *Modern Law Review* 430, 443. See also A Murray, 'Pre-Nuptials, LSPs and Compensation Guidance: Before and After the Law Commission Report' [2014] *Family Law* 491.

[320] *Radmacher* at [81]-[82] (Lord Phillips).

[321] *Radmacher v Granatino* [2010] UKSC 42 [75].

KEY CASE *KA v MA (Prenuptial Agreement Needs)* [2018] EWHC 499

At the time that they married, the husband (MA) and wife (KA) had one child together and the husband had three adult children from a previous marriage. The parties entered into a prenuptial agreement which provided that the husband, who had assets of £32 million at the start of the marriage, would pay the wife an index-linked £600,000 lump sum, periodical payments of £2,000 per month, and child maintenance. The wife owned a couple of properties that she rented out and was a full-time mother. The parties lived very comfortably, spending about £1 million per year and living in a home worth £3.35 million.

Both parties had independent legal advice before signing the agreement. The wife's solicitors had noted her unhappiness with the terms and the fact that she wanted to get married for the benefit of their son, and that the husband required a prenuptial agreement to do so. They had advised against signing it on the basis that the provision was too low.

On divorce, the wife sought to depart from the nuptial agreement on the basis that it did not meet her needs, which she assessed at £6 million. She accepted that she had no claim under the sharing principle.

Roberts J upheld the nuptial agreement partially. She held that the parties had freely entered into the nuptial agreement. The husband's position that he wanted a prenuptial agreement before he married did not create duress or exploitation of a dominant position in this case. They were mature adults, each of whom had been married before. The wife had an established professional career was financially independent prior to the marriage. Although the agreement was entered into before the Supreme Court decision in *Radmacher*, the wife had been clearly advised that she may well be bound by the agreement and that this was 'the direction of travel' of the case law.

Roberts J departed from the agreement to meet the wife's needs, which she found to be £1.35m to meet her housing needs in the local area and a *Duxbury* fund of almost £1.6m (as a lump sum in lieu of lifetime spousal maintenance), on top of which she was capable of earning up to £20,000 per year from employment. The wife's need was for a home that was comfortable and safe for her and for their child, when he lived with her during boarding school holidays. The judge held that there was no basis for generosity in assessing needs when the source of the award was non-matrimonial assets that the husband had specifically entered into the agreement to protect.

And now our fictional scenario.

SCENARIO 3

Illustration 4: Mary and Steve

We have considered what the range of fair settlements might look like for this wealthy couple. Steve has had a successful career as a rock musician and he came into the marriage with considerable assets. It is therefore very possible that he would have wanted a prenuptial agreement. What effect would this have on Mary's claims?

The answer, as you now know, depends upon two things:

1. The procedural aspect: Was the agreement freely entered into by each party with a full appreciation of its implications?
2. The substantive aspect: What prevailing circumstances might mean that it was unfair to hold the parties to their agreement?

Unless Mary challenges the prenuptial agreement the parties will simply invite the court to make an order that reflects its terms. Although the judge has to consider all the s25 factors, the existence of a nuptial agreement is part of all the circumstances of the case. In reality, though, the judge is likely to give it little consideration unless it is manifestly unfair. It is really only if Mary seeks not to be held to the agreement that the court will scrutinise it, just as it did in *KA v MA*.

4.8.2 Application of these criteria to different kinds of nuptial agreement

The majority in *Radmacher* thought that *Macleod* was wrong to draw a distinction between prenuptial and postnuptial agreements. The key issue is not what the type of agreement is, but the parties' circumstances when it was made compared to those prevailing at the end of the marriage. At the beginning of this section, we noted that it is useful to visualise nuptial agreements on a continuum. As we move along the continuum towards the end of the marriage, the courts' approach to nuptial agreements becomes increasingly strict and towards the *Edgar* approach. A party wishing to resile from an agreement made close to the end of the marriage (and that could include a prenup of the marriage was short) would therefore need strong justification for doing so: if it does not meet their current needs, why did they so recently enter into it? For such cases, the stricter *Edgar* approach of looking for a change in circumstances since they entered into the agreement is appropriate. Assuming that they freely entered into the agreement, what has changed to cause them to now object to something they previously agreed to?

Where the agreement was made well before it came into effect (such as a prenuptial agreement made before a long marriage, or a postnuptial agreement made early in such a marriage), then a change of circumstances more likely to have rendered the agreement unfair. For example, one party may have become ill or disabled, careers and fortunes made or lost, or children born who were not foreseen at the time of drawing up the agreement. A court may well find more reason to depart from the terms to some extent. However, the stricter *Edgar* approach of may still be appropriate where the agreement was drawn up to protect assets acquired before the marriage, i.e. non-matrimonial property, rather than to deviate from a fair division of the matrimonial assets. As we have seen at 4.7.3.1, non-matrimonial assets are not usually subject to the sharing principle and thus are susceptible to inclusion only to meet needs or compensation in the way outlined in *Radmacher*.

For all types of agreement, *Radmacher* prevails. Whoever seeks to resile from an agreement faces a considerable uphill struggle.

FOCUS Think Critically

Should parties be able to decide for themselves?

In her dissent in *Radmacher*, Lady Hale noted that this was 'a complicated subject upon which there is a large literature and knowledgeable and thoughtful people may legitimately hold differing views'.[322] The majority decision was based on respect for individual autonomy: the freedom to control, insofar

---

[322] *Radmacher v Granatino* [2010] UKSC 42 [135].

as possible, one's own future. Part of this is the freedom to enter into contracts governing aspects of one's life, both public and private. Why should an adult not enter into such a contract? Part of being an autonomous adult is the freedom to make bad decisions and live with the consequences. There are other arguments in favour of enforceable marital agreements. They may reduce litigation and costs. Given the high divorce rate and the uncertainty of the existing law, the ability to enter into an enforceable agreement may even encourage more people to marry—particularly, perhaps, those who have been married before and who have property from that marriage that they want to preserve. Fehlberg and Smyth found that binding nuptial agreements in Australia tended to be used by defined groups, namely couples with a significant asset difference between them, second marriages, those with family businesses, and those who had previous experience of the family courts.[323] These are all understandable reasons for wishing to regulate the consequences of marriage.

Yet the Court in *Radmacher* did not hold that such contracts were automatically enforceable. While it certainly moved in that direction, it provided a number of safeguards. Given that in other areas of life the law provides very limited relief to those who enter into unwise contracts, is there something special about the marital context that justifies this different approach?

There are three main arguments, which are strongest when it comes to prenuptial agreements rather than agreements at the end of a marriage:

1. *People in relationships need protecting*
Parties enter into prenuptial agreements when—one assumes—they are in the full flush of love. 'The court . . . should not be blind to human frailty and susceptibility when love and separation are involved'.[324] The economically weaker party may not have equal bargaining power, or the clarity, foresight, and conviction to 'make rational choices in the same way that businessmen can'.[325] Notwithstanding a 42 per cent divorce rate,[326] they may not believe that the prenuptial agreement will ever be triggered or they may not anticipate a future change in circumstances—a career change; the birth of children; an illness or disability; years out of the job market—that renders it less favourable. In such circumstances, is it appropriate for the law to intervene to protect that party? There are examples of laws framed so as to 'redress inequality of bargaining power in other long running relationships, notably between landlord and tenant, employer and employee. Are they not a closer analogy with marriage than an ordinary commercial bargain between economic equals?'[327] Or is this patronising, as the majority of the Supreme Court considered?

2. *The wider social interest in marriage*
A second argument is that the court is not merely ensuring fairness between the parties but representing a wider societal interest in ensuring that the parties cannot bargain their way out of supporting one another. As the House of Lords said in *Hyman*, the parties' claims are 'a matter of public concern which they cannot barter away'. By marrying, the parties 'contract into the package which the law of the land lays down'. The state recognises your marriage and provides certain legal advantages to married couples that it does not provide for the unmarried. One cannot pick and choose among these rights and responsibilities. If marriage 'simply means what the parties want it to mean'[328] there is no justification for privileging marriage in law.

3. *The gender dimension*
As Lady Hale recognised in her dissent in *Radmacher*, women are usually the economically weaker party,[329] and the purpose of a prenuptial agreement is to deny that person the 'provision to which

[323] B Fehlberg and B Smyth, 'Binding Prenuptial Agreements in Australia: The First Year' (2002) 16 *International Journal of Law, Policy, and the Family* 127.
[324] *NG v KR (Pre-Nuptial Contract)* [2008] EWHC 1532 [129] (Baron J).
[325] *Radmacher v Granatino* [2010] UKSC 42 [135] (Baroness Hale).
[326] Office of National Statistics, *Divorces in England and Wales 2017* (ONS 2018).
[327] Lady Hale, 'Equality and Autonomy in Family Law' (2011) 33(1) *Journal of Social Welfare and Family Law* 3, 12.
[328] J Herring (2010) 'On the Death Knell of Marriage', 160(7441) *New Law Journal* 1551.
[329] *Radmacher* was unusual in that it was the wife who was the wealthier.

she . . . would otherwise be entitled'[330] at the end of the marriage. In other words, it is about the autonomy to contract out of concepts such as equality, partnership, and marriage as a joint endeavour in which each contributes equally and supports the other—'standards that are intended to be of universal application throughout our society'.[331] As Herring points out, 'there is no other area of discrimination law you can contract out of'.[332] Indeed, the autonomy that the majority was concerned about is, as the Law Commission pointed out, 'not simply the freedom to make an agreement' but also 'the freedom to force one's partner to abide by an agreement when he or she no longer wishes to do so . . . it is therefore freedom to use a contract to restrict one's partner's choices.'[333] It is troubling that the steps towards gender equality that the Supreme Court took in *White* and *Miller/ McFarlane*—decisions that had potentially lifelong real-world consequences for those divorcing after them—were put at risk by the decision in *Radmacher*. Will it be, as Lady Hale wondered, 'a retrograde step likely only to benefit the strong at the expense of the weak'?

4.9 Orders after a foreign divorce

Under Part III Matrimonial and Family Proceedings Act 1984 (MFPA) a person who was validly divorced (or judicially separated or whose marriage was annulled) outside England and Wales can apply for a financial remedy order here in certain circumstances *even though* a court or authority in another jurisdiction has made their equivalent of a financial remedy order.

Prior to the MFPA, the Law Commission had identified the hardship caused by situations in which England/Wales recognised a foreign divorce and related financial settlement as valid and replacing their own jurisdiction, even though the foreign court or authority may have made no or inadequate provision for one party.[334] The purpose behind the legislation was—said the Supreme Court in the leading case of *Agbaje v Akinnoye-Agbaje*—to alleviate these 'adverse consequences'.[335] The power under the MFPA is thus not about which jurisdiction should prevail: it gives our domestic courts jurisdiction *despite* prior valid judicial or other proceedings in another jurisdiction.[336]

The MFPA applies to those in same-sex marriages including those entered into abroad, and schedule 7 to the Civil Partnership Act 2004 contains mirror provisions in respect of those who entered into a civil partnership or foreign equivalent.

In order to proceed with a claim:

1. The person wanting to make an application cannot have remarried.

2. The person wanting to make an application must seek permission to do so from the English/Welsh court and show:

   a. sufficient connections to England and Wales. This can be demonstrated by either spouse being domiciled in England and Wales on the date when the foreign divorce took effect or the date of the application for financial provision; or

---

[330] *Radmacher v Granatino* [2010] UKSC 42 [137].
[331] *F v F* [1995] 2 FLR 45, 66 (Thorpe J).
[332] J Herring (2010) 'On the Death Knell of Marriage', 160(7441) *New Law Journal* 1551.
[333] Law Commission, *Matrimonial Property Agreements* (Law Com CP No 198, 2011) para 5.31.
[334] Law Commission, *Financial Relief after Foreign Divorce* (Law Com No 117, 1982).
[335] [2010] UKSC 13 [71].
[336] See Lord Collins at [50].

habitually resident for 12 months ending on either of those dates; or by virtue of one or both parties having a beneficial interest at the date of the application in a dwelling house in England or Wales that had been the matrimonial home.[337]

b.   that there are substantial grounds for making the application, which is more burdensome than another standard—'a good arguable case'—commonly required for applications in other areas of law. It is helpful if the applicant can show that the foreign order has led to injustice or caused hardship (some jurisdictions provide very limited provision for women, for example), but this is not a prerequisite for permission. In *Juffali v Juffali*, the wife applied following a *talaq* divorce pronounced by the husband in Saudi Arabia (recognised as valid in this country) which entitled her to no financial provision whatsoever for herself and her daughter.[338]

c.   Whether in all the circumstances it would be appropriate for an order to be made, taking into account all the circumstances of the case. The court is directed to a series of considerations set out in s16; these include the parties' connection with England and Wales and the other country; any orders made in that foreign jurisdiction and whether they have been complied with; and the length of time that has elapses since the date of the divorce.

If the application proceeds, the courts have the full range of financial remedy powers outlined in 4.4 available to them. There is one exception to this: if the jurisdiction is based solely on the presence of a marital home in England or Wales, then the claim is limited to the value of that property.

When determining the quantum of the financial provision to be made, the Supreme Court, in the leading case *Agbaje v Akinnoye-Agbaje*,[339] identified three principles: (1) that primary consideration must be given to the welfare of any children of the marriage; (2) that it will never be appropriate to make an order that gives the applicant more than he or she would have been awarded if all the proceedings had taken place within this jurisdiction; and (3) that, where possible, provision should be made for the reasonable needs of each spouse. All of the factors in s25 Matrimonial Causes Act 1973 (or the Civil Partnership Act equivalent) apply, along with the case law principles discussed in this chapter.

4.10 After a financial remedy order is made

Obtaining the order is not the end of matter. There is further work for the lawyers and the parties to do.

4.10.1 Implementing the terms

First, if they have not already done so, the parties must obtain decree absolute. They may have paused the divorce proceedings at decree nisi stage and not applied for decree absolute so as to enable them to remain married while financial matters were resolved. (A spouse is in a much stronger position than an ex-spouse if one of the parties dies in the interim.) The

---

[337] Section 15.
[338] *Juffali v Juffali* [2016] EWHC 1684 (Fam).
[339] [2010] UKSC 13.

parties then have to implement the terms of the order. This may mean transferring title to a house, closing joint bank accounts, transferring shares, making lump sum payments, or starting to make regular payments to the former spouse.

4.10.2 Enforcement

The Law Commission has estimated that on average 9 per cent of financial remedy orders will be the subject of enforcement action, and this does not include those orders being breached but where there is no enforcement action.[340] The court has a range of powers to compel compliance with an order. What is appropriate will depend on the aspect of the order that needs to be enforced. Methods include:

1. General enforcement of an order for the payment of money such as a lump sum order. This can specify the method of enforcement sought, or leave it to whatever method the court deems appropriate; the latter is more common practice.[341] This will result in the court making an order summoning the debtor to court for the purposes of being questioned on oath about his or her means, and to produce specified documents. A penal notice is attached to the summons.

The following items numbers 2 to 5 inclusive, can be part of a general enforcement application or freestanding.

2. Oral examination under Part 71 Civil Procedure Rules. As above, this also orders the debtor to attend court for questioning.

3. Attachment of earnings order. This obliges the debtor's employer to deduct a specified amount from the debtor's earnings. This is useful for maintenance orders (as it could be done, for example, on a monthly basis) but can also be used for lump sums. The amount is limited by law.

4. Third party debt order which order money owed to the debtor by a third party to be redirected to the creditor. This can include money held by the debtor in a bank account as this is money owed to the debtor by the bank. It is unfortunately only effective on the day it is served on the third party, so would not work if the bank account was empty on that day.

5. A charging order. This imposes a charge on the property of the debtor, which can include both real property (land/houses) and investments/shares. It can only be used for an order to pay a sum of money, not to effect the transfer of a property, but once a charge is obtained an order for sale can be sought. (Note that where a party refuses to sign documents to effect a house sale or transfer, a judge can do this instead.)

6. A judgment summons. This can result in a deliberate non-payer's imprisonment for contempt of court. This can only be used for certain types of maintenance order

---

[340] Law Commission, *Enforcement of Family Financial Orders* (Law Com No 370, 2016) para 1.21.
[341] According to R Harrison QC, speech to the Bloomsbury Family Law Conference, London, 25 June 2019.

listed in Schedule 8 Administration of Justice Act 1970. This is not part of a general enforcement application.

7.   Warrants of control over assets.[342] This involves bailiffs seizing belongings of the debtor which they then sell, putting the proceeds towards the debt.

8.   A Hadkinson order, named for the case *Hadkinson v Hadkinson*, which is an order barring someone from participating in existing or further legal proceedings (such as pursuing an appeal) unless they comply with an existing order.[343] Sir Ernest Ryder has said that 'Such an order is draconian in its effect because it goes directly to a litigant's right of access to a court. It is not and should not be a commonplace. As developed in case law, it is a case management order of last resort in substantive proceedings (for example for a financial remedy order) where a litigant is in wilful contempt rather than a species of penalty or remedy in committal proceedings for contempt.'[344] A court considering whether to make a Hadkinson order will therefore need to find that (1) the respondent is in contempt; (2) the contempt is deliberate and continuing; (3) as a result there is an impediment to the course of justice (4) there is no other realistic and effective remedy; (5) the order is proportionate to the problem and goes no further than necessary to remedy it.[345]

9.   A passport order, as per *Bayer AG v Winter and Others*.[346] This prevents a person from leaving the country. It is useful leverage where there are no obvious assets to go after. For an example of it in action in the financial remedy context, see *Young v Young*.[347]

On the basis that prevention is better than cure, the Law Commission has recommended that judges are directed to consider whether any terms as to enforcement should be included whenever a family financial order is made.[348] Thus, the court could make a secured periodical payments order rather than an unsecured one, so that in the event of non-payment the secured property is sold.

Enforcement methods available for overseas assets are outside the scope of this book and can be highly complex, as demonstrated by the series of enforcement steps across multiple jurisdictions in *Akhmedova*, which started life as *AAZ v BZZ*, discussed at 4.7.1.[349]

4.10.3 Appeals and applications to set aside an order

The principle that there should be finality of litigation weighs heavily on the court. Nevertheless, the parties can appeal (within strict time limits) on the following grounds.

---

[342] See S Oliver, D Brown, and G Schofield, *Enforcing Family Finance Orders* (2nd edn, Jordans 2017). See also the methods discussed by Z Saunders in a series of articles: [2016] *Family Law Journal* 740; 787; 931.

[343] [1952] 2 All ER 567. For a summary of the history of such orders see *C v C (Appeal: Hadkinson Order)* [2011] 1 FLR 434.

[344] *Assoun v Assoun [No 1]* [2017] EWCA Civ 21, [3].

[345] *de Gafforj v de Gafforj* [2018] EWCA Civ 2070 [11] (Peter Jackson LJ).

[346] [1986] 1 WLR 497.

[347] [2012] Fam. 198.

[348] Law Commission, *Enforcement of Family Financial Orders* (Law Com No 370, 2016) Chapter 18.

[349] *Akhmedova v Akhmedov and Others* [2016] EWHC 3234 (as *AAZ v BBZ*); [2018] EWFC 23 (Fam); [2019] EWHC 1705 (Fam).

Where the order is wrong

An appeal will be successful if the judge was wrong with respect to what the law is, whether statutory or case law, or has misunderstood the facts, although there are limitations to this.[350] Where a decision is an exercise of judicial discretion such as deciding an appropriate financial settlement, it is difficult for a judge to be wrong in their exercise of that discretion—it essential requires the judge to have given far too much weight to one factor at the expense of another, or ignoring certain factors.[351]

In *Andrew C v Rebecca C*, Booth J said

> The Appeal Courts have deliberately refused to define 'wrong' but in this context it essentially means this: either the District Judge has ordered something that he had no power to order, or arrived at a conclusion on the basis of no evidence, those being two examples, or in exercising the discretionary powers under the Matrimonial Causes Act in identifying the parties' assets and incomes and in carrying out the re-distributed phase of the exercise, he has come to a conclusion that is so wide of the mark as to be outside the wide ambit of reasonable conclusions that would amount to a fair outcome. It is not sufficient that I might have reached a different conclusion—that is no test of the measure of the order being wrong.[352]

For misrepresentation, fraud, duress, or mistake

'Even innocent misrepresentation as to a material fact can be a vitiating factor if the undisclosed fact was material to the decision which the court made at the time and/or if it undermines the basis on which the order was made.'[353] The parties can challenge an order either by way of an appeal or by way of an application to a first instance judge to set aside the order.

Supervening events

Sometimes, the rationale for the order has been invalidated by a supervening event. In the leading case, *Barder v Barder (Caluori Intervening)*, the order provided that the matrimonial home be retained by the wife for herself and the two children.[354] Approximately one month after the consent order was approved, the wife killed herself and the children, and the husband applied for leave to appeal out of time against the terms of the order. The House of Lords set four conditions for a successful application out of time: (1) new events have occurred since the making of the order which invalidate the basis, or fundamental assumption, upon which the order was made, so that, if leave to appeal out of time were to be given, the appeal would be certain, or very likely, to succeed; (2) the new events should have occurred within a relatively short time of the order having been made; (3) the application for leave to appeal out of time should be made reasonably promptly in the circumstances of the case; (4) the grant of leave to appeal out of time should not prejudice

---

[350] *Piglowska v Piglowski* [1999] UKHL 27.

[351] *N v N (Financial Orders: Appellate Role)* [2011] EWCA Civ 940.

[352] *Andrew C v Rebecca C* [2015] EWFC B236 per Booth J. This is a rare example of a reported modest asset case.

[353] *AB v CD* [2016] EWHC 10 (Fam) (Roberts J). See also, for deliberate fraud, *Sharland v Sharland* [2015] UKSC 60 and *Gohil v Gohil* [2015] UKSC 61.

[354] [1988] AC 20.

third parties who have acquired, in good faith and for valuable consideration, interests in property which is the subject matter of the relevant order.

Note that a common type of mistake—mistake as to the value of an asset—is no longer regarded as falling within the *Barder* principle. Fluctuations in the value of assets such as shares and houses are normal and predictable, even if the consequences can be severe: in *Myerson v Myerson (No. 2)*, a fall in the value of the shares taken, willingly, by the husband as the bulk of his settlement meant that the split of the assets went from 43 per cent to the wife to the equivalent of 105 per cent to the wife by the time of the husband's unsuccessful appeal.[355]

FOCUS Think Critically

What Conception of Fairness Underlies Financial Remedy Law?

The objective that courts have identified—to do that which is fair, just and reasonable between the parties in rearranging the family finances[356]—has developed over decades of case law. Fairness itself is not mentioned in the Matrimonial Causes Act 1973 or its antecedents. Yet the idea that a financial settlement should be fair is not contentious. As a concept, it has considerable 'rhetorical force'.[357]

However, as we have seen, pinning down what fairness requires has proven extremely difficult. As Lord Nicholls recognised in *Miller/McFarlane*, it 'is grounded in social and moral values [that] change from one generation to the next'.[358] Faced with an almost total absence of legislative input, the courts have sought to identify and expound on underlying principles to ensure that financial remedy decisions continue to be made 'in a climate which reflects society's current attitudes'.[359] In the case law considered in this chapter, we can see four different conceptions of fairness at work: fairness as responsibility to provide for dependants (pre-*White*); fairness as valuing different roles equally (*White*); fairness as acknowledging the different consequences of those roles (*Miller/McFarlane*); and, most recently, fairness as autonomy (*Radmacher*). We have moved from responsibility towards others to responsibility for oneself.

As far back as the Poor Laws, the state sought to look first and foremost to the resources within the family to provide for all members of the family, rather than the burden falling on the state—'an ethic of family responsibility'.[360] So, too, divorce laws reflected a social interest in the wife's continued economic needs being met, however inadequately, by the husband rather than the state. Marriage is 'its own little security system' . . . '[t]he more the private family can look after its own, the less the state will have to do so.'[361]

As recently as *Dart*, the court's judgment was still 'firmly located within the traditional discourse of the provider's responsibility to his dependant—to meet needs'[362] (for what were reasonable

[355] *Myerson v Myerson (No 2)* [2009] EWCA Civ 282.

[356] *Page v Page* [1981] 2 FLR 198 (CA) 206 (Wood J), which, ironically, had an extraordinarily unfair outcome by modern standards.

[357] A Diduck, 'Ancillary Relief: Complicating the Search for Principle', (2011) 38(2) *Journal of Law and Society* 272, 273.

[358] *Miller v Miller/McFarlane v McFarlane* [2006] UKHL 24 [4].

[359] *Co v Co (Ancillary Relief: Pre-Marriage Cohabitation)* [2004] EWHC 287 (Fam) [43] (Coleridge J).

[360] J Eekelaar, 'Family Law and Social Control', in J Eekelaar and J Bell (eds), *Oxford Essays in Jurisprudence* (Clarendon Press 1987).

[361] Lady Hale, 'Equality and Autonomy in Family Law' (2011) 33(1) *Journal of Social Welfare and Family Law* 3, 4.

[362] A Diduck, 'What Is Family Law For?' (2011) 64 *Current Legal Problems* 287, 295.

requirements but moderately assessed needs?).[363] 'The idea that a wife might have a little extra to save for a rainy day or to leave to her family if she died was seen as going beyond what she reasonably required.'[364] As Alison Diduck points out, that is the role of the provider,[365] and the wife is not the provider—on the contrary:

> in the breadwinner/dependant ideology of marriage the claimant wife (and approximately seventy per cent of claimants are wives) comes to law not as the autonomous rights-bearing individual, but as dependant and supplicant (or potential plunderer of her husband's fortune). . . . It was as if the courts felt similar to the way in which many husbands and wives feel when they are negotiating ancillary relief – that it is the husband's money and assets that are being dealt with.[366]

White 'altered the narrative'[367] in its language—the 'yardstick of equality', 'no place for discrimination between husbands and wives', 'no bias in favour of the money-earner'—and the idea that a non-financial contribution could be equal to a financial one. Fairness here meant equality. In *Miller/McFarlane*, equality had three strands.

First, it involved understanding that formal equality of division is not the same as substantive equality if decisions made by the parties during the marriage have disparate consequences post-divorce: 'Giving half the present assets to the breadwinner achieves a very different outcome from giving half the assets to the homemaker with children.'[368] Second, both parties are responsible for these disparate consequences—'mutual dependence begets mutual obligations of support'.[369] This is a new responsibility ethic to replace the responsibility of the breadwinner to his dependant, but it has old roots in the idea that parties should look first to one another and not to the state. Third, marriage is an equal partnership (albeit one in which the parties can retain non-matrimonial property), at the end of which each party is *entitled* to a fair share of the available property.

Yet we also see another theme emerging: autonomy, individual choice. We can see it in the statutory encouragement of a clean break. We see it in Lady Hale's reference to giving each party 'an equal start on the road to independent living'.[370] We see it in Mostyn J's attacks on compensation: 'No one forced her to give up work . . . what cannot be disputed is that the reason Mrs McFarlane gave up work was because she, and intelligent liberated autonomous adult woman, decided to give up work.'[371] 'In the new discourse the individual becomes responsible for herself and her familial choices.'[372] We see it too in *Radmacher*, with its explicit statement that there should be respect for individual autonomy. Here, once more, we see responsibility: this time, responsibility for oneself. Anne Barlow situates such decisions in a social context in which adult couples are increasingly given the 'liberty jointly to exercise their autonomy around decision-making', such as with the 'replacement of statutory child support obligations with parent-negotiated child maintenance; strong regulatory encouragement for family mediation; and rejection of calls for family law regulation of cohabitant separation'.[373]

---

[363] See discussion by Lord Nicholls in *White v White* [2001] 1 AC 596, 607; 608.

[364] Lady Hale, 'Equality and Autonomy in Family Law' (2011) 33(1) *Journal of Social Welfare and Family Law* 3, 8.

[365] A Diduck, 'What Is Family Law For?' (2011) 64 *Current Legal Problems* 287, 295.

[366] A Diduck, 'Fairness and Justice for All? The House of Lords in *White v White*' (2001) 9 *Feminist Legal Studies* 173, 175.

[367] A Diduck, 'What Is Family Law For?' (2011) 64 *Current Legal Problems* 287, 303.

[368] *Miller v Miller/McFarlane v McFarlane* [2006] UKHL 24 [136] (Lady Hale).

[369] *Miller v Miller/McFarlane v McFarlane* [2006] UKHL 24 [11] (Lord Nicholls).

[370] *Miller v Miller/McFarlane v McFarlane* [2006] UKHL 24 [144] (Lady Hale). In 'Equality and Autonomy in Family Law' (2011) 33(1) *Journal of Social Welfare and Family Law* 3, she asks whether equality of opportunity is the key.

[371] *SA v PA* [2014] EWHC 392 (Fam) [28].

[372] A Diduck, 'What Is Family Law For?' (2011) 64 *Current Legal Problems* 287, 306–8.

[373] A Barlow, 'Solidarity, Autonomy and Equality: Mixed Messages for the Family?' (2015) 27(3) *Child and Family Law Quarterly* 223.

So, is this what fairness is now? Lady Hale thought that respecting individual autonomy reflects a different kind of equality.[374] But we must be careful with autonomy. On the face of it, it is a very attractive principle.[375] But it underestimates the gendered social, economic, and structural constraints affecting decision-making in a marriage. Even if this were not the case, would we want people to act as autonomous individuals rather than as families?

4.11 Conclusion

In this chapter we have taken a detailed look at a complex area, financial remedy law, in which a small number of Supreme Court cases have established important principles for lower courts to follow. A number of objections to the current law are apparent and are not ignored by judges, for among the case law we see a number of judicial statements about the rationale for a principle, the difficulties in application, and indeed, reference to academic research itself. You may very well take the view that the interrelationship between the different principles and the statutory factors make the law extremely difficult for students to understand—and if law students, with their background in legal method, cannot understand the law, it surely is not sufficiently accessible to the person attempting to understand the law for his or her own case. Ours is a discretionary system and it lacks predictability and accessibility. This is the price of individualised fairness, although you may wonder at the fairness of some of the cases.

For us, the discussion is academic. But the Wachtels, the Darts, the Whites, the Millers and McFarlanes, the Radmachers and Granatinos saw their marriages reduced, years hence, to footnotes to a textbook. For them, the law's reasoning is anything but academic: judgments in their cases directed the future course of their lives and those of others. The theories and principles we consider were their lived experience.

 KEY POINTS

- At the end of a marriage, it is necessary to consider the practical and financial arrangements for the parties' future. The parties may reach agreement between themselves and invite the court to turn that into an order. If they cannot agree a fair settlement then courts have the power to impose a settlement on them.

- Courts have wide powers to redistribute assets according to what is fair. In Key Case *White v White*, the House of Lords held that there was no place for discrimination between the money-earner and the homemaker/child-carer and in the conjoined Key Cases of *Miller* and *McFarlane*, the Supreme Court set out three rationales for redistributing assets on divorce: to meet the parties' needs, to compensate for relationship-generated disadvantage, and to share the fruits of the marital partnership.

---

[374] *Radmacher v Granatino* [2010] UKSC 42 [178].
[375] A Barlow, 'Solidarity, Autonomy and Equality: Mixed Messages for the Family?' (2015) 27(3) *Child and Family Law Quarterly* 223, 225.

- It is common (but not essential) to take a starting point of equal sharing and then consider whether the principles of needs or compensation, or practical reasons such as the nature of the assets, justify a move away from equal division. A person receives the greater of the award under the sharing principle, needs, or compensation.

- In Key Case *Radmacher v Granatino* the Supreme Court held that 'the court should give effect to a nuptial agreement that is freely entered into by each party with a full appreciation of its implications unless in the circumstances prevailing it would not be fair to hold the parties to their agreement'. This involves two aspects, the procedural aspect (was the agreement freely entered into by each party with a full appreciation of its implications?) and the substantive aspect (what prevailing circumstances might mean that it was unfair to hold the parties to their agreement?).

- In the case law considered in this chapter, we can see four different conceptions of fairness at work: fairness as responsibility to provide for dependants (pre-*White*); fairness as valuing different roles equally (*White*); fairness as acknowledging the different consequences of those roles (*Miller/McFarlane*); and, most recently, fairness as autonomy (*Radmacher*).

 # FURTHER READING: SOME STARTING POINTS

- Good sources of statistics on financial remedy cases and household economies can be found in the Ministry of Justice, *Family Court Statistics Quarterly England and Wales* series, and the Office of National Statistics' regular Statistical Bulletins including *Families and Households in the UK*. The British Social Attitudes survey is a goldmine of useful information and is analysed by Park et al. at *British Social Attitudes: The 30th Report* (NatCen Social Research 2013) which is online at https://www.bsa.natcen.ac.uk/.

- The Law Commission's *Matrimonial Property, Needs and Agreements* (Law Com No 343, 2014) is a comprehensive overview of financial remedy law and there is a very good summary. Both of those documents can be found on the Law Commission website at https://www.lawcom.gov.uk/project/matrimonial-property-needs-and-agreements/. Useful overviews of financial remedy law can be found in the Family Justice Council, *Guidance on 'Financial Needs' on Divorce* (Ministry of Justice 2016). Ira Ellman considers the underlying rationale for spousal maintenance in 'The Theory of Alimony' (1989) 77(1) *California Law Review* 1, as does John Eekelaar in 'Property and Financial Settlement on Divorce – Sharing and Compensating' [2006] *Family Law* 754.

- For the economic impact of divorce, see Hayley Fisher and Hamish Low, 'Who Wins, Who Loses and Who Recovers from Divorce?' in Jo Miles and Rebecca Probert (eds), *Sharing Lives, Dividing Assets: An Inter-Disciplinary Study* (Hart 2009). The same authors have also written 'Finances after Divorce in the Short and Long Term' [2018] *Family Law* 1533; and 'Recovery from Divorce: Comparing High and Low Income Couples' (2016) 30 *International Journal of Law, Policy, and the Family* 338. Gillian Douglas and Alison Perry, 'How Parents Cope Financially on Separation and Divorce – Implications for the Future of Ancillary Relief' (2001) *Child and Family Law Quarterly* 67 is also recommended.

- For discussions of the underlying principles of fairness and the impact of responsibility, equality, and autonomy, read Lady Hale, 'Equality and Autonomy in Family Law' (2011) 33(1) *Journal of Social Welfare and Family Law* 3; three articles by Alison Diduck at (2011) 64 *Current Legal Problems* 287, (2001) 9 *Feminist Legal Studies* 173, and (2011) 38(2) *Journal of Law and Society* 272; Gillian Douglas, 'Simple Quarrels? Autonomy v Vulnerability' in Rebecca Probert and Chris Barton (eds), *Fifty Years in Family Law: Essays for Stephen Cretney* (Intersentia 2012); and Anne Barlow, 'Solidarity, Autonomy and Equality: Mixed Messages for the Family?' (2015) 27(3) *Child and Family Law Quarterly* 223.

- The Key Cases discussing these concepts are *White v White* [2001] 1 AC 596 and *Miller v Miller/McFarlane v McFarlane* [2006] UKHL 24. For a really useful case that explains *Miller/McFarlane* and covers stellar contribution, read *Charman v Charman (No 4)* [2007] EWCA Civ 503 and the excellent discussion by

Jo Miles, 'Charman v Charman: Making Sense of Need, Compensation and Equal Sharing after *Miller/McFarlane*' [2008] *Child and Family Law Quarterly* 378. A useful illustration of the application of the s25 criteria to an average-asset case is *W v H (Divorce: Financial Remedies)* [2020] EWFC B10.

- On nuptial agreements, the Key Case is *Radmacher v Granatino* [2010] UKSC 42 and the chapter lists a number of subsequent cases applying or distinguishing those principles. Joanna Miles, 'Marriage and Divorce in the Supreme Court and the Law Commission: For Love or Money?' (2011) 74(3) *Modern Law Review* 430 is a good discussion.

 Visit the **online resources** to watch a video of Polly Morgan discussing this chapter topic, and to check your understanding of this chapter with self-test questions and scenario questions.

5 Cohabitants and Remedies Not Dependent on Marriage

LEARNING CHECKLIST

By the end of this chapter, you should be able to:

* *Explain* the main rights and responsibilities of cohabitants and compare these to the position of married couples

* *Explain* the legal tests to establish a successful trusts of land claim under common intention constructive trust or resulting trust principles, or under the principles of proprietary estoppel and *critically discuss* how and why applicants may struggle to be successful

* *Explain* what the requirements are for making a valid Will and how property is distributed when a person dies with a Will or under the rules of intestacy when a person dies without a Will

* *Critically evaluate* whether or not the law should be reformed to enable cohabitants to inherit under the intestacy rules

* *Describe* the powers available to courts on an application under the Inheritance (Provision for Family and Dependants Act 1975) and *evaluate* how the Act decides what is reasonable provision for an applicant

* *Critically discuss* how cohabitants can protect their position and why they often do not do so, by reference to differing levels of knowledge

* *Critically evaluate* arguments about whether cohabitants should have 'divorce style' rights and the practical issues that would need to be resolved in order to *create* a suggested scheme for cohabitants, taking inspiration from existing models.

SCENARIO 1

Fiona and Ishan

Fiona (aged 60) and Ishan (aged 68) dated for several years before deciding that it was time to move in with one another. After some discussion, they decided to move into the house that Ishan already owns. Ishan told Fiona that he wanted to take care of her and that the house would be a home for them both. Fiona sold her existing property and used the equity to undertake some improvements to the house. It is now five years after they started living together, and Fiona has sought legal advice. She and Ishan are no longer getting on well together, and she wants to know what would happen if they split up. She is particularly worried about the house, and whether Ishan could claim maintenance from her because she is still working whereas he is retired. She is also expecting an inheritance as her mother is seriously ill and not expected to recover. She and Ishan are not married to one another.

SCENARIO 2

Helen and Cherry

Helen and Cherry bought a house in 1997. It is in their joint names. There is no express declaration of the beneficial interest. During the relationship, Helen worked and Cherry was been a homemaker. Helen died last month. Cherry needs advice on what to expect next. She is worried that Helen's children have inherited half of the house. Helen did not have a Will, and she and Cherry were not married.

SCENARIO 3

Rhys, Laila, and Rhys's mother Tina

Rhys and Laila have been living together in rented accommodation for five years. They have saved up to buy a house, but could not afford it until Rhys's mother, Tina, gave Rhys £20,000 towards the deposit. Laila is bankrupt, and they therefore agree to put the house in Rhys's sole name. They are planning to get married.

5.1 Introduction

People have always lived together without marriage. Current figures indicate that about 13.4 per cent of the population of England and Wales aged over 16 are living with a partner to whom they are not married. This compares with 38.75 per cent who are living with a spouse or civil partner, and 38.4 per cent who are living either by themselves or with friends or family.[1]

Of those who are cohabiting (that is, living with someone to whom they are not married), some will have previously been married or in a civil partnership, and are now divorced, but most will never have been. The number of people who live with a partner and who have never been in a marriage or civil partnership increased by over 1.4 million people in the decade from 2009 to 2019.[2] Across all age groups, acceptance of cohabitation has risen.[3]

That is not to say that cohabitation has ever rivalled marriage. Even today, when it is more widespread than ever before, married families significantly outnumber unmarried ones. Probert, who has traced the development of cohabitation over the centuries, has

---

[1] Office of National Statistics, *Population Estimates by Marital Status and Living Arrangements, England and Wales 2019* (July 2020). Table 2 in the underlying dataset.
[2] Office of National Statistics, *Population Estimates by Marital Status and Living Arrangements, England and Wales 2019* (July 2020). Table 2 in the underlying dataset.
[3] Anne Barlow, Simon Duncan, Grace James, and Alison Park, 'Just a Piece of Paper? Marriage and Cohabitation', in Alison Park and National Centre for Social Research (eds), *British Social Attitudes: Public Policy, Social Ties: The 18th Report* (Sage 2001).

looked at the number of births outside marriage as an indicator of unmarried relationships over those centuries in which reliable contraception was not available. She found that unmarried relationships 'accounted for only a small proportion of such births until relatively recently', and that even 'in the supposedly liberated 18th century it barely crept above 5 per cent'.[4] Cohabitation was, says Frost, the exception rather than the rule.[5]

Cohabitation has, therefore, always been a choice for some, an undesired necessity for some, and an unintended status for others. As we see in Chapter 2 when we look at the history of marriage law, for many centuries there were significant problems in knowing whether a valid marriage had been created, the status and effect of informal or so-called 'common law' marriages, and attempts to bypass the legal restrictions relating to the formation of valid marriages. Even these days, some situations, particularly surrounding non-qualifying religious ceremonies, still give rise to uncertainty. But these couples were not choosing cohabitation over marriage: even if they got the procedures wrong, sometimes deliberately, marriage was the relationship form that they wanted others to recognise them as having.

Nevertheless, regardless of the reasons for cohabitation, and how 'marriage-like' a particular relationship may seem to those involved in it or to external observers, there is a stark difference between the position of cohabitants and those of married couples when a relationship breaks down. There is no worse meeting for a family lawyer than one in which the lawyer advises their client that notwithstanding their relationship of thirty years' duration, they have no viable claims at the end of that relationship.

In the next sections, we will look at what those differences are, and what remedies are currently available to those who lived together or had children together but who have never married one another.

5.2 The legal status of cohabitants

In 1965, Lord Devin wrote that 'a man and a woman who live together outside marriage are not prosecuted under the law, but they are not protected by it. They are outside the law. Their union is not recognised, no legal obligation is implicit in it, and an express obligation will not be enforced by the law.'[6]

Although he was writing more than 55 years ago, it is still the case that in England and Wales there is no set of legal rights and duties between an unmarried couple or between them and the state. For almost all purposes, the individuals in a couple are seen as independent actors. There are some exceptions. Cohabiting relationships are recognised for certain purposes advantageous to the state, such as the payment of state welfare benefits. Express obligations by way of cohabitation agreements are enforceable subject to some exceptions. Parents have financial obligations towards their children which are not dependent on cohabitation or remarriage, but upon parental status—again, this is advantageous

---

[4] R Probert, 'Cohabitation: Current Legal Solutions' (2009) 62(1) *Current Legal Problems* 316, 319. See also R Probert, *Marriage Law and Practice in the Long Eighteenth Century: A Reassessment* (Cambridge UP 2009).
[5] Ginger S Frost, *Living in Sin: Cohabiting as Husband and Wife in Nineteenth-Century England* (Manchester University Press 2008/2011) 225.
[6] P Devlin, *The Enforcement of Morals* (OUP 1965).

to the state because it reduces the state's child support obligations. But noting these ad hoc remedies is a long way from saying that unmarried couples are protected by law.

Table 5.1 sets out the considerable differences between being married or civilly partnered on the one hand, and living or breaking up with someone to whom you have never been married.

TABLE 5.1 Comparison of the respective positions of married and unmarried couples

Married or civilly partnered	Unmarried
During the relationship	
Mutual obligation of support enforceable through the Domestic Proceedings and Magistrates' Courts Act 1978.	No mutual obligations of support
At the end of the relationship	
On divorce, the court has wide powers to redistribute the parties' assets in accordance with what is fair, based on the principles of needs, compensation, and sharing, and irrespective of legal or beneficial ownership. Pensions can be shared, capital divided, shares transferred, houses and other property transferred, and one party can be required to pay the other spousal maintenance, potentially for as long as they both are alive. While debts cannot be transferred, the court can make an order that takes account of one party's indebtedness and provides enough for them to pay the debt off. The relevant statutes are the Matrimonial Causes Act 1973 for married couples, or the Civil Partnership Act 2004.	On the breakdown of an unmarried relationship, the court has no power to redistribute property according to what is fair. There is no power to share a pension, to order spousal maintenance, to divide capital, or to order to transfer of any assets. The court has no power to address debts.
	If a family home is owned jointly, then it is very likely that each party will receive a share of its value. If it is in the sole name of one party, then the other party would need to make a claim under the Trusts of Land (Appointment of Trustees) Act 1996, asserting that a trust has arisen or that the owner is estopped from denying them an interest in the house. These are exceptionally difficult claims.
Claims for an interest in property under the Trusts of Land (Appointment of Trustees) Act 1996 or a claim for financial provision for the children under Schedule 1 to the Children Act 1989 are possible but almost always unnecessary because of the availability of the courts' financial remedy powers.	If there are children, it is possible to have the use of a house for the children's dependency only, under Schedule 1 to the Children Act 1989.
Rights to occupy the family home	
By virtue of the marriage, a spouse (or civil partner) has 'home rights', the right to occupy the matrimonial home whether or not they have a legal or beneficial interest in it. A court can restrict or terminate this right through use of an occupation order under the Family Law Act 1996. See Chapter 7.	An unmarried cohabitant has no legal right to occupy the family home by virtue of the cohabitation, but may have that right by virtue of an interest in the property. (If the interest is beneficial, it may not be quickly proved in urgent situations.) While the courts can make an occupation order permitting them to occupy the home, the courts' powers are more limited, and the test more stringent, for those who are not married and have no interest in the property. See Chapter 7.

Protection from domestic abuse

Under the Family Law Act 1996 a court may exclude a party from the family home. The courts' powers are wider and the legal tests easier where the parties are married and therefore have 'home rights'. See Chapter 7.	Under the Family Law Act 1996 a court may exclude a party from the family home, but the courts' powers are weaker and the legal tests more stringent if the parties are not married or not beneficial owners. See Chapter 7.

On the death of one party

On the death of one party to the marriage, their widow or widower is in a preferential position if the deceased died intestate (without a Will). They will receive most or all of the deceased's estate (assets). If the deceased had a private pension, the widow or widower may receive a spouse's pension payment each month.	If one partner in an unmarried relationship dies, the survivor is in a relatively weak position if the deceased died intestate (without a Will). The Intestacy Rules, which set out what will happen to the deceased's assets, do not mention a cohabitant at all, so they will only inherit if they make a successful application under the Inheritance (Provision for Family and Dependants) Act 1975. A Will is therefore essential to protect cohabitants. Not all private/occupational pensions provide for the survivor of an unmarried relationship.

Taxation

Married couples can benefit from a range of tax advantages including in relation to inheritance tax and married couples' tax allowance.	Unmarried couples cannot benefit from the tax advantages available to married couples.

Parental responsibility

A father who is married to the mother of his children, or marries her later, has automatic parental responsibility for her children. The same applies to married second female parents.	A father who is not married to the mother of his children has to acquire parental responsibility for them and does not acquire it automatically. See Chapter 8.

Child maintenance

If there are children, it is possible to have the use of a house for the children's dependency only, under Schedule 1 to the Children Act 1989. That schedule also provides for lump sums of periodical payments to be made for the benefit of the children. This statutory power is limited by the child maintenance scheme. However, where the parties are divorcing, the claims for financial provision on divorce are likely to be more valuable. Such a claim would be indirect through the award to the parent with primary carer, or directly for the benefit of the children under s27 Matrimonial Causes Act. Irrespective or marital status, a parent with primary care of a child can apply to the Child Maintenance Service for a regular amount of child maintenance to be paid by the other parent. See Chapter 6.	If there are children, it is possible to have the use of a house for the children's dependency only, under Schedule 1 to the Children Act 1989. That schedule also provides for lump sums of periodical payments to be made for the benefit of the children. This statutory power is very limited by the child maintenance scheme. See Chapter 6. Irrespective or marital status, a parent with primary care of a child can apply to the Child Maintenance Service for a regular amount of child maintenance to be paid by the other parent. See Chapter 6.

Contractual freedom	
Private contracts such as prenuptial agreements cannot be enforced without court approval. See Chapter 4.	Private contacts are likely to have force like any other commercial contract, subject to the general vitiating factors, and some exceptions.
Perception of rights	
Although there is no such thing as 'next of kin status' (see 5.12.4) most people will respect the views and perceived rights of a spouse or civil partner.	Whether or not someone will respect the views and perceived rights of an unmarried cohabitant in relation to their partner is uncertain and situation-dependent. As the number of cohabitants grows, acceptance will increase, but the dearth of actual legal rights can cause difficulties in the event of a dispute.

Table 5.1 shows us that during a cohabiting relationship there are no mutual obligation of support and at the end of the relationship no divorce-style claims can be made. On death, a cohabitant is in a much weaker position than a widow or widower—and indeed there is no status for a bereaved cohabitant, either linguistically or legally. If there are children, then the combination of the child support scheme and the residual powers of the court, particularly under Schedule 1 to the Children Act, may provide some financial support including, in some cases, the use of accommodation while the children are minors (see Chapter 6). A cohabitant may be able to establish a beneficial interest in the family home. We will see that this is not always easy, because the house may not be in their legal name, and there may be no evidence that they are entitled to share in its value.

Compare this to the position of married couples who are divorcing. As we see in Chapter 4, they can rely on a comprehensive set of legal powers encompassing the redistribution of income, capital, property of all kinds, and pensions, according to what was fair and with little regard to legal or beneficial ownership. That is the consequence of entry into marriage. Yet, at the end of a cohabiting relationship, the parties still have exactly the same needs as a married couple: they need somewhere to live, and enough money to live on. But they do not have access to a package of rights and remedies designed for them. In order for us to evaluate whether unmarried couples should have such rights, we need to begin by evaluating the current remedies available to them. We start by looking at claims for an interest in the family home, known as a trusts of land claim, and what happens to a person's property when they die.

SCENARIO 1

Illustration 1: Fiona and Ishan

We can now begin to see the legal position of Fiona and Ishan.

This is a couple in older middle age. It is likely that their pensions constitute a valuable asset. The court has no power to share these in order to adjust for any differences in value. Ishan is retired and presumably living on his pension. He may be receiving some financial support from Fiona, who is still working. The court has no power to order that she pays spousal maintenance to him.

The house is in Ishan's sole name, because he owned it before he and Fiona moved in together. Fiona will need to rely on the law of trusts to establish that she is entitled to a share of the property, or she may assert that Ishan is estopped from denying her interest in the property. We consider these claims at 5.3 onwards.

If Ishan asks Fiona to leave the property, she has no home rights that would enable her to stay. She could apply for an occupation order under the Family Law Act 1996, which would enable her to stay in the house temporarily, as long as she satisfied the stringent legal tests.

SCENARIO 2

Illustration 1: Helen and Cherry

Helen and Cherry have a house in joint names, where there is no express declaration of the beneficial interest. Helen has now died without a Will. We call this 'dying intestate'. Her estate will be divided between her blood relatives in accordance with a statutory list of priorities. Cherry, as an unmarried partner, will not inherit any share of Helen's property, and that would be the case even if they had spent a lifetime together. Cherry's remedies are:

1. To see if Helen's occupational pension scheme provides post-death benefits to surviving co-habitants, or if there is a lump sum payable for death in service that Helen told the pension company that Cherry should have.
2. To establish that she is beneficially entitled to a share of the property. Fortunately, this is much easier to do when a house is in joint names than if it had been in Helen's sole name, as we shall see. But even if she establishes an interest in the house, she does not inherit Helen's share. There will therefore be a practical problem: those of Helen's relatives who inherit from her under the rules of intestacy may seek to sell the home she shared with Cherry, leaving Cherry homeless unless she can raise the funds to buy them out.
3. To make a claim under the Inheritance (Provision for Family and Dependants) Act 1975 for financial provision out of Helen's estate on the grounds that the intestacy rules did not make reasonable financial provision for her and that in the circumstances that failure was unreasonable. We will consider Cherry's eligibility, and what she needs to show, at 5.13.

5.3 Trusts and the family home

In this section, we look at how a cohabitant can establish an interest in the family home by asserting that a constructive or resulting trust has arisen, or that a party is 'estopped' from asserting their strict legal rights (for example to exclude the claimant from an interest in the house). As we shall see, this area of law is uncertain and complex. It was not designed for cohabitants or the way in which people in intimate relationships organise their lives.

It is very important to note that a trust of land or estoppel claim is equally available to married couples. Indeed, many of the older cases involve married couples as a consequence of the law at that time. Nowadays, these remedies are less favourable than remedies available to divorcing couples under the Matrimonial Causes Act 1973. This means that most married couples will apply under that Act instead.

We begin by looking at legal and beneficial ownership of homes and how they come into existence.

5.3.1 Legal title and beneficial interests

A deed is necessary to convey or create a *legal* interest in land (s52 Law of Property Act 1925). Unless it has been destroyed, there is thus always a document setting out the legal ownership of a property.

Alongside legal title, and in co-existence with it, we have beneficial title, which is sometimes referred to as having an 'equitable interest'. Beneficial title is hard to define, but easiest to think of in terms of entitlement to share in the proceeds of sale of a particular property. The legal owners of a property hold the property on trust for the beneficiaries, who own the beneficial or equitable title. A trust of land is the name given to a trust over property which consists of or includes land.[7]

In most cases the legal owner(s) and beneficial owner(s) are the same and not much thought, if any, is given to the concept of beneficial ownership until a dispute arises.

There are two ways to hold the beneficial interest in a property jointly with another person, as 'tenants in common' or as 'joint tenants'. The word tenancy in this context does not denote a rented property: these are ways of *owning* the beneficial interest in a property. Let us use the example of a fictional unmarried couple, Adam and Bella.

- If you hold a property as beneficial tenants in common, you and your co-owner(s) will each hold a specified share in the property. For example, Adam and Bella might own 50 per cent-50 per cent ('tenants in common in equal shares'), or 60 per cent-40 per cent, or 73 per cent-27 per cent ('tenants in common in unequal shares'). The percentages can be anything as long as they add up to 100 per cent.

- If you hold a property as beneficial joint tenants, however, you do not hold separate shares. Instead, all the joint tenants hold the same undivided 100 per cent between them. Adam and Bella together own 100 per cent, not A 50 per cent and B 50 per cent.

Remember that the legal owner(s) hold the property on trust for the beneficial owner(s). In the above examples the legal ownership may lie with Adam or Bella or both, or different people altogether: the legal ownership can be different to the beneficial ownership. It is just that in most cases the legal and beneficial titles will be held by the same person(s).

As we will see, an express written declaration of the beneficial ownership of land is definitive. However, disputes may arise where the house is in joint legal names but there is no express declaration of whether the parties hold as joint tenants or tenants in common and, if the latter, in what shares.

In this situation, the law operates a presumption that 'equity follows the law'—that the beneficial ownership reflects the legal ownership. Thus, where a house has one legal owner, the presumption is that that person is also the sole beneficial owner. Where a house is in joint names, the presumption is that the parties are beneficial joint tenants (not tenants in common). The maxim that equity follows the law 'simply describes the initial location of

---

[7] Section 1(1) Trusts of Land (Appointment of Trustees) Act 1996.

the burden of proof'.[8] Without a written express declaration, the burden lies on the person who seeks to rebut the presumption by showing (on the balance of probabilities) that the beneficial title is held differently to the legal title. That person faces an uphill struggle.

FOCUS Know-How

Consequences of tenancy in common and joint tenancy

There are a number of consequences of holding as tenants in common as opposed to joint tenants.

On the death of a joint tenant, the surviving co-owner(s) inherit the property under the survivorship rules. Remember our example of unmarried couple, Adam and Bella. If Adam and Bella together own a single undivided 100 per cent share, and Adam dies, then Bella is now the sole owner of that 100 per cent share. Adam will not be able to leave his share in the property to anyone else and if he makes a Will and tries to do that, that provision will not have any effect. If Adam does not want Bella to inherit, he will need to 'sever the joint tenancy' by serving written notice on her. This will convert them from joint tenants to tenants in common in equal shares (never unequal shares). Bankruptcy of one party causes automatic severance, and the share belonging to the bankrupt will vest in the trustee in bankruptcy.

On the death of a tenant in common, the deceased person's interest in the property forms part of their estate. It does not automatically belong to the surviving co-owner(s). Thus if Adam held a 50 per cent interest and Bella held a 50 per cent interest, then Bella retains her 50 per cent interest but Adam's 50 per cent is part of his estate and passes to whoever inherits the estate pursuant to his Will or (if he has no Will) pursuant to the intestacy rules. That could be Bella, but it might not be. Let us say that Adam left a Will and that Will left the entirety of his estate to his good friend Mike. The effect of that would be that the beneficial interest in the house is now owned 50 per cent by Bella and 50 per cent by Mike. If Mike wanted to realise this share by turning it into cash, then either the house is sold and the proceeds divided 50-50 in accordance with their shares, or one of them buys the other out. If Bella wishes to continue living there, she would need to buy Mike's 50 per cent of the property from him.

For most young people, it is more likely that they will split up than that they will separate. When tenants in common separate, each is entitled to their share of the property. When two joint tenants separate, their 100 per cent share is divided and each is entitled to 50 per cent of the equity.

The consequences of the different ways to hold the beneficial title should be explained by the conveyancer acting for the parties on their house purchase. However, sometimes this information is buried in a long document, or explains what will happen on death without explaining the more likely situation of the parties splitting up. Douglas, Pearce, and Woodward gathered together sets of standardised written advice provided by conveyancers to prospective joint purchasers. They found that they:

> varied enormously in content, quality and comprehensibility. . . . most put more emphasis on the consequences of death than on the lifetime implications. Some gave no explanation of declarations of trust, one did not mention the question of the respective shares at all, and several did not mention what would happen on sale or separation, nor mention any particular issues for cohabitants.[9]

Accordingly, it is not uncommon for parties to seek legal advice from a family lawyers because they are unhappy when they realise the consequences of their relationship ending. As we shall see, the law does not always help them.

---

[8] L Maniscalco, 'Common Intentions and Constructive Trusts: Unorthodoxy in Trusts of Land' [2020] 2 *The Conveyancer and Property Lawyer* 124.

[9] G Douglas, J Pearce, and H Woodward, 'Cohabitation and Conveyancing Practice: Problems and Solutions' [2008] 5 *The Conveyancer and Property Lawyer* 365, 371.

5.3.2 **Express declarations of the beneficial interest**

A beneficial interest can be written or unwritten. In this section we look at written documents, which are express declarations of trust. While a deed is required to convey a *legal* interest in land, only a signed document[10] is necessary to create any other type of interest in land (s53 Law of Property Act 1925) including a beneficial interest. This written document may be within one of the conveyancing forms completed on a house purchase (the TR1) or it may be that a separate written document has been prepared. Unfortunately, however, it is not always clear to third parties whether an express declaration has been made. This means that a beneficial interest may be hidden.

In registered land, it may be possible to tell whether someone is a joint tenant or tenant in common by looking at the office copies filed at the Land Registry. However, while legal ownership will be recorded there, not all beneficial interests will be recorded. In Figure 5.1, for example we have no idea whether any beneficial interests have arisen that are not recorded by the Land Registry.

The information on the Office Copies comes from the conveyancing documentation. When a person or persons buy a property they will sign a Land Registry form TR1 *Transfer of Whole of Registered Title*. This form will record the names of the legal owners of the property. As you can see from Figure 5.2, it also has a box for the parties to set out the beneficial ownership of the property where there is to be more than one legal owner, indicating whether they will be joint tenants or tenants in common in equal shares; or will hold the property on trust, either for themselves as tenants in common in unequal shares or on trust for another person. It is possible to simply write that they are to hold the property on trust for themselves in accordance with a separate declaration of trust. The TR1 is signed as a deed.

Completing the relevant box in the TR1 or signing a separate declaration of trust are both *express declarations* of the beneficial interest—they are written. An express declaration by the parties is determinative as to their interest, unless there is duress, undue influence, mistake, or fraud:

> The court must give effect to it. (*Gissing v Gissing*, 1971)[11]

> There is no room for the application of the doctrine of resulting, implied, or constructive trusts. (*Goodman v Gallant*, 1986)[12]

> If the property in question is land there must be some . . . conveyance which shows how it was acquired. If that document declares . . . in whom the beneficial title is to vest that necessarily concludes the question of title as between the spouses for all time, and in the absence of fraud or mistake at the time of the transaction the parties cannot go behind it at any time thereafter. (*Pettitt v Pettitt*, 1970)[13]

In other words, if you have an express (written) declaration, then it is binding on the parties unless one of the standard contract vitiating factors is present, such as fraud or mistake, in which case the documentation can be rectified. The only way for the parties to alter a deed is by a further deed. Other documents or verbal agreements are ineffective.

[10] A deed is not necessary for any non-legal interest, but is sensible because it avoids issues with consideration.
[11] [1971] AC 886 (HL).
[12] [1986] 2 WLR 236 (CA).
[13] [1970] AC 777 (HL).

So far, so simple. Difficulties can be avoided by expressly stating how the property is to be held—just by ticking a box! Unfortunately, completion of the box on the transfer form is not mandatory despite the House of Lords in *Stack v Dowden* recommending that it be a mandatory requirement.[14] As a clearly frustrated Wall J said in *Carlton v Goodman*, 'Perhaps conveyancers do not read the law reports. I will try one more time: *always try to agree on and then record how the beneficial interest is to be held*. It is not very difficult to do.'[15] In *Oxley v Hiscock* however, it was not the poor conveyancer who was to blame: despite stating the risks to Ms Oxley quite clearly, Ms Oxley declined to have an express declaration of trust, on the basis that she felt that she knew Mr Hiscock 'well enough not to need written legal protection in this matter'.[16] That we know her situation from a law report indicates how badly that turned out for her.

These failings mean that it is sometimes unclear whether a sole legal owner is also the sole beneficial owner, or whether joint legal owners hold the beneficial interest as tenants in common, and if so in what shares, or as joint tenants.

SCENARIO 2

Illustration 2: Helen and Cherry

Helen and Cherry have a house in joint names, where there is no express declaration of the beneficial interest. We are told that they bought in 1997, and at this time box 10 was not on the TR1 form, so it is possible that the parties were not encouraged to consider the beneficial interests. Even if they were, the research we discuss at 5.14.2 shows that this discussion may have had little effect on them.

Our first issue in helping Cherry is to identify whether she and Helen as the legal owners held the property on trust for themselves as joint tenants or as tenants in common.

Example of an office copy entry for a sole legal owner

REGISTERED PROPRIETOR(S): Janet Jones of 13 Lambeth Street, London SW1 5EN

Example of an office copy entry for joint legal owners who own as beneficial joint tenants

REGISTERED PROPRIETOR(S): Janet Jones and Ian Jacobs of 8 Churchill Avenue, Stoke on Trent ST4 8AB

Example of an office copy entry for joint legal owners who hold as beneficial tenants in common

REGISTERED PROPRIETOR(S): Janet Jones and Ian Jacobs of 8 Churchill Avenue, Stoke on Trent ST4 8AB

NOTICES AND RESTRICTIONS

No disposition by a sole proprietor of the registered estate (except a trust corporation) under which capital money arises is to be registered unless authorised by an order of the court.[17]

FIGURE 5.1 Example of office copies entries

---

[14] [2007] UKHL 17.

[15] *Carlton v Goodman* [2002] 2 FLR 259, 273 (Wall LJ). Emphasis is the judge's own.

[16] [2004] EWCA Civ 546 at [9].

[17] This strange set of words is called a 'Form A' restriction. The purpose of the restriction is to ensure that, on the death of one proprietor, the property cannot automatically be sold by the survivor on his own without the survivor showing that they are solely entitled to the legal and beneficial interests in the property. It also alerts third parties to the existence of a tenancy in common.

> 10 Declaration of trust. The transferee is more than one person and
>
>   ■ they are to hold the property on trust for themselves as joint tenants
>
>   ■ they are to hold the property on trust for themselves as tenants in common in equal shares
>
>   ■ they are to hold the property on trust.

FIGURE 5.2 Extract from the TR1 form

5.3.3 Introducing constructive and resulting trusts and estoppel

Although we have seen that there may be express written declarations of the beneficial interest, s53 Law of Property Act 1925 also says that requirements of a deed for legal interests and a signed document for other interests do not affect 'the creation or operation of resulting, implied or constructive trusts'. That means that a trust over the beneficial interest can arise without being expressly written. We call this an implied trust, and we are concerned with two types of implied trust, the resulting trust and the common intention constructive trust.

These trusts can arise as a result of discussions between the parties or the parties' conduct as well as by virtue of financial contribution. Therefore, they may arise in situations where the parties have not specifically sat down and discussed the beneficial ownership. This means that they can arise without the parties understanding them. In fact, they may not have given the matter any thought at all.

While many different types of people may cohabit—friends become housemates, extended families may pool resources to live together, business partners may share commercial property—our discussion in this chapter is concerned with the domestic context rather than commercial context (i.e., the family home), and with two main situations relevant to couples who split up:

1. *Joint legal owner situations* in which the house is in joint legal names but there is no express declaration of how the beneficial interest is to be shared. This means that when a couple separates, or one of them dies or becomes bankrupt[18] there is uncertainty about their respective shares. The principles of a resulting or constructive trust will be applied to determine what shares the parties intended.

2. *Sole legal owner situations.* Where the house is in the legal name of one person, their former cohabitant, who is not a legal owner of the property, may seek to establish that they have a beneficial interest in the property by virtue of a resulting or constructive trust, albeit that this is unwritten.

As we shall see, it is the common intention constructive trust that is considered most appropriate to the domestic context.

An application under the Trusts of Land (Appointment of Trustees) Act 1996 ('TLATA') is the mechanism to establish that a constructive or resulting trust of land has arisen. An

---

[18] Bankruptcy causes the assets of the bankrupt to be vested in the trustee in bankruptcy. It will be necessary to identify what interest a bankrupt has in a house and what has vested in the trustee. The trustee may then seek to force the sale of the family home to realise the bankrupt's share of the proceeds of sale, and pass these onto creditors.

application under TLATA can be made by any person who is a trustee of land (such as a legal owner) or who asserts an interest in land (such as a beneficiary or a creditor whose debt is secured on the property, or a trustee in bankruptcy). Section 14 says that the court can 'declare the nature and extent of a person's interest in a property' subject to a trust. A successful claim will entitle the claimant to a proportion of value of the property. The court can then order the sale of the property under s15.[19] While in practical terms, one party may wish to buy out the other's interest, the court has no jurisdiction to order that. As we discuss at 5.4.7, the court can also deal with rights of occupation and the payment of 'occupation rent'.

We are also going to look at estoppel. Estoppel arises where assurances or representations made by one party, in relation to a property, have been relied on by another party to his or her detriment. In this situation, the person giving the assurances may be estopped (prevented) from going back on their assurances because to do so would be unconscionable.

5.4 **Common intention constructive trusts**

A common intention constructive trust arises from an agreement, arrangement or understanding based on the parties' common (i.e., shared) intention and detrimental reliance.

There are two stages to the enquiry:

1. Stage One: Establishing that a trust has arisen.

    a. Is there a common intention that the claimant has a beneficial interest in the property?

    b. Has the claimant relied on that common intention, by changing his or her position to their detriment?

2. Stage Two: Quantification of the interest under the constructive trust.

We will look at each stage in turn, starting by considering how one may establish a common intention.

5.4.1 **Establishing a common intention**

A common intention is an intention that is common to both parties; that is, the claimant must persuade the court that s/he and the respondent *both* have an intention that the claimant has a beneficial interest in the property that is the subject of the application.

The court has to take an objective view as to what the parties' intentions were. As Lord Diplock said in a leading case, *Gissing v Gissing*:

> the relevant intention of each party is the intention which was reasonably understood by the other party to be manifested by that party's words or conduct notwithstanding that he did not consciously formulate that intention in his own mind or even acted with some different intention which he did not communicate to the other party.[20]

Inevitably, the reason a dispute is in court is because the parties are at odds over this. Such claims are therefore evidentially extremely challenging, as we shall see.

---

[19] See *Bagum v Hafiz and Another* [2015] EWCA Civ 801.
[20] [1971] AC 886, at 906[B]-[C].

5.4.2 Common intention in joint legal name situations

Where the house is in joint legal names, there is a presumption (a starting point) that the legal owners hold the beneficial title as joint tenants:

> a conveyance into joint names indicates both legal and beneficial joint tenancy, unless and until the contrary is proved (*Stack v Dowden*).[21]

> if the property is purchased in joint names by parties in a domestic relationship the presumption of joint beneficial ownership applies (*Marr v Collie*).[22]

The presumption is that if the house is owned legally by two or more people, they are also the beneficial joint tenants, which means they hold the house together in one undivided share. If Adam and Bella, our couple from 5.3.1, are both legal owners, the presumption is that they are beneficial joint tenants. On sale, the proceeds would be divided equally. If either of them disagrees with this, then that person will have to persuade the court, on the balance of probabilities, that they *both* intended to hold in defined unequal shares.

Note that this presumption of joint tenancy applies in the domestic context, i.e., to the family home. It does not apply in the commercial or business context, or in those situations in which couples or family members enter into business together (as in Key Case *Laskar v Laskar*).

KEY CASE *Stack v Dowden* [2007] UKHL 17

Mr Stack and Ms Dowden had lived together for 20 years and had four children.

Their first home was bought in Ms Dowden's sole name. She funded the purchase from savings from an account in her sole name and a mortgage in her sole name. She was able to buy the house at a good price under the terms of a relative's Will. Mr Stack said that he contributed to the down-payment by putting money in Ms Dowden's bank account. The parties did a lot of improvements to the property, which they lived in for ten years. They then sold the property and bought a new one in their joint names. However, they did not make any express declaration of the beneficial interest.

This second house was funded using the proceeds of sale of the first house, Ms Dowden's savings, and a mortgage in joint names. They made regular lump sum payments to the mortgage in addition to their monthly payments, and through this paid off the mortgage. The lump sums were paid by both of them, but Ms Dowden paid more than half of the amount. When they separated, Mr Stack sought an order for the sale of the property and half of the proceeds. Ms Dowden argued that the proceeds should be split 65 per cent/35 per cent in her favour to reflect her greater financial contribution to the acquisition of the house.

The House of Lords, by a majority, held that:

- 'At least in the domestic consumer context, a conveyance into joint names indicates both legal and beneficial joint tenancy, unless and until the contrary is proved.'[23]
- 'In a joint names case the questions are not simply, "what is the extent of the parties' beneficial interests?"' but, 'did the parties intend their beneficial interests to be different from their legal interests?' and 'if they did, in what way and to what extent?'[24]
- 'In identifying the extent of the parties' beneficial interests in a property, the court was seeking to ascertain the parties' shared intentions, actual, inferred or imputed, with respect to the property, in the light of their whole course of conduct in relation to it.'[25]

---

[21] *Stack v Dowden* [2007] UKHL 17, [58].
[22] *Marr v Collie* [2017] UKPC 17.
[23] Para [58] (Lady Hale).
[24] Para [66] (Lady Hale).
[25] Para [60] (Lady Hale).

- 'The burden will be on the person seeking to show that the parties did intend their beneficial interests to be different from their legal interests, and in what way.'[26] Per Lady Hale:

This is not a task to be lightly embarked upon. In family disputes, strong feelings are aroused when couples split up. These often lead the parties, honestly but mistakenly, to reinterpret the past in self-exculpatory or vengeful terms. They also lead people to spend far more on the legal battle than is warranted by the sums actually at stake. A full examination of the facts is likely to involve disproportionate costs. In joint names cases it is also unlikely to lead to a different result unless the facts are very unusual. . . . It cannot be the case that all the hundreds of thousands, if not millions, of transfers into joint names . . . are vulnerable to challenge in the courts simply because it is likely that the owners contributed unequally to their purchase.[27]

Per Lord Walker:

In the ordinary domestic case where there are joint legal owners there will be a heavy burden in establishing to the court's satisfaction that an intention to keep a sort of balance-sheet of contributions actually existed, or should be inferred, or imputed to the parties. The presumption will be that equity follows the law.[28]

On establishing whether the parties intended to hold other than as beneficial join tenants:

- 'The court should undertake a survey of the whole course of dealing between the parties and take account of all conduct which threw light on the question what shares were intended.'[29]
- 'Many more factors than financial contributions may be relevant to divining the parties' true intentions. These include: any advice or discussions at the time of the transfer which cast light upon their intentions then; the reasons why the home was acquired in their joint names; the reasons why (if it be the case) the survivor was authorised to give a receipt for the capital moneys; the purpose for which the home was acquired; the nature of the parties' relationship; whether they had children for whom they both had responsibility to provide a home; how the purchase was financed, both initially and subsequently; how the parties arranged their finances, whether separately or together or a bit of both; how they discharged the outgoings on the property and their other household expenses.'[30] ('The paragraph 69 factors').
- 'When a couple are joint owners of the home and jointly liable for the mortgage, the inferences to be drawn from who pays for what may be very different from the inferences to be drawn when only one is owner of the home. The arithmetical calculation of how much was paid by each is also likely to be less important. It will be easier to draw the inference that they intended that each should contribute as much to the household as they reasonably could and that they would share the eventual benefit or burden equally.'[31]
- 'The parties' individual characters and personalities may also be a factor in deciding where their true intentions lay. In the cohabitation context, mercenary considerations may be more to the fore than they would be in marriage, but it should not be assumed that they always take pride of place over natural love and affection.'[32]
- 'There are differences between sole and joint names cases when trying to divine the common intentions or understanding between the parties. . . . the decision to put the property into joint names would almost always have been a conscious decision.'[33]

---

[26] Para [68] (Lady Hale).
[27] Paras [68]-[69] (Lady Hale).
[38] Para [33] (Lord Walker).
[29] Paras [61] (Lady Hale) and [145] (Lord Neuberger).
[30] Para [69] (Lady Hale).
[31] Para [69] (Lady Hale).
[32] Para [69] (Lady Hale).
[33] Para [66] (Lady Hale).

- The search is still for the result which reflects what the parties must, in the light of their conduct, be taken to have intended '[and the court could not] abandon that search in favour of the result which the court itself considers to be fair'.[34] Although the parties' joint intentions might change over time, at any one time they must be the same for all purposes.[35]

On quantification:

- When quantifying an established beneficial interest, the court should take 'a wide view of what contributions were to be taken into account, while remaining sceptical of the value of alleged improvements that were really insignificant, or elaborate arguments, suggestive of creative accounting, as to how the family finances were arranged'.[36]

On the facts of this case:

- 'This is . . . a very unusual case. There cannot be many unmarried couples who have lived together for as long as this, who have had four children together, and whose affairs have been kept as rigidly separate as this couple's affairs were kept. This is all strongly indicative that they did not intend their shares, even in the property which was put into both their names, to be equal (still less that they intended a beneficial joint tenancy with the right of survivorship should one of them die before it was severed). Before the Court of Appeal, Ms Dowden contended for a 65% share and in my view she has made good her case for that.'[37]

Stack is therefore a case in which the Court emphasises the difficulty of attempting to rebut a presumption of joint tenancy but on the facts, which the judges thought were 'very unusual'[38] and 'exceptional', found that the presumption had been rebutted.

Key Case Stack v Dowden established some important new principles:

- Buying a domestic property in joint names indicated both legal and beneficial joint tenancy, unless and until the contrary was proved.
- The burden will be on the person seeking to show that the parties did intend their beneficial interests to be different from their legal interests, and in what way.
- The court should undertake a survey of the whole course of dealing between the parties and take account of all conduct which threw light on the question what shares were intended.
- Many more factors than financial contributions may be relevant to divining the parties' true intentions.

Prior to *Stack*, the concentration on financial contribution to the acquisition price and on quantifying the parties' shares by reference to that meant that there was no presumption that they were beneficial joint tenants but instead tenants in common with possibly

---

[34] Para [61] (Lady Hale).
[35] Para [62] (Lady Hale). Note this last sentence because it is relevant to ambulatory trusts and the Key Case of *Jones v Kernott*.
[36] Para [34] (Lord Walker).
[37] Para [92] (Lady Hale). Ms Dowden had in fact paid more than 65 per cent but this was the figure that she contended for in court.
[38] Lady Hale at [92] and Lord Walker at [33].

unequal shares.[39] In Key Case *Jones v Kernott*, Lord Walker and Lady Hale identified two reasons for the new presumption of beneficial joint tenancy:

> the presumption of a beneficial joint tenancy is not based on a mantra as to 'equity following the law' (though many non-lawyers would find it hard to understand the notion that equity might do anything else). There are two much more substantial reasons (which overlap) why a challenge to the presumption of beneficial joint tenancy is not to be lightly embarked on. The first is implicit in the nature of the enterprise. If a couple in an intimate relationship (whether married or unmarried) decide to buy a house or flat in which to live together, almost always with the help of a mortgage for which they are jointly and severally liable, that is on the face of things a strong indication of emotional and economic commitment to a joint enterprise. That is so even if the parties, for whatever reason, fail to make that clear by any overt declaration or agreement. . . .
>
> The notion that in a trusting personal relationship the parties do not hold each other to account financially is underpinned by the practical difficulty, in many cases, of taking any such account, perhaps after 20 years or more of the ups and downs of living together as an unmarried couple. That is the second reason for caution before going to law in order to displace the presumption of beneficial joint tenancy.[40]

Lady Hale emphasised in *Stack* that rebutting the presumption of beneficial joint tenancy was 'not a task to be lightly embarked upon'. There will be evidential problems and a significant risk that the costs involved would exceed the property's value. That is because these are civil procedure claims and, as is usual for civil cases, the losing party will be ordered to pay the winner's costs unless at trial they 'beat' any Part 36 settlement offer they made by being awarded more than they would have settled for receiving outside court.

SCENARIO 2

Illustration 3: Helen and Cherry

Helen and Cherry have a house in joint names, where there is no express declaration of the beneficial interest. *Stack v Dowden* gives us a presumption that they hold as joint tenants; i.e., that she and Helen together held one single undivided 100 per cent share of the beneficial interest in the property. This is good news for Cherry, as the surviving cohabitant. As a joint tenant, the survivorship rule operates. It means that the surviving co-owner inherits the property absolutely. It does not fall into Helen's estate and cannot therefore be inherited by her relatives under the intestacy rules.

Although the presumption of joint tenancy in joint names cases can be rebutted, Helen's relatives would need to adduce evidence in order to rebut this presumption and *Stack* makes clear how difficult that would be. It would be hard enough when the parties are alive, but with Helen dead they have evidential problems. They would take an enormous costs risk in litigating this as if they lost the normal civil procedure costs consequence is that the loser would pay the winning party's costs. Of course, a mere threat to litigate would be distressing for Cherry and may incur pre-emptive legal costs.

You may be sympathetic to Cherry if this is a long-term relationship. Would your feelings be different if the parties had recently cohabited and Helen had contributed most, if not all, of the purchase funds? In such a case, the evidence to rebut the presumption of joint tenancy is stronger, but the outcome is by no means clear.

---

[39] As Thompson and George have pointed out, judges do occasionally still talk of a presumption of joint legal owners having 'equal shares'. Following *Stack*, this is technically incorrect: it is a tenancy in common that involves each party having shares. It could be that this imprecision in language is intended to apply to what happens once a beneficial joint tenancy is established which is that if the house is sold one has to have a way of dividing the proceeds of that single undivided share—which is to divide the proceeds up equally. See MP Thompson and M George, *Thompson's Modern Land Law* (6th edn, OUP 2012) at p295.

[40] Paras [19] and [22].

While *Stack* was unusual in that there was no beneficial joint tenancy on the facts, the most likely outcome of cases subsequent to *Stack* is that a claimant will not be able to rebut the presumption of beneficial joint tenancy even if the parties' respective financial contributions have been unequal. This was the situation in Key Case *Fowler v Barron*.

> **KEY CASE** *Fowler v Barron* [2008] EWCA Civ 377
>
> The house was bought by Mr Barron but placed in joint legal names with his cohabitant Miss Fowler. There was no express declaration of the beneficial interest. As they were joint legal owners, the presumption was that the parties held as beneficial joint tenants.
>
> For his part, Mr Barron had an intention that despite the house being in joint legal names Miss Fowler should not have a share. He did not communicate this. The Court of Appeal held that 'any secret intention of Mr Barron . . . does not provide the evidential basis for rebutting the presumption, since it is not evidence of the parties' shared intention.'[41]
>
> Mr Barron argued that their conduct rebutted the presumption of joint tenancy because he had paid the mortgage and the bills, as well as the acquisition cost. However, the Court found Miss Fowler's income was used for their children and that this was 'her contribution to household expenses for which both parties were responsible'. The division of who paid for what 'was perfectly logical if . . . she did most of the shopping for the children'. The Court inferred that 'the parties intended that it should make no difference to their interests in the property which party paid for what expense. . . . the parties simply did not care about the respective size of each other's contributions.'[42]
>
> Mr Barron was therefore not successful in rebutting the presumption of a joint tenancy.

5.4.3 Common intention in sole legal name situations

As we have seen, the maxim 'equity follows the law' tells us that when a house is in one person's sole name that person is presumed to be the sole beneficial owner too. But this presumption can be rebutted by evidence to the contrary. The claimant will have to establish that they have a beneficial interest in the property. Depending on the facts, this may be easy to do or extremely difficult. If they succeed in establishing that they do have an interest, the court will proceed to quantify the extent of that interest.

Where the house is in one party's sole name, the claimant will need to show that there is a common intention to share the beneficial interest. Lord Diplock tells us in *Gissing v Gissing* that 'the relevant intention of each party is the intention which was reasonably understood by the other party to be manifested by that party's words and conduct'.[43]

---

41 [2008] EWCA Civ 377 at [37] (Arden LJ).
42 [2008] EWCA Civ 377 at [41] (Arden LJ).
43 [1971] Act 886, 906 (Lord Diplock).

There are two ways in which this common intention can be found, which are described by Lord Bridge in Key Case *Lloyds Bank v Rosset*. Either:

1. 'There has been an agreement, arrangement or understanding reached between them that the property is to be shared beneficially. . . . based on evidence of express discussions between the partners.'[44] This is known as *Rosset I*.

Or

2. The common intention can be inferred from the parties' conduct (*Rosset II*).

KEY CASE *Lloyds Bank v Rosset* [1991] 1 AC 107

The husband and wife bought a derelict home for themselves and their children using money from the husband's Swiss family trust. The trust insisted that the house be in the husband's sole name. The house was renovated by builders paid using money raised by a mortgage with Lloyds Bank. During the renovation, Mrs Rosset painted, decorated, and ordered materials for the builders.

After the parties separated, the mortgage repayments were not made and the bank sought to repossess the house. The wife defended the proceedings by asserting that she had a beneficial interest under a constructive trust which constituted an overriding interest under s70(1)(g) Land Registration Act 1925 as she had been in actual occupation of the property at the relevant date. An overriding interest would be binding on the bank.

The only substantive judgment is by Lord Bridge, with whom the other Lords agreed. His discussion of the principles of a constructive trust have become well known:

The first and fundamental question which must always be resolved is whether, independently of any inference to be drawn from the conduct of the parties in the course of sharing the house as their home and managing their joint affairs, there has at any time prior to acquisition, or exceptionally at some later date, been any agreement, arrangement or understanding reached between them that the property is to be shared beneficially. The finding of an agreement or arrangement to share in this sense can only, I think, be based on evidence of express discussions between the partners, however imperfectly remembered and however imprecise their terms may have been. Once a finding to this effect is made it will only be necessary for the partner asserting a claim to a beneficial interest against the partner entitled to the legal estate to show that he or she has acted to his or her detriment or significantly altered his or her position in reliance on the agreement in order to give rise to a constructive trust or a proprietary estoppel.

In sharp contrast with this situation is the very different one where there is no evidence to support a finding of an agreement or arrangement to share, however reasonable it might have been for the parties to reach such an arrangement if they had applied their minds to the question, and where the court must rely entirely on the conduct of the parties both as the basis from which to infer a common intention to share the property beneficially and as the conduct relied on to give rise to a constructive trust. In this situation direct contributions to the purchase price by the partner who is not the legal owner, whether initially or by payment of mortgage instalments, will readily justify the inference necessary to the creation of a constructive trust. But, as I read the authorities, it is at least extremely doubtful whether anything less will do.[45]

---

[44] *Lloyds Bank v Rosset* [1991] 1 AC 107.
[45] Pages 132E–133A.

> The House of Lords held that Mrs Rosset did not have a beneficial interest at the relevant time needed to establish an overriding interest, which was when the house was bought. Moreover, she did not acquire a beneficial interest later through her work. Her conduct in decorating and ordering was 'so trifling as to be de minimis' and thus was insufficient to support an inference that a common intention existed.
>
> *Rosset* is an example of why a claimant who is married to the legal owner may need to establish her interest outside divorce proceedings. Many of the cases in this chapter actually involve married couples, either because of third party involvement or because of the state of matrimonial property law in past decades.

Rosset I cases

Under *Rosset I*, the claimant must prove, on the balance of probabilities, that there has:

> at any time prior to acquisition, or exceptionally at some later date, been any agreement, arrangement or understanding reached between them that the property is to be shared beneficially. . . . The finding of an agreement or arrangement to share in this sense can only, I think, be based on evidence of express discussions between the partners, however imperfectly remembered and however imprecise their terms may have been.[46]

A discussion would not constitute an express declaration of trust, as it is not in a signed written document. However, remember that lack of a signed document does not prevent a trust from arising by way of a constructive trust, and a discussion can support the existence of a constructive trust as long as the other requirements are met. For claims under *Rosset I* no financial contribution to the purchase price or mortgage payments is needed. The intention is evidenced by the discussion.

The difficulty here may be what the discussions were about. Parties, mostly ignorant of constructive trust principles, may not talk in terms of ownership. Nevertheless, the conversation must be referrable to ownership rather than, to example, a right to occupy or general words of comfort. As Waite J said in *Hammond v Mitchell*:

> The primary emphasis accorded by the law in cases of this kind to express discussions between the parties ('however imperfectly remembered and however imprecise their terms') means that the tenderest exchanges of a common law courtship may assume an unforeseen significance many years later when they are brought under equity's microscope and subjected to an analysis under which many thousands of pounds of value may be liable to turn on fine questions as to whether the relevant words were spoken in earnest or in dalliance and with or without representational intent. This requires that the express discussions to which the court's initial inquiries will be addressed should be pleaded in the greatest detail, both as to language and as to circumstance.[47]

Some other examples of intention based on express discussions:

- In *Rowe v Prance*, the respondent bought a yacht in his sole name.[48] An agreement to share the beneficial interest was inferred from express discussions: the respondent had

---

[46] *Lloyds Bank v Rosset* [1991] 1 AC 107.

[47] [1991] 1 WLR 1127.

[48] [1999] All ER (D) 496.

referred to the yacht as 'our yacht', and the court held that this was intended by him to be understood by Mrs Rowe as indicating her beneficial interest; he said that her interest in the yacht was her security; and that the only reason it was registered in his sole name was because she did not have an Ocean Master's Certificate.

- In *Eves v Eves* the respondent had told the female claimant that the only reason why the property was to be acquired in his sole name was because she was under 21 and that, but for her age, he would have had the house put in their joint names.[49] He admitted in evidence that this was simply an excuse and the court found that he had no intention of ever doing this. Lord Denning MR decided that the respondent 'should be judged by what he told her—by what he led her to believe—and not by his own intent which he kept to himself.' At first glance this seems strange: how can there be a common intention (i.e., an intention in both their minds) that they both have an interest in the property when one is deliberately trying to prevent the other from having that interest? The answer is that the court found that his statement amounted to a recognition that she would have an interest in the house, presumably because if it was not in his mind that she had an interest in the house he would not have had to come up with an excuse.

- In *Grant v Edwards*, the house, which was intended to be a home for Ms Grant and Mr Edwards, was conveyed into the sole name of Mr Edwards and his brother although Ms Grant contributed half of the costs of acquisition.[50] The court found that Mr Edwards simply did not want her to acquire an interest in the house. However, what he told her was that the house should not be in her name because she was going through a divorce. This led Ms Grant to believe that once those proceedings were over her name would be put on the legal title.

- In *Drake v Whipp*,[51] the parties both contributed financially to the purchase of a barn to convert into their home. It was put into Mr Whipp's sole name. Ms Drake had thought it was to be in joint names, and when she found out that it was not Mr Whipp promised to 'put it right' but kept saying that he was too busy to get around to it. Mr Whipp conceded that by 'putting it right' he meant that since he was using her money, she would get a percentage of the value of the property.

As you can see from *Eves v Eves* and *Grant v Edwards*, the giving of a false excuses to the claimant is a small but not uncommon feature of constructive trusts cases. *Hammond v Mitchell* is another example. In that case, the husband said to his new partner that he had to put the house in his sole name both because he was going through a divorce and because he had problems with the tax authorities arising from his (soon to be ex-)wife having burnt all his accounts. The reality is that there was no intention on the part of the respondents in these three cases to share the equitable interest. If there had been, they would not have had to come up with false excuses to avoid joint registration. But remember the statement of Lord Diplock in *Gissing v Gissing*: 'the relevant intention of each party is the intention which was reasonably understood by the other party to be manifested by that party's

---

[49] [1975] 1 WLR 1338.
[50] [1986] Ch 638 (CA).
[51] [1996] 1 FLR 826.

words and conduct'.[52] In these cases, the respondents had led the claimants to believe that they had a beneficial interest in the property.[53]

Rosset II cases

The second category of situations that Lord Bridge identified in *Rosset* are those in which a common intention can be inferred from the parties' conduct. He indicated that conduct cases were 'very different' to those in which there was an agreement or arrangement to share. He thought that the only type of conduct that would allow a court to infer a common intention to share the beneficial interest would be a direct contribution to the purchase price or the mortgage:

> In this situation direct contributions to the purchase price by the partner who is not the legal owner, whether initially or by payment of mortgage instalments, will readily justify the inference necessary to the creation of a constructive trust. But, as I read the authorities, it is at least extremely doubtful whether anything less will do.

Note that the court cannot impute (attribute to the parties) an intention that did not exist, even if that would be fair. Instead, the court is using their behaviour as evidence that a common intention actually existed, even if the parties never spoke about it. As Lord Diplock said in *Gissing v Gissing*:

> In drawing such an inference, what [the parties] said and did which led up to the acquisition of a . . . home and what they said and did while the acquisition was being carried through is on a different footing from what they said and did after the acquisition was completed. Unless it is alleged that there was some subsequent fresh agreement, acted upon by the parties, to vary the original beneficial interests created when the . . . home was acquired, what they said and did after the acquisition was completed is relevant [only if it can explain why at the time of the purchase they had that] particular common intention as to how the beneficial interests should be held. . . . The conduct of the [parties] in relation to the payment of the mortgage instalments may be no less relevant to their common intention . . . than their conduct in relation to the payment of the cash deposit. . . .
>
> Even where there has been no initial contribution by the [claimant] to the cash deposit and legal charges but she makes a regular and substantial direct contribution to the mortgage instalments it may be reasonable to infer a common intention of the spouses from the outset that she should share in the beneficial interest or to infer a fresh agreement reached after the original conveyance that she should acquire a share. . . .
>
> Where the wife has made no initial contribution to the cash deposit and legal charges and no direct contribution to the mortgage instalments nor any adjustment to her contribution to other expenses of the household which it can be inferred was referable to the acquisition of the house, there is in the absence of evidence of an express agreement between the parties no material to justify the court in inferring that it was the common intention of the parties that she should have any beneficial interest . . . merely because she continued to contribute out of her own earnings or private income other expenses of the household.[54]

[52] [1971] Act 886, 906 (Lord Diplock).
[53] [2015] EWCA Civ 404.
[54] [1971] AC 886, 906[D]-[H] and 908[B]-[C] (Lord Diplock).

This seriously limited the use of the constructive trust in situations in which there were no express discussions. As Sloan explains:

> [the *Rosset*] focus on express discussion or direct financial contributions clearly prejudiced those legal non-owning cohabitants who could not point to express discussions and had made only indirect financial or purely domestic contributions, particularly where those contributions in substance facilitated the acquisition of the equity in the home by the other party to the relationship, often through the payment of one particular regular bill (i.e. the mortgage).[55]

However, while not assisting as regards non-financial contributions, it appears that *indirect* financial contributions to the purchase price or mortgage may be sufficient evidence of common intention. In *Gissing v Gissing*, the House of Lords suggested that payment of the household bills could be regarded as a financial contribution to the purchase price, *if* that contribution to the joint expenses of the household enabled the respondent to pay the mortgage out of his own money, on the basis, presumably, that he would not have committed to so large a mortgage unless it was intended that the applicant contribute financially to the mortgage or other expenses. Per Lord Reid:

> As I understand it, the competing view is that when the wife makes direct contributions to the purchase by paying something either to the vendor or to the building society which is financing the purchase, she gets a beneficial interest in the house although nothing was ever said or agreed about this at the time: but that, when her contributions are only indirect by way of paying sums which the husband would otherwise have had to pay, she gets nothing unless at the time of the acquisition there was some agreement that she should get a share. I can see no good reason for this distinction and I think that in many cases it would be unworkable. Suppose the spouses have a joint bank account. In accordance with their arrangement, she pays in enough money to meet the household bills and so there is enough to pay the purchase price instalments and their bills as well as their personal expenses. They never discuss whose money is to go to pay for the house and whose is to go to pay for other things. How can anyone tell whether she has made a direct or only an indirect contribution to paying for the house? It cannot surely depend on who signs which cheques.[56]

Gissing predates *Rosset*, but insofar as *Rosset* may be drawing the test more narrowly than *Gissing* this may have been unintended: Lord Bridge's explanation of the *Rosset II* test starts by stating that he understands his explanation to be what the previous authorities say, implying that he did not intend to alter the law. More recently, in *LeFoe v LeFoe*,[57] Mostyn J, citing *Gissing*, held that the claimant had a beneficial interest in the property by virtue of her indirect financial contributions, and that Lord Bridge had not intended to exclude that possibility in *Rosset*.[58] He noted that if his interpretation was incorrect, 'these cases would be decided by reference to mere accidents of fortune, being the arbitrary allocation of financial responsibility as between the parties', i.e., who paid what out of which account. That may be, a matter of simple convenience between the parties rather than indicative of their intention. Remember, though, that it is intention that is key.

[55] B Sloan, 'Keeping Up with the *Jones* Case: Establishing Constructive Trusts in "Sole Legal Owner" Scenarios', (2015) 35(2) *Legal Studies* 226.
[56] *Gissing v Gissing* [1971] Act 886, 896F–897B.
[57] [2001] 2 FLR 970, 980–2.
[58] See M Pawlowski, 'Beneficial Entitlement – Do Indirect Contributions Suffice?' [2002, March] *Family Law* 190.

Note that there can be no common intention to share a property if the evidence shows that the financial contribution in question was a gift or a loan (which demands repayment of capital not a share in a house): both are incompatible with a constructive trust. (However, a loan at an uncommercial rate of interest could count as detrimental reliance.[59])

Is there a broader approach to inference post-*Stack*?

Rosset is clear that what is necessary to show common intention in the absence of express discussions is a financial contribution that directly or indirectly pays the deposit or the mortgage. Following *Stack v Dowden*, the situation is more unclear. In that case, the House of Lords said that the search was on 'to ascertain the parties' shared intentions . . . in the light of their whole course of conduct in relation to it'.[60] The list of relevant considerations cited by Lady Hale at paragraph 69 were not all referable to financial contribution. Lord Walker, too, thought 'the law has moved on [since *Rosset*] and your Lordships should move it a little more in the same direction'.[61] That seems to indicate that the Court was taking a broader, more flexible approach to evidence from which an intention to share could be inferred. 'Indeed', Sloan says, 'the whole rationale of the majority approach in *Stack* was a recognition that a narrow focus on matters such as direct financial contributions was inadequate as a means of ascertaining common intention in this context.'[62] *Stack*, however, was a case in which the house was in joint legal names so the issue was not *whether* the claimant had an interest in the property but the quantification of that interest. This has left some commentators wondering whether this broader approach applies to sole name cases too, or whether the more restrictive approach of financial contribution still prevails.

In support of the idea that the Court was widening the *Rosset II* test for sole owners are the statements in *Stack* to the effect that Lord Bridge's comments were obiter, and that he had 'set [the] hurdle rather too high'.[63] The judges in *Abbott v Abbott*, which was a single owner case, thought that the law had 'moved on' since Lord Bridge's remarks in *Rosset*, and that the parties' whole course of conduct in relation to the property must be taken into account in determining their shared intentions as to its ownership provided that the conduct was still 'in relation to property'.[64] Although *Abbott* was heard by Supreme Court judges, crucially, it is a Privy Council case and thus not of direct precedential value. In Key Case *Jones v Kernott* Lord Walker and Lady Hale's joint speech can be interpreted as suggesting that the paragraph 69 *Stack* factors may be applicable inferring conduct in sole names cases but, as Sloan says, 'unfortunately the matter is not clear cut and there are interpretative arguments to be made on either side'.[65] As there have been no Supreme Court case since *Stack* which deal with the single owner situation, position is not as certain as it could be. While we may assume that a Supreme Court hearing a sole names case would

---

[59] *Levi v Levi* [2008] 2 P & CR DG1 (Ch).
[60] [2007] UKHL 17 at [60] (Lady Hale).
[61] [2007] UKHL 17 at [26] (Lord Walker).
[62] B Sloan, 'Keeping Up with the *Jones* case: Establishing Constructive Trusts in "Sole Legal Owner" Scenarios', (2015) 35(2) *Legal Studies* 226.
[63] [2007] UKHL 17 at [63] (Lady Hale).
[64] [2007] UKPC 53.
[65] B Sloan, 'Keeping Up with the *Jones* case: Establishing Constructive Trusts in "Sole Legal Owner" Scenarios', (2015) 35(2) *Legal Studies* 226.

adopt the same viewpoint manifested in its obiter comments, without such a judgment we cannot be certain as to the scope of relevant considerations in sole name cases.

Sloan suggests that post-*Jones* courts have taken a mixed approach to widening the scope of conduct capable of founding a common intention, albeit that the Court of Appeal has been more ready to do so than the lower courts.[66] *Jackson's Matrimonial Finance*, for example, notes that 'it is now widely accepted that whether or not Lord Bridge's dicta were reconcilable with the speeches in *Gissing* the law has moved on and his analysis as to conduct is too narrow. The question of what conduct will be required to establish a common intention is the subject of ongoing debate.'[67] The authors do not suggest what conduct may be necessary. John Wilson QC notes that 'the cases subsequent to *Stack* do little to clarify how much wider the test should be, indicating—see *Thomson v Humphrey*—that this enquiry must be approached on a case-by-case basis, and where precisely the line should be drawn is unclear.'[68] In *Thomson v Humphrey* the judge simply says that 'Accepting that matters have moved on since Lord Bridge's restrictive requirement that there needs to be a direct contribution in terms of the mortgage payments, it is not sensible to attempt to say what will and will not be enough.'[69]

This uncertainty presents a real risk to anyone contemplating litigation, especially when the costs are considered.[70]

Imputation versus inference

A second issue arising from *Stack* and subsequent cases is whether it is possible to impute a common intention to the parties, or whether it had to be inferred from conduct in the absence of express discussions. As Lord Neuberger explained in a strong dissent in *Stack*, 'Imputation involves concluding what the parties would have intended, whereas inference involves concluding what they did intend.' A court engaged in imputation is 'constructing an intention where none existed at the time', but which the court thinks ought to have existed if the parties were being fair to one another. Lord Neuberger has called this process 'difficult, subjective, and uncertain'.[71] Inference, in contrast, requires some evidence that they did actually intend to share the beneficial interest, even if that evidence is rather vaguely adduced from conduct in the face of one party's assertions that there never was any such intention.

Following *Jones v Kernott*, it is clear that it is *not* possible to impute a common intention to the parties—one must be inferred in order for a constructive trust to arise. Nevertheless, both routes involve degrees of artifice, and there can be a very fine line between inference and imputation. Etherton has suggested that where the evidence of inferred intention is so tenuous as to merge with imputation, the evidence will not meet the requisite standard required to rebut the presumption that equity follows the law.[72]

---

[66] B Sloan, 'Keeping Up with the *Jones* Case: Establishing Constructive Trusts in "Sole Legal Owner" Scenarios', (2015) 35(2) *Legal Studies* 226. See, for example, *Geary v Rankine* [2012] EWCA Civ 555.

[67] *Jackson's Matrimonial Finance* at Chapter 14.

[68] John Wilson QC, *Cohabitation Claims: Law, Practice and Procedure* (2nd edn, Family Law Week 2015) at 4.76.

[69] [2009] EWHC 3576 (Ch) at [29].

[70] See section 5.10 of this chapter.

[71] *Stack v Dowden* [2007] UKHL 17 [127].

[72] T Etherton, 'Constructive Trusts and Proprietary Estoppel: The Search for Clarity and Principle' [2009] 2 *The Conveyancer and Property Lawyer* 104, 108.

Inference and imputation arise again at stage two of the constructive trust enquiry (5.5.7), when we look at quantification of a successful claimant's interest. This is because at this second stage, even if not at the first, we can impute what shares the parties intended.

5.4.4 Post-acquisition intention

It is possible for the parties' common intention to change post acquisition. In *Stack*, Lord Neuberger comments that 'The fact that the ownership of the beneficial interest in a home is determined at the date of acquisition does not mean that it cannot alter thereafter.'[73]

As Lord Bridge made clear in *Rosset* when he referred to an agreement made 'at any time prior to acquisition, *or exceptionally at some later date*' (emphasis added), this is likely to be unusual. It could happen where one party moves into a home in the sole name of the other, or where the parties are joint owners but their common intention as to their respective beneficial shares changes during the period of cohabitation. Such a change in intention would need to be:

- in writing, signed, per s53(1)(c) Law of Property Act 1925; or
- because a constructive (or resulting) trust has arisen per s53(2), which may be the result of express discussions (*Rosset I*) or inferred from conduct (*Rosset II*).

In *James v Thomas*, the Court took the view that courts 'will be very slow to infer from conduct alone that parties intended to vary existing beneficial interests established at the time of acquisition'.[74] Etherton refers to 'a fairly clear policy of the court that it is considerably more difficult to prove a change from sole to shared beneficial entitlement after the acquisition of the property than to prove there was a common instruction constructive trust on its acquisition'.[75] This is problematic as when one party moves in with another they may be even less likely to have express discussions referable to their ownership of the property than at the point of acquisition.

A person who moves into a house already owned by their partner is thus likely to face an uphill struggle to show that there was a common intention that they should have a beneficial interest in the property. It will be easier to show if they have made a substantial improvement to the property so as to increase its value. In *Bernard v Josephs* Griffiths LJ gave the example of a situation in which 'the man bought the house in the first place and the woman years later used a legacy to build an extra floor to make more room for the children. In such circumstances, the obvious inference would be that the parties agreed that the woman should acquire a share in the greatly increased value of the house produced by her money'.[76]

---

[73] *Stack v Dowden* [2007] UKHL 17 [138].
[74] [2008] 1 FLR 1598 at [24] (Chadwick LJ).
[75] T Etherton, 'Constructive Trusts and Proprietary Estoppel: The Search for Clarity and Principle' [2009] 2 *The Conveyancer and Property Lawyer* 104, 113.
[76] [1982] 1 Ch 391, 404 (CA). See also the discussion in *Burns v Burns* [1984] FLR 216.

SCENARIO 1

Illustration 2: Fiona and Ishan

The house is in Ishan's sole name. The presumption is that equity follows the law and that Ishan as the sole legal owner is also the sole beneficial owner. In order to show that a constructive trust has arisen, Fiona will need to show that she has any interest at all. First, she must prove on the balance of probabilities that she and Ishan had a common intention that she would have an interest in the property. She will need to adduce evidence of express discussions (*Rosset I*) or invite the court to infer a common intention from their conduct (*Rosset II*). If we were acting for Fiona, we would therefore need to interview her in detail about any discussions that they had, and about the way that they behaved in relation to the property.

We've been told that Ishan owned the house prior to Fiona moving into it. As we have seen, this is not fatal to her claim, but it will be exceptional for the court to find an intention to share the beneficial interest arising post-acquisition, especially in those cases under *Rosset II*. It would be very helpful if we found that Fiona contributed towards the mortgage or household bills, or that the parties otherwise mingled their finances.

There are two key facts that jump out: the statements made by Ishan and the improvements paid for by Fiona. Ishan told Fiona that he wanted to take care of her and that the house would be a home for them both. It is unclear whether these assurances manifest an intention to share the beneficial interest. It could be an expression of an intention to offer financial support for the duration of the relationship or even in relation to inheritance if he died. The improvements are a direct contribution to the house, but not to the purchase price. The amount spent and the nature of the improvements will be important as this will help the court to determine whether Fiona undertook this work because she understood that she was to have an interest in the house. It is to this point that we will return when we consider whether she has relied on these statements to her detriment.

5.4.5 Ambulatory trusts

The parties' interests under a trust may be ambulatory, meaning that their respective interests are capable of being quantified at any given time, but have changed over time. Piška argues that 'the ambulatory constructive trust goes further than simply recognising that the beneficial interests may subsequently change; it provides that until quantified the parties' interests may change over time to take into account changing circumstances, in particular respective contributions'.[77] In this way it is somewhat analogous to a floating charge.

It is unclear what sort of events may justify a finding of an ambulatory trust. In Key Case *Jones v Kernott*, the parties' interests in their jointly owned house changed to take into account the increasing contribution of Ms Jones and the ending of Mr Kernott's contributions. In that case, the cashing in of a life insurance policy and Ms Jones taking responsibility for making all the mortgage payments was sufficient, but, Piška asks, 'what about those cases where there is clearly a change of circumstances but not so dramatic an event, such as a change in contributions?'[78] We do not yet know.

---

[77] N Piška, 'Ambulatory Trusts and the Family Home: *Jones v Kernott*' (2010) 1 *Trusts Law International* 87.
[78] N Piška, 'Ambulatory Trusts and the Family Home: *Jones v Kernott*' (2010) 1 *Trusts Law International* 87.

KEY CASE *Jones v Kernott* [2011] UKSC 53

Ms Jones and Mr Kernott were joint legal owners of 39 Badger Hall Avenue. There was no express declaration of trust setting out the beneficial interest.

When they separated, Ms Jones stayed in the home. Mr Kernott bought another property using the proceeds of a joint life insurance policy that they cashed in. Some years later, Mr Kernott claimed that he was entitled to half of the value of Badger Hall Avenue.

Where a house is in joint legal names, the presumption is that equity follows the law (see 5.3.1) so that the parties hold the property as beneficial joint tenants. In this case, there was no evidence to displace that presumption. Had Mr Kernott sought to realise his interest in the property at the time of separation, he would therefore have received 50 per cent of the proceeds of sale.

However, he did not do so, and Ms Jones argued that when she and Mr Kernott separated, their common intention changed so that his interest in the property crystallised at that moment, so that he was not entitled to any increase in its value from that point onwards but would instead have the sole benefit of any increase in value in his new house. In support of this, she pointed out that they had cashed in their joint life insurance policy and the whole of the proceeds of it had been used by Mr Kernott to use to rehouse himself, and that from separation he did not pay the mortgage, endowment policy or other outgoings on Badger Hall Avenue. He could not have afforded to do so alongside the payments on his new house.

The Supreme Court held that although the parties had started as beneficial joint tenants, their intentions changed on separation, and this could be inferred from their conduct. Their common intention at separation was that Mr Kernott's interest in the property should crystallise.

Importantly, however, *Jones v Kernott* was a house in joint legal names with no express declaration of the beneficial interest, so there was a presumption that Mr Kernott had a beneficial interest. The issue was what that interest was. It would be much more difficult to show an ambulatory constructive trust in sole legal name situations.

5.4.6 Detrimental reliance and unconscionability

It is not enough that there should be a common intention to share the beneficial interest. The claimant must also have relied upon this intention by changing their position to their detriment.[79] The requirement of detriment applies whether the claim is based on *Rosset I* (express discussions) or *II* (inferred from conduct). In *Chan Pui Chun v Leung Kam Ho* the Court of Appeal rejected the submission that detriment is not required when there is an express oral agreement[80] that the beneficial interest would be shared.[81] Nevertheless, some have suggested that such detriment may be quite minor in joint names and *Rosset I* situations.

Detrimental reliance requires that the claimant has engaged in 'conduct on which she cannot reasonably have been expected to embark unless she was to have an interest in the house'.[82] The respondent must have known that the claimant engaged in that conduct in

---

[79] Remember that these stages only apply where there is no express declaration of the beneficial interest.
[80] If it were written. it would be a written declaration of trust and we would not have to be looking at *Rosset* at all.
[81] [2002] EWCA Civ 1075, at [93].
[82] *Eves v Eves* [1975] 1 WLR 1338.

reliance on that intention. Equity then 'acts on the conscience of the legal owner to prevent him from acting in an unconscionable manner by defeating the common intention'.[83]

The claimant's change in position does not have to be wholly in reliance on the common intention; part reliance is sufficient.[84] However, it must be causally linked to the common intention. This is because it is combination of the shared intention and the claimant's subsequent behaviour that effectively completes the bargain to which the constructive trust gives effect. Thus, if the claimant's detriment or change of position occurred before the common intention existed, the claim cannot succeed.

What, therefore can be detriment? That the detriment does not have to be financial was made clear in *Gillett v Holt*, in which Robert Walker LJ said that:

> the authorities also show that it is not a narrow or technical concept. The detriment need not consist of the expenditure of money or other quantifiable financial detriment, so long as it is something substantial. The requirement must be approached as part of a broad enquiry as to whether repudiation of an assurance is or is not unconscionable in all the circumstances.[85]

Sometimes—perhaps quite a lot of the time—the evidence used as to show a change of position will be the same evidence on which a common intention based on conduct can be inferred. However, the scope of the former is wider: *Grant v Edwards* tells us that as far as detriment is concerned any conduct relating to the parties' joint lives is sufficient *provided that* the claimant would not have otherwise changed their position (the causal link):

> once it has been shown that there was a common intention that the claimant should have an interest in the house, any act done by her to her detriment relating to the joint lives of the parties is, in my judgment, sufficient detriment to qualify. The acts do not have to be inherently referable to the house.[86]

However, as the court made clear in *G v G (Matrimonial Property: Rights of Extended Family)*,

> a change of position ranks in terms of 'detriment' or 'sacrifice' only if it results in a net disadvantage to the individual concerned. A claimed detriment must hurt, and claims of constructive trust tend to fail to the extent that the claimant has already benefited from the effort alleged.[87]

In *H v M (Property Occupied by Wife's Parents)*, for example, the wife's parents were in financial difficulties. The husband and wife bought the parents' farm and permitted them to remain living there. The parents spent money renovating the farm and on her divorce the wife claimed that her parents were the beneficial owners. The court found no detriment by the parents; on the contrary the purchase of the farm enabled them to avoid bankruptcy and stay in their home.

If the benefits weigh equally with the detriment there is no net loss. The weighing up benefits and detriments is not an exercise in financial accounting, as they encompass more

---

[83] *Grant v Edwards* [1986] Ch 638 (CA) at 656F-H (Lord Browne-Wilkinson).
[84] *Amalgamated Investment & Property Co v Texas Commerce International Bank* [1982] QB 84.
[85] [2001] Ch 210 (CA) at 232D. This was an estoppel case, but the same concept applies.
[86] *Grant v Edwards* [1986] Ch 638 (CA).
[87] [2005] EWHC 1560 (Admin).

than financial considerations. In *Parris v Williams* the court observed that 'whether in any particular case the claimed acts of detriment are or are not sufficient is essentially a matter of judgment for the judge concerned to hear the matter. That will involve a consideration of all the circumstances.'[88] For that reason, we must be cautious about saying that a particular type of conduct is detrimental: in the circumstances it may have been counterbalanced by a benefit or not causally linked to the common intention, or *de minimis* (too small a detriment to matter). However, to give an idea of the courts' approach, the following have, in their respective circumstances, been *capable of* constituting detriment:

- Payment of the deposit for the purchase of the house.
- Direct payment of the mortgage.
- Payments to the household expenses where these enable the respondent to pay the mortgage (*Grant v Edwards*).[89]
- Painting the outside of the house, extensive internal decoration and cleaning, wielding a 14lb sledgehammer to break up concrete covering the whole of the front garden and putting the rubble into a skip then preparing the garden for turfing; and demolishing a shed and putting up a new one (*Eves v Eves*; hence it is often referred to as 'the sledge-hammer case').[90]
- Reducing work as a barrister to supervise and manage renovations. Barristers are self-employed and dependent on their reputation, so this resulted in a significant reduction in the claimant's income and professional standing (*Cox v Jones*).[91]
- Improvements to a house in the sole name of the respondent (*Grant v Edwards*).[92]

However, consider some unsuccessful examples:

- Conduct stemming from a desire to live in a comfortable home (as this would not be referable to a common intention to share the beneficial interest). In *Rosset* Lord Bridge had 'considerable doubt' about whether Mrs Rosset's assistance with renovating work would amount to detriment or a significant alteration of position when 'it would seem the most natural thing in the world for any wife' to assist with such work.[93]
- Undertaking DIY as a husband: 'he should not be entitled to a share in the house simply by doing the "do-it-yourself" jobs which husbands often do' (*Button v Button*).[94]
- Undertaking internal decorative work, building a wardrobe, laying a lawn, and constructing an ornamental well and side wall in the garden (*Pettitt v Pettitt*). The House of Lords held that the husband's claim failed because he had 'merely . . . done in his leisure time jobs which husbands normally did; and the improvements carried out were nearly all of an ephemeral character'.[95]

---

[88] *Parris v Williams* [2008] EWCA Civ 1147.
[89] [1986] Ch 638 (CA).
[90] *Eves v Eves* [1975] 1 WLR 1338.
[91] [2004] EWHC 1486 (Ch).
[92] [1986] Ch 638 (CA). See also M Pawlowski, 'Constructive Trusts and Improvements to Property' [2009, August] *Family Law* 680.
[93] [1991] 1 AC 107 (HL).
[94] [1968] 1 W.L.R. 457, 461 (Lord Denning MR).
[95] [1970] AC 777 (HL).

- Doing the sort of things a wife does for the benefit of the family: 'The wife does not get a share in the house simply because she cleans the walls or works in the garden or helps her husband with the painting and decorating. Those are the sort of things which a wife does for the benefit of the family without altering the title to, or interests in, the property' (*Button v Button*).[96]

- Giving up a career at the bar to focus on building an equestrian centre with the respondent (*Walsh v Singh*). The court rejected the claimant's assertion that she would not have done this except in reliance on a common intention, finding that her motivation was her commitment to the respondent, whom she was intending to marry. The decision to give up the bar was essentially a joint decision that suited them both, for different reasons. The claimant's actions were not in reliance on their common intention to share the beneficial interest.[97]

- Working in the respondent's business and living with him, contributing her labour to improvements to the property (*James v Thomas*). The court held that the claimant did this because she and the respondent were making their life together as man and wife. The claim failed because she had not relied on their common intention. 'The cottage was their home: the business was their livelihood. It is a mistake to think that the motives which lead parties in such a relationship to act as they do are necessarily attributable to pecuniary self-interest.'[98]

- The mere fact of cohabitation itself: 'The law is not so cynical as to infer that a woman will only go to live with a man to whom she is not married if she understands that she is to have an interest in their home (*Grant v Edwards*).[99]

- Giving up her job and leaving her home, effectively losing employment prospects (*Thomson v Humphrey*). The judge found that 'she had a poorly paid part-time job with no prospects. The giving up of a job is referable, in my judgment, not to an expectation that she would own or have a share in the property, but to the assurance that she would be looked after. Now, that may or may not be an assurance that she now regards as having been breached, but even if she does, I am not satisfied that her move can be seen as having been in any way in reliance on the prospect of ownership of the property.'[100]

The common issue in some of these cases is that the conduct by the claimant was something that she—it is usually a she—would have done anyway and thus not referable to a common intention that she should have an interest in the property, or which is short-lived or minimal.

You will have noted that a number of gender stereotypes have crept into the judicial assessment of detriment. Housekeeping and painting will not be sufficient, but if a woman also uses a 14lb sledgehammer to break up concrete, the law believes that she has done this only in reliance on a belief that she had a beneficial interest. A man's interest in DIY is simply a manly pursuit, the sort of thing done by a man whether or not he believes that

---

[96] [1968] 1 W.L.R. 457, 462 (Lord Denning MR).
[97] [2009] EWHC 3219 (Ch).
[98] [2008] 1 FLR 1598.
[99] [1986] Ch 638 (CA).
[100] [2009] EWHC 3576 (Ch).

he has a beneficial interest. Would the outcome of *Eves* have been different if, as Lawson questions, Ms Eves had been a heavy muscular woman who enjoyed mud-wrestling and discus-throwing?[101] What if the man undertaking DIY is less robust, and the work therefore more arduous? We do not know and the most recent cases do not talk in gendered terms, at least explicitly. More seriously, what we do not know is whether or not the particular skills and characteristics of the individual claimant are relevant to whether this is conduct on which the claimant cannot reasonably have been expected to embark unless they were to have an interest in the house.

There have been some assertions that detrimental reliance is no long a requirement of a constructive trust, given that it went unmentioned in three of the leading Supreme Court/ Privy Council cases *Stack*, *Abbott*, and *Jones*.[102] This assertion was dismissed in no uncertain terms by the Court of Appeal in *Curran v Collins*,[103] as indeed it had been by the Court of Appeal in the slightly earlier case of *Smith v Bottomley*,[104] in which the judges held that detrimental reliance was 'a critical element' to a successful constructive trust claim. But the first three cases were all joint names cases, and the latter two both sole legal owner cases. Does this mean that detriment is an element of sole names cases but not joint names cases? Probably not. There is no indication that the judges in *Stack* intended to dispense with detriment in joint names cases through their assertion that joint legal names creates a presumption of joint tenancy. As Sloan points out, 'it would be difficult to justify the intervention of equity in the absence of such reliance due to the need for some form of unconscionability.'[105]

Where a common intention has been found, and the claimant has relied upon that to his or her detriment, it will almost always be unconscionable to deny the claimant a remedy. Not doing so would mean that the respondent had become unjustly enriched at the expense of the claimant. It is the reliance which completes the formation of the constructive trust because 'for a trust to be created the court has to be satisfied that it would be unconscionable for the legal owner to assert his legal interest in the property to the exclusion of the alleged beneficiaries.'[106] Thus unconscionability is 'closely bound up with' with detrimental reliance.[107]

There are a small number of cases in which it is not unconscionable to deny a remedy even when there has been a common intention and detrimental reliance. This is when the situation involves an illegality of purpose in which the claimant is implicated. Constructive trusts are, after all, creatures of equity, and as such the parties have to come to equity with 'clean hands'. The courts will not help a claimant whose cause of action is based on an illegal or immoral act. As the maxim says, *ex turpi causa non oritur actio* (no action arises from a dishonourable cause). In *Q v Q*, the transfer of a house from father to son was intended to avoid inheritance tax, but the father later sought to assert that the property continued to belong to him beneficially. The court held that this was both

---

[101] A Lawson, 'The Things We Do for Love: Detrimental Reliance in the Family Home' (1996) 16 *Legal Studies* 218.

[102] See, for example T Etherton, 'Constructive Trusts and Proprietary Estoppel: The Search for Clarity and Principle' [2009] 2 *The Conveyancer and Property Lawyer* 104.

[103] [2015] EWCA Civ 404.

[104] [2013] EWCA Civ 953.

[105] B Sloan, 'Keeping Up with the *Jones* case: Establishing Constructive Trusts in "Sole Legal Owner" Scenarios', (2015) 35(2) *Legal Studies* 226.

[106] *De Bruyne v De Bruyne* [2010] EWCA Civ 519.

[107] *De Bruyne v De Bruyne* [2010] EWCA Civ 519.

a constructive trust and (because the son had done a great deal of work to the home) an estoppel situation.[108]

FOCUS Know-How

Other types of constructive trust

In this chapter, we have discussed constructive trusts that have arisen as a result of a common intention coupled with detrimental reliance. There are different situations in which a constructive trust may arise without detrimental reliance playing a part.

Archibald and Another v Alexander concerned three adult children and their mother.[109] They agreed that they would buy a house together, using the mother's money, for the mother to live in. This plan was intended to reduce the inheritance tax liability on the mother's death. As it happened, two of the children were not available to sign the paperwork, so the house was transferred into the sole name of one daughter, Patsy. After the mother's death, Patsy claimed to be the sole beneficial owner of the house. The court held that the lack of detriment on the part of the other children was not fatal to the claim that a constructive trust had arisen, because the constructive trust arose as a result of the terms on which the property was transferred and the unconscionability of Patsy treating the property as her own, rather than the presence of common intention plus detriment. Similarly, in *De Bruyne v De Bruyne*, the Court of Appeal held that no detrimental reliance was needed as long as there were other circumstances rendering it unconscionable not to provide a remedy:

> In common intention constructive trusts the equity arises because it would be unconscionable for the owner of the property to be allowed to deny the cohabitee the interest which it was agreed or understood that he or she would have and in reliance on which the cohabitee acted to his or her detriment. In a case like *Lloyds Bank plc v Rosset* where the husband purchased the house with money from his own family trust, and the wife made no financial contribution to its acquisition but relied instead on works of improvement which she carried out to the property, some causal link is necessary in order to connect the work done to the agreement or understanding that the ownership should be shared and so deprive the husband of absolute ownership of a property which he had paid for. This requirement of detrimental reliance is closely bound up with the question of unconscionability . . .

> There are, however, a number of situations in which equity will hold the transferee of property to the terms upon which it was acquired by imposing a constructive trust to that effect. These cases do not depend on some form of detrimental reliance in order to re-balance the equities between competing claimants for the property. They concentrate instead on the circumstances in which the transferee came to acquire the property in order to provide the justification for the imposition of a trust. The most obvious examples are secret trusts and mutual wills in which property is transferred by will pursuant to an agreement that the transferee will hold the property on trust for a third party. In neither case does the intended beneficiary rely in any sense on the agreement (he may not even be aware of it) but, in both cases, equity will regard it as against conscience for the owner of the property to deny the terms upon which he received it. It is not necessary in such cases to show that the property was acquired by actual fraud (although the principle would apply equally in such cases). The concept of

108 *Q v Q* [2008] EWHC 1874 (Fam); see M Pawlowski, 'Constructive Trusts, Illegal Purpose and Locus Poenitentiae' [2009] 2 *The Conveyancer and Property Lawyer* 145. Cf. *Archibald* where the transfer, although also to save inheritance tax, was not a sham in that the mother did not continue to assert she held the beneficial interest.
109 [2020] EWHC 1621 (Ch).

fraud in equity is much wider and can extend to unconscionable or inequitable conduct in the form of a denial or refusal to carry out the agreement to hold the property for the benefit of the third party which was the only basis upon which the property was transferred. This is sufficient in itself to create the fiduciary obligation and to require the imposition of a constructive trust. The principle is a broad one and applies as much to *inter vivos*[110] transactions as it does to wills.[111]

In the situations described in the second paragraph of *De Bruyne*, the constructive trust is not a common intention constructive trust of the type we are discussing in this chapter, where detrimental reliance is an essential component. It is instead a different type of constructive trust which has arisen by virtue of the circumstances in which the transferee came to acquire the property and the unconscionability of them denying the reasons for that transfer. As far as we are concerned, as between cohabitants in the kinds of situations outlined in the scenarios in this chapter, detriment is an essential element.

There is an exception to this. Where the claimant does not have to rely on his illegal or immoral purpose to assert his claim—for example, because that purpose has not been carried out—then the claim will not fail for an illegal purpose. This is more likely to apply in resulting trust situations where the presumption of a resulting trust in situations where one party makes a contribution to the purchase price of another's property can make the reasons for that contribution irrelevant.

SCENARIO 1

Illustration 3: Fiona and Ishan

In addition to proving that there was a common intention that she was to acquire an interest in the house, it is necessary for Fiona to show that she relied on that common understanding to her detriment. Detrimental reliance requires that the claimant has engaged in 'conduct on which she cannot reasonably have been expected to embark unless she was to have an interest in the house'.[112]

The detriment that Fiona may plead is likely to be twofold: first, that she would not have sold her home if not for those representations; and second, that she made improvements to the home. One problem is that when she sold her existing property she would have received the sale proceeds. That is not a detriment unless we invite the court to find that doing so substantially weakened her position: the argument would be that leaving owner-occupation for an uncertain position with Ishan was detrimental. It is doubtful that this will be sufficient.

A stronger argument is that of the improvements. Unless they are very minimal, or purely decoration, improvements would count as detriment. They have to be causally linked to the common intention so the court must decide whether Fiona has financed improvements to the property in reliance on an understanding that she had an interest in the property, as opposed to being about her personal comfort in Ishan's house.

As you can see, the detriment here comprises the same evidence on which Fiona can argue that there was a common intention—and that is often the case.

---

[110] *Inter vivos* means 'between the living'.
[111] *De Bruyne v De Bruyne* [2010] EWCA Civ 519.
[112] *Eves v Eves* [1975] 1 WLR 1338.

5.4.7 Constructive trusts stage two: Quantification

If the claimant has been found to benefit from a constructive trust, the issue then becomes what share they are entitled to. The quantification of the parties' shares depends on their intention as found by the court, because a common intention constructive trust arises to give effect to those intentions.

Where the house is in joint names, the starting point is, as we have seen, that the parties hold as beneficial joint tenants and thus on sale of the property their single undivided share is realised as an equal division of the proceeds of sale. If the presumption of joint tenancy has been successfully rebutted, as in *Stack*, the court will base the division on the different common intention that it has found.

In sole names cases, where the constructive trust is based on *Rosset I*—that is, on express discussions—the discussions should enable the court to identify what shares were intended. Thus, if the discussion supports equal sharing, the court will quantify the shares equally. If the discussion supports sharing based on the parties' respective financial contributions, the shares will be in accordance with those contributions. The same applies to cases decided under *Rosset II*, but the absence of express discussions may make this task more difficult.

But what of those cases in which the court is able to find that the parties intended to share the beneficial interest but is unable to discern *how* they intended to share it? The principle derived from *Oxley v Hiscock* is that if the court cannot, despite its best endeavours, infer what shares the parties intended from their discussions or conduct, then it can impute to the parties an intention to be fair. Of course, this is a fictional intention—if the parties had an intention then the court would have been able to infer what it was; the whole point of imputation (as we discussed at 5.5.3) is that it attributes to the parties an intention that they did not have. Despite Lord Neuberger's forceful criticisms this in *Stack*—and Lady Hale's similar doubts—in *Jones v Kernott* the Supreme Court reiterated the *Oxley* solution of imputing what was fair.[113]

In undertaking the task of imputation, the court will look at the whole course of dealing between the parties in relation to the property.[114]

The Court of Appeal in *Oxley* noted that even where there were direct contributions to the purchase price, and thus 'an interference that each party should have some beneficial interest', this did not necessarily mean 'that their respective shares should be proportionate to the amount of their direct contributions'.[115] There may be reasons why that would not be fair. (Despite this statement, the Court did, however, only look to financial contributions in *Oxley*, both direct and indirect and before and after acquisition.) In *Jones v Kernott* their Lordships thought that '"the whole course of dealing . . . in relation to the property" should be given a broad meaning enabling a similar range of factors to be taken into account as may be relevant to ascertaining the parties' actual intentions'.[116] In other words, they referred back to the paragraph 69 factors that Lady Hale had suggested in

---

[113] *Jones v Kernott* [2011] UKSC 53.
[114] *Oxley v Hiscock* [2004] EWCA Civ 546.
[115] [2004] EWCA Civ 546 at [40].
[116] *Jones v Kernott* [2011] UKSC 53 [51(4)] (Lord Walker and Lady Hale).

Stack were relevant to the first hurdle, rebutting a presumption of joint tenancy in joint names cases:

> Many more factors than financial contributions may be relevant to divining the parties' true intentions. These include: any advice or discussions at the time of the transfer which cast light upon their intentions then; the reasons why the home was acquired in their joint names; the reasons why (if it be the case) the survivor was authorised to give a receipt for the capital moneys; the purpose for which the home was acquired; the nature of the parties' relationship; whether they had children for whom they both had responsibility to provide a home; how the purchase was financed, both initially and subsequently; how the parties arranged their finances, whether separately or together or a bit of both; how they discharged the outgoings on the property and their other household expenses.[117]

Despite the broad nature of the paragraph 69 enquiry, in cases since *Jones v Kernott*, though, judges have tended to steer clear of the highly discretionary and unpredictable quantification that the non-financial *Stack* paragraph 69 factors would yield, and instead have tended to focus on the parties' more easily quantifiable financial contributions to the acquisition of the house, the mortgage, and the household economy. As we shall see, this is closer, although not quite the same as, a resulting trust analysis.

It is important to understand the scope of the paragraph 69 enquiry. The factors noted by Lady Hale relate to the way in which they dealt with the property. The court is not creating a divorce-style outcome by the back door. It cannot look at fairness more widely than in relation to the property in question. In *Graham-York v York (Personal Representative of the Estate of Norton Brian York) and Another*, the Tomlinson LJ said:

> It is essential, in my judgment, to bear in mind that, in deciding in such a case what shares are fair, the court is not concerned with some form of redistributive justice. Thus it is irrelevant that it may be thought a 'fair' outcome for a woman who has endured years of abusive conduct by her partner to be allotted a substantial interest in his property on his death. The plight of Miss Graham-York attracts sympathy, but it does not enable the court to redistribute property interests in a manner which right-minded people might think amounts to appropriate compensation. Miss Graham-York is 'entitled to that share which the court considers fair having regard to the whole course of dealing between them in relation to the property'. It is these last words, which I have emphasised, which supply the confines of the enquiry as to fairness.[118]

As such, even a successful claimant on a trusts claim may on balance remain financially harmed by the relationship when other factors, such as giving up work to care for children, are taken into account.

As we see at 5.4.3, we cannot use imputation to establish that a trust has arisen in the first place.[119] It is only once it has been established both that the claimant does have an interest and that the court cannot identify what the parties actually intended their shares to be that the court can make a fair division. If it *can* find what the parties intended their shares to be, whether from express discussions or inference, there is no room to impute a different split even if the court thinks that would be fairer.

---

[117] *Stack v Dowden* [2007] UKHL 17 [69].
[118] [2015] EWCA Civ 72.
[119] *Capehorn v Harris* [2015] EWCA Civ 955 and *Barnes v Philips* [2015] EWCA Civ 1056.

SCENARIO 1

Illustration 4: Fiona and Ishan

Let us assume that the court in this case has found both a common intention and detrimental reliance. How is the court to quantify Fiona's interest? The answer lies in what the court has found to be their common intention. Here there are several possibilities. The court could have found that they intended to share the property equally. On the facts—post-acquisition intention, significantly different financial contributions—this is pretty unlikely. A more probable outcome would be to find that the parties intended that Fiona should have some interest in the house, but proportional to her financial contribution. If the court finds common intention but cannot discern the relevant proportions that the parties intended, then the court can impute an intention to be fair, decide what would be fair, and impose that outcome. Again, it is likely that the court would see fairness in this case as related to financial contribution.

However, this scenario is very different to situations in which the parties are together at the time when the property was placed in one party's sole name, or in which there is a long history of pooled financial resources in which both have contributed directly or indirectly to the household bills and mortgage, or in which there are children. In such a case, the survey of the whole course of dealing that *Stack* requires would be likely to yield very different results.

Equitable accounting

Equitable accounting is a doctrine under which a beneficiary under a trust may be required to pay an 'occupation rent' to a beneficiary who has been excluded from the property. It is therefore an adjustment that happens *after* the parties' respective interests in the property have been determined.

As Lady Hale indicated in *Stack v Dowden*, the doctrine has now been replaced by the provisions of the Trusts of Land (Appointment of Trustees) Act 1996, albeit that the outcomes of each may be the same. As an equitable remedy, courts have a discretion as to whether to permit it.

Section 12 TLATA governs the right of a beneficiary to occupy a property and s13 enables the trustees—the legal owners—to exclude one or more of the beneficiaries (but not all of them) from occupation of the property or restrict their occupation. They cannot exclude a beneficiary unreasonably or to an unreasonable extent, but can impose reasonable conditions on the beneficiary's occupation. For example, the trustees can require a beneficiary to pay outgoings or expenses in relation to the land or assume any other obligation in relation to the land or to any activity which is or is proposed to be conducted there. They can also require the beneficiary to make payments by way of compensation to the beneficiary who has been excluded or restricted, or to forgo any payment or other benefit to which he would otherwise be entitled under the trust.

In relation to separating couples, this comes into play when one party remains in the property to the exclusion of the other post-separation. It does not matter whether they are beneficial joint tenants or tenants in common, and exclusion can be constructive. In *Jones v Kernott*, the court held that accounting would be disproportionate to the assets in the case and did not allow it. However, but for that fact, the court would have allowed Mr Kernott to claim for occupation rent against Ms Jones, and Ms Jones to cross-claim against Mr Kernott for the mortgage instalments he had not made.[120] However, subject to the very real problem of accurately and cost-effectively undertaking the calculation, if the person in occupation has paid the mortgage, the court will often treat any interest payments as wiping out any 'occupation rent' payable to the excluded party,[121] and insofar as there have been capital repayments, the payer should be entitled to half of the credit of those. In relation to renovations, a person in occupation who does improvements to the property with the consent of the owner(s) should be credited with their share of the increase in the property value, or one half of the expenditure, whichever is lesser. These are not, however, hard and fast rules and the position post-*Kernott* is still uncertain. The objective, however, is to do justice to the parties, having regard to the statutory considerations now governing occupation rent.[122]

5.5 Resulting trusts

The classic definition of a resulting trust comes from the judgment of Lord Browne-Wilkinson in *Westdeutsche Landesbank Girozentrale v Islington London Borough Council*, a judgment whose length has haunted many a law student:

> Under existing law a resulting trust arises . . . where A makes a voluntary payment to B or pays (wholly or in part) for the purchase of property which is vested either in B alone or in the joint names of A and B. [In this situation] there is a presumption that A did not intend to make a gift to B: the money or property is held on trust for A (if he is the sole provider of the money) or in the case of a joint purchase by A and B in shares proportionate to their contributions. It is important to stress that this is only a *presumption*, which presumption is easily rebutted either by the counter-presumption of advancement or by direct evidence of A's intention to make an outright transfer . . .[123]

As Lord Browne-Wilkinson indicates, where a person makes a contribution to the acquisition costs of a house in someone else's name, or in joint names with someone else, there is a presumption that the contributor intended to obtain a beneficial interest in the house commensurate with their contribution and not to make a gift.

The presumption of resulting trust is rebuttable by evidence that:

- The contributor intended a different share to that which is proportionate to the amount of their contribution. 'The courts will always strive to work out the real intention of the [contributor] and will only give effect to presumptions of resulting trust . . . where the intention cannot be fathomed and a "long stop" or "default" solution is needed.'[124]

- That the contribution was, in fact, a gift (and thus nothing was expected in return).

- The contribution was a loan (to be repaid with money, not a share in the house).

The relevant intention is the subjective intention of the contributor not, as would be the case with a constructive trust, an intention common to both parties. It appears that

---

[120] See [49] of the judgment of Lord Nicholls and Lady Hale.

[121] As in *Murphy v Gooch* [2007] EWCA Civ 603. See Elizabeth Cooke 'Accounting Payments: Please Can We Get the Maths Right?' [2007] *Family Law* 1024.

[122] *Murphy v Gooch* [2007] EWCA Civ 603; see also *Rowland v Blades* [2021] EWHC 426 (Ch).

[123] [1996] AC 669 at 708.

[124] *Kyriakides v Pippas* [2004] 2 FCR 434, [74].

this intention does not have to be communicated to the other party. The courts' role is to search for this intention, starting from the position that the contributor intended to have a share commensurate with his contribution. The burden of proving differently lies with the person saying that the presumption does not apply.[125]

As Lord Phillips MR explained in *Lavelle v Lavelle*:

> Where one person, A, transfers the legal title of a property that he owns or purchases to another, B, without receipt of any consideration, the effect will depend on his intention. If he intends to transfer the beneficial interest in the property to B, the transaction will take effect as a gift and A will lose all interest in the property. If he intends to retain the beneficial interest for himself, B will take the legal interest but will hold the property in trust for A.

> Normally there will be evidence of the intention with which a transfer is made. Where there is not, the law applies presumptions. . . . there will be a presumption that A does not intend to part with the beneficial interest in the property and B will take the legal title under a resultant trust for A. . . .

> In these cases equity searches for the subjective intention of the transferor. It seems to me that it is not satisfactory to apply rigid rules of law to the evidence that is admissible to rebut the presumption of advancement. Plainly, self-serving statements or conduct of a [contributor], who may long after the transaction be regretting earlier generosity, carry little or no weight. But words or conduct more proximate to the transaction itself should be given the significance that they naturally bear as part of the overall picture . . . [126]

Where the contribution is made by a person who is traditionally under an equitable obligation to support another person, it is presumed to be a gift. You may see references to this presumption, known as the presumption of advancement. It is, says Blackham, 'best regarded as a rule of evidence that shifts the burden of proof in certain cases', so that the donor will have to prove that the contribution was not a gift.[127]

Traditionally, it applied to payments made by father to their child; husbands to their wives; and engaged men to their fiancées: the obligation of support was gendered. Section 199 of the Equality Act 2010 would have abolished the presumption, but this section is not yet in force so the presumption remains although courts have now treated it gender neutrally, applying it between mother and child, for example.[128] However, this is subject to several important caveats. First, most familial arrangements will be domestic and thus fall into the remit of constructive trusts rather than resulting trusts (see 5.6). Second, the presumption has been described as 'relatively weak' and 'capable of being rebutted on comparatively

---

[125] *Tribe v Tribe* [1996] Ch 107.

[126] [2004] 2 FCR 418.

[127] A Blackham, 'The Presumption of Advancement: A Lingering Shadow in UK Law?' (2015) 21(7) *Trusts and Trustees* 786; my thanks to Dr Brian Sloan for suggesting this very clear article.

[128] In *Patel v Mirza* the Supreme Court referred to the presumption arising from mother to child: see [2016] UKSC 42 at [18] (Lord Toulson). It was also applied (although rebutted) in Key Case *Laskar*. In *Close Invoice Finance v Abaowa*, the High Court also took it to apply to mother and child on the basis that 'our society recognises fathers and mothers as having similar obligations in relation to provision for their children and . . . similar degrees of affection for them': [2010] EWHC 1920 (QB).

slight evidence'.[129] There will almost always be other evidence capable of showing that the contribution was a gift, or that it was not, and this means that it is little used.[130]

Under a resulting trust, therefore, the contributions are likely to determine both the existence of a resulting trust and the quantification of the parties' shares. If A contributes 60 per cent of the acquisition cost, the presumption is that he is entitled to 60 per cent of the equity in the house.[131]

The acquisition costs have been taken to include:

- The cash down payment.[132]
- Expenses connected with the purchase, such as conveyancing fees and stamp duty land tax.[133]
- A right to buy discount, wherein a long-term council tenant is able to buy the home they rent at a substantial discount below market value. This is treated as a contribution of cash.[134]
- Mortgages: money raised by way of a mortgage are usually treated as a contribution by the person(s) who took out the mortgage. Where the mortgage is in joint names, this would constitute equal contributions as they are jointly and severally liable.[135]

They do not include the costs of furnishing a property, fitting it out, or renovating it.

Let us now consider the issue of mortgage repayments. As it is likely that one partner may move into a home that the other purchased, on the face of it no resulting trust should apply: the house has already been purchased without a financial contribution by the person moving in. In principle, the parties may at that time have a changed intention: that from the point of cohabitation the person who moved in will acquire an interest proportionate to their contribution. In *Jones v Kernott*, the Supreme Court preferred—for reasons we discuss at 5.6—a constructive trust approach rather than a resulting trust, so a claimant who has made mortgage repayments may have a remedy, but it almost certainly not by virtue of a resulting trust.

Given that a resulting trust is concerned with a contribution to the acquisition costs of a property, you will have identified that there is a crossover with constructive trusts where the common intention may also be evidenced by contribution to acquisition. It is this issue to which we now turn.

---

[129] Lord Upjohn in *Pettitt v Pettitt* [1970] 1 AC 777 at 814, discussed by the much more recent Key Case *Laskar*.
[130] Blackham has traced its current use: A Blackham, 'The Presumption of Advancement: A Lingering Shadow in UK Law?' (2015) 21(7) *Trusts and Trustees* 786.
[131] The equity in a property is the value of the property after the mortgage, any other secured debts, and costs relating to the sale of the property are paid. It is the amount that the owner(s) would actually realise from selling the property. For more information on mortgages see Chapter 4.
[132] In *Midland Bank v Cooke* [1995] 4 All ER 562, a wedding gift from the husband's parents which they put towards the deposit was deemed a gift to both in equal shares.
[133] *Re Densham* [1975] 1 WLR 1519.
[134] *Springette v Defoe* [1992] 2 FLR 388 (CA) and *Laskar v Laskar* [2008] EWCA Civ 247.
[135] In *Stack*, Lord Neuberger was doubtful that this way of treating a mortgage was justified by principle or authority. Nevertheless, in *Laskar*, he said, 'there was a strong case for apportioning the mortgage equally between the parties when it comes to assessing their respective contributions to the purchase price', but in that case the mortgage payments had been made from the rental income, not from one or other party.

KEY CASE *Laskar v Laskar* [2008] EWCA Civ 347

Most council or housing association tenants are entitled to buy the houses that they rent with a discount commensurate to the amount of time they have lived there. This is known as 'right to buy'.[136]

In *Laskar*, mother exercised her right to buy the council house that she had been renting. As she had lived there for some time, she was entitled her to a substantial discount on what would have been the market value of the house. She bought the house for this discounted price by obtaining a mortgage in joint names with her daughter, and both mother and daughter contributed a modest down-payment in virtually equal proportions. The house was put into their joint legal names but with no express declaration of the beneficial interest. The house was then rented out to tenants with the mortgage being paid from the rental income.

As this was a commercial arrangement, the court rejected the notion that they were presumed to be joint beneficial owners under a constructive trust and instead held that a resulting trust existed, so that their shares would be in proportion to their payment towards the purchase price. There was no evidence as to any discussions that could rebut this. The mortgage loan was in joint names, and the cash deposits were almost equal between the mother and daughter. However, the discount to which the mother was entitled was a contribution that she had made, and when this was taken into account the mother was entitled to two-thirds of the value of the property as against the daughter's one-third.

The court rebutted the presumption of advancement—that the mother had intended to make a gift—for several reasons, including that there was a wide disparity in their respective contributions and it could not presumed that the mother would intend to make a gift of such a size to only one of her several children.

SCENARIO 3

Illustration 1: Rhys, Laila, and Rhys's mother Tina

This scenario involves a house bought in Rhys's sole name with money contributed by Laila and Tina. It is very common for parents to help finance properties for their children, and even more common for their children to subsequently separate from their partners.

Traditionally, a contribution would have been dealt with under resulting trust principles, with the presumption of advancement serving to place the burden on Tina to show that she did not intend her contribution to be a gift to Rhys. Post-*Stack*, this situation should be resolved under constructive trust principles as the house was intended as a home for Rhys and Laila and not (for example) as house to rent out to tenants.

The starting point is that Rhys is the sole beneficial owner because he is the sole legal owner. Laila and Tina will need to rebut this presumption by showing that the three of them held the property as tenants in common in shares commensurate to their contributions, or alternatively that as between Tina on the one hand and Rhys and Laila on the other there was an intention to share in proportion to their financial contributions, and as between Rhys and Laila there was an intention to share what was left equally.

---

[136] See https://www.gov.uk/right-to-buy-buying-your-council-home and https://righttobuy.gov.uk/am-i-eligible/eligibility-quiz/ accessed 1 November 2020.

> Would there be much difference between a resulting and constructive trust outcome? As between Tina and the others, probably not. It is very likely that under a constructive trust Tina's financial contribution (which is evidence of common intention and detriment) would give her no more than a share commensurate with her contribution. Her weakness in this, as with a resulting trust, is whether the court will infer an intention to share the beneficial interest when the relationship is one of parent and child. She may have intended a gift. Of course, if Rhys and Laila split up, Tina may argue that it was a loan or a resulting trust, but what we are concerned with is what their intention was at the time of purchase (or exceptionally some later time), not what, in light of experience, they wish they had intended.

5.6 Which one—resulting or constructive trust?

Although the intention of the parties is key under both a resulting and constructive trust, they take different approaches. Under a resulting trust, the parties' shares depend upon their financial contributions to the acquisition costs. Under a constructive trust, the court looks at the whole course of dealing between the parties rather than simply the costs of acquisition. In some cases, the parties' intentions under a constructive trust will be to share in accordance with their financial contributions to the acquisition costs of the property, in which case there will be no difference between the outcomes under resulting or constructive trust principles. But in many cases, the broader scope of the constructive trust enquiry yields a different outcome.

In *Stack v Dowden*, the majority view was that a constructive trust should apply in the domestic context, i.e., in respect of family homes. They thought that the resulting trust was more appropriate for a commercial context, such as arrangements between business partners or family members who had entered into a commercial arrangement with one another (such as buying a 'buy to let' property). In reaching this view, the Court was influenced by several factors outlined by Lady Hale, with whom the other judges—Lord Neuberger excepted—agreed.

First, Lady Hale noted that constructive and resulting trusts were being used by cohabiting couples because more of them owned houses as a result of the huge expansion in home ownership that had taken place since the Second World War and the introduction of 'right to buy' legislation in the 1980s. This, combined with house price inflation, meant that 'it is almost always more advantageous for someone who has contributed to the acquisition of the home to claim a share in its ownership rather than the return of the money contributed, even with interest'.[137] Disputes between cohabitants were 'increasingly visible in recent years as more and more couples live together without marrying' and thus without access to the courts' wide powers of property redistribution on divorce.[138] Yet, Lady Hale points out, citing the research by Barlow et al. referred to at 5.14.2 of this chapter, there is widespread belief in common law marriage—the myth that cohabitants have access to divorce-style rights against one another at the end of a relationship.[139]

---

[137] At para [41].
[138] Para [44]. See Chapter 4.
[139] At [45].

The upshot of this is that more disputes between cohabiting couples are coming before the courts. However, she argued that an approach based on a resulting trust was inappropriate. The behaviour of those cohabiting in an intimate relationship was different to those in commercial situations and 'an outcome which might seem just in a purely commercial transaction may appear highly unjust in a transaction between husband and wife or co-habitant and cohabitant'.[140] In particular, 'the importance to be attached to who paid for what in a domestic context may be very different from its importance in other contexts or long ago . . . in law, context is everything'.[141] For the majority of the Lords, therefore, a constructive trust approach was more likely to reflect what the parties actually intended.

In the subsequent case of *Jones v Kernott*, the joint speech of Lord Walker and Lady Hale reiterated that 'In the context of the acquisition of a family home, the presumption of a resulting trust made a great deal more sense when social and economic conditions were different'. In particular, the presumption of advancement applied so that 'the breadwinner husband who provided the money to buy a house in his wife's name, or in their joint names, was presumed to be making her a gift of it, or of a joint interest in it.' As we see at 5.5, however, the presumption was abolished by the Equality Act 2010 although this provision is not yet in force. For Lord Walker and Lady Hale, in its place 'the tool which equity has chosen to develop law is the "common intention" constructive trust. Abandoning the presumption of advancement while retaining the presumption of resulting trust would place an even greater emphasis upon who paid for what, an emphasis which most commentators now agree to have been too narrow.'[142]

Nevertheless, the division between an investment/commercial arrangement (resulting trust) and a familial one (constructive trust) is not clear-cut. In the resulting trust Key Case *Laskar v Laskar*, the arrangement was a profit-making once, but the parties were related. In *Wodzicki v Wodzicki*, the parties were stepmother and stepdaughter who were not close; this too was a resulting trust situation.[143] In *Gallarotti v Sebastianelli* a common intention constructive trust was applied when the parties were not family members or in a relationship but were simply friends.[144] Most notably, in *Marr v Collie* the Privy Council held that it was not the intention of *Stack* or *Laskar* to limit constructive trusts only to domestic contexts, and that constructive trusts may arise between couples who purchase a buy-to-let property. The proper approach is to look at what the parties intended:

> If it is the unambiguous mutual wish of the parties, contributing in unequal shares to the purchase of a property, that the joint beneficial ownership should reflect their joint legal ownership, then effect should be given to that wish. If, on the other hand, that is not their wish, or if they have not formed any intention as to beneficial ownership but had, for instance, accepted advice that the property be acquired in joint names, without considering or being aware of the possible consequences of that, the resulting trust solution may provide the answer.[145]

---

[140] At [42].
[141] At [69].
[142] *Jones v Kernott* [2011] UKSC 53 [24].
[143] [2017] EWCA Civ 95.
[144] [2012] EWCA Civ 865.
[145] *Marr v Collie* [2017] UKPC 17 at [54] (Lord Kerr).

The approach in *Marr v Collie* therefore was to look at the parties' intentions in determining whether a resulting or constructive trust should be applied, not (as had been the case previously) to look at the *purpose* for which the property had been acquired, which was 'if for habitation, the CICT doctrine applied; if for investment, the resulting trust doctrine instead'.[146] These intentions would take precedence over the presumption that a house in joint names presumes joint tenancy, or the presumption of a resulting trust, as presumptions 'exist to fill evidentiary gaps' and when their intention is known there are no gaps.[147] This would require a court to consider intention before they then determined whether to apply a constructive or resulting trust analysis.[148]

Sloan has suggested that:

> the difficulty or, depending on one's perspective, the beauty, of the *Marr* emphasis on common intention is that, by the time one has used the common intention to determine the starting point, perhaps one may as well also use it to determine the end point . . . . On that basis, it arguably does not much matter whether one starts with a resulting trust and varies it according to common intention, or starts with a presumption that equity follows the law and grafts a common intention constructive trust onto that (whatever the possible difficulties of doing that in light of the distinction between 'sole name' and 'joint name' cases).[149]

It is unfortunate that *Marr* caused this confusion, but you may well be of the view that many aspects of trusts of land are confusing. It is not uncommon for judges to confuse the concepts and conflate the requirements. *Marr v Collie* is a Privy Council decision and, unlike *Stack*, is not directly binding on the courts below. Nor has it had much impact beyond the sphere of trusts law academics.[150] We can now assume that there is no firm dividing line between commercial and domestic spheres, as the facts of some cases straddle the two. But it is less clear whether we should be looking at intention or looking at the purpose for which a house was purchased. In default of clarification, *Stack*'s purposive approach remains the binding precedent.[151]

5.7 Proprietary estoppel

Proprietary estoppel is an equitable claim in which a party is prevented—estopped—from asserting his or her strict legal rights because of a contrary promise or representation that they have made to the claimant. It is a claim against the conscience of the promisor. As Wilson explains 'The conceptual foundation of proprietary estoppel is the prevention of unconscionable conduct by the legal owner.'[152]

---

[146] AYS Georgiou, '*Marr v Collie*: The Ballooning of the Common Intention Constructive Trust' (2019) 82(1) *Modern Law Review* 145.

[147] L Maniscalco, 'Common Intentions and Constructive Trusts: Unorthodoxy in Trusts of Land' [2020] 2 *The Conveyancer and Property Lawyer* 124.

[148] George and Sloan consider the implications of this: M George and B Sloan, 'Presuming Too Little about Resulting and Constructive Trusts? *Marr v Collie* [2017] UKPC 17' [2017] 4 *The Conveyancer and Property Lawyer* 303.

[149] B Sloan, 'Constructive of Resulting Trusts: Does It Matter?' [2020] 1 *The Conveyancer and Property Lawyer* 82.

[150] See AYS Georgiou, '*Marr v Collie*: The Ballooning of the Common Intention Constructive Trust' (2019) 82(1) *Modern Law Review* 145.

[151] See discussion of the *Marr* uncertainty and precedent in *Rowland v Blades* [2021] EWHC 426 (Ch) at [96].

[152] J Wilson QC, *Cohabitation Claims: Law, Practice and Procedure* (2nd edn, *Family Law* 2015) at 4.156.

The elements of a proprietary estoppel claim are:

- A 'clear enough' ('sufficiently clear') promise or assurance made by the respondent relating to property.[153]
- The claimant relying on that promise or assurance to his or her detriment. 'It is the detrimental reliance which makes the promise irrevocable and leads to the conclusion, at the end of a broad enquiry, that repudiation of the assurance is unconscionable.'[154]
- The conclusion that the combination of promise and reliance makes it unconscionable for the respondent promisor to assert their strict legal rights.

5.7.1 The nature of the assurances

The first element of estoppel is the existence of promise, representation, or assurance. The promise does not need to relate to ownership of a property but could, for example, relate to being able to occupy a property (as in Key Case *Southwell*) or to all of the respondent's assets (such as assurances that the promisee would inherit their estate).

The promise must be 'sufficiently clear and unequivocal'.[155] Whether a promise is sufficiently clear and unequivocal depends on its context. In a commercial context, Martin J Dixon writes, 'there might well have to be a very clear and certain assurance, but in a family situation a different path could be trod'.[156] As we will see in the discussion of *Thorner v Major* at 5.8.3, the finding that the parties were 'taciturn and undemonstrative men committed to a life of hard and unrelenting physical work' was relevant to the way in which the promises or representations were made and the way they were understood.

In *Walton v Walton*, Hoffman LJ said that 'taken in its context, it must have been a promise which one might reasonably expect to be relied upon by the person to whom it was made'.[157] It is an objective test whether the promisor intended the promisee to rely on his assurances. If it was reasonable for the promisee to rely on them, then it would not generally be open to the promisor to say that he did not intend the promisee to rely on those assurances.[158] This means that estoppel may provide a remedy when the claimant is under a unilateral belief that he or she will acquire rights even if the promisor did not intend that, as long as the promisor either encouraged this belief by his representations or did not correct any belief of which he was aware. In this way, it is possible for estoppel to be created through acquiescence alone.

5.7.2 Detrimental reliance and unconscionability

The second element is that the promisee has relied on the promise or assurance to his detriment. The detriment must be sufficiently causally linked to the promise made, and this is judged when the promisor seeks to repudiate the promise.[159] In *Coombes v Smith*, the

---

153 *Thorner v Major* [2009] UKHL 18.
154 *Southwell v Blackburn* [2014] EWCA Civ 1347.
155 *Thorner v Major* [2009] UKHL 18.
156 MJ Dixon, 'Proprietary Estoppel: A Return to Principle?' [2009] 3 *The Conveyancer and Property Lawyer* 260, 265.
157 *Walton v Walton* [1994] Lexis Citation 3926 at [16].
158 *Thorner v Major* [2009] UKHL 18 at [17] (Lord Scott).
159 *Gillett v Holt* [2001] Ch 210, 232.

claimant's pleaded detriment included that she had left her husband and 'allowed herself' to become pregnant by the respondent. The court rejected this both as detriment and for lack of even a partial causal link with assurances made: she had moved into the property and become pregnant by the respondent because she wanted to do so.[160] In *Southwell* the court considered and disregarded the ebb and flow of benefits and detriments where those were consequences of the parties' relationship rather than the assurances made.

The detriment does not need to be financial but must be substantial. In *Jennings v Rice*, it was caring for an elderly woman for some years in reliance on her promise that the claimant would inherit her house.[161] Whether or not it is substantial is assessed 'as part of a broad inquiry as to whether repudiation of an assurance is or is not unconscionable in all the circumstances.'[162] This may involve weighing the detriment found to have been suffered against any benefits that the claimant enjoyed because of that reliance.[163] Many couples will receive—and not tally up—the benefits of a relationship (such as love and affection, housekeeping done for you, receipt of financial and practical support) and detriments (having to do the housekeeping, providing financial support, and a million other things that family lawyers can tell you about). Where these are not causally connected to the assurances, or where they connected but are roughly equal between the parties, they do not constitute detriment. The claimant's expectation, which has come about by virtue of the assurances made, should be proportional to the detriment suffered[164]— otherwise it would not be unconscionable to deny a remedy. As Hoffman LJ said in *Walton v Walton*, equitable estoppel 'does not look forward into the future and guess what might happen. It looks backwards from the moment when the promise falls due to be performed and asks whether, in the circumstances which have actually happened, it would be unconscionable for the promise not to be kept.'[165]

As can be seen, at each stage proportionality is important. That reflects the equitable nature of the estoppel claim. As Lord Scott said in *Thorner v Major*, while the three elements 'would, I think, always be necessary [they] might, in a particular case, not be sufficient'.[166] A representation or assurance may not have been sufficiently clear, the reliance might not have been reasonable in the circumstances, and the detriment might not be sufficiently substantial to justify the intervention of equity, which only provides a remedy where it would be unconscionable not to do so.

While the three elements are the essential components of an estoppel claim, the courts have rejected the idea that they constitute 'watertight compartments'.[167] Whether it was reasonable to rely on the promise or assurance will depend on the quality of the assurance; and the second and third elements, detriment and unconscionability, are closely entwined. The court will test the detriment by ascertaining 'whether, in particular individual circumstances, it would be unconscionable for a party to be permitted to deny that

---

[160] [1986] 1 WLR 808.
[161] [2002] EWCA Civ 159.
[162] *Davies & Anor v Davies* [2014] EWCA Civ 568 at [30] (Floyd LJ).
[163] [2010] UKPC 3 at [51].
[164] *Jennings v Rice* [2002] EWCA Civ 159, [36] (Aldous LJ).
[165] [1994] Lexis Citation 3926. Cited with approval in *Thorner v Major* and *Southwell v Blackburn*.
[166] *Thorner v Major* [2009] UKHL 18 at [15] (Lord Scott).
[167] *Gillett v Holt* [2001] Ch 210.

which, knowingly, or unknowingly, he has allowed or encouraged another to assume to his detriment [rather] than to enquiring whether circumstances can be fitted within the confines of some preconceived formula serving as a universal yardstick for every form of unconscionable behaviour.'[168]

SCENARIO 1

Illustration 5: Fiona and Ishan

Could estoppel assist Fiona? Here we have some assurances from Ishan that he wanted to take care of her and that the house would be a home for them both. Estoppel promises must relate to property, but do not have to be related to ownership of property. Here, these assurances—assuming they have been proven to have been made—could relate to inheritance of property (to which estoppel can apply) or to financial support more generally.

The first thing to consider is whether the assurances are sufficiently clear in the context in which they were made. Specifically, were they promises or assurances upon which one might reasonably expect the claimant to rely? We need more evidence relating to the circumstances surrounding Fiona moving in with Ishan.

Estoppel also requires detrimental reliance. Here, Fiona moved in with Ishan, sold her own house, and financed improvements to the property. She may have moved in because she wanted to do so, irrespective of the assurances made. The improvements once again count as detriment, but she would still need to show a causal link between the detriment and the assurances made and that the work was not so minimal as to be out of proportion compared to the assurance made. What we are looking to discern is it is or is not unconscionable in all the circumstances for Ishan to deny her an interest in the house (or inheritance, if that is the promise made).

Fiona may have benefited from her relationship to Ishan. This—and any benefits to him—must be weighed against the detriment she alleges that she has suffered.

As we see below, the remedy is to award the minimum necessary to do justice. In this case, the court may award Fiona an interest in the house commensurate with her contribution or it may award her the value of her improvements. Is her situation comparable to that of Mrs Blackburn in *Southwell v Blackburn*? She gave up a secured tenancy; Fiona has given up a house. But, crucially, she has received the sale proceeds. Her detriment, therefore, is the expenditure on the improvements. An award of that amount would seem the minimum necessary to do justice in our scenario.

5.7.3 Remedies

Proportionality is also important at the remedy stage, as the court will award the minimum necessary to do justice.[169] The court cannot go further than this. There are two approaches. One approach is to give effect to the promise made. If the promise was that the claimant could occupy a property for life, then, assuming she has relied on that to her detriment, an entitlement to occupy for life may be the remedy unless that is considered disproportionate when considering the extent of the detriment. If it would be disproportionate to give effect to the promise made, the court may instead compensate the claimant

---

[168] *Taylors Fashions Limited v Liverpool Victoria Trustees Co Ltd* [1982] 1QB 133.
[169] *Crab v Arun District Council* [1976] Ch 179 and *Pascoe v Turner* [1979] 1 WLR 431.

for the detriment that she has suffered as this would be the lesser remedy. The former approach is based on expectation loss as in contract law; the latter, reliance loss, as in tort.[170] In *Culliford and Lane v Thorpe*, the judge, HHJ Paul Matthews, suggested that in cases that satisfy a common intention constructive trust (as well as estoppel) the court should give effect to the agreement made rather than provide compensation for the detriment, as this would be the effect of a constructive trust approach.[171]

Several of the leading estoppel cases involve quite extraordinary circumstances in which the promisee has provided free labour over a number of years in exchange for assurances that he would receive a share in a property. In the House of Lords case of *Thorner v Major*[172] the claimant, David Thorner, worked on his cousin Peter's farm for an extraordinary *29 years without pay* on understanding he would inherit it. When Peter died, it was revealed that he had no Will and consequently the law of intestacy (see 5.12.2 of this chapter) was applied to mean that Peter's children, and not the claimant, inherited the farm. Evidentially, the promise aspect of the case was difficult. Both claimant and cousin were referred to as 'taciturn and undemonstrative men committed to a life of hard and unrelenting physical work'.[173] Nevertheless the court found that Peter had 'encouraged the expectation which David had formed that David would be would be Peter's successor to [the farm] upon his death and encouraged David to continue with his very considerable unpaid help to Peter there; and those remarks were reasonably understood and relied upon by David in that way'.[174] The Court gave effect to the promise, and ordered that the farm be transferred to David.

Similarly, in *Gillett v Holt*,[175] Mr Gillett worked on Mr Holt's farm for more than four years. During those years, the judge found that Mr Holt had made seven public assurances in similar terms, to the effect that 'all this will be yours'. In reliance on those assurances, 'Mr Gillett and his wife devoted the best years of their lives to working for Mr Holt and his company, showing loyalty and devotion to his business interests, his social life and his personal wishes, on the strength of clear and repeated assurances of testamentary benefits' at the expense of their own financial well-being. Mr Gillett was awarded a proportion of the farm, 'as the parties would have contemplated it during the period when the assurances were given and down to the time when those assurances were repudiated'. As Mr Holt had not died when the claim was made, there was a reduction in the award to take account of the fact that Mr Gillett was receiving early what he expected to receive only on Mr Holt's death.

Although these cases are factually dramatic, proprietary estoppel has been used in more common scenarios between cohabiting couples. In *Pascoe v Turner*, for example, Mr Pascoe and Ms Turner lived together in a home paid for by, and in the sole name of, Mr Pascoe. When he moved out, Mr Pascoe told Ms Turner that the house was all hers. Miss Turner then spent one quarter of her savings on repairs, improvements and redecoration. When Mr Pascoe then sought to evict her, the court held that he had made a clear

---

[170] *Culliford and Lane v Thorpe* [2018] EWHC 426 (Ch).
[171] *Culliford and Lane v Thorpe* [2018] EWHC 426 (Ch).
[172] [2009] UKHL 18.
[173] *Thorner v Major* [2009] UKHL 18 at [59] (Lord Walker).
[174] *Thorner v Major* [2009] UKHL 18 at [40] (Lord Walker reciting the findings of the judge at first instance).
[175] [2001] Ch 210 (CA).

statement that he had gifted the house to her, and she had relied on that to her detriment by spending what was, to her, quite a lot of money on the house. The court therefore ordered the transfer of the house to her. In this way proprietary estoppel provided a remedy that—as the court could not infer a common intention—a constructive trust approach could not.

In Key Case *Southwell v Blackburn* estoppel also provided a remedy where there was no common intention and thus no possibility of a constructive trust.

As *Southwell* shows, even a successful claimant may receive only a modest award. So too in *Liden v Burton*, where the claimant gave £500 per month to Mr Burton in the belief that she would obtain an interest in a property. Her award of the minimum required to do justice was her money back with interest, reflecting that if she had known her payments would not have achieved an interest in the house, she would have invested the money in an interest-bearing account.[176]

Like constructive trusts, estoppel cases are evidentially risky. They involve adducing evidence that may take the form of vague recollections of verbal assurances given years previously. The credibility of the witnesses and whatever contemporaneous evidence exists are therefore enormously important. Even then, a party may be honestly mistaken, or ascribe meaning to something that had no such meaning at the time. Looking back at a past relationship, particularly in light of the strong feelings accompanying the end of a relationship, can give 'a distorted view',[177] especially when one tries to reframe decisions made out of love and affection into legal categories. As with trusts of land applications, therefore, the risks are significant and, given the stringent approach to remedies, the changes of winning may be easily outweighed by the costs risk involved.

KEY CASE *Southwell v Blackburn* [2014] EWCA Civ 1347

Following her divorce, Mrs Blackburn and her daughters lived in a housing association home under a secure tenancy.[178] She had spent between £15,000 and £20,000 of her divorce settlement of £25,000 on fitting out and furnishing that property as their long-term home. After she began a relationship with Mr Southwell, he and Mrs Blackburn agreed to live together. Mr Southwell bought a house in his sole name. He paid the down payment, and the mortgage was in his sole name. He made the mortgage payments and paid most of the household bills. Mrs Blackburn paid £4,000 to £5,000 as her contribution to the setting up of the new home (which was potentially all that she had left from her divorce settlement) and she and her children moved in. The court found that she was vulnerable, 'taking a big risk, moving from a secure rented house on which she had spent a lot of money, leaving her job and moving her children'.

The court found that Mr Southwell did not want to marry Ms Blackburn in case it gave her a claim to his (much greater) assets. Given his personality, which was shrewd, cautious and guarded, the court could find no clear promise that she would become an equal owner in the house. But, while the assurances involved in estoppel cases have to be referable to property, they do not have to be referable to *ownership*.

---

[176] [2016] EWCA Civ 275.

[177] *Lissimore v Downing* [2003] 2 FLR 308, [47] (HHJ Norris).

[178] It is not easy to evict someone from a secure tenancy. Thus a secure tenancy is a thing of value because it means that the tenant is much less subject to the whims of landlords and the vagaries of the rental market.

The court found that Mr Southwell had said to Mrs Blackburn that 'she would always have a home and be secure in this one', that he was taking on a 'long-term commitment to provide her with a secure home', and otherwise led her to believe that she would have 'the sort of security that a wife would have, in terms of accommodation at the house, and income.' Mr Southwell argued that this meant that he was offering a home only for the duration of the relationship. The Court of Appeal rejected that, holding that these statements were inconsistent with accommodation only for the duration of the relationship. Rather, these were entitlements which would be recognised in the event of breakdown of the relationship, just as the contribution of a wife to the assets of a marriage would be recognised in the event of marital breakdown. (Hayward criticises the judicial consideration of the meaning of these statements, and what it was reasonable for them to convey to Mrs Blackburn, as lacking analytical rigour.[179])

The Court found that these statements had been necessary to persuade Mrs Blackburn to move herself and her children to live with him, as without them she would not have done so. Accordingly, he knew that she would rely on them.

The detriment to Mrs Blackburn 'was not that she embarked upon a relationship with [Mr Southwell] but that she abandoned her secure home in which she had invested and invested what little else she had in a home to which she had no legal title. It is the detrimental reliance which makes the promise irrevocable and leads to the conclusion, at the end of a broad enquiry, that repudiation of the assurance is unconscionable.'

While she had benefited from the arrangement by being able to live rent free and with Mr Southwell's financial support, Mr Southwell was able to benefit from the support of Mrs Blackburn with housekeeping whilst he was furthering his career. His earnings had risen and the house had risen in value significantly. The various asserted benefits, flowing in both directions, were the incidents of the relationship whilst it successfully subsisted rather than direct consequences of reliance upon the promise as to security. In contrast, the assurances that he made were what induced her to move in with him. The Court held that it was unconscionable for him to go back on these.

Remember that the remedy is the minimum necessary to do justice. Here, the court chose to give Mrs Blackburn enough to put her in the equivalent position that she was in before she moved in with Mr Southwell, adjusted for inflation. That was around £28,500.

FOCUS Think Critically

Estoppel or a constructive trust?

The elements of an estoppel claim may sound to you rather like a constructive trust. At some points, it has looked as though the two concepts might be merged, most notably as a result of *Gissing v Gissing*,[180] which has been called 'proprietary estoppel in the guide of a common intention constructive trust'.[181] Indeed, it has been said that 'every common intention constructive trust contains the elements of proprietary estoppel. Another way of putting it would be to say that common intention constructive trust is a sub-set of proprietary estoppel. But that is not how the case law has developed'.[182] In fact, despite their similarities, proprietary estoppel and constructive trusts have run on parallel but unmerged lines. The differences between them may render one more suitable than the other in a particular case.

---

[179] A Hayward, 'Cohabitants, Detriment, and the Potential of Proprietary Estoppel: *Southwell v Blackburn*' [2015, September] *Child and Family Law Quarterly* 303.

[180] *Gissing v Gissing* [1971] Act 886.

[181] D Hayton, 'Constructive Trusts of Homes – A Bold Approach' (1993) 109 *Law Quarterly Review* 485.

[182] *Culliford and Lane v Thorpe* [2018] EWHC 426 Ch (HHJ Paul Matthews).

A constructive trust relates to ownership of property, whereas estoppel is wider; it must relate to property but that does not have to be ownership thereof. In some of the leading cases it relates to the right to inherit property. That is incompatible with the idea of a constructive trust, which is founded on a current common intention that the beneficial interest is already owned by the claimant as well as the respondent. Second, in a constructive trust situation, the interest is being found by the court based on the parties' common intention; estoppel is 'more of a remedy which comes into existence from the date when it is declared by the court'.[183] No intention common to the parties is necessary.

As we see from the estoppel case of *Southwell v Blackburn*, the courts have used both types of claim to address the vulnerabilities of cohabitants. Some commentators have argued that estoppel should have been developed in preference to the expansion of the constructive trust by *Stack v Dowden*. Neither is better than a comprehensive regime of property claims for cohabitants. Nevertheless, estoppel claims may be more useful for many cohabitation disputes in which verbal assurances of some kind have been made, assuming that a causal link between those and the detriment can be shown. Hayward argues that this is because the greater degree of ambiguity of representation or assurance that estoppel tolerates offers 'some judicial recognition and accommodation of the unstructured informality of dealings in this context'.[184] Cohabitants may make representations or assurances over a period of time, and they may use ambiguous language. 'Lovers are more likely to promise in vague terms that they will love and take care of each other forever than to specify the precise benefits which their eternal love will confer.'[185] They may make no representations at all that are referable to property ownership. Rather than engage in consideration of whether a court can impute intention to the parties under a constructive trust, where no such intention can be inferred, a longstanding discussion, estoppel proffers a solution that avoids that issue altogether.

5.8 Statutory remedies under the 1882 and 1970 Acts

So far, we have considered an approach under the Trusts of Land (Appointment of Trustees) Act 1996. However, there are two earlier statutes that can provide assistance in specific situations: the Married Women's Property Act 1882 and the Matrimonial Proceedings and Property Act 1970. We will take each in turn.

5.8.1 Married Women's Property Act 1882

This is the crucially important piece of legislation that gave married women property rights at the end of the nineteenth century, as discussed in Chapter 4. As the name suggests, it is applicable primarily to married people or those who were married, but it applies also to those who were engaged to be married provided that the engagement or marriage ended fewer than three years ago.

---

[183] M Pawlowski, 'Constructive Trusts, Illegal Purpose and Locus Poenitentiae' [2009] 2 *The Conveyancer and Property Lawyer* 145.

[184] A Hayward, 'Cohabitants, Detriment, and the Potential of Proprietary Estoppel: *Southwell v Blackburn*' [2015, September] *Child and Family Law Quarterly* 303.

[185] J Mee, *The Property Rights of Cohabitees* (Hart 1999) 102. Quoted by Hayward, 'Cohabitants, Detriment, and the Potential of Proprietary Estoppel: *Southwell v Blackburn*' [2015, September] *Child and Family Law Quarterly* 303.

Under s17, the court can resolve any disputes over possession of property or ownership of real or personal property (or sale proceeds thereof) but cannot alter those interests, merely declare what they already are. The court applies the same trust principles discussed in this chapter. When assessing the claimant's beneficial interest, the court can take into account any *substantial* contribution in money or money's worth that they have made to the improvement of the property, as long as the court is satisfied that the contributor believed that they had or would as a result acquire an interest in the property. Clearly, whether or not something is a substantial improvement is somewhat subjective and it will be for the claimant to adduce evidence as to the extent and cost of the work and any increase in the property's value. The court will then look at the value of the property prior to the improvement work, and the value afterwards, and credit the claimant with the gain.[186]

The court can injunct a party from disposing of property that is the subject of a pending application.

5.8.2 Matrimonial Proceedings and Property Act 1970

Like the Married Women's Property Act 1882, the Matrimonial Proceedings and Property Act 1970 applies to engaged and formerly engaged couples as well as to married couples. Section 37 states that where a claimant contributes in money or money's worth to the improvement of real or personal property the claimant will be treated as having acquired a share of the beneficial interest (or increased their existing share). The claimant's contribution must be of a substantial nature.

This provision was introduced to reverse the effect of a case called *Pettitt v Pettitt*.[187] Section 65 Civil Partnership Act 2004 provides identical provisions for civil partners.

5.9 Other assets on separation

Chattels—personal belongings, furniture, etc.—are divided in accordance with the same principles of beneficial ownership described in this chapter, starting with the same presumption that the legal owner is the sole beneficial owner. However, while we have seen that an interest in land must be in writing (albeit that this does not prevent a resulting or constructive trust from arising), there are no formalities necessary to create a trust in respect of assets other than land. This means that an express trust can be established verbally. If, despite that, no express declaration exists, then the court will look at *Rosset I* and *II* for a constructive trust, or contribution for a resulting trust. (Contrast this with the position under the Matrimonial Causes Act where the court has wide powers on divorce to redistribute property irrespective of ownership.)

Litigation about chattels is not ideal. In many cases the costs of pursuing a claim are likely to be out of proportion with the value of the chattels in question.

An example of a successful claim for a relatively valuable chattel is found in *Rowe v Prance*, in which the respondent bought a yacht.[188] The claimant did not contribute to the purchase price, but an agreement to share the beneficial interest was inferred from express

---

[186] *Re Nicholson* [1974] 1 WLR 476.
[187] *Pettitt v Pettitt* [1970] AC 777 (HL).
[188] [1999] All ER (D) 496.

discussions (*Rosset I*). She suffered detriment in reliance on that, by giving up her rented home and putting her furniture into storage so they could live in the boat and sail the world together. They broke up before this happened, and she was held to be a beneficial co-owner.

There is a presumption that money in a bank or building society account that is held in joint names will be divided in equal shares, regardless of who put what amount of money in. As a consequence, anything bought using money from the joint account will also be regarded as jointly owned. The presumption can be rebutted by evidence to the contrary. Where an account is in the sole name of one party, the presumption is that they are the sole beneficial owner, and again this presumption can be rebutted by evidence to the contrary. In *Paul v Constance*, Mr Constance was the sole legal owner of a bank account into which damages for personal injury had been paid.[189] He often repeated, however, to Ms Paul, his cohabitant, that 'the money is as much yours as mine'. This was held to be an express declaration of trust, which—as we see in the section above—does not have to be in writing unless it relates to land. Although Scarman LJ describes the case as borderline—not to mention evidentially difficult as Mr Paul had died—the Court of Appeal upheld this finding on appeal in light of the surrounding circumstances. Remember that where there is an express declaration of trust, no detriment is needed.

5.10 Bringing it together: Problems with family property

As we have seen, a cohabitant or former cohabitant seeking to establish a claim in relation to property faces a difficult and expensive route. In this section, we bring together some of the problems and concerns that the chapter has highlighted.

'When a person acts in an unconscionable way towards another, how should a court, in seeking to achieve "practical justice", balance and reconcile values of certainty, consistency arising from precedent, overall coherence in the structure of the law, deference to Parliament on policy issues, and the provision of a remedy appropriate to reverse or prevent harm to the innocent party?'[190] There is no easy answer to that. Ideally, Parliament could have legislated to create a unified, coherent regime applicable to the domestic sphere. But it has not done so. In the absence of legislative action, the House of Lords and its successor the Supreme Court have stepped in (in much the same way as the latter did with nuptial agreements). In widening the scope of constructive trusts, the courts have engaged in what John Dewar has termed the 'familialisation' of family property.[191] By this, he means that the courts have developed a set of trusts principles applicable to family property but not to the commercial context. We see this in the rejection of the resulting trust, and in the approach to inference and the paragraph 69 *Stack* factors, and the move away from the primacy of financial contribution. Hayward argues that familiarisation has

---

[189] [1977] 1 WLR 527.
[190] T Etherton, 'Constructive Trusts and Proprietary Estoppel: The Search for Clarity and Principle' [2009] 2 *The Conveyancer and Property Lawyer* 104.
[191] J Dewar, 'Land, Law, and the Family Home', Chapter 13 in S Bright and J Dewar (eds), *Land Law: Themes and Perspectives* (OUP 1998).

occurred 'inductively', with no clear judicial policy underlying it. It is also piecemeal, as is perhaps inevitable in a common law system. Nevertheless, in her speech in *Stack*, Lady Hale explicitly referred to the social context: the increase in cohabiting relationships and the rise in house ownership. More recently, in *Jones v Kernott*, Lord Walker and Lady Hale state in their joint speech that when a couple purchase a property to live in, this is 'a strong indication of emotional and economic commitment to a joint enterprise'.[192] This is the language of family law.

Whether deliberate or not, even a familialised version of trusts law provides a deeply flawed mechanism for the resolution of property disputes between cohabitants.[193] We are dependent on case law in all its inconsistency. Development is incremental and depends on the right case reaching the higher courts, and on the judges giving clear guidance. However clearly expressed the judgments in our Key Cases are, there are gaps, and important points are obiter. Why no mention of detrimental reliance in *Stack*, *Jones*, or *Abbott*? Does the whole course of dealing apply to intention as well as quantification, as we think? What exactly counts as the domestic sphere to which constructive trusts apply in preference to resulting trusts? How much has the scope of evidence of a common intention inferred from conduct widened since *Rosset*? To what extent are domestic contributions considered—and are they given enough weight? Is the distinction between inferring intention and imputing it simply artificial when couples do not discuss these issues? The factual basis is likely to be heavily disputed. Many years may have passed by since the house in question was bought. It takes a great deal of nerve—or desperation—for a claimant to issue proceedings given these uncertainties, and just as much nerve to defend them. Mr Kernott lost his case: his share of the house was eaten up entirely by his own legal costs and those of the successful Ms Jones. That is because these are civil procedure claims and, as is usual for civil cases, the losing party will be ordered to pay the winner's costs unless at trial they 'beat' any Part 36 settlement offer they made by being awarded more than they would have settled for receiving.

It is certainly the case that, as Hayward points out, the 'current trust framework embraces many elements redolent of family law, including the de facto application of judicial discretion, direct engagement with the concept of fairness and an increasing recognition of relationship dynamics'.[194] However, the requirements surrounding express and inferred common intention are premised on certain assumptions about how cohabiting couples behave, assumptions that are questionable.

Let's just remind ourselves of some of the key findings from the studies discussed at 5.2.2. Hibbs, Barton, and Beswick found that 74 per cent of those living together in their partner's house said they had a claim on the property.[195] Despite this, Douglas, Pearce, and

---

[192] [2011] UKSC 53, [19].

[193] For an extremely interesting discussion of how trusts law may in some cases provide a better outcome for a claimant than a system based on the Matrimonial Causes Act or benefit and loss, see S Gardner, 'Problems in Family Property' (2013) 72(2) *Cambridge Law Journal* 301.

[194] A Hayward, '"Family Property" and the Process of "Familialisation" of Property Law' (2012) 24 *Child and Family Law Quarterly* 284.

[195] M Hibbs, C Barton, and J Beswick, 'Why Marry? Perceptions of the Affianced' [2001] *Family Law* 197, 201.

Woodward found that they had given little thought to the implications of legal ownership, sometimes deliberately:

> cohabitant purchasers show little interest in the significance of joint (or sole) ownership, being more pre-occupied with completing the purchase and the practical details. . . . at the very time that they were making the decision to live together, couples could not simultaneously envisage anything going wrong with their relationships and instinctively did not want to 'plan for failure'. Moreover, several perceived it as unromantic or awkward to make legal provision, for example to protect larger contributions to property purchase.[196]

It is clear that the paragraph 69 list of considerations set out by Lady Hale in *Stack* as being relevant to their whole course of conduct in relation to the property were designed to enable the courts to undertake a holistic analysis of how the parties managed money, so that the court could discern their intentions. In that way, it sought to deviate from the financially-focused prior law to reflect the realities of cohabitants' lives. As Lawson says, 'to make their rights dependent upon their expressed common intention, about a matter they would not usually have thought it necessary to consider, is unrealistic and the cause of frequent and sometimes severe injustice.'[197] The apparently wider post-*Stack* approach to inferring common intention from conduct is therefore to be welcomed. But this is not simple to do. Cohabitants have a range of different models of money management, from joint pooling of money, partial pooling, to no pooling, from equal financial contributions to those proportional to the parties' incomes.[198] They are, as we have seen, a diverse group. As Wong says,

> a cohabiting relationship has to demonstrate that it possesses marriage-like qualities as proof of the requisite commitment in order to warrant legal protection. To assess this, we often see factors such as the length of cohabitation, the nature of the relationship, and the nature and extent of financial arrangements being reproduced in statutes for the court's consideration. However, given the multifarious nature of married and cohabiting relationships, these factors are no more than blunt instruments for shedding light on the complex and nuanced interrelations of couples.[199]

The parties' selection of who pays for what may say nothing about their property intentions. For example, a woman may pay less towards the bills than her partner in light of his greater income and her childcare responsibilities: it does not follow that she would expect a lesser share of a jointly owned house at the end of the relationship. In any case, the lack of legal assistance on the breakdown of a relationship means that the principles expounded in these cases are unknown to the people involved. Instead, couples are finding their own rationales for splitting assets and Tennant et al. found that the most obvious influence when they did so was ownership.[200] This means that the non-financial contributions

---

[196] G Douglas, J Pearce and H Woodward, 'Cohabitants, Property and the Law: A Study of Injustice' (2009) 72(1) *Modern Law Review* 24, 39.

[197] A Lawson, 'The Things We Do for Love: Detrimental Reliance in the Family Home' (1996) 16 *Legal Studies* 218.

[198] C Vogler, 'Managing Money in Intimate Relationships: Similarities and Differences Between Cohabiting and Married Couples' Chapter 4 in J Miles and R Probert (eds), *Sharing Lives, Dividing Assets: An Inter-Disciplinary Study* (Hart 2009).

[199] S Wong, 'Shared Commitment, Interdependency and Property relations: A Socio-Legal Project for Cohabitation' (2012) 24 *Child and Family Law Quarterly* 60.

[200] R Tennant, J Taylor, and J Lewis, *Separating from Cohabitation: Making Arrangements for Finances and Parenting* (Department for Constitutional Affairs research series 2006).

that a party has made to the family which we recognise on divorce and which have economic consequences—child-raising, home-making, caring for an elderly relative—are not weighted in the balance sufficiently, but are dismissed as the sort of things a man or woman does around the house.

5.10.1 Should we reform trusts law?

You may have realised that courts have repeatedly sought to clarify principles so as to enable their better utilisation by cohabitants. The presumption that putting the family home in joint legal names creates a beneficial joint tenancy is also a device. The paragraph 69 factors in *Stack* enable courts to conduct a relatively wide enquiry, albeit constrained by the fact that they must be referable to the house. The Supreme Court was explicit about its rationale: the rise in home ownership and the plight of cohabitants. The preference for a constructive trust rather than a resulting trust in domestic situations give more protection for those who contribute in non-financial terms.

Nevertheless, we have seen that asserting a trust of land or estoppel claim is difficult and expensive, compounded by the uncertain state of law. We therefore need to consider whether we could reform the law in this area to make it more user-friendly. One easy step would be to require parties to complete an express declaration of the beneficial interest in the TR1, although this would not help when one party moves into another's existing home. We could, as have some cases in New Zealand, look at the parties' reasonable expectations, objectively determined. Gardner suggests that the nature of the parties' relationship, rather than their intentions, should be key.[201] This would avoid the need to try to find the parties' intentions and to engage in the sorts of manipulations of intentions evidenced by the false excuse cases. The principles of unjust enrichment could help us here. A claimant would be entitled to restitution based on the retained advantage of the respondent at the claimant's expense.

But a reform of trusts of land would not help cohabitants in relation to other financial consequences arising from the relationship such as loss of earning capacity. They do not present an alternative to a comprehensive scheme of cohabitants' rights. That does not preclude some consideration of whether the any of the principles of trusts law or unjust enrichment should be used as the basis of a cohabitation claim: indeed, some jurisdictions do use unjust enrichment arising from a relationship as the basis of a scheme that looks not merely at real property but also losses and gains arising from other aspects of the relationship.

Of course, a relationship may not break down. It may end with one party's death. Before we consider how we could protect cohabitants, let us consider their position, compared to married couples, when one of them dies.

5.11 Death and inheritance

In this chapter, we have identified the much weaker position of cohabitants compared to married couples at the end of a relationship. As we shall see, this continues when we consider the position when someone in a cohabiting relationship dies without a

---

[201] S Gardner 'Rethinking Family Property' (1993) 109 (April) *Law Quarterly Review* 263.

Will. First, we are going to look at why making a Will is so important and the limits on testamentary freedom, before turning to consider what claims may be made against a deceased person's estate when the deceased has not made reasonable provision for them from their assets.

5.11.1 Making a Will

Different jurisdictions have different rules about how to make a Will. If you do not follow these rules, the resulting Will may be invalid, in which cases the default statutory provisions for those who die without a valid Will (known as the rules of intestacy) will determine who is to inherit.

In England and Wales, the Wills Act 1837 requires that a Will must be in writing and signed by the testator (the person making the Will) in the presence of two adult witnesses who have a clear line of sight of the signing and who are not beneficiaries under the Will or the spouses or civil partners of beneficiaries. In 2020, as a result of the COVID-19 pandemic, the Act was amended to permit Wills to be signed in the virtual presence of two adult witnesses instead of their physical presence. This amendment is intended to be temporary, lasting for two years, although it can be extended.[202]

It should deal with all assets of the testator. The Will may include pecuniary legacies (fixed sums of money to a specified person), specific legacies of a particular chattel, and/or charitable legacies. It should include a residual legacy—what happens to the rest of the estate once the other kinds of legacy (if any) have been distributed. If the Will does not provide for a residuary gift, the residue will be distributed according to the rules of intestacy.

A Will revokes any previous Wills made by the testator. It is not necessary to actively destroy a previous Will, but this is often done. It is not possible to amend a Will just by crossing aspects out. It will require either a new Will to be executed or a codicil to be drawn up and executed in the same way as a Will.

Many Wills are drafted by solicitors, legal executives or probate practitioners. All three are qualified, regulated, and insured. However, drafting a Will is not a 'reserved legal activity' that only lawyers can do. This means that some will writers are unregulated, unqualified, and/or do not carry professional indemnity insurance, although many people do not realise this. While consideration was given to making such work a reserved legal activity, the government declined to do so, citing consumer choice. Some people draft their own Will, and it is possible to purchase precedent kits from stationers for this purpose. However, the risk is that the Will may cause interpretation problems, be wrongly executed (and thus not valid), or not provide the executors (the people charged with carrying out the Will's provisions after the testator's death) with all the powers that they need.

---

[202] Wills Act 1837 (Electronic Communications) (Amendment) (Coronavirus) Order 2020. See Ministry of Justice, *Guidance on Making Wills Using Video-Conferencing* (2020). Available at https://www.gov.uk/guidance/guidance-on-making-wills-using-video-conferencing accessed 8 November 2020.

5.11.2 Testamentary capacity and testamentary freedom

The phrase 'testamentary capacity' refers to the legal and mental ability of a person to make a Will. A person's ability to do so may be affected by their age (minors lack legal capacity), the existence of undue pressure or duress, or a physical or mental disability (mental capacity).

If the testator is physically unable to sign a Will but has mental capacity to make a Will, then the document can be signed at their direction when they are in the same room. If a person has lost mental capacity, for example due to a brain injury or dementia, the Court of Protection (the court that makes decisions about arrangements for people without mental capacity) can authorise the execution of a Statutory Will. This is a Will for someone who cannot make their own, and is useful to assist with tax planning, replacing deceased beneficiaries, and to avoid the effect of an out-of-date Will or the intestacy rules. In deciding whether a Statutory Will should be permitted, the Court of Protection will consider whether the Will is in the person's best interests, a determination that is guided by a checklist of factors set out in s4 Mental Capacity Act 2005.

However, it is not always easy to assess whether a person has the mental capacity to make a Will. The test for determining this is set out in the nineteenth century case of *Banks v Goodfellow*. The cases *Walker v Badmin* and *James v James and others* confirm that this test was not changed by the Mental Capacity Act 2005.[203]

KEY CASE *Banks v Goodfellow* (1870) LR 5 QB 549

The testator's niece challenged the validity of Mr Banks' Will, made in 1863. In 1841 he had been 'confined as a lunatic' and he continued to suffer from delusions that he was being pursued by a man who was dead, and by evil spirits whom he believed to be visibly present, as well as having epileptic fits. Evidence as to his capacity to manage his business affairs was contradictory.

The court held that in order to have testamentary capacity a testator must be able to:

- Understand the nature of the act of making a Will and its effect. However, it is not necessary that he should view his Will with the eye of a lawyer and comprehend its provisions in their legal form.
- Understand the extent of the property of which he is disposing.
- Comprehend and appreciate the claims to which he ought to give effect. (This means that he must be able to identify the people whom he could benefit and their relationship to him.)

'A degree or form of unsoundness which neither disturbs the exercise of the faculties necessary for [the above three points], nor is capable of influencing the result, ought not to take away the power of making a will.'

The fact that those left behind may view a Will as unfair, inappropriate, and hurtful does not matter. If he has testamentary capacity he 'may disinherit . . . his children, and leave his property to strangers to gratify his spite, or to charities to gratify his pride'.[204]

---

[203] [2014] EWHC 21 (Ch) and [2018] EWHC 43 (Ch) respectively.
[204] *Boughton v Knight* (1873) LR 3 P&D 64, 66 (Sir J Hannen).

The issue is whether the testator had capacity, i.e., whether the criteria set out in *Banks v Goodfellow* are satisfied. It is therefore necessary to distinguish between decisions that are the result of mental incapacity and decisions that are simply the result of the testator being 'moved by capricious, frivolous, mean or even bad motives'.[205] The latter does not render the Will invalid. As the court said rather pithily in *Sharp v Adam*,[206] 'an intentional, unjust and unfair will must be upheld if the testator has the capacity to make a rational, just and fair one; but it cannot be upheld if he did not'.

Behind this is the concept of testamentary freedom, the idea that in this jurisdiction, unlike in some others, a person is entitled to leave his estate to whomever he chooses, however his family and friends may feel about that. This is what Cretney has referred to as 'a necessary and desirable incident of the economic power inherent in the ownership of property'.[207] As such, it has, as Brook has shown, 'evolved slowly over time, as people gained greater control over both real and personal property'.[208]

There are, as we shall see, some limitations on testamentary freedom, namely the ability of a family member or dependant of the deceased is a claim under the Intestacy (Provision for Family and Dependants) Act 1975 (see 5.13) in cases where deceased made no reasonable provision for them. In the normal way, 'the instincts and affections of mankind, in the vast majority of instances, will lead men to make provision for those who are the nearest to them in kindred and who in life have been the objects of their affection'.[209] But this is not a requirement of the law.

Of course, a manifestly unfair or surprising Will may invite challenge from unhappily disinherited family and friends, as in *Rea v Rea*.[210]

KEY CASE *Rea v Rea* [2019] EWHC 2434 (Ch)

In 2015, Mrs Rea made a leaving £1,000 each to her three sons, and the rest of her estate, including a house worth £750,000, to her daughter. In 2009 the latter had returned to live with and care for her mother, which she did until the mother died in 2016. The Will stated:

> I declare that my sons do not help with my care and there ha[ve] been numerous calls from me but they are not engaging with any help or assistance. My sons have not taken care of me and my daughter has been my sole carer for many years. Hence should any of my sons challenge my estate I wish my executors to defend any such claim as they are not dependent on me and I do not wish for them to share in my estate save what I have stated in this Will.

---

[205] JR Martyn, A Learmonth, JE Gordon, C Ford, and T Fletcher, *Theobald on Wills* (18th edn, 2016, 1st supplement, Sweet & Maxwell 2018) at Part B, Ch3, Section 1.
[206] *Sharp v Adam [2005] EWHC 1806 (Ch)* at [152]; dictum approved by the Court of Appeal at [2006] EWCA Civ 449 [79].
[207] S Cretney 'Dividing Family Property on Death: Approaches to Reform of Intestacy', Chapter 10 in *Law, Law Reform and the Family* (OUP 1998) 247.
[208] J Brook, 'Testamentary Freedom: Myth or Reality' [2018] 1 *The Conveyancer and Property Lawyer* 19.
[209] *Banks v Goodfellow* (1870) LR 5 QB 549.
[210] [2019] EWHC 2434 (Ch).

The 2015 Will revoked an earlier Will leaving the estate to the four children equally. The brothers challenged the 2015 Will, arguing that their mother could not adequately understand English, did not know or approve of the contents of the Will, and that the Will was the result of undue pressure by the daughter and/or fraudulent calumny (a wonderfully named claim that alleges that the daughter poisoned the testator's mind against her brothers by 'casting dishonest aspersions' on their character so they are cut out of the Will).[211]

The brothers' case failed because there was no evidence to support the claims of undue influence or fraudulent calumny, and the burden of proof was on them. On the contrary, the mother's solicitor had obtained a medical report confirming Mrs Rea's capacity before the Will was signed, which is good practice when it is foreseeable that a Will may be challenged. Both the doctor and lawyer testified that she knew her own mind and understood the Will.

For an example of a successful claim of calumny, see *Christodoulides v Marcou* [2017] EWHC 2632 (Ch).

5.12 Administration of the estate

When a person dies, it is necessary to administer their estate (the assets that they own). These may include properties, unincorporated business interests, shares, investments, bank accounts, cash, and personal chattels such as cars, antiques, furniture, and other household contents and personal belongings. The estate may need to receive the proceeds of life insurance or other policies or monies due under a pension scheme that includes a lump sum payment on death (such as a death in service benefit).

Once the assets of the estate have been established, any debts of the deceased will be paid out of the estate. If the estate is insolvent, then the creditors will be paid in a specific order of priority (residual beneficiaries last) and when the estate runs out of money any debts still not fully paid will never be paid. Debts in the sole name of the deceased cannot be inherited. Debts held jointly with another person, such as a mortgage, credit card, or overdraft, become the sole responsibility of the survivor. Many people carry life insurance for this reason. There may also be taxes to pay on the estate, such as inheritance tax or outstanding lifetime taxes such as capital gains or income tax.

After the debts are paid, what is left, if anything, is distributed in accordance with the deceased's Will or, if there is no Will, in accordance with rules set down by statute.

5.12.1 Dying with a Will

It is usual to appoint two people in the Will as its executors, tasked with the job of administering the deceased person's estate.[212] In order for the executors to have the power to do this work, they will almost always have to obtain a grant of probate from a court. (There is an exception if the estate is worth less than £10,000 or if the deceased owned everything

---

[211] *Re Edwards* [2007] EWHC 1119 (Ch) contains a description of fraudulent calumny.
[212] Two is usual, one is possible but risky (what if they die first?), four is the maximum. Many people appoint a family member and/or friend as well as a professional executor such as a solicitor or probate practitioner.

as a beneficial joint tenant so that it passes to the survivor automatically). Executors owe a fiduciary duty to the creditors and beneficiaries of the estate.

A person who has been named as executor can renounce their appointment as long as they have not started to administer the estate. The court will grant letters of administration to authorise a person to administer an estate when there is a Will but no executor is acting.

There are a number of rules that help executors where the Will does not accurately reflect the assets at the time of death. For example, if the testator made more specific legacies than he could afford then the legacies abate (are reduced) in equal proportions. If the testator left an item as a gift but did not possess it at the time of their death, then the gift will fail: it is not within the estate and cannot be bequeathed. It is already owned by someone else.

5.12.2 Dying intestate

When a person dies without leaving a Will, we call this dying intestate. It is not up to the surviving family who gets what. The estate must be distributed to the relations of the deceased in a strict order of priority set out in a statutory list known as the intestacy rules, found in Parts 3 and 4 of the Administration of Estates Act 1925 as amended. The current rules order of priority is set out in Figure 5.3.

Testamentary freedom or capacity are therefore not relevant where the deceased has made no Will. Inheritance depends on whether the deceased person was married at the time of their death, and what surviving blood relations they have. The intestacy rules reflect not the wishes of the deceased specifically, but are a set of default rules that are generally reflective of majority public opinion on the respective moral and practical entitlements of the various family members of the deceased.

Rather than obtaining a grant of probate, it will be necessary for the person nearest the top of the intestacy list to apply to court for letters of administration which give the applicant the right to administer the estate. Where there is more than one person able to apply, then it depends on who makes the application first. As with a Will, all the assets of the deceased are 'called in' and any debts paid before the estate is distributed.

Under the intestacy rules, when a married person dies without a Will, their spouse or civil partner inherits the first £270,000.[213] If there are no children, they take the entire estate. They also receive all of the deceased's personal possessions. These are defined in s55(1) Administration of Estates Act 1925 as tangible moveable property other than property consisting of money or securities for money, or that which was used solely or mainly for business purposes or solely as an investment. If the deceased also had children, the children together receive half of the value of the estate over £270,000.

When an unmarried/widowed person dies, the children inherit the entire estate. If there are no children, then the estate goes to any surviving parents of the deceased. If there are none, the estate goes in turn to other relations: surviving siblings or their issue;[214] if none then to surviving half-siblings or their issue; if none, then to any surviving grandparents; and so on down a list. Ultimately, if a deceased person living in England or Wales had no relations, the estate is bona vacantia: it passes to the Crown and is used by the government.

---

[213] Administration of Estates Act 1925 (Fixed Net Sum) Order 2020. The amount changes periodically.

[214] Direct descendants such as children and grandchildren.

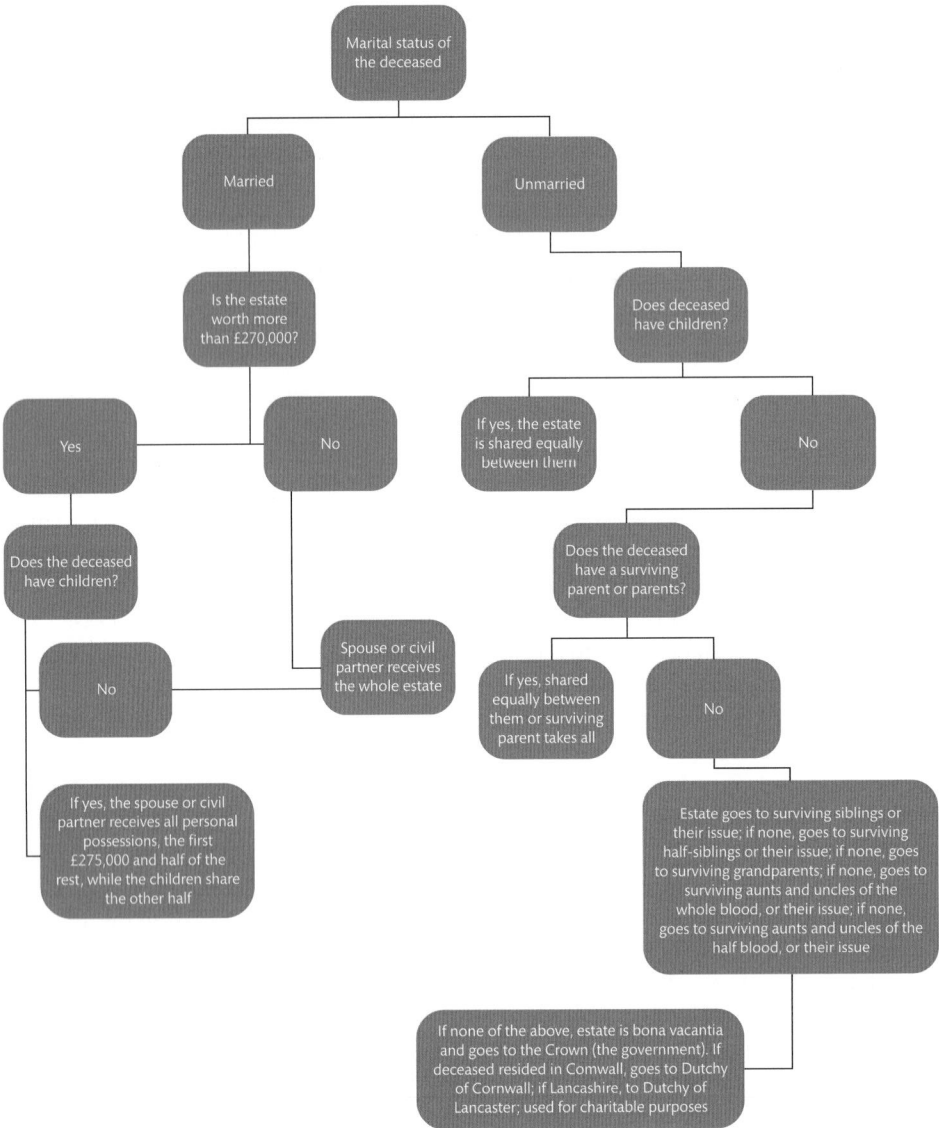

FIGURE 5.3 Intestacy order of priority

If the deceased died in Cornwall or Lancaster, however, the estate passes not to the Crown but to the Duchy of these areas, who use the sums locally for charitable causes. It is very rare for a person to die with no relatives in the statutory list, and in the year 2017–2018 the Crown received only £12,215,000 in this way for deaths in England and Wales.[215]

---

[215] HM Procurator General and Treasury Solicitor, *Accounts for the Crown's Nominee for the year ended 31 March 2019* (HC 2178). Available at https://www.gov.uk/government/publications/crown-nominee-account-2018-to-2019 accessed 2 February 2020.

5.12.3 Intestacy: The state's choice

The intestacy rules provide a default set of entitlements. However, it is by no means clear what principles underlie the choices that the state has made about who inherits. No rationales or objectives are evident from legislation. Cooke argues that it is not possible or desirable to separate out the various potential aims of the law.[216] Nevertheless, the inclusion of certain categories and the exclusion of others reflects certain values.

Early intestacy provisions, rather like early divorce laws, addressed the preoccupations of landowning families. As Burns explains, they 'reflected the desire to maintain a family dynasty and retain property within the family, emphasising the inheritance and well-being of legitimate children, primarily male children, as immediate heirs'.[217] As such, intestacy was based on the idea of providing an endowment for future generations. It has only been since 1925 that the position of spouses has been stronger than that of children. By that time, Burns says, dynastic inheritance down the male line 'was no longer considered an appropriate justification because it adversely affected widows and did not accord with expectations about how inheritance ought to work.' Mid-twentieth-century intestacy rules were drawn up by reference to what people usually did in their Wills so that they reflected the majority view of society. A survey of Wills submitted to probate showed that a spouse-focused scheme was likely to reflect the subjective intentions of most intestate people.[218] But improving the lot of spouses meant that provision for children would be reduced, and this was the subject of some concern.

We have not so far spoken of the position of cohabitants. That is because the intestacy rules reflect marital and blood relationships only.

FOCUS Think Critically

The position of cohabitants

You may have noticed that Figure 5.1 does not feature cohabitants at all. That is because the intestacy rules do not mention cohabitants: on the death of a partner the unmarried cohabitant receives nothing. Only blood relations (and persons legally adopted into the family) inherit. This is a hangover from the Administration of Estates Act 1925. In 2011 the Law Commission recommended that certain cohabitants be brought into intestacy provision because of the growing number of cohabitants, greater public acceptance of cohabitation, and concern about the lack of awareness of the consequences of intestacy.[219] They suggested the inclusion of unmarried couples who had cohabited for at least five years or, if they have a child or children together, had been living in the same household for at least two years. However, while most of the Law Commission's recommendations were implemented by the Inheritance and Trustees' Powers Act 2014, this aspect of the intestacy rules was not altered.

---

[216] Elizabeth Cooke, 'Wives, Widows and Wicked Step-Mothers: A Brief Examination of Spousal Entitlement on Intestacy' (2009) 21(4) *Child and Family Law Quarterly* 423.
[217] F Burns, 'Surviving Spouses, Surviving Children and the Reform of Total Intestacy Law in England and Scotland: Past, Present and Future' (2013) 33 *Legal Studies* 85, 88.
[218] F Burns, 'Surviving Spouses, Surviving Children and the Reform of Total Intestacy Law in England and Scotland: Past, Present and Future' (2013) 33 *Legal Studies* 85, 96.
[219] Law Commission, *Intestacy and Family Provision Claims on Death* (Law Comm No. 331, 2011) Part 8.

The Commission also recommended that provision for spouses and civil partners change in two ways. First, it recommended that a spouse without children should be able to retain the whole of the deceased's estate rather than the first £450,000 plus half of the rest, with the other half going to the next in line of intestacy after children. Second, where there were children, the spouse would receive the first £250,000 (as it then was) and only a life interest in half of what was over that. Both of these things were amended by the 2014 Act, so that, as is the case now, spouses without children retain the whole estate, and those with children take half of anything above £250,000 (now £270,000) absolutely. The intention behind the Law Commission's proposals was therefore an improvement in the position of both spouses and cohabitants at the expense of other relations. The legislative outcome was an improvement in the position of spouses only. Yet, for many, the family tree is complex, with divorce, remarriage, cohabitation, stepchildren, and half-siblings. The intestacy rules do not reflect this complexity, privileging spouses and direct descendants over others who may, in terms of affection, have been closer to the deceased.

The rules do not take into account the closeness of a relationship, need, or the many different ways in which people may conduct their relationships.

Research has shown that most people believe that cohabitants should inherit in the event of intestacy.[220] Subsequently, various members of the House of Lords concerned with cohabitation reform have attempted unsuccessfully to reform the law relating to intestacy.[221]

Imagine, now, that you are unaware of the legal differences in the position of married couples and cohabitants, as many people are.[222] You and your partner are also like the majority of adults in the United Kingdom, in that neither of you has a Will.[223] Perhaps this is because you believed the common law marriage myth, or you and your partner always intended to make a Will but simply did not get around to it.

On the death of your partner, you are in for a terrible, distressing, shock. You get nothing.

You may resort to a claim under the Inheritance (Provision for Family and Dependants) Act 1975, if you qualify. You may be able to assert a constructive or resulting trust over the family home, although we have seen how difficult that is. But would it not have been better if your partner had simply got around to making a Will?

5.12.4 Legal consequences of death

Now that we have seen how a person's estate is administered on their death, we need to consider other consequences arising from this death, both legal and practical.

Who is next of kin?

When a person is married, it may be common to refer to their spouse or civil partner as next of kin and respect that person's right to make decisions if their spouse is unable to do so. But, with the exception of some situations relating to children, naming someone as

---

[220] E.g. C Williams, G Potter, and G Douglas, 'Cohabitation and Intestacy: Public Opinion and Law Reform' [2008, December] *Child and Family Law Quarterly* 499; and A Barlow, C Burgoyne, E Clery, and J Smithson, 'Cohabitation and the Law: Myths, Money and the Media', in A Park, J Curtice, K Thomson, M Phillips, MC Johnson, and E Clery (eds), *British Social Attitudes: The 24th Report* (Sage 2008).

[221] For example, Lord Marks' and Lord Lester's cohabitation bills, discussed at 5.14.5.

[222] See 5.14.2 of this chapter.

[223] Figures vary by survey from about 54 per cent to about 60 per cent of adults without a Will.

your 'next of kin' creates no rights for that person because it is not a recognised legal status in England and Wales. Nevertheless, there are some situations when references to 'next of kin' are often used, such as in medical settings and on death.

The naming of a person on hospital or care home records as 'next of kin' creates no particular rights for that person, although it acts as consent to the hospital or home to disclose information about the patient to the person named. If a person wants to nominate someone to make decisions when they cannot do so, then they may, if they have legal capacity to do so, make a lasting power of attorney appointing their chosen person as attorney, able to make decisions pertaining to their health and well-being. This is subject to the safeguard that medical professionals may refer the issue to court if there is disagreement about what is in the person's best interests. Similarly, a person can appoint a property and financial affairs attorney to deal with their assets. Where a person has already lost mental capacity to make a decision, then the court can appoint a 'deputy' to manage their affairs. Those acting under powers of attorney or deputyships must act in the best interests of the person concerned. The Court of Protection oversees this, and rules on any disputes.

On death, one person may deal with the funeral directors, coroner, or other official organisations. Generally, this work will fall to the closest relation, but there is no law requiring that. Taking on this role confers no rights or responsibilities and has no effect on inheritance, which falls to be dealt with under a Will (by the executor) or the intestacy rules. If there is a dispute about a body, then a court would become involved. The relevant law is as set out by Hale J in *Buchanan v. Milton*:

> There is no right of ownership in a dead body. However, there is a duty at common law to arrange for its proper disposal. This duty falls primarily upon the personal representatives of the deceased. An executor appointed by will is entitled to obtain possession of the body for that purpose even before the grant of probate. Where there is no executor, that same duty falls upon the administrators of the estate, but they may not be able to obtain an injunction for delivery of the body before the grant of letters of administration.[224]

Sometimes, alongside a Will, the deceased leaves a written document setting out how they would like a funeral to happen. These are not binding in law, although those left may consider them morally binding.

Jointly owned property on death

At 5.3.1 we discussed that one can hold the beneficial interest in a jointly owned property as either tenants in common or joint tenants. As described in that section, on the death of a joint tenant, the surviving co-owner inherits the entirety of the property, and it does not get distributed under a Will or the intestacy rules. In the case of a tenant in common, the deceased's share does fall under their Will to whomever they have named as their beneficiary. If they die intestate then it passes under the intestacy rules.

---

[224] [1999] 2 FLR 844, 845-6, references omitted. Citing *Williams v Williams* (1881) 20 ChD 659; *Rees v Hughes* [1946] KB 517; *Sharp v Lush* (1879) 10 ChD 468, 472; *Dobson v North Tyneside Health Authority and Another* [1997] 1 FLR 598, 602, obiter). For an example of difficulties making arrangements for the disposal of the body of notorious Moors murderer Ian Brady, see *Oldham Metropolitan Borough Council & Ors v Makin & Ors* [2017] EWHC 2543 (Ch).

The situation is the same for other assets held as beneficial joint tenants such as a joint bank account. Here, the contents of the account would usually pass under the survivorship rule to the remaining joint owner, and not fall under a Will or the intestacy rules. It is possible for a person to claim that the parties held the account not as beneficial joint tenants but as tenants in common, or on trust for the deceased only, and that a proportion of the money in the account, or perhaps all of it, falls to be distributed and does not pass by survivorship.[225]

SCENARIO 2

Illustration 4: Helen and Cherry

Let's return to Helen and Cherry. Helen has died, and Cherry, her cohabitant, is worried. Helen did not have a Will. The effect of the intestacy rules will be that Helen's children inherit the whole of Helen's estate between them: This includes money in her bank accounts, investments, her car, her furniture, her personal belongings such as jewellery: even her toothbrush, her clothes, her photographs and mementos. All of this can be taken by her children.

Fortunately, in this scenario Cherry and Helen held as beneficial joint tenants and the survivorship rule operates so that the house does not fall into Helen's estate and is not passed to the children. Any bank accounts in joint names would also pass to Cherry. But this is, as you know, a fictional scenario. In reality, Helen may have held the house as sole legal owner, meaning that Cherry would have to establish a constructive trust or estoppel to stay there.

This is the result of a cohabitant dying without a Will. For want of a few hundred pounds, or even the cost of a Will kit from a stationer, Helen has done incalculable harm to the woman she loved.

Death and taxes

Inheritance tax is a tax on the assets of the deceased person. The tax is currently 40 per cent and is paid only on the value of the estate above a certain threshold, currently £325,000. It is usually paid by the deceased's estate before the estate is distributed to the heirs.

Inheritance tax can be contentious. Newspapers have run campaigns against it and political parties promised to reduce or abolish it.[226] However, it is a contribution to public funds. Gifts to spouses and civil partners are not subject to inheritance tax, and nor is some business property, agricultural property, and charitable gifts. As a result, in 2017–2018 only 3.9 per cent of estates need to pay the tax.[227] This was lower than the previous year's figure of 4.6 per cent because a new exemption introduced for main residences in certain circumstances reduced the number of estates exceeding £350,000.

Although the proportion of inheritance tax payers is small, it is sensible to do some tax planning in preparation for old age, particularly if a person may need to pay for their personal care or care home fees. Tax planning may involve making gifts while alive so as to reduce or avoid inheritance tax. There are strict rules surrounding this, and people cannot

---

[225] For an example, see *Drakeford v Cotton & Another* [2012] EWHC 1414 (Ch).

[226] See, for example E Agyemang, 'Inheritance Tax: What Does the Future Hold?' (*Financial Times*, 11 July 2019).

[227] The latest available statistics are for 2017–2018 and can be found at https://www.gov.uk/government/statistics/inheritance-tax-statistics-commentary accessed 7 November 2020.

intentionally deprive themselves of assets so as to avoid care fees, for example. Some tax may also be payable on gifts (depending on their value) if the deceased does not survive for at least seven years after making the gift.

The effect of death on guardianship of children

It is possible for a person with parental responsibility[228] to appoint a guardian or guardians to look after their children in the event of their death. This must be done in writing and is often done in a Will. The guardian will have parental responsibility for the children. If the person appointing the guardian changes his or her mind, they can revoke the appointment.[229] It is possible for a person who has been appointed as a guardian to refuse their appointment within a reasonable period of time after the appointment takes effect.[230]

The appointment of a guardian will not take effect where there is any other person with parental responsibility still alive, unless there was an order in force that named the deceased person as the person with whom the children lived (which could be under a child arrangements order, previous guardianship order, or special guardianship order). If one of these orders was in place, the guardianship takes effect and the guardian shares parental responsibility with the existing holders of parental responsibility. In the event of a conflict between those who hold PR, it will be necessary to make an application to court for an order such as a child arrangements order, prohibited steps order, or specific issues order, all of which fall under s8 Children Act 1989.[231]

If the deceased person was the only person with parental responsibility for the child, and either they made no Will or they did but failed to appoint a guardian, then someone will need to make an application to court for parental responsibility. This could be an application for parental responsibility by a father (s4 Children Act 1989), second female parent (s4ZA) or step-parent (s4A), or an appointment under s5 for guardianship. All of these will give parental responsibility.[232] Although parental responsibility can be obtained by someone with whom the child lives under a child arrangements order, that kind of parental responsibility only lasts for the duration of the order and may thus be less desirable in the circumstances. If the child has no person able to care for them, then the state will step in.[233] In the interim, s3(5) Children Act 1989 gives a general power to any person who does not have parental responsibility for a child but who has care of that child to do 'what is reasonable in all the circumstances of the case for the purpose of safeguarding or promoting the child's welfare'.

Note that an appointment of the deceased's spouse or civil partner as guardian is automatically revoked when the parties cease to be spouses on the granting of a divorce decree absolute, or on annulment, unless the document appointing the guardian says otherwise.

---

[228] This could be a parent, existing guardian, or a Special Guardian (see Chapter 12).
[229] Section 6 Children Act 1989. Even if the appointment was made by Will, revocation does not require the making of a new Will.
[230] Section 6(5) Children Act 1989.
[231] See Chapter 10.
[232] Parental responsibility and its acquisition is discussed in Chapter 8.
[233] See Chapters 11 and 12.

Effect of marriage or divorce on a Will

It is sensible to make a new Will on marriage and on divorce. Unless a Will is expressed to be in contemplation of marriage, subsequent marriage will automatically revoke the Will. Unless a new Will is made, the intestacy rules will apply.

When decree absolute is obtained on divorce, any appointment of the former spouse or civil partner as trustee or executor is void. Any legacy to them also takes effect as though the former spouse or civil partner had died on the day of decree absolute, meaning that the legacy skips them and falls into the residue of the estate. However, it is possible to make a Will that specifically says that those provisions are to survive divorce.

5.12.5 Contentious probate

It is increasingly common to challenge the validity of a Will. For lawyers, this type of work is called 'contentious probate'. In 2018, there were 86 contested probate cases filed, up 8 per cent from the number seen in 2017 (80 cases)[234] and this figure does not include related actions such as applications to remove trustees or executors or Inheritance Act applications (see 5.13). In fact, the proportion of challenges remains small compared to the number of estates subject to probate—there are about a quarter of a million grants of representation (probate or letters of administration) each year—even when we take into account that many more cases will have settled without court proceedings being commenced and are not therefore counted within the statistics. Nevertheless, contested probate is an area of growth in legal practice.[235]

There are several potential reasons this.

1. It may in part be attributable to the increasing numbers of people who live with dementia, as this this can raise questions about that person's capacity to execute a Will ('testamentary capacity'), their understanding of its contents, or their susceptibility to be influenced by another person or be the victim of fraud.

2. More people are divorcing and remarrying, or living as without marriage as cohabitants. There may be half-siblings, stepchildren, and assorted other relatives. The complexity of the family tree may give more scope for rival claims and bad feelings.

3. People may be becoming more litigious.

4. Estates may be more valuable and thus worth fighting over. If the deceased owned a property in London, for example, the value may be considerable.

5. People may be relying on inheritance to address their own financial weaknesses, such as if they have inadequate pension provision in later life, or to help get young relations on the property ladder.

---

[234] Ministry of Justice, *Family Court Statistics Quarterly, England and Wales: Annual 2018 including October to December 2018* (March 2019). This data is not included in more recent releases.

[235] An article that shows the variety of different types of probate disputes including Will validity and claims against an estate is 'Top 10 Contentious Trust and Probate Cases of 2018' (Kingsley Napley blog 15 January 2019). Available at https://www.kingsleynapley.co.uk/insights/blogs/dispute-resolution-law-blog/top-10-contentious-trust-and-probate-cases-of-2018 accessed 7 November 2020.

6. Some people make homemade Wills, perhaps using a precedent kit purchased from a stationery shop. These may be drafted in a way that is ambiguous or unclear.

7. More contentious probate cases are reported in the newspapers. This may encourage people to make applications.

8. People may allow their beliefs about fairness to lead them into litigation that they are bound to lose, because they disagree that people's wishes 'can be unexpected, inexplicable, unfair, and even improper' but still be valid.[236]

The intestacy rules themselves cannot be challenged. It is possible to challenge the *applicability* of them to certain people in the statutory list by doubting someone's blood relationship or the validity of a marriage, or by locating a missing Will.

If the Will is valid, or relationships cannot be challenged, there is one further route that can be taken, which is to make a claim under the Inheritance (Provision for Family and Dependants) Act 1975, commonly known as the Inheritance Act. This is not a challenge to the validity of a Will or its applicability to relatives. It is a claim that the deceased did not provide adequately for the applicant, and should have done so.

5.13 Inheritance Act claims

An application under the Inheritance (Provision for Family and Dependants) Act 1975 is an application that the applicant should receive financial provision from a deceased person's estate because the deceased's Will or the intestacy rules failed to make reasonable financial provision for them *and* that failure is unreasonable. The public policy behind this is that the law should not cast onto the public purse obligations which ought to be met by other family members.[237]

The Act's predecessor was the Inheritance (Family Provision) Act 1938, and that was introduced, repeatedly, as a private member's bill before obtaining government support and passing with very little objection.[238] Members of Parliament seem to have been primarily concerned with what they saw as unjust dispositions neglecting meritorious applicants: women whose husbands had run off with another woman, sons who had worked the family farm, small shopkeepers who 'build up a small fortune, and one of the things that occurs is a second marriage in old age, or an old man's caprice, or some kind of injustice is committed', but in respect of which 'they bury their heads in poverty and go on suffering, while all the world supposes that there must be some valid reason for the disinheritance.'[239] Interestingly, these calls to fairness are not reflected in interpretations of the current law, as discussed.

The objections, such as they were, were founded on its interference with testamentary freedom: that an award of money under the Act 'can only be obtained by taking it away

---

[236] *Gill v Woodall* [2010] EWCA Civ 1430 at [28] (Lord Neuberger MR).
[237] We also see the same policy objective cited as a reason for judicial scrutiny of nuptial agreements. See Chapter 4's discussion of the case of *Hyman v Hyman*.
[238] See *Hansard* 28 June 1937 vol 325, col 1758.
[239] Miss Rathbone, *Hansard* 05 November 1937 vol 328, col 1308.

from someone whom the testator definitely wished to receive it' and thus 'thwart[ed] a testator's dying wish.'[240] But this is not always the case, for two reasons. First, the Inheritance Act applies equally to those who dies intestate. Second, given the rising number of blended families, remarriages, and divorces, the deceased's Will may have become out of date and thus not reflect what the testator would have wanted at the time of his death. Note that the deceased must have been domiciled in England for a claim to be made.

It seems to have been anticipated that the numbers of such disputes likely to come before the courts would be few in number. While accurate statistics on the current levels of Inheritance Act disputes are hard to obtain, it appears that the number of claims is growing.[241] This may in part be due to the widening of the categories of applicants on several occasions.

Before making any claim, it is sensible to note the litigation risk involved, particularly the costs risk. Unlike in many family cases, such disputes fall under the Civil Procedure Rules and as such the starting point under CPR 44.3(2)(a) is that costs follow the event, i.e., that the losing party pays (most of) the winner's costs. In inheritance disputes, the losing applicant's costs may be paid from the deceased's estate instead if the applicant successfully persuades the court that the need for litigation was caused by the conduct of the deceased and the circumstances afford reasonable grounds for investigation. However, this is by no means certain and anyone contemplating litigation takes a significant financial risk. This perhaps explains why mediation and arbitration are popular means of avoiding court in this area.[242]

5.13.1 What provision can be made?

Under s2, the court can:

- Order the deceased's net estate to pay the applicant periodical payments for any specified term.[243]
- Order the deceased's net estate to pay the applicant a lump sum.
- Order the transfer of property to the applicant (or order the applicant to buy property for this purpose).
- Order the settlement of property on trust for the benefit of the applicant (or order the applicant to buy property for this purpose).
- Vary an ante-nuptial or postnuptial settlement made in the deceased's marriage (including such a settlement made by Will) if that variation is for the benefit of the surviving spouse, any child of that marriage, or any person who was treated by the

[240] Major Dower, *Hansard* 05 November 1937 volume 328, col 1302.
[241] This is because both the family and chancery courts have jurisdiction and claims may be heard at many different locations, and many disputes will never get to court, but are resolved through negotiation. For a fuller explanation of why accurate statistics are hard to obtain, see B Rich, 'Statistics and Headlines in Legal News: Controlling the Surges' (*Transparency Project* 25 August 2017). Available at http://www.transparencyproject.org.uk/statistics-and-headlines-in-legal-news-controlling-the-surges/ accessed 9 February 2020.
[242] The episode titled 'Mediation' of the BBC Radio 4 series 'Behind Closed Doors' provides a realistic dramatisation of a mediation in an inheritance dispute.
[243] Net means after payment of tax and other debts owed by the estate.

deceased as a child of the family in relation to that marriage. There are identical provisions for civil partnerships.

- Vary an existing order varying the trusts on which the deceased's estate is held, whether under the Will or intestacy provisions. (This may apply where the deceased's estate is held on trust for a minor.)

5.13.2 Who can apply?

Under s1(1) of the Act, an application can only be made by the deceased's:

- *Spouse or civil partner: s1(1)(a).* A party to a void marriage or civil partnership would not inherit under the intestacy rules as those relate to valid marriages and partnerships only. However, they can make a claim under this Act as long as they entered into the void marriage 'in good faith' (s25(4)) and their purported marriage had not been recognised by as void by a court before the death.

- *Former spouse or civil partner (s1(1)(b))* who has not remarried/repartnered, as long as there is no clean break in their financial remedy order on divorce. Clean break provisions are those which terminate the parties' claims against one another under the Inheritance (Provision for Family and Dependants) Act 1975. Where one party is receiving spousal maintenance from another at the time of the latter's death, there will be no clean break of the recipient's claims, so the recipient may seek to replace the spousal maintenance that is lost on the payer's death by making a claim under this Act.

- *Children of the deceased (s1(1)(c)).* This refers to the relationship between the deceased and the applicant, and not the age of the applicant: a child can be an adult child. An illegitimate child (that is, one born outside marriage) is included (s25(1)), as is a child *in utero* at the time of the parent's death. A child adopted by the deceased can claim, as he or she is treated for all purposes as if he was the child of the adopters.[244] It follows that a child who is adopted out of the family is no longer a child of the biological parent and would not fall within this subsection.

- *A person treated by the deceased as a child of the family: s(1)(1)(d).* A child of the family is a child who, although not the genetic child of the deceased, is part of a family formed by a marriage or civil partnership of the deceased—i.e., stepchildren. In 2014, the section was widened to include any child 'in which the deceased at any time stood in the role of a parent'. This can include situations in which the family comprised only two people: the applicant and the deceased person. A child may be a child of the family in relation to more than one family.

- *Cohabitants of more than 2 years: s1(1)(ba).* Whereas the intestacy rules make no provision for cohabitants, the 1975 Act does do so. Protection for cohabitants was added by s2 Law Reform (Succession) Act 1995, following a recommendation by the Law Commission in its report *Family Law: Distribution on Intestacy*.[245] It aligned the Act with those cohabitants entitled to bring actions under the Fatal Accidents Act 1976.

---

[244] Sections 66 and 67 of the Adoption and Children Act 2002.
[245] Law Commission, *Family Law: Distribution on Intestacy* (Law Com No 187, 1989).

In order to be eligible, the applicant has to have been living in the same household as the deceased; in *Gully v Dix*, the Court of Appeal held that 'household' had the same meaning as in the divorce case of *Santos v Santos* (see Chapter 3).[246] They must also have been living as though they were the husband or wife or civil partner of the deceased for the whole of two years ending immediately before the date when the deceased died. This does not require marriage or civil partnership; rather, it describes a relationship akin to that of spouses. We can see this from Neuberger J's judgment in Key Case *Re Watson*.

- *A person being maintained (s1(1)(e))*. Anyone who, immediately before the death of the deceased, was being maintained, either wholly or partly, by the deceased may make a claim, but this section applies only to those who do not fall under any of the other classes of applicant. A person is being maintained if the deceased 'was making a *substantial contribution* in money or money's worth towards the reasonable needs of the applicant other than a contribution made for full valuable consideration pursuant to an arrangement of a commercial nature'.[247] An example of an arrangement of a commercial nature would be if the applicant was the lodger or paid carer of the deceased. If that is the case, then it will be necessary to consider whether they gave full valuable consideration for what they received from the deceased: if they did so, they were not maintained.

The contribution made by the deceased must be to the reasonable needs of the applicant (such as housing, groceries, bills, etc.) and not to frivolities.

KEY CASE *Re Watson (Deceased)* [1999] 1 FLR 878

The applicant, Miss Griffiths, had 30-year relationship with Mr Watson, but they did not live together until 1985 when their respective parents had died and thus no longer needed their care. At that time, Ms Griffiths moved in with Mr Watson. Their arrangement was that Mr Watson would continue working and Ms Griffiths would be responsible for the housekeeping, washing, shopping, cooking and gardening, and for paying roughly half of the utility bills. He had promised marriage but she declined, saying that she wanted to keep her independence. While their relationship had in the early years been sexual, it was no longer so. In 1990 Miss Griffiths bought a house using her savings and inheritance, which remained empty.

After ten years of cohabitation, the deceased died intestate and his estate was bona vacantia (see Figure 5.1). Miss Griffiths brought a claim based on having been maintained by Mr Watson, or in the alternative that she had, for more than two years, lived in the same household as Mr Watson 'as the wife of the deceased'. Do not forget that this does not require marriage or civil partnership but describes a relationship akin to that of spouses.

Neuberger J held that:

- 'When considering whether two people are living together as [though they were] husband and wife, it would be wrong to conclude that they do so simply because their relationship is one which a husband and wife could have. If the test were as wide as that, then, bearing in

---

[246] *Gully v Dix* [2004] EWCA Civ 139; *Santos v Santos* [1972] Fam 247.
[247] Section 1(3) as amended by the Inheritance and Trustees' Powers Act 2014 and relating to deaths after 1 October 2014.

mind the enormous variety of relationships that can exist between husband and wife, virtually every relationship between a man and a woman living in the same household would fall
within s1(1A). . . . the court should ask itself whether, in the opinion of a reasonable person
with normal perceptions, it could be said that the two people in question were living together as husband and wife; but, when considering that question, one should not ignore the
multifarious nature of marital relationships.'

· 'I have reached the conclusion that Miss Griffiths did live "as the . . . wife" of Mr Watson. From the
time they met until Mr Watson's death, a period of over 30 years, each appears to have enjoyed a
relationship with the other which was . . . closer than with any other person . . . . For over the last
10 years of that relationship, they lived alone together. . . . It is not unusual for a happily married
husband and wife in their mid-fifties . . . not merely to have separate bedrooms, but to abstain
from sexual relations. . . . The fact that Mr Watson proposed marriage and Miss Griffiths rejected
it does not materially assist the contrary argument. It confirms that the relationship was both
sufficiently close to justify a proposal of marriage and strong enough for the parties to remain
living together for a substantial time notwithstanding its rejection.'

He therefore held that Miss Griffiths did meet the cohabitation requirement and also held that the
lack of provision from Mr Watson's estate had not been reasonable (see 5.12.3). This meant that she
was entitled to provision from his estate. The court considered the factors in s3 of the Act. She could
sell the house she owned, but as she was 67 years old her reasonable need was a for a bungalow,
which would be more expensive. She would need a top-up of capital for the bungalow purchase
and for fitting it out. Although she lived very frugally, she also reasonably needed an extra £2,500
per year to top up her income.

As she fell under the Act as a cohabitee, it was not necessary to consider whether she was also
being maintained. However, Neuberger J did go on to address this, holding that she was partly
maintained because he was providing her with a home, free of charge, save to the extent that she
contributed towards the outgoings that she also used. However, he was not making 'a substantial contribution . . . towards the reasonable needs' of Miss Griffiths because she owned an empty
house in the same town. She did not therefore succeed on this part of her claim.

5.13.3 Reasonable financial provision

Section 1(1) provides that the applicant may apply to the court for an order 'on the ground
that the disposition of the deceased's estate effected by his Will, or the law relating to
intestacy, or the combination of his Will and that law, is not such as to make reasonable
financial provision for the applicant'.

Thus, in order to determine whether a claim should be successful, it is first necessary
to establish that the Will or intestacy did not make reasonable financial provision for the
applicant. This is inherently tied up with what could have been made, and this depends
upon the nature of the applicant's relationship with the deceased.

For all applicants other than spouses and civil partners, the court can order that they
receive 'such financial provision as would be reasonable in all the circumstances of the
case for the applicant to receive for his/her maintenance'. In assessing whether the Will
or intestacy made reasonable provision, the standard is whether they received what was
reasonable in all the circumstances for his/her *maintenance*.

Maintenance is not defined in the Act. It includes a person's everyday living costs, such
as the cost of rent or mortgage, bills, and food. 'The level at which maintenance may be

provided for is clearly flexible and falls to be assessed on the facts of each case. It is not limited to subsistence level' but nor can it 'extend to any or every thing which it would be desirable for the claimant to have'.[248] In *Lewis v Warner*, the court held that maintenance could also refer to 'other forms of assistance with the requirements of daily life. If, therefore, a person is in want of a particular thing to sustain a reasonable quality of life, the provision of it could possibly represent "maintenance" regardless of his financial means.' In that case, the applicant, who was in poor health, was 'in want of' the right to buy, for market value, the home that he had shared with his deceased partner because it meant that he could remain in the area in which he had always lived, near to shops, and near to a neighbour who was a doctor and who checked on him every morning.[249]

Spouses and civil partners are in a better position. The court can order that they receive 'such financial provision as it would be reasonable in all the circumstances of the case for them to receive, *whether or not* that provision is required for his/her maintenance' (s1(2)(a)). This preferential position also applies to those who were judicially separated but where at the date of death the separation was not continuing. The court also has a discretion to apply the more generous standard to those who fall within s14 of the Act, a category that includes spouses and former spouses (and civil partners) where the deceased died within a year of decree absolute, nullity, or judicial separation but where no financial remedy order had been made.

The burden of proof is on the applicant to show that the provision made by the Will or intestacy was unreasonable in the circumstances. It could be that although the provision made was ungenerous by the above standards, that lack of generosity was objectively reasonable when one turns to the factors set out in s3(1) of the Act. This section contains a list of factors to which the court *must* have regard in determining, first, whether reasonable financial provision was made, and second, if reasonable financial provision was not made, what should be made. The court assesses these criteria as they exist at the date of the hearing.[250]

These criteria are:

(a) the financial resources and financial needs which the applicant has or is likely to have in the foreseeable future;

(b) the financial resources and financial needs which any other applicant for an order under s2 of this Act has or is likely to have in the foreseeable future;

(c) the financial resources and financial needs which any beneficiary of the estate of the deceased has or is likely to have in the foreseeable future;

(d) any obligations and responsibilities which the deceased had towards any applicant for an order under the said s2 or towards any beneficiary of the estate of the deceased;

(e) the size and nature of the net estate of the deceased;

---

[248] Key Case *Ilott v Blue Cross* at [14]–[15] (Lord Hughes).
[249] [2016] EWHC 1787 (Ch).
[250] Section 3(5).

(f) any physical or mental disability of any applicant for an order under said s2 or any beneficiary of the estate of the deceased;

(g) any other matter, including the conduct of the applicant or any other person, which in the circumstances of the case the court may consider relevant.

When assessing a person's financial resources and financial needs, the court must, under s3(6), consider their earning capacity and their financial obligations and responsibilities. The standard of living is not mentioned in the Act but is nevertheless relevant to assessing what would constitute reasonable financial provision.

Additional criteria for spouses and former spouses

When assessing a claim by a spouse or civil partner or former spouse or civil partner there are three additional criteria set out in s3(2): the age of the applicant; the duration of the marriage or civil partnership; and the contribution made by the applicant to the welfare of the family, including any contribution made by looking after the home or caring for the family. You may be familiar with this wording as it mirrors that in s25 Matrimonial Causes Act 1973—the list of factors the court must consider in relation to financial remedy applications on divorce.

In addition to this, the court must also consider the 'deemed divorce fiction'. This involves cross-checking the outcome proposed in the inheritance case against what the spouse would have received if, at the date of death, the marriage had been terminated by divorce instead. Section 25 Matrimonial Causes Act 1973 and the Key Cases discussed in Chapter 4 are therefore relevant. The intention behind this provision was to ensure that a widow or widower would not be worse off on the death of their partner spouse than on divorce.[251] Nevertheless, it does not set an upper or lower limit on what the court might order under the 1975 Act.[252] It is only one of the criteria to be considered and is, in many cases, not a particularly helpful one as more assets may be available on death than on divorce, such as the proceeds of a life insurance policy.[253]

Additional criteria for cohabitants

Section 3(2A) requires the court to have regard not only to the s3(1) criteria but also to the age of the applicant; the length of the period during which the applicant lived as the husband or wife or civil partner of the deceased and in the same household as the deceased; and the contribution made by the applicant to the welfare of the family of the deceased, including any contribution made by looking after the home or caring for the family.

Additional criteria for children

Section 3(3) applies to applications by children of the deceased or children who were not children of the deceased but were children of the family. It states that in addition to the s3(1) criteria set out above, the court must consider the manner in which the applicant

---

[251] That this was the mischief the section was intended to address is stated by Lord Hughes in Key Case *Ilott v Blue Cross* at para [13]. A widow or widower cannot bring a claim under Matrimonial Causes Act 1973 on the death of their spouse; they would use the Inheritance (Provision for Family and Dependants) Act instead.

[252] Para 3(2) confirms this. It was inserted by the Inheritance and Trustees Powers Act 2014 Sch 2 para 5(2).

[253] A point made by A Francis, *Inheritance Act Claims: Law, Practice and Procedure* (Jordan 2003/Issue 33 of 2019) at Chapter 8.

was being or in which he might expect to be educated or trained. Thus if the intention was for a young child to attend private school, then reasonable provision could include private school fees. There is no specific limit on age or educational level and so it is possible to claim for the costs of tertiary education or even postgraduate education or training.

In the case of children of the family, it must also consider whether the deceased maintained or assumed responsibility for maintaining the applicant and, if so, the extent, basis (why did the deceased maintain the applicant?) and duration, and whether the applicant did so knowing that the applicant was not his own child. The court must also consider the liability of any other person—such as a biological parent—to maintain the applicant.

It used to be considered that for adult children to succeed on a claim there had to be—in the words of Oliver J in *Re Coventry*—'some sort of a moral claim' by the applicant to be maintained by the deceased or at the expense of his estate beyond the mere fact of a blood relationship'.[254] In Key Case *Ilott v Blue Cross* the Supreme Court held that this was not a prerequisite, but that 'in the case of a claimant adult . . . capable of living independently, something more than the qualifying relationship is needed to found a claim' and this may be a moral claim to part of the deceased's estate.

Additional criteria for people being maintained

When the court considers claims by persons being maintained by the deceased, it must, by virtue of s3(4), consider the length of time over which the applicant was maintained, the extent of the contribution made, and the basis for this (i.e., why the deceased did so). This could be because of the deceased's love and affection for the applicant, or it could be because they were caring for the deceased's children, for example.

The court must also consider whether and to what extent the deceased assumed responsibility for the maintenance of the applicant. Since 2014, it has not been necessary to show this as a precondition of a successful claim. Nevertheless, it remains a relevant consideration.

SCENARIO 2

Illustration 5: Helen and Cherry

We know that Helen's death has left Cherry in a difficult position. She has a potential claim under the Inheritance (Provision for Family and Dependants) Act 1975 if she can show that the operation of the intestacy rules mean that Helen did not make reasonable financial provision for her, and that this provision was unreasonable.

As they are unmarried, Cherry will need to show that she has not received 'such financial provision as would be reasonable in all the circumstances of the case for the applicant to receive *for her maintenance*'. Any award she receives will comprise what is reasonable for her maintenance and no more than that (whereas if they had been married, the award would not be capped at the level of maintaining Cherry).

---

[254] *Re Coventry (Deceased)* [1979] 2 WLR 853 at 865.

Cherry is eligible to make this claim by virtue of being a cohabitant for more than two years. The court will consider:

(a) the financial resources and financial needs which Cherry has or is likely to have in the foreseeable future;

(b) the financial resources and financial needs which any other applicant for an order under s2 of this Act has or is likely to have in the foreseeable future;

(c) the financial resources and financial needs which any beneficiary of Helen's estate has or is likely to have in the foreseeable future;

(d) any obligations and responsibilities which Helen had towards Cherry or any other applicant, or towards any beneficiary of the estate;

(e) the size and nature of Helen's net estate;

(f) any physical or mental disability of any applicant for an order under said s2 (including Cherry) or any beneficiary of Helen's estate

(g) any other matter, including the conduct of Cherry or any other person, which in the circumstances of the case the court may consider relevant.

As she is claiming as a cohabitant, Section 3(2A) requires the court to also have regard to Cherry's age, the length of the period during which Cherry lived as though she was Helen's wife and in the same household as Helen; and the contribution Cherry made to the welfare of the Helen's family, including any contribution made by looking after the home or caring for the family. (This must be a humiliating element to the case, to prove your relationship's value.)

Depending on the financial arrangements between them, it is also possible that Cherry was being maintained by Helen; that is, that Helen 'was making a *substantial contribution* in money or money's worth towards the reasonable needs of the applicant other than a contribution made for full valuable consideration pursuant to an arrangement of a commercial nature'. Under this category of claim, the court will need to consider the length of time over which Cherry has been maintained, the extent of the contribution made, and why Helen maintained her, as well as the factors listed at s3(1).

It may be that because Helen's share of the house has passed to Cherry as the surviving joint tenant,[255] reasonable financial provision has been made for her. We can see from Key Case *Re Watson* that one issue might be whether the house that Cherry now owns wholly is suitable for her. The court must consider what housing would be suitable for Cherry, whether she could or should be required to downsize, and whether, as she ages, she needs a more expensive house (bungalows are usually more expensive than storied houses). Even if the house is suitable, reasonable financial provision is what is needed for her maintenance, and housing is merely one part of Cherry's maintenance, which encompasses not only her living costs but, per *Lewis v Warner*, 'other forms of assistance with the requirements of daily life'.[256]

5.13.4 Assessing reasonableness

Assessing whether the financial provision made by the deceased or lack thereof was reasonable involves a value judgment. Section 3 does not really assist in this regard. As the Court of Appeal said in Key Case *Ilott v Blue Cross*, it:

> provides no guidance about the relative importance to be attached to each of the relevant criteria. . . . the jurisprudence reveals a struggle to articulate, for the benefit of the parties

---

[255] See Illustration 4 of this scenario.
[256] [2016] EWHC 1787 (Ch).

in a particular case and of practitioners, how that value judgment has been, or should be, made on a given set of facts.[257]

This means that 'in a given factual situation, there is often room for a wide divergence of legitimate views about the value judgments which have to be made under the Act'.[258] This renders the outcome difficult to predict.

It would be easy to assume that a value judgment as to reasonableness inherently involves considerations of fairness. That is not quite correct. The process is not about whether someone else in the same circumstances would have been more generous in the provision made. Andrew Francis writes that:

> the commonest misconception among laymen, and to an extent even among lawyers, who may be unfamiliar with the terms of the 1975 Act, is that the jurisdiction is in some way designed to correct acts of unfairness, or to alter dispositions which are unreasonable, or to reward the just and deserving, or even to correct wills which are in some way 'perverse'. It is sometimes said that there ought to be 'fair' division of an estate under the 1975 Act. But this is wrong. The 1975 Act is not an instrument by which an imbalance between beneficiaries may be corrected.[259]

Instead of being about whether it might have been reasonable for the deceased to have been more generous, the test is as set out by Oliver J in *Re Coventry*:

> It is not the purpose of the Act to provide legacies or rewards for meritorious conduct. Subject to the court's powers under the Act and to fiscal demands, an Englishman still remains at liberty at his death to dispose of his own property in whatever way he pleases or, if he chooses to do so, to leave that disposition to be regulated by the laws of intestate succession. In order to enable the court to interfere with and reform those dispositions it must, in my judgment, be shown, not that the deceased acted unreasonably, but that, looked at objectively, *his disposition or lack of disposition produces an unreasonable result in that it does not make any or any greater provision for the applicant*—and that means, in the case of an applicant other than a spouse, for that applicant's maintenance. It clearly cannot be enough to say that the circumstances are such that if the deceased had made a particular provision for the applicant, that would not have been an unreasonable thing for him to do, and therefore it now ought to be done. The court has no carte blanche to reform the deceased's dispositions or those which statute makes of his estate to accord with what the court itself might have thought would be sensible if it had been in the deceased's position.[260]

This was explicitly approved by the Supreme Court in Key Case *Ilott v Blue Cross*.

5.13.5 Quantification

If the assessment of whether the applicant received reasonable financial provision shows that they did in fact do so, then they have no claim. All parties may very have strong feelings about this. Nevertheless, the test is an objective one.

---

[257] The Court of Appeal in *Ilott v Blue Cross* [2012] 2 FLR 170 at [88] (Black LJ).

[258] Sidney Ross, *Inheritance Act Claims* (4th edn, Sweet & Maxwell 2017), at the foreword by Henderson LJ.

[259] A Francis, *Inheritance Act Claims: Law, Practice and Procedure* (Jordan 2003/Issue 33 of 2019) at Chapter 1.

[260] *Re Coventry (Deceased)* [1979] 2 WLR 853, 864. Emphasis added.

KEY CASE *Ilott v Blue Cross* [2017] UKSC 17

Heather Ilott's mother, Mrs Jackson, cut her out of her life when, aged 17, Heather left home secretly to live with a boyfriend of whom Mrs Jackson did not approve. Heather went on to marry her boyfriend, with whom she had five children.

This estrangement between mother and daughter lasted 26 years until Mrs Jackson's death. Although there had been various attempts at reconciliation, these had not succeeded. Mrs Jackson did not make any provision for Mrs Ilott in her Will, leaving her estate to various charities including the Blue Cross (an animal welfare charity). She explained this decision in various Wills made over the years as being the result of Mrs Ilott's behaviour in leaving home, which she had never forgiven. At first instance the district judge had found that Mrs Jackson's decision to exclude her daughter from her Will was harsh and unreasonable.

At the time of the first instance hearing (which is the relevant date for considering the financial position), Mrs Ilott had four children at home including one who worked and financially contributed. Mr Ilott earned very little, Mrs Ilott even less. The family received various benefits and tax credits. These benefits were means-tested by reference to income and to capital and would be lost if Mrs Ilott was awarded capital of more than £16,000. Their annual net income from all sources was £20,387. They lived within their means albeit that these were almost wholly derived from public funds. They did not have sufficient money to replace old household equipment or furnishings, or the family car, let alone pay for extra-curricular activities for the children or holidays.

The district judge awarded Mrs Ilott £50,000 which he arrived at by calculating what Mrs Ilott would need for her maintenance. This was an extra £4,000 per year, which he then converted into a single lump sum based on achieving a specific rate of interest and Mrs Ilott's statistically average likely life expectancy.[261]

The case bounced back and forth between the High Court and the Court of Appeal repeatedly, with the Court of Appeal substituting a more generous award. Ultimately the case came before the Supreme Court, which unanimously restored the district judge's decision. The judgment of the Court is given by Lord Hughes:

- 'Unlike some other systems, English law recognises the freedom of individuals to dispose of their assets by will after death in whatever manner they wish. There are default succession rules in the event of intestacy, but by definition those only come into play if the deceased left no will. Otherwise the law knows of no rule of automatic succession or forced heirship. To this general rule, the statutory system of family provision imposes a qualification. It has provided since 1938 for the court to have power in defined circumstances to modify either the will or the intestacy rules if satisfied that they do not make reasonable financial provision for a limited class of persons. . . . The present statute is the Inheritance (Provision for Family and Dependants) Act 1975.'[262]

- The two questions to be considered are usually: '(1) did the Will/intestacy make reasonable financial provision for the claimant and (2) if not, what reasonable financial provision ought now to be made for him?'[263]

- 'Reasonable financial provision is, by section 1(2), what it is "reasonable for [the claimant] to receive", either for maintenance or without that limitation according to the class of claimant. These are words of objective standard of financial provision, to be determined by the court.'[264]

---

[261] The *Duxbury* basis: see Chapter 4.
[262] Paragraph [1].
[263] Para [23].
[264] Para [16].

- 'The Act does not say that the court may make an order when it judges that the deceased acted unreasonably. . . . Nevertheless, the reasonableness of the deceased's decisions are undoubtedly capable of being a factor for consideration within section 3(1)(g), and sometimes section 3(1)(d).'[265] The estrangement was a relevant consideration that reduced the award (even though it was principally Mrs Jackson's fault), but 'care must be taken to avoid making awards under the 1975 Act primarily rewards for good behaviour on the part of the claimant or penalties for bad on the part of the deceased'.[266]
- It is not the case that once there is a qualified claimant and a demonstrated need for maintenance, the testator's wishes cease to be of any weight. They may of course be overridden, but they are part of the circumstances of the case and fall to be assessed in the round together with all other relevant factors.[267]
- 'The right test was well set out by Oliver J in *Re Coventry*', i.e., that it must be shown, 'not that the deceased acted unreasonably, but that, looked at objectively, his disposition or lack of disposition produces an unreasonable result in that it does not make any or any greater provision for the applicant'.[268]

The order made by the district judge was within the generous ambit of judgment available to him. Accordingly, it should be restored.

Lady Hale agreed with this, but wrote a separate judgment with which Lords Wilson and Kerr agreed in order to highlight 'the unsatisfactory state of the present law, giving as it does no guidance as to the factors to be taken into account in deciding whether an adult child is deserving or undeserving of reasonable maintenance'.[269] She points out that 'a respectable case could be made for at least three very different solutions' that were open to the district judge:

(1) 'He might have declined to make any order at all. The applicant was self-sufficient, albeit largely dependent on public funds, and had been so for many years. She had no expectation of inheriting anything from her mother. She had not looked after her mother. She had not contributed to the acquisition of her mother's wealth. Rather than giving her mother pleasure, she had been a sad disappointment to her.'

(2) 'He might have decided to make an order which would have the dual benefits of giving the applicant what she most needed and saving the public purse the most money.'

(3) 'He might have done what in fact he did for the reasons he did. He reasoned that an income of £4,000 per year would provide her with her "share" of the household's tax credit entitlement and capitalised this in a rough and ready way, taking into account some future limited earning potential, at £50,000.'[270]

Remember that an appeal will only succeed if the judge was wrong, not simply because a different judge making a value judgment that is highly discretionary would have decided differently.

If this assessment shows that they did not receive financial provision or the financial provision was unreasonable, the issue then becomes what financial provision ought now to be made for them. Where the claimant is a spouse or civil partner, remember that the award can be more generous and the court thus needs to ask 'What provision would it be

---

[265] Para [16]–[17].
[266] Para [47].
[267] Para [47].
[268] Para [18]; *Re Coventry (Deceased)* [1979] 2 WLR 853 at 865.
[269] Para [66].
[270] Para [65].

reasonable in all the circumstances of the case for the spouse to receive, whether or not for his maintenance?' Do not forget, though, that unless the parties are or were married or civilly partnered, they are entitled only to what is reasonable *for their maintenance*. Thus for all others, the question is 'What provision would it be reasonable in all the circumstances of the case for the claimant to receive for his maintenance?'

Just as the considerations discussed at 5.12.3 are relevant to determining whether the provision made was reasonable, so too are they relevant to quantifying what provision should be made where the claim is successful. The aim is to identify and achieve reasonable provision.

5.14 **Protecting cohabitants**

So far, we have considered the implications of being in an unmarried cohabiting relationship. In Chapter 6 we look at financial support where there are children, although the powers there relate to support for the children not personal entitlements of their parents. We have seen that there are stark differences between the remedies available at the end of a marriage (whether by death or separation) and those available to unmarried couples, even those whose relationships are long-lasting and committed. In this section, we consider whether and how cohabitants can protect themselves, and how the law could implement a scheme to do so.

5.14.1 **Can cohabitants protect themselves?**

Some cohabitants choose to regulate their property matters through the use of private contracts such as cohabitation or 'living together' agreements, or (as we have seen) express declarations of trust in relation to property. You can see some suggested contracts on websites such as Advice Now.[271]

Traditionally, courts declined to enforce agreements seen to promote sexual immorality, of which living together without marriage was part. In *Fender v St John-Mildmay* Lord Wright said that the law would not enforce an immoral promise 'such as a promise between a man and a woman to live together without being married or to pay a sum of money or to give some other consideration in return for an immoral association'.[272] But that was a 1938 case and more recently, in *Sutton v Mishcon de Reya*, Hart J accepted that 'there is nothing contrary to public policy in a cohabitation agreement governing the property relationship between adults who intend to cohabit or who are cohabiting for the purposes of enjoying a sexual relationship.'[273]

This provides an indication that cohabitation contracts would be enforceable subject to the usual requirements for contractual validity, including that

- the parties must have intended to create legal relations (There is, as Pawlowski points out, 'a presumption is against legal relations where the contract is of a domestic or family nature'[274]);

---

[271] https://www.advicenow.org.uk/guides/how-make-living-together-agreement accessed 8 November 2020.
[272] [1938] AC 1, 42 (Lord Wright).
[273] [2003] EWHC 3166 (Ch).
[274] M Pawlowski, 'Cohabitation Contracts – The Sutton Case' [2004] *Family Law* 199 citing *Jones v Padavatton* [1969] 1 WLR 328.

- the terms are sufficiently certain to be given effect; and
- there is consideration unless the agreement takes the form of a deed.

Thus, Fiona and Ishan, our couple in Scenario 1, could have entered into a cohabitation contract which made provision for what would happen if they broke up. The content of cohabitation contracts can vary. Some precedent agreements have clauses dealing with many different aspects of living together such as responsibility for bills. There is nothing to stop them from voluntarily assuming certain responsibilities towards the other, assuming that the contract was otherwise valid. Helen and Cherry in Scenario 2 could also have written an express declaration of trust regulating ownership of their home, and this could also include how a potential sale of the house might be managed. Subject to the usual principles that render any contract void, an express declaration of trust is a valid contract, and as it is usually expressed as a deed no consideration is required. To provide one another with rights on death, the parties could make Wills that contained complementary provisions. Not all of the rights that married couples have can be shared by private contract with cohabitants. There is no power to share a pension, for example, but nothing to stop a person contracting to pay a proportion of their income to another. There is no right to claim spousal maintenance, but nothing to stop someone from agreeing to financially support another. These voluntary assumptions of responsibility are not subject to the limitations of nuptial agreements between married couples: as we see in Chapter 4, under the Matrimonial Causes Act 1973 the parties do not have absolute freedom of contract. Cohabitants do.

There are, however, a number of caveats to this. First, there are very few modern cases dealing with the enforcement of cohabitation contracts that go beyond simple declarations of trust in relation to property. Rebecca Probert suggests that this could be because few such contracts are made, or because such contracts are not litigated out of fear of the uncertain result or because the parties simply apply the terms of the agreement.[275] This means that cohabitation contracts are largely untested.

Secondly, claims made by or on behalf of children, as discussed in Chapter 6, cannot be terminated by agreement between the parties, as a matter of public policy. You cannot contract out of your obligation other than by ceasing to be a legal parent.

Finally, it is important to make a distinction between contracts which relate to cohabitation, but happen to be between a couple engaged in a sexual relationship, and contracts for sexual services. The latter are still unenforceable for public policy reasons. In *Sutton v Mishcon de Reya* itself, the contract was unenforceable despite the general principle that Hart J espoused. That is because it involved a master-slave relationship premised on consensual financial domination and submission, in which the slave transferred all his assets to the master. While the financial aspects themselves would have been enforceable subject to consideration (or a deed) and the absence of duress, here they were inseparable from the sexual elements of the relationship so the whole agreement was unenforceable.[276]

---

[275] R Probert, 'Cohabitation Contracts and Swedish Sex Slaves' (2004) 16 *Child and Family Law Quarterly* 453.
[276] [2003] EWHC 3166 (Ch) 1.

5.14.2 Why don't cohabitants protect themselves?

Given that adults are free to organise their own property matters as they wish, why do they not do so? In July 2002, the Law Society's Family Law Committee published *Cohabitation: The Case for Clear Law*.[277] This identified four different types of unmarried couple: informed, uninformed, reluctant, and no-choice. This categorisation is useful way of demonstrating the diversity of cohabiting relationships and how a divorce-style scheme may affect them.

Informed cohabitants

Sometimes 'both parties are fully aware of the limited rights that they may have and have come to a conscious and informed decision that they wish to live together without marriage and without entering into financial responsibility for each other.'[278] Some may be treating cohabitation as a 'trial run' for marriage and thus are rejecting the legal consequences of marriage *at this time*. Some may be saving up for a big wedding. In Barlow's study, there was 'clear evidence that for many cohabitation was indeed a prelude to marriage' as 59 per cent of cohabitants had gone on to marry the person they lived with. In 2006, 80 per cent of brides and grooms gave the same home addresses on their marriage notices.[279] Given the rise in cohabitation, this figure may be even higher now. For such couples, a regime of protection for cohabitants would be unwanted. As Ruth Deech argues, it is 'evidently unfair to impose the penalties of a failed marriage on persons who were experimenting precisely in order to avoid that sort of outcome'. . . . The law is converting the relationship into marriage *ex post facto*.'[280]

Informed cohabitants may also comprise those who are opposed to marriage—those for whom cohabitation is a desired state rather than a precursor to marriage. Some dislike marriage because of its history of oppression of women or what they perceive as expectations around marriage. Such couples may—unlike the trial run cohabitants—want equivalent rights and responsibilities even though they do not want the name of marriage. This group could enter into a civil partnership now that this status is available to different as well as same-sex couples. As we see in Chapter 2, campaigners for opposite-sex civil partnerships see civil partnerships as more modern and indicative of equality between the parties than marriage.[281]

Some informed cohabitants may reject marriage because of previous bad experiences or because they see marriage as idealised and fear not being able to live up to it.[282] Cohabitation with a new partner often follows the breakdown of a marriage, and this may

---

[277] The Law Society, *Cohabitation: The Case for Clear Law: Proposals for Reform* (July 2002).
[278] The Law Society, *Cohabitation: The Case for Clear Law: Proposals for Reform* (July 2002).
[279] J Haskey, 'Spouses with Identical Residential Addresses before Marriage: An Indicator of Pre-Marital Cohabitation' (1997) 89 *Population Trends* 13.
[280] R Deech, 'The Case against the Legal Recognition of Cohabitation' (1980) 29(2/3) *International and Comparative Law Quarterly* 480, 483–4. For her views some 19 years later, see R Deech, 'Cohabitation' [2010, January] *Family Law* 39.
[281] See also the website of the campaign for Equal Civil Partnerships http://equalcivilpartnerships.org.uk/ accessed 2 July 2018.
[282] A Barlow, S Duncan, G James, and A Park, 'Just a Piece of Paper? Marriage and Cohabitation', in A Park and National Centre for Social Research (eds), *British Social Attitudes: Public Policy, Social Ties: The 18th Report* (Sage 2001).

influence the decision not to marry. They may be happy as cohabitants precisely because it brings greater freedom to define and exit the relationship. Depending on the reason, they may or may not want cohabitation to attract legal consequences.

There is one final sub-group here, and that is those for whom the issue is simply not important. They are not rejecting marriage but consider themselves to be 'as good as' married. The formality of getting married is 'seen more as an expectation, sometimes a rather vague and ideal expectation, for some future date. . . . For these cohabitants . . . the legal side of getting married formally—just like the legal side of not being married—remained peripheral'.[283] They know they have limited rights but are not overly concerned about remedying that.

Uninformed cohabitants

This group comprises those who do not think they need to get married. It is probable, says the Law Society, that 'neither have given the matter much thought and probably have common misconceptions about what their legal position may or may not be.'[284]

The 'common misconception' to which the Law Society refers is the prevalence of the 'common law marriage' myth. As discussed in Chapter 2, the 2001 British Social Attitudes Survey found that only 34 per cent per cent of those surveyed believed correctly that the legal effects of marriage and cohabitation were different, with 56 per cent believing that unmarried couples definitely or probably had the same rights.[285] Hibbs, Barton, and Beswick surveyed a number of people engaged to marry and found that 41 per cent of them thought marriage would not change the legal nature of their relationship with their partner, and 37 per cent thought it would not have legal consequences with regard to their present or future children.[286] Conversely, most of them (60 per cent) thought that living together had legal consequences and that rights accrued over a period of time. Many were mistaken about the consequences of dying without a Will. James et al. found that apart from minor differences, these misconceptions transcended age, social class, geographical region, and religious belief.[287]

As we shall see when we come to discuss the current remedies available to cohabitants, it is particularly troubling that these misunderstandings also relate to the family home, and even in situations where the cohabitants have bought together and thus received legal advice or information. Hibbs et al. found that 74 per cent of those living together in their partner's house said they had a claim on the property, which is almost certainly not the case. Douglas, Pearce, and Woodward found that:

> Not only did most cohabitants in [our] study know little about their legal position as cohabitants, they were also ignorant or ill-informed as to the legal consequences of the way in which they held the family home. . . . Most cohabitants could not recall what, if any,

---

[283] S Duncan, A Barlow, and G James, 'Why Don't They Marry? Cohabitation, Commitment and DIY Marriage' (2005) 17 *Child and Family Law Quarterly* 383.

[284] The Law Society, *Cohabitation: The Case for Clear Law: Proposals for Reform* (July 2002).

[285] A Barlow, S Duncan, G James, and A Park, 'Just a Piece of Paper? Marriage and Cohabitation', in A Park and National Centre for Social Research (eds), *British Social Attitudes: Public Policy, Social Ties: The 18th Report* (Sage 2001).

[286] M Hibbs, C Barton, and J Beswick, 'Why Marry? Perceptions of the Affianced' [2001] *Family Law* 197, 201.

[287] G James, A Park, and A Barlow, *Cohabitation, Marriage and the Law: Social Change and Legal Reform in the 21st Century* (1 ed, Hart 2005).

legal advice they had been given. . . . Our conveyancer interviewees confirmed that cohabitant purchasers show little interest in the significance of joint (or sole) ownership, being more pre-occupied with completing the purchase and the practical details. . . . at the very time that they were making the decision to live together, couples could not simultaneously envisage anything going wrong with their relationships and instinctively did not want to 'plan for failure'.[288] Moreover, several perceived it as unromantic or awkward to make legal provision, for example to protect larger contributions to property purchase.[289]

Tennant, Taylor, and Lewis studied a group of former cohabitants on behalf of the Department for Constitutional Affairs. They had begun to cohabit because they wanted to be together; because of a specific event such as a pregnancy; or they had just drifted into it without explicit discussion. Whatever the reason, they had generally given little thought to the legal implications. It may be that it is only when a relationship ends that much thought is given to the matter. Even then, Tennant et al.'s cohabitants often did not get legal advice. Sometimes this was because the breakup was amicable or straightforward. For some, legal advice was cost prohibitive or they were unaware that advice to cohabitants was available. The researchers noted that 'there was a sense that getting advice involved a degree of risk, where an individual suspected their rights may be limited or that the advice would be biased against them'.[290] This suggests that people are afraid of the certainty of knowing they lacked remedies. Of course, what this meant was that people with successful claims did not necessarily receive their full legal entitlement.

If you are not aware that you lack legal protections, you do not know that you need to take positive steps to acquire them. Our uninformed cohabitants are a group for whom a regime of divorce-style rights could make a real difference. However, such a scheme would need to be opt-out or mandatory rather than opt-in, because if they have not taken steps to protect their position to date then it is unlikely that they would opt into any alternative scheme.

Reluctant cohabitants

In this group one person wishes to marry but the other does not. The Law Society explains that:

> It could be that this relationship started out as [informed or uninformed] and that one party (possibly the one with the economic disadvantage such as the partner who has given up work to look after the children) begins to recognise their lack of rights. It may be that one of the parties is naïve or uninformed and their partner makes use of that. However, the other party does not wish to marry perhaps because they are fully aware of the obligations they would be taking on. . . . He or she therefore reluctantly remains in the relationship, as the alternative is even less attractive.[291]

This is because, as Hibbs, Barton, and Beswick phrase it, 'one spouse's right is the other's duty'.[292] As we see in Chapter 3, marriage is a package deal in which the principles of needs,

---

[288] This also explains why so few people who marry enter into prenuptial agreements.

[289] G Douglas, J Pearce, and H Woodward, 'Cohabitants, Property and the Law: A Study of Injustice' (2009) 72(1) *Modern Law Review* 24, 39.

[290] R Tennant, J Taylor, and J Lewis, *Separating from Cohabitation: Making Arrangements for Finances and Parenting* (Department for Constitutional Affairs research series 2006).

[291] The Law Society, *Cohabitation: The Case for Clear Law: Proposals for Reform* (July 2002).

[292] M Hibbs, C Barton, and J Beswick, 'Why Marry? Perceptions of the Affianced' [2001] *Family Law* 197, 201.

compensation and sharing on divorce play a role in ameliorating the effect of gendered division of labour or the incapacity of one party to meet his or her needs independently.

Lady Hale has observed that given the financial remedies available to a court on divorce

> most women ought to regard the financial and proprietary remedies available to married people as a very good reason to marry. Only women who are richer or more successful than their husbands (admittedly a growing proportion), and who can be confident that this will not change even if they have children, should prefer to cohabit. For the same reason, most men ought to regard them as very good reasons not to marry.[293]

No-choice cohabitants

These couples are unable to marry. Perhaps one is already married or civilly partnered to someone else, and simply informally separated. They may be within the prohibited degrees of relationship so the law does not allow them to be married. For many years, this 'no choice' category would have included all same-sex couples. To be able to make a choice between cohabitation and marriage was a privilege not afforded to everyone.

5.14.3 Should cohabitants have greater rights and responsibilities?

A number of different but interlinked arguments have been made about whether we should provide rights for cohabitants. These relate to:

- The right of a person to make choices about what is right for them, by choosing to marry or choosing not to do so
- Society's interest in marriage and the benefits of marriage
- Society's interest in people being in committed relationships and the law's role in encouraging this
- Whether we should recognise that relationships take different forms, or encourage a preferred form (the form and function debate)

Let us explore these arguments further.

Individual choice and the existence of marriage

We have noted that some people—such as those who are using cohabitation as a trial for marriage—will not want any consequences at all to stem from their relationship. People may choose to cohabit rather than marry precisely because they want freedom from obligation.[294] There are already two schemes for those couples who wish to acquire rights: marriage and civil partnership. People who choose not to marry have rejected the package of rights and responsibilities that the state has already created for them for just this purpose. If they want to provide a package of rights and responsibilities outside marriage, they can enter into cohabitation contracts, giving them the autonomy to arrange their personal affairs as they see fit.

---

[293] B Hale, 'Unmarried Couples in Family Law' [2004] *Family Law* 419.
[294] S McRae, *Cohabiting Mothers: Changing Marriage and Motherhood* (Policy Studies Institute 1993).

Given these options, why should the law impose regulation on those who do not want it? Should there 'be a corner of freedom for such couples to which they can escape and avoid family law', as Deech argues?[295] Surely we should uphold the rights of individuals to regulate their own personal affairs. As Bailey-Harris says, 'the respect accorded to individual self-determination in contemporary society requires that the choice to be different be given meaning.'[296]

Those who propose a scheme of rights for cohabitants would make several responses to these arguments. First, they would say that freedom to determine the outcomes of one's relationships ignores the economic and emotional power differential that may exist between partners and the compromises or sacrifices that people often make for the benefit of the family at their own personal expense. This is an argument we have touched on previously, when we considered in Chapter 4 whether nuptial agreements should be binding. Paternalism and the state's own interest in the outcomes of relationship and the raising of children militate against unrestricted private ordering. Second, those who marry or cohabit are not necessarily making an informed choice, because as we have seen many are ignorant of the legal differences. Given that Hibbs et al. found that engaged couples were not particularly interested in finding out about the consequences of marriage *even though they were about to get married*, we may be asking too much to expect cohabitants to do so.[297] It may be that people simply assume that the law will 'provide fair and appropriate remedies for all family situations', which of course is not the case.[298]

State and social interest

Law is 'society's agent'.[299] In divorce cases, the principle of meeting the parties' needs reflects the clear public interest in ensuring that assets are split between the parties so as to minimise dependence on the state. Although Schedule 1 Children Act 1989 and the Child Support Act 1991 have provided remedies on the breakdown of a relationship in which there are children, these are not as favourable as those remedies available under the Matrimonial Causes Act. Accordingly, there is a greater risk that at the end of a cohabiting relationship one or both parties and any children will be left homeless or in difficult financial circumstances. Given the research by Tennant et al. that suggests that cohabitants on separation look at legal ownership of assets over principles used on divorce, such as equal sharing, need, or compensation, legally-imposed powers of asset redistribution could play a role in protecting cohabitants from the harmful consequences of the way in which they have conducted their relationships.[300] Without this, relationship breakdown has greater

---

[295] R Deech, 'The Case against the Legal Recognition of Cohabitation' (1980) 29(2/3) *International and Comparative Law Quarterly* 480, 483. She repeats this statement in 'Cohabitation' [2010, January] *Family Law* 39.

[296] R Bailey-Harris, 'Law and the Unmarried Couple – Oppression or Liberation?' [1996] *Child and Family Law Quarterly* 137.

[297] M Hibbs, C Barton, and J Beswick, 'Why Marry? Perceptions of the Affianced' [2001] *Family Law* 197.

[298] A Barlow, S Duncan, G James, and A Park, 'Just a Piece of Paper? Marriage and Cohabitation', in A Park and National Centre for Social Research (eds), *British Social Attitudes: Public Policy, Social Ties: The 18th Report* (Sage 2001).

[299] R Bailey-Harris, 'Law and the Unmarried Couple – Oppression or Liberation?' [1996] *Child and Family Law Quarterly* 137.

[300] R Tennant, J Taylor, and J Lewis, *Separating from Cohabitation: Making Arrangements for Finances and Parenting* (Department for Constitutional Affairs research series 2006).

economic consequences for the state, both directly (such as by providing welfare benefits) and indirectly (through the social consequences of poverty and social marginalisation). Providing cohabitants with rights against one another may reduce the costs to the state.

There is a correlation between marriage and positive outcomes such as better educational outcomes for children, lower criminality, and reduced poverty.[301] But, as we pointed out in Chapter 2, the correlation between outcomes for children and marriage are not necessarily causative. In fact, the research shows that they have more to do with who gets married rather than the legal or social consequences of marriage. Crawford et al.'s study of why children born to married couples exhibited better cognitive and socio-emotional development on average than those born into other relationship forms concluded that parents who marry before their child is born are different in terms of ethnicity, education level, and socio-economic status, relationship stability, and relationship quality to those who are unmarried.[302] Specifically, married couples are more highly educated, more highly paid, and more securely housed than others. If we made cohabitation more like marriage, would these positive correlations also apply to cohabitation? Crawford et al. think not. Their research suggests that the differences between married couples and those in other relationship forms largely reflect the selection of different types of people into marriage. There is little, if any, benefit for children's cognitive and socio-emotional development arising from the fact of their parents' marriage in and of itself.

Commitment

Fitzgibbon argues that those who marry 'form a relationship which embraces obligation as a fundamental component'.[303] To Scott, this creates 'in the individual spouse a sense of obligation to behave as expected, stimulated in part by the recognition that violations result in sanctions in the form of both self-imposed guilt and of disapproval by the spouse and other members of the community'.[304] Legal obligations—most readily apparent at the end of a marriage—serve to reinforce and enforce these socially recognised commitments.[305] One major objection to divorce-style rights is that these may disincentive the parties from getting married and thereby risk 'undermining the deliberate act of commitment that is the bedrock of stability' (i.e., marriage) so that 'with less intentional commitment, we risk creating ever more family breakdown'.[306] In other words, the act of commitment inherent in marriage creates obligation; and breach of this obligation attract social opprobrium, creating a deterrent effect that reinforces marital stability.

---

[301] See C Crawford, A Goodman, E Greaves, and R Joyce, 'Cohabitation, Marriage and Child Outcomes: An Empirical Analysis of the Relationship between Marital Status and Child Outcomes in the UK using the Millennium Cohort Study' (2012) 24 *Child and Family Law Quarterly* 176 for a lengthy list of studies.

[302] C Crawford, A Goodman, E Greaves, and R Joyce, 'Cohabitation, Marriage and Child Outcomes: An Empirical Analysis of the Relationship between Marital Status and Child Outcomes in the UK using the Millennium Cohort Study' (2012) 24 *Child and Family Law Quarterly* 176.

[303] S Fitzgibbon, 'Marriage and the Good of Obligation' (2002) 47 *American Journal of Jurisprudence* 41.

[304] ES Scott, 'Social Norms and the Legal Regulation of Marriage' (2000) 86 *Virginia Law Review* 1901.

[305] The sharing principle is discussed in Chapter 4 in the context of financial provision on divorce.

[306] H Benson, 'Why Cohabiting Couples Should Not Get the Same Rights as Married Couples' (Marriage Foundation Blog, 30 August 2018). Available at https://marriagefoundation.org.uk/cohabiting-couples-not-get-rights-married-couples/ accessed 1 March 2020.

Marriage stability, it is argued, is important because within a stable relationship individual interests are sacrificed to the greater good. Couples can engage in role specialisation—such as one being a breadwinner and the other a home-maker—in a way that minimises the risks involved to the latter.[307] This is important because specialisation has social (principally economic) benefits. This is why at the end of a marriage assets are redistributed in such a way that the differential impact of role specialism during the marriage is mitigated. But role specialisation exists in both marital and cohabiting relationships. The argument here not against cohabitation, but about relationship insecurity. Just as divorce laws are alleged to provide security for role specialisation within a marriage, so too could cohabitation laws be used to make what Bailey-Harris calls 'social policy statements about the values to be accorded to differing roles within the family'.[308] In other words, if we made cohabitation more like marriage, would cohabiting families act like married families?

As we see in Chapter 3 when we consider fault-based divorce, it is by no means clear that law is able to influence people to behaved differently in their private lives. Given that the divorce rate is 42 per cent, one may well take the view that social opprobrium no longer holds marriages together or determines what happens at the end. It does not necessarily follow that supporting cohabitation undermines marriage either, both because many cohabitants go on to marry and because those that do not may reject marriage irrespective of whether a regime for cohabitants is implemented. It is not always about the money.

Form or function?

The form or function argument is about whether the law should protect families because of their function (what they do) or because of their form (the legal status of being married or not being married). The former approach would identify that married and unmarried couples share similar—but not identical—characteristics and needs for protection and therefore there is no reason why the law should continue to privilege marriage by giving married couples enhanced legal rights. The latter approach would hold that a distinction between married and unmarried couples is justified as the former alone had elected into those rights and responsibilities.

Anne Barlow and Grace James argues that 'In the past, form and function coincided almost universally, allowing the law to develop its privileging of patriarchal marriage, to protect the economically weaker partner using functional justifications.'[309] The law reflected the functioning of families, because almost all families involved married parents. This meant that it could address inequalities arising from the way people had conducted their relationships simply by providing for a right to maintenance during the marriage, a right to a financial settlement on the breakdown of the marriage, and statutory protections for the widow(er) on death. However, the lack of such rights for unmarried couples and the rise in unmarried cohabitation means that the law no longer protects every family. The legal remedies available to unmarried couples are grossly inadequate if judged by

---

[307] AM Parkman, 'Mutual Consent Divorce', Chapter 4 in AW Dnes and R Rowthorn (eds), *The Law and Economics of Marriage and Divorce* (Cambridge University Press 2010).
[308] R Bailey-Harris, 'Law and the Unmarried Couple – Oppression or Liberation?' [1996] *Child and Family Law Quarterly* 137.
[309] A Barlow and G James, 'Regulating Marriage and Cohabitation in 21st Century Britain' (2004) 67(2) *Modern Law Review* 143.

their capacity to protect the vulnerable, support role specialisation, promote the welfare of children, and minimise the costs to the state.

The issue, therefore, is whether, 'as society becomes increasingly diverse, socially, religiously and in its personal morality and value-systems, the law is obliged to recognise diversity by giving legal status to a range of different family relationships which individuals choose for themselves', or whether the law should prefer some types of relationship over others.[310]

5.14.4 What might a cohabitation scheme look like?

There are a number of potential models for a scheme of protection for cohabitants, by which we mean the availability of a coherent scheme rather than a series of ad hoc powers, and which provides for *at least some* of the powers available under the Matrimonial Causes Act (such as lump sum, periodical payments, property adjustment, and pension sharing). A scheme could be default, capturing all people who met certain criteria without them taking any steps to acquire these rights or responsibilities, with or without the ability to opt out. Alternatively, it could take the form of an opt-in domestic partnership scheme similar to marriage or civil partnership although not necessarily attracting the same rights and responsibilities. In England and Wales, civil partnership represents just such a scheme, but one that attracts virtually the same rights and responsibilities.

Most schemes that exist in other countries establish rights and responsibilities on relationship breakdown, and many also include inheritance and succession protections when a person's cohabitant dies.

In his excellent article 'The Rights of Cohabitants: When and How Will the Law Be Reformed?', Edward Hess identifies a number of practical considerations that need to be addressed when designing a scheme of divorce-style rights for cohabitants, as well as a number of issues of principle.[311] We now turn to address these points.

How do we define cohabitation?

With marriage, there is a clear starting point: the date of the wedding. It is not as simple with cohabitation. As Lady Hale has said, 'unlike marriage or registered partnerships, these relationships do not define themselves'.[312] People may drift into living with one another without a clear commencement date. At what point does staying over with one's boyfriend or girlfriend become cohabiting with them? When one stays two, three, or four days per week, or only full-time? What if the other party retains their own separate flat but is only there occasionally? Is it about the degree of mutual dependency, or payment of bills for one household, shared children or childcare, or domestic chores? Is a sexual relationship a prerequisite? While a marriage can be annulled on the basis of non-consummation, a sexual relationship is not a prerequisite to marriage. Should we recognise as cohabitants within a legal scheme those people who are related to one another or who are platonic friends?

---

[310] R Bailey-Harris, 'Law and the Unmarried Couple – Oppression or Liberation?' [1996] *Child and Family Law Quarterly* 137.

[311] [2009, May] *Family Law* 405.

[312] Brenda Hale, 'Unmarried Couples in Family Law' [2004] *Family Law* 419.

As it is not always clear when a relationship of cohabitation exists, it may be necessary for the court to resolve this issue in the event of a dispute, and this would require consideration of the parties' lives and degree of integration. But the lack of a clear definition of cohabitation is not an insurmountable hurdle. The Inheritance (Provision for Family and Dependants) Act 1975 allows claims by cohabitants, as does the Fatal Accidents Act 1976. The Law Commission has referred to 'living together in a joint household'. A private member's bill by Lord Lester, discussed at 5.14.5, simply uses the phrase 'living together as a couple'.[313] Many schemes around the world have also successfully resolved this issue. In Australia, the law on 'de facto' relationships refers to the parties as living together 'on a genuine domestic basis'.[314] Scotland refers to living together 'as if husband and wife' or civil partners.[315]

What cohabiting relationships should give rise to legal remedies?

Most people would agree that not all cohabiting relationships should give rise to legal remedies. This is because cohabiting relationships vary in duration, quality, and commitment to a much wider degree than marriage. As we have discussed at 5.14.3, people may initially cohabit because they do not want to acquire rights. We could exclude such couples by providing that cohabitants acquire rights only after a specific period of time or on the happening of certain events.

If we accept the cohabitants should *not* acquire rights on day one of their cohabitation, the issue becomes *when* such rights should be acquired. Some schemes require a minimum number of years of cohabitation, most commonly two, three, or five years, before rights are acquired. (Of course, it may be uncertain when that period started to run for the reasons set out above). Cohabiting relationships are on average shorter than marriages, with only a small percentage lasting for ten years or more as cohabitees; most will either marry or break up. However, Barlow et al. found that 'if we compare like with like, for example young secular childless couples, or older couples in a long-term union with children, there would probably be little difference between separation rates of cohabiting and married couples.'[316] This implies that there is no justification based on relationship length for limiting access to divorce-style rights: if we let married couples in short relationships seek financial remedies, why not cohabitants? But this ignores one key difference between married and unmarried couples: cohabiting couples without children are more likely to keep their finances separate than are married couples and may not, therefore, be mutually dependent in the same way. In fact, Vogler found that men in childless cohabiting relationships are more than 20 times more likely than married fathers to keep their finances at least partly separate.[317]

---

[313] Cohabitation Bill [HL] 2008–09. The text of the bill can be found at https://publications.parliament.uk/pa/ld200809/ldbills/008/2009008.pdf accessed 9 November 2020.

[314] See 5.14.5.

[315] See 5.14.5.

[316] É Beaujouan and M Ní Bhrolcháin, *Cohabitation and Marriage in Britain since the 1970s*: Population Trends No. 145 (Office of National Statistics 2011).

[317] C Vogler, 'Managing Money in Intimate Relationships: Similarities and Differences Between Cohabiting and Married Couples' Chapter 4 in J Miles and R Probert (eds), *Sharing Lives, Dividing Assets: An Inter-Disciplinary Study* (Hart 2009).

Some schemes make an exception to the number of years if there are children. The presence of children may create dependency and inequality in the parties' respective financial positions. Perhaps because they recognise this, cohabiting couples with children are more likely to pool their resources in the same way that married couples do (whether or not they have children). However, at the end of a cohabiting relationship, there is little evidence that the parties split their assets in a way that adjusts for inequalities in their respective financial positions. Tennant et al. found that:

- The most obvious influence on financial arrangements made on separation was ownership. Financial and non-financial contributions made by non-owners tended not to be recognised if they were inconsistent with the legal title. There were cases where financial contributions had been made by the non-owner but notions of ownership overrode them.

- Financial dependency during the relationship was rarely recognised in arrangements on separation. Consideration of the needs of children or adults played little part in the arrangements made. (This is of course starkly different to the approach of a court on divorce where children are the first consideration and the parties needs must must be met.)

- 'Unmet needs, or reliance on the state and on families, were evident amongst cohabitants who had been financially dependent on their partner, and particularly where they were the main carers of children postseparation. The clearest disadvantage occurred where women with children lived in the man's house and had to leave it when the relationship came to an end. Here people had to move into rented accommodation, were often dependent on benefits and experienced a substantial drop in their living standards.'[318]

This indicates that divorce-style rights for cohabitants that focus on need or on future limitations to earning capacity would particularly assist those who are likely to be the primary carer of children post-separation (usually the mother) and those who are in a weaker financial position during the relationship (again, usually the female partner).[319]

Some schemes look at the effect of the relationship upon the parties' future lives, such as whether at the end of the relationship there is economic disparity between the parties that is attributable to the way that they ran their lives together. A scheme based on economic disparity may look at whether one party has left the relationship with a continuing benefit, such as the economic benefit in terms of earning capacity or home equity, or whether the other has a continuing economic disadvantage from the relationship, such as because they are caring for children. This is not dissimilar to the concept of unjust enrichment which we discussed at 5.10.1 in the context of reforming trusts of land or the principle of compensation in financial remedy law.

---

[318] R Tennant, J Taylor, and J Lewis, *Separating from Cohabitation: Making Arrangements for Finances and Parenting* (Department for Constitutional Affairs research series 2006).
[319] See also M Maclean and J Eeekelaar, 'Perceptions of Risk-Taking Associated with Formal and Informal Partners Relationships' (2005) 17(2) *Child and Family Law Quarterly* 247.

Where economic disparity or the presence of children is the basis, no minimum number of years of cohabitation is necessary, although some schemes use a combination of these criteria. The reason why no minimum number of years is necessary is because you capture the same people under both methods: those for whom the cohabitation has consequences. Naturally the economic disparity is likely to be greater in the case of longer relationships than shorter relationships, and ongoing loss is greater when there are children to be looked after. Scotland does not have a minimum period, and in *Gow v Grant* Lady Hale noted research showing that this had not proved a problem and that in fact very few cases had involved short relationships.[320] Similarly, Miles et al. found that imposing a minimum duration of two years 'would have made hardly any difference' to the number of potential cases seen by solicitors in Scotland.[321]

What financial remedies should be available?

Now that we have decided who the law should protect, we must turn to considering how. Should the remedies available to cohabitants be the same as those available to married couples who are divorcing, or less generous? The remedies that you may consider appropriate are likely to depend on your view of the purpose of protection for cohabitants and your views on the degree to which marriage should remain privileged, as much as on practical considerations such as the extent of financial enmeshment between the parties. What does a just and equitable outcome look like, bearing in mind the competing considerations of financial need, individual choice, and state interest?

Many schemes provide the same rights to cohabitants as they do to married couples, but some schemes provide lesser remedies, choosing to treat marriage preferentially in an attempt to encourage parties to marry. For example, the scheme may restrict provision to lump sums only, or offer a range of potential remedies such as transfer or settlement or property, 'spousal' maintenance, and pension sharing. As we will see, in Scotland the court can only order a lump sum payment from one party to another. Scottish lawyers saw it this as limiting the scheme's usefulness because if a party cannot raise a lump sum there is no remedy, and for many people income rather than capital is their most valuable asset.[322] Moreover, if there is a disparity between pension values then the availability of a lump sum does not mitigate the effects of the inability to share a pension, because the cost of buying an equivalent pension with a lump sum may be too high.

Limitation period

The next issue is whether there should be a limitation period for bringing an action for financial support at the end of a cohabiting relationship. Most schemes allow a claim to be brought only within a relatively short period of the relationship ending. In Scotland,

---

[320] [2012] UKSC 2 at [52], Lady Hale citing F Wasoff, J Miles, and E Mordaunt, *Legal Practitioners' Perspectives on the Cohabitation Provisions of the Family Law (Scotland) Act 2006* (Centre for Research on Families and Relationships 2010). Available at http://www.crfr.ac.uk/cohabitation/

[321] J Miles, F Wasoff, and E Mordaunt, 'Cohabitation: Lessons from Research North of the Border?' (2011) 23 *Child and Family Law Quarterly* 302.

[322] J Miles, F Wasoff, and E Mordaunt, 'Cohabitation: Lessons from Research North of the Border?' (2011) 23 *Child and Family Law Quarterly* 302.

it is one year. Without such a limitation period it would be difficult to have any certainty, particularly if one had an unfortunate romantic history with lots of unsuccessful cohabiting relationships. For marriage, as we see in Chapter 4, there is no limitation period if the parties do not remarry and have not obtained a clean break of their respective claims. However, most people do not enter into marriages as often as they might cohabit.

Opt-in or opt-out?

There are two ways a scheme of rights for cohabitants could operate. One is for the scheme to capture all couples by default (subject to them having lived together for certain period or there being qualifying events such as the birth of children or retained economic benefit or loss). This would protect the most vulnerable in society who may be the least likely to take positive steps to acquire rights. An information campaign by the government designed specifically to address the common law marriage myth was unsuccessful in getting couples to enter into cohabitation agreements, mostly because one party in a couple refused to do so or they suffered from a belief that the relationship would not break down—and that was among those who were aware of the legal position.[323] 'A presumptive scheme is therefore the only way of reaching the vast majority of cohabiting couples'.[324]

We could then, if we thought it appropriate, allow couples the option of opting out of the default scheme. One of the proposed schemes for England and Wales, that of Lord Marks (see 5.14.5) permits the parties to opt out only if they have legal advice to ensure that they know whether it is in their interests to do so.

Conversely, you could have an opt-in scheme, i.e., one that the parties had to take steps to join. This could be a form of registration process giving rise to a registered partnership. An opt-in scheme is very much like marriage: it may or may not have different rights and responsibilities to marriage but it is still a form of state-recognised partnership. There is no firm dividing line between a domestic partnership scheme and marriage—only the name and any religious significance parties attribute to the latter. In Australia, the parties can register their 'de facto' relationship for convenience, but registration is not necessary: the parties acquire rights and responsibilities by default. Compare this to the French pacs, a registration-only scheme albeit one that allows a choice of rights and responsibilities.

Table 5.2 sets out the respective advantages and disadvantages of each style of scheme. The key issue is how we should balance personal autonomy and people's freedom to avoid state-imposed obligations, on the one hand, with the fact that most people are ignorant of the different treatment of cohabitants and married couples and do not therefore take necessary steps to protect their position.

5.14.5 Potential model schemes

Let us now look to look at some of the schemes that are in operation around the world and various proposals that have been made in this country.

---

[323] A Barlow, C Burgoyne, and J Smithson, *The Living Together Campaign—An Investigation of Its Impact on Legally Aware Cohabitants* (Ministry of Justice 2007).
[324] R Probert, 'The Cohabitation Bill' [2009, February] *Family Law* 150, 151.

TABLE 5.2 Advantages and disadvantages of opt-in and -out schemes

Advantages to a scheme that people have to opt into	Advantages to a default scheme that captures everyone unless they specifically opt out
A regime that is there only when people choose to use it respects individual autonomy. People should be free to avoid state-imposed obligations.	People are ignorant of the legal differences between marriage and cohabitation, and without an understanding of the precarious legal position of cohabitants they will not know that they need to take steps to acquire rights until it is too late.
	Research by Tennant et al. suggests that placing responsibility on cohabitants to act to acquire legal rights, 'is not consistent with how couples behave'.[325]
If those in relationships wanted rights, then they have a solution: marriage. The fact that they have not chosen to marry indicates that they do not want to grant one another financial rights.	It is wrong to assume that the fact that people have not married means they do not want to protect the other person. There are many reasons why people may not have married.
Many politicians and religious figures want to make a clear distinction between marriage and other relationship forms, and privilege marriage.	Now that civil partnerships are open to both different-sex and same-sex couples, there is already an alternative to marriage. Why should the state provide another scheme just because people have not taken advantage of what is already available?
It places the onus on a couple to opt out.	People who are particularly vulnerable are unlikely to take the steps required to opt into a scheme. This means that a scheme that applies by default protects them better. What value are legal protections if those who are most vulnerable have no access to them because they did not know to opt in?

Scotland

Scotland has had a scheme for cohabitants since the Family Law (Scotland) Act 2006. Section 25 defines a cohabitant as a member of a couple who live or lived together as if they were husband and wife or civil partners. In determining whether two people are cohabitants, the court must consider the nature and duration of their relationship and any financial arrangements between them during that period. It does not require a minimum period of cohabitation as it is designed on the basis of retained economic advantage and disadvantage.

At the end of the relationship, the Act provides for household good acquired during (but not before) the cohabitation to be divided equally with the exception of money, securities [investments], cars, and pets. It presumes that these goods are jointly owned, unless there

---

[325] R Tennant, J Taylor, and J Lewis, *Separating from Cohabitation: Making Arrangements for Finances and Parenting* (Department for Constitutional Affairs research series 2006).

is proof that the parties contributed to their acquisition in unequal shares or they were gifts or inheritances.

The court can also order one party to pay the other a lump sum (a) that takes account of any economic burden of caring, after the end of the cohabitation, for a child of whom the cohabitants are the parents; or (b) is because one party has derived economic advantage from contributions made by the other, or one party has suffered economic disadvantage in the interests of the other. 'Economic advantage' includes gains in capital, income, and earning capacity. The court takes into account the extent to which any economic advantage derived by one cohabitant is offset by the economic disadvantage suffered by the other. In *Gow v Grant*, the Supreme Court held unanimously that the overriding principle was one of fairness in the 'assessment of compensation for contributions made or economic disadvantages suffered in the interests of the relationship', having regard to where the parties were at the beginning of their cohabitation and where they were at the end. 'This is more practical than asking whether either the [respondent] has derived a net economic advantage from the contributions of the applicant or the applicant has suffered a net economic disadvantage in the interests of the [respondent] or any relevant child.' The relevant provisions were 'designed to correct imbalances arising out of a non-commercial relationship where parties are quite likely to make contributions or sacrifices without counting the cost or bargaining for a return'.[326]

In her concurring judgment in *Gow v Grant*, Lady Hale commented that

> The main lesson from this case, as also from the research so far, is that a remedy such as this is both practicable and fair. It does not impose upon unmarried couples the responsibilities of marriage but redresses the gains and losses flowing from their relationship. As the researchers comment, "The Act has undoubtedly achieved a lot for Scottish cohabitants and their children".[327] English and Welsh cohabitants and their children deserve no less.[328]

A claim must be brought within one year. The parties can opt out of the scheme at any time. If a cohabitant dies without a Will, then the surviving cohabitant may bring a claim for a share of their estate (capital or transfer of property) within six months.

The Law Commission's proposals

In 2007, the Law Commission published its report *Cohabitation: The Financial Consequences of Relationship Breakdown*.[329] This contained recommendations for the introduction of a default regime dealing with the property consequences of the breakdown of a cohabiting relationship. The Law Commission proposals have multiple eligibility criteria including a minimum cohabitation period (they suggest between two and five years) or having a child together. In addition to this, the applicant must have made a 'qualifying contribution' to the relationship. A 'qualifying contribution' is any contribution arising from the cohabiting relationship which is made to the parties' shared lives or to the welfare of members of their families, and includes future contributions such as caring for children.

---

[326] [2012] UKSC 2 at [33] and [50] (Lord Hope) and Lady Hale at [54]. Lord Hope delivers a unanimous decision; Lady Hale a majority; they concur with one another and use the same terms.

[327] This is a reference to F Wasoff, J Miles, and E Mordaunt, *Legal Practitioners' Perspectives on the Cohabitation Provisions of the Family Law (Scotland) Act 2006* (Centre for Research on Families and Relationships 2010).

[328] Para [56].

[329] Cm 7182, Law Com No 307, 2007).

Once a qualifying contribution had been established, it would be necessary to show that the respondent has, as a result, retained a benefit at the end of the relationship or the applicant has suffered or will suffer a continuing economic disadvantage. The scheme therefore rejected the matrimonial principle of need. Law Commissioner Stuart Bridge explained this was because:

> It is difficult to define what is meant by 'needs' in the abstract, in particular, whether 'need' is an objective concept, or whether it is variable according to the parties' standards of living. It may also be thought difficult to justify meeting an individual's needs (at least in broad terms, e.g., regardless of their source) where no legal commitment, epitomised by marriage or by civil partnership, has been entered into.[330]

The choice of the phrase 'retained benefit' over the Scottish equivalent of 'economic advantage' was a deliberate attempt 'to exclude protracted analysis of what might be called "water under the bridge": every past gain and loss over the course of a long relationship, regardless of whether they have any enduring impact at the point of separation'.[331] An 'economic equality ceiling' would prevent either party from claiming against the other if their positions at the end of the relationship were roughly equal, even if one would have been much better off if they had not made a qualifying contribution. In this way, the scheme looks to the future rather than the past (in contrast, for example, to trusts of land claims).

The scheme provided for a two-year period in which the applicant could claim a lump sum, property transfer order, property settlement, order for sale, and pension sharing. Periodical payments would not be available except in respect of childcare costs, although the child support scheme would run alongside. It is therefore, with this exception, a clean break scheme. The Commission felt that 'the arguments in favour of a clean break which apply to divorcing couples are even stronger for separating cohabitants, who have not entered into any legal commitment to support each other financially'.[332] In this way, the Commission sought to make a clear distinction from those rights available to divorcing couples. It did so too by providing what marriage does not: the availability of an opt-out. However, their opt-out could be overridden if enforcing it would be manifestly unfair or there had been an unforeseen change in circumstances since the parties had opted out.

The government announced in 2011 that it would not be bringing forth legislation that reflected the Law Commission proposals, citing other legislative priorities.[333] To date, this position has not changed.

Lord Lester's Cohabitation Bill

This private member's bill[334] was first introduced in 2008 and has never progressed past a certain stage. It is an opt-out scheme, formulated with the support of Resolution, the

[330] S Bridge, 'Financial Relief for Cohabitants: How the Law Commission's Scheme Would Work' [2007, November] *Family Law* 998; summarising the Law Commission report at 4.18ff.

[331] J Miles, F Wasoff, and E Mordaunt, 'Cohabitation: Lessons from Research North of the Border?' (2011) 23 *Child and Family Law Quarterly* 302.

[332] Para 4.98.

[333] House of Commons, Written Ministerial Statement on the Government Response to the Law Commission Report, 6 September 2011, *Hansard* HC col 16WS.

[334] Cohabitation Bill [HL] 2008–09. The text of the bill can be found at https://publications.parliament.uk/pa/ld200809/ldbills/008/2009008.pdf accessed 9 November 2020.

organisation for family lawyers. The scheme applies to those living together as a couple who are not within the prohibited degrees of relationship[335] and who are not married or civilly partnered. Eligibility depends on either cohabitation for at least two years or there being a child of them both or a joint 'live with' order in respect of a child. The court must consider it just and equitable to make an order.

While he proposes quite a wide range of powers—lump sums, property adjustment orders, periodical payments, and pension sharing—he would restrict this to meeting the applicant's reasonable needs, and with the aim that the parties should be self-supporting as soon as possible. Periodical payments can be ordered for up to three years. It can be ordered for longer only if necessary to avoid exceptional hardship that would otherwise arise in consequence of them having lived as a couple or to meet the costs of appropriate childcare to enable the primary carer 'to care for any relevant child whilst maintaining gainful employment'.

There is a list of factors, similar to that contained in s25 Matrimonial Causes Act 1973, for the court to consider, and an application must be made within two years of separation unless there are exceptional circumstances. This scheme is well considered, in that the wide range of powers means flexibility and it specifically addresses the costs of raising children. Part of its flexibility is the fact that it is highly discretionary, meaning that outcomes may be less predictable but that outcomes can be tailored to the parties' precise situation.[336] Notably, the bill preserves the privilege of marriage. Whereas an outcome for divorcing couples under the Matrimonial Causes Act would meet needs generously interpreted as well as apply principles of compensation (to the extent that this has not been attacked by case law) and sharing, in this scheme the award is the less generous 'reasonable needs'.

To opt out, the parties must have received independent legal advice as to the effect of doing so; this opt-out may be varied or ignored by the court if manifestly unfair because of the circumstances at the time the opt-out was entered into, or because of an unforeseen change in circumstances since the parties had opted out.[337]

Lord Marks' Cohabitation Rights Bill

This is another private member's bill and was introduced into the House of Lords in 2017.[338] It applies to cohabiting couples who are not married or civilly partnered or within the prohibited degrees of relationship. Eligibility is based on the parties having lived together for two years, having a child together, or one party being pregnant by the other at the time of separation.

The applicant must have made a 'qualifying contribution' to the relationship. This may be financial or in terms of contribution to the parties' shared lives or the welfare of members of their families, and can be a past or future contribution.

As a result of that qualifying contribution, the respondent must have retained a benefit or the applicant be at continuing economic disadvantage. A 'retained benefit' is a financial benefit which has been acquired, retained, or enhanced by or for the respondent during

---

[335] I.e., too closely related to one another to be permitted to marry. See Chapter 2.
[336] See Chapter 4's discussion about the respective merits of certainty and discretion.
[337] See R Probert, 'The Cohabitation Bill' [2009, February] *Family Law* 150 for a discussion of this bill.
[338] Cohabitation Rights Bill [HL] HL Bill 34 of 2017–19. The text of the bill is at https://services.parliament.uk/bills/2017-19/cohabitationrights.html accessed 9 November 2020.

the parties' cohabitation or in contemplation of the parties' cohabitation, whether in the form of capital assets of any kind, income, whether actual or potential, or earning capacity; and an 'economic disadvantage' is a past, present, or future financial loss, burden, or cost. The aim of the legislation is to reverse that gain or loss insofar as it is reasonable and practicable to do so. The court can award a lump sum; property transfer, settlement, or sale; and/or pension sharing. There are a number of discretionary factors that the court should consider when deciding what to do.

The bill also seeks to amend the Inheritance (Provision for Family and Dependants) Act 1975 and include cohabitants within the intestacy rules so that they would inherit if their partner died without a Will.

The parties can enter into an opt-out agreement or a deed of trust. They must have legal advice first, so that they understand what they are giving up. Claims must be brought within two years unless there are exceptional circumstances justifying a late application.

Australia

Australia recognises 'de facto' relationships, that is those cohabiting relationships that exist in fact (rather than those formed by law, which are 'de jure'). The Family Law Act 1975[339] defines a de facto relationship as one between two people who are not related or married to one another who live together on a genuine domestic basis.[340] This encompasses same-sex couples: indeed, Australia provided equivalent protections for same-sex couples well before it introduced same-sex marriage.

If a de facto relationship breaks down, the court has the power to make a financial order if:

- The relationship lasted for at least two years; or
- There is a child or children of the relationship; or
- One party has made substantial financial or non-financial contributions to the other person's property, and a serious injustice would be caused to one party as a home-maker or parent if property was not divided; or
- The de facto relationship was registered in a state or territory or the parties were living together on a genuine domestic basis.

Most Australian states and territories enable people to register their de facto relationship although this is not a requirement. Having a registration certificate is a proof of the existence of the relationship. If there is no registration, in determining whether a couple is living together on a genuine domestic basis, the courts look at the length of the relationship, whether it was sexual in nature, the degree of mutual commitment to a shared life, the degree of financial dependency, the arrangements for care and support of children, and property ownership and use, as well as the public aspects of the relationship such as how the relationship is perceived. It is possible to be married to one person and in a de facto relationship with another person at the same time and even to be in more than one de facto relationship at the same time.

---

[339] In Western Australia the applicable law is the Family Law Act 1997 (WA). There are some differences between this territory and others.

[340] See S Leigh and D Barry, 'Cohabitation: Compare and Contrast the Australian System' [2011, April] *Family Law* 404.

The courts can divide any property whether joint or solely owned and whenever acquired. This includes pension sharing and there is also a power to order 'spousal' maintenance as well as child maintenance. The court will consider the parties' needs and their financial and non-financial contributions and will not make an order unless it is just and equitable to do so. The remedies available for de facto couples are almost identical to those available to married couples, and on death a de facto cohabitant has the same rights as a married person, including receiving a share of their estate if the deceased died without a Will.

The parties can enter into a binding financial agreement similar to a prenuptial agreement if they wish to avoid these consequences.

France

In France, couples may marry or enter into a Pacte Civil de Solidarité ('pacs'), which is an opt-in registration scheme. Outside these two options there is no formal regime for cohabitants, although they do have some social and welfare rights.

Introduced in 1999, the pacs contract (and any later amendments) must be registered by a notary or the head clerk of a tribunal d'instance in order to be binding. The scheme is open to same-sex and opposite-sex couples. In fact, prior to the introduction of same-sex marriage in 2013 pacs was the only scheme of legal protections available to same-sex couples. A pacs provides some default protections for the parties but they can contract out of these, choosing to adopt more or less onerous provisions. This gives it a flexibility not available to marriage and there is some evidence that couples are choosing more responsibilities than fewer. Parties can dissolve a pacs by unilateral or joint written declaration to the notary or head clerk, so it is much easier than divorce.

While marriage is still the preferred status, attracting a range of rights and responsibilities, the pacs is a popular option, especially among the young. In 2015, there were 188,947 pacs as against 222,664 marriages.[341] Nevertheless, there is evidence that a pacs may be a precurser to marriage rather than a replacement for it: around 40 per cent of pacs are brought to an end so the parties can marry. This explains why pacs rates are particularly high among the young, and why the average age of marriage is into the thirties.

What can we learn from these schemes?

The schemes have a number of different features. Some set prerequisites for eligibility based on the length of the relationship or the presence of children. This is not, in fact, necessary if you use a retained advantage/disadvantage approach as it will naturally be the case that where there are children or a longer relationship the level of comparative advantage and disadvantage will be higher, so you capture those for whom the relationship has had a significant impact. Some schemes provide very similar types of remedy as on divorce, such as enabling pensions to be shared, while others are more limited (France, Scotland). This reflects a desire for there to be a bright line between the benefits of marriage and those of the cohabitation/domestic partnership regime. Marriage is therefore still advantaged. An alternative way of privileging marriage would be to allow the same types of order on the end of a cohabiting

---

[341] Institut national d'études démographiques. https://www.ined.fr/en/everything_about_population/data/france/marriages-divorces-pacs/marriage-nuptiality/#r177 accessed 9 November 2020. There are no more recent statistics for pacs.

relationship as on divorce but on a less favourable basis. Lord Lester QC's bill does this, limiting claims to reasonable needs. Scotland, the Law Commission, and the two private members' bills are all opt-out albeit with safeguards; Australia enables the parties to enter into a binding alternative agreement. France is an opt-in scheme. All demonstrate that a workable scheme is possible and show the variety of ways in which one could be achieved.

5.15 Conclusion

The significant rise in cohabitation over the last decade has brought into focus the very different position of married couples and those who cohabit without marriage. In this chapter, we have considered how very difficult it is to establish a successful trusts of land claim and how those who live together without marriage may find themselves, as a result of relationship breakdown or their cohabitant's death, with very limited legal remedies indeed. If you need a reminder of what the differences are, look back at Table 5.1.

Parliament could seek to reform trusts of land or inheritance laws to mitigate the harms potentially caused to cohabitants, but such reform would be piecemeal compared to what it could do, which is provide a package of divorce-style rights and responsibilities for those who are not married or civilly partnered. Such a package could take the form of a domestic partnership regime that people elected into, or a scheme for those who live together but have taken no steps to protect their positions. Research shows that cohabitants are a diverse group who do not take steps to protect themselves even in the ways that they can do, such as by making an express declaration of the beneficial interest in the family home or making a Will. A number of different schemes exist around the world and several workable schemes have been suggested for this jurisdiction. While the government appears to have no current intention to reform the law in this area, we may yet follow other countries in providing a coherent scheme for unmarried couples.

 KEY POINTS

The Position of Cohabitants

- There is a stark legal difference between the position of cohabitants and those of married couples. During a cohabiting relationship, there is no mutual obligation of support and at the end of a relationship no divorce-style claims can be made. The principal remedy available to cohabitants is to establish a beneficial interest in the family home by asserting a constructive or resulting trust. It is now generally accepted that where a property is bought as a family home, the former will be the appropriate mechanism.

- Trusts of land claims are exceptionally difficult. There are many areas of legal uncertainty and the factual basis is likely to be heavily disputed. As is usual for civil cases, the losing party will be ordered to pay the winner's costs. These can be considerable. All of this could be avoided if the parties had made an express written declaration of trust.

- To establish that the constructive trust has arisen, it is necessary to show that the parties had a common intention that the claimant has a beneficial interest in the property and that the claimant relied on this to his or her detriment. At stage two, the interest (if proven) is quantified.

- In most cases where A makes a contribution to the purchase price of a property in the sole name of B or jointly with B, the law presumes that they intended A to have a beneficial interest proportionate to the contribution. This is a resulting trust.

- Proprietary estoppel is an equitable claim in which a party is prevented from asserting his or her strict legal rights because of a contrary promise or representation that they have made to the claimant. While there are similarities between estoppel and constructive trusts there are some key differences as the case law has run on parallel but unmerged lines.

- Trusts principles can be applied to other assets on separation. While an interest in land has to be in writing, an express trust over non-land can be established verbally.

- In England and Wales, a Will must be in writing and signed by the testator in the presence of two adult witnesses who are not beneficiaries under the Will or the spouses or civil partners of the beneficiaries. If a person dies without a Will, we call this dying intestate. In this situation the estate must be distributed to the relations of the deceased in an order of priority set out in the statutory intestacy rules. Cohabitants receive nothing under the rules.

- Certain categories of individual can apply under the Inheritance (Provision for Family and Dependants) Act 1975 for financial provision from a deceased person's estate on the basis that the deceased's Will or the intestacy rules failed to make reasonable financial provision for them and that failure is unreasonable.

- People may cohabit for a variety of reasons. Some will be fully aware of the limited rights that they have. Some will be unaware and may believe in the common law marriage myth. They may not take positive steps to protect themselves.

- When considering whether cohabitants should have divorce-style rights at the end of a relationship or on the death of a partner, a number of factors need to be considered including individual choice; the availability of marriage and civil partnership; the risks to the state; the need for the law to reflect important social values; the demographic of cohabitants; and state paternalism.

 # FURTHER READING: SOME STARTING POINTS

- Much good research has been done by Anne Barlow and her colleagues into the nature and extent of cohabitation why some cohabit rather than marry. See, for example 'Just a Piece of Paper? Marriage and Cohabitation', in Alison Park and National Centre for Social Research (eds), *British Social Attitudes: Public Policy, Social Ties: The 18th Report* (Sage 2001); 'Why Don't They Marry? Cohabitation, Commitment and DIY Marriage' (2005) 17 *Child and Family Law Quarterly* 383; and 'Regulating Marriage and Cohabitation in 21st Century Britain' (2004) 67(2) *Modern Law Review* 143.

- For some excellent commentary on whether there should be a regime for cohabitants and what that may look like, see Rebecca Probert, 'Cohabitation: Current Legal Solutions' (2009) 62(1) *Current Legal Problems* 316; Ruth Deech, 'The Case against the Legal Recognition of Cohabitation' (1980) 29(2/3) *International and Comparative Law Quarterly* 480 and 'Cohabitation' [2010, January] *Family Law* 39; and Edward Hess, 'The Rights of Cohabitants: When and How Will the Law Be Reformed?' [2009, May] *Family Law* 405. The Law Commission's cohabitation report is *Cohabitation: The Financial Consequences of Relationship Breakdown* (Cm 7182, Law Com No 307, 2007).

- On trusts, look at the Key Cases to trace the development of the law, but be careful to check that the older cases remain correct statements of the law by checking later cases and/or a respected practitioner guide. There are a great many commentaries and articles on each of them. Those on *Stack* could file a filing cabinet but a brief but very clear explanation is Luke Barnes, 'Stack v Dowden: The Principles in Practice' (*Family Law Week* 2007). Some good articles are Andrew Hayward, 'Cohabitants, Detriment, and the Potential of Proprietary Estoppel: *Southwell v Blackburn*' [2015, September] *Child and Family Law Quarterly* 303; and Brian Sloan, 'Keeping Up with the *Jones* Case: Establishing Constructive Trusts in "Sole Legal Owner" Scenarios', (2015) 35(2) *Legal Studies* 226. For the confusion between constructive and resulting trusts, see Sloan's 'Constructive or Resulting Trusts: Does It Matter?' [2020] 1 *The Conveyancer and Property Lawyer* 82; AYS Georgiou, '*Marr v Collie*: The Ballooning of the Common Intention Constructive Trust' (2019) 82(1) *Modern Law Review* 145, and the other articles footnoted at 5.6.

- For discussions of trusts law problems and reform, see Gillian Douglas, Julia Pearce, and Hilary Woodward, 'Cohabitation and Conveyancing Practice: Problems and Solutions' [2008] 5 *The Conveyancer and Property Lawyer* 365; Andrew Hayward, '"Family Property" and the Process of "Familialisation" of Property Law' (2012) 24 *Child and Family Law Quarterly* 284; Terence Etherton, 'Constructive Trusts and Proprietary Estoppel: The Search for Clarity and Principle' [2009] 2 *The Conveyancer and Property Lawyer* 104; Simon Gardner, 'Problems in Family Property' (2013) 72(2) *Cambridge Law Journal* 301 and 'Rethinking Family Property' (1993) 109(April) *Law Quarterly Review* 263; and Anne Lawson, 'The Things We Do for Love: Detrimental Reliance in the Family Home' (1996) 16 *Legal Studies* 218.

- On death and inheritance, an excellent starting point is Stephen Cretney 'Dividing Family Property on Death: Approaches to Reform of Intestacy', Chapter 10 in *Law, Law Reform and the Family* (OUP 1998), which draws on two articles which you could read instead, at [2004] *Denning Law Journal* 35; and (1995) 111(1) *Law Quarterly Review* 77. Apart from Key Case *Ilott*, there are two important Law Commission reports, *Family Law: Distribution on Intestacy* (Law Com No 187, 1989) and *Intestacy and Family Provision Claims on Death* (Law Com No. 331, 2011). Several articles trace the history of inheritance laws and discuss the proposals in these two reports. We suggest Elizabeth Cooke, 'Wives, Widows and Wicked Step-Mothers: A Brief Examination of Spousal Entitlement on Intestacy' (2009) 21(4) *Child and Family Law Quarterly* 423; and Fiona Burns, 'Surviving Spouses, Surviving Children and the Reform of Total Intestacy Law in England and Scotland: Past, Present and Future' (2013) 33 *Legal Studies* 85. The episode titled 'Mediation' of the BBC Radio 4 series 'Behind Closed Doors' provides a realistic dramatisation of a mediation in an inheritance dispute.

 Visit the **online resources** to watch a video of Polly Morgan discussing this chapter topic, and to check your understanding of this chapter with self-test questions and scenario questions.

6 Financial Support for Children

LEARNING CHECKLIST

By the end of this chapter, you should be able to:

- *Critically discuss* the history of financial support for children and *evaluate* the weaknesses of the various schemes that have existed
- *Describe* the current child support scheme and how maintenance is calculated
- *Critically discuss* why some parents do not pay child maintenance and the public views on how maintenance should be calculated
- *Describe* the interrelationship between the child support scheme and residual judicial powers
- *Describe* the courts' powers under Schedule 1 Children Act 1989 and how the courts go about deciding what order to make, by reference to the statutory provisions and the case law
- *Identify* some of the more controversial aspects of Schedule 1 and *evaluate* how Schedule 1 may be of use to parties at different ends of the economic spectrum.

SCENARIO

Melissa and Frank

Melissa and Frank have two children. They are an unmarried couple who have recently separated. The children will be living with Melissa primarily, but regularly spending time with Frank. Frank has a child from a previous relationship who lives with her mother. As they were unmarried, Melissa is concerned about her lack of financial remedies. In particular, she does not know how she is going to house the children. Frank is moderately wealthy. The house that they lived in during the relationship is in Frank's sole name, and Melissa has been advised by solicitors that she is unlikely to be successful on a trusts of land claim. She is interested to know whether she is entitled to any support from Frank because of the children.

6.1 Introduction

All those who are legal parents have the obligation to maintain their child. This obligation is not limited to those with parental responsibility. It ceases only as a result of the child ceasing to be their child, such as on the making of a surrogacy parental order or an adoption order; or on the child reaching adulthood—and sometimes not even then.

There are three main sources of financial support for children:

1. The scheme established by the Child Support Act 1991 and amended subsequently. This calculates child maintenance as a percentage of the gross weekly income of the non-resident parent. This scheme is open to separated parents whether or not they were married.

2. Matrimonial Causes Act 1973. This is the primary piece of legislation dealing with the financial outcomes of divorces, called 'financial remedy'.[1] Claims for financial support for children can be made in divorce proceedings between the parents; by definition this applies to formerly married couples only. There are mirrored provisions for civil partners in the Civil Partnership Act 2004.

3. Schedule 1 to the Children Act 1989. This provides a comprehensive set of financial provision for children.

In this chapter, we are going to consider each of these in turn. As we shall see, the introduction of the child support scheme established by the Child Support Act 1991 has limited the courts' powers considerably, although the latter remain important in ameliorating the flaws in the scheme.

6.2 A brief history of financial support for children

Historically, child support involved no enforceable obligation owed by a parent to the primary carer or the child himself.[2] Indeed, for many centuries there were no laws specifically providing for child maintenance. Instead, the poor laws required parishes to support paupers in their area, including children—the Poor Law Act 1575 referred to such children as 'the great burden' of the parish. Parents and grandparents could be required to support their children and grandchildren, the aim being to recoup the costs that the parish had expended on maintaining the child. Child support was not, therefore, an independent jurisdiction but an aspect of a punitive regime for the poor.

Wikeley—whose survey of the history of child support informs this section—writes that 'between 1601 and 1834 a series of measures were enacted with the twin goals of seeking to discourage procreation outside wedlock and to ensure that the parents, not the parish, bore financial responsibility for illegitimate children'.[3] (Legitimate children were in theory protected by obligations of spousal support during marriage.) The 1601 Poor Relief Act allowed parishes to remove people who might become financially dependent on the parish, and there are examples of pregnant women being forcibly removed to a neighbouring parish. In 1718, magistrates were given the power to seize land and chattels belonging to absconding fathers. Several pieces of 'bastardy' legislation allowed unmarried mothers who were dependent on the parish to be gaoled.[4] Given that these rules and

---

[1] This topic is dealt with extensively in Chapter 4.
[2] G Douglas, 'Can't Pay? Won't Pay!' Chapter 5 in *Obligation and Commitment in Family Law* (Hart 2018).
[3] N Wikeley, *Child Support: Law and Policy* (Hart 2006) 47.
[4] A 'bastard' being the term for an illegitimate child.

sanctions related only to those dependent on the parish, it is difficult to see these measures as being about anything other than the financial benefit of the state. They do not constitute legal recognition of any moral obligation to maintain one's children.

The nineteenth century poor laws were a response to concern about increasing financial costs associated with administering the existing laws and a belief that it was necessary to make receipt of poor relief less favourable than working, hence the introduction of workhouses. Married women whose husbands had deserted them were provided with modest financial support; the parish could recover its expenditure from the husband. The new divorce jurisdiction enabled the wealthy to bring private law suits for maintenance for the wife. Financial support for the children (if she was able to have custody of them, as this was the right of the husband) was 'treated as parasitic upon the spousal right to maintenance' that existed where the wife was morally innocent of wrongdoing.[5]

In parallel to this divorce jurisdiction, the so-called bastardy laws continued to operate in respect of unmarried mothers. Beliefs that a woman who had children outside of wedlock would falsely name the wealthiest person she could find as the father led in 1834 to stringent legal and evidential requirements upon an unmarried mother seeking financial support from a putative father, including corroboration of her evidence. It was not until 1844 that unmarried mothers were able to seek maintenance directly from the children's father, and this was not dependent on whether she was claiming poor relief. Nevertheless, the difficult evidential requirements of the so-called 'bastardy laws' remained, and from 1844 to 1868 the poor law authorities were prohibited from bringing proceedings instead. After that time, the authorities could once more use pursue those failing to maintain their children.

The poor laws and their siblings the vagrancy Acts and bastardy laws continued to operate into the twentieth century notwithstanding the introduction of a number of pieces of welfare-focused legislation in the early twentieth century (old age pensions, free school meals, national insurance). After the second world war, the old laws were finally abolished by the National Assistance Act 1948. With the establishment of the welfare state, child maintenance ironically became a purely private law issue, and remained so until the Child Support Act 1991.

6.3 Financial support under the child support scheme

Child maintenance under the scheme is a percentage of the non-resident parent's income. It bears no relation whatsoever to the costs of actually raising a child. The Child Poverty Action Group estimates that the raising a child to the age of 18 costs £185,000 for a single parent (including the costs of childcare) and £151,000 for a couple.[6]

---

[5] N Wikeley, *Child Support: Law and Policy* (Hart 2006) 75.
[6] D Hirsch, *The Cost of a Child in 2019* (Child Poverty Action Group 2019).

6.3.1 History and controversy

The Child Support Act 1991 came about for several reasons. At the time, child mainte-nance was dealt with by the courts, or through private agreement between the parents. There were a number of problems associated with this. It was highly discretionary and thus outcomes were unpredictable and inconsistent. Enforcement was expensive and be-cause of that often disproportionate to the amounts of maintenance in question. Courts had no power to trace parents who could not be found. Only one third of children enti-tled to receive child maintenance actually received it regularly, something that Margaret Thatcher, who was prime minister until 1990, thought scandalous. Many primary carers could not afford to work because they could not afford childcare. Child poverty was (and indeed, still remains) widespread. There were therefore good practical reasons for the creation of a statutory agency—the Child Support Agency (CSA)—that would address these problems.

There was also an ideological rationale. In the 1980s and early 1990s, there was con-siderable political rhetoric around so-called 'absent fathers' and the costs to the state as-sociated with single parenthood. By 1989 there were 770,000 single parents in receipt of income support, but only 22 per cent were receiving child maintenance.[7]

> The whole story of policy-making in the 80s was to try and find ways of saving money on social security, and all ways of saving money on social security are politically unattractive. Child support was seen as the politically more attractive way of doing it.[8]

The Act reflected a particular view of personal responsibility that was attractive to many politicians because single parenthood was seen as a moral problem and the solution was a punitive. Single parents were seen as part of an underclass that contributed to delinquency and crime, happily dependent on state benefits and teenagers getting pregnant specifically so that they received a council flat.[9] It was for these reasons that the scheme established by the 1991 Act enabled the state to recoup the cost of benefits provided to single-parent families from the child maintenance they received on a pound-for-pound basis.

The Child Support Agency started work in April 1993. It was, however, extremely un-popular among the general public, for all sorts of reasons. It calculated child support based on a percentage of the non-resident parent's net income and the children's ages, requiring over 100 pieces of information.[10] Calculations were so complex that one court was prompted to refer to the figure as 'a rate fixed by mathematically obtuse calcula-tions in innumerable unintelligible schedules'.[11] The scheme was inflexible, unlike the discretion inherent in a judicial process, with no scope for variations to allow for special

[7] Lord Chancellor's Department, *Children Come First: The Government's Proposals on the Maintenance of Chil-dren* Cm 1264 vol 1 (1990).
[8] Michael Whippman, Policy Director, Department of Social Security, 1994–1998 speaking to a Channel 4 docu-mentary 'Can't Pay, Won't Pay' (1999). Cited by L McCarthy-Cotter, *The 1991 Child Support Act: Failure Foresee-able and Foreseen* (Springer 2018).
[9] L McCarthy-Cotter, *The 1991 Child Support Act: Failure Foreseeable and Foreseen* (Springer 2018) 41–2.
[10] House of Commons Work and Pensions Committee, *The Performance of the Child Support Agency: Second Re-port of Session 2004–05* Volume I (HMSO 2014). For some worked examples, see G Davis, N Wikeley, and R Young, *Child Support in Action* (Hart 1998).
[11] *Re C (A Minor) (Contribution Notice)* [1994] 1 FLR 111, 117 (Ward J).

circumstances. This occasionally gave rise to some rather odd outcomes. Jane Fortin gives as an example the case of *Phillips v Peace*, an application for financial support from a millionaire father under Schedule 1 to the Children Act. The CSA had assessed Mr Peace's maintenance liability as nil, as under the scheme rules it could not take into account his income from shares dividends, which enabled him to live in a house worth £2.6 million and own vehicles valued at £189,000.[12] Over 90 per cent of CSA staff time was spent on calculations and recalculations as benefits rates changed, leaving scant time for addressing arrears.[13] Unpredictable ever-changing assessments caused uncertainty, stress, and worry to both paying and recipient parents. Arrears accrued easily because the CSA timed liability from the point of its request for information but then spent months making the assessment, so when it requested funds arrears already existed. Use of the CSA was mandatory if the parent with care was on benefits. This was usually the mother, and she was forced to name her children's father(s) or face a 'swingeing' 40 per cent deduction in her benefits for up to three years.[14] Many men did not believe that the application had not been made voluntarily and viewed CSA involvement as a punishment visited by their ex partners.[15] The fact that the maintenance calculation expressly included an element for the expenses of the primary carer meant that many payers felt that they were being asked to support their former partner rather than the children.[16] The costs associated with supporting any other children in the payer's new family was not sufficiently taken into account. In one study, by Davis, Wikeley and Young, 40 per cent of parents reported their post-separation relationship had worsened since the CSA became involved.[17] There were allegations that the scheme had a role in some payers' suicides.[18] And it did nothing to help children escape poverty: the rule requiring parents on benefits to apply to the CSA, and the consequent deduction of those benefits from any child support received, meant that the family had the same income as before, and only the state saved money. Where the maintenance received did add to the family income, it could cause them to lose certain passport benefits such as free school meals, putting them in a worse position than before. In 1993, its first year of operation, the Child Support Agency received more than 1,000 complaints.

Subsequent reform

The Child Support Act 1995 simplified the assessment calculation and introduced some flexibility into the assessments enabling variations from the formula in certain circumstances. Nevertheless, the new scheme was equally unpopular. Many assessments continued to be wrong. There was little evidence that it was helping to remove children

---

[12] [1996] 2 FLR 230; see J Fortin, *Children's Rights and the Developing Law* (2nd edn, Cambridge University Press 2005) 296.

[13] Department for Social Security, *A New Contract for Welfare: Children's Rights and Parents' Responsibilities*, (Cm 4349, 1999).

[14] J Fortin, *Children's Rights and the Developing Law* (2nd edn, Cambridge University Press 2005) 295.

[15] G Davis, N Wikeley, and R Young, *Child Support in Action* (Hart 1998).

[16] J Fortin, *Children's Rights and the Developing Law* (2nd edn, Cambridge University Press 2005) 297.

[17] G Davis, N Wikeley, and R Young, *Child Support in Action* (Bloomsbury 1998).

[18] For example, that of Graham Clay. See S Midgley, 'Father Killed Himself after Child Payout Was Tripled: Divorced Man Struggled to Pay Maintenance (*The Independent*, 22 December 1993). Available at https://www.independent.co.uk/news/uk/father-killed-himself-after-child-payout-was-tripled-divorced-man-struggled-to-pay-maintenance-1469049.html accessed 15 February 2020.

from poverty. The National Audit Office recorded that in the financial year 2001-2002 an estimated 36 per cent of receipts from non-resident parents and 81 per cent of maintenance assessment debts were incorrect—and that was an improvement on previous years.[19] Research commissioned by the Department for Work and Pensions found, perhaps unsurprisingly, that if the system was fairer and easier to understand, more people might be minded to cooperate with assessments.[20]

In 2003 a new scheme established by the Child Support, Pensions and Social Security Act 2000 came into force. This simplified the calculation further and based support on a simple percentage of the non-resident parent's net income, and reducing the amount of money recouped out of the maintenance when state benefits were received. The 1999 Child Support White Paper commented: 'With hindsight, we can see that the problem lies with the way that the child support system was designed. The complex rules do not fit either with the lives of separated families or with other systems that provide support for families.'[21] It suggested that 'simpler rules, tougher sanctions and better enforcement of maintenance will mean that at least 80% of maintenance due will be paid under the new scheme'.[22] It was also predicted that it would do more to lift children out of poverty.[23] One significant problem occurred in practice, however: the Agency's £456 million new computer system was unable to communicate with the old computer system, meaning that cases could not be transferred easily from the original scheme to the new scheme, so two schemes had to be administered in parallel. This perhaps explains why it cost the CSA £323 million to collect only £601 million', as a House of Commons select committee noted when referring to the Agency's performance as 'woefully inadequate'.[24]

By 2005 the government had conceded that the CSA was in meltdown. An estimated £3.5 billion of arrears were outstanding and 60 per cent of that was deemed to be uncollectable.[25] But, as Key Case *R (on the application of Kehoe) v Secretary of State for Work and Pensions* shows, enforcement was purely a matter for the service and an individual primary carer could not enforce the child maintenance obligation themselves.

---

[19] Comptroller and Auditor General, *Child Support Agency Client Funds Account 2001–2002* (National Audit Office 2002).

[20] N Wikeley, S Barnett, J Brown, G Davis, I Diamond, T Draper, and P Smith, *National Survey of Child Support Agency Clients*: DWP Research Report no. 152 (CDS 2001).

[21] Department for Social Security, *A New Contract for Welfare: Children's Rights and Parents' Responsibilities*, (Cm 4349, 1999) at p1.

[22] Department for Social Security, *A New Contract for Welfare: Children's Rights and Parents' Responsibilities*, (Cm 4349, 1999) chapter 2 para 24.

[23] G Paull, I Walker, and Y Zhu, 'Child Support Reform: Some Analysis of the 1999 White Paper' (2000) 21(1) *Fiscal Studies* 105.

[24] House of Commons Work and Pensions Committee, *The Performance of the Child Support Agency: Second Report of Session 2004–05* Volume I (HMSO 2014) 9.

[25] National Audit Office, *Child Support Agency—Implementation of the Child Support Reforms* (The Stationery Office 2006).

KEY CASE *R (on the application of Kehoe) v Secretary of State for Work and Pensions* [2005] UKHL 48

This was a judicial review suit brought by Mrs Kehoe, a mother who had sought maintenance for her children through what was then the Child Support Agency. The father of the children was her former husband Mr Kehoe. For over ten years, Mr Kehoe provided what Lord Bingham described as 'significant sums of money' to the Agency for the support of the children, but 'the process of obtaining payment was protracted and difficult and substantial arrears built up from time to time. Mrs Kehoe strongly feels, perhaps rightly, that direct action by her against her former husband would have yielded more satisfactory results.'

Mrs Kehoe argued that as she had a right to financial support for the children, the provisions of the Act that provided for enforcement by the Secretary of State (via the CSA) and denied her a directly power of enforcement against Mr Kehoe were inconsistent with the right of access to a court guaranteed by Article 6 of the European Convention on Human Rights. She therefore sought a declaration under s4 Human Rights Act 1998 that the Child Support Act was incompatible with Article 6, and damages.

The House of Lords held (Lady Hale dissenting) that:

- The 1991 Act did not confer any right on a parent in the position of Mrs Kehoe. The right to recover maintenance was vested in the CSA.
- If national law had given Mrs Kehoe the right to recover maintenance directly, then Article 6 would apply and guarantee her access to a court. However, national law did not give her that right and Art 6 did not create a substantive right of access to a court that had no legal basis in national law, only procedural rights. Accordingly, Art 6 was not engaged at all, and so it was not capable of being breached.
- Mrs Kehoe's only remedy was to bring judicial review proceedings if the Child Support Agency was to refuse to enforce *as a result of a mistake of law*.

As Wikeley has noted, the majority saw this as an issue of statutory construction. In contrast, Lady Hale's dissent is 'a child-centred analysis', constructing the right to maintenance as a right belonging to a child rather than a parent with care.[26] She held that the right to enforce was procedural and thus capable of protection under Art 6. She took the view that children as children have a civil right to be maintained by their parents, Article 6 was engaged.[27] She went on to note that:

> Even in benefit cases, where the state does have a direct interest in enforcement, it is not the sort of interest which stems from needing enough money to feed, clothe and house the children on a day to day basis. Only a parent who is worrying about where the money is to be found for the school dinners, the school trips, the school uniform, sports gear or musical instruments, or to visit the 'absent' parent, not only this week but the next and the next for many years to come, has that sort of interest. A promise that the Agency is doing its best is not enough. Nor is the threat or reality of judicial review.

---

[26] N Wikeley, 'A Duty but Not a Right: Child Support after *R (Kehoe) v Secretary of State for Work and Pensions*' (2006) 18(2) *Child and Family Law Quarterly* 287.

[27] David Burrows notes that 'a strange and uncomfortable cohabitation exists between family (private), and administrative (public), in respect of the 1991 Act and that three judges at three different stages of the *Kehoe* case who held that there was an Art 6 right were all family lawyers': D Burrows, 'Public v Family' (2008) 158(7311) *New Law Journal* 357.

The lack of any legal mechanism under which a parent could enforce maintenance was particularly galling in light of the significant and increasing arrears which they had not collected, and this contributed to strong negative feelings about the CSA on the part of both the paying and receiving parents.

The Henshaw Report

The 2006 Henshaw Report, named for its lead author, described the CSA as unfit for purpose.[28] Henshaw found that the system cost more money to run than it obtained and spent significant resources seeking and transferring relatively small amounts of money between parents. The policy of requiring primary carers on benefits to use the CSA incentivised non-cooperation. He recommended that parents should be encouraged to make their own arrangements, so that the state could focus on the more difficult cases and on enforcement. It was, said Wikeley, about carrots and sticks: the carrots related to the removal of the recoupment of benefits and the sticks related to the greater enforcement mechanisms.[29] Henshaw's principal recommendation was the abolition of the CSA on the basis that it was 'not capable of the radical shift in business model, culture and efficiency required', and its replacement with a new agency. That agency was the Child Maintenance and Enforcement Commission (CMEC) born under the Child Maintenance and Other Payments Act 2008.

Child Maintenance and Enforcement Commission

The Child Maintenance and Enforcement Commission was a short-lived public body, accountable to the Secretary of State for Work and Pensions, that existed from July 2008 to its replacement in July 2012. It had three principal functions:

1. To promote the financial responsibility that parents have for their children. It did this by trying to increase awareness of child maintenance issues among those who provided services to parents and children, including those who work with the most vulnerable groups in society.[30]

2. To provide information and support on the different maintenance options available, which it did through a website and call centre called Child Maintenance Options. Ireland et al. found that use of the child maintenance options service did correlate with positive results in the number of child maintenance arrangements reached.[31]

3. To provide an efficient statutory Child Maintenance Service with effective enforcement (known, once again, as the Child Support Agency). It therefore separated out information provision and advice that helped parents to reach their own decision from its role in dealing with uncooperative parents.

---

[28] D Henshaw, *Recovering Child Support: Routes to Responsibility* (Cm 6894, 2006).

[29] N Wikeley, 'Child Support: Carrots and Sticks' [2008] *Family Law* 1102.

[30] CMS, *Annual Report and Accounts 2010/11* (HC1193, 2011).

[31] E Ireland, E Poole, and C Armstrong, with J Hall, P Keogh, and S Purdon, *Evaluation of the Child Maintenance Options Service* (CMEC Research Report 3, 2011).

In 2012, CMEC was itself abolished and replaced with the Child Maintenance Service (CMS). The ostensible rationale for this change was that it would enable parents to make this own arrangements on the basis that this is 'better for everyone involved', with the state's involvement being restricted to those situations in which parents were unable to come to their own decision, thus achieving value for money for the taxpayer while sending a message that both parents take responsibility for their children.[32] In this way, the message was not so different to the responsibility focused messages in previous iterations of the Service, but greater emphasis was given to private ordering.

6.3.2 The current (2012) scheme

The establishment of the Child Maintenance Service brought with it a shift in tone to one of private ordering: getting parents to agree their own maintenance rather than (as was originally the case) compulsory intervention when parents were on benefits. But this was simply responsibility in a different form: responsibility to the state had been replaced with a responsibility to make one's own arrangements free of the state.

The 2012 scheme changed from a calculation based on the non-resident parent's net income to one based on gross income i.e., before tax and national insurance. The description in this chapter about how maintenance is calculated is based on this 2012 scheme. We generally avoid discussing precise percentages in our scenario because of the risk that they may change, and they necessarily simplify complex rules. We therefore recommend that you look for the most up-to-date information on the government website.[33]

6.3.3 Defining a qualifying child

Child maintenance under the scheme is paid to the primary carer of a 'qualifying child', which is a child or young person:

- aged under 16; or
- aged under 20 and in full-time non-advanced education.[34] This means education that is not higher than A Levels or their equivalent;

and for which the primary carer is eligible to receive child benefit.

Child benefit is payable in respect of almost all children but there are some exceptions such as if the child is in prison or residential care for a certain period of time, or if the child is married or civilly partnered.

---

[32] Department for Work and Pensions, *Strengthening Families, Promoting Parental Responsibility: The Future of Child Maintenance* (Cm 7990, 2011).
[33] Child Maintenance Service, *How We Work Out Child Maintenance: A Step by Step Guide* (2018) available at https://www.gov.uk/government/publications/how-we-work-out-child-maintenance accessed 26 September 2020.
[34] Regulation 76, which cross-refer to s142(2) of the Social Security Contributions and Benefits Act 1992 and its statutory instruments 2006/223, 2007/2150, 2008/1879 and 2009/3268.

6.3.4 Who pays maintenance?

Child support is paid *to* the person with primary care of the child. This is presumed to be the person who receives the child benefit; by default, child benefit is paid to the mother in the absence of evidence that she is not the primary carer.[35]

The child maintenance is paid *by* the non-resident parent. Legal parenthood is a necessary condition but extends beyond biological parenthood to encompass parenthood acquired through a surrogacy parental order or other forms of assisted reproduction. No assessment can be made against someone who is not a legal parent, even if they have played a parental role as (for example) many step-parents or foster parents do. The scope of the liability is therefore narrower than under the Matrimonial Causes Act 1973 (which gives courts the power to order maintenance for any child of the family, not merely biological children) or Schedule 1 to the Children Act 1989 (some sections of which enable an order to be made against a step-parent). The term 'non-resident parent' is defined by the Child Support Maintenance Calculation Regulations 2012 as a person who provides day-to-day-care to a lesser extent than the other parent, and in a different household, although in fact the child may live with them for part of the time.[36]

If the parents have an exactly equal division of the child's time, then no child maintenance would be paid: neither is the non-resident parent. However, over the course of a year it is almost certain that there will be a slight inequality in time such as to create a liability. Even a modest adjustment of time may make a considerable difference.

Sometimes parents do not have to pay maintenance. Parents who will be assessed at the nil rate of maintenance are those:

- Who have a gross weekly income of less than £7
- Are aged under 16, or under 20 if in full-time non-advanced education or on a government-approved training course
- Are 16 or 17 years old and in receipt of certain benefits such as income support or jobseekers' allowance, or who are included in their partner's claim for these
- Are in prison or in a care home or independent hospital and are getting help with fees.

With the exception of these categories, all non-resident parents are liable to make a contribution whatever their level of income.

If a person denies that they are the parent of a child, then the Child Maintenance Service will ask for DNA test results from an approved company or a court declaration that the person is not the child's parent. Otherwise, they will assume that the person is the parent. This means that they will still make a child maintenance assessment and any arrears that accrue will only be cancelled if the person turns out not to be the parent. The service can presume parentage in certain situations familiar to you from Chapter 8, such as where the father is married to the mother, or because a person refuses a DNA test. If a DNA test is not appropriate, for example because the child is adopted or born via assisted reproduction, then a court declaration will be needed.

---

[35] Child benefit is a state payment to help with the costs of raising a child. It is paid to a child's primary carer; by default this is assumed to be the mother. The current rate is £20.30 per week for the first child, and £13.40 for each subsequent child. It is paid in respect of all children aged under 16 (or up to 19 if in full-time education or training).

[36] SI 2012/2677.

6.3.5 Making and receiving payments

The maintenance liability is a percentage of the non-resident parent's gross weekly income, with some adjustments. It is not based on the child's needs (unlike the courts' approach) but was designed to reflect the standard of living of the non-resident parent.[37]

The current scheme is designed to encourage parents to reach their own agreements as to child maintenance without the involvement of the service. The service refers to this as a 'family-based arrangement', in that separated families make their own arrangements independently, but perhaps using a maintenance calculator or other tools on the service website.

There are likely several reasons for this emphasis on parties reaching their own agreements. First, where agreement is reached, the implication is that both parents are relatively happy with the figure, and thus more likely to abide by it. This will have the advantage of regular, consistent payments for the benefit of the child, and hopefully minimise conflict. Second, the current Conservative government's ideological approach is based on small government and private ordering: individuals reaching their own agreement fits with this.

If a family-based arrangement breaks down, or if the maintenance cannot be agreed, then either parent can apply to the Child Maintenance Service, which offers the following services:

- Direct pay, in which the service calculates the amount of child maintenance to be paid, and the non-resident parent then pays the primary carer directly. There is a one-off fee of £20 for this service, which is waived for victims of domestic abuse.

- Collect and pay, in which the service calculates the amount of child maintenance, and then collects it from the non-resident parent and pays it to the primary carer. This attracts a fee: there is an initial £20 charge and then the service will charge the non-resident parent an extra 20 per cent on top of the maintenance for its administration costs and deduct 4 per cent from the maintenance due to the primary carer. This is applied to every payment received.

- Enforcement, discussed at 6.3.6.

Note that arrears made under family-based arrangements cannot be subject to enforcement action. If a person breaches a family-based arrangement, the remedy is to make an application for collect and pay.

Between May and July 2019, 44,800 parents spoke to Child Maintenance Options, the government helpline that discusses which of the above services may be appropriate. 5,800 of went on to make family-based arrangements but most used the Child Maintenance Service.[38]

As at March 2020, some 737,700 children are covered by Child Maintenance Service arrangements, breaking down as 471,700 children covered through Direct Pay, 261,200

---

[37] Department for Social Security, *A New Contract for Welfare: Children's Rights and Parents' Responsibilities*, (Cm 4349, 1999).

[38] Department for Work and Pensions, *Child Maintenance Arrangements Made after Speaking to Child Maintenance Options* (2020). Data from customers calling up to July 2019, surveyed in November 2019. Available at https://assets.publishing.service.gov.uk/government/uploads/system/uploads/attachment_data/file/884677/child-maintenance-arrangements-made-after-speaking-to-cm-options-may-to-july-2019.pdf accessed 26 September 2020.

through Collect and Pay, and 4,800 not yet assigned to a service.[39] 68 per cent of parents due to pay child maintenance through Collect and Pay paid some maintenance in the three months January to March 2020.

The introduction of fees for use of the service was controversial and the government had originally wanted the application fee to be £100, although it reduced this in the face of strong opposition. Nevertheless, the fee serves several purposes. First, it is designed to financially support the Child Maintenance Service. Second, it is designed to reduce use of the service for both practical and ideological reasons. To Douglas, 'family-based, i.e., private, arrangements have come to reflect the moral superiority attached private ordering and agreement, which are characterised as more civilised forms of dispute resolution likely to reduce conflict and thus benefit the child.'[40] As Steve Webb MP, then a minister with the Department of Work and Pensions explained:

> The £20 fee strikes a balance. It is meant to get people to pause and think — 'Hang on, I've got to pay for this. What am I getting for it? Could I do it for myself?' — rather than simply defaulting to the statutory scheme. If it were free, the danger is that all 1 million cases, or the best part of them, would simply go straight from one system to another, and we would be exactly where we started. The £20 fee is a stop and think fee, and is not intended as an insurmountable barrier for those who cannot make a family-based arrangement.[41]

The ideological reason for the introduction of the fee is about individuals reaching their own agreements without state involvement. As Gingerbread, the campaign group for single parents, notes:

> the encouragement of Direct Pay arrangements is meant to 'engender co-operation' between parents, by nudging parents towards a maintenance arrangement that doesn't require the state to intervene for payments to flow. . . .Collect and Pay charges are intended to encourage Direct Pay compliance – the principle being that a paying parent can only avoid Collect and Pay charges if maintenance is paid in full and on time, and they remain in the Direct Pay service where there are no ongoing fees. . . . Maximising lighter touch Direct Pay arrangements ensures CMS running costs are kept to a minimum . . . For receiving parents, the 4 per cent Collect & Pay deduction is intended to ensure 'that both parents have an incentive to work together and to try Direct Pay'.[42]

While introduction of collection charges raised a significant amount for the government (albeit only a modest proportion of the running costs of the service), Gingerbread goes on to argue that there is little evidence of a nudge effect in action. The charges have little bearing on the decision to move onto Collect and Pay because for the receiving parent, there is no choice but to move onto Collect and Pay if the payer is not paying. Rabindrakumar found that among such parents there was 'a very strong, common feeling that charges . . . were unfair—a double penalty, coming on top of the other parent's non-compliance'.[43]

---

[39] Department for Work and Pensions, *Child Maintenance Service statistics: Data to March 2020* (June 2020). Available at https://www.gov.uk/government/publications/child-maintenance-service-statistics-data-to-march-2020-experimental/child-maintenance-service-statistics-data-to-march-2020-experimental accessed 26 September 2020.
[40] G Douglas, 'Can't Pay? Won't Pay!' Chapter 5 in *Obligation and Commitment in Family Law* (Hart 2018) 159.
[41] Second Delegated Legislation Committee, *Draft Child Support Fees Regulations 2014*, HC Monday 3 February 2014 *Hansard* vol 575, col 8.
[42] S Rabindrakumar, *Direct Pay Child Maintenance: Innovation or Failure?* (Gingerbread, March 2019) 6. Sources omitted.
[43] S Rabindrakumar, *Direct Pay Child Maintenance: Innovation or Failure?* (Gingerbread, March 2019) 9–10.

SCENARIO ILLUSTRATION 1

Melissa and Frank

Our scenario is that Melissa and Frank have two children. If they are living with Melissa primarily this makes Frank liable to pay child maintenance. Parties are encouraged to reach their own agreement: a 'family-based arrangement'. They could do this by inputting information about Frank's income into the child support calculator on the government website. If they cannot agree a figure, or if Frank won't disclose this information, then either can apply for 'direct pay' (where the service calculates the amount of child maintenance for a one-off fee of £20 but then leaves the parties to set up a payment arrangement themselves), or collect and pay (where the money is also collected by the Child Maintenance Service for an ongoing charge to both parties). They could also use the service if any family-based agreement breaks down.

6.3.6 Calculating child maintenance

There are several steps to calculating child maintenance under the scheme.[44]

Step One: Calculate the payer's gross weekly income

The payer's gross weekly income means their income before the payment of income tax and national insurance. Income includes earnings from employment, self-employed profits, and personal or occupational pensions, as well as from benefits (other than tax credits, student grants, and student loans, which are not counted as income). Details of the payer's income can be obtained from HM Revenue and Customs (HMRC) who will hold these records in the self-assessment tax return of those who are self-employed or in the 'pay as you earn' records for those who are employed. The Child Maintenance Service will deduct any contributions made by the non-resident parent to a registered pension scheme, which could be an occupational pension or a private pension. This means it is possible for a non-resident parent to reduce the gross weekly income figure, and thereby their maintenance liability, by increasing their pension contributions, although a variation is possible if the amount of contributions is excessive in the circumstances.

Under the pre-2012 schemes, maintenance was calculated on the net income of the payer after tax and national insurance as well as pension contributions, not the gross income. The decision to change to gross income enabled the service to use HMRC information and thereby obtain more accurate information and do so faster.[45] The figures that HMRC provides relate to the last tax year for which records are available, not the current tax year (tax years run April to April). The child maintenance calculation will therefore be based on this figure not any current figure, unless the non-resident parent's current income is

---

[44] The best guide to this is Child Maintenance Service, *How We Work out Child Maintenance: A Step by Step Guide* (2018) available at https://www.gov.uk/government/publications/how-we-work-out-child-maintenance accessed 26 September 2020.

[45] Department for Work and Pensions, *A New System of Child Maintenance—Summary of Responses to the Consultation* (Cm 7061, 2007). The change to gross income was accompanied by a reduction in the percentage of income paid by the non-resident parent, 'to match the new calculations as closely as possible in cash terms with the current assessments, thereby smoothing the transition': James Plaskitt MP testifying to the Public Bill Committee on Tuesday 9 October 2007.

different by at least 25 per cent (and they can prove this), or the historical income is zero, or the information is not available.[46]

The service assesses a weekly amount of maintenance so it will take the annual figures, divide them by 365 days per year and multiply by seven. This will average out any fluctuations in income. The final figure is the 'gross weekly income'.

If the non-resident parent does not cooperate with an assessment, the service can either assess the maintenance at a default rate, or it can make an assessment based on the best evidence it does have combined with general statistical information about how much people in certain jobs earn. It is a criminal offence not to provide information when requested or to supply information that they know is untrue.

Step Two: Apply deductions for other children

The service looks at whether there are other children the non-resident parent or their partner support, meaning for which they receive child benefit (thus for which they are the primary carer(s)). This could include a partner's children from a previous relationship, or children from the new relationship. If there are, and the paying parent has a gross weekly income of £200–£3,000, then the service will reduce the gross weekly figure from step one by certain percentages.

No deduction is made at this stage:

- If there are other children in the household but the paying parent has a gross weekly income between £100 and £200: a deduction is made later in the calculation process (meaning that it affects the outcome differently).

- For other children of the payer that do not live with him, and for which he is therefore liable for maintenance. This is taken into account later in the calculation process.

Step Three: Apply the relevant payment rate

The rate of maintenance payable varies according to the gross weekly income established by the end of step two. These are set out in Table 6.1.

TABLE 6.1 Child maintenance rates

Gross weekly income	Rate	Weekly amount to be paid
Unknown or not provided	Default	£38 if there is one qualifying child
		£51 for two qualifying children
		£61 for 3 or more qualifying children[47]
Below £7	Nil	£0 (irrespective of number of children)
£7 to £100, or if the non-resident parent receives certain benefits	Flat	£7 (irrespective of number of children)

[46] The 25 per cent was set so as to only take account of significant fluctuations in income and thereby provide greater certainty to the parties and be operationally efficient: see written answer to Parliamentary Question 218234 (15 December 2014).
[47] These figures are contained in the Child Support Maintenance Calculation Regulations 2012. Information correct as at February 2020.

£100.01 to £199.99	Reduced	The payer pays a fixed amount of £7 (irrespective of the number of children) as the assessment on the first £100 of their gross weekly income.
		They then pay a percentage of their income for any amount over £100:
		17% for one qualifying child
		25% for two qualifying children
		31% for three or more qualifying children
£200 to £800	Basic	12% of non-resident parent's gross weekly income where there is one qualifying child
		16% if there are two qualifying children
		19% if there are three or more qualifying children
£800.01 to £3,000	Basic Plus	The following basic rate is applied to the first £800 of gross weekly income:
		12% of non-resident parent's gross weekly income where there is one qualifying child
		16% if there are two qualifying children
		19% if there are three or more qualifying children
		The following percentages are applied to any gross weekly income above £800:
		9% of non-resident parent's gross weekly income where there is one qualifying child
		12% if there are two qualifying children
		15% if there are three or more qualifying children
£3000.01+		Apply basic plus rate; on application under Children Act 1989 Schedule 1 the court can order an additional 'top-up'

Step Four: Other things affecting the assessment

We mentioned above that the service will take account of other children supported by the payer.

Where the children live with the payer, we saw that this is done at step two in many cases. However, it is done at the present stage—by applying a different percentage of gross weekly income that takes into account the other children—when the paying parent has a gross weekly income of between £100 and £200.

So far, the deductions we have made relate to the presence of other children in the payer's household. However, sometimes the payer may have several qualifying children from different relationships for whom he is not the primary carer. Where there are several children in different homes that need to be maintained by the payer, the service will calculate the maintenance as above for all of the children, and then split it between the primary carers in accordance with the number of children each has. This means that if the payer is on the basic rate, and has two children with ex-partner A and three with ex-partner B, then the payer's assessment is for five children: the rate is 31 per cent of the payer's gross weekly income. This is divided as to two-fifths to A and three-fifths to B. The result is that each recipient primary carer receives less than if the payer had fewer children: the share of the payer's income is capped at 31 per cent no matter how many children he or she has, and is then divided between their households.

For example, if the payer has children from a previous relationship with person A but is not their primary carer, and from a previous relationship with person B but is not their primary carer, and there are children in the payer's current household with new partner C, then there is a deduction for children of C, and then the maintenance liability for the children with A and B is split between A and B in accordance with the number of children each has.

The service will also make a deduction (after any apportionment) where the child stays overnight at the same address as the non-resident parent and when they do so are being looked after by them. If the child is at boarding school or in hospital, those nights count if the child would, but for that, be with the no-resident parent. The amount deducted from the assessment depends upon the number of overnights. It is presently a one-seventh reduction in the assessment for every 52 nights that the payer has the child (i.e., equivalent to one night per week), up to a maximum of a 50 per cent reduction. The service will look at any agreements or court orders that set this out, or any pattern already established. There is no reduction for shared care where the flat rate is paid.

Remember that if there is exactly equal division of the child's time, there is no liability at all.

FOCUS Think Critically

Public views on child maintenance

The British Social Attitudes Survey 30 (2012) asked over 3,000 participants about child maintenance, using a number of scenarios based on female recipients and male payers.[48] Two-thirds of respondents agreed that the state should force a parent to pay child maintenance and a similar number agreed that the law should set a minimum amount rather than leave it to the parents to decide. Although men and women agreed this to different extents, this view was the majority view of both men and women. When asked how much maintenance should be paid, most people indicated a figure about one third higher than the current statutory formula, and thought that it should encompass not merely the child's necessities but also amenities for the child to the extent that the father's income allowed. Bryson, Ellman, McKay and Miles' report on the survey results concludes that 'the public clearly does not believe the function of maintenance is limited to keeping children from poverty. This is clear, because their favoured maintenance amounts continue to increase with paternal income beyond the point at which the child's household income is above any plausible "poverty line" (such as 60 per cent of median income).'[49]

Most survey respondents thought that both mothers' and fathers' income should be taken into account when setting the amount that the father should pay, and that if the mother's income was lower than that of the father, he should pay a greater *proportion* of his income: not simply a greater amount to reflect the fact that his income was higher, but a greater proportion of his income too.

[48] You can find all the British Social Attitudes Surveys at https://www.bsa.natcen.ac.uk/.
[49] C Bryson, IM Ellman, S McKay, and J Miles, *Child Maintenance: How Would the British Public Calculate What the State Should Require Parents to Pay?* (Nuffield Foundation 2015).

This view was consistent among both male and female respondents. To Ellman et al., this suggests that the public believe that 'children of higher-income fathers should enjoy some of the amenities the father is capable of providing, but which the mother is not'. In contrast, the American public would keep the proportion of the father's income the same irrespective of his wealth.[50] Both countries, though, would make the father pay a higher rate the more the mother's income declined.

What is interesting about these studies is the way in which they reflect, or do not reflect, the systems in place. In England and Wales, payers in the higher income parts of the basic plus rate do pay an additional rate, but the increase in rate is not proportional to the increased income. Thus a father of one child would pay 12 per cent of income up to £800 per week but only 9 per cent on income above that to the £3,000 mark when the courts regain jurisdiction to make a top-up order.

Quite how the percentages to be paid have been reached is somewhat unclear. The 1999 command paper, *A New Contract for Welfare: Children's Rights and Parents' Responsibilities*, noted that 'the proposed base rate of 15 per cent of their income [which was the percentage at the time for a payer with two children] is roughly half the average that an intact two-parent family spends on a child'.[51] That suggests that an intact family would spend 30 per cent of their income on their children. Of course, as Ellman points out, this does not make sense: if parents spend 30 per cent of their income pre-separation on their children, then when they are separated, they would each need to continue to spend 30 per cent of their own individual incomes on the children,[52] although with the costs of running two households this would be less affordable. In an intact household, children indirectly benefit from the joint financial position of the parents but post-separation their individual financial positions may be very different to one another. Meeting the costs of children by providing child maintenance makes the children cost-neutral (assuming the child maintenance is at the correct level, which ignores the reality of the grey area between child-related expenses and the expenses of their carer). But it does not compensate for the other problem of having children, which is the way in which they prevent the primary carer from financially bettering her position. If the parties were married, the principles of needs and compensation on divorce may do so, but even these do not compensate adequately.[53] Thus, Ellman explains, 'translating estimates of parental expenditures on children in intact families, into required support amounts in a child support guideline applied to separated families, is a tricky business involving many policy choices. It requires more than arithmetic.'[54] Moreover, as we discuss in our next Focus Box, the degree to which the system is perceived as fair affects the level of compliance and therefore any system of child maintenance needs to have public support in order to fulfil its aims.

Special expenses variation

A variation is an alteration to the assessed figure based on factors that are not otherwise taken into account. In this way, it permits a modicum of discretion into what is otherwise a fixed formula, albeit nowhere near the level of discretion that courts have in their residual jurisdiction. A variation has to be specifically requested by either the paying or recipient parent and can result in either an increase or a decrease in the sum payable.

---

[50] IM Ellman, S Mckay, J Miles, and C Bryson, 'Child Support Judgments: Comparing Public Policy to the Public's Policy' (2014) 28 *International Journal of Law, Policy and the Family* 274.

[51] Department for Social Security, *A New Contract for Welfare: Children's Rights and Parents' Responsibilities* (Cm 4349, 1999).

[52] IM Ellman, S Mckay, J Miles, and C Bryson, 'Child Support Judgments: Comparing Public Policy to the Public's Policy' (2014) 28 *International Journal of Law, Policy and the Family* 274 at endnote 28.

[53] See Chapter 4.

[54] IM Ellman, S Mckay, J Miles, and C Bryson, 'Child Support Judgments: Comparing Public Policy to the Public's Policy' (2014) 28 *International Journal of Law, Policy and the Family* 274.

The following can vary the maintenance upwards:

- Any unearned income of the payer, such as dividends, rental income, or any income generated from the ownership of assets that individually have a net worth more than £31,250.[55] The Child Maintenance Service will attribute to the payer a weekly income at the judgment debt rate which is currently 8 per cent per year.[56]

- Pension contributions made by the payer to the extent they are 'excessive' compared to the payer's personal circumstances.

- The payer having earnings as well as receiving certain benefits that have automatically led to an assessment at the nil rate or flat rate.

- A conclusion that the non-resident parent has diverted income, i.e., that they have not truthfully declared the extent of their income.

It is possible to reduce the amount of maintenance payable if the payer incurs certain 'special expenses':

1. The payer can ask for costs associated with having contact with the children to be considered. This could include, for example, costs of travel to contact or overnight accommodation if the children live far away.

2. The boarding element (only) of any boarding school fees paid by the non-resident parent can be taken into account.

3. If the payer has another child in their household who has a long-term illness or disability that results in extraordinary costs being incurred, it may be possible to take these into account.

Note that the above expenses cannot be taken into account of the paying parent is receiving benefits or has a gross income of less than £7 per week.

SCENARIO ILLUSTRATION 2

Melissa and Frank

To calculate Frank's liability for child support, the service will first calculate his gross income using information from HMRC. They will deduct any contributions he makes to a pension scheme, but not tax or national insurance. Let us assume that Frank's gross weekly income is £1,600 before tax and national insurance but after he has made his pension contributions. That makes his salary around £87,360 if he pays 5 per cent into his pension.

We make no deduction at this stage for the other child of Frank's from an earlier relationship, because that child is not in his household. This means that Frank is assessed in the Basic Plus category. But as he has three children in total, his assessment will be 19 per cent of his gross weekly income for the first £800 of his income, and 15 per cent on anything above that (coincidentally another £800).

---

[55] See Income Tax (Trading and Other Income) Act 2005 and Child Support Maintenance (Calculation) Regulations 2012.

[56] 8 per cent divided by 52 weeks per year.

This gives us a total liability of £272 per week or £90.66 per child. This will be split two-thirds to Melissa and one third to the mother of Frank's other child.

Frank can reduce his liability (after any apportionment) where a child stays overnight with him. If he has his two children by Melissa overnight for 52 or more nights per year (equivalent to one night per week), that is a one-seventh reduction in the payments to Melissa. If he drops below 52 nights per year even slightly, then he gets no deduction.[57]

Remember that if the parties use the Collect and Pay service, they will charge Frank an additional 20 per cent on top of his payments and deduct 4 per cent from the amount received from him before the balance is divided between the mothers.

6.3.7 Appeals

As with state benefits, the first step to challenge a child maintenance assessment is to request a Mandatory Reconsideration by the Child Maintenance Service. This can be done by either party but can be done only once per case.

The reconsideration is of the child support decision, which includes how much maintenance is payable, any default maintenance decision, any decision to refuse to revise a calculation in light of changed circumstances, any variation decision, or a refusal to vary. It is not possible to appeal against a payment schedule such as how long it takes to pay off any arrears.

Appeal from a mandatory reconsideration lies to the Social Security and Child Support Tribunal, and must be lodged within one month.

6.3.8 Enforcement

As we see in Key Case *Kehoe*, enforcement is a matter for the Secretary of State through the Child Maintenance Service (and its predecessors) rather than the parents concerned.

If arrears have accumulated, the non-resident parent can try to negotiate a repayment plan. In deciding its response, the service will consider the welfare of any child likely to be affected by payment in instalments, including both the qualifying child and any other children such as those within the current household of the non-resident parent. They also take into account the hardship of both households. There is usually no time limit for seeking payment of arrears. However, do note that they can decide to accept part payment in full and final satisfaction of what is owed, and can write off arrears in a number of situations.[58]

---

[57] The deduction is one-seventh per child, so if one child stayed over, the payment for that child £90.66 would be reduced by one-third and the payment for the other would stay at £90.66.

[58] See Tim Jarrett, *Child Maintenance: The Multi-Billion Pound Write-Off of Arrears on Child Support Agency Cases* (House of Commons Library Briefing Paper CBP-7776, March 2019).

If arrears are not being cleared, then the service may turn to one of a number of different mechanisms to enforce payment:

1. Take money directly from the paying parent's bank or building society account, including any joint accounts they have with another and some types of business accounts (sole trader, and partnership without limited liability/unlimited partnership). The services does not require court permission to do this and can recoup the amount owed either as a one-off lump sum payment or in regular instalments. This can be used both for arrears and for any future payments. Appeal lies to a magistrates' court.

2. Where the non-payer is employed, the service can require their employer to deduct the amount owed from the non-payer's earnings. The employer must comply with the terms or they may be prosecuted, but they can charge the non-payer for this work. Up to 40 per cent of the non-payer's income can be taken this way. Again, this does not require court permission, but appeal is to a court.

3. Deduction from state benefits or pension. The amount that can be taken this way is capped.

4. Deduction from a deceased payer's estate—this is a debt that should be paid when the estate is administered (see Chapter 5).

5. They could apply to court for a liability order which legally recognises the debt as owing.[59] This is a step usually only taken if the above methods have not been successful or so much money is owed that those methods are inappropriate. Once an order is obtained, as with any other commercial debt, the service may:

   a) Instruct bailiffs to seize the non-payer's goods and possessions, which they then auction to raise money to pay the debt. Bailiffs also add on their own fees to the sum owed.

   b) Seek a charging order securing the debt against any property owned by the non-payer and then seek an order of sale and take the debt from the proceeds of sale. (Where the property is jointly owned, the liability attaches to the debtor's share only, but it is still on the title to the whole property.)

   c) Inform a credit reference agency of the existence of the debt. This will reduce the non-payer's credit rating and thus their ability to borrow either at all or at a low interest rate.

   d) Seek an order to set aside any dispositions of property/assets that the debtor has transferred to a third party for less than full value in an attempt to rid themselves of assets that could be used to pay the order. It is also possible to obtain a freezing order to prevent anticipated disposal.

6. Apply for a committal order. The debtor will be summoned to a court hearing at which the court will consider whether they have wilfully refused to pay maintenance—inability to pay is a different matter. This power is only used as a last resort and the

---

[59] No liability order can be granted after 12 July 2006 for maintenance that was owed before 12 July 2000.

court must first consider the welfare of any child likely to be affected. On a committal application the court can do any of the following:

a)   Send the non-payer to prison for up to six weeks for breach of the liability order.

b)   Pass a sentence of imprisonment but suspend it if the debt is paid.

c)   Suspend the non-payer's driving licence for up to two years.

d)   Remove their passport (possible since December 2018 and similar to the civil writ *ne exeat regno*).

The committal order does not end any liability. The debt is still owing and further enforcement action can be taken if the debt is not paid. If the debt is paid, or partly paid, then the debtor can ask for the sanction to be lifted.

There is a power lying on the statute book to make an administrative liability order, i.e., one that does not require court involvement. This power has not been brought into force.[60] While there is a power to require the debtor to make penalty payments to the government, which has been brought into force, no regulations have been passed explaining how this may happen. Finally, there are also powers under the 2008 Act to impose a curfew on a non-payer, but these is not in force.

As at the end of September 2019:

- 49,700 deductions from earnings orders and requests were in place
- 3,700 liability orders were in process
- 5,700 enforcement agent referrals were in process
- 3,500 regular and lump sum deduction orders were in process.[61]

FOCUS Think Critically

Why do some parents not pay child maintenance?

Part of the controversy surrounding the child support service and its predecessors is their failure to get to grips with the very significant arrears that have accrued but which have not been collected. It appears that little effort seems to be going to enforcement of arrears still outstanding from under the 1993 and 2003 schemes.[62] Although the children concerned will have grown up, that money is still owed to their primary carer who has disproportionately carried the financial burden of the children. Indeed, since December 2018 the service has had the power to write-off arrears that accumulated under the legacy 1993 and 2003 schemes if no payment towards those arrears were made in a three-month period. That is a potential write-off of £3.7 billion.

[60] Child Maintenance and Other Payments Act 2008.

[61] Department for Work and Pensions, *Child Maintenance Service statistics: Data to September 2019, Great Britain* (December 2019). 'In process' means, to the Child Maintenance Service, ongoing. The statistical breakdown may be found in the data tables at https://www.gov.uk/government/statistics/child-maintenance-service-statistics-data-to-september-2019-experimental accessed 23 February 2020.

[62] See National Audit Office, *Child Maintenance: Closing Cases and Managing Arrears on the 1993 and 2003 Schemes* (HC 1054 2016–17, 28 March 2017).

The service's own research shows that when the service had made the calculation of the appropriate figure, which it does in direct pay cases, it was only in approximately half of cases that the payer had met their obligation fully.[63] That said, in about 44 per cent of cases, the amount owed is below £500.[64]

In 2015 the Department of Work and Pensions commissioned some research into self-employed non-resident parents paying (or not paying) child maintenance.[65] This research, by Connors and Fu, found that for some parents:

- There was mistrust about how the child maintenance paid by the paying parent was being spent by the receiving parent. There was a perception that the payments were not being spent on the child. [The counter argument to this is that if the money is coming into the primary carer's household, it doesn't matter whether it is spent directly on the child or on paying the central heating bill: the child benefits indirectly. Even in cases where the money is spent on (for example) alcohol or cigarettes for the recipient parent, that person still has to buy food for the child. Only when the amount being contributed exceeds half of the costs of raising the child can a complaint about expenditure be legitimate—in all other cases the resident parent is absorbing the extra costs themselves.]
- There were concerns that calculations did not take account of payments and other forms of support made outside the scheme (such as when the non-resident parent bought clothes or nappies).
- The scheme was viewed by many non-resident parents as a form of punishment imposed by the primary carer. As Connors and Fu write, 'This background of conflict and tension underplays paying parents' responses to the statutory system itself—as their relationships with ex-partners could influence their response to the CSA/CMS, potentially reducing motivation to comply.
- Some non-resident parents were unable to afford the payments due to a low or fluctuating income. Some also prioritised other bills especially those relating to 'survival' such as rent and heating, work-related expenses, or bills with high costs for non-compliance. Connors and Fu note that this 'seemed linked to a perception that the cost of non-compliance was low; respondents felt that response from the [service] after non-payment was often delayed or unpredictable'.
- Some parents perceived that the calculations and payment schedules were unfair, especially as self-employed persons may experience variable income flow or periods of sickness.
- Some had had negative experiences with the service and its staff, including system errors and what they felt was a judgmental approach. There was a perception that paying parents were 'treated as criminals' and assumed to be at fault, even when they were willing to pay. 'Many parents thus felt morally justified in "fighting back" with non-compliance.' There was also a degree of resentment about government interference in personal affairs.

Maclean and Eekelaar found that some fathers felt that their liability should reduce when the mother repartnered; a passing of responsibility to another man.[66] They also saw a connection between child support and child contact. While child support is more often paid in situations where there *is* contact, this may not be a causal relationship as much as indicative of cooperative parenting. While the law does not see the two as connected, some parents may well object to contributing to the household of a primary carer who is not, in their view, supportive of contact. Bryson et al.

[63] Department for Work and Pensions, *Survey of Child Maintenance Service Direct Pay Clients* (December 2016).
[64] HC Work and Pensions Committee, *Child Maintenance Service* (2017) para 59, cited by G Douglas, 'Can't Pay? Won't Pay!' Chapter 5 in *Obligation and Commitment in Family Law* (Hart 2018).
[65] Caitlin Connors and Emily Fu, *Attitudes and Behaviours of Self-Employed Child Maintenance Clients and Barriers to Paying Child Maintenance* (Department for Work and Pensions 2015).
[66] M Maclean and J Eekelaar, *The Parental Obligation: A Study of Parenthood Across Households* (Hart 1997).

similarly found that there is a connection between child maintenance and contact in the public mind: their research using the British Social Attitudes Survey showed that most people would reduce child maintenance if the mother unreasonably stopped a father from seeing his child, but made no deduction if the father refused to see the child.[67]

There is one other way of conceptualising a failure to pay child support, and that is that for some payers it is experienced or intended as a form of economic abuse. Rather than failing to pay because they cannot afford it, the non-resident parents make a positive choice not to pay, or to pay late, or to lie about their financial circumstances in order to harm their former partners (and children). We have acted for a woman whose former husband paid her maintenance by cheque each month, always late and always leaving her wondering whether that would be the month in which she could not pay the mortgage and thereby keep herself and her daughter housed. He could have paid by direct payment: presumably the irritation of having to write an unwanted cheque each month was outweighed by his pleasure at causing her to wait for it.

Natalier has argued that behaviour such as this is the 'post-separation equivalent of denying women access to household resources, money to cover necessities, and financial information in co-habiting relationships'.[68] The women in her study 'understood their former partner's behaviours not as singular incidents with temporally and financially bounded effects but as strategies of ongoing control over their present and future lives'. For Natalier, this is a form of gendered, state-facilitated abuse of women.

As you can see, there are a variety of reasons for non-compliance by self-employed parents, the basis of which does not appear to include a principled objection to supporting one's children. The objections often have much more to do with a feeling of being treated unfairly and oppressively by a government agency that has a very poor history of accurate and timely administration. For some payers and receivers, child support will, as with all interactions with a former partner, also be a way of perpetuating abuse or imposing punishment.

Research such as those discussed in this focus box serves an important purpose. By understanding reasons for non-payment, schemes can be reformed in such a way that they address barriers for compliance and thereby do a better job of helping children. Wikeley has referred to this as the 'holy grail' of child support schemes.[69]

6.4 Residual judicial powers for child maintenance

There are a number of usual powers to order different forms of financial provision for children contained in various statutes:

- The Matrimonial Causes Act 1973 contains powers of financial remedy on divorce, nullity, or judicial separation; this includes provision for children. In the case of civil partners there are almost identical powers in the Civil Partnership Act 2004.
- Where the parties are not separated, then the Domestic Proceedings and Magistrates' Courts Act 1978 provides an obligation of maintenance during marriage.

[67] C Bryson, IM Ellman, S McKay, and J Miles, *Child Maintenance: How Would the British Public Calculate What the State Should Require Parents to Pay?* (Nuffield Foundation 2015).
[68] K Natalier, 'State-Facilitated Economic Abuse: A Structural Analysis of Men Deliberately Withholding Child Support' (2018) 26 *Feminist Legal Studies* 121.
[69] N Wikeley, 'Child Support: Carrots and Sticks' [2008] *Family Law* 1102.

- Schedule 1 to the Children Act 1989 contains a number of comprehensive powers to order a child's parents to provide financially for him or her, including in some cases into adulthood, and against step-parents. Importantly, this is not dependent on the parties' marital status and is therefore very useful in the case of unmarried persons for whom the Matrimonial Causes Act is not available.

- Finally, as we have seen, in Chapter 5, the Inheritance (Provision for Family and Dependants) Act 1975 enables claims to be made from the estate of a deceased person and again this is not dependent on marital status nor on age.

The Matrimonial Causes Act and Schedule 1 to the Children Act 1989 are the subject of separate sections within this chapter.

There are important limits on these judicial powers. The effect of the introduction of the child support scheme was to curtail the courts' powers to deal with financial support for children. Section 8 Child Support Act 1991 says that courts do not have jurisdiction in any case where the Child Maintenance Service has jurisdiction, but lists some exceptions. The result is an 'awkward division of function' between different legislation.[70]

Situations in which courts do have residual jurisdiction are:

- Where one or both parties is outside the jurisdiction. The Child Maintenance Service only has jurisdiction where both parents are habitually resident in the UK, with certain exceptions. If the parties are unmarried, a Schedule 1 application can be made; if married then an application under the Matrimonial Causes Act 1973 (if the parties are divorcing) would be appropriate.

- As a top-up above the maximum Child Maintenance Service assessment in the case of those earning more than £3,000 per week: s8(6) Child Support Act 1991. The top-up is by virtue of an application under Schedule 1 to the Children Act 1989, and it is necessary to obtain a maximum assessment before one can apply to court.[71] In *TW v TM*, Mostyn J held that the amount that a non-resident parent should pay in addition to the Child Maintenance Service calculation should, as a starting point, be the same percentage as the CSA used for amounts below £3,000.[72]

- For educational expenses such as school fees or the costs of attending education or training: s8(7).

- For expenses relating to a child's disability: s8(8). Such an application can be made under Matrimonial Causes Act or under Schedule 1, and the child may be aged over 18.

- Where the child is over 16 but *not* in full-time education or training (and thus not within the scope of the service), an application can be made under Schedule 1 or under the Matrimonial Causes Act 1973. The child may be an adult aged over 18.

- Where the child is in *tertiary* education or training, such as at university, an application can be made under Schedule 1 or under the Matrimonial Causes Act 1973 as again, the statutory scheme does not apply, and again this may be in respect of an adult child.

---

[70] G Davis, S Cretney, and J Collins, *Simple Quarrels* (Clarendon Press 1994), 36.
[71] *Dickinson v Rennie* [2014] EWC 4306 (Fam).
[72] *TW v TM (Minors)* [2015] EWHC 3054 (Fam).

- When financial support is being ordered against a parent with care, because the child support scheme only applies against non-resident parents: s8(10). This is very rare, and the only reported successful case is *Re S (Child Financial Provision)*.[73] This is perhaps because it may be a claim for financial support for the applicant parent, in disguise as a claim for the non-resident child, as in *N v C*.[74]

- Where the order is against a stepchild. The Matrimonial Causes Act 1973 applies to children of the family as defined in s52, and is not limited to the biological children of the divorcing couple. Conversely, the child support scheme only applies to the payer's legal children.[75]

There is one final, important, exception, which is parents can enter into (temporarily binding) maintenance agreements. A maintenance agreement under s9(1) the Child Support Act 1991 is 'an agreement for the making of or securing of periodical payments by way of maintenance to or for the benefit of a child'. By definition it requires agreement between the parties although all that is necessary is that they agree a nominal amount because they can then invite the court to vary it up and the court has jurisdiction, by virtue of that agreement, to set the quantum.[76] The effect of a maintenance agreement is to oust the jurisdiction of the Child Maintenance Service for 12 months from the date of the order.[77] After that time, either payer or recipient can apply to the Child Maintenance Service and any calculation under this scheme will replace the maintenance agreement; the resulting assessment may be an increase or a decrease in maintenance payable, thus the risks of that are to be borne in mind. One way around the '12-month rule' is to express the payments as a lump sum or sums for school fees as these are not within the Child Maintenance Service's powers and thus cannot not be replaced by their assessment.

As we shall see, neither maintenance agreements nor any financial remedy order between the parents are capable of ousting the jurisdiction of the court under Schedule 1 to the Children Act, although they are a relevant consideration (see Key Case *Morgan v Hill*). The usual rule that you cannot litigate through different channels on the same legal issue does not apply to children cases 'particularly when dealing with the developing needs of a child. The requirements of children, as they grow, require for the court to preserve its jurisdiction for the protection of the child. No adult compromise can oust that jurisdiction.'[78]

---

[73] [2004] EWCA Civ 1685.

[74] [2013] EWHC 399 (Fam).

[75] Where an application is made in relation to a child of the family who is a stepchild, s25(4) provides a list of additional factors that the court must consider in addition to those in s25(3).

[76] This way of doing things is called a '*V v V* order'.

[77] This applies to orders dated after 3rd March 2003. Section 4(10)(aa) Child Support Act 1991.

[78] *MB v KB* [2007] EWHC 789 (Fam).

6.5 Financial support under the Matrimonial Causes Act 1973

Where the child's parents are married, an application under the Matrimonial Causes Act is almost always preferable to those available under the Children Act 1989 because the powers are wider.[79] Usually, financial support for children is absorbed into the claims of the spouse who has primary care, forming part of the assessment of their needs. However, in s23 there are specific powers to make financial provision for children, albeit, as we discuss, these are now strongly restricted by the child support scheme:

- Order a party to pay the other a lump sum or sums.[80] In this context, a lump sum could be used to pay school fees, private health insurance, or any other capital need.

- Order a party to make periodical payments for the benefit of a child. Remember that s8 Child Support Act restricts the use of this (see 6.4).

- Order the transfer of property to the child or to a specified person for the benefit of the child. This is known as a property adjustment order; 'property' in this context means any type of asset, not merely 'real property' (houses).

- Order the sale of property and decide how the proceeds should be shared out.

- Order that property be held on trust for the benefit of a child.

- Vary a prenuptial or postnuptial agreement for the benefit of the children of the family.

- An application under s35 (maintenance agreements).

The nature of each of these powers is discussed in Chapter 4. Note that there are mirrored powers in relation to civil partnerships under the Civil Partnership Act 2004, so all references to married couples here apply just as much to civil partners.

Under s27, there is also the power to apply to court on the grounds that the other party to the marriage has failed to provide, or to make a proper contribution towards, reasonable maintenance for any child of the family. The court can make orders in relation to periodical payments, secured periodical payments, and lump sum orders. This does not appear to be dependent on the marriage having broken down.[81]

6.5.1 Deciding what provision to make

When considering whether to make an order for financial provision for children, the court must consider s25(3):

(a) the financial needs of the child;

(b) the income, earning capacity (if any), property and other financial resources of the child;

---

[79] What we say is also relevant to the mirror provisions in the Civil Partnership Act 2004.

[80] Unlike the position in relation to adults, more than one order for lump sum can be made: *Rayden and Jackson on Divorce and Family Matters* (18th edn) at para 17.240.

[81] *H v H* [2015] EWHC B24 (Fam). For capitalisation of child maintenance, see *AZ v FM (Rev 1)* [2021] EWFC 2.

(c) any physical or mental disability of the child;

(d) the manner in which he was being and in which the parties to the marriage expected him to be educated or trained; and

(e) the considerations mentioned in s25 in relation to the parties to the marriage themselves: their income and financial resources; needs, obligations and responsibilities; standard of living; and any physical or mental disability that they have.

Note that periodical payments under the Matrimonial Causes Act 1973, including by way of child maintenance, are in any event not enforceable if more than 12 months old without the consent of the court.[82]

6.5.2 Duration

With some exceptions, set out in s29(3), no order for periodical payments, lump sums, or transfer of property can be made in favour of a child who has attained the age of 18. Periodical payments and secured periodical payments must end on the first birthday that the child has after the date when compulsory schooling ends,[83] unless the court considers that in the circumstances of the case the welfare of the child requires that it should extend to a later date. In any event, periodical payments cannot extend beyond his or her 18th birthday.

The exceptions are where the court finds that:

- the child is, or will be, or if an order were made, receiving instruction at an educational establishment or undergoing training for a trade, profession or vocation, whether or not he is also, or will also be, in gainful employment; or
- there are special circumstances which justify the making of an order.

In these situations, the court can make an order into adulthood.

6.6 Financial support under Schedule 1

Schedule 1 to the Children Act 1989 gives courts the power to order different types of financial provision for children. At 6.4 we identified that Schedule 1 is one of the residual court powers that (mostly) survived the passing of the Child Support Act 1991. In this section we are going to look at what those powers are, and when it is appropriate to use them.

Schedule 1 (which is linked to s15 of the Act) tells us that financial provision is available where the parties have children. The parents' marital status is not important: the remedy is available irrespective of that. However, its use is primarily by those who have never been married to the other parent. This reflects the fact that other legal provisions available to married couples, most notably those of the Matrimonial Causes Act 1973, offer more generous outcomes.

---

[82] Section 32 Matrimonial Causes Act 1973.

[83] A child ceases to be of compulsory school age on the last Friday in June in the academic year in which he reaches the age of 16 or if he reaches 16 after the last Friday in June but before the start of the new school year.

If the parties were married and had a financial remedy order under the 1973 Act, this does not preclude a later application under Schedule 1.[84] However, in that situation Key Case *Morgan v Hill* tells us that this agreement would influence the court unless it was found to be inadequate. It is certainly possible for an outcome in divorce proceedings to meet needs at the point of divorce but not to do so subsequently: growing children may require a larger house, for example.

6.6.1 Applicants and respondents

The process for making a Schedule 1 application is very close to that of a financial remedy application under the Matrimonial Causes Act (see Chapter 4), and must also be preceded by a mediation information and assessment meeting (MIAM) unless one of the exceptions applies. In addition to mediation, arbitration and early neutral evaluation may be appropriate as ways of resolving issues without contentious court proceedings. These are discussed in Chapter 1.

Where the child for whom financial provision is sought is a minor, the application can be made by a parent, guardian or special guardian, as well as any person who is named in a s8 child arrangements order as a person with whom the child is to live. In fact, while an application is usually made on a freestanding basis, the court can make an order under Schedule 1 at any time it makes, varies or discharges a special guardianship order or any provision in a 'live with' child arrangements order.[85] An application to vary a periodical payments order can be made by the child himself once he reaches the age of 16: para 6(4).

The respondents to the application are one or both parents. In respect of claims under Schedule 1 paragraph 1 (but not paragraph 2), a claim can also be made against a step-parent in respect of whom the child was a child of the family. That means someone who was married or civilly partnered to the other parent, not a parent's unmarried partner. In this way, Schedule 1 is similar to the Matrimonial Causes Act 1973, which makes the welfare of a child of a family the first consideration irrespective of whether there is a biological relationship. Under paragraph 2, an adult may apply for financial provision from his or her parents (but not a step-parent) as long as the parents are living in different households from one another.

Schedule 1 can be used where one parent lives abroad as long as the other parent is within the jurisdiction, i.e., in England or Wales. Usually, the applicant parent is the one in England and Wales but the courts also have jurisdiction where the respondent is here but the child is not. Similarly, the courts have jurisdiction where the child lives outside England and Wales, but at least one parent is within the jurisdiction.[86]

---

[84] *MB v KB* [2007] 2 FLR 586.

[85] Para 1(6).

[86] *Re S (Child) (Financial Provision)* [2004] EWCA Civ 1685. The relevant paragraph, 14 to Schedule 1, was subsequently amended, but from 31 December 2020 (Brexit) is being reinstated in the form referred to in *Re S*.

6.6.2 What provision can be made?

Paragraphs 1 and 2 of Schedule 1 set out what financial support can be provided. The court's powers differ depending upon whether the 'child' is a minor or an adult. These are set out in Table 6.2. You can see that the courts' powers are wider in respect of a minor child than in respect of an adult child.

Periodical payments

Periodical payments are regular payments made by the respondent to the applicant for the benefit of the child, or to the child directly. They do not have to be repaid. If there are concerns about compliance with the order, they can be secured against an asset of the respondent, and that asset may be sold if the respondent fails to make the payments.

TABLE 6.2 Comparison of powers under Schedule 1 paragraphs 1 and 2

	Paragraph 1	Paragraph 2
Age	Child aged under 18	'Child' aged over 18 and • receiving instruction at an educational establishment or undergoing training for a trade, profession or vocation, whether or not while in gainful employment (or would be if order made); or • where there are special circumstances such as a disability that justify an order being made but not if immediately before he reached the age of 16, a periodical payments order was in force with respect to him.[87]
Remedy	• periodical payments • secured periodical payments • a lump sum The order will direct that the respondent make the payment(s) to the applicant for the benefit of the child or to the child him or herself. • settlement of property for the benefit of the child • transfer of property to the child or to the applicant for the benefit of the child.	• Periodical payments • Lump sum
Against	One or both parents as well as any step-parent who has treated the child as a child of the family	One or both parents (cannot be against a step-parent) The parents must be living in different households from one another: para 2(4).

---

[87] This means a periodical payments order under section 23 or 27 of the Matrimonial Causes Act 1973; the Domestic Proceedings and Magistrates' Courts Act 1978; or the Civil Partnership Act 2004.

In *GW v RW*, Mostyn J took the view that when a court made a child maintenance order the appropriate starting point:

> should almost invariably be the figure thrown up by the new child support rules. The Government's express policy in making awards of child maintenance susceptible to abrogation and replacement by a maintenance calculation by the CSA . . . was that child maintenance orders should be negotiated 'in the shadow of the CSA. All parties will know that either parent can turn to the CSA in future, and that it will therefore be sensible to determine child maintenance broadly in line with CSA assessment rates.'

> If a child maintenance order, whether made by consent or after a contest, is markedly at variance with the calculation under the new regime then there will be a high temptation for one or other party after the order has been in force for a year, and after giving 2 months' notice, to approach the CSA for a calculation. Quite apart from the obvious acrimony that this would engender, a calculation in a different amount to the figure originally negotiated or awarded may cast doubt on the fairness of the original ancillary relief settlement between the parties, leading to further litigation. These spectres should be avoided at all costs.[88]

Note that the use of periodical payments under Schedule 1 is curtailed by the Child Support Act 1991. They are available only when the service has no jurisdiction (for example because one parent is outside England and Wales), or in situations in which s8 Child Support Act 1991 has preserved court jurisdiction, such as the power to order a top-up to a child maintenance assessment when the payer is earning more than £3,000 per week. A periodical payments order under Schedule 1 ceases to have effect if a maintenance calculation is made by the Child Maintenance Service.[89]

An order for periodical payments under paragraph 1 will end on the child's 17th birthday unless the court 'thinks it right in the circumstances of the case to specify a later date' and, if so, that later date cannot extend beyond the child's 18th birthday unless:

- the child is, or would, if the order was made, be receiving instruction at an educational establishment or undergoing training for a trade, profession or vocation, whether or not while in gainful employment; or
- there are special circumstances which justify the making of an order.

In other words, the court can make an order for financial provision into adulthood (theoretically without limitation) if the child is in education or training, or special circumstances apply. The education ground includes tertiary education (university). Some courts have been willing to include a gap year before university. It may be hard to persuade a court to order the funding of postgraduate education even if vocational, although this does not appear without precedent.[90]

---

[88] *GW v RW* [2003] 2 FLR 108 at [74] quoting the White Paper, *A New Contract for Welfare: Children's Rights and Parent's Responsibilities* (Cmnd 4349,1989) at para 25.

[89] Child Support Act 1991 s10(1)(a).

[90] See the comments of the authors in A Bagchi et al., *Applications under Schedule 1 to the Children Act 1989* (2nd edn, Lexis Nexis 2018) at 7.8.

The special circumstances ground relates to the circumstances of the child rather than his parents.[91] In *Re N (A Child) (Financial Provision; Dependency)* Munby J made it clear that

> it is not enough . . . that increasing numbers of legally emancipated adults are continuing to live at home rent free with their parents, or that . . . the particular child in question is likely . . . to go on living after majority with one or other parent. It is not for the courts to impose legally binding obligations on unwilling parents merely because some parents choose . . . voluntarily to assume a financial burden which the law of England does not . . . impose upon the parent of an adult child with legal capacity.[92]

In many special circumstances cases the circumstance is the child's disability. What is appropriate provision for a disabled child will depend on the nature and severity of the child's disability. In *C v F (Disabled Child: Maintenance Orders)*, the Court of Appeal took 'the broadest view of such expenses', and the needs of the seriously disabled adult child in that case included 'the costs associated with, for example, additional help, feeding such additional help, a larger house, heating, clothing, running a car and respite care.'[93]

Any periodical payments will end on the death of the payer, and where the order requires periodical payments are to be made to the other parent for the benefit of the child (as opposed to the child directly) this ceases to have effect if the parents live together for more than six months. Note that the child may have a claim against the estate of a deceased parent, something that is discussed in Chapter 5.

Transfer or settlement of property

A minor cannot own the legal title to land, and no transfer to a child over 18 is permitted by paragraph 2 (see Table 6.2 for the powers under each paragraph). While a property can be transferred to an applicant parent or guardian for the benefit of a child, there are no reported cases in which this has happened, and in *A v A (A Minor) (Financial Provision)* [1994] 1 FLR 657, Ward J stated provision of a home should be by way of settlement (a trust) rather than an outright a transfer of property order. The usual structure, therefore, is for the property to be held on trust for the benefit of the child and on the happening of certain events the beneficial title to the house is transferred back to the respondent.[94] Any settlement of property will end in the same circumstances as periodical payments, i.e., by 18 at the latest unless education or special circumstances apply.

This means, effectively, that the use of the house is borrowed for the duration of the child's dependency. As Bailey-Harris points out, 'it is therefore not a vehicle for asset distribution between unmarried partners in their own right, and is not used to achieve a

---

[91] *T v S (Financial Provision for Children)* [1994] 2 FLR 883. See also *MT v OT (Financial Provision: Costs)* [2008] 2 FLR 1311 (wealth of father not a special circumstance).
[92] [2009] EWHC 11.
[93] [1998] 2 FLR 1.
[94] If the house was already the family home before the Schedule 1 application then it may be that the applicant, as well as the respondent, has an interest in it, and is entitled to a share of its value at the end of the trust.

fair result between the adult parents in the light of their role-division during the relationship'.[95] As such, it is less favourable than a spousal claim under the Matrimonial Causes Act, but may be the only remedy if the parties are unmarried and there is no likelihood of a successful Trusts of Land or estoppel claim (discussed in Chapter 5).

In *K v K*, the Court of Appeal confirmed that it had the power under Schedule 1 to transfer a secured tenancy into the sole name of the primary carer.[96] It may be necessary to injunct the non-resident parent from giving notice to terminate the tenancy while the Schedule 1 application is being considered.

Lump sums

The court may order a lump sum either to be paid as a one-off or in instalments (para 5(5)). Lump sums can only be used to meet capital needs, as they cannot be used as a way around the restrictions on periodical payment orders.[97] (There are, however, some examples of this restriction being somewhat loosely interpreted.[98]) Examples of appropriate uses of lump sums may include to furnish a new property, to cover expenses relating to accommodations for a disability, and for a car to transport the child. A lump sum can be for future use or to pay for costs already incurred, including in costs uncured in connection with the child's birth.[99] It does not have to be repaid.

Schedule 1 Children Act applications can be costly. It was accepted in *Re S (Child: Financial Provision)* that the court had power to award the resident parent a lump sum that included money to cover their legal fees on the basis that the application, and thus the fees, were for the benefit of the child.[100]

SCENARIO 1

Illustration 3: Melissa and Frank

So far, we have seen that the Child Maintenance Service would assess Frank's income at £90.66 per child per week. Melissa cannot apply for periodical payments under Schedule 1 because the Child Maintenance Service has jurisdiction. However, she can apply for some types of remedy that CMS does not cover, such as a lump sum or settlement of property.

---

[95] R Bailey-Harris, 'Law and the Unmarried Couple – Oppression or Liberation?' [1996] *Child and Family Law Quarterly* 137.
[96] [1992] 2 FLR 220.
[97] *Philips v Peace* [1996] 2 FLR 230.
[98] *DE v AB (Financial Provision for Child)* [2011] EWHC 3792 (Fam), for example, and *CF v KM (Financial Provision for a Child: Costs of Legal Proceedings)* [2011] 1 FLR 208. For a discussion, see A Bagchi et al., *Applications under Schedule 1 to the Children Act 1989* (2nd edn, Lexis Nexis 2018) at 11.14.
[99] Para 5(1).
[100] *Re S (Child: Financial Provision)* [2005] 2 FLR 94; see also and *M-T v T* [2007] 2 FLR 925 and *CF v KM (Financial Provision for a Child: Costs of Legal Proceedings)* [2011] 1 FLR 208.

6.6.3 Deciding what provision to make

Under Schedule 1 para 4, when considering whether to make an order, the court must consider 'all the circumstances' including:

- The income, earning capacity, property and other financial resources of the applicant and the parents
- The financial needs and obligations of the applicant and the parents
- The financial needs of the child
- The child's earning capacity (if any), property and resources
- Any disability, physical or mental, of the child
- The manner in which the child is being, or is expected to be, educated or trained.

This list is similar to the s25 factors in the Matrimonial Causes Act but it is narrower in scope in that it does not include conduct or contribution, for example.[101]

When an application is made against a step-parent, there are additional factors. The court must consider whether the step-parent has assumed responsibility for the child's maintenance and, if so, the extent to which and the basis on which that was assumed and the length of the period during which s/he met that responsibility; whether s/he did so knowing that was not his child; and the liability of anyone else to maintain the child. These phrases will be familiar to you from our discussion of claims under the Inheritance (Provision for Family and Dependants) Act 1975 in Chapter 5.

Although not explicitly mentioned, courts do look at the standard of living of the parties. This is clear from Key Case *J v C*. Although this case discusses some important points of principle, it is also useful to read the full judgment for its clear application of the s4 criteria to the facts of the case.

> **KEY CASE** *J v C (Child Financial Provision)* [1999] 1 FLR 152
>
> The child was born to unmarried parents whose relationship broke down while the mother was pregnant. When she was 18 months old, the father won £1.4 million on the National Lottery. The applicant mother lived in rented accommodation and was in receipt of housing benefit, council tax benefit, income support and child benefit. The mother had two other daughters who also lived with her and the child; they had a different father.[102] She owed debts incurred buying Christmas presents and there was a county court judgment against her for water rates. In response to the mother's application under Schedule 1, the father argued that the child had been unwanted.
>
> Per Hale J:
>
> - While the welfare of the child was not the paramount consideration in Schedule 1 cases,[103] nor first consideration as it would be under s25 Matrimonial Causes Act 1973, it nevertheless 'must be one of the relevant circumstances to be taken into account when assessing whether and how to order provision'.

---

[101] *PG v TW (No 2) (Child: Financial Provision)* [2014] 1 FLR 923.

[102] The father also had children by other relationships who could also have made Schedule 1 claims although, as Hale J points out, not necessarily to the same value.

[103] Because s105 Children Act 1989 excludes maintenance from the definition of upbringing to which s1 relates.

- 'Although paragraph 4(1) requires a judge to consider all the circumstances, no great weight should be attached to whether she was wanted or the length or quality of the parents' relationship. As a general proposition, children should not suffer because their parents are irresponsible or uncaring towards them.'
- 'Paragraph 4(1) does not include any reference to the standard of living enjoyed by the family before the breakdown of the marriage. This is not surprising as in cases concerning children of unmarried parents there may not have been any cohabitation between them at all. Nevertheless, the child is entitled to be brought up in circumstances which bear some sort of relationship with the [non-resident parent's] current resources and present standard of living. Parents are responsible for their children throughout their dependency. The fact that such riches as they have came after the breakup of the relationship cannot affect that.'
- As a matter of public policy, where resources allow, the family obligation should be used to reduce, or even eliminate, the need for children to be supported by public funds.
- The father is not responsible for the child's two half-sisters. 'However, the child needs to live with her mother and her mother has to provide for the sisters too, and in human terms she needs to grow up with her sisters. It would clearly be greatly to her benefit for her to do so. In taking that view I draw some support from *A v A* where there were two other children who were not the responsibility of the father.[104] Ward J held that this was immaterial because their needs did not greatly affect the cost of keeping a roof over the head of the relevant child and her carer.'

The judge ordered the father to purchase a modest four-bedroomed house for the child to live in with her mother and two sisters, and this was to be held on trust for the child's benefit until such time as she reached the age of 21 or completed full time education, whichever came later. After that, the house would revert to the father and the mother and children would need to vacate the property. Any future cohabitation or remarriage of the mother should not result in the reversion of the property to the father as this would not affect the child's need for her mother to care for her.

The father was also required to pay the mother enough money for her to buy a reasonable family car and carpets and furnishings for the house, and to refund her for some of her past expenditure on the child.

The principles set out in this case were endorsed by the Court of Appeal in Key Case *Re P (Child: Financial Provision)*.

KEY CASE *Re P (Child Financial Provision)* [2003] EWCA Civ 837

The respondent father was an immensely successful international businessman who told the court that he could 'raise and pay any sum which the court may order'. He had an intermittent four-year relationship with the applicant, as a result of which they had a daughter. Child maintenance was assessed at £152 per week, although this bore no relation to the father's true assets, and accordingly the mother made a Schedule 1 application.[105] At first instance, the judge awarded the mother £450,000 for a house, £30,000 for furnishings, £20,000 for a car to be replaced every four years,

---

[104] *A v A (A Minor: Financial Provision)* [1994] 1 FLR 657 (Fam).

[105] If you are wondering on what basis the court had jurisdiction to make a periodical payments order when the Child Maintenance Service assessed the father at less than £3,000 per week, very well done. The answer is that this case preceded the case confirming that the Child Maintenance Service had to have assessed at the maximum level possible in their assessment, which is *Dickinson v Rennie* [2014] EWC 4306 (Fam).

periodical payments of £35,360 per annum (to be reduced by £9,333 on the child's seventh birthday and end on completion of her secondary education), and backdated maintenance of £7,500 for 26 months. While this may sound generous, remember that this is a 'big money case' and that the child is entitled to be brought up in circumstances which bear some sort of relationship with the non-resident parent's current resources and present standard of living, and £450,000 does not buy much in central London.

The mother appealed. To succeed on appeal, she had to show that the first instance judge was wrong, meaning that his decision was outside the ambit of his discretion.

Per Thorpe LJ:

- The principles discussed in *J v C* were correct.
- The court takes a broad-brush approach when considering the amount of the claim: 'it is not for the court to specify the precise amounts of each category of the claim, but to take an overall sum to make provision for the components that are referred to'.
- While the welfare of the child is clearly embraced within the court's general duty to 'have regard to all the circumstances', welfare must be not just 'one of the relevant circumstances' but a constant influence on the discretionary outcome.
- In a big money case, the starting point for the judge should be to decide the home that the respondent must provide for the child. The home will be required during the child's minority or until further order. 'The appropriate legal mechanism is therefore a settlement of property order.' Since the respondent will receive the house back when the child is older, he must have some right to veto an unsuitable investment.
- 'In most cases the lump sum meets the cost of furnishing and equipping the home and the cost of the family car.' Once the housing costs have been determined, the amount of the lump sum should be easier to judge. 'The value, the size, and the location of the home all bear upon the cost of furnishing and equipping it as well as upon future income needs.'
- 'Once those issues are settled, the judge can proceed to determine what budget the mother reasonably requires to fund her expenditure in maintaining the home and its contents and in meeting her other expenditure external to the home, such as school fees, holidays, routine travel expenses, entertainments, presents, etc. . . . What is required is a broad common-sense assessment.'
- It is not wrong for the court to increase the periodical payments order to include an allowance for the mother, especially if the mother is unable to work because she has to look after the child. 'There is an inevitable tension between the two propositions, both correct in law, first that the applicant has no personal entitlement, secondly, that she is entitled to an allowance as the child's primary carer. Balancing this tension may be difficult in individual cases. In my judgment, the mother's entitlement to an allowance as the primary carer may be checked but not diminished by the absence of any direct claim in law. The court must recognise the responsibility, and often the sacrifice, of the unmarried parent (generally the mother) who is to be the primary carer for the child, perhaps the exclusive carer if the absent parent disassociates from the child.'
- 'In order to discharge this responsibility the carer must have control of a budget that reflects her position and the position of the father, both social and financial. On the one hand she should not be burdened with unnecessary financial anxiety or have to resort to parsimony when the other parent chooses to live lavishly. On the other hand, whatever is provided is there to be spent at the expiration of the year for which it is provided. There can be no slack to enable the recipient to fund a pension or an endowment policy or otherwise to put money away for a rainy day. In some cases it may be appropriate for the court to expect the mother to keep relatively detailed accounts of her outgoings and expenditure in the first and then in succeeding years of receipt. Such evidence would obviously be highly relevant to the determination of any application for either upward or downward variation.'

Per Bodey J:

- The overall result should be fair, just and reasonable taking into account all the circumstances.
- 'It is in quantifying the mother's reasonable needs as carer of the child that a tension emerges in such cases as this where the father is very wealthy. This tension is between seeking to achieve that the child has a standard of living bearing 'some sort of relationship with the father's current resources and standard of living', yet that the mother is not in the process provided for just the same as if she and the father had undertaken the commitment of marriage. Such tension is unlikely to emerge where the father is of lesser means, as (i) his lifestyle will be more modest as a comparative factor and (ii) his own needs will place a curb on the amount which he can reasonably be expected to pay.'
- It is not possible to create a formula to maintain the distinction between the mother in her capacity as carer and the mother in her own right. The 'grey areas of indirect benefit to the child . . . justify the . . . desirability of a broad budgetary approach by the court in bigger money cases.'
- 'In cases where the father's resources permit and the mother lacks significant resources of her own, she will generally need suitable accommodation for herself and the child, settled for the duration of the child's minority with reversion to the father; a capital allowance for setting up the home and for a car and income provision with the expense of the child's education being taken care of, generally by the father, direct with the school.'

The mother succeeded on her appeal and was awarded £1 million for a house, £100,000 for internal decoration of it, and periodical payments of £70,000 per annum (less state benefits), as well as backdated maintenance of £40,000.

Although *Re P* sets out the approach to be taken in 'big money' cases, it is useful in all cases because of the process it suggests: start by identifying an appropriate house, and the other expenses come from the costs of living there, or the standard of living that the house indicates.

6.6.4 Millionaires and mistresses?

You may wonder whether all Schedule 1 cases involve male millionaires and women at the opposite end of the economic spectrum.

At the top end of the spectrum, awards can be very generous in light of the principle outlined in *J v C* that the child's upbringing should bear some relation to the lifestyle of the non-resident parents. As Thorpe J said in *F v F (Ancillary Relief: Substantial Assets)*, it 'it is important as a matter of principle that the court should endeavour to determine reasonableness according to the standards of the ultra-rich and to avoid confining them by the application of scales that would seem generous to ordinary people'.[106] In big money cases, an allowance for the primary carer in her capacity as primary carer has been permitted. Nevertheless, any benefits to her are not the same as the claims one would have at the end of a marriage, and involve no principles of compensation or sharing, and include needs only insofar as they reflect the role of the primary carer *as primary carer*. Accordingly, there is no power to take into account the future needs of the carer at the conclusion of the relevant child's dependency: *Re A (A Child) (Financial Provision: Wealthy Parent)*.[107] The fact that the home for the applicant and child is by way of settlement during the child's minority rather

---

[106] [1995] 2 FLR 45, [50].
[107] [2015] Fam 277. See also *CA v DR (Schedule 1 Children Act 1989: Pension Claim)* [2021] EWFC 21.

than outright transfer also serves as a reminder that Schedule 1 is about financial provision for children. Once the children are no longer dependent, at age 18 (or later if in education or special circumstances) the property reverts to the settlor and the maintenance ceases. At that time, the person who was the children's primary carer is potentially in some financial difficulties. With her earning ability having been hindered by the presence of children, she may not have had the opportunity to build up her own asset base. Many women suffer irreparable significant long-term detriment to their earning capacity as a result of being the primary carer, detriment that is not often suffered by the men involved.[108] The end of the children's dependency may therefore mark a period of financial difficulty for the mother.

While the cases we have considered so far have all been cases in which the respondent non-resident parent is wealthy, Schedule 1 is useful in low or moderate asset cases. It is just that moderate and low asset cases are often not litigated to appeal level because of the costs involved, and thus are often not reported in the law reports.

As discussed at 6.6.2, the courts' residual top-up jurisdiction in relation to periodical payments is only for non-resident parents with gross incomes of more than £3,000 per week. In low or modest asset cases, there is thus no jurisdiction to make a periodical payments order and the applicant must apply to the Child Maintenance Service instead. The only exceptions are where the service has no jurisdiction, such as where the parent lives abroad and here *SW v RW* indicates that the child maintenance is likely to be set at the level that the Child Maintenance Service would have applied if they had jurisdiction.[109]

Nevertheless, the courts' jurisdiction for lump sums and property may be useful in low and moderate asset cases. The significance that a Schedule 1 claim may have on the finances of a couple of modest means is apparent by looking at the case of *DE v AB*.[110] The mother had a good job, as a result of which she was able to raise a large mortgage of £600,000 on a house in London. She lost her job and became pregnant. The mortgage payments were too large to cope with, and she fell into debt. By the time of the hearing, she had net equity of £98,000 and debts of £111,385, not counting the mortgage. The father had net equity in his home of £364,000 and an income of around £100,000 per year. He was ordered to pay £250,000 towards housing for the mother and child, and a lump sum of £40,000. He had to sell his house to achieve this. He could then rehouse himself on his remaining £68,000 plus his (not inconsiderable) mortgage capacity. Although the house bought by the mother with the money would revert to him when his child was no longer dependent, at the time the child was a toddler so this was a long way ahead. The mother could rehouse herself using the £250,000 and a more affordable mortgage which would make up the shortfall between what each could provide and what a house cost.

Where a non-resident parent has other children with other partners, the court will have to balance their needs and standard of living, seeking to achieve an outcome that is fair, just and reasonable. In *Re M-M (A Child)*, the court ordered the father—who was married to someone else, with whom he had three children—to pay the mother a lump sum sufficient to pay her credit card debts.[111] This equated to about a third of the father's savings,

---

[108] See Chapter 5.
[109] [2008] EWHC 73 (Fam). This principle also applies to periodical payments as a top-up: see *GW v RW* [2003] 2 FLR 108.
[110] [2011] EWHC 3792 (Fam).
[111] [2014] EWCA Civ 276. The father was also ordered to make periodical payments, the court having jurisdiction because the father lived abroad.

and the rationale for this was that if the mother was able to get out of debt she could spend her future income on improvements to the house or buying herself a car.[112]

In looking at those cases in which the primary carer is on benefits, it is essential to understand the impact on means-tested benefits where receipt of a lump sum or certain income level can result in benefits being reduced or stopped. It is, however, also necessary to consider the principle reiterated by Lady Hale in *J v C*, namely that where resources allow, the obligation to maintain a child should be met by family so as to reduce, or even eliminate, the need for children to be supported by public funds. (This principle is equally applicable in cases involving financial settlements on divorce.)

SCENARIO

Illustration 4: Melissa and Frank

Let us assume that Melissa has applied for a lump sum and settlement of property to ensure that she and the children are appropriately housed. Start by considering the value, size, and location of the home that child needs. The court is likely to start by considering the costs of housing in the area in which the children currently live, and what mortgage Melissa and Frank could each raise. Once an appropriate level of housing has been determined, the costs of running the house can be more easily estimated. Although Frank is wealthy, we are some way from super-rich here, and there will be real limits to what is possible.

In determining how housing and a car should be funded, the court must consider 'all the circumstances' including:

- The income, earning capacity, property and other financial resources of the applicant and the parents. The court will therefore look at Frank's and Melissa's earnings, what they are capable of earning (which in Melissa's case is going to depend on childcare availability), and their financial resources. For example, what mortgage borrowing capacity do each of them have? What savings?
- The financial needs and obligations of the applicant and the parents. What other obligations do they have? For example, does Frank also have children by another person as well as Melissa? Is furniture needed? A car is likely to be necessary.
- The financial needs of the child. What do the children need to live on? This is linked to the parties' standard of living, even if they have never lived together. Note, though, that we cannot use Schedule 1 to bypass the Child Maintenance Service. The CMS has assessed Frank's liability for day-to-day costs of the children and he does not earn above their maximum of £3,000 per week, so there is no jurisdiction for the court to order periodical payments and we must only concentrate on capital costs.
- The child's earning capacity (if any), property and resources. This is likely to be not applicable in the vast majority of cases, although it is possible that a child may be the beneficiary of a trust.
- Any disability, physical or mental, of the child. This is closely linked to the child's financial needs. A disabled child may have significant financial needs such as for personal care, adapted houses, and/or specialist equipment.
- The manner in which the child is being, or is expected to be, educated or trained. Is there an expectation that the children should be privately educated?

What is the structure of the arrangement to be? As we have seen, settlement of property is much more likely than outright transfer, and any other payments will need to be made as lump sums for capital expenditure rather than periodical payments.

---

[112] For a discussion of low and moderate asset cases, see A Mehta, 'Schedule 1 to the Children Act 1989: Not Just For WAGS' (*Family Law Week* 6 June 2015).

6.6.5 Variations to prior agreements or orders

As we have seen, a person's liability to their children is potentially open-ended, with no statutory age limit where the child is disabled or in education. An applicant may apply to increase the periodical payments (called 'varying them up') and a respondent to decease the payments; such applications may be made where circumstances change.[113] An order can also be suspended and then revived.[114] When varying a periodical payments order, the court can also order a lump sum. Lump sums themselves can be paid in instalments, and the regularity of those instalments varied.[115] However, the court cannot make more than one settlement or transfer of property order against the same person in respect of the same child.[116]

One of the potential reasons for a respondent payer to seek to reduce his or her liability is the cohabitation of the primary carer. In divorce proceedings, when dealing a former spouse's own entitlements, cohabitation may be a valid reason to reduce spousal maintenance payable, although this is by no means certain (see Chapter 4). Under Schedule 1, however, we are not dealing with the claims of a former spouse but with the claims of a child. Accordingly, it is much less likely that the cohabitation of the primary carer will lead to any variation in capital provision. As Lady Hale indicated in *J v C*, any future cohabitation or remarriage of the mother should not result in the reversion of the property to the father as this would not affect the child's need for her mother to care for her. Similarly, Singer J held in *F v G (Child: Financial Provision)*, that the mother's cohabitation and the financial gifts she may receive from her cohabitant does not detract from the value of the contribution the mother will be making to the child's upbringing. However, the income element of any provision could be susceptible to variation 'when any adult relationship of the mother's has a settled impact on her domestic economy'. That is not because the cohabitant assumes any legal responsibility for the child—they do not—but it is another bill-payer in the household. If that relationship breaks down, then the periodical payments could be varied upwards again.

Key Case *Morgan v Hill* tells us that an application for a variation is approached in the same way as a new application.

KEY CASE *Morgan v Hill* [2006] EWCA Civ 1602

Mr Morgan (who is described as 'immensely rich') and Ms Hill had an affair, the result of which was the birth of a child, Mark, who lived with Ms Hill and a child she had by another relationship, Mary. The parties reached an agreement about financial support. However, this was not converted into a court order and four years later Ms Hill applied under Schedule 1.

---

[113] Paragraph 1(4).
[114] Paragraph 6(2).
[115] Para 5(6).
[116] Paragraph 1(5)(b).

The Court of Appeal considered the importance of the agreement previously reached, and whether by providing for Mark Mr Morgan was effectively being asked to subsidise Mary. It held that:

- Under Schedule 1 paragraph 10(3)(b) the court is empowered to alter an agreement if satisfied that it 'does not contain proper financial arrangements with respect to the child'. The resulting alteration must, however, 'be just having regard to all the circumstances'. The previous agreement may be a very significant circumstance. However, in this case it was inadequate for several reasons.
- The approach of the court is the same whether a fresh application is made under paragraph 1 of Schedule 1 or a variation application is made under paragraph 10. The agreement is one of the crucial circumstances of the case for the purposes of paragraph 4. 'It represents the starting point. It is powerful evidence of what the circumstances of the case require by way of provision for the child, and usually it will be the best evidence of it. Ordinarily it will be not only the starting point, but also the finishing point, unless there is established one of the two grounds set out in paragraph 10 for varying it, that is to say either that a change in circumstances (foreseen or unforeseen) since the agreement was made calls for a change in provision, in which event the change of circumstance is both the occasion for and normally the measure of the variation, or it is established that the agreement does not make proper financial arrangements for the child.'
- It is in practical terms difficult to separate out costs and expenses relating to Mary from those relating to Mark. Direct costs, such as food clothing and holidays, may be capable of identification. However, such practical difficulties do not allow the judge to gloss over the fact that the courts have no jurisdiction to make an order against Mr Morgan for the benefit of Mary. However, Mary may derive incidental benefit from the fact that she lives in the same house as Ms Hill and Mark, and this does not mean that Mr Morgan is being ordered to support her.

6.6.6 Bringing it all together

From the cases discussed in this chapter, we can collate some useful guidance.

The nature of the parties' relationship:

- Although paragraph 4(1) requires a judge to consider all the circumstances, no great weight should be attached to whether she was wanted or the length or quality of the parents' relationship: *J v C*.
- In *F v G (Child: Financial Provision)*, the court considered *J v C* and *Re P* and held that while the length and nature of the parents' relationship and whether or not the child was planned were generally of little, if any, relevance, since the child's needs and dependency are the same regardless, the extent to which the unit of primary carer and child have become accustomed to a particular level of lifestyle can impact legitimately on an evaluation of the child's needs.[117]

---

[117] [2004] EWHC 1848 (Fam).

The process and structure:

- Start by considering the value, size, and location of the home that child needs. This will help decide on the cost of furnishing and equipping it. Then decide on an appropriate lump sum for this and for a car. Finally, look at what budget the mother reasonably requires to run the home and meet other expenditure such as school fees, holidays, routine travel expenses, entertainments, presents, etc: *Re P*. This approach was called 'very wise' by Lewison LJ in *Re A (A Child) (Financial Provision: Wealthy Parent)*.[118]

- Consider a lump sum for any costs already incurred by the primary carer, for example relating to the birth of the child or raising the child so far.

- The parents will need to provide the court with details of suitable properties and schedules of monies needed, which the other parent will no doubt challenge. The court will determine what amount is appropriate.

- The home will ordinarily be transiently required during the child's minority or until further order. The appropriate legal mechanism is therefore a settlement of property order.

- Outright transfer of the house by way of a property adjustment order should not ordinarily be made to provide benefits for the child after he or she had attained independence. This approach is supported by the way claims under the Inheritance (Provision for Family and Dependants) Act are treated: *A v A (A Minor: Financial Provision)*.[119]

The extent to which the primary carer may benefit from the award made:

- The primary carer has no entitlement to financial support on her own behalf under s1. However, she is entitled to support as the primary carer: *Re P*.

- In big money cases, it is not wrong for the court to augment the periodical payments order for a child to include an allowance for the mother, especially if the mother has to give up work or is unable to work because she has to look after the child: *Re P*, following *Haroutunian v Jennings*.[120] In most cases the carer's element will not be specifically quantified but a broad-brush approach taken.

- The maintenance must be not only for food, clothing, heat, light and housing and so on but for care for a young child. The fact that the money goes to the child and may eventually find its way into the pocket of the mother paying her for caring for the child is something which the father cannot pray in aid to bring down the amount of the order: *Haroutunian v Jennings*.

- The courts will interpret 'for the benefit of the child' loosely. In *H v C* (2009) private health insurance for the mother was part of the award under Schedule 1.[121]

- However, there is no power to take into account the future needs of the carer at the conclusion of the relevant child's dependency on the basis that knowing that his or

---

[118] [2015] Fam 277.
[119] [1994] 1 FLR 657.
[120] (1980) 1 FLR 62.
[121] [2009] EWHC 1527 (Fam).

her parent is not going to be rendered 'destitute' is of emotional benefit to the child: *Re A (A Child) (Financial Provision: Wealthy Parent).*[122] It is therefore not akin to the matrimonial principle of compensation, discussed in Chapter 4.

- In practical terms, it is also difficult to disentangle the indirect costs (such as running a car or paying the gas bill) pertaining to each individual in the household: *Morgan v Hill.*

- At least as far as big money cases are concerned, the court must therefore take a 'broad-brush' approach, in the same way that it does to financial remedy claims between spouses: *Re P.*

- The primary carer will almost always be required to keep receipts for expenditure of the sums provided under Schedule 1 to show that none is going to the personal or exclusive benefit of the parent (as opposed to indirectly for the benefit of the child in their capacity as carer): *Re P* and *Re N (A Child) (Financial Provision; Dependency).*

6.7 Conclusion

Most people accept that a scheme that requires parents to support their children is required. The issue is what that should look like. In this chapter, we have considered two main schemes—one run by the Child Maintenance Service, and one run by courts applying Schedule 1 Children Act 1989—as well as a number of lesser used powers.

The courts retain a discretion that enables them to do justice in an individual situation rather than simply apply a formula, but the scope of judicial powers has been limited by the existence of the child support scheme. Although Schedule 1 Children Act 1989 can be used by those at all ends of the economic spectrum, the reality is that many cases concern applications against wealthy individuals and this reflects the costs of going to court as well as the limits imposed by the scheme. If a person's main asset is his income, which is the case for many of us, the fact that courts retain the power to order periodical payments only where CMS does not have jurisdiction, or as a top-up for the wealthy, means that much of the advantage of Schedule 1 has gone. While the Child Maintenance Service is more accessible than court, and in theory more consistent (both reasons for the passing of the Child Support Act 1991), it is not necessarily a better solution.

The Child Maintenance Service inherited a system that had been so flawed that it had lost public confidence. Even though the formula has been much simplified since the early days of the Child Support Agency, it is still complex, and improvements to the scheme designs have been incremental and have come far too late for some. Arrears remain significant, and parents' powers to challenge incorrect assessments or force enforcement by the CMS are very limited. This can create a vicious circle in which faults with the scheme cause non-compliance, and the effects of non-compliance, such as arrears, cause people to lose faith in the scheme and thereby trigger further non-compliance. Government attempts to rewrite the schemes and to address the issues with public perception by replacing the agencies concerned have not addressed all of the problems associated with them.

---

[122] [2015] Fam 277.

KEY POINTS

- All those who are legal parents have the obligation to maintain their child. This obligation is not limited to those with parental responsibility.

- There are three main sources of financial support for children: (1) The scheme established by the Child Support Act and amended subsequently, which establishes maintenance as a percentage of the non-resident parent's income (2) The Matrimonial Causes Act 1973 for formerly married couples only (3) Schedule 1 to the Children Act 1989.

- The child support scheme was established by the Child Support Act 1991. It assesses maintenance as a percentage of the non-resident parent's income. It bears no relation whatsoever to the costs of actually raising a child and at the time of its drafting only one third of children entitled to receive child maintenance actually received it regularly and there was considerable political rhetoric around so-called 'absent fathers' and the costs to the state associated with single parenthood.

- The initial child support scheme administered by the Child Support Agency (CSA) led to outcomes that were unpredictable, and unfair, and there were constant variations in assessments. Its design meant that it did not alleviate poverty. Although it was amended in 1995, similar problems occurred under the newer scheme. The 2006 Henshaw Report described the Child Support Agency as unfit for purpose. This report led to the replacement of the Child Support Agency with the Child Maintenance and Enforcement Commission. In 2012, that too was abolished.

- The 2012 scheme is the current scheme. Parents are encouraged to make 'family-based arrangements' without the involvement of the Child Maintenance Service. Where the parents cannot agree, the service can assess the amount of child maintenance and collect the money, but it charges a collection fee for this. Maintenance is based on a percentage of the payer's gross income after deduction of pension contributions. Allowances are made for other children, and for special expenses. Research has shown that the public would on average increase the amount of child maintenance above the levels set by the Child Maintenance Service formula.

- There are various enforcement mechanisms. There are many reasons why some people do not pay child maintenance, including relationship with child contact, lack of money, variable income, domestic abuse, perceptions about unfairness, and scheme inflexibility.

- The introduction of the Child Support Act limited the courts' powers to make financial provision for children. On divorce, financial support for children is usually absorbed into the claims of the spouse who has primary care, forming part of the assessment of their needs. Where the parties are not separated, the Domestic Proceedings and Magistrates' Courts Act 1978 provides an obligation of maintenance during marriage. Schedule 1 to the Children Act 1989 contains a number of comprehensive powers to order a child's parents to provide financially for him or her, including in some cases into adulthood, and against step-parents.

- Under Schedule 1 Children Act 1989 the court can order periodical payments (except where the Child Maintenance Service has jurisdiction), lump sums, and transfer or settlement of property. The court must consider all the circumstances including a statutory list of considerations and the standard of living of the parties.

- Where the claim is for property, start by considering the value, size, and location of the home that child needs. This will help decide on the cost of furnishing and equipping it and the costs associated with living there. While the courts will interpret 'for the benefit of the child' loosely, the primary carer has no entitlement to financial support on her own behalf under Schedule 1, but is only entitled to support in her capacity as the primary carer.

FURTHER READING: SOME STARTING POINTS

- Nick Wikeley has written widely about the statutory child support scheme. A comprehensive account of the history of child support, its moral and legal basis, and the development and operation of the child support scheme can be found in his book *Child Support: Law and Policy* (Hart 2006). A very interesting chapter is 'Financial Support for Children after Parental Separation: Responsibility and Responsible Parenting', Chapter 15 in Rebecca Probert, Stephen Gilmore and Jonathan Herring (eds), *Responsible Parents and Parental Responsibility* (Hart 2009). These books do not, by virtue of their publication date, cover the 2012 scheme. Wikeley has also written a number of articles, only a small proportion of which we have included in this chapter. Any research on child support should therefore start with this writer.

- Information about the different services offered by the Child Maintenance Service can be found at https://www.gov.uk/making-child-maintenance-arrangement. The 2012 scheme is described in the Child Maintenance Service publication *How We Work out Child Maintenance: A Step by Step Guide* (2018) available at https://www.gov.uk/government/publications/how-we-work-out-child-maintenance. This takes you through a calculation with examples.

- For sources of statistics, you may want to read Donald Hirsch, *The Cost of a Child in 2019* (Child Poverty Action Group 2019); and Caroline Bryson, Ira Mark Ellman, Stephen McKay, and Joanna Miles, *Child Maintenance: How Would the British Public Calculate What the State Should Require Parents to Pay?* (Nuffield Foundation 2015). A discussion of the implications of this is IM Ellman, S Mckay, J Miles, and C Bryson, 'Child Support Judgments: Comparing Public Policy to the Public's Policy' (2014) 28 *International Journal of Law, Policy and the Family* 274. You can find all the British Social Attitudes Surveys at https://www.bsa.natcen.ac.uk/. They are a fantastic research resource. The Department for Work and Pensions publishes regular statistics on the performance of the Child Maintenance Service, which can be found at https://www.gov.uk/government/publications/child-maintenance-service-statistics-data-to-march-2020-experimental/child-maintenance-service-statistics-data-to-march-2020-experimental.

- For criticisms of the scheme and research into non payers, see Leanne McCarthy-Cotter, *The 1991 Child Support Act: Failure Foreseeable and Foreseen* (Springer 2018); Gillian Douglas, 'Can't Pay? Won't Pay!' Chapter 5 in *Obligation and Commitment in Family Law* (Hart 2018); Caitlin Connors and Emily Fu, *Attitudes and Behaviours of Self-Employed Child Maintenance Clients and Barriers to Paying Child Maintenance* (Department for Work and Pensions 2015), and some of the judicial comments in *R (on the application of Kehoe) v Secretary of State for Work and Pensions* [2005] UKHL 48.

- A good practitioner guide on Schedule 1 is A Bagchi et al., *Applications under Schedule 1 to the Children Act 1989* (2nd edn, Lexis Nexis 2018). *Re P (Child: Financial Provision)* [2003] EWCA Civ 837 establishes how, in practical terms, courts should approach an application under Schedule 1, and the principles are also addressed in *J v C (Child: Financial Provision)* [1999] 1 FLR 152 and *Morgan v Hill* [2006] EWCA Civ 1602. An excellent case note on *Re P* is by Stephen Gilmore, '*Re P (Child) (Financial Provision)* - Shoeboxes and Comical Shopping Trips—Child Support from the Affluent To Fabulously Rich' (2004) 16 *Child and Family Law Quarterly* 103. A good article on the use of Schedule 1 in lower and moderate asset cases is A Mehta, 'Schedule 1 to the Children Act 1989: Not Just For WAGS' (*Family Law Week* 6 June 2015).

- If you would like to look at an order relating to financial provision for children, there are precedents drafted by the Family Orders Project on the Judiciary website at https://www.judiciary.uk/publications/practice-guidance-standard-children-and-other-orders/

 Visit the **online resources** to watch a video of Polly Morgan discussing this chapter topic, and to check your understanding of this chapter with self-test questions and scenario questions.

Domestic Abuse

LEARNING CHECKLIST

By the end of this chapter, you should be able to:

- *Critically discuss* the types of behaviours that might constitute domestic abuse, the family violence and feminist theories that seek to explain its causes, and the differential impact of domestic abuse on men and women

- *Describe* what international human rights instruments say about domestic abuse and *critically discuss* what Articles of the ECHR are engaged and how

- *Describe* the different legal powers available to protect victims of domestic abuse and *evaluate* their strengths and weaknesses by reference to research and academic commentary

- *Apply* the occupation order provisions in the Family Law Act 1996 to a fictional scenario by reference to the parties' respective entitlements to occupy.

SCENARIO 1

Kelly and Niall Hill

Kelly and Niall are married. They live in a house in the sole name of Niall. From a few months into the relationship, Niall has sought to control Kelly. Each time that she gets a job he seems to find some way to sabotage it. He has forced her to open several credit cards which he uses and she does not know how much debt has been incurred. He reads all her emails and text messages, and he has a tracking device on her mobile. He has punched and thrown Kelly on a number of occasions, and she has been treated in hospital although she told the nurse that she had fallen in the garden. She has left in the past but returned because Niall apologised, and for a short time, things were better. However, recently things have got worse again and last week a neighbour called the police after hearing her screaming, and Niall was arrested for assault. Kelly is now staying in a refuge and wants to return to the family home, but only if Niall is not there.

SCENARIO 2

Alex and Frances

Alex and Frances are not married, but they have a child together. Their relationship broke down when Alex developed a drinking problem, and became verbally abusive towards Frances and started to throw things in the house and punch the walls. Since separation, Alex has sent Frances a series of text messages calling her names and threatening to come around and kick the door in. Their house is in joint names. Frances does not feel safe in the property and wishes to prevent Alex from returning to it.

7.1 **Introduction**

Domestic abuse or intimate partner violence was seen for many centuries as a private matter within the family that only rarely attracted criminal or civil sanction. Indeed, it was perfectly lawful for a husband to beat, imprison, and rape his wife, to deprive her of access to resources or her children, and to force her to live with him. Only in extreme cases would the law intervene. In *Re Cochrane* (1840), the court held that 'the husband hath by law power and dominion over his wife and may keep her by force within the bounds of duty, and may beat her, but not in a violent or cruel manner'.[1] It was not until *R v Jackson* (1891) that the Court of Appeal held that a man had no right to beat or imprison his wife, and it was only in 1991 that it was held that a man could be capable in law of raping his wife. Prior to that, the wife's consent to marriage constituted consent to sex.[2] Women's violence or abuse in same-sex relationships, were not subject to any attention. The law did not merely ignore domestic abuse, but for centuries gave it official sanction.

Although many people would argue that the state's response to domestic abuse is still inadequate in practice, there are now statutory powers that seek to provide support and protection for victims of domestic abuse and increasingly serious penalties for the perpetrators. In the 1970s, growing recognition of the nature and consequences of domestic abuse led to specific legislation aimed at protecting victims including the Domestic Violence and Matrimonial Proceedings Act 1976 and the Domestic Proceedings and Magistrates Court Act 1978. These remained the principal sources of protection until the Family Law Act 1996 and the Protection from Harassment Act 1997. While these pieces of legislation have attempted to address domestic abuse, like their predecessors they have done so with only partial success, and for that reason have been subject to numerous amendments designed to address specific weaknesses. As this book is published, a new Act—the Domestic Abuse Act 2021—has just received Royal Assent and seeks yet again to improve protection for victims.

In this chapter, we consider the nature and effect of domestic abuse and how the law has sought to address it. Although domestic abuse may be present in a wide range of familial relationships, and some of the legal powers discussed below can be used by a wider category than simply domestic partners, in this chapter we focus primarily on intimate partner abuse.

There are two main reasons why family solicitors will want to know about domestic abuse. First, your client may need you to take protective actions such as applying for a non-molestation order or refer them to appropriate services. As a family solicitor, you will know what resources are available locally. Secondly, the effect of domestic abuse will be

---

[1] 8 Dow PC 630.
[2] [1891] 1 QB 671; *R v R* [1991] 4 All ER 481.

felt even if you are not directly involved in taking protective steps. Sometimes it will be an obvious aspect of the case, as in some child contact situations discussed in Chapter 10. At other times, it may play a part in your client's decision-making without being obvious. In order to be able to advise your client properly, you will need to be aware of this.

First, let us start by establishing a definition of 'domestic abuse' and some of the terms used in this chapter.

7.2 Defining domestic abuse

Our understanding of what domestic abuse looks like has changed over time. We now recognise that physical violence, or the threat thereof, may be only one component of an abusive relationship or indeed not present in relationships that are nevertheless abusive in other ways.

In Key Case *Yemshaw v Hounslow London Borough Council*, the Supreme Court interpreted the term 'domestic violence' within the Housing Act 1996 as capable of encompassing non-physical acts of abuse that caused harm.

KEY CASE *Yemshaw v Hounslow London Borough Council (Secretary of State for Communities and Local Government and another intervening)* [2011] UKSC 3

Mrs Yemshaw left the matrimonial home with her two young children and was refused accommodation by the local authority on the basis that she was intentionally homeless. She would not be intentionally homeless if it was probable that remaining in the house would lead to domestic violence or other violence against her. However, while her husband had shouted at and belittled her so that she felt not 'like a human', he had never hit her or threatened to do so, so housing officers classed her as intentionally homeless. Her judicial review of this decision failed, but her case succeeded in the Supreme Court, which held (per Lady Hale) that:

'Violence' is a word very similar to the word 'family'. It is not a term of art. It is capable of bearing several meanings and applying to many different types of behaviour. These can change and develop over time. . . . The purpose of the legislation would be achieved if the term 'domestic violence' were interpreted [as including] 'physical violence, threatening or intimidating behaviour and any other form of abuse which, directly or indirectly, may give rise to the risk of harm'.

   Was this, in reality, simply a case of marriage breakdown in which the Appellant was not genuinely in fear of her husband; or was it a classic case of domestic abuse, in which one spouse puts the other in fear through the constant denial of freedom and of money for essentials, through the denigration of her personality, such that she genuinely fears that he may take her children away from her however unrealistic this may appear to an objective outsider? This is not to apply a subjective test. . . . The test is always the view of the objective outsider but applied to the particular facts, circumstances and personalities of the people involved.[3]

The case was remitted back to the local authority to make the decision afresh in light of the case's definition of domestic violence.

---

[3] Paragraphs [27], [28], and [36].

Soon after *Yemshaw*, the government adopted a definition of domestic abuse across all of its services, which explicitly included non-physical forms of abuse. The Domestic Abuse Act 2021 places this definition on a statutory footing. It defines domestic abuse as a single incident or a course of conduct comprising physical or sexual abuse; violent or threatening behaviour; coercive or controlling behaviour; economic abuse; and psychological, emotional or other abuse. This definition only applies where the perpetrator and victim are both aged 16 or over.

To fall within the domestic sphere, the abuse must be between 'personally connected' persons. Section 2 of the Domestic Abuse Act defines what this means. Two people are personally connected if they are or have been married, civilly partnered, or engaged; are or have been in an intimate, personal relationship with one another; have or had a parental relationship by being parents or having parental responsibility for the same child; or they are relatives within the meaning of the s63 Family Law Act 1996. It therefore recognises a much wider category of abusive relationships than intimate partner violence, as it covers most familial relationships in which both parties are aged over 16. As Madden Dempsey writes, 'focusing on the nature of the relationship between the parties is the most common way of differentiating domestic violence from generic violence in US and English law'.[4]

The Act does not fail to recognise that children aged under 16 are victims of domestic abuse. At s3, the Act includes as a victim of abuse any child (i.e., a person under the age of 18) who sees or hears, or experiences the effects of, the abuse, and is related to the victim or perpetrator through parenthood or parental responsibility or the s63 Family Law Act category of relatives. Moreover, there a number of criminal offences that cover child abuse.

Finally, the Act also recognises (at s1(5)) that the perpetrator may behave abusively towards the victim by directing their conduct at another person such as their child.

STATUTORY EXTRACT *s1 Domestic Abuse Act 2021*

Definition of 'domestic abuse'

(1) This section defines 'domestic abuse' for the purposes of this Act.
(2) Behaviour of a person ('A') towards another person ('B') is 'domestic abuse' if

   (a) A and B are each aged 16 or over and are personally connected to each other, and
   (b) the behaviour is abusive.

(3) Behaviour is 'abusive' if it consists of any of the following:

   (a) physical or sexual abuse;
   (b) violent or threatening behaviour;
   (c) controlling or coercive behaviour;
   (d) economic abuse (see subsection (4));
   (e) psychological, emotional or other abuse;

   and it does not matter whether the behaviour consists of a single incident or a course of conduct. . . .

---

[4] M Madden Dempsey, *Prosecuting Domestic Violence: A Philosophical Analysis* (Oxford University Press 2009) 111.

Although the Act includes a general catch-all ('other abuse') it refers specifically to some terms which merit further explanation. These terms are not defined in the Act (with the exception of economic abuse) but are commonly understood to encompass certain behaviours. Here is a non-exhaustive list of examples.

- Physical abuse may include kicking, punching, slapping, dragging, pinning, or pinching the victim; scratching or biting; scalding or burning them; and choking or strangling them (the latter being a significant predictor of the victim's future death at the hands of the perpetrator).[5] The perpetrator may or may not use weapons. Violence may be used or threatened towards other family members and pets. Physical abuse may also involve controlling access to food; or controlling access to medication either by withholding it or forcing medication (or indeed, illegal drugs, on the victim). Female genital mutilation is another form of physical abuse, and we discuss the law's response to this at 7.5.9 and 7.5.10.

- Sexual abuse may involve rape or other forced sexual activities, exceeding or ignoring the limits of the victim's consent. It can involve forced prostitution or sexual exploitation; using sexually degrading language or forcing the victim to watch or make pornography; revenge porn (the release to others of intimate photographs of the victim); rough sex contrary to the victim's consent; and tricking or forcing the victim into having unsafe sex. This can include refusing or sabotaging contraception, or lying about using contraception or having a clean bill of sexual health.

- Violent or threatening behaviour may take a number of forms. The perpetrator may make threats to the life or safety of the victim or someone they care for, including pets. They may threaten to harm themselves if the victim leaves, or say that the victim will not be able to see their children again if they leave. They may throw or damage objects or the victim's possessions; shout or yell; or cause the victim to fear being assaulted. They may send harassing or abusive messages or encourage others to do so.

- Controlling or coercive behaviour occurs when one person engages in a range of acts designed to make the victim dependent on them or subordinate and regulates their day-to-day life.[6] These can include economically abusive acts that deprive the victim of the financial or practical means of escape, isolate them from sources of support, or exploit the victim in financial or other ways. It may involve behaviour such as controlling where the victim goes, who they see, using spyware to monitor their whereabouts; reading their emails or text messages; controlling how they dress, and forbidding them from doing certain things or leaving the house without the perpetrator; or removing their passport or other essential documents. The perpetrator may use threats, humiliation, punishment, or intimidation as well as or instead of physical violence to ensure compliance. The perpetrator may also force the victim to engage in criminal acts such as shoplifting and use the fear of prosecution as a way of enforcing compliance.

---

[5] N Glass et al., 'Non-Fatal Strangulation is an Important Risk Factor for Homicide of Women' (2008) 35(3) *The Journal of Emergency Medicine* 329. See also S Edwards, 'The Strangulation of Female Partners' [2015] 12 *Criminal Law Review* 949 on the difficulties in prosecuting strangulation.

[6] P McGorrery and M McMahon, 'Prosecuting Controlling or Coercive Behaviour in England and Wales: Media Reports of a Novel Offence' (2019) *Criminology and Criminal Justice* 1 describes the nature of the coercive and controlling behaviour found in prosecutions for the specific offence of this name.

While there is now a criminal offence of engaging in coercive and controlling behaviour (which we discuss at 7.5.3), not all coercive and controlling behaviour will satisfy the requirements of that particular criminal offence which requires that the perpetrator's conduct causes the victim to fear violence on at least two occasions or cases them serious alarm or distress which has a substantial adverse effect on their usual day-to-day activities.

- Economic abuse is defined in s1(4) of the Act as 'behaviour that has a substantial adverse effect on [the victim's] ability to acquire, use or maintain money or other property, or obtain goods or services'. The charity Surviving Economic Abuse says that 'economic abuse is designed to reinforce or create economic instability. In this way it limits women's choices and ability to access safety. Lack of access to economic resources can result in women staying with abusive men for longer and experiencing more harm as a result.'[7] Specific acts of economic abuse may involve taking or hiding money; putting assets into their name only; interfering with the victim's ability to work or acting in a way that gets them into trouble at work; refusing access to necessities; using the victim's credit or causing them debt; and requiring them to account for every purchase.

- For families with connections in other countries, trans-national marriage abandonment involves stranding a spouse abroad without access to the resources to return to the UK. It is a feature of some child contact cases and is mentioned specifically in Practice Direction 12J which covers domestic violence and harm in the family courts. We discuss PD12J and how family courts approach children cases in which domestic abuse is an issue at length in Chapter 10.

- Psychological and emotional abuse may involve humiliating or criticising the victim; verbally abusing them; threatening to keep or take their children from them if the victim leaves; threatening to commit suicide if the victim leaves; threatening to 'out' them if they are gay; behaving jealously or possessively; and stalking or harassing the victim online or in person. The Protection from Harassment Act 1997 gives examples of stalking behaviour including following, contacting or attempting to contact a person; publishing statements or materials about them or pretending to be them; monitoring their internet use; loitering, watching, and spying.

- Although forced marriage is not explicitly mentioned in the Act it falls within the definition of domestic abuse because it is likely to involve physical abuse and imprisonment; coercive and controlling behaviour; harassment and stalking and other forms of emotional abuse; and (if the marriages takes place) rape and other forms of sexual abuse. Similarly, while so-called 'honour-based' violence is not mentioned in the Act it too encompasses a range of domestic abuses up to and comprising murder of the victim.

As you can see, these forms of abuse are often connected and overlapping. Physical and sexual violence may be part of a coercive and controlling relationship, because the perpetrator seeks to use all methods of controlling the victim that they can. The relationship may also involve psychological or emotional abuse as part of isolating the victim from

---

[7] See https://survivingeconomicabuse.org/economic-abuse/what-is-economic-abuse/ accessed 29 November 2020.

support. A woman who is forced into prostitution for the financial gain of their abuser experiences physical and sexual abuse, economic abuse, and coercive and controlling behaviour. While the definition includes single incidents, it is unlikely that abuse will occur on one occasion only.

7.2.1 Prevalence

It is difficult to accurately gauge the extent of domestic abuse, because it depends on how you define it and whether people recognise whether they have been victims. The Crime Survey for England and Wales estimated that 7.3 per cent of women and 3.6 per cent of men aged 16 to 74 experienced domestic abuse in 2019. Since the age of 16, 27.6 per cent of women and 13.8 per cent of men have experienced abuse.[8] These statistics are based on self-reporting by those interviewed for the survey, which asks about physical, sexual and non-sexual abuse, financial and emotional abuse, and threats to hurt the survey respondent or someone close to them, as well as forms of stalking and unwanted obscene communications.

Where crimes are recorded (and there are in excess of three-quarters of a million domestic abuse-related crimes per year, accounting for some 11 per cent of all crimes), 74 per cent of victims are female.[9] Abuse by a partner is more common than abuse by another family member, and the victims of partner abuse are overwhelmingly female.[10] 77 per cent of domestic homicide victims are female.[11] According to the femicide census, 62 per cent of all women killed by men were killed by a current or former partner and in most cases there was a known history of abuse.[12] We explore gender in domestic abuse at 7.3.1.

Part of the difficulties in identifying the prevalence of domestic abuse is that not all victims of abuse will realise at the time that they are in a domestically abusive relationship. A perpetrator or victim of jealousy, verbal abuse, monitoring of movements or text messages, and turning up unannounced may attempt to explain this behaviour away as indicative of their love for the victim or as being romantic. As the 1960s song goes, 'If he didn't care for me, I could have never made him mad'.[13] A number of pieces of research also suggest that women tend to under-report domestic violence perpetrated against them and over-report their own violence.[14]

---

[8] Office for National Statistics, *Domestic Abuse Prevalence and Victim Characteristics* Appendix Table 1: Prevalence of domestic abuse among adults aged 16 to 74, by type of abuse and sex, year ending March 2020 (2020).
[9] Office for National Statistics, *Domestic Abuse Victim Characteristics, England and Wales: Year Ending March 2020* (2020). In 2019 the police recorded 758,941 domestic abuse crimes in England and Wales, but these statistics do not include Greater Manchester which was upgrading its reporting IT system at the time.
[10] Office for National Statistics, *Domestic Abuse Prevalence and Victim Characteristics* Appendix Table 1: Prevalence of domestic abuse among adults aged 16 to 74, by type of abuse and sex, year ending March 2020 (2020).
[11] Office for National Statistics, *Domestic Abuse Victim Characteristics, England and Wales: Year Ending March 2020* (2020).
[12] J Long et al., *Femicide Census: UK Femicides 2009–2018* (2020).
[13] 'He hit me, and it felt like a kiss', by Jerry Goffin and Carole King, was recorded by the Crystals in 1962 and describes the explanation given by their babysitter of her boyfriend's abuse.
[14] See the discussion in RP Dobash and R Emerson Dobash, 'Women's Violence to Men in Intimate Relationships: Working on a Puzzle' (2004) 44 *British Journal of Criminology* 324.

The charity Safe Lives estimates that each year more than 100,000 people in the UK are at high and imminent risk of being murdered or seriously injured as a result of domestic abuse.[15] Of those referred to MARAC, a multi-agency risk assessment conference for high-risk cases, 99.9 per cent are women, and there are 124,569 children in households where a person is the subject of a MARAC referral.

Abuse type and frequency varies according to a range of victim demographics including age and ethnicity.[16] 15.7 per cent of victims in MARAC cases were Black or minority ethnic, 6.6 had a disability, and 1.3 per cent involved victims who identify as lesbian, gay, or bisexual.[17]

FOCUS Think Critically

Domestic abuse and the pandemic

The COVID-19 pandemic and associated restrictions correlate with an increase in the number of reports of domestic abuse made to the police. The Office for National Statistics reports that 'In April, May and June roughly one-fifth (21%, 20% and 19%) of all offences recorded by the police were flagged as domestic abuse-related, which represents an increase of around five percentage points compared with the same period in previous years.'[18] The number of reports has been rising annually, so it is unclear to what extent the pandemic itself (or its consequences) is responsible. The number of non-molestation and occupation orders has fluctuated above and below the usual levels but does appear to be linked to the imposition of restrictions on movement and the subsequent easing of those restrictions, with an increase in applications around the time that the first lockdown period was eased in May 2020.

Women's Aid's preliminary research into the effects of the pandemic found that 67.4 per cent of those who were experiencing abuse said that it had worsened since the pandemic started, and 71.7 per cent said that their abuser now had more control over their life. Although there is a specific exemption from lockdown for those fleeing abuse, 78.3 per cent said that it had made it harder for them to leave their abuser. This is likely for a variety of reasons. Lockdown has caused practical difficulties for domestic abuse support services and increased demand, and victims may have difficulties accessing support at all, or safely.[19]

7.2.2 The costs of domestic abuse

Domestic abuse can have a long-lasting and profound effect on victims, including on children who witness domestic abuse. Victims may experience physical injury; loss of hope and self-esteem; financial harm; homelessness; mental illness, shame and self-blame, depression, anxiety, trauma related symptoms or post-traumatic stress disorder; and loss of

---

[15] SafeLives, *Getting It Right First Time: Policy Report* (SafeLives 2015).

[16] Office for National Statistics, *Percentage of adults aged 16 to 59 years who were victims of domestic abuse in the last year, by ethnic group, year ending March 2014 to year ending March 2019, Crime Survey for England and Wales* (2019); and *Domestic Abuse Victim Characteristics, England and Wales: Year Ending March 2020* (2020).

[17] 'Gender of Victims Discussed at MARAC': MARAC Dataset 2019/20. Available at https://safelives.org.uk/practice-support/resources-marac-meetings/latest-marac-data accessed 29 November 2020.

[18] Office for National Statistics, *Domestic Abuse during the Coronavirus (COVID-19) Pandemic, England and Wales: November 2020* (2020).

[19] For access to the Women's Aid research, see https://www.womensaid.org.uk/covid-19-resource-hub/#1588 945125706-690bb10f-d6d4 accessed 7 December 2020.

trust.[20] Golding found that abused women experienced depression or anxiety disorders at three times the rate of those in the general population.[21] A third of all female suicide attempts can be attributed to the effects of past and present domestic abuse.[22] Abused men are statistically much more likely than non-abused men to experience depression and psychological distress.[23]

It is possible to calculate the economic costs of this, including by putting a figure on the victim's loss of quality of life. The government estimates the cost of domestic abuse as approximately £66 billion per year, comprised of the costs of trying to prevent abuse; costs that result from abuse happening including lost wages, healthcare costs, rehousing, and property damage as well as reduction in the victim's quality of life; and costs of legal responses.[24] The latest figures, which are from 2016/17, are broken down in Table 7.1.

In Chapter 10, where we focus on child contact against a background of domestic abuse, we discuss multiple studies showing that children who had witnessed abuse were more likely to be fearful and inhibited and show symptoms of anxiety, depression, and trauma.[25] Children who see domestic abuse are also more likely to use aggression as a way of addressing problems and this fits with the situational couple violence type of domestic abuse discussed at 7.3.1. The presence of domestic abuse within a household is the most common reason that children are in need of child protection measures, although victims may be reluctant to seek support for fear of their children being removed from them.

7.2.3 Terminology used in this chapter

As our understanding of domestic abuse has changed over the years, so too has the terminology used to describe it. You may have heard the terms 'battered women' or 'battered women's syndrome'.[26] Those who argue that both men and women are equally violent have

TABLE 7.1 The economic and social costs of domestic abuse

Costs in anticipation	Costs as a consequences				Costs in response				Total
	Physical and emotional harm	Lost output	Health services	Victim services	Police costs	Criminal legal	Civil legal	Other	
£6m	£47,287m	£14,098m	£2,333m	£724m	£1,257m	£336m	£140m	£11m	£66,192m

[20] E Crawford, H Liebling-Kalifani, and V Hill, 'Women's Understanding of the Effects of Domestic Abuse: The Impact on Their Identity, Sense of Self and Resilience. A Grounded Theory Approach' (2009) 11(2) *Journal of International Women's Studies* 63; S Lloyd, 'The Effects of Domestic Violence on Women's Employment' (1997) 19(2) *Law and Policy* 139.
[21] JM Golding, 'Intimate Partner Violence as a Risk Factor for Mental Disorders: A Meta-Analysis' (1999) 14(2) *Journal of Family Violence* 99.
[22] E Stark and A Flitcraft, *Women at Risk: Domestic Violence and Women's Health* (Sage 1996).
[23] DA Hines and K Malley Morrison, 'Psychological Effects of Partner Abuse against Men: A Neglected Research Area' (2001) 2(2) *Psychology and Men and Masculinity* 75.
[24] R Oliver, B Alexander, S Roe, and M Wlasny, *The Economic and Social Costs of Domestic Abuse: Research Report 107* (Home Office, 2019).
[25] JL Edleson 'Children's Witnessing of Adult Domestic Violence' (1999) 14(8) *Journal of Interpersonal Violence* 839.
[26] LE Walker, *The Battered Woman* (Harper and Row 1979) and *The Battered Woman Syndrome* (Springer 1984).

referred to 'battered husbands'.[27] The phrase 'domestic violence' has been reconceived as domestic abuse to reflect our greater understanding of coercive and controlling behaviour and other non-physical forms of abuse. Some writers prefer to refer to those who have experienced abuse as survivors rather than victims, arguing that this 'makes visible women's and children's resistance'.[28] The terms 'intimate partner violence' or 'couple violence' are often used to distinguish abuse perpetrated on a domestic partner from other forms of intrafamily abuse such as elder abuse, child abuse, or abuse by those who have status within a particular family.

In this chapter, when we refer to 'abuse' we mean conduct that may be physical but is not exclusively so, and where we refer to 'violence' we mean physical violence or the use of force. This is the approach also taken by Michelle Madden Dempsey.[29] We have kept the terms used by the researchers that we cite but where they refer to violence and are not limiting this only to physical violence but mean what we have termed 'abuse', we have clarified that.

We have used the terms victims (as not all victims survive) and perpetrators, but do remember that when we discuss the legal powers these are alleged victims and alleged perpetrators unless and until a court finds abuse to have occurred.

7.3 **What causes domestic abuse?**

Nobody knows for certain what causes domestic abuse, and a number of different theories have been advanced with varying degrees of credibility. It is likely that there is not one single cause but a combination of factors including the individual characteristics of the parties and their relationship as well as wider social factors.[30] However, there are two main schools of thought: the family violence perspective and the feminist perspective.[31]

Family violence theorists see abuse as a method of resolving conflict within the family, especially for those who lack other resources or skills in resolving conflict. In this way, domestic abuse is not caused by aberrant behaviour; it is inevitable and normal. Intimate partner abuse is simply one type of family abuse. As Kurz, explains, proponents of the family violence approach believe that families are 'subject to serious stresses from difficult working conditions, unemployment, financial insecurity, and health problems, which cause family members to be violent to one another.'[32] As behaving abusively attracts few sanctions, the benefits outweigh the detriments (to the perpetrator, at least). Accordingly, if domestic abuse is to be reduced, it is necessary to impose harsher legal and social consequences in order to increase the costs compared to the benefits.

[27] SK Steinmetz, 'The Battered Husband Syndrome' (1977) 2 *Victimology* 499.
[28] L Kelly and J Radford, 'Nothing Really Happened: The Invalidation of Women's Experiences of Sexual Violence' (1990) 10 *Critical Social Policy* 39.
[29] M Madden Dempsey, *Prosecuting Domestic Violence: A Philosophical Analysis* (Oxford University Press 2009) 109.
[30] J Miles, 'Domestic Violence' in J Herring (ed.), *Family Law: Issues, Debates, Policy* (Willan 2001).
[31] D Kurz, 'Social Science Perspectives on Wife Abuse: Current Debates and Future Directions' (1989) 3(4) *Gender and Society* 489. Another excellent summary is J Lawson, 'Sociological Theories of Intimate Partner Violence' (2012) 22(5) *Journal of Human Behaviour in the Social Environment* 572.
[32] D Kurz, 'Social Science Perspectives on Wife Abuse: Current Debates and Future Directions' (1989) 3(4) *Gender and Society* 489.

In contrast to this perspective, feminist scholars such as Dobash and Dobash position gender centrally within their understanding of the causes of domestic abuse. In particular, they see inter-partner abuse as an expression of patriarchal domination and thus different to other kinds of family abuse.[33] In this way it departs from the family violence perspective, which sees intimate partner abuse as simply one type of family abuse. For feminist theorists, domestic abuse is about men controlling women and is rooted in structural gender inequality that seeks to subordinate women.[34] As Madden Dempsey writes, 'domestic violence cannot exist in a society without patriarchy'.[35] Patriarchal power is the core element of domestic violence.

7.3.1 Gender differences and types of abuse

The differences between family violence theorists and feminist scholars extend to the role of women as perpetrators of abuse. The former argue that women use physical violence to the same extent as men and for the same reason: as a way to resolve conflict. It is 'mutual combat'.[36] They point to studies that show that specific acts are done by both men and women at about the same rate.[37]

In contrast, feminist scholars argue that the nature of abuse and physical violence by men is different to violence that by women. When women are violent it is more likely to be as a form of self-defence—they are responding to violence with violence, rather than instigating it.[38] Women are much more likely to be the victims of coercive and controlling behaviour or sexual abuse compared to men,[39] and the studies that family violence theorists rely upon ignore the context of the acts reported and ignore these other forms of abuse altogether. Dobash and Dobash found in a study of 95 couples on a court-mandated programme in Scotland that women did not tend to use intimidation or coercive or controlling behaviour.[40] Feminist scholars also argue that women are more likely to be injured than men and subject to prolonged and serious violence, and this is why they are more likely to contact the police or seek domestic violence support services than men.[41] Collins and Banyard found that women experience an average 35 physical assaults before

---

[33] RP Dobash and RE Dobash, *Violence against Wives: A Case against the Patriarchy* (Free Press 1979).

[34] E Schneider, *Battered Women and Feminist Lawmaking* (OUP 2000).

[35] M Madden Dempsey, *Prosecuting Domestic Violence: A Philosophical Analysis* (Oxford University Press 2009) 218. For a critique of Madden Dempsey's views, see S Cowan, 'Motivating Questions and Partial Answers: A Response to *Prosecuting Domestic Violence* by Michelle Madden Dempsey' (2014) 8 *Criminal Law and Philosophy* 543.

[36] MA Straus, 'The Controversy over Domestic Violence by Women: A Methodological, Theoretical, and Sociology of Science Analysis', in X Arriaga and S Oskamp (eds), *Violence in Intimate Relationships* (Sage 1999).

[37] M Straus and G Hotaling (eds), *The Social Causes of Husband-Wife Violence* (University of Minnesota Press 1980); and M Straus, 'Victims and Aggressors in Marital Violence' (1980) 3 *American Behavioral Scientist* 681.

[38] See DS Saunders, 'Are Physical Assaults by Wives and Girlfriends a Major Social Problem? A Review of the Literature' (2002) 8(12) *Violence against Women* 1424 and the works he cites.

[39] DS Saunders, 'Are Physical Assaults by Wives and Girlfriends a Major Social Problem? A Review of the Literature' (2002) 8(12) *Violence against Women* 1424.

[40] RP Dobash and R Emerson Dobash, 'Women's Violence to Men in Intimate Relationships: Working on a Puzzle' (2004) 44 *British Journal of Criminology* 324.

[41] M Hester 'Who Does What to Whom? Gender and Domestic Violence Perpetrators in English Police Records' (2013) 10(5) *European Journal of Criminology* 623.

accessing services, although Musgrove and Grove found that the figure was more than 60.[42] Dobash and Dobash found that women were more likely to describe their experiences as frightening, or say that they felt helpless or trapped, whereas most men reacted dismissively to the physical violence they had suffered.[43] Domestic abuse should be seen as part of a pattern that has the purpose of establishing and maintaining control over the female partner (or former partner), and of which physical violence is only one part. This suggests that male-on-female abuse is qualitatively and quantitatively more severe than female-on-male abuse.

Is it possible to reconcile these two approaches? Joan Kelly and Michael Johnson have argued that each theory addresses different forms of violence and the proponents of each theory are talking about different things.[44] They argue that there are four different categories of abuse, which affect men and women differently:

1. Coercive controlling violence, which involves intimidation, coercion and control coupled with physical violence. It is characterised by a need for power and control over the victim, escalates over time, and is marked by the use of multiple forms of control.[45] This type of abuse, Kelly and Johnson argue, is primarily (but not exclusively) by male perpetrators on female victims and this asymmetry explains why women use domestic abuse services such as shelters, or make reports to the police, more often than men. A number of studies show high rates of injury and one of the major predictors of continued physical violence is the presence of coercive behaviours. The psychological effects on the victim can be very great. Perpetrators are much less likely to respond to interventions.

2. Situational couple violence, which is the most common type of inter-partner abuse. It is not a less serious form of coercive controlling violence but a different type of violence with different causes. Rather than being about power and control over a partner, it results from situations or arguments between the parties that erupt into physical violence by one or both parties. Such violence is usually (but not always) less serious (e.g. pushing, shoving, or grabbing) than that which is present in coercive controlling violence and does not tend to result in any physical injuries. Cafcass, the Children and Family Court Advisory and Support Service, recognises situational couple violence, noting that 'persistent "low-severity" abuse is very likely to cause significant emotional harm to children who have to live with this, and violence that carries a high risk of severe harm can still be used in a context where neither partner has (yet) established a pattern of control over the other.'[46]

[42] J Collins and K Banyard, *Women and the Criminal Justice System* (Fawcett Society 2004); A Musgrove and N Groves, 'The Domestic Violence, Crime and Victims Act 2004: Relevant or "Removed" Legislation?' (2008) 29(3) *Journal of Social Welfare and Family Law* 233.
[43] RP Dobash and R Emerson Dobash, 'Women's Violence to Men in Intimate Relationships: Working on a Puzzle' (2004) 44 *British Journal of Criminology* 324.
[44] JB Kelly and MP Johnson, 'Differentiation among Types of Intimate Partner Violence: Research Update and Implications for Interventions' (2008) 46(3) *Family Court Review* 476.
[45] MP Johnson, 'Patriarchal Terrorism and Common Couple Violence: Two Forms of Violence against Women' (1995) 57 *Journal of Marriage and the Family* 283.
[46] Cafcass, Situational Couple Violence Toolkit. Available at https://www.cafcass.gov.uk/grown-ups/professionals/ciaf/resources-for-assessing-domestic-abuse/ accessed 28 November 2020.

While there are similarities in the use of verbal aggression and jealousy, these are not part of a pattern of controlling behaviours and abuse is less likely to escalate over time. Notably, it is inflicted by both men and women equally. Rates are higher among teenagers and young adults than older adults, and among the young adult group women are more likely to be situationally violent than men. Perpetrators may respond to intervention programs.

3. Separation-instigated violence, which, as the name suggests, involves violence which occurs for the first time at the point of separation. It is therefore different to coercive controlling violence because one party has not sought to control the other during the relationship. It is more likely to be perpetrated by the partner who is being left. Kelly and Johnson suggest that it is triggered by a traumatic separation, perhaps involving public humiliation and resulting in a loss of control by the perpetrator on one or two occasions. As we see in Chapter 10, when we discuss child contact, for about 15 per cent of victims violence occurred for the first time after separation.[47] It is important to be able to distinguish temporary separation-instigated violence (which is more likely to be halted by a domestic abuse protection orders of some kind) from behaviours which are an escalation of an existing pattern of coercive and controlling behaviour where separation can result in very serious risks to the victim.

4. Violent resistance. This type of violence is reactionary, an immediate response to an assault, and is primarily perpetrated by women on men. When some researchers say that women are more likely to use violence in self-defence, they are referring to Johnson's category of violent resistance. However, some women do, of course, use violence for reasons other than resistance: they may be coercively controlling, for example.

SCENARIO 1

Illustration 1: Kelly and Niall Hill

If we apply Kelly and Johnson's categories to Kelly and Niall we would categorise Niall as exercising coercive and controlling abuse over Kelly. This is marked by a need to control multiple aspects of her life including work, money, and who she socialises with or contacts. He is physically violent and uses this to obtain compliance, but physical violence is only one part of the abuse that Kelly is suffering.

SCENARIO 2

Illustration 1: Alex and Frances

Alex's conduct is not separation-instigated as they were abusive before, but separation has marked an escalation. This is probably situational violence. However, these categories are only useful if they help us to understand how to prevent or minimise the risk of abuse to victims in general or Frances in particular.

---

[47] T Hotton, 'Spousal Violence after Marital Separation' (2001) 27(7) *Juristat* 1.

Johnson argues that family violence theorists and feminist scholars are referring to different categories of abuse and are therefore not talking about the same thing.[48] He argues that the former concentrate on situational couple violence, which is rooted in conflict and not in patriarchal domination (although sexism in society and gender inequalities may still play a role), and that violent resistance helps explain why women report using violence as much as men in some studies that concentrate on identifying acts of violence. Feminists concentrate on coercive and controlling violence which is overwhelmingly experienced by women and which is a pattern of abuse of which physical violence is only one part.

These categories help us to understand what interventions might successfully reduce domestic abuse. The way in which domestic abuse is thought about affects how police forces and individual police offers attending a domestic abuse incident react. As Saunders points out, if domestic abuse is seen primarily as 'mutual combat' (to use Straus' phrase) then both parties are more likely to be arrested.[49] If an incident is seen as isolated, the overall pattern will be missed, and the effects on the victim underestimated. Hester has argued that part of the problem is that 'the criminal justice system is incident-focused, and decisions about the risks, charges and prosecutions are assessed in relation to an individual incident reported to the police.'[50]

7.3.2 Same-sex couples and domestic abuse

You may wonder where same-sex couples sit within these theories. Domestic abuse within same-sex couples is generally considered to be at or above the level experienced by different-sex couples. However, there are a number of differences. Being part of a minority group may exacerbate the stresses which can contribute to domestic abuse under the family violence theory.[51] LGBQ victims studied by Donovan and Hester saw domestic abuse 'as a heterosexual, gendered phenomenon, primarily physical in nature' and this prevented them from identifying themselves as victims of domestic abuse until after the relationship had ended.[52] They suggest that to those in their first same-sex relationship, 'lack of knowledge about what same-sex relationship could be like, what they could expect, or what love might be in a same-sex relationship, were often given in explanation for the lack of recognition, at the time, of the relationship as domestically violent.'[53] There are also practical impediments to same-sex couples accessing services which is that many domestic violence services are same-sex, elevating a risk of the perpetrator gaining access to the victim, and

---

[48] MP Johnson, 'Patriarchal Terrorism and Common Couple Violence: Two Forms of Violence against Women' (1995) 57 *Journal of Marriage and the Family* 283.

[49] DS Saunders, 'Are Physical Assaults by Wives and Girlfriends a Major Social Problem? A Review of the Literature' (2002) 8(12) *Violence against Women* 1424.

[50] M Hester 'Who Does What to Whom? Gender and Domestic Violence Perpetrators in English Police Records' (2013) 10(5) *European Journal of Criminology* 623.

[51] L Rollè, G Giardina, AM Caldarera, E Gerino, and P Brustia, 'When Intimate Partner Violence Meets Same Sex Couples: A Review of Same Sex Intimate Partner Violence' (2018) *Frontiers in Psychology* 1506.

[52] C Donovan and M Hester, '"I Hate the Word 'Victim'": An Exploration of Recognition of Domestic Violence in Same Sex Relationships' (2010) 9(2) *Social Policy and Society* 279. LGBQ is the description used by Donovan and Hester.

[53] C Donovan and M Hester, '"I Hate the Word 'Victim'": An Exploration of Recognition of Domestic Violence in Same Sex Relationships' (2010) 9(2) *Social Policy and Society* 279.

a victim may be reluctant to seek services if they feel that the services may discriminate against them or they are not publicly 'out'. While Donovan and Hester's study did not cover transgender individuals other than those identifying within the LGBQ categories, research by the Scottish Trans Alliance suggests that 80 per cent of trans individuals experience some form of physical, sexual, or emotional abuse or control, although only 60 per cent of them would categorise this as domestic abuse.[54]

7.3.3 Assessing domestic abuse risk

Many family solicitors and other professionals (such as police officers, social workers and health workers) will screen clients for domestic abuse. The purposes of screening are:

- to assess the risk that the perpetrator poses;
- to enable appropriate services to be offered to the victim;
- to better target appropriate interventions at the perpetrator; and
- to understand the influence that the abuse may have on decision-making by the victim.

As each of the categories identified by Kelly and Johnson have different risks and respond differently to intervention, it is necessary to understand the nature and level of the risk that a specific victim faces. There are a number of toolkits that are designed to assess risk, none of which will be entirely accurate at predicting harm. Most toolkits ask about whether the abuser is jealous or possessive, telling the victim what to wear, and who they can see, and accusing the victim of flirting with others or cheating; whether the abuser controls the family money; whether the abuser belittles, humiliates, criticises or plays 'mind games'; whether the abuser monitors, or follows the victim or uses tracking software; whether the abuser forces the victim to do things they do not want to do including sexual acts, or prevents them from going to college or work; and whether the victim feels isolated from friends and family and in fear of making the abuser angry. These would be indicative of coercive controlling abuse.

The most widely used in the UK is the *Domestic Abuse, Stalking and Harassment and Honour Based Violence (DASH) Risk Identification and Assessment and Management Model* used by the Association of Chief Police Officers and Cafcass. This particular toolkit is designed to enable an assessment of the level of risk posed by the alleged abuser. If the DASH score is high, the victim will be referred to MARAC, a multi-agency risk assessment conference which enables information-sharing about high-risk cases. MARAC members may include the police, children's social services, NHS representatives; probation officers; council housing officers; Cafcass officers, and representatives from the voluntary sector. Neither the victim nor the perpetrator attends the meeting. MARAC does not only deal with known abusive relationships. As we see at 7.5.4, one of its roles is to consider whether to disclose a person's history of violence to a new partner who may be at risk of abuse starting.

---

[54] A Roch, G Ritchie, and J Morton, *Out of Sight, Out of Mind? Transgender People's Experiences of Domestic Abuse* (Scottish Trans Alliance 2010).

7.4 **Domestic abuse as a human rights issue**

As domestic abuse often arises as an issue in the family law context, and some of the protective steps outlined at 7.5 of this chapter fall within the remit of family lawyers, domestic
abuse is often seen as a family law issue. However, there is an objection to this: by making
it part of the private sphere, we seem to minimise its importance as a public concern, a
human rights issue, and a criminal issue.

In this section we consider the human rights implications of domestic abuse and what
this means for the state's response to domestic abuse.

7.4.1 **Recognition of domestic abuse as a human rights issue**

A number of international legal instruments recognise domestic violence as an infringement of human rights. The 1979 UN Convention on the Elimination of All Forms of
Discrimination against Women (known as CEDAW or the Women's Convention') is one
such. While this document did not explicitly identify domestic abuse as a form of discrimination against women, this was remedied by subsequent guidance.[55] The United
Kingdom ratified the Convention in 1986 but, unlike the ECHR, it does not form part
of our domestic law. While the treaty is binding on the UK, and the UK must report on
its progress in meeting the Convention's aims, there is no remedy for the individual. The
Convention is part of the remit of the UN Human Rights Commissioner. Article 2 of the
1994 Declaration on the Elimination of Violence against Women explicitly recognises

> Physical, sexual and psychological violence occurring in the family, including battering,
> sexual abuse of female children in the household, dowry-related violence, marital rape,
> female genital mutilation and other traditional practices harmful to women, non-spousal
> violence and violence related to exploitation.[56]

Secondly, the Council of Europe Convention on Preventing and Combating Violence
against Women and Domestic Violence (known as the Istanbul Convention) is also extremely important. It is ratified by the UK which must produce annual reports about its
level of compliance with the requirements of the convention.

These two conventions, together with the guidance, declarations, and statements associated with them, recognise that domestic abuse is a form of gender-based violence and
gender discrimination.

We now turn to consider the ECHR which is part of our domestic law.

7.4.2 **Domestic abuse and the ECHR**

There are several Articles of the ECHR that are relevant.

Article 2

Article 2 ECHR is the right to life. Key Case *Opuz v Turkey* tells us that this may be
breached if the state knew of a real and imminent risk to the life of the victim and failed

---

[55] The UN Committee on the Elimination of Discrimination against Women, *General Recommendation 19* (1992).
[56] Resolution adopted by the UN General Assembly A/RES/48/104 of 23 February 1994.

to take steps designed to protect them. However, the judgment specifically recognises that there are limits on the state's obligation. It is only when the state knows or ought to have known of the risk that the obligation to take protective measures arises.

In a separate but concurring judgment in the later case of *Valiuliene v Lithuania*, Judge Pinto de Albuquerque questioned whether the test of imminent risk was sufficient in cases of domestic violence: 'Realistically speaking, at the stage of an "immediate risk" to the victim it is often too late for the State to intervene. In addition, the recurrence and escalation inherent in most cases of domestic violence makes it somehow artificial, even deleterious, to require an immediacy of the risk. Even though the risk might not be imminent, it is already a serious risk when it is present.'[57]

Article 3

Article 3 states that no one shall be subjected to torture or to inhuman or degrading treatment or punishment. Domestic abuse can reach the level of engaging Article 3. In *Valiuliene v Lithuania* the European Court of Human Rights recognised that 'the ill treatment of the applicant, which on five occasions caused her physical injuries, combined with her feelings of fear and helplessness, was sufficiently serious to reach the level of severity under Article 3 of the Convention and thus raise the Government's positive obligation under this provision.'[58]

The Court also stated that it could not 'turn a blind eye to the psychological aspect of the alleged ill-treatment'.[59] This gives support to the suggestion made by Choudhry and Herring back in 2006 that physical violence is not an essential prerequisite for Article 3[60] although in practical terms cumulative psychological harm may be less likely to come to the attention of the state and thereby trigger the state's positive obligations.

While Article 3 is an absolute right permitting no interference where it applies, it does not always apply. The state will not breach this right unless it failed to take reasonably available measures which could have had a real prospect of altering the outcome of mitigating the harm. It is not necessary to show that the harm would not have occurred without the state's failings, but it does require that the state know or ought to know about the abuse.[61] If it does so then Article 3 requires the implementation of 'adequate criminal-law mechanisms' to 'deter the commission of offences against personal integrity, backed up by law-enforcement machinery for the prevention, suppression and punishment of breaches of such provisions, and this requirement also extends to ill-treatment administered by private individuals.'[62]

Article 8

Article 8 is already familiar to you: it is the right to private and family life. Most commonly, this Article is engaged by an act of a state which interferes with family life, and it is in

---

[57] No paragraph or page references are provided for the concurring judgment.
[58] App no. 33234/07, judgment of 26 March 2013 perfected 26 June 2013 at para 70.
[59] Para 69. For an excellent commentary on this case, see RJA McQuigg 'The European Court of Human Rights and Domestic Violence: *Valiuliene v Lithuania*' (2014) 18(7–8) *The International Journal of Human Rights* 756.
[60] S Choudhry and J Herring, 'Domestic Violence and the Human Rights Act 1998: A New Means of Legal Intervention?' [2006] *Public Law* 752.
[61] *E v United Kingdom* (Application No.33218/96 judgment 26 November 2002) at para 99.
[62] Paras 73 and 75.

that context that we consider Article 8's role in adoption cases in Chapter 12, for example. This is because Article 8 imposes a positive obligation on the state to protect family life where it exists. In domestic abuse cases, Article 8 can be used to support arguments against victimless prosecutions—those criminal prosecutions where the victim does not wish to cooperate—or against third parties being able to apply for protective orders for a victim contrary to their wishes. Intervention against the wishes of the victim, it is argued, constitute an interference with her autonomy. It is all the more important to protect the victim's autonomy in view of the fact that her right to self-determination has already been limited by the domestic abuse itself.

But Article 8 also has a further element to it, as the right to private life has been held to encompass a right to psychological and physical integrity[63] and a right to establish and develop relationships including with the world outside the home.[64] Domestic abuse can interfere with these aspects of Article 8 and the state is under a positive obligation to protect individuals in order to promote this aspect of their right. However, Article 8 is not an absolute right like Article 3, and therefore even when it is engaged it can be subject to interference where necessary, and where the rights and interests of two or more people are engaged those rights must be balanced against one another to see whose should prevail. In the context of domestic abuse, the perpetrator's rights are also engaged. Criminal prosecution and civil protective actions are capable of ending the relationship by prohibiting further contact, and capable of excluding the abuser from this or her property. Where the victim is not willing to support prosecution, continuing in her absence reduces the defendant's ability to challenge that evidence, and this may affect their Article 6 right to a fair trial. The Crown Prosecution Service Inspectorate has noted that 'such points are not infrequently prayed in aid by the defence, when arguing that the prosecution is not justified, or an abuse of process.[65]

Choudhry and Herring argue that in this balancing exercise, the rights of the victim should be weighed more heavily for several reasons.[66] First, they argue that even if a victim does not wish to cooperate with the prosecution, their decision may not be free of outside influence. They may worry about retaliation, they may wonder about the practical and financial effects of prosecution, and they may believe that the law will not adequately protect them anyway. But protecting the victim's freedom not to cooperate means exposing her to abuse and therefore infringing her right to psychological and physical integrity as statistically she is likely to be abused again.

However, by removing victims' choice of prosecution/protection, we may reduce the extent to which the perpetrator blames them, although this is by no means certain. Second, Choudhry and Herring argue that 'the interests of children and the wider community need to be taken into account'.[67] Victimless prosecutions send a message about

---

[63] *X and Y v Netherlands* (1985) 8 EHRR 235; *Pretty v United Kingdom* (App. No. 2346/02, judgment 29 April 2002).

[64] *Burghartz v Switzerland* (1994) 18 EHRR 101; *Friedl v Austria* (1996) 21 EHRR 83; *Pretty v United Kingdom* (App. No. 2346/02, judgment 29 April 2002).

[65] HM Crown Prosecution Service Inspectorate, *Violence at Home: A Joint Thematic Inspection of the Investigation and Prosecution of Cases Involving Domestic Violence* (2004) at para 7.20.

[66] S Choudhry and J Herring, 'Righting Domestic Violence' (2006) 20 *International Journal of Law, Policy and the Family* 95.

[67] S Choudhry and J Herring, 'Righting Domestic Violence' (2006) 20 *International Journal of Law, Policy and the Family* 95, 102.

the unacceptability of domestic abuse. A number of international agreements beyond the ECHR recognise domestic abuse as a human rights issue, and, as we saw at 7.2.2, domestic abuse comes at significant costs to the state and there is therefore a state interest in stopping it. Thirdly, children are involved in many incidents of domestic abuse and there is strong evidence that they are harmed by this in the long term.[68] They too are entitled to protection, including under the ECHR, and as we see in Chapter 9 their rights are given particular weight in the balancing exercise. Finally, Jane Fortin has argued that the underlying philosophy of the ECHR is the promotion of the good life, and on that basis we should interpret rights under the ECHR consistently with what is in the rights-holder's interests. No one, she says, has the right 'to be treated in a way that fundamentally harms them.'[69]

Article 13

Article 13 provides that 'everyone whose rights and freedoms as set forth in this Convention are violated shall have an effective remedy before a national authority notwithstanding that the violation has been committed by persons acting in an official capacity'. In the context of domestic abuse, this imposes a positive obligation on the state to provide an effective remedy including where the breach of the human rights has been caused by an individual rather than the state itself. The remedy in question could be protective steps designed to reduce or avoid harms to a victim.

Article 14

Article 14 is the parasitic right: it has to be coupled with a substantive right. It states that the rights and freedoms contained in the ECHR 'shall be secured without discrimination on any ground such as sex, race, colour, language, religion, political or other opinion, national or social origin, association with a national minority, property, birth or other status.' Domestic abuse is both gendered and has different risk levels according to age and race. In Key Case *Opuz v Turkey* the European Court of Human Rights recognised that insufficient protections by the state were a form of discrimination against women and girls.[70]

> **KEY CASE** *Opuz v Turkey* (Application no. 33401/02, ECtHR 9 June 2009)
>
> The facts of this case are very distressing. Nahide Opuz was married to a man, Huseyin Opuz, who abused her, and they had three children. She had reported him to the police several times and there were contemporaneous medical records of her injuries. On one occasion he attacked Ms Opuz and her mother (who is not named in the judgment) with a knife, causing them injuries that rendered them unable to work for several days. The state declined to prosecute. On another occasion he drove his car into Ms Opuz and her mother, causing the latter life-changing injuries. He was fined for that. Mrs Opuz and her mother sought protection from the police but ultimately withdrew their

---

[68] JL Edleson 'Children's Witnessing of Adult Domestic Violence' (1999) 14(8) *Journal of Interpersonal Violence* 839.
[69] J Fortin, 'Accommodating Children's Rights in a Post Human Rights Act Era' (2006) 69(3) *Modern Law Review* 299.
[70] See commentary by M Burton, 'The Human Rights of Victims of Domestic Violence: *Opuz v Turkey*' (2010) 22 *Child and Family Law Quarterly* 131.

complaints that he had tried to kill them. A prosecution for making death threats against them was dropped. In the face of his threats, Ms Opuz brought but withdrew divorce proceedings.

Three years later, he stabbed Ms Opuz seven times in front of the children, and again was fined for that. He made further death threats which the state declined to prosecute. Ms Opuz moved in with her mother. The mother told the police that Opuz had been coming to her house every day with a knife or gun and threatening her, Ms Opuz and the children with death. When they decided to leave the area to escape him, Mr Opuz forced the mother's removal van off the road and shot her dead. He was sentenced to fewer than 16 years' imprisonment, which had been reduced for good behaviour during the trial and provocation: he had argued that he had committed a crime of honour against his mother-in-law for her role in taking his wife away from him and exposing her to an immoral way of life. He was released pending appeal and issued further threats towards Ms Opuz and her new boyfriend. Again no protective steps were taken. When Ms Opuz complained to the ECHR, the photograph and fingerprints of Mr Opuz were distributed to police stations so that they could arrest him if he appeared near her home.

Ms Opuz argued that the Turkish state had violated her rights under Article 2 (the right to life), Article 3 (the prohibition on torture and inhuman or degrading treatment) and Article 14 (non-discrimination in the application of the other rights).

The European Court of Human Rights unanimously found that Turkey had violated the mother's right to life. It held that states were under an obligation to put in place provisions to prevent and deter offences and punish offenders. The obligation extends 'in appropriate circumstances to a positive obligation on the authorities to take preventive operational measures to protect an individual whose life is at risk from the criminal acts of another individual.'[71] Article 2 will be breached if the authorities:

> knew or ought to have known at the time of the existence of a real and immediate risk to the life of an identified individual or individuals from the criminal acts of a third party and that they failed to take measures within the scope of their powers which, judged reasonably, might have been expected to avoid that risk. Furthermore, having regard to the nature of the right protected by Article 2, a right fundamental in the scheme of the Convention, it is sufficient for an applicant to show that the authorities did not do all that could be reasonably expected of them to avoid a real and immediate risk to life of which they have or ought to have knowledge.[72]

Turkey argued that Ms Opuz and her mother had withdrawn their complaints and that under Turkish law a victimless prosecution was not possible. The ECHR (again unanimously) held that:

> there seems to be no general consensus among States Parties regarding the pursuance of the criminal prosecution against perpetrators of domestic violence when the victim withdraws her complaints. . . . Nevertheless, there appears to be an acknowledgement of the duty on the part of the authorities to strike a balance between a victim's Article 2, Article 3 or Article 8 rights in deciding on a course of action. . . . there are certain factors that can be taken into account in deciding to pursue the prosecution: the seriousness of the offence; whether the victim's injuries are physical or psychological; if the defendant used a weapon; if the defendant has made any threats since the attack; if the defendant planned the attack; the effect (including psychological) on any children living in the household; the chances of the defendant offending again; the continuing threat to the health and safety of the victim or anyone else who was, or could become, involved; the current state of the victim's relationship with the defendant; the effect on that relationship of continuing with the prosecution against the victim's wishes; the history of the relationship, particularly if there had been any other violence in the past; and the defendant's criminal history, particularly any previous violence.

[71] Para 128.
[72] Para 130.

> It can be inferred from this practice that the more serious the offence or the greater the risk of further offences, the more likely that the prosecution should continue in the public interest, even if victims withdraw their complaints.[73]
>
> Ms Opuz argued that her husband's conduct amounted to torture under Article 3 and that 'it was as though the violence had been inflicted under state supervision. The insensitivity and tolerance shown by the authorities in the face of domestic violence had made her feel debased, hopeless and vulnerable'.[74] The Court held that the state was under a positive obligation 'to take measures designed to ensure that individuals within their jurisdiction are not subjected to torture or inhuman or degrading treatment or punishment, including such ill-treatment administered by private individuals.'[75] The abuse in this case reached the level to fall under Article 3. Turkey was in violation because it had failed to take sufficient steps to protect Ms Opuz, including of its own volition where she had withdrawn a complaint, and because the steps it had taken were ineffective (including very light punishments that had no effect in deterring Mr Opuz).
>
> The Court also unanimously found a breach of Article 14, in that the failure of the state to protect the women's Article 2 and 3 rights was gendered: 'The applicant has been able to show, supported by unchallenged statistical information, the existence of a *prima facie* indication that the domestic violence affected mainly women and that the general and discriminatory judicial passivity in Turkey created a climate that was conducive to domestic violence.'[76]

7.4.3 Consequences for policing and prosecution

The application of these human rights has consequences for policing and prosecution of domestic abuse and for the civil remedies that may be available to victims. Domestic abuse crimes have a high rate of attrition (fall-off), much higher than other types of crimes, notwithstanding that victims of domestic abuse can identify their abuser so there is always someone who could be prosecuted. Attrition means that a progressively smaller proportion of cases proceed at each of the following stages: calling the police, identifying in a police report that what has happened is a crime, arresting an alleged perpetrator, charging them, and conviction. Hester studied attrition rates of cases dealt with by Northumbria Police over three months and found that of 869 recorded domestic violence incidents, 222 resulted in arrest, 60 people were charged, and 31 convicted.[77] Most of those convicted received fines or community rehabilitation orders (which may include attending a perpetrator programme); only four received a custodial sentence.

In a number of cases in Hester's study, the Crown Prosecution Service had reduced the charge from its original level, presumably as they thought the higher charge was less likely to result in conviction. Issues with evidence help explain the attrition rate.[78] Hester found that evidence such as photographs of injuries which could have helped the prospects of successful conviction were not being collected. In its much larger investigation, the Crown Prosecution Service Inspectorate also found that 'the absence in many cases of

---

[73] Paras 138 and 139.
[74] Para 155.
[75] Para 159.
[76] Para 198.
[77] M Hester, 'Making It through the Criminal Justice System: Attrition and Domestic Violence' (2005) 5(1) *Social Policy and Society* 79.
[78] ES Buzawa and CG Buzawa, *Domestic Violence: The Criminal Justice Response* (Sage 2003).

corroborative evidence (reflecting poor investigation at the scene and subsequently) leads to a reliance upon the victim's statement and willingness to pursue the complaint.'[79] If they are not willing, charges are more likely to be dropped.

One attempt to address this is through victimless prosecutions which rely not on victim testimony but on evidence such as officers' body-worn cameras, recordings of 999 calls, or admissions by the perpetrator.[80] But lack of victim cooperation does not adequately explain the attrition rate. The availability of victimless prosecutions demonstrates that it is possible to prosecute some, perhaps many, cases without their cooperation. The reasons why so few successful prosecutions occur must lie elsewhere, perhaps with a belief—not present in other types of crimes—that whether or not prosecution occurs is a matter for the victim[81] or because 'dominant police culture depicted violence in the home as "just another domestic"—a nuisance call to familiar addresses that rarely resulted in a satisfactory policing outcome'.[82]

The human rights dimension not only affects the criminal justice response to domestic abuse but also the civil and family law response. As we see in Chapter 10, courts have not often approached domestic abuse in child context cases in a way that sufficiently protects the victims. One of the key issues is the lack of a coherent package of support for victims of domestic abuse.

As Hester writes, 'Generally, criminal justice interventions are unlikely to be effective on their own, and are most effective when carried out in a context of wider support and advocacy for those victimised.'[83] The new Domestic Abuse Commissioner may help in this regard, but at present the law provides a mixed bag of different legal powers, stemming from numerous pieces of legislation and subject to many amendments, and backed up by insufficient resources that largely depend upon assistance from voluntary organisations and charities.

7.5 Protection offered by the law

Domestic abuse may involve commission of a number of criminal offences, such as common assault, actual or grievous bodily harm, or murder. There are also offences specifically designed for the domestic context, and relate to harassment, stalking, coercive and controlling behaviour, forcing someone to marry against their will, and subjecting a girl to female genital mutilation. If a person is worried that they, or someone close to them, is in a relationship with someone who has a history of violence, they can seek information from the police that may help a victim make an informed decision about whether to continue in the relationship.

---

[79] At para 1.17.
[80] A visceral example of the aftermath of domestic abuse seen through officers' body camera footage can be found in the BBC Panorama documentary *Domestic Abuse: Caught on Camera* (first broadcast 8 December 2014).
[81] C Hoyle and A Sanders, 'Police Response to Domestic Violence: From Victim Choice to Victim Empowerment?' (2000) 40 *British Journal of Criminology* 14. See also L. Ellison, 'Prosecuting Domestic Violence without Victim Participation' (2002) 65(6) *Modern Law Review* 834.
[82] HM Crown Prosecution Service Inspectorate, *Violence at Home: A Joint Thematic Inspection of the Investigation and Prosecution of Cases Involving Domestic Violence* (2004) at p6.
[83] M Hester, 'Making It through the Criminal Justice System: Attrition and Domestic Violence' (2005) 5(1) *Social Policy and Society* 79.

Alongside criminal offences, there are a number of civil remedies covering similar grounds. A civil injunction or order can be sought to prevent harassment, forced marriage, female genital mutilation, and molestation. Although these orders are civil in nature, breach can result in imprisonment. As occupation of the family home may be a real concern to a victim of domestic abuse, the courts also have the power under the Family Law Act 1996 to exclude a person from the family home. This may be used alongside or subsequently to the more temporary but immediate issue of a domestic violence protection notice or order which may also exclude an alleged perpetrator.

These remedies rarely interconnect. They were conceived at different times and while there may be some overlap in respect of who can apply and the kinds of behaviour that are covered, they are disparate. In this and subsequent sections of this chapter, we look at each of them in turn.

7.5.1 The Domestic Abuse Act 2021

At the time of writing, the Domestic Abuse Act 2021 has just received Royal Assent and has therefore entered into law.

The Act has:

- Put the government's definition of domestic abuse on a statutory footing.
- Abolished domestic violence protection orders and notices and replace them with domestic abuse protection notices and orders which are wider in scope. The government has said that it is their intention 'that DAPOs will become the "go to" protective order in cases of domestic abuse.'[84]
- Created the position of Domestic Abuse Commissioner for England and Wales with responsibility for oversight of domestic abuse services; encouraging good practice; and making recommendations about how services can be improved. The Commissioner will be independent but will only have the power to submit reports to Parliament. In Wales, the Commissioner will have a reduced role as a result of devolution.
- Placed a duty on local authorities in England to provide refuges another safe accommodation, and improve support for homeless domestic abuse victims.
- Prohibited alleged perpetrators from cross examining alleged victims (and vice versa) in person in the civil and family courts. An advocate can be instructed at public expense for this purpose.
- Placed the domestic violence disclosure scheme (Clare's Law) on a statutory footing.
- Created an offence of non-fatal strangulation or suffocation, given that these acts often predict future homicide.

7.5.2 Harassment and stalking under the Protection from Harassment Act 1997

There are a number of offences under the Protection from Harassment Act 1997, of which we are concerned with harassment (s2); harassment that puts a person in fear of violence

---

[84] Home Office, *Domestic Abuse Protection Notices/Orders Factsheet* (August 2020).

(s4); harassment which involves a course of conduct that amounts to stalking (s2A(1); stalking involving a fear of violence (s4A(1)(b)(i)); and stalking involving serious alarm or distress (s4A(1)(b)(ii)). In 2019, police in England and Wales recorded 176,837 offences relating to stalking or harassment.[85]

Harassment

Section 1 of the Protection from Harassment Act 1997 provides that 'a person must not pursue a course of conduct which amounts to harassment of another, and which he knows or ought to know amounts to harassment'. A person ought to know that he is committing harassment 'if a reasonable person in possession of the same information would think the course of conduct amounted to or involved harassment. Under s2, an offence is committed if a person engages in a course of conduct amounting to harassment. There must be at least two occasions of harassment to constitute a course of conduct, and conduct can include speech (s7). Section 4 involves a course of conduct that causes another to fear, on at least two occasions, that violence will be used against them.

Stalking

Under s2A a person commits an offence if they engage in a course of conduct which constitutes harassment and amounts to stalking. Subsection (3) gives examples of stalking behaviour including following, contacting or attempting to contact a person; publishing statements or materials about them or pretending to be them; monitoring their internet use; loitering, watching, and spying. Section 4A covers stalking that causes another person to fear violence against them on at least two occasions or causes them serious alarm or distress which has a substantial adverse effect on the victim's usual day-to-day activities.

Acquadro Maran and Veretto haves estimated that the average period for which someone is domestically stalked is 16.6 months.[86]

The Crown Prosecution Service has reported that between April 2019 and March 2020, there were some 2,288 prosecutions for stalking offences in England and Wales, and 84 per cent of a randomly selected sample of these involved a former partner, often with a background of domestic abuse. They note that of 50 completed prosecutions in April to June 2020:

> In every case involving an ex-partner, victims were bombarded with unwanted and often threatening phone contact and were physically stalked at their home or place of work. Social media was cited as a significant factor in 17 cases, with offenders usually creating multiple Facebook and Instagram accounts to get around being blocked by their victims. Three cases involved the disclosing of private sexual images - so-called "revenge porn", with one woman's photos sent to her manager by an ex. In two cases, trackers were put on the victims' cars and one involved an attempted abduction.[87]

[85] Office for National Statistics, *Domestic Abuse Prevalence and Victim Characteristics* Appendix Table 18: Table 18: Number of domestic abuse-related stalking and harassment offences recorded by the police, by offence, year ending March 2020 (2020).
[86] D Acquadro Maran and A Veretto, 'Psychological Impact of Stalking on Male and Female Health Care Professional Victims of Stalking and Domestic Violence' (2018) 9 *Frontiers in Psychology* 321.
[87] Crown Prosecution Service, 'Stalking analysis reveals domestic abuse link' (4 December 2020). Available at https://www.cps.gov.uk/cps/news/stalking-analysis-reveals-domestic-abuse-link accessed 7 December 2020.

The National Stalking Helpline, run by Suzy Lamplugh Trust, has suggested that the lock-downs caused by the COVID-19 pandemic exacerbated stalking behaviours.[88]

Injunctions and restraining orders under the Act

When sentencing a person for committing an offence under the Act, the courts can issue a *civil* restraining order under s5 to prevent the defendant from harassing the victim. Indeed, under s5A—a later addition to the Act—a restraining order can also be issued when a defendant is acquitted if the court considers it necessary to do so in order to protect the victim from harassment by the defendant.[89] The consent of the victim is not necessary and an order is subject to appeal.

As the order is civil, the necessity criterion is determined on the balance of probabilities. This means that a person can be found to be responsible for domestic abuse to the civil standard, justifying the making of an order, but not guilty before the same court in criminal proceedings where the standard of proof is beyond reasonable doubt. The scope is also wider than the behaviour for which the perpetrator has been charged, in that since 2009 judges can issue them on conviction for any offence. Breach is a criminal offence and police can arrest without a warrant.

The courts can also issue injunctions under 3A to restrain a named person from pursuing any conduct which amounts to harassment.[90] This may be used either where harassment is taking place or where harassment is anticipated.

7.5.3 The criminal offence of coercive and controlling behaviour

Section 76 of the Serious Crime Act 2015 made controlling or coercive behaviour in an intimate or family relationship illegal from 29 December 2015. Breach of the provision can result in a significant fine or up to 5 years in prison. It was amended by the 2021 Act as follows.

STATUTORY EXTRACT *s76 Serious Crime Act 2015*

Controlling or coercive behaviour in an intimate or family relationship:

(1) A person (A) commits an offence if

    (a) A repeatedly or continuously engages in behaviour towards another person (B) that is controlling or coercive,

    (b) at the time of the behaviour, A and B are personally connected, (see subsection (6))

    (c) the behaviour has a serious effect on B, and

    (d) A knows or ought to know that the behaviour will have a serious effect on B.

---

[88] Crown Prosecution Service, 'Stalking analysis reveals domestic abuse link' (4 December 2020). Available at https://www.cps.gov.uk/cps/news/stalking-analysis-reveals-domestic-abuse-link accessed 7 December 2020.

[89] This was added by the Domestic Violence, Crime and Victims Act 2004.

[90] This was added by the Serious Organised Crime and Police Act 2005.

(4) A's behaviour has a 'serious effect' on B if

    (a) it causes B to fear, on at least two occasions, that violence will be used against B, or

    (b) it causes B serious alarm or distress which has a substantial adverse effect on B's usual day-to-day activities.

(5) For the purposes of subsection (1)(d) A 'ought to know' that which a reasonable person in possession of the same information would know.

(6) A and B are "personally connected" if any of the following applies:

    (a) they are, or have been, married to each other;

    (b) they are, or have been, civil partners of each other;

    (c) they have agreed to marry one another (whether or not the agreement has been terminated);

    (d) they have entered into a civil partnership agreement (whether or not the agreement has been terminated);

    (e) they are, or have been, in an intimate personal relationship with each other;

    (f) they each have, or there has been a time when they each have had, a parental relationship in relation to the same child (see subsection (6A));

    (g) they are relatives.

It is a defence for A to show that A believed that he or she was acting in B's best interests, and the behaviour was in all the circumstances reasonable, although this is not a defence in relation to behaviour that causes B to fear that violence will be used against her.

The introduction of this offence marks the increasing recognition that domestic abuse can be pernicious without involving actual physical violence, and that non-physical harms can severely affect victims. The Act sought to address the limitations of the Protection from Harassment Act by covering those in romantic and family. It is sensible when referring to coercive and controlling behaviour to be clear whether you refer to the nature of the harm or the specific offence.

One research study commissioned by a law firm in 2018 found that 53 per cent of respondents reported having experienced some kind of bullying or controlling behaviour at the hands of their partner. There was no difference between the genders as to the number experiencing such behaviour although there were differences in the nature of the behaviour reported. While it is unclear whether this study defines coercive and controlling behaviour in the same way that the law does, it suggests that many relationships are marked by a degree of controlling behaviour.[91]

The offence also does not apply where B is below the age of 16 and A is a person with parental responsibility for them, a liability to maintain them, or who has care of them. However, this is because there are already a number of criminal offences that cover the same ground in relation to acts against children.

As s76(1) says, the behaviour must be engaged in 'repeatedly' or 'continuously' and must have a serious effect on the victim, defined as causing them to fear violence on at least two occasions or having a substantial adverse effect on their usual day-to-day activities. The Crown Prosecution Service guidance gives examples of stopping or changing the way the victim socialises, causing a change in their home routine, work patterns, college attendance,

---

[91] K Ryan, 'More Than a Third of Men and Women in UK Admit to Being in a Coercive Relationship' [2019, July] *Family Law* 723.

employment status or route to work, or a victim putting in place measures to safeguard themselves at home, as well as a deterioration in the victim's physical or mental health.[93]

SCENARIO 1

Illustration 2: Kelly and Niall Hill

We have previously suggested that Niall's behaviour fits the pattern of coercive and controlling domestic abuse under the Kelly and Johnson categories. But does it fit the criminal offence of coercive and controlling behaviour? It would appear so. The parties are personally connected. Niall's behaviour seems to have had a serious effect on Kelly, under both legs of subsection (4) and a reasonable person ought to have known that physical abuse and his other forms of control would have a serious effect on Kelly.

There have been a few prosecutions under the new offence although numbers are increasing.[94] McGorrey and McMahon identified 145 cases in England and Wales between 29 December 2015 when the law came into effect and 30 April 2018. Of the 108 cases in which they had sufficient information for analysis, 107 defendants were convicted and sentenced. Ninety-nine per cent of offenders were male and 90 per cent of victims were current or former intimate partners. More than 20 per cent of convicted offenders had prior convictions for family violence. In most cases, physical abuse was present.[95]

There may be several reasons why there have been so few prosecutions. It may reflect evidential difficulties, as much coercive control is hidden,[96] and prosecutions are extremely unlikely to be successful without victim testimony.[97] There may also be issues with interpretation of the Act. The Crown Prosecution Service's guidance notes that 'there might be confusion about where the "appropriate" dynamic of a relationship ends and where unlawful behaviour begins', noting that coercive and controlling relationships are marked out by the consequences for the victim of non-compliance with the perpetrator's rules.[98] It may be that perpetrators are prosecuted for associated behaviours, such as physical violence, which the police or prosecutors may feel are safer legal ground.

7.5.4 Domestic violence disclosure scheme

In February 2009, four months after ending her relationship with George Appleton, 36-year-old Clare Wood was murdered by him. Appleton had a history of violence against

---
[93] Crown Prosecution Service, *Controlling or Coercive Behaviour in an Intimate or Family Relationship Legal Guidance* (2017).

[94] Office for National Statistics, *Domestic Abuse and the Criminal Justice System*—Appendix Tables (2020).

[95] P McGorrery and M McMahon, 'Prosecuting Controlling or Coercive Behaviour in England and Wales: Media Reports of a Novel Offence' (2019) *Criminology and Criminal Justice* 1.

[96] See C Bishop, 'Why it's so hard to prosecute cases of coercive or controlling behaviour' (The Conversation, 31 October 2016).

[97] JR Tolmie, 'Coercive Control: To Criminalize or Not to Criminalize?' (2018) 18(1) *Criminology and Criminal Justice* 50.

[98] Crown Prosecution Service, *Controlling or Coercive Behaviour in an Intimate or Family Relationship Legal Guidance* (2017).

women. He had threatened to kill an ex-girlfriend's dog, throw acid in her face, and burn her alive. He had been jailed for three years in 2002 for harassing another woman and for six months in 2001 after breaching a restraining order (presumably made under the Protection from Harassment Act 1997). Clare did not know this at the time she entered into the relationship.

Clare Woods' death was the impetus for the introduction of the domestic violence disclosure scheme, or Clare's Law, which enables certain people to receive information about their partner's previous history of abuse so that they can make an informed decision about whether to continue with the relationship or extricate themselves early and safely. This is based on evidence that some people are serial perpetrators of domestic abuse.[99] Clare Woods' father, who campaigned for the introduction of the scheme, believed strongly that she would not have entered into a relationship had she known about Appleton's past.[100]

Despite its name Clare's Law initially had no statutory basis, and derived its authority from the police's common law power to disclose information where it is necessary to prevent crime.[101] It provides a framework within which disclosure can be considered and made, and which considers the parties' rights under data protection law and the ECHR. However, the new Domestic Abuse Act 2021 does place the scheme on a statutory footing.

There are two aspects: the right to ask and the right to know.

- The 'right to ask' enables a person (A) to ask the police about their partner (B)'s previous history of domestic violence or violent acts. It is also possible for someone to ask about the partner of a close friend of family member. Any information may be provided directly to the person best placed to safeguard A (for example, the parent of a minor who is in a risky relationship) or, if different, A him or herself.

- The 'right to know' allows police to proactively disclose information that has come to them and leads them to be concerned that B presents a risk to A. They may have received this information from third party safeguarding partners, intelligence sources, or through their own investigations.

Deciding whether to disclose

The decision about whether information can be disclosed to A is made by a multi-agency team, ideally MARAC, the Multi-Agency Risk Assessment Conference. Until the Secretary of State issues new guidance under s77 of the 2021 Act, disclosure should only be made if:

- it is reasonable to conclude that such disclosure is necessary to protect A from being the victim of a crime;

- there is a pressing need for such disclosure; and

- interfering with the rights of B, including B's rights under Article 8 of the ECHR to have information about his/her previous convictions kept confidential, is necessary and proportionate for the prevention of crime.[102]

---

[99] Home Office, *Together We Can End Violence against Women and Girls* (2009).

[100] J Meikle, 'Women May Be Warned Of Partners' Violent Pasts under New "Clare's Law"' (*The Guardian*, 17 July 2011).

[101] Home Office, *Domestic Violence Disclosure Scheme (DVDS) Guidance* (2016).

[102] Home Office, *Domestic Violence Disclosure Scheme (DVDS) Guidance* (2016) 18.

The guidance notes that this determination 'involves balancing the consequences for B if his/her details are disclosed against the nature and extent of the risks that B poses to A' and that it may be possible for information to be disclosed without full details of the offences being provided.

The conference will also need to consider whether B should be told that information may be disclosed to A. Whether or not this is appropriate depends on whether telling B increases the risk of harm to A.

What information may be disclosed?

The scheme is designed to permit the disclosure of convictions, cautions, or final warnings for offences of violence or abuse. The type of offences that may cause concern are listed in the scheme guidance, and comprise a wide range of offences relating to violence (not necessarily against a partner or family member), harassment, false imprisonment, and child abduction.[103] Research in Wales found that serial domestic abuse perpetrators 'are more likely than non-serial domestic abuse perpetrators to have [be involved in] past assault of family and stranger/acquaintance violence, recent escalation in violence, past use of weapons and denial of spousal assault'.[104] This suggests that evidence of non-domestic offences may be indicative of an elevated risk of partner abuse.

However, it is not merely previous convictions that can trigger disclosure. Cases not proceeded with, or intelligence about offences, and concerning behaviour towards previous partners may all be disclosed if they reasonably lead the police or MARAC to believe that there is a risk of harm to A.

Use of the scheme

In the first year of operation, commencing March 2014, at least 1,335 disclosures were made across England and Wales and 3,760 applications were made.[105] However, the scheme is not particularly well known. In the year ending March 2019, which marks five years of the scheme's existence, there were 6,496 'right to ask' applications and disclosure was made in 40 per cent of cases, and 7,252 'right to know' applications of which 55 per cent resulted in disclosure.[106] The higher percentage for right to know applications may results from the fact that if the police are proactively considering disclosure they are particularly concerned.

7.5.5 Domestic violence protection orders and notices

At present, if the police arrest a suspected perpetrator of domestic abuse, or bail them pending a charging decision by the CPS, the perpetrator can be remanded in custody or bailed with certain conditions, breach of which would result in arrest.

[103] Home Office, *Domestic Violence Disclosure Scheme (DVDS) Guidance* (2016).

[104] A Robinson, A Clancy, and S Hanks, *Prevalence and Characteristics of Serial Domestic Abuse Perpetrators: Multi Agency Evidence from Wales* (National Offender Management Service Wales 2014).

[105] J Grierson, '"Clare's Law" Saves 1,300 Women from Violent Partners in First Year' (*The Independent*, 26 January 2015). Available at https://www.independent.co.uk/news/uk/crime/clare-s-law-saves-1-300-women-violent-partners-first-year-10001781.html accessed 25 November 2020.

[106] Data from 36 police forces in right to know and 39 in right to ask. See Home Office, *Domestic Violence Disclosure Scheme Factsheet* (August 2020).

Yet there is a considerable disparity between the number of arrests and the number of prosecutions. What if the perpetrator is released with a caution or no further action, or arrested but not charged? Or what if they are released under investigation, or bailed but with no prohibition on contacting the alleged victim?[107] In these situations, there was a need for some measure to give the alleged victim the opportunity to think about the future of the relationship and take legal steps such as to seek a non-molestation order without the alleged perpetrator being able to pressure them or there being a risk of further harm (separation is often accompanied by an escalation in abusive behaviour).[108] It was also hoped that this 'breathing space' might help victims to permanently escape their abusers and support prosecutions against them.

Domestic violence protection orders and notices were designed to fill this gap, and were modelled on a number of similar schemes available in other European countries. They were introduced by the Crime and Security Act 2010 and rolled out nationally on 8 March 2014 following a successful pilot. However, they were abolished by the new Domestic Abuse Act 2021. At 7.5.6 we describe the similarities and differences between the old and new schemes.

STATUTORY EXTRACT *s24 Crime and Security Act 2010* (now abolished)

Power to issue a domestic violence protection notice:

(1) A member of a police force not below the rank of superintendent ('the authorising officer') may issue a domestic violence protection notice ('a DVPN') under this section.
(2) A DVPN may be issued to a person ('P') aged 18 years or over if the authorising officer has reasonable grounds for believing that
   (a) P has been violent towards, or has threatened violence towards, an associated person, and
   (b) the issue of the DVPN is necessary to protect that person from violence or a threat of violence by P.

Where the police had reasonable grounds for believing that a person has used or threatened violence towards someone, and that person is at risk of future violence or threats of violence, s24 Crime and Security Act 2010 enabled the police to issue a domestic violence protection notice (DVPN), provided they had the authorisation of an officer at superintendent rank.

A DVPN was specifically designed for situations where the alleged victim and perpetrator were associated persons within the meaning of the Family Law Act 1996, which encompasses a range of romantic, parenting, or familial relationships (the list is at 7.5.11). It prohibited the alleged perpetrator from 'molesting' the person named in the notice (s24(6)), by a general prohibition on molestation and/or by prohibiting certain molesting acts.

---

[107] The 'super-complaint' against the police by the Centre for Women's Justice criticised the use of release under investigation rather than bail as placing women at risk. Centre for Women's Justice, *Super-Complaint: Police Failure to Use Protective Measures in Cases Involving Violence against Women and Girls* (19 March 2019). Available at https://www.centreforwomensjustice.org.uk/policy-research accessed 26 November 2020.
[108] See Home Office, *Domestic Violence Protection Notices (DVPNs) and Domestic Violence Protection Orders (DVPOs) Guidance* (2016).

Where they lived together, the notice could exclude the alleged perpetrator from the family home and/or prevent them from coming within a certain distance of it (s24(7)). It lasted for 48 hours only. Breach of the notice could result in arrest without warrant.

Within this 48-hour period the police had to, under s27(1), apply for a domestic violence protection order (DVPO) from the magistrates, which lasted from a minimum of 14 to a maximum of 28 days (s28(10)). As with a DVPN, the order had to prohibit general or specific non-molestation and could exclude the alleged perpetrator from the family home, and breach may result in arrest without a warrant. Before making a DVPO, the magistrates must have been satisfied on the balance of probabilities (not the criminal standard of beyond reasonable doubt) that the perpetrator had been violent towards, or threatened violence towards, the victim; and that the DVPO was necessary to protect them from violence or a threat of violence. Somewhere between 90 and 95 per cent of DVPOs applied for were granted.[109]

Before making a DVPN or DVPO, the police or magistrates had to consider the welfare of any person aged under 18 whose interests may be affected by the notice or order, the opinion of the alleged victim, and any representations from the alleged perpetrator. However, in each case, although their views must be considered, the consent of the alleged victim was not required (s24(5) and 28(5)). The DVPO was therefore an example of a step being taken to protect victims whether or not they agree, with the police acting as the applicant. This may reduce the risk to the victim because they may not be blamed for it, but the arguments about victim disempowerment that are applicable to victimless prosecutions are applicable here.

SCENARIO 1

Illustration 3: Kelly and Niall Hill

Following Niall's arrest, the police could issue a DVPN which would exclude Niall from the family home for up to 48 hours and apply for a DVPO. Kelly's views on this are relevant but not determinative. The magistrates will need to be satisfied on the balance of probabilities that he has used or threatened violence towards her. The evidence from the police's attendance at their home will be useful here, but remember that the case does not need to be proven beyond reasonable doubt for a DVPO to be issued. As the DVPO will only last for a maximum of 28 days, Kelly will need to use this time to take further legal steps such as applying for a non-molestation order.

The efficacy of DVPNs and DVPOs was dependent on two things: the police's willingness to use them; and the use that the victim made of the breathing space provided. Between their introduction nationally in March 2014 and January 2015, courts granted 2,220 domestic violence protection orders (DVPOs).[110] In the year ending March 2019, five years after the notices and orders were rolled out nationally, 4,349 DVPNs were issued (data from 24 forces) and 5,859 DVPOs were made (data from 39 forces).[111] Considering the

---

[109] Office for National Statistics, *Domestic Abuse and the Criminal Justice System*—Appendix Tables (2020).

[110] Home Office, *Memorandum to the Home Affairs Committee: Post-Legislative Scrutiny of the Crime and Security Act 2010* (Cm 9185, 2015).

[111] Home Office, *Domestic Abuse Protection Notices/Orders Factsheet* (August 2020).

number of incidents of domestic abuse in this period, this is a low rate of use. The pilot scheme showed that only a modest proportion of victims applied for a non-molestation order following the issue of a notice or order. It is unclear whether this was because they did not want a non-molestation order (they may have not wanted their abuser to be excluded from the home) or because their assets exceeded the public funding threshold to obtain legal aid, or—because the scheme does not include any follow-up by support services—because they did not have sufficient information about their options.[112] Burton argues that 'barring orders do not operate in a vacuum; in addition to the broader legal context, the level of nonlegal support for victims is essential to assessing their effectiveness as a protective measure.'[113]

7.5.6 Replacement of orders and notices by the Domestic Abuse Act 2021

The Domestic Abuse Act 2021 abolished DVPNs and DVPOs and replaced them with domestic abuse protection notices (DAPNs) and orders (DAPOs).

Like their predecessors, they permit police to issue a notice that lasts for up to 48 hours during which time the police must apply for the order, and the victim's consent is not required. The court will need to be satisfied that the order is necessary and proportionate to protect the victim from domestic abuse or the risk of domestic abuse.

However, there are a number of key differences:

1. Criminal, family, and civil courts will also be able to make a DAPO of their own volition during existing court proceedings and those proceedings do not need to be specifically related to domestic abuse.

2. Victims will also be able to apply for a DAPO and like the police will not require leave to do so (such an application would be made to a family court). There may be authorised third party applicants such as local authorities who also will not require leave, but it will also be possible for any third party to apply with leave. Legal aid will be available to victims applying for an order.

3. They can last indefinitely (s38(3)), and be varied over time as the situation changes.

4. DAPOs will be able to impose positive obligations on the perpetrator, not merely prohibitions. For example, they may require them to attend a domestic abuser perpetrator programme or seek substance abuse treatment or a mental health assessment. There will be an agency responsible for supervising compliance and reporting any breaches (s36(2)), but which agency is not yet known.

5. Perpetrators can be subject to electronic monitoring (tagging) (s35(6)) and will have to report any changes in their address to the police.

---

[112] Mandy Burton, 'Emergency Barring Orders in Domestic Violence Cases: What Can England and Wales Learn from Other European Countries?' (2015) 27(1) *Child and Family Law Quarterly* 25.

[113] Mandy Burton, 'Emergency Barring Orders in Domestic Violence Cases: What Can England and Wales Learn from Other European Countries?' (2015) 27(1) *Child and Family Law Quarterly* 25.

Breach of a DAPO is a criminal offence as well as a contempt of court. The DAPO is therefore a hybrid: a civil order with criminal consequences. It is not the first such, as both non-molestation orders and harassment and stalking restraining orders are of the same ilk, but it is the most significant for several reasons. First, it can be made by both civil/family and criminal courts, and this will help with problems caused by different courts dealing with different matters relating to the same couple, such as non-molestation applications during pending criminal proceedings. Second, it imposes potentially significant requirements upon the perpetrator and monitors compliance. In this sense it goes much further than other civil orders which simply prevent the perpetrator from doing something and is potentially capable of enabling long-term behavioural change. Whether in fact it does so will be down to the resources available to perpetrators and the willingness of courts to make such orders.

7.5.7 Criminal offence of forced marriage

Despite the existence of forced marriage protection orders, the Anti-Social Behaviour, Crime and Policing Act 2014 created a criminal offence of using violence, threats or any other form of coercion for the purpose of causing another person to enter into a marriage, where the perpetrator believes, or ought reasonably to believe, that the conduct may cause the other person to enter into the marriage without free and full consent. We discuss this, and the controversy surrounding whether criminalisation helped victims or not, in Chapter 2.

7.5.8 Forced marriage protection orders

The Forced Marriage (Civil Protection) Act 2007 created forced marriage protection orders, a type of civil injunction, breach of which enables the police to arrest. These orders are described in detail in Chapter 2.

7.5.9 Criminal offence of female genital mutilation

Female genital mutilation (FGM) is the act of partially or totally removing or otherwise injuring a woman or girl's external genitalia. There are four main types of FGM, the most serious of which (Type I) is the partial or total removal of the clitoris and at the least serious (Type IV) 'pricking, piercing, incising, scraping and cauterizing the genital area'.[114] It is practised in approximately 30 countries, most of them in Africa but also in certain areas of the Middle East and Asia. There are no health benefits and considerable health risks. It can cause severe bleeding, problems urinating, cysts, infections, complications in childbirth where the vaginal opening has been almost completely sewn up, and increased risk of newborn deaths. FGM is often done by people who have no medical training and without anaesthetic or proper surgical equipment. It can cause deaths from shock and blood loss. About 200 million women worldwide have suffered it, usually before puberty.[115]

---

[114] These are the categories used by the World Health Organization.
[115] World Health Organization, *Health Risks of Female Genital Mutilation*. Available at https://www.who.int/teams/sexual-and-reproductive-health-and-research/key-areas-of-work/female-genital-mutilation/health-risks-of-female-genital-mutilation accessed 22 November 2020.

Female genital mutilation is a form of violence against women and girls. In *K v Secretary of State for the Home Department*, Lady Hale noted that FGM:

> is a human rights issue, not only because of the unequal treatment of men and women, but also because the procedure will almost inevitably amount either to torture or to other cruel, inhuman or degrading treatment within the meaning, not only of Article 3 of the European Convention on Human Rights, but also of Article 1 or 16 of the Convention against Torture and other Cruel, Inhuman or Degrading Treatment or Punishment, Article 7 of the International Covenant on Civil and Political Rights, and Article 37(a) of the Convention on the Rights of the Child.[116]

In the UK, it is also criminal, under the Female Genital Mutilation Act 2003 (in Scotland, the Prohibition of Female Genital Mutilation (Scotland) Act 2005). The 2003 Act makes it an offence to:

- excise, infibulate or otherwise mutilate the whole or any part of a girl's labia majora, labia minora or clitoris
- aid, abet, counsel or procure a girl to excise, infibulate or otherwise mutilate the whole or any part of her own labia majora, labia minora or clitoris
- aid, abet, counsel or procure a person who is not a United Kingdom national or United Kingdom resident to do a relevant act of female genital mutilation outside the United Kingdom.

These offences can be committed both inside the UK and outside the UK and a person convicted of any of the above can be imprisoned for up to 14 years.

Where a child aged under 16 is subjected to FGM, an offence is also committed by any person who has parental responsibility for her and frequent contact with her; or who is aged 18 or over and 'has assumed (and not relinquished) responsibility for caring for the girl in the manner of a parent' (s3A). A person convicted of this offence can be imprisoned for up to seven years. It is a defence for the defendant to show that they did not think there was a significant risk of FGM where they could not reasonably have been expected to be aware of the risk or they took 'such steps as he or she could reasonably have been expected to take to protect the girl from being the victim of a genital mutilation offence' (s3A(5)).

7.5.10 Female genital mutilation protection orders

Section 5A and Schedule 2 of the Act create female genital mutilation protection orders, which came into force from 17 July 2015 (by virtue of the Serious Crime Act 2015). These orders are directed against those who may be involved in the actual or intended FGM of a particular child. They are modelled on forced marriage protection orders and are civil in nature although breach is a criminal offence as well as a contempt of court.

Applications can be made by the girl to be protected, a relevant third party, or (with the leave of the court) any other person. Applications can be made on notice or *ex parte*. Local authorities are 'a relevant third party' by virtue of the Female Genital Mutilation Protection Order (Relevant Third Party) Regulations 2015 and a significant proportion of

---

[116] [2007] 1 AC 412 at [94].

applications are made by local authorities as part of their child protection work.[117] In 2019, there were 107 applications for an order, of which 105 were in relation to someone aged under 17. Of these applications, 65 were made by local authorities, none by the girl to be protected, and the rest by other agencies (such as the Official Solicitor) or the voluntary sector.[118]

A court can make an order either to protect a girl from future FGM or to protect an existing victim. In deciding whether to make an order, the court must 'have regard to all the circumstances, including the need to secure the health, safety and well-being of the girl'. The order itself can include a number of different elements, such as prohibiting the respondent from:

- Arranging, attempting to arrange, or otherwise instructing or encouraging any other person to subject the person to be protected to any procedure involving female genital mutilation and the excision, infibulation or mutilation of the whole or any part of the person's labia majora, labia minora or clitoris;

- Instructing or otherwise encouraging the person to be protected to undergo FGM or facilitating, allowing or otherwise permitting them to do so

- Using or threatening violence, intimidating, harassing or pestering the person to be protected or otherwise instructing or encouraging any other person to do so.[119]

In *Re E (Children) (Female Genital Mutilation: Protection Orders)*, the court made an order to protect three Nigerian girls living in the UK. The application was made by the mother and there was compelling evidence that the father had made plans to subject the girls to FGM.[120] The order included provisions preventing the father from coming within 100 metres of the children's home or school or removing them from England and Wales. What provisions are appropriate will depend on the situation. In *Re X (Female Genital Mutilation Protection Order) (No 2)*, the Court said that it should 'concentrate on the reasonable and proportionate management of risk, having regard also to the very considerable harm which is being guarded against'.[121]

A breach of an order can be dealt with either within the Family Court as a contempt (with a penalty of up to two years' imprisonment), or through prosecution in a Criminal Court (up to five years' imprisonment).

7.5.11 Non-molestation orders

Hunter has suggested that 'survivors of violence may make strategic choices about whether or not to seek an injunction based on rational assessments as to whether or not it is likely to increase their safety'.[122] But, as we have seen so far, a number of powers

---

[117] SI 2015/1442

[118] Ministry of Justice, *Family Court Statistics Quarterly* (Underlying Dataset) (2020).

[119] Adapted from the Compendium of Standard Orders issued by the Courts and Tribunals Judiciary, which can be found at https://www.judiciary.uk/publications/practice-guidance-standard-children-and-other-orders/ accessed 22 November 2020.

[120] [2015] EWHC 2275 (Fam).

[121] [2019] EWHC 1990 (Fam).

[122] R Hunter, 'Doing Violence to Family Law' (2011) 33(4) *Journal of Social Welfare and Family Law* 343.

are out of the victim's hands. The victim has no role in deciding whether the police should apply for a DVPN or the court should grant a Protection from Harassment Act restraining order. Therefore, if a victim seeks legal advice, the most likely recommendation will be to seek a non-molestation order although this may well change as the Domestic Abuse Act 2021's domestic abuse protection orders appear to offer stronger protections.

Non-molestation orders were introduced by the Family Law Act 1996. While that Act's no-fault divorce provisions never came into force and were repealed as we see in Chapter 2, Part IV of the Act is well used. It contains two principal legal powers: a power to make an occupation order, which we discuss at 7.6.2, and a power to make a non-molestation order. This is an order that prohibits the respondent from behaving towards the applicant in certain ways. 'Molestation' itself is (deliberately) not defined in the Act, and can encompass a wide range of different behaviours. In *C v C*, Sir Simon Brown P said that it 'implies some deliberate conduct which is aimed at a high degree of harassment of the other party, so as to justify the intervention of the court'.[123]

The order may refer to molestation in general or particular acts of molestation, so it could (for example) prevent the respondent from sending text messages to the applicant. Commonly, it will prohibit the abuser from using or threatening violence against the applicant; harassing, pestering or intimidating her; or encouraging another to do so. Orders often also prohibit the respondent from coming within a certain distance of where the applicant is living or working on the basis that doing so would constitute molestation, although there is some uncertainty over whether an exclusion order should be an exercise of the inherent jurisdiction rather than part of a non-molestation order.[124] Either way, an exclusion order can be useful where an occupation order does not apply because the applicant's home is not the family home.

If made final, the order will usually last for 6–12 months or until further order, and may be renewable. Breaches of a non-molestation orders were criminalised by the Domestic Violence, Crime and Victims Act 2004, but can also be punished as a contempt of court. Around one quarter of perpetrators are prosecuted for breach a non-molestation order[125] and the total number of breaches is likely to be much higher. Bates and Hester suggest that this is due partly to the police lacking knowledge of the orders and partly because since breach was criminalised they have become confused about their role in enforcing the orders.

In the year ending March 2019, 27,787 non-molestation orders were made.[126] The rate has fluctuated over time and is increasing, but not significantly so.

The parties to the application

The applicant must be associated with the respondent. This has the meaning set out in s63(3) Family Law Act. If the respondent is not an associated person, the Act cannot be used.

---

[123] [1998] 2 WLR 599 (HC).
[124] See the discussion in *Re T (A Child: Murdered Parent)* [2011] EWHC B4 (Fam).
[125] L Bates and M Hester, 'No Longer a Civil Matter? The Design and Use of Protection Orders for Domestic Violence in England and Wales' (2020) 42(2) *Journal of Social Welfare and Family Law* 133.
[126] Office for National Statistics, *Family Court Statistics Quarterly April to June 2020* Table 16: Applications and orders made for domestic violence remedies in England and Wales 2003 to 2019 (2020).

FOCUS Know-How

What does a non-molestation order look like?

Here is an example non-molestation order for Kelly Hill, which is given for educational purposes only. It assumes that the order was initially made ex parte and then the application and order served on the respondent, with a return date listed. We have omitted the clauses relating to service, and the prominent warning that breach of the order is a criminal offence or a contempt of court.

It is ordered:

1. The respondent, Niall Hill, must not intimidate, harass, pester, use or threaten violence against the applicant, Kelly Hill, and must not instruct, encourage or in any way suggest that any other person should do so.
2. The respondent, Niall Hill, must not contact or attempt to contact the applicant, Kelly Hill, by any means (including electronic or online social media) except through his solicitors.

STATUTORY EXTRACT s63(3) Family Law Act 1996

(3) For the purposes of this Part, a person is associated with another person if

    (a) they are or have been married to each other;

      (aa) they are or have been civil partners of each other;

    (b) they are cohabitants or former cohabitants;

    (c) they live or have lived in the same household, otherwise than merely by reason of one of them being the other's employee, tenant, lodger or boarder;

    (d) they are relatives;[127]

    (e) they have agreed to marry one another (whether or not that agreement has been terminated);[128]

      (ea) they have or have had an intimate personal relationship with each other which is or was of significant duration;

        (eza) they have entered into a civil partnership agreement (as defined by section 73 of the Civil Partnership Act 2004) (whether or not that agreement has been terminated);[129]

    (f) in relation to any child, they are both persons falling within subsection (4); or

    (g) they are parties to the same family proceedings (other than proceedings under this Part).

(4) A person falls within this subsection in relation to a child if—

    (a) he is a parent of the child; or

    (b) he has or has had parental responsibility for the child.

[Further provisions relating to adoptive children or children placed for adoption are omitted.]

---

[127] Defined in s63(1) as (a) the father, mother, stepfather, stepmother, son, daughter, stepson, stepdaughter, grandmother, grandfather, grandson or granddaughter of [the applicant] or of that person's spouse, former spouse, civil partner or former civil partner, or (b) the brother, sister, uncle, aunt, niece, nephew or first cousin (whether of the full blood or of the half blood or by marriage or civil partnership of [the applicant] or of that person's spouse, former spouse, civil partner or former civil partner).

[128] The claim has to be brought within three years of the end of the engagement: s33(2).

[129] A civil partnership agreement is the unromantic term for the engagement of a couple who intend to enter into a civil partnership.

The court will look at all the circumstances including the need to secure the health, safety and well-being of the applicant or the person for whose benefit the order would be made or of any relevant child (s42(5)).

Of course, there is a significant crossover here with the criminal law, as many of these acts would also be criminal anyway, and the order is an order that they therefore not commit a crime. The order can also exclude the abuser from coming within a certain distance of the property, although this may not be upheld on appeal (no cases on this) or from communicating with the other party at all.

FOCUS Think Critically

Should third parties be able to make applications?

Section 60 Family Law Act 1996 enables rules to be made that would allow applications for non-molestation orders (and occupation orders) to be made by authorised third parties. These could be the police, the local authority (social services or housing authority) or voluntary sector organisations such as Women's Aid. However, this section has never been brought into force. Advantages to third party applications being allowed include addressing problems relating to affordability/funding; enabling victims to deflect the perpetrator's blame for the application; and sending a message that domestic violence is a serious matter in which the state had an interest. It therefore had 'symbolic advantages as well as tangible and practical benefits'.[130] While it may further disempower victims, Humphreys and Thiara found that 60 per cent of victims would prefer somebody else to make an application for a remedy on their behalf.[131] While the new Domestic Abuse Act does not bring s60 into force, it does enable third parties to apply (with leave or as authorised persons) for a new domestic abuse protection order.

The application process

Typically, an application will be made *ex parte*; that means without notice to the other side. The alleged abuser will be served with it, and there will be a return court date at which the court will consider whether the order should stand once it has considered the evidence.

The court may accept a party's undertaking (solemn promise to the court) not to molest the other party, rather than making an order. Breach of an undertaking is a contempt of court, just the same as a breach of order is a contempt of court. However, the court cannot accept an undertaking if the respondent has used or threatened violence and a non-molestation order is necessary.

7.6 Occupation of the family home

The right to remain in the family home, and the possibility of excluding an abuser may be extremely important considerations for someone considering whether to seek to end an abusive relationship. The Family Law Act 1996 sets out two important forms of protection,

---

[130] M Burton, 'Third Party Applications for Protection Orders in England and Wales: Service Providers' Views on Implementing Section 60 of the Family Law Act 1996' (2003) 25(2) *Journal of Social Welfare and Family Law* 137.
[131] C Humphreys and RK Thiara, 'Neither Justice nor Protection: Women's Experiences of Post-Separation Violence' (2003) 25(3) *Journal of Social Welfare and Family Law* 195.

non-molestation orders, which we have already discussed, and occupation orders which regulate occupation of the family home. Occupation orders can require an abuser to leave the family home whatever their legal interest in it, and can give a victim exclusive occupation irrespective of whether they have a legal interest in it (although the courts' powers vary depending on the parties' respective entitlements). They are a response to concerns that victims were not leaving abusive relationships because they feared homelessness for themselves and any children.

Before we look at occupation orders, we need to start by considering the legal concept of home rights, as these are relevant to the courts' powers to make an occupation order.

7.6.1 Home rights

Section 30 Family Law Act 1996 provides for 'home rights', the rights of a spouse or civil partner to occupy the matrimonial/partnership home irrespective of whether they have a legal or beneficial interest in it. Home rights are personal occupation rights, and confer no legal or beneficial interest in the property. They do not apply to unmarried cohabitants or other family members.

Home rights only relate to properties that:

- Are a dwelling house, defined in s63(1) as any building, or part of a building which is occupied as a dwelling, or any caravan, house-boat or structure which is occupied as a dwelling, and any yard, garden, garage or outhouse belonging to it and occupied with it.
- Have at any time been or been intended to be the couple's matrimonial/partnership home, a concept familiar from financial remedy law but not defined anywhere in statute. In the event of dispute, whether or not a particular property was or was intended to be the couple's home falls to be objectively determined.

While it is possible to have home rights in respect of more than one property simultaneously, the right can only be asserted in respect of one at a time.[132]

Effect of a home right

Where a person (let us call them Niall, as in Scenario 1) is entitled to occupy the home either because they have a legal or beneficial interest in it, or are otherwise entitled to live there (for example pursuant to a tenancy agreement) then s30 gives their spouse or civil partner (we will call her Kelly) the right not to be evicted or excluded from the home or any part of it, except by a court order made under s33. If Kelly is not in occupation of the property then the court can give her permission to enter into and occupy it. Her home rights operate as a charge on Niall's estate or interest (s31). That is why Niall must have a right of occupation of the property as a prerequisite for Kelly claiming home rights.

Home rights only operate to give Kelly a right of occupation that she does not otherwise have: if she and Niall are the joint owners of the matrimonial home, for example, then she cannot assert home rights, but instead has a right to occupancy through her legal title. However, if Kelly's interest is solely a beneficial one, she will be treated as not being

---

[132] Sch 4 para 2 Family Law Act 1996.

entitled to occupy so will be able to assert her home rights (s30(9)). This is useful because it would be exceptionally difficult to prove the existence of an unwritten beneficial interest in the timescales needed to assert home rights.

Home rights therefore have several purposes. They prevent the spouse of someone entitled to occupy from ejecting them from the property or preventing them from returning. An application for an occupation order can be made under s33 by the possessor of home rights as an 'entitled applicant' which gives the court stronger powers to regulate occupation of the home than would be the case if the applicant was unentitled. They also, as discussed at 7.6.10, bind third parties wishing to deal with the property who have notice of the rights. This offers valuable protection for the applicant when the house in question is owned rather than rented, as third parties will not want to buy or lend on the property, thereby altering the parties' assets. As such, while home rights can be asserted at any point during the marriage or civil partnership, they are usually asserted when the marriage breaks down, and for many solicitors are asserted routinely whenever it becomes clear that the matrimonial or partnership home is in the other party's sole name.

SCENARIO 2

Illustration 2: Alex and Frances

While Kelly has home rights by virtue of her marriage, Alex and Frances are not married. Frances does not have home rights because they are not married, and in any event she is a co-owner of the house and therefore does not need to derive an occupancy right from Alex.

Duration of home rights

Home rights exist as long as the marriage or civil partnership exists and are therefore terminated by decree absolute[133] or by the death of a party. Under s33(5) they can be extended by the court through the mechanism of an occupation order where the court considers it just and reasonable in all the circumstances to do so. This would mean that if Niall died, Kelly's home rights could continue. Such an application must be made during the period in which the marriage or civil partnership is in existence.[134] It is also possible for someone to release/waive their own home rights.[135]

As Kelly derives her home rights from Niall, if his entitlement to occupy the property ends, so does the home right of Kelly in relation to that property. If the house is rented rather than owned, and Niall served notice to quit, Kelly would need to take other legal steps to protect herself.[136] The situation is different where Kelly has a legal or beneficial interest in the property. Kelly's home rights can be registered as a charge at the Land Registry. The effect of registration[137] is to notify a potential buyer of the property or a

---

[133] Section 31.
[134] This is implied wording of section 33(5).
[135] Sch 4 para 5(1) Family Law Act 1996.
[136] These are described in *Bater v Greenwich London Borough Council* [1999] 2 FLR 993 and are outside the scope of this book.
[137] For unregistered land, this is a Class F land charge.

lender/mortgagee that someone other than Niall has a right and thereby bind them so that they take subject to Kelly's interest. Her consent will thus be needed for any mortgage or sale of the property.

Home rights do not prevent mortgagees from seeking a possession order in relation to the property, but they do require Kelly to be served with notice so that she can be joined into the proceedings. It may be that she can demonstrate her ability to make the mortgage payments instead of Niall. Note that if she makes a makes a payment towards the rent, mortgage payments or other outgoings on the home, then these payments are treated as having been made by Niall. This means that a mortgagee cannot seek repossession for non-payment by the mortgagor themselves. The same goes for tenancies: the landlord could not evict for non-payment by Niall if Kelly is paying, as any payments made by her are treated as payments by him.

It may occur to you that where the property is owned by Niall, some payments by Kelly, particularly towards a mortgage, may become relevant under a constructive trust claim in relation to the property, but s30 anticipates that and specifically provides that such payments will not be relevant to any claim that she might assert to an interest in the home (although as against Niall she should claim under the Matrimonial Causes Act 1973 in preference).

7.6.2 Occupation orders

An occupation order is a court order made under section 33, 35, 36, 37, or 38 Family Law Act 1996 that regulates the occupation of the family home. It does this by enabling the victim to enter into or remain in the property, either by declaring that they have an existing entitlement to do so or by granting them an entitlement to do so when they have none. At the same time, the order can suspend or restrict the occupation rights of another person, including a person who is the sole owner of the property.

Occupation orders are intended to be a relatively short-term form of protection that enables the applicant time to secure alternative accommodation, make an application to court under the Trusts of Land (Appointment of Trustees) Act 1996 (see Chapter 5), Schedule 1 Children Act 1989 (Chapter 6), or, in the case of married or civilly partnered couples only, the Matrimonial Causes Act 1973 or the Civil Partnership Act 2004. An application for an order can be made on a freestanding basis or coupled with family proceedings. Most commonly, they are coupled with an application for a non-molestation order (see 7.5.11).

Note that occupation orders can only be made in respect of domestic dwelling-houses, not commercial properties. 'Dwelling-house' has the same meaning as for home rights, that given in s63(1).

Who can apply?

The respondent to the application must be a person who is 'associated' with the applicant within the meaning of s63(3) Family Law Act 1996 (see 7.6.11). An occupation order cannot be made where the parties are not within these categories or where the parties *only* have a commercial relationship with one another such as landlord and tenant or home-owner and lodger.

Note that, as discussed at 7.6.1, the spouse or civil partner of a person who owns the home is entitled to live in the matrimonial as an entitled person even if they themselves have no beneficial interest in that property, unless or until the court suspends that through an occupation order. This home right does not extend to cohabiting couples.

Declaratory and regulatory orders

There are two kinds of orders, which can be made together or separately.

A declaratory order that declares that the applicant has an existing right to occupy the property or which confers or extends occupation rights.[138] A person with an existing right of occupation will be an 'entitled applicant'. An existing right to occupy may have arisen as the result of the applicant:

- being a legal owner of the property
- being a tenant or otherwise having a contractual right to occupy such as a licence,
- having a beneficial interest in the property[139]
- having a right of occupancy by virtue of a successful estoppel claim[140]
- having a home right.[141]

A respondent can be entitled or not entitled in the same way. In some cases, neither party will have an existing right of occupation, although this is unusual.

If the court is being asked to make a declaratory order that merely says that a person has an existing right to occupy, then the only issue for the court to determine is whether they do in fact have that right. The court can extend a home right beyond the death of the applicant's spouse/civil partner (e.g., if the deceased's beneficiaries are trying to oust the widow/widower, provided that the respondent is an associated person), or their divorce or dissolution (e.g., if they have decree absolute before resolving financial claims), if it is just and reasonable to do so.

A regulatory order regulates the existing rights of occupation of the property. It may do this by enforcing the applicant's existing rights of occupation and/or terminating, suspending, or otherwise restricting the respondent's occupation. Occupation orders can also grant a right of occupation to a person without an existing right (an 'unentitled applicant'). The court will need to consider firstly whether to make an order, and, if so, what the order should contain.

The court may:

- Enforce the applicant's entitlement to remain in occupation, such as by forbidding the respondent from changing the locks or physically preventing them from living in the property
- If the applicant has left the property, require the respondent to permit the applicant to return to live there
- Prohibit, suspend, or restrict any existing rights that the respondent has to occupy the property, including home rights

---

[138] Law Commission, *Domestic Violence and the Occupation of the Family Home* (Law Comm No 207, 1992) para 4.1.
[139] See Chapter 5.
[140] See Chapter 5.
[141] See 7.5.1 of this chapter.

- Decide when the parties can live in the property, for example by making one party move out part-time so that the other parent re-enters the property for contact with the children
- Require the respondent to leave the home to live elsewhere
- Require the respondent to stay out of certain areas of the home all or some of the time
- Exclude the respondent from a defined area in which the house is included (for example, the street).

When deciding whether to make a regulatory order, the court must consider all the circumstances, including the specific factors set down in the statute, such as the balance of harm test discussed at 7.6.4.

FOCUS Know-How

What does an occupation order look like?

Here are some of the common provisions for an occupation order under s33, adapted for Kelly Hill. It is provided is given for educational purposes only. We have omitted the clauses relating to service, and the prominent warning that breach of the order is a criminal offence or a contempt of court.

It is ordered:

1. The court declares that the applicant is entitled to occupy the property at 10 Mulberry Way, Diss IP21 4EQ ('the family home') as her home.
2. The respondent must allow the applicant to occupy the family home.
3. The respondent must leave the family home within 36 hours of this order being personally served on him or of him being made aware of the terms of this order whether by personal service or otherwise.
4. Having left the family home the respondent must not return to, enter or attempt to enter or go within 100 metres of it.

7.6.3 Overview of occupation order provisions

The courts' powers vary according to the section of the Family Law Act 1996 under which the application is made, and this depends upon the respective entitlements of the applicant and respondent. An entitled applicant is in a much stronger position than non-entitled applicant.

- S33 concerns an applicant who is entitled to occupy and a respondent who may or may not be so entitled. Under s33 the court has wider and more long-term powers than under the other sections. Almost all currently married or civilly partnered couples should fall into this category by virtue of home rights, whether or not they are legal or beneficial owners of the property. In contrast, only those cohabitants who are legal or beneficial owners or otherwise have a legal right of occupancy will fall into s33. This means that as far as occupation orders are concerned, cohabitants are often in a weaker position than those who are married.
- S35 is for applicants who is the former spouse or civil partner of the respondent and who do not have a legal or beneficial interest in the home and are thus not entitled to

occupy the home. (As former spouses, their home rights will have ended on decree absolute.) The respondent here must be entitled to occupy.

- S36 is for applicants who are cohabitants or former cohabitants of the respondent and who do not have a legal or beneficial interest in the home and are therefore not entitled to occupy it. The respondent here must be entitled to occupy.

The dwelling house either has to be or have been the home of the parties, or have been intended to be their home. Note that at the same time it makes an occupation order or at any later time the court can impose obligations relating to the repair and maintenance of the house, use of furniture and payments of outgoings. This is considered further at 7.6.6.

- S37 is for unentitled spouses or former spouses, as against an unentitled respondent. It will be rare for there to be an unentitled current spouse due to the existence of home rights.
- S38 is for situations where the applicant and respondent are or were cohabitants and where neither is entitled to occupy. This situation typically involves those living in the property under a bare licence or who are squatters.

As with the earlier sections, the property must be dwelling house. For ss37 and 38, however, the application can only be made in respect of a property which is or was the home of the parties, not a property that was merely intended to be their home. Note also that there are no powers under ss37 and 38 to make an order in relation to the repair and maintenance of the house, use of furniture, or payments.

Which section to use?

Under s39, if the court find that the applicant has applied under the wrong section, it can nevertheless still make an order under a different section.

If your client has a choice between two or more sections, you would always choose the more favourable, the one with the lowest section number. As occupation orders are typically made urgently, to resolve an immediate issue, in some situations it may not be possible to prove in time that the applicant falls into the more favourable category. For example, where the applicant is not a legal owner of the property and wishes to assert a beneficial interest under the principles of a constructive or resulting trust, unless there is a written express declaration of trust the claim may well take some considerable time to resolve. In the interim, the applicant would need to apply under a less favourable category and reapply as an entitled applicant under s33, the more favourable category, once the claim has been established. Under s39(4) the fact that they called themselves an unentitled applicant for the purposes of the application does not prejudice any later claim to a legal or beneficial interest.

Note that a former spouse or civil partner who has either a beneficial intertest in the property or who is entitled to a share of the proceeds of sale of the property (e.g., under a financial remedy order) is classed as not entitled to occupy unless they have a legal interest.[142] This means that they fall within s35 not s33.

---

[142] Section 35(11).

SCENARIO 2

Illustration 3: Alex and Frances

Alex and Frances are co-owners of the house. Section 33 applies to them because both Frances and Alex are entitled occupants by virtue of their legal interests in the house. If the house was in Alex's sole name, Frances would not be able to assert home rights (as they are not married) nor use s33 unless she could clearly evidence a beneficial interest. It is more likely that she will need to apply under s36 as an unentitled applicant against an entitled respondent.

7.6.4 The balance of harm test

The balance of harm test requires the court to identify whether the applicant or a relevant child is likely to suffer significant harm attributable to the conduct of the respondent if it does not make a regulatory order, and balance this against any likely significant harm to the respondent or a relevant child if the order was made. If the applicant's harm is greater, the court *must* make an order if the court is applying sections 33, 35, or 37.

The court is under no duty to make an order if either:

- the harm does not reach the level of being significant (significant in this context has the same meaning—considerable, noteworthy, or important—as it has under the Children Act 1989);[143] or
- the harm is not attributable to the conduct of the respondent.

In these situations, the court has a discretion to make the order, rather than a duty. To decide whether or not to exercise this discretion, the court will need to consider the 'general factors': the parties' and any relevant child's housing needs; the parties' resources; the likely effect of making or not making the order on the parties or a relevant child's health, safety, or well-being; and the conduct of the parties.

Note that under sections 36 and 38, the potential harm of making or not making an order is merely one consideration among other factors so the court is under no duty to make an order. It always simply has a discretion to do so.

The Key Case of *Chalmers v Johns* tells us the steps that should be taken when considering the balance of harm test in s33, 35, or 37. This is set out in diagrammatic form in Figure 7.1.

KEY CASE *Chalmers v Johns* [1999] 1 FLR 392

Ms Chalmers and Mr Johns had lived together for 25 years, but had a mutually violent relationship fuelled by Ms Chalmers' drinking problem. On several occasions the police were called out. When they eventually separated, Ms Chalmers left the home with the parties' 7-year-old daughter and both she and Mr Johns applied for occupation orders under s33 in relation to the house which they rented in their joint names. Ms Chalmers was successful in her application for an interim order,

---

[143] Per Otton LJ in Key Case *Chalmers v Johns* [1999] 1 FLR 392 at 398.

which required Mr Johns to vacate the house to enable her and the daughter to move back in. Mr Johns appealed against the interim order.

The Court of Appeal allowed the appeal.

The first instance judge had conflated the significant harm test under subsection (7) with the discretionary factors under subsection (6) rather than considering them separately in turn.

When considering an application under s33, the court has to first ask whether the applicant or any relevant child is likely to suffer significant harm attributable to the conduct of the respondent if an order is not made (subsection (7)). If so, then the court 'must make the order unless balancing one harm against the other, the harm to the respondent or a child is likely to be as great' or greater. 'If, however, the court answers the question in the negative, then it enters the discretionary regime provided by subsection (6).' This means that the court has a discretion, having regard to all the circumstances of the case including the list contained in subsection (6), such as housing needs and financial resources, to decide to make an order anyway.

The judge was wrong to find that there had been significant harm attributable to the respondent because 'this was, in the range of domestic violence, a very slight case'. That meant that she did not have a duty to make the order under subsection (7), but could exercise its discretion to do so under subsection (6). This does not require the judge to find that any significant harm is involved or that any harm be attributable to the respondent. Nevertheless, an occupation order is a draconian one. The judge was wrong to exercise her discretion to make such a 'draconian' order on an interim basis given that the substantive hearing would take place within a few weeks and other injunctive measures such as a non-molestation order could adequately protect Ms Chalmers in the meantime.

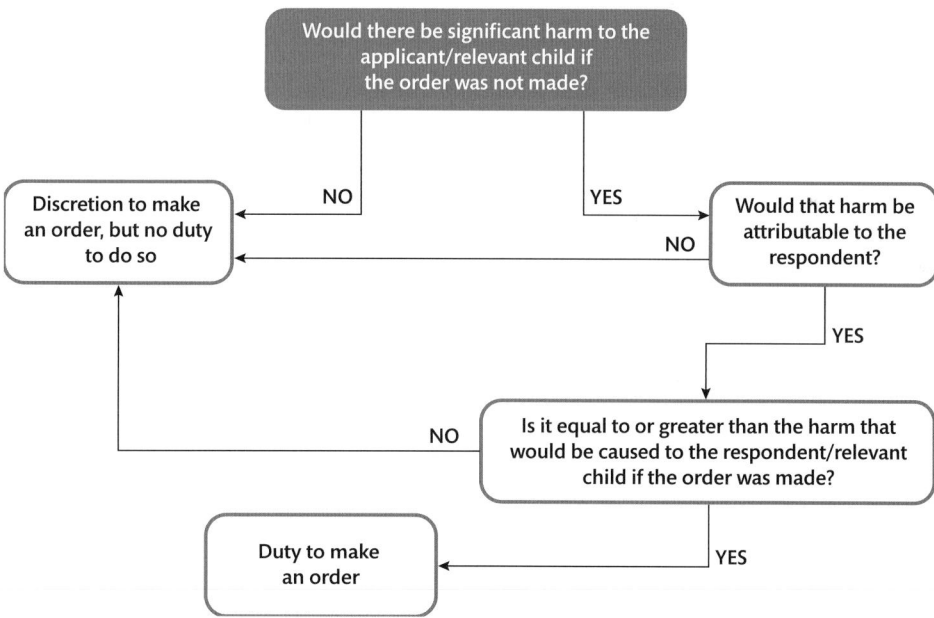

FIGURE 7.1 Balance of harm test under ss33, 35, and 37

What harm is necessary?

Harm is defined in s63(3) as ill-treatment or the impairment of physical or mental health in relation to adults. The definition of harm does not, therefore, require that there be physical violence although this is often the context in which occupation orders are used. The Law

Commission deliberately avoided a requirement of physical violence, and chose to place 'an emphasis on the need for a remedy rather than on the conduct which gave rise to that need'.[144] In *Chalmers* the violence was relatively minor. In *Dolan v Corby*, there was no physical violence at all.[145] The only basis on which an application could be made was that Ms Dolan suffered from mental health problems, but as these were not attributable to Mr Corby's conduct, the court was not under a duty to make the order. The court went on to consider whether to exercise its discretion to make an order anyway, and after considering the general factors, did so because the vulnerability of Ms Dolan. Court of Appeal held that

> an order requiring a Respondent to vacate the family home and overriding his property rights is a grave or draconian order and one which would only be justified in exceptional circumstances, but exceptional circumstances can take many forms and are not confined to violent behaviour on the part of the Respondent or the threat of violence.[146]

This case is merely one of a number in which judges have reiterated the occupation orders are 'draconian' and that exceptional situations are required to justify the courts' interference with property interests.[147] Another exceptional situation can be found in *Grubb v Grubb*.

KEY CASE *Grubb v Grubb* [2009] EWCA Civ 976

Mrs Grubb brought (defended) divorce proceedings against Mr Grubb on the fact of his behaviour. She also sought an occupation order in respect of the matrimonial home which was a house that had been in Mr Grubb's family for a long time and which was part of an estate that he saw as being his to steward.

The judge made an occupation order against Mr Grubb on the basis of his conduct, housing need, and other factors in s33(6) while at the same time not holding that Mrs Grubb or their children would suffer significant harm if the order was not made (s33(7). Mr Grubb appealed.

The Court of Appeal held that 'an occupation order is always serious, and no doubt can sometimes be particularly serious when it relates to a spouse's removal from what one might almost call his ancestral home. But the occupation order is likely to carry its greatest level of seriousness when it is made against a spouse to whom alternative accommodation is not readily available.' However, Mr Grubb had significant resources including other properties available that he could live in, whereas he had refused to allow Mrs Grubb to live in one of them. This justified the order, especially as a short-term measure pending longer term solutions in their divorce case.

Relevant children

It is not merely the harms to adults that the court must consider. As part of the balance of harm test it must also look at the effect of making/not making an order on any 'relevant child'. A relevant child is defined in s62(2) as:

(a) any child who is living with or might reasonably be expected to live with either party to the proceedings;

---

[144] Law Commission, *Domestic Violence and the Occupation of the Family Home* (Law Comm No 207, 1992) para 4.34.

[145] [2011] EWCA Civ 1664.

[146] [2011] EWCA Civ 1664 at [27] (Black LJ).

[147] See, e.g., *Re Y (Children) (Occupation Order)* [2000] 2 FCR 470 and *Re L (Children) (Occupation Order: Absence of Domestic Violence)* [2012] EWCA Civ 721. This term 'draconian' was first used in *Chalmers v Johns* [1999] 1 FLR 392; one of our Key Cases.

(b) any child in relation to whom an order under the Adoption Act 1976, the Adoption and Children Act 2002 or the Children Act 1989 is in question in the proceedings; and

(c) any other child whose interests the court considers relevant.

For children, the definition of harm is the same as that used in s31 Children Act 1989, i.e., ill-treatment or the impairment of health or development, and a comparison can be made with what could be expected of a similar child. 'Ill-treatment' includes forms of ill-treatment which are not physical and, in relation to a child, includes sexual abuse.[148] Given the parallel with significant harm under s31, a judicial finding of significant harm in relation to an occupation order is 'a serious matter'[149] because if the local authority was to take the view that the occupation order did not resolve the harm, it could apply for a care order.

An example of harm to a child determining the outcome of the case is *B v B (Occupation Order)*.

KEY CASE *B v B (Occupation Order)* [1999] 1 FLR 715

The husband and wife were both tenants of a council house in which they lived with their new baby and the husband's son from a previous relationship, who was aged 6. The husband was found to have committed 'substantial violence' against the wife, as a result of which she and the baby left the house and were rehoused by the council in temporary bed and breakfast accommodation. She applied for an occupation order under s33 as well as a non-molestation order.

At first instance, the judge made the occupation order. The husband appealed successfully. The Court of Appeal held that the respondent's son would suffer significant harm if the order was made to exclude the husband from the house, and this was greater than the significant harm that would be suffered by the wife and baby. This was because the husband would be classed by the council as intentionally homeless and therefore eligible only for temporary housing for himself and his son, whereas the wife and baby were classed as priority need and would be rehoused permanently in a few weeks. Both children were relevant children, and the balance of harms lay in enabling the son, and thus the father, to remain in the house. It was therefore under no duty to make an order, and declined to exercise its discretion to do so. The judge, Butler-Sloss LJ, was at pains to point out that the case was unusual because the son was the child of only one party, and no one other than his father could care for him.[150] While the local authority could offer the son temporary accommodation by himself under s20 Children Act 1989 (see Chapter 11), separation from his father was not in his interests.

In *Re L (Children) (Occupation Order: Absence of Domestic Violence)*, the judge found that the children would suffer significant harm if an order was not made, but the harm was not attributable to the respondent father's conduct but rather to the level of (non-physical) conflict between both parents as their marriage fell apart.[151] Absent attributability, the court was under no duty to make an order. Given the level of harm, however, the judge exercised his discretion to make an order excluding the father from the home on the basis

---

[148] Presumably the sexual abuse of adults would be considered ill-treatment or causing harm to their physical or mental health, so why the section refers separately only to the sexual abuse of children is unclear.
[149] *Re L (Children) (Occupation Order: Absence of Domestic Violence)* [2012] EWCA Civ 721.
[150] Although blended families have become much more common in the more than 20 years since this case was decided, so the situation will not now be as uncommon as thought.
[151] [2012] EWCA Civ 721.

that the mother was the primary carer and should therefore remain with the children. As an alternative, given the large size of the house, the judge could have simply excluded each parent from some areas of the house so they stayed apart, or provided that the parents each used the whole house at different times, but the Court of Appeal declined to overturn the decision on that basis.

7.6.5 Discussion of the key sections

The powers available to the court depend upon the applicant's and respondent's respective entitlements to occupy.

Section 33

This is the most favourable category, because it concerns an applicant with an entitlement to occupation who simply wishes to enforce that right against the respondent. An order made under this section is potentially indefinite in duration. Because the applicant has a right to occupy, the court will make a declaratory order to that effect. However, the applicant may also need the court to enforce that right and/or seek to suspend or restrict the occupation of the respondent. In deciding whether to do this, the court will use the 'balance of harm test' outlined at 7.6.4.

SCENARIO 1

Illustration 4: Kelly and Niall Hill

As an entitled applicant against an entitled respondent, Kelly has access to the most favourable provision, s33. Here, the court must make an order excluding Niall if the balance of harm test is satisfied, in that Kelly is likely to suffer significant harm attributable to Niall's conduct if the order is not made and that this harm is greater than or equal to the harm caused to him if the order was made. Unless there is some significant harm to Niall that we do not know about, this test is almost certainly satisfied, but even if it was not, the court would still have a discretion to make an occupation order in Kelly's favour after considering the general factors set out in Table 7.2.

TABLE 7.2 Occupation orders under s33 Family Law Act 1996

Section 33	
Applicant	Those who are entitled to occupy the house: • A person with a legal or beneficial interest in the home • A person who has a contract entitling them to occupy, such as a tenancy agreement • A person in respect of whom there is an enactment giving him the right to occupy • A person who has home rights. The respondent may be entitled or not entitled.
The home	A dwelling-house 'that is or at any time has been the home of the applicant and of another person with whom he is associated, or was at any time intended by the applicant and any such other person to be their home'

What the court can do	Declaratory order under subsection (4) that the applicant is entitled to occupy or has home rights.
	Order under subsection (3):
	• Enforce the applicant's entitlement to remain in occupation as against the other person ('the respondent'); or require the respondent to permit the applicant to enter and remain in the home or part of it
	• If the respondent is entitled to occupy, prohibit, suspend or restrict that entitlement or terminate his or her home rights
	• Regulate the occupation of the home by the parties
	• Require the respondent to leave the home or part of it, or exclude the respondent from a defined area in which the house is included (for example, the street).
	• If the parties are married or civilly partnered, provide that home rights are not brought to an end by the death of the other or the termination of the marriage or civil partnership. The court may exercise this power where it considers that in all the circumstances it is just and reasonable to do so.
Duration	The order may be made for a specified period, until the occurrence of a specified event, or until further order.
Legal tests	The balance of harm test:
	The court *must* include a subsection (3) provision if the applicant or any relevant child is likely to suffer significant harm attributable to conduct of the respondent if it does not make the order, *unless*
	• the respondent or any relevant child is likely to suffer significant harm if the provision *is* included; and
	• this harm is as great as or greater than the harm attributable to the conduct of the respondent which is likely to be suffered by the applicant or child if the provision is not included.
	If this test is not met, subsection (6) says that the court still has a discretion to make a subsection (3) order. In deciding whether to do so the court shall have regard to all the circumstances including:
	• the housing needs and housing resources of each of the parties and of any relevant child
	• the financial resources of each of the parties
	• the likely effect of any order, or of any decision by the court not to exercise its powers, on the health, safety or well-being of the parties and of any relevant child
	• the conduct of the parties in relation to each other and otherwise
	These are known as the 'general factors'.

Section 35

Section 35 relates to former spouses and civil partners. If the court decides to make an order there are certain mandatory provisions it must include. Because the applicant is non entitled, the court will need to give the applicant a right to occupation and suspend or limit the right of the entitled respondent. In considering whether to make the order, the court must consider all the circumstances including the general factors familiar from s33 and a number of additional factors. As with section 33, the balance of harm test applies, so the court follows the steps set out in Figure 7.1 and Table 7.3.

Where the court is considering whether to exercise its discretion, one of the relevant considerations is the length of time that has elapsed since the parties stopped living

TABLE 7.3 Occupation orders under s35 Family Law Act 1996

Section 35	
Applicant	A former spouse or civil partner who has no existing right to occupy but was married/partnered to an entitled respondent.
The home	A dwelling-house that was at any time their matrimonial/civil partnership home or was at any time intended by them to be.
What the court can do	If the court decides to make an order, it must include the following: • If the applicant is in occupation, the order *must* give the applicant the right not to be evicted or excluded from the dwelling-house or any part of it by the respondent and prohibit the respondent from evicting or excluding the applicant during that period. • If the applicant is not in occupation, the order must give the applicant the right to enter into and occupy the dwelling-house and require the respondent to permit this. The order may also (under subsection (5)): • regulate the occupation of the dwelling-house by either or both of the parties; • prohibit, suspend or restrict the respondent's right to occupy • require the respondent to leave the dwelling-house or part of it; or • exclude the respondent from a defined area in which the dwelling-house is included. These are known as 'subsection (5) provisions'.
Duration	The order: • may not be made after the death of either of the former spouses/civil partners and ceases to have effect on the death of either of them. • cannot last for more than six months but may be extended on one or more occasions for a further period not exceeding six months.
Legal tests	In deciding whether to make an order the court shall have regard to all the circumstances including: The general factors: • the housing needs and housing resources of each of the parties and of any relevant child • the financial resources of each of the parties • the likely effect of any order, or of any decision by the court not to exercise its powers, on the health, safety or well-being of the parties and of any relevant child • the conduct of the parties in relation to each other and otherwise Plus: • the length of time that has elapsed since the parties ceased to live together • the length of time that has elapsed since the marriage or civil partnership was dissolved or annulled; and • the existence of any pending proceedings between the parties, for property adjustment on divorce/dissolution; under Schedule 1 Children Act; or relating to the legal or beneficial ownership The balance of harm test: If the court decides to make an order, it *must* include a subsection (5) provision if the applicant or any relevant child is likely to suffer significant harm attributable to conduct of the respondent if it does not make the order, *unless*

- the respondent or any relevant child is likely to suffer significant harm if the provision *is* included; and
- this harm is as great as or greater than the harm attributable to the conduct of the respondent which is likely to be suffered by the applicant or child if the provision is not included.

If this test is not met, the court still has a *discretion* to make a subsection (5) order. In deciding whether to do so the court shall have regard to all the circumstances including:

- the housing needs and housing resources of each of the parties and of any relevant child
- the financial resources of each of the parties
- the likely effect of any order, or of any decision by the court not to exercise its powers, on the health, safety or well-being of the parties and of any relevant child
- the conduct of the parties in relation to each other and otherwise
- the length of time that has elapsed since the parties ceased to live together

together. The longer this is, the weaker the application, although this is only one of several factors that the court must consider.

Note that whereas an order made under s33 is potentially indefinite in duration, an order made under this section is time-limited, albeit that it can be extended on multiple occasions.

Section 36

Section 36 covers current or former cohabitants without an existing right to occupy, against a respondent who does have a right to occupy. Section 62 defines 'cohabitants' as two persons who are neither married to each other nor civil partners of each other but are living together as husband and wife or as if they were civil partners. As the applicant is not (at the time they make the application) entitled to occupy, the order gives the applicant the right to occupy (including letting them re-enter the property if necessary) and may restrict or suspend the respondent's right.

The balance of harm test here is different to that under ss 33 and 35. In those sections, the court must include a subsection (5) provision if the test is satisfied, whereas under s36 it does not have to do so. It considers significant harm merely as one of several considerations.

An order made under s36 last for only six months and (unlike s35) it can only be extended once, as shown in Table 7.4.

TABLE 7.4 Occupation orders under s36 Family Law Act 1996

Section 36	
Applicant	A person who has no existing right to occupy but is the cohabitant or former cohabitant of an entitled respondent.
The home	A dwelling-house in which they cohabit, cohabited at any time, or in which they at any time intended to cohabit.

What the court can do	If the court decides to make an order:
	• If the applicant is in occupation, the order must give the applicant the right not to be evicted or excluded from the dwelling-house or any part of it by the respondent[152] and prohibit the respondent from evicting or excluding the applicant during that period (subsection (3)).
	• If the applicant is not in occupation, the order must give the applicant the right to enter into and occupy the dwelling-house and require the respondent to permit this (subsection (4)).
	The order may also (under subsection (5)):
	• regulate the occupation of the dwelling-house by either or both of the parties;
	• prohibit, suspend or restrict the respondent's right to occupy
	• require the respondent to leave the dwelling-house or part of it; or
	• exclude the respondent from a defined area in which the dwelling-house is included.
	These are known as 'subsection (5) provisions'.
Duration	The order:
	• may not be made after the death of either of the former spouses/civil partners and ceases to have effect on the death of either of them.
	• cannot last for more than six months but may be extended on one occasion for a further period not exceeding six months.
Legal tests	In deciding whether to make an order under subsections (3) or (4) the court shall have regard to all the circumstances including:
	• the housing needs and housing resources of each of the parties and of any relevant child
	• the financial resources of each of the parties
	• the likely effect of any order, or of any decision by the court not to exercise its powers, on the health, safety or well-being of the parties and of any relevant child
	• the conduct of the parties in relation to each other and otherwise
	• the nature of the parties' relationship and in particular the level of commitment involved in it
	• the length of time during which they have cohabited
	• whether there are or have been any children who are children of both parties or for whom both parties have or have had parental responsibility
	• the length of time that has elapsed since the parties ceased to live together
	• the existence of any pending proceedings between the parties, under Schedule 1 Children Act or relating to the legal or beneficial ownership
	In deciding whether to include a subsection (5) provision, the court shall have regard to all the circumstances including:
	• the housing needs and housing resources of each of the parties and of any relevant child
	• the financial resources of each of the parties
	• the likely effect of any order, or of any decision by the court not to exercise its powers, on the health, safety or well-being of the parties and of any relevant child

[152] It does not protect against a landlord who is not the respondent.

- the conduct of the parties in relation to each other and otherwise
- whether the applicant or any relevant child is likely to suffer significant harm attributable to conduct of the respondent if the subsection (5) provision is not included in the order; and whether the harm likely to be suffered by the respondent or child if the provision is included is as great as or greater the harm attributable to the conduct of the respondent which is likely to be suffered by the applicant or child if the provision is not included.

SCENARIO 2

Illustration 4: Alex and Frances

We have said that Frances would need to apply under s36 if she was not a co-owner of the house, as s36 refers to unentitled cohabitants of entitled persons. The occupation order would need to give her a right to occupy as she does not have one currently, and she would also want the court to make an order suspending Alex's right of occupation. The order can only last for six months and be extended once for six months so within this time Frances will need to either bring an application under the Trusts of Land (Appointment of Trustees) Act 1996 (see Chapter 5), make a claim under Schedule 1 Children Act 1989 for financial provision, including housing, for their child, negotiate a settlement of such claims, or simply fall back on her own resources to rehouse herself.

In order for the court to make an order that includes a provision excluding Alex, the court will need to consider the factors set out in Table 7.4 as the subsection (5) criteria. This includes the harm to Frances and their child as one of a number of considerations.

Section 37

Section 37 relates to married or formerly married or civilly partnered couples and their former matrimonial/partnership home, but where neither of them has a right of occupation. As such, the order has to provide the applicant with a right to occupy that she does not have at the point of application. The balance of harm test applies as set out in Figure 7.1, so that the court must make an order if significant harm attributable to the respondent will be suffered by the applicant or a relevant child if the order is not made, and that harm is greater than the harm that would be suffered by the respondent and any relevant child. This reflects the fact that the interests of the parties in remaining in the house are legally equal: neither is entitled, so it comes down to harm. If the test is not satisfied, then the court has a discretion to make the order based on all the circumstances of the case, as shown in Table 7.5.

TABLE 7.5 Occupation orders under s37 Family Law Act 1996

Section 37	
Applicant	Where the parties are or were married or civil partnered, but neither is entitled to remain in occupation.
The home	A dwelling-house which they occupy which is or was the matrimonial/civil partnership home.

What the court can do	Regulatory order under subsection (3) may include the following: • require the respondent to permit the applicant to enter and remain in the dwelling-house or part of the dwelling-house; • regulate the occupation of the dwelling-house by either or both • require the respondent to leave the dwelling-house or part of the dwelling-house; or exclude the respondent from a defined area in which the dwelling-house is included.
Duration	The order cannot last for more than six months but may be extended on one or more occasions for a further period not exceeding six months.
Legal tests	The court *must* make an order if the applicant or any relevant child is likely to suffer significant harm attributable to conduct of the respondent if it does not make the order, *unless* • the respondent or any relevant child is likely to suffer significant harm if the provision *is* included; and • this harm is as great as or greater than the harm attributable to the conduct of the respondent which is likely to be suffered by the applicant or child if the provision is not included. If this test is not met, the court still has a *discretion* to make an order. In deciding whether to do so the court shall have regard to all the circumstances including: • the housing needs and housing resources of each of the parties and of any relevant child • the financial resources of each of the parties • the likely effect of any order, or of any decision by the court not to exercise its powers, on the health, safety or well-being of the parties and of any relevant child • the conduct of the parties in relation to each other and otherwise.

Section 38

Section 38 concerns cohabitants or former cohabitants neither of whom have a right to occupy. As these parties are both in legally weak positions in relation to the house, the courts' powers are more limited that under the other sections. Section 38 orders are regulatory—there is no existing entitlement to declare—and can only last for six months with a maximum of one further six-month extension, as shown in Table 7.6.

The balance of harm test is in a modified form compared to that found in ss 33 and 35. Even if the test is met because the harm to the applicant would be greater than the harm to the respondent, the court is not compelled to make the order: that finding is just one of the factors it must consider.

TABLE 7.6 Occupation orders under s38 Family Law Act 1996

Section 38	
Applicant	Where the parties are or were cohabitants and occupy the home, but neither is entitled to remain in occupation.
The home	A dwelling-house which is the home in which they cohabit or cohabited

What the court can do	Regulatory order under subsection (3) may include the following: • require the respondent to permit the applicant to enter and remain in the dwelling-house or part of the dwelling-house • regulate the occupation of the dwelling-house by either or both of the parties • require the respondent to leave the dwelling-house or part of the dwelling-house; or exclude the respondent from a defined area in which the dwelling-house is included.
Duration	The order cannot last for more than six months but may be extended on one occasion for a further period not exceeding six months.
Legal tests	In deciding whether to make an order the court shall have regard to all the circumstances including: • the housing needs and housing resources of each of the parties and of any relevant child • the financial resources of each of the parties • the likely effect of any order, or of any decision by the court not to exercise its powers, on the health, safety or well-being of the parties and of any relevant child • the conduct of the parties in relation to each other and otherwise • whether the applicant or any relevant child is likely to suffer significant harm attributable to conduct of the respondent if the order is not made and whether the harm likely to be suffered by the respondent or child if the provision is included is as great as or greater the harm attributable to the conduct of the respondent which is likely to be suffered by the applicant or child if the provision is not included.

7.6.6 Obligations relating to the house

When the court makes an order under sections 33, 35, or 36 (or at any time thereafter), section 40 gives it the power to impose obligations in relation to the property. It can require one or both parties to repair or maintain the house or pay the rent, mortgage or other out-goings on it. This does not depend on whether they are the person in occupation or excluded from the property. This is a very useful provision, as it means that if one party cannot pay the mortgage by themselves (such as a full-time mother), the other party can still be required to pay. The court can also require the party in occupation of whole or part of the property to pay the other party periodical payments as compensation for their exclusive use of that space, if the other party would (but for the order) be entitled to occupy the home.

It can also grant either party possession or use of the furniture or other contents of the house or order them to take reasonable care of these, and/or to keep the house and its contents secure.

In deciding whether and, if so, how to exercise its powers under this section, the court shall have regard to all the circumstances of the case including:

• the financial needs and financial resources of the parties; and
• the financial obligations which they have, or are likely to have in the foreseeable future, including financial obligations to each other and to any relevant child.

An order under this section is tied to the occupation order, so ceases to have effect when the occupation order ceases to have effect. Section 40 does not apply to sections 37 and 38 because these are situations in which neither party has a right of occupation.

7.6.7 The application process

Occupation orders do not have to be made alongside non-molestation orders, but a person who is at risk of domestic abuse or harm in the family home may well make both applications at the same time. However, while courts routinely make non-molestations on an *ex parte* basis (*ex parte* means without prior notice to the respondent), that is not the case with occupation orders even though s45 gives them the power to do so. This reflects the seriousness of the interference with the property interests involved. Thus, even if one files the application without serving it on the respondent, the court will not usually make an order then, but only issue the application and list a hearing known as the 'return date'. The application will then need to be served on the respondent. On the return date, the court will consider evidence from both parties before deciding whether the order should be made. The consequence of this is that the respondent may well be at the family home in the interim and thus the applicant may need to find somewhere safe to stay at least until the return date.

In considering whether to make an *ex parte* occupation order, the court must consider all the circumstances including:

- any risk of significant harm to the applicant or relevant child, attributable to the conduct of the respondent, if the order is not made immediately
- whether it is likely that the applicant will be deterred or prevented from pursuing the application if an order is not made immediately
- whether there is reason to believe that the respondent is aware of the proceedings but is deliberately evading service and that the applicant or a relevant child will be seriously prejudiced by the delay involved in effecting the substituted service.[153]

These reasons will need to be included by the applicant in the witness statement that they write that accompanies the application for an occupation order.[154] The court must also bear in mind the guidance in Key Case *R v R (Family Court: Procedural Fairness)*.

KEY CASE *R v R (Family Court Procedural Fairness)* [2014] EWFC 48

Mr R returned from work to the home that he had shared with his wife of 20 years and their six children. Later that evening he was served with an occupation order which prevented him from entering or attempting to enter the street in which the house was situated. Mrs R had sought an occupation order on an *ex parte* basis on the basis that he was controlling and verbally abusive. While the judge had declined to make an order excluding him from the house without notice to him, she had erroneously included a provision that prevented him from accessing the very street in which the house was situated. His appeal was upheld by Peter Jackson J, who set out guidance for courts as to when a court should make an occupation order on an *ex parte* basis:

1. The default position of a judge faced with a without notice application should always be 'Why?' not 'Why not?' As has been repeatedly stated, without notice orders can only be made in exceptional circumstances and with proper consideration for the rights of the absent party.

---

[153] Section 45(2) paras (i)–(iii).
[154] Family Procedure Rules 2010 rule 10.2 (4).

2. The court should use its sweeping powers under the Family Law Act 1996 with caution, particularly at a one-sided hearing. Where an order is made, it is the responsibility of the court (and, where applicable, the lawyers) to ensure that it is accurately drafted. This consideration applies with special force when a breach of the order will amount to a criminal offence.

3. Extra injunctive provisions such as exclusion areas and orders prohibiting any direct communication between parties should not be routinely included in non-molestation orders. They are serious infringements of a person's freedom of action and require specific evidence to justify them.

4. The power to penalise non-compliance with case management orders should be used firmly but fairly, in a way that supports the overriding objective rather than defeating it.

5. The court should be on guard against the potential for unfairness arising from the Legal Aid, Sentencing and Punishment of Offenders Act 2012, whereby the applicant is entitled to legal representation as a result of unproven allegations, while the respondent is not.'

7.6.8 Breach of an occupation order

A power of arrest can be attached to an occupation order. This will enable the police to arrest (without a warrant) a person whom the police have reasonable cause to suspect is in breach of the order. Without this, it will be necessary to apply to the court for a warrant or for a power of arrest to be added in case of further breach. Under s47, the court must attach a power of arrest to one or more provisions in the occupation order 'if it appears to the court that the respondent has used or threatened violence against the applicant or a relevant child' unless the court is 'satisfied that in all the circumstances of the case the applicant or child will be adequately protected without such a power of arrest'.

7.6.9 Undertakings

Undertakings are solemn promises to the court. We have discussed them before in Chapter 4, as they are often used in financial remedy orders. In the occupation order context, s46 allows a court to accept the respondent's undertaking to leave the home or permit the applicant to live there rather than make an occupation order. For the applicant, this saves the expense of a fully contested hearing and the need to give evidence about potentially distressing matters. For the respondent, this has the advantage of requiring no admission or finding about prior behaviour or risk, and also avoids the potential reputational harm of being subject to an occupation order. A breach of an undertaking is a contempt of court just as if the same content had been included in the body of an order, but no power of arrest can be attached. This means that the court must not accept an undertaking in any case where a power of arrest has to be attached.

7.6.10 Occupation orders and third parties

Applications for occupation orders must be served on landlords or mortgagees so that they can make representations at the return date if they wish to do so.[155] As an occupation

---

[155] Family Procedure Rules r10.3(3).

order is an order regulating occupation between the applicant and respondent, it does not affect any rights or powers that a third party, such as a landlord, may have in relation to the property although, as discussed at 7.5.1, home rights that operate as a charge on the property may do so. A beneficiary of an occupation order who is also a connected person[156] will in some circumstances be entitled to be joined to any application by a mortgagee to repossess the property.

Section 60 Family Law Act 1996 enables rules to be made that allow a third party to apply for an occupation order (or non-molestation order) on behalf of the victim of the domestic abuse. However, while this power exists, it has never been brought into force.

7.7 Conclusion

In this chapter we have looked at an area that has profound consequences for family life and is a large part of the work of many family lawyers. We do not know why some people are domestically abusive. What we do know is that the law has found domestic abuse difficult to address for a variety of reasons. The legal powers available are piecemeal, overlapping, and not always accessible to victims of abuse. The police and prosecution responses have been lacking. Rates of domestic abuse remain high and each week people die because of it. The Domestic Abuse Act 2021 has the potential enhance protections for domestic abuse victims. It remains to be seen how successful this will be.

KEY POINTS

- Although a number of causes of domestic abuse have been suggested, there are two main theories, the family violence theory and the patriarchal/feminist theory. Kelly and Johnson have suggested that domestic abuse can properly be placed into four categories: situation couple violence, separation instigated violence, coercive controlling violence, and violent resistance. They argue that many of the differences in the theories about the root causes of domestic abuse can be explained by the fact that different theorists are talking about different forms of violence with different prevalence rates between men and women and characterised by different behaviours.

- A number of international legal instruments recognise that domestic abuse is a form of gender discrimination against women and girls and have placed responsibilities upon states to address this. Within the UK, the ECHR can be used to both protect abusers and to require the state to protect those at risk of violence. In a number of cases, the European Court of Human Rights recognised that states have positive obligations to protect people from violence whether or not they seek protections for themselves, although there are limits to state obligations. This has consequences for the policing and prosecution of domestic violence, an area of the criminal law which has a high attrition rate for a variety of reasons.

- The law has provided a number of civil and criminal law options to those seeking protection from domestic violence or those acting on their behalf. These include protection against behaviours including harassment and stalking; coercive and controlling behaviour; molestation; forced marriage; female genital mutilation; and where the victim wishes to remain in the family home and exclude the abuser.

---

[156] Section 54(5) defines connected persons as spouses, former spouses, civil partners, former civil partners, cohabitants or former cohabitants of the mortgagor.

- The Domestic Abuse Act 2021 provides a statutory definition of domestic violence, establishes a domestic abuse Commissioner, and creates domestic abuse protection orders, a hybrid civil criminal order providing enhance protections for victims. The success or otherwise of this new order remains to be seen.

 # FURTHER READING: SOME STARTING POINTS

- The Office for National Statistics holds statistics on prevalence of domestic violence, prosecutions, and victim and perpetrator characteristics. The Ministry of Justice's Court Statistics Quarterly give the figures for types of order made. The MARAC Dataset 2019/20 can be found at https://safelives.org.uk/practice-support/resources-marac-meetings/latest-marac-data. The costs of domestic abuse can be found at R Oliver, B Alexander, S Roe and M Wlasny, *The Economic and Social Costs of Domestic Abuse: Research Report 107* (Home Office, 2019), which draws on previous research.

- On the nature, effects, and potential causes of domestic abuse, see M Madden Dempsey, *Prosecuting Domestic Violence: A Philosophical Analysis* (Oxford University Press 2009); RP Dobash and RE Dobash, *Violence against Wives: A Case against the Patriarchy* (Free Press 1979); DS Saunders, 'Are Physical Assaults by Wives and Girlfriends a Major Social Problem? A Review of the Literature' (2002) 8(12) *Violence against Women* 1424 and the works he cites; RP Dobash and R Emerson Dobash, 'Women's Violence to Men in Intimate Relationships: Working on a Puzzle' (2004) 44 *British Journal of Criminology* 324; JB Kelly and MP Johnson, 'Differentiation among Types of Intimate Partner Violence: Research Update and Implications for Interventions' (2008) 46(3) *Family Court Review* 476; DA Hines and K Malley-Morrison, 'Psychological Effects of Partner Abuse against Men: A Neglected Research Area' (2001) 2(2) *Psychology and Men and Masculinity* 75; and M Hester 'Who Does What to Whom? Gender and Domestic Violence Perpetrators in English Police Records' (2013) 10(5) *European Journal of Criminology* 623.

- For coercive and controlling behaviour, see P McGorrery and M McMahon, 'Prosecuting Controlling or Coercive Behaviour in England and Wales: Media Reports of a Novel Offence' (2019) *Criminology and Criminal Justice* 1, which describes the nature of the coercive and controlling behaviour found in prosecutions for the specific offence of this name, and the Crown Prosecution Service guidance, *Controlling or Coercive Behaviour in an Intimate or Family Relationship Legal Guidance* (2017).

- For the attrition rate and issues with policing and prosecution, see M Hester, 'Making It through the Criminal Justice System: Attrition and Domestic Violence' (2005) 5(1) *Social Policy and Society* 79; HM Crown Prosecution Service Inspectorate, *Violence at Home: A Joint Thematic Inspection of the Investigation and Prosecution of Cases Involving Domestic Violence* (2004); and C Hoyle and A Sanders, 'Police Response to Domestic Violence: From Victim Choice to Victim Empowerment?' (2000) 40 *British Journal of Criminology* 14.

- There are a number of very good documentaries on domestic violence. A visceral example of the aftermath of domestic abuse seen through officers' body camera footage can be found in the BBC Panorama documentary *Domestic Abuse: Caught on Camera* (first broadcast 8 December 2014). Others include *Love You to Death* (BBC2 16 December 2016) and *Behind Closed Doors: Fear and Control* (ITV Tonight Show 18 February 2016).

 Visit the **online resources** to watch a video of Polly Morgan discussing this chapter topic, and to check your understanding of this chapter with self-test questions and scenario questions.

8 Parenthood and Parental Responsibility

LEARNING CHECKLIST

By the end of this chapter, you should be able to:

- *Identify* the legal parents of a child and where this may differ from biological reality
- *Describe* the criteria for the making of a surrogacy parental order and *critically discuss* how judges have interpreted these requirements
- *Evaluate* the arguments for and against reforming the laws surrounding surrogacy
- *Describe* how a person may acquire parental responsibility and how parental responsibility differs from legal parentage
- *Critically discuss* how statute and case law address parental responsibility for fathers who are not married to their child's mother, and limitations on the exercise of parental responsibility.

SCENARIO 1

Peter and Jasmine and children Freddy (10) and Mabel (7)

Peter and Jasmine are a divorced couple. Following difficulties in conceiving a child during their marriage, their son Freddy, now aged 10, was conceived using donor sperm. Unexpectedly, a few years later Jasmine became pregnant a second time, and gave birth to Mabel, who is now 7. Peter and Jasmine are now divorced, and the situation is not amicable. Peter has sought your advice because he is concerned that he is not Mabel's biological father and wants to know what this means.

SCENARIO 2

Rhys and Hardeep and baby Anji (2 months)

Rhys and Hardeep are a gay male couple who desperately wanted a child. They entered into a surrogacy arrangement in India, as a result of which their daughter Anji has just been born. They are currently in India and have sought your advice on whether they will be recognised as Anji's parents in England.

SCENARIO 3

Sara and Haruto and son Kenzo (5)

Sara is mother to Kenzo, a 5-year-old boy. Kenzo's father is her on-again off-again boyfriend, Haruto. She has been referred to you for some advice by a local domestic abuse charity. Haruto is not currently living with Sara, but frequently turns up at the house and sometimes 'kicks off' if Sara is busy. He is now threatening to take Kenzo. Sara wants to know whether he can do this.

8.1 Introduction

In previous centuries, the identity of a child's mother was almost always clear, with disputes being exceptionally rare. It was not necessary for the law to define motherhood, for it was evident from the fact of childbirth. Advances in reproductive technologies mean that it is now possible for a woman to gestate, nourish, and give birth to a child to whom she has no genetic relationship at all. It is also possible for a person to be legally male and conceive, carry, and birth a child. As a result, the law has had to identify what aspects of conception or birth make someone a mother.

Fatherhood has always been less clearly manifested, but with most births taking place within marriage, presumptions of legitimacy—that the child was the biological child of husband and wife—served to ensure that most children had legally recognised parentage. Now, at the beginning of the twenty-first century, most children in England and Wales are born to unmarried parents. Given the frequency of family breakdown and the impermanence of many relationships, children may grow up within blended families: those that are made up of children with different biological and legal relationships to one another and a range of adults in parenting roles. A child may view as their parent—that is, as performing the social role of parenting—someone to whom they have no legal or genetic relationship at all. We have separated the biological reality of parentage from the legal status of parenthood, and legal status from the social reality of parenting—what Lady Hale, drawing on an influential work by Goldstein, Freud, and Solit, referred to in *Re G (Children)* as social and psychological parenthood, as opposed to genetic or gestational parenthood.[1] This disaggregation of the parental role has been termed the 'fragmentation of parenthood'.[2]

In recognition of this, the Children Act 1989 differentiates between legal parenthood and the act of parenting. It does so by creating 'parental responsibility', a legal status held by some, but not all parents, and capable of being held by others who are not legally or genetically related to the child. Parental responsibility recognises the act of parenting as distinct from parentage.

---

[1] *Re G (Children)* [2006] UKHL 43. J Goldstein, A Freud and A Solnit's seminal work is *Beyond the Best Interests of the Child* (New York Free Press 1973).
[2] See, e.g., B Neale and C Smart, *Family Fragments* (Polity Press 1998).

In this chapter, we look at how the law has defined parentage. We consider what repro-ductive technologies and various permutations of conception mean when we ask, 'Who is a child's mother?' 'Who is a child's father?' We then turn to parental responsibility before concluding by looking at the position of unmarried fathers.

8.2 Legal parenthood

In a series of cases, Sir James Munby has had to determine the parentage of children born through assisted reproduction. The allocation of parentage is, he noted, 'a question of most fundamental gravity and importance. What, after all, to any child, to any parent, never mind to future generations and, indeed, to society at large, can be more important, emo-tionally, psychologically, socially and legally, than the answer to the question: who is my parent? Is this my child?'[3] Yet the reasons why he was called upon to identify the legal relationship between parent and child was because the law has separated the conception of a child from the act of bearing a child, and the act of bearing a child from the act of raising that child. How, then, does the law identify who is a child's mother and who is the child's father?

8.2.1 Who are a child's legal parents?

At common law, the woman who has given birth to a child has always been regarded as that child's mother, although it is safe to say that the question of maternal attribution has not often come before a court.[4] The act of childbirth itself has evidenced the maternal status of the woman concerned. In the *Ampthill Peerage* case, for example, the House of Lords simply noted that 'Motherhood, although also a legal relationship, is based on a fact, being proved demonstrably by parturition' [childbirth].[5] The child's genetic father has al-ways been his legal father, and where the mother was married it was presumed that her husband was that person. Now, too, in assisted reproduction, the father is not necessarily the person donating the sperm, and some children have no legal father at all. Thus, since the Act was passed, the development of techniques of assisted reproduction have meant that it is now possible for the woman who gives birth to a child to be genetically unrelated to him, and indeed for the mother not to be a woman at all, but a male mother. It has there-fore become essential that we define what is meant by these terms in a way that is consis-tent and enables those with a tie to the child to be easily recognised. This is not a simple task. Although the Births and Deaths Registration Act 1953 requires the registration of a child's birth, the Act does not define what is meant by the terms 'mother' and 'father' other than in respect of an adopted child, where they refer to the 'natural' father or mother.

As Table 8.1 shows, a number of different people involved in the conception or raising of the child could argue for recognition as a parent. The law prescribes who can do so, and who cannot. This allocation of parenthood by the legal system can be founded on a

---

[3] *Re Human Fertilisation and Embryology Act 2008 (Cases A, B, C, D, E, F, G and H)* [2015] EWHC 2602 (Fam).

[4] One example is *Slingsby v Attorney-General* (1916) 33 TLR 120, discussed in S Cretney, *Family Law in the Twen-tieth Century* (Oxford University Press 2003), at 529.

[5] *The Ampthill Peerage Case* [1977] AC 547 at 577 (Lord Simon).

TABLE 8.1 Permutations of Conceptual Arrangements

Recipient of Reproductive Material or Services	Contributed Reproductive Material or Services
1. Single *woman* may conceive with . . .	
	a) donated sperm alone to fertilise recipient's own egg; she carries the embryo
	b) donated sperm to fertilise recipient's own egg; surrogate carries embryo (surrogate has no genetic connection)
	c) donated sperm to fertilise donated egg; recipient carries the embryo
	d) donated sperm to fertilise donated egg (from someone other than surrogate); surrogate carries embryo (surrogate has no genetic connection)
	e) donated sperm to fertilise surrogate's egg; surrogate carries embryo (surrogate has genetic connection)
2. Single *man* may conceive with . . .	
	a) surrogate's eggs; surrogate carries embryo (surrogate has a genetic connection)
	b) donated egg; embryo created with recipient's sperm is carried by surrogate who is someone other than egg donor (surrogate has no genetic connection)
	c) donated sperm to inseminate surrogate (surrogate has a genetic connection)
	d) donated sperm to fertilise donated egg; surrogate carries embryo (surrogate has no genetic connection)
3. *Heterosexual [different-sex]* couple may conceive with . . .	
	a) their own sperm and eggs; female partner carries embryo
	b) donated sperm (used to fertilise female partner's egg); female partner carries embryo
	c) donated egg (male partner's sperm used to fertilise); female partner carries embryo
	d) donated sperm to fertilise donated egg; female partner carries embryo
	e) donated sperm to fertilise donated egg; surrogate (someone other than egg donor) carries embryo (surrogate has no genetic connection)
	f) donated sperm to inseminate surrogate (surrogate has a genetic connection)
	g) male partner's sperm used to inseminate surrogate (surrogate has a genetic connection)
4. *Female* partners may conceive with . . .	
	a) donated sperm to inseminate one partner; that partner carries embryo
	b) donated sperm to fertilise the egg of one partner; other partner carries embryo
	c) donated sperm to fertilise the egg of one partner; surrogate carries embryo (surrogate has no genetic connection)

	d) donated sperm used to fertilise donated egg; embryo is carried by 1 partner
	e) donated sperm used to fertilise donated egg; embryo is carried by surrogate (surrogate is someone other than egg donor, and has no genetic connection)
	f) donated sperm used to inseminate surrogate (surrogate has a genetic connection)
5. *Male* partners may conceive with . . .	
	Options are the same as in block 2, above, pertaining to a single man.

From Angela Campbell, 'Conceiving Parents through Law' (2007) 21 IJLPF 2, 242.

number of different claims, such as biological identity, the parties' intentions, and the act of parenting. As Angela Campbell writes, these three factors 'commonly blend together in analyses regarding where and how to locate parental status.'[6] Different jurisdictions may take different approaches. In this jurisdiction, the roles of parent identified by Lady Hale in *Re G (Children)*—genetic, gestational, and social-psychological—are capable of being held by different people, but only one will be the legal parent.

All children are born with a legal mother. Under s33(1) Human Fertilisation and Embryology Act 2008, the mother of a child born through assisted reproduction is 'the woman who is carrying or who has carried a child' i.e., the woman who was pregnant and gave birth to the child. This reflects the position at common law. It follows that where the child is conceived using an embryo created with a donor egg and implanted into a woman, the egg donor is not the child's mother.[7] In *Re G (Children)*, Lady Hale observed that while the attribution of motherhood to the person bearing the child 'may be partly for reasons of certainty and convenience, it also recognises a deeper truth: that the process of carrying a child and giving him birth (which may well be followed by breast-feeding for some months) brings with it, in the vast majority of cases, a very special relationship between mother and child, a relationship which is different from any other.'[8] This also serves a helpful practical purpose, in that someone identifiable must have responsibility for the child. That relationship is recognised from the moment of birth.[9]

The situation for fathers is more complicated and depends on consent, marital status, and method of conception. At common law, the child's legal father is the person who is the child's biological father, but there is no route to the easy attribution of paternity by third parties as there is with the act of childbirth. The advent of assisted reproduction has further complicated matters. In the case of births post-dating the coming into force of the

---

[6] Angela Campbell, 'Conceiving Parents through Law' (2007) 21(2) *International Journal of Law, Policy and the Family* 242.
[7] For the position of transgender persons, see 8.2.3.
[8] *Re G (Children)* [2006] UKHL 43. For a discussion of this case see A Diduck, 'If Only We Can Find the Appropriate Terms to Use the Issue Will Be Solved: Law, Identity and Parenthood' (2007) 19(4) *Child and Family Law Quarterly* 458.
[9] *Marckx v Belgium* App No. 6833/74 (ECtHR, 13 June 1979).

Human Fertilisation and Embryology Act 2008 on 6 April 2009, the position is that *the child's biological father will be his legal father in all situations except:*

- Where he donated his sperm to a licensed clinic for use in women other than his partner: s41. An anonymous sperm donor does not become a legal parent of the child born in this way, but note the requirement that the donation is via a licensed clinic. Sperm donation outside a licensed setting can result in the donor being the legal father of any child.

- If a woman uses donor sperm to become pregnant through a licensed clinic:

  a) *Married different-sex couples:* If the mother is married or civilly partnered to a man, her husband will be the child's father *unless* he does not consent to the placing in her of the embryo/sperm/eggs/artificial insemination (s35 Human Fertilisation and Embryology Act 2008). This requires artificial insemination, not sex. The father's consent will be recorded on a specific form held by the clinic concerned.

     In *Leeds Teaching Hospitals AHA v A* Mr and Mrs A sought treatment together, as did Mr and Mrs B. In error, Mrs A's eggs were fertilised by Mr B's sperm, a matter only discovered because the parties were of different races. Mrs A was the mother of the resulting twins, as she had given birth to them. Under s35, Mrs A's husband was to be treated as the father unless he did not consent to the placing in her of the embryos. The court held that Mr A had only consented to his wife's treatment with his own sperm, not that of someone else, and so he was not the father. (Even though he later wanted to be treated as such, his consent was to be objectively ascertained by the court). Instead, Mr B was the father. This was because the relevant section that provided that those donating sperm to others were not the legal fathers of any resulting children did not apply to this situation because Mr B had not consented to donating to others at all.[10] Had Mr B consented not only to treatment with his wife but to donating sperm to other women, he would have the protection of the provision and would not be the father of any children born to those other women. As he fell outside the provision, however, the common law rule applied to mean that as he was the biological father so, too, was he the legal father.

  b) *Unmarried different-sex couples:* If the mother is not married or civilly partnered but seeks treatment with a man, he will be the child's father if the 'agreed fatherhood provisions' are met (s36). That is the case even if donor sperm is used. The 'agreed fatherhood provisions' relate to consent and are discussed at 8.2.2.

  c) *Married same-sex couples:* If the mother is married or civilly partnered to a woman, that woman will be the child's second female parent unless she does not consent to the placing in the mother of the embryo/sperm/eggs/artificial insemination (s35 Human Fertilisation and Embryology Act 2008). If a child is deemed to have a second female parent, no man is to be treated as the father of the child (s45).

---

[10] [2003] EWHC 259.

d) *Unmarried same-sex couples:* If the mother is not married or civilly partnered and seeks treatment with another woman, the latter will be the second female parent of the child, if the 'agreed female parenthood provisions' are met (see 8.2.2), and there will be no father.

e) *Unmarried woman:* If an unmarried woman seeks treatment by herself, there will be no father as she will utilise anonymous donor sperm.

f) Outside a clinic setting, the situation can be different:

g) *Married different-sex couples:* If a woman becomes pregnant through assisted reproduction otherwise than through a licensed clinic (for example via home insemination using a turkey baster), and she is married or civilly partnered to a man, then he will be the child's father even if the sperm was not his, *unless* he does not consent to the placing in her of the embryo/sperm/eggs/artificial insemination (s35 Human Fertilisation and Embryology Act 2008).

h) *Unmarried different-sex partners:* The father is the man whose sperm was used.

i) *Married same-sex couples:* If a woman becomes pregnant through assisted reproduction otherwise than through a licensed clinic (for example via home insemination using a turkey baster) and she is married or civilly partnered to a woman, then that woman will be the child's second female parent even though the sperm will be from a known or unknown donor, *unless* the second female parent does not consent to the placing in her of the embryo/sperm/eggs/artificial insemination (s35 Human Fertilisation and Embryology Act 2008). If a child is deemed to have a second female parent, no man is to be treated as the father of the child (s45).

j) *Unmarried female same-sex couples:* The father is the man whose sperm was used; there is no second female parent.

k) *Unmarried male same-sex couples:* The father is the man whose sperm was used; the mother is the woman who gives birth (remember, there always has to be a mother), and the second man has no legal status. However, if this is a surrogacy arrangement, a parental order can be made which terminates the motherhood of the woman and any partner, and provides that the two men are the child's parents.

As you can see in Table 8.2, the marital status of the parties and the method and location of conception are important determiners. In all situations falling outside the Human Fertilisation and Embryology Act, the biological father is the legal father. This includes when the mother becomes pregnant through assisted reproduction otherwise than through a licensed clinic and she is not married; and when the mother becomes pregnant through sex, whether or not she is married.[11]

---

[11] For an extremely messy example of a dispute as to whether the child was conceived through sex or assisted reproduction, see *M v F & H* [2013] EWHC 1901 (Fam).

TABLE 8.2 Identifying the parent

	Mother married or civilly partnered to a man	Mother married or civilly partnered to woman	Mother in unmarried relationship with man	Mother in unmarried relationship with woman
Conception is via sexual intercourse with a man	The biological father is the legal father. The *pater est* presumption is that this person is her husband; this is rebuttable by evidence that another man is the biological father.	The biological father is the legal father.	The biological father is the legal father.	The biological father is the legal father.
Assisted reproduction at home e.g. turkey baster. Not conceived via sex.	Her husband will be the father, whether or not donor sperm is used, unless he does not consent to the placing in her of the embryo/sperm/eggs/ artificial insemination (s35 HFEA 2008).	The wife is the second female parent unless she does not consent to the placing in the mother of the embryo/sperm/ eggs/artificial insemination (s42 HFEA 2008). Where there is a second female parent, there is no father.	The biological father is the legal father.	The biological father is the legal father.
Assisted reproduction through a licensed clinic. Not conceived via sex.	Her husband will be the father, whether or not donor sperm is used, unless he does not consent to the placing in her of the embryo/sperm/eggs/ artificial insemination (s35 HFEA 2008).	The wife is the second female parent unless she does not consent to the placing in the mother of the embryo/sperm/ eggs/artificial insemination (s42 HFEA 2008). Where there is a second female parent, there is no father.	Her boyfriend will be the father, whether or not donor sperm is used, provided the Agreed Fatherhood Provisions are met (i.e., that he consents and there is no consenting spouse): s37 HFEA 2008.	The girlfriend is the second female parent if the Agreed Female Parenthood Conditions are met (i.e., that she consents and there is no consenting spouse): s44 HFEA 2008. Where there is a second female parent, there is no father.

SCENARIO 1

Illustration 1: Peter and Jasmine and children Freddy (10) and Mabel (7)

Peter and Jasmine's son Freddy was conceived using donor sperm. Although now divorced, at the time they were married.

Jasmine is Freddy's mother because she was pregnant and gave birth to him. This is the position both at common law and under the 2008 Act.

Is Peter Freddy's father? This depends upon the method of conception. If Jasmine became pregnant by having sex with another man, Peter would not be Freddy's father even if this was with Peter's blessing and only for the purposes of conception. We must consider how a presumption of legitimacy affects this.

If Peter and Jasmine instead used a syringe or turkey baster to insert the sperm, whether at home or at a fertility clinic, then Peter will be the father unless he did not consent at the time to her being inseminated. It would be different if Peter and Jasmine were unmarried.

Mabel was conceived through sex, although Peter is unsure whether he is her biological father. Mabel's legal father will be her biological father. As we shall see, the law presumes that the biological father is the mother's husband, but this is capable of being rebutted.

SCENARIO 2

Illustration 1: Rhys and Hardeep and baby Anji (2 months)

Rhys and Hardeep are a gay male couple who desperately wanted a child. They entered into a surrogacy arrangement in India, as a result of which their daughter Anji has just been born. Under the law in England and Wales, the mother of Anji is the surrogate that they used, who is Daya. The father of Anji will depend upon Daya's marital status. Surrogacy always involves assisted reproduction rather than conception by sexual intercourse (otherwise it is not surrogacy). This means that Daya's husband, if she has one, will be the child's father unless he did not consent to her surrogacy. This is the case even if the sperm used belonged to either Rhys or Hardeep.

The situation under the relevant Indian laws may well be different, but Rhys and Hardeep wish to return to the UK and it is under the law of England and Wales that they will need their position to be recognised.

8.2.2 The agreed fatherhood and female parenthood provisions

As we have seen, where the mother is married or civilly partnered to a man, he will be the father of the child unless he did not consent to the placing in her of the embryo/sperm/eggs or her artificial insemination (s35 HFEA 2008). Similarly, where the mother is married or civilly partnered to a woman, that partner will be the second female parent, unless it can be shown that the partner did not consent (s42). This applies irrespective of whether the assisted reproduction takes place at a licensed clinic or somewhere else.

Where the mother is unmarried, her partner can acquire the status of parent of a child born to her. In the case of male partners, this happens when the 'agreed fatherhood conditions' contained in ss36-37 are satisfied and in the case of a female partner, that woman can become the child's second female parent when the 'agreed female parenthood' conditions are satisfied (ss43-44). These provisions only apply when a licensed clinic is providing treatment and not to home insemination situations (cf married parties).

The agreed fatherhood provisions require the intended father to give signed notice in writing confirming that he consents to being treated as the father of any child resulting from the treatment provided to the mother under the clinic's licence, and the mother gives a notice that she consents to this. Either party can withdraw their consent prior to insemination. The parties cannot be within the prohibited degrees of relationship. The agreed female parenthood provisions in s44 mirror the agreed fatherhood provisions.

Within a clinic, the relevant forms are Form WP ('Your consent to your partner being the legal parent') for the mother and Form PP ('Your consent to being the legal parent') for the father or second female parent. In nearly forty cases, clinics have failed to obtain proper signatures to the correct forms at the correct time, meaning that the legal parenthood of the child born subsequently has been uncertain and required a court application to resolve. These cases started with *AB v CD v The Z Fertility Clinic*, in which the mother's partner, who was not biologically related to the child, was held not to be a second parent as the relevant forms were not completed by the clinic prior to treatment as required, and there was no informed consent as required by the terms of the clinic's licence. This meant that the treatment was not provided pursuant to the licence and the female parenthood conditions could not apply. The cases continued, from *Re A* to *Re Z* to *Re AA* to (at the time of writing) *Re AJ*.[12] While the mistakes were fatal to acquisition of parentage in *AB v CD*, the courts have established that mistakes that are 'obvious on the face of the document and it is plain what was meant' can be rectified: *In the matter of HFEA 2008 (Cases A-H, Declaration of Parentage)*.[13] An example of such a mistake would be each party signing in the other's spot on the form. This is because such correction does not constitute a legal change: it reflects the parties' intentions which Munby P held 'finally and irrevocably crystallised at the moment when the embryo or the sperm and eggs were placed in the mother, or the mother was artificially inseminated, and this treatment resulted in the birth of the child'.[14] In *Re O*, the parents had adopted their child, having been told that this was the only way to give them both the legal parenthood they had intended; the judge revoked the adoption and issued a declaration of parentage.[15]

FOCUS Know-How

Why are there no second male parents?

At law, a child can only have two legal parents. That is the common law position and the way in which the Human Fertilisation and Embryology Act 2008 is drafted.[16] As a child will always have a mother, it is not possible for both parties in a male couple to be a child's parent at the point of birth, unless one of them is a female to male transgender person who has given birth: male mothers are possible, as we see in 8.2.3. Apart from this exceptionally rare situation, the only ways in which a male couple can both become legal parents are through either the making of a surrogacy parental order or adoption order in their favour, both of which terminate the mother's parenthood.

---

[12] [2017] EWHC 3351 (Fam); see [2016] EWHC 2273 (Fam) for background.

[13] [2015] EWHC 2602 (Fam).

[14] See *Re Y, Z, AA, AB and AC* [2017] EWHC 784 (Fam). Subsequent conduct does not change this: *PQ v RS and Others (Legal Parenthood: Written Consent)* [2019] EWFC 65.

[15] [2016] EWHC 2273 (Fam). See also Chapter 12's discussion on revoking adoption orders.

[16] See *R (K) v Secretary of State for the Home Department* [2018] EWHC 1834 (Admin).

8.2.3 The position of transgender and intersex people

In Chapter 2 we discussed the ability of a person to change legal sex through the acquisition of a gender recognition certificate. Although many people who are transgender or who have both male and female sexual characteristics do have gender confirmation surgery, this is not a prerequisite of the obtaining of a certificate. This means that it is possible to be legally male but retain a womb and/or ovaries and fallopian tubes, or to be legally female but retain a penis and testicles, although hormone treatment can make a trans person infertile. While the usual position under the Gender Recognition Act 2004 is that a person's acquired gender becomes their legal gender for all purposes, s12 states that this does not affect the status of a person as the mother or father of a child. In *R (On the application of JK) v The Registrar General (The Secretary of State for the Home Department and others intervening)*, a transgender woman (a person who transitions from male to female) was the biological father of two children born to her wife and conceived through sex; she subsequently obtained a gender recognition certificate showing her gender as female. The effect of s12 was that she remained the father to both children, albeit henceforth a female father.[17]

In Key Case *McConnell*, the situation was slightly different. This concerned a female to male transgender man who retained female organs and was able to become pregnant and give birth to a little boy. The issue was whether he was a male mother or a pregnant father.

The outcome of the case, is that the law recognises male mothers and female fathers.

A male to female transgender person who obtains a gender recognition certificate will remain the father or any children born prior to the issue of her certificate. While she will not be able to gestate a child, she may become the child's second female parent if she seeks assisted reproductive treatment with a woman who carries the child, or she may become the child's parent through a surrogacy parental order or adoption. If she retains the ability to produce sperm, then she may be the child's biological father.

A female to male transgender person who obtains a gender recognition certificate will remain the mother of any child born prior to the issue of his certificate and any child that he gestates that is born afterwards. If he seeks assisted reproductive treatment with a woman who becomes pregnant, he will be recognised as that child's father if the agreed fatherhood conditions are met or they are married.

> **KEY CASE** *R (on the Application of McConnell) v The Registrar General for England and Wales and others* [2019] EWHC 2384 (Fam) and [2020] EWCA Civ 559
>
> In 2018, a transgender man, Freddy McConnell, became pregnant and gave birth to a son. He brought an application for a declaration that the Registrar General of Births should permit him to be registered on the child's birth certificate as his father, rather than his mother. McConnell was not automatically the child's mother because the Human Fertilisation and Embryology Act 2008 refers to the mother as 'the woman' who gives birth and he is not a woman. But nor did he satisfy any of the criteria for fatherhood under the Act. This was the first time on which a court had had to determine what constituted motherhood, and it 'required no fewer than 58 pages to provide an answer'.[18]

---

[17] [2015] EWHC 990 (Admin). See P Dunne, 'Recognising Transgender Parenthood on Birth Certificates: *R (JK) v Secretary of State for the Home Department*' [2015] *International Family Law* 230.

[18] C Fenton Glynn, 'Deconstructing Parenthood: What Makes a "Mother"?' [2020] *Cambridge Law Journal* 34.

The starting point was the common law position, as set out in the *Ampthill Peerage* case, that motherhood was proven by childbirth.[19] The judge, McFarlane P, then went on to consider whether the common law position had been changed by legislation. He found that it had not. Although McConnell had a gender recognition certificate and was thus male, he was nevertheless the child's mother, because neither s12 nor any other provision in the Gender Recognition Act altered the common law position that the person who gives birth is the mother:

> There is a material difference between a person's gender and their status as a parent. Being a 'mother', whilst hitherto always associated with being female, is the status afforded to a person who undergoes the physical and biological process of carrying a pregnancy and giving birth. It is now medically and legally possible for an individual, whose gender is recognised in law as male, to become pregnant and give birth to their child. Whilst that person's gender is 'male', their parental status, which derives from their biological role in giving birth, is that of 'mother'.[20]

Section 12 did not operate prospectively to change a person's status as a parent in respect of children born after the parent obtained a gender recognition certificate, just as it did not—as in *JK*—affect the parent's status where the child was born prior to the certificate.

The effect of this was that McConnell would be identified on his son's birth certificate as his mother. McConnell argued that this breached his human rights. He argued that by identifying him as male, and as a mother, his transgender status was revealed in breach of his Article 8 ECHR right to private life and that his motherhood conflicted with his and the child's lived reality. McFarlane rejected this argument, holding that any interference was justified by the legitimate aim of a coherent regime of birth registration and by the interests of the child to know the person who carried him.

McConnell's appeal was unsuccessful. The Supreme Court has declined to hear the case.

8.3 **Birth registration**

Birth registration is enormously important. Article 24 of the United Nations' International Covenant on Civil and Political Rights recognises a right to birth registration. The UN Convention on the Rights of the Child also holds birth registration to be a human right at Article 7: 'The child shall be registered immediately after birth and shall have the right from birth to a name, the right to acquire a nationality and, as far as possible, the right to know and be cared for by his or her parents.' By identifying a child as being born, and identifying that child's links to others—his identity—the child has status: his existence within society is recognised.

This is because a number of consequences flow from birth registration, including being entitled to a nationality, having access to healthcare, schooling, state housing, welfare benefits, and national insurance and thus the right to work. Having identification enables a person to obtain a passport, and enables the state to capture accurate demographic data and control citizenship.[21] As Andrew Bainham has explained, the state also has an

---

[19] *The Ampthill Peerage Case* [1977] AC 547.

[20] *R (On the Application of TT) v The Registrar General for England and Wales and Others* [2019] EWHC 2384 (Fam), known on appeal as *R (on the Application of McConnell) v The Registrar General for England and Wales and others* [2020] EWCA Civ 559.

[21] A Bainham, 'What Is the Point of Birth Registration?' (2008) 20(4) *Child and Family Law Quarterly* 449.

interest in identifying *someone* to take responsibility for the child from the moment of birth. The state, he says, 'has no particular interest in biological certainty': 'what matters is that someone presenting himself as the parent accepts this responsibility and thereby relieves it of the substitute care it would otherwise have to provide and the financial liability it would otherwise incur.' Birth registration serves the purpose of ascribing legal and financial responsibility.

It follows that lack of registration makes a child more at risk of child trafficking, child labour, and exploitation, because they lack the papers necessary to work or travel legitimately.[22] As UNICEF, the United Nations Children's Fund, has observed, 'The right to be recognized as a person before the law is a critical step in ensuring lifelong protection and is a prerequisite for exercising all other rights.'[23] While in England and Wales only about 20 births per year are not registered in the first 12 months,[24] there are an estimated 230 million children worldwide—a quarter of all those aged under 5—whose birth is unregistered, and who do not, therefore, officially exist, with all the consequences that flow from that. Some areas of the world, such as South Asia (36 per cent of births registered) and sub-Saharan Africa (37 per cent), have very low rates of registration[25] and there is a correlation between this and poor growth and developmental outcomes for young children.[26]

In addition to the practical benefits of birth registration, a second important benefit is the sense of identity that it gives to the child. The Supreme Court has recognised that

> For the parent, perhaps particularly for a father, the knowledge that this is 'his' child can bring a very special sense of love for and commitment to that child which will be of great benefit to the child . . . For the child, he reaps the benefit not only of that love and commitment, but also of knowing his own origins and lineage, which is an important component in finding an individual sense of self as one grows up. The knowledge of that genetic link may also be an important (although certainly not an essential) component in the love and commitment felt by the wider family, perhaps especially grandparents, from which the child has so much to gain.[27]

While the ECHR does not explicitly address birth registration, the European Court of Human Rights held in *Marckx v Belgium* that an unmarried mother and her child were a family within the protections of Article 8, and they were entitled to legal recognition of that from the point of birth.[28] In a surrogacy case, *Mennesson v France*, the Court held that Article 8 EHCR protects a person's ability to establish the substance of his or her identity, including the legal parent–child relationship.[29] In Key Case *R (On the Application of*

---

[22] UNGA, 'Report of the Office of the United Nations High Commissioner for Human Rights' (27th session, UN Doc A/HRC/27/22 (2014).

[23] https://data.unicef.org/resources/birth-registration-for-every-child-by-2030/.

[24] Response by the General Register Office to a freedom of information enquiry, 13 June 2011, at https://www.whatdotheyknow.com/request/what_is_the_maximum_penalty_for.

[25] Plan, *Count Every Child: The Right to Birth Registration* (2009).

[26] J Jeong, A Bhatia, and G Fink, 'Associations between Birth Registration and Early Child Growth and Development: Evidence from 31 Low- and Middle-Income Countries' (2018) 18 *BMC Public Health* 673.

[27] *Re G (Children)* [2006] UKHL 43 (Lady Hale).

[28] App No. 6833/74 (ECtHR, 13 June 1979).

[29] App No. 65192/11 (ECtHR, 26 June 2014).

McConnell), discussed at 8.2.3, the President of the Family Division noted that a child's Article 8 rights 'must normally include the right to know who gave birth to them'.[30]

Birth registration also involves the selection of a name for the child, and this too has implications for the child's sense of identity:

> One of the first questions asked by friends and relatives following the birth of a child is 'what is the baby's name?' . . . The name given to a child ordinarily evolves over the months of the pregnancy through a bundle of cultural, familial and taste influences. The forename finally chosen forms a critical part of his or her evolving identity. The sharing of a forename with a parent or grandparent or bearing a forename which readily identifies a child as belonging to his or her particular religious or cultural background, can be a source of great pride to a child and give him or her an important sense of 'belonging' which will be invaluable throughout his or her life.
>
> If a baby cannot be brought up by his or her parents, often the forename given to him or her by their mother is the only lasting gift they have from her. It may be the first, and only, act of parental responsibility by his or her mother. It is likely, therefore, to be of infinite value to that child as part of his or her identity.[31]

Some countries have very strict rules around child names, often aimed at preserving national identity.[32] Generally, however, the selection of a name is treated as an act of parental responsibility within the discretion of the parents, however much a name may cause the child to be teased or bullied. Only exceptionally have courts intervened at the point of birth (as opposed to a later dispute between parents about a change of name). The quote above comes from one such case, *Re C (Children)*, in which the court prevented the mother from naming her daughter Cyanide (the name of a deadly poison) on the grounds that it would cause the child significant emotional harm, the threshold for care proceedings.[33]

8.3.1 The law in England and Wales

In England and Wales, a nationwide scheme of birth registration was first introduced in 1836 with the creation of the General Register Office, although parents were not legally required to their children's birth until 1874. The relevant legislation now is the Births and Deaths Registration Act 1953 (as amended), s1(1) of which requires that the birth of a child born in England and Wales is to be registered and s2 of which specifies that this must be done in 42 days. There are special provisions for late registration and for stillbirths. A fully completed birth certificate will include:

* the child's name, sex, place and date of birth;
* the parents' names and addresses, places and dates of birth, and jobs;
* the date, if any, of the parents' marriage or civil partnership; and
* the mother's maiden name.

---

[30] *R (On the Application of TT) v The Registrar General for England and Wales and Others* [2019] EWHC 2384 (Fam) (McFarlane P).
[31] *Re C (Children)* [2016] EWCA Civ 374 at [40]–[41] (King LJ).
[32] See 'Who, What, Why: Why Do Some Countries Regulate Baby Names?' (*BBC News* 1 February 2013).
[33] [2016] EWCA Civ 374.

The inclusion of a surname for the child is mandatory. A first name does not have to be entered, although one can be added or altered within the first 12 months.

The duty to register a child's birth lies with the child's father and mother. Where the mother is married or civilly partnered, either she or her spouse (whether same-sex or different-sex) may register the birth. They can do this together or one of them can do it on their own. By virtue of the marriage or civil partnership, the identity of both parents can be registered. This includes where the child is born as a result of assisted reproduction, even if donor sperm or eggs were used.

Sometimes, of course, a mother will be married but the child's father will be someone other than her husband. She cannot jointly register with that man without some proof to rebut the *pater est* presumption that her husband is the child's father (see 8.3.2), and this is required even if all parties, including the husband, agree on the father's identity.

Section 10 Births and Deaths Registration Act 1953 states that where the mother is not married or in a civil partnership with the child's father, he cannot be named as the father without her consent, and she cannot name a man as the father without his consent. While they can register the birth jointly, if only one of them attends the register office then they will need to bring evidence of the consent of the other. This usually takes the form of a statutory declaration by each party as to the identity of the father, but can include certain kinds of court order, such as an order under s4 Children Act 1989 which relates to parental responsibility for a father. Note that the unmarried mother is under no obligation to name the father and the space on the form for his name can be left blank. If there is a dispute about parentage or the father wishes to be registered against the mother's wishes, he would need to seek a declaration of parentage from the court. The consequences of this for unmarried fathers are discussed at 8.3.3.

Where the birth of a child to parents who are not married or civilly partnered to one another has been the result of assisted reproduction, the consent forms required by the Human Fertilisation and Embryology Act 2008 and a certificate of a registered medical practitioner as to the medical facts will be evidence enabling the registrar to enter the name of the legal father or second female parent.

If the parents are dead or otherwise unable or unwilling to register the child's birth, then registration can be done by any 'qualified informant'. This could be a person present at the birth (such as a midwife), an occupier of the house in which the child was born, or any person having charge of the child. The Registrar may serve notice on qualified informants to register the birth, and the Registrar's office will know about almost all births because the NHS notifies them. A failure to register is not only a breach of the 1953 Act but may also raise child protection concerns and is likely to be part of a wider pattern of concerning behaviour. In *London Borough of Tower Hamlets v M, F and T*, the parents' refusal to register T's birth was part of a set of beliefs sometimes known as 'sovereign citizenship', in which a person refuses to acknowledge the state as having any powers to regulate his life.[34] The act of birth registration was seen by the father as something that enabled the state to control his son. The local authority, in whose favour there was an interim care order over T, was held to be a qualified informant able to register his birth.

---

[34] [2019] EWHC 1572 (Fam).

8.3.2 The *pater est* presumption

The law operates a presumption that where the mother is married or in a civil partnership with a man, that man is the child's biological father. This is known as the *pater est* presumption. The presumption applies even if the parties have separated or are divorcing, or have divorced so recently that the child could have been conceived during the marriage.

The presumption not only reflects the likelihood that a child is legitimate, but also the desirability of them being so. In the days before DNA testing, when illegitimacy—being born outside wedlock—attracted social stigma and illegitimate children lacked legal protections and inheritance rights, it meant that most children born to a married woman would be considered legitimate. As Jackson has written, 'A child's mother or "father" may both know that another man is the true biological father, but the presumption enables them to conceal the extra-marital conception. This common-law rule works, therefore, not to promote truth about a child's origins, but rather to safeguard the traditional family unit.'[35] Section 38(2) of the Human Fertilisation and Embryology Act 2008 preserves this common law presumption. This means that it also applies to situations where the child is conceived using assisted reproduction, including in those cases in which the insemination takes place outside a licensed clinic.

The presumption is rebuttable by evidence, proven on the balance of probabilities, that someone else is the biological father and thus the legal father (s26 Family Law Reform Act 1969). The burden of proof is on the person who seeks to rebut the presumption.

Note that there is no presumption in the case of unmarried couples, however long their relationship.

8.3.3 Disputed paternity and declarations of parentage

Most of the time, fatherhood is not an issue and no one will look beyond the father, if any, listed on the birth certificate, because birth certificates are meant to tell the truth about who a child's father is. Where assisted reproduction is concerned, the Human Fertilisation and Embryology Act 2008 defines who is a parent, so that it does not necessarily reflect biology.[36]

It is a criminal offence under the Perjury Act 1911 for either the mother or alleged father to register a man as the father when they know that he is not (rather than simply have doubts), even if the mother is married and the *pater est* presumption applies. Nevertheless, studies have shown between 1 and 29 per cent of all children have the 'wrong father' on their birth certificate. Although a more accurate figure is probably fewer than 10 per cent, this is still a substantial number.[37]

---

[35] E Jackson, 'What Is a Parent?' in A Diduck and K O'Donovan (eds), *Feminist Perspectives in Family Law* (Routledge Cavendish 2006) 59.

[36] An interesting discussion of this is A Bainham, 'Arguments about Parentage' (2008) 67(2) *Cambridge Law Journal* 322.

[37] M A Bellis, K Hughes, S Hughes, and JR Ashton, 'Measuring Paternal Discrepancy and Its Public Health Consequences' (2005) 59 *Journal of Epidemiology and Community Health* 749.

Where there is a dispute over the paternity of a child, an application to court for a declaration of parentage can be made under s55A Family Law Act 1986. The application must be made by a person with 'sufficient personal interest' in the matter, or by someone who is a parent or alleged parent of the child or the child himself. The Secretary of State for Work and Pensions may also apply for the purposes of the Child Support Act 1991 (see Chapter 6). The child is not automatically a party to the case, but if they become one then they will have a guardian appointed for them unless they are competent to instruct their own solicitor.

Under s20 Family Law Reform Act 1969, the court can order DNA testing. However, a person's consent is required for them to be tested (s21). A minor who is over the age of 16 is able to give their own consent, and there appears to be no provision for non-consensual testing: they are in the same position as an adult.

For those under the age of 16 the consent can be given by 'the person who has the care and control of him', and if that person does not consent then the court can order the test if it is in the child's best interests (part of which will involve consideration of the child's wishes and feelings about that). In *Re D (Paternity)* the court said that 'such interests should not receive any precise definition but range as widely and as deeply as the individual facts of a case required it to do.'[38] Sometimes, the court will hold that determining the application is not in the child's best interests. In *MS v RS and BT (Paternity)* the mother's husband had surreptitiously undertaken a DNA test of the children and then sought a declaration that he was not their father. The mother and the man alleged to be the biological father gave unclear evidence and kept changing their story, so it seemed that they may have something to hide. Nevertheless, the court declined to make a declaration of parentage when the children, who were aged 15 and 13, opposed it strongly. (In any case, if they were *Gillick*-competent, the court could not have ordered them to be DNA tested without their consent.)[39]

More commonly, courts find that it is best for a child to know his or her genetic heritage in the long term. As Smart says, the tendency is for courts 'to assume that (genetic) truth is better than (relational) fiction' and that 'the addition of more genetic kin through these means is inevitably seen as producing a positive outcome for children (and possibly for adults).' Yet, as she points out, 'children live in webs of relationships that are delicately interconnected and adding more relatives may disrupt and even break some of these links.'[40] The truth can be highly disruptive to the child's existing family structure and beliefs. Courts may need to balance the immediate impact that this may have against what many judges consider to be the long-term benefits of truth. In *Re D (Paternity)* Hedley J ordered DNA testing of an 11-year-old boy, considering certainty to be in his long-term best interests even though the child was currently strongly opposed, but indefinitely stayed the order until he was mentally in a better place.[41] By that time, he had, as Fortin points out, already been unsettled by the claim being made.[42] The court cannot, however, find on the

---

[38] *Re D (Paternity)* [2006] EWHC 3545 (Fam).

[39] [2020] EWFC 30. For the concept of *Gillick* competence, see Chapter 9.

[40] C Smart, 'Law and the Regulation of Family Secrets' (2010) 24(3) *International Journal of Law, Policy, and the Family* 397.

[41] [2006] EWHC 3545 (Fam).

[42] J Fortin, 'Children's Right to Know Their Origins – Too Far, Too Fast?' (2009) 21(3) *Child and Family Law Quarterly* 336.

one hand that testing is in the child's best interests and decide to make a declaration of parentage but then defer this until, pursuant to a s8 Children Act specific issues order, the child is told of their parentage.[43]

The adult parties may not share the same interests as the child. As Fortin says, declarations of parentage 'can be exploited by adults [claiming to be the child's father] to promote their own claims, driven by what may be false assumptions about the overriding significance to children of their biological links with their parents'.[44] The consequence of a declaration of parentage may well be that the father concerned seeks parental responsibility for the child and/or an order that the child spend time with them. In *Re H and A (Children)* the mother's husband, Mr A, was the primary carer of young twins, and believed himself to be their father. When another man, with whom the mother had had an affair, claimed to be the father, the court refused that man's application for a declaration of parentage after hearing evidence that Mr A would not be able to cope if the children were found not to be his, and would leave the family. Ultimately, as the case was remitted by the Court of Appeal for rehearing, we do not know whether the judge decided that the child's best interests lay in knowing the biological reality of their parentage, or in retaining their primary carer.[45]

While an adult such as a putative father can refuse a DNA test, that does not prevent the court from being able to determine the truth. For one thing, if there is another man putting himself forward as the father, he would presumably undertake a DNA test willingly. The standard of determining parentage is the balance of probabilities: is it more likely than not that this man is the father? The fact that a man refuses to have a DNA test and therefore a clear determination of whether or not he is the father enables the court to infer that he believes that he is the father—why else would he refuse the test, which involves simply swabbing the inside of his cheek?

This was the situation in which Mr Jones found himself in Key Case *Secretary of State for Work and Pensions v Jones*.

Jones tells us that an inference of paternity from a refusal to consent to a DNA sample is 'virtually inescapable' even if would have the effect of rebutting the presumption of legitimacy. The court agreed with the statement of Waite LJ in *Re A (A Minor) (Paternity: Refusal of Blood Test)* that in order to avoid an inference, the father would 'certainly have to advance very clear and cogent reasons for his refusal to be tested—reasons that it would be just and fair and reasonable for him to be allowed to maintain.'[46]

If a declaration of paternity is obtained, the court should forward this to the General Registry Office, which will re-register the birth under ss14 and 14A Births and Deaths Registration Act 1953. Alternatively, an application to the Registrar General can be made by the mother, the biological father, any man wrongly named on the birth certificate, or a person with parental responsibility for the child, producing evidence such as a DNA test from an approved tester, or an affidavit. The name of any previous man is not deleted, but a correction to the register is made in the margins.

---

[43] *Re F Paternity: Registration* [2011] EWCA Civ 1765.

[44] J Fortin, 'Children's Right to Know Their Origins – Too Far, Too Fast?' (2009) 21(3) *Child and Family Law Quarterly* 336. Cf the arguments in this article with Fortin's earlier view in her comment '*Re F*: "The Gooseberry Bush approach"' (1994) 57 *Modern Law Review* 296.

[45] [2002] EWCA Civ 383.

[46] *Re A (A Minor) (Paternity: Refusal of Blood Test)* [1994] 2 FLR 463, 473 (Waite LJ), cited with approval in *Jones*.

KEY CASE *Secretary of State for Work and Pensions v Jones* [2003] EWHC 2163

The child's mother was separated from her husband and living with her lover, Mr Jones, when the child was conceived. She later returned to her husband, registering him as the child's father on the birth certificate. Some years later, the mother sought child support from Mr Jones. The Child Support Agency wrote to Mr Jones and asked him if he was the father. On a CSA form, Mr Jones ticked *yes* to being the father, but then wrote *maybe* and put a question mark next to this. However, he refused to undergo a DNA test.

Butler-Sloss LJ issued a declaration that Mr Jones was the child's father. She held that there were two routes for doing so, which had been satisfied. First, the mother's evidence that Mr Jones was the only person with whom she had sexual relations in the conception period combined with Mr Jones' answer on the CSA form, his refusal to undergo DNA testing, and his refusal to attend court together meant that it was more likely than not that he was the father and rebutted the *pater est* presumption that her husband was the child's father. Second, even without these factors, Mr Jones' refusal to be tested led *by itself* to the 'virtually inescapable' inference that he was the father of the child.

SCENARIO 1

Illustration 2: Peter and Jasmine and children Freddy (10) and Mabel (7)

The *pater est* presumption applies to Mabel's birth, so that the starting point is that she is a legitimate child, i.e., that Peter is indeed her biological father. The fact that Peter and Jasmine had previously had difficulty conceiving is evidence that may rebut the presumption of legitimacy. However, there is a simple solution: a DNA test. If the court was asked to make a declaration of paternity, then it would decide whether it was in Mabel's best interests to know the truth about her paternity, whatever that is.

While the court can order that Mabel be DNA tested, it has no such power to order Peter to be tested. If, however, he refuses, *Jones* tells us that the court is very likely to infer that he believes himself to be the father—only clear and cogent reasons for refusing to consent to the test would prevent this virtually inescapable conclusion being drawn. In the event, in our fictional scenario the court finds that it is in Mabel's best interests to know the truth, and DNA testing of both her and Peter show that, to a very high degree of accuracy, Peter is her father.

SCENARIO 3

Illustration 1: Sara and Haruto and son Kenzo (5)

We're concerned here with whether Haruto can follow through on his threat to remove Kenzo from Sara's care. The first thing to establish is whether in fact Haruto is the father of Kenzo. If he is not, then any attempt to remove Kenzo from his mother's care would constitute child abduction. Sara tells you that Haruto is named on Kenzo's birth certificate as his father. She and Haruto attended the registrar together. Unless and until paternity is successfully challenged, Haruto is the child's legal father.

8.3.4 **Losing parenthood**

It is possible to lose one's status as a parent. This will only happen in one of three ways. First, it may be that the paternity of a child was misattributed and that a declaration of paternity has been made in favour of another person. This would mean that any person previously recognised as the child's legal father would no longer be their father. Second, when a child is adopted, the child becomes the child of the adopter(s) for all purposes and this terminates the parental status of the birth parents. Finally, where the child is born as a result of a surrogacy arrangement, it is possible to terminate the status of the surrogate and, if she has one, her spouse/civil partner, and make a parental order recognising the commissioning parent(s) as the legal parent(s). It is to this that we turn next.

8.4 **Surrogacy**

Surrogacy involves a woman (the surrogate) who bears a child on behalf of another person or couple (the commissioning parents) who then raise the child. Surrogacy differs from adoption in that the child is conceived at the instigation of the commissioning parents, with the surrogate and the commissioning parent(s) all having the intention that the child will become the child of the commissioners. To recognise this underlying intention, the commissioning parents are often known as the 'intended parents' and it is this term that we use in this chapter.

Most of those who enter into surrogate arrangements do so because they are unable to birth a child themselves, either because they are biologically male (a single man or a gay couple) or because they are biologically female but unable to carry a pregnancy to term. For some parents, therefore, surrogacy is the only way in which they can have a child who is genetically related to them.

There are two types of surrogacy.

1. In traditional surrogacy, the surrogate is artificially inseminated with the intended father's semen. This may happen at a clinic or at home. The baby will therefore be conceived using the surrogate's egg.

2. In gestational surrogacy, the surrogate's eggs are not used, so she will have no genetic link to the child. The eggs may be those of the intended mother or donor eggs. The sperm may be that of the intended father or donor sperm. Because gestational surrogacy involves in-vitro fertilisation (IVF), it is necessary for it to take place in a clinic setting.

The legal treatment of surrogacy arrangements varies considerably across the world. In some countries, surrogacy arrangements are unlawful, whereas in others they fall within a legal scheme. In some countries they exist in a legal grey area, not unlawful but certainly frowned upon. Treatment of the contract between the surrogate mother and the intended parents also varies from being enforceable (so that the surrogate must hand over the child to the intended parents) to being unenforceable as a matter of public policy. In some countries, the surrogate cannot be paid, so the surrogate acts altruistically rather than for financial benefit; in other countries the arrangement is commercial, in that the surrogate is paid an amount in excess of her losses or expenses, and an agency or fertility clinic may be involved on a for-profit basis. This variation in practice and law across the globe can cause enormous difficulties for transnational surrogacy arrangements.

8.4.1 Surrogacy in England and Wales

In England and Wales, surrogacy is lawful but heavily circumscribed. This approach has been described as based on tolerance rather than positive acceptance.[47]

As we have seen, the legal mother of a child is the person who gives birth to that child, meaning that the surrogate mother is always the first legal mother whether or not she is genetically related to the child. In England and Wales, the law provides that the surrogate can give up her status as parent—along with her husband if he is the legal father—in favour of the intended parent or parents, who then become the child's parents at law. This is achieved by the making of a parental order after the birth of the child. Do not confuse this order with a parental responsibility order or an adoption order—it is an order specific to surrogacy. Prior to the introduction of parental orders by the Human Fertilisation and Embryology Act 1990, it was only possible for the intended parents to become the child's parents by adopting him or her.

We do not know how many surrogacy arrangements there are each year involving couples from the UK. We only know that 442 parental orders were made in England and Wales in 2019, although there is some doubt about this figure as it varies with that of the Registrar General.[48] The tight regulation of surrogacy within the UK (set out in two main statutes, the Surrogacy Arrangements Act 1985 and the Human Fertilisation and Embryology Act 2008) can cause problems for those who find themselves non-compliant with the legal requirements. There are likely to be other arrangements where the intended parents have not or cannot apply for a parental order because they do not know that they should or because they have not complied with the criteria necessary for the court to make a parental order, which are set out in ss54 and 54A Human Fertilisation and Embryology Act 2008.

Before we consider the details of the sections, there are a few key points to note.

First, while it is lawful to enter into a surrogacy arrangement, the arrangement is not enforceable in this jurisdiction. The surrogate is free to change her mind, in which case she will remain the child's mother. In these circumstances, or if she cannot be found, the court cannot make a parental order although it can order that the child live with the intended parent(s) under a s8 Children Act child arrangements order, rather than with the surrogate. While there is no legal obligation on the intended parents to make a parental order application, the effect is that without this they will not be recognised in this jurisdiction as the child's parents. While it is likely that on a day-to-day basis this will not affect

---

[47] J Baker, 'Eastern and Western Perspectives of Surrogacy: Out with the Old, In with the Best Interests?' [2016] *International Family Law* 338.

[48] Ministry of Justice, *Family Court Statistics April to June 2020* (2020). Table 4 gives the figures for preceding full years. For a discussion of the data uncertainties, see Chapter 2 in Surrogacy in the UK Working Group on Surrogacy Law Reform, *Surrogacy in the UK: Myth Busting and Reform—Report of the Surrogacy UK Working Group on Surrogacy Law Reform* (2015).

their situation (because those they come into contact with generally do not ask about how a child was conceived), it is very possible that at some point—either relating to inheritance, or a serious issue relating to parental responsibility or health—the fact that the parents have no legal relationship with the child will cause serious problems and much distress.

Second, our model of surrogacy is altruistic and not commercial. Those involved in the surrogacy arrangement cannot make a profit from it. This has important consequences for the availability of legal advice, and a number of criminal offences can be committed in undertaking surrogacy-related work. While advising on the law of surrogacy is not unlawful, s2(1) of the Surrogacy Arrangements Act 1985 makes it a criminal offence to offer certain services on a commercial—i.e., profit-making—basis, although these offences do not apply to the surrogate mother herself or the intended parents.

It is also an offence for a commercial organisation to broker or negotiate a surrogacy arrangement or match a surrogate with someone looking to use her, advertise that it is willing to do so, or receive payment for arranging surrogacy, although non-profit making organisations are able to assist in making surrogacy arrangements and recover reasonable costs for doing so. These offences are aimed not at the surrogate herself or at the intended parents, but at others who may exploit. This means that solicitors, who should be able to help ensure that the surrogacy arrangement is legally compliant, are limited in what they can do before the child is born. Some organisations exist to support surrogates and intended parents, including Surrogacy UK and Childlessness Overcome Through Surrogacy (COTS), but they have to limit their activities.

Although no one has been prosecuted so far, the High Court referred the 'British Surrogacy Centre' to the police in the case *J v G*.[49]

8.4.2 The criteria for a parental order

Once the child is born, the intended parents can apply for a parental order. In this section, we consider the criteria for making this order, which are set out in ss54 and 54A Human

---

Statutory Extract *s2 Surrogacy Arrangements Act 1985*

Negotiating surrogacy arrangements on a commercial basis, etc.
(1) No person shall on a commercial basis do any of the following acts in the United Kingdom, that is—
  (a) initiate any negotiations with a view to the making of a surrogacy arrangement,
  (aa) take part in any negotiations with a view to the making of a surrogacy arrangement,
  (b) offer or agree to negotiate the making of a surrogacy arrangement, or
  (c) compile any information with a view to its use in making, or negotiating the making of, surrogacy arrangements;
  and no person shall in the United Kingdom knowingly cause another to do any of those acts on a commercial basis.

---

[49] [2013] EWHC 1432 (Fam).

Statutory Extract *s54 Human Fertilisation and Embryology Act 2008*

Parental orders: two applicants

(1) On an application made by two people ('the applicants'), the court may make an order providing for a child to be treated in law as the child of the applicants if –

    (a) the child has been carried by a woman who is not one of the applicants, as a result of the placing in her of an embryo or sperm and eggs or her artificial insemination,

    (b) the gametes of at least one of the applicants were used to bring about the creation of the embryo, and

    (c) the conditions in subsections (2) to (8) are satisfied.

(2) The applicants must be –

    (a) husband and wife,

    (b) civil partners of each other, or

    (c) two persons who are living as partners in an enduring family relationship and are not within prohibited degrees of relationship in relation to each other.

(3) Except in a case falling within subsection (11), the applicants must apply for the order during the period of 6 months beginning with the day on which the child is born.

(4) At the time of the application and the making of the order –

    (a) the child's home must be with the applicants, and

    (b) either or both of the applicants must be domiciled in the United Kingdom or in the Channel Islands or the Isle of Man.

(5) At the time of the making of the order both the applicants must have attained the age of 18.

(6) The court must be satisfied that both –

    (a) the woman who carried the child, and

    (b) any other person who is a parent of the child but is not one of the applicants (including any man who is the father by virtue of section 35 or 36 or any woman who is a parent by virtue of section 42 or 43),have freely, and with full understanding of what is involved, agreed unconditionally to the making of the order.

(7) Subsection (6) does not require the agreement of a person who cannot be found or is incapable of giving agreement; and the agreement of the woman who carried the child is ineffective for the purpose of that subsection if given by her less than six weeks after the child's birth.

(8) The court must be satisfied that no money or other benefit (other than for expenses reasonably incurred) has been given or received by either of the applicants for or in consideration of –

    (a) the making of the order,

    (b) any agreement required by subsection (6),

    (c) the handing over of the child to the applicants, or

    (d) the making of arrangements with a view to the making of the order,unless authorised by the court.

Fertilisation and Embryology Act 2008. Section 54 relates to two people applying for a parental order together, and the more recent addition s54A relates to a sole applicant, but is in similar terms. As we shall see, judges have been willing to interpret some of these provisions with a degree of flexibility not apparent in the wording of the statute itself.

The criteria we will discuss in turn are:

- The child's best interests
- The eligibility of the applicants
- The need for a genetic link to the child

- Conception not via sexual intercourse
- The applicants' ages
- The applicants' domicile
- The time limit for making an application
- The applicants' living arrangements
- The consent of the first legal parents
- The requirement that the arrangement be non-commercial.

The child's best interests

The Human Fertilisation and Embryology (Parental Orders) Regulations 2010 state that whenever a court is coming to a decision relating to the grant of a parental order, the paramount consideration is the welfare of the child, throughout his or her life.[50] This means that even if all of the other criteria are fulfilled, the court will not make a parental order unless it is in the child's best interests to do so. Prior to 2010, the child's welfare was not paramount, and its elevation has led courts in almost all cases to make an order if it is in the interests of the child even if not all of the other criteria have been met.

Before an order can be made, a parental order reporter (an officer of Cafcass, the Children and Family Court Advisory and Support Service) must prepare a report for the court about whether the parental order is indeed in the child's best interests and whether the legal requirements for the order have been met.[51] This 'requires a similar degree of care and caution as that to an application for adoption'. The parental order reporter must see the child with the applicants 'unless there are compelling and exceptional reasons based on the child's welfare why such observations cannot take place or where there is sufficient independent evidence pertaining to the child's welfare from an alternative source'.[52]

The eligibility of the applicants

Until recently, the applicants for a parental order, i.e., the intended parents, had to be a couple, either married to one another, civil partners, or in an enduring family relationship not within the prohibited degrees of relationship.[53] Sole applicants could not apply, and the only way a single intended parent could terminate the status of the surrogate as legal mother and become parent instead was to adopt the child. In a Parliamentary debate prior to the passing of the 2008 Act, Dawn Primarolo MP, a health minister, explained that the couple requirement

> recognises the magnitude of a situation in which a person becomes pregnant with the express intention of handing the child over to someone else, and the responsibility that

---

[50] Although this Regulation has been superseded, this provision remains. Note that the child's welfare throughout his life is the phrasing also found in the welfare principle in the Adoption and Children Act 2002, whereas the Children Act 1989 principle does not explicitly mention 'throughout his life'.

[51] A useful explanation of the reporter's role can be found at https://www.cafcass.gov.uk/grown-ups/parents-and-carers/surrogacy/ accessed 25 April 2020.

[52] *Re Z (Foreign Surrogacy: Allocation of Work: Guidance on Parental Order Reports)* [2015] EWFC 90 (Russell J).

[53] The prohibited degrees relate to close blood relationships. For the purposes of the 2008 Act, two people are within the prohibited degrees of relationship if one is the other's parent, grandparent, sibling (including half-siblings), aunt or uncle. See Chapter 2.

that places on the people who will receive the child. There is an argument, which the Government have acknowledged in the Bill, that such a responsibility is likely to be better handled by a couple than a single man or woman. . . . single people are able to adopt and to receive IVF, so why can they not get a parental order over surrogacy? The difference is this: adoption involves a child who already exists and whose parents are not able to keep the child, for whom new parents are sought. That is different, which is why there is no parallel. IVF involves a woman becoming pregnant herself and giving birth to her child—there is not a direct parallel. Surrogacy, however, involves agreeing to hand over a child even before conception.[54]

There have, however, been some case law developments since the Act was first in force. In Key Case *A v P (Surrogacy: Parental Order: Death of Applicant)*, Theis J, who is the lead judge for surrogacy cases in the High Court, was willing to treat the requirement of two applicants as satisfied when the child's intended father (who was also the child's biological father) had died between the making of the joint application and the hearing.

Although *A v P* involved death, in *Re X* the intended parents were separated at the time the application was issued. Munby P held that, as they were not divorced, they remained 'husband and wife' within the meaning of the section, and that as they had in any event made the application jointly, it was an application 'made by two people'.[55]

By this point, the courts had therefore interpreted the requirement of 'two applicants' as not necessitating two living and living-together applicants. However, in *Re Z (A Child: Human Fertilisation and Embryology Act: Parental Order)*[56] Munby P was not willing to go a step further and interpret the requirement for there to be two applicants as requiring only one applicant. The applicant in this case was a single man who had conceived a child using his own sperm and a donor egg, with the resulting embryo implanted in an unmarried surrogate mother located in the United States. After the child's birth, he returned to the UK and applied for a parental order. Munby P refused the application but issued a declaration that the requirement in section 54(1) that an application for a parental order could only by two people was incompatible with the applicant's Art 8 right to private and family life read in conjunction with Article 14, the right to non-discrimination in the application of that right.

As a result, the law was changed from January 2019. A new s54A was created which sets out the criteria for a single applicant to obtain a parental order.[57] The conditions set out in this section are the same as those found in s54, save that the sole applicant must fulfil each criterion by themselves, such as being genetically linked to the child, being over 18, and being domiciled in the UK, the Channel Islands, or the Isle of Man.

The need for a genetic link to the child

At least one of the intended parents *must* be genetically related to the child. This means that the sperm of the intended father and/or the intended mother's eggs have been used. Where there is a sole applicant, that person must therefore be fertile to the extent necessary

---

[54] Dawn Primarolo, Minister of State, Department of Health, HL Deb 13 June 2008 cols 248–9.
[55] *Re X (A Child) (Surrogacy: Time Limit)* [2014] EWHC 3135 (Fam) at [66]–[67].
[56] [2015] EWFC 73.
[57] Human Fertilisation and Embryology Act 2008 (Remedial) Order 2018, which came into force on 3 January 201, inserts a new s54A into the 2008 Act.

KEY CASE *A v P (Surrogacy Parental Order Death of Applicant)* [2011] EWHC 1738 (Fam)

The application for a parental order was made by Mr and Mrs A, a husband and wife, following a traditional surrogacy arrangement in which the surrogate mother was impregnated with sperm from Mr A. As the intended parents, Mr and Mrs A made the application jointly, but in between the application being made and the application being heard, Mr A died of cancer.

Theis J held that the cause of action survived his death because an application for a parental order was essentially declaratory in nature and conferred a fundamental status on an applicant and on the child, B. She then went on to consider whether the requirements for the making of a parental order in Mrs A's favour were met. While the Act required that there be more than one applicant, which there was, there was no requirement that they both be alive at the point of determination.

She then looked at whether it was in B's best interests for a parental order in favour of both Mr and Mrs A to be made rather than another kind of order, such as for adoption or a s8 Children Act child arrangements order that he live with Mrs A. She found that the consequences of not making an order were that:

- without a parental order there would be no legal relationship between B and Mr A, his biological father who was also the intended father, and B would be denied the social and emotional benefits of recognition of that relationship;
- B was already disadvantaged by the death of his biological father Mr A;
- B would potentially be financially disadvantaged (in terms of inheritance) by there not being an order recognising him as his son; and
- B would not have a legal reality which matched his day to day reality.

In her judgment, Theis J drew on both the ECHR and the UNCRC to explain why a parental order was preferable to any other order that would enable Mrs A to continue to raise the child:

> The primary aim of s54 is to allow an order to be made which has a transformative effect on the legal relationship between the child and the applicants. The effect of the order is that the child is treated as though born to the applicants. It has clear implications as regard the right to respect for family life under Article 8 [ECHR]. Family life exists in this case . . . The effect of not making an order will be an interference with that family life in that the factual relationship will not be recognised by law. . . .
>
> No other order or combination of orders will recognise B's status with both Mr and Mrs A equally. Article 8 is engaged and any interference with those rights must be proportionate and justified. In the particular circumstances of this case the interference cannot be justified as no other order can give recognition to B's status with both Mr and Mrs A in the same transformative way as a parental order can.
>
> Article 8 of the United Nations Convention of the Rights of the Child requires the State to protect the child's right to identity. . . If the consequences of a purposive construction of s54(4) is that the child's identity with his biological father is preserved and the child's identity is linked to both Mr and Mrs A the court may consider itself bound to arrive at such a conclusion on the combined reading of Article 8 ECHR and Article 8 of the UNCRC.

She therefore made a parental order in favour of Mr and Mrs A, in spite of Mr A's death. That meant that B was in the same position as any other child whose father had died.

for their biological contribution. Where the applicant is a single woman, the only way to achieve a compliant surrogacy arrangement, therefore, would be for the surrogate to be implanted with an embryo created from in-vitro fertilisation using the applicant's egg. This is a more expensive procedure and presents a difficult hurdle to those who are using surrogacy because they have difficulties conceiving rather than having difficulty carrying a pregnancy to term.

Conception not via sexual intercourse

The pregnancy must not be the result of sexual intercourse, as that is not a surrogacy situation whatever the parties' intentions.

The applicants' ages

The intended parent(s) must be aged over 18. There is no maximum age specified in the Act, but their age may be relevant to the determination of whether the making of a parental order is in the child's best interests, in that it may go to their ability to care for the child.

SCENARIO 2

Illustration 2: Rhys and Hardeep and baby Anji (2 months)

Rhys and Hardeep are currently in India and are experiencing difficulties in bringing Anji into the UK. This is a common issue with international surrogacy. They will need to seek a parental order for in order to terminate the parental status of Daya and her husband (if she has one) and become Anji's legal parents. There will need to be a parental order report by a Cafcass officer and the making of the parental order must be in Anji's best interests. There must also be a genetic relationship between one of the applicants—so either Rhys or Hardeep—and the baby. Without this, no parental order can be made.

The applicants' domicile

The intended parents, or at least one of them, must be domiciled in the UK, the Channel Islands, or the Isle of Man. Domicile is a legal term. A person's usual domicile is the domicile of their father (if he is married to their mother) or their mother (if unmarried).[58] This is known as their domicile of origin. Even if a person becomes habitually resident in another country, they do not lose that domicile of origin unless they intend to reside in the new country—their domicile of choice—as their sole or principal permanent home. Simply moving to live abroad, without that intention, is insufficient to change domicile. Indeed, a person may have homes in multiple countries, but can only have one domicile.[59] In *Re A (A Child) (Parental Order: Surrogacy Arrangement)*, for example, the applicant father was British but lived and worked in a number of other countries. It was held that he retained his domicile of origin in England because of his strong family links and his intention to

---

[58] *Udny v Udny* (1869) LR 1 Sc & Div 441 (HL).
[59] A discussion of the law relating to domicile can be found in *Z and Another v C and Another* [2011] EWHC 3181 (Fam).

return to England on his retirement.[60] Compare this to *Re G (Surrogacy: Foreign Domicile)*, in which the intended parents were Turkish and lived in Turkey. The short time they spent in the UK pursuing the surrogacy was insufficient to change domicile because they had no intention to adopt England as their domicile of choice.[61]

In *A and B v SA (Parental Order: Domicile)*, one of the two intended fathers, A, was born in Poland but resident in the US from the age of 17. His partner, B, was American. The parties moved to the UK in 2008, and had a baby in 2012 using an Indian surrogate. A's domicile of origin was therefore Poland, and B's was the United States. It was not necessary to determine whether A's domicile had changed on moving to the US as a minor, because both A and B had acquired a domicile of choice in the UK by the time they made their application for a parental order. They satisfied the domicile requirement because their move to the UK was intended to be permanent, motivated in large part by the greater legal recognition of their same-sex relationship in the UK and the protection this would accord themselves and any future children.[62] This was also a key issue for the intended fathers in *Re G and M (Parental Orders)*.[63]

The time limit for making an application

The order must be made within six months of the child's birth: s54(3). In *Re X (Children) (Parental Order: Foreign Surrogacy)*[64] the judge noted that 'no specific reason can be ascertained' for the choice of six months, which had been first set out in the Human Fertilisation and Embryology Act 1990, and in the similarly-named *Re X (A Child) (Surrogacy: Time Limit)* the court recorded that 'the Parliamentary debates are silent as to any policy underpinning' the choice of six months as opposed to any other, equally arbitrary period.[65]

However, the six months limit has been interpreted loosely. *Re X (A Child) (Surrogacy: Time Limit)* concerned a British married couple who entered into a surrogacy agreement in India, and who were unaware of the requirements of English surrogacy law, the existence of parental orders, the time limits involved, or the fact that under English law the child's legal parents were the surrogate mother and (as he consented to her implantation) her own husband, and not either intended parent. By the time the matter was heard in court, over two years had elapsed since the child was born. Although the applicants could have adopted the child, Munby P held that it would be 'nonsensical' to refuse a parental order in the circumstances: 'Parliament has not explained its thinking, but given the transcendental importance of a parental order, with its consequences stretching many, many decades into the future, can it sensibly be thought that Parliament intended the difference between six months and six months-and-one-day to be determinative and one day's delay to be fatal?'[66] Subsequently, in *D v ED (Parental Order: Time Limit)* Russell J made an order in respect of children aged 8 and 5 years respectively, on the basis that 'it would be manifestly unjust to give a delay that was innocently wrought, even a very long

---

[60] [2015] EWHC 1756 (Fam).
[61] *Re G (Surrogacy: Foreign Domicile)* [2007] EWHC 2814 (Fam).
[62] [2013] EWHC 426 (Fam).
[63] [2014] EWHC 1561 (Fam).
[64] [2008] EWHC 3030 (Fam).
[65] [2014] EWHC 3135 (Fam).
[66] [2014] EWHC 3135 (Fam) at [55].

one such as this, greater weight than the welfare of these children'.[67] In *A v C*, she made a parental order where the children concerned were 13 and 12 but the parents ignorant as to the need for an order in this jurisdiction.[68] While this does not mean that time limits are now non-existent, and the need for a case-by-case approach has been emphasised, it is likely that the children's welfare interest in the making of a 'transformative' parental order sufficiently outweighs the arbitrary statutory deadline.[69] This is one effect of the elevation of the child's welfare to paramount status.

Once started, an application takes on average around 9 to 12 months before the parental order is made.[70]

The applicants' living arrangements

At the time of the making of the parental order, s54 requires that the child's home must be with the applicants. Yet 'the concept of home must and should be construed flexibly'.[71] In *Re X (A Child) (Surrogacy: Time Limit)*, Munby P made a parental order even though the applicants were separated and the child living between two houses, on the basis that

> 'X had his "home" with the intended parents, with both of them, albeit that they lived in separate houses. He plainly did not have his home with anyone else. His living arrangements were split between the intended father and the intended mother. It can fairly be said that he lived with them.'[72]

He went on to explain that even if that interpretation was not right, he had to interpret legislation compatibly with the ECHR where possible, and in *Kroon v The Netherlands*, the European Court of Human Rights had accepted that family life existed between two parents and their children even though the parents had never married, did not cohabit, and lived in separate houses.[73] He noted that this interpretation involved 'a lesser degree of reading down' than was required in *A v P*.[74] In a further flexible interpretation, in *KB & RJ v RT*, Pauffley J held that a child lived with her parents because of the level of Skype contact she had with them, and their directing her day to day care, despite the parents being in the UK and the child, for reasons of immigration difficulties caused by the lack of a parental order, being stranded in India.[75]

The consent of the first legal parents

The surrogate mother must give free, full, and unconditional consent for the parental order to be made and for her legal parenthood to be extinguished. Her consent will be ineffective if given fewer than six weeks after she has given birth.[76] She is free to refuse to

---

[67] [2015] EWHC 911 (Fam).
[68] [2016] EWFC 42. The parents had entered into a surrogacy arrangement in the US and been recognised as the legal parents in that jurisdiction.
[69] See also a comment by Gillian Douglas at (2016) 46 (October) *Family Law* 1225.
[70] Law Commission Consultation Paper 244 (June 2019) at para 3.79.
[71] *KB & RJ v RT* [2016] EWHC 760 (Fam) at [45] (Pauffley J).
[72] *Re X (A Child) (Surrogacy: Time Limit)* [2014] EWHC 3135 (Fam) at [67].
[73] *Kroon and Others v The Netherlands* (Application No 18535/91) [1994] ECHR 35.
[74] *Re X (A Child) (Surrogacy: Time Limit)* [2014] EWHC 3135 (Fam) at [60]. 'Reading down' means, in this context, interpreting the Act in a way that renders it compatible with the ECHR.
[75] *KB & RJ v RT* [2016] EWHC 760 (Fam).
[76] The same restriction applies where a birth mother gives consent to her newborn being adopted.

consent, in which case a parental order cannot be made and she will remain the child's legal mother. In this jurisdiction, surrogacy agreements are unenforceable. Where the surrogate is married or in a civil partnership, or the relevant fatherhood or parenthood conditions are satisfied, the surrogate's spouse or partner will be the child's father (or second female parent as the case may be), meaning that their consent is also required.

However, where they do not consent to the parental order, the court may nevertheless make a child arrangements order under s8 Children Act 1989 that provides that the child live with the intended parents. This is what happened in our next Key Case, *Re H*.

KEY CASE *Re H (A Child) (Surrogacy Breakdown)* [2017] EWCA Civ 1798

The intended parents were a gay male couple, A and B. They mixed their sperm and this was used to fertilise an egg donated by a third party which was implanted into an experienced surrogate, C, at a clinic in Cyprus. DNA testing revealed that it was the sperm of A which had fertilised the egg, and so he was the child's biological father, but not the legal parent. The legal parents were C, because she gave birth to the child, even though she had no genetic connection to her, and D. D was C's husband, and he was the child's legal father because he consented to her surrogacy (s35), even though he also had no genetic link to the child.

At some point thereafter, C and D fell out with A and B and refused consent to the making of a parental order. The result of this was that a parental order could not be made, and C and D remained the legal parents. However, A and B sought to have the child live with them. This was opposed by C and D, who wanted to care for the child themselves.

At first instance, Theis J held that the intended parents, A and B, would not seek to exclude the surrogate and her husband from the child's life, whereas C and D would, if they had care of the child, seek to exclude A and B. The child's best interests therefore lay with living with A and B. She made a s8 child arrangements order that the child live with A and B and spend time with C and D six times per year. As a result of this, A and B obtained parental responsibility, but C and D remained the legal parents. Theis J then made a s8 prohibited steps order that limited the exercise of C and D of their parental responsibility, so that they had no decision-making powers.

C and D appealed, arguing that this was tantamount to a parental order by the back door.

Upholding Theis J's approach in the Court of Appeal, McFarlane LJ noted that the case was 'another example of the consequences of not having a properly supported and regulated framework to underpin arrangements of this kind.'[77] He held that the order made by Theis J was not tantamount to a parental order in that it did not have the same transformative effect.

A and B then sought a declaration that fact that the child's genetic father (A) could not be named on her birth certificate (because D was the child's legal father) breached the child's rights under Articles 8 and 14 ECHR.[78] Lieven J dismissed the application, holding that the interference with the child's Article 8 rights was justified, in that it pursued a number of legitimate aims:

- that there should be legal certainty as to who a child's parents are;
- the importance of not forcing gamete donors to be parents by making them automatically parents; and
- that if the genetic father could require himself to be named on the birth certificate in place of the husband then that would tip the balance towards a more enforceable, or at least

---

[77] [2017] EWCA Civ 1798.

[78] Art 14 is not a freestanding claim. It is of discrimination in the application of another ECHR right.

> compellable, position for the intended parents, contrary to the principle of non-enforceability of surrogacy agreements.
>
> She noted that 'surrogacy raises intensely difficult moral and ethical issues, where complex balances have to be drawn in any legal scheme. Those balances must seek to protect the interests of the children concerned, and take into account the wider ethical dimensions.' The current law was a proportional response to the legitimate aims that she had identified, and the interference in the child's rights was also mitigated by the fact that A and B would be able to explain her genetic heritage to her.

The outcome of *Re H* would not have been satisfying to any of the parties. The child lives with a biological parent, but not a legal parent; and the legal parents' involvement in her life was significantly curtailed. As H grows up, the effect of this situation on her will become apparent. However, the alternative is that surrogacy arrangements be commercially enforceable. Would that have been any better for the child?

Given that many applications before the courts of England and Wales relate to surrogacy arrangements effected abroad, there have been cases where the surrogate mother has handed over the child, but then cannot be found again in order to sign the necessary consent. It has been held that if all reasonable steps have been taken to try to locate the surrogate mother, a parental order can still be made absent her consent.[79] In *Re D*, however, the court could not determine whose consent was required and was thus unable to make a parental order. The Georgian surrogate's marital position could not be established as she could not be found; the agency variously described her as married, divorced, and single, but not in that order, and there was some doubt as to her identity. While the court made a s8 order that the child live with the intended parents, the child's legal parents are unknown and unlocated, a situation which will inevitably cause problems at some future point.[80]

The requirement that the arrangement be non-commercial

Under s54(8), the court must be satisfied that no money or other benefits have changed hands as consideration for the arrangement, the handing over of the child to the intended parents, the parental order itself, or the surrogate's consent to the order. These reflect the fact that surrogacy in this country must be altruistic and not commercial. However, when it makes the parental order the court can authorise payments for expenses reasonably incurred as well as other payments that fall outside the above categories, such as payments for egg donation or medical treatment.[81] There is no case that tells us what is reasonable, and the amount varies significantly by country.

---

[79] *Re D (Children) (Surrogacy: Parental Order)* [2012] EWHC 2631 (Fam). The clinic responded to enquiries made in the court proceedings with a single piece of paper on which an offensive gesture had been drawn.
[80] [2014] EWHC 2121 (Fam).
[81] *Re C (Parental Order)* [2013] EWHC 2408 (Fam) establishes that payments to egg donors or for medical treatment abroad do not fall within the 2008 Act's restrictions.

When considering sums paid, the court will take the approach set out by Theis J in Key Case *Re WT (A Child).*

In *Re A, B, and C (Infants)* the amount paid by the applicants to their three surrogates were £13,192.80, £12,477.61, and £15,000 respectively. Nevertheless, while these amounts were agreed without reference to actual expenses, the surrogates incurred a range of different costs including mattress and bedding, medications and hygiene products, maternity clothing, a mobility scooter required for a difficult pregnancy, loss of earnings, travel to hospital including for prenatal appointments, childcare for their own children when attending the ante-natal appointments, a cleaner when unable to clean due to pregnancy-triggered sciatica, takeaway meals for their children when they were unable to cook due

KEY CASE *Re WT (A Child)* [2014] EWHC 1303 (Fam)

The intended parents, who were British, used an Indian surrogate contracted by an Indian fertility clinic. They did not choose her, nor were they permitted to meet her, and information about her that the clinic provided was lacking in several respects. They paid the clinic nearly $28,000 plus some additional legal fees. Of this the surrogate herself received about $4,600.

Theis J drew together principles first established in *Re X and Y (Foreign Surrogacy)* [2008] EWHC 3030 (Fam) and *Re S (Parental Order)* [2009] EWHC 2977 (Fam) and concluded that:

- The question whether a sum paid is disproportionate to 'reasonable expenses' is a question of fact in each case. What the court will be considering is whether the sum is so low that it may unfairly exploit the surrogate mother, or so high that it may place undue pressure on her with the risk, in either scenario, that it may overbear her free will.
- The principles underpinning section 54(8), which must be respected by the court, is that it is contrary to public policy to sanction excessive payments that effectively amount to buying children from overseas.
- However, as a result of the changes brought about by the Human Fertilisation and Embryology (Parental Orders) Regulations 2010, the decision whether to authorise payments retrospectively is a decision relating to a parental order and in making that decision, the court must regard the child's welfare as the paramount consideration.
- As a consequence, 'it is difficult to imagine a set of circumstances in which, by the time an application for a parental order comes to court, the welfare of any child, particularly a foreign child, would not be gravely compromised by a refusal to make the order'. As a result: 'it will only be in the clearest case of the abuse of public policy that the court will be able to withhold an order if otherwise welfare considerations support its making', per Hedley J in *Re L (A Child) (Parental Order: Foreign Surrogacy).*[82]
- Where the applicants for a parental order are acting in good faith and without 'moral taint' in their dealings with the surrogate mother, with no attempt to defraud the authorities, and the payments are not so disproportionate that the granting of parental orders would be an affront to public policy, it will ordinarily be appropriate for the court to exercise its discretion to give retrospective authorisation, having regard to the paramountcy of the child's lifelong welfare.

---

[82] [2010] EWHC 3146 (Fam) at [10].

to nausea or sickness caused by pregnancy, and holidays to enable them to recuperate from the pregnancies. The judge authorised the payments, noting that 'any amount that [the surrogates] may have been left with at the end would have been modest if not insignificant and could not be said to approach a commercial agreement.'[83]

Re A, B, and C (Infants) concerned a UK-based arrangement, but the reality is that many surrogacy arrangements have an international element, with the surrogate mother living in a country in which commercial surrogacy is either permitted or not expressly prohibited. In these situations the surrogate may have been paid a rate above her expenses or compensation for loss of earnings during the pregnancy, and/or a profit-making agency may have levied a fee on its own behalf. Even within the UK, lack of certainty and difficulties in obtaining legal advice can cause problems. Courts are therefore often faced with a position in which the child's welfare supports the parental order being made, yet the arrangement falls foul of domestic law by having been commercial. Despite this, courts have tended to retrospectively authorise the payments and make a parental order. Indeed, some fairly large sums have been retrospectively approved, albeit after close scrutiny. The Russian surrogacy agency in *AB v DE* charged €50,000, about standard for the Russian market, of which half went to the agency and half—equivalent to one or two years' average wage in Russia—went to the surrogate. In *Re W*, the US-based surrogate received $38,500 above the agency fees of $22,000 and her expenses for carrying triplets. The court held that while this $38,500 was not for reasonable expenses, it did not constitute an inducement such as to overbear the surrogate's will, nor was it outside the amounts paid in other US surrogacy arrangements. (What is a modest amount by one country's standards maybe so great in the surrogate's country as to overbear her free will.) Indeed, there was an altruistic element to the surrogate's actions, bearing in mind the health risks in bearing triplets.[84] It did not, therefore, fall foul of public policy.

Even though courts do ask for detailed schedules of expenses and some are clearly not true expenses, there have been no cases in which a parental order was refused due to the level of payments being made. In *Whittington Hospital NHS Trust v XX*, the Supreme Court was even prepared to award the costs of international surrogacy as part of the claimant's negligence award for loss of fertility, holding that this was not contrary to public policy provided that it was reasonable for the claimant to seek the foreign commercial arrangement rather than an arrangement within the UK (although the country should have a well-established system in which the interests of all involved, including the child, were properly safeguarded).[85] The courts' task, therefore, is to police the financial arrangement with a view to considering whether it contravenes the underlying aim of the section—that it involves the purchase of a child within a jurisdiction where there is little regulation or independent oversight, and thus to ensure that the court does not approve arrangements 'in favour of people who would not have been approved as parents on welfare grounds under any set of existing law such as adoption for example if the age of the commissioning parents would have excluded them as potential adopters and/or they have previously been turned down for adoption'.[86]

[83] [2016] EWFC 33 at [22] (Russell J).
[84] [2013] EWHC 3570 (Fam).
[85] [2020] UKSC 14.
[86] *Re Z (Foreign Surrogacy: Allocation of Work: Guidance on Parental Order Reports)* [2015] EWFC 90 (Russell J).

SCENARIO 2

Illustration 3: Rhys and Hardeep and baby Anji (2 months)

As Rhys and Hardeep entered into an international surrogacy arrangement, this would almost certainly have been commercial in nature. This means that they would have paid the surrogate and the clinic or organising agency. Their payments would be a mixture of expenses incurred for the medical treatment, expenses incurred by the surrogate, and profit for the clinic and surrogate. Under English law, only the former is strictly permitted. However, the cases indicate that what the courts are really concerned about is whether the arrangement is tantamount to buying a child and whether the level of the money involved constituted an inducement such as to overbear the surrogate's will. The court will therefore consider the payments made in that light, bearing in mind that their paramount consideration is the child's welfare. This means that it is very likely to be in the child's interests to make the order even if the amounts exceed expenses by some margin. There appear to be no reported cases where a parental order has been refused purely because of the money involved.

(Note that as of the end of 2018 India banned commercial and foreign surrogacy because it had become such a popular destination.)

8.4.3 Problems with surrogacy law

At the time that the 1985 Act was passed, IVF was relatively new: the first child born through IVF was Louise Brown in 1978. The first gestational surrogacy arrangement—that is, one not using the surrogate's egg—happened in the same year. The development of these techniques presented new difficulties for the law. The 1982 Warnock committee thought that all surrogacy arrangements were 'liable to moral objection' irrespective of whether money changed hands, and were thus at pains not to encourage it. In particular they were concerned about the risk that the surrogate might be exploited.[87] That committee considered the regulation of assisted reproduction in considerable detail, and the Human Fertilisation and Embryology Act 1990 was the result of considerable work. It was, as Alghrani and Griffiths point out, one of the very first comprehensive legal regimes for assisted reproduction in the world. However, the Surrogacy Arrangements Act 1985 was a different beast, an 'ad hoc, knee jerk reaction'.[88] It was the outcome of moral panic over the birth, to a surrogate, of 'Baby Cotton', in January of that year. Outraged newspapers referenced that the surrogate had received £6,500, which she hoped to use to decorate her home. 'Sold for carpets and curtains', was one headline. 'Born to be sold', said another.[89]

The result was that while surrogacy was legally recognised, the circumstances in which this could happen were tightly constrained and although the surrogate and the intended parents were not criminalised, others involved in commercial surrogacy were at risk of

---

[87] M Warnock, *Report of the Committee of Inquiry into Human Fertilisation and Embryology* (Cmnd 9314, 1984).
[88] A Alghrani and D Griffiths 'The Regulation of Surrogacy in the United Kingdom: The Case for Reform' (2017) 29(2) *Child and Family Law Quarterly* 165.
[89] See K Gander, 'UK'S First Surrogate Mother on Carrying Someone Else's Baby and How the Law Must Change', *The Independent*, 23 March 2017.

committing an offence. The 1998 Brazier report supported the continuation of criminal sanctions but further recommended that a parental order be refused if payments in excess of expenses had been made. This would, the committee thought, incentivise people to comply with the parental order requirements (assuming that they were aware of them). The report did not lead to any legal changes.[90] Ten years later, the Human Fertilisation and Embryology Act 2008 decriminalised not-for-profit agencies but, apart from that, the 1985 criminal sanctions are still in place.

While tight regulation of surrogacy was meant to protect those involved—especially the children—from exploitation and harm, the result of over regulation and criminalisation has not been the ending of surrogacy or even of commercial surrogacy. On the contrary, surrogacy numbers are increasing. For some people it is their only method of having a child to whom they are genetically related. In particular, surrogacy is an attractive way forward for some gay couples, whereas in previous decades same-sex couples had difficulty in accessing reproductive technologies of any kind. The problem is that the laws circumscribing surrogacy have caused people to enter into international arrangements which are incompatible with our current laws. 'The reality is there is a legal commercial framework which is driven by supply and demand.'[91]

In the next sections, we look at the problems with current law and practice.

Issues relating to legal knowledge

Many legal difficulties arise because people are ignorant of domestic law until it is too late, or are trying to find ways around the limitations of our current law. One of the reasons for lack of awareness is that while advising on the law of surrogacy is not itself unlawful, negotiating a surrogacy arrangement is, and because of the risks involved many firms choose to steer away from surrogacy work altogether. The principal source of advice is non-profit organisations run by small groups of non-legally qualified, unregulated, volunteers, and sometimes they can seriously misunderstand the law with significant consequences, as in *Re X and Y (Foreign Surrogacy)*.[92] Although some of these organisations specifically suggest surrogates and intended parents consult solicitors, the parties often do not do this. This means, as Theis J has said, the intended parents may be 'inadvertently sleepwalking into an uncertain legal future for their much-wanted child. That uncertainty is very likely to be detrimental to that child's long-term welfare'.[93]

Issues with the altruistic model of surrogacy

One of the reasons for the criminalisation of certain aspects of surrogacy work is to avoid the perception (and reality) that children are being sold. However, our particular model also enables the surrogate to change her mind and remain the child's legal mother. While some will see this as an important safeguard, it may be devastating to the intended parents.

---

[90] M Brazier, *Surrogacy: Review for Health Ministers of Current Arrangements for Payments and Regulation* (Cm 4068, 1998). For a detailed discussion of this report see J Wallbank, 'Too Many Mothers? Surrogacy, Kinship and the Welfare of the Child' (2002) 10 *Medical Law Review* 271.

[91] *Re PM* [2013] EWHC 2328 (Fam).

[92] [2008] EWHC 3030 (Fam).

[93] *Re A and B (No 2 Parental Order)* [2015] EWHC 2080 (Fam).

It will also be devastating to the surrogate if the court makes a child arrangements order that the child live with the intended parents in the face of the surrogate's refusal to consent to a parental order.[94] For those surrogates who do not perceive themselves as mothers, the gap of time between the child's birth and the making of a surrogacy parental order some months later causes difficulties: the child will be living with the intended parents but at least one of them will not have parental responsibility for the child let alone be recognised as their parent. A different problem has arisen at the time of writing during the COVID-19 quarantine, which is that surrogates are unable to hand the child over to the intended parents due to lockdown and the cessation of most international travel.[95] They have been left caring for a baby that they intended to hand over much earlier, with all the associated practical and emotional problems that may bring.

International surrogacy risks

The increase in international surrogacy arrangements reflects the perceived delays and obstacles in using UK-based clinics and the associated costs compared even to commercial arrangements in some other countries. In Australia, a study of intended parents showed that domestic arrangements were less popular due to the length of the legal process and fears that the surrogate would change her mind, something less likely in the commercial context.[96] Fenton Glynn and Scherpe argue that the number of commissioning parents who are now travelling to other jurisdictions to undertake surrogacy arrangements is 'the strongest evidence that the law is outdated'. They point out that in 2015, 156 of 281 parental orders were made concerning children who were born outside the UK and surrogacy is a specific category on UK passport applications. To them, 'The increasing challenges to, and derogations from, the law indicate that it is increasingly out of date and fails to reflect current societal attitudes towards surrogacy arrangements.'[97]

International surrogacy brings with it a new set of potential risks. One of these is lack of adherence to ethical norms within the UK. A number of surrogacy situations involve UK-based surrogates travelling abroad so that they can be impregnated in a clinic outside the UK. Although there may of course be benefits relating to costs or the availability of more advanced treatment techniques abroad, the reason for this may also be because of the availability of procedures that are not ordinarily lawful in the UK, such as gender selection.

If the child is born abroad, there may well legal difficulties relating to immigration and nationality that can trap intended parents and the child abroad. Some intended parents

---

[94] In *R v Harris (Lian)* [2019] EWCA Crim 1678 a surrogate mother was jailed for repeatedly breaching a non-molestation order that protected the intended parents who had care of the child.

[95] S Kale, 'Surrogates Left Holding the Baby as Coronavirus Rules Strand Parents', *The Guardian* (London, 14 May 2020). Available at https://www.theguardian.com/lifeandstyle/2020/may/14/surrogates-baby-coronavirus-lockdown-parents-surrogacy accessed 14 May 2020.

[96] SG Everingham, MA Stafford-Bell and K Hammarberg, 'Australians' Use of Surrogacy' (2014) 201(5) *Medical Journal of Australia* 1.

[97] C Fenton-Glynn and J Scherpe, 'Surrogacy: Is the Law Governing Surrogacy Keeping Pace with Social Change?' (2017). Available at https://www.law.cam.ac.uk/sites/www.law.cam.ac.uk/files/images/www.family.law.cam.ac.uk/documents/cambridge_family_law_submission.pdf accessed 10 May 2020.

have been unable to get permission to return to the UK with the child until they are recognised as the parents, and/or because the child is seen by the country they are presently in as being the child of the surrogate alone. In *Re X and Y (Foreign Surrogacy)* the intended parents used a surrogate living in Ukraine. The Ukrainian government refused the children Ukrainian passports on the basis that the children were deemed British under Ukrainian law, which allows surrogacy, but the children were initially unable to enter the UK because, without a parental order, the children were seen by the British immigration authorities as Ukrainian. This meant that until the issue was resolved by permitting entry to the UK outside the normal immigration rules, the children were stateless.[98] Even if the intended parents are recognised as parents in the country in which the arrangement is made, they may not realise that they are not so recognised in the UK and that they have to apply for a parental order here.

Some intended parents have been caught by unanticipated and sudden changes to the law. India, which had become a popular location for international surrogacy, banned all foreign intended parents in late 2018 and provided that surrogates could bear a child only on a non-commercial basis and only for their relatives. Thailand banned commercial surrogacy after a series of high-profile scandals, including the abandonment by the intended parents of a child with Downs Syndrome.[99]

Where intended parents from other countries come to the UK for a surrogacy arrangement here, they are unable to satisfy the domicile requirements for a parental order without a permanent intention to settle here. They may not be able to take the child abroad to adopt the child in their home country because the Adoption and Children Act 2002 prohibits the removal of a British citizen child from the UK for the purposes of adoption unless certain conditions are satisfied.[100]

Risks relating to exploitation

There is a risk, particularly in commercial arrangements, that the surrogate mothers are being exploited, i.e., that the health risks that she is undertaking by becoming pregnant outweighs the financial or other benefit to her, and/or that she is not exercising her free will. This is by no means universal and many surrogates carry babies because they take pleasure from doing so notwithstanding the physical risks and irrespective of payment. Nevertheless, there are real concerns about so-called 'baby mills' involving women who are trafficked or otherwise intensely vulnerable. In 2018, 33 pregnant women in Cambodia were imprisoned for being surrogates for Chinese couples. One surrogate told *The Guardian* that she had entered into the arrangement out of financial need, not knowing that commercial surrogacy had become illegal in Cambodia. She could not afford to raise the baby, but complying with the surrogacy agreement could lead to a 20-year prison sentence.[101] Even domestically, exploitation can occur: in *Re Z (Surrogacy Arrangements)*

---

[98] *Re X and Y (Foreign Surrogacy)* [2008] EWHC 3030 (Fam). The making of a parental order, where at least one of the intended parents is a British citizen intended parent, means that the child has British citizenship.

[99] 'Couple who abandoned baby Gammy will be allowed to keep twin sister Pipah', *The Guardian* (London, 8 November 2014).

[100] See the Adoptions with a Foreign Element Regulations 2005 (SI 392/2005).

[101] See, for example, 'Pregnant Cambodian women charged with surrogacy and human trafficking', *The Guardian* (London, 7 July 2018) and '"I will not give them the baby": the plight of Cambodia's detained surrogates', *The Guardian* (London, 2 October 2018).

(Child Arrangement Orders), for example, the surrogate mother had severe learning difficulties and it was unlikely that she understood the process at all, let alone was capable of giving free and full consent.[102] There is evidence that intended parents do factor ethics into their selection of the country in which their surrogacy arrangement is to take place.[103] However, there have been situations where the agency concerned has failed to respond to the intended parents' enquiries about the surrogate's health and well-being.

Some intended parents use surrogacy because they would never be approved for adoption. In the Thai case mentioned above, the intended father had convictions for child sex offences. While the parental order reporter should be able to discover this, not all surrogacy arrangements result in a parental order application.

The ethical dimension

Last, but not least, surrogacy is seen by some as immoral, or involving the unethical commodification of women's bodies, reducing women to their wombs and desirable physical attributes. Others see it as the sale and human trafficking of children, or consider that it is innately harmful to them.[104]

Not everyone would agree that surrogacy is wrong. Some argue that it is an example of reproductive liberty in which the surrogate freely chooses to bear a child and on what terms. Some surrogates, perhaps many, take pleasure from giving a child to another couple; the intended parents gain a much-wanted child. Whether a surrogate bears a child for altruistic or practical reasons (or both, for they are not mutually exclusive), surrogacy is a form of work; it is literally labour. As such, the argument goes, it should be treated no differently to other forms of work. As Harris and Erin have argued, it is unclear 'why, for example, the use of a uterus for profit is undignified whereas the use of a brain for profit, or a hand for profit, is not.'[105]

Somewhere in between these two positions lie those who believe that 'the good ought to be encouraged and the bad discouraged'.[106] The law's difficulties are in how precisely to achieve this distinction.

While it is impossible to say that all surrogacy situations are happy and safe, a longitudinal study by Cambridge's Centre for Family Research found that surrogacy had no effect on the relationship between the child and their intended parent, or on their well-being.[107] While the children concerned were the result of UK-based 'altruistic' arrangements, a US study of children born to gay male intended parents who would have entered into a commercial arrangement found that the children 'were functioning as well or better than

---

[102] [2016] EWFC 34.

[103] Working Group on Surrogacy Law Reform, *Surrogacy in the UK: Myth Busting and Reform—Report of the Surrogacy UK Working Group on Surrogacy Law Reform* (2015).

[104] A suggestion of sources on the ethics of surrogacy can be found in the further reading list at the end of this chapter.

[105] J Harris and CA Erin, 'An Ethically Defensible Market in Organs' (2002) 325 *British Medical Journal* 114.

[106] J Wallbank, 'Too Many Mothers? Surrogacy, Kinship and the Welfare of the Child' (2002) 10 *Medical Law Review* 271.

[107] S Golombok, E Illioi, L Blake, G Roman, and V Jadva, 'A Longitudinal Study of Families Formed Through Reproductive Donation: Parent-Adolescent Relationships and Adolescent Adjustment at Age 14' (2017) 53 *Developmental Psychology* 1966.

children in the general population'.[108] (This is true of the children of same-sex parents generally, perhaps because such children are always planned for and therefore wanted.) Although these are small-scale studies, they suggest that the fact a child was conceived through surrogacy does not, in and of itself, negatively affect him.

FOCUS Think Critically

Ethics in assisted reproduction

In this chapter, we have highlighted the various ways in which a parent who is not otherwise able to conceive or carry a child can use assisted reproduction to become a parent. One in 80 children in the UK is born using assisted reproduction of some sort. We have also looked at the ways in which a person's legal status as a mother or a father may differ from their legal gender, and the law's creation of a new status, that of second female parent.

As our use of assisted reproduction technologies grows, and we recognise new statuses for those who play a part in a child's life, we need to revisit the underlying ethical considerations. The 1982 Warnock report did engage with the underlying ethical dimension—Baroness Warnock, the committee's chair, was a philosopher—but since then the law has struggled to keep up with innovations in assisted reproduction and surrogacy and the changing reasons why people are using these technologies, such as the increase in the number of same-sex couples seeking to have a child, or individuals of both sexes choosing to have children without a partner. These technologies are no longer the preserve of infertile, heterosexual, couples—although rates of infertility are increasing.[109] How should we distribute access to reproductive technologies more evenly? The costs of such treatment and their rationing or unavailability on the NHS means that those with money have access to treatments not available to everyone. Should we screen intended surrogate parents before they commission a child? How can we guard against exploitation of surrogates—or is it a job like any other? Should the clinic used by Freddy McConnell have provided him with treatment, given that he is legally male? (There are some comments about this at paragraph 124 of the judgment.) What effect, if any, do the circumstances of conception have on the children? We do know that such children are deeply loved and wanted—their parents go to enormous lengths to have them—and that (for example) there are particularly warm relationships between mothers and children born with donated sperm.[110] But that is a far cry from saying that we understand the long-term social or psychological effects. But these again will vary according to the environment in which such children are raised and the normalisation of different technologies. Despite the Human Fertilisation and Embryology Act 1990 being modernised by the 2008 Act of the same name, the fact that the Act still refers to 'the woman who gives birth' rather than 'the person who gives birth' illustrates the ways in which both law and medicine have moved on again.

There are, inevitably no easy solutions. As Fasouliotis and Schenker have observed, 'it is very difficult to find solutions to the ethical problems in reproductive technologies that are acceptable in pluralistic society'.[111] People tend to have strong views on reproductive matters, including the extent to which they are the business of the state.

[108] RJ Green, RJ Rubio, ED Rothblum, K Bergman, and KE Katuzyn, 'Gay Fathers by Surrogacy: Parenting and Well-Being of Female and Male Children' (2019) 6(3) *Psychology of Sexual Orientation and Gender Diversity* 269.
[109] V Ravitsky and S Kimmins, 'The Forgotten Men: Rising Rates of Male Infertility Urgently Require New Approaches for Its Prevention, Diagnosis and Treatment' (2019) 101(5) *Biology of Reproduction* 872.
[110] L Owen and S Golombok, 'Families Created by Assisted Reproduction: Parent–Child Relationships in Late Adolescence' (2009) 32(4) *Journal of Adolescence* 835.
[111] SJ Fasouliotis and JG Schenker, 'Ethics and Assisted Reproduction' (2000) 90(2) *European Journal of Obstetrics & Gynecology and Reproductive Biology* 171.

8.4.4 Reforming the law

At the time that the Surrogacy Arrangements Act 1985 was passed, surrogacy did not have the level of acceptance that it does today, but neither did any family form other than the traditional heterosexual conjugally-based nuclear family. When the Human Fertilisation and Embryology Act 1990 established parental orders in place of what had previously been necessary (adoption orders over a surrogate-born child), there were significantly fewer surrogacy arrangements than there are today, and they were principally used by infertile different-sex couples. Since then, families have changed in myriad ways. Same-sex couples are not subject to the same level of disapproval and can marry or enter into a civil partnership. Single parenthood is more widespread and accepted. Blended families involving children from prior relationships are common. A number of celebrities have used surrogates without attracting condemnation. Scientific advances have been made in the areas of fertility and conception. While the 2008 Act updated the 1990 Act and made important changes such as permitting non-profit agencies and providing for unmarried couples, Ghevaert and Cabeza argue that it did not go far enough and that our surrogacy law 'remains rooted in the early 1990s, designed to cater for small numbers of altruistic arrangements involving a friend or family member.'[112] As we have seen, judges have made orders in situations not envisaged when the statute was passed, such as where the applicants are separated or where one has died, where a commercial arrangement has been made, where the child has never entered the UK, and where the time limits elapsed many years ago. This is because the child, who is much wanted and loved, is already living with and attached to the surrogates, and the making of a parental order very much in the child's interests. As Fenton Glynn and Scherpe have said, 'couples seeking a child can easily sidestep domestic restrictions, presenting English courts with a *fait accompli*: the presence in the UK of the child whose welfare is paramount and effectively trumps all other considerations'.[113]

This also demonstrates, however, that the law is not currently achieving its aims. Indeed, what we consider the aims of a law on surrogacy should be may have changed. The legal regulation of surrogacy poses a dilemma. Should the law:

- Ban legal surrogacy, with the consequence that while this would reduce surrogacy, it would not end it altogether but would push people towards countries lacking effective safeguards to screen and protect the parties and the child?

- Continue to permit surrogacy within a tight framework such as by allowing altruistic arrangements only, in the knowledge that the judiciary have utilised various methods of statutory interpretation to mitigate the risks of non-compliance? The danger here is that without sufficient public information, not everyone will comply with the regulations and they may not be able to obtain a parental order contrary to the child's

---

[112] L Ghevaert and R Cabeza, 'Surrogacy, Egg Donation and Assisted Reproduction: Payments and the Conflict of Law and Policy' [2014, February] *Family Law* 215.

[113] C Fenton-Glynn and J Scherpe, 'Surrogacy: Is the Law Governing Surrogacy Keeping Pace with Social Change?' (2017). Available at https://www.law.cam.ac.uk/sites/www.law.cam.ac.uk/files/images/www.family.law.cam.ac.uk/documents/cambridge_family_law_submission.pdf accessed 10 May 2020.

interests. Only recently did the government provide guidance to all those who might be involved in surrogacy arrangements.[114]

- Be reformed to reflect the reality of modern surrogacy? This could include, for example, enabling intended parents to become the legal parents from the moment of birth, and permitting for-profit arrangements. This approach would allow greater freedom of reproductive choice and would address some of the reasons why intended parents seek arrangements abroad. We could even make surrogacy arrangements enforceable. However, this may be seen as unethical or harmful.

A working paper published by the surrogacy organisation Surrogacy UK in 2015 made a number of recommendations for reform of the law.[115] These included the pre-authorisation of parental order arrangements, so that the intended parents would obtain parenthood as soon as the child was born and would then register the birth, and the removal of the requirement of a biological link with the intended parent or one of them. This would better recognise the intention of the parties.[116] These particular recommendations were adopted by the Law Commission in its 2019 consultation paper *Building Families through Surrogacy: A New Law.*[117] It proposed the creation of a regulator to oversee surrogacies and surrogacy organisations under the auspices of the Human Fertilisation and Embryology Authority. Surrogacy organisations, as opposed to fertility clinics, are not currently regulated. It also proposed the creation of a 'new pathway'. This would apply to *domestic surrogacy arrangements only*, meaning those in which all stages take place in the UK.

The pathway would work as follows.

- The surrogate and the intended parents would need to meet certain eligibility criteria prior to conception in order to take advantage of the new pathway. If they were unable to do so, such as for safeguarding reasons, the new pathway would not apply and the situation would be addressed under a reformed parental order process. The criteria would be (1) they all receive independent legal advice; (2) they all seek counselling about the implications, as does the surrogate's spouse or civil partner, if any; (3) all parties, including the surrogate's spouse or civil partner, would be medically screened and (4) subject to criminal records checks. This would constitute an advance assessment of the welfare of the future child.

- The parties would sign a written surrogacy agreement.

- If the eligibility criteria were met, the intended parents would become the legal parents of the child from the moment of the child's birth and would be able to register that birth as the parents. The surrogate would be able to lodge a written objection within 35 days (one week fewer than the 42 days in which a birth must be registered) and if

---

[114] This was the result of a working group report set up by the surrogacy organisation Surrogacy UK. Working Group on Surrogacy Law Reform, *Surrogacy in the UK: Myth Busting and Reform—Report of the Surrogacy UK Working Group on Surrogacy Law Reform* (2015).
[115] Surrogacy UK Working Group on Surrogacy Law Reform, *Surrogacy in the UK: Myth Busting and Reform—Report of the Surrogacy UK Working Group on Surrogacy Law Reform* (2015).
[116] For an interesting article on the role of intention v gestation, see K Horsey, 'Challenging Presumptions: Legal Parenthood and Surrogacy Arrangements' (2010) 22(4) *Child and Family Law Quarterly* 449.
[117] Law Commission Consultation Paper 244 (June 2019).

she does so then legal parenthood and parental responsibility would revert to her. Where an intended parent would be a legal parent at birth under the current law (for example, as a sperm donor of an unmarried surrogate), then he would continue to be the legal parent, together with the surrogate. The surrogate's own spouse would have no rights or responsibilities (no status) capable of being transferred and recalled. The justification is that the current requirement as to spousal/partner consent 'sends an unwelcome message about a woman's bodily autonomy'.[118] However, he or she would need to satisfy the safeguarding requirements.

- Where 'for medical (whether physical or mental) or biological reasons, the single intended parent is, or both intended parents are, unable to gestate a foetus to term, or deliver a healthy baby', the requirement for a genetic link between the child and at least one intended parent would be removed. (In the case of a different-sex couple, the woman would need to be unable to gestate the child to term; the man is obviously unable to gestate a child himself. Even if he could do so, for example by retaining female organs if transgender, as in Freddy McConnell's case, he may be unable to so as this would affect his gender identity and thus harm his mental health.)

- The requirement of domicile be retained but people who are not domiciled in the UK but who are habitually resident here would also be permitted to use the pathway or apply for a parental order.

- Information about the surrogate, the intended parents, and any sperm or egg donors would be recorded on a national surrogacy register so that in due course the child could access information about their conception and birth.

Table 8.3 compares the proposed new pathway to the current system of parental orders.

Any arrangement involving other countries would not be eligible for the new pathway but would be addressed under a reformed parental order process. The requirement of a

TABLE 8.3 Comparison of the parental order route v the proposed new pathway

	Proposed new pathway	Existing parental orders route
Covers both traditional and gestational surrogacy	Yes	Yes
Allows international surrogacy arrangements	No	Yes
Permits independent surrogacy arrangements outside clinics	Yes	Yes
Compulsory safeguards before conception	Yes	No
Post-birth welfare assessment	No	Yes
Surrogate can object to acquisition of parental status by intended parents	Yes	Yes
Post-birth court hearing needed	No	Yes
Access to the new national register of surrogacy arrangements	Yes	Yes

Source: Adapted from a table on page 14 of the Law Commission's *Summary of Consultation Paper* (2019).

---

[118] Law Commission, *Building Families through Surrogacy: A New Law* (Consultation Paper 244, June 2019) para 8.9.

genetic link would remain. Additionally, there would be unified guidance on immigration and nationality, as well as provision for the legal recognition of parenthood across borders, so as to address the problem of children stranded oversees or stateless.

The Law Commission was much less clear about fees and costs. Describing the issue as one on which people have 'strongly held and opposing views', they did not make any provisional proposals.[119] Instead, they broke down different types of payment into groups, such as gifts, compensation for loss of wages, pregnancy expenses, compensation for pain and inconvenience, and a surrogacy fee, so that consultees could make responses about which groups of payment should be permitted. The outcome of the consultation is not expected until 2022.

8.5 Parental responsibility

The history of parental rights is, for the most part, a history of paternal rights or 'father-right'. Until the nineteenth century, when a child was born to a married couple, the father had sole legal authority for that child. Writing in 1770, Blackstone notes that the mother was 'entitled to no power, but only to reverence and respect'.[120] The father alone was able to decide how the child was raised, albeit that where a child was illegitimate—born to parents who were not married to one another—the mother alone had parental authority. If a woman separated from her husband, she had no right to a continuing role in her child's life. The 1839 Custody of Children Act finally gave mothers the right to petition for access to their children under the age of 7, assuming that she was of good character (not adulterous) and, of course, that she had the funds necessary to bring suit.[121] This was later expanded to encompass children under 16 and then 21, the then age of majority.

The sole authority model was convenient. It was easy to tell who had decision-making power in relation to a child, and it avoided the need for courts to act as arbiters in family disputes, something courts strongly resisted. In *Re Curtis* (1859), for example, the judge, Sir Richard Kindersley, said, that 'if it be the case . . . That the judge is armed with the authority to determine what the custody of the children of the marriage shall be, simply with reference to what is most for their interests, I can only stay that there is no such jurisdiction in this court.' He went on to describe this situation as being happy because 'If such jurisdiction existed, I suspect that the peace of half the families in this country would be disturbed.'[122] Similarly, in the now-notorious[123] case *Re Agar-Ellis* (1883), the court upheld a decision by the father to send his daughter to be cared for by clergymen over her

---

[119] Law Commission, *Building Families through Surrogacy: A New Law* (Consultation Paper 244, June 2019) para 14.1.

[120] W Blackstone, *Commentaries on the Law of England* (Clarendon Press 1770), Vol 1, Ch 16.

[121] One of the main campaigners for the Act was Caroline Norton, who, deprived of her own children unless she entered into a financial agreement favourable to her husband, wrote *Observations on the Natural Claim of a Mother to the Custody of her Children as Affected by the Common Law Right of the Father* (1837).

[122] (1859) 28 L.J.Ch. 458.

[123] Lord Upjohn described *Re Agar-Ellis* as 'dreadful' in *J v C* [1970] AC 668 and in *Hewer v Bryant* [1970] 1 QB 370 Lord Denning said 'I would get rid of the rule in *Re Agar-Ellis*. . . . The common law can, and should, keep pace with the times'. In *Gillick v West Norfolk and Wisbech Area Health Authority*, Lord Scarman referred to it as 'horrendous': [1986] AC 112, 183E.

boarding school holidays rather than by her mother, on the basis that 'the father knows far better as a rule what is good for his children than a court of justice can'.[124]

As Neale explains, it was only with the development of a discourse of child welfare that the notion of father-right gradually lost its potency.[125] The Guardianship of Infants Act 1925 was the beginning of the end for father-right, at least as far as legitimate children were concerned. (The Legitimacy Act 1959 equalised the position in relation to illegitimate children.) However, as Brophy demonstrates, those supporting the Act were equally at pains to reject the idea that maternal rights were at play.[126]

It is, as McFarlane P has written, hard to underestimate the importance of the 1925 Act.[127] It meant that if the parents divorced, the court had the power to determine with whom the child should live and other matters relating to the child's upbringing and the administration of the child's estate. Section 1 required courts to 'regard the welfare of the infant as the first and paramount consideration' and explicitly stated that they 'shall not take into consideration . . . the claim of the father, or any right at common law possessed by the father, in respect of such custody, upbringing, administration or application [to be] superior to that of the mother, or the claim of the mother [to be] superior to that of the father.' It therefore introduced into legislation, for the first time, the idea that decisions about children should be based not on parental rights or preference, but on what was best for the child. This principle, known as the welfare principle, is a fundamental element of child law, and the subject of Chapter 9. Nevertheless, the Act did not apply while marriages were in existence, and as Chapter 3 shows, divorces were not common at this time although numbers were rising. This meant that a married mother still had no ability to make decisions about her child, whether important decisions or inconsequential issues of daily parenting. Her position was only equalised by the Guardianship of Minors Act 1973, which gave both parents of legitimate children certain rights and authorities in relation to their child and gave courts the power to determine issues relating to children, including what was then termed custody and access, irrespective of their parents' marital status. Apart from the father's ability to apply to court, however, the Act did not change the position that as far as illegitimate children were concerned the mother alone had parental authority. Ironically, in relation to illegitimate children, the mother's position remained much stronger than that of the father for much longer.

In 1989, the Children Act created a new legal status: that of being a person with parental responsibility.

8.5.1 What is parental responsibility?

Parental responsibility is the 'conceptual building block' of the Children Act.[128] Most of the rights and obligations a parent has regarding a child are not because he or she is a legal parent,

---

[124] (1883) LR 24 Ch D 317, CA.

[125] B Neale, 'Theorising Family, Kinship and Social Change', CAVA Workshop Paper 6. Available at https://www.leeds.ac.uk/cava/papers/wsp6.pdf accessed 23 May 2020.

[126] Dr Julia Brophy's doctoral thesis traces the development of the law: *Law, State, and the Family: The Politics of Child Custody*. Thesis submitted to the University of Sheffield (1985).

[127] A McFarlane, 'Making Parental Responsibility Work' [2014] *Family Law* 1264.

[128] B Hoggett, The Children Bill—The Aim' [1989] *Family Law* 217.

but because he or she has parental responsibility (PR). It 'is more, much more, than a mere lawyer's concept or a principle of law. It is a fundamentally important reflection of the realities of the human condition, of the very essence of the relationship of parent and child'.[129]

The scope of PR is, as Black J said *Re D (Contact and Parental Responsibility: Lesbian Mothers and Known Father) (No 2)*, 'intangible and difficult to define precisely'.[130] Section 3(1) Children Act 1989 says that a person with parental responsibility has 'all the rights, duties, powers, responsibilities and authority which by law a parent of a child has in relation to the child and his property' without defining precisely what those are. Nevertheless, it is possible to come up with a non-definitive list derived from previous cases and specific statutory powers:

- Parental responsibility gives holders the right to make certain decisions about the child's upbringing, such as to decide the child's name,[131] where the child should live and whether he or she can leave the jurisdiction; the right to decide the child's religious upbringing and education; and the right to discipline the child.

- Parental responsibility gives holders a right to consent to, or refuse to consent to, medical treatment or assessment of the child; to child being voluntarily accommodated by the local authority under s20 (and to remove the child from that accommodation in some circumstances); to the child being interviewed by the police; and to the child's marriage or civil partnership if they are aged 16 or 17.[132]

- Parental responsibility gives holders the right to take certain legal steps or gives status in certain legal proceedings, such as the right to apply to discharge a care order (s39). It includes the right to agree to or veto the issue of a passport for the child; the right to administer the child's property and to enter into contracts relating to the child; and a right to make certain court applications without the prior permission of the court. It gives a right of access to the child's medical and educational records and even the right to determine disposal of a child's body after his death.[133]

As it is possible for a non-parent to also acquire parental responsibility, these rights and obligations may be held by non-parents.

8.5.2 Parental responsibility versus legal parenthood

Relatively few consequences stem from legal parenthood alone. These are:

- The right to make an application under s8 Children Act 1989 (specific issues, prohibited steps, and child arrangements) without prior permission from the court. Those who are PR holders but not parents may also make such applications.

- The right to reasonable contact with a child in care under s34 Children Act 1989, unless the court orders otherwise. This also applies to non-parents with PR. Note that there is no general right to contact with one's child (or parent).

---

[129] *Re H-B (Children) (Contact: Prohibition on Further Applications)* [2015] EWCA Civ 389, [72] (Sir James Munby P).
[130] [2006] EWHC 2 (Fam).
[131] For a case in which the naming of a child as an act of PR was overruled for child protection reasons, see *Re C (Children)* [2016] EWCA Civ 374.
[132] Marriage Act 1949 s3(1A).
[133] Note that these rights and duties are not absolute. This is discussed at 8.7.3.

- The right to be consulted by a local authority who is looking after a child pursuant to a care or interim care order or a s20 arrangement. This also applies to non-parents with PR.

- The duty to ensure that a child receives education that is enshrined in the Education Act 1996 applies both to parents and those with parental responsibility.

- The obligation to financially support the child. All legal parents are required to financially support the child whether or not they have parental responsibility. (Conway has called the separation of the obligation to maintain from PR 'a neat piece of legal casuistry practised only to simultaneously benefit the public purse and to score a political point'.[134]) Conversely, non-parents are not obliged to maintain the child (save for step-parents in some circumstances) even if they have PR.[135]

- A right of succession under the intestacy rules or to make an application under the Inheritance (Provision for Family and Dependants Act) 1975.

There are some powers that require *both* legal parenthood and parental responsibility. When the court wishes to make a placement or adoption order, for example, it will need the consent of those parents with parental responsibility (although it can dispense with that consent).

The division of rights and responsibilities between those with PR and those with legal parenthood may seems somewhat arbitrary, and has led John Eekelaar to ask what point there is in having a separate concept of parental responsibility.[136] Why not simply stick to legal parenthood, or make legal parenthood consequence-free and all the powers and duties incidents only of parental responsibility?

One reason for the division between PR and parenthood is that at the time that the Children Act was passed the nuclear family was no longer the dominant family form. Between the passing of the 1973 Act and the passing of the Children Act 1989, the number of divorces each year nearly doubled. As a result, many children were living in households headed by one parent only, with or without the involvement of the non-resident parent.[137] Other adults—step-parents, same-sex partners, grandparents—might be involved in the act of parenting, but without accompanying rights or responsibilities. The Children Act 'invented the concept of parental responsibility precisely to disaggregate parental status from the important role that adults—usually parents—fulfilled in the lives of children'.[138] It did this by enabling those who undertook the function of parenting to acquire parental responsibility even when they were not the child's legal parent. Nevertheless, some things were seen as so important that they required the consent of parents too, whether or not they had PR.

But the ability to give non-parent carers rights and responsibilities was matched by a significant policy decision: that fathers who were not married to their child's mother were not to acquire parental responsibility automatically. We will return to this topic once we have considered who does have parental responsibility, and how.

---

[134] H Conway, 'Parental Responsibility and the Unmarried Father' (1996) 146(6746) *The New Law Journal* 782.
[135] See Chapter 6.
[136] J Eeekelaar, 'Rethinking Parental Responsibility' [2001] *Family Law* 426.
[137] M Maclean and J Eekelaar, *The Parental Obligation: A Study of Parenthood across Households* (Hart 1997).
[138] C Lind and T Hewitt, 'Law and the Complexities of Parenting: Parental Status and Parental Function' (2009) 31(4) *Journal of Social Welfare and Family Law* 391.

8.5.3 Who has parental responsibility?

More than one person may have parental responsibility for a child at the same time (s2(5) Children Act 1989). As we shall see, not all parents have PR, and some people who are not parents can acquire it. As a result of reforms since the Children Act was passed, a wide range of people can now obtain PR, including step-parents, second female parents, and those with whom the child spends time but does not live.

A person who has PR for a child does not stop having that responsibility just because someone else acquires it. There is no maximum number of people who can have parental responsibility for a child, although it will become practically difficult to exercise when there are too many holders.

There are two groups of PR holder:

1.   Those who have it automatically by operation of law, and cannot lose it except by losing their status as parents; and

2.   Those who have to take steps to acquire parental responsibility and can lose it

Let us look at these in turn.

Those who have it automatically by operation of law

PR holders in this category can only lose PR by losing their status as parents.

a)   The child's gestational mother (the person pregnant with the child), who is also the child's legal mother, always has parental responsibility for the child: ss2(1) and 2(2)(a) Children Act 1989. In *R (on the Application of McConnell) v The Registrar General for England and Wales and others* (discussed at 8.2.3), one of the reasons given by the Court of Appeal for refusing to permit the transgender male mother to be registered as his child's father was that the fact of giving birth granted the mother automatic parental responsibility from the moment of birth and that 'someone must have parental responsibility for a newly born child, for example, to authorise medical treatment and more generally to become responsible for its care'.[139]

b)   The child's legal father acquires PR if he is married to the child's mother at the time of the child's birth. If the parents marry after the child's birth that child is legitimated by this later marriage (s2 Legitimacy Act 1976), and s1(3)(b) Family Law Reform Act 1987 says that persons legitimated are to be treated as though they were born to married parents. This would mean that the father falls into s2(1) Children Act 1989 as the married father of a child, and obtains PR because of that. Under s9 Legitimacy Act they should in fact re-register the birth even if the father is already named on the birth certificate, although this requirement is more honoured in the breach, and re-registration would also give the father parental responsibility for a child born after 1 December 2003.[140] Note that this parental responsibility is not lost on divorce.

---

[139]   [2020] EWCA Civ 559 at [64].
[140]   Legitimacy Act 1976 s9.

c) Second female parents who are married/civilly partnered to the birth mother acquire PR automatically. They also acquire it on later marriage. It is not lost if they divorce.

d) Adoptive parents obtain parental responsibility through the adoption order.

e) In surrogacy, the intended parents of the child obtain parental responsibility through the making of a parental order.

Those who have to take steps to acquire parental responsibility

All of the people in this category can lose their parental responsibility as described at 8.7.1.

a) A child's biological father, who is not married to the mother, has to take steps to acquire parental responsibility.

    i) He will acquire PR if he is named as the father on the child's birth certificate, as long as the child was born after 1 December 2003. This is the date on which the provision saying this (inserted into the Children Act by the Adoption and Children Act 2002) came into effect. If his name appears on the birth certificate of a child born before this date, he does not acquire PR in this way. This means that a father may have two children, one born before 1 December 2003 and one born after, and be named on both birth certificates, but (assuming he has taken no other steps to acquire PR) will only have PR for the younger child.

    ii) Where the entry on the birth certificate is the result of re-registration of the birth, the father will obtain PR only if no father has been previously named and the re-registration is with the mother's consent (s10A Births and Deaths Registration Act 1953), and the child was born after 1 December 2003. Where the re-registration is the result of an application to court for a declaration of parentage, which implies a lack of consent by the mother, parental responsibility is not automatically conferred because the relevant provision—s14 of the 1953 Act—is not listed in the Children Act as having this effect. It appears that the misattributed father would continue to have parental responsibility until this is specifically terminated by the court (a declaration of parentage would not achieve this), but there is no case law in relation to that point.

    iii) By entering into a parental responsibility agreement with the mother.[141] This is a simple one-page form in which the mother signs her agreement to the other parent having parental responsibility. The form is then filed at court. No hearing is necessary and there is no fee payable.

    iv) By making a successful court application for a parental responsibility order under s4 Children Act 1989. See 8.5.4.

    v) By being named in a child arrangements order as a person with whom the child will live or spend time (in the latter situation the power to grant PR is discretionary).

---

[141] Parental Responsibility Agreement Regulations 1991. (SI1991/1478).

b) Second female parents who are not married or civilly partnered to the mother (but who are second female parents because they sought assisted reproductive treatment with the mother and consented to this status) can acquire parental responsibility under ss4ZA Children Act 1989[142] through the same methods as an unmarried father, or by later marriage to the mother or civil partnership to the mother. Remember that there is no such thing in law as a second male parent.

c) A child's step-parent can obtain parental responsibility for him either through agreement with the other parent(s) with parental responsibility (via the completion of a simple form) or by the making of a court order. This could be a court order under s4A (which specifically relates to step-parents) or as a consequence of the making of a s8 child arrangements order in the step-parent's favour.

d) When the court makes a child arrangements order, any person who is named as a person with whom the child will live will get parental responsibility for the child, as the court *must* make a parental responsibility order in this situation. This lasts only for the duration of the order. However, where the person with whom the child is to live is their legal parent (including second female parent) then the parental responsibility is granted under s4 or 4ZA, which means that it will last beyond the duration of the living arrangements and can only be ended by an order specifically terminating it.

e) When the court makes a child arrangements order, any person who is named as a person with whom the child will spend time *may* get parental responsibility at the court's discretion. Thus Keehan J made an order that a 16-year-old girl's aunt have PR when the child was living with her father but seeing her aunt three times per week, the mother having died.[143] Such PR will last only for the duration of the underlying child arrangements order. However, where the person with whom the child is to spend time is their legal parent (including second female parent) then the parental responsibility is granted under s4 or 4ZA, which means that it will last beyond the duration of the child arrangements order and a specific application would need to be made to terminate it.

f) Institutional parental responsibility is acquired by the local authority on the making of an interim care order, a care order (see Chapter 12), or an emergency protection order (see Chapter 11). This PR lasts only for the duration of the order.

g) A 'special guardian' under s14C Children Act 1989 acquires parental responsibility through the making of a special guardianship order. This is important because a special guardian will be the person with whom the child lives. This legal status is discussed in Chapter 12.

h) A guardian appointed by a person with parental responsibility under his or her Will obtains parental responsibility for the child upon the death of the appointer if the appointment takes effect. It will not take effect where there is any other person with parental responsibility still alive, unless there was an order in force that named the

---

[142] This was inserted by the Human Fertilisation and Embryology Act 2008.
[143] [2018] EWHC 3834 (Fam).

deceased person as the person with whom the children lived. The court can also appoint a guardian under s5 Children Act. This is discussed further in Chapter 5.

i) The prospective adopters of a child acquire parental responsibility for the child as soon as the child is placed with them, placement being a specific legal status.[144]

SCENARIO 3

Illustration 2: Sara and Haruto and son Kenzo (5)

We have previously established that Haruto is named on Kenzo's birth certificate. As Kenzo is only aged 5, this means that he was born after 1.12.2003 and therefore being named on the birth certificate has given Haruto parental responsibility. However, as we can see, he is in the category of parents who can lose parental responsibility by court order.

FOCUS Think Critically

The position of unmarried fathers

As we have seen, fathers who are not married to their child's mother do not acquire parental responsibility automatically (the same is true of unmarried second female parents). So, part of the disaggregation of 'parenthood as a question of *fact* from parenting as an on-going child-raising *act*'[145] is that only some fathers will have PR. The law does not assume that a father who is not married to the child's mother is an appropriate person to have parental responsibility for this child. Unmarried fathers have to prove themselves in a way that mothers and married fathers do not.

That the law was constructed in this way was, of course, a deliberate policy decision. Even before the introduction of parental responsibility, unmarried fathers were unable to acquire parental rights. Underlying these concerns was the idea that whereas the mother has shown commitment to the child by gestating and giving birth to her, 'the position of the natural father may be infinitely variable', ranging from the married father to the case where there was 'only the single act of intercourse (possibly even rape)' to connect the father to the child.[146] The Law Commission had considered giving them such rights automatically in its 1982 report *Illegitimacy*, and rejected the idea principally out of concern that 'unmeritorious' fathers should not have any parental rights, a position favoured by a significant number of respondents to its consultation.[147]

Given that 'considerable social evils might have resulted if the father at the bottom end of the spectrum had been automatically granted full parental rights and duties,'[148] the Children Act

---

[144] Adoption and Children Act 2002, s25.

[145] PG Harris and RH George, 'Parental Responsibility and Shared Residence Orders: Parliamentary Intentions and Judicial Interpretations' (2010) 22(2) *Child and Family Law Quarterly* 151.

[146] *Re H (Minors) (Local Authority: Parental Rights) (No 3)* [1991] Fam 151, sub nom *Re H (Minors) (Rights of Putative Fathers)* (Balcombe LJ).

[147] Law Commission, *Family Law: Illegitimacy* (Law Com No. 118, 1982). For an argument that is largely against the acquisition of parental responsibility for unmarried fathers, see R Deech, 'The Unmarried Father and Human Rights' (1992) 4 *Journal of Child Law* 3.

[148] *Re H (Minors) (Local Authority: Parental Rights) (No 3)* [1991] Fam 151, sub nom *Re H (Minors) (Rights of Putative Fathers)* (Balcombe LJ).

continued this approach, so that an unmarried father, unlike the mother or his married counterparts, would need to persuade either the mother or the court that he was a suitable person to have PR.[149] In *McMichael v UK*, the European Court of Human Rights held that 'there exists an objective and reasonable justification for the difference in treatment between married and unmarried fathers with regard to the automatic acquisition of parental rights' and accordingly there was no breach of Article 8.[150]

In fact, most fathers were completely unaware that the concept of parental responsibility existed anyway. Research by Ros Pickford found that three-quarters of fathers, whether married or unmarried, were not aware that there was a difference in status between married and unmarried fathers. Many fathers were exercising parental responsibility—child-raising, decision-making, taking responsibility and exercising powers—without actually having it.[151] Proportionately few fathers took the steps necessary to obtain parental responsibility. As Sheldon notes, 'in 1996 there were 649,485 births registered in England and Wales, of which 35.8% were outside marriage. In the same year the courts made only 5,587 parental responsibility orders, and only around 3,000 parental responsibility agreements'.[152] This implies that parental responsibility did not matter very much—they had not been alerted to their lack of PR, so it could not be important to their daily lives. While this may have been true—and may still be true—of many people, the problem is that it is only when something terrible happens and they need that PR that they are told they do not have it. A few days after the death of a young mother, we had to tell her fiancé, the child's father, that he did not have parental responsibility for their child, and that we would need to seek an urgent order. The fact that he had unwittingly done without PR before did nothing to lessen his anger and bafflement, and his feeling of somehow being reduced in his role. When informed of the legal position, the fathers in Pickford's study felt similarly.

Pickford's research—which came too late for our client's child—was instrumental in changing the law. The Adoption and Children Act 2002 provided that if the father of a child was named on the child's birth certificate, he would acquire parental responsibility for that child. The relevant provisions came into effect on 1 December 2003 and are not retrospective, so apply only to children born on or after that date. It therefore follows that a father may have parental responsibility for one child, but not for another.

As most children's fathers are named on their birth certificate, the 2002 reforms did significantly increase the numbers of fathers with PR. Nevertheless, there remained a small proportion of birth registrations—about 7 per cent—in which the mother attended the registrar by herself and did not name a father.[153] These mothers were more likely to be younger than those who register jointly, with low incomes, low educational attainment, mental health difficulties, and insecure housing.[154] The government found that they made the decision to register solely based on a combination of factors to do with 'the rights of the child, involvement in parenting and the relationship between

---

[149] References to an unmarried father mean a father not married to his child's mother; he may of course be married to someone else.
[150] (1995) 20 EHRR 205.
[151] R Pickford, *Fathers, Marriage and the Law* (Family Policy Studies Centre 1999). This is also available in A Bainham, S Day Sclater and M Richards, *What Is a Parent? A Socio-Legal Analysis* (Hart 1999).
[152] S Sheldon, 'Unmarried Fathers and Parental Responsibility: A Case for Reform?' (2001) 9 *Feminist Legal Studies* 93. See also Lord Chancellor' Department, *Procedures for the Determination of Paternity and on the Law on Parental Responsibility for Unmarried Fathers* (HMSO 1998). 1996 is the last year on which statistics on PR agreements were collected.
[153] Department for Work and Pensions and Department for Children Schools and Families, *Joint birth registration: Recording Responsibility* (Cm 7293, 2008), at para 36.
[154] Department for Work and Pensions and Department for Children Schools and Families, *Joint birth Registration: Recording Responsibility*, (Cm 7293, 2008), at paras 40–4.

the parents', such as finance, the parents' own life experiences, experience with older children, the perceived suitability of the father, the religion of both parents, cultural expectations and the naming of the child.'[155] It was not specifically out of a desire to exclude the fathers.[156]

In 2009, the Welfare Reform Act would have made joint registration mandatory, which would have had the effect that all fathers would be registered and thus attain parental responsibility whether or not they—or the mother—wanted it. There were some exceptions to naming the father: as we have seen, under the Human Fertilisation and Embryology Act 2008, not all children have legal fathers; and some mothers may not know the father's identity or whereabouts. Some fathers will have died or lacked capacity, and some mothers may be in fear for their own or their child's safety if the father is contacted.[157] In the event, this reform was never brought into force, apparently because of opposition by registrars who did not want the role of inquisitor of reluctant parents.[158]

The rationale for mandatory joint registration was made explicit by the title of the preceding green paper, *Joint Birth Registration: Promoting Parental Responsibility*. It was hoped that having parental responsibility for the child would 'help embed a cultural norm that fathers should reach the birth of their child with an expectation that they have a clear responsibility for their child'[159] and 'encourage parents to have an ongoing relationship with their children'. It was part of a wider discourse about 'feckless fathers', the breakdown of the nuclear family, and sole parent households.[160] Joint registration was seen, at least in part, as a solution to these issues and demonstrated what Sheldon has referred to as a 'significant policy optimism' about the capacity of policy to achieve social aims.[161]

Thus, while joint birth registration would give unmarried fathers the legal status to mirror their biological contribution, it was also 'an educative device'[162] designed to cause both fathers and mothers to undertake the act of co-parenting in accordance with social norms. As McFarlane LJ said in *Re W (Direct Contact)*:

> Whether or not a parent has parental responsibility is not simply a matter that achieves the ticking of a box on a form. It is significant matter of status as between a parent and a child, and just as important, as between each of the parents. By stressing the 'responsibility' which is so clearly given prominence in the Children Act 1989 . . . it is hoped that some parents may be encouraged more readily to engage with the difficulties that undoubtedly arise when contemplating post separation contact than may hitherto have been the case.[163]

[155] Department for Work and Pensions and Department for Children Schools and Families, *Joint birth registration: recording responsibility*, Cm 7293 (HMSO, 2008) para 47.

[156] For evidence that mothers do not generally seek to exclude fathers, see J Graham, C Creegan, M Barnard, A Mowlam, and S McKay, *Sole and Joint Birth Registration: Exploring the Circumstances, Choices and Motivations of Unmarried Parents*. Department for Work and Pensions Research Report No 463 (HMSO 2007).

[157] On this, the mother's word was not taken: if the child was conceived through rape, a conviction would support a refusal to register the further; if registration was not in the child's interests a social worker or medical professional could provide the evidence required.

[158] For a discussion of the registrars' role and position, see C Barton, 'Joint Birth Registration: "Recording Responsibility" Responsibly?' [2008, August] *Family Law* 789 and A Bainham, 'What is the point of Birth Registration?' (2008) 20(4) *Child and Family Law Quarterly* 449.

[159] Department for Work and Pensions and Department for Children Schools and Families, *Joint Birth Registration: Recording Responsibility*, Cm 7293 (HMSO, 2008) at paras 19 and 23.

[160] J Wallbank. '"Bodies in the Shadows": Joint Birth Registration, Parental Responsibility, and Social Class' (2009) 21(3) *Child and Family Law Quarterly* 267. For the rhetoric of the absent father in child support, see Chapter 6, and for an explanation of the Baby P case, see Chapter 11.

[161] S Sheldon, 'From "Absent Objects of Blame" to "Fathers Who Want to Take Responsibility": Reforming Birth Registration Law' (2009) 31(4) *Journal of Social Welfare and Family Law* 373.

[162] J Wallbank. '"Bodies in the Shadows": Joint Birth Registration, Parental Responsibility, and Social Class' (2009) 21(3) *Child and Family Law Quarterly* 267.

[163] [2012] EWCA Civ 999.

It is no coincidence that the naming of the child's father gave convenient help to the Child Support Agency because the idea was first mooted by a Department of Work and Pensions white paper on child maintenance. By framing the problem as one of irresponsible parenthood, the government constructed the solution as lying at the hands of individual parents and was, perhaps deliberately, entirely blind to the state's role in child poverty and social marginalisation. In fact, in nearly half of sole registration cases, the father was nonetheless in regular contact with the child, and may well have been exercising parental responsibility without legally having it, and paying child support. While this is much higher proportion of no-contact than the national figure of 13 per cent of all fathers,[164] the problem lies in the assumption that joint birth registration can encourage and socially engineer successful (and safe) *acts* of co-parenting. Indeed, Sheldon has noted that the proposals paid little attention to 'a concern which was highly significant in earlier family law and policy: the potential adverse impact of recognising the genetic father on the social family unit in which a child may live with his mother and her new partner'.[165]

8.5.4 Freestanding applications for PR

If the child's legal father is not married to the mother, then he does not have parental responsibility automatically. While many fathers obtain PR by virtue of being named on the child's birth certificate, if this has not happened and the mother refuses to enter into a PR agreement, then the father's route is to apply to court for parental responsibility under s4 Children Act 1989. A second female parent who is not married to the child's mother can acquire parental responsibility under similar provisions in s4ZA.

When deciding whether the father (or second female parent) should have PR, the child's welfare is the court's paramount consideration (s1 Children Act 1989), meaning that the court will do what is best for the child. This welfare principle is the subject of our next chapter.

When working out whether it is best for the child that the parent should have PR or not, the court is guided both by statutory checklist and by previous case law. In particular, the court will consider three considerations identified by Balcombe LJ in *Re H (Minors) (Local Authority: Parental Rights) (No 3)*:

1. the degree of commitment the applicant has shown towards the child;
2. the degree of attachment between applicant and child; and
3. the reasons why the applicant is applying for the order.[166]

These three considerations are not exhaustive, and there may be other factors relevant in a given case. They are, however, 'undoubtedly, the starting-point for the making of an order'.[167]

---

[164] Eloise Poole, Svetlana Speight, Margaret O'Brien, Sara Connolly, and Matthew Aldrich, 'What Do We Know about Non-Resident Fathers?' (2013). Briefing paper available at http://www.modernfatherhood.org/wp-content/uploads/2013/11/Briefing-paper-Non-resident-fathers.pdf accessed 5 April 2019.
[165] S Sheldon, 'From "Absent Objects of Blame" to "Fathers Who Want to Take Responsibility": Reforming Birth Registration Law' (2009) 31(4) *Journal of Social Welfare and Family Law* 373.
[166] [1991] Fam 151, sub nom *Re H (Minors) (Rights of Putative Fathers)*.
[167] *Re RH (A Minor) (Parental Responsibility)* [1998] 2 FCR 89 (Butler-Sloss LJ).

The court must also consider the 'welfare checklist' contained in s1 Children Act 1989. Indeed, it is required to do so by the phrasing of s1. Again, the welfare checklist is not exhaustive and not every element of it will be relevant to the application, but it does focus the court's attention on the effect of the application on the child.

Finally, there is a statutory presumption applicable to applications for PR by fathers and second female parents, the presumption of involvement.[168] This requires courts to presume, unless the contrary is shown, that involvement of both parents in the life of the child concerned will further the child's welfare. The presumption does not always apply: it does not apply where there is evidence before the court that involvement of any kind would put the child at risk of suffering harm, and even if it does apply, it can be rebutted.[169]

Objections to the making of an order are likely to be of two kinds. Firstly, the mother may argue that the father is likely to use parental responsibility to disrupt the child's primary care rather than intervene in a way that benefits the child. Secondly, it may be that the father's existing conduct demonstrates that if he received PR he would misuse it.[170] If the father's purpose in applying is 'demonstrably improper and wrong'[171] then it may be appropriate to refuse parental responsibility, although it is possible to grant it and then restrict its use. It is important to distinguish misuse of PR from those situations in which the father may simply have a different viewpoint to that of the mother, which is an entirely legitimate consequence of parental responsibility.

The case law has shown that courts generally approach applications for PR favourably. Indeed, this was the case even before the presumption of involvement was introduced in 2014. For example, in *Re G (A Minor) (Parental Responsibility Order)*, Balcombe LJ said:

> I am quite prepared to accept that the making of a parental responsibility order requires the judge to adopt the welfare principle as the paramount consideration. But having said that, I should add that, of course, it is well established by authority that, other things being equal, it is always to a child's welfare to know and, wherever possible, to have contact with both its parents, including the parent with whom it is not normally resident, if the parents have separated.

> Therefore, prima facie, it must necessarily also be for the child's benefit or welfare that it has an absent parent sufficiently concerned and interested to want to have a parental responsibility order. In other words, I approach this question on the basis that where you have a concerned although absent father, who fulfils the other test about which I spoke in *Re H*, namely having shown a degree of commitment towards the child, it being established that there is a degree of attachment between the father and the child, and that his reasons for applying for the order are not demonstrably improper or wrong, then prima facie it would be for the welfare of the child that such an order should be made.[172]

There has also been a series of cases in which courts have talked about PR as a natural consequence of parentage, and thus something that all parents should have. The

---

[168] The Children and Families Act 2014 inserted a new s1(2A) into the Children Act 1989.
[169] The presumption is explained in Chapter 10.
[170] S Gilmore, 'Parental Responsibility and the Unmarried Father – A New Dimension to the Debate' (2003) 15 *Child and Family Law Quarterly* 21.
[171] *Re C and V (Contact and Parental Responsibility)* [1998] 1 FLR 392 (Ward LJ).
[172] [1994] 1 FLR 504 (CA) 508A (Balcombe LJ).

main proponent of this viewpoint has been Wall LJ. In *Re S (Parental Responsibility)*, for example, he said:

> It is wrong to place undue and therefore false emphasis on the rights and duties and the powers comprised in 'parental responsibility' and not to concentrate on the fact that what is at issue is conferring upon a committed father the status of parenthood for which nature has already ordained that he must bear responsibility. There seems to me to be all too frequently a failure to appreciate that the wide exercise of s8 orders can control the abuse, if any, of the exercise of parental responsibility which is adverse to the welfare of the child. Those interferences with the day-to-day management of the child's life have nothing to do with whether or not this order should be allowed.
>
> There is another important emphasis I would wish to make. I have heard, up and down the land, psychiatrists tell me how important it is that children grow up with good self-esteem and how much they need to have a favourable positive image of the absent parent. It seems to me important, therefore, wherever possible, to ensure that the law confers upon a committed father that stamp of approval, lest the child grow up with some belief that he is in some way disqualified from fulfilling his role and that the reason for the disqualification is something inherent which will be inherited by the child, making her struggle to find her own identity all the more fraught.[173]

In *Re C and V (Contact and Parental Responsibility)* Thorpe LJ used language taken from *Re S* to emphasise his view that PR was 'designed not to do more than confer on the natural father the status of fatherhood which a father would have when married to the mother' and that 'it is important that wherever possible, the law should confer on a concerned parent that stamp of approval'.[174]

The tendency for courts to treat parental responsibility as a natural corollary to parenthood has been the subject of some trenchant criticism. Harris and George, for example, question how it can be considered wrong 'to place emphasis on the rights and duties and powers of parental responsibility when those are the precise terms in which the Children Act defines parental responsibility'.[175] The granting of PR based on legal fatherhood defeats the purpose of parental responsibility, which was 'designed to separate out parenthood as a question of *fact* from parenting as an on-going child-raising *act*'.[176]

A second strand of criticism relates to the use of parental responsibility as a symbolic gesture rather than reflecting its function.[177] This is what Helen Reece has termed parental responsibility as 'legitimation' or 'therapy' for the benefit of the father:

> In relation to the allocation of parental responsibility, an increasingly significant element of the meaning of parental responsibility is 'a pat on the back, official confirmation' . . . Since the Children Act 1989 there has been a shift in the reasons given by the courts for granting unmarried fathers parental responsibility. In the earlier cases, the main reason. . .

---

[173] [1995] 2 FLR 648 (CA) 657 (Wall LJ).

[174] [1998] 1 FLR 392.

[175] PG Harris and RH George, 'Parental Responsibility and Shared Residence Orders: Parliamentary Intentions and Judicial Interpretations' (2010) 22(2) *Child and Family Law Quarterly* 151.

[176] PG Harris and RH George, 'Parental Responsibility and Shared Residence Orders: Parliamentary Intentions and Judicial Interpretations' (2010) 22(2) *Child and Family Law Quarterly* 151.

[177] John Eeekelaar, 'Rethinking Parental Responsibility', [2001] *Family Law* 426.

was to give him decision-making power. In the more recent cases, the reasons are less to do with decision-making and more to do with feelings and emotions. . . . The courts are on occasion deciding parental responsibility on the basis of adults' need for recognition. . . . Truly, this is parental responsibility as legitimation.[178]

The danger of this approach, say Harris and George, is that parental responsibility 'is increasingly granted to men who are going to play no real part in their children's upbringing, primarily as a means of placating them.'[179] It conflates the child's best interests with those of the father and assumes that the child will benefit from the granting of parental responsibility to an interested father. That may be the case. It may be that the father is able to exercise parental responsibility to the child's advantage and that the granting of PR encourages the father to play a continuing role in this child's life—after all, it is his child, not the exclusive possession of the mother. At worst, though, it may open the door to years of friction and contested court proceedings which may stress the child.[180]

Even if the court refuses to make an order giving the father parental responsibility, this does not necessarily mean that the father will have no involvement in the children's lives. There are cases where the father's conduct is such that it is not in the best interests of the child for there to be any contact with him for the same reasons that he should not have parental responsibility (or vice versa), but the court should address the issue of contact separately from the issue of PR even if the applications themselves are often coupled.[181] Some fathers will have contact even where they have been refused parental responsibility, as in *Re P (Parental Responsibility)*. In that case, the father was given supervised contact (because of a fear that he may sexually groom the children) but was refused PR because the court found he intended to use it abusively to undermine the mother's care.[182]

8.6 Exercising parental responsibility

Given that multiple people can have parental responsibility for a child at the same time, there is considerable scope for disagreement about the exercise of parental responsibility. The person who has day-to-day care of the child has the most scope to exercise PR, but each party may act unilaterally in most situations, and it is possible for a person to delegate his parental responsibility to another person.

8.6.1 Delegated parental responsibility

Section 2(9) states that a person with parental responsibility cannot surrender or transfer any part of their parental responsibility. However, it is possible for a person to delegate the

[178] Helen Reece, 'The Degradation of Parental Responsibility', in S Gilmore, J Herring, and R. Probert (eds), *Responsible Parents and Parental Responsibility* (Hart Publishing 2009).
[179] PG Harris and RH George, 'Parental Responsibility and Shared Residence Orders: Parliamentary Intentions and Judicial Interpretations' (2010) 22(2) *Child and Family Law Quarterly* 151.
[180] J Ashley, 'Parental Responsibility – A New Deal or a Costly Exercise?' [1999, March] *Family Law* 175.
[181] *Re W (Parental Responsibility Order: Inter-Relationship with Direct Contact)* [2013] EWCA Civ 335.
[182] [1998] 2 FLR 96.

exercise of their parental responsibility (or an aspect of it) to another person. For example, if a child's grandparents are taking her away on holiday, a document recording that a holder of parental responsibility delegates that to the grandparents for the duration of the holiday would enable the grandparents to authorise medical treatment in an emergency. The document could be time-limited, and limited as to its scope (for example, saying that it was to be exercised only for medical treatment, and only when the parents could not be reached).

8.6.2 Acts by those without PR

Some of those who undertake a parenting role towards a child will not have parental responsibility for them. This is something we discuss at 8.5.3 with particular reference to unmarried fathers who have not taken steps to acquire PR. From a legal standpoint, any actions taken which would ordinarily constitute an exercise of PR are protected by s3(5) Children Act 1989, which enables any person who does not have parental responsibility for a child but who has care of him to do 'what is reasonable in all the circumstances of the case for the purpose of safeguarding or promoting the child's welfare'. This section applies not only to parents without PR but to any adult who has care of a child, such when he is playing at a friend's house and trips over, or when a teenager seeks refuge with a friend's family after an argument with their parents. What is reasonable is situation dependent and must be for the purposes of safeguarding the child, or of promoting their welfare. Thus it would be reasonable to affix a plaster on the child's knee or accommodate a teenager overnight rather than let them sleep rough, but not to try to authorise non-urgent elective medical treatment, for example.

8.6.3 Unilateral actions and a duty to consult?

Although several people may have parental responsibility for a particular child, the Children Act contains few requirements that they agree. Indeed, s2(7) of the Act states that each PR-holder can act independently of any other.

The effect of this is that unless the Act or another statute provides otherwise, they can act unilaterally in exercising their PR.

There has been some academic discussion about whether or not there is, or should be, a duty to consult other PR holders on certain decisions. The Act makes no mention of this at all. Potter and Williams point out that a duty to consult was explicitly rejected by the Law Commission in its 1988 *Review of Child Law*, a precursor to the Children Act 1989,

> **Statutory Extract** *s2 Children Act 1989*
>
> (1) Where more than one person has parental responsibility for a child, each of them may act alone and without the other (or others) in meeting that responsibility; but nothing in this Part shall be taken to affect the operation of any enactment which requires the consent of more than one person in a matter affecting the child.

on the grounds that it would be unworkable and undesirable.[183] A duty to consult would certainly be difficult to enforce. The law would first have to decide what appropriate consultation looked like. For practical reasons, it would need to be limited only to certain important decisions. While the Law Commission thought that a duty to consult was important to preserve the equal status of parents, the reality is that a parent with day-to-day care—usually the mother—has much greater scope to exercise PR than a person who sees the child less often. As Eekelaar has pointed out, if the father is often involved with the child, and things are amicable, consultation will naturally occur anyway.[184] But what would happen if another person with parental responsibility could not be found, or where consultation simply provides a further opportunity for argument? The exercise of PR by more than one person only benefits the child if the parents can work together, even where they initially disagree. Otherwise there is a risk that it becomes a stick with which to beat the other parent.

Exceptions to unilateral exercise

There are only a few statutory exceptions to unilateral action. Where a s8 'live with' order is in force, no person may change the child's surname or remove the child from the UK (save that the person with whom the child lives may do so for up to one month).[185] When a child is the subject of a care order, the local authority has parental responsibility for him or her. In Chapter 12 we explain that this PR can be used to overrule that of the parents, but that nevertheless there are some aspects of PR that the local authority cannot exercise without court sanction, including renaming the child and consenting to serious medical treatment.

Despite the clear language of s2(7), in *Re J (Specific Issues Orders: Child's Religious Upbringing and Circumcision)* Butler-Sloss LJ listed several other situations not provided for in statute where in the Court of Appeal's view parental responsibility should not be exercised unilaterally and where the consent of all PR-holders or a court order is necessary.[186] These are:

- Decisions to consent to the sterilisation of the child. In reality, this would never be done by any surgeon without prior court approval, even if the PR holders agree. To do so would be to invite criminal and tortious liability. A court will only approve sterilisation if it was in the young woman's best interests, such as where she was unable to understand pregnancy and would be harmed by one, but no less invasive and permanent contraceptive options would work.

- Changing the child's surname. While a s8 'live with' order is in force, s13 says that no person may change a child's name, but *Re PC (Change of Surname)* extended this to all situations.[187]

---

[183] Garfield Potter and Catherine Williams, 'Parental Responsibility and the Duty to Consult: The Public's View' (2005) 17(2) *Child and Family Law Quarterly* 207; Law Commission, *Review of Child Law: Guardianship and Custody*, Law Com No 172 (HMSO, 1988), at para 2.10.

[184] John Eekelaar, 'Rethinking Parental Responsibility', [2001] *Family Law* 426.

[185] Sections 12 and 13 Children Act 1989. See Chapter 10.

[186] [2000] 1 FLR 571.

[187] [1997] 2 FLR 730. For a comment on this case, see J Eekelaar, 'Do Parents Have a Duty to Consult?' (1998) 114 *Law Quarterly Review* 337.

- Circumcision of a male child. Circumcision of a female child is more commonly known as female genital mutilation and is a criminal offence in this jurisdiction. Male circumcision is lawful.

The case of *Re C (Welfare of Child: Immunisation)* added immunisation to this list.[188]

If the PR-holders are unable to agree, the appropriate remedy is to apply to court for a prohibited steps or specific issues order under s8 Children Act 1989. The court will then determine the issue on the basis of the welfare principle—what is in the best interests of the child. It is not uncommon for courts to deal with applications about the above issues.

Some exercises of PR are, however, irreversible: a child cannot be un-immunised, for example. Judges can be extremely disapproving of some unilateral actions, such as changing a child's school. A parent who anticipates that the other parent may take a particular step should seek a prohibited steps order to prevent them from doing so, before the court is presented with an act it cannot undo.

Sometimes, a parent or other PR holder cannot be found, and this presents a real obstacle where a decision needs to be made by all PR holders. Family lawyers will be familiar with receiving telephone calls from parents who are unable to obtain a passport for their child because the Passport Office requires a signature from a parent whose location is unknown or who does not respond to contact. In this situation—usually urgent as the holiday has been booked—the only option is to apply to court for a s8 specific issues order.

SCENARIO 3

Illustration 3: Sara and Haruto and son Kenzo (5)

Both Sara and Haruto have parental responsibility for Kenzo. As Kenzo lives with Sara, she has much more scope to make everyday decisions such as when he goes to bed, or whether he can join a particular kindergarten trip to the zoo. These little things are all manifestations of parental responsibility and they can all be done unilaterally. But this does not mean that her parental responsibility is more important or more powerful. She and Haruto are completely equal in their rights and responsibilities to him.

It therefore follows that if she wishes to vaccinate or circumcise Kenzo, or change his name, then she would need Haruto's consent; and if that consent was not forthcoming then she would need to make an application to court for a specific issues order.

Haruto may be concerned that Sara may exercise her PR unilaterally about something he disagrees with, such as choice of primary school, or he may want something to happen, such as Kenzo circumcised. The only 'deal breaker' if they cannot agree is to seek a specific issues order (to decide an issue) or prohibited steps order (to prevent Sara from an exercise of her PR, temporarily while the court decides the issue, or permanently). These types of disputes would ideally be resolved out of court, perhaps with the help of a mediator.

---

[188] [2003] EWCA Civ 1148.

8.7 Removing or restricting PR

Parental responsibility will last until the child is an adult (aged 18). There are a number of exceptions to this. PR which is solely an incidence of certain orders (such as a child arrangements order specifying where the child is to live, or a special guardianship order) lasts only as long as the order is in effect. Where a child attains *Gillick* competency, a concept discussed in Chapter 9, the powers of those with parental responsibility are, in some circumstances, limited by the child's capacity to make his or her own decisions.

In this section, we look at what happens when a parent is unable or unwilling to exercise PR in a way that benefits the child.

8.7.1 Losing PR

Those who acquired parental responsibility automatically can only lose it by losing their very status as parents, i.e., when the child is adopted by a third party, or, in the case of surrogacy, the gestational mother will lose her parental responsibility to the intended parents when a parental order is made. *Apart from this, there is no way that a birth mother or married father can lose PR, however terrible they are as parents.* (Note that PR acquired through marriage to the mother is *not* lost on divorce.)

SCENARIO 1

Illustration 3: Peter and Jasmine and children Freddy (10) and Mabel (7)

Peter and Jasmine are now divorced, but their children were born during their marriage. As we have established that Peter is indeed their legal father, the position is that Peter has parental responsibility for the children. If Peter was to use his parental responsibility in a way that harmed the children, the court could restrict his use of it, wholly or in part, but, as he was married to the children's mother, it cannot be removed from him.

However, the courts *can* remove PR from those who acquired it other than automatically by operation of law: s4(2A) Children Act 1989. It can therefore be removed from all those listed at 8.5.3 as needing to take steps to acquire PR. This group notably includes fathers who are not married to the child's mother. An application to remove a person's parental responsibility is not a common application and is usually made against a background of seriously harmful behaviour by that person. In this section, we look at the leading cases, all of which involve the removal of PR from fathers as opposed to any other category of PR holder. We start with Key Case *Re P*.

Re P tells us that applications to terminate a person's PR require 'solid grounds', and that the court will consider the same factors as on an application to obtain PR. Part of this includes considering whether there is any element of PR that the parent in question would be able to exercise in a way that benefits the child. If they cannot, then removal of PR is appropriate.

KEY CASE *Re P (Terminating Parental Responsibility)* [1995] 1 FLR 1048

The child, when only nine weeks old, suffered life-threatening injuries that rendered her perma-nently disabled. The parents were not married, but the mother entered into a PR agreement with the father, giving him PR as a tactical step in the subsequent care proceedings.[189] Sometime later, the father was found to have been the perpetrator of the injuries and was subsequently gaoled. From prison, the father made an unsuccessful application for contact with the child and the mother brought an application for an order terminating his PR. Singer J terminated the PR, holding that:

· The starting point is that wanting and exercising PR is 'a laudable desire which is to be en-couraged rather than rebuffed'. Once obtained, PR 'should not be terminated in the case of a non-marital father on less than solid grounds, with a presumption for continuance rather than for termination.' The ability of a mother to make such an application therefore should 'not be allowed to become a weapon in the hands of the dissatisfied mother'.

· Applications to terminate PR should be dealt with in the same way as applications to acquire PR, so the welfare principle applies and the court should consider the parent's evidence of attachment and degree of commitment to the child. In this case, the child was only nine weeks old and any 'degree of attachment for good or for bad which the child may have felt towards her father is now a purely theoretical thing of no practical consequence. To describe anything that the father has done in relation to this child as demonstrative of a commitment to her is an abuse of language'.

· It is pertinent to consider how the court would deal with the case if the father was mak-ing an application for PR rather than having it already. It is difficult to imagine why a court would make a parental responsibility order in this case. There 'is no element of the bundle of responsibilities that make up parental responsibility which this father could in present or foreseeable circumstances exercise in a way which would be beneficial for the child.' It would be unsettling to the mother and the foster parents if the father retained his PR.

· The father has 'forfeited responsibility' for the child.

Although only a first instance decision, Singer J's approach has been highly influential. In *Re M (Minors)* the father had two convictions for threatening to kill the mother and had indecently assaulted her in front of the children. The Court of Appeal approved the ap-proach taken in *Re P*, noting that 'it would be appropriate, following the grant of parental responsibility to the father, to evaluate how he has gone about meeting that responsibility since the order was made and what benefit the children have derived from it or may be expected to derive from it in the future.' The father in that case would continue to under-mine the mother's ability to care for the children, so removal was in their best interests.[190]

In *CW v SG* (also known as *Re D*) the father was imprisoned for sexual offences against his partner's 9- and 10-year-old daughters, following which the mother applied for an order terminating his PR in respect of the 8-year-old son, D, that they had together.

---

[189] Fathers without PR are not automatically parties to care proceedings, and their consent is not needed to an adoption. Giving the father PR therefore makes him a party and requires a court wishing to approve an adoption to satisfy the legal test to dispense with the requirement that he consents. See Chapter 12.

[190] *Re M (Minors)* 11 October 1995, unreported. Discussed by S Gilmore, 'Withdrawal of Parental Responsibility: Lost Authority and a Lost Opportunity' (2015) 78(6) *Modern Law Review* 1042.

She argued that the father's continued involvement in the family would be harmful.[191] Baker J followed *Re P*, holding that 'if the father did not have parental responsibility it is inconceivable it would now be granted to him' and that 'there is no element of the bundle of responsibilities that make up parental responsibility which this father could, in present or foreseeable circumstances, exercise in a way which would be beneficial for D'. The Court of Appeal endorsed this approach, emphasising that:

> the concept of parental responsibility describes an adult's responsibility to secure the welfare of their child which is to be exercised for the benefit of the child not the adult. The all-encompassing nature of the responsibility underpins one of the principles of the Act which is the 'no order' principle in section 1(5) CA 1985: the expectation that all other things being equal parents will exercise their responsibility so as to contribute to the welfare of their child without the need for a court order defining or restricting that exercise. [It is] difficult to see how . . . the father can be said to be capable of exercising 'with responsibility' his parental rights, duties, powers, responsibilities and authority.[192]

While in these cases the fathers had been sexually abusive, albeit not necessarily to the child subject to the application, the removal of PR has not been restricted to such cases. In *C v D and Another*, the High Court terminated the parental responsibility of a man whose appalling bullying of the mother and autistic child affected the child's care so seriously that the child was placed on a child protection plan.[193]

As both *CW v SG* and *C v D* were heard after the ECHR was incorporated into domestic law, the courts concerned had to consider the human rights implications of removal. After all, removal of PR is 'more draconian in effect than a care order', in that even when a child is in care because they have suffered or are likely to suffer significant harm, the parents nevertheless retain parental responsibility.[194] The European Court of Human Rights' Commission[195] had previously considered this issue, in the Key Case *Smallwood v UK*.

In reliance on the Commission's findings that the removal of PR was capable of being objectively justified, the courts in *CW v SG* and *C v D* both held that removal was a proportional response to the situation notwithstanding the availability of alternatives restricting the scope of PR, something that is discussed in the next section.

However, the domestic stages of the decision in *Smallwood* were heard before most of the other cases on removal of PR, and the decision to remove his PR is perhaps the weakest successful application to be reported. It would be wrong to interpret *Smallwood* as suggesting that courts will remove parental responsibility on less than solid grounds. The other cases have involved a higher high level of misconduct on the part of the father.

---

[191] [2013] EWHC 854 (Fam).

[192] On appeal as *Re D (A Child)* [2014] EWCA Civ 315.

[193] [2018] EWHC 3312 (Fam). For child protection plans, see Chapter 11.

[194] S Gilmore, 'Withdrawal of Parental Responsibility: Lost Authority and a Lost Opportunity' (2015) 78(6) *Modern Law Review* 1042. Care proceedings are discussed in Chapter 12.

[195] When it existed, the Commission was a gatekeeper for the Court. Only if the Commission found that the complaint was well-founded could it proceed to the full Court.

KEY CASE *Smallwood v UK* (App No 29779/96) (1999) 27 EHRR CD 155

Mr Smallwood was an unmarried father whose parental responsibility was removed by court order. The judge looked at whether the father would have been granted parental responsibility if he was now applying for it by considering his commitment, attachment, and motives. He failed Mr Smallwood on all three elements, finding in particular that he 'was intending to use parental responsibility not for good, well-intentioned rational reasons but to have a disruptive effect, to oppose the mother's decisions and to prove that he was always right'. This decision was upheld on appeal, albeit with some hesitation, and he was refused permission to apply to the House of Lords.

Mr Smallwood then appealed to the European Court of Human Rights, arguing that the removal of his parental responsibility was a breach of his right to family life under Article 8. He also argued that had he been an unmarried mother his parental responsibility would be incapable of termination and that consequently he was discriminated against in the application of his Article 8 rights (Articles and 14 together) by reason of his status as a father.

The Commission found that there was no breach of Article 8, because although there was an interference with his right to family life, this was justified by reference to Article 8(2) as being a proportionate response to a legitimate aim. They also found that there was no breach of Article 8 combined with Article 14, because the differential treatment of unmarried mothers and unmarried fathers had been previously held to not fall foul of the Convention rights.

This is a reference to two cases previously decided by the European Court. In *Marckx v Belgium*, the Court had found that an unmarried mother and her child were a family within the protections of Article 8, and they were entitled to legal recognition of that from the point of birth.[196] However, in *Lebbink v Netherlands*, the Court held that a father who was not married to their child's mother did not automatically have family life with that child. Whether or not he did so was a question of fact 'depending upon the real existence in practice of close personal ties'. Only if family life exists as a fact are the protections of Article 8 triggered.[197] Mere biological kinship is by itself insufficient.

8.7.2 Restricting the exercise of parental responsibility

The cases we have discussed so far are those cases in which the court had the power to remove a person's parental responsibility. But that is not always the case. The parental responsibility of a mother, or of a father or second female parent who is married to the mother, cannot be removed unless that person loses their status as parent through the child being adopted, the making of a surrogacy parental order, or parentage has been misattributed. This is the case even if that person's conduct is horrendous, as in *H v A (No 1)*, a case in which the father had attempted to kill the mother and children, first by driving a flaming car into their house and then by attempting to hire a hitman.[198]

Where it is not possible to remove a person's PR, the courts may instead choose to restrict that person's exercise of it. This may also be appropriate for those situations in

---

[196] *Marckx v Belgium* App No. 6833/74 (ECtHR, 13 June 1979).
[197] *Lebbink v Netherlands* [2004] 3 FCR 59.
[198] [2015] EWFC 58.

which PR *could* be removed, but where this may be a disproportionately severe response, or where a court is determining that PR should be granted but there is nonetheless some legitimate concern that it may be misused.[199]

The mechanisms for restricting a person's PR are s91(14) orders and specific issues and prohibited steps orders under s8.

A s91(14) order prevents a person from proceeding with an application without the prior permission of a judge, who decides whether the application is to be issued (see 10.7.4). This is designed to filter out applications that are without merit or which are vexatious (designed to cause trouble), thereby reducing the stress to the respondent.

A specific issues order is an order resolving a particular issue that those with PR cannot agree, such as whether the mother should be able to take the child to France for a holiday (or permanently), what school a child should attend, or whether a child should be vaccinated. A prohibited steps issue covers the same ground, but it does so by prohibiting a person from the exercise of PR that they intend. For example, a parent may be ordered not to remove a child from a certain school, or vaccinate a child. The court can make a specific issues application on an application for a prohibited steps order, and vice versa, and which of the two is appropriate largely depends upon whether the person seeking the order is for or against the act proposed. In the context of misuse of PR, a prohibited steps order can be used to circumscribe what that person can do. This could be single-issue or it could relate to certain aspects of a child's life, or it could be tantamount to the complete removal of PR. In *H v A*, the court had no power to remove the murderous father's PR but the court made a comprehensive order that the mother did not have to consult the father about any exercise of parental responsibility, and forbidding anyone from giving him information about the mother or child. The consequence of this was that although the father retained PR, he was not able to exercise it in any way. The judge held that this interference in the father's human rights to family life was proportionate and necessary.

A prohibited steps order has also been used to help preserve the integrity of the primary family unit, in the interests of the child. *Re D (Contact and PR: Lesbian Mothers and Known Father) (No.2)* concerned, as the name suggests, a lesbian couple who had a child using sperm donated by a man that they had sought for that purpose.[200] Unfortunately, he and the two women had different understandings of the role that he would play in the child's life. The father sought PR, which was resisted by the couple. The court granted PR, because the father was committed and attached to the child, but restricted his use of it so that he was unable to make decision in relation to two aspects that had proven controversial: the child's medical treatment and schooling. This prevented him from undermining the child's day-to-day carers.

[199] *Re M (A Child)* [2013] EWCA Civ 969.
[200] [2006] EWHC 2.

SCENARIO 3

Illustration 4: Sara and Haruto and son Kenzo (5)

Sara and Haruto have not been married and Haruto is in the category of people whose PR can be removed by court order.

Given the case law that we have discussed, an application to remove Haruto's PR would need a solid foundation. It would not succeed purely on the ground that he disagreed with Sara over parenting decisions, as he is entitled to do so. The fact he turns up unannounced, and may be unpleasant when he does so, is disruptive. It may well be contrary to Kenzo's best interests. But it does not come close to justifying a removal of PR. A more proportionate approach would be to seek either a non-molestation order (see Chapter 7) or to seek a s8 order, or both. A section 8 order could provide that Kenzo live with Sara and this could be coupled with an order setting out when she was to make Kenzo available to spend time with Haruto. A prohibited steps order could also prevent Haruto from removing him from Sara's care other than at those times. A section 8 order would only be made if in Kenzo's best interests. That is the 'welfare principle' that we discuss in the next chapter.

8.7.3 Is parental responsibility absolute?

In this chapter, we have explained how parental responsibility differs from the status of being a legal parent, and how it was designed to disaggregate 'parenthood as a question of *fact* from parenting as an on-going child-raising *act*'.[201] In so doing, it moved away from notions of parental authority and emphasised the responsibility involved in raising a child. In introducing the Children Bill in Parliament, the then Lord Chancellor, Lord Mackay of Clashfern, noted that the concept of PR 'emphasises that the days when the child should be regarded as a possession of his parent – indeed when in the past they had a right to his services and to sue on their loss – are now buried forever. The overwhelming purpose of parenthood is the responsibility for caring for and raising the child to be a properly developed adult both physically and morally'.[202]

The term was therefore chosen to emphasise 'the practical reality that bringing up children is a serious responsibility'.[203] Again and again, government policy and court judgments have reiterated this and sought to use PR as a mechanism by which to improve parenting quality.[204] Yet the statutory definition of PR mentions and includes parental rights. This, says Nigel Lowe, 'immediately throws one back to the rights and duties which

[201] PG Harris and RH George, 'Parental Responsibility and Shared Residence Orders: Parliamentary Intentions and Judicial Interpretations' (2010) 22(2) *Child and Family Law Quarterly* 151.

[202] 502 HL Official Report (5th Series) Col 490.

[203] B Hoggett, 'The Children Bill – The Aim' [1989] *Family Law* 217.

[204] See L Fox Harding, '"Parental Responsibility": A Dominant Theme in British Child and Family Policy for the 1990s' (1994) 14(1/2) *International Journal of Sociology and Social Policy* 84; and J Eeekelaar, 'Parental Responsibility: State of Nature or Nature of the State?' (1991) 13(1) *Journal of Social Welfare and Family Law* 37.

"responsibility" was meant to replace'.[205] Our list of the consequences of PR also comprises mainly rights and powers.

These rights and powers are not absolute. They are subject to different kinds of interference and limitations. For example, a PR holder can discipline a child, but there are legal boundaries beyond which a parent may commit a criminal offence or his child made the subject of a care order. A PR holder can decide *how* a child is to be educated but not *whether* they are educated. Thus, a parent can select the child's school from those available or home-school the child, but is under a legal duty to provide an education and if they do not do so then the child protection functions of the state will intervene.

There are other brakes on parental authority. Holders of parental responsibility may exercise their PR unilaterally but both the Children Act 1989 and case law have identified areas of PR which require court scrutiny and/or unanimous consent. All of those with PR are equal, albeit that there is more scope for those with day-to-day care to exercise their PR than those who see the child less frequently. If PR holders disagree, and make an application under s8 Children Act 1989 for the matter to be resolved by way of a specific issues or prohibited steps order, then the determining factor will be what is best for the child, rather than what is desired by the adults. This is the welfare principle, and the paramountcy of the child's welfare in court applications is the subject of Chapter 9. It is a significant limit to the scope of parental authority, albeit only in litigated cases.

Chapter 9 will also consider a further limitation on parents' rights, namely the rights of the child. The death of the *Re Agar-Ellis* construction of parental rights was not parental responsibility in the 1989 Act, but the 1985 House of Lords decision in *Gillick v West Norfolk and Wisbech Area Health Authority*.[206] Citing Blackstone's statement that 'the power of parents over their children is derived from... their duty' and exists partly 'to enable the parent more effectually to perform his duty, and partly as a recompense for his care and trouble in the faithful discharge of it',[207] the Lords specifically disapproved *Re Agar-Ellis*, variously saying that it was 'so out of line with present day views that it should no longer be treated as having any authority' and calling it 'horrendous'.[208] Instead, the Lords returned to Blackstone's eighteenth-century *Commentaries on the Laws of England* to hold that parental rights 'exist for the benefit of the child and they are justified only in so far as they enable the parent to perform his duties towards the child'.[209] Parental rights are 'derived from parental duty'.[210] Rights encompass concomitant duties, existing for the benefit of the child, to better enable a parent to care for him. The consequence of this was that as a child attained sufficient understanding, the parental obligation was no longer needed, and she was able to exercise something akin to an autonomy right—although, as we shall see, there has been some retreat from the full implications of this.

---

[205] N. V. Lowe, 'The Meaning and Allocation of Parental Responsibility – A Common Lawyer's Perspective' (1997) 11 *International Journal of Law, Policy and the Family* 192.
[206] [1986] AC 112.
[207] W Blackstone, *Commentaries on the Laws of England* (17th edn, 1830), vol 1, p452.
[208] Lord Fraser at p173A.
[209] Lord Fraser at p170E.
[210] Lord Scarman at p184A.

Human rights law, too, serves to limit parental rights and authorities. The child is a rights-holder under both the UN Convention on the Rights of the Child and under the Human Rights Act 1998 which incorporates the European Convention on Human Rights into domestic law. In Chapter 9, we consider to what extent the twin influences of parental responsibility and the welfare principle serve to limit the child's development as an autonomous individual.

8.8 Conclusion

In this chapter, we have considered how someone is identified as the legal mother or father of a child and how new reproductive technologies, or changes of gender, have affected this assignation. As technologies develop further, and as we splinter the role of parent into different aspects, we may experience further difficulties in finding the language needed to identify what relationship someone has to a child, legally, biologically, and socially. We have also looked at the differences between being a legal parent and having parental responsibility, and seen that the law makes a distinction between married and unmarried couples in both areas. Yet many people are unaware of the nature and consequences of each status and the ways in which parenthood and parental responsibility can be lost or restricted. Depending on your age as you read this book, you may discover that a parent of yours does not have parental responsibility for you, or that you do not have parental responsibility for your children. You may agree or disagree with how the law ascribes parental responsibility, but now understand its practical significance and the messages that the law sends about the role of parents and others in raising a child. In the next chapter, we consider to what extent parents have rights over children and whether children have rights over themselves and others.

 KEY POINTS

- All children are born with a legal mother. At common law and under the Human Fertilisation and Embryology Act 2008, the child's mother is the woman who gave birth to her. At common law, the child's legal father is the biological father but there are exceptions in the Human Fertilisation and Embryology Act 2008. Where the mother is married or seeks reproductive treatment with another woman, that person may be the child's second female parent. It is only possible to lose one's status as a legal parent through the making of a surrogacy parental order or the child being adopted.

- In England and Wales, a child's birth should be registered in the first 42 days. A mother who is not married to the baby's father can choose whether to name him on the birth certificate. His consent will be sought. Where there is a dispute over paternity a court can order DNA testing of the child if it is in the child's best interests.

- Surrogacy involves a woman (the surrogate) who bears a child on behalf of another person or couple (the commissioning or intended parent(s)) who then raise the child. In England and Wales, surrogacy is lawful but heavily circumscribed. The surrogate can give up her status as parent—along with her husband if he is the legal father—in favour of the intended parent or parents, through the making of a parental order after the birth of the child. There is no consensus about how the law should regulate surrogacy.

- In 1989, the Children Act created a new legal status: that of being a person with parental responsibility. PR disaggregates 'parenthood as a question of fact from parenting as an on-going child-raising act'. Not all legal parents have PR, and it can be held by non-parents.

- All mothers, irrespective of marital status, have parental responsibility automatically. Fathers who are married to the mother also acquire parental responsibility through operation of law. Those who acquired parental responsibility automatically can only lose it by losing their very status as parents.

- Fathers who are not married to their child's mother do not acquire parental responsibility automatically but can attain it by being named on the child's birth certificate (for a child born after 1 December 2003); by entering into a PR agreement with the mother; by making a freestanding application to court for PR; or by being named in a child arrangements order a person with whom the child will live. The court can remove PR from those who acquired it other than automatically by operation of law.

 # FURTHER READING: SOME STARTING POINTS

- On the permutations by which a child can be conceived, see A Campbell, 'Conceiving Parents through Law' (2007) 21(2) *International Journal of Law, Policy and the Family* 242. The definition of a mother was addressed at length in *R (on the Application of McConnell) v The Registrar General for England and Wales and others* [2019] EWHC 2384 (Fam) and [2020] EWCA Civ 559.

- For a discussion of genetic truth v legal fiction, see A Bainham, 'Arguments about Parentage' (2008) 67(2) *Cambridge Law Journal* 322; E Jackson, 'What is a Parent?' in A Diduck and K O'Donovan (eds), *Feminist Perspectives in Family Law* (Routledge Cavendish 2006); and J Fortin, 'Children's Right to Know Their Origins – Too Far, Too Fast?' (2009) 21(3) *Child and Family Law Quarterly* 336. Cf the arguments in this article with Fortin's earlier view at (1994) 57 *Modern Law Review* 296.

- On surrogacy, see A Alghrani and D Griffiths 'The Regulation of Surrogacy in the United Kingdom: The Case for Reform' (2017) 29(2) *Child and Family Law Quarterly* 165; the report by the Working Group on Surrogacy Law Reform, *Surrogacy in the UK: Myth Busting and Reform* (2015) and the Law Commission's Consultation Paper 244 (June 2019). This is an ongoing project for the Law Commission so you should look at their website for consultation responses and their final recommendations. Dr Kirsty Horsey has written widely on surrogacy, including 'Challenging Presumptions: Legal Parenthood and Surrogacy Arrangements' (2010) 22(4) *Child and Family Law Quarterly* 449.

- We have space here for only a few recommendations on the ethics of surrogacy, but they will lead you on to further sources. We recommend R A Posner, 'The Ethics and Economics of Enforcing Contracts of Surrogate Motherhood' (1989) 5 *Journal of Contemporary Health Law and Policy* 21; A Niekerk and L van Zyl, 'The Ethics of Surrogacy: Women's Reproductive Labour' (1995) 21 *Journal of Medical Ethics* 345 and response to it at (1997) 23 *Journal of Medical Ethics* 344; M Freeman, 'Is Surrogacy Exploitive?' in S McLean (ed), *Legal Issues in Human Reproduction* (Dartmouth 1989); and SAM McLean, 'Mothers and Others: The Case for Surrogacy' in E Sutherland and A McCall Smith (eds), *Family Rights: Family Law and Medical Ethics* (Edinburgh University Press 1990).

- One of the most influential writers on parental authority and responsibility is John Eekelaar. In 'Rethinking Parental Responsibility' [2001] *Family Law* 426 he discusses the differences between PR and legal parenthood, and in 'Parental Responsibility: State of Nature or Nature of the State?' (1991) 13(1) *Journal of Social Welfare and Family Law* 37 he discusses the underlying rationale for the status. To his critiques, we should add that of Helen Reece. If you cannot get hold of 'The Degradation of Parental Responsibility', in S Gilmore, J Herring, and R Probert (eds), *Responsible Parents and Parental Responsibility* (Hart Publishing 2009), look for her subsequent article 'Parental Responsibility as Therapy' [2009, December] *Family Law* 1167.

- On the differential treatment of unmarried fathers, see Ros Pickford, *Fathers, Marriage and the Law* (Family Policy Studies Centre 1999), also in A Bainham, S Day Sclater and M Richards, *What Is a Parent? A Socio-Legal Analysis* (Hart 1999) and in summary on the Joseph Rowntree Foundation website at https://www.jrf.org.uk/report/fathers-marriage-and-law. Both Sally Sheldon and Julie Wallbank have written widely on birth registration and the position of parents: see Wallbank at (2009) 21(3) *Child and Family Law Quarterly* 267; and Sheldon at (2009) 31(4) *Journal of Social Welfare and Family Law* 373. Andrew Bainham's article 'What Is the Point of Birth Registration?' (2008) 20(4) *Child and Family Law Quarterly* 449 is very clear. John Clifton has summarised some of the research into unmarried fatherhood in an article at [2014] *Family Law* 050. Finally, Gillian Douglas has provided an overview of PR and shared care in her essay 'Commitment-Based Parenting: Parental Responsibility in English Law' in G Douglas, M Murch, V Stephens (eds.), *International and National Perspectives on Child and Family Law* (Intersentia 2018).

 Visit the **online resources** to watch a video of Polly Morgan discussing this chapter topic, and to check your understanding of this chapter with self-test questions and scenario questions.

9 Children's Rights and Welfare

LEARNING CHECKLIST

By the end of this chapter, you should be able to:

- *Explain* the welfare principle: its meaning, when it applies, and its effect on decisions relating to children's upbringing
- *Identify* and *evaluate* alternatives to the welfare principle
- *Critically evaluate* whether and to what extent children in England and Wales can be said to have moral and/or legal rights, and in what respects, by reference to academic commentary, case law, and conventions
- *Discuss* some leading cases involving children's rights
- *Explain* to what extent children have a right to decide on their own medical treatment, and *analyse* whether the approach taken by courts is compatible with interests and/or rights
- *Critically evaluate* whether there is a conflict or incompatibility between rights-based and welfare-based decision-making and the different processes involved.

SCENARIO 1

Frank and Laura and Amanda (child arrangements case)

Frank and Laura are the parents of Amanda, aged 12. Following their separation, Frank and Laura have been unable to agree where Amanda should have her primary home, or whether her time should be shared between them. Frank has now applied to court for a child arrangements order under s8 Children Act 1989.

SCENARIO 2

Mishal and Lee (medical treatment case)

Mishal is the mother of Lee, aged 17. Lee is suffering from an aggressive form of brain cancer. Neither of them want Lee to be treated with radiotherapy or chemotherapy because they believe that they have very harmful side effects. The hospital has applied to court under the inherent jurisdiction for a declaration that it would be lawful to provide this treatment.

SCENARIO 3

Claudia (judicial review)

Claudia is 15 years old and has applied for judicial review of her school's refusal to permit her to wear a 'purity ring', a symbol of her desire to stay celibate until marriage. The school does not permit students to wear jewellery. She asserts that her rights under Article 9 European Convention on Human Rights (freedom of thought, conscience, and religion) have been breached.

9.1 Introduction

In Chapter 8, we considered the concept of parental responsibility. What we did not consider, however, was the basis on which parental responsibility should be exercised. Just how should those with parental responsibility make decisions? Do adults always know best? And what about the child's views in all this? Most decisions that holders of parental responsibility make which are exercises of their parental responsibility are made outside court. Where they are unable to agree on a way forward, or a third party such as a hospital trust is concerned about a decision, courts may be asked to decide what should happen. Sometimes, courts are required to decide matters of life and death and a number of the cases discussed in this chapter are distressing because of this.

In this chapter, we are going to consider the legal principle on which most cases relating to children are decided, the welfare principle. We will consider whether this principle is compatible with an approach that respects children's rights. In Chapter 10, we look at how courts apply these principles to private law disputes about children.

9.2 The welfare principle

When court decide cases that deal with the upbringing of a child, or the administration of a child's property, s1 Children Act 1989 tells us that 'the child's welfare shall be the court's paramount consideration'. This is the welfare principle, sometimes called the paramountcy principle or the best interests test. It is a fundamentally important part of child law.

STATUTORY EXTRACT *s1 Children Act 1989*

(1) When a court determines any question with respect to—
   (a) the upbringing of a child; or
   (b) the administration of a child's property or the application of any income arising from it, the child's welfare shall be the court's paramount consideration.

The child's welfare is 'synonymous with his or her "wellbeing" and "interests"'.[1] The paramountcy of these means that they determine the outcome of the case, even in the face of other strong considerations. They are 'the trump card'.[2]

The implications of the child's welfare being paramount were discussed by the House of Lords in Key Case *J v C* (1970). Although that case predates the welfare principle as written in the Children Act 1989, it interpreted a similar paramountcy requirement in the Guardianship of Infants Act 1925.

KEY CASE *J v C* [1970] AC 668

In 1958, a child was born in England to Spanish parents. At only a few days' old, he was taken into foster care as a result of his mother's hospitalisation for tuberculosis. Once the mother recovered, the child (who is simply referred to in the decision as 'the child' or 'the infant') went back to her and the family returned to Spain. Seventeen months later the child, who was ill from malnutrition caused by the parents' poverty, returned to live with the foster parents at his mother's request. In 1963, when the child was five, the foster mother wrote 'a tactless and most unfortunate letter' to the parents about how integrated and English the child had become, and as a result of this letter the parents notified the local authority that they wanted the child back. The child was made a ward of court, meaning that no important decision could be made about him without court approval. The issue of where the child should live was not resolved by the court until 1965, when a judge decided that he should remain under the 'care and control' of the foster parents, but required them to bring him up as a Roman Catholic, like his parents, and instruct him in the Spanish language.

In 1967, the foster parents applied for the child to be raised in the Church of England so that he could join a church school choir and thereby obtain a scholarship. In response, the parents brought an application for the return of the child. The judge applied s1 Guardianship of Infants Act 1925, which required him to make the child's welfare his 'first and paramount' consideration. He decided that the child's prospects would be better in the UK than in Spain, in that he was English in his ways, close to one of his foster brothers, and that the chances of his successful adjustment in Spain were in the circumstances slight and there was a risk to his emotional stability and happiness. Even though no criticisms could be levied at his parents' ability to provide for him (their financial and health positions being significantly improved), his best interests lay with remaining with under the care and control of the foster family.

This decision was upheld by the Court of Appeal and the parents appealed again, to the House of Lords. They argued that courts should presume that a child's welfare was best served by living with his parents unless they were 'unfitted by character, conduct or position in life to have this control'. As the parents were not unfit, the court should give care and control to them.

The Lords dismissed the parents' appeal. It was impossible to say that the first instance judge had been wrong, which is a requirement of a successful appeal. By this time, the child was ten and had not seen his parents since he was three.

In a much-quoted passage, Lord MacDermott said that the requirement to regard the welfare of the child as the first and paramount consideration

> must mean more than that the child's welfare is to be treated as the top item in a list of items relevant to the matter in question. I think they connote a process whereby, when all the

---

[1] *Re B (A Minor) (Wardship: Sterilisation)* [1987] 2 WLR 1213.
[2] *Re S (A Child)* [2003] 2 FCR 577 at [62] (Hale LJ).

> relevant facts, relationships, claims and wishes of parents, risks, choices and other circum-
> stances are taken into account and weighed, the course to be followed will be that which
> is most in the interests of the child's welfare as that term has now to be understood. That
> is the first consideration because it is of first importance and the paramount consideration
> because it rules upon or determines the course to be followed.[3]
>
> The Lords held that the rights and wishes of parents were something to be assessed and weighed in
> the balance.[4] This was the approach whether the case was between parents, between parents and
> legal strangers, or between strangers only.

J v C tells us that the paramountcy of the child's interests requires that those interests determine the outcome of the case. Although in some, perhaps many, cases, the parents' wishes will be followed, that is not automatic. Another option may be best for the child. This conflict with parental rights and interests is something to which we will return later in this chapter, when we discuss the case of the terminally ill infant Alfie Evans.

The judge's decision about what is best is an objective assessment: he or she is not bound to adopt the positions of either party or the child himself. 'It is the role and duty of the court to do so and to exercise its own independent and objective judgment'.[5] This means that the judge will take all of the child's interests and needs into account and weigh up the advantages and disadvantages of each course of action until it can decide what is best for the child.[6] As we shall see, there are no limits on what these interests and needs may be.

9.2.1 When does the welfare principle apply?

The welfare principle only applies in situations relating to the upbringing of a child (defined by s105 as including the care of the child but not his maintenance) or the administration of a child's property.

It is not always clear whether an issue before the court is one that pertains to a child's upbringing sufficiently to bring it within the scope of s1 or whether the child's upbringing is tangential to the main issue. In *Re Z (A Minor) (Identification: Restrictions on Publication)*, the court was concerned with a mother's decision that her daughter—who had special educational needs and was the subject of considerable media attention—could appear in a documentary. It held that 'a question of upbringing is determined whenever the central issue before the court is one which relates to how the child is being reared'.[7] Deciding that this decision was one that related to childrearing, the court determined under the welfare principle that it was not in the child's best interests to appear in the documentary and made a s8 prohibited steps order preventing her participation. In the later case of

---

[3] 710G-H (Lord Macdermott).
[4] 715A (Lord MacDermott).
[5] *Kings College Hospital NHS Trust v Thomas and Haastrup* [2018] EWHC 127 (Fam).
[6] *Re A (Children) (Conjoined Twins: Surgical Separation)* [2001] Fam 147 (CA).
[7] *Re Z (A Minor) (Identification: Restrictions on Publication)* [1997] Fam 1, 29.

Re X (A Child) (Injunctions Restraining Publication), the terms 'upbringing' and 'rearing' were described as connoting:

> the bringing up, care for, treatment, education and instruction of the child throughout childhood by its parents or by those in loco parentis. Upbringing thus involves a process in which the parent, or other person in loco parentis, is the subject and of which the child is the object. . . . Section 1(1)(a) of the 1989 Act therefore applies only to those processes or actions of which the child is the object, and not to those in which the child is the subject.[8]

This encompasses properly made applications for a child arrangements, prohibited steps, or specific issues order under s8, applications for parental responsibility, and applications to take a child into care or for the adoption of the child (although in the latter two situations other tests in addition to the child's welfare have to be met).

The idea that we do what is best for a child also applies to the courts' exercise of the inherent jurisdiction, although the court is not applying s1 Children Act. That is because the inherent jurisdiction is a residual, non-statutory power.

FOCUS Know-How

What is a s8 order?

There are three kinds of section 8 order:

- A child arrangement order, which regulates with whom the child lives and when and with whom they spend time. This order was formerly known as a residence and contact order.
- A specific issues order, which decides a point of dispute relating to the exercise of parental responsibility, such as the medical treatment of a child.
- A prohibited steps order which controls the exercise of parental responsibility and can thus be used to prevent a PR holder from doing something such as removing the child from school.

We will discuss s8 applications in detail in Chapter 10.

FOCUS Know-How

What is the inherent jurisdiction and wardship?

Wardship is the power of the High Court to make a child a 'ward of court' so that no important step in the child's life can be taken without the court's consent. It is thus exercised to 'cast its cloak of protection over minors whose interests are at risk of harm'[9] and its use is potentially long-term. A child is made a ward of court by the making of an application not its determination, in contrast to other orders.[10] Any person with an interest in the child's welfare can start proceedings. The jurisdiction can be exercised in any High Court proceedings relating to children, including of the court's own motion.

---

[8] *Re X (A Child) (Injunctions Restraining Publication)* [2000] All ER (D) 1403.
[9] *Re Z (A Minor) (Identification: Restrictions on Publication)* [1997] Fam 1, 23 (Ward LJ).
[10] Senior Courts Act 1981, s41(2).

The wardship power derives from a king or queen's ancient obligation to protect their subjects—the *parens patriae* jurisdiction. This royal obligation arose because the child owed a corresponding duty of allegiance to the sovereign.[11] As Lord Esher MR has explained:

> It was a paternal jurisdiction, a judicially administrative jurisdiction, in virtue of which the Chancery Court was put to act on behalf of the Crown, as being the guardian of all infants, in the place of a parent, and as if it were the parent of the child, thus superseding the natural guardianship of the parent.[12]

As from the application, parental responsibility for the child lies with the court,[13] and the court must act in his best interests.[14] The parental responsibility of others is removed.

Prior to the Children Act 1989, wardship was often used by local authorities to deal with some of the deficiencies in child protection law. The Act reduced the use of wardship by making it incompatible with the making of a care or supervision order: the local authority and the courts cannot both be decision-makers for the child, and wardship would remove parental responsibility that a local authority has pursuant to a care order, just as it removes the PR of other holders.[15] These days, its primary use is where there is an international element to the case. It can be used to protect children abducted or taken abroad where it is feared they will come to harm such as forced marriage or female genital mutilation.[16] However, where the child is outside the country wardship orders should be made only with 'extreme circumspection'[17] where a 'very high threshold' of justification is met.[18]

Despite the mention by Lord Esher that wardship places the court 'in the place of a parent' the powers of the court in respect of a ward are not limited to things within the scope of parental responsibility.[19] This is because it is part of the inherent jurisdiction, the High Court's residual powers 'to make any order or determine any issue in respect of a child, . . . where it would be just and equitable to do unless restricted by legislation or case law'.[20] In other words, the inherent jurisdiction is able to fill legislative gaps. Its only limitations are where statute or case law have excluded its use.

For example, s100 Children Act 1989 explicitly prevents the High Court from exercising its inherent jurisdiction to place a child in care or supervision or local authority accommodation[21] or make a child in care a ward of court or to give a local authority the power to determine an issue of parental responsibility. It cannot therefore be used to bypass the statutory regime set out in Parts III and IV of the Children Act. On any other issue, local authorities also require leave (permission) from the court to make an application for wardship or to invoke the inherent jurisdiction. The courts can only grant leave under s100(4) if (a) the result cannot be achieved under any statutory provision that the local authority could apply under, and (b) there is reasonable cause to believe that if the inherent jurisdiction is not exercised the child is likely to suffer significant harm. In many situations, there will be a statutory provision that the local authority could use, as it can apply for a s8 prohibited steps or specific issues order with the court's permission.

---

[11] *Re P(GE) (An Infant)* [1965] Ch 568 at 587.
[12] *R v Gyngall* [1893] 2 QB 232, 23 (Lord Esher MR). For a description of the origins of wardship, see J Seymour, 'Parens Patriae and Wardship Powers: Their Nature and Origins' (1994) 14(2) *Oxford Journal of Legal Studies* 159.
[13] *T v S (Wardship)* [2011] EWHC 1608 (Fam).
[14] *Re B (A Minor) (Wardship: Sterilisation)* [1988] AC 199.
[15] S100 Children Act 1989.
[16] See, e.g., *Re S (Wardship: Peremptory Return)* [2010] EWCA Civ 465.
[17] *Al Habtoor v Fotheringham* [2001] EWCA Civ 186 at [42] (Thorpe LJ).
[18] *Re B (A Child) (Habitual Residence: Inherent Jurisdiction)* [2015] EWCA Civ 886 at [53] (Black LJ).
[19] *Re R (A Minor) (Wardship: Consent to Treatment)* [1992] Fam 11. This case is discussed at 9.5.3.
[20] Family Procedure Rules 2010, r2.3.
[21] Although a child can be made a ward if they are already voluntarily accommodated by the local authority under s20 Children Act 1989.

The limitations on applications only apply to local authorities. A hospital—another common applicant—is not limited in this way. In *Re NY (A Child)*, the Supreme Court held that where there was a choice between a s8 application (which can be heard by any family court) and invocation of the inherent jurisdiction (High Court only), the latter should hear cases of particular complexity or urgency, or where there was a need for a judge with particular expertise in cross-border cases.[22] In *Re Y (Risk of Young Person Travelling to Join IS) (No 1)*, wardship was used to prevent a 16-year-old boy from travelling abroad where it was thought he intended to join IS, Islamic State.[23] Hayden J said that wardship enabled the court 'to tailor bespoke solutions to complex and challenging situations'.[24] Although wardship itself ends when the child reaches the age of 18, the inherent jurisdiction can be utilised to protect a vulnerable adult just as it can a child, and the court's use of that in this case enabled it to protect the child into adulthood.[25]

Shortly after the decision in *Re Y*, the Court of Appeal had to deal with another case involving radicalisation in *Re M (Children)*. In that case, which was much reported in the news, a group of adults and children had left the UK to travel to Syria to join IS. They were stopped in Turkey, and eventually returned to the UK. The children were made wards of court on the local authority's application. Munby P observed 'that cases such as this demonstrate the continuing need for a remedy which, despite its antiquity, has shown, is showing and must continue to show a remarkable adaptability to meet the ever emerging needs of an ever changing world.'[26]

In addition to radicalisation cases, the inherent jurisdiction is most commonly used to make decisions about medical treatment of children, on applications brought by hospitals where the child's parents do not consent to the treatment proposed or the hospital believes that life-sustaining treatment should be withdrawn. We take a look at some of these at section 9.6.4.

The welfare principle does *not* apply:

- to situations not pertaining to the child's upbringing or property. Later in this chapter, we will look at how children have asserted their human rights under the ECHR, often through the mechanism of judicial review. Such cases are about the lawfulness of a policy or act by a public body and do not pertain to a child's upbringing.

- Where a statute lays down different criteria. One example is the requirement under the Matrimonial Causes Act 1973 that courts approaching the division of family property on divorce give 'first consideration' to the welfare of the child. First consideration is not the same as paramount consideration: it does not elevate the child's welfare above other considerations.[27] Under the Family Law Act 1996, a court, when considering whether to exclude an occupier from the family home, must consider the health and well-being of any child, but again this is not the paramount criterion.

- To a local authority's obligations under Part III Children Act towards children in its area under (see Chapter 11). If an authority had to act in the best interests of every individual child in the exercise of its duties towards all children, this would have overwhelming resource implications and issues with clashes of interests.

---

[22] [2019] UKSC 49.

[23] [2015] EWHC 2098 (Fam).

[24] *Re Y (Risk of Young Person Travelling to Join IS) (No 2)* [2015] EWHC 2099 (Fam).

[25] *In re Y (A Minor) (Wardship: Assistance on Transition to Adulthood); Practice Note* [2018] 1 WLR 66. See also Munby P's *Guidance: Radicalisation Cases in the Family Courts* [2015] Lexis Citation 240.

[26] [2015] EWHC 1433 (Fam).

[27] In *M v H* [1998] 3 WLR 485, Lord Brandon indicated that first consideration was the same as first and paramount; however, other judges and academics have drawn a clear distinction between paramountcy and first consideration.

- Although the welfare of the child may be greatly affected by the decision, the principle does not apply to decisions about whether to imprison a parent for breaching a court order.[28] If it did so, then courts would rarely make an order against a primary carer, thus seriously limiting the courts' ability to enforce compliance.
- If a person needs permission to make an application about a child's upbringing, the welfare principle does not apply to the permission application even though it would apply to the substantive application.[29]

Finally, note that outside court proceedings there is no mechanism to require parents to act in their child's best interests. When parents resolve matters themselves, which is the vast majority of the time, they may make decisions that are contrary to the interests of the child, or which focus on the child's welfare as only one in a list of relevant considerations. There are limitations, as we see in Chapter 8, such as laws on child protection and criminal law. However, outside the court process there is no obligation or mechanism to require parents to do what is best for their children and such a requirement would be unenforceable. In contrast, in a court decision under the welfare principle the child's interests never come second.

SCENARIO 1

Illustration 1: Frank and Laura and Amanda (child arrangements case)

This is the scenario that concerns Frank's application for a child arrangements order in respect of his 12-year-old daughter Amanda. As you will now know, this application will be dealt with under the welfare principle, because it pertains to Amanda's upbringing. This means that the court's role is to look at what is best for her. As we shall see, this is not always straightforward.

SCENARIO 2

Illustration 1: Mishal and Lee (medical treatment case)

This scenario concerns the opposition of 17-year-old Lee and his mother to him being treated with chemotherapy and radiotherapy. The hospital has made an application under the inherent jurisdiction of the court, but in fact the approach is the same as under the welfare principle—the court must determine whether it is in Lee's best interests to be treated against his will.

SCENARIO 3

Illustration 1: Claudia (judicial review)

Claudia has applied for judicial review of her school's refusal to permit her to wear a 'purity ring'. However, this is not a situation to which the welfare principle applies. It does not pertain to her upbringing. It is a review of the lawfulness of the school's policy, reviewable because the school is a public body.

---

[28] See Chapter 10 at 10.7.2.
[29] *Re A* [1992] 2 FLR 154.

9.2.2 How do we know what is best for a child?

The Children Act does not tell us what is meant by an evaluation of a child's best interests. Indeed, it would be difficult to do so. What is best for one child may not be what is best for another, so it depends upon the individual child. At s1(3) there is, however, a checklist of things that the courts should consider in reaching a decision. This is known as the 'welfare checklist' and it is discussed in detail in Chapter 10. The welfare checklist says that courts 'shall have regard to':

(a) the ascertainable wishes and feelings of the child concerned (considered in the light of his age and understanding);

(b) his physical, emotional and educational needs;

(c) the likely effect on him of any change in his circumstances;

(d) his age, sex, background and any characteristics of his which the court considers relevant;

(e) any harm which he has suffered or is at risk of suffering;

(f) how capable each of his parents, and any other person in relation to whom the court considers the question to be relevant, is of meeting his needs;

(g) the range of powers available to the court under this Act in the proceedings in question.

This is a non-exhaustive list and is not in any hierarchical order of importance. Which of these considerations is most important in a particular case will depend on the situation. For example, the ability of each parent to offer a child a home that meets their *physical* needs is unlikely to be the subject of much discussion in the case of a child who is not disabled, but the importance of this is likely to be greater in the case of a physically disabled child.

While the weighting of the factors may differ from case to case, consideration of the checklist is a requirement: s1(3) says the court 'shall' have regard to it. That does not necessarily mean that a judge has to go through it in his or her judgment, as long as they bear it in mind,[30] but if they do discuss the factors explicitly their decision will be very hard to appeal. As Stephen Gilmore has said, 'the Children Act retains a wide discretion while providing a structure to the exercise of discretion by introducing a checklist of factors in s1(3)'. Some judges find it helpful to draw up a balance sheet of pros and cons of different options.[31]

But—rather like the s25 criteria for financial provision on divorce[32]—the checklist tells the judge what to consider, but not why or what relative importance each consideration has in deciding the child's best interests. It is, says Peter Jackson LJ, 'obligatory, flexible and open-ended, providing the decision-maker with a workbench and tools with which to devise a proper welfare outcome'.[33]

---

[30] *Re G (Children)* [2006] UKHL 2305 at [40] (Lady Hale).
[31] As in *Re A (Medical Treatment: Male Sterilisation)* [2000] 1 FCR 193.
[32] See Chapter 4.
[33] *Re A (A Child)* [2018] EWCA Civ 2240, [14] (Peter Jackson LJ).

In reaching this welfare determination, the court is not limited only to considering certain aspects of the child's welfare such as where he will be physically better off:

> the welfare of a child is not to be measured by money only, nor by physical comfort only. The word welfare must be taken in its widest sense. The moral and religious welfare of the child must be considered as well as its physical well-being. Nor can the ties of affection be disregarded.[34]

In fact, it has been held that 'It would be undesirable and probably impossible to set bounds as to what is relevant to a welfare determination'.[35] This means that cases are fact-specific: when one considers the whole life of the child, his physical and emotional needs, his safety, his opportunities for development, what he wants himself, the approaches of each of his parents, his social and cultural opportunities, etc., no two cases are the same.

This also means that there are relatively few judgments that engage with the theoretical underpinnings of the welfare principle. The leading case doing so is Key Case *Re G (Children) (Religious Upbringing)*.

KEY CASE *Re G (Children) (Religious Upbringing)*
[2012] EWCA Civ 1233

The mother and father were part of the Hasidic Jewish community, an ultra-Orthodox branch of Judaism in which communities are tight-knit and largely closed to non-observers, and for whom religious observance governs every aspect of their lives including their food, dress, education, culture, and heritage.

Following their divorce, the mother moved away from the Hasidic way of life, but still considered herself to practise Orthodox Judaism: still highly conservative, but less so than Hasidism. For example, the mother said she might permit the children to watch television; the father, in common with most Hasidic communities, did not. With their mother they could associate with other children; with their father they could not associate with non-Hasidic children. There were contested proceedings about whether the children should live with the mother or the father. The judge at first instance made an order in favour of the mother. This meant that when the children were with their mother they practised Orthodox Judaism and when they were with their father for contact they practised Hasidic observance.

The parties also disagreed about whether their children should go to a Hasidic or Orthodox school. The Orthodox school favoured by the mother took both boys and girls, whereas the Hasidic Talmudic school was single sex. In the Talmudic school, boys did not take secular qualifications beyond GCSE, only religious qualifications. The expert evidence given to the court was that girls were educated to be mothers and not to go to university. Career opportunities for boys were very limited and for girls non-existent. The mother wanted the children to have opportunities she and the father did not have to study for A levels, go to university, and support themselves through employment.

At first instance, the court held that the children should go to the Orthodox school and made a s8 specific issues order in those terms. The basis of this decision was that the Orthodox school would avail the children of far greater opportunities in life. The Cafcass officer had 'tried to assess in which situation the children will have the most choices about relationship with both parents in the future, and the most choice about how they wish to live in the future'. The judge agreed with

---

[34] *Re McGrath (Infants)* [1893] 1 Ch 143, 148 (Lindley LJ).
[35] *Re S (Adult Patient: Sterilisation)* [2001] Fam 15, 30.

the Cafcass officer that it would cause emotional confusion for them to depend upon their mother for love and care, yet have her choices presented as undesirable, and that the Orthodox community may be more understanding of the fact the parents were separated and the religious differences between them.

The father appealed to the Court of Appeal, where the court's judgment is delivered by Munby LJ, with whom Kay LJ and Sir Stephen Sedley agreed. He discusses the meaning of welfare:

> Evaluating a child's best interests involves a welfare appraisal in the widest sense, taking into account, where appropriate, a wide range of ethical, social, moral, religious, cultural, emotional and welfare considerations. Everything that conduces to a child's welfare and happiness or relates to the child's development and present and future life as a human being, including the child's familial, educational and social environment, and the child's social, cultural, ethnic and religious community, is potentially relevant and has, where appropriate, to be taken into account. The judge must adopt a holistic approach. . . .
>
> I have referred to the child's happiness. Very recently, J Herring and C Foster have argued persuasively that behind a judicial determinations of welfare there lies an essentially Aristotelian notion of the 'good life'. What then constitutes a 'good life'? There is no need to pursue here that age-old question. I merely emphasise that happiness, in the sense in which I have used the word, is not pure hedonism. It can include such things as the cultivation of virtues and the achievement of worthwhile goals, and all the other aims which parents routinely seek to inculcate in their children.
>
> I have also referred to the child's familial, educational and social environment, and his or her social, cultural, ethnic and religious community. The well-being of a child cannot be assessed in isolation. Human beings live within a network of relationships. . . . As Herring and Foster comment, relationships are central to our sense and understanding of ourselves. Our characters and understandings of ourselves from the earliest days are charted by reference to our relationships with others. It is only by considering the child's network of relationships that their well-being can be properly considered. So a child's relationships, both within and without the family, are always relevant to the child's interests; often they will be determinative.
>
> . . . A child's welfare is to be judged today by the standards of reasonable men and women in 2012, not by the standards of their parents in 1970,[36] and having regard to the ever changing nature of our world: changes in our understanding of the natural world, technological changes, changes in social standards and, perhaps most important of all, changes in social attitudes. . ..
>
> At this point a fundamental issue has to be grappled with. What in our society today, looking to the approach of parents generally in 2012, is the task of the ordinary reasonable parent? What is the task of a judge, acting as a 'judicial reasonable parent' and approaching things by reference to the views of reasonable parents on the proper treatment and methods of bringing up children? What are their aims and objectives? These are questions which, in the forensic forum, do not often need to be asked or answered. But in a case such as this they are perhaps unavoidable.
>
> In the conditions of current society there are, as it seems to me, three answers to this question. First, we must recognise that equality of opportunity is a fundamental value of our society: equality as between different communities, social groupings and creeds, and equality as between men and women, boys and girls. Second, we foster, encourage and facilitate

---

[36] This is a reference to *J v C*, which was decided in 1970.

> aspiration: both aspiration as a virtue in itself and, to the extent that it is practical and reason-
> able, the child's own aspirations. Far too many lives in our community are blighted, even to-
> day, by lack of aspiration. Third, our objective must be to bring the child to adulthood in such
> a way that the child is best equipped both to decide what kind of life they want to lead—what
> kind of person they want to be—and to give effect so far as practicable to their aspirations.
> Put shortly, our objective must be to maximise the child's opportunities in every sphere of life
> as they enter adulthood. And the corollary of this, where the decision has been devolved to a
> 'judicial parent', is that the judge must be cautious about approving a regime which may have
> the effect of foreclosing or unduly limiting the child's ability to make such decisions in future.
>
> As the Orthodox school would avail the children of greater opportunities, it was in the interests of
> the children to go there. The Court of Appeal dismissed the father's appeal.

Munby thus equates well-being with opportunity and bringing the child to adulthood 'in such a way that the child is best equipped both to decide what kind of life they want to lead'. This is close to a philosophical argument advanced by Joel Feinberg and discussed at 9.3.1. Feinberg argues that children have the right to an open future, which means that we should not foreclose children's opportunities.

As *Re G* also demonstrates, the courts' determination of what is in the children's best interests is extremely wide: it encompasses 'everything that conduces to a child's welfare and happiness or relates to the child's development and present and future life as a human being'. The problem with this, is that 'if welfare is concerned with the full development of the child as a human being, there is no logical reason to place temporal or content-based limits on the extent of the welfare enquiry; anything that may affect that development is potentially relevant'.[37] That means that a decision must encompass a huge scope of thought. Taylor argues that 'to expect a judge to evaluate "everything that conduces to a child's welfare and happiness or relates to the child's development and present and future life as a human being, including the child's familial, educational and social environment, and the child's social, cultural, ethnic and religious community" for the next 90 years is breathtakingly ambitious.'[38] Is it something that judges, limited for time, and limited by what they know, can really do?

We now turn to consider this and other concerns about the welfare principle, before asking whether, for all its faults, there is any better basis for making decisions about children.

9.2.3 Some issues with the welfare principle

On the face of it, there are many reasons why we should do what is best for children. As a legal concept, the welfare principle it is easy to understand and those parents (and others) drawn into children proceedings are almost always supportive of it as the decision-making basis.

However, a number of through-provoking criticisms have been made.

---

[37] R Taylor, 'Secular Values and Sacred Rights: *Re G (Education: Religious Upbringing)*' (2013) 25(3) *Child and Family Law Quarterly* 336.

[38] R Taylor, 'Secular Values and Sacred Rights: *Re G (Education: Religious Upbringing)*' (2013) 25(3) *Child and Family Law Quarterly* 336.

The welfare principle's indeterminacy

In a highly influential article, Robert Mnookin has argued that judicial decisions about arrangements for children are indeterminate—incapable of being accurately resolved. He says that children cases are different to other kinds of adjudication because the parents' parties' 'attitudes, dispositions, capacities, and shortcomings' are relevant in a way that would not be the case in, for example, a commercial dispute. In contrast to other types of dispute, where the focus is on past acts and facts, children cases involve the prediction of future events:

> Applying the best-interests standard requires an individualized prediction: with whom will this child be better off in the years to come? . . . [This] depends in part on the future behavior of the parties. Because these parties will often interact in the future, this probable interaction must be taken into account in deciding what the outcome is to be. . . . Most disputes resolved by adjudication do not require predictions involving appraisals of future relationships where the "loser's" future behavior can be an important ingredient.[39]

In order for a judge to determine whether it is better for the child to live with his mother or father, Mnookin argues that the judge would need to know:

- how each parent had behaved in the past, how this had affected the child, and the child's present condition;
- the future behaviour and circumstances of each parent if the child were to remain with that parent and the effects of this behaviour and these circumstances on the child;
- the behaviour of each parent if the child were to live with the other parent and how this might affect the child;
- if the decision would require removing the child from his present circumstances, school, friends, and familiar surroundings, the effects these changes would have on the child;
- the probability of various outcomes; and
- the seriousness of possible benefits and harms associated with each.[40]

Elster has pointed out that these factors need to be known even if there are only two possible outcomes—the child lives with his mother or the child lives with his father.[41]

The behaviour of the parties during the legal proceedings also affects the outcome. 'By making certain claims, or by acceding to certain proposals, one can reveal oneself to have a character that has a bearing on the resolution of the dispute.'[42]

Mnookin ultimately concludes that while 'there are numerous competing theories of human behaviour', 'no theory at all is considered widely capable of generating reliable

---

[39] R Mnookin, 'Child Custody Adjudication: Judicial Functions in the Face of Indeterminacy' (1975) 39(3) *Law and Contemporary Problems* 226.

[40] R Mnookin, 'Child Custody Adjudication: Judicial Functions in the Face of Indeterminacy' (1975) 39(3) *Law and Contemporary Problems* 226.

[41] J Elster, *Solomonic Judgements: Studies in the Limitation of Rationality* (Cambridge University Press 1989). For an example of a case in which the parents' characters were key see *M v H (A Child) (Educational Welfare)* [2008] EWHC 324 (Fam); and Key Case *S v G* [2015] EWFC 4 in Chapter 10.

[42] J Elster, 'Solomonic Judgments: Against the Best Interest of the Child' (1987) 54 *University of Chicago Law Review* 1.

predictions about the psychological and behavioral consequences of alternative dispositions for a particular child'. In other words, no judge can accurately gauge what is in the best interests of a child in many if not all of the cases before her, because the judge lacks accurate information. Experts are often needed to help determine what is best, because this includes considerations of the parties' psychology. This comes at financial cost and delay.

It therefore follows that judicial determinations of best interests are limited by what is possible. The answer to the question in the title to this section, 'How do we know what is best for a child?', is that it is impossible to know.

SCENARIO 1

Illustration 2: Frank and Laura and Amanda (child arrangements case)

Applying Mnookin's argument to this case, the court would need to be able to predict all the possible outcomes of a decision that Amanda should live with her father or her mother. This involves predictions—based largely on the parties' personalities and past conduct—about what sort of life she would lead with each of them. But do not forget that a likely outcome whoever she lives with is that she would see the other parent for some period of time. That factor will change how she experiences life too. So do factors such as whether a parent moves house or changes job; the degree to which she can retain a friendship group or happily make new friends; whether she is destined to suffer an illness or disability; and whether a parent will repartner. Then we have to account for the fact that the decision itself will change the parties' relationships with one another. So, whatever variables are in play now, other variables will be in play in the future.

The role of discretion and values in assessing welfare

Even if, by some supernatural force, accurate prediction of all the possible consequences of the options open to the judge could be made, these do not help the judge with her ultimate problem: 'What set of values should a judge use to determine what is in a child's best interests? . . . [She] must have some way of deciding what counts as good and what counts as bad.' In *Re G*, Munby LJ defined the goal of welfare-based decisions as keeping a child's opportunities open and thereby maximising his potential as an adult. He was influenced by an article by Herring and Foster which argued that behind judicial determinations of welfare, 'at least in England and Wales, there lies an essentially Aristotelian notion of the "good life"' and that 'a judge's job in determining best interests can more accurately be described as maximising the flourishing of the human in question' rather than transient happiness or unhappiness.[43] (We will return to this notion of the good life when we consider, at 9.3, children's moral rights.)

However, Munby LJ could just as easily have decided that a different value best reflected the children's interests, such as respect for the children's own views, or (as in *Re Agar-Ellis*) that father knows best. That is because the decision in a children case is an exercise of judicial discretion: a different judge may have made a different decision on the same facts, because they attributed different weight or importance to the various factors. '[S]o long as

---

[43] J Herring and C Foster 'Welfare Means Rationality, Virtue and Altruism' (2012) 32 *Legal Studies* 480.

he or she does not claim to be applying it as a conclusive rule of law, the judge can consider almost any factor which could possibly have a bearing or a child's welfare and assign to it whatever weight he or she chooses'.[44] Yet decisions which are exercises of discretion are very hard to appeal because the appellant will struggle to show that the discretion was exercised wrongly.

The advantage of discretion is that it focuses on what is best for *this* child in *these* unique circumstances, but it does so at the expense of predictability and uniformity. As Herring has observed, 'it is not so much that judges improperly impose their own views on people, but, rather, that the welfare principle is so vague that it leaves a judge with little to go on but her or his own moral values, or those of experts.'[45] A judge may believe that young children are best with their mothers,[46] or that children are best raised by their natural parents, or any number of things about child-raising which may or may not accord with research or be shared by the wider public.[47] To repeat a wonderful phrase: 'judges are tied by the invisible threads of their own convictions'.[48] In her seminal critique of the welfare principle, Helen Reece gives an example of the case of *May v May*, in which the judge had to choose between two parents, both of whom were fit to care for the child. The mother was easy-going, having a relaxed approach to homework and television, whereas the father saw academic achievement, punctuality, the undertaking of chores and tidiness as more important. The judge saw the father's approach as better for the children, a decision that was upheld on appeal.[49] A different judge may have seen the mother's less pressured household as better. As Eekelaar has written, 'The concept of the "welfare of the child" conceals very difficult value judgments, both about our ideas about individual happiness, fulfilment and moral character and also about the organisation of our society.'

Helen Reece argues that 'the indeterminacy of children's welfare has allowed other principles and policies to exert an influence from behind the smokescreen of the paramountcy principle. Its strength 'lies in its apparent neutrality; it is a principle to which everyone can pay lip service but which can at the same time be used to justify any decision'.[50]

This has two consequences.

Firstly, it is very difficult to identify any principles that would enable parents who are thinking about going to court to predict how the courts may approach similar fact situations. People 'bargain in the shadow of law': they reach agreements outside courts by assessing what their chances are if the dispute went to court.[51] If there was more predictability, the argument is that the parties would know enough about the likely outcome of proceedings to be able to negotiate a resolution outside the court process.

---

[44] J Eekelaar, *Regulating Divorce* (Oxford University Press 1991) 125.

[45] J Herring, 'Farewell Welfare?' (2005) 27(2) *Journal of Social Welfare and Family Law* 159.

[46] See the discussion of *Brixey v Lynas* in Chapter 10.

[47] See *Re G (Children) (Residence: Same-Sex Partner)* [2006] UKHL 2305 and an excellent case note on it by Leanne Smith at (2007) 29(3/4) *Journal of Social Welfare and Family Law* 307.

[48] The Canadian judge Justice Southin in *Rockwell v Rockwell* (1998) 43 RFL 450 (BCCA) at 460; cited by S Choudhry and J Herring, *European Human Rights and Family Law* (Hart 2010) 113.

[49] [1986] 1 FLR 325. Cited by H Reece, 'The Paramountcy Principle: Consensus or Construct?' (1996) 49(1) *Current Legal Problems* 267.

[50] H Reece, 'The Paramountcy Principle: Consensus or Construct?' (1996) 49(1) *Current Legal Problems* 267.

[51] RH Mnookin and L Kornhauser, 'Bargaining in the Shadow of the Law: The Case of Divorce' (1979) 88(5) *Yale Law Journal* 950.

Second, the extent of judicial discretion enables a judge to make a decision on the basis of values that are prejudiced or not acceptable in our society and disguise these by using other justifications for their decision.[52] In a somewhat notorious US case, *Ireland v Smith*, the court initially ordered the transfer of a 3½-year-old child from her happy and stable life with her mother to her father's home because the mother wanted to put her in daycare while she attended college: the father was not planning to care for the child himself, however, but rather intended that his own mother care for the child. In *Re W (A Minor)* the judge transferred care of a 2-year-old girl from her father and his fiancée to her mother on the basis that 'it was the general view of the courts that a young child ought to be with the mother, other things being equal'.[53] Research from Australia shows that courts favour parents who accord to gendered stereotypes over those who challenge stereotypical assumptions of what it is to be a good mother or father.[54] However, just as discretion permits judges to impose their own values, there is also a risk associated with any attempts to circumscribe the exercise of this, such as by introducing a presumption (starting point) that a particular thing is in a child's interests. For example, the presumption that the involvement of both parents in the life of a child (discussed in Chapter 10) has been criticised on the basis that a similar provision in Australian law reduced the parties' and the courts' focus on what was best for the child.[55] As Herring writes:

> Presumptions, then, when they bite, have the effect of requiring a judge to make an order which he or she would otherwise not believe promotes the welfare of the child. It assumes an abstract assessment of what we can say about children generally should carry more weight than an individual assessment of the facts by an experienced judge, with evidence about a particular child.[56]

The cultural context of welfare

Our views of a child's best interests are affected by our own experiences, as well as the culture in which we were raised. Each culture has its own understanding of what is in a child's best interests. The preservation of cultural or ethnic traditions or religious beliefs may be more important to marginalised groups than to those in majority groups. As Gilmore has written:

> the manner in which children's welfare is promoted is contingent on a vast array of historical and political decisions relating to how we are governed, for example our individualist approach to child-rearing as opposed to a collectivist one, and Parliament's preference for 'significant harm' rather than a simple welfare criterion as a precondition to State intervention to protect children. These choices form the backdrop against which specific welfare decisions are taken. How the welfare of a particular child is viewed may differ considerably depending on whether the decision is taken in a society which

---

[52] H Reece, 'The Paramountcy Principle: Consensus or Construct?' (1996) 49(1) *Current Legal Problems* 267.

[53] (1983) 13 *Family Law* 47.

[54] See *Focus: Think Critically: Are the courts biased against fathers?* in Chapter 10.

[55] Helen Rhoades, 'Legislating to Promote Children's Welfare and the Quest for Certainty' (2012) 24(2) *Child and Family Law Quarterly* 158.

[56] J Herring, 'The Welfare Principle and the Children Act: Presumably It's about Welfare?' (2014) 36(1) *Journal of Social Welfare and Family Law* 14. This is a good discussion of presumptions around the welfare principle.

considers that family privacy and autonomy should be prized highly and thus sees a minimal role for the State or one that sees a more enlarged and very public role for the State in child-rearing.[57]

At 9.4 of this chapter, we consider several important international conventions or laws protecting children. One criticism often made of them is that they reflect the dominant Western ideas about children's welfare.[58] Le Blanc has written that 'The discussions surrounding the formulation of international conventions of human rights have been notoriously beset by significant, and culturally based, differences of moral and political outlook'.[59] Even within Western countries there is not necessarily agreement about what is best for a child.

We can see this by considering two issues across two countries: first, applications by one parent to remove a child from New Zealand or England/Wales, contrary to the wishes of the other parent; and secondly, approaches to the circumcision of boys in the US and UK.

FOCUS Think Critically

The child's best interests across different cultures

The legal systems in New Zealand and in England and Wales both use the child's welfare as the basis of court decisions by one parent to take the child to live abroad (known as international relocation). In England and Wales, this is a s8 application and that is why the welfare principle applies.

Rob George researched the way in which such applications were treated in both jurisdictions. He found that 'when practitioners in England and New Zealand analysed three hypothetical relocation disputes, significant variation was seen between the two groups' of lawyers. English lawyers were more likely to be swayed by the way in which the well-being of the primary carer who wishes to re-locate will impact upon the children if relocation is refused. In New Zealand, greater weight seemed to be given to the importance of continuing family relationships, which geographical separation makes much more difficult. George concluded that 'making the welfare principle the main guide to relocation cases is no guarantee that different countries will apply similar reasoning or reach similar outcomes in actual cases.'

He went on to consider what may account for these differences:

One possible explanation of the findings of this research might be that each country is using a coherent but different version of the welfare principle, each highlighting different elements relevant to best interests. These different applications of the welfare principle may stem from different contexts in which that principle is being applied. Equal or near-equal shared care is more frequent in New Zealand than in England (though that may be changing), which is likely to affect views on what arrangements best meet a child's best interests. In the relocation context, geography may also be a significant difference between England and New Zealand:

---

[57] Stephen Gilmore, 'A Critical Perspective on the Welfare Principle', in Lesley-Anne Cull and Jeremy Roche (eds), *The Law and Social Work* (Palgrave Macmillan 2001). References in this extract have been omitted.

[58] For a discussion on Western ideas and the Universal Declaration of Human Rights, see J Gumbis, V Bacianskaite, and J Randakeviciute, 'Do Human Rights Guarantee Autonomy?' (2008) 62/63 *Cuadernos Constitucionales de la Cátedra Fadrique Furió Ceriol* 77.

[59] LJ LeBlanc, *The Convention on the Rights of the Child: United Nations Lawmaking on Human Rights* (University of Nebraska Press 1995).

whereas international moves from England vary from just a few miles (to France or Ireland, say) to intercontinental locations, most moves from New Zealand involve a long-haul flight. On the other hand, New Zealand courts seem willing to stop even very short relocations, and many English cases involve long-distance relocations to Australasia, North America or the Far East. It is not clear, therefore, the extent to which geographic differences provide an explanation for the variation seen.

George's study suggests that our understanding of the welfare principle varies from country to country and that, although many countries agree that the children's welfare should be relevant to or determinative of the decision, that does not result in similar trends across different jurisdictions.

A second example of different approaches is the issue of non-therapeutic male circumcision. In England and Wales, this pertains to the child's upbringing and can be the subject of a s8 specific issues or prohibited steps application (depending on whether the applicant seeks to circumcise the child or prevent it). While each case is dealt with on its own merits, the tendency in this jurisdiction is to hold that circumcision is not in the child's best interests. Circumcision is not a cultural norm in this jurisdiction. Only about 15.8 per cent of men are circumcised, a high proportion of whom were born abroad.[60] Cases tend to come before the courts only when circumcision is sought for religious reasons (Jewish or Muslim). In a number of reported cases, judges have taken the approach that the child's best interests lie in allowing him to make his own decision in the future and in keeping his options open in the meantime. (This is an approach based on the philosophical idea that a child has the right to an open future, as we discuss at 9.3.1.[61]) In the United States 55 per cent of men are circumcised[62] and religion alone does not account for this frequency.

Why is there such disparity? The medical benefits and risks are the same in each jurisdiction, but our assessment of the relative importance of each of these is different. Darby argues that 'The ubiquity of routine infant circumcision in the United States was . . . the result, not of any clinical trials or other research demonstrating the value of circumcision in improving child health, but of a power play within the medical profession and the temptations of technology.' The way in which the medical professions developed in each country explains the difference in approach.[63] This has led in the US to circumcision becoming a cultural norm.

Earp and Shaw point out that 'even when there is widespread agreement about what constitutes a harm or benefit, the *weight* to be assigned to the outcome may still differ from person to person'.[64] Different people—judges or parents—may weight certain types of risk more heavily than others. Similarly, the desire to conform to a prevailing cultural norm will vary from person to person. In support of this, Earp and Shaw refer to the work of psychologist Dan Kahan who has argued that 'individuals gravitate toward perceptions of risk that advance the way of life to which they are committed'.[65] Thus, Earp and Shaw conclude, 'moral concern guides not only response to risk, but also guides the basic faculty of risk perception'. An individual selectively filters risk to support their worldview, and that is mediated by the culture in which they exist.

---

[60] SS Dave, KA Fenton, CH Mercer, B Erens, K Wellings, and AM Johnson, 'Male Circumcision in Britain: Findings from a National Probability Sample Survey' (2003) 79 *Sexually Transmitted Infections* 499.

[61] R Darby, 'The Child's Right to an Open Future: Is the Principle Applicable to Non-Therapeutic Circumcision?' (2013) 39 *Journal of Medical Ethics* 463.

[62] AA Leibowitz, K Desmond, and T Belin, 'Determinants and Policy Implications of Male Circumcision in the United States' (2009) 99(1) *American Journal of Public Health* 138.

[63] R Darby, 'Targeting Patients Who Cannot Object? Re-Examining the Case for Non Therapeutic Infant Circumcision' (2016, April-June) *SAGE Open* 1.

[64] BD Earp and DM Shaw, 'Cultural Bias in American Medicine: The Case of Infant Male Circumcision' (2017) 1(1) *Journal of Pediatric Ethics* 8.

[65] DM Kahan, 'Cultural Cognition as a Conception of the Cultural Theory of Risk', in S Roeser et al. (eds), *Handbook of Risk Theory* (Springer Netherlands 2012) 725, 728.

Of course, in centuries past, we would not be having an argument about whether we should ban smacking, as has recently happened in Scotland. But society's views about what is best for children have changed dramatically. In the 1930s, the belief that fresh air was essential for children led to the development of the 'baby cage' for tenement blocks, a small cage that could be dangled outside a window several storeys up, with a baby inside. Utilising such a device would now result in emergency child protection intervention. In the 1950s, the new attachment theory held that a child needed, for his own future development, to securely attach to one adult. Even in recent years this has led to the refusal of shared parenting time or overnight stays for the other parent, but it is now thought that children may attach to more than one person at once. In the 1970s, the welfare principle was used to justify the removal of children from gay parents to prevent the children being teased at school or influenced by their carers' sexuality: concern about tearing children away from their primary carers was less significant than concern about 'the risk of children, at critical ages, being exposed or introduced to ways of life which . . . may lead to severance from normal society, to psychological stresses and unhappiness and possibly even to physical experiences which may scar them for life'.[66]

As social values and norms change, decisions made under the welfare principle can adapt to those changed views without any need for the wording of the legislation to be altered. The principle simply continues to develop 'by reflecting and adopting the changing views, as the years go by, of reasonable men and women, the parents of children, on the proper treatment and methods of bringing up children; for after all that is the model which the judge must emulate for . . . he must act as the judicial reasonable parent'.[67]

This flexibility has enabled the welfare principle to stand the test of time. But it reflects dominant discourses about welfare that may clash with the views expressed by minority groups. We can see the conflict between secular values and religious beliefs in another Key Case concerning ultra-Orthodox Jewish communities, *J v B and the Children*.

KEY CASE *J v B and the Children (Ultra-Orthodox Judaism: Transgender)* [2017] EWFC 4; *appealed as Re M* [2017] EWCA Civ 2164

The family were members of the ultra-Orthodox Charedi Jewish community, which is very close-knit with strict rules around religious observance, and membership of that community is all-encompassing.

In 2015, the father separated from the mother in order to transition gender from male to female. As a result, the father was rejected by the community, which she left. The mother would not permit the father to see the children and resisted the father's application for contact on the basis that the father's identity as a transgender woman would cause the children to be ostracised by fellow members of the Charedi community so that other children would not be allowed to socialise with her and the mother and children may be forced to leave the community and therefore everything they knew.

---

[66] H Reece, 'The Paramountcy Principle: Consensus or Construct?' (1996) 49(1) *Current Legal Problems* 267.
[67] Per Lord Upjohn in Key Case *J v C*.

At first instance, Peter Jackson J, a very experienced and careful judge, found that

> The best possible outcome would be for the children to live with their mother, grow up in the community, and enjoy a full relationship with their father by regular contact. The worst outcome, I find, would be for the mother and children to be excluded from the community. The question is whether, in striving for the best outcome, the court would instead bring about the worst.

With the benefit of a number of expert reports, the judge found that the community *would* ostracise the children if the father had direct contact and that this ostracisation would harm them. He identified a number of formidable arguments in favour of direct contact but ultimately ordered only indirect contact, which the community would tolerate. He found that 'the likelihood of the children and their mother being marginalised or excluded by the ultra-Orthodox community [was] so real, and the consequences so great, that this one factor, despite its many disadvantages, must prevail over the many advantages of contact.'[68]

The father successfully appealed, with the Court of Appeal noting that the community may yet be encouraged to tolerate direct contact, that there was further work to be done with the children in reintroducing their father, and that the court, as a public body, had to bear in mind its obligation under the Equality Act 2010. The leading judgment was by Munby P, who drew on his judgment in *Re G*, reiterating that

> the judge in a case like this is to act as the 'judicial reasonable parent', judging the child's welfare by the standards of reasonable men and women today, 2017, having regard to the ever changing nature of our world including, crucially for present purposes, changes in social attitudes, and always remembering that the reasonable man or woman is receptive to change, broadminded, tolerant, easy-going and slow to condemn.

He thought that Peter Jackson J should have considered:

> 'directly and explicitly challeng[ing] the parents and the community with the possibility that, absent a real change of attitude on their part, the court may have to consider drastic steps such as removing the children from the mother's care, making the children wards of court or even removing the children into public care' and 'explicitly confront[ing] the mother and the community, which professes to be law abiding, with the fact that its behaviour is or may be unlawfully discriminatory'.

It is possible to read both Peter Jackson J's judgment and that of the Court of Appeal and agree with each in turn, even though they come to different conclusions. As Dunne writes, 'it is difficult to locate the alleged vulnerabilities in Peter Jackson J's reasoning . . . Section 1 CA does not permit family courts to sacrifice individual child welfare in the pursuit of social progress.'[69] Ultimately, the two judgments take different approaches to welfare. The first instance judgment focuses on the (serious) consequences of the children having to leave their community, their friends, their school, and the life that they know. The appeal judgment concentrates on a wider conception of welfare which is grounded in the child being a part of a tolerant, diverse, society and the relevance of human rights in considerations about welfare. For Dunne, 'there are legitimate doubts' that the welfare of

---

[68] Para 187.
[69] P Dunne, 'In the Matter of M (Children): A Collision between Two Unconnecting Worlds?' (2018) 40(2) *Journal of Social Welfare and Family Law* 234.

the children 'could be adequately promoted through legitimising transphobia-inspired community norms'.[70]

The coda to this case is that after the appeal court judgment, the case was remitted back to the High Court (Hayden J) for further consideration. In 2020 it was reported that the father had withdrawn her application for contact. Whatever your view on the 'right' outcome, it brings to the fore the difficulties of identifying where children's welfare lies, and how that welfare fits in with opposing social values.

The competing interests of multiple children

The welfare principle can encounter significant difficulties when faced with more than one child. Consider a situation in which the court is resolving a disagreement about when three children, aged 15, 12, and 5, should see their father. Each child has differing views and the respective weight to be given to those views reflects their respective ages and understanding. The 15-year-old should be able to travel to her father's house by public transport without difficulty, but wants to spend evenings with her friends and has various after-school obligations. The 12-year-old wants to spend each weekend with his father, but is dependent on being driven. He is on the autistic spectrum, and a consistent routine is in his best interests. The 5-year-old wants to stay with his mother, but it is in his best interests to spend some time with his father, albeit not whole weekends, and he is jealous of the attention that the 12-year-old requires. In practical terms, the arrangements for one will have an effect on the arrangements for the others. For example, the 5-year-old cannot be left unattended, so if the mother has to take the 12-year-old to his father's house, he has to be in the car too and therefore misses joining an art class that he wants to take. In such a situation, it is impossible for the court to make an order that is individually in the best interests of each child, even though that is what is required. Compromise is inevitable. On an everyday basis, parents cannot, and do not do what is in the best interests of each child, all of the time.

This is a relatively trivial example, but consider this more serious one: *Birmingham City Council v H* concerned a 15-year-old girl who was in care, and who had given birth to a child, also in care.[71] The local authority sought an order under s34(4) Children Act 1989 authorising it to refuse contact between the mother and baby, because social workers were concerned by the mother's rough handling of the baby and propensity to violence. The mother opposed this application, and there was evidence that she might self-harm if she was prevented from having contact with her child. The interests of mother and baby were therefore in opposition, and both were minors. But whose welfare was paramount?

The Court of Appeal held that the respective interests of the mother and child should be weighed in the balance, and this led to an outcome that the mother should have contact, albeit closely monitored. This was overturned by the House of Lords, which held that under s34 'the child in respect of whose upbringing a question is to be determined by the court is the son or daughter of the parent named in the order and it is that child's welfare which is to be paramount'. The case did not concern the upbringing of the mother so, although she was herself a child, and the decision contrary to her best interests, her welfare was not the paramount consideration. Similarly, in *Re T and E*, it was in T's interests for her to leave

[70] P Dunne, 'In the Matter of M (Children): A Collision between Two Unconnecting Worlds?' (2018) 40(2) *Journal of Social Welfare and Family Law* 234.
[71] [1994] 2 AC 212 (HL).

care and live with her father; but in her half-sister E's interests to be placed for adoption as a pair with T.[72] The children's interests were considered separately. As the application before the court was T's father's application for her to live with him, the court considered only her interests, albeit with 'extreme reluctance' because 'it was highly unsatisfactory that the vital question of children's welfare should depend on the vagaries of procedure'.[73]

One could also argue that the scope of the best interests decision in these cases was too narrow, and that the courts should have given more weight the interests of the child in being part of a family and community, and in sacrificing individual self-interest for the benefit of others. This is something we discuss at 9.2.4. But it is not the basis of the decisions that were made, which asked whether one child's interests should be considered at all and answered the question by a narrow reading of the statute. They are uncomfortable decisions because they harmed some of the children involved. The welfare principle offered them no protection. To Reece, this approach 'emphasizes the futility of the search for a rational justification for the paramountcy principle.'[74] If children are worth protecting, why are they not all protected?

In his speech in *Birmingham*, with which the other Lords agreed, Lord Slynn implied that if the case had involved the upbringing of the mother as well as that of the child, the Court of Appeal's approach of balancing their respective interests might be appropriate as the welfare of both would be paramount. In *Re S (Relocation: Interests of Siblings)* the judge similarly suggested that if the upbringing of two children was the subject of the application, the proper approach would be to come to the decision which involved 'the least risk to their collective welfare'.[75] That is how a court would have to resolve the transport problem discussed above.

One situation that presented the most profound difficulties was that of *Re A (Conjoined Twins: Surgical Separation)*. In this case, the court was presented with a situation in which two children were the subject of the application, but their collective welfare involved the death of one of them.

KEY CASE *Re A (Children) (Conjoined Twins: Surgical Separation)* [2001] Fam 147

This case concerned two babies, Jodie and Mary,[76] whose bodies were joined at the pelvis, their spines and spinal cords fused although they had separate heads, legs, and arms.[77] Jodie was the stronger of the twins and Mary the weaker. Mary's brain and lungs were underdeveloped, and she relied on Jodie's heart to pump blood around her body as her own heart was not functioning correctly. Without

[72] *Re T and E (Proceedings: Conflicting Interests)* [1995] 1 FLR 581.
[73] At pp588 and 589 (Wall J).
[74] H Reece, 'The Paramountcy Principle: Consensus or Construct?' (1996) 49(1) *Current Legal Problems* 267.
[75] [2011] EWCA Civ 454.
[76] These were not their real names. See 'Separated twin is now living a full life, says judge who ordered the operation that killed her conjoined sister' (*Daily Mail*, 4 October 2014). Available at https://www.dailymail.co.uk/news/article-2780371/Separated-twin-living-life-says-judge-ordered-operation-killed-conjoined-sister.html accessed 1 August 2020.
[77] One of the issues in the case is whether the babies were one legal person or two. For a discussion of this, see the judgment at p181; and A Sharpe, *Foucault's Monsters and the Challenge of Law* (Routledge 2010).

the support offered by Jodie's organs, Mary could not survive. But the pressure on Jodie's heart could not be sustained for more than a few months, after which both would die. As an article in one medical journal noted at the time, Mary 'lived on borrowed time, all of which was borrowed from Jodie'.[78] The issue was whether they should be surgically separated. The awful dilemma was that if Mary and Jodie were not separated, both would die in a few months. In the intervening period, their lives would be marked by pain caused by them pulling at one another as they moved. However, the act of separation would cause the immediate and premature death of Mary. (This is why you may be familiar with this case from studies of criminal law, for it also concerns whether this would constitute murder.)

The parents refused consent to the surgery on religious grounds. It thus fell to the courts to decide, under the inherent jurisdiction, whether it was in the children's best interests to be separated.

The Court of Appeal held that it was in Jodie's best interests to be separated, because that would save her life and she had the prospects of living 'a relatively normal life' with a relatively normal lifespan. What of Mary? Ward LJ wrote that:

> The only gain I can see is that the operation would, if successful, give Mary the bodily integrity and dignity which is the natural order for all of us. But this is a wholly illusory goal because she will be dead before she can enjoy her independence and she will die because, when she is independent, she has no capacity for life. . . . I am satisfied that Mary's life, desperate as it is, still has its own ineliminable value and dignity. . . .

> The question is whether this proposed operation is in Mary's best interests. It cannot be. It will bring her life to an end before it has run its natural span. It denies her inherent right to life. There is no countervailing advantage for her at all. It is contrary to her best interests. Looking at her position in isolation and ignoring, therefore, the benefit to Jodie, the court should not sanction the operation on her.

The principle on which the whole of child law is predicated, that of doing what is best for a child, offered no solution at all in this context. What, then, was the correct approach?

For Ward LJ, it was 'impossible not to put in the scales of each child the manner in which they are individually able to exercise their right to life'. Mary had life only because she was able to use Jodie's heart and this was going to cause Jodie's death. He held that:

> Into my scales of fairness and justice between the children goes the fact that nobody but the doctors can help Jodie. Mary is beyond help.

> Hence I am in no doubt at all that the scales come down heavily in Jodie's favour. The best interests of the twins is to give the chance of life to the child whose actual bodily condition is capable of accepting the chance to her advantage even if that has to be at the cost of the sacrifice of the life which is so unnaturally supported. I am wholly satisfied that the least detrimental choice, balancing the interests of Mary against Jodie and Jodie against Mary, is to permit the operation to be performed.[79]

Mary and Jodie's case demonstrates the limits of the welfare principle. Where the interests of two children are separate, but they themselves are indivisible, it offers no assistance. The interests of one had to give way to the interests of the other, even—or perhaps especially—when the matter was life or death. The court was forced to balance their interests, and

[78] JJ Paris and AC Elias-Jones, ' "Do We Murder Mary to Save Jodie?" An Ethical Analysis of the Separation of the Manchester Conjoined Twins' (2001) 77 *Postgraduate Medical Journal* 593.

[79] This case is fictionalised in Ian McEwan's novel *The Children Act*, as is Key Case *Re E (A Minor) (Wardship: Medical Treatment)* [1993] 1 FLR 386, and there is a discussion of the origins of the book at a dinner with the judge, Sir Alan Ward, at 9.3.2.

choose the least bad option, an option that resulted in the death of one child, but not the death of two.[80]

Both Mary and Jodie were the subject of this application, and it was their interests that were considered. We now turn to consider whether there is any room at all for the interests of the child's family or others.

The rights and interests of others

Under the welfare principle, others' interests are relevant, but only insofar as they have an effect on the child's well-being.[81] Where the interests of the child are closely linked to that of another person, harm to that person may affect the child's well-being. In *Re Y (Mental Incapacity: Bone Marrow Transplant)*, an adult woman lived in a residential home for those with serious learning disabilities.[82] Because she lacked the capacity to make decisions about her own healthcare, decisions about her were made on the basis of her best interests—just like the welfare principle that would have applied had been a child. Y's sister developed leukaemia and a bone marrow transplant from a compatible donor gave her the best chance of survival. Only two unrelated donors in the UK matched, but the best chance of survival was if the donor was a blood relation. Y was a match. The issue was whether it was in Y's best interests to undergo the general anaesthetic, pain and discomfort of donating marrow to her sister. On one approach to best interests, it is not in Y's interests to donate. The surgery brings her no medical benefits. On the contrary, it involved medical risk and pain. However, Y's sister was important to her. Her death would harm Y by depriving her of love and companionship. Their mother would be so distressed that the evidence indicated that she would be unable to visit Y as often, and this too would harm her. But medical best interests are not the end of the matter. From an emotional, psychological, and social perspective, the donation was in Y's best interests. It was not altruistic: helping her sister benefited Y.

There is no doubt that the interests of children are often closely linked to that of their family, especially their primary carer. The whole idea of the welfare principle 'presupposes that we can separate the interests of children from their parents' when in reality they are often closely entwined.[83] An argument often made by a primary carer wishing to relocate abroad, for example, is that if they remained in this country they would be so unhappy that this would affect their care of the child in a way that was contrary to the child's best interests.[84] As Barbara Bennett Woodhouse has written, 'A truly child-centred perspective would . . . expose the fallacy that children can thrive while their care-givers struggle, or that the care-givers' needs can be severed from the child, which can lead to the attitude that violence, hostility and neglect toward the care-giver are somehow irrelevant in the best interests calculus'.[85] The danger lies in any assumption that the child's interests are

---

[80] For another case in which the court chose the least bad option, in that case relating to schooling, see *M v H (A Child) (Educational Welfare)* [2008] EWHC 324 (Fam).

[81] See *Re P (Contact) (Supervision)* [1996] 2 FLR 314.

[82] [1996] 2 FLR 787; see D Feenan, 'Good Harvest – *Re Y (Mental Incapacity: Bone Marrow Transplant)*' (1997) 9 *Child and Family Law Quarterly* 30.

[83] J Herring and C Foster 'Welfare Means Rationality, Virtue and Altruism' (2012) 32 *Legal Studies* 480.

[84] See, for example, *Re H (Children) (Residence Order)* [2001] 2 FLR 1277.

[85] B Bennett Woodhouse, 'Hatching the Egg: A Child-Centered Perspective on Parents' Rights' (1993) 14 *Cardozo Law Review* 1747 at 1825.

always the same as those of the parents, and the risk of parents manipulating the court by running an argument that unless they get what they want, the child will be harmed. This is a particular concern because children almost always have no independent direct voice in proceedings relating to them. In most cases, their views will be filtered through the adults.

But: do we want children's interests to prevail in all circumstances, irrespective of the effect on others' well-being and rights? Is it in the interests of society for the interests of others to be ignored? One of the main criticisms that Reece has made of the welfare principle is that it elevates the interests of children above those of adults. She argues that while children may require more protection than adults, that does not mean that we should prioritise their interest above the competing (and perhaps more important/consequential) interests of others. What is the point of growing into a successful adult, she asks, if from adulthood your interests are sacrificed to those of children?[86] Do we want to live in a society in which individual self-interest is the aim—especially given that the people that a child's interests are most likely to impact are those who are closest to the child, the very people on which the child relies for his care? But, equally, is it right to require parents to subordinate 'any legitimate expression of their own individual needs or rights'[87] below those of their children?

We turn now to considering alternatives or modifications to the welfare principle, including approaches that better reflect the child's position as part of his family and society.

9.2.4 Is welfare the best criterion?

So far, we have discussed the scope of the welfare principle and the advantages and disadvantages of it. But is there really any better basis on which to make decisions about children?

Some suggestions are:

- In the event of a dispute about where the child should live, the existing primary caretaker should be preferred. This, O'Kelly writes, 'is based upon the premise that the intimate interaction between young children and their primary caretakers creates a unique psychological bond between them'.[88] Breaking that bond would harm the child.[89] In most cases, the existing primary caretaker in intact families is the mother, so this is a close relation to the maternal preference approach, which says that courts should prefer to place children with their mother.

- A return to the historical position wherein fathers automatically held the right to make decisions about their children including whether or not they could see their mother ('father-right'). This was based on the belief that the father knew best what was good for the child.

- A starting point that the child's time should be shared equally between the parents. We discuss shared parenting time in Chapter 10, including the research on the

---

[86] H Reece, 'The Paramountcy Principle: Consensus or Construct?' (1996) 49(1) *Current Legal Problems* 267.

[87] A Diduck, *Law's Families* (Lexis Nexis 2003) 91.

[88] M O'Kelly, 'Blessing the Tie That Binds: Preference for the Primary Caretaker as Custodian' (1987) 63(4) *North Dakota Law Review* 481.

[89] This approach was influenced by a seminal book, J Goldstein, A Freud, and A Solnit, *Beyond the Best Interests of the Child* (Free Press 1973). It was these authors who coined the term 'psychological parenthood'.

circumstances in which it can be beneficial to a child and the circumstances when it is likely to be contrary to the child's interests.

- That the parties should toss a coin to resolve a dispute or adopt another randomised outcome generator.
- An approach based on the outcome that gives the greatest good to society (a utilitarian approach). It is certainly the case that if we wanted to improve the position of as many children as possible, an approach based on the potentially conflicting welfare of each individual child would not work. Some children's interests would have to defer to the interests of other children who (for example) had greater need for resources.
- Modifications of the welfare principle that give greater weight to the importance of the child as part of a family and community.
- An approach that weighs the child's interests against those of others affected, which is the proper approach under the ECHR (see section 9.4.1).
- Letting the child decide.

Elster points out that the chosen criterion is capable of affecting behaviour prior to separation, although it is not clear to what extent. In theory, if courts were to adopt a maternal preference approach or equal shared time, there would be little incentive for either parent to take extra care of the child during the relationship, because in most cases doing so would not change the outcome of a post-separation dispute. Contrast this with a preference for the primary caretaker, which would incentivise each parent to spend the most time with the child prior to separation if they wanted to be the primary caretaker post-separation (although research has shown that the quality of parenting time, rather than the quantity, is what is important to children).[90]

Let us take a closer look at some of these suggestions.

Replacing the welfare principle

Mnookin has suggested that we should accept that children cases are indeterminate and in preference adopt a more determinate system—such as tossing a coin or using a random outcome generator like a lottery machine—in situations in which both parents are suitable carers and thus the detriment to the child of either outcome is limited. All you would need to do before the coin toss would be to determine that neither parent is unfit.[91]

You might consider such an approach to be callous, to which there are two responses. First, the current method of considering the parties' characters and abilities is capable of harming them, even if that process is accurate (which it is not). It would mean that there would be no prolonged court battles with accordant stress to the whole family. Family courts would be less busy, with more time for more complex cases. If we extended this to less finely balanced situations, a party may find they have better odds by tossing a coin than by marshalling their arguments. A randomised system favours no participant, and the parties' respective arms are equal, something important given the number of parties who cannot afford legal representation and are unable to access legal aid. Second,

---

[90] See Chapter 10.
[91] J Elster, 'Solomonic Judgments: Against the Best Interest of the Child' (1987) 54 *University of Chicago Law Review* 1.

Mnookin points out, states have taken far more serious decisions on a randomised basis, such as military draft by lottery.[92] Ultimately, most people would be uncomfortable with the abdication of responsibility that comes from randomisation of decisions about children. They would need to accept that our existing methods of determining best interests are so deeply flawed that randomisation is equally justifiable. This may be impossible to persuade them of (and may not be true).

John Eekelaar has suggested an approach that paid attention to the potential 'extreme adverse effects of certain outcomes on the well-being of particular individuals'. To him, the 'best solution is surely to adopt the course that avoids inflicting the most damage on the well-being of any interested individual', even if this means that the well-being of the child takes second place. This approach is not quite the same as the approach taken in Key Case *Re A (Children) (Conjoined Twins: Surgical Separation)* because that case concerned the interests of two children, and what Eekelaar is proposing is an approach that weighs the interests of adults into the balance too. He writes:

> The methodology can be illustrated in this way. Suppose one could assign a value to the degree of benefit and detriment to the well-being of all interested parties under various possible solutions. The following would be a simple case. C is the child. X and Y are adult participants. Minus values indicate an outcome that has more detriment than benefit for the party:
>
> Solution 1: C (+15); X (+10); Y (−30).
>
> Solution 2: C (+10); X (+10); Y (−20).
>
> Solution 3: C (+5); X (-5); Y (−10).[93]

Under Eekelaar's approach, solution 1 would be the outcome of a decision under the welfare principle, because it gives the outcome that scores most highly for the child, C. However, it is seriously detrimental to one of the adult participants (Y), although the welfare principle will ignore that. Solution 2 is utilitarianism: it provides the greatest good for the greatest number when compared to the other two solutions (the total score being 0, as against −5 and −10 respectively). Solution 3 is the solution for which Eekelaar advocates: it is not as good for the child as the other solutions, but it avoids great harm to others.

SCENARIO 1

Illustration 3: Frank and Laura and Amanda (child arrangements case)

How might this case be decided if not under the welfare principle? A primary caretaker presumption would assume that the child's welfare was met by remaining with her mother. But what if the price of that is that the child does not sustain a successful relationship with her father, perhaps because mother Laura is not supportive of contact, or father Frank has a tendency to criticise Laura to Amanda whenever she visits?

---

[92] R Mnookin, 'Child Custody Adjudication: Judicial Functions in the Face of Indeterminacy' (1975) 39(3) *Law and Contemporary Problems* 226.

[93] J Eekelaar, 'Beyond the Welfare Principle' (2002) 14 *Child and Family Law Quarterly* 237.

> Would it be fair to let 12-year-old Amanda decide? Certainly, under the welfare checklist her view attracts some weight given her age. But children do not always make decisions in their own best interests and are not always (ever?) free of influence. Is it fair to make her choose between her parents in this way, or is it a situation in which the court is acting in her best interests by taking the decision out of her hands?
>
> What if we used Eekelaar's suggestion and tried to calculate the benefit and harm to each party of each potential course of action? Perhaps not seeing Amanda will plunge Frank into a depression. In such a situation, is it right that Amanda should be required to see her father to prevent that harm to him? The welfare principle would disregard that risk except to the extent that his depression would have a knock-on effect on Amanda herself. But Amanda is part of a family. Is it in her interests to have those to whom she is closest happy?

Modifying the welfare principle

Using Eekelaar's framework, let us consider an option that provides no benefit to the child, or even harms them slightly, but which benefits another person in their family enormously. We will call this solution 4:

Solution 4: C (–5); X (+25); Y (0).

In this example, the proposed way forward involves minimal harm to the child (–5), but great advantage to one of the adult participants, X. That adult may be someone close to the child, with whom they have a bond or on whom they rely. Should, or would, we want the child to experience some sacrifice in return for that person having great benefit?

Under the welfare principle, we would need to persuade the court that it was in the child's interests for X to be benefited. We could do this, as in *Re Y (Mental Incapacity: Bone Marrow Transplant)*, by reframing the benefits to X as indirectly or directly of benefit to C. If we can persuade the court of this, then the welfare principle allows this outcome.

Let us take things a step further. Should we allow the interests of C to cede to those of X where there is a significant advantage to X, even when we cannot identify any benefit—medical, psychological, emotional—to C? Herring would do so. He proposes that the interests of a child are promoted when the child has a fair and just relationship with each parent, in which each family's interests are respected.[94] This can only happen where the rights and interests of others are considered and, occasionally, this requires sacrifices on the part of the child. Herring terms this 'relationship-based welfare'[95] because it reflects the position of the child as part of a family and a part of society. After all, would we want children who are selfish, interested only in pursuing their own well-being at the expense of others?

This does, in fact, better accord with the way in which decisions are made in families outside court. Many types of major decisions made by parents, such as moving house or changing jobs, are likely to be for the benefit of the family unit as a whole rather than a particular child within the family who may have to change school or leave his friends behind.

---

[94] J Herring, 'The Welfare Principle and the Rights of Parents' Chapter 5 in A Bainham, S Day Sclater and M Richards (eds), *What is a Parent: A Socio-Legal Analysis* (Hart 1999).

[95] J Herring, 'The Human Rights Act and the Welfare Principle in Family Law – Conflicting or Complementary?' (2009) 11(3) *Child and Family Law Quarterly* 223.

As Diekema has written, 'there are few situations in which society actually requires parents to always act in a way that is optimal for their children. In seeking to optimize family welfare, parental decisions may commonly subjugate the interests of individual children.'[96] The state does not intervene in these kinds of decisions unless the parents are causing the child significant harm, the threshold for a child protection intervention. Yet when someone with sufficient standing makes an application to court in private law proceedings, the court imposes the best interests of the individual child on the child's family.

9.3 **Children's moral rights**

Any discussion of children's rights must start by making a distinction between rights that are recognised by law, and moral rights, which are those recognised by philosophical theories about rights. In many cases, we would expect a child's moral rights to be reflected in their legal rights, but this is not always the case.

There are two main theories of what it means to have a moral right, the will or choice theory, and the welfare or interest theory.

Under the will or choice theory, all people have liberty rights, or what Hart termed the 'equal right of all men to be free'.[97] A liberty right gives the rights-holder the freedom to do something, but not a duty to do it. All other rights are aspects of this liberty right, and thus manifestations of each individual's personal autonomy: their right to make choices about their life.

Under this theory, my having this right imposes a corresponding duty upon you. In that sense, it is a claim-right. It makes a claim upon you. My right to life, for example, imposes a duty on you not to kill me. It gives me the right to control that duty; I am a 'small-scale sovereign'.[98] I can choose to enforce or waive that duty (although the law may reflect a different approach and prevent me from doing so, for example by providing that I cannot consent to my own murder). While I can prevent you from doing something that would interfere with my right to life, I can also require you to do something, such as to provide me with food. (In reality, it may be impossible to meet the positive rights of every person as it depends on the resources available.)

The will theory suggests that those who do not have the capacity to control another's duty cannot be said to be holders of rights. As Hart said, 'It is hard to think of rights except as capable of exercise.'[99] This has particular implications for children cases, because children—especially very young children—may lack the capacity to make rational choices, hold others to duties, or waive those duties. This also applies to those adults who are unconscious or who lack mental capacity. As Campbell has pointed out, under the will theory 'the distinctive thing about children's rights is that there are none.'[100] Indeed, the

---

[96] DS Diekema, 'Parental Refusals of Medical Treatment: The Harm Principle as Threshold for state Intervention' (2004) 25(4) *Theoretical Medicine and Bioethics* 243.

[97] HLA Hart, 'Are There Any Natural Rights?' (1955) 64(2) *The Philosophical Review* 175.

[98] HLA Hart, *Essays on Bentham: Studies in Jurisprudence and Political Theory* (Clarendon Press 1982).

[99] HLA Hart, *Essays on Bentham: Studies in Jurisprudence and Political Theory* (Clarendon Press 1982).

[100] TD Campbell, 'The Rights of the Minor: As Person, as Child, as Juvenile, as Future Adult' (1992) 6 *International Journal of Law and the Family* 1.

will theory risks allowing those who can assert their rights (the powerful) to dominate those that cannot (the vulnerable, including children).

Many people would find it morally objectionable to treat such vulnerable people as not having any rights. Some will theorists respond that although children may be incapable of exercising their rights themselves, they still have rights, albeit that those must be exercised for them by adults acting as their proxies, acting not in the child's best interests but in the way that the child would act if he was able to make a rational decision. In many of the cases about children's rights discussed in this chapter, for example, the child was not the applicant, or, if they were, they had the help of adults to bring their case. As the child becomes older, they will need adult proxies less and less.

In contrast to the will or choice theory, there is the interest theory. This sees the purpose of rights as the protection and promotion of fundamental human interests. The philosopher John Finnis identified seven fundamental human interests: life itself; the acquisition of knowledge (as an end in itself); play/recreation (for its own sake); friendship and sociability; aesthetic experience (knowing and experiencing beauty); practical reasonableness (the ability to reason correctly about what is best for yourself, and to act on those decisions); and spiritual or religious experience.[101] These are aspects of what Aristotle termed 'the good life', a life of 'virtuous activity in accordance with reason'.

Joseph Raz argues that not all interests are rights, and that 'a right exists only if an interest of the right-holder—i.e., an aspect of her well-being—is of sufficient importance to hold others to be under a duty'.[102] As the interest is important, the corresponding duty cannot be waived. As Goodin and Gibson write, 'It does not matter that rights-holders are not in a position to assert rights . . . all that is strictly required is that one have interests which are recognisable by others who are duly empowered, by the moral community more generally, to press those claims on one's behalf.'[103] Under the interest theory, therefore, as all humans have fundamental interests, they are all rights-holders, including children. We know their interests, and so we can protect their rights even though they are unable to articulate them, something that is a weakness of the will/choice theory.[104]

The above summary is a very simplified explanation of how the will and interest theories attempt to explain the function of rights. They each have different answers to the question of whether children have rights and the purpose of rights. Criticisms can be made of both theories. As Wenar has commented, they 'are both inadequate to our understanding of rights, the weakness of each being the strength of the other'. Thus the will theory gives rights and imposes duties that do not confer benefits on the rights-holder, while the interest theory 'accepts rights that confer benefits, but rejects rights whose holders do not benefit from holding them'.[105] Many highly intelligent people have spent centuries arguing about which theory is correct, and suggesting alternatives or adaptations, and continue to do so.

---

[101] J Finnis, *Natural Law and Natural Rights* (Clarendon Press 1980).
[102] J Raz, 'On the Nature of Rights' 93 *Mind* 194.
[103] RE Goodin and D Gibson, 'Rights, Young and Old' (1997) 17(2) *Oxford Journal of Legal Studies* 185.
[104] RE Goodin and D Gibson, 'Rights, Young and Old' (1997) 17(2) *Oxford Journal of Legal Studies* 185.
[105] L Wenar, 'The Nature of Rights' (2005) 33(3) *Philosophy and Public Affairs* 223.

To Freeman, 'the most fundamental of rights is the right to possess rights.'[106] But some philosophers argue that children do not have human rights at all, even if the law chooses to give them some legal rights. They argue that fact that we may owe children duties—moral obligations—does not presuppose that they have human rights. Griffin, for example, argues that the vulnerability of children and their future potential as autonomous decision-makers in search of the good life explain our obligations to children, but do not mean that they can be said to have either the human rights of adults or a narrower class of rights specific to children.[107] O'Neill argues that for most children, 'the rhetoric of rights is merely one indirect way of reminding others of some of their obligations' towards children. To her, children's the remedy for a lack of rights is to grow up.[108]

In the next section, we will try to locate what rights do or children should have, and whether these are different to the rights of adults.

9.3.1 A right to an open future?

You may recall that in Key Case *Re G (Children) (Religious Upbringing)* Munby LJ draws on Aristotle's notion of a 'good life' to decide that the children who were the subject of the case should go to the school that gave them the greatest opportunities for adulthood. He said that the judge's objective:

> must be to bring the child to adulthood in such a way that the child is best equipped both to decide what kind of life they want to lead—what kind of person they want to be—and to give effect so far as practicable to their aspirations. Put shortly, our objective must be to maximise the child's opportunities in every sphere of life as they enter adulthood. . . . the judge must be cautious about approving a regime which may have the effect of foreclosing or unduly limiting the child's ability to make such decisions in future.

This is very close to a concept developed by the legal philosopher Joel Feinberg. In an influential chapter, he argued that there are four categories of rights:

1. A-rights, held by adults and older children only, such as to choose or reject a religion.
2. C-rights, held by children or dependent adults only, such as the right to be provided with food and shelter. Macleod suggests that C-rights could include the right to be loved.[109]

The rights held only by adults or only by children are rights that that group has by virtue of a specific moral capacity, attribute, or interest not held by the other group. As children

---

[106] M Freeman, 'Why It Remains Important to Take Children's Rights Seriously' (2007) *15 International Journal of Children's Rights* 5.

[107] J Griffin, 'Do Children Have Rights?', in D Archard and CM Macleod (eds), *The Moral and Political Status of Children* (OUP 2002).

[108] O O'Neill, 'Children's Rights and Children's Lives' (1992) 6 *International Journal of Law and the Family* 24. O'Neill's article can also be found in (1988) 98 *Ethics* 445.

[109] CM Macleod, 'Are Children's Rights Important?' Chapter 9 in E Brake and L Ferguson (eds), *Philosophical Foundations of Children's and Family Law* (OUP 2018).

need protection, their rights are directed towards protecting their interests rather than towards liberty rights.

3. A-C rights, held by both adults and children, such as a right not to be killed.

4. Right-in-trust: rights held in trust for the child but which he does not attain until he is an adult. These rights may be violated before the child reaches adulthood by closing off opportunities for the child and thereby limiting the scope of his adult autonomy.

Feinberg argues that as every child is a potential adult, it is the role of parents and/or the state to ensure that the child's options are left open until such time as they can make their own choices. Feinberg calls this the right to 'an open future'.[110] This right would be breached by the state, the parent, or the child themselves making decisions that limit the child's future options. Thus one of the consequences of keeping options open for adulthood is that the child's current autonomy is limited. As it would reduce scope for the child's future decisions, refusing life-saving medical treatment, leaving school without qualifications, or even eating sugary foods that worsen health would breach the child's rights. As Feinberg said, 'Respect for the child's future autonomy as an adult often requires preventing his free choice now'. The child's autonomy as a child takes second place to their future autonomy as an adult. But it is by no means clear, writes Brennan, that the best way to protect children is to ignore their current preferences: after all—'we want to teach our children to be good choosers and we do that, in part, by letting them try out the business of choosing'.[111] Only by making mistakes will children understand how to make sensible decisions.

Claudia Mills has argued that it is unrealistic to think that we are always able to give children an open future. Opportunities 'close every day, as we make choices to spend our time this way rather than that, to pursue x rather than y'.[112] It would be impractical and exhausting to try to do everything, and probably impossible. It would mean that children led frenetic lives and were unable to enjoy childhood because they were too busy maximising their potential for adulthood. That would be, Griffin argues, 'a thoroughly dubious policy for raising sane and healthy children'.[113] They might never fulfil their potential to excel at one thing because they were busy with lots of things. Then there is the issue of resourcing. If the child's right is a positive one, then the state and/or parents would be under a duty to provide the goods and services needed to keep their options open. Even if it were a negative duty—a duty not to interfere with the child's interests—then that would be easily breached. Millum gives the example of a parent who moves to a new city for a good job, but the school there does not offer music lessons and offers one less foreign language.[114] By moving, the parent has closed doors to the child—but can it really be said that the child's rights have been breached? Even if we decided that they had, would we want the child's rights to prevail over those of others in all situations?

---

[110] J Feinberg, 'The Child's Right to an Open Future', in RC Curren (ed.), *Philosophy of Education: An Anthology* (Blackwell 2007); also in W Aiken and H LaFollette (eds), *Whose Child? Children's Rights, Parental Authority, and State Power* (Littlefield, Adams, and Co. 1980).

[111] S Brennan, 'Children's Choices or Children's Interests: Which Do Their Rights Protect?' Chapter 4 in D Archard and C Macleod (eds), *The Moral and Political Status of Children* (OUP 2002).

[112] C Mills, 'The Child's Right to an Open Future?' (2003) 34 *Journal of Social Philosophy* 499.

[113] J Griffin, 'Do Children Have Rights?', in D Archard and CM Macleod (eds), *The Moral and Political Status of Children* (OUP 2002).

[114] J Millum, 'The Foundation of the Child's Right to an Open Future' (2014) 45(4) *Journal of Social Philosophy* 525.

SCENARIO 2

Illustration 2: Mishal and Lee (medical treatment case)

This scenario concerns the opposition of 17-year-old Lee and his mother to him being treated with chemotherapy and radiotherapy. As we have seen, what is best for Lee will determine the outcome of the court proceedings. But let us think about how Lee's moral rights might affect this issue.

Lee is 17 and that would be important to his assertion of rights under the will theory, because we assume that at this age he is capable of rational choices. Under the interest theory, he is also a rights-holder as the interests that are engaged are fundamental. On the one hand, we have his autonomy—the right to make his own choices. On the other hand, by making a choice to refuse treatment, he is seriously risking his future, and under Feinberg's proposal he should not be allowed to do this. We therefore have a conflict between his interests and his autonomy.

What we have not considered is whether his right to life can require another to provide him with costly medical treatment. If that is a positive right—one that imposes a positive duty on another to do something as opposed to not do something—there are significant resource implications.

9.3.2 Autonomy interests

Feinberg's idea of an open future is closely related to John Eekelaar's description of developmental interests, the idea that 'all children should have an equal opportunity to maximize the resources available to them during their childhood (including their own inherent abilities) so as to minimize the degree to which they enter adult life affected by avoidable prejudices incurred during childhood.'[115] In addition to developmental interests, Eekelaar identifies two other categories of interest held by children, basic interests in obtaining physical, emotional and intellectual care (a necessary prerequisite for adult self-fulfilment); and autonomy interests, i.e., the right of a child to make decisions about his own life. Most people would agree that the law should protect children's basic interests. The law reflects this view by requiring parents to meet their children's need for food, shelter, clothing etc., and if the parents are not willing or able to do this then the state steps in. The child protection system and the welfare benefits system are both ways in which the state tries to ensure that children's basic needs are met (although a significant proportion of children nevertheless live in poverty). Children's developmental interests are also partly protected by law. The UN Convention on the Rights of the Child gives children a number of rights in this area, albeit these rights are loosely expressed.

The most controversial category is children's autonomy interests. When people refer to children's rights, this is often what they mean: the capacity to choose for themselves. As Freeman says, 'To respect a child's autonomy is to treat that child as a person and as a rights-holder.'[116] Some, perhaps many, people are uncomfortable with the idea that a child might have a right of autonomy or self-determination. Behind the discomfort with children's autonomy lies two concerns. First, most people would argue that children lack the

---

[115] J Eekelaar, 'The Emergence of Children's Rights' (1986) 6(2) *Oxford Journal of Legal Studies* 161.
[116] M Freeman 'Taking Children's Rights More Seriously' (1992) 6 *International Journal of Law and the Family* 52.

experience, foresight, or cognitive capacity to make particular decisions. Our fear is that a child may decide 'wrongly'. As Sir Thomas Bingham has said:

> a child is after all a child. The reason why the law is particularly solicitous in protecting the interests of children is that they are liable to be vulnerable and impressionable, lacking the maturity to weigh the longer term against the shorter, lacking the insight to know how they will react and the imagination to know how others will react in certain situations, lacking the experience to match the probable against the possible.[117]

Second, they may worry about the impact that the child's autonomy may have on others. In many situations, a child's autonomy rights will constrain the rights of those closest to him—his parents.[118]

One way to address these concerns, Feinberg suggests, is to give children fewer rights. For example, we do not allow children to drive, vote, buy alcohol, or marry or consent to sexual relations below a certain age. We require the education of children and we limit the hours in which children can work. Certain occupations are denied to them (such as joining the army or going down a mine). These limitations reflect a view that children need protection. We have not abandoned children to their autonomy rights, irrespective of the consequences.[119] Instead, we have prevented them from making short-term choices that harm them (or others), thereby protecting their potential for long-term autonomy.[120] Eekelaar would allow children to make an increasing number of decisions as they grew older (i.e., to exercise their autonomy rights), as long as these did not interfere with their developmental or basic interests. This would enable children to be brought 'to the threshold of adulthood with the maximum opportunities to form and pursue life-goals which reflect as closely as possible an autonomous choice'.[121] He calls this 'dynamic self-determination'.

Samantha Brennan also argues for an approach of graduated autonomy. For her, enabling a child to make an increasing number of decisions means that they 'move gradually from having their rights primarily protect their interests to having their rights primarily protect their choices. This reflects the transition of the child from being a creature whose interests are of moral concern, and hence deserve the protection of rights, to being a creature who can choose for herself.'[122] Such an approach also addresses the false dichotomy between adults, whom we see as autonomous and responsible, and children, whom we see as incompetent and irrational.[123] She gives the example of where the child lives. When the child is younger, courts determine what is best for the child by reference to her best

---

[117] *Re S (Minor) (Independent Representation)* [1993] 2 FCR 1.

[118] See A McCall Smith, 'Is Anything Left of Parental Rights?' Chapter 1 in E Sutherland and A McCall Smith (eds), *Family Rights: Family Law and Medical Advance* (Edinburgh University Press 1991).

[119] BC Hagen, 'Children's Liberation and the New Egalitarianism: Some Reservations about Abandoning Youth to Their "Rights"' (1976) 3 *BYU Law Review* 605. I would not have found this source without the reference in M Freeman 'Taking Children's Rights More Seriously' (1992) 6 *International Journal of Law and the Family* 52.

[120] J Fortin, 'Children's Rights: Are The Courts Taking Them More Seriously?' (2004) 15 *King's College Law Journal* 253.

[121] J Eekelaar 'The Interests of the Child and The Child's Wishes: The Role of Dynamic Self-Determination' (1994) 8 *International Journal of Law and the Family* 42, 53.

[122] S Brennan, 'Children's Choices or Children's Interests: Which Do Their Rights Protect?' Chapter 4 in D Archard and C Macleod (eds), *The Moral and Political Status of Children* (OUP 2002). Brennan also points out that some children who are severely disabled will never be able to exercise autonomy, yet we would still consider them to have interests that should be protected.

[123] M Minnow, 'Rights for the Next Generation: A Feminist Approach to Children's Rights (1986) 9 *Harvard Women's Journal* 15.

interests, but when older those interests include 'some elements of choice for the child in terms of who provides the care'.

However, not everybody believes that children should have more limited rights than adults, even when very young. Child liberationists believe that children should have the rights that adults have, and that children's lack of capacity should not prevent this.[124] They do not see the purpose of rights as being to protect individuals. Indeed, they argue that giving rights to children helps them to develop the capacity required to make their own decisions. They point out that a person does not suddenly, the age of 18, become better able to make decisions than the day previously. Adulthood is a long period, yet immediately that a person reaches 18 we allow them to make decisions that can impact them negatively for the entire course of their life. Adults frequently make poor choices.

Certainly, the division between adulthood and childhood is arbitrary. All age-related rights are arbitrary. Why should we make 10 the age of criminal responsibility, allow a child to join the army at 16 with parental consent, but only allow adults to buy a glass of beer?

SCENARIO 2

Illustration 3: Mishal and Lee (medical treatment case)

The implications of an arbitrary assignment of capacity to refuse treatment will be all too clear. Lee is 17; when he turns 18, as we will see at 9.5.1, he has the ability to refuse treatment.

While we can recognise that the acquisition or attribution of rights at the age of 18 (or in some cases younger) is arbitrary, most people would take the view that it is necessary to have a point at which rights are acquired. Brennan argues that because the state cannot consider the effects of each child's decision on him or her individually, it has to set some generalised rules applicable to categories of children, and it tends to do so by reference to age. Thus, she concludes, 'some legal rules may need to be applied on the basis of coarse lines even if the moral facts are more complex'. We need some system to easily prevent those who are least likely to be able to make a rational, informed decision about the issue to be protected, and while being a blunt tool, age-related criteria are easier than individually assessing the state of knowledge of each child. This explains why states are justified in setting ages for drinking alcohol or for leaving school.

We can see the effect of this division between childhood and adulthood in the case *Re E*.

KEY CASE *Re E (A Minor) (Wardship: Medical Treatment)* [1993] 1 FLR 386

E was a 15¾ -year-old boy with leukaemia. He and his parents were members of the Christian denomination Jehovah's Witnesses. In 1945, the legislative body of the Witnesses declared that the Bible effectively prohibited the use of blood products, including receiving a blood transfusion, with

---

[124] E.g. J Holt, *Escape from Childhood: The Needs and Rights of Children* (Ballantine Books 1974).

the penalty for doing so being disfellowshipped and prevented from attaining eternal life. Most Witnesses will refuse blood transfusions, even of their own blood. As a result of this belief, E and his parents refused blood transfusions as part of his treatment.

Had he been able to have conventional treatment the hospital assessed that he had an 80–90 per cent chance of remission. Although the hospital used an alternative treatment plan, this was not as successful. When E's haemoglobin levels were either hours or a few days away from being so low that he might have a heart attack, stroke, or become blind, the hospital sought a declaration that it would be lawful for them to treat him with blood products. E and his parents opposed the application, arguing that E had sufficient knowledge and understanding to make his own decision and that he was nearly 16, an age when he attained the right to consent to treatment under s8 of the Family Law Reform Act 1969.

Ward J held that although E understood that he would die, he did not 'have any sufficient comprehension of the pain he has yet to suffer, of the fear that he will be undergoing, of the distress not only occasioned by that fear but also—and importantly—the distress he will inevitably suffer as he, a loving son, helplessly watches his parents' and his family's distress'. He held that E did not have the capacity give informed consent and that his will was not sufficiently free: 'his volition has been conditioned by the very powerful expressions of faith to which all members of the creed adhere.' He concluded that 'court should be very slow to allow an infant to martyr himself' and made the declaration sought by the hospital.

This decision reflected the best interests of E, balancing his views and religious convictions against his life and enabling his life to be saved. But while the legal proceedings ended there, the story does not. The writer Ian McEwan includes E's case in fictionalised form in his book *The Children Act*. The idea for the book arose after he attended a dinner party hosted by Ward J, who told him what happened next:

> Months later, Ward took the boy (now in good health) and his father to a football match, which they watched from the directors' box. The young man was able to meet his football heroes. The gleam of joy in his eyes, his excitement at being alive, was a sight the judge would never forget. The court's decision was vindicated. But the story did not end there. A few years later the young Witness was readmitted to hospital and needed another blood transfusion. By then, he was old enough to make an independent decision. He refused treatment and died for his beliefs.[125]

The final outcome, therefore, was that when E became old enough to exercise his own autonomy, he chose the option that resulted in his death. Adults are free to make 'wrong' decisions—that is, decisions that others think are not in their best interests. Only when an adult lacks the mental capacity to make a decision for themselves does the law intervene. As McFarlane LJ said in *PC v City of York*, 'there is a space between an unwise decision and one which an individual does not have the mental capacity to take and . . . it is important to respect that space, and to ensure that it is preserved, for it is within that space that an individual's autonomy operates'.[126]

Consider, though, the extent to which E was really able to exercise free choice. Parents inevitably guide and steer their children towards what, in their view, are more desirable

---

[125] I McEwan, 'The Law Versus Religious Belief' *The Guardian*, 5 September 2014. Available at https://www.theguardian.com/books/2014/sep/05/ian-mcewan-law-versus-religious-belief accessed 13 July 2020.
[126] *PC v City of York* [2013] EWCA Civ 478, [54].

options for education, religion, careers, friends, and they do this even if the child has (in theory) the ability to choose between options. Brought up by his parents within the religion, he may have only known the values of that religion. Was his decision an exercise of his autonomy, or the inevitable consequence of child-raising choices made over the course of his life by his parents? Would a decision made by a judge be any different—or simply replace the values prioritised by the child and his parents with judicial values, or the values of a larger section of society, instead?[127]

9.4 Children's legal rights

So far, we have considered children's moral rights. The law may reflect one or more of the views on moral rights set out above. But, as Freeman points out, 'the passing of laws is only a beginning. It is a signal that must be taken up by society.'[128] A right, even one embodied by law, is not worth much if it cannot be enforced.

There are four key sources of children's legal rights applicable to children in England and Wales:

1. Domestic law

2. The European Convention on Human Rights and Fundamental Freedoms (the ECHR)

3. The United Nations Convention on the Rights of the Child (the UNCRC)

4. European Union law, to the extent (following the UK's departure from the EU) that it is reflected in domestic law.

These different sources are interrelated. When the UK was a member state of the EU some types of EU law were directly applicable in the UK without the necessity of incorporation and some were directly effective so can be enforced in domestic courts. Our domestic law therefore frequently has its origins in EU law. All EU member states are also signatories to both the ECHR and the UNCRC. The ECHR was incorporated into domestic law by the Human Rights Act 1998. This means that claims of human rights breaches can be brought in our domestic courts and not merely by bringing a case in the European Court. The UNCRC, while not part of our domestic law, still forms part of our international obligations, to which we are accountable to the UN. It has also influenced domestic law, notably in the duties on local authorities imposed by the Children Act 2004. In the next section, we take a closer look at what these sources mean for children in England and Wales.

9.4.1 The European Convention on Human Rights

The European Convention for the Protection of Human Rights and Fundamental Freedoms (ECHR) is a treaty of the Council of Europe. The Treaty entered into force in 1953. Although often mistaken for part of the European Union, the Council is a separate

---

[127] For a discussion of parents' instruction of their children and parental rights, see C M Macleod, 'Conceptions of Parental Autonomy' (1997) 25(1) *Politics and Society* 117.
[128] MDA Freeman, *The Rights and Wrongs of Children* (Frances Pinter 1983) 33.

supranational organisation whose aim is to uphold human rights, democracy and the rule of law across 47 member states. While all EU member states are also Council Members, the Council has much wider membership, including several former Soviet states. All Council of Europe member states have ratified the ECHR.

The ECHR sets out a number of rights and freedoms. Some of these are absolute, meaning that it is not lawful to breach the right. More commonly, the rights and freedoms are subject to limitations—they are conditional. We have seen in previous chapters that Article 8, the right most commonly cited in family situations, is a conditional right.

FOCUS Know-How

Determining whether an ECHR right has been breached

There are a number of questions that must be answered before it is possible to determine whether a right has been breached.

1. *Does a certain measure fall within the scope of the article?*

First of all, the applicant—the person asserting that their rights have been breached—must show that the decision or law that is alleged to breach the ECHR falls within the scope of the article. We saw in Chapter 8 that the relationship between an unmarried father and his child is not protected by Article 8 unless family life already exists as a fact. The relationship between a mother and her child is no longer protected by Article 8 once that child is adopted by others. In Key Case *Williamson*, the Supreme Court held that Article 9 protected the manifestation only of those beliefs that were consistent with basic standards of human dignity or integrity. If the measure does not fall within the scope of the article, then there is no claim.

Note that non-activity on the part of the state can found a claim, because states are under a positive obligation to safeguard a right as well as a negative obligation (not to breach rights).

If the measure does fall within the scope of the article, then consider:

2. *Does the measure interfere with one of the rights protected by the article?*

If not, there is no claim. The burden of proof is again on the applicant. If it does interfere with a right, there will be a breach unless the interference is permitted. Most ECHR rights are not absolute—they allow interference in prescribed circumstances.

3. *Is the interference permitted by the article?*

The burden of proof at this stage lies with the state to show that the interference is permitted by the article. In respect of Article 8, it is paragraph (2) that permits interference that is in accordance with law.

　　a. The first sub-question, therefore, is whether there is a law or legal rule (including common law) that authorises the measure. Related to this are two further sub-questions: Is the law adequately accessible? Is the law or rule formulated with sufficient precision to enable the citizen to regulate his conduct, i.e., to foresee the consequences?[129]

　　b. It is not enough for Article 8's purposes that the interference be in accordance with law. It also has to be necessary in a democratic society. In *Pretty v United Kingdom*, the Court held that the 'notion of necessity implies that the interference corresponds to a pressing social need'[130]

129　*The Sunday Times v United Kingdom* (App no. 6538/74) (26 April 1979).
130　*Pretty v United Kingdom* (2002) 35 EHRR 1, 38, para [70].

We must ask, therefore, whether the measure pursues a legitimate aim—a pressing social need. Article 8 specifies that those may be related the interests of national security, public safety or the economic well-being of the country, the prevention of disorder or crime, the protection of health or morals, or the protection of the rights and freedoms of others.

Where the rights and interests of one person conflict with those of another, these must be weighed against each other to determine whose rights will prevail in the circumstances before the court. We discuss how this affects parents and children at 9.6.1.

> c. Even if the Article does have a legitimate aim, the measure must be a suitable way of achieving that aim. If it is not, then it can hardly be a necessary interference. It must also be a proportionate way of achieving that aim. If the same aim could be achieved by means that constituted less of an interference then the interference cannot be necessary.

Note that states have a margin of appreciation or discretion in to how to address certain issues, particularly those issues where there is no consensus among states. This means that states may differ in how they uphold a particular right. As Milanovic has written,

> The method that the Court uses, . . . [is] to refer to a moral consensus among the . . . European states, and to leave them a margin of appreciation when such a consensus is lacking. Hence, because it relies on this deferential comparative method, the Court generally tends to follow, rather than lead. Once a consensus emerges, it will probably impose it on the recalcitrant members of its interpretative community. . . . But until that happens, it will leave the democratic processes in diverse European societies to come up with their own solutions.[131]

This is why states may be in compliance with an Article on a particular issue and, without changing the law at all, later be out of compliance as the consensus on what protecting that right involves shifts across signatory countries.

Where a person believes that a state entity or public body has breached his or her rights as set down in the Convention, they can bring proceedings in the European Court of Human Rights in Strasbourg, France. The ECHR was incorporated into the domestic law of England and Wales by the Human Rights Act 1998, meaning that domestic courts can deal with claims of rights infringements against public authorities, including actions for damages. Given that the ECHR is part of our domestic law, the courts are also under a duty to interpret domestic legislation in a way that is incompatible with Convention rights, when resolving any ambiguity. Unfortunately, domestic courts' approach to the Human Rights Act has been described as 'extraordinarily haphazard'.[132]

Although children are not the focus of the ECHR, the provisions of the Convention apply to them as well as to adults. This means that children are rights-holders under the ECHR. However, when compared to the UN Convention on the Rights of the Child, the scope of the ECHR is much narrower. Whereas the former allows for the special nature of childhood and for a range of social justice rights, the early focus of the ECHR was on parents' rights, not children's rights.[133] Only more recently has this changed. The Convention has been particularly influential in two specific areas of child law, education and juvenile

---

[131] Dr Marko Milanovic, 'No Right to Same-Sex Marriage under the ECHR' (EJIL Talk, 24 June 2010). Available at https://www.ejiltalk.org/no-right-to-same-sex-marriage-under-the-echr/ accessed 28 October 2020.
[132] J Fortin, 'Accommodating Children's Rights in a Post Human Rights Act Era' (2006) 69(3) *Modern Law Review* 299.
[133] A Levy, 'Do Children Have Human Rights?' (2002) 32 *Family Law* 204.

justice. It has also been utilised in important cases relating to children's freedom of expression, freedom of religion, participation in legal proceedings, and privacy. The latter concerned the right of a teenage mother, Angela Roddy, to tell her life story.

> **KEY CASE** *Re Roddy (A Child) (Identification: Restriction on Publication)* [2004] 2 FLR 949
>
> When Angela Roddy was 12 years old, she became pregnant by a boy of a similar age. There were allegations in the newspapers that the Catholic Church had provided her with financial support to dissuade her from having an abortion and a number of lurid headlines such as 'Cardinal's cash will buy us pram—Dad of girl, 12, welcomes church aid'. A care order was made in respect of both Angela and the baby. Although Angela later returned home to her parents, the baby was later adopted against Angela's wishes. The court made an order preventing the identity of Angela and the father; this also indirectly protected the baby from identification.
>
> When she was 16, Angela approached Associated Newspaper Groups, publisher of the *Mail on Sunday*. She wanted an article about her experiences to be published and for her to be named and photographed for it. This required the lifting of the injunction.
>
> Munby J approached the issue by considering Angela's rights under the ECHR:
>
> > What we are actually talking about here is the extent to which we are prepared to recognise the autonomy of the 16-year-old; in particular, the extent to which we are prepared to recognise that 16-year-olds have rights to freedom of expression secured to them by Articles 8[134] and 10.
>
> He took as the starting point the issue of *Gillick* competence,[135] namely the principle that Angela had sufficient understanding and maturity to decide whether to tell her story to the newspapers:
>
> > The courts must face reality. We must, as Lord Scarman said, be sensitive to human development and social change. Angela may not yet be quite 17 years old but she is a young woman with a mind of her own and, as her solicitor B has said, a mature and articulate young person. We no longer treat our 17-year-old daughters as our Victorian ancestors did, and if we try to do so it is at our—and their—peril. Angela, in my judgment, is of an age, and has sufficient understanding and maturity, to decide for herself whether that which is private, personal and intimate should remain private or whether it should be shared with the whole world.
>
> > In my judgment (and I wish to emphasise this) it is the responsibility—it is the duty—of the court not merely to recognise but . . . to *defend* . . . the *right* of the child who has sufficient understanding to make an informed decision, to make his or her own choice.[136]
>
> Having held that Angela's Article 8 and 10 rights were engaged, he then balanced them against the rights of the baby and the baby's minor father to keep their private lives private and preserve and protect the family life they enjoyed with their respective families. (At 9.6.1 of this chapter, we consider how competing rights are balanced under the ECHR.) He considered that it would be a proportional interference with their rights and the competing rights of Angela to lift the injunction in relation to Angela, but continue to prohibit the identification of the baby or its father.

---

[134] Article 8 here is engaging not only a right to privacy but (Munby J says) a right to choose to share 'what would otherwise be private with others or, indeed, with the world at large . . . So the right to communicate one's story to one's fellow beings is protected not merely by Art 10 but also by Art 8'.

[135] We discuss *Gillick* competence at 9.5.2.

[136] Emphasis in the original.

It is important to note that the welfare principle did *not* apply this case, as it did not pertain to Angela's upbringing (see 9.2.1). This means that the welfare principle did not dictate the outcome and thereby prevented the court from engaging with the children's rights.

Another case which did not pertain to a child's upbringing, although it related to something profoundly important to the young woman concerned, is Key Case *Begum*. This was a judicial review case brought by a schoolgirl against her school's uniform policy, on the basis that it breached her rights under Article 9 ECHR.

> **KEY CASE** *R (on the application of Begum) v Headteacher and Governors of Denbigh High School* [2006] UKHL 15
>
> Shabina Begum was a pupil at Denbigh High School. There were three uniform options, one of which was a salwar kameez. This comprised a shirt and tie worn under a square-necked pinafore dress with loose trousers underneath and, weather permitting, a jumper and blazer. Shabina argued that the school had breached her Article 9 right to freedom of thought, conscience and religion by not permitting her to wear a jilbab, a long, loose-fitting, outer garment that she said better reflected her religious mandate to dress modestly in a mixed-sex setting, but which some other Muslim pupils would have refused to wear.
>
> The Supreme Court held by a majority that there was no interference with Article 9, in that she was free to attend a different school with different school uniform options, or which was single-sex. Article 9 does not give a right to a person to manifest their religion at any time and place of their choosing, nor does it protect every act motivated or inspired by a religion.
>
> Unanimously, all judges held that even if there had been an interference with her Article 9 rights, in that wearing the jilbab was a manifestation of her religion, it would have been justified under Article 9(2), which permits limitations on the Article 9 right that are 'prescribed by law and are necessary in a democratic society in the interests of public safety, for the protection of public order, health or morals, or for the protection of the rights and freedoms of others'. Here, the school uniform policy had the legitimate purpose of protecting the rights and freedoms of others.

It is important to consider whether and to what extent the young people concerned in these two cases were really able to articulate their rights without assistance. In *Re Roddy* the proceedings were brought on Angela's behalf by a newspaper publisher with a financial interest in telling her story. Asserting her legal rights was the means to an end that the publisher sought. But the judgment makes clear that she had a mind of her own and had approached the newspaper in the first place. Shabina Begum was only 13 when she first raised the issue with the school and 17 by the time of the Supreme Court hearing. Both of her parents had died, and asserting her rights in such circumstances was a considerable achievement. She too had help, in this case from her brother and other members of their community. But, like Angela Roddy, her rights were taken seriously. Although they ceded to the rights and interests of others, she was a rights-holder.

But these cases which engage children's rights are rare for the fact that the children in question were the instigators of the claims. As Fortin notes, it is more common for cases that concern children's rights to be brought by adults, either as proponents of children's rights[137] or by asserting adults' rights against those of children.[138] Key Case *Williamson* is a good example of the latter. This was a judicial review of the banning of corporal punishment in schools. While the subject matter involved children's well-being, it did not in fact involve children as parties at all.

Williamson addressed the rights of adults, and although the ultimate outcome was that the legislation had the legitimate aim of protecting the rights and freedoms of children, the children's rights and interests were articulated as a reason to interfere with the parents'

KEY CASE *R (On the application of Williamson and others) v Secretary of State for Education and Employment* [2005] UKHL 15

In 1986, following a decision of the European Court of Human Rights in *Campbell and Cosans v United Kingdom*[139] the Education (No 2) Act 1986 prohibited the corporal punishment of children in state schools. The Education Act 1996 extended this to private schools. The claimants in *Williamson* were a group of Christian headteachers, teachers, and parents who objected to the ban on corporal punishment in private schools. They asserted that it unlawfully interfered with their rights under Article 9 ECHR to manifest their religion, arguing that 'part of the duty of education in the Christian context is that teachers should be able to stand in the place of parents and administer physical punishment to children who are guilty of indiscipline' and thereby 'help form godly character'. They argued that certain passages of the Bible justified and required this.

The Lords held that when a parent authorised a child's teacher to administer corporal punishment it was a manifestation of the parents' beliefs. Although many people would see corporal punishment as always wrong, 'a free and plural society must expect to tolerate all sorts of views which many, even most, find completely unacceptable.'[140] However, while the Article 9 right to *hold* a belief was absolute, the right to *manifest* that belief was not. It was implicit in Article 9 that it protected the manifestation only of those beliefs that were consistent with basic standards of human dignity or integrity. This requirement was satisfied only where the corporal punishment inflicted was of a mild nature and was not administered with such severity or in such circumstances as to adversely affect a child's physical and moral integrity.

In this case, the corporal punishment at issue was capable of being protected by Art 9(1) because it was 'of a mild nature'. However, Article 9(2) permitted interference with Art 9(1) where that interference was in accordance with law (as it was, under the Education Act 1996), and where necessary i.e., where it was a proportional response to a legitimate aim such as to protect the rights and freedoms of others. In the case of children, 'it has long been held . . . that the rights and freedoms of the child include his interests'.[141] The legislation was held to be a proportional response to the aim of promoting children's well-being by protecting them 'against the distress, pain and other harmful effects this infliction of physical violence may cause'. Accordingly, the breach of the applicants' Article 9(1) rights were justified by the rights and interests of the children, so the applicants' claim failed.

---

[137] Fortin gives the example of the Official Solicitor taking the UK to the European Court of Human Rights in relation to the Supreme Court decision in *X and Others v Bedfordshire County Council* that councils were not vicariously liable for abuse perpetrated by foster parents.

[138] J Fortin, 'Children's Rights - Flattering to Deceive?' (2014) 26(1) *Child and Family Law Quarterly 51*.

[139] (1982) 4 EHRR 293.

[140] Lady Hale at [77].

[141] Lady Hale at [80], referring to the cases of *Hendriks* and *Johansen* discussed at 9.6.1.

rights, rather than being given prominence. In part, this was due to the process itself, as Lady Hale explains:

> My Lords, this is, and has always been, a case about children, their rights and the rights of their parents and teachers. Yet there has been no one here or in the courts below to speak on behalf of the children. No litigation friend has been appointed to consider the rights of the pupils involved separately from those of the adults. No non-governmental organisation, such as the Children's Rights Alliance, has intervened to argue a case on behalf of children as a whole. The battle has been fought on ground selected by the adults.[142]

Note too that while this was a case in respect of the ECHR, Lady Hale—albeit alone—draws on the UNCRC to explain why the state was entitled to prohibit all corporal punishment in schools: 'Above all, the state is entitled to give children the protection they are given by an international instrument to which the United Kingdom is a party, the United Nations Convention on the Rights of the Child.'[143] We turn next to the UNCRC.

SCENARIO 3

Illustration 2: Claudia (judicial review)

Claudia has applied for judicial review of her school's refusal to permit her to wear a 'purity ring'. She is a practising Christian and to her this is an expression of her personal faith and her belief that sex should only occur in a married relationship. The school uniform policy prohibits all jewellery other than a single set of plain stud earrings. In Claudia's case the school argues that the ring is representative of a moral view rather than being a necessary symbol of Christian faith. It says that by not permitting jewellery it fosters a sense of school identity and cohesion; it reduces displays of wealth and status that might cause some students to feel pressured or be bullied; and it promotes high standards of conduct as well as protecting health and safety.

A state school is a public body. The Human Rights Act 1998 s6(1) makes unlawful for a public body to act in a way which is incompatible with a Convention right. Claudia is claiming a breach of Article 9, the freedom of thought, conscience and religion, which includes a right to manifest that religion or belief.

However, as we have seen from *Begum* and *Williamson*, this is not an absolute right. Applying *Begum*, we know that Article 9 does not give a right to a person to manifest their religion at any time and place of their choosing, nor does it protect every act motivated or inspired by a religion (for example, in *Williamson*, the corporal punishment).

Claudia does not succeed in her claim for judicial review. The court holds that she was not manifesting her belief by wearing the ring because she was not religiously mandated to do so, and therefore Article 9 was not engaged at all (cf *Begum*, where the majority held they were engaged). Had she succeeded on this point, then she may still have lost on the basis that the interference was proportionate and pursued a legitimate aim.

The facts of this scenario are adapted from *R (on the application of Playfoot) v Governing Body of Millais School* [2007] EWHC 1698 (Admin).

---

[142] Lady Hale at [70].
[143] Lady Hale at [80]. Since this case, Scotland has banned smacking generally, not merely in schools, and the definition of physical punishment is that used by the UN Committee on the Rights of the Child.

9.4.2 **The UN Convention on the Rights of the Child**

The 1989 UN Convention on the Rights if the Child (UNCRC) is a core UN human rights treaty and the most ratified international convention of them all, with only one UN member—the United States—electing not to be bound by it.

The Convention encompasses 54 articles, divided into children's rights to provision, to protection, and to participation. Alston has called it 'by far the most detailed and comprehensive (in terms of the rights recognized, as opposed to the categories of persons covered) of all of the existing international human rights instruments'.[144] Article 4 states that by ratifying the Convention, a state commits to proactively implementing the rights contained it, which apply to all those under the age of 18.[145] The UK ratified the Convention in 1991.

Some of the key Articles are:

- Article 3: 'In all actions concerning children, whether undertaken by public or private social welfare institutions, courts of law, administrative authorities or legislative bodies, the best interests of the child shall be a primary consideration.'

FOCUS Think Critically

Article 3 of the UNCRC

Let us pause here for a moment. To make a child's best interests the paramount consideration, as s1 Children Act does, is to make it determine the outcome of the case. To make a child's interests *the* primary consideration is to make it one consideration among others, but the most important one. What Article 3 does is to make the child's best interests '*a* primary consideration', i.e., one consideration among others, but an important one. Alston describes this as a deliberate choice:

> It is clear that the drafters' preference for the indefinite ['a'] rather than the definite article ['the'] in this phrase is intended to indicate that the child's best interests are not to be considered as the single overriding factor. The objective implicit in opting for the word 'a' is to ensure that there is sufficient flexibility, at least in certain extreme cases, to enable the interests of those other than the child to prevail.[146]

As he points out, this was sensible given the broad scope of the UNCRC and the 'very wide range of situations' in which children's rights may be in consideration. It moved away, however, from the wording of the earlier Declaration of the Rights of the Child adopted by the UN in 1959, which had referred to the interests of the child as 'the paramount consideration'.

As Parker notes, it is unclear whether Article 3 was intended to protect children as a class or individual children.[147] The Article refers to 'all actions concerning children' and does not limit these to judicial actions in relation to individual children. However, an interpretation which obliged all decision-makers to do what is individually best for each child would be impossible when children have such different needs and contrasting interests, and state resources are limited.

---

[144] P Alston, 'The Best Interests Principle: Towards a Reconciliation of Culture and Human Rights' (1994) 8 *International Journal of Law and the Family* 1.

[145] G Lansdown, 'Implementing the UN Convention on the Rights of the Child in the UK' (1995) 7(3) *Child and Family Law Quarterly* 122.

[146] P Alston, 'The Best Interests Principle: Towards a Reconciliation of Culture and Human Rights' (1994) 8 *International Journal of Law and the Family* 1.

[147] S Parker, 'The Best Interests of the Child - Principles and Problems' (1994) 8 *International Journal of Law, Policy, and the Family* 26.

- Article 5: 'States Parties shall respect the responsibilities, rights and duties of parents . . . to provide, in a manner consistent with the evolving capacities of the child, appropriate direction and guidance in the exercise by the child of the rights recognized in the present Convention.'

- Article 9: 'States Parties shall ensure that a child shall not be separated from his or her parents against their will, except when competent authorities subject to judicial review determine, in accordance with applicable law and procedures, that such separation is necessary for the best interests of the child. . . .'

- Article 12: 'States Parties shall assure to the child who is capable of forming his or her own views the right to express those views freely in all matters affecting the child, the views of the child being given due weight in accordance with the age and maturity of the child. . . .'[148]

- Article 18: 'States Parties shall use their best efforts to ensure recognition of the principle that both parents have common responsibilities for the upbringing and development of the child. Parents or, as the case may be, legal guardians, have the primary responsibility for the upbringing and development of the child. The best interests of the child will be their basic concern.'

- Article 21: 'States Parties that recognize and/or permit the system of adoption shall ensure that the best interests of the child shall be the paramount consideration. . . .'

Note that both Articles 9 and 21 render the child's best interests the determining factor in respect of compulsory separation from parents and adoption, whereas in all other situations Article 3 applies and makes these interests a primary consideration.

Many of the articles create positive obligations on the state and parents. These can be grouped into three main categories: those that provide for children's basic needs; those that protect the child from neglect, abuse, and exploitation; and those that provide for children's participation in their families and communities. Many of the articles reflect what Eekelaar called 'developmental rights'; that is, rights to maximise one's opportunities rather than granting autonomy rights (liberty rights) to children. Thus Article 12, for example, gives children the right to express their views, but not the freedom to make choices. As Gilmore points out, 'the child's right to be heard on matters affecting them is not the same as giving the child right to make his or her own choice. It is simply right to have an opportunity to try to influence the decision maker'.[149] Alderson refers to these as 'halfway-to-autonomy rights'. She notes that:

> The Convention states that 'the best interests of the child shall be a primary consideration' (Articles 1, 3, 21). Rights are affected by the 'evolving capacities of the child', the 'responsibilities, rights and duties of parents' (Article 5) and the national law. Rights cannot be exercised in ways which would harm the child or other people, and right holders must 'respect the rights and reputations of others', as well as 'national security and public order, health and morals' (Article 13).[150]

---

[148] This is not limited to those who are *Gillick*-competent: see J Fortin, 'The *Gillick* Decision - Not Just a High Water Mark', Chapter 11 in S Gilmore, J Herring, and R Probert (eds), *Landmark Cases in Family Law* (Bloomsbury 2016).
[149] S Gilmore, 'Use of the UNCRC in Family Law Cases in England and Wales' (2017) 25 *International Journal of Children's Rights* 500.
[150] P Alderson, 'UN Convention on the Rights of the Child: Some Common Criticisms and Suggested Responses' (2000) 9 *Child Abuse Review* 439.

In these ways, she concludes, the Convention 'repeatedly qualifies children's rights'. O'Neill goes further: 'Mere insistence that certain ideals or goals are rights cannot make them into rights', she argues. 'None of these "rights" is well formed as an enforceable claim, but they can be seen as ideals that should inform the construction of institutions that secure enforceable claims.'[151] While the Convention has—as Brighouse says—been 'enormously influential on the thinking of policy-makers, welfare agencies, non-governmental organizations, and even child welfare workers',[152] that is a far cry from saying that the Convention has established enforceable, universal children's rights.

While on the face of it the number of ratifications indicates a significant level of world-wide support for children's rights, not every article is specific. Some are open to differing interpretations or leave states a significant margin of discretion in how to implement the right in question. For example, Article 27 says that children have the right to 'a standard of living adequate for the child's physical, mental, spiritual, moral and social development' and that 'the parent(s) or others responsible for the child have the primary responsibility to secure, within their abilities and financial capacities, the conditions of living necessary for the child's development'. This could potentially make a significant economic difference to children and their carers (usually their mothers).[153] Yet the Convention does not define what an adequate standard of living looks like, beyond directing states to 'take appropriate measures to assist parents and others responsible for the child to implement this right' and in cases of need to 'provide material assistance'. It then caveats that any such assistance should be 'in accordance with national conditions and within [the state's] means', so that states can decide how and to what extent to provide assistance. The overall effect is that the article is aspirational: its lack of definition means it is unenforceable. Fortin suggests, however, that this partly explains why the Convention is so popular.[154]

Freeman has written that 'laws which recognise rights are only as good as those that administer them'.[155] Unfortunately, UNCRC implementation mechanisms are weak. The UN Committee on the Rights of the Child is the body that oversees state compliance with the Convention and (if ratified) the Protocols. Every five years, each state will report to the Committee about its progress in implementing the terms of the Convention and the Committee will recommend changes that should be made within the next five-year period. The most recent UK report and Committee comments date from 2016.[156] In response to it, the Committee made wide ranging recommendations, the most significant of which related to the use of physical restraint and solitary confinement of detained children, increasing the number of social workers and removing children from their families only as a last resort, reducing school exclusions, improving outcomes for

---

[151] O O'Neill, 'Children's Rights and Children's Lives' (1992) 6 *International Journal of Law and the Family* 24 and footnote 17 thereof.

[152] H Brighouse, 'What Rights (If Any) Do Children Have?' Chapter 3 in D Archard and C Macleod (eds), *The Moral and Political Status of Children* (OUP 2002).

[153] F Olsen, 'Children's Rights: Some Feminist Approaches to the United Nations Convention on the Rights of the Child' (1992) 6 *International Journal of Law and the Family* 192.

[154] J Fortin, 'Children's Rights - Flattering to Deceive?' (2014) 26(1) *Child and Family Law Quarterly* 51.

[155] MDA Freeman, *The Rights and Wrongs of Children* (Frances Pinter 1983) 33.

[156] Committee on the Rights of the Child, *Concluding Observations on the Fifth Periodic Report of the United Kingdom of Great Britain and Northern Ireland* (June 2016). Available at https://www.niccy.org/media/2536/un-concluding-observations-june-2016.pdf accessed 30 June 2020.

children with disabilities or of lower socio-economic backgrounds, and further developing comprehensive services to support children who are victims or at risk of sexual exploitation and abuse.

In addition to the Convention, there are three optional protocols, one on the Sale of Children, Child Prostitution and Child Pornography (2000); one on the Involvement of Children in Armed Conflict (2000); and one, the Communications Procedure (2011), which established a process enabling individuals to take their complaints about violations not resolved at national level to the UN's Committee on the Rights of the Child for a non-binding determination.

In the UK, conventions that are ratified do not automatically become part of domestic law but require legislation to have effect. In contrast to the ECHR, the UNCRC has never been incorporated wholesale into the domestic law of any part of the UK, although in Wales and Scotland some general duties on ministers and public authorities have. Moreover, as the UK has not ratified the Communications Procedure Protocol, individuals in the UK who allege violation cannot bring their complaint directly to the UN. There are, however, independent children's commissioners in each nation of the UK who are required by statute to have regard to the UNCRC. In England, this role was created by the Children Act 2004.

Given that the UNCRC is not part of our domestic law, it is necessary to consider what role it does play domestically. In *R (SG and Others) v Secretary of State for Work and Pensions*,[157] Lord Hughes identified three ways in which the UNCRC may be used:

1. If the construction (i.e., meaning) of UK legislation is in doubt, the court may conclude that it should be construed, if otherwise possible, on the footing that this country meant to honour its international obligations.

2. International treaty obligations may guide the development of the common law.

3. The UNCRC may be relevant in English law to the extent that it falls to the court to apply the ECHR via the Human Rights Act 1998. The European Court of Human Rights has sometimes accepted that the Convention should be interpreted, in appropriate cases, in the light of generally accepted international law in the same field, including multilateral treaties such as the UNCRC.[158]

Gilmore has identified many examples of the UNCRC being used by English family courts 'to confirm a particular interpretation of the law or to assist in resolving an ambiguity'.[159] We have already mentioned Article 12, which our next Key Case, *Mabon*, involves. Article 3 is also much cited, with the obligation on public authorities to promote the welfare of children embodied in s11 Children Act 2004 in 'spirit, if not the precise language'.[160]

---

[157] [2015] UKSC 16, [137].

[158] For an example of the third category, see *R (P) v Secretary of State for the Home Department* [2001] EWHC Admin 357 (QBD).

[159] S Gilmore, 'Use of the UNCRC in Family Law Cases in England and Wales' (2017) 25 *International Journal of Children's Rights* 500.

[160] *ZH (Tanzania) v Secretary of State for the Home Department* [2011] UKSC 4 at [23] (Lady Hale).

KEY CASE *Mabon v Mabon* [2005] EWCA Civ 634

Three brothers, aged 17, 15, and 13, were the subject of s8 child arrangements proceedings brought by their parents. They disagreed with the position of the guardian appointed to represent their best interests, and applied for permission to become parties and to instruct their own solicitor, as that person would represent their viewpoint. Although the welfare principle does apply to s8 cases, it does not apply to applications for permission to become a party. This meant that the boys' welfare was not the court's paramount consideration at this stage.

The boys relied on Article 12 UNCRC to argue that they had a right to express their views freely, including in judicial proceedings relating to them, and that their right to a private and family life under Art 8 ECHR required respect for their personal autonomy and participation in the court's decision-making process.

The Court of Appeal held that rule 9.2A Family Procedure Rules said that leave *must* be granted if the children demonstrated sufficient understanding to take part in the proceedings, and that this rule was:

> sufficiently widely framed to meet our obligations to comply with both Art 12 of the United Nations Convention and Art 8 of the ECHR, providing that judges correctly focus on the sufficiency of the child's understanding and, in measuring that sufficiency, reflect the extent to which, in the 21st century, there is a keener appreciation of the autonomy of the child and the child's consequential right to participate in decision making processes that fundamentally affect his family life.

Thorpe LJ went on:

> Unless we in this jurisdiction are to fall out of step with similar societies as they safeguard Art 12 rights, we must, in the case of articulate teenagers, accept that the right to freedom of expression and participation outweighs the paternalistic judgment of welfare.

Mabon is also a Key Case in Chapter 10, when we discuss children's participation in private law disputes about their upbringing.

9.4.3 European Union law

Under EU law, children's rights have tended to be ancillary to the rights and protections offered to adults, such as free movement of workers. However, since 2009, children's rights have received more explicit attention. The EU Charter of Fundamental Rights (which has had the force of a treaty since 2009) refers specifically to children's rights at Article 24:

1. Children shall have the right to such protection and care as is necessary for their well-being. They may express their views freely. Such views shall be taken into consideration on matters which concern them in accordance with their age and maturity.

2. In all actions relating to children, whether taken by public authorities or private institutions, the child's best interests must be a primary consideration.

3. Every child shall have the right to maintain on a regular basis a personal relationship and direct contact with both his or her parents, unless that is contrary to his or her interests.

In addition to this, Art 14 protects free compulsory education, Article 21 prohibits age-related discrimination and Art 32 protects young people at work. The Lisbon Treaty, also

2009, states that the 'protection of the rights of the child' is an EU objective. This has led to a number of initiatives relating to the protection of children, particularly in the areas of trafficking and sexual exploitation. Several institutions of the EU, including the Council and the Commission have adopted guidelines or set agendas which relate to the promotion of children's rights across member states.

As the UK has left the EU, we must now rely only on those EU-derived rights that form part of our domestic law. What this means for children is currently unknown. It may well be that the close relationship between EU law and the UNCRC and ECHR mean that most rights are preserved to some or other extent.

9.4.4 How these laws fit together

The ECHR, the UNCRC, and the EU Charter are closely interrelated. As all member states of the EU are signatories to both the UN Convention and the ECHR, 'the EU is bound to adhere to the principles and provisions enshrined therein, at least in relation to matters that fall within the scope of the EU's competence (as defined by the EU treaties).'[161] Article 3 UNCRC, which makes the best interests of the child a primary consideration in all actions concerning children, is closely mirrored by the requirement in by Article 24.2 of the EU Charter to make the child's best interests a primary consideration in all actions 'relating to' children. 'The word "concerning" in Article 3.1, like the phrase "relating to" in Article 24.2, encompasses actions with indirect, as well as direct, effect upon children.'[162] This means that public bodies in the UK must consider the child's best interests in its decision-making on matters affecting children, even indirectly. Remember, though, that where the decision directly affects the child's upbringing, the welfare principle applies instead, elevating the child's interests to become the paramount consideration rather than a primary consideration.[163]

As between the ECHR and other treaties, the Grand Chamber observed in *Neulinger and Shuruk v Switzerland* that the ECHR 'cannot be interpreted in a vacuum but must be interpreted in harmony with the general principles of international law . . . and in particular the rules concerning the international protection of human rights.'[164] This includes the UNCRC. In *HH v Deputy Prosecutor of the Italian Republic, Genoa*, Lord Wilson noted that 'the rights of children under Article 8 [ECHR] must be examined through the prism of Article 3.1 [UNCRC]'.[165] This meant, said Lady Hale, that '[i]n making the proportionality assessment under Article 8, the best interests of the child must be a primary consideration. This means that they must be considered first. They can, of course, be outweighed by the cumulative effect of other considerations.'[166] In discovering what those interests are, the child's views must be determined; just as is required by Article 12 UNCRC.

---

[161] European Union Agency for Fundamental Rights and Council of Europe, *Handbook on European Law Relating to the Rights of the Child* (2015) 27.
[162] *ZH (Tanzania) v Secretary of State for the Home Department* [2011] UKSC 4 at [26] (Lady Hale).
[163] *ZH (Tanzania) v Secretary of State for the Home Department* [2011] UKSC 4 at [25] (Lady Hale).
[164] App no 41615/07; judgment 6 July 2010 at para [131]. A good example of the way in which domestic law, the ECHR, and the UNCRC all meet in Key Case *Axon*.
[165] *IIII v Deputy Prosecutor of the Italian Republic, Genoa* [2012] UKSC 25 at [155].
[166] *ZH (Tanzania) v Secretary of State for the Home Department* [2011] UKSC 4 at [33] (Lady Hale).

9.5 **Medical treatment of children**

The rights of both parents and children, and the relationship between rights-based claims and the welfare principle come to the fore in cases concerning medical treatment of children. In the vast majority of situations, children's medical treatment is not contentious and doctors are able to work alongside the child and his family in order to agree appropriate treatment (if there is a treatment available) or, if the child is desperately ill, the withdrawal of life support.

If there is a dispute or uncertainty about what is best for the child, then the issue should be put before a court. The hospital may be seeking a declaration about whether a particular course of treatment is lawful or whether it is lawful to restrain a patient in order to provide treatment, or they may be arguing that treatment should end and palliative care only be given. A parent or PR holder may conversely seek an application preventing the hospital from withdrawing treatment by arguing that such treatment is in the child's best interests.

A number of applications do come before the courts and while often reported in the media they generally attract little attention. The mechanism for an application is either an application under the inherent jurisdiction of the High Court or as an application for a specific issues or prohibited steps order under s8 Children Act 1989.[167] The court will grant a declaration that treatment in accordance with the hospital's plans would be lawful because such treatment is in the child's best interests, or would not be lawful because it is not in the child's best interests.

It is settled law that hospitals can make applications in relation to children. In *Tafida Raqeeb v Barts NHS Foundation Trust*, MacDonald J explained that

> The jurisdiction of the court to make such an order arises where a child lacks the capacity to make the decision for him or herself, in the context of a disagreement between those with parental responsibility for the child and those treating the child (*An NHS Trust v MB* [2006] EWHC 507 (Fam)). The court has no power to require doctors to carry out a medical procedure against their own professional judgment.[168]

Whether the application is made under the Children Act or under the inherent jurisdiction, the court's decision is based on what is in the child's best interests. The child will be represented by an independent guardian. The ability of hospitals to challenge parents' decisions about their children's medical treatment is contentious, because the state usually intervenes only when a child is at risk of significant harm, and does so through child protection processes. In a medical treatment case, this threshold is not always met. We will discuss this further when we look at four of the most controversial cases of recent years, those of Alfie Evans, Charlie Gard, Ashya King, and Tafida Raqeeb.

Before we consider these, let's consider the legal position and the Key Case, *Gillick*.

9.5.1 **The position in relation to adults**

Those who are aged over 18 are entitled to consent to or refuse medical treatment and their wishes must be respected unless they have been assessed as lacking the mental capacity to make the decision in question. 'Even when his or her own life depends on receiving

---

[167] For discussion of which, see *Re JM (A Child)* [2015] EWHC 2832 (Fam).
[168] [2019] EWHC 3320 (Admin).

medical treatment, an adult of sound mind is entitled to refuse it.'[169] This is the case even if others believe that the adult's decision is irrational, short-sighted, or fails to balance the relevant considerations in the way they themselves would. In *Re T (Adult: Refusal of Treatment)* Lord Donaldson observed that:

> An adult patient who . . . suffers from no mental incapacity has an absolute right to choose whether to consent to medical treatment, to refuse it or to choose one rather than another of the treatments being offered . . . This right of choice is not limited to decisions which others might regard as sensible. It exists notwithstanding that the reasons for making the choice are rational, irrational, unknown or even non-existent.[170]

In *Kings College Hospital NHS Foundation Trust v C and V*, MacDonald J noted that:

> this position reflects the value that society places on personal autonomy in matters of medical treatment and the very long-established right of the patient to choose to accept or refuse medical treatment from his or her doctor. . . . "Over his or her own body and mind, the individual is sovereign" (John Stuart Mill, *On Liberty*, 1859).[171]

Any assessment of capacity starts from the position that the patient has capacity. This presumption may be rebutted by evidence that she cannot understand, retain, weigh up, or communicate the information relevant to the decision, these being the requirements of capacity under s3 Mental Capacity Act 2005. A person may have the capacity to make a relatively simple decision but not a more complex one where the information is more difficult to understand.

Kings College concerned a woman, C, who declined the kidney dialysis that was required to save her life as she wanted to die. Media attention was based on evidence that C only wanted to die because she felt that she had 'lost her sparkle' (with the implication that this was not a sufficient reason).[172] But C had capacity. She was able to understand the information she was given about her prognosis and treatment options and determine what weight to give this relative to other information required to make the decision. The fact that another person may have weighed that information differently did not change the fact that C was a capacitous adult and therefore was free to choose to die.

Where a patient is assessed as not having capacity, the court must act in the adult patient's best interests, just as the welfare principle requires the court to do what is best for a child. In determining what is in her best interests, the court takes a holistic approach, just as it does with children. In *Aintree University Hospital NHS Trust v James*, the Supreme Court said that:

> [I]n considering the best interests of this particular patient at this particular time, decision-makers must look at his welfare in the widest sense, not just medical but social and psychological; they must consider the nature of the medical treatment in question, what it

[169] *St George's Healthcare NHS Trust v S* [1999] Fam 26.
[170] [1993] Fam 95.
[171] [2015] EWCOP 80.
[172] C Coleman, 'Why Woman Who Lost Her Sparkle Was Allowed to Die' (*BBC News* 2 December 2015). Available at https://www.bbc.co.uk/news/uk-34985442 accessed 18 July 2020. O Boycott, 'Court Grants Woman Right to Die after "Losing her Sparkle"' (*The Guardian*, 2 December 2015). Available at https://www.theguardian.com/uk-news/2015/dec/02/court-grants-impulsive-self-centred-mother-permission-to-die accessed 18 July 2020. Note that this characterisation of the decision as being about a right to die is incorrect; it is about a right to refuse consent; *The Guardian's* url is rather telling about the reporting.

involves and its prospects of success; they must consider what the outcome of that treatment for the patient is likely to be; they must try and put themselves in the place of the individual patient and ask what his attitude towards the treatment is or would be likely to be; and they must consult others who are looking after him or are interested in his welfare, in particular for their view of what his attitude would be.

. . . The purpose of the best interests test is to consider matters from the patient's point of view. That is not to say that his wishes must prevail . . . But insofar as it is possible to ascertain the patient's wishes and feelings, his beliefs and values or the things which were important to him, it is those which should be taken into account because they are a component in making the choice which is right for him as an individual human being.[173]

Thus any decision about the patient's best interests takes into account what they would have wanted had they had the capacity to decide for themselves, and weighs that in the mix. There is a 'strong presumption' in favour of life and the preservation of life, but this is rebuttable, for example where the person's quality of life is poor and their suffering great.[174]

When the court has decided what is in the patient's best interests, it will issue a declaration as to what is lawful. The courts' powers in relation to medical treatment do not extend to ordering doctors to treat the patient ('The court has no power to require doctors to carry out a medical procedure against their own professional judgment'[175]) or to offer particular treatments that are not otherwise available, but merely authorise the doctors to do what is accordance with their clinical judgment and within the scope of the courts' determination of what is in the patient's best interests. This protects medical staff from what would otherwise be criminal acts of assault upon the patient's body. Where treatment is not in the patient's best interests the consequence of this is that it would *not* be lawful to give that treatment, and once again the courts' declaration protects medical staff from the consequences of that, which may include the death of the patient.

We must now consider whether the law treats children's capacity to consent to medical treatment differently.

9.5.2 Children's right to consent

In many situations those with parental responsibility for a seriously ill child will reach agreement with doctors about what is best for him or her. In the event of a disagreement, the courts strongly encourage mediation. If the matter still cannot be resolved, the court may grant a declaration that a particular treatment is or is not in the child's best interests.[176] However, as with adults, the court cannot force doctors to carry out any medical procedure that is contrary to their professional judgment. The determination of the child's best interests is not limited to the child's *medical* best interests, but takes the same holistic approach that is set out in *Aintree*.

---

[173] *Aintree University Hospital NHS Trust v James* [2013] UKSC 67.
[174] *Airedale NHS Trust v Bland* [1993] AC 789 at 894.
[175] *Barts NHS Foundation Trust v Shalina Begum, Muhmamed Raqeeb and Tafida Raqeeb (by her Children's Guardian)* [2019] EWHC 2531 (Admin) and [2019] EWHC 2530 (Fam) at [115] (MacDonald J).
[176] *Re B (A Minor) (Wardship: Medical Treatment)* (1982) 3 FLR 117.

The law treats those aged 16 or 17 differently to younger children. Section 8 Family Law Reform Act 1969 gives 16- and 17-year-olds the legal capacity to consent to medical treatment including steps to diagnosis. Parental consent is not required.

STATUTORY EXTRACT *s8 Family Law Reform Act 1969*

Consent by persons over 16 to surgical, medical and dental treatment

(1) The consent of a minor who has attained the age of sixteen years to any surgical, medical or dental treatment which, in the absence of consent, would constitute a trespass to his person, shall be as effective as it would be if he were of full age; and where a minor has by virtue of this section given an effective consent to any treatment it shall not be necessary to obtain any consent for it from his parent or guardian.

(2) In this section "surgical, medical or dental treatment" includes any procedure undertaken for the purposes of diagnosis, and this section applies to any procedure (including, in particular, the administration of an anaesthetic) which is ancillary to any treatment as it applies to that treatment.

(3) Nothing in this section shall be construed as making ineffective any consent which would have been effective if this section had not been enacted.

Legal capacity means that the law grants a particular status: here, the power to consent to treatment. Mental capacity means the ability to understand and make decisions, and the tests as to whether or not an adult or a 16- or 17-year-old has mental capacity is set down in the 2005 Act. The effect of s8 is that 16- and 17-year-olds have the legal capacity to consent to medical treatment unless and until it is proven that they lack mental capacity under the Mental Capacity Act 2005.

There is no such equivalent for those aged under 16. Accordingly, the issue of whether such children could give valid consent to medical treatment has fallen to be determined by case law. The Key Case on this is *Gillick v West Norfolk and Wisbech Area Health Authority*.

KEY CASE *Gillick v West Norfolk and Wisbech Area Health Authority* [1986] 1 AC 112

In 1980, the Department of Health issued guidance to the effect that doctors could lawfully provide contraceptive advice and treatment to a girl aged under 16 without parental consent as long as the doctor 'was acting in good faith to protect her against the harmful effects of sexual intercourse'. It further noted that while the girl should be encouraged to talk to her parents, doctor-patient confidentiality applied to the situation.

Victoria Gillick was the mother of five girls aged under 16. She wrote to the health authority attempting to forbid them to provide advice or contraception to her daughters without her consent. When the authority refused, she sought a declaration that the Department of Health guidance was unlawful because it breached her parental rights and caused or encouraged sexual intercourse with a minor contrary to the Sexual Offences Act 1956. (Technically, this was not a judicial review claim (although it could have been) but an ordinary action for infringement of her rights under private law, although this is not important for our purposes.)

The House of Lords decided against Mrs Gillick by a majority of three to two. The leading judgments are by Lords Scarman and Fraser, with whom Lord Bridge agreed.

Citing Blackstone's statement that 'the power of parents over their children is derived from. . . their duty' and exists partly 'to enable the parent more effectually to perform his duty, and partly as a recompense for his care and trouble in the faithful discharge of it',[177] Lord Fraser held that:

> [P]arental rights to control a child do not exist for the benefit of the parent. They exist for the benefit of the child and they are justified only in so far as they enable the parent to perform his duties towards the child, and towards other children in the family.[178]

And that:

> Once the rule of the parents' absolute authority over minor children is abandoned, the solution to the problem in this appeal can no longer be found by referring to rigid parental rights at any particular age. The solution depends upon a judgment of what is best for the welfare of the particular child. Nobody doubts, certainly I do not doubt, that in the overwhelming majority of cases the best judges of a child's welfare are his or her parents. But, as I have already pointed out, Mrs Gillick has to go further if she is to obtain the first declaration that she seeks. She has to justify the absolute right of veto in a parent. But there may be circumstances in which a doctor is a better judge of the medical advice and treatment which will conduce to a girl's welfare than her parents.[179]

Lord Scarman said that:

> Parental rights clearly do exist, and they do not wholly disappear until the age of majority. The principle of the law, as I shall endeavour to show, is that parental rights are derived from parental duty and exist only so long as they are needed for the protection of the person and property of the child.[180] . . .

> The principle is that parental right or power of control of the person and property of his child exists primarily to enable the parent to discharge his duty of maintenance, protection, and education until he reaches such an age as to be able to look after himself and make his own decisions. . . .

> In the light of the foregoing I would hold that as a matter of law the parental right to determine whether or not their minor child below the age of 16 will have medical treatment terminates if and when the child achieves a sufficient understanding and intelligence to enable him or her to understand fully what is proposed. It will be a question of fact whether a child seeking advice has sufficient understanding of what is involved to give a consent valid in law. Until the child achieves the capacity to consent, the parental right to make the decision continues save only in exceptional circumstances. Emergency, parental neglect, abandonment of the child, or inability to find the parent are examples of exceptional situations justifying the doctor proceeding to treat the child without parental knowledge and consent: but there will arise, no doubt, other exceptional situations in which it will be reasonable for the doctor to proceed without the parent's consent.[181]

---

[177] W Blackstone, *Commentaries on the Laws of England* (17th edn, 1830), vol 1, p452.
[178] Page 170D.
[179] Page 171.
[180] Page 184.
[181] Page 189.

Gillick is one of the most important cases in child law. If you saw a doctor by yourself when you were under the age of 16, *Gillick* is to thank for it. However, its effect has been felt beyond its immediate scope, which was the provision of advice on contraception. It gave us the *Gillick* test: that a child can give a consent valid in law 'when the child achieves a sufficient understanding and intelligence to enable him or her to understand fully what is proposed'. This is known as '*Gillick* competence'. The point at which a child attains this level varies from child to child and according to the complexity of the decision that needs to be made. A child may be competent to decide a simple matter before they become able to decide a complex one.

However, there are two ways to look at *Gillick*.

Lord Fraser's view is couched in the language of the child's interests—sometimes the better decision-maker of what is in a child's best interests is a doctor not a parent. It is not about children's rights. A third party can make decisions about a child both where the child consents to that decision and where it is in the child's best interests. It is difficult to view his speech as suggesting an autonomy right.

Compare this to Lord Scarman's view that parental rights terminate on the child reaching sufficient age and understanding to consent for themselves, and that where this happens the parents' consent or refusal has no effect, i.e., the child has an autonomy right. Scarman also says that parental rights do not entirely disappear until the age of majority, but this is not incompatible with the idea that they may disappear sooner where the child is competent. It is simply that adulthood marks the point at which parental 'rights' must cease to exist: if there was a young person who was not *Gillick*-competent by the time they attained adulthood then the law in relation to incapacitous adults will apply—parents do not simply go on making decisions for their adult children.

Lord Bridge—forming the majority together with Lords Fraser and Scarman—agreed with both judgments, and Scarman agreed with Lord Fraser despite the differences in their judgments. This has created uncertainty about whether the Scarman view that parental rights do not survive the child attaining *Gillick* competency was the majority view.[182]

KEY CASE *R (on the application of Axon) v Secretary of State for Health and the Family Planning Association* [2006] EWHC 37 (Admin)

Ms Axon was the mother of five children. She sought to challenge 2004 Department of Health guidance that stated that those aged under 16 had the same right to medical confidentiality as adults unless a risk to the health, safety or welfare of the child was so serious as to outweigh her right to privacy; and that a doctor or other medical professional was able to provide reproductive health advice and treatment to a child aged under 16 without parental knowledge or consent, where the child had sufficient understanding and it was in her best interests. Ms Axon alleged that this breached her Art 8(1) right to family life because she would want to know if her daughters sought an abortion.

---

[182] For a clear discussion of the judgments and reaction to them, see J Fortin, 'The *Gillick* Decision - Not Just a High Water Mark', Chapter 11 in S Gilmore, J Herring, and R Probert (eds), *Landmark Cases in Family Law* (Bloomsbury 2016).

Silber J dismissed her application for a number of reasons, holding that Ms Axon 'does not—and because of *Gillick*, cannot—claim any right to exercise authority over what treatment her competent children receive on contraception.' Where a young person was *Gillick*-competent, no Article 8 right of the parent existed.

He held that:

- The decision of the majority in *Gillick* 'shows that they had impliedly rejected the submission that a medical professional was obliged to inform the young person's parents'. Both Lord Fraser and Lord Scarman had adopted the statement that 'the parent's right is a dwindling right'.
- 'The European Convention and the UN Convention [on the Rights of the Child] show why the duty of confidence owed by a medical professional to a competent young person is a high one and which, therefore, should not be overridden except for a very powerful reason.' Per *Yousef v Netherlands*, in 'judicial decisions where the rights under Art 8 of parents and of a child are at stake, the child's rights must be the paramount consideration'.
- 'There is nothing in the Strasbourg jurisprudence which persuades me that any parental right or power of control under Article 8 is wider than in domestic law.'
- 'As a matter of principle, it is difficult to see why a parent should still retain an Article 8 right to parental authority relating to a medical decision where the young person concerned *understands* the advice provided by the medical professional and its implications.'
- Limits on the right to confidentiality 'might well be inconsistent with the keener appreciation of the autonomy of the child and the child's consequential right to participate in decision-making processes that fundamentally affect his family life'.

He refers to Articles 5, 12, 16 and 18 UNCRC, and the Key Cases of *Williamson* and *Mabon*, the latter illustrating 'that the right of young people to make decisions about their own lives by themselves at the expense of the views of their parents has now become an increasingly important and accepted feature of family life'.

The later similar-fact Key Case of *Axon* takes *Gillick* as authority for the proposition that parental rights do not survive. However, this is only a High Court decision.

As you can see, while *Gillick* predated the ECHR's incorporation into our domestic law and the UK's ratification of the UNCRC, and does not mention these documents at all, *Axon* engages directly with both and neatly demonstrates the ways in which they are utilised to support one another. In *PD v SD and Others*, which concerned a declaration that the local authority which accommodated a 16-year-old transgender boy should not consult his parents, Keenan J agreed with Silber J's approach.[183]

Neither *Gillick* nor *Axon* were cases pertaining to a child's upbringing and thus the welfare principle did not apply. They were challenges to policies. That means that the court was concerned only with rights-based arguments rather than welfare-based ones. That is not the case with decisions relating to the appropriate medical treatment for a particular child, where the court must determine what is in the child's best interests. If we were to follow Lord Scarman's view in *Gillick* that parental rights terminate when a child attains sufficient understanding and apply it to a medical treatment case, we can immediately see a potential conflict between the child's *Gillick* autonomy rights and their best interests. A child with sufficient understanding could make a decision that was injurious to them, and there would be no parental rights still in existence to change that. The implications of this were brought

---

[183] [2015] EWHC 4103 (Fam).

starkly to the fore in two cases that Gillian Douglas termed the 'retreat from *Gillick*'. They concerned the rights of a child to *refuse* treatment rather than—as in *Gillick*—the rights of a child to *consent* to treatment. However, they also discuss whether or not a court can override the consent of a *Gillick*-competent child or a 16- or 17-year-old to consent.

9.5.3 Children's right to refuse?

When it provides those aged 16 or 17 with a right to consent to treatment, the Family Law Act 1969 also states (at s8(3)) that this does not make ineffective 'any consent which would have been effective if this section had not been enacted'. This left open whether there remained a parental right to consent to treatment opposed by the child himself, and thus whether a child had a one-sided right: a right to consent, but not to refuse if their parents consented to them being treated.

Re R (A Minor) (Wardship: Consent to Treatment) concerned a 15-year-old girl who suffered from a mental illness characterised by psychosis, violence, and suicidal behaviour interspersed with lucid periods. In those periods, she indicated that she did not consent to being medicated, although the medication prevented her from relapsing into psychosis. The Court of Appeal held that where a child refuses treatment, such treatment can be given lawfully provided that a person with parental responsibility consents or there is a court order. Although R herself was judged not to be *Gillick*-competent, the Court held that a parental and court right to consent existed irrespective of whether the child was *Gillick*-competent. This means if a *Gillick*-competent child under 16 refuses treatment she can be treated against her will as long as at least one person with PR consents, or the court exercises its powers. In his judgment, Lord Donaldson MR suggests that Lord Scarman had not, in *Gillick*, intended to suggest that a child with sufficient understanding had an *exclusive* right to determine treatment and that if this is what he had meant it was *obiter* and therefore nor binding on the courts below.[184]

Some months later, the Court of Appeal had to decide whether this also applied to a 16- or 17-year-old.[185] *Re W (A Minor) (Medical Treatment: Court's Jurisdiction)*[186] concerned a 16 year-old with the eating disorder anorexia whose refusal to eat would cause imminent brain damage and infertility. Did the fact that she had a statutory right to consent to treatment entitle her to refuse treatment? The court held that it did not. Whether or not a child is *Gillick*-competent, whether or not she has a statutory right to consent, the court (whose powers were 'theoretically limitless' and extended beyond the powers of the natural parent) or a person with parental responsibility could override her refusal to consent to treatment.

Lord Donaldson MR—who noted the academic criticism of this decision in *Re R*—said:

- 'Section 8 of the Family Law Reform Act 1969 gives minors who have attained the age of 16 a right to consent to surgical, medical or dental treatment. Such consent cannot be overridden by those with parental responsibility for the minor. It can, however, be overridden by the court.'

---

[184] [1992] Fam 11.

[185] *Re W (A Minor) (Medical Treatment: Court's Jurisdiction)* [1993] Fam 64.

[186] For a clear comment on this case, see J Eekelaar, 'White Coats or Flak Jackets? Children and the Courts - Again' (1993) 109(April) *Law Quarterly Review* 182.

- 'A minor of any age who is *Gillick*-competent in the context of particular treatments has a right to consent to that treatment which again cannot be overridden by those with parental responsibility, but can be overridden by the court.'

- 'No minor of whatever age has power by refusing consent to treatment to override a consent to treatment by someone who has parental responsibility for the minor and a fortiori a consent by the court. Nevertheless, such a refusal is a very important consideration in making clinical judgments and for parents and the court in deciding whether themselves to give consent. Its importance increases with the age and maturity of the minor.'[187]

He used an analogy of a 'flak jacket', holding that consent is the flak jacket that protects doctors from breaching criminal and civil law when they provide medical care. The doctor only needs one flak jacket to proceed.[188]

Thus, says Freeman, 'the law now discriminates and does so on grounds of age when the clear intention of the highest court in *Gillick* was to adopt a functional [i.e., capacity-based], rather than a status-based, approach'.[189] The Children Act 1989, passed soon after *Gillick*, introduced the concept of parental responsibility but did not include any clarification of the concept of *Gillick* competence or areas of uncertainty in the decision.

The effect of the retreat cases is thus that, as Sir James Munby said in *An NHS Trust v X*,[190] 'in relation to medical treatment neither the decision of a *Gillick*-competent child nor the decision of a child 16 years old or more is determinative in all circumstances':

- The consent of a *Gillick*-competent child aged under 16, or a 16- or 17-year-old, cannot be overridden by a PR holder but can be overridden by a court.

- The refusal of treatment by a *Gillick*-competent child aged under 16, or a 16- or 17-year-old, can be overridden by either a PR holder or a court.

However, he does suggest that in some medical contexts where treatment may be particularly invasive, a *Gillick*-competent child's decision may be determinative; and he also comments that in relation to some non-medical matters, the child's decision may be determinative if it is not objectively foolish or irrational, citing his own decisions in *Mabon* and *Re Roddy* in support.[191] Given that the inherent jurisdiction is theoretically limitless in scope, it may be that what he means is not that the court has no power in such a situation to override the child's decision, but that in these types of situation the child's best interests will always lie in upholding their autonomy.

The case law therefore makes a distinction between the right to consent and a right to refuse, albeit that the Court of Appeal did say that in the circumstances of a dispute between the parents and child the matter should be put before the court. (Department of Health guidance is also sceptical about the wisdom of relying on the consent of a PR

---

[187] At p83.
[188] At p78.
[189] M Freeman, 'Rethinking Gillick' (2005) 13 *International Journal of Children's Rights* 201.
[190] [2021] EWHC 65 (Fam.).
[191] See para [30].

holder against the refusal of a competent minor.)[192] This is an artificial distinction; the selection of one type of treatment may involve a refusal to consent to another alternative type. Abortion is a medical treatment, yet the intention surely cannot have been to enable a child to consent to abortion but to be unable to prevent her parent forcing abortion on her.[193] (Indeed, in *An NHS Trust v X*, Sir James Munby gives a child's refusal to consent to abortion as an example of a situation in which the decision of a *Gillick*-competent child would be treated as determinative). Moreover, as Gilmore and Herring have argued, even if the child lacks capacity in relation to one treatment about which he has sufficient understanding, she may not have sufficient understanding in relation to another treatment.[194] Despite a partial defence by Gilmore and Herring, the majority of commentators have treated the reasoning of the retreat cases harshly, describing the distinction between consent and refusal as 'absurd'[195] and 'palpable nonsense'.[196] Looking at the subsequent cases which have involved children refusing treatment, the strong pattern is for any refusal of treatment to be overridden by the court, either by holding that the child or young person is not *Gillick*-competent or by saying even if she is, it is in her best interests to override that refusal. Downie has criticised this as meaning that any assessment of the child's competency is a pretence undertaken with the aim of finding the child incompetent in order to legitimise the court overriding his wishes.[197] In at least one case, a 14-year-old girl was held not to be able to make an informed decision—but had not been given the information necessary to enable her to do so.[198] Freeman too also used the word 'pretence', arguing that 'it is clear that competence is irrelevant where the really important questions are addressed'.[199]

The distinction between a right to consent and a right to refuse is difficult to understand from the perspective of the child's autonomy. If the child has sufficient understanding to make their own decision, why should the law say that only a decision to consent should be respected? Should greater weight be given to the effect on a child of forcing medical procedures on them that they do not consent to, at the expense of their bodily integrity? On one hand, the current approach is understandable: the disputes that come before the court have serious implications, often life and death. Ward J's comment in Key Case *Re E* that the courts should be slow to allow a child to martyr himself reflect a discomfort that a child might choose to die or otherwise close off their future opportunities—in *Re W*,

---

[192] E.g. Department of Health, *Code of Practice: Mental Health Act 1983* (The Stationery Office 2008); cited by J Fortin, 'A Decade of the HRA and Its Impact on Children's Rights' [2011, February] *Family Law* 176.

[193] In reality, no doctors would perform an abortion without the consent of the young woman or a court order that it was in her best interests, but that is a matter of defensive practice rather than law. Lord Donaldson MR acknowledges this issue in *Re W* at p79.

[194] S Gilmore and J Herring, '"No" Is the Hardest Word: Consent and Children's Autonomy' (2011) 23(1) *Child and Family Law Quarterly* 3. See also 'Children's Refusal of Medical Treatment: Could *Re W* be Distinguished?' [2011, July] *Family Law* 715, by the same authors.

[195] J Urwin, '*Re R*: The Resurrection of Parental Powers?' (1992) 8 *Professional Negligence* 69, 72.

[196] J Harris, 'Consent and End of Life Decisions' (2003) 29 *Journal of Medical Ethics* 10, 15.

[197] See, e.g., *Re L (Medical Treatment: Gillick Competency)* [1998] 2 FLR 810, discussed by A Downie at 'Consent to Medical Treatment: Whose View of Welfare?' [1999, Dec] *Family Law* 818.

[198] *Re L* [1998] 2 FLR 810.

[199] M Freeman, 'Rethinking Gillick' (2005) 13 *International Journal of Children's Rights* 201.

even if W had eventually eaten, it may not have been in time to save her fertility and brain function. The autonomy rights of the child can conflict with the child's right to an open future, or in some cases, to any future at all.

SCENARIO 2

Illustration 4: Mishal and Lee (medical treatment case)

We are now clearer about the legal position of Lee. At the age of 17 he has a statutory right to consent to medical treatment although he cannot force doctors to provide him with treatment that they consider not appropriate in their professional judgment. He can consent even if his mother refuses; this is the effect of the 1969 Act.

However, he cannot refuse consent if Mishal consents. We know from the retreat cases that the consent of a *Gillick*-competent minor can be overridden. However, the hospital would be exceptionally unwise to treat Lee in reliance on Mishal's consent, whatever the 'retreat' cases say, because of the uncertainty about the interpretation of *Gillick*; and indeed there will be practical issues because he may need restraining. An application to court should therefore be made, although good practice would certainly be to try to negotiate between Mishal and Lee, perhaps with the aid of a mediator. The case would be dealt with on the basis of Lee's best interests, with his views and those of his mother having weight, particularly given his weight, but, as you can see from the case law, the likely outcome, if the treatment has a good chance of saving his life, is to authorise the treatment.

The outcome may be different if the treatment was more experimental or the risks and benefits more finely balanced. However, there is a strong presumption in favour of a course of action that will prolong life, but that presumption is rebuttable.[200]

Now consider the position of Lee. He has a strong view. Is this view to be respected, or to be overruled? It would be a terrible thing to physically force him. Do not forget that when he turns 18 he can refuse treatment and provided that he has mental capacity the fact that others may think that catastrophically unwise will have no effect, as in Key Case *Re E*. But is his choice really free of influence, and fully informed? Should we save him from himself? Or allow him a dignified death, insofar as that is possible? You decide.

9.6 Rights and welfare in conflict?

A number of consequences arise from the fact that children are rights-holders.

1. As we have seen, the rights of a child as set out in law may conflict with their best interests and the requirement under English law that decisions relating to their upbringing be taken on the basis of the welfare principle.

2. The child may have several rights which need to be balanced against one another, or an absolute right that prevails over a non-absolute one. For example, in relation to the circumcision of a male child, the child's freedom to manifest his religion (Article 9) may conflict with his own right to physical integrity, which is an aspect of Article 8's right to private life. As neither article is absolute, and can thus be interfered

---

[200] *Wyatt v Portsmouth Hospitals NHS Trust* [2005] EWCA Civ 1181.

with, the relative importance of each article to the child's situation will need to be considered before one right is determined to prevail. In a child protection context, the rights of a child to private and family life with his birth parents (Article 8) may conflict with his Article 3 right to not to be subjected to torture or to inhuman or degrading treatment or punishment. As Article 3 is absolute, if the child protection concerns attain the requisite level of severity to engage Article 3, that article must prevail and in such a situation clearly also protects his interests.

3. The rights of a child as set out in law may conflict with the rights and interests of others.

In this section, we consider how the European Court of Human Rights and our domestic courts have dealt with these consequences.

9.6.1 Conflicting rights and interests under the ECHR

At 9.4.1 we saw that under the ECHR, in the event of a conflict the rights of each person concerned must be weighed to determine whose rights will prevail in the circumstances before the court. For example, in adoption, the Article 8 rights to family life of the child, the rights of the birth parents and (if this exists as a fact, because the child has been with them for some time) the rights of the potential adopters must all be balanced (Chapter 12). In this chapter, the Key Cases of *Williamson* and *Roddy* both involved the court in balancing the rights of children v parents, and child v child respectively.

Balancing the parties' respective rights and interests may be easy in some cases and difficult in others. Balancing is closely linked to consideration of the proportionality of the interference compared to the interests involved, the need for states to consider competing interests, and the margin of appreciation given to state authorities.[201] However, the European Court has repeatedly emphasised that the rights and interests of the child will be accorded significant weight in the balancing exercise:

* *Hendriks v Netherlands*: 'where . . . there is a serious conflict between the interests of the child and one of its parents which can only be resolved to the disadvantage of one of them, the interests of the child must, under Article 8(2), prevail.'[202]
* *Hokkanen v Finland*: 'the rights and freedoms of all concerned must be taken into account, and more particularly the best interests of the child and his or her rights under Article 8 of the Convention. Where contacts with the parent might appear to threaten those interests or interfere with those rights, it is for the national authorities to strike a fair balance between them.'[203]
* *Johansen v Norway*: 'a fair balance has to be struck between the interests of the child . . . and those of the parent . . . In carrying out this balancing exercise, the Court will attach particular importance to the best interests of the child, which, depending on their nature and seriousness, may override those of the parent. In particular, . . . the parent cannot be entitled under Article 8 of the Convention to have such measures

---

[201] B Cali, 'Balancing Test: European Court of Human Rights (ECtHR)', *Max Planck Encyclopedia of International Law* (2018).
[202] App no 8427/78; (1983) 5 EHRR 223.
[203] App no 19823/92; (1995) 19 EHRR 139.

taken as would harm the child's health and development.'[204] In this case, the court rejected the position of Norway, which had argued that the court should, in judging necessity, attach paramount importance to the best interests of the child rather than attempting to strike a fair balance.

- *Scott v United Kingdom*: 'consideration of what is in the best interests of the child is always of crucial importance'.[205]
- *Elsholz v Germany*: 'The Court further recalls that a fair balance must be struck between the interests of the child and those of the parent and that in doing so particular importance must be attached to the best interests of the child which, depending on their nature and seriousness, may override those of the parent. In particular, the parent cannot be entitled under Article 8 of the Convention to have such measures taken as would harm the child's health and development.'[206] (It thus cites *Johansen*.)
- *Yousef v Netherlands*: 'the court reiterates that in judicial decisions where the rights under Article 8 of parents and those of a child are at stake, the child's rights must be the paramount consideration. If any balancing of interests is necessary, the interests of the child must prevail'.[207]
- *Hoppe v Germany*: 'In determining whether the impugned measure was "necessary in a democratic society", the Court has to consider whether, in the light of the case as a whole, the reasons adduced to justify this measure were relevant and sufficient for the purposes of para.2 of Article 8 of the Convention. Undoubtedly, consideration of what lies in the best interest of the child is of crucial importance in every case of this kind. . . . The Court further recalls that a fair balance must be struck between the interests of the child and those of the parent and that, in striking such a balance, particular importance must be attached to the best interests of the child which, depending on their nature and seriousness, may override those of the parent.'[208] (It cites *Elsholz* as authority.)

With the exception of *Hendriks* and *Yousef*, these cases emphasise the importance of the child's rights and interests but do not go as far as to make these determine the outcome of the case. *Yousef* in particular is an outlier among the other cases in referring to paramountcy. It cites as authority *Elsholz*, but that is not what *Elsholz* says, as *Elsholz* reiterates the approach set out in *Johansen*.[209] It is possible that the *Yousef* court did not intend to change the law, given its use of the word 'reiterates'.[210] It is *Johansen* that has been followed with its statement that the rights and interests of the parties should be balanced, with the children's rights prevailing dependent on their nature and seriousness. This has led

---

[204] App no 17383/90; (1997) 23 EHRR 33.
[205] *Irene M Scott v the United Kingdom* App no 34745/97; [2000] 1 FLR 958.
[206] App no 25735/94; (2002) 34 EHRR 58.
[207] App no 33711/96; [2003] 1 FLR 210.
[208] App no 28422/95; (2004) 38 EHRR 15.
[209] See S Choudhry, 'The Adoption and Children Act 2002, the Welfare Principle and the Human Rights Act 1998 – A Missed Opportunity?' [2003] *Child and Family Law Quarterly* 119. As Choudhry notes, while precedent does not work in the European Court same way as it does in common law jurisdictions, the Court still strives for consistency.
[210] S Choudhry and J Herring, *European Human Rights and Family Law* (Hart 2010) 233.

Choudhry and Herring to conclude that 'the ECHR has been far more comfortable with the notion that parents have rights over their children than the English courts have'.[211] Indeed, many of the cases listed above involved claims by parents for family life with their children, not claims by children themselves.

9.6.2 The domestic approach

Our domestic courts have strained to say that the welfare principle is compatible with the ECHR. In *Re KD (A Minor) (Ward: Termination of Access)*, Lord Oliver said that:

> Such conflict as exists, is, I think, semantic only and lies only in differing ways of giving expression to the single concept that the natural bond in the relationship between parent and child gives rise to universally recognised norms which ought not to be gratuitously interfered with and which, if interfered with at all, ought to be so only if the welfare of the child dictates.[212]

They have, for example, treated decisions made under the welfare principle that also interfere with an Article 8 right as satisfying the Article 8 requirement that the interference be 'necessary'.

Domestic courts often refer to the UNCRC and the ECHR in support of decisions they have actually made under the welfare principle, where the outcome under each approach would be the same. However, this skirts over the potential that the child's welfare will conflict with the rights and interests of others in other cases. In *Johansen* itself the European Court emphasised that the ultimate aim of care proceedings was to reunite the natural parent and the child and thereby emphasised the importance of that natural bond—but held nevertheless that 'a fair balance has to be struck between the interests of the child in remaining in public care and those of the parent in being reunited with the child.'

That being the case, most legal commentators disagree with Lord Oliver and take the view that there is a difference between making a decision that is in the child's best interests and the interfering with a person's rights because it is necessary to do so:

- A decision made under the welfare principle does not have to be necessary, just slightly better for the child than the alternative. That is a different, lower, standard than necessity under the ECHR.

- Under the welfare principle the child's interests will always prevail; under the ECHR they may not. They provide a reason to interfere with another's rights[213] and are given particular importance, but they do not automatically determine the outcome in all cases. The rights and interests of those concerned are balanced and the rights and interests of the child may cede to those of others. This leaves open the possibility that despite the interests of the child being given particular importance, there may be a case in which the rights of the parent prevail against those of a child. This is the *Johansen* approach and Tolson has suggested that it 'remains the proper approach required by

---

[211] S Choudhry and J Herring, *European Human Rights and Family Law* (Hart 2010) 225.

[212] [1988] AC 806.

[213] Protecting the rights and interests of children is a legitimate aim eg under Article 8(2): *Olsson v Sweden (No 1)* (1988) 10 EHRR 259, at [64ff].

the Convention. It is materially, and none too subtly, different from section 1 of the Children Act 1989. It ought to produce different results in some cases.'[214]

- The processes for reaching the outcome are different. The ECHR starts with a right and then looks at whether there are justified and permissible reasons for interference with it. You can see this when you consider Key Cases *Williamson* or *Begum*, for example. The welfare principle asks only what option is best for the child.

- In discussing cases relating to the naming of children in the media (such as Key Case *Re Roddy*), Helen Fenwick has argued that the courts have held that such cases do not relate to a child's upbringing—and therefore do not engage the welfare principle—precisely so that they can avoid having to address the direct conflict between the rights of media freedom of expression and the child's welfare.[215] As Peter Harris writes:

  > If, as is the practice of the courts, both Article 8 and the welfare principle are applied to determine which, if any, order to make, commentators argue that either the court must balance the interests of everybody affected (albeit giving the child's interests especial weight when that is necessary and proportionate) or simply focus on what is best for the child, taking into account the interests of others only in so far as they affect the child's welfare. The courts cannot, they argue, apply both rules when deciding which, if any, order to make and without creating a potential for conflict.[216]

- In private law proceedings such as those relating to contact with a child, a rights-based approach would consider the Article 8 rights of parents and children to family life with one another before considering whether interference with that right would be justified under Article 8(2) in the interests of, inter alia, health or morals or the rights and interests of others. Only if the interference was a necessary and proportionate response to one or more of these legitimate aims would the court stop short of ordering contact.[217] In a welfare-based decision, the child's interests in contact would be considered and would determine the outcome.

9.6.3 Reconciling the incompatibility

In our discussion of children's moral rights at 9.3, we identified that under the will theory, all rights are aspects of a single liberty right, the right to make choices and thereby exercise autonomy. It is autonomy rights which present us with the most difficulties when it comes to reconciling rights and interests.

Fortin suggests that *Gillick* competency should be a required of a child before he or she is able to assert autonomy rights. A child would not have rights under the will theory without having sufficient understanding to exercise their choices rationally. Such an approach

---

[214] Robin Tolson QC, 'The Welfare Test and Human Rights: Where's the Beef in the Sacred Cow?' *Family Law Week* 3 May 2005. Available at http://www.familylawweek.co.uk/site.aspx?i=ed307 accessed 19 August 2020.

[215] H Fenwick, 'Clashing Rights, the Welfare of the Child and the Human Rights Act' (2004) 67 *The Modern Law Review* 889.

[216] P Harris, 'Article 8 of the European Convention and the Welfare Principle: A Thesis of Conflict Resolution' [2014, March] *Family Law* 331.

[217] See S Choudhry and H Fenwick, 'Taking the Rights of Parents and Children Seriously: Confronting the Welfare Principle under the Human Rights Act' (2005) *Oxford Journal of Legal Studies* 453.

would fit with the will theory which denies rights to children only because they lack the capacity to make reasoned choices. During the period of incapacity, adults act as proxies making decision on children's behalf.

In Key Case *Re Roddy*, Munby seems to take the approach of using *Gillick* competency as a gateway to the exercise of Angela Roddy's autonomy rights under two articles of the ECHR, the Article 8 right to private and family life and the Article 10 freedom of expression. Munby J 'skilfully inserted the test of *Gillick* competence into the interpretation of [Angela Roddy's] position under the Convention', Fortin writes, and 'in this way Munby J made clear his view that certain Convention rights are only available to *Gillick*-competent children.'[218] Similarly, in Key Case *Axon* Silber J mapped *Gillick* competence onto the ECHR, holding that no Article 8 right outlasted the child attaining sufficient understanding, and thereby treating the child as holding Article 8 rights—and her mother as not holding those rights—from the point when the former became competent to decide the issue in question for herself.

Of course, this does not help us with the issue of children exercising autonomy in a way that harms them even when they are *Gillick*-competent. Do not forget that a person may have sufficient understanding of an issue but still choose unwisely or in a way that others may consider to be catastrophically contrary to their interests. One way to address this is to prevent children from making decisions that foreclose their future options, as we discuss at 9.3.2. In doing so, we protect their future autonomy rights, but at the expense of their current autonomy rights.

If we turn to the interest theory of rights, the position is different. Under this theory, all children, whether or not of rational understanding, are rights-holders and their rights exist to protect their fundamental interests, albeit that not all interests are of sufficient importance to give rise to a right. Jane Fortin argues that the rights contained in the ECHR are 'formulations of aspects of the good life and should be interpreted in a way that enhances a person's life'. On that basis, she says, as 'neither adults nor children have a "right" to be treated in a way that fundamentally harms them. . . . it follows that a child's welfare cannot be inconsistent with his rights'.[219] This means that we should interpret rights under the ECHR consistently with what is in the rights-holder's interests. There is no incompatibility between the two.

Where there are competing interests between adults and children, Fortin suggests that the court should continue to balance these rights against one another, 'with the various items of evidence relating to the child's welfare being absorbed into the balancing process. Only if the balancing act produces no obvious answer will the child's interests prevail' over those of the adults.[220] If a wider approach to the welfare principle was adopted, one which better reflected the child's position in a nexus of relationships (such as Herring's relationships-based welfare, which we discuss at 9.2.4) then this may not be necessary in many cases. There would be fewer clashes between the respective interests of adults and children because the child's interests would include the happiness and well-being of those around him.

---

[218] J Fortin, 'The *Gillick* Decision - Not Just a High Water Mark', Chapter 11 in S Gilmore, J Herring, and R Probert (eds), *Landmark Cases in Family Law* (Bloomsbury 2016).
[219] J Fortin, 'Accommodating Children's Rights in a Post Human Rights Act Era' (2006) 69(3) *Modern Law Review* 299.
[220] J Fortin, 'Accommodating Children's Rights in a Post Human Rights Act Era' (2006) 69(3) *Modern Law Review* 299.

Peter Harris suggests a different approach. He proposes that Article 8 should provide parameters within which courts could make decisions rather than being the decision-making criterion. Courts would be precluded from exercising their powers in a way that disproportionately interfered with the Article 8 rights of the parties, but the welfare principle (or any other principle we decided to apply) would be the basis of the decision. A court could make any decision that was in the child's welfare as long as it did not interfere with the child's or others' Article 8 rights. This, Harris argues, has three main advantages. First, it would avoid any conflict between the ECHR and the welfare principle having to be adjudicated. Second, this approach better reflects the way in which the Convention provides states with a margin of appreciation—a discretion in how it goes about upholding an individual's rights. Finally, it would 'advance the policy which lay at the heart of the Children Act 1989, namely defending families against unwarranted interventions by the state'.[221]

9.6.4 The cases of Charlie Gard and Alfie Evans

In recent years there have been several very high-profile cases in which the parents of terminally ill children have fought to prolong the child's life while doctors seek a declaration that withdrawal of life support is in the child's best interests. These cases, concerning the little boys Alfie Evans and Charlie Gard, both of whom were terminally ill, bring together a number of issues that we have discussed in this chapter, including the children's welfare, parents' and children's rights, state interference in family life, and the difficulties in deciding what is in a child's best interests. We are now going to discuss two such cases. These cases involved parents fighting desperately against what they perceived to be medical professionals, supported and permitted by the state, murdering their children. Indeed, Alfie Evans' father threatened to bring a private murder prosecution against the doctors involved, and there were sizeable public protests at each hospital and considerable involvement from foreign-based campaign organisations.

The first case we will discuss is that of Alfie Evans.

KEY CASE *Alder Hey Children's NHS Foundation Trust v Evans and Another* (the Alfie Evans case)

Alfie Evans was born in May 2016. A few months later, he suffered a number of seizures and was hospitalised. It became clear that he had a degenerative brain condition: his brain was turning into water and cerebral-spinal fluid, and he was placed on a ventilator to help him breathe. Scans in February 2018 showed that Alfie had no capacity to hear, touch, taste, or see. The hospital made a court application for a declaration that continued ventilation was not in his best interests. By this time Alfie was completely dependent on mechanical ventilation and continued to have frequent seizures. It was unlikely that he felt pain or discomfort. Alfie's parents argued that he should be taken abroad to a country which would keep him ventilated and thus alive, albeit that there was no prospect of recovery.

---

[221] P Harris, 'Article 8 of the European Convention and the Welfare Principle: A Thesis of Conflict Resolution' [2014, March] *Family Law* 331.

Hayden J found that continued ventilation was medically futile (because there was no possibility of Alfie's position ever improving)[222] and that it compromised his dignity and autonomy. It was in Alfie's best interests to withdraw ventilation and provide palliative care for Alfie for the short period of time between the removal of that life support and his death.

Alfie's parents appealed successively to the Court of Appeal, the Supreme Court (which refused permission to appeal on the basis that there was no arguable point of law), and the European Court of Human Rights (which declared the application inadmissible because there was no evidence of any human rights violation) and on each occasion they were unsuccessful. While the Supreme Court declined to hear the appeal, they did note that Alfie's best interests were the 'gold standard' against which decisions about him had to be made. Drawing on their earlier decision in *Aintree University Hospital NHS Trust v James*,[223] they said that if treatment was not in the patient's best interests then it followed that it would not be lawful to give that treatment, because doing so would be contrary to the patient's best interests.

On 23 April 2018 ventilation with withdrawn from Alfie, and five days later he died.

The reports of this case can be found at: [2018] EWHC 308 (Fam) (20 February 2018); [2018] ECHR 297 (28 March 2018) European Court of Human Rights (application number 14238/18); [2018] EWHC 818 (Fam) (11 April 2018); [2018] EWCA Civ 805 (16 April 2018); Supreme Court Permission to appeal refused with reasons[224] (20 April 2018); [2018] ECHR 357 (23 April 2018) European Court of Human Rights (application number 18770/18); and [2018] EWCA Civ 984 (25 April 2018).

The Alfie Evans case came soon after the case of Charlie Gard, another highly controversial case that attracted much attention internationally as well as in the UK.

KEY CASE *Great Ormond Street Hospital v Yates and Others (the Charlie Gard case)*

Charlie suffered from an incurable and rare mitochondrial depletion syndrome which caused progressive brain damage and seizures. His parents sought permission to remove him for an experimental, unproven treatment in the United States. They did not believe that the prognosis was as bad as suggested. In contrast to the Alfie Evans case, Charlie's parents did not seek to prolong his life indefinitely, but wanted to switch to palliative care only once the experimental US treatment had been given a chance. The High Court made a declaration that it was not in Charlie's best interests to undergo the suggested treatment in the US because such treatment was futile—there was no evidence that the treatment was capable of crossing the blood/brain barrier. The court also found that Charlie was probably capable of feeling pain, and held that it was not in his best interests for artificial ventilation to continue; and that it was in his best interests for ventilation to be withdrawn. Apparently mindful of the international attention the case had caused, Francis J noted that:

In this country children have rights independent of their parents. Almost all of the time parents make decisions about what is in the best interests of their children and so it should be.

---

[222] Medically futile means there is 'no real prospect of curing or at least palliating the life-threatening disease or illness from which the patient is suffering'. The Court of Appeal in *Gard* considered whether the law should consider whether some treatment 'may bring some benefit to the patient even though it has no effect on the underlying disease or disability', i.e., would nonetheless be medically futile.

[223] [2013] UKSC 67.

[224] https://www.supremecourt.uk/docs/in-the-matter-of-alfie-evans-court-order.pdf.

Just occasionally, however, there will be circumstances such as here where a hospital and parents are unable to decide what is in the best interests of a child who is a patient at that hospital. It is precisely because the hospital does not have power in respect of that child that this hospital makes an application to the court, to an independent judge, for a determination of what is in that child's best interests. In circumstances where there is a dispute between parents and the hospital, it was essential that Charlie was himself independently represented and a guardian was therefore appointed to represent Charlie so that there was someone who could independently report to the court as to what was in his best interests.[225]

Like Alfie's parents, Charlie's parents repeatedly appealed and applied to the European Court of Human Rights which held the application to be inadmissible. In its judgment the European Court referred explicitly to the UNCRC and the EU Charter of Fundamental Rights in support of its decision.

Charlie died on 28 July 2017.

The reports of this case can be found at [2017] EWHC 972 (Fam) (11 April 2017); [2017] EWCA Civ 410 (23 May 2017) Supreme Court permission to appeal refused with reasons (8 June 2017);[226] [2017] ECHR 559 (13 June 2017) European Court of Human Rights (application no. 39793/17); Supreme Court permission to appeal refused with reasons (19 June 2017);[227] [2017] ECHR 605 (27 June 2017) European Court of Human Rights (application no. 39793/17); [2017] EWHC 1909 (Fam) (24 July 2017) and directions (26 and 27 July 2017).[228]

Significant harm or best interests?

The parents' arguments for prolonging the boys' lives were held not to be in their best interests. As a response to this, Charlie Gard's parents sought to argue that courts should not intervene in parenting decisions unless the child was at risk of significant harm[229]—the threshold for making a care application—and that the court intervening and making decisions on the basis simply of Charlie's best interests was an unjustified interference in their parental rights under Article 8. While they accepted that the court had jurisdiction in relation to the lawfulness of the treatment by Great Ormond Street Hospital, they argued that the court had no jurisdiction to determine whether they could take Charlie abroad for treatment unless that would cause Charlie significant harm or there was a dispute between PR holders. They argued that without either of these the courts could not intervene in the parents' exercise of their PR. They argued that if the court obtained jurisdiction:

simply by a party approaching the court and raising questions as to what is in the best interests of a child that would erode the whole concept of parental responsibility; in fact it would shift the responsibility from parents to the state.[230]

---

[225] [2017] EWHC 1909 (Fam) (24 July 2017) at [18] (Francis J).
[226] An oral judgment was delivered and can be found at https://www.supremecourt.uk/news/permission-to-appeal-hearing-in-the-matter-of-charlie-gard.html accessed 17 August 2020.
[227] There is no judgment to cite, but the statement of reasons can be found at https://www.supremecourt.uk/news/latest-judgment-in-the-matter-of-charlie-gard.html accessed 17 August 2020.
[228] A copy of the order can be found at https://www.judiciary.uk/wp-content/uploads/2017/07/cg-order.pdf but is not otherwise reported.
[229] In fact, it was found—although Francis J's judgment could have made it clearer—that Charlie was suffering significant harm. A clear discussion of the facts can be found in N Hammond-Browning, 'When Doctors and Parents Don't Agree: The Story of Charlie Gard' (2017) 14 *Bioethical Inquiry* 461.
[230] This is taken from a transcript of the parents' QC's arguments prepared by Rachel Taylor for her article 'Parental Decisions and Court Jurisdiction: Best Interests or Significant Harm?' [2020] *Child and Family Law Quarterly* 141.

The argument that parents have a right to harm their children as long as it is not significant seems, in the context of this case—the prolongation of a life of suffering—to be singularly unedifying, but as we see in Chapter 12 the state does only take children into care if they are suffering or likely to suffer (meaning that there is a real possibility of them suffering) *significant* harm. As Taylor has written, 'From the parents' perspective, if the court's jurisdiction could be invoked without firm and clear limits, parental responsibility would essentially be held on gift from the state, a gift that could be revoked at any point.'[231] Indeed, the children's parents are not alone in arguing that in medical cases relating to children the courts should follow the parents' wishes, subject to some safeguards, as medical ethicists Diekema and Gillon have separately argued as much.[232]

The argument that court involvement should be limited only to significant harm situations was rejected both by the Court of Appeal ('the sole principle is that the best interests of the child must prevail and that must apply even to cases where parents, for the best of motives, hold on to some alternative view'[233]) and the Supreme Court. In *Gard*, the Supreme Court stated that:

> parents are not entitled to insist upon treatment by anyone which is not in their child's best interests. Furthermore, although a child can only be compulsorily removed from home if he is likely to suffer significant harm, the significant harm requirement does not apply to hospitals asking for guidance as to what treatment is and is not in the best interests of their patients.[234]

If, as Lord Fraser held in *Gillick*, 'parental rights to control a child do not exist for the benefit of the parent' but instead for the benefit of the child, then a parent does not have a right to make a decision that is contrary to the welfare of the child. Both the inherent jurisdiction and s10 Children Act (applications for a s8 order with leave) enable an application to be made by others even where the PR holders are not in dispute with one another. Taylor points out that if state intervention was limited to situations of significant harm, this would hardly be conducive to any ongoing relationship between the doctors and the parents and an acrimonious relationship will impede rather than help the care of the child.[235]

Moreover, the concept of harm encompasses more than physical pain and suffering. As Poole J said in *Guy's and St Thomas' Children's NHS Foundation Trust v Pippa Knight*, the absence of pain is not the same as the absence of harm, and an unconscious child may nonetheless experience a burden upon their person even if they are unconscious:

> Her condition and the treatment it necessitates are significant burdens. Even if one discounted these factors in the welfare assessment, on the grounds that Pippa has no conscious awareness of them, they ought to be taken into account in the broad assessment of

---

[231] R Taylor, 'Parental Decisions and Court Jurisdiction: Best Interests or Significant Harm?' [2020] *Child and Family Law Quarterly* 141.

[232] DS Diekema, 'Parental Refusals of Medical Treatment: The Harm Principle as Threshold for State Intervention' (2004) 25(4) *Theoretical Medicine and Bioethics* 243; R Gillon, 'Why Charlie Gard's Parents Should Have Been the Decision-Makers about Their Son's Best Interests' (2018) 44 *Journal of Medical Ethics* 462.

[233] [2017] EWCA Civ 410 (McFarlane LJ).

[234] The *Gard* decision of 8 June, at https://www.supremecourt.uk/news/permission-to-appeal-hearing-in-the-matter-of-charlie-gard.html accessed 17 August 2020.

[235] R Taylor, 'Parental Decisions and Court Jurisdiction: Best Interests or Significant Harm?' [2020] *Child and Family Law Quarterly* 141. See also J Bridgeman, '"Leaving No Stone Unturned": Contesting the Medical Care of a Seriously Ill Child' [2017] *Child and Family Law Quarterly* 63.

her interests. It must be relevant to any assessment of her interests that she has such grave loss of function and requires such intensive and intrusive treatment to preserve her life.[236]

Since their sons' deaths, the parents of both Charlie and Alfie have continued to argue for the introduction of laws in their children's names that would substitute the best interests test with one permitting court intervention only where the child was at risk of significant harm, thereby strengthening parental rights. Such a move would frustrate both children's rights and their interests,[237] and it would bring additional problems, such as that it would place the UK at odds with international law. Moreover, given that doctors cannot be compelled to offer treatment against their clinical judgment, such a change would have no effect on medical practice unless accompanied by a requirement that doctors had to carry out any treatment that parents desired irrespective of efficacy.[238] That would cause significant resourcing issues for the NHS, and create a situation where there was no judicial scrutiny and no separate representation to protect the interests of the child. However, Iowa—not bound by either the ECHR or the UNCRC—has recently passed a law preventing doctors from going to court to seek permission to withdraw live-sustaining treatment, even if that treatment is medically futile.[239] This leaves the best interests of the child in the hands of the child's parents.

We now turn to look at a more recent case, that of Tafida Raqeeb, in which the interests of the child did indicate a continuation of life-sustaining treatment.

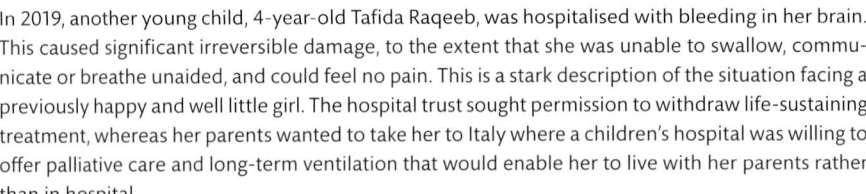

KEY CASE *Barts NHS Foundation Trust v Shalina Begum, Muhhamed Raqeeb and Tafida Raqeeb (by her Children's Guardian)* [2019] EWHC 2531 (Admin) and [2019] EWHC 2530 (Fam) (the Tafida Raqeeb case)

In 2019, another young child, 4-year-old Tafida Raqeeb, was hospitalised with bleeding in her brain. This caused significant irreversible damage, to the extent that she was unable to swallow, communicate or breathe unaided, and could feel no pain. This is a stark description of the situation facing a previously happy and well little girl. The hospital trust sought permission to withdraw life-sustaining treatment, whereas her parents wanted to take her to Italy where a children's hospital was willing to offer palliative care and long-term ventilation that would enable her to live with her parents rather than in hospital.

Reviewing the principles laid down in the Alfie Evans and Charlie Gard cases, MacDonald J held that it was in her best interests to be treated in Italy:

- 'In circumstances where T is not in pain, where the burden of the treatment is low, where there is a responsible body of medical opinion that considers that she can and should be maintained on life support with a view to her being cared for at home on ventilation by her family in the same manner in which a number of children in a similar situation to Tafida are

[236] [2021] EWHC 25 (Fam) at [76]–[78] (Poole J).

[237] E Cave and E Nottingham, 'Who Knows Best (Interests)? The Case of Charlie Gard' (2017) 26(3) *Medical Law Review* 500.

[238] DI Benbow, 'An Analysis of Charlie's Law and Alfie's Law' (2019) 28(2) *Medical Law Review* 223.

[239] Medica Futility Blog, 'Iowa Enacts Strongest Simon's Law in the World – Parents May Demand Futile Treatment' (Bioethics.net, 5 July 2020). Available at http://www.bioethics.net/2020/07/iowa-enacts-strongest-simons-law-in-the-world-parents-may-demand-futile-treatment/ accessed 26 October 2020.

treated in this jurisdiction, where there is a funded care plan to this end, where Tafida can be safely transported to Italy, where the continuation of life-sustaining treatment is consistent with the religious and cultural tenets by which Tafida was being raised and having regard to the sanctity of Tafida's life, this case *does* in my judgment lie towards the end of the scale where the court should give weight to the reflection that in the last analysis the best interests of every child include an expectation that difficult decisions affecting the length and quality of the child's life will be taken for the child by a parent in the exercise of their parental responsibility. . . .'[240]

- 'Further, whilst I did not hear detailed submissions on the import of Article 8 of the ECHR in the context of this case, and whilst the Article 8 rights of the parents are subordinate to the best interests of the child where the two conflict, in the circumstances I have just summarised there is in my judgment a cogent argument that the making of orders the effect of which would be to override the choice made by the parents in the exercise of their parental responsibility would not constitute a necessary and proportionate justification for the interference in their Art 8 rights that would thereby occur.'[241]
- 'Within this context, whilst not determinative, the Article 9 rights of the parents and of Tafida to freedom of thought, conscience and religion fall for consideration in this case and in my judgment must be accorded weight in the balancing exercise in circumstances where the parents' beliefs, which beliefs would have influenced Tafida, included the belief that to withdraw life sustaining treatment from Tafida would be a sin in circumstances where they believe that where the breath of life subsists so too the soul.'[242]
- 'Absent the fact of pain or the awareness of suffering, the answer to the objective best interests tests must be looked for in subjective or highly value laden ethical, moral or religious factors extrinsic to the child, such as futility (in its non-technical sense), dignity, the meaning of life and the principle of the sanctity of life, which factors mean different things to different people in a diverse, multicultural, multifaith society.'[243]

One aspect of the *Raqeeb* case is the reasonableness of the parents' decision. In an earlier case, *Re Ashya King*, the court permitted the parents to take the child to Prague for proton therapy treatment, saying that the parents' proposal was reasonable and accordingly it was not the place of the court to stand in the way of their exercise of PR.[244] In *Gard*, McFarlane LJ said:

in the end it is the judge who has to choose the best course for a child. Where, as in the case of *Re King* before Mr Justice Baker, there really was nothing to choose as between the benefits and detriments of the two forms of radiotherapy, the court readily stood back and allowed the parents to make their choice.[245]

The apparent differences between *Gard* and *Evans* on the one hand, and *King* and *Raqeeb* on the other is the extent to which, in the latter two cases, the course of treatment proposed by the parents was supported by a reasonably body of medical opinion. It may therefore

---

[240] At [182].
[241] At [182].
[242] At [184].
[243] At [191].
[244] [2014] EWHC 2964 (Fam).
[245] [2017] EWCA Civ 410 at [96].

be that the courts will only uphold parental discretion where the parents are selecting between choices both of which are supported by a reasonable body of medical practice and which are therefore finely balanced.

The ECHR rights of the parents and child

We have mentioned that in *Gard* the parents argued that court involvement breached their Article 8 rights to private and family life when done on the basis of best interests rather than significant harm. In reply, the Supreme Court noted that 'the European Court of Human Rights has firmly stated that in any judicial decision where the rights under Article 8 of the parents and the child are at stake, the child's rights must be the paramount consideration. If there is any conflict between them the child's interests must prevail.' Thus Charlie's rights provided a legitimate reason for interference under Article 8(2) with the parents' rights.

As we have seen earlier in this chapter, the Supreme Court's reference to paramountcy as being part of the ECHR is not an entirely accurate statement as the ECHR case law is somewhat inconsistent on this. Indeed, when the parents did appeal to the European Court of Human Rights, the admissibility decision notes that:

> the decisive issue is whether the fair balance that must exist between the competing interests at stake—those of the child, of the two parents, and of public order—has been struck, within the margin of appreciation afforded to States in such matters, taking into account, however, that the best interests of the child must be of primary consideration. . . . The Court has also reiterated that there is a broad consensus—including in international law—in support of the idea that in all decisions concerning children, their best interests must be paramount. . . .[246]

This suggests that when states are considering how to implement the obligation to balance the rights of parent and child in such a way that the rights of the child are a primary consideration, the paramountcy principle is an approach that falls within the margin of discretion because it has such widespread support.

As to the parents' arguments that their own Article 8 rights were breached by interference on the basis of best interests rather than significant harm, the Court 'recalls that there is a broad consensus—including in international law—in support of the idea that in all decisions concerning children, their best interests must be paramount' before noting that there was no ECHR jurisprudence on this particular point. However, the issue was moot, in that it had been held that there was a risk of significant harm to Charlie.[247]

Finally, the European Court noted the Supreme Court's comments about the existence of a conflict of interest between the parents seeking to displace what was best for the child by asserting their own Article 8 rights and bringing an action on behalf of the child for breach of his rights. The Court suggested, but did not find it necessary to decide, that the parents did not have standing to bring a complaint on behalf of Charlie because of this conflict of interest.

---

[246] [2017] ECHR 605 (27 June 2017).
[247] [2017] ECHR 605 (27 June 2017).

The conflation of the child's ECHR rights with those of the parents was also an element in *Raqeeb*. A main element of the parents' argument was that Article 9 ECHR required that the court respect their religious beliefs which included the sanctity of life. While not determinative because such views form only part of a holistic evaluation of a person's best interests, they did provide a tipping point towards the perpetuation of life-sustaining treatment, with MacDonald J holding that, in the context of a finely balanced case, refusing the parents' treatment proposals would constitute a disproportionate interference in their own and Tafida's Article 9 rights. However, note that in this case the parents' and child's Article 9 rights were treated as 'closely aligned'.[248] Tafida was being raised by Muslim parents in accordance with the Islamic faith. The judge therefore attributed to her a wish to live in a minimally conscious state, without pain, in the care of her parents because the sanctity of life is a tenet of Islam. As Cave, Brierly, and Archard point out, it is problematic to attribute a belief in the sanctity of life to such a small child, although of course she may well have grown up sharing her parents' views. It is an even greater reach to suggest that a belief that life is precious can equate to a wish that oneself live in a minimally conscious state for ever more. To Cave et al., therefore, 'the *Raqeeb* case gives a consideration to parental preferences that blurs the distinction between the child's point of view and that of her parents'.[249]

9.7 Conclusion

This chapter has at once covered a narrow and broad spectrum of issues. On the one hand, it has addressed only two legal ideas, the welfare principle, and rights. Yet within our discussions there are multiple considerations, theories, and contradictions. Theorists have been unable to agree on a definition of rights, the purpose of rights, or the nature of rights. This renders discussion of children's moral rights somewhat difficult even before we think about whether children should have different rights to adults. A principle which at first seems uncontentious—the welfare principle—has shown itself to have multiple and significant flaws: but then so have the alternatives suggested. A conflict has arisen between the rights of parents and the rights and interests of children, and between domestic law and our international convention obligations.

Lady Hale has memorably said, 'The modern tendency of the law is to recognise that children are indeed people'.[250] Despite this, you may well be left with the impression that children's rights are heavily contingent on not being at odds with their welfare, and that the situations in which children have truly asserted their autonomy rights successfully are few and far between.

---

[248] E Cave, J Brierly, and D Archard, 'Making Decisions for Children—Accommodating Parental Choice in Best Interests Determinations' (2020) 28(1) *Medical Law Review* 183.
[249] E Cave, J Brierly, and D Archard, 'Making Decisions for Children—Accommodating Parental Choice in Best Interests Determinations' (2020) 28(1) *Medical Law Review* 183.
[250] As Hale J in *Kingston upon Thames Royal London Borough Council v Prince and another* [1998] All ER (D) 670 (CA).

KEY POINTS

- When it decides a case that deals with the upbringing of a child, or the administration of a child's property, s1 Children Act 1989 tells us that 'the child's welfare shall be the court's paramount consideration'. *Re G (Children) (Religious Upbringing)* [2012] EWCA Civ 1233 says that best interests encompasses 'everything that conduces to a child's welfare and happiness or relates to the child's development and present and future life as a human being'.

- While the welfare principle attracts a high level of support, a number of through-provoking criticisms have been made of it. It is indeterminate, unpredictable, hard to appeal because of the level of discretion, and yet at risk of judicial bias or assumptions about how children should be raised. There are a number of suggests for alternatives to the welfare principle such as a primary caretaker or maternal presumption; tossing a coin; utilitarianism; or modifying the principle to give weight to the interests of others.

- In many cases, we would expect a child's moral rights to be reflected in their legal rights, but this is not always the case. The legal philosopher Joel Feinberg has argued that children have the right to an open future—to have their options left open until such time as they can exercise their autonomy by making their own choices.

- Some, perhaps many, people are uncomfortable with the idea that a child might have a right of autonomy or self-determination. Samantha Brennan argues for an approach of graduated autonomy: that is that a child grows older they can 'move gradually from having their rights primarily protect their interests to having their rights primarily protect their choices'.

- There are four key sources of children's legal rights applicable to children in England and Wales: (1) domestic law; (2) the European Convention on Human Rights and Fundamental Freedoms (the ECHR); (3) the United Nations Convention on the Rights of the Child (the UNCRC); and (4) European Union law. These sources are interrelated.

- In a series of cases including *Re Roddy (A Child) (Identification: Restriction on Publication)* [2004] 2 FLR 949; *R (on the application of Begum) v Headteacher and Governors of Denbigh High School* [2006] UKHL 15; *Mabon v Mabon* [2005] EWCA Civ 634; and *R (On the application of Williamson and others) v Secretary of State for Education and Employment* [2005] UKHL 15, domestic courts have had to address children's ECHR rights. The welfare principle did not apply to these cases because they did not pertain to the children's upbringing; accordingly, there was no conflict with the welfare principle.

- In *Gillick v West Norfolk and Wisbech Area Health Authority* [1986] 1 AC 112 the House of Lords held that a young person aged under 16 had the right to consent to medical treatment without the knowledge or consent of her parents [now, a person with parental responsibility] provided that she had sufficient understanding of what was proposed and doctors believed that the treatment was in her interests. This is known as attaining '*Gillick* competence'. In his judgment, Lord Scarman suggests that parental rights only exist as long as they are needed and that they terminate if and when the child reaches competency. The implications of this were brought starkly to the fore in two cases that Gillian Douglas termed the 'retreat from *Gillick*'. They concerned the rights of a child to *refuse* treatment rather than—as in *Gillick*—the rights of a child to *consent* to treatment.

- Under the ECHR, in the event of a conflict the rights of each person concerned must be weighed to determine whose rights will prevail in the circumstances before the court. However, the European Court has repeatedly emphasised that the rights and interests of the child will be accorded significant weight. Our domestic courts have strained to say that the welfare principle is compatible with the ECHR. Many legal commentators disagree with this, arguing that there is a difference between starting with a right and then considering whether any infringement is necessary, and doing what is in the child's best interests.

FURTHER READING: SOME STARTING POINTS

- For the meaning, philosophy, or underlying rationale of the welfare principle, see J Herring and C Foster 'Welfare Means Rationality, Virtue and Altruism' (2012) 32 *Legal Studies* 480. That article influenced the judgment in *Re G (Children) (Religious Upbringing)* [2012] EWCA Civ 1233. See also *J v B and the Children (Ultra-Orthodox Judaism: Transgender)* [2017] EWFC 4; appealed as *Re M* [2017] EWCA Civ 2164. Good case notes are at (2013) 25(3) *Child and Family Law Quarterly* 336; (2014) 77(1) *Modern Law Review* 101; and (2018) 40(2) *Journal of Social Welfare and Family Law* 234.

- There are several very influential articles on the merits and demerits of the welfare principle, including R Mnookin, 'Child Custody Adjudication: Judicial Functions in the Face of Indeterminacy' (1975) 39(3) *Law and Contemporary Problems* 226; J Elster, 'Solomonic Judgments: Against the Best Interest of the Child' (1987) 54 *University of Chicago Law Review* 1; and an expansion of Elster's discussion at in J Elster, *Solomonic Judgements: Studies in the Limitation of Rationality* (Cambridge University Press 1989). Helen Reece's article 'The Paramountcy Principle: Consensus or Construct?' (1996) 49(1) *Current Legal Problems* 267 is also much cited, and there are clear discussions of the issues in a trio of articles by Jonathan Herring at (2005) 27(2) *Journal of Social Welfare and Family Law* 159; (2014) 36(1) *Journal of Social Welfare and Family Law* 14; and in A Bainham, S Day Sclater, and M Richards (eds), *What Is a Parent? A Socio-Legal Analysis* (Hart 1999).

- On medical treatment cases, the most important case of them all is *Gillick v West Norfolk and Wisbech Area Health Authority* [1986] 1 AC 112. There are many discussions of this case and its legacy, but start with J Fortin, 'The *Gillick* Decision - Not Just a High Water Mark', Chapter 11 in S Gilmore, J Herring, and R Probert (eds), *Landmark Cases in Family Law* (Bloomsbury 2016); and M Freeman, 'Rethinking *Gillick*' (2005) 13 *International Journal of Children's Rights* 201.

- On children's moral rights there are writings of varying complexity. Three good books are MDA Freeman, *The Rights and Wrongs of Children* (Frances Pinter 1983), which is considered a classic; D Archard and CM Macleod (eds), *The Moral and Political Status of Children* (OUP 2002), especially the chapters by Brennan and Brighouse; and E Brake and L Ferguson (eds), *Philosophical Foundations of Children's and Family Law* (OUP 2018). O'Neill's article 'Children's Rights and Children's Lives' (1992) 6 *International Journal of Law and the Family* 24 has prompted various responses including M Freeman, 'Taking Children's Rights More Seriously' in the same volume at p52, and Brighouse, as above. O'Neill's article can also be found in (1988) 98 *Ethics* 445. We spent some time discussing Feinberg's influential chapter 'The Child's Right to an Open Future', which can be found both in RC Curren (ed.), *Philosophy of Education: An Anthology* (Blackwell 2007) and in W Aiken and H LaFollette (eds), *Whose Child? Children's Rights, Parental Authority, and State Power* (Littlefield, Adams, and Co. 1980).

- Jane Fortin is a leading writer on children's rights; see 'Accommodating Children's Rights in a Post Human Rights Act Era' (2006) 69(3) *Modern Law Review* 299 and other articles footnoted. See also the works by H Fenwick, P Harris, and S Choudhry and H Fenwick footnoted. You may also want to look at the European Union Agency for Fundamental Rights and Council of Europe *Handbook on European Law Relating to the Rights of the Child* (2015). S Choudhry and J Herring's *European Human Rights and Family Law* (Hart 2010) is a clear and thorough discussion of the issues.

- Finally, Ian McEwan's novel *The Children Act* is based on two of the Key Cases discussed in this chapter, *Re A (Children) (Conjoined Twins: Surgical Separation)* [2001] Fam 147 and *Re E (A Minor) (Wardship: Medical Treatment)* [1993] 1 FLR 386.

 Visit the **online resources** to watch a video of Polly Morgan discussing this chapter topic, and to check your understanding of this chapter with self-test questions and scenario questions.

10 Private Law Decisions about Children

LEARNING CHECKLIST

By the end of this chapter, you should be able to:

- *Explain* the use and purpose of s8 applications and the court process
- *Identify* the principles that the court will apply to s8 applications and *analyse* how they may apply in particular situations
- *Describe* the different types of contact and *critically discuss* the research on shared parenting time
- *Identify* the tools that courts have at their disposal to encourage compliance with orders or sanction non-compliance, and *critically evaluate* how successful these are
- *Critically discuss* both domestic and ECHR case law on the importance of contact and *evaluate* whether there can be said to be a human right to contact
- *Describe* why a child or his primary carer may be fearful of or otherwise opposed to contact by reference to the research literature on domestic abuse and alienation respectively; and *critically evaluate* how successfully (nor not) courts have addressed these high-risk, high-conflict situations
- *Explain* when a parent can remove a child from the jurisdiction lawfully and when removal may constitute child abduction, and *critically discuss* the use of the Hague Convention and the Brussels II revised Regulation and defences available to summary return orders.

SCENARIO 1

Al, Ruth, and son Daniel (12 weeks old)

Al and Ruth are the parents of baby Daniel, who is just 12 weeks old. They separated when Ruth was pregnant and intend to divorce. Al has parental responsibility for Daniel by virtue of being married to Ruth, irrespective of whether or not he is named on the birth certificate (see Chapter 8). Both Al and Ruth are Jewish. However, for Ruth one of the reasons for their marriage breaking down was because Ruth has recently lost her faith and no longer wishes to practise Judaism, whereas Al's faith remains strong. He wishes to bring Daniel up in the Jewish faith, whereas Ruth wishes to bring Daniel up without a faith.

There are now several applications before the court. Al has applied for a child arrangements order that Daniel live with him for some of the time. Ruth opposes this application and has also applied for a prohibited steps order that Al not arrange for or permit their son to be circumcised.

SCENARIO 2

Molly, Mark, and daughter Katie (6)

Molly and Mark are an unmarried couple who separated a few months ago. Mark moved out of the family home, and Molly has stayed living there with their 6-year-old daughter Katie. Molly and Mark are both determined to make the transition as smooth as possible for Katie, but they disagree about a number of issues, such as the time that Katie should spend with Mark. Molly believes that Katie should see Mark every other weekend, and is concerned that midweek contact might disrupt Katie's routine and make her unsettled for school. Mark is upset because he is no longer seeing Katie every day and does not want the role of 'weekend dad'.

Mark is not named on Molly's birth certificate so he does not have parental responsibility for her. He has not acquired parental responsibility through any of the other possible methods outlined in Chapter 8.

SCENARIO 3

Claire, Ellie, and son Jacob (10)

Claire and Ellie are a married same-sex couple who lived with their son Jacob (aged 10). Jacob was conceived using donor sperm though a licensed clinic, so he has no legal father. Claire is his biological and gestational mother, and Ellie (who met Claire after his birth) is his stepmother.[1] She does not have parental responsibility, as she and Claire have not entered into a parental responsibility agreement.[2] Last year, Claire and Ellie separated and Ellie moved out. Jacob holds Ellie responsible for the breakdown of the relationship and does not want to see her. Ellie brought an application that Claire make Jacob available to spend time with her on two Saturdays per month.

Since the order was made, there have been four Saturdays when contact has not taken place. On one occasion, it was because Claire said that Jacob was unwell. On the second and third occasions, Claire said that Jacob was upset and did not want to see Ellie. On the fourth occasion, Ellie arrived at Claire's house to collect Jacob but no one was home. Ellie now needs to apply to enforce the order. Claire, in turn, applies to bring contact to an end, saying that it should be up to Jacob when he sees Ellie.

SCENARIO 4

Sarah, Phil, and children Bill (11), Ben (8), and Bella (4)

Sarah and Phil have three children, Bill, Ben, and Bella. Sarah separated from Phil by obtaining a non-molestation order and an occupation order to exclude him from the family home and allow her to stay there with the children. She then issued divorce proceedings on the fact of Phil's behaviour, citing several incidents of physical and sexual abuse of her by Phil, and allegations that Phil had shouted at and threatened to hit the children. She has also alleged that Phil has a drinking problem and occasionally uses recreational drugs.

---

[1] Ellie could have been a second female parent to Jacob if she and Claire had met earlier. Where a child is conceived in a licensed clinic, s42 Human Fertilisation and Embryology Act 2008 would make the mother's wife a second female parent unless she does not consent to the placing in the mother of the embryo/sperm/eggs/artificial insemination. This part of the Act came into force in April 2009.

[2] S4A Children Act 1989 provides for step-parent parental responsiblity by agreement or court order.

In the last few months since the divorce, Phil has spent some time with the two younger children, but they are increasingly refusing to see him and Bella has been developing stomach aches on days when she is due to see Phil, which may be caused by stress. The oldest child, Bill, strongly refuses to see Phil. Phil is now seeking an order that the children live with him, which Sarah opposes. Phil is accusing Sarah of alienating the children against him and of having a mental illness that means she is unfit to care for them.

10.1 Introduction

Every day, parents and other caregivers make decisions about the upbringing of children. In Chapter 9, we saw that when courts become involved, they make decisions on the basis of what is in the child's best interests. This chapter should be read in conjunction with Chapter 9, because that chapter explains *why* we do what is best for a child, and this chapter shows how courts go about that. We consider how such cases work and some common types of application that come before the courts. In particular, we are going to consider applications about where a child should live and when they should spent time with a non-resident parent, as well as more difficult cases involving allegations of domestic violence, breaches of existing court orders, and situations in which a child has become alienated from a parent. We finish by looking at cases involving relocating across jurisdictions or child abduction.

These types of dispute, usually between parents but occasionally involving others, are known as 'private law proceedings'. In contrast, proceedings in which the state—through the local authority children's services department—is a party are known as 'public law proceedings'.[3]

There are approximately 50–56,000 new private law applications every year.[4] We do not, however, know what proportion of families turn to the family courts. Figures from 10 per cent of separating couples to 38 per cent have been suggested.[5] Each application takes on average six months to reach final order.[6] However, some simple cases take much less time and some complex cases can involve years of litigation.

10.2 Introducing s8 applications

Most private law applications which relate to a child's upbringing are brought under s8 Children Act 1989. There are three types of s8 application:

1. An application for a child arrangements order (formerly known as residence and contact orders)

2. An application for a prohibited steps order, preventing someone from exercising their parental responsibility in a specified way

3. An application for a specific issues order, resolving an issue relating to the child's upbringing.

---

[3] Public law proceedings are about the state intervening to protect a child.

[4] Ministry of Justice, *Family Court Statistics Quarterly, England and Wales, April to June 2020* (September 2020).

[5] See Sir Andrew McFarlane, 'Living in Interesting Times', keynote speech to the Resolution Annual Conference 2019, Manchester 5 April 2019, and the comment by K Reeve, 'Custody Fights Blight Four in Ten Break Ups' – A Word of Caution?' (*The Transparency Project* 2 July 2019) Available at http://www.transparencyproject.org.uk/custody-fights-blight-four-in-ten-break-ups-a-word-of-caution/ accessed 14 November 2020.

[6] Ministry of Justice, *Family Court Statistics Quarterly, England and Wales, April to June 2020* (September 2020).

> **STATUTORY EXTRACT** *s8(1) Children Act (as amended)*
>
> In this Act 'child arrangements order' means an order regulating arrangements relating to any of the following
>
> (a) with whom a child is to live, spend time or otherwise have contact, and
> (b) when a child is to live, spend time or otherwise have contact with any person;
>
> 'a prohibited steps order' means an order that no step which could be taken by a parent in meeting his parental responsibility for a child, and which is of a kind specified in the order, shall be taken by any person without the consent of the court; and
>
> 'a specific issue order' means an order giving directions for the purpose of determining a specific question which has arisen, or which may arise, in connection with any aspect of parental responsibility for a child.

We are going to consider each of these types of application in turn, starting with prohibited steps and specific issues orders.

10.2.1 Prohibited steps orders and specific issues orders

When parents and/or those with parental responsibility disagree about an issue relating to a child's upbringing, they can make an application to court for a judge to decide that issue by way of a specific issues or prohibited steps order. Section 10.2.4 explains who can make an application.

A prohibited steps order prevents someone with parental responsibility from exercising an aspect or aspects of that responsibility. For example, if one parent fears that the other is likely to permanently remove the child from his or her school, they could seek an order that the other parent be prohibited from doing that. In extreme cases, the order can be used to prevent any exercise whatsoever of parental responsibility by a person. Common types of specific issues order relate to which school a child should attend, whether a child should leave the jurisdiction to go on holiday with one parent, contrary to the wishes of the other, and whether a child should have a particular form of medical treatment. It can therefore be seen that specific issues applications and prohibited steps orders cover the same situations: they are two sides of the same coin. If you are opposed to something you could apply for either; if you are in favour of something only the former. The court can make a specific issues order on an application for a prohibited steps order, and vice versa, or can make either order without an application, simply of its own volition during other children proceedings.

However, the application must relate to the exercise of parental responsibility for the child and cannot, therefore, be used for issues that are not related to parental responsibility, even if they have an indirect effect on the child, such as the consequences of a certain kind of financial settlement between a divorcing couple, or whether a non-molestation order should be made under the Family Law Act 1996.

SCENARIO 1

Illustration 1: Al and Ruth and son Daniel (12 weeks old)

One of the applications before the court is Ruth's application for a prohibited steps order that Al not arrange for or permit their son to be circumcised. A prohibited steps order curtails what would be an exercise of Al's parental responsibility, albeit one that falls into the category of situations in which the consent of both parents ought to be obtained (see Chapter 8). Al could alternatively have applied for a specific issues order that Daniel be circumcised. The principles are the same, so it does not matter which one has brought the application. The outcome will be that the court prohibits or permits the circumcision.

10.2.2 Child arrangements orders

For many years, an order stating with whom a child should live was known as a custody order, and an order stating when a non-resident parent (a parent who does not live with the child) would see the child was an access order. These terms, custody and access, carry connotations of possession or ownership of the child by one parent who then acts as a gatekeeper to the other parent's time with the child. The Children Act 1989 replaced these terms with 'residence', to describe the person with whom the child was to live, and 'contact' to describe time spent with a non-resident parent or other person named in the order (such as a grandparent). This was part of the Children Act's reconceptualisation of the social principles underlying the state's involvement in family life (see Chapter 11). Contact and residence were designed to be neutral concepts that emphasised co-parenting and parental responsibility rather than rights. Underlying it all was the welfare principle.

However, in 2014, the Children and Families Act amended the Children Act, changing the terms used. The government felt that 'residence' and 'contact' had also acquired a possessive meaning, so the term 'child arrangements order' was introduced as a neutral alternative.

There are two types of child arrangement order, reflecting the functions of the previous residence and contact orders:

1. A 'live with' order is an order that a child lives with a person either all the time or for a specified period of time. A live with order can be made in favour of more than one person—either people who live together or separately. We will discuss this when we look at common types of child arrangement orders.

2. A 'spend time' with order requires the person with whom the child lives (the resident parent) to make sure that the child spends time with a named person.

Much of the leading academic research and writing predates these 2014 changes and thus refers to 'contact' and 'residence'. This research is still valid today as the 2014 changes did not do much to change the courts' approach. In this chapter we will also often use these old terms, simply because it is easier to know what exactly we are talking about. However, we should properly referring to contact orders as orders that a person 'spends time or otherwise has contact' with a child, and residence orders as 'an order saying with whom the child is to live'.

10.2.3 When a s8 order ceases to have effect

Under s9(6–7) Children Act 1989, the court can only make an order that lasts past the child's 16th birthday in exceptional circumstances or where the order varies or discharges an existing order. Any existing s8 orders cease to have effect once the child turns 16, unless (a) the order is solely a 'live with' order, or (b) the court has specified that it is to last past that birthday.

A child arrangements order between parents will also cease to apply if the parents later live together for a continuous period of more than six months. In the case of a live with order, this cessation only applies if both parents have parental responsibility.[7]

10.2.4 Who can apply for a s8 order

Section 10(1) Children Act 1989 defines who can apply for a s8 order. This comprises:

1. those who are *entitled* to apply; of which there are
   a. those who are entitled to apply for any kind of s8 order;
   b. those who are entitled only to apply for certain types of application;
   c. those who are entitled to apply provided that they have certain consents; and
2. those who have obtained prior *leave* (permission) from the court to apply.

These categories, and those who fall within them, are set out in Table 10.1. Note too that if the court is dealing with one type of application in family proceedings (such as a parental responsibility application), s10(1)(b) enables the court to make any s8 order of its own volition even though no formal application for one is before the court.

SCENARIO 1

Illustration 2: Al, Ruth, and son Daniel (12 weeks old)

Al has made an application for a child arrangements order. As Daniel's father, Al can apply for any s8 order. He has parental responsibility for Daniel but the right of a parent to apply for a s8 order does not depend on this.

SCENARIO 2

Illustration 1: Molly, Mark, and daughter Katie (6)

We are told that Mark and Molly are an unmarried couple with a 6-year-old daughter. As Molly's father, Mark can apply for any s8 order. He does not have parental responsibility for Molly, but the right of a parent to apply for a s8 order does not depend on parental responsibility. (If his application succeeds, the court will consider whether to give him parental responsibility.)

---

[7] Section 11(5) and (6).

TABLE 10.1 Who can apply for a s8 order

Any s8 order	· Any parent, guardian, or special guardian of the child. Note that parent is not limited to those with PR, but they must be an existing parent (so not a person whose child has been adopted away from them) · Any person with parental responsibility by virtue of s4A (step-parents) · Any person with whom the child lives pursuant to a child arrangements order
A child arrangements order only	All of the above, plus · Any party to a marriage or civil partnership (even if no longer in existence) in relation to whom the child is a child of the family · Any person with whom the child has lived for at least three of the last five years. This period does not need to have been continuous, but must not have ended more than three months ago · If there is a 'live with order' already, any person who has the consent of the persons named in that order as the person(s) with whom the child lives · Where there is a care order, any person who has the consent of the local authority · In any case (other than where there is a live with order or a care order), anyone who has the consent of all of those who have parental responsibility · Anyone with PR under s12(2A) (parental responsibility given to someone with whom the child spends time but who is not a parent)
A child arrangements: 'live with' order only	All of the above, plus · A local authority foster parent with whom the child has lived for at least one year immediately preceding the application · A grandparent, brother, sister, uncle, aunt (including in-laws and of the half-blood) or step-parent with whom the child has lived for at least one year immediately preceding the application.
Variation or discharge of a s8 order only	All of the above, plus · Anyone who was the applicant in the order that they are trying to vary or discharge · Anyone named in an order as a person with whom the child was to spend time or otherwise have contact
Requires leave of the court to make any s8 application at all	· Everyone else. This includes the child himself. · Note, however, that where a foster carer has fostered the child within the last six months, they are further restricted.

SCENARIO 3

Illustration 1: Claire, Ellie, and son Jacob (10)

Ellie brought an application for a child arrangements order. She is a step-parent of Jacob but does not have parental responsibility. She could not therefore apply as a parent, or as someone with PR. However, she was able to apply as a 'party to a marriage or civil partnership (even if no longer in existence) in relation to whom the child is a child of the family'. This category of applicant can only apply for a child arrangements order. To apply for a specific issues or prohibited steps order, she would need the court's permission.

Any person not named in Table 10.1 as able to make an application will need to seek the leave (permission) of the court before they can proceed with an application.

Where a person needs leave, their proposed application is considered by a judge who decides whether it can proceed. Section 10(9) requires the judge to have particular regard to—

(a) the nature of the proposed application for the section 8 order;

(b) the applicant's connection with the child;

(c) any risk there might be of that proposed application disrupting the child's life to such an extent that he would be harmed by it; and

(d) where the child is being looked after by a local authority—

    (i) the authority's plans for the child's future; and

    (ii) the wishes and feelings of the child's parents.

The court can also take into account the overall merits of the substantive application and its prospects of success. The judge does not need to decide whether the application *will* succeed or even that they are likely to succeed, merely whether the applicant has 'some realistic possibility of success'.[8] If they do not, permission will be refused. It may be necessary to hear oral argument or even witness evidence about this and also the risk that the application, if allowed to proceed, might disrupt the child's life 'to such an extent that he would be harmed by it'.

Those who require leave include three notable categories of potential applicant.

The child himself

In complex cases, the court may make the child a party. The child's interests will be represented by a litigation guardian (a guardian ad litem) who will in turn instruct a solicitor. This always happens in care cases, for children of any age. However, an older child may very well want to bring their own application or join an existing application that is relevant to them, not least because the child may have a different view to the guardian about what is best for them. However, even if the case is about them, they must first get leave (permission). This type of application should be heard by the High Court, which must grant leave if the child has sufficient understanding to participate as a party, i.e., they are *Gillick*-competent (see Chapter 9) to instruct their own solicitor.[9] If a child is given leave to instruct their own solicitor, there is no further role for the guardian.[10] We consider how children's voices are heard, whether or not they have a guardian or their own solicitor, at 10.3.2.

Grandparents

Most grandparents do not fall within any of the categories of entitlement set out in Table 10.1, and therefore need the court's leave to pursue an application. A number of

---

[8] *Re F and R (Section 8 Order: Grandparents' Application)* [1995] 1 FLR 524.
[9] Rule 9.2A(6).
[10] Rule 9.2A Family Procedure Rules.

> **KEY CASE** *Mabon v Mabon* [2005] EWCA Civ 634
>
> We first considered this Key Case in Chapter 9 as an example of children asserting their rights under the ECHR and the UNCRC. You may recall that the parents of three boys, aged 17, 15, and 13, were involved in s8 proceedings about the arrangements for them. They sought leave to become parties and to instruct their own lawyer to represent them in place of a guardian who would act in what he or she saw as their best interests. The Court of Appeal held that rule 9.2A Family Procedure Rules said that leave *must* be granted if the children demonstrated sufficient understanding to take part in the proceedings. However:
>
> > If direct participation would pose an obvious risk of harm to the child arising out of the nature of the continued proceedings, and if the child was incapable of comprehending that risk, then the judge was entitled to find that sufficient understanding had not been demonstrated. But judges had to be equally alive to the risk of emotional harm that might arise from denying the child knowledge of and participation in the continuing proceedings.
>
> In this case, the children were given permission to instruct their own solicitor and to become parties to the case.

grandparent rights organisations argue that all grandparents should be entitled to make applications without requiring leave first. In 2011, the Family Justice Review 2011 considered this, but ultimately recommended to the government that the requirement for leave should remain as 'this prevents hopeless or vexatious applications that are not in the interests of the child.'[11]

Local authority foster carers

Local authority foster carers require leave unless they fall into one of the other categories in Table 10.1. Note that they cannot apply for leave unless they have the consent of the local authority, or are a relative of the child, or are a person with whom the child has lived for at least one year. This is to prevent foster carers disrupting the local authority's care plan.

10.3 Principles for deciding s8 applications

Now that we know who can apply, we need to think about on what basis a court might decide the application. There are a number of statutory principles found in section 1 Children Act 1989.

10.3.1 The welfare principle

In Chapter 9, we saw that when the court makes a decision relating to a child's upbringing or the administration of his property, it must do what is best for the child. This is because s1(1) Children Act 1989 applies and that makes the child's welfare the paramount consideration.

---

[11] D Norgrove, *Family Justice Review Final Report* (Ministry of Justice 2011) para 4.46.

The decisions described in this chapter, such as if or when a child should see a non-resident parent, or whether a parent should have permission to move a child to live abroad, are decisions about the child's upbringing. The court must therefore do what is in the child's best interests.

10.3.2 The welfare checklist

In Chapter 9 we also saw that s1(3) Children Act 1989 provides a non-exhaustive list of things the court 'shall have regard to' when deciding what is in a child's best interests. This is the welfare checklist.

STATUTORY EXTRACT *s1(3) Children Act 1989*

(3) In the circumstances mentioned in subsection (4), a court shall have regard in particular to
    (a) the ascertainable wishes and feelings of the child concerned (considered in the light of his age and understanding);
    (b) his physical, emotional and educational needs;
    (c) the likely effect on him of any change in his circumstances;
    (d) his age, sex, background and any characteristics of his which the court considers relevant;
    (e) any harm which he has suffered or is at risk of suffering;
    (f) how capable each of his parents, and any other person in relation to whom the court considers the question to be relevant, is of meeting his needs;
    (g) the range of powers available to the court under this Act in the proceedings in question.
(4) The circumstances are that—
    (a) the court is considering whether to make, vary or discharge a section 8 order, and the making, variation or discharge of the order is opposed by any party to the proceedings; or
    (b) the court is considering whether to make, vary or discharge a special guardianship order or an order under Part IV [care and supervision orders].

Let us consider these further.

The child's wishes and feelings

The wishes and feelings of a child may be heard in several ways, depending on the nature and complexity of the case. As we see at 10.2.4, a child who is *Gillick*-competent may instruct his own solicitor. In particularly complex cases where a child cannot instruct his own solicitor, or does not wish to do so, a litigation guardian may be appointed to represent his interests. But these are not common. In most cases, the child's views will be filtered through the adult parties to the case and the child is not directly represented at all.

However, giving the child the opportunity to be heard is a requirement:

- of Article 23(b) of the Brussels II Revised Regulation that relates recognition of other countries' judgments, which says that: 'A judgment relating to parental responsibility shall not be recognised by Member States if it was given, except in case of urgency, without the child having been given an opportunity to be heard, in violation of fundamental principles of procedure of the Member State in which recognition is sought.'[12]

- of Art 8 European Convention on Human Rights, as an aspect of the right to private and family life (albeit that 'it would be going too far to say that domestic courts are always required to hear a child in court on the issue of access to a parent . . . but this issue depends on the specific circumstances of each case, having due regard to the age and maturity of the child concerned').[13]

- of Art 12 of the UN Convention on the Rights of the Child, which says that 'Every child has the right to say what they think in all matters affecting them, and to have their view taken seriously.'

Of course, the child's age and level of understanding is relevant to the weight to be given to their wishes and feelings. The older the child, the harder it will be for the court to decide that it is in the child's best interest to ignore what they want. There is no precise age which child's wishes will be determinative of the outcome of the application, as children develop at different rates, but the psychiatrists Sturge and Glaser have suggested that 'as a rough rule' the wishes of those aged above 10 years of age should 'considerable weight', with those aged 6 to 10 being given 'intermediate' weight and the views of those aged under 6 seen as 'often indistinguishable in many ways from the wishes of the main carer (assuming normal development)'.[14] Quite often, the child's views are obtained by a Cafcass family court adviser who meets with the child to prepare either a brief report as to his wishes and feelings or, if requested to do so by the court, a longer report with recommendations under s7 Children Act.

FOCUS Know-How

What is Cafcass?

Cafcass is the Children and Family Court Advisory and Support Service, an independent body established by the Parliament (Criminal Justice and Court Services Act 2000). Cafcass family court advisers will become involved in family court proceedings at the request of the judge and their role is to safeguard and promote the welfare of children in family proceedings. Before the establishment of Cafcass, this work was done by the Family Court Welfare Service, the Guardian ad Litem Service, and the children's section of the Official Solicitor's Office. Cafcass is independent of the courts and the local authority. The Welsh equivalent is Cafcass Cymru.

A right to be heard is not the same as a right to determine the outcome. The court's decision must still be based on what is best for the child, and what the child wants is only one element in the welfare checklist. As Sherwin points out, the Children Act makes the child's welfare paramount, not his or her wishes and feelings.[15] This means that the court

---

[12] Brussels II Revised is European Union Regulation (EC) No 2201/2003 concerning jurisdiction and the recognition and enforcement of judgments in matrimonial matters and the matters of parental responsibility. As a Regulation, it is directly applicable in member states, including the UK, without needing to be implemented by domestic legislation. We consider it in more detail at section 10.10.5.

[13] *Sahin v Germany* (Application No 30943/96 [2003] 2 FLR 671 [73]).

[14] C Sturge and D Glaser, 'Contact and Domestic Violence – The Experts' Court Report' (2000) 30 *Family Law* 365.

[15] M Sherwin, 'The Law in Relation to the Wishes and Feelings of the Child', Ch 1 in R Davie, G Upton, and V Varman (eds), *The Voice of the Child: A Handbook for Professionals* (Falmer Press 1996).

will only be able to do what the child wants if that coincides with what is in his or her best interests.

For some children being heard will be very important. For others, communicating a viewpoint that will make one parent unhappy may be an emotional burden.[16] There may be situations when the court takes the view that what the child says he or she wants does not reflect their true feelings, or thinks that the child's view is coloured by the wishes of a parent. This creates a tension between the idea that a growing child has a '"developmental trajectory" towards competence' . . . and the child's specific circumstances.[17] We particularly see this in the cases discussed at 10.8.4, when we look at some children's unjustified opposition to contact. As McFarlane LJ observed in *Re A (A Child)*, 'The evaluation of the weight to be given to the expressed wishes and feelings of a teenage child in situations where the parent with care is intractably hostile to contact is obviously not a straightforward matter, no matter how consistently and firmly those wishes are expressed.'[18]

In *Re L (A Child)*, the court refused to allow an appeal on the basis that the 8-year-old had not been asked explicitly about the possibility of moving from living with his mother and grandmother to living with his father, because the child was emotionally torn to such a degree that it was not in his interests to ask him for a view, and such a view would not be reliable given the pressure he was under.[19]

We have said that in particularly difficult cases, a litigation guardian may be appointed to represent the child's interests. Practice Direction 16A gives suggestions of situations in which it may be appropriate to make the child a party (either via a guardian or, if they have capacity, directly), including 'where the child has a standpoint or interest which is inconsistent with or incapable of being represented by any of the adult parties'; 'where there is an intractable dispute over residence or contact, including where all contact has ceased, or where there is irrational but implacable hostility to contact or where the child may be suffering harm associated with the contact dispute'; 'where an older child is opposing a proposed course of action'; and situations of particularly complexity, such as those which have an international dimension or where there are multiple children whose welfare is in conflict with one another.[20] Paragraph 7.6 of Practice Direction 16A says that:

> It is the duty of a children's guardian fairly and competently to conduct proceedings on behalf of the child. The children's guardian must have no interest in the proceedings adverse to that of the child and all steps and decisions the children's guardian takes in the proceedings must be taken for the benefit of the child.

Guardians are usually Cafcass officers and in turn they will be represented by a solicitor whom they instruct. They are often known as 'Rule 16.4 guardians' because it is under this provision of the Family Procedure Rules that they are appointed.

As in Key Case *Mabon v Mabon*, there is no continuing role for a guardian if the children have permission to represent themselves. Whereas the guardian will always advance

[16] See C Piper, 'Barriers to Seeing and Hearing Children in Private Law Proceedings' [1999] *Family Law* 394.

[17] AL James, A James, and S McNamee, 'Constructing Children's Welfare in Family Proceedings' [2003, December] *Family Law* 889.

[18] [2013] 2 All ER 62, [68]. Discussed in A Inglis, 'Dear Judge: Children's Wishes and Feelings in Court Applications' [2014, October] *Family Law* 1450.

[19] *Re L (A Child)* [2019] EWHC 867 (Fam).

[20] Para 7.2.

what they see as the child's best interests, a child representing himself may form a different view as to what is in his best interests.

Some judges are willing to see children in their chambers although the relevant guidelines make it clear that this is not in order to gather evidence, but 'to enable the child to gain some understanding of what is going on, and to be reassured that the judge has understood him/her' while being clear that 'decisions in the case are the responsibility of the judge, who will have to weigh a number of factors, and that the outcome is never the responsibility of the child'.[21]

SCENARIO 3

Illustration 2: Claire and Ellie and son Jacob (10)

Ellie brought an application that Claire make Jacob available to spend time with her, and Claire says that Jacob does not want to see her. His wishes and feelings will be taken into account, but the court will need to consider whether his views are his own or whether they have been influenced by Claire's hostility to Ellie, and whether his views are rational. Even then, the court may think that it is in his interests to see Ellie.

Claire is arguing that it should be up to Jacob when he sees Ellie. The court is unlikely to be attracted to that idea—after all, parents do not leave it up to their children whether they go to school, because going to school is in the child's best interests.

SCENARIO 2

Illustration 2: Molly, Mark, and daughter Katie (6)

Katie is aged 6. This is an age at which her wishes and feelings will be accorded very little weight.

The child's physical, emotional, and educational needs

A key advantage to the welfare principle is that it sees each child as an individual with his or her own unique needs and personality, and it focuses the court on those. While all children have certain needs in common, such as for food and shelter, there may be situations where the child's physical needs are more complex, such as where child is disabled. In many cases, each parent will be able to meet a child's physical needs, but there may be differences in their capacity to meet the child's emotional needs. This was the situation in *RO v Local Authority*, in which Keenan J had to decide whether a 6-year-old girl should live with her aunt and uncle, or her father and his partner, following the death of her mother (from whom the father was separated). Keenan J held that the child was in desperate need of a mother figure, stability and 'very sensitive and very devoted care and attention with carers who are particularly attuned to her special emotional needs .' The father was, the judge found, unable to demonstrate any understanding of what those needs were, nor how

---

[21] Family Justice Council and the President of the Family Division, 'Guidelines for Judges Meeting Children Who Are Subject to Family Proceedings' [2010] 2 FLR 1872.

he could meet them. In contrast, the aunt and uncle had 'the skills, the determination and the emotional empathy to meet F's complex emotional needs . . . [for] a warm, loving, caring, secure and stable family home.'[22] The child therefore went to live with them.

The child's needs are therefore closely linked to the parents' capability to meet his needs, and any harm that the child is at risk of suffering. In a particularly acrimonious set of proceedings, the parents may lose sight of the child's needs altogether and get caught up in their own disputes.

The likely effect of a change of circumstances

This provision requires the court to pay attention to the benefits of the *status quo* compared to the benefits of a change in situation. For example, a child who moves to live with his other parent may experience disruption to his routine, schooling, and friendship groups, as well as his home and emotions. As the Supreme Court has said, 'Many of the familiar aspects of his life which anchor his stability and sense of security would be changed.'[23] The court has to consider this when determining what is in the child's best interests.

Clearly, there are situations in which short-term disruption is outweighed by the advantages of a change over the short or long term. However, research from the Ministry of Justice indicates that the *status quo* is 'the principle guiding the courts' when deciding where a child should live, 'unless grave concerns are expressed over the child's wellbeing'.[24] It is therefore a powerful factor. This is a particularly important thing to note when it comes to the issue of whether the courts are biased against fathers, which we discuss at 10.5.5. In intact families, most of the everyday parenting role is taken by the mother. When parents separate, it is more commonly the father who moves out of the family home. This may be for the best of reasons, such as to enable the children to remain in a familiar place. What it does do, however, is create a status quo that then positions the father as the applicant in the vast majority of children proceedings and therefore the person who is disrupting the child's routine.

The child's characteristics

The child's age may be relevant to their welfare, and not merely because it affects the weight that it to be given to their own views. In *Re G (A Child: Intractable Contact)*, the child's age, character, and gender had to be seen in the context of the parenting style of the father. In that case, the judge, HHJ Bellamy, referred to the child as being 'at an age when she is moving from dependence to independence, from accepting the need to comply with the directions of her parents to questioning and challenging those directions and testing boundaries'. This was important, given her father's tendency to become aggressive and controlling (as he was found to have been with the mother).[25]

Background and characteristics can become particularly important in cases involving religious or ethnic minorities. A child's religious and ethnic heritage is part of who they are, and important to their sense of identity. It is therefore an aspect of their welfare—but

---

[22] *RO v Local Authority* [2013] EWHC B31 (Fam).
[23] *Re B* [2009] UKSC 5 [42] (Lord Kerr).
[24] E Giovannini, *Outcomes of Family Justice: Children's Proceedings—a Review of the Evidence* (Research Summary 6/11, Ministry of Justice 2011).
[25] *Re G (A Child: Intractable Contact)* [2013] EWHC B16 (Fam).

may be at odds with other aspects of their welfare, such as a continuing relationship with their non-resident parent, as in *J v B and the Children (Ultra-Orthodox Judaism: Transgender)* (appealed as *Re M*), which is discussed at length in Chapter 9.[26]

Any harm which he has suffered or is at risk of suffering

The Children Act 1989 defines harm to mean 'ill-treatment or the impairment of health or development including, for example, impairment suffered from seeing or hearing the ill-treatment of another'.[27] It therefore encompasses not only physical harm to the child and other kinds of harm such as emotional abuse and neglect, but also witnessing harm suffered by others, such as through domestic abuse. The court cannot merely work on the basis of suspicions that harm has occurred or could occur, but must make a finding (on the balance of probabilities).

Harm is often linked to parental capacity to meet the child's needs, in that failure to meet needs may result in the child suffering harm. For example, if a parent is unable to get the child to go to school, the child's education will be harmed. If the child has medical needs for a certain type of care—such as an autistic child's need for routine and consistency or perhaps quiet—then they may be harmed by a chaotic and noisy family home. Where a parent is hostile towards the other parent and badmouths that parent in front of the child, they may harm the child's relationship with that parent which may well be contrary to his or her best interests. In some cases, the harm may be 'significant', in which case the case may cease being a private law dispute within the family and instead become a child protection case.

SCENARIO 1

Illustration 3: Al and Ruth and son Daniel (12 weeks old)

One part of this application is whether or not Daniel should be circumcised. The parents will need to argue that circumcision is in the child's best interests or not, depending on their position. Al may argue that circumcision has health benefits that outweigh the harm caused by the physical removal of Daniel's foreskin, which will cause him temporary pain that he will not remember when older, and that circumcision will give him the benefit of a sense of belonging to the Jewish faith community. Ruth, on the other hand, is likely to argue that the procedure is harmful, in that it is painful and associated with risks, and this coupled with the fact that the procedure is medically unnecessary outweighs any advantage that circumcision would bring to Daniel's likely future faith.

In *Re J (Child's Religious Upbringing and Circumcision)*, which concerned the circumcision of a 5-year-old boy, the judge goes through each element in the welfare checklist in turn, considering issues such as the child's religious and cultural heritage, the medical and psychological effects, the capacity of each parent to support the circumcision, the fact that the child was too young to express any valuable wishes and feelings, and the effect on his relationships with his parents and his religious community.[28]

[26] [2017] EWFC 4; [2017] EWCA Civ 2164.
[27] Section 31(9).
[28] [1999] 2 FCR 34.

SCENARIO 4

Illustration 1: Sarah, Phil, and children Bill (11), Ben (8), and Bella (4)

Sarah may allege that the children are at risk of physical and/or emotional harm if they live with or spend time with Phil. She may also allege that the children have experienced harm through witnessing Phil's abuse of her. There is a Practice Direction which sets out how allegations of domestic abuse should be addressed by the court and the consequences of the allegations being shown to be true or false. This is discussed in detail at 10.8.2.

How capable the adults are of meeting his needs

Once the needs of the child have been determined under s1(3)(b) above, it is necessary to look at how capable each of the parties is in meeting those needs. In Key Case *S v G*, the court held that the child's physical and educational needs would be met by either parent. However, there was a key difference in the parents' ability to meet his long-term needs. The court held that the mother's 'energetic self-reliance' would provide the child with more opportunities if he lived with his mother than if he lived with his father.

This provision also refers to the capability of 'any other person in relation to whom the court considers the question to be relevant'. This could include applicants who are not parents (such as grandparents) or it could mean people with whom the parents live or with whom they are closely involved, such as a parent's new spouse or partner. (Such people may contribute to the day-to-day parenting of the child but would necessarily not have parental responsibility.)[29]

FOCUS Think Critically

Is there a presumption in favour of biological parents?

Given the diversity of family forms, it is possible that a child may be surrounded not merely by parents and grandparents, but also by step-family or half siblings; they may have same-sex parents or transgender parents. Their father may or may not have ever lived with their mother: indeed, they may have a mother and a second female parent but no legal father; they may (through adoption or surrogacy) have two legal fathers. The person they consider as their primary carer may not be biologically related to them. Courts have recognised that a person may be important to a child despite there being no biological tie. As we have seen, ultimately anyone can apply for a s8 order, although some of them will require prior leave and the court will consider their connection with the child, their prospects of success, and the risk of their application causing disruption to the child's life. But what is the status of a person who is not biologically related to the child, when in dispute with someone who is so related?

---

[29] Sections 12 and 12A Children Act 1989.

In *Re G (Children: Same-Sex Partners)* the House of Lords considered whether the children should live with the woman who was their biological and legal mother, or her female former partner, who was a psychological parent to the child but not a legal or biological one. Lord Nicholls said that:

> 'The [children's] welfare is the court's paramount consideration. In reaching its decision the court should always have in mind that in the ordinary way the rearing of a child by his or her biological parent can be expected to be in the child's best interests, both in the short term and also, and importantly, in the longer term. I decry any tendency to diminish the significance of this factor. A child should not be removed from the primary care of his or her biological parents without compelling reason. Where such a reason exists the judge should spell this out explicitly.'[30]

Lord Nicholls makes it easy to be misunderstood as meaning that there is a presumption in favour of a biological parent that can only be overcome by 'compelling reason'. However, a more generous interpretation of what he actually means is that the decision is to be made simply on what is best for the child, but as the advantages of the biological parent are significant, thus the factors outweighing them will need to be significant too. As Lady Hale notes, if the mother continued to frustrate contact, it may then become in their best interests to move them to live with the partner.[31] The loss of the relationship with the partner would be capable of outweighing the benefits of the children living with their mother.

It is perhaps unsurprising that the issue came before the Lords again. *Re B (A Child)* involved a residence dispute between the father of a 4-year-old boy and the grandmother with whom he had been living. While the magistrates made a residence order in favour of the grandmother, this decision was, in light of *Re G*,[32] overturned by the High Court, with the Court of Appeal upholding the latter decision. In the Supreme Court, Lord Kerr made it clear that *Re G* had been misunderstood. 'In the ordinary way one can expect that children will do best with their biological parents' but 'it is only as a contributor to the child's welfare that parenthood assumes any significance'.[33] In this particular case, the child's best interests lay with the grandmother, who could offer a higher standard of care to that of the father.

There is therefore no presumption that a child should be with his or her biological parent—but there is admittedly a fine line between saying that children generally do better with a biological parent and this becoming the starting point for decision-making.

SCENARIO 3

Illustration 3: Claire, Ellie, and son Jacob (10)

We should apply the principles from these *Re B* and *Re G* to Ellie's situation. Claire is Jacob's biological parent as well as his psychological parent. As Lady Hale said in *Re G*, 'in the overall welfare judgment, that must count for something in the vast majority of cases. Its significance must be considered and assessed'. However, there is no principle that Ellie should not see Jacob or that he could not live with her just because she is a step-parent. The court will consider what benefits having a continuing relationship with her would bring to Jacob. As a psychological parent she may have a very important role to play and he may grieve if she is not available to him, even if he seems not to want to see her. This will of course depend on the length of time that she has known and co-parented him, as indicators of the quality of their previous relationship. It may be that these factors outweigh the biological tie.

---

[30] [2006] UKHL 43 [2].
[31] [2006] UKHL 43 [43–44].
[32] See extract from the High Court judgment (HHJ Richards) at para 18 of the HL decision.
[33] [2009] UKSC 5.

The court's powers

Although the court may be dealing with one particular application, this does not prevent the court from making other kinds of orders. For example, on an application for a child arrangements order, the court also has the power to make a parental responsibility order and it would not matter that no formal application for that had been made. The court could make such an order of its own volition or at the request of one of the parties or an expert advising the court. In determining whether to make an order, the court also needs to consider the no order principle, which is the principle that no order should be made unless it is better for the child to do so (see 10.3.5).

Bringing it all together: The welfare checklist in action

We have previously noted at 9.2.2 that the welfare checklist is a non-exhaustive list and is not in any hierarchical order of importance. Which of these considerations is most important in a particular case will depend on the situation. For example, the ability of each parent to offer a child a home that meets their *physical* needs is unlikely to be the subject of much discussion in the case of a child who is not disabled, but the importance of this is likely to be greater in the case of a physically disabled child.

We have also previously noted that while the weighting of the factors may differ from case to case, consideration of the checklist is a requirement: s1(3) says the court 'shall' have regard to it. That does not necessarily mean that a judge has to go through it in his or her judgment, as long as they bear it in mind,[34] but if they do discuss the factors explicitly their decision will be very hard to appeal. Some judges find it helpful to draw up a balance sheet of pros and cons of different options.[35]

But what does a judgment by reference to the welfare principle and checklist look like? There is an excellent example in the case *S v G*. In his judgment Peter Jackson J explicitly discusses each element of the checklist in turn.

> **KEY CASE** *S v G* [2015] EWFC 4
>
> This was an application by the Russian mother to take her 2½-year-old son, Daniel, to live with her in Russia. The British father opposed the application and sought to have the child live with him solely or for some of the time (which would have meant the mother had to go with Russia without the child, or remain in the UK).[36]
>
> - Daniel's feelings are captured in his father's description: 'he is enjoying life'.
> - Daniel's background is as a child of a transnational marriage with a strong heritage and cultural identity in each country. Neither heritage has presumptive precedence.
> - Daniel's physical and educational needs will be met, whatever course is taken. His emotional need is for a fulfilling childhood with meaningful relationships with both parents and with his wider family on both sides, so that he grows up with direction in life and a proper experience of his dual heritage.

---

[34] *Re G (Children)* [2006] UKHL 2305 at [40] (Lady Hale).
[35] As in *Re A (Medical Treatment: Male Sterilisation)* [2000] 1 FCR 193.
[36] We consider the law on relocation at 10.9.

- As to parental capacity, it is important to have regard to short- and long-term aspects of the question. In the short term, both parents have broadly equal capacity to meet Daniel's needs. However, my assessment is that there is a distinct difference between them in terms of their capacity to meet his longer term needs. . . . She would, I find, show Daniel an example of energetic self-reliance, offering him a wider field of possibilities for his future than he would receive in the father's care or in shared care in England. . . . [The judge then expands on this.]
- In considering the likely effect of a change in circumstances, one must look at the realistic options for Daniel's future. On the one hand, there is the mother's proposal to move to Moscow. On the other hand, there would be an arrangement in England under which Daniel would live with both of his parents in some way. . . .
- In the short term, much the greatest loss to Daniel is entailed in a move to Moscow. He would experience the loss of his regular time with his father and the disruption accompanying the move. . . . However, I consider that he would adapt to his new circumstances. While the amount of time that he has spent with his father and paternal family since June has strengthened these relationships to the point that Daniel would miss them, it also means that they have reached the stage where they can be sustained by means of regular contact.
- If Daniel moves to Moscow, his mother will become his sole carer. No adverse comment has been made about her plans for him, which are practical and realistic. She is capable of organising accommodation, schooling and contact. She would also be in a position to achieve her personal goals in a way that she could not in England. Having come here in the mistaken belief that she and the father could make a fulfilling life together, the mother would feel trapped and isolated if she was forced to remain here for the rest of Daniel's childhood after such a short and unsuccessful attempt to live as a family. . . . To require the mother to remain in England for at least the next 15 years would leave her with a justifiable sense of bitterness that is not in Daniel's interests.
- The powers of the court extend internationally under the 1996 Convention, providing for recognition, registration and enforcement. There can be no guarantee that an order for contact will be complied with, but I consider the treaty powers to be a significant reinforcement to the already robust probability that the mother will honour her obligations.

It is interesting to note that the judge was particularly impressed by what he called the mother's 'energetic self-reliance' and thought that this would give the child greater opportunities in later life, which was in his best interests. Although not referred to in the judgment, this tallies with the court's approach in the religious schooling Key Case *Re G (Children) (Religious Upbringing)* and with Robert Mnookin's criticisms of the way in which the welfare principle relies on parental character, both of which are discussed in Chapter 9 as part of our discussion of what welfare means.[37]

10.3.3 The presumption of involvement

Section 1(2A) Children Act 1989 says that in specified circumstances the court 'shall' presume that 'involvement of a parent in the life of the child concerned will further the child's welfare'. There is quite a lot to unpack in this brief statement.

---

[37] *Re G (Children)* [2012] EWCA Civ 1233.

What is the presumption?

A presumption gives us a starting point in favour of one side of the argument. We have to assume that a certain thing is correct, unless there is evidence to the contrary. Here, the assumption is that involvement of a parent in the life of the child will further the child's welfare, i.e., will be best for the child. This applies only to the involvement of a parent, not of other applicants such as grandparents. To rebut the presumption will require evidence that 'involvement of that parent in the child's life would put the child at risk of suffering harm whatever the form of the involvement',[38] i.e., that there is no form of involvement that is without risk. As long as there is at least one form of involvement that would not put the child at risk, the presumption applies. This means that the presumption will apply to the vast majority of eligible applications, because in all but the most serious cases there will be some form of involvement, however minor, that is without risk.

Where the presumption does not apply, the starting point for the court's deliberations is neutral.

What is involvement?

If the presumption does apply to a particular case, we are still left with the question of what 'involvement' means. The Children Act 1989 does not define it, except to say that it does not mean any particular division of a child's time. While it certainly could be interpreted to mean some form of time with the child, it could equally mean another form of contact with the child, such as telephone calls, or it might not mean contact with the child at all—being 'involved' could simply mean being consulted about major decisions relating to the child. Therefore, even when the presumption does apply, it still does not mean that the applicant will get the level or type of involvement that they seek. It depends entirely on what is in the child's best interests.

To what type of cases does the presumption apply?

It applies only to certain types of application, namely where the court is dealing with:

- a contested s8 application, i.e., a specific issues, prohibited steps, or child arrangements application (discussed in this chapter);
- a special guardianship application (Chapter 12);
- an order under Part IV Children Act, which deals with care and supervision applications (Chapter 12);
- an application for parental responsibility by an unmarried father or unmarried second female parent (Chapter 8); and
- an application to remove parental responsibility, where this is legally possible (Chapter 8).[39]

It does not apply to applications for an adoption order, which are dealt with under the Adoption and Children Act 2002, or applications under the inherent jurisdiction. Moreover, while it does apply to specific issues and prohibited steps orders, the involvement of a parent may not be relevant to the decision that needs to be taken. If, for example,

---

[38] Section 1(6)(b) Children Act 1989.
[39] Sections 1(4) and (7) Children Act 1989.

the dispute is about which school a child should attend, or whether a child should be vaccinated, the presumption is unlikely to assist.

While the presumption does not technically apply to applications to remove a child from the jurisdiction under s13 Children Act 1989, because such an application may alternatively be made under s8, courts have tended to import the welfare checklist and presumption into such cases, as we discuss at 10.9.2.

SCENARIO 2

Illustration 3: Molly, Mark, and child Katie (6)

Mark is the father of Katie, and this is a s8 application to which the presumption applies. Accordingly, the law will presume that it is in Katie's best interests for him to continue to be involved in her life. The exception to this is if Molly can prove, on the balance of probabilities ('more likely than not') that any involvement would put Katie at risk of harm. As she cannot do so, the presumption applies.

However, the presumption does not mean a particular division of Katie's time. It therefore reinforces his importance in her life, but does not help him with the issue of when and how much time he should spend with Katie.

SCENARIO 3

Illustration 4: Claire, Ellie, and son Jacob (10)

Ellie is not the mother of Jacob: she is a stepmother. As such, the presumption does not apply. The court starts neutrally in considering what is in Jacob's best interests.

SCENARIO 4

Illustration 2: Sarah, Phil, and children Bill (11), Ben (8), and Bella (4)

Phil is the children's father, and the presumption applies to parents. However, Sarah has made allegations of domestic abuse by Phil against herself and the children. The presumption does not apply where there is evidence before the court that 'involvement of that parent in the child's life would put the child at risk of suffering harm whatever the form of the involvement'.[40] The court will therefore need to consider (a) are the allegations made by Sarah true? If so, (b) is there any form of contact that would *not* put the children at risk of harm? There may or may not be a form of involvement—not necessarily direct contact—that would be free from harm, in which case the presumption applies. However, the court may find that despite there being a non-risky form of contact, it is still not in the children's best interests to have any involvement with their father, and even if the court thinks there should be some involvement, this does not mean there will be direct contact.

---

[40] S1(6)(b) Children Act 1989.

The clause is poorly drafted. Remember that the presumption applies:

- only in certain types of case
- only to parents
- only if the parent can be involved in the child's life in some way that does not put the child at risk of suffering harm and that involvement has a potentially wide meaning but does not lead to a specific division of the child's time.

Given that courts have sent strong messages about the importance of both parents in the life of a child, and make orders in the vast majority of applications for parental responsibility or contact (even in cases where there has been domestic abuse), you may wonder why the presumption was introduced at all.

In introducing the legislation that inserted the presumption, the children's minister, Tim Laughton, argued that the presumption would address the widespread perception that courts were biased against contact and thus against fathers. He did in fact acknowledge that this was an inaccurate perception, which rather indicates that the presumption was more about sending a message than about changing the law. Second, he argued that inserting a presumption would make the law clearer and encourage people to resolve their contact disputes outside court.

However, a similar presumption in Australian law had not had this effect. Making the legal outcomes more predictable through the use of a presumption of a 'meaningful relationship' between the child and both parents had actually led to an increase in court litigation in Australia as parents held out for what they saw as their entitlement rather than the arrangement that was best for the child.[41] This is because the presumption had been commonly understood as being about the amount of time spent with a child. 'In practice, Australian trial judges have tended to measure the notion of a meaningful relationship in temporal terms, creating a de facto assumption or at least a yardstick of shared care',[42] and as a result the number of 'shared parenting arrangements' increased from 4 to 34 per cent of orders.[43] Protection for domestic violence victims was also weakened: about a quarter of these orders involved a family history of domestic abuse.[44] In short, the Australia presumption distracted attention from the court's proper focus on the child. It was for such reasons that in this country the Family Justice Review (2012) had ultimately rejected any presumption that could dilute the welfare principle.[45] The government's rejection of their conclusions was based on a questionable belief that as long as they avoided

---

[41] An excellent summary of the Australian experience is at H Rhoades, 'Legislating to Promote Children's Welfare and the Quest for Certainty' (2012) 24(2) *Child and Family Law Quarterly* 158.

[42] *Family Justice Review Final Report* (2011) para 4.35, quoting a consultation response from Professor Helen Rhoades that can be found in full at Annex G, p115, to the report.

[43] R Kaspiew, M Gray, R Weston, L Moloney, K Hand, and L Qu, *Evaluation of the 2006 Family Law Reforms* (Australian Institute of Family Studies 2009). Available at https://aifs.gov.au/sites/default/files/publication-documents/evaluationreport.pdf accessed 18 March 2019.

[44] R Kaspiew, M Gray, R Weston, L Moloney, K Hand, and L Qu, *Evaluation of the 2006 Family Law Reforms* (Australian Institute of Family Studies 2009). Available at https://aifs.gov.au/sites/default/files/publication-documents/evaluationreport.pdf accessed 18 March 2019.

[45] F Kaganas, 'A Presumption that "Involvement" of Both Parents Is Best: Deciphering Law's Messages' (2013) 25(3) *Child and Family Law Quarterly* 270.

the term 'shared parenting' they could insert a presumption that the involvement of both parents within the best interests of the child without experiencing the same problems as Australia. This ignored the fact that the Australian legislation did not mention shared parenting either.

The presumption can be seen as one of several ways in which the Children Act seeks to influence parental behaviour. The message to parents from both the courts and—especially after the introduction of the presumption of involvement—the legislature is that constructive and unselfish co-parenting is expected.

10.3.4 The 'no delay' principle

Section 1(2) Children Act 1989 tells us that the court 'shall have regard to the general principle that any delay in determining the question is likely to prejudice the welfare of the child'. Some delay may be necessary to enable evidence to be gathered, but proceedings can take a long time in the life of a child and delays can make it impossible to change the status quo without significant disruption. Serious delays could breach Article 8 ECHR, the right to private and family life, as *Görgülü v Germany* established that 'effective respect for family life requires that future relations between parent and child not be determined by the mere passage of time'.[46] Such delays could also result in a breach of Article 6 ECHR, which says that 'In the determination of his civil rights and obligations or of any criminal charge against him, everyone is entitled to a fair and public hearing within a reasonable time by an independent and impartial tribunal established by law.'

10.3.5 The 'no order' principle

Section 1(5) Children Act 1989 tells us that the court should not make an order 'unless it considers that doing so would be better for the child than making no order'. In her role as Law Commissioner during the drafting of what would become the Act, Brenda Hoggett (Lady Hale), argued that the purpose of the 'no order' principle was to 'seek to keep compulsory intervention to minimum' and thus 'reinforce rather than to undermine parental responsibility'.[47] However, where parties have been unable to agree themselves and have turned to the court, it is nearly always in the child's best interests for the court's decision to be embodied in an order, even if the parties end up agreeing what should happen. This is because a conflict has arisen that was sufficiently serious to merit court involvement, and without an order further conflict may arise.

10.4 The court process in private law cases

In this section, we look at the process for determining a s8 application, from before an application is made until final disposal. The process is set out in Figure 10.1.

---

[46] *Görgülü v Germany* [2004] 1 FLR 894.
[47] B Hoggett, 'The Children Bill: The Aim' [1989] *Family Law* 217, 218–9.

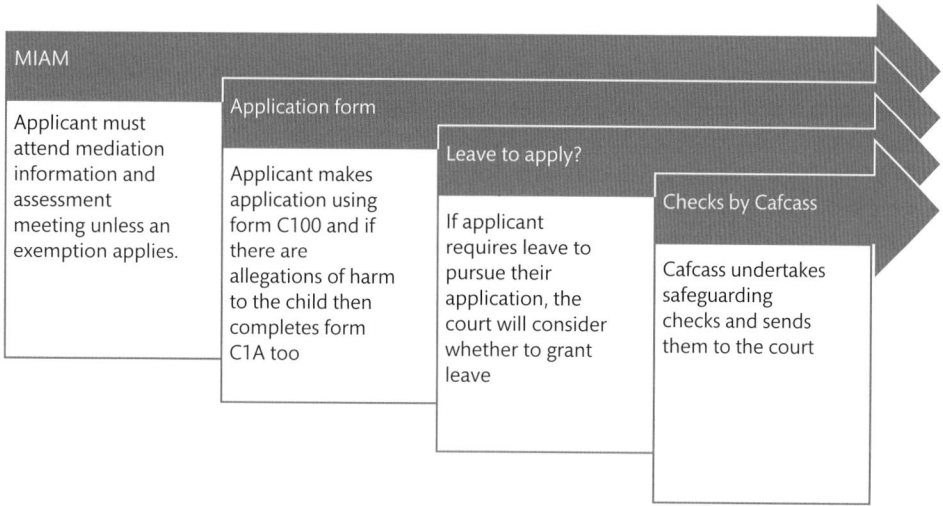

MIAM

Applicant must attend mediation information and assessment meeting unless an exemption applies.

Application form

Applicant makes application using form C100 and if there are allegations of harm to the child then completes form C1A too

Leave to apply?

If applicant requires leave to pursue their application, the court will consider whether to grant leave

Checks by Cafcass

Cafcass undertakes safeguarding checks and sends them to the court

FIGURE 10.1 Procedure for making a s8 application

10.4.1 Mediation and legal aid

Before making a s8 application, the applicant must usually attend a Mediation Information and Assessment Meeting (MIAM).[48] This is a meeting with a mediator who will explain the benefits of mediation and determine whether the case is suitable for mediation. Attendance at a MIAM does not compel a party to mediate; the obligation is simply to find out about it. Where the mediator does not think the case is suitable for mediation, they will sign a form to say that. This may happen if there is a significant power imbalance between the parties.

There are exemptions to obtaining a MIAM, including where an application is urgent,[49] made within existing proceedings or by consent, where mediation has been tried within the last 4 months, where a mediator is unavailable, or because the applicant asserts that there is domestic abuse and can evidence this.[50]

Since 2013, legal aid has not been available for most private law disputes about children. There are two situations in which legal funding is still available. First, it is available for family mediation. Second, it is still available to a party who is a victim of domestic abuse or who alleges that the child who is the subject of the application is at risk of harm from someone else.[51] It will be necessary for the person seeking legal funding to provide evidence that they are a victim of domestic abuse or that there is risk to the child. Only certain types of evidence are allowed. In both cases, a person will only be able to get legal aid if they also pass the means and merits tests. This means that the person applying for legal aid will need to, first, demonstrate that their case has merit, meaning that they have

---

[48] Practice Direction 3A *Family Mediation Information and Assessment Meetings* (MIAMS) para 12.
[49] As defined by the Family Procedure Rules Part 3, Non-Court Dispute Resolution.
[50] Family Procedure Rules r3.8(1)(a). The full list of exemptions can be found in Practice Direction 3A.
[51] This includes situations in which a child is abducted or wrongfully retained abroad by a parent.

a (usually 50 per cent) chance of winning their case and that the costs are reasonable and proportionate compared to the benefit of winning. Note that a person may initially receive legal funding but lose that if an experts' report such as a Cafcass report is not favourable to them, as this will mean their case is unlikely to succeed and therefore does not have merit. Second, their income and assets must be below a certain level.

In many cases a party will simply earn too much or have too many assets to be able to receive any legal aid even if they struggle to afford to pay solicitors' fees. This means that people are increasingly likely to represent themselves, even in the most difficult cases. In the three month period April to June 2020, neither party had legal representation in 36 per cent of cases, one party was represented in 44 per cent of cases (31 per cent applicant and 13 per cent respondent), and in 21 per cent both parties were represented.[52] As a result, cases 'now typically involve longer hearings and return to court more frequently'.[53]

SCENARIO 2

Illustration 4: Molly, Mark, and child Katie (6)

Mark has tried mediation but it has not been successful. Provided that the mediation broke down within the last four months, the mediator will sign to say that he is exempt from the requirement of a further MIAM. If it is more than four months ago, then he will need to attend another MIAM (unless he is exempt for any other reason) but there is no obligation on him or on Molly to agree to mediate. His obligation is purely to attend the MIAM.

SCENARIO 4

Illustration 3: Sarah, Phil, and children Bill (11), Ben (8), and Bella (4)

Sarah has obtained a non-molestation order and an occupation order from the court. These are forms of protection order and are evidence that enable her to access legal aid, provided that she also passes the means and merits tests.

She is exempt from the requirement to attend a MIAM. Her protection orders are her evidence that the case is not suitable for mediation.

10.4.2 Safeguarding

Prior to the first hearing, the court will send a copy of the application Cafcass, who will then contact the local authority children's services team and the police to find out whether they are aware of any safeguarding issues relating to the parties, and will in turn relay this

[52] Ministry of Justice, *Family Court Statistics Quarterly, England and Wales, April to June 2020* (September 2020).
[53] Sir Andrew McFarlane, 'Living in Interesting Times'. Keynote speech to the Resolution Annual Conference 2019, Manchester 5 April 2019.

information to the court. This could include domestic violence callouts to the family home or child protection investigations. They will also telephone the parties to find out if either party has concerns about the safety and well-being of the children.

Concerns about the children may also come to the attention of the court through the filing of form C1A, colloquially known as the 'harm form'. This provides the applicant (or respondent) with an opportunity to describe previous court proceedings relating to domestic abuse, such as non-molestation proceedings under the Family Law Act 1996, or to note incidents of harmful behaviour. The purpose of the safeguarding checks and the harm form is simply to alert the court issues that may require attention and thereby enable the court to make appropriate directions for how the case is to proceed.

10.4.3 At court

At the first hearing and dispute resolution appointment (FHRDA) the judge will determine what the case is about and what needs to be done before the case can be decided. The judge will therefore give directions about the filing of evidence, such as that the parties can file witness statements and perhaps other kinds of evidence such as letters from the child's school. The appropriate evidence will depend on what the case is about.

Simple cases in which there are no concerns about harm may be settled at this hearing: being at court can focus the parties' minds on reaching agreement. In some courts, there may be a Cafcass officer available to talk to the parties to see if an agreement can be reached then and there, with their assistance. If the parties reach agreement, they can ask the judge to make that into an order, and the case will be over.

However, where there is evidence of risk or harm to a child or one of the parties that has become apparent from the applications or the safeguarding checks, Practice Direction 12J requires courts to be very careful about approving interim or final agreements reached without the court being fully apprised of the facts.[54] The court may therefore hold a 'fact-finding hearing' at which it will hear evidence about the allegations and decide whether or not some or all of the allegations are true, before it decides the application. Inevitably, it takes time to prepare witness statements and gather evidence, especially if experts' reports are required. Cases can take a long time in the life of a child and may even result in the complete breakdown of a precarious relationship between the child and that parent, or in one of the parties succeeding by default.

In some cases, a fact-finding hearing may not be necessary. Where a party has a criminal conviction for an offence that relates to the same incident that the family court is considering, the allegation has already been proven to a higher standard (beyond reasonable doubt) than that used in the family courts (on the balance of probabilities). In such cases there may be arguments over what effect that incident should have on the outcome, but the underlying facts cannot be disputed. Alternatively, the court may not hold a fact-finding hearing if it believes that the allegations, taken at their highest, are not sufficient to have an effect on arrangements for the child.

---

[54] See 10.8 of this chapter.

10.4.4 The role of experts

The court's role is to determine what is in the best interests of the child or children who are the subject of the application. As we have seen, this includes considering a range of different factors contained in the welfare checklist. In many cases, it will be possible to resolve the case with little or no expert involvement, as in Scenario 2. In more complex cases, the court may take the view that it is necessary to have the help of experts either to ascertain facts (for example, the cause of an injury or whether drugs are present in a parent's hair) or to explain the implications of those facts or to make recommendations to the court. In the latter situation it may be necessary to have a fact-finding hearing first, so that the expert can prepare her report on the basis of the facts found by the judge.

Section 7 reports

The most commonly used resource is for the court to direct Cafcass to prepare a report about the family under s7 Children Act 1989. This could be limited to simply finding out what the child's wishes and feelings are, but could be wider and involve the Cafcass family court adviser meeting the parties, the child, and other people who are important in the child's life, observing the child with each parent, and recommending what should happen. This takes about three to four months to prepare, causing delay in the case, but can provide very useful information to the judge. A study commissioned by Cafcass found that in 75 per cent of cases courts followed the recommendations of the Cafcass officer, rising to 90 per cent where the court schedules a further review date.[55]

Where the issues raised in the case are so serious that the court thinks that the child may be suffering or likely to suffer significant harm, the court can ask the local authority to prepare a report under s37 Children Act 1989 (see 10.7.3). This requires the authority to consider whether it should apply for a care or supervision order or provide assistance to the child in accordance with their statutory obligations towards children in need. In this way, serious cases may leave the private law sphere and turn into public law child protection cases.

Other experts

Where necessary to resolve the case, the court may also give permission to a party (or the parties jointly) to instruct a psychiatrist or psychologist to assess a parent or child. This may be appropriate where there are concerns that a child's opposition to contact is irrational.[56] Experts may also be required for issues that are outside the scope of normal judicial knowledge. In Key Case *Re G (Children) (Religious Upbringing)* (discussed in more detail in Chapter 9) the court had to decide whether the children, who were Jewish, should attend a Hasidic Jewish school or an Orthodox Jewish school. It heard evidence from a senior religious figure and the headteachers of each proposed school, who outlined the nature of each school's curriculum and environment.[57] In cases with an international

---

[55] C Baksi, 'Family Judges Backing Court Welfare Reports', *Law Society Gazette* (London, 13 December 2012). The likelihood of the report being followed means that a publicly funded party will lose their legal aid if the Cafcass report is contrary to their position as they no longer pass the merits test.

[56] See 10.8.4.

[57] [2012] EWCA Civ 1233.

element, an expert on the law of the other country may be needed. Depending on the issues in the case, paternity testing, or testing for substance misuse (hair strand testing or liver function) may be ordered. This may be undertaken via the party's GP or there are specialist companies that will undertake this work and provide a report to the court. All of these must be funded by the parties (or their legal aid) and can be very expensive.

SCENARIO 1

Illustration 4: Al, Ruth, and son Daniel (12 weeks old)

The court may well want expert evidence on the issue of circumcision. In *Re J (Child's Religious Upbringing and Circumcision)*, the court heard from a consultant paediatrician and read the General Medical Council and British Medical Association Guidelines.[58]

SCENARIO 2

Illustration 5: Molly, Mark, and daughter Katie (6)

The issue in this case is not whether Mark should see Katie but how frequently. Molly believes that Katie should see Mark every other weekend, and is concerned that midweek contact might disrupt Katie's routine and make her unsettled for school. Mark is upset because he is no longer seeing Katie every day and does not want the role of 'weekend dad'. This case requires the application of common sense and a focus on what is best for this little girl. This is exactly the type of case where mediation should have succeeded. Now that it is in court, a judge will decide on the basis of his or her views on what is best for a child of this age. If there is a Cafcass officer available at court to talk to the parties, this may help them reach agreement. It is very unlikely indeed that the court will require an expert report. If Katie was older, it may be appropriate to ask her wishes and feelings but at the age of 6 these are unlikely to be given much weight.

SCENARIO 4

Illustration 4: Sarah, Phil, and children Bill (11), Ben (8), and Bella (4)

This is a much more complex case, with Sarah alleging abuse by Phil and that he has a drinking and drugs problem and Phil alleging that Sarah is mentally unwell and therefore not able to look after the children. The court will need to make sense of this by working out what is true before it can decide what is best for the children. If we were acting for Sarah, we would want a fact-finding hearing so that we can produce our evidence that Phil is abusive. We would consider whether there was any

---

[58] [1999] 2 FCR 34.

independent supporting evidence contained in medical records (such as reports of injury or a report of abuse that predates these proceedings). Have any friends witnessed any incidents? Have the police been called out to the house because of a reported violent incident?

One practical problem is that some victims of domestic abuse will not have any form of independent evidence. They may have tried to hide what was happening or been isolated from their friends and sources of help. Sarah's testimony on the witness stand is a form of evidence and the judge will use this opportunity to form a view on her credibility as a witness, and on Phil's credibility. Phil has a harder job because it is hard to prove a negative (although the burden of proof is on Sarah as she is the person asserting the abuse). He will look for evidence that is inconsistent with Sarah's allegations.

As there are allegations of alcohol and drug misuse, Sarah may seek an order that Phil undergo tests that show this. If Phil denies these allegations he may seek permission to file a report that shows (for example) no damage to his liver from alcohol or no drugs present in his hair strands. Phil is asserting that Sarah is too unwell to care for the children. If there is some prima facie evidence of illness, then the court may order a psychiatric report.

Finally, the children may have some important evidence. It is unlikely that the parents will want the children to give testimony and at least two of the children are likely to be seen as too young to do that. However, they may be interviewed in an age-appropriate way by a social worker, Cafcass officer, or child psychiatrist. At a minimum, it is likely that a Cafcass officer will meet with them, and observe contact between them and Phil.

10.4.5 Final hearings (disposal)

Once the judge has all the information necessary to make a decision, he or she will look to make a final order. This does not prevent the parties from returning to court in the future by making a fresh application. After all, children grow, and it is inevitable that the arrangements that worked for a 5-year-old do not work for a 10- or 15-year-old.

10.5 Child arrangements orders in detail

A child arrangements order may specify with whom the child will live. This may be with one person or with more than one person. If the order is in favour of more than one person, then:

- Where the people that the child lives with are in separate households (such as divorced mum and dad) this is known as a 'shared' live with order.
- Where these people live together (such as mum and stepdad) the order is a 'joint' live with order.

It is not usually necessary to name both the parent and their new partner in a live with order. However, naming a person in a child arrangements order as a person with whom the child lives will give that person parental responsibility, and this may be useful if the parent is working away or not always available in emergencies.

Section 8 uses the phrase 'spend time or otherwise have contact' in describing arrangements that would previously have constituted a contact order. Courts have broad powers to decide when, where, and how contact is to take place, and to place conditions that require actions by both the resident and non-resident parent.

Spending time with a child may involve:

- Daytime only contact (unsupervised, supported, or supervised)
- Overnight staying contact, whether one night at a time or several nights (what is appropriate will depend on the age of the child)
- Telephone or videocalling contact
- Letters or emails
- A combination of the above.

At 10.5.5, we note that there is a point at which spending time with a parent becomes living part-time with that parent, and the consequences of whether the order is expressed as a live with order or a spend time with order.

While most children will have direct contact with a parent by spending in-person time with them, it may be in their best interests to supplement this with additional contact by telephone, skype, or email/letter, especially if there is a significant (for the child) amount of time between visits. As relationships become increasingly international, children may live in a different country to a parent or other person who is important to them, and video calls, such as via skype or facetime, can be very important in maintaining a relationship. Because the court likes to anticipate any potential areas for future disagreement, the court may also specify the arrangements for key dates such as religious holidays, birthdays, and mother's/father's day, and include a general 'catch all' clause that the parties are free to agree 'such other or additional contact' on top of that which is ordered.

Where a child's relationship with their non-resident parent has broken down, or there has been a long (in the life of the child) period since contact last took place, it may be appropriate for contact to take place in a supported environment, such as a contact centre, or in the presence of a responsible adult such as a family friend or relative, at least until a relationship has developed. A contact centre is a place where children can meet a non-resident parent and spent time with them. They are often church or village halls staffed by volunteers, and filled with toys, and many parents and children may be there at any one time. As a result of funding difficulties, many contact centres have closed, but they are a precious resource. While a child will become bored with contact in a centre after a while, they are a safe space for a relationship to be rebuilt. They can also be used as a neutral handover venue, where one parent arrives with the child, and the child is handed over to the other parent via a volunteer, so that the parents do not meet. This can be appropriate in situations where there have been arguments at the point of handover but the non-resident parent is permitted to take the child out.

Where direct contact is in the child's best interests but there are nevertheless risks to him or her, contact may need to be closely supervised. In *Re S (A Child)* the judge declined to make a direct contact order because the supervision would need to be long-term. The father had been convicted of downloading pornographic images of teenage girls, although a risk assessment showed that the risk to his own daughter, aged 8, was small. The refusal was overturned on appeal, on the basis that long-term supervision was not by itself a reason to refuse direct contact.[59] Nevertheless, there are real difficulties relating to the cost

---

[59] [2015] EWCA Civ 689.

of long-term supervision, especially if the supervision cannot be by a family member and a professional agency has to be paid to provide the supervision. Contact centres do not provide close supervision so are not appropriate in this situation.

While in *Re S* the Court of Appeal was much influenced by the statements we consider at 10.6.2 about the importance of contact, there will be some cases in which only indirect contact, such as the sending of letters, emails, or gifts, is the child's interests. In Key Case *Re O (Contact: Imposition of Conditions)* Sir Thomas Bingham MR said that the object of indirect contact is to build up a relationship between the absent parent and the child.[60] This means that indirect contact may lead in due course to direct contact, although in some cases the risks as such that the contact will never be direct.

KEY CASE *Re O (Contact Imposition of Conditions)*
[1995] 2 FLR 124 (CA)

The parents of a 2¼-year-old boy had separated. The mother was implacably hostile to the father being involved in the child's life. The father agreed not to pursue direct contact at that time, but the court made an order that the mother send him regular photographs and nursery reports, tell him about any significant illnesses of the child, and give the child any letters and gifts he sent. Given the boy's age, the mother had to read the letters out loud to the child. She argued that the court had no power to require her to do any of these things.

The leading judgment is by Sir Thomas Bingham MR:

· 'It cannot be emphasised too strongly that the court is concerned with the interests of the mother and the father only insofar as they bear on the welfare of the child.

· Where parents of a child are separated and the child is in the day-to-day care of one of them, it is almost always in the interests of the child that he or she should have contact with the other parent. . . . [T]he separation of parents involves a loss to the child, and it is desirable that that loss should so far as possible be made good by contact with the non-custodial parent, that is the parent in whose day-to-day care the child is not.

· The courts should not at all readily accept that the child's welfare will be injured by direct contact. Judging that question the court should take a medium-term and long-term view of the child's development and not accord excessive weight to what appear likely to be short-term or transient problems.

· In cases in which, for whatever reason, direct contact cannot for the time being be ordered, it is ordinarily highly desirable that there should be indirect contact so that the child grows up knowing of the love and interest of the absent parent with whom, in due course, direct contact should be established.

· The object of indirect contact is to build up a relationship between the absent parent and the child.

· If the caring parent puts difficulties in the way of indirect contact . . . then such parent must understand that the court can compel compliance with its orders; it has sanctions available and no residence order is to be regarded as irrevocable.

· Neither parent should be encouraged or permitted to think that the more intransigent, the more unreasonable, the more obdurate and the more uncooperative they are, the more likely they are to get their own way.'

---

[60] *Re O (Contact: Imposition of Conditions)* [1995] 2 FLR 124, 130 (CA).

10.5.1 Conditions attached to child arrangements orders

Under s11(7) Children Act 1989 the court also has the power to detail how the child arrangements are 'to be carried into effect'. This enables the court to impose conditions on an order that must be complied with by a named person who may be a person in whose favour the order is made; a parent of the child or someone with parental responsibility for him; or a person with whom the child is living. Note, therefore, that this power can be enforced against more people than simply parents.

Common inclusions in orders are to:

- Detail when and where the child is to be handed over from one parent to the other, and who is to be present at handover (perhaps not a parent's new partner if this is likely to cause acrimony). In cases where the parties find it very difficult to communicate directly, handover may take place at a neutral venue or be facilitated by a third party.

- Require a parent to do a positive act to promote contact, such as read a letter from the non-resident parent to the child where the child is too young to read himself or forward school reports.[61]

- Require a parent not to do something, such as to be abstinent from alcohol or drugs in the period running up to and during their time with the child.

- Make contact conditional on certain things such as 'contact shall only take place if the mother provides a negative breathalyser sample at the start of any contact session when requested to do so'.[62] (Some judges have sent the parties to the car accessories shop Halfords to buy breathalysers.) Such conditions must be enforceable. In *B v B (Custody: Conditions)* the court awarded what was then 'custody' of the children to the mother on condition that she should not go out to work until the children were in full time education and that each child had to be in bed by 6.30pm. The Court of Appeal held that the conditions were 'too onerous and hardly practicable to enforce'.[63]

FOCUS Know-How

What might a child arrangements order look like?

This is what a 'live with' order in favour of the mother, combined with a 'spend time with' (contact) order in favour of the father, may look like. This order also contains a condition relating to drugs and alcohol. We have adapted this from precedents produced by the judiciary's Family Orders Project, which lawyers are meant to use, and the headings and definitions of the order have been omitted.

1. The children shall live with the applicant mother as a final order.
2. The applicant mother must make sure that the children spend time with or otherwise have contact with the respondent father as follows:
   a. Each Wednesday from 4pm to 7pm

---

[61] *Re O (Contact: Imposition of Conditions)* [1995] 2 FLR 124 (CA) is authority for the courts' power to require a positive step to promote contact.

[62] Children Act Proceedings Master Copy Orders (January 2016). Available at https://www.lawsociety.org.uk/practice-areas/family-children/cap-master-orders/ accessed 23 October 2018.

[63] [1980] 1 FLR 385, 390.

   b. On alternate weeks from Saturday at 11am to Sunday at 4pm

   c. On intervening weeks, by telephone, the applicant to telephone the respondent's house between 11am and 12 noon on the Saturday.

3. The following conditions shall apply:

   a. Handover at the start of contact will be at the applicant's house with the respondent to collect the children.

   b. Handovers at the end of contact will be at the respondent's house with the applicant to collect the children.

   c. The respondent shall not drink alcohol or use non-prescription drugs for a period of 24 hours before or at any time while seeing the children.

An order that provided only for indirect contact may say something like:

1. The respondent must make sure that the children have indirect contact with the applicant to take the form of letters, cards, and gifts to be sent to the children by the applicant which must be passed or read to the children by the respondent.

2. Such communications must be sent no more frequently than fortnightly or as set out in the schedule to this order.

3. The respondent must encourage the children to respond to communications sent.

4. The respondent must send to the applicant school reports and photographs and updating medical information when received.

10.5.2 Effect of a child arrangements order

There are several important consequences to a child arrangements order, which can be found in sections 12 and 13 Children Act 1989.

Surname

When a child arrangements order is in force, nobody can change the child's surname without either a court order (which would be the result of a specific issues application) or the consent of everyone with parental responsibility.

Removal from the UK

When a child arrangements order is in force, nobody can remove the child from the United Kingdom (note: this is wider than our jurisdiction, England and Wales) without either a court order or the consent of everyone with parental responsibility (s13). To do so may constitute the crime of child abduction. However, where there is a 'live with' order in place, the person in whose favour that was made can remove the child from the UK for up to one month. The effect of this is that a parent who had a 'spend time with' order cannot remove the child from the UK for a holiday without consent, whereas a parent with a 'live with' order can do so.

We consider child abduction and applications to permanently remove a child from the jurisdiction to live abroad at 10.9 and 10.10.

Parental responsibility

As we discussed in Chapter 8, all mothers will have parental responsibility for a child, but not all fathers or second female parents will, and the child may also live with or spend time with a non-parent. It may therefore be necessary to give parental responsibility to the person named in a 'live with' or 'spend time with' order. Under s12:

1. Where the court makes an order that the child live with his father or second female parent, the court *must* make a parental responsibility order under ss4 or 4ZA Children Act 1989. This is understandable: if the child lives with someone, that person will need to have certain powers and duties in order to be able to make day-to-day decisions.

2. Where the court makes an order that the child spends time or otherwise has contact with his father or second female parent, the court *can* make a parental responsibility order under ss4 or 4ZA Children Act 1989 if it thinks it appropriate.

3. Where the court makes an order that the child live with someone who is not his parent, the court *must* make a parental responsibility order. However, this is not an order under ss4 or 4ZA Children Act 1989, which is permanent (albeit removable) parental responsibility. Instead, s12(2) provides that the person will have parental responsibility only for as long as the 'live with' order remains in force.

4. Where the court makes an order that the child spends time or otherwise has contact with someone who is not his parent, the court *can* make a parental responsibility order if it thinks it appropriate, and s12(2) provides that the person will have parental responsibility only for as long as the 'spend time with' order remains in force.

On a day to day basis, the person with whom the child lives has much greater scope to exercise their parental responsibility. They will be the person who is available to sign school permission slips and take the child to the doctor and ensure the child is safe and fed. However, this does not mean that the 'live with' order operates as a kind of trump card giving them greater rights or responsibilities than anyone else with parental responsibility. That is not the case: all those with parental responsibility are equal and in most cases can exercise that responsibility unilaterally. Indeed, s2(8) Children Act 1989 makes it clear that parental responsibility cannot be exercised in a way that is incompatible with a child arrangements order.

Guardianship

A parent can appoint a guardian to look after the child in the event of their death. Such an appointment does not take effect where there is any other person with parental responsibility still alive *unless* the person who died was a person with whom the child lived under a child arrangements 'live with' order. If so, the guardianship takes effect and the guardian shares parental responsibility with any other remaining parental responsibility holders, who could include the other, non-resident, parent.

Note that this type of guardian is not the same as a litigation guardian.

SCENARIO 4

Illustration 5: Sarah, Phil, and children Bill (11), Ben (8), and Bella (4)

Both Sarah and Phil have parental responsibility: Sarah, as mother, has it automatically and Phil has it by virtue of having been married to her. In the event of her death, the appointment of a guardian for the children would not come into effect because Phil is a person with parental responsibility who is still alive.

However, if there was a child arrangements order saying that the children lived with Sarah, then the appointment of the guardian would come into effect and the guardian would share the parental responsibility with Phil. In the event of a dispute about where the children should live, one of them would have to apply to court and the court would determine this on the basis of the welfare principle.

SCENARIO 2

Illustration 6: Molly, Mark, and daughter Katie (6)

Consider what would happen if Molly, as the sole adult with parental responsibility for Katie, died. She could appoint a guardian and her appointment of that guardian would come into effect because there is no one else with parental responsibility. Mark would need to apply for parental responsibility and, if the guardian disagreed that Katie should live with him, a child arrangements order.

Consent to marriage

A person aged 16 or 17 can marry with the permission of all those with parental responsibility (or the consent of the court), as described in Chapter 2. However, where there is a 'live with' order in force, only the permission of the person with whom the child lives is required.[64]

Care orders

A child arrangements order is incompatible with a care order and therefore if a child arrangements order is made it will discharge the care order.[65] This is one way in which a person who wishes to care for a child can potentially intervene in the care process, as without a child arrangements order they would not have the status to make an application to discharge the care order. Conversely, if a care order is made it discharges any existing child arrangements order. This is discussed further in Chapter 12.

Voluntary accommodation

Under s20 Children Act 1989 the local authority has certain powers and duties to accommodate children, something we discuss in Chapter 11. The status of a person seeking to challenge that depends in part upon whether they have parental responsibility or not.

10.5.3 When does contact work?

Setting out in black and white what the court *can* do does not help with what it *should* do, or what arrangements are best for the children. Even with the best intentions in the world, parents may struggle to reach agreement. Very often, feelings about the other person run high. Agreements may be negotiated against a background of heartbreak, anger, and grief. Third parties, new partners, and wider family may also express strong views. There may

---

[64] Marriage Act 1949, s3.
[65] Children Act 1989 s9.

be practical issues to do with housing or bills that get caught up in discussions about parenting. The parents may have different styles and underlying beliefs about bringing up children and these can assume prominence after separation. Even if the parties seek the court's assistance, an order is not a cure for a strained relationship, nor—despite the drafter's best efforts—can it resolve all issues between the parties that may arise.

In their report *Making Contact: How Parents and Children Negotiate and Experience Contact after Divorce*, Trinder, Beek, and Connolly identified a number of factors that determined whether contact 'worked', which they defined as safe, committed, and positive for everyone.[66] They found that there were direct determinants of the quality of contact, as well as mediating factors. Direct determinants included commitment to contact, role clarity and relationship quality, the nature of the relationship and breakup; challenges, such as the nature of the separation, new adult partners, money, logistics, parenting style and quality, and safety issues. Mediating factors—those factors that had an effect on the determining factors—included beliefs about contact, relationship skills, the involvement of family, friends and external agencies, and the educational qualifications and income of the parents. Given the variety of factors that influence the parties' approach to post-separation parenting, it is clear that resolving one issue does not necessarily make contact work.

10.5.4 What patterns of care are most common?

Imagine that you are representing yourself at court on an application to 'spend time with' your child, or to have the child live with you for some of the time. How will you know what to ask for? If you ask to share the child's time equally between you and your ex-partner, will you be laughed out of court—or will you be asking too little if you ask for two nights per week? Parents 'need reference points in this strange terrain'.[67] Some judges have issued guidance on their expectations and approaches, and these are likely to be very useful for people representing themselves. But there is one major problem with these: they assume typical cases when there is no such thing.

A common pattern has been for a child to see the non-resident parent once per week after school (but not overnight) and every second weekend with an overnight stay between the Saturday and Sunday. The fact that this pattern is common does not mean that it is the best pattern. An appropriate child arrangements pattern will depend on a number of variables such as the age of the child and the proximity of the parents' homes and is therefore individual to that family. A number of studies have also shown that the frequency of contact depends upon the non-resident parent's social class and income, as well as gender. Contact between father and daughter, for example, is more likely to break down than contact between father and son.[68]

---

[66] L Trinder, M Beek, and J Connolly, *Making Contact: How Parents and Children Negotiate and Experience Contact after Divorce* (Joseph Rowntree Foundation 2002).

[67] S Bennett and S Armstrong Walsh, 'The No Order Principle, Parental Responsibility and the Child's Wishes' [1994, February] *Family Law* 91.

[68] See E Giovannini, *Outcomes of Family Justice: Children's Proceedings—a Review of the Evidence* (Research Summary 6/11, Ministry of Justice 2011) for a discussion.

We know that the non-resident parent is much more likely to be the father rather than the mother. Researchers for the Modern Fatherhood project found that:

- 38 per cent of fathers visit, see, or have contact with the children several times a week

- 21 per cent visit, see, or have contact with the children once a week

- 28 per cent visit, see, or have contact with the children less than weekly but at least a few times a year

- 13 per cent report that they have no contact with their non-resident children. This equates to 129,000 men in the UK.[69]

These figures should be taken as approximate only, as there is evidence that resident and non-resident parents will each describe the level of the non-resident parent's contact differently. The figures above represent the level of contact that non-resident fathers describe.

10.5.5 Should care be shared equally?

When the Children Act was drafted, the government thought that 'shared residence orders' (as they were then called) would be rare because in most cases there would not be a genuinely equal division of a child's time.[70] It is certainly true that in this jurisdiction such an exact split is currently uncommon, although the fathers' rights group Fathers for Justice have argued that there should be 'a legal presumption of 50/50 shared parenting after separation'.[71] Other groups, including some MPs, have shied away from equal division, but argued for a legal presumption that it is in a child's best interests to spend substantial amounts of time with each parent.[72] Such arrangements, known as 'shared time parenting' or 'shared care', are more common than exact equal division. Accurate figures are hard to come by, although Peacey and Hunt found that about 9-12 per cent of children had a shared care arrangement that is equivalent to least three nights per week.[73]

In this section, we will be referring to shared care arrangements as encompassing anything from a 35/65 split to a 50/50 split of the child's time, which is the range used by a

---

[69] E Poole, S Speight, M O'Brien, S Connolly, and M Aldrich, 'What Do We Know about Non-Resident Fathers?' (2013). Briefing paper available at http://www.modernfatherhood.org/wp-content/uploads/2013/11/Briefing-paper-Non-resident-fathers.pdf accessed 5 April 2019.

[70] Lord Mackay, *Hansard*, House of Lords Deb vol 501, col 127–8; cited by PG Harris and R H George, 'Parental Responsibility and Shared Residence Orders: Parliamentary Intentions and Judicial Interpretations' (2010) 22(2) *Child and Family Law Quarterly* 151, 156.

[71] Fathers for Justice website, 'Our Mission' page. Available at https://www.fathers-4-justice.org/our-campaign/our-mission/ accessed 22 October 2018.

[72] See, e.g., the Shared Parenting Orders Bill (HC Bill 56) introduced by Brian Binley MP in 2010, which created a presumption that the child should spend 'a substantial and significant amount of time with both parents', and the Children (Access to Parents) Bill 2010–12 introduced by Charlie Elphicke MP, which sought to create a presumption 'that the child's welfare is best served through having reasonable access to and contact with both parents unless exceptional circumstances are demonstrated that such access and contact is not in the best interests of the child'.

[73] V Peacey and J Hunt, *Problematic Contact after Separation or Divorce* (Gingerbread/Nuffield Foundation 2009).

number of different studies on shared care. If reached through a court process, a shared care pattern could be expressed either as:

- An order that the child *lives with* A and *spends time with* B (for example from Thursday to Sunday), which would previously have been known as a 'residence and contact' order; or

- An order that the child *lives with* A from Monday to Wednesday and *lives with* B from Thursday to Sunday (or any other pattern involving substantial time with each parent such as one week with A and the next with B). This would previously have been known as a 'shared residence' order.

SCENARIO 2

Illustration 7: Molly, Mark, and daughter Katie (6)

Mark could seek an order that Katie *lives with* him for some or all of the time. 'Katie shall live with Mark until further order' would mean that Katie lived with him all the time, but the order could alternatively specify a part-time arrangement that 'Katie shall live with Mark from Monday at 9am to Wednesday at 5pm' (or whatever pattern they agreed or the judge ordered). A 'live with' order made in favour of two people who live separately, like Mark and Molly, would be a 'shared live with order'.

Alternatively, he could agree that Katie will live with Molly for much of the time and seek an order that he *spends time with* Katie (a 'contact order'). For enforceability (see 10.7.2) this would be phrased to require Molly to act: 'Molly must make sure that Katie spends time with Mark from Monday at 9am to Wednesday at 5pm and has contact with him by telephone on Saturday at 3pm'.

The amount of time is likely to determine whether the order is expressed as 'living (part-time) with' or 'spending time with'. Where the time that Katie spends with Mark is significant and includes overnight stays, then either expression would be suitable.

Some judges and lawyers have used the difference between these formulations as a mechanism to send a message to the parents about their post-divorce roles. Establishing that the child 'lives with' each parent for different periods of time can imply an equality that writing an order that the child 'lives with' one parent and 'spends time with' the other does not, even if the actual amount of time is no different. As Harris-Short has pointed out, 'labels matter, but they matter because of the messages they send'.[74] Harris and George see the use of shared residence orders as linked to the courts' tendency to make parental responsibility orders more often than in the past (see Chapter 8).[75] Thus, just as Helen Reece has argued that parental responsibility orders are being made 'as therapy' for non-resident parents, principally in a line of cases determined by Ward LJ, so too has that judge argued that shared residence orders are 'of practical therapeutic importance . . . and reflect the need for [the father] to be given some status'.[76] This view is not universal, however, and

---

[74] S Harris-Short, 'Resisting the March towards 50/50 Shared Residence; Rights, Welfare, and Equality in Post-Separation Families' (2010) 32(3) *Journal of Social Welfare and Family Law* 257, 262.

[75] PG Harris and RH George, 'Parental Responsibility and Shared Residence Orders: Parliamentary Intentions and Judicial Interpretations' (2010) 22(2) *Child and Family Law Quarterly* 151, 166.

[76] H Reece, 'Parental Responsibility as Therapy' (2009) 39 *Family Law* 1167, discussing *Re S* [1995] 2 FLR 648; *Re H (Shared Residence: Parental Responsibility)* [1995] 2 FLR 883 (CA), 889.

some judges insist that almost any unequal division of time is expressed as 'live with' and 'spend time with'. They may take the view that the child's welfare interest in consistency and familiarity may lie in having a clearly identified primary carer, usually the mother because in most cases she is the primary carer prior to separation.[77]

Despite the variation in judicial views, it appears that 'current case-law is significantly more supportive of shared care than either the current policy framework or the existing research base'.[78] This is because the research that has been done on shared care arrangements has found no evidence that shared care *in and of itself* improves outcomes for children. Amato and Gilbreth's meta study found that what non resident parents do when they are with the child is more important than the frequency in which they see them.[79] Shared care also risks exacerbating hostility between the parties by raising expectations on one parent's part that such an order will force the other parent to respect them more.[80] The Australian experience of shared care has not been positive.[81]

There is a real risk that shared parenting arrangements are about the parents' desires, not what is best for the child. In particularly acrimonious situations, substantial time with each parent simply provides an opportunity to expose the children to greater conflict. If imposed upon parties who cannot get on with one another, who are rigid in ensuring they get 'their' time, and who have practical difficulties moving the child between houses it is more likely to break down.

So, while 'several studies have shown that contact with non-resident fathers following divorce is associated with positive outcomes among children when parents have a cooperative relationship, [it] is associated with negative outcomes when parents have a conflicted relationship'.[82] As the more acrimonious cases are precisely those that are likely to end up in court, they are cases in which shared parenting may be the least appropriate. But courts have made shared care orders even in acrimonious cases. For example, Newnham has criticised the decision in *A v A (Shared Residence)*[83] to make a shared residence order as a method of containing the parents' 'virtual state of war' and the suggestion in subsequent cases 'that a "harmonious relationship" between the parents is no longer a prerequisite for shared residence, but an expected result.'[84]

---

[77] Interestingly, Dermott has argued that some fathers are creating a new form of fatherhood that does not emulate motherhood and which is based on an intimate emotional engagement with the child but not the labour involved in day-to-day parenting. E Dermott, *Intimate Fatherhood: A Sociological Analysis* (Routledge 2008).

[78] L Trinder, 'Climate Change? The Multiple Trajectories of Shared Care Law, Policy and Social Practice' (2014) 26(1) *Child and Family Law Quarterly* 30, 30–1.

[79] PR Amato and JG Gilbreth, 'Non-Resident Fathers and Children's Wellbeing: A Meta Analysis' (1999) 61(3) *Journal of Marriage and the Family* 557. A meta study is a statistical analysis of other studies on the same subject, bringing together the results of those studies in an attempt to find common themes/results.

[80] S Harris-Short, 'Resisting the March towards 50/50 Shared Residence; Rights, Welfare, and Equality in Post-Separation Families' (2010) 32(3) *Journal of Social Welfare and Family Law* 257, 262.

[81] H Rhoades, R Graycar, and M Harrison, 'The Family Law Reform Act 1995: The First Three Years' (2001) 15(1) *The Australian Family Lawyer* 1; H Rhoades, 'The Dangers of Shared Care Legislation: Why Australia Needs (Yet More) Family Law Reform' (2008) 36(3) *Federal Law Review* 279.

[82] PR Amato and JG Gilbreth, 'Non-Resident Fathers and Children's Wellbeing: A Meta Analysis' (1999) 61(3) *Journal of Marriage and the Family* 557.

[83] *A v A (Shared Residence)* [2004] EWHC 142 (Fam), [2004] 1 FLR 1195, at paras [20] and [23].

[84] *Re R (Residence: Shared Care: Children's Views)* [2005] EWCA Civ 542, [2006] 1 FLR 491, [11] (Thorpe LJ). Cited in A Newnham, 'Shared Residence: Lessons from Sweden' (2011) 23(2) *Child and Family Law Quarterly* 251, 252.

We know that successful arrangements tend to have certain features:

- They are likely to be negotiated by the parties themselves rather than forced on them.
- The parents mutually respect one another.
- The parents are willing to respond positively to changes in the child's wishes and needs over time.
- The parents are more likely to have university-level education and flexible working arrangements (that enable them to collect the children from school for example).
- The parents have sufficient money to afford houses near one another that are big enough for the children to be comfortable in.
- The children tend to be of primary school age.
- The children feel at home in each house.[85]
- The fathers tend to have been involved in the children's daily care prior to separation.

In short, successful arrangements are 'likely to work well when arrangements are child-focused, flexible, and cooperative'[86] so that practical impediments can be overcome, and the parents tend to be within a specific demographic grouping that is not typical of most separating parents. These are exactly the features that cannot be created by court order.

FOCUS Think Critically

Gender bias in the family courts

The most common type of application made by a father is an application for his child to spend time with him. This reflects the fact that most children of separated parents live with their mother. The vast majority of such applications are successful, in that they result in an order for contact.[87] However, this does not explain what level of contact the fathers have, and whether this is more or less than they wanted. For example, they may have sought but been refused an order that the child live with them, or they may have sought substantially shared time but achieved weekend time only. It also does not tell us anything about whether the mother complies with the order, which is something that we consider at 10.7 of this chapter.

The fact that most fathers' applications result in contact does not accord with public perception. This has two implications. First, it may mean that those who have good cases (a category that includes most fathers) may be discouraged from making an application if they think that their application will be unsuccessful (although there may also be financial or other barriers to them applying). Second, although most disputes are addressed outside the court process, parties negotiate 'in the

---

[85] Drawn from B Fehlberg, B Smyth, M Maclean, and C Roberts, 'Legislating for Shared Time Parenting after Separation: A Research Review' (2011) 25(3) *International Journal of Law, Policy, and the Family* 318; National Board of Health and Welfare of Sweden, *Alternating Residence: To Live with Dad and Mum Even When They Are Not Living Together* (2004); and C Smart, 'Equal Shares: Rights for Fathers or Recognition for Children?' (2004) 24 *Critical Social Policy* 487.

[86] B Fehlberg, B Smyth, M Maclean, and C Roberts, 'Legislating for Shared Time Parenting after Separation: A Research Review' (2011) 25(3) *International Journal of Law, Policy, and the Family* 318.

[87] E Giovannini, *Outcomes of Family Justice: Children's Proceedings—a Review of the Evidence* (Research Summary 6/11, Ministry of Justice 2011).

shadow of law'.[88] This means that they assess their prospects of success, and therefore what they are willing to concede in negotiation or mediation, based on whether they would do better or worse by going to court, and the costs (financial, practical, and emotional) of doing so. If fathers believe that they will not get what they want at court, then they may be willing to settle outside court for less too. In this way, children may be deprived of a relationship that, in most (but not all) cases, is in their best interests.

The fact that most applications are successful also does not prevent gender from influencing the outcomes. We can see this when we turn to applications that relate to young children.

The case *Brixey v Lynas* concerns whether there is a preference or presumption that very young children should live with their mother.[89] The parents, who were themselves young, were each living with their own parents, and they each sought to have primary care of the child. The baby was 'happy, healthy and well cared for' by the mother. The sheriff found that the father, who was 'comfortably middle class', could give the baby 'all the advantages of comfort, education and a strong and stable moral framework', whereas the mother 'had none of the educational and social advantages which he had' and her lifestyle was 'not particularly stable'. Although the sheriff described the case as Solomonic in its difficulty, he felt that he could not deprive the baby of the advantages of her paternity, and ordered that the baby live with the father. On appeal, the decision was reversed. The father then appealed to the House of Lords, which was the final court of appeal for Scotland.

The Lords held that:

> Nature has endowed men and women with very different attributes and it so happens that mothers are generally better fitted than fathers to provide for the needs of very young children. This is no more discriminatory than the fact that only women can give birth. . . . the advantage to a very young child of being with its mother is a consideration which must be taken into account in deciding where lie its best interests in custody proceedings in which the mother is involved. It is neither a presumption nor a principle but rather recognition of a widely held belief based on practical experience and the workings of nature. . . . where a very young child has been with its mother since birth and there is no criticism of her ability to care for the child only the strongest competing advantages are likely to prevail.

Brixey suggests, therefore, that if a similar case was to be determined in England or Wales, a father would face an uphill struggle to persuade the court that a very young child should live with him where there was no criticism of the quality of the mother's care.

Indeed, courts are generally wary of taking a young child away from his mother for more than brief periods. There is some (disputed) evidence that overnight shared care of children under about four years of age can be detrimental to their development and behaviour because they may experience separation anxiety. This has led some courts, including the writer's local court, to be wary of making orders for overnight staying contact for young children. Given that most contact applicants are fathers, this equates to a maternal preference for young children. Cashmore and Parkinson argue that it is not overnight staying per se that causes issues, but being away from the other parent for too long.

---

[88] RN Mnookin and L Kornhauser, 'Bargaining in the Shadow of the Law: The Case of Divorce' (1979) 88 *Yale Law Journal* 950.

[89] [1998] 2 FLR 499 (HL, Scotland). Although it related to interpretation of a Scottish law, the relevant legal principle was the best interests of the child, and the case was determined by the House of Lords, which was the final court of appeal for Scotland just as it was for England and Wales. This means that although the decision is not binding in England and Wales, it is influential.

They argue that, as with older children, it is the particular child and his or her family circumstances that determine whether the arrangement is good or bad for the child.[90]

Lawrie Moloney has looked at when Australian courts make 'live with' orders in favour of fathers. Australia also uses the best interests of the child as the basis for its decisions. Moloney excluded those cases which involved allegations of child abuse, abduction, or violence and concentrated only on those cases in which both parties were 'functioning as good or at least adequate parents', meaning that the cases were closely contested. He found that in the judgments he analysed the most pervasive theme 'either directly or indirectly, linked behaviours and future outcomes with the gender of the litigants'. Specifically, he found that:

> mothers were likely to be successful if they appeared to conform to a maternal stereotype of self-sacrifice on behalf of their children. Generally, fathers were successful when mothers were judged to be in some way inadequate—that is, fathers tended to be successful by default. Notwithstanding parenting awards [i.e., decisions] in favour of fathers in a little under half the cases, there is also evidence of judicial scepticism concerning their capacity to parent without the assistance of a mother figure, and/or scepticism about fathers' plans to reduce their commitment to the paid work force.[91]

In those cases where the children were placed with the mother, the judge tended to view her as willing to place their needs first and emotionally connected with them (i.e., self-sacrificing, nurturing), while the father was described in less emotional language as solid and reliable or having a breadwinning role. In those cases in which the court placed the child with their father, Lawrie found that the courts' described the mother in ways that implied that she was not self-sacrificing, not committed, was promiscuous or immoral or absent, or had a physical or mental illness, and thus transgressed stereotypes of what a mother should be. In contrast, the father in such cases had played a pre-existing primary carer role—but his chances of success were boosted if he had help from his family or a new female partner. In this way, both mothers and fathers suffered from gender stereotyping. Although we cannot map these findings neatly to this jurisdiction as gender perceptions may differ across jurisdictions, it is an interesting study nonetheless.

Julie Wallbank has argued that gender bias acts against women in family courts in this jurisdiction by characterising women who are opposed to contact, or who have concerns about it, as 'wilful' or 'hostile' rather than legitimately worried about the children's welfare.[92] Similarly, Felicity Kaganas has looked at the language used in judgments about contact and found that they often characterise good parents as those who understand the importance of contact and bad parents as those who obstruct or fail to promote it.[93] As Barnett has argued, 'Images of "safe family men" and "implacably hostile mothers" continue to influence the perceptions of professionals.'[94] This is particularly important when there are allegations of domestic abuse as it may cause courts to ignore or underappreciate risks around contact.

The research therefore suggests that our perceptions of what is in a child's best interests are innately tied up with gender stereotypes. It is not as simple as saying that most fathers get contact. Stereotypes operate against both men and women and obscure the best interests of the child.

---

[90] J Cashmore and P Parkinson, 'Parenting Arrangements for Young Children: Messages from Research' (2011) 25 *Australian Journal of Family Law* 236.

[91] L Moloney, 'Do Fathers "Win" or Do Mothers "Lose"? A Preliminary Analysis of Closely Contested Parenting Judgments in the Family Court of Australia' (2001) 15(3) *International Journal of Law, Policy, and the Family* 363.

[92] J Wallbank, 'Castigating Mothers: The Judicial Response to "Wilful" Women in Disputes over Paternal Contact in English Law' (1998) 20(4) *Journal of Social Welfare and Family Law* 357.

[93] F Kaganas, 'Regulating Emotion: Judging Contact Disputes' (2011) 23(1) *Child and Family Law Quarterly* 63.

[94] Adrienne Barnett, '"Like Gold Dust These Days": Domestic Violence Fact-Finding Hearings in Child Contact Cases' (2015) 23 *Feminist Legal Studies* 47, 53.

SCENARIO 1

Illustration 5: Al and Ruth and son Daniel (12 weeks old)

Daniel is just 12 weeks old. Al has applied for a child arrangements order that Daniel live with him for some of the time. Ruth opposes this application. However, *Brixey* indicates that the court is likely to be reluctant to remove Daniel from his mother's primary care, given his age, unless there are 'the strongest competing' reasons that 'outweigh any advantage in maintaining the natural maternal link or the status quo.' This does not mean that there will be no contact but it means that his time with Al is likely to be broken up into short periods.

10.6 Is there a human right to contact?

Numerous cases in the European Court of Human Rights have emphasised that 'the mutual enjoyment by parent and child of each other's company is a fundamental element of family life' and thus protected by Article 8.[95]

Effective respect for family life imposes a positive obligation on the state (including the courts as institutions of the state) to take 'necessary measures to safeguard [the] right . . . Such measures may be judicial.'[96] In the context of Article 8, this involves 'a right for parents to have measures taken with a view to their being reunited with their children, and an obligation for the national authorities to take such measures.'[97] (Although the Court refers here to a right for parents, it is also a right of children, who are equally protected by Article 8: 'it is in a child's interest for its family ties to be maintained, as severing such ties means cutting a child off from its roots, which can only be justified in very exceptional circumstances.')[98]

Courts are therefore under positive duty to take measures to reunite parents and children, and this can include both judicial sanctions and practical pro-contact measures. This obligation applies not only to public law cases (those in which the state is a party, such as care cases) but also to private law disputes such as child arrangements cases.[99]

However, there are important limitations to this right.

10.6.1 Limitations on the positive obligation

First, Article 8 ECHR does not apply to all familial relationships. As we see in Chapter 8, a father–child relationship does not automatically attract the protection of Article 8 but depends upon whether the father is married to the child's mother. If he is not, then whether

---

[95] See, e.g., *W v United Kingdom* (1988) 10 EHRR 29 (Application no. 9749/82, judgment 8 July 1987); *McMichael v United Kingdom*, (1995) 20 EHRR 205 (Application no. 16424/90, judgment 24 February 1995). *McMichael* is discussed in Chapter 9.

[96] J-F Akandji-Kombe, *Positive Obligations under the European Convention on Human Rights* (Directorate General of Human Rights, Council of Europe 2007).

[97] *Gnahoré v France* (2002) 34 EHRR 967, [50].

[98] *Görgülü v Germany* [2004] 1 FLR 894, [48].

[99] *Kosmopoulou v Greece* [2004] 1 FLR 800, [43–4].

family life exists is a question of fact (*Lebbink v Netherlands*).[100] Similarly, a parent whose child has been adopted from them no longer has family life with the child (*Seddon*).[101] That is a consequence of our transplant model of adoption, which involves the complete overriding of the biological relationship and the severing of all legal ties, including the parents' status as parent. Where family life does not exist, Article 8's protections are not triggered.

Second, even where Article 8 does apply, the right is not absolute and can be interfered with as set out in Article 8(2):

STATUTORY EXTRACT *Article 8 ECHR*

(1) Everyone has the right to respect for his private and family life, his home and his correspondence.
(2) There shall be no interference by a public authority with the exercise of this right except such as is in accordance with the law and is necessary in a democratic society in the interests of national security, public safety or the economic wellbeing of the country, for the prevention of disorder or crime, for the protection of health or morals, or for the protection of the rights and freedoms of others.

This allows a public authority (such as a court) to interfere with the right to have measures taken to reunite the family where this is necessary to protect the child's well-being. Specifically, *S and G v Italy* tells us that 'a parent cannot be entitled under Article 8 . . . to have such measures taken as would harm the child's health and development'.[102] However, as the Court said in *Gnahoré v France*, the child's interests have a 'double aspect'.

> On the one hand, there is no doubt that ensuring that the child grows up in a healthy environment falls within this interest and that Article 8 cannot in any way entitle a parent to have such measures taken as would harm the child's health and development.

> On the other hand, it is clear that it is nevertheless in the child's interest that the links between him and his family should be maintained except where the family is shown to be especially unworthy for that purpose; to break that link amounts to cutting the child off from his roots. It follows that the child's interest necessitates that only wholly exceptional circumstances may lead to a breaking of the family bond and that everything should be done to maintain personal relations and, where possible and when the occasion arises, to 'reconstitute' the family.[103]

Although the Court in *Gnahoré* referred to 'exceptional circumstances', it does so in the context of 'a breaking of the family bond'. States have a wider margin of discretion if the restrictions on the parent–child relationship are lesser. For example, there is a wide discretion in determining with whom a child should live. Where, however, the court is considering limiting or terminating contact, or failing to enforce contact despite finding that it is in the best interests of the child, *C v Finland* tells us that 'stricter scrutiny is called

---

[100] *Lebbink v Netherlands* [2004] 3 FCR 59.
[101] *Seddon v Oldham Metropolitan Borough Council (Adoption: Human Rights)* [2015] EWHC 2609 (Fam).
[102] [2000] 2 FLR 771, [169].
[103] *Gnahoré v France* (2002) 34 EHRR 967, [59].

for', because a breakdown here would potentially mean a complete cessation of the parent–child relationship.[104]

There are several other ways in which states can breach the ECHR.

1. Where there is no functioning mechanism for a child arrangements case to be decided. Article 13 requires states to have 'an effective remedy before a national authority' for breaches of the Convention. Article 6, the right a fair and public hearing within a reasonable time, includes the right to access a court[105] although as we will see with s91(14) orders this is not an absolute right (see 10.7.4).

2. Where the court has decided that contact is in the child's best interests, failure to enforce a child arrangements order can cause the court to breach Article 8. As Akandji-Kombe writes when he discusses state obligations under the ECHR:

> The state becomes responsible for violations committed between individuals because there has been a failure in the legal order, amounting sometimes to an absence of legal intervention pure and simple, sometimes to inadequate intervention, and sometimes to a lack of measures designed to change a legal situation contrary to the Convention.[106]

The state's obligation is based on whether it has taken 'all necessary steps to facilitate contact as can reasonably be demanded in the special circumstances of each case',[107] not whether such measures were ultimately successful.[108] In *Hansen v Turkey*, the domestic court fined the father for failing to comply with a contact order in favour of the child's mother. The European Court held that this was inadequate and that the domestic court should have considered other measures, such as seeking the assistance of psychologists or locating the children when they were absent for contact sessions.[109] The court can even use coercive measures against the children, although these are 'not desirable'.[110] However, not all measures will be appropriate in every case, and a failure to use an undesirable mechanism does not necessarily place the state in breach. Note also that failure to enforce a judgment is a potential breach of Article 6.[111]

3. Delays in the court processes can also breach Article 6, the right a fair and public hearing within a reasonable time. These delays can be in hearing the case initially or in subsequently failing to address enforcement issues in a timely manner. As we discuss at 10.3.4, delays can result in the case being resolved not by what is best for the child but through the continuation of the status quo. 'The adequacy of a measure is to be judged by the swiftness of its implementation, as the passage of time can have irremediable consequences for relations between the child and the parent who does not live with him or her'.[112] However,

---

[104] *C v Finland* (2008) 46 EHRR 485, [2006] 2 FLR 597, [60].

[105] *Golder v United Kingdom* (Application no. 4451/70, judgment 21 February 1975), [32].

[106] J-F Akandji-Kombe, *Positive Obligations under the European Convention on Human Rights* (Directorate General of Human Rights, Council of Europe 2007).

[107] *Glaser v United Kingdom* (2001) 33 EHRR 1.

[108] *Prizzia v Hungary* (Application no. 20255/12, judgment 13 June 2013), [35].

[109] [2003] 3 FCR 97.

[110] *Shaw v. Hungary* (Application no. 6457/09, judgment 26 July 2011), [67].

[111] *Hornsby v Greece* (Application no. 18357/91, judgment 19 March 1997), [40].

[112] *Sylvester v Austria* (Application nos. 36812/97 and 40104/98 judgment 24 April 2003).

in some cases a degree of delay will be reasonable. For example, if there has been a long lapse in the relationship between parent and child then a gradual reintroduction may be appropriate.[113]

10.6.2 The ECHR and domestic case law

Although the impact of the ECHR can be felt within the domestic jurisprudence (note, for example, the reference to 'strict scrutiny' in the domestic decision in Key Case *Re C (Direct Contact: Suspension)*, the courts of England and Wales have had a pro-contact approach for a long time. In 1971, in *B v B*, the court held that 'to deprive a good parent completely of access to his child is to make a dreadful order. . . . the impact on both parent and child must have lifelong consequences.'[114] In 1973, the court emphasised that contact may cause upset to the child but these are

> heavily outweighed by the long-term advantages to the child of keeping in touch with the parent concerned . . . save in exceptional circumstances to deprive a parent of access is to deprive a child of an important contribution to his emotional and material growing up in the long term.[115]

The Children Act 1989 is 'premised' on the proposition that it is in the interests of a child 'to retain contact with the parent with whom the child does not reside'.[116] And in some judgments we can see the impact of both the ECHR and Article 9 of the UN Convention on the Rights of the Child, which provides the child with a right to 'maintain personal relations and direct contact with both parents on a regular basis, except if it is contrary to the child's best interests':

- *Re O (Contact: Withdrawal of Application)*: 'Unless there are cogent reasons against it, the children of separated parents are entitled to know and to have the love and society of both their parents. In particular, the courts recognise the vital importance of the role of non-resident fathers in the lives of their children, and only make orders terminating contact when there is no alternative.'[117]

- *S (Contact: Promoting Relationship with Absent Parent)*: 'Whatever the difficulties, however scant the prospects of success, the courts must not relent in pursuit of the restoration of what had been a natural relationship between father and daughter, absent compelling evidence that the welfare of the child requires respite.'[118]

- *Re P (Children)*: 'In my judgment contact should not be stopped unless it is the last resort for the judge.'[119]

The ways in which the Strasbourg jurisprudence and the domestic case law come together are particularly clear in the judgment of Munby LJ in *Re C (Direct Contact: Suspension)*.

---

[113] *Sobota-Gajic v Bosnia and Herzegovina* (Application no. 27966/06, judgment 6 November 2007).
[114] [1971] 1 WLR 1493 (Edmund Davies LJ).
[115] *M v M (Child: Access)* [1973] 2 All ER 81, 88 (Latey J).
[116] [1993] 1 FCR 973, 984 (Butler-Sloss P).
[117] [2004] 1 FLR 1258, [6] (Wall LJ).
[118] [2004] EWCA Civ 18, [47] (Thorpe LJ).
[119] [2008] EWCA Civ 1431, [38] (Ward LJ).

KEY CASE *Re C (Direct Contact Suspension)* [2011] EWCA Civ 521 (Fam)

A 3-year-old girl lived with her father under a residence order. The issue was what contact, if any, the mother should have with her daughter. There were concerns about whether the mother's serious mental health difficulties were such that she posed an emotional risk to the child.

At first instance, HHJ Henderson said 'My presumption is strongly in favour of face-to-face contact between a parent and child and that presumption will only be displaced by powerful evidence. I have considered the welfare check list of the Children Act, the Human Rights Act and the UN Convention on the Rights of the Child in my analysis of this case.' Nevertheless, applying the welfare principle, he made an order for indirect rather than direct contact, and the mother appealed.

In his appeal judgment, Munby LJ identified six principles drawn from the case law:

1. Contact between parent and child is a fundamental element of family life and is almost always in the interests of the child.
2. Contact between parent and child is to be terminated only in exceptional circumstances, where there are cogent reasons for doing so and when there is no alternative. Contact is to be terminated only if it will be detrimental to the child's welfare.
3. There is a positive obligation on the State, and therefore on the judge, to take measures to maintain and to reconstitute the relationship between parent and child, in short, to maintain or restore contact. The judge has a positive duty to attempt to promote contact. The judge must grapple with all the available alternatives before abandoning hope of achieving some contact. He must be careful not to come to a premature decision, for contact is to be stopped only as a last resort and only once it has become clear that the child will not benefit from continuing the attempt.
4. The court should take a medium-term and long-term view and not accord excessive weight to what appear likely to be short-term or transient problems.
5. The key question, which requires 'stricter scrutiny', is whether the judge has taken all necessary steps to facilitate contact as can reasonably be demanded in the circumstances of the particular case.
6. All that said, at the end of the day the welfare of the child is paramount; 'the child's interest must have precedence over any other consideration.'

An appeal judge can only interfere with the decision of a lower court judge if that judge was plainly wrong. Munby LJ dismissed the appeal, saying that the judge had borne in mind the welfare checklist, and given the case 'strict and anxious scrutiny'. There was no need for him to have set out the ECHR and domestic case law, as he would have had these in mind.

It is perhaps because of the paramountcy of the child's welfare that the domestic courts have generally 'avoided the language of rights' when discussing the benefits of contact to the child. As we see in Chapter 9, these are not the same thing. However, as Choudhry and Herring point out, even if they did refer to Article 8, this right is not absolute.[120] Moreover, there is no apparent power to compel an unwilling non-resident parent to see a child they do not want to see. The duty is imposed upon the resident parent: a 'spend time with order' requires the resident parent to 'make sure that the children spend time or otherwise have

---

[120] Shazia Choudhry and Jonathan Herring, *European Human Rights and Family Law* (Hart 2010).

contact with' the other parent. What we have instead in relation to non-resident parents is 'a moral and potentially legal obligation on the parent with care to facilitate a relationship where the non-residential parent wants this'.[121]

10.6.3 What if the non-resident parent does not want contact?

There is no power in law to compel a parent to see their children. The order is phrased to require the resident parent to 'make sure' that the children spend time with the other parent when required by the order. This means that the resident parent must make the children available, but it places no obligation on the non-resident parent to attend contact.

Some resident parents have made applications for child arrangements orders to settle the time that the non-resident parent sees the children even though that parent does not appear committed to doing so. This may be because the children are upset if contact is arranged and then cancelled, or a parent is inconsistent in their attendance. The application's purpose is to embarrass the non-resident parent into committing to a specific, written, pattern. This tactic may or may not work.

10.7 Tools for enforcement and encouragement of contact

Most child arrangements disputes take place against a background of inter-parental hostility, although the degree of this can vary considerably. After all, if the parties were able to agree arrangements, they would not need to go to court. The courts have at their disposal some positive tools designed to promote and encourage contact. These are:

- Activity directions and conditions
- Family assistance orders

In most cases, neither of these tools will be required.

There may also be situations in which one parent is refusing to abide by the terms of an order. A breach of a court order is a prima facie contempt of court. Therefore, in addition to the positive tools, the court has a range of sanctions to use against parents who breach the terms of an order. These are:

- Committal to prison, as breaching a court order is a contempt of court
- Enforcement orders (unpaid work requirement)
- Compensation for financial loss
- Monitoring orders

Finally, there are two other important powers which are not sanctions, but which may well be seen by one party as such. These are:

- A section 37 direction
- Moving the child to live with the other parent.

---

[121] Family Justice Council Children in Families Committee, *The Use of Shared Residence Orders: A Discussion Paper* (2010).

10.7.1 Tools for encouragement

These tools are designed to constructively assist in making contact work well.

Activity directions and conditions

An activity direction is an order that a party to child arrangements proceedings 'take part in an activity that would, in the court's opinion, help to establish, maintain or improve the involvement in the life of the child' of either that party or another party. Such orders can be made because a party has previously failed to comply with a child arrangements order or in preparation for the court deciding what child arrangements order to make. When the order is made during proceedings, it is called a direction, and when it is made at the end of proceedings, it is a condition.

The court must determine that the proposed activity is appropriate to the case, identify which organisation will provided the activity (local providers are commissioned by Cafcass), and ensure that the party can reasonably be expected to travel to the location of the proposed activity. In doing so, the court must consider any conflict with the person's religious beliefs or the times at which they normally work or attend education. An activity direction cannot be made to require someone to undergo medical or psychiatric examination, assessment, or treatment or take part in mediation (s11A(6)). All the court can do in such cases is use persuasion.

An order cannot be made against a child, even if the child is made a party, unless the child is actually the parent of another child who is the subject of the proceedings, nor can it be made against someone who is not habitually resident in England or Wales. The orders are most commonly directed at parents. Three common types are:

1. A 'separated parents information programme', a half-day course designed to help parents communicate after separation. Participants may watch a video of a separated family having difficulty communicating amicably, and the effect of this on the children, and then discuss how their communication could be improved.[122]

2. A domestic violence perpetrator programme, a 60-hour course aimed at helping participants resolve disputes non-abusively.

3. A 'child contact intervention'. Gabrielle Jan Posner has called this 'the most effective sub-species of activity direction'.[123] It involves Cafcass or another accredited provider supervising up to 12 hours of contact. This is particularly useful in those cases where contact has broken down and there is hostility to contact on the part of the resident parent and/or the children. Court approaches to such difficult cases are considered at 10.8.

Family assistance orders

A family assistance order (FAO) (s16 Children Act 1989) directs Cafcass or the child's local authority to appoint an officer to 'advise, assist, and befriend' the persons named in the order, who could be the child himself, his parent, guardian, or special guardian, and/or

---

[122] See https://www.cafcass.gov.uk/grown-ups/parents-and-carers/divorce-and-separation/separated-parents-information-programme/ accessed 21 October 2020.

[123] GJ Posner, 'Child Contact Interventions: An Underused Resource' (*Family Law Week*, 11 November 2017).

anyone with whom he is living or who is named in a child arrangements order as a person with whom he is to live, spend time, or otherwise have contact. Although the child may be named in the order as someone to be befriended, unlike the similar supervision order in care proceedings, there is no child protection element.

FAOs were designed as a form of 'focused, short-term help to a family to help overcome the problems and conflict associated with parents' separation'.[124] An order therefore has what Ward LJ has called a 'peace-keeping purpose'.[125] The original *Children Act Guidance* anticipated that assistance 'may well be focused more on the adult rather than the child'.[126] This has been borne out in practice: Sturgeon-Adams and James found that only 55 per cent of FAOs involved work with children, something that Trinder and Stone attribute to professionals' belief that 'support for children was best achieved through improving adult relationships'.[127]

There is, therefore, some overlap with what can be achieved under an activity direction, although family assistance orders are rarer. In 2019, there were 259 children named in FAOs, which is a tiny fraction of the overall number of children involved in proceedings.[128] A previous requirement that such orders had to be made only in 'exceptional' cases was removed by the Children and Adoption Act 2006, following research that showed confusion what this meant.[129] However, the persons named (other than the child) must agree to the order being made, notwithstanding the *Making Contact Work* report's recommendation that the consent requirement be removed.[130] This means, that the FAO is a 'curious beast, targeted at families where there is some disagreement requiring an order, but not enough to prevent consent being given'.[131]

An order can be made in any proceedings in which the court could make a s8 order, and at any point in the proceedings including at the conclusion. Orders are for a maximum of twelve months.[132] Although capable of renewal, 'the court will lean against simply making FAO after FAO for a substantial period of time'.[133] Cafcass itself reports that the most effective orders include a defined plan of work lasting between three and six months only.[134]

---

[124] *Children Act 1989 Guidance and Regulations Vol 1: Court Orders and Pre-Proceedings* (Department for Education 2014) para 11.

[125] *Re M* [1999] 1 FLR 75 (Ward LJ). Cited by Richard Little, 'Family Assistance Orders: Rising to the Challenge' [2009] *Family Law* 435, 436.

[126] *Children Act 1989 Guidance and Regulations Vol 1: Court Orders* (1991 edition) at para 2.50.

[127] L Sturgeon-Adams and AL James, *The Use of Family Assistance Orders in Divorce and Separation Cases: Joseph Rowntree Foundation JR Findings 579* (1999); L Trinder and N Stone, 'Family Assistance Orders - Professional Aspiration and Party Frustration' [1998] *Child and Family Law Quarterly* 291.

[128] Ministry of Justice, *Family Court Statistics Quarterly April to June 2020: CSV Data: Children Act National Child Count* (2020).

[129] L Sturgeon-Adams and AL. James, 'Assisting Families – Section 16 Orders under the Children Act 1989' [1999] *Family Law* 471; L Sturgeon-Adams and AL James, 'Understanding Exceptionality: Differing Perceptions of the Family Assistance Order' (2000) 5 *Child and Family Social Work* 177.

[130] Lord Chancellor's Advisory Board on Family Law Children Act Sub-Committee, *Making Contact Work: A Report to the Lord Chancellor on the Facilitation of Arrangements for Contact between Children and Their Non-Residential Parents and the Enforcement of Court Orders for Contact* (Lord Chancellor's Department 2001) para 11.9.

[131] L Trinder and N Stone, 'Family Assistance Orders - Professional Aspiration and Party Frustration' [1998] *Child and Family Law Quarterly* 291.

[132] Extended from six months.

[133] *Re E (Family Assistance Order)* [1999] 2 FLR 512, 518 (Bennett J).

[134] Cafcass, *Family Assistance Order Guidance* (2016). Available at https://www.cafcass.gov.uk/wp-content/uploads/2017/12/Family-Assistance-Orders-guidance-flow-chart.pdf accessed 25 October 2018.

While the approval of Cafcass or the local authority is not needed, they should be consulted beforehand 'about whether it would be in the best interests of the child in question for a family assistance order to be made and, if so, how the family assistance order could operate and for what period'.[135] There are financial costs involved, which compete with child protection work for scarce resources. While an order can still be made without local authority or Cafcass consent, and they would have to comply with the order, realistically there is very little that a court can do in the face of protests by these organisations about lack of funding but refuse to make the order. As Johnson J said in *Re C (Family Assistance Order)*, he could attach a penal notice and imprison the director of social services for any subsequent breach, but 'that would be totally contrary to the best interests of the boy and the childcare system as a whole'.[136] That said, 'if an order [i]s made at the outset, it might, just might, prevent the situation from becoming intractable' and save the parties and the court system—including Cafcass—further 'time, effort and money'.[137]

10.7.2 Tools for enforcement

Child arrangements orders are directed at the resident parent(s) and require them to 'make sure that the children spend time or otherwise have contact with' the other parent in whatever pattern is set out in the order.[138] A child arrangements order will note prominently on the first page[139] that 'If you do not do what the child arrangements order says you may be sent to prison and/or fined, made to do unpaid work or pay financial compensation. . . . A penal notice is attached to parts of this order. That means that if you do not do what those parts of the order say you may be sent to prison, fined and/or your assets may be seized.'[140] It also warns about the consequences of taking a child out of the jurisdiction or changing the child's name.

It therefore follows that an individual may be in breach of the order where they do not 'make sure' that the children spend time with the other parent when required by the order. If the individual *could not* have complied for reasons outside their control, this is not a breach.[141] 'For example, if a parent taking a child for contact is prevented from going on or is delayed by unforeseen and insuperable transport or weather problems – one thinks of the sudden and unexpected grounding of the nation's airlines by volcanic ash – then there will be no breach'.[142] Even if it was in their power to have complied with the child arrangements order, they may not be in breach if they have 'a reasonable excuse' for not

---

[135] Practice Direction 12M. Note that local authority consent *will* be required if the child does not live in their area: s16(7).

[136] *Re C (Family Assistance Order)* [1996] 1 FLR 424, 425.

[137] GJ Posner, 'In Praise of Family Assistance Orders' [2000] *Family Law* 435, 437.

[138] Children Act Proceedings Master Copy Orders (January 2016). Available at https://www.lawsociety.org.uk/practice-areas/family-children/cap-master-orders/ accessed 23 October 2018. Note that there is no order that requires a non-resident parent to spend time with the child even if that would be in the child's best interests. The law has no remedy where a parent is not interested in their child.

[139] As required by CPR 81.9.

[140] Children Act Proceedings Master Copy Orders (January 2016). Available at https://www.lawsociety.org.uk/practice-areas/family-children/cap-master-orders/ accessed 23 October 2018.

[141] *Re LW (Children) (Enforcement and Committal: Contact)* [2010] EWCA Civ 1253.

[142] *Re LW (Children) (Enforcement and Committal: Contact)* [2010] EWCA Civ 1253, [40].

complying. 'A typical case might be where a child suddenly falls ill and the defendant, reasonably in the circumstances, takes the child to the doctor rather than going to contact.'[143]

When a court finds a breach proved and there is no reasonable excuse, it has a range of responses, the most serious being to send the person who has breached the order to prison for contempt of court. As an alternative, a court may make an enforcement order requiring him or her to undertake unpaid work, or require them to pay financial compensation to any party who has incurred financial loss as a result of their breach. Whatever the outcome, it must be a proportionate response, aimed both at punishing for the breach and at deterring further breaches.

Sometimes, particularly in children cases, situations change and arrangements will need to be revisited. For example, as a child grows older, their preferences about a pattern of contact may change, or social or academic activities require an alteration to the schedule. Where this happens, the parties can seek to amend the court order either by consent or following a contested process. Simply breaching the order leaves them open to an enforcement application.

Committal to prison

A committal application is an application to commit a person to prison for breaching the terms of an order. It is an application that is most likely to be made by one parent against the other. Clearly, this has significant consequences: that person has a criminal record, may lose their job and thus their income, and the child is deprived of their care, which may well harm the child. It may not be clear who can look after the child during the period of imprisonment either.[144] Committal—or even the threat of it—may also irreparably damage the relationship between the children and the parent who is applying to enforce the order. In *Churchyard v Churchard*, the judge noted that imprisonment of the mother would mean that she

> would be taken away from [the children] for a time and their father would be branded in their eyes as the man who had put their mother in prison. That is a brand from which no parent in my experience can ever hope to recover. It is the most deadly blow a parent can inflict on his children.[145]

Committal to prison for contempt of court does not fall under the Children Act 1989 as pertaining to a child's upbringing, so the welfare principle does not apply to make the children's interests paramount. Nevertheless, their welfare is a relevant consideration and judges are therefore reluctant to use imprisonment other than a last resort.[146] Thus, although courts can and do send parents to prison, this tends to be for persistent and blatant failure to comply in the face of repeated warnings. This reluctance can leave the courts open to criticism that they do not do enough to secure compliance with their orders. In *Re LW (Children) (Enforcement and Committal: Contact)*, Munby LJ noted that 'the threat, or if need be the actual implementation, of a very short period of imprisonment—just a day or two—may

---

[143] *Re LW (Children) (Enforcement and Committal: Contact)* [2010] EWCA Civ 1253, [40].
[144] The child may be wholly alienated from the other parent and the court will be cautious about simply handing the child over to that parent because of the distress it may cause the child.
[145] [1984] FLR 635, 638.
[146] *A v N (Committal: Refusal of Contact)* [1997] 1 FLR 533.

at an earlier stage of the proceedings achieve more than the threat of a longer sentence at a much later stage in the process. I do not suggest this as a panacea—this is an area in which there is no panacea—but it is something which, I suggest, is worth keeping in mind.'[147]

As a committal application may have a criminal consequence, prison, the alleged breach must be proved to the usual criminal standard—beyond reasonable doubt. The Article 6 ECHR right to a fair trial is engaged and the person alleged to be in breach is entitled to legal representation. He or she may defend the allegation by saying either that there was no breach of that they had a reasonable excuse for breaching the order. Part 37 of the Family Procedure Rules and the associated Practice Direction 37A sets out the process.

Enforcement orders

An enforcement order (s11J Children Act 1989) requires the person against whom the order is made to undertake a specified number of hours of unpaid work as punishment for breaching a child arrangements order. This work, overseen by the Probation Service, can include picking up litter, removing graffiti, decorating public buildings, or working in a charity shop. It is therefore the same as what we would, in the criminal law context, call 'community service'. The minimum number of hours that can be ordered is 40, the maximum 200. The order can be made on a suspended basis, triggered in the event of further breaches.

An enforcement order can only be made on an application and not of the court's own volition. Section 11J(5) sets out potential applicants, who include the resident parent, a non-resident parent named in the order as having time with the child, and (with prior permission from the court) the child himself. The court must be satisfied beyond reasonable doubt that the person who is alleged to have breached the child arrangements order has in fact done so. Even if they have, the court may not make an enforcement order if satisfied that the person can show on the balance of probabilities that they have a reasonable excuse for their breach (s11J(3)).

Trinder et al.'s 2013 study of enforcement showed that courts 'made very limited use of the new provision for unpaid work, primarily as few cases required a punitive approach. Courts made greater use of unpaid work as a threat—whether in the form of assessment or as a suspended order—rather than as a punitive sanction'.[148] Indeed, in 2019 it appears that only two such orders were made.[149]

Compensation for financial loss

Under s110 Children Act 1989 the court can order a party who is in breach of an order to pay compensation to another party who has, as a result of the breach, been caused financial loss. For example, if the non-resident parent has bought tickets for a trip to a theme park, and the resident parent does not then make the child available for contact, the latter may be ordered to pay the non-resident parent for the cost of the tickets (or any lesser amount). It does not provide for a further penalty sum or 'damages' on top of that.

[147] *Re LW (Children) (Enforcement and Committal: Contact)* [2010] EWCA Civ 1253, [106].
[148] L Trinder, J Hunt, A Macleod, J Pearce, and H Woodward, *Enforcing Contact Orders: Problem-Solving or Punishment?* (University of Exeter/Nuffield Foundation 2013).
[149] Ministry of Justice, *Family Court Statistics Quarterly April to June 2020: CSV Data: Children Act National Child Count* (2020).

In deciding the amount, the court has to take into account the financial circumstances of the person who has breached the order and the welfare of the children who are the subject of the application—after all, the likely result of the order is to take money out of the household in which the children are living. The breach has to be proven on the balance of probabilities, which is a lower standard than that required for a committal or an enforcement order. As with these, it is a defence that the individual had a 'reasonable excuse' for not complying with the order. Once an order for compensation is made, it can be enforced in the same way as any other debt. In 2019, no compensation orders were made.[150]

Monitoring orders

A monitoring order under s11H Children Act 1989 is a request by the court that Cafcass monitors compliance by the parties with the terms of a child arrangements order and report any difficulties to the court. This will enable the court to decide what further steps to take to ensure compliance. The Act does not specify the details of what the monitoring may involve, but Cafcass guidance indicates that it is likely to take the form of telephone contact with the parties and, where the children are of sufficient age and understanding, with the children. Each order lasts for a maximum of 12 months, but this may be during or after proceedings, and, unlike a family assistance order, the parties to the case do not need to agree to the order being made.[151] The order is framed as a request because of the resource implications of this work by Cafcass. The number of monitoring orders made each year is not known, as neither Cafcass or the Ministry of Justice appears to record that information.[152]

SCENARIO 3

Illustration 5: Claire, Ellie, and son Jacob (10)

Ellie has brought an enforcement application based on alleged breaches of the order. The fact that Claire has not made sure that Jacob was available for contact is, on the face of it, a breach, but the court must determine whether that is the case. The standard of proof differs between the civil standard (on the balance of probabilities) to the criminal standard (beyond reasonable doubt) depending on the potential sanction. If Ellie is seeking committal to prison, or an enforcement order (the unpaid work requirement) then the breach has to be proven beyond reasonable doubt. The court also has to consider whether there is any defence.

Even if the breach is proven, and there is no defence, the court may be reluctant to imprison Claire or order her to undertake unpaid work. These will indirectly affect Jacob and although the welfare principle does not apply to the issue of sanction, the court will be mindful that such sanctions are unlikely to endear Ellie to Jacob or build a more positive relationship between the mothers. The court may prefer to consider positive tools at its disposal and may choose not to impose a sanction or to suspend a sanction to come into effect only if there are further breaches. This kind of approach has attracted criticism that orders can be flouted with impunity.

---

[150] Ministry of Justice, *Family Court Statistics Quarterly April to June 2020: CSV Data: Children Act National Child Count* (2020).

[151] *Section 11A–P (Children Act 1989) Guidance (for Cafcass Practitioners)* (2008).

[152] Response by Cafcass to a freedom of information request made by barrister Lucy Reed at https://www.whatdotheyknow.com/request/prevalence_of_contact_monitoring (2013).

10.7.3 Other strategies

While the tools for encouragement and enforcement set out at 10.7.1 and 10.7.2 are those designed specifically for these purposes, there are two further options which may have a similar effect but are not designed for that purpose. These are for the court to make a s37 direction, or to remove the child from a parent who is impeding the child's relationship with their non-resident parent.

Section 37 directions

Sometimes, a court deciding a set of family proceedings can become so concerned about a child's welfare that thinks it may be appropriate for a care or supervision order to be made. It could be that such strong allegations have been made by one party against the other that, rather than help a party 'win' their case, the situation is no longer suitable for the private law sphere at all, but triggers the child protective role of the state. Under s37 Children Act 1989 the court can direct the local authority to investigate the child's circumstances and consider whether they should make an application for a care or supervision order, provide services to the child or his family, or take any other action about the child. After its investigations the local authority will report their decision and proposals, if any. While, as Scott Baker J said in *Re H (A Minor) (Section 37 Direction)*, it forces the local authority 'to apply its mind to the specific problem of whether a care or supervision order is necessary', the court has no power to order the local authority to apply for either order.[153]

Moving the child to live with the other parent

When a resident parent has been found to have repeatedly breached court orders, one option is to make a child arrangements order in favour of the other parent. An order like this cannot be made to punish the resident parent (although they may perceive it as such), but only when the child's welfare is best served by the move: the welfare principle applies. Not all non-resident parents will be able to willing or able to assume a primary care role, and the child's wishes and feelings will be relevant alongside the other welfare checklist factors. However, subject to this the court may find that where only one parent will promote a relationship with the other parent, the child should live with that parent: only then will they have the benefit of both parents.

Of course, while that is the hope, there is no evidence about whether or not a change of residence will have the desired effect of enabling the child to have relationships with both parents. If repeated court orders have been breached, the situation between the parents is likely to be highly fraught and entrenched. The child may have become alienated from the parent that they are now to live with, or not know them very well. It may be necessary for him or her to spend a period of time with foster parents in between the parents' homes, in order to adjust to what is happening and be free of influence. Rather than the transfer simply causing the child short-term distress that is outweighed by the long-term benefits, there is a possibility that the transfer has come too late for any relationship between parent and child to be repaired. In *Re S (A Child)*, for example, the court made an order transferring residence of the 12-year-old child from the mother to the father, whom he called

---

[153] *Re H (A Minor) (Section 37 Direction)* [1993] 2 FLR 541 (Scott Baker J). On the powers of the court, see comments by Wall J in *W v Wakefield City Council* [1995] 1 FLR 170.

a monster. While he was in transition foster care, he would sit with his head in his lap and fingers in his ears at all contacts with his father. Ultimately, the father abandoned his attempts and the court made an order that the child live with the mother, be supervised by the local authority, and have indirect contact with the father through the provisions of photos and school reports. We will never know whether or not this child—whether as a child or as an adult—regained his relationship with his father or remained permanently estranged despite the efforts of the court and the father himself.[154] It is this kind of experience that means that 'orders transferring children from one parent to another are 'more often threatened than carried out'[155] and 'usually only taken as a last resort'.[156] In *Re A (Residence Order)* Coleridge J called it an 'essential weapon or tool . . . . It may indeed be a case of putting a gun to a parent's head to force him or her to rethink', but cautioned that any 'apparent volte-face' by the current resident parent needed to be fully tested to determine whether it was genuine. He thought that if the resident parent now accepted that contact should happen and their parenting was otherwise of an acceptable standard, then 'the remedy of last resort needs to be deployed with great care'.[157]

However, the 'last resort' approach has been recently criticised by the current President of the Family Division, McFarlane P. In *Re L (A Child)*, he heard an appeal by the mother of a decision that an 8-year-old boy should move from the household of his mother and grandmother to live with his father. The mother and grandmother had falsely accused the father of sexual abuse and continued to speak negatively about the him in the presence of the child. Against that background, McFarlane P held that a change of residence was not premature:

> Use of phrases such as 'last resort' or 'draconian' cannot and should not indicate a different or enhanced welfare test. What is required is for the judge to consider all the circumstances in the case that are relevant to the issue of welfare, consider those elements in the s1(3) welfare check list which apply on the facts of the case and then, taking all those matters into account, determine which of the various options best meets the child's welfare needs.[158]

The approach of the mother and grandmother was causing the child emotional harm and risked further emotional harm. In that context, the child's welfare lay in the child living with his father with whom he had—when he saw him—'a highly positive, close and fun relationship'. The test to be adopted is thus the welfare principle without any gloss or requirement of exceptionality: is it better for the child to live with person A or person B?

10.7.4 Restricting further applications

Under s91(14) Children Act 1989, the court can make an order requiring a party to seek permission from the court before making specified kinds of further application about the child. The making of an application is not completely prevented, but a hurdle imposed: the judge determines whether the application is to be issued and will only do so if the

---

[154] [2010] EWCA Civ 325. The first instance report is *TE v SH and S* [2010] Fam Law 1182 (aka *Warwickshire CC v TE*).
[155] Ward LJ in *Re C (Residence Order)* [2008] 1 FLR 211.
[156] Wall LJ in *In the Matter of R (A Child)* [2009] EWCA Civ 1316.
[157] [2010] 1 FLR 1083 [21].
[158] [2019] EWHC 867 (Fam). For a recent interesting discussion, see *Re X, Y and Z (Children: Agreed Transfer of Residence)* [2021] EWFC 18.

applicant has 'an arguable case with some chance of success'[159] and (per s91A, inserted by the Domestic Abuse Act 2021) whether there has been a material change in circumstances since the s91(14) order was made. This means that the respondent is not stressed by an application unless it has merit. As it 'does nothing to prevent a meritorious application',[160] it is compatible with Article 6 ECHR, the right to a fair trial.

A new s91A inserted by the Domestic Abuse Act 2021 expands the use of s91(14) orders so that they can be used where the court is satisfied that the making of an application would put either the child or another individual at risk of harm. However, the primary purpose of a s91(14) restriction is as a 'a useful weapon of last resort in cases of repeated and unreasonable applications'[161] or 'where there is evidence of one party not taking the

---

KEY CASE *Re P (Section 91(14) Guidelines) (Residents and Religious Heritage)* [2000] Fam 15

The child, N, who had Down's Syndrome, was born to Orthodox Jewish parents who were unable to care for her. She was placed in foster care for what was initially intended to be a short period of time. No Orthodox Jewish foster carers could be found for her, so she was cared for by Catholic foster carers who undertook to adhere to certain Orthodox tenets. Over time, N's parents remained unable to care for her and the foster carers became deeply attached to her. The parents, however, made several applications for N's return and these were unsuccessful with the courts making a residence order in favour of the foster carers. Although the court held that these applications were not unreasonable, they were motivated by a rejection of the courts' previous decisions and the prospect of further applications caused a strain on the foster carers. The Court of Appeal considered whether to make a s91(14) order preventing the parents from making further applications without the leave of the court.

Butler-Sloss LJ issued the following guidance:

- Section 91(14) of the Act of 1989 should be read in conjunction with section 1(1), which makes the welfare of the child the paramount consideration.
- 'The power to restrict applications to the court is discretionary and in the exercise of its discretion the court must weigh in the balance all the relevant circumstances. An important consideration is that to impose a restriction is a statutory intrusion into the right of a party to bring proceedings before the court and to be heard in matters affecting his/her child. The power is therefore to be used with great care and sparingly, the exception and not the rule. It is generally to be seen as a useful weapon of last resort in cases of repeated and unreasonable applications.
- In suitable circumstances (and on clear evidence), a court may impose the leave restriction in cases where the welfare of the child requires it, although there is no past history of making unreasonable applications. In [such] cases . . ., the court will need to be satisfied first that the facts go beyond the commonly encountered need for a time to settle to a regime ordered by the court and the all too common situation where there is animosity between the adults in dispute or between the local authority and the family and secondly that there is a serious risk that, without the imposition of the restriction, the child or the primary carers will be subject to unacceptable strain.
- . . . The degree of restriction should be proportionate to the harm it is intended to avoid.'

---

[159] *Re P (Section 91(14) Guidelines) (Residents and Religious Heritage)* [2000] Fam 15.
[160] *Re R (Residence: Contact: Restricting Applications* [1998] 1 FLR 749 (CA) 761 (Evans LJ).
[161] *Re P (Section 91(14) Guidelines) (Residents and Religious Heritage)* [2000] Fam 15.

Applying these principles to the facts, she held that 'In the highly charged atmosphere of this case and with the clear evidence of the impact of the litigation so far on the [foster carers], this is, in my judgment, a clear case for imposing a section 91(14) restriction on the parents, in the interests of the child, in respect of future residence applications and without limit of time. They will of course have the right without restriction to make suitable applications for any variation of contact.'

court's decision and not taking no for an answer and acting unreasonably by continuing to make applications to the court which in turn cause detriment to the child involved'.[162] However, in Key Case *Re P (Section 91(14) Guidelines) (Residents and Religious Heritage)*, the Court of Appeal held that s91(14) was not limited to such situations.

As we can see from these judicial statements, s91(14) must be read in conjunction with the s1 welfare principle, so that the judge considers whether 'the best interests of the child require interference with the fundamental freedom of a parent to raise issues affecting the child's welfare before the court as and when such issues arise.'[163] Nevertheless, the draconian nature of the order has been repeatedly emphasised by judges. In *B v B (Residence Order: Restricting Applications)* Waite LJ called it 'a substantial interference with the fundamental principle of public policy enshrined in our unwritten constitution that all citizens enjoy a right of unrestricted access to the Queen's courts'.[164]

A s91(14) order can be made of the court's own volition or on an application by a party or on behalf of the child. An order can be permanent but is more commonly made for a limited period, typically a year or two.

FOCUS Think Critically

How common are breaches?

A study of enforcement applications and mechanisms by Trinder, Hunt, Macleod, Pearce, and Woodward[165] found that there are about 1,400 applications for enforcement per year (0.036 per cent of all children involved in cases). These applications were usually brought within a year of the contact order being made and in 70 per cent of cases it was because in that time contact had completely broken down. (The remaining 30 per cent involved 'ongoing partial compliance'.)[166] As may be expected from the fact that most resident parents are mothers, most applicants for enforcement are fathers.[167]

Trinder et al. reported that

- 'The most common type of case involved parents whose conflicts with each other prevented them from making a contact order work reliably in practice.'

---

[162] *Re R (Residence: Contact: Restricting Applications)* [1998] 1 FLR 749 (CA) 755 (HHJ Coltart, quoted by Wilson J).
[163] *B v B (Residence Order: Restricting Applications)* [1997] 1 FLR 139 (CA) 146F.
[164] [1997] 1 FLR 139 (CA) 147A.
[165] L Trinder, J Hunt, A Macleod, J Pearce, and H Woodward, *Enforcing Contact Orders: Problem-Solving or Punishment?* (University of Exeter/Nuffield Foundation 2013).
[166] L Trinder, J Hunt, A Macleod, J Pearce, and H Woodward, *Enforcing Contact Orders: Problem-Solving or Punishment?* (University of Exeter/Nuffield Foundation 2013) 25.
[167] L Trinder, J Hunt, A Macleod, J Pearce, and H Woodward, *Enforcing Contact Orders: Problem-Solving or Punishment?* (University of Exeter/Nuffield Foundation 2013) 21.

- The second largest group comprises cases 'with significant safety concerns', the vast majority of which had actually been addressed earlier in the proceedings (but not to the satisfaction of one of the parties).
- The third largest group comprised cases in which 'older children themselves wanted to reduce or stop contact'.[168]

Breaches of contact orders are therefore often indicative of more profound mistrust or lack of cooperation between the parties, for which both parties may hold a degree of responsibility. They may also indicate that the contact arrangement is wrong for the child.

Only 4 per cent of cases involved the resident parent's unreasonable implacable hostility to contact or the child becoming alienated from the non-resident parent, which is a smaller proportion than may popularly be thought. We look at alienation at section 10.10 of this chapter.

Some cases will combine a number of these features: the categorisation reflects the main issue in the case.

10.8 High-risk, high-conflict child arrangements cases

It is natural for a child to prefer time spent with one parent over the other, for example because of 'temperament, age, gender, shared interests, parents preferred by siblings, and parenting practices'.[169] It is also normal for a child caught up in parental separation to feel a degree of sadness, anger, and blame which may lead them to support one parent and reject the other. In most of these cases, a relationship with both parents is both possible and desirable, although it will require flexibility in adapting to a pattern that works for everyone.

There are situations in which a continuing relationship between parent and child is at risk. There may be several possible reasons for this. If the arrangements are not child focused and the parties have lost sight of the child's perspective and interests, then they may break down. If the child has witnessed inter-parental domestic abuse, or a parent's struggles with substance abuse, their refusal to see a parent is likely to be rational and proportionate. Indeed, contact may be unsafe for the child and his resident parent, so that it is not in his best interests. In other cases, the breakdown in the parent–child relationship may have more to do with mutual hostility between the parents from which the child has not been protected.

Key Case *Re T (A Child)* involved highly acrimonious proceedings over a 4-year-old girl, LT. Wall LJ finished his judgment in the case by explaining the potential harm to LT of her parents' long-running dispute.

Rarely, a case may involve certain features that fit the controversial psychological phenomenon of 'alienation'. 'Alienation' is a term coined by psychiatrist Richard Gardner to describe those situations in which a child strongly identifies with and idealises one parent [the primary carer], but profoundly rejects and denigrates the other parent [the

[168] L Trinder, J Hunt, A Macleod, J Pearce, and H Woodward, *Enforcing Contact Orders: Problem-Solving or Punishment?* (University of Exeter/Nuffield Foundation 2013) 8.
[169] JR Johnston, 'Parental Alignments and Rejection: An Empirical Study of Alienation in Children of Divorce' (2003) 31 *Journal of the American Academy of Psychiatry and the Law* 158, 159.

KEY CASE *Re T (A Child)* [2009] EWCA Civ 20

Per Wall LJ:

'I cannot part with this appeal without addressing a few words directly to L's parents. The judge was plainly right to find that both parents love L, and that, in turn, she loves them and is "happy with either". However, the judge was also right, in my view, to find that there is a risk to L if her parents "continue to be at loggerheads". Indeed, I would put the matter more strongly. If the parents retain their current hostility to each other, they will undoubtedly cause L serious emotional harm.

L is a child of mixed heritage, and in my judgment it is essential that she benefits from both parts of it. What matters, in my view, is that L should have love and respect for each of her parents and should be able to move easily between them. To achieve this, the parents must have respect for each other.

Each parent represents 50 per cent of L's gene pool. Children, moreover, learn about relationships between adults from their parents. In twenty years' time it will not matter a row of beans whether or not L spent x or y hours more with one parent rather than the other: what will matter is the relationship which L has with her parents, and her capacity to understand and engage in mutually satisfying adult relationships. If she is given a distorted view of adult relationships by her parents, her own view of them will be distorted, and her own relationships with others—particularly with members of the opposite sex—will be damaged.

L must therefore be able to appreciate that even though her parents are separated, they have respect for each other. Most disputes about children following parental separation have nothing to do with the children concerned: they are about the parents fighting all over again the battles of the past, and seeking retribution for the supposed ills and injustices inflicted on them during the relationship. This case shows every sign of going that way.

The father and the mother share equal responsibility for this state of affairs, and the father in particular should not regard the outcome of this appeal as a victory: it is, in reality, a defeat for both parties, who have been unable to resolve their differences by sensible agreement. They are fortunate in having a daughter whom they both love and who loves them. Each must fully appreciate the role the other has to play in L's life, and the current hostility between them must cease. Otherwise, in my judgment, the emotional damage to L will be serious and lasting.'

non-resident parent] even if the relationship between the child and the alienated parent was previously good. The concept is controversial because of the implication that this situation is caused by the resident parent influencing the child. This is why it is sometimes known as 'parental alienation syndrome', although we will discuss why this is a controversial phrase for a controversial concept at 10.8.4.

10.8.1 Getting to grips with what is happening

Ultimately, the words used to describe what is happening are neat labels for complex relationships. But as lawyers know, words hold power. The label 'parental alienation syndrome, for example, has been likened to a "nuclear weapon" that can be exploited within the adversarial legal system'.[170] In Key Case *Re LVMH*, the expert psychiatrists preferred

---

[170] J Doughty, N Maxwell, and T Slater, *Review of Research and Case Law on Parental Alienation* (Cardiff University Children's Social Care Research and Development Centre/Cafcass Cymru 2018) citing Andrew Schepard, 'Editorial Notes' (2001) 39 *Family Court Review* 243.

the term 'implacable hostility' for high-conflict cases, because it allowed for a range of possible explanations.[171] Others have used the phrase 'children resisting contact'.[172] But this too has been criticised as implying that the problem is those resisting contact when in fact there may be good reasons for their opposition, such as domestic abuse or the non-resident parent's behaviour.

It is essential that the court tries to get to grips with what is occurring: is it a justified or unjustified opposition to contact based on the child's best interests? Are allegations of abuse true or false? Is it an opposition to contact based on what is normal for that age, such as a young child's anxiety about being separated, however temporarily, from a primary carer, or the non-resident parent's parenting style?[173] Is it because the child perceives that the parent is not really interested in them, or dislikes a new partner?[174] Is it because they would rather be doing something else, such as seeing their friends (as in *Re O (Contact: Withdrawal of Application)*), or because the journey to the other parent's house is too long?[175] As part of its determination of what is happening, the judge will need to undertake what HHJ Bellamy described as

> an assessment of whether the child's views are rational (when judged against any findings the court may have made in respect of parental behaviour), congruent (when judged against what is known about the child's overall presentation and functioning) and genuine (when judged against any findings the court may have made concerning factors such as enmeshment, alienation and the emotional ties of loyalty the child may have to the resident parent).[176]

The court may be faced with a case in which, in order to defend themselves against allegations that they are abusive, the non-resident parent is accusing the resident parent of alienating the child.[177] In turn, the resident parents may respond that their own and their child's opposition to contact is simply a rational and proportionate response to the non-resident parent's past or present conduct, or a justified fear that the child would be harmed or abducted if direct contact took place.[178] Conversely, a resident parent may be perceived by professionals as implacably hostile to contact when in fact he or she is demonstrating 'appropriate protectiveness'.[179] We will see at 10.8.2 that contact can give

---

[171] C Sturge and D Glaser, 'Contact and Domestic Violence – The Experts' Court Report' (2000) 30 *Family Law* 365.
[172] E.g. BJ Fidler and N Bala, 'Children Resisting Postseparation Contact with a Parent: Concepts, Controversies, and Conundrums' (2010) 48(1) *Family Court Review* 10.
[173] JB Kelly and JR Johnston, 'The Alienated Child: A Reformulation of Parental Alienation Syndrome' (2001) 39(3) *Family Court Review* 249.
[174] J Fortin, J Hunt, and L Scanlan, *Taking a Longer View of Contact: The Perspective of Young Adult who Experienced Parental Separation in Their Youth* (University of Sussex/Nuffield Foundation 2012).
[175] [2003] EWHC 3031 (Fam).
[176] *Re G (A Child: Intractable Contact)* [2013] EWHC B16 (Fam) 83 (HHJ Bellamy).
[177] JR Johnston, 'Parental Alignments and Rejection: An Empirical Study of Alienation in Children of Divorce' (2003) 31 *Journal of the American Academy of Psychiatry and the Law* 158, 158–9.
[178] Note that most alienated parents have never been abusive and most resident parents who are victims of domestic abuse do not alienate children from the abusers, so although abusers may be more likely to engage in some alienating behaviours, domestic abuse does not itself predict alienation: JR Johnston, 'Children of Divorce Who Reject a Parent and Refuse Visitation: Recent Research and Social Policy Implications for the Alienated Child' (2005) 38(4) *Family Law Quarterly* 757.
[179] C Harrison 'Implacably Hostile or Appropriately Protective? Women Managing Child Contact in the Context of Domestic Violence' (2008) 14(4) *Violence against Women* 381.

an abuser the opportunity to continue abuse, and that sometimes abuse worsens (or even starts) after separation. Indeed, abusers themselves have alienated children against their victims 'as a smokescreen for their own abusive behaviour'.[180] Only when the court determines what is going on can the court proceed effectively. Different findings by the court merit different responses.

In sections 10.8.2 to 10.8.4, we consider two areas in detail: first, how the courts approach cases involving allegations of domestic abuse, which can present a justified reason for refusing contact, and other risky situations; and second cases in which a child and/or their primary carer is implacably hostile to contact for a reason that is not justified.

10.8.2 Domestic abuse in child arrangements cases

One of the most contentious issues facing the family courts is what to do when there are allegations of domestic abuse in a case relating to a child. In this section we will look at how courts adjudicate allegations of domestic abuse that are raised in child arrangements proceedings and what effect proven domestic abuse may have on the outcome.

What is domestic abuse?

The Domestic Abuse Act 2021 defines domestic abuse as physical or sexual abuse, violent or threatening behaviour, controlling or coercive behaviour, economic abuse, or psychological, emotional, or other abuse.[181] It may be a single event or a course of conduct. To fall within the domestic sphere, the abuse must be between connected persons, a category including relatives, co-parents, and people who have been in an intimate relationship among others. The definition also recognises children as victims of domestic abuse, defining a child victim as someone aged under 18 who 'sees or hears, or experiences the effects of the abuse'.

The Act does not spell out what abuse may look like, although we explore this in Chapter 7. The previous definition used by government was follows:

> any incident or pattern of incidents of controlling, coercive or threatening behaviour, violence or abuse between those aged 16 or over who are or have been intimate partners or family members regardless of gender or sexuality.

> This can encompass, but is not limited to, psychological, physical, sexual, financial, or emotional abuse.[182]

Practice Direction 12J, *Child Arrangements and Contact Orders: Domestic Violence and Harm*, notes that this definition also includes 'culturally specific forms of abuse including, but not limited to, forced marriage, honour-based violence, dowry-related abuse and transnational marriage abandonment', whereby a spouse is stranded abroad without access to resources.

---

[180] BJ Fidler and N Bala, 'Children Resisting Postseparation Contact with a Parent: Concepts, Controversies, and Conundrums' (2010) 48(1) *Family Court Review* 10.
[181] The Domestic Abuse Bill 2019–21. Available at https://services.parliament.uk/bills/2019-21/domesticabuse.html accessed 15 November 2020.
[182] Home Office, Information for Local Areas on the Change to the Definition of Domestic Violence and Abuse (2013); and https://www.gov.uk/government/news/new-definition-of-domestic-violence accessed 15 November 2020.

The abuse that we are discussing, therefore, may or may not be physical abuse. But abuse of any kind can have serious effects on children, whether they are direct victims or witnesses to the abuse of another.

Effect of abuse on victims

There is considerable evidence that being in a household in which abuse takes place causes long-term harm to children. Adult-on-adult domestic abuse raises the risk of adult-on-child domestic abuse: parents who are physically violent to each other are 3 to 9 times more likely to be violent to their children than in non-violent families.[183] Domestic abuse may also be coupled with other risks to the child. Research by the Children's Commissioner for England found that 420,000 children (3.6 per cent of all children in England) are in household where domestic abuse, substance abuse, and mental illness (the so-called 'toxic trio') are all present to a moderate or severe extent.[184]

After separation, the risks arising from abuse do not diminish. Humphreys and Thiara's study of female domestic violence victims found that 45 out of 49 women with contact arrangements with an abusive ex-partner experienced problems with post-separation violence, some of it long-term.[185] Hotton found that post-separation violence tended to be more severe and more likely to be witnessed by children than pre-separation violence. Indeed, for some people—about 15 per cent—violence occurred for the first time after separation, not before, perhaps as retaliation for leaving.[186] In one US study, three quarters of women hospitalised because of domestic violence were already separated or divorced from their abuser.[187] It is therefore 'at the most dangerous juncture in their relationship' that contact applications occur.[188] Even when proceedings are over, and even in situations where violence has not previously been present, contact may be a flashpoint for the use of violence against a former partner. Hardesty and Chung suggest that this is because child contact may constitute the only time former partners are together.[189] Contact can also provide the opportunity for non-physical abuse such as verbal abuse, using financial support to try to control contact, stalking behaviours, interrogation of the child about the resident parent's life or their location, failure to return the child from contact (or deliberately returning them late in order to create a fear of abduction) and attempts to undermine the child's relationship with their primary carer. Hester and Radford shockingly described fathers involving their children in plans to kill their mother as 'a common complaint'.[190]

---

[183] TE Moffitt and A Caspi, 'Implications of Violence between Intimate Partners for Child Psychologists and Psychiatrists' (1998) 39(2) *Journal of Child Psychology and Psychiatry* 137, 142.

[184] H Chowdry, *Estimating the Prevalence of the 'Toxic Trio': Evidence from the Adult Psychiatric Morbidity Survey, Vulnerability Technical Report 2* (Children's Commissioner for England, July 2018) 10.

[185] C Humphreys and RK Thiara, 'Neither Justice Nor Protection: Women's Experiences of Post-Separation Violence' (2003) 25(3) *Journal of Social Welfare and Family Law* 195.

[186] T Hotton, 'Spousal Violence after Marital Separation' (2001) 27(7) *Juristat* 1.

[187] J Zorca, 'How Abused Women Can Use the Law to Help Protect Their Children', in E Peled, PH Jaffe, and JL Edleson (eds), *Cycles of Violence* (Sage 1995).

[188] JL Hardesty, 'Separation Assault in the Context of Postdivorce Parenting: An Integrative Review of the Literature' (2002) 8(5) *Violence against Women* 597, 603.

[189] JL Hardesty and GH Chung, 'Intimate Partner Violence, Parental Divorce, and Child Custody: Directions for Intervention and Future Research', (2006) 55 *Family Relations* 200, 201.

[190] M Hester and L Radford, *Domestic Violence and Child Contact Arrangements in England and Denmark* (Joseph Rowntree Foundation/Policy Press 1996) 28.

Even if a child is not is not the person being hit, raped, controlled, or threatened, seeing a parent or other family member being abused in this way, or witnessing the aftermath of this, is likely to be very traumatic for the child. And, of course, the resident parent's anxieties or psychological distress about contact may negatively affect the child.[191] (Sometimes a court may decline to make a child arrangements order because of the resident parent's distress outweighs the advantages of contact. Such distress must of course affect the children's welfare in order to be a relevant consideration.) Jeffrey Edleson's meta study[192] found that children who had witnessed abuse were more likely to be fearful and inhibited and show symptoms of anxiety, depression, and trauma. They were more likely to behave aggressively as a way of coping with problems, because that is the behaviour that was modelled for them, and they were generally less socially competent and more likely to engage in antisocial acts. Where the child witnessed physical abuse or the use of weapons in the home, this strongly increased the risk that the child would go on to commit an act of serious violence. These effects lasted into adulthood.[193] Indeed, men who witnessed their mothers being physically abused by their fathers were statistically more likely to be violent towards their own wives; and women who saw their mothers abused were more likely to suffer higher rates of violent victimisation by their own husbands in adulthood.[194]

How should courts approach cases involving alleged abuse?

As with all decisions about child arrangements, the paramount consideration is the child's welfare. There is therefore no presumption or starting point that there should be no contact, as there are cases where some form of contact, whether direct or indirect, will be in the child's interests despite a background of domestic abuse or other seriously harmful behaviour. This was made clear in Key Case *Re LVMH*.

KEY CASE *Re LVMH (Contact Domestic Violence)* [2000] 2 FLR 334 (CA)

This was an appeal by four fathers in four different cases (Re L, Re V, Re M, and Re H). Each father had committed serious domestic abuse against their child's mother and the courts had refused them direct contact.

The leading judgment is given by Butler-Sloss P:

- 'Where allegations of domestic violence are made which might have an effect on the outcome, those allegations must be adjudicated upon and found proved or not proved.'
- 'Violence to a partner involves a significant failure in parenting – failure to protect the child's carer and failure to protect the child emotionally.'
- Even if domestic abuse is proven, there is no presumption against contact. 'The court always has the duty to apply s1 of the Children Act 1989 that the welfare of the child is paramount.'

---

[191] C Shalansky, J Ericksen, and A Henderson, 'Abused Women and Child Custody: The Ongoing Exposure to Abusive Ex-Partners' (1999) 29(2) *Journal of Advanced Nursing* 416.

[192] A meta study is a statistical analysis of other studies on the same subject, bringing together the results of those studies in an attempt to find common themes/results.

[193] JL Edleson 'Children's Witnessing of Adult Domestic Violence' (1999) 14(8) *Journal of Interpersonal Violence* 839.

[194] Statistics Canada, *Violence against Women Survey* (Statistics Canada 1993).

> The court weighs the seriousness of the domestic violence, the risks involved and the impact on the child against the positive factors (if any), of contact.
>
> · 'The ability of the offending parent to recognise his past conduct, be aware of the need to change and make genuine efforts to do so, will be likely to be an important consideration.'
>
> The court's amicus curiae instructed child psychiatrists Dr Claire Sturge and Dr Danya Glaser to provide expert advice on the effect of witnessing domestic violence on the children involved. The court drew on this report, *Contact and Domestic Violence—The Experts' Court Report*,[195] and a report to the Lord Chancellor by his Children Act Sub-Committee, on *Contact between Children and Violent Parents*.[196]

Re LVMH emphasised the importance of making findings of whether abuse had occurred before the court decided what, if any, contact to order. The best way to do this is through a 'fact-finding' hearing, which is a hearing at which the court hears evidence from the parties and any other witnesses and decides what has happened or not happened (see 10.4.3). Fact-finding hearings are often referred to as '*Re L* hearings', after this case. Only when it knows 'the truth' can the judge move on to deciding what the arrangements for the children should be.

Despite this, a 2015 study of the practices of five county courts by Harding and Newnham found that fact-finding hearings were held in fewer than 10 per cent of cases in which domestic abuse allegations were raised.[197] In a few cases, the hearing did not proceed because the allegations were admitted or withdrawn. However, there is evidence that courts (and lawyers) have not held hearings because they consider allegations of abuse to be irrelevant. For example, they may treat allegations as 'historical' and ignore that such incidents may be examples of continuing risk.[198] They may view incidents as minor even in those situations in which an objective observer would consider them rather serious. Barnett notes that 'it appears from the reported cases that the approach of the lower courts is to ignore allegations of domestic violence altogether if they consider that they are not serious enough to warrant a separate fact-finding hearing'.[199]

Whether or not a fact-finding hearing was held, even in those cases in which domestic violence was proven to have happened, contact was denied by judges only 1 per cent of the time.[200] Judges' and professionals' response to the new 2008 Practice Direction 12J *Child Arrangements and Contact Orders: Domestic Violence and Harm*, which requires courts to consider risk, was to consider *what* contact should be ordered, not *whether* it should be ordered. Thus, as Harding and Newnham found, 'the question of domestic

---

[195]   (2000) 30 *Family Law* 615.

[196]   Advisory Board on Family Law, Children Act Sub-Committee, *A Report to the Lord Chancellor on Contact between Children and Violent Parents* (TSO 2000).

[197]   M Harding and A Newnham, *How Do County Courts Share the Care of Children?* (Nuffield Foundation 2015).

[198]   A Barnett, 'Contact at all Costs? Domestic Violence and Children's Welfare' (2014) 26(4) *Child and Family Law Quarterly* 439.

[199]   A Barnett, '"Like Gold Dust These Days": Domestic Violence Fact-Finding Hearings in Child Contact Cases' (2015) 23 *Feminist Legal Studies* 47, 67.

[200]   H Saunders, *Twenty-Nine Child Homicides* (Women's Aid 2004).

violence tended to be reconceptualised as being primarily about reducing the risk to the child and facilitating as much contact as was possible in the circumstances'.[201] Yet the impetus for the publication of PD12J was a Women's Aid report entitled *Twenty-Nine Child Homicides*, which argued that over a ten year period the deaths of 29 children were the result of either court ordered or informally arranged contact when there was a history of domestic abuse.

Let us consider one example. In *Re M (Children)*, the judge at first instance found that the mother had been a victim of prolonged domestic abuse by the father, witnessed by the children who had themselves been the victims of what the court called 'inappropriate chastisement' by him. The judge found that the mother had 'a real terror' of the father and that the father would destabilise the mother and children because he had not changed his ways. She declined to order contact. On appeal, however, the Court of Appeal held that refusal of contact was draconian and not be proportionate and necessary:

> the order . . . can only be lawful within the meaning of art 8(2) of the Convention if the order for no direct contact is necessary in a democratic society for the protection of the right of the mother, and consequently the minor children in her care, to grow up free from harm. In order to reach that conclusion the court must consider and discard all reasonable and available avenues which may otherwise promote the boys rights to respect for family life, including, if in the interests of promoting their welfare during minority, contact with their discredited father.

> In the circumstances . . . I am not satisfied that the order is demonstrated to be proportionate to the legitimate end which the judge pursued in ensuring the viability and stable placement of the children with their mother.[202]

The Court of Appeal remitted the case back to the lower courts to consider whether supervised contact would be appropriate.

Barnett found that this approach—of concentrating on what contact should be ordered, rather than whether it should be ordered—influenced lawyers acting for the alleged victims of abuse. Barnett found a perception that only 'recent, extremely serious physical violence would lead to no contact being ordered'.[203] Believing that contact would be ordered in any event, the lawyers advised their clients not to oppose contact, which in turn meant the judges were not faced with opposition.[204] One domestic abuse victim in a focus group for the Ministry of Justice's 2020 report *Assessing Risk of Harm to Children and Parents in Private Law Children Cases* reported that

> My lawyer totally empathised and said 'I totally understand but the system is how it is, and your husband would have to be a murderer to not get contact with his children'. . . I was confident because of previous ABH they wouldn't hand over my children and she said,

[201] M Harding and A Newnham, *How Do County Courts Share the Care of Children?* (Nuffield Foundation 2015).
[202] [2013] EWCA Civ 1147.
[203] A Barnett, '"Like Gold Dust These Days": Domestic Violence Fact-Finding Hearings in Child Contact Cases' (2015) 23 *Feminist Legal Studies* 47.
[204] Cf R Bailey-Harris, J Barron, and J Pearce, 'From Utility to Rights? The Presumption of Contact in Practice' (1999) 13 *International Journal of Law, Policy, and the Family* 111 and A Barnett, 'Contact at all Costs? Domestic Violence and Children's Welfare' (2014) 26(4) *Child and Family Law Quarterly* 439.

'I'm not being funny love but I've seen fathers who have multiple records of ABH who have unsupervised contact, you're not going to win this case today'.[205]

In not opposing contact, it is quite possible that the lawyers were trying to prevent their clients from being perceived as hostile to contact, as that perception could lead the courts to compensate for that perceived hostility by ordering even more contact to the abusive parent or even making a 'live with' order in their favour. But this created what Bailey-Harris et al. have referred to as a presumption of contact, not embodied in law, but in the actions and beliefs of legal professionals, and 'displaced only in the very rarest circumstances'.[206]

FOCUS Think Critically

The death of Jack and Paul Sykes

Following the separation of Claire Throssell and Darren Sykes in 2014, their two children Jack (aged 12) and Paul (aged 9) moved with Claire to her own mother's house but spent time with Darren at the former family home. Although this contact had been agreed, Claire later told a social worker that she felt bullied into it by Darren. Over the next few months:

1. Paul told a teacher that Darren had dragged him along by the throat and punched him in the stomach. (There is conflicting evidence about whether Claire herself was ever physically abused by Darren in addition to psychological/emotional abuse during the marriage which included monitoring her whereabouts constantly).
2. Darren came and forcibly removed the children from the grandmother's house when they were not due to see him.
3. Darren came over to Claire's mother's house and threw Claire's belongings out.

The police undertook a Domestic Abuse, Stalking and Honour Based Violence (DASH) risk assessment, grading the situation as 'standard risk' domestic abuse.[207]

As a result of these incidents, Claire applied for a child arrangements order that the children should live with her, and a prohibited steps order that Darren should not see the children until the local authority children's services team had assessed the situation. However, only a week after Claire made this application, she agreed to the court making an interim order that Darren should have contact twice each week. Claire told a later Serious Case Review that 'she had been advised by her legal representative that the court was unlikely to agree to father having no contact, which is what she had requested, and because of this she accepted the proposal of contact twice each week.'

When making the order, the court had access to a record from a social worker that showed 'allegations of abuse, the children's fear of their father and their statements that they wanted contact to continue'. However, it was not until after contact had been agreed that Cafcass undertook safeguarding checks. The Cafcass officer 'probably did not read the application in its entirety' and did not spot that Darren had told Claire that he understood why fathers kill their children. The Cafcass officer

---

[205] R Hunter, M Burton, and L Trinder, *Assessing Risk of Harm to Children and Parents in Private Law Children Cases* (Ministry of Justice 2020) at 7.3.

[206] R Bailey-Harris, J Barron, and J Pearce, 'From Utility to Rights? The Presumption of Contact in Practice' (1999) 13 *International Journal of Law, Policy, and the Family* 111, 118.

[207] The *Domestic Abuse, Stalking and Harassment and Honour Based Violence (DASH) Risk Identification and Assessment and Management Model* is a risk assessment used by the Association of Chief Police Officers and Cafcass to identify the risk level in a particular situation.

filed a report suggesting a s7 report on contact be prepared but did not suggest suspending contact in the meantime. Meanwhile, the local authority social services team indicated that as the matter was in the hands of the court, their further involvement would not affect the outcome.

On 20 October 2014, a different Cafcass officer met with Darren. She asked him questions in relation to hurting or harming his children and he was adamant that he would never do such a thing. . . . [She] brought the meeting to a close because she felt that [Darren] was becoming 'agitated and unreasonable' . . . [Darren] did not want the interview to end and barred the door while he expressed his view that Cafcass believed his ex-wife and sons rather than him.'

On 22 October, during contact at the former family home, Darren locked the children in the attic, barricaded the doors, doused the house with petrol, and set fire to it, killing Jack and Paul as well as himself.

In this case, although the children's deaths could not have been predicted, we see a number of very concerning features about the risks surrounding contact:

- delays in getting information from social services to Cafcass before the first hearing;
- lack of competent safeguarding work by Cafcass;
- apparent legal advice given to Claire that contact would be granted, which as we have seen may have influenced her agreement to it;
- contact being agreed by Claire despite her fears. Cafcass and Women's Aid have found that contact is agreed at the first hearing in 89 per cent of cases where there are allegations of domestic abuse. This may be 'indicative of a context of coercion or fear'.[208]
- the court accepting the agreement for contact despite the allegations and without investigating them;
- the court taking into account the children's wishes. While this is not in itself inappropriate—the children's wishes and feelings are a contact checklist factor—research shows courts can take a 'selective approach', taking children's views into account if they say they want contact but disregarding them if they do not.[209]

Claire has since become a campaigner on the laws surrounding contact and domestic abuse.

The Throssell case is one example of a high-profile child death linked to contact. As we have seen, it was not the first such situation. Nor was it the last: Women's Aid followed their 2004 report *Twenty-Nine Child Homicides* with *Nineteen Child Homicides* in 2016.[210] These reports, 12 years apart, both argued that the pro-contact approach of the courts was exposing both children and their resident parents to further abuse and that the court process itself was being used by abusers to further coerce and control the other parent, such as by making applications designed purely to cause distress and expense rather than out of genuine care for the child.

Legal aid and domestic abuse

The potential to misuse the legal system was worsened by the loss of legal aid in 2014. While alleged victims of domestic abuse are—subject to evidence and the means and merits tests—eligible for legal aid, alleged perpetrators are not. Someone accused of these acts

[208] Cafcass/Women's Aid, *Allegations of Domestic Abuse in Child Contact Cases* (2017). For a useful critique of this report, see http://www.transparencyproject.org.uk/joint-research-cafcass-and-womens-aid/.
[209] S Holt (2011) 'Domestic Abuse and Child Contact: Positioning Children in the Decision-Making Process' (2011) 17(4) *Child Care in Practice* 327.
[210] Women's Aid, *Nineteen Child Homicides* (2016).

has the right to defend themselves, and to challenge the evidence against them. It is part of the Article 6 ECHR right to a fair trial. Yet if they cannot afford a lawyer, they will have to conduct their own cases. In criminal rape trials, the alleged perpetrator cannot cross-examine the alleged victim directly, but must use a barrister. In the family courts, where domestic abuse may include rape alongside other severely harms, there was until recently no such rule. The Domestic Abuse Act 2021 now creates an automatic ban on victim-perpetrator cross-examination, enabling the court to appoint a publicly funded advocate to cross-examine the parties where there there is evidence of domestic abuse or where lack of advocate would diminish the quality of witness evidence or cause significant distress to a witness or party.

Even if a person is a victim of domestic abuse, and has the evidence necessary to show that, they may nonetheless earn too much to be eligible for legal aid. That may not in fact be much at all, and certainly not enough to fund representation throughout or experts' reports. Harwood studied the effect of austerity on access to justice in the family courts and found that:

- Litigants in person may not mention matters which the court would consider to be of importance, and judges 'do not know what they do not know'.
- In particular, in domestic violence matters, allegations were often generalised rather than specific and alleged victims are unable to 'package this information in a format accessible to a court'. As a result, courts may direct litigants making allegations to particularise a small number of allegations, and this may prevent courts from having an accurate view of the risks involved.
- There were differing views on the extent to which courts should tease out information that if the parties had been represented would have been raised by the lawyers
- Even if a party has legal aid, it can be difficult to obtain legal aid funding for experts' reports.[211]

These factors, both in isolation and together, mean that judges will struggle to reach correct, safe, decisions.

The current practice direction and reform of the law

By 2016, the year in which *Nineteen Child Homicides* was published, criticism of the courts' approach was mounting, from academics, practitioners, victims, the media,[212] and (notwithstanding the responsibility it held for a situation caused in part by the removal of legal aid) Parliament itself.[213]

As a result of this, a new version of Practice Direction 12J was issued in October 2017. Figure 10.2 shows the impact of key reports on the different versions.

---

[211] J Harwood, '"We Don't Know What It Is We Don't Know": How Austerity Has Undermined the Courts' Access to Information in Child Arrangements Cases Involving Domestic Abuse' (2019) 31(4) *Child and Family Law Quarterly* 321.

[212] S Laville, 'Revealed: How Family Courts Allow Abusers to Torment Their Victims' (*The Guardian,* 22 December 2016).

[213] All-Party Parliamentary Group on Domestic Violence, *Domestic Abuse, Child Contact and the Family Courts* (April 2016).

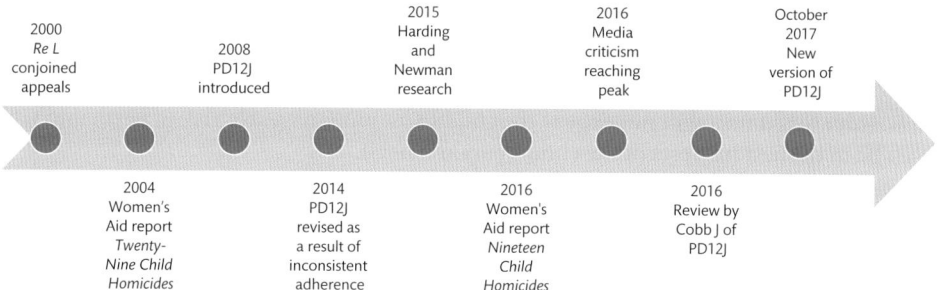

FIGURE 10.2 Timeline of changes to domestic abuse practice direction

While the previous iterations of Practice Direction 12J provided mandatory directions to courts hearing domestic abuse cases,[214] the new version of Practice Direction 12J is written in more directive language to try to reduce non-compliance or non-application. It also widens the definition from 'violence' to 'abuse' and adopts the government's current definition, adding transnational abandonment as a form of abuse.

The Practice Direction requires courts to consider 'at all stages of the proceedings, and specifically at the first hearing' whether domestic abuse is raised as an issue. The court must not proceed without the results of safeguarding checks. Even if an order is agreed by the parties, the court must carefully scrutinise it.

The key elements of the Direction are:

- The court must consider whether the presumption of involvement applies (paragraph 7).

- The court may make special arrangements to protect the party or child attending any hearing, such as by having separate waiting areas and arrangements for entering and exiting the court building (paragraph 10).

- 'The court must not generally make an interim child arrangements order, or orders for contact, in the absence of safeguarding information, unless it is to protect the safety of the child' (paragraph 12). This acts as a presumption against making interim contact orders in cases of alleged abuse.

- While not being able to prevent alleged perpetrators cross-examining alleged victims— the Practice Direction will need to be updated now that this is possible by virtue of the 2021 Act—it does provide that parties could identify questions in advance and that judges may undertake the cross-examination of an alleged victim (paragraph 28).

- The court should consider whether it needs a social work, psychiatric, psychological or other assessment (including an expert safety and risk assessment), and whether it should make a contact activity order such as a domestic violence perpetrator

---

[214] 'The practice direction is (still) mandatory - there is stronger language: "the court is required". . . (although the previous wording "the court should" could be argued in that sense)': M Crawford, 'The Revised Practice Direction 12J: Child Arrangements & Contact Orders: Domestic Violence and Harm' (*Family Law Week* 17 November 2017). For mandatory elements, see paras 8, 14, 15, 18, 22, and 29.

programme or (with consent) a direction for treatment or another kind of intervention (paragraphs 33 and 34).[215]

- 'When deciding the issue of child arrangements the court should ensure that any order for contact will not expose the child to an unmanageable risk of harm and will be in the best interests of the child' (paragraph 35).

- 'The court should make an order for contact only if it is satisfied that the physical and emotional safety of the child and the parent with whom the child is living can, as far as possible, be secured before during and after contact, and that the parent with whom the child is living will not be subjected to further domestic abuse by the other parent' (paragraph 36).

- In assessing whether contact is in the child's best interests, the court should consider 'the conduct of both parents towards each other and towards the child and the impact of the same'. In particular, the court should consider the effect of the abuse and the motivations of an abuser in making an application, as well as (per *Re L*) 'the capacity of the parents to appreciate the effect of past domestic abuse and the potential for future domestic abuse' (paragraph 37).

- 'Where a risk assessment has concluded that a parent poses a risk to a child or to the other parent, contact via a supported contact centre, or contact supported by a parent or relative, is not appropriate' (paragraph 38). A court may therefore look at managing risk through the use of an expert third party, such as an independent social worker, which can be expensive.

- The court must record any admissions of domestic abuse; any findings of fact (these are to be attached as a schedule to the order) (paragraph 15); and its reasons why, if it orders contact, it believes the order made will not expose the child to risk of harm and is beneficial to the child (paragraph 40).

Note that the Practice Direction now requires that courts 'ensure' that a contact order will not 'expose the child to an *unmanageable risk of harm* and *will be in the best interests of the child*'. This indicates that harms may exist, but if contact is otherwise in the best interests of the child the issue is simply whether and how those harms can be managed. The risk here is that courts will continue to focus on how contact should happen, not whether it should happen.

However, the Practice Direction also improves protection for the resident parent compared to its earlier versions. Whereas prior versions referred only to the physical and emotional safety of the child, the current version refers also to the need to secure the safety of both the child *and the parent with whom the child is living*. This marks a recognition of the use of contact as a way to continue domestic abuse.

In 2020, the Ministry of Justice published a report entitled *Assessing Risk of Harm to Children and Parents in Private Law Children Cases*.[216] The report made a series of recommendations about reform. It identified four main problems:

1. Lack of resources. Additional investment was needed in the courts, Cafcass, contact centres, specialist support services, and provision of legal aid.

---

[215] Note that treatment requires consent; some other forms of intervention such as a contact activity direction or condition do not. See para 34.
[216] R Hunter, M Burton, and L Trinder, *Assessing Risk of Harm to Children and Parents in Private Law Children Cases* (Ministry of Justice 2020).

2. The pro-contact culture and how this affected domestic abuse cases (the report recommends revisiting the presumption of involvement).

3. Lack of joined-up working, meaning that the criminal courts and family courts worked separately in domestic abuse cases. The report recommended better integration. One way of achieving that might be what it called a 'one family one judge' approach 'in which certain concurrent family and criminal proceedings involving domestic abuse are heard by the same cross-ticketed judge, with the aim of reducing the need for victims to re-tell their stories and promoting a more joined up approach to the handling of such cases between the jurisdictions'.[217]

4. The adversarial nature of the system, which positioned parents against one another and limited the child's involvement. The report recommended that courts adopt a more investigative role, and work is ongoing on what that might look like.

SCENARIO 4

Illustration 6: Sarah, Phil, and children Bill (11), Ben (8), and Bella (4)

Sarah is alleging that Phil uses drugs, is physically and sexually violent to her, and has threatened the children with violence. Phil is alleging that Sarah has alienated the children against him and is mentally unfit to care for the them. The court should have been alerted to these issues allegations through the filing of a harm form (whether by the applicant or the respondent) or through Cafcass' safeguarding checks, which should take place prior to the initial court hearing.

The court's first job is to consider what effect, if any, the allegations and counter-allegations may have if proven. Some allegations may not be sufficiently serious or relevant to affect the outcome of the case. That is not the case here: these are serious allegations and this is a situation in which the court is going to need to determine the truth of the allegations before it can decide what further steps to take to resolve the applications. (However, as discussed there is evidence that courts have had a tendency to dismiss allegations as 'historical' or irrelevant without determining the truth of them. With the revised practice direction that *ought* to not happen any more.)

It therefore highly likely that a fact-finding hearing will need to be held and the court will determine 'the truth' on the balance of probabilities. That will include findings about whether there has been domestic abuse. Sometimes the court will immediately go on to decide what should happen, but it is more probable that they will first adjourn the case to allow time for some expert reports to be prepared. Here, at least one of the children is refusing to see Phil, so the court may want a Cafcass officer to determine why that is, and the children's other wishes and feelings. As discussed in section 10.3.2, these will not be determinative and the weight of their wishes will depend on their age and understanding. The court may alternatively consider ordering a report from a psychiatrist or psychologist if necessary to help it resolve the matter. The expert will rely on the facts found proven by the judge, so if Phil is proven to have been abusive and continues to deny that, then the expert and the court may well consider that he is of high risk of that abuse continuing. Conversely, if the situation is that Sarah is unjustifiably blocking contact, then the court's approach would be different to a situation in which the children's objections are rational and proportionate.

---

[217] *Assessing Risk of Harm to Children and Parents in Private Law Children Cases Implementation Plan* (Ministry of Justice 2020). Judges are able to hear cases in the areas of law for which they are 'ticketed'.

Phil's application is for the children to live with him. If the allegations of abuse are found to be true, it is extremely unlikely indeed that such an application would succeed. The court would have to be satisfied that there would be no further risk of harm notwithstanding the existence of past harm. But whether there should be a 'spend time with' order in his favour is a more complex issue.

As we discovered at Illustration 1, this is a case in which the presumption of involvement will not apply if the allegations of domestic abuse are found to be true and there is no form of contact that would not put the children at risk of harm. The Children Act defines harm as seeing or hearing the ill-treatment of another (s31) and Practice Direction 12J tells us that the court should make an order for contact 'only if it is satisfied that the physical and emotional safety of the child *and the parent with whom the child is living* can, as far as possible, be secured before during and after contact, and that the parent with whom the child is living will not be subjected to further domestic abuse by the other parent.' That means that the court needs to consider whether there is some form of contact that is safe.

10.8.3 Other risky situations

The Practice Direction focuses on the harms caused by domestic abuse, but there are other potential harms to children. How should the court approach a case in which a parent has a conviction for possession of child pornography downloaded from the internet, for example? What if a parent has a conviction for a serious offence of violence to someone outside the family? What if a parent has a substance abuse problem, or serious mental illness affecting their ability to care for the children safely? In these sorts of situations, it will be necessary to assess whether there is a risk to the child or resident parent. (It does not automatically follow that someone with a sexual interest in children of a certain age is always a risk to their own children, or children of a different age or gender.) The case is unlikely to be resolved without expert advice, and there are agencies that specialise in carrying out risk assessments like this. In resolving the case, courts are likely to take an approach very similar to that set out in PD12J, namely that there is no presumption against contact but if contact is in the child's best interests it must not expose the child to an unmanageable risk of harm. That may result in there being no contact; indirect contact only; or supervised contact, depending on the level of risk. In these situations, of course, the resident parent may exhibit understandably high levels of anxiety about contact. Sometimes this anxiety on the part of the primary carer may affect the child to such an extent that it outweighs the benefits of contact and means that it is no longer in the child's best interests.

10.8.4 Unjustified opposition to contact

In some situations, a child and/or their resident parent may be opposed to contact for no good or proportionate reason. In the most severe cases, the child might strongly identify with and idealise one parent, but profoundly reject and denigrate the other parent even if the relationship between the child and the alienated parent was previously good. The child's rejection of the parent is 'a severe distortion on the child's part of the previous parent–child relationship'.[218] Some psychologists will call this situation 'alienation'. Some

---

[218] JB Kelly and JR Johnston, 'The Alienated Child: A Reformulation of Parental Alienation Syndrome' (2001) 39(3) *Family Court Review* 249, 254.

prefer the term 'parental alienation syndrome' because they believe the situation is caused by the resident parent, although the reality appears to be much more complex. The psychiatrist Richard Gardner coined the term 'alienation' and considered it to be a psychological syndrome, based on a number of features common to alienated children:

- A strong alignment or enmeshment with one parent (the favoured parent) from whom they fear separation,[219] and behaving in ways that they think will please that parent (including through rejection of the non-resident parent).

- Vehement rejection of the other (non-resident) parent that is 'almost phobic'[220] and includes a refusal to see or speak to the other parent; this can extend to other members of that parent's family.

- Not calling the non-resident parent 'dad' or 'mum' but instead, without guilt, referring to them abusively,[221] and similarly behaving rudely—in a way that they would never usually behave—towards professionals in the court process that they perceive as being on the non-resident parent's 'side'.

- Using language that is not typical for a child their age. 'The language through which the child portrays such information includes such phrases as: "He touches me inappropriately", or "He has penetrated me". These are borrowed scenarios from the alienating parent.'[222]

- Referring to matters that are outside their direct knowledge, but which they have picked up from the alienating parent. Weir gives as an example 'He threw my mum down the stairs when she was pregnant with me . . . I know because I was there.'[223]

- Making serious complaints about weak, frivolous, or absurd matters to do with the non-resident parent ('They said that their maternal grandmother was not their grandmother anymore "because she forces us to eat sweets and be silly"').[224]

- Not remembering any happy times with the non-resident parent but remembering or exaggerating only negative memories.

Much of the literature on alienation will refer to an 'alienating parent' in the belief that the resident parent is deliberately or inadvertently causing the alienation. Alienating behaviours may include:

- Denigrating the non-resident parent in the child's hearing, responding negatively to any positive comments about the non-resident parent, or suggesting that the non-resident parent is dangerous or has abandoned the child.

- Withholding information from the non-resident parent about the child's health or schooling.

---

[219] JR Johnston, 'Parental Alignments and Rejection: An Empirical Study of Alienation in Children of Divorce' (2003) 31 *Journal of the American Academy of Psychiatry and the Law* 158, 158–9.
[220] S Whitcombe, 'Parental Alienation or Justifiable Estrangement? Assessing a Child's Resistance to a Parent in the UK' [2017] *Seen and Heard* 27.
[221] LF Lowenstein, 'Implacable Hostility Leading to Alienation' (2008) 172 *Criminal Law and Justice Weekly* 185.
[222] LF Lowenstein, 'Implacable Hostility Leading to Alienation' (2008) 172 *Criminal Law and Justice Weekly* 185.
[223] K Weir, 'A Guide to the "Parental Alienation Syndrome"' (2009). Unpublished.
[224] Example from *Re M (Children)* [2012] EWHC 1948 (Fam) [17].

- Preventing or frustrating direct contact and/or showing extreme anxiety around contact.

- Allowing the child a choice about contact with the other parent, placing the responsibility on them.[225] Lowenstein says that 'It is often not what the alienator says but how it is said by saying nothing positive about the absent parent. Such statements as: "Father/Mother would like to take you out, do you want to go?" is likely to provide an answer which is negative from the child because the child expects the custodial parent to feel that is what is expected of him/her.'[226]

- Making false allegations of abuse or neglect, either deliberately or in the wrong belief that abuse has occurred.[227]

A child who is firmly opposed to contact may well assert that their views are true, rational, proportionate, and not influenced by anyone else, and become angry and entrenched when it is suggested otherwise.[228] The child psychiatrist Kirk Weir has also argued that a child's opposition to contact may be 'a false solution to the conflict of loyalty created by the prolonged conflict between their parents'.[229] For this reason, courts may be sceptical of their expressed wishes and feelings, believing them to be either the product of external influence or not a truthful account of their feelings. In *Re S (Transfer of Residence)*, for example, HHJ Bellamy said that:

> I cannot and do not ignore S's expressed wishes. However, in the light of [the expert's] evidence, it would be inappropriate for me to proceed on the basis that those expressed wishes and feelings should be taken at face value. The impact of alienation on the reliability of those wishes and feelings and the signs (albeit modest) that they may not reflect his true feelings are matters to be taken into account when assessing the weight to be attached to them.[230]

Alienating a child from his parents can constitute emotional harm. There have been cases in which the child has been made the subject of a care or supervision order to reflect the fact that they are being caused significant harm.[231]

A warning about the concept of alienation

Now that we have outlined what alienation may look like, it is necessary to give a warning. Although much as been written about alienation, it is a contentious concept: it is not a psychiatric condition listed in the *Diagnostic and Statistical Manual of Mental Disorders* (DSM) published by the American Psychiatric Association. Some professionals avoid the term

[225] S Whitcombe, 'Parental Alienation or Justifiable Estrangement? Assessing a Child's Resistance to a Parent in the UK' [2017] *Seen and Heard* 27.

[226] LF Lowenstein, 'Implacable Hostility Leading to Alienation' (2008) 172 *Criminal Law and Justice Weekly* 185.

[227] BJ Fidler and N Bala, 'Children Resisting Postseparation Contact with a Parent: Concepts, Controversies, and Conundrums' (2010) 48(1) *Family Court Review* 10, 11.

[228] S Friedlander and M Gans Walters, 'When a Child Rejects a Parent: Tailoring the Intervention to Fit the Problem' (2010) 48(1) *Family Court Review* 98, 102. See also JR Johnston, 'Children of Divorce Who Reject a Parent and Refuse Visitation: Recent Research and Social Policy Implications for the Alienated Child' (2005) 38 *Family Law Quarterly* 757.

[229] K Weir, 'High-Conflict Contact Disputes: Evidence of the Extreme Unreliability of Some Children's Ascertainable Wishes and Feelings' (2011) 49(4) *Family Court Review* 788.

[230] [2010] EWHC 192 [70] (Fam).

[231] E.g. *Re M (Intractable Contact Dispute: Interim Care Order)* [2003] EWHC 1024 (Fam). See Chapter 12.

'alienation' altogether, preferring to use 'implacable hostility' or 'unjustified estrangement'. That is not to say that the situations described here do not exist: all family lawyers have seen such cases. It's just that not all psychiatrists believe that it should be described as a collection of psychological symptoms or as a quasi-medical 'Parental Alienation Syndrome'.[232]

We must also be cautious about the use of 'alienation experts'. There are legitimate criticisms to be made of this small group, the limits of their research, and a real risk of confirmation bias, i.e., that they see alienation precisely because they are used to doing so. Parents who feel they have been alienated may find support among other alienated parents, but this again does not indicate that what they are experiencing is indeed alienation, as opposed to a justified opposition to contact: it is perhaps too easy to blame the other parent rather than look at one's own behaviour.

There is also a dispute between experts as to the role of the resident parent in alienating the child. It may be family conflict that is causing the 'alienated behaviours' rather than the actions of the other parent. For one thing, the *non-resident* parent can influence the child in becoming estranged from them through their own conduct. For example, if they respond to the conflict by withdrawing, the child may interpret this as evidence that the parent does not love them, when in fact it may be due to lack of funds to continue litigation, or stress and anxiety, or a belief that the courts are unable to help. Some non-resident parents may also have an overly harsh or rigid parenting style, or behave angrily or dismissively towards the child, or in a way that is immature and self-centred.[233] They may not be very good parents. In *Re O'Connell*, the children's rejection of their father was caused solely by his behaviour towards their mother.[234] The judge described him as 'conducting a campaign' against her, becoming 'obsessed with his unfounded view' that she was abusively mistreating the children' and being 'blind to the children's needs insofar as they came second to his own plans'. 'The fact that Mr. O'Connell was not enjoying contact with them was entirely his own fault, and nobody else's', he concluded.

Allegations that the other parent is alienating the child can also be the response of someone who is abusive, a way of disguising or diminishing the effect of their own behaviour. There is a gendered element to this—most (but not all) domestic abusers in family cases are male, and alienation is an allegation made against the resident parent who is usually the mother. Alienation allegations have been seen as a way of silencing abuse victims and deflecting attention from the best interests of the child.[235] In such situations, the child's opposition has a rational basis.

---

[232] See RA Gardner, 'Parental Alienation Syndrome vs. Parental Alienation: Which Diagnosis Should Evaluators Use in Child-Custody Disputes?' (2002) 30 *The American Journal of Family Therapy* 93, in which Gardner, who 'founded' the concept, argues that it is a syndrome.

[233] JB Kelly and JR Johnston, 'The Alienated Child: A Reformulation of Parental Alienation Syndrome' (2001) 39(3) *Family Court Review* 249. See also S Friedlander and M Gans Walters, 'When a Child Rejects a Parent: Tailoring the Intervention to Fit the Problem' (2010) 48(1) *Family Court Review* 98. It therefore follows that the alienated parent will need to reverse these behaviours to help overcome alienation: see EM Ellis, 'Help for the Alienated Parent' (2005) 33(5) *American Journal of Family Therapy* 415.

[234] [2006] EWCA Civ 1199.

[235] See, for a critique, see 'Collective Memo of Concern to the World Health Organisation re Inclusion of "Parental Alienation" as a "Caregiver-Child Relationship Problem" Code QE52.0 in the *International Classification of Diseases 11th Revision*', 13 May 2019. Available at http://www.learningtoendabuse.ca/collective-memo-of-concern-to-WHO-about-parental-alienation.html accessed 14 May 2019.

Even in high-conflict separations where it is common for each parent to express neg-ative sentiments about the other parent to the child, most children continue to long for and seek contact with both parents' even if they say the opposite.[236] Labelling a situation as 'alienation' may entrench the parties further, when what is needed is cooperation by both parents.[237]

There is also some evidence that children can become estranged from a parent without being exposed to the parental behaviours listed above.[238] So why then do some children become estranged while others in similar situations do not? The answer is that we do not know for certain. Kelly and Johnston have suggested that it is a response to 'complex and frightening dynamics within the divorce [or separation] process itself, to an array of parental behaviours, and also to their own vulnerabilities that make them susceptible'.[239] These may include the child's age and temperament, the level of hostility or humiliation in the parents' separation and the parents' reactions and personalities. Different factors may combine in such a way to trigger a profound breakdown in the relationship.

Addressing unjustified opposition to contact

Courts are understandably reluctant to allow a recalcitrant parent to block contact that they believe to be in the child's interests and may well use a combination of positive and negative tools (including enforcement mechanisms) to get contact going. There are a num-ber of strategies to address a situation where a child or their resident parent has a profound and unjustified opposition to contact, although Doughty et al. have been critical of the lack of robust evaluation of the options.[240] Most strategies discussed by alienation researchers involve psycho-educational approaches with the children and their parents. Garber, for example, recommends specialised therapeutic intervention, to redirect the parents' needs, avoid blame, and restore the child's healthy role within the family.[241] Children can some-times be resistant to this because they feel that the problems that have arisen are caused by adult(s) and not by them.[242] There is, however, no power to compel parents to under-go 'medical treatment', although the court can apply persuasion and can require parents to attend parenting classes as a form of activity direction (see 10.7.1). Simply waiting for spontaneous resolution or letting the child decide if and when to spend time with the other parent is unlikely to work,[243] although some alienated children do seek out their estranged parent when they are older.

---

[236] BJ Fidler and N Bala, 'Children Resisting Postseparation Contact with a Parent: Concepts, Controversies, and Conundrums' (2010) 48(1) *Family Court Review* 10, 11.

[237] See, for example, the nuanced position taken by Cohen J in *PA v CK and Others* [2018] EWHC 2004(Fam).

[238] BJ Fidler and N Bala, 'Children Resisting Postseparation Contact with a Parent: Concepts, Controversies, and Conundrums' (2010) 48(1) *Family Court Review* 10, 11.

[239] JB Kelly and JR Johnston, 'The Alienated Child: A Reformulation of Parental Alienation Syndrome' (2001) 39(3) *Family Court Review* 249.

[240] J Doughty, N Maxwell, and T Slater, *Review of Research and Case Law on Parental Alienation* (Cardiff Univer-sity Children's Social Care Research and Development Centre/Cafcass Cymru 2018) 25.

[241] B Garber, 'Parental Alienation and the Dynamics of the Enmeshed Parent–Child Dyad: Adultification, Paren-tification, and Infantilisation' (2011) 49(2) *Family Court Review* 322.

[242] K Weir, 'Clinical Advice to Courts on Children's Contact with Their Parents following Parental Separation' (2006) 11(1) *Child and Adolescent Mental Health* 40.

[243] K Templer, M Matthewson, J Haines, and G Cox, 'Recommendations for Best Practice in Response to Parental Alienation: Findings from a Systematic Review' (2016) *Journal of Family Therapy* 1.

Weir argues that it is crucial that contact continues or restarts immediately, and is not deferred until after such therapy has taken place.[244] As we discussed at section 10.7.2, if the child arrangements order is breached, the court can impose sanctions including fines, imprisonment, and unpaid work requirements, on the resident parent. Lowenstein found that the combination of therapy backed up by court sanctions was effective.[245] Judicial continuity and active case management are therefore likely to be important.[246]

SCENARIO 3

Illustration 6: Claire, Ellie, and son Jacob (10)

Contact has broken down. If the court believes that spending time with Ellie is in Jacob's best interests (the most important issue!), then it will need to be mindful that the longer the court delays the more difficult it will be to restart contact (see 10.3.4 on the 'no delay' principle). There are, on the facts of this scenario, no allegations of harm, but the relationship breakdown has caused bad feeling and upset. The court may want to take a carrot-and-stick approach, using a combination of positive tools to try to help the parties to come to terms with the new situation but set out clear expectations with sanctions for non-compliance.

SCENARIO 4

Illustration 7: Sarah, Phil, and children Bill (11), Ben (8), and Bella (4)

Let us take a different approach now: what would happen if the court found that Sarah's opposition to contact or the children's opposition is genuine but disproportionate? Perhaps the abuse allegations have been found to be exaggerated rather than completely untrue, or the court believes that the risk of future harm is manageable. In such a case, the court may take the view that it is in the children's best interests for there to be contact, but faces serious practical difficulties. It is essential to the rule of law that people comply with court orders, but court orders do not win over people. The court may be attracted to using a positive tool such as a family assistance order alongside a contact order. Ultimately, the court would need to decide whether a genuine but disproportionate rejection of Phil is sufficiently against the children's best interests as to justify some of the more serious enforcement mechanisms.

In the most severe cases, or cases in which the above strategies have not succeeded, it may be appropriate to remove the child from the resident parent (perhaps via foster care) to live with the parent from whom they are estranged. *Re R (A Child)*, for example, involved

---

[244] K Weir, 'Clinical Advice to Courts on Children's Contact with Their Parents following Parental Separation' (2006) 11(1) *Child and Adolescent Mental Health* 40.

[245] LF Lowenstein, 'Parental Alienation Syndrome: A Two Step Approach toward a Solution' (1998) 20 *Contemporary Family Therapy* 505.

[246] M Shaw and J Bazley QC, 'Effective Strategies in High Conflict Contact Disputes' (2011) *Family Law* 1129.

KEY CASE *Re M (Children)* [2012] EWHC 1948 (Fam)

Two boys, aged 10 and 8, lived with their mother and had contact with their father under a child arrangements order. After contact broke down, the father applied for an order that the children live with him.

The judge, Peter Jackson J, found that the mother did not believe the children should have any relationship with their father or his wider family. She had moved hundreds of miles away from the father, taking the children with her, without telling anyone where they had gone, and unilaterally changed the children's surnames from that of their father. She was influencing the children to speak negatively about their father and refuse contact. Over time, their relationship with their father had progressed from hugging him to saying that they wanted him dead. They were acting out of loyalty to their mother.

The judge made a conditional residence order in favour of the father: the condition was that the children would move to live with him if, and only if, the mother breached the contact order again. A further breach would tip the scales towards it being in their best interests to live with their father.

a long-running child arrangements case in which there are many examples of alienated behaviour by the 11-year-old child, and some behaviour by the resident mother that could be called alienating.[247] The child's interests were represented by a Litigation Guardian and a child psychologist also prepared a report. Contact with the non-resident father was taking place, but while there was evidence that the child enjoyed the contact, he was unable to admit that. The Guardian took the view that the mother was unable to separate her feelings about the father from the needs of their child. The judge held that it was in his best interests to move to live with his father and stepmother, with the mother having contact time.

Even if a court is not minded to transfer residence, judges may use the threat of transfer as leverage for future compliance, as in Key Case *Re M (Children)*. As with all other transfers of residence that we discussed at 10.7.3, this must be because it is in the child's best interests for them to have a relationship with both parents, rather than as a form of punishment for the child and resident parent, although they may well experience it as such.

Templer et al. reviewed a number of studies and concluded that a change of residence was 'an effective strategy for improving parent–child relationships and reducing distress', even though the child is being removed from the care of their favoured parent.[248] That this is an appropriate route is, however, contested by the very distinguished signatories to one paper, who argue that 'we do not know much, if anything, about the impact of removal of children from their preferred parent' but that 'removing children from preferred primary-care parents is contrary to research on child resilience, recovery from trauma and accepted child development principles'.[249] Even if it is in the child's best interests, it may not be practically possible if the non-resident parent is unable to assume primary care.

---

247 [2009] EWHC B38 (Fam). See also *Re X, Y and Z (Children: Agreed Transfer of Residence)* [2021] EWFC 18.

248 K Templer, M Matthewson, J Haines, and G Cox, 'Recommendations for Best Practice in Response to Parental Alienation: Findings from a Systematic Review' (2016) *Journal of Family Therapy* 1.

249 'Collective Memo of Concern to the World Health Organisation re Inclusion of "Parental Alienation" as a "Caregiver-Child Relationship Problem" Code QE52.0 in the *International Classification of Diseases 11th Revision*', 13 May 2019. Available at http://www.learningtoendabuse.ca/collective-memo-of-concern-to-WHO-about-parental-alienation.html accessed 14 May 2019.

In the short term, continued attempts at establishing contact can cause the child to experience real distress and physical symptoms, such as stomach aches, triggered by that distress. The child is likely to feel that he or she has not been listened to. A change of residence may involve a change of school or friends. Many judges are reluctant to adopt a firm approach for fear of causing distress to the child, and may instead proceed cautiously over a period of time. They may, for example, start with appointing a guardian to represent the child's interest independently of the parents,[250] or try different patterns or methods of contact in an attempt to find one that works. But, if they do not address the situation firmly, it may get worse. Some studies argue that in adulthood, as well as in childhood, a child who has unjustifiably rejected a parent may suffer from low self-esteem, self-hatred, lack of trust, depression, and substance abuse problems; and in due course they are much more likely to become estranged from their own children.[251] (We need to take these studies with a pinch of salt because we do not know what other factors may be influencing the situation.[252]) Courts have to balance increased short-term upset and disruption against the existing emotional harm to the child of being alienated and the risk of further long-term adverse effects. There are, ultimately, no easy solutions—and not many hard ones either.

Alienation is a controversial subject which has attracted considerable research, but where criticism that can be made of the methods used in that research and where there are great gaps in the knowledge base. That does not make it easy for judges, lawyers—or students. The reality is that 'alienation' is a phrase that gets bandied around a great deal and probably in many cases where the situation is far more nuanced. Finally, although *allegations* that one party has alienated the child against the other are relatively common, the research shows that actual findings of alienation are relatively rare. Although estimates are difficult because of the lack of an agreed definition, Cafcass Cymri found alienation in only 3 of 25 of its most serious cases[253] and Trinder found that 'implacably hostile parents who unreasonably refused all contact' accounted for only 4 per cent of enforcement applications.[254] They are, though, among the most complex cases in family law.

10.9 Relocating with children

It is not uncommon for a parent to seek to remove a child from the jurisdiction to live permanently in another country. The increasing ability of people to move freely in a global marketplace means that people move more commonly for work or study or to join with

[250] Family Procedure Rules 2010, r16.4.

[251] See AJL Baker, 'The Long-Term Effects of Parental Alienation on Adult Children: A Qualitative Research Study' (2005) 33(4) *The American Journal of Family Therapy* 289; JJ Harman, S Leder-Elder, and Z Biringen, 'Prevalence of Parental Alienation Drawn from a Representative Poll' (2016) 66 *Children and Youth Services Review* 62.

[252] See, for a critique, see 'Collective Memo of Concern to the World Health Organisation re Inclusion of "Parental Alienation" as a "Caregiver-Child Relationship Problem" Code QE52.0 in the *International Classification of Diseases 11th Revision*', 13 May 2019. Available at http://www.learningtoendabuse.ca/collective-memo-of-concern-to-WHO-about-parental-alienation.html accessed 14 May 2019.

[253] S Parsons and J Doughty, Podcast: 'Parental Alienation: What It Is and How It's Different from Implacable Hostility' (5 September 2018). Available at https://www.communitycare.co.uk/2018/09/05/parental-alienation-different-implacable-hostility/. See also testimony to the Welsh Assembly by Cafcass at 10.38.04 minutes (Nigel Brown) http://record.assembly.wales/Committee/4755#A43065 which explains how they arrived at that figure.

[254] L Trinder, J Hunt, A Macleod, J Pearce, and H Woodward, *Enforcing Contact Orders: Problem-Solving or Punishment?* (University of Exeter/Nuffield Foundation 2013).

romantic partners that they have met online. Prior to the UK's departure from the EU, there was free movement of workers between the UK and EU. Relocation may bring economic or practical benefits. It may enable a child to understand another part of his or her heritage or see more of the world. It may involve relocation to the country of origin. Perhaps this was always the plan, or perhaps the parent seeking to relocate is doing so because they feel isolated in the UK and want to be closer to their family in the country of origin.

If a family wishes to move together, that is not a child law problem. They simply move abroad, obtaining visas and permits and leave to remains if they require it. The family unit is together.

The problem arises when one parent in a separated family wishes to move abroad with the child or children, and the other parent opposes this. In the vast majority of relocation cases, it is the mother who is the parent wishing to relocate (this is because the vast majority of resident parents are women). For that reason, and for clarity and convenience, we are going to simply say 'she' for the parent wishing to relocate and 'he' for the father of the children who wishes to stop them leaving the country.

In this section, we consider both international relocations and internal relocations within the UK. While the former can present a considerable logistical difficulty to continuing contact, so can the latter, because it is possible to move further within the UK than between certain parts of the UK and the continent. As Henaghan says, 'relocation cases challenge the dominant solution to parental separation', which is that both parents should play a significant continuing role in their children's lives.[255]

10.9.1 The legal framework for international relocation

The consent of all those with parental responsibility is needed to remove a child from the UK, whether permanently or temporarily. If this consent is not forthcoming, then either the parent seeking to relocate will need to apply for leave to remove the children from the jurisdiction by way of a specific issues application under s8 Children Act 1989 or the person seeking to prevent relocation will need to apply for a s8 prohibited steps order. Removal of the children without the necessary consents may mean that the relocating parent commits a criminal offence under Child Abduction Act 1984 and if an existing order is in place may be in contempt of court.

If the relocating parent is the only person with parental responsibility, no other consents are required. However, there are two important caveats. First, a parent who wishes to block relocation can apply for a prohibited steps order and if this is the father he does not need prior leave to make an application even if he does not have parental responsibility. Second, even when the parent seeking to relocate is the sole person with parental responsibility, the Hague Convention on Child Abduction, which is a common mechanism for forcing a return, looks at whether the parent seeking return is exercising rights of custody, and the left behind parent may be doing so even if he does not have PR.

Where there is a child arrangements order in force stating with whom the child is to live (formerly known as a residence order) s13 Children Act 1989 enables the resident

---

[255] M Henaghan, 'Relocation Cases – The Rhetoric and the Reality of a Child's Best Interests – A View from the Bottom of the World' (2011) 23(2) *Child and Family Law Quarterly* 226.

parent to remove the child from the UK for up to one month without the consent of all those with PR or the leave of the court. Where the parent wishes to remove the child for longer, or permanently, an application can therefore be made for leave under s13 as an alternative to s8. Removal or retention for longer than one month without court approval or others' consent could constitute child abduction. Technically, the welfare checklist does not apply to applications under s13, but, as Black LJ said in Key Case *Re C (A Child) (Internal Relocation)*

> the courts have nonetheless treated it as if it were . . . This is sensible and unsurprising because the welfare checklist is a useful *aide memoire* and because any other approach would lead to an artificial situation in which the outcome of a case might depend upon the precise form of the application made initiating it, whether for leave under s13 or for a s8 order.[256]

10.9.2 The traditional approach to international relocation

As this is an issue which affects the upbringing of a child, the court will apply the welfare principle contained in s1 Children Act 1989 and (as observed in Key Case *Re C*) the welfare checklist. The presumption of involvement will apply, either because the court will be considering a s8 application or on the same basis as the welfare checklist.

The traditional approach gives considerable weight to the wishes of the relocating parent in the decision about whether or not it is in the best interests of the children to move abroad. We can see this in two early cases.

In *Poel v Poel*, the mother and father had a 2-year-old son, but were divorced. The father saw the child for several hours per week.[257] The mother had remarried. She and her husband sought to relocate to New Zealand where the latter had good job prospects. At first instance, the judge refused the relocation application. However, the Court of Appeal held that the mother should be allowed to take the child to New Zealand. Winn LJ considered that 'the child's happiness is directly dependent not only upon the health and happiness of his own mother but upon her freedom from the very likely repercussions, of an adverse character, which would result' from a decision to refuse permission. Such refusal would affect 'her relations with her new husband and her ability to look after her family peacefully and in a psychological frame of ease'. Similarly, in *Chamberlain v de la Mare*, which concerned a mother's application to relocate to New York for her new husband's job, Griffiths LJ said:

> The welfare of young children is best served by bringing them up in a happy, secure family atmosphere. When, after divorce, the parent who has custody of the children remarries, those children then join and become members of a new family and it is the happiness and security of that family on which their welfare will depend. However painful it may be for the other parent, that parent has got to grasp and appreciate that fact.
>
> If a step-father, for the purposes of his career, is required to live elsewhere, the natural thing would be that he will wish to take his family, which now includes his step-children, with him, and if the court refuses to allow him to take the step-children with him, . . . that

256 [2015] EWCA Civ 1305At [21].
257 [1970] 1 WLR 1469 (CA).

may well spill over into a sense of resentment against the step-children who have so interfered with his future career prospects. If that happens it must reflect upon the happiness and possibly even the stability of this second marriage.[258]

The *Poel* and *Chamberlain* approaches therefore treat what is best for the child as being what is best for the primary carer and her new family, in that it would affect the child's welfare if the adults with whom they lived were unhappy or destabilised. *Poel* is a case from 1970 and *Chamberlain* from 1983. They influenced a lengthy line of subsequent cases in which relocation applications were likely to be successful.

In 2001, when society looked somewhat different, the Court of Appeal decided the case *Payne v Payne*. Until recently, this was the leading case on relocation.

KEY CASE *Payne v Payne* [2001] EWCA Civ 166

The mother was a New Zealander resident in the UK who, post-divorce, sought permission to relocate back to New Zealand with her 4-year-old daughter, Sophie. The evidence showed that the mother had struggled as a single parent whose family and friends were not close by. She and Sophie lived in a one-bedroom flat and Sophie spent long days at nursery while the mother worked. The father saw her regularly and she had a strong relationship with him and with her paternal grandmother.

At first instance, the mother's application to relocate was successful. The father appealed.

The mother argued that there was a presumption that a primary carer would be permitted to relocate unless the court concluded that this would be incompatible with the welfare of the children. The father argued that the approach taken in *Poel* and *Chamberlain* could not survive the Human Rights Act 1998 and the ECHR case law which required the rights of each parent and the child to be balanced, with the child's interests being paramount.[259]

The Court of Appeal held:

- The welfare of the child was the paramount consideration under s1 Children Act 1989 and the welfare checklist applied. Article 8 ECHR required the rights of the parties to be balanced and any interference had to be proportionate, but domestic law was not incompatible with this.[260]
- There was no presumption in favour of relocation. However, 'the underlying principles in *Poel v Poel*, as explained in *Chamberlain v de la Mare*, have stood the test of time and give valuable guidance as to the approach the court should adopt in these most difficult cases.'[261] The 'reasonable proposals of the parent with a residence order wishing to live abroad carry great weight'.[262] 'The effect upon the applicant parent and the new family of the child of a refusal of leave is very important.'[263]
- The proposals 'have to be scrutinised with care and the court needs to be satisfied that there is a genuine motivation for the move and not the intention to bring contact between the child and the other parent to an end.'[264] The effect upon the child of the denial of contact

---

[258] (1983) 4 FLR 434 (CA).
[259] This is discussed at 9.6.1.
[260] At [82] (Butler-Sloss P).
[261] At [83] (Butler-Sloss P).
[262] At [85] (Butler-Sloss P).
[263] At [85] (Butler-Sloss P).
[264] At [85] (Butler-Sloss P).

with the other parent and in some cases his family is very important, as is the opportunity for continuing contact.[265]

Thorpe LJ used his judgment to provide a set of guidelines designed to guard against 'too perfunctory an investigation resulting from too ready an assumption that the mother's proposals are necessarily compatible with the child's welfare'. These are known as the 'Payne Discipline':

(a) 'Is the mother's application genuine in the sense that it is not motivated by some selfish desire to exclude the father from the child's life? Then ask, is the mother's application realistic, by which I mean founded on practical proposals both well researched and investigated? If the application fails either of these tests, refusal will inevitably follow.

(b) If, however, the application passes these tests then there must be a careful appraisal of the father's opposition: is it motivated by genuine concern for the future of the child's welfare or is it driven by some ulterior motive? What would be the extent of the detriment to him and his future relationship with the child were the application granted? To what extent would that be offset by extension of the child's relationships with the maternal family and homeland?

(c) What would be the impact on the mother, either as the single parent or as a new wife, of a refusal of her realistic proposal?[266]

(d) The outcome of the second and third appraisals must then be brought into an overriding review of the child's welfare as the paramount consideration, directed by the statutory checklist in so far as appropriate.'[267]

The Court of Appeal held that the first instance judge had approached the case correctly and his decision was upheld.

Even though *Payne* tells us that there is no legal presumption in favour of relocation, *Payne* follows the approach taken in the earlier cases by giving significant weight to the happiness of the primary carer who wishes to relocate family at the expense of the child's relationship with the non-resident parent and the potentially significant impact on contact. It invites a strategy wherein the primary carer emphasises to the court how refusal of what she wants will have a harmful effect upon the child. In this way, the child's welfare is subsumed into that of his primary carer.

10.9.3 The current approach to international relocation

Poel, *Chamberlain*, and *Payne* all involved mothers as primary carers in situations in which the fathers had contact but not daily care. Our next Key Case, *K v K (Children: Permanent Removal from Jurisdiction)*, involved a shared residence situation. In this case, the Court of Appeal held that there should be no difference in approach between cases in which the person wishing to relocate was the primary carer and those in which care was shared between the parties to a greater extent.

This case, rather than *Payne*, now represents the starting point for international relocation cases.

---

[265] At [85] (Butler-Sloss P).
[266] The later conjoined cases *Re B (Children) (Removal from Jurisdiction)* and *Re S (A Child) (Removal from Jurisdiction)* [2003] EWCA Civ 1149 also considered the effect of refusal on a step-parent.
[267] Para [40] (Thorpe LJ).

KEY CASE *K v K (Children Permanent Removal from Jurisdiction)*
[2011] EWCA Civ 793

There were two children. Following the parents' divorce, the court made a shared residence order (which would now be called a shared 'live with' order) under which the children spent five nights with the father and nine with the mother each fortnight. The parents each worked only part-time, enabling this arrangement. The mother was Canadian and sought permission under s13 to remove the children to Canada. The Cafcass officer recommended against granting permission but at first instance the mother was successful. The father appealed.

The Court of Appeal allowed the appeal.

Per Moore-Blick LJ at [86]:

The only principle of law enunciated in *Payne v Payne* is that the welfare of the child is paramount; all the rest is guidance. Such difficulty as has arisen is the result of treating that guidance as if it contained principles of law from which no departure is permitted. Guidance of the kind provided in *Payne v Payne* is, of course, very valuable both in ensuring that judges identify what are likely to be the most important factors to be taken into account and the weight that should generally be attached to them. It also plays a valuable role in promoting consistency in decision-making. However, the circumstances in which these difficult decisions have to be made vary infinitely and the judge in each case must be free to weigh up the individual factors and make whatever decision he or she considers to be in the best interests of the child.

Per Black LJ at [142]-[143]:

Whilst [the paramountcy of the child's welfare] is the only truly inescapable principle in the jurisprudence, that does not mean that everything else—the valuable guidance—can be ignored. It must be heeded for all the reasons that Moore-Bick LJ gives but as guidance not as rigid principle or so as to dictate a particular outcome in a sphere of law where the facts of individual cases are so infinitely variable.

Furthermore, the effect of the guidance must not be overstated. Even where the case concerns a true primary carer, there is no presumption that the reasonable relocation plans of that carer will be facilitated unless there is some compelling reason to the contrary, nor any similar presumption however it may be expressed.

As *K v K* was a Court of Appeal decision and *Payne* a House of Lords decision, the former cannot overrule the latter and is bound by it. However, the Court of Appeal interpreted Payne as simply providing guidance and not presumptions. In *Re F (International Relocation)*, Ryder LJ suggested that a judgment that included

selective or partial legal citation from *Payne* without any wider legal analysis is likely to be regarded as an error of law. In particular, a judgment that not only focuses solely on *Payne* but also compounds that error by only referring to the [*Payne* discipline] is likely to be wholly wrong.[268]

---

[268] [2015] EWCA Civ 882 at [27].

In *Re C (Internal Relocation)* Vos LJ said that:

> one of the valid concerns about the Payne factors is that they do not adequately reflect the gender-neutral approach to these problems that the court will now adopt in every case. Whilst the *Payne* principles may still be of some utility in some cases, they are no part of the applicable test for the applicable principles. In some circumstances, the judge may find them useful. In others, the judge may not, If the judge finds them a useful guide to some of the factors that he should consider, he will be doing so only as part of the multi-factorial balancing exercise that is required.[269]

Following *K v K*, therefore, the proper approach is that the child's welfare is the paramount consideration. *Payne* may be helpful in providing guidance as to what factors courts should look at. However, a proper welfare determination involves an assessment of all factors relevant to the child's welfare and these will be case-specific. *Payne* is not to be used to suggest that some factors, such as the effect of refusal on the parent wishing to relocate, are automatically more important. The importance of the factors will vary from case to case.

10.9.4 Relevant considerations pertaining to the child's best interests

If, as a lawyer, you are acting for a person who is making an application to relocate, you will need to persuade the court that relocation is in the children's best interests. It is therefore very helpful to have a careful plan for housing and for the children's future education and medical care. The court will want to know that the proposals are realistic and not speculative. It will also be essential for the relocating parent to make proposals for contact with the parent left behind and any relevant other members of the family. This could be in-person contact, such as during school holidays if the relocation distance is great, and/or contact by telephone or videocalling. It may be relevant to consider whether, where relocation is international, the country to which the applicant wishes to move will reciprocally enforce a contact order and/or whether a mirror order—an order in the same terms but made in the foreign court—is necessary. With some exceptions, once a child becomes habitually resident in another country, our domestic courts will no longer have jurisdiction.[270]

A key aspect of relocation cases is the effect on the adults of the granting or refusal of permission. This is only relevant insofar as it affects the children. A parent seeking to prevent removal may emphasise the loss of a particular heritage or culture. As we have already noted, the welfare of the child is often tied to that of their primary carer and a lawyer acting for that person will wish to emphasise the negative effect that refusal would have on their ability to care for the child. As many parents move for economic reasons, the benefits to the child of greater financial security, which can include better outcomes on a range of different criteria including education, are also relevant. Remember, though, that at 9.2.3 we discussed the different trends in relocation approvals in England and Wales compared

---

[269] [2015] EWCA Civ 1305.
[270] Under Brussels II Revised, the original state of habitual residence retains jurisdiction for the first three months. This Regulation is discussed at 10.10.5.

to courts in New Zealand, highlighting that welfare-based appraisals are seen through the prism of the culture of the home country.

There is not necessarily a straight decision between remaining and relocating. An application to relocate may trigger (or be a response to) an application by the other parent to increase their level of time with the child. A court may therefore need to decide with whom the child should live: should it be with parent A in the UK; with parent B in the UK; or with parent B in country X?

At 10.3.2, we used the judgment in Key Case *S v G* to illustrate how a judge may undertake the task of determining where the child's welfare lies by reference to the welfare checklist. That was a relocation case, so you may wish to turn to 10.3.2 to remind yourself of it. The authors of *Relocation: A Practical Guide* have suggested that the judgment of Baker J in *Re S (Relocation: Pakistan)* also provides 'a good explanation' of how the court should approach a holistic welfare analysis.[271]

FOCUS Think Critically

Effect of relocation on the children and their parents

In 2009, Marilyn Freeman published a review of the effect of relocation decisions on the parties and the children in the two-year period following the decision.[272] She found that:

- 'Children are regularly "lost" to left-behind parents through the relocation decisions made by the United Kingdom courts. . . . Many parents complained that there were constant problems in exercising the contact that had been ordered by the court granting permission to relocate.'[273]
- 'Several parents reported that indirect contact, which is often part of a contact order and is designed to supplement the infrequent physical visits between a parent and child, rarely happens and cannot be relied upon as a method of maintaining contact.'[274]
- 'Many left-behind parents spoke of the devastation that the relocation has brought to their lives. . . . Depression is a common experience for such parents.'[275]
- The usual feedback from relocating mothers is that the move has worked well for them and their children.[276]

Note that this study attracted predominantly fathers who had unsuccessfully sought to stop relocation so does not provide a full picture of the benefits to the mothers or the children concerned, or those fathers who did not previously have a close relationship with their children.

A different perspective on relocation would be that parents who wish to relocate are in search of a better life. Some are returning to their country of origin where they have family who are able to provide support. Some are taking advantage of greater economic prospects in a new country which

---

[271] [2015] EWHC 3288. R George, F Judd QC, D Garrido QC, and A Wormwood, *Relocation: A Practical Guide* (2nd edn, *Family Law* 2016).
[272] M Freeman, *Relocation: The Reunite Research* (Reunite and the Ministry of Justice 2009). There are several reports by Professor Freeman on the same issue.
[273] Page 14.
[274] Page 14.
[275] Page 26.
[276] Page 26.

would, economically at least, benefit the children concerned. As such, as Behrens argues, 'restrictions on relocation operate unfairly against the person who is likely to be providing the majority of care to a child. In doing so, they compound the social and economic disadvantages that accompany the provision of care, particularly where the caregiver is a woman'.[277]

A study by Horsfall and Kaspiew in Australia found that the 'research evidence on the positive or negative impact of relocation on parent and child well-being and outcomes can be said to be equivocal at best'. The positive attitude of the relocating parent was a key factor in children's ability to positively adapt to the move.[278]

10.9.5 Internal relocation

While we have looked at international relocation at length, not all international relocation cases involve moving as far away as is it is possible to move internally within the UK. A parent who moves from Norfolk to Scotland, for example, is removing a child further away from the other parent than if they move from Norfolk to the Netherlands, and travel between the two for the purposes of contact may be more difficult. Neither the Hague Convention or Brussels II Revised, which assist in international relocation cases, apply between the constituent states of the UK or its dependents, which are treated as one state for the purposes of those agreements.

Where the child has been moved to another part of the United Kingdom, the Isle of Man or Jersey (but not the other Channel Islands), the Family Law Act 1996 provides for the recognition and enforcement throughout these countries of any order specified in Part I of the Act, which include section 8 orders, special guardianship orders, orders for contact during placement for adoption and post-adoption, care or supervision orders, orders under the Child Abduction and Custody Act 1985, and 'orders made by a court in England and Wales in the exercise of the inherent jurisdiction of the High Court with respect to children'. Any person who is the beneficiary of one of these orders can apply to register that order in another part of the UK. However, there is no summary return procedure.[279]

Given the potential disruption to the relationship between the children and the parent left behind, we need to look at whether the courts approach internal relocation cases in the same way as international relocation cases.

The traditional position is that the courts will not usually stand in the way of a parent wishing to relocate internally nor impose conditions on the move. Such conditions might be under s11(7) Children Act 1989 or by way of s8 specific issues or prohibited steps order.

As Butler-Sloss LJ said in *Re E (Residence: Imposition of Conditions)*, 'a restriction upon the right of the carer of the child to choose where to live sits uneasily with the general understanding of what is meant by residence order' and that 'where the parent is entirely suitable and the court intends to make a residence order in favour of that parent, a condition of residence is in my view an unwarranted imposition upon the right of the parent to choose where he/she will live within the UK or with whom.'[280] In *Re S (A Child)(Residence*

---

[277] J Behrens, '*U v U*: The High Court on Relocation' [2003] *Melbourne University Law Review* 572, 584.
[278] B Horsfall and R Kaspiew, 'Relocation in Separated and Non-Separated Families: Equivocal Evidence From the Social Science Literature' (2010) 24 *Australian Journal of Family Law* 34.
[279] *Re R* [2016] EWCA Civ 1016.
[280] [1997] EWCA Civ 3084 at [21].

Order: Condition), Clarke LJ said that a condition should only be imposed 'in genuinely exceptional cases' and that 'no case will be exceptional unless the absence of such a condition would be incompatible with the welfare of the child'.[281] However, *Re S* was, on the facts, an exceptional case because of the combination of the child's disability and medical problems, the limits of her understanding, her foreshortened life expectancy, and the practicalities of travel between south London and Cornwall.[282]

In Key Case *Re C (A Child) (Internal Relocation)* Black LJ said that she could see no rational basis for treating internal and external relocation cases differently.

KEY CASE *Re C (A Child) (Internal Relocation)* [2015] EWCA Civ 1305

C, who was aged 10, lived with her mother in London and spent two nights per week and every other weekend with her father, who lived close by. The mother wanted to move to Cumbria (about 300 miles from London) where she had family. This would have meant the father and daughter saw one another less often. The father applied for a shared 'live with' order under s8 Children Act, and the mother a specific issues order permitting her to move the child's school to one in Cumbria.

The leading judgment is by Black LJ, who notes that:

> I have not been [able] to identify a convincing explanation for the position that has been adopted, whereby the freedom of a parent to move appears to have been accorded greater weight in internal relocation cases than in external relocation cases. It might be argued that there is greater ease of enforcement of, say, an order providing for the child to spend time with the other parent after relocation if the move is within the UK than if it is not. However, I do not find this argument compelling in the light of the enforcement provisions of Brussels II [revised] and the 1996 Hague Convention. [24] . . . I am at a loss to identify any other obvious justification for keeping internal and external relocation cases in separate compartments.

After reviewing the line of cases on internal relocation, she held that:

> Given the central thread of welfare that runs through all these authorities, and with the reasoning in *K v K* very much in mind, I would not interpret the cases as imposing a supplementary requirement of exceptionality in internal relocation cases. It is no doubt the case, as a matter of fact, that courts will be resistant to preventing a parent from exercising his or her choice as to where to live in the United Kingdom unless the child's welfare requires it, but that is not because of a rule that such a move can only be prevented in exceptional cases. It is because the welfare analysis leads to that conclusion. One can see from the authorities, and indeed from this case, that the courts are much pre-occupied in relocation cases, whether internal or external, with the practicalities of the child spending time with the other parent or, putting it another way, with seeing if there is a way in which the move can be made to work, thus looking after the interests not only of the child but also of both of his or her parents. Only where it cannot, and the child's welfare requires that the move is prevented, does that happen.

She concluded that the same approach should be taken to internal relocation cases as to international relocations following Key Case *K v K*, namely that the single relevant consideration is the child's welfare with no presumptions as to exceptionality.

---

[281] [2001] EWCA Civ 847 at [35]-[37].

[282] This case was remitted after the first appeal and the decision made the second time was appealed a second time at [2002] EWCA Civ 1795.

In *BB v CC* a first instance decision to make a shared residence order with the condition that the mother relocate to be closer to the father was upheld on appeal.[283]

10.10 Child abduction

Most abductors of children are those children's mothers. The Child Abduction Act 1984 and the Children Act 1989 both create specific offences relating to the abduction of children. In addition to that, there are two important international agreements which seek to provide fast resolutions to child abductions by returning the children from the state to which they have been abducted back to their country of habitual residence.

10.10.1 Abduction under the Child Abduction Act 1984

The Child Abduction Act 1984 creates criminal offences of removing a child from the UK without the appropriate consent or removing or detaining a child from a person who has lawful control of him. Note the reference to the UK—it is not abduction to remove a child to Scotland or Northern Ireland even though they are separate legal jurisdictions to England and Wales.

Section 1 offences and defences

> **STATUTORY EXTRACT** *s1 Child Abduction Act 1984*
>
> Offence of abduction of child by parent, etc.
> (1) Subject to subsections (5) and (8) below, a person connected with a child under the age of sixteen commits an offence if he takes or sends the child out of the United Kingdom without the appropriate consent.

Under s1 an offence is committed by a connected person, not a stranger. A connected person, i.e., the person who can commit an offence, is defined in s1(2) as a parent; guardian; special guardian; a person named in a child arrangements order as a person with whom the child is to live; a man who is not married to the mother but in respect of whom there are reasonable grounds for believing that he is the father; or someone who has custody of the child. Unlike kidnapping, therefore, child abduction relates exclusively to those abductors who fall into specified categories of relationship to the child. However, note that an offence can be committed by someone who 'sends' the child out of the UK, such as with a person who is not connected.

The appropriate consent means the consent of each of the child's mother; a father with parental responsibility; any guardian or special guardian; any person named in a child arrangements order as a person with whom the child is to live; and any person who has custody of the child (who may include a local authority if the child is in care); or the leave of the court. A person shall be treated as having custody of a child 'if there is in force an order of a court in the United Kingdom awarding him (whether solely or jointly with another person)

---

[283] Unreported other than on Westlaw, [2018] 10 WLUK 627.

custody, legal custody or care and control of the child'. The consent of the court will also be needed prior any removal from the jurisdiction where the child is a ward of court.

It is a defence to a s1 abduction if the abductor believes that the other person(s) have consented or would consent if aware of all the relevant circumstances, or where the abductor has taken all reasonable steps to communicate with the other person but has been unable to communicate with him; or the other person has unreasonably refused to consent.

Unless the court says otherwise, s13 Children Act 1989 permits a person with whom a child lives under a child arrangements order to remove the child from the UK for up to one month without others' consent; the period is three months for special guardians.[284] In these situations no offence would be committed under s1 providing that the child was returned within these periods. Where there is no 'live with' or special guardianship order, a person can only remove the child from the UK with the consent of all of the other PR holders, or the court's permission by way of a s8 specific issues application. This is the case whether removal is temporary, such as for a holiday, or permanent. It is not uncommon in practice to be contacted by primary carers who have booked a holiday and only found out subsequently that they need the consent of the other parent, and sometimes that person cannot be found. In this situation, a court application will need to be made in preference to relying on a defence under the Child Abduction Act. It is not sensible to risk arrest or prosecution. However, many parents do not realise that taking a child abroad without the other parent's permission may constitute child abduction.

SCENARIO 4

Illustration 8: Sarah, Phil, and children Bill (11), Ben (8), and Bella (4)

Let us alter this scenario and suppose that Sarah wishes to move permanently to another jurisdiction with the children. As she was married to Phil, as the children's father he has parental responsibility for them. This means that she would need either the court's permission or Phil's permission to relocate.

What if she did not get consent and just moved? As we have seen, this would be child abduction under the 1984 Act. She is a connected person, and she has removed the children from the UK without appropriate consent. A number of defences are available to her.

Section 2 offences and defences

STATUTORY EXTRACT *s2 Child Abduction Act 1984*

Offence of abduction of child by other persons
(1) Subject to subsection (3) below, a person, other than one mentioned in subsection (2) below, commits an offence if, without lawful authority or reasonable excuse, he takes or detains a child under the age of sixteen
   (a) so as to remove him from the lawful control of any person having lawful control of the child; or
   (b) so as to keep him out of the lawful control of any person entitled to lawful control of the child.

---

[284] Section 1(4) Child Abduction Act 1984 amended; see also s13 Children Act 1989.

Section 2 makes it an offence if, without lawful authority or reasonable excuse, a person removes or detains a child from a person having lawful control of him (whether or not they take them out of the UK). Unlike under s1, this offence can therefore be committed by any person. Indeed, no s2 offence is committed by a person who is a s1 connected person. It is a defence to show that the person who has abducted the child is the child's father (not being married to the mother) or someone who at the time of the offence had reasonable grounds to believe he was the father; or that the defendant believed that the child was aged 16 or over.

Section 3 provides that a person takes a child if they cause or induce the child to accompany them, which is a question of objective fact.[285] In *R v Pringle*, the defendants were aged 20 and 18 and had taken two 13-year-old girls, who had truanted from school, to a nearby woodland, thus removing them from the lawful control of the girls by their school.[286]

10.10.2 Abduction of a child from care

There is a separate offence, within the Children Act 1989, of abducting a child from care. Section 49 makes it an offence to 'knowingly and without lawful authority or reasonable excuse' take a child away from the 'responsible person'; keep the child away from the responsible person; or induce, assist or incite a child to run away or stay away from the responsible person. The offence only applies in relation to a child who is in care, the subject of an emergency protection order, or under s46 police protection.[287] The responsible person is the person who for the time being has care of the child by virtue of a care or emergency protection order or s46.

An offence under s49 is most likely to arise where a parent whose child has been removed by the police or the local authority simply removes the child or retains them after contact. Note that where the child is accommodated under s20 Children Act 1989 the state has no power to prevent the parent from removing the child and doing so would not be abduction. The local authority in such a situation would need to apply for a care order.

10.10.3 Preventing child abduction

There are several legal and practical steps that can be taken to prevent an anticipated abduction from taking place or an attempted abduction from being successful.

Preventing travel

Where removal is anticipated, the person wishing to prevent the removal could apply for a prohibited steps order forbidding the potential abductor from removing the children from the jurisdiction or a particular locality. This is a s8 Children Act application and breach without reasonable excuse would be contempt of court. An application could be made on notice or, if the abduction was feared to be imminent, could be on an *ex parte* basis.

---

[285] *R v Mousir* [1987] Crim LR 561.
[286] [2019] EWCA Crim 1722.
[287] For care orders, see Chapter 12. For emergency protection orders and police protection, see 11.8.

The court can also order a person to surrender up their own or the children's passports, or make an order preventing the issue of a passport to the child (which is only helpful if the children are not holders of a passport from another country over whom the courts of England and Wales have no jurisdiction). There may be difficulties in serving the order if the abducting parent has already disappeared.

Alternatively, making an application for the child to become a ward of court would immediately prohibit the child's removal from the UK and wardship comes into effect as soon as an application is made rather than when an application is decided.

There is also an 'all ports warning system'. The police can contact the National Border Targeting Centre which notifies officials at all departure points from the UK so that the children can be prevented from leaving. This is used where the risk of abduction is real and imminent. A Child Rescue Alert can also be issued to local media.

Child abduction warning notices

Where the concern is that the child is associating with a person who may keep them from their carer, rather than necessarily abducting them from the jurisdiction, a child abduction warning notice (CAWN) may be given to the person or persons at risk of withholding the child. This has no statutory basis, but is a tool used by police to try to prevent contact between a child and someone they believe to be harmful to that child. One of its most significant uses is to try to prevent child sexual exploitation including grooming, or running away from home to be with a potential predator. Until recently they were known as 'harbourers' warnings'. After obtaining a statement from the child's carer the police will issue the warning, which confirms that the person has no permission to associate with or contact the child.

As a CAWN has no statutory basis, breach of one is not a criminal offence. The CAWN is both preventative and, if unsuccessful, will help in any prosecution. That could be for an offence under the Child Abduction Act 1984—the defendants in *R v Pringle* had been served with one—or under other legislation such as s49 Children Act.

FOCUS Think Critically

The effect of child abduction on children

We have already drawn on Professor Marilyn Freeman's research on relocation cases. In 2015, a further study by Professor Freeman involved interviewing a small group of 34 people who had been abducted as children. She found that:

- Eighteen (53 per cent) of the interviewees had observed or experienced domestic violence before their abduction. However, it was difficult to definitively link the incidence of domestic violence with the occurrence of abduction.
- 35 per cent of those interviewed reported actual or attempted multiple abductions.
- 65 per cent of abductees had no contact with their other parent whilst abducted.
- 'Some of the interviewees reported planning to kill their abductor so that they could return home again. Feelings of loss and confusion were regularly reported by the interviewees, with many having to deal with complete culture changes. Several also spoke about their depression and suicidal thoughts or attempts.'

- 'Anger towards the left-behind parent for not coming to find them was a further commonly reported theme although many interviewees also described how they grew to accept the abductor's account of the left-behind parent.'
- 'Several interviewees reported feeling that their voice was not heard during the legal process. They also discussed the issues that the legal process does not deal with and what happens after it has concluded. It was suggested that to simply return the child to their country of habitual residence was not enough. Support and follow-up was required and this was often lacking.'[288]

10.10.4 The Hague Convention on the Civil Aspects of International Child Abduction

The Hague Convention of 25 October 1980 is an international agreement. At the time of writing, 101 countries are party to the Convention, including the UK (it was incorporated into domestic law by the Child Abduction and Custody Act 1985).

Article 1 states that the Convention's objectives are

a) to secure the prompt return of children wrongfully removed to or retained in any Contracting State; and

b) to ensure that rights of custody and of access under the law of one Contracting State are effectively respected in the other Contracting States.

Wrongful removal and retention

The Convention establishes a procedure for the swift return of a child abducted from one state to another. It applies when a child under 16 is habitually resident in one contracting state prior to the removal or retention but has been *wrongfully removed* to or *wrongfully retained* in another contracting state.

The removal or retention must have taken place after the Convention came into force between the UK and the country to which the child has been taken.

Under Article 3, a removal or retention is wrongful where

- It is in breach of rights of custody attributed to a person, an institution or any other body, either jointly or alone, under the laws of the state in which the child was habitually resident immediately before the removal or retention; and

- At the time of removal or retention those rights were actually exercised, either jointly or alone, or would have been so exercised but for the removal or retention.

While removal involves taking the child to another state, retention involves keeping the child in that second state. A lawful removal may become an unlawful retention, for example where a child is not returned to the UK at the end of an agreed foreign holiday or where a person with whom the child lives pursuant to a s8 order keeps the child abroad for longer than the month permitted in s13.

---

[288] M Freeman, 'Parental Child Abduction: The Long-Term Effects' [2015] *Family Law* 219. See also an American study: GL Greif and RL Hegar, 'Impact on Children of Abduction by a Parent: A Review of the Literature' (1992) 62(4) *American Journal of Orthopsychiatry* 599.

The underlying rationale is that decisions about a child's upbringing are best made in the place of the child's habitual residence and not by a court in the country to which the child has been abducted, both for practical reasons and to disincentivise abductions by depriving abductors of an intended benefit of their abduction. As Lady Hale said in *Re M (Children) (Abduction)*, 'The message should go out to potential abductors that there are no safe havens among the contracting states.'[289] However, it is important to understand that return to the country of habitual residence is not a decision about which parent the children should live with or any other matters relating to the child's upbringing (see Article 19). That would be for the courts of habitual residence to determine. It may well be that the children and abducting parent return together and continue to live together.

The process for summary return

An application for a return order can be made by any person, institution, or other body that claims the child has been removed or retained in breach of custody rights (Article 8). Every contracting state has a central authority which deals with applications under the Convention. In the UK this is the Lord Chancellor, who delegates responsibility to the Ministry of Justice's International Child Abduction and Contact Unit. The Unit deals with both outgoing cases (where the child is abducted from the UK) and incoming cases (where the child has been abducted to the UK). They assist those within and outside the UK who seek the return of their child, including by referring individuals to specialist solicitors.

The central authority will request the child's return under the Convention. In response, the state to which the child has been taken should take steps to return the child. This state does not get involved in any substantive decision-making about the child's future, but simply considers whether the removal or retention was wrongful, i.e. in breach of rights of custody, and whether there are any defences to a return.

Legal aid is available for advice and court applications in child abduction cases, including for foreign nationals whose children have been abducted into the UK.

Habitual residence

The return is to the state in which the child was habitually resident prior to their removal. Habitual residence is a question of fact (rather than being a legal concept such as domicile).

In *A v A (Children: Habitual Residence) (Reunite International Child Abduction Centre Intervening)* Baroness Hale, with whom the majority agreed, held that habitual residence had the same meaning in the Hague Convention, the European Convention, and domestic law.[290] This is the definition given by the Court of Justice of the European Union in *Re Proceedings Brought by A*. It is:

> the place which reflects some degree of integration by the child in a social and family environment'. To that end, in particular the duration, regularity, conditions and reasons for the stay on the territory of a Member State and the family's move to that State, the child's nationality, the place and conditions of attendance at school, linguistic knowledge and the family and social relationships of the child in that State must be taken into consideration.[291]

---

[289] [2008] 1 FCR 536.
[290] [2013] UKSC 60.
[291] Case C-523/07 (judgment 2 April 2009) [2010] Fam 42.

Where the child is very young, the integration to be considered is that of those caring for him. It therefore follows that a child who is abducted does not become habitually resident in the country of abduction if they are on the run, i.e., their integration has been impeded by the need to hide or move regularly. It is possible to have more than one habitual residence at a time, and to have none, although this will be rare.[292]

Rights of custody

The judge deciding the return application (in the state to which the child has been abducted) must decide whether the claimant had rights of custody within the meaning of the Convention, and whether he was exercising them. Article 5 says that 'For the purpose of this convention, rights of custody shall include rights relating to the care of the person of the child and, in particular, the right to determine the child's place of residence.' In *Hunter v Murrow*, Thorpe LJ set out a two-step process:

> The first task is to establish what rights, if any, the Applicant had under the law of the state in which the child was habitually resident immediately before his or her removal or retention. I shall refer to this as 'the domestic law question'. This question is determined in accordance with the domestic law of that state. It involves deciding what rights are recognised by that law, not how those rights are characterised. . . .

> The next question is whether those rights are properly to be characterised as 'rights of custody' within the meaning of arts 3 and 5(b) of the Convention. . . . This is a matter of international law and depends on the application of the autonomous meaning of the phrase 'rights of custody'.[293]

Thus what constitutes a right of custody depends not on the domestic law of either state involved but on the autonomous law of the Convention. Section 8 Child Abduction and Custody Act 1985 enables a person to apply to the High Court for a declaration that the removal was wrongful. It is also possible under Article 15 for the state hearing the return application to seek a declaration from the home state as to whether the applicant had rights of custody. In *Re D (A Child) (Abduction: Rights of Custody)*, the House of Lords held that an Article 15 declaration from the foreign court was conclusive as to whether the applicant was exercising rights of custody because 'the foreign court is much better placed than the English to understand the true meaning and effect of its own laws in convention terms. Only if its characterisation of the parent's rights is clearly out of line with the international understanding of the convention's terms . . . should the court in the requested state decline to follow it.'[294]

Practice Direction 12F notes at paragraph 2.17 that

> In England and Wales a father who is not married to the mother of their child does not necessarily have 'rights of custody' in respect of the child. An unmarried father in England

---

[292] *Re B* [2016] UKSC 4. For a discussion of the line of cases between *Re A* and *Re B*, see D Williams QC, M Gration, and M Wright, 'Habitual Residence and the 'Parens Patriae' jurisdiction after *Re B* [2016] UKSC 4' [2016] *International Family Law* 239.

[293] *Hunter v Murrow* [2005] EWCA Civ 976. Note in *Re D* the Lords held that the outcome of *Hunter* was correct but the reasoning was not; the extract here is still good law.

[294] [2006] UKHL 51 at [44] (Lady Hale).

and Wales who has parental responsibility for a child has rights of custody in respect of that child. In the case of an unmarried father without parental responsibility, the concept of rights of custody may include more than strictly legal rights and where immediately before the removal or retention of the child he was exercising parental functions over a substantial period of time as the only or main carer for the child he may have rights of custody.[295]

In England and Wales, a person is held to be exercising rights of custody when he has parental responsibility; or where he is named in a court order with respect to the child or has made an application which is yet to be determined; and potentially where he has exercised parental functions over a substantial period of time as the only or main carer (even if he does not have PR or an order). Whether or not someone is exercising those rights is generally interpreted widely. In the recent decision in *Re A (A Child) (Abduction: Exercise of Rights of Custody)*, which is a useful survey of the interpretation of the exercise requirement, the judge noted that

> neither counsel was able to refer me to any case in which a parent with rights of custody has been found by the court to be '*not actually exercising*' those rights. It is of course possible to conceive that such a case may arise. However, that such a finding has yet to be made in the 35 years since the Convention was incorporated into English law, reflects perhaps that a parent who could be said to be '*not actually exercising*' any rights of custody is inherently unlikely to react to the removal or retention of their child by bringing a Hague Convention application.[296]

Defences

There are various defences to an application for summary return, which are found in Articles 12 and 13.

Article 12 says that if the application is brought within 12 months of the wrongful removal or retention, the court 'shall' (i.e., must) order the return of the child *unless* one of the Art 13 defences apply, in which case under Article 18 the court has a discretion to order return.

If the application is brought after 12 months the court shall return the child unless the child is 'now settled in its new environment'. In *Re N (Minors Abduction)* Bracewell J held that 'now' meant when proceedings for his return are started, rather than the time of the hearing, and that 'the word "settled" in this context has two constituents. First, it involves a physical element of relating to, being established in, a community and an environment. Secondly, . . . it has an emotional constituent denoting security and stability.'[297] The new environment refers to the child's place, home, school, people, friends, activities, and opportunities. The rationale for Article 12 is that if the child has become settled in the new country the home court may no longer be the best place to resolve issues relating the child. Do not forget, though, that this simply means that the courts of the country to which the child has been abducted assume jurisdiction to decide substantive issues relating to the

---

[295] Family Procedure Rules Part 12, Practice Direction 12F International Child Abduction. Available at https://www.justice.gov.uk/courts/procedure-rules/family/practice_directions/pd_part_12f accessed 12 November 2020.

[296] [2020] EWHC 2784 (Fam) at [74] (Richard Harrison QC). Emphasis in the original.

[297] *Re N (Minors) (Abduction)* [1991] 1 FLR 413, 417–18.

child. That may include deciding, after hearing all the evidence, that the child should live with the parent from whom he has been abducted and thus return to the home country. Success on an Article 12 or 13 defence is not equivalent to success overall.

If a defence under Articles 12 or 13 is not made out, then the fact that the welfare of the child may be better served by remaining in the country of abduction is not a reason to refuse return. Indeed, even if a defence is made out so that the court is not required to order return, it has a discretion to order return anyway, under Article 18.

> **STATUTORY EXTRACT** *Article 13 Hague Convention*
>
> Notwithstanding the provisions of the preceding Article, the judicial or administrative authority of the requested State is not bound to order the return of the child if the person, institution or other body which opposes its return establishes that:
>
> a) the person, institution or other body having the care of the person of the child was not actually exercising the custody rights at the time of removal or retention, or had consented to or subsequently acquiesced in the removal or retention; or
> b) there is a grave risk that his or her return would expose the child to physical or psychological harm or otherwise place the child in an intolerable situation.
>
> The judicial or administrative authority may also refuse to order the return of the child if it finds that the child objects to being returned and has attained an age and degree of maturity at which it is appropriate to take account of its views.
>
> In considering the circumstances referred to in this Article, the judicial and administrative authorities shall take into account the information relating to the social background of the child provided by the Central Authority or other competent authority of the child's habitual residence.

Let us consider each of these.

Defence of consent or acquiescence

The parent alleged to have abducted the children may argue that the removal of the children was with the consent of those whose consent was required. In many cases the only consent required will be that of the father. Consent must be clear and unequivocal and not based on misrepresentation or fraud, and nor must it have been withdrawn prior to the removal.[298]

The burden is on the alleged abducting parent to prove, on the balance of probabilities, that the removal was by consent.[299] Even if the removal was by consent, a parent may have retained the children beyond the period for which consent was given. For example, if the father agrees to the mother taking the children from the UK to Poland for two weeks to visit family, the initial removal is lawful. However, the mother's retention of the children after two weeks would constitute wrongful retention because there is no consent to that longer period.

---

[298] *Re P-J (Children) (Abduction: Consent)* [2009] EWCA Civ 588.
[299] *Re P (Abduction: Consent)* [2004] 2 FLR 1057.

Sometimes, the left behind parent may acquiesce to the children's removal or retention and only later seek their return. Whether he has acquiesced depends on his subjective state of mind, which is something that the court must discover.[300] It is not an objective test of how others perceived his intention, with one exception:

> Where the words or actions of the wronged parent clearly and unequivocally show and have led the other parent to believe that the wronged parent is not asserting or going to assert his right to the summary return of the child and are inconsistent with such return, justice requires that the wronged parent be held to have acquiesced.... However this is exceptional.[301]

The burden of proof of showing acquiescence is on the abducting parent. The fact that a father may enter into negotiations about the child remaining in the country of abduction or about seeing them there is not acquiescence but may be a pragmatic response to the situation.[302] I would suggest judges should be slow to infer an intention to acquiesce from attempts by the wronged parent to effect a reconciliation or to reach an agreed voluntary return of the abducted child.

Defence of a grave risk of harm

This is the most used defence, and it is that there is a grave risk that the child's return would expose the child to physical or psychological harm or otherwise place the child in an intolerable situation. In *Re C (Abduction: Grave Risk of Psychological Harm)* Thorpe LJ explained that there must be

> clear and compelling evidence of the grave risk of harm or other intolerability which must be measured as substantial, not trivial, and of a severity which is much more than is inherent in the inevitable disruption, uncertainty and anxiety which follows an unwelcome return to the jurisdiction of the court of habitual residence.[303]

The burden lies with the person asserting the defence, i.e., the abducting parent. This may include findings as to violence or abuse, although the court is dealing with a summary return application not a substantive one and thus the evidence before the court is likely to be limited. The risk must be of harm to that specific child and their carer, not a general risk of harm attributable to being in that country. In *Re S (Abduction: Custody Rights)* the Court of Appeal held that the risk of terrorist attacks in Israel were not sufficient to meet the Article 13 defence.[304] The risk must have reached sufficient seriousness to be considered to be 'grave' as opposed to simply being a risk that exists.

In *Re D (Abduction) (Rights of Custody)* Hale held that 'Intolerable' is a strong word, but when applied to a child must mean 'a situation which this particular child in these

---

[300] *Re H and Others (Minors) (Abduction: Acquiescence)* [1998] AC 72.
[301] *Re H and Others (Minors) (Abduction: Acquiescence)* [1998] AC 72, 90 (Lord Browne-Wilkinson).
[302] *P v P* [1998] 2 FLR 835.
[303] [1999] 1 FLR 1145.
[304] [2002] EWCA Civ 908.

particular circumstances should not be expected to tolerate'.[305] Sometimes the risks may relate to the conduct of the parent left behind. But return to the country from which the child was removed is not a return that parent, and it is common for the parent left behind to help defeat an Article 13(b) defence by offering undertakings that will ameliorate risk, such as that he will vacate the matrimonial home to enable the other parent and children to live there. The court will also look at other measures that could be taken such as obtaining a non-molestation order.[306] In England and Wales the President's Practice Guidance on *Case Management and Mediation of International Child Abduction Proceedings* makes it clear that investigation of protective measures should be done at the earliest opportunity.[307]

Occasionally a parent may say that they will refuse to return with the child, and that their non-availability as a future carer will cause the child grave harm. Courts are extremely reluctant to allow such an argument to succeed as it would 'drive a coach and four through the Convention'.[308]

As such, the Article 13(b) defence 'represents a high hurdle',[309] compounded by the fact that even if a defence is made out, under Article 18 the court retains a discretion to order return. In *Re M (Abduction: Intolerable Situation)* the existence of protective measures in the home country of Norway were considered sufficient to cause the defence to fail even though the father was being released from prison after serving a sentence for murder of a man he believed to be having an affair with the mother, and the mother was therefore genuinely terrified.[310]

The child's objection to return

It is a defence that the child objects to being returned and has attained an age and maturity at which it is appropriate to take account of his or her views. The younger the child is, the less likely it is that he or she will have the maturity for the court to take his or her objections into account,[311] but there is no set age after which which the views must be taken into account. In considering the child's views, the court will need to determine whether the child's objection is actually of return to the country or return to the other parent. A Hague Convention return is a return to the country only, not necessarily a return to the other parent although in some cases they will be inextricably linked, such as if the abducting parent refuses to return with the child so that the parent left behind will assume care of the child.[312] They may also be linked in the child's minds to an extent that they count as an objection even to return to the country.[313] The court will need to weigh the nature of

---

[305] [2006] UKHL 51.

[306] *TB v JB (Abduction: Grave Risk of Harm)* [2001] 2 FLR 515.

[307] Issued 13 March 2018. Available at https://www.judiciary.uk/publications/practice-guidance-case-management-and-mediation-of-international-child-abduction-proceedings/ accessed 12 November 2020.

[308] *C v C* [1989] 1 WLR 654 (Butler-Sloss LJ).

[309] *TB v JB (Abduction: Grave Risk of Harm)* [2001] 2 FLR 515.

[310] [2000] 1 FLR 930.

[311] *Re R (Child Abduction: Acquiescence)* [1995] 1 FLR 716.

[312] *Re M (A Minor)(Child Abduction)* [1994] 1 FLR 390, 395 (Butler-Sloss LJ).

[313] As in the leading case on objection which is *Re M (Children) (Republic of Ireland) (Child's Objections) (Joinder of Children as Parties to Appeal)* [2015] EWCA Civ 26.

the child's objection and the strength of it against the purpose of the Convention, which includes respect for the home country's processes.[314]

However, taking account of the child's views does not require a court to follow those views, even if the court finds they are the child's genuine views and not the product of the influence of the abducting parent.[315] As with the other defences, even if the court is satisfied that the child objects and that he is of sufficient age and maturity for his objection to considered, the court still has a discretion under Article 18 to order return.

FOCUS Know-How

Use of the Hague Convention

The Hague Conference on Private International Law publishes regular statistics about use of the Convention. The most recent analysis is from 2015.[318] This found that 73 per cent of alleged abductors were mothers, 24 per cent were fathers and the remaining 3 per cent comprised grandparents, institutions or other relatives. 80 per cent of the alleged abductors were either primary carers or joint primary carers, and most travelled to a state of which they were a national rather than to a state where they had no prior links.

Around 3,000 children were involved in return applications in 2015, across all contracting states. 17 per cent of cases were resolved by voluntary return and 28 per cent by court order. If the matter ended up in court as opposed to voluntary return or a compromise, the courts ordered return 65 per cent of the time. The most common reason for refusal was Article 13(1)(b), the grave risk of harm. The average length of time taken to reach a court decision was 158 days.

SCENARIO 4

Illustration 9: Sarah, Phil, and children Bill (11), Ben (8), and Bella (4)

It is very likely that the courts of the country to which the children have been abducted by Sarah deem that Phil was exercising rights of custody, and this would be the advice given by the UK if an Article 15 request had been made. He is a parent with parental responsibility and there may be a child arrangements order in force that the children spend time with him. On the face of it, therefore, summary return is indicated unless an Article 12 or 13 defence applies. Has there been a delay by Phil in bringing the application? Do the children object to return? Bella is too young to express a view, but the views of Ben and especially Bill will be relevant although not determinative because the court could nevertheless order return under Article 18. Is there a grave risk of harm to the children? Return to the UK is not necessarily return to Phil, although there may be an existing contact order. Can the UK put in place measures to secure the children's safety? Perhaps in the child arrangements proceedings the court already did so—or did not consider Sarah's allegations to be true.

---

[314] *Zaffino v Zaffino* [2005] EWCA Civ 1012.

[315] *Re D (A Child) (Abduction: Rights of Custody)* [2006] UKHL 51.

[316] N Lowe and V Stephens, *A statistical analysis of applications made in 2015 under the Hague Convention of 25 October 1980 on the Civil Aspects of International Child Abduction—Global report. Preliminary Document No 11 of September 2017 Part I* (2015). Available at https://www.hcch.net/en/publications-and-studies/details4/?pid=6598 accessed 11 November 2020.

10.10.5 The Brussels II Revised Regulation

Article 11 of the Revised Regulation[317] has the effect of modifying the application of the Hague Convention where both countries involved are within the EU. Among EU member states, therefore, it takes precedence over the Hague Convention.

The Regulation provides for a swift return of the child to the state of his habitual residence utilising the Hague Convention process. The Regulation, however, provides that where a child has been abducted, the courts of the home state retain jurisdiction *unless* the child has become habitually resident in the abducting state and either certain other conditions are satisfied, such as acquiescence or lapse of time (Article 10). (A defence to return is therefore found within Article 10; note that these are narrower than under Hague.)

STATUTORY EXTRACT *Article 10 Brussels II Revised Regulation*

Jurisdiction in cases of child abduction

In case of wrongful removal or retention of the child, the courts of the Member State where the child was habitually resident immediately before the wrongful removal or retention shall retain their jurisdiction until the child has acquired a habitual residence in another Member State and:

(a) each person, institution or other body having rights of custody has acquiesced in the removal or retention; or

(b) the child has resided in that other Member State for a period of at least one year after the person, institution or other body having rights of custody has had or should have had knowledge of the whereabouts of the child and the child is settled in his or her new environment and at least one of the following conditions is met:

(i) within one year after the holder of rights of custody has had or should have had knowledge of the whereabouts of the child, no request for return has been lodged before the competent authorities of the Member State where the child has been removed or is being retained;

(ii) a request for return lodged by the holder of rights of custody has been withdrawn and no new request has been lodged within the time limit set in paragraph (i);

(iii) a case before the court in the Member State where the child was habitually resident immediately before the wrongful removal or retention has been closed pursuant to Article 11(7);

(iv) a judgment on custody that does not entail the return of the child has been issued by the courts of the Member State where the child was habitually resident immediately before the wrongful removal or retention.

Courts should act expeditiously in dealing with return applications under Hague and only in exceptional circumstances should they issue a judgment more than six weeks after the return application (Article 11(3)). The Regulation gives greater importance to the voice of

---

[317] Brussels II *Bis* (Revised) is European Union Regulation (EC) No 2201/2003 concerning jurisdiction and the recognition and enforcement of judgments in matrimonial matters and the matters of parental responsibility. It repealed Regulation (EC) No 1347/2000 and had effect from 1 March 2005. As a Regulation, it is directly applicable in member states, including the UK, without needing to be implemented by domestic legislation.

the child than Hague, in that Article 11(2) says that states must ensure that children are 'given the opportunity to be heard during the proceedings unless this appears inappropriate having regard to his age and degree of maturity.' As Richard Harrison has commented, 'this creates an effective presumption in favour of at least ascertaining the views of the child.'[318] It does not give any particular indication of how those views should be ascertained, so it is not a requirement that the child be made a party.

Article 11(4) also modifies the application of Hague in the EU by providing that 'a court cannot refuse to return a child on the basis of Article 13(b) of the 1980 Hague Convention [grave risk of harm] if it is established that adequate arrangements have been made to secure the protection of the child after his or her return.'

Even if an Article 13 defence is made out, so that the courts of the country to which the child had been abducted decline to make a return order, the left behind parent can nevertheless bring proceedings in the home country and enforce these in the abducting country, which *must* give effect to the order even though that country had come to its own decision not to order return. There are no defences to reciprocal enforcement of the home country's decision even if that decision involves the child's return to the home state, unless there has been a procedural unfairness such as a failure to serve the application or hear the parties or child.[319] This is the effect of Article 11(8) read with Article 42. Thus, when the UK was a member of the EU, a parent who was left behind in England or Wales could apply for a s8 live with order and the court would consider the best interests of the child under the welfare principle in making its determination, as it would in any other s8 application, and when the court had made an order it would be enforced in the other jurisdiction. In *Re S (Abduction—Hague Convention or BIIa)*, the Court of Appeal considered that the home country should not usually pre-empt the abducting country's decision by making such an order unless the country of abduction had already declined to order return:

> absent a good reason to the contrary, the better course is for the court to defer making a return order until an application under the 1980 Convention has been determined in the other Member State. . . . Once such a determination has been made the court can then decide what order to make pursuant to Article 11(8) of BIIa.

> Apart from this being the 'expected' route, it has certain real advantages. First, a higher degree of direct assistance is likely to be provided by the authorities in the requested state to a party bringing an application under the 1980 Convention than in respect of an application for the enforcement of an order. Secondly, there is a specific obligation on states to determine applications under the 1980 Convention within 6 weeks. There is no such specific requirement in respect of the enforcement of parental responsibility orders. Thirdly, Article 11 provides what is to happen if a non-return order is made. There is, therefore, a tailor-made procedure through which the courts of the respective Member States engage with the case and engage with each other. Additionally, any subsequent return order has an

---

[318] R Harrison, 'The Views of Children in Child Abduction Cases under the Hague Convention' (*Family Law Week* 2 June 2005).

[319] As in *Re D (A Child) (Recognition and Enforcement of a Romanian Order)* [2016] EWCA Civ 12.

expedited enforcement procedure . . . 'without any possibility of opposing its recognition if the judgment has been certified in the Member State of origin in accordance with' Article 42(2). The making of a summary return order does not necessarily lead to the expeditious return of a child.[320]

The preferred process is therefore for the abducting state courts to deal with a Hague Convention return before the domestic courts make their own return order and seek recognition of that in the abducting state.

Although the powers under the Regulation seem great, Beaumont, Walker and Holliday have shown that even when Article 11(8) is used, the child is not usually returned to the home state.[321]

Note that the Regulation does not apply in Denmark. After Brexit, the operation of Brussels II, which had direct effect, was revoked within the UK by virtue of the Jurisdiction and Judgments (Family) (Amendment etc) (EU Exit) Regulations 2019.[322] The Hague Convention, which was incorporated into domestic law, will remain. Any court of a member state which is already seised of the matter before 1 January 2021 will remain seised.

10.10.6 Non-Hague Convention abductions

The High Court can exercise its inherent jurisdiction to order the return of a child abducted to the UK from a non-Convention country. Obtaining the return of a child who has been abducted from the UK to a non-Hague country can be exceptionally difficult. While an application for wardship of the child can be made notwithstanding the child's removal from the jurisdiction, it may be that the left behind parent will have to bring proceedings in the state to which the child has been abducted. The charity Reunite International assists many parents whose children have been abducted.[323]

10.10.7 Reciprocal enforcement of children orders generally

Both the Hague Convention and the Brussels II Revised Regulation provide mechanisms for reciprocal enforcement of other states' decisions relating to the exercise of parental responsibility. The latter is no longer applicable but in relation to the former procedural requirements for recognition and enforcement in England and Wales are found at Part 31 Family Procedure Rules and the accompanying Part 31 Practice Direction.

---

[320] [2018] EWCA Civ 1226 at [47ff] (Moylan LJ).
[321] P Beaumont, L Walker, and J Holliday, 'Not Heard and Not Returned: The Reality of Article 11(8) Proceedings' [2015] *International Family Law* 124.
[322] SI 2019/519. See also N Lowe, 'What are the Implications of the Brexit Vote for the Law on International Child Abduction?' [2017] *Child and Family Law Quarterly* 253, although note the date.
[323] https://www.reunite.org/ accessed 13 November 2020. See also K Beevers, 'Non-Convention Child Abduction—Consideration of Welfare and Undertakings' (2003) 6(4) *Contemporary Issues in Law* 303.

Under Article 23(1) of the Hague Convention 'the measures taken by the authorities of a Contracting State shall be recognised by operation of law in all other Contracting States', with the defences set out in Article 23(2).

A further Hague Convention, the Hague Convention of 19 October 1996 on Jurisdiction, Applicable Law, Recognition, Enforcement and Co-operation in respect of Parental Responsibility and Measures for the Protection of Children also provides for the advance recognition of contact orders and this will continue to apply post-Brexit and applies to children up to the age of 18 rather than 16. Although Nash has said that the 1996 Convention 'has not really taken hold as one might have expected', its continuation post-Brexit may mean that it gains in importance to cases relating to the UK.[324]

Where the state is not a party to any of the above, our common law may nevertheless recognise the foreign order, although whether or not another state will recognise an English or Welsh order will depend on their own laws.

10.11 Conclusion

In this chapter, we have built on the knowledge of parental responsibility and children's welfare and rights to look at how courts approach applications under the welfare principle. This has included consideration of some of the most difficult cases before the family courts—those relating to domestic abuse and those in which the relationship between the child and one of her parents has wholly broken down. We have looked at the court's powers to make orders and the way in which they go about doing so by reference to the welfare checklist, expert assistance, and guidance from the higher courts. We have noted that the European Convention on Human Rights and our domestic case law both emphasise the importance of a continuing relationship between a non-resident parent and his child, while noting the tension that may exist between this and the child's welfare. Courts have not always successfully protected children and their resident parents from harms, but equally courts have not always been successful in enforcing contact where contact is in the best interests of the child. We have seen that both mothers and fathers accuse the court system of bias against them and that the reality is very complex. Private law decisions about children represent difficult and messy area of law in which principles give way to practicalities and the welfare of the child is not easily ascertained.

---

[324] E Nash, 'Recognition under the 1996 Hague Convention' [2015] *International Family Law* 264.

KEY POINTS

- There are approximately 50–56,000 new private law applications every year. Most such applications will be brought under s8 Children Act 1989. There are three types of section 8 application: an application for a child arrangements order, which determines where a child lives and when they spend time with a non-resident parent or other person; an application for a prohibited steps order preventing someone from exercising their parental responsibility in a specified way; and an application for a specific issues order, resolving an issue relating to the child's upbringing.

- When the court decides an application under s8, it will apply the principles set out in s1 Children Act 1989: the welfare principle, the welfare checklist, the presumption of involvement (where it applies), the principle that delay is likely to prejudice the welfare of the child, and the principle that the court should make no order unless it is better for the child than not making an order.

- A child arrangements order may specify with whom the child will live. Such an order can be made in favour of more than one person, either in one household or more than one household. A child arrangements order may also (or only) make arrangements for the child to spend time with named individuals. Although there are common patterns of child contact and shared care, the sole criterion is what arrangement is in the best interests of the child concerned.

- Numerous cases in the European Court of Human Rights have emphasised that the mutual enjoyment by parent and child of each other's company is a fundamental element of family life under Article 8. Courts are therefore under a positive duty to take measures to reunite parents and children where family life is held to exist. Our domestic case law also indicates a pro-contact approach reflective of the ECHR jurisprudence but also reflecting assumptions that children of separated parents are entitled to know and to have the love and society of both their parents. Courts have a number of tools to promote and encourage contact as well as enforcement powers. Research shows that there are very few enforcement applications each year and the most common type of case involves parents whose conflicts with one another prevent them from making the contact order work in practice.

- Sometimes the child and/or their primary carer may be opposed to contact. It is crucial for the courts to ascertain why, and whether the opposition is genuine and rational. There is a significant body of research showing that contact can be a point for the continuation of domestic abuse or even when domestic abuse starts. Not all harms to children relate to domestic abuse. Whatever the nature of the risk, courts will need to identify and assess the level of risk to children before they can determine whether contact is in the child's best interests. Some children may become estranged or alienated from the non-resident parent, but how and why this happens is controversial.

- It is increasingly common for parents to seek to relocate outside the jurisdiction with children. Unless the relocating parent is the sole holder of parental responsibility, he or she will need the consent of all other holders or the court. A key consideration will be the effect on the relationship between the left-behind parent and the children. Where a parent removes the children from the UK without the requisite consents, this may constitute child abduction.

- When a child has been abducted outside the UK, there are two legal agreements which may help. Within the European Union, the Brussels II (Revised) Regulation provides a swift return mechanism. It varies the Hague Convention on the Civil Aspects of Child Abduction within the EU. The Hague Convention is a widely signed international agreement that provides for summary return of children to their country of habitual residence unless certain defences apply.

FURTHER READING: SOME STARTING POINTS

- The main source of statistics on use of the family courts is the Ministry of Justice's Family Court Statistics Quarterly, England and Wales. These can be found at https://www.gov.uk/government/collections/family-court-statistics-quarterly. The underlying datasets are also useful. Some analyses of the cases are

Elena Giovannini, *Outcomes of Family Justice: Children's Proceedings—a Review of the Evidence* (Research Summary 6/11, Ministry of Justice 2011); and Maebh Harding and Annika Newnham, *How Do County Courts Share the Care of Children?* (Nuffield Foundation 2015).

- To see what a s8 order may look like, see the omnibus of precedent orders, Children Act Proceedings Master Copy Orders (January 2016). Available at https://www.lawsociety.org.uk/practice-areas/family-children/cap-master-orders/.

- Two excellent analyses of courts' approach to child arrangements cases and the risks of gender bias are Felicity Kaganas, 'A Presumption that "Involvement" of Both Parents Is Best: Deciphering Law's Messages' (2013) 25(3) *Child and Family Law Quarterly* 270 and Lawrie Moloney, 'Do Fathers "Win" or Do Mothers "Lose"? A Preliminary Analysis of Closely Contested Parenting Judgments in the Family Court of Australia' (2001) 15(3) *International Journal of Law, Policy, and the Family* 363.

- For shared residence, start with some good summaries such as Sonia Harris-Short, 'Resisting the March towards 50/50 Shared Residence; Rights, Welfare, and Equality in Post-Separation Families' (2010) 32(3) *Journal of Social Welfare and Family Law* 257; Belinda Fehlberg et al., 'Legislating for Shared Time Parenting after Separation: A Research Review' (2011) 25(3) *International Journal of Law, Policy, and the Family* 318; and Liz Trinder, 'Shared Residence: A Review of Recent Research Evidence' (2010) 22(4) *Child and Family Law Quarterly* 475. We also recommend the writings of Helen Rhoades and Harris & George cited in the footnotes.

- For a discussion of the effect of domestic abuse on children and critique of the courts' approach, see Jeffrey L. Edleson 'Children's Witnessing of Adult Domestic Violence' (1999) 14(8) *Journal of Interpersonal Violence* 839; Christine Harrison, 'Implacably Hostile or Appropriately Protective? Women Managing Child Contact in the Context of Domestic Violence' (2008) 14(4) *Violence against Women* 381; and Humphreys and Thiara's 'Neither Justice Nor Protection: Women's Experiences of Post-Separation Violence' (2003) 25(3) *Journal of Social Welfare and Family Law* 195. Adrienne Barnett's research has been significant in this area: see (2015) 23 *Feminist Legal Studies* 47 and (2014) 26(4) *Child and Family Law Quarterly* 439. Finally, there is Rosemary Hunter et al., *Assessing Risk of Harm to Children and Parents in Private Law Children Cases* (Ministry of Justice 2020) and accompanying implementation plan and a literature review by Adrienne Barnett. All of these documents can be found at https://www.gov.uk/government/consultations/assessing-risk-of-harm-to-children-and-parents-in-private-law-children-cases.

- For alienation, there is much written by relatively few people. We recommend that you start with Joan B Kelly and Janet R Johnston, 'The Alienated Child: A Reformulation of Parental Alienation Syndrome' (2001) 39(3) *Family Court Review* 249; and Julie Doughty, Nina Maxwell, and Tom Slater, *Review of Research and Case Law on Parental Alienation* (Cardiff University Children's Social Care Research and Development Centre/Cafcass Cymru 2018).

- On the human rights implications of contact, see Shazia Choudhry and Jonathan Herring, *European Human Rights and Family Law* (Hart 2010), which is very clear. The principal study on enforcement is Liz Trinder, Joan Hunt, Alison Macleod, Julia Pearce, and Hilary Woodward, *Enforcing Contact Orders: Problem-Solving or Punishment?* (University of Exeter/Nuffield Foundation 2013).

- The topic of relocation is heavily case-based, but a good overview of the current law by recognised experts in the area is Rob George et al., *Relocation: A Practical Guide* (2nd edn, Family Law 2016). The research of Marilyn Freeman is also very useful: M Freeman, 'Parental Child Abduction: The Long-Term Effects' [2015] *Family Law* 219; as is that of Horsfall and Kaspiew: 'Relocation in Separated and Non-Separated Families: Equivocal Evidence from the Social Science Literature' (2010) 24 *Australian Journal of Family Law* 34.

 Visit the **online resources** to watch a video of Polly Morgan discussing this chapter topic, and to check your understanding of this chapter with self-test questions and scenario questions.

11 Child Protection: State Support for Children

LEARNING CHECKLIST

By the end of this chapter, you should be able to:

- *Explain* the responsibilities that local authorities have to safeguard and promote the welfare of children
- *Critically discuss* the ethos and ideologies underlying Part III to V of the Children Act, and compare this to pre-Children Act approaches, using academic commentaries to support your views
- *Critically discuss* to what extent the law has struck the right balance between the intervention of the state and the autonomy of the parents to bring up their children by themselves in the way they choose
- *Describe* the options open to local authorities seeking to protect a child at risk of harm
- *Identify* areas of law or practice that could be reformed, supporting your views by reference to research, case law, and academic commentary.

SCENARIO 1

Andrzej and grandmother Lena

Andrzej is 9 years old. He has cerebral palsy, which causes him to have muscle spasms and seizures. He uses a wheelchair, has difficulties eating and swallowing, and has a learning disability. As Andrzej's parents are deceased, he is cared for by his grandmother, Lena, who is finding it increasingly difficult to meet Andrzej's needs as she gets older. She has parental responsibility for Andrzej as Andrzej's mother's Will appointed her as his guardian.

SCENARIO 2

Maya

Maya is 15 years old. She has repeatedly run away from home after arguments with her mother, who has parental responsibility for her (her father is in prison). Maya is increasingly being drawn into local gang culture and petty criminality, and was recently found by police on the streets high on drugs. Her mother does not want her to return home, telling social workers that Maya is too much of a handful.

11.1 Introduction

In Chapters 8 and 9, we looked at the welfare principle and private law decisions about children. The relevant legal provisions are found in Parts I and II of the Children Act 1989. In this chapter, we consider how the Children Act also provides a legal framework within which the state can support children to remain with and their families through difficult situations and intervene to protect them when they face unacceptable risks. These are Parts III, IV, and V of the Act. In Chapter 12, we go on to consider the compulsory powers of the state in the form of applications for care and supervision orders, and the potential outcomes of such proceedings, including adoption. As we shall see, the numbers of children involved with social services teams is rising exponentially, although this is not largely indicative of greater need.

Let us look first at the history of child protection and the inherent tension in protecting children while aspiring to support their lives with their families.

11.2 A brief history of child protection law

Child protection has not always been a social concern. Its existence is predicated on both acceptance of childhood as a recognisable period that deserves special protection, and on a view that the welfare of children is a matter of public interest justifying intervention in families.

The first iterations of child protection in its more familiar forms occurred in the nineteenth century. The 1839 the Infant Custody Act 1839 gave separated mothers of good moral character the right to petition a court to see their children, and to seek custody of children under the age of 7. A high-profile case in the United States, regarding the serious abuse of Mary Ellen Wilson, led directly to the founding of the New York Society for the Prevention of Cruelty to Children in 1875. This led in turn to the founding of the National Society for the Prevention of Cruelty to Children (NSPCC) in England in 1889, and, in the same year, the Prevention of Cruelty to Children Act. In this period, however, child protection functions were largely the concern of charitable and campaigning organisations and churches, rather than being part of the functions of the state. The rhetoric was one of child rescue: of working in impoverished communities to save children from morally deviant parents.

Over the next few decades, the emphasis changed from child rescue to one of promoting children's physical, mental, and educational development. Children were seen as a social asset requiring protection and development in the national interest. Multiple Acts were passed regulating children's work in factories, shops, and mines, and requiring their education. The focus on paternal rights evidenced by the case *Re Agar-Ellis* (1883), with its support for family privacy, therefore gave way to a more welfare-based approach. This simultaneously provided greater rights to mothers (e.g., the Guardianship of Infants Act 1925). Such developments were not without concern, in case they might 'involve so much interference with parental control as to lead to dangerous results'[1] but, Piper has suggested, the development of children simply became seen as too important to be left to families.[2]

---

[1] Lord Herschell (1894), quoted in *Hansard* vol 24, col. 1609. Quoted by Piper.
[2] C Piper, 'Moral Campaigns for Children's Welfare in the Nineteenth Century', Chapter 1 in H Hendrick (ed.) *Child Welfare and Social Policy* (Policy Press 2005).

The period from approximately 1920 through to the Second World War was not one of great development of the position of children, with the exception of the approach taken to juvenile justice. However, there were several reasons why public attention turned to children during wartime. First, the mass evacuation of children from inner cities to the country highlighted the extremely impoverished slum conditions in which some children had been living. Second, a solution was needed for the many children orphaned by the war, and at the time, foster carers were in short supply. Third, there was a political will to abandon all traces of the Elizabethan and Victorian Poor Laws. In 1944 there were still 27,000 children in the care of poor law authorities, including some in workhouses. Finally, and by no means least, in 1945, 12-year-old Dennis O'Neill was starved and beaten to death by his foster carer, a man with whom he had been placed by authorities but who had not been subject to proper screening for suitability and who had a history of violence. Dennis's parents, an unemployed labourer and his wife, had been imprisoned for neglect of their 11 children, having been raising them on a poverty level income of £2 pounds per week. The subsequent Monckton Report on Dennis's death identified confusion between two local authorities about his well-being, coupled with staff shortages that meant his welfare had gone unmonitored.[3] Subsequently, the Curtis Report identified significant problems in the care offered to children who could not live at home.[4] These factors combined to ensure that the issue of children's welfare became politically urgent. Shortly thereafter, the Children Act 1948 was passed.

The 1948 Act 'has long been seen as a landmark in the history of the public care of children, and as a major element in the creation of the post-World War II welfare state'[5] alongside its ideological siblings the National Health Service and free comprehensive education. Its focus was on preventing family breakdown. As Cretney explains, the Curtis Committee 'recommended that every effort should be made to keep the child in the family home, but if this was not possible the aim should be to find something "much better"'.[6] For those children who could not be cared for by their families, including those orphaned in wartime, local authority children's officers should be appointed whose role was to screen potential foster carers for suitability, and regularly visit children in their foster placements. However, it was not until the Local Authority Social Services Act 1970 that specific social services departments were introduced. Times were changing, and 'the new service, and the profession which was to be its hallmark, aspired to be community-based, flexible and creative in approach, was positive about those it was working with and optimistic about what could be achieved.'[7]

---

[3] Home Office, *Report by Sir William Monckton on the Circumstances Which Led to the Boarding Out of Dennis and Terence O'Neill at Bank Farm, Minsterly and the Steps Taken to Supervise Their Welfare* (Cmd 6636, 1945).
[4] M Curtis, *Report of the Care of Children Committee* Cmd 6922, 1946).
[5] S Cretney 'The State as a Parent: The Children Act 1948 in Retrospect', Chapter 9 in *Law, Law Reform and the Family* (OUP 1998).
[6] Cretney explains that to the Curtis Committee this much better option was adoption, but that this was not included in the Children Act 1948 'because that bill was regarded as primarily concerned with child welfare and not legal status'. This is, he goes on, 'a remarkable illustration of the way in which policy may effectively be determined by considerations of legal classification and departmental responsibility'. S Cretney 'The State as a Parent: The Children Act 1948 in Retrospect', Chapter 9 in *Law, Law Reform and the Family* (OUP 1998). The quote 'much better' is taken from the Curtis Report at para 447.
[7] N Parton, 'Social Work, Child Protection and Politics: Some Critical and Constructive Reflections' (2014) 44 *British Journal of Social Work* 2042.

The history of child protection law is also the history of the children it has failed. Those whom the law has helped do not attract the same attention. In 1973, 'the optimism that had been evident in social work [was] dealt a major blow by one significant event', the death of 7-year-old Maria Colwell, who was kicked to death by her stepfather after years of starvation and abuse.[8] At the time of her death, Maria had been the subject of a number of reports to social services by teachers and neighbours. In fact, social workers, health visitors, NSPCC workers, police and housing officers had, between them, visited Maria's family 50 times, yet inter-agency communication had been lacking and multiple reports not followed up. The impact of Maria's death on 'day-to-day policy and practice was considerable'. The inquiry into her death criticised social workers' concentration on family support, resulting afterwards in a 'greater emphasis on substitute care and on protecting children from their families'.[9] This involved the establishment of child protection committees, which brought together a number of agencies involved in safeguarding children, as well as the compilation of child protection registers, which listed children who were at risk of harm.

Despite these efforts, Maria was not the last high-profile child death, as you can see from Figure 11.1. To name only a few tragic victims, Jasmine Beckford,[10] Tyra Henry,[11] and Heidi Koseda[12] were all killed in 1984 alone, and Kimberley Carlisle[13] died in 1986. While the circumstances surrounding their deaths were different, there were common themes: a lack of coordination between agencies including police, social workers, and the NHS; a failure to see the children in person; manipulation by parents; and uncertainty about the cultural and racial context. Packman and Jordan also attribute social workers' (and other agencies') failings to the prevailing ethos of the time:

> The implicit basis of child care practice up to that point was that no fundamental conflicts of interest between parents and children, or between families and the state, were at stake in such interventions. Thus statutory removal of children was perceived as exceptional, and good practice aimed at minimizing it. Substitute care was seen as supporting parents as well as providing for children's needs, and practical assistance as preserving the family unit. The recognition of parents who intentionally harmed their children could not be easily accommodated within the understanding of what these services were there to do: the scandals and the subsequent enquiries revealed time and again that social workers could not see what to lay people was painfully obvious, and what lawyers and other professionals (with the benefit of hindsight) constructed to be their duty to recognize . . . Far from perceiving social work as too adversarial, [major inquiries into child deaths] insisted that it remained too bland, welfarist and optimistic in its assumptions and operational strategies with potentially abusive parents.[14]

---

[8] N Parton, 'Social Work, Child Protection and Politics: Some Critical and Constructive Reflections' (2014) 44 *British Journal of Social Work* 2042.

[9] H Hendrick, 'Children and Social Policies', Chapter 2 in H Hendrick (ed.) *Child Welfare and Social Policy* (Policy Press 2005) 47.

[10] London Borough of Brent, *A Child in Trust: The Report of the Panel of Inquiry into the Circumstances Surrounding the Death of Jasmine Beckford* (1985).

[11] London Borough of Lambeth, *Whose Child? The Report of the Public Inquiry into the Death of Tyra Henry* (1987).

[12] London Borough of Hillingdon, *Report of the Review Panel into the Death of Heidi Koseda* (1986).

[13] L Blom-Cooper, *A Child in Mind: Protection of Children in a Responsible Society: The Report of the Commission of Inquiry into the Circumstances surrounding the Death of Kimberley Carlile* (London Borough of Greenwich and Greenwich Health Authority 1987).

[14] J Packman and B Jordan, 'The Children Act: Looking Forward, Looking Back' (1991) 21(4) *British Journal of Social Work* 315.

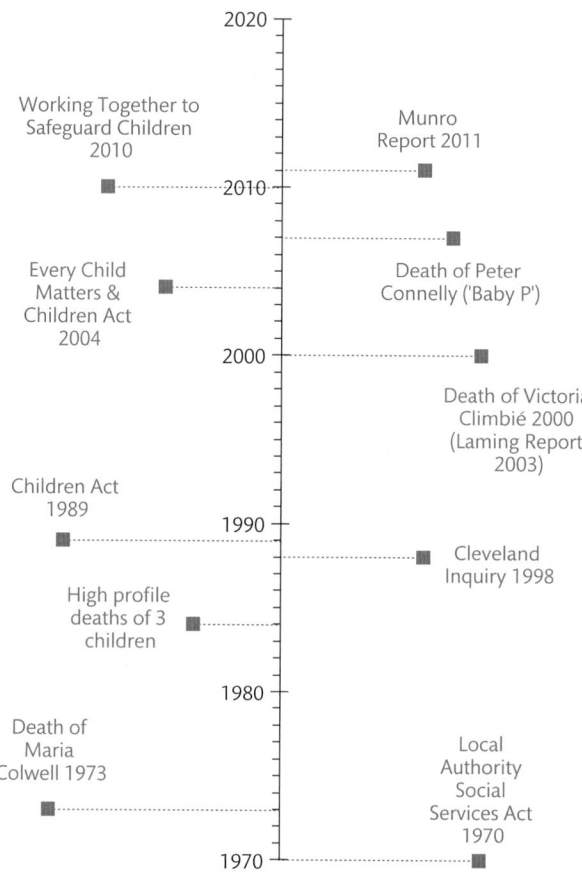

FIGURE 11.1 Timeline of key developments in the last 50 years

Here we see the tension between approaches designed to protect children from harm by their parents, and those that sought to preserve the family unit as *usually* the best place in which to raise a child. From this point, practice tilted towards the protection of children from harm by their parents: there was a significant increase—from 7,622 in 1985 to 29,766 by 1987—in the numbers of children who were on child protection registers or subject to 'place of safety orders' removing them from their families for up to 28 days. Social workers were fearful of not taking action and leaving children in dangerous situations. This meant that the coercive powers of the state were focused on preventing harm to children, without much if any attention paid to the harms of child removal.

But the pendulum had swung too much towards intervention, and this was all too evident in 1987 when, during a five-month period, 121 children from 57 homes in Cleveland were removed from their families under 28-day 'place of safety orders' (now abolished). So many children were removed that, without sufficient foster carers, some children had to be accommodated on hospital wards. Although some of these children were legitimately at risk or in concerning family situations,[15] the trigger for their removal was

---

[15] Ninety-eight of the children eventually returned home.

a diagnosis that the children had been sexually abused, based on a deeply flawed anal dilation test carried out by two paediatricians. When the parents attracted media and political attention, the government ordered an inquiry. Chaired by Butler-Sloss J, it was critical of everyone involved for treating the children as isolated objects of concern, not people within their families, and for ignoring the parents' interests and well-being.[16] But it demonstrated

> that family support and child protection were not two necessarily conflicting and incompatible priorities: both required similar attitudes, approaches, and skills. Even parents who were suspected of abuse retained a sense of responsibility for their children which should be nurtured, not crushed; and even the implementation of legal powers required respect, communication, the willingness to listen, and the desire to reach agreements—not least with the victims themselves.[17]

It was following the Cleveland scandal and subsequent inquiry that the Children Act 1989 was born. Although Cleveland was undoubtedly 'the catalyst which persuaded the government of the need for legislation',[18] reform was not reactionary or ill-considered. The groundwork had already been laid by the Law Commission[19] and a considerable body of academic research. It is simply that Cleveland came as 'the culmination of a fifteen-year period in which the care of children had become a major political concern, the focus of media attention and public outrage, and an ideological battleground for rival pressure groups and experts'.[20]

The consideration given to the contents of the Act, and the research that informed it, help to explain why the Act has remained remarkably current and resilient even thirty years later. However, like all legislation, it is only as good as those utilising it, and insofar as the Act contains obligations on local authorities and other agencies, it is only as good as the funding and training received to implement it. We can see this by considering yet another child death, that of 8-year-old Victoria Climbié in 2000. Victoria was tortured and killed by her great-aunt and her great-aunt's boyfriend. Originally from the Ivory Coast, Victoria had no other family in the UK. She was well-known to four different local authorities' social services teams, two hospitals, several police child protection teams, several churches, the NSPCC, and several housing departments. Twelve chances to intervene to save her were missed. Different agencies thought wrongly that the other was following up; signs of torture were mistaken for scars caused by a medical condition (scabies); the family moved around and obfuscated investigation; social workers mistook the child's fear of her great-aunt for culturally appropriate respect; and social services teams were in disarray—under-resourced, overworked, and inadequately supervised.[21] These were all

---

[16] *Report of the Inquiry into Child Abuse in Cleveland 1987* (Cm 412, 1988).
[17] J Packman and B Jordan, 'The Children Act: Looking Forward, Looking Back' (1991) 21(4) *British Journal of Social Work* 315.
[18] B Hale, 'In Defence of the Children Act' (2000) 83(6) *Archives of Disease in Childhood* 463.
[19] Law Commission, *Review of Child Law, Guardianship and Custody* (Law Comm No. 172, 1988).
[20] J Packman and B Jordan, 'The Children Act: Looking Forward, Looking Back' (1991) 21(4) *British Journal of Social Work* 315.
[21] Lord Laming, *The Victoria Climbie Inquiry: Report of an Inquiry by Lord Laming* (Cmd 5730, 2003).

familiar issues: as with the death in 1945 of Dennis O'Neill, her death was not down to poor legislation but poor practice.

A subsequent report by Lord Laming emphasised the importance of multi-agency working, appropriate training and supervision, and good record-keeping. Many of his recommendations found their way into 2004's *Every Child Matters*, the government's framework for the organisation of services to children (see Figure 11.1), and the Children Act 2004, which is premised on the idea that 'child protection cannot be separated from policies to improve children's lives as a whole'. Section 11 of the 2004 Act also placed duties on a range of organisations, agencies, and individuals (including NHS trusts, the police and probation services, as well as local authorities), to ensure that 'their functions are discharged having regard to the need to safeguard and promote the welfare of children'.[22] The tendency of legislation subsequent to the Children Act has been to add to the state's duties towards children, especially children leaving local authority care as young adults.

But first, let us look at how the Children Act 1989 aims to protect children.

11.3 The ethos and function of the Children Act 1989

The Act was 'intended to establish a balance between the family and the state which reflected community views about the need for child protection and for supported families'.[23] It makes a distinction between services for children and their families (Part III of the Act) and compulsory intervention (Parts IV and V). Although cases can cross from supporting families under Part III to intervening in them under Part IV or vice versa, each Part is distinct.

11.3.1 Support for families under Part III (sections 16B to 30A)

As Lady Hale—a principal architect of the Children Act before her judicial career[24]— has argued, 'Any civilised society has to start from the proposition that children are best brought up in their own families: it is the bedrock of society that children belong in families and not to the state.'[25] The Act explicitly states (at s1(5)) that no order should be made unless it would be better for the child to make an order. The Act therefore 'assumes that bringing up children is the responsibility of their parents and that the state's principal role is to help rather than to interfere'.[26]

Part III of the Act contains broad powers and duties given to local authorities to enable them to provide services designed to meet children's needs, promote their upbringing by

---

[22] HM Government, *Every Child Matters* (Cm 5860, 2003).

[23] J Masson, 'The State as Parent: The Reluctant Parent: The Problem of Parents of Last Resort?' (2008) 35(1) *Journal of Law and Society* 52.

[24] At the time she was the Law Commissioner in charge of family law and a principal architect of the Act, as well as a member of the Interdepartmental Review of the Child Care Law (1985).

[25] B Hale, 'In Defence of the Children Act' (2000) 83(6) *Archives of Disease in Childhood* 463.

[26] B Hoggett [Lady Hale], 'The Children Bill: The Aim' [1989] *Family Law* 217.

> **FOCUS** Know-How
>
> **Powers versus duties**
>
> Before we go further, let us consider the difference between two words used in this description of the Act: 'powers' and 'duties'. A *power* to do something is the ability to do so lawfully; it does not mean that a court or local authority must take that action. In the case of a local authority, a decision about whether to exercise a particular power may be partly determined by available resources and the needs of others. In the case of the court, it may be because other options are in the child's best interests. In contrast, a *duty* to do something is a requirement or an obligation: the local authority must do this because the law says it has to. Duties are often discernible from powers by use of the word 'shall'.

their families, and ameliorate the need for compulsory intervention under Part IV. To Packman and Jordan, it is here that the Act

> takes a quantum leap from the old, restricted notions of 'prevention', to a more positive outreaching duty of 'support for children and families' . . . 'Prevention' is recast in terms of preventing harm, preventing offending and preventing the need for compulsory intervention in families' lives through court orders: but no longer as preventing children being 'looked after' on their parents' behalf.[27]

Preventative work was to be done by social workers acting in partnership with families because, in the words of June Thoburn, 'the Act recognises that a child's welfare cannot be considered independently of his or her family'.[28] As part of this, local authorities are required to identify children in their area who are in need (*children in need*) and by virtue of s17 offer them services designed to meet those needs. *Section 20* also gives local authorities the power (and sometimes the duty) to accommodate children and young people who cannot live at home.

Part III also establishes the status of being a *looked after child*—a child who is accommodated by or in the care of a local authority, whether in an emergency, temporarily, or in the longer term. Section 22 sets out certain duties that local authorities have towards looked after children. These duties may last beyond the period in which the child is looked after and well into adulthood. Over the thirty years of the Act's operation, it is this set of obligations that have been expanded and made more onerous on local authorities, in light of poor outcomes for children who leave local authority care.

11.3.2 Care and supervision orders under Part IV (sections 31 to 42)

The broad powers of Part III were matched by tight controls on compulsory intervention by the state. Only when a child was at unacceptable risk should the state compulsorily intervene and any such intervention would be subject to review and safeguards.[29] Local

---

[27] J Packman and B Jordan, 'The Children Act: Looking Forward, Looking Back' (1991) 21(4) *British Journal of Social Work* 315.

[28] J Thoburn, The Children Act 1989: Balancing Child Welfare with the Concept of Partnership with Parents' (1991) 13(5) *Journal of Social Welfare and Family Law* 331, 332.

[29] Law Commission, *Review of Child Law, Guardianship and Custody* (Law Comm No. 172, 1988) at para 2.1.

authorities would be able to make an application for a care or supervision order, but as we see when we discuss these orders in Chapter 12, parental responsibility is not removed when the state intervenes, although its exercise is be restricted.[30]

11.3.3 Investigations and emergency powers under Part V (sections 43 to 52)

Where a local authority has serious concerns about the welfare of a child, it will undertake a *s47 investigation*. This section places the authority under a duty to 'make or cause to be made such enquiries as they consider necessary to enable them to decide whether they should take any action to safeguard or promote the child's welfare'. If necessary, the authority can seek a *child assessment order* under s43 to provide it with the information it needs to the information needed to determine whether or not the child is suffering or likely to suffer significant harm.

Part V also gives very short-term *police emergency powers* to protect children, and enables a local authority to apply to court for an *emergency protection order*. But, as with the other part of the Act which give coercive powers to the state, they are strictly time-limited, much shorter in duration than the previous 28-day place of safety orders, and in the case of emergency protection orders require the scrutiny of a court. As Lord Mackay said when introducing the Act in the House of Lords, the Act

> seeks[s] to strike a balance between the need to protect children from harm and the need to allow aggrieved parents to challenge action taken in respect of their children—the need for which was graphically illustrated by what happened in Cleveland. . . . As recommended in the Jasmine Beckford report, local authorities and other agencies will be required to co-operate in support of a more active investigative responsibility placed on social services departments.[31]

To Packman and Jordan, the Act 'treads a tightrope between children and parents, the state and families, courts and local authorities, and where power is unequal it tries to safeguard the weak.'[32]

FOCUS Think Critically

Ideological perspectives in the Children Act 1989

In order to assess the success of the Children Act 1989, or any other child protection measure, we have to first identify what it was intended to achieve. That involves a philosophical discussion about the role of the state in family life. As we have seen, different events have tended to influence law and practice in different directions and even a single piece of legislation may reflect a number of different viewpoints about the role of the state, the status, rights, and interests of parents and children, and the nature of childhood.

---

[30] 'Parenthood is a matter of responsibility rather than rights': Law Commission, *Review of Child Law, Guardianship and Custody* (Law Comm No. 172, 1988) at para 2.1.

[31] Lord Mackay of Clashfern LC at the second reading of the Children Act Bill, *Hansard*, HL vol 502, col 492 (December 6, 1988).

[32] J Packman and B Jordan, 'The Children Act: Looking Forward, Looking Back' (1991) 21(4) *British Journal of Social Work* 315.

For Lorraine Fox Harding, laws and policies about children reflect one or more of four different ideological perspectives, which she described in two articles published in 1991, just as the Children Act 1989 came into force.[33] These value perspectives offer an important contribution to how we think about the state's role. Fox-Harding describes them as follows:

1. **Laissez-faire and patriarchy.** The state's role is one of minimal intervention with the privacy and sanctity of the family being respected except in extreme cases. This is premised on a belief that undisturbed family life, with parents bringing up their children how they want, is best for adults and children. This is a patriarchal approach in that minimal intervention in the family allows power within the family to lie where it falls, which 'will tend to enhance patriarchy in a society where adult males are powerful in relation to women and children'.[34] In its most extreme form, interference with the family would be possible only in limited circumstances, such as where harm to a child was proven to the criminal standard (rather than, as presently, the civil standard). Where it does occur, state intervention should be strong and authoritative, placing the child into a new family which will then be subject to the same privacy and sanctity. An example of this approach is found in the nineteenth century when courts deferred issues of child raising to fathers.

2. **State paternalism and child protection.** This approach favours more extensive state intervention to protect children from inadequate parental care, and the removal of the child from the birth family may be justified on a much lower threshold or a much wider definition of abuse or harm than in the *laissez-faire* approach. The welfare of the child is paramount, but this is construed as requiring protection from parental inadequacy. The birth family's rights and any bonds the child has with the birth family are given much reduced weight compared to the child's interests in having a new permanent home where good quality care will be provided. The child is therefore seen as a separate individual rather than part of a birth family unit. As Featherstone et al. write, 'A language of child protection situates the idealised child separately from his/her family. This is extremely dangerous, especially in very unequal societies.'[35] In the past, this approach has led to children being removed from their families and even sent abroad, sometimes because of their ethnic heritage. Examples of this include the plight of the 'stolen generations' of Aboriginal children in Australia, the forced removal of First Nations Canadians, and the more than 130,000 British children, mostly from deprived backgrounds or in state care, who were sent to Australia and Canada, from the 1920s to the 1970s. This perspective has considerable resource implications and the risk is that without proper resources it simply results in inadequate substitute care.[36]

3. **Defence of the birth family and parents' rights.** This viewpoint emphasises the importance of psychological and biological bonds within the family and thus sees the family as (usually) the best place in which to raise children. The state does intervene extensively, but not in a predominantly coercive way. Instead, the role of the state is preventative: it is to positively support birth families by offering services designed to support the family functioning well and remaining together. This is the viewpoint that dominated social care practice in the 1960s. The effects of poverty, class, and deprivation 'are seen as important elements in child care, explaining much of what appears to be inadequate parenting while the (usually coercive) response of the state is disproportionately directed to lower class and

---

[33] LM Fox Harding, 'The Children Act 1989 in Context: Four Perspectives in Child Care Law and Policy' Part I: (1991) 13(3) *Journal of Social Welfare and Family Law* 179 and Part II: (1991) 13(4) *Journal of Social Welfare and Family Law* 285. Fox Harding developed these ideas in *Perspectives in Child Care Policy* (Longman 1995). Quotes are from these articles unless otherwise stated.

[34] LM Fox Harding, 'The Children Act 1989 in Context: Four Perspectives in Child Care Law and Policy' Part I: (1991) 13(3) *Journal of Social Welfare and Family Law* 179, 181.

[35] B Featherstone, K Morris, and S White, 'A Marriage Made in Hell: Early Intervention Meets Child Protection' (2014) 44(7) *British Journal of Social Work* 1735.

[36] LM Fox Harding, 'The Children Act 1989 in Context: Four Perspectives in Child Care Law and Policy' Part I: (1991) 13(3) *Journal of Social Welfare and Family Law* 179, 189.

deprived families'.[37] Substitute care by the state is seen as a last resort, and comes with its own problems. If the child does have to be separated from the birth family, ties should be maintained. Fox Harding remarks that while government may 'in its rhetoric support "the family", this is done mainly from a *laissez-faire* stance', rather than a defence of the birth family viewpoint, in that 'it is the family's autonomy and internal responsibilities which are stressed, not its claim to state material support'.[38]

4. **Children's rights and child liberation.** This perspective sees the child as a separate rights-bearing entity entitled to autonomy. This perspective does not, therefore, see childhood as an innately different state to adulthood. 'The strengths and competence of children, and their similarity to adults, are emphasised, rather than their vulnerability; children are not seen as in need of protection, but empowerment.'[39] Parental and state control over children is seen as benefiting adults only. This, says Fox Harding, calls into question 'the very existence of a guardianship role for the state, involving decisions about where children should live and who should have rights over them'.[40] The state's role is not to make decisions *about* children, but to enable children to exercise their freedoms by granting them the normal rights of citizenship. At its most extreme, therefore, the child liberation approach would be deeply problematic. It would involve a reconceptualized view that childhood does not require a special need for protection, which might be considered as troubling to many people. Fox Harding argues that such an approach would risk greater harms for children: 'without a protective machinery backed by the force of the law it seems highly like that much abuse, neglect and poor child care could not be stopped'.[41] However, as we see in Chapter 9, it may be possible to reconcile a child's right to self-determination with their welfare.

Fox-Harding identifies all four perspectives in the Children Act 1989 to differing extents. The no order principle in s1(5) is an example of a *laissez-faire* approach although this is not a 'dominant motif' in the Children Act. To Fox Harding, paternalism and defence of the birth family are the most dominant themes. They are conflicting viewpoints: one cannot simultaneously protect the birth family's autonomy and give the state a paternalistic role. State paternalism underlies the power to make a care or supervision order on the basis of anticipated harm (which was not the case before the Children Act 1989), the existence of child assessment orders (see 11.5.3) and the state's obligations to support former looked after children. We can see the defence of the birth family and the role of the state in supporting families in the obligations on local authorities to identify and provide services for children in need. Fox Harding observes that 'on the face of it, there is more in the Children Act that leans to a pro-parent emphasis than there is on the child protection side', citing parental powers to challenge emergency protection orders, greater rights to contact with a child in care than had been the case previously, and the introduction of shorter time restrictions on certain orders, as examples.[42] She attributes this approach to the influence of active family rights lobbying during the 1980s and, in particular, the impact of the Cleveland scandal. Finally, while the more extreme end of the child liberation movement is not reflected in the Children Act, the Act does require courts to consider the wishes and feelings of the child. While children's views are more often filtered through their

---

[37] LM Fox Harding, 'The Children Act 1989 in Context: Four Perspectives in Child Care Law and Policy' Part I: (1991) 13(3) *Journal of Social Welfare and Family Law* 179, 181.

[38] LM Fox Harding, 'The Children Act 1989 in Context: Four Perspectives in Child Care Law and Policy' Part II: (1991) 13(4) *Journal of Social Welfare and Family Law* 285, 287–8.

[39] LM Fox Harding, 'The Children Act 1989 in Context: Four Perspectives in Child Care Law and Policy' Part I: (1991) 13(3) *Journal of Social Welfare and Family Law* 179, 182.

[40] LM Fox Harding, 'The Children Act 1989 in Context: Four Perspectives in Child Care Law and Policy' Part II: (1991) 13(4) *Journal of Social Welfare and Family Law* 285, 295.

[41] LM Fox Harding, 'The Children Act 1989 in Context: Four Perspectives in Child Care Law and Policy' Part II: (1991) 13(4) *Journal of Social Welfare and Family Law* 285, 296.

[42] LM Fox Harding, 'The Children Act 1989 in Context: Four Perspectives in Child Care Law and Policy' Part II: (1991) 13(4) *Journal of Social Welfare and Family Law* 285, 292.

parents, Cafcass, or a litigation guardian, the Act was passed only a few years after the *Gillick* case and does enable children adjudged to have sufficient understanding to instruct their own solicitors, make their own applications, use local authority complaints procedures, and refuse to cooperate with a child assessment order.

Fox Harding concludes by wondering whether the Children Act's inclusion of all four viewpoints could be an attempt to strike a balance, 'strengthening parents' powers in some areas, children's rights in others, and the scope for action of courts and social workers in other areas again. It may be argued that what is achieved is genuinely more effective balance, correcting tendencies to both over- and under-react'.[43]

Fox Harding was writing just as the Act was coming into force and noted that 'much would depend on how the Act is interpreted and resourced'.[44] In 2018, Roger Smith returned to the four value perspectives in light of the Act's operation and more recent policy developments.[45] He noted that government support for adoption was aligned with a *laissez-faire* perspective in which state intervention is limited but authoritative and final. Increasing numbers of child protection interventions (discussed at 11.5.1) reflect the state paternalism and child protection viewpoint, as did the Conservatives' troubled families initiative.[46] In contrast, Labour's Sure Start programme, which provides community-based services for families and which has been the subject of considerable budget cuts,[47] was 'effecting an accommodation between family support [defence of the birth family] and child protection'.[48] The effect of austerity has also been, Smith argues, to hinder the recognition of children's rights.

He concluded that the *laissez-faire* and child protection viewpoints had 'gained in authority and influence, and in parallel, family support and children's rights advocates have been weakened, both materially and in terms of their presence in policy debates'.[49] While *laissez-faire* and paternalism 'may disagree as to whether the "family" or the "child" is the focal point for intervention, and . . . differ over the nature and extent of intervention, they are', Smith argues 'effectively bound by their shared commitment to coercive, one-sided and authoritarian modes of determining family structures and parental behaviour'.[50]

11.4 Duties towards children in need under Part III

Section 17(1) Children Act 1989 imposes a general duty on local authorities to 'safeguard and promote the welfare of children within their area who are in need' and, 'so far as is consistent with that duty, to promote the upbringing of such children by their families, by providing a range and level of services appropriate to those children's needs'.

The general duty to children in need is supplemented by specific obligations in Schedule 2 to the Act, such as to take reasonable steps, through the provision of services under Part

---

[43] LM Fox Harding, 'The Children Act 1989 in Context: Four Perspectives in Child Care Law and Policy' Part II: (1991) 13(4) *Journal of Social Welfare and Family Law* 285, 300.

[44] LM Fox Harding, 'The Children Act 1989 in Context: Four Perspectives in Child Care Law and Policy' Part II: (1991) 13(4) *Journal of Social Welfare and Family Law* 285, 299.

[45] R Smith, 'Reconsidering Value Perspectives in Child Welfare' (20180 48 *British Journal of Social Work* 616.

[46] This 2011 initiative involved local authority intervention in families with at least two of these three criteria: children involved in criminal offences, certain levels of school exclusion and truancy, and at least one parent who was in receipt of out-of-work benefits.

[47] See House of Commons Library Briefing Paper 7257, *Sure Start (England)* (2017). For a discussion of the approaches of the Labour and subsequent coalition governments, see B Featherstone, K Morris, and S White, 'A Marriage Made in Hell: Early Intervention Meets Child Protection' (2014) 44(7) *British Journal of Social Work* 1735.

[48] R Smith, 'Reconsidering Value Perspectives in Child Welfare' (20180 48 *British Journal of Social Work* 616, 630.

[49] R Smith, 'Reconsidering Value Perspectives in Child Welfare' (20180 48 *British Journal of Social Work* 616, 629.

[50] R Smith, 'Reconsidering Value Perspectives in Child Welfare' (20180 48 *British Journal of Social Work* 616, 629.

III to prevent children within their area suffering ill-treatment or neglect (para 4(1)); and to take reasonable steps to minimise the need for compulsory state intervention including care applications and criminal cases against children (para 7).

There were 389,260 children in need in England at 31 March 2020.[51] The number and rate of children in need fluctuates only slightly from year to year, in contrast with the number of children subject to child protection investigations. Let us look at what is meant by a 'child in need'.

11.4.1 When is a child in need?

Section 17(10) Children Act 1989 defines a child as being in need if:

(a) he is unlikely to achieve or maintain, or to have the opportunity of achieving or maintaining, a reasonable standard of health or development without the provision for him of services by a local authority under this Part;

(b) his health or development is likely to be significantly impaired, or further impaired, without the provision for him of such services; or

(c) he is disabled.[52]

Section 19 defines 'development' as physical, intellectual, emotional, social or behavioural development; and 'health' as physical or mental health. A disabled child is one who is 'blind, deaf or dumb or suffers from mental disorder of any kind or is substantially and permanently handicapped by illness, injury or congenital deformity or such other disability as may be prescribed'.

The local authority must identify which children are in need[53] and assess those needs.[54] The current statutory guidance for all organisations who work with children is called *Working Together to Safeguard Children*.[55] This provides guidance on the purpose of an assessment, namely to analyse whether the child is in need, the nature of any services required (and whether further specialist assessments are required. This means looking at:

* the nature of the welfare concerns
* the family's strengths and weaknesses
* the vulnerability and resilience of the child
* factors that help protect the child from harm
* the family history (for example, is there a history of inter-generational poor parenting)
* the ability of the parents and wider family to safeguard and promote the child's welfare
* the risks to the child and how they should be managed.

---

[51] Department for Education, *Characteristics of Children in Need: 2020* (2020).
[52] Disabled children may also be provided with services under Services for disabled children under s2 Chronically Sick and Disabled Persons Act 1970.
[53] Schedule 2 para 1(1).
[54] HM Government, *Working Together to Safeguard Children* (2018).
[55] HM Government, *Working Together to Safeguard Children: A Guide to Inter-Agency Working to Safeguard and Promote the Welfare of Children* (2015, revised 2018).

Each area will have a Local Safeguarding Children Board which will publish the criteria it uses to determine whether a child's situation merits a referral to the local authority for an assessment of whether the child meets the criteria in s17. The definition of 'need' was kept deliberately wide so as to 'reinforce the emphasis on preventative support and services to families'.[56] The only way to challenge a decision that a child is not in need, apart from by complaining to the local authority or ombudsman, is on the principle of *Wednesbury* unreasonableness: that no local authority could have rationally reached the conclusion that the child was not in need. That is a high standard. The local authority will identify and record the cause of the child's primary need. As Figure 11.2 shows, abuse or neglect is by far the most common primary need, followed by family dysfunction and a child's disability. Local authorities also track additional factors that they identify during the assessment which have contributed to the child being in need. Of these, the single most common factor is domestic abuse, whether directed at the child, a parent or carer, or other adult in the household. The second most common factor is mental ill health, followed by emotional abuse, drug and alcohol abuse, and neglect.[57] Some of these factors may be experienced in combination.

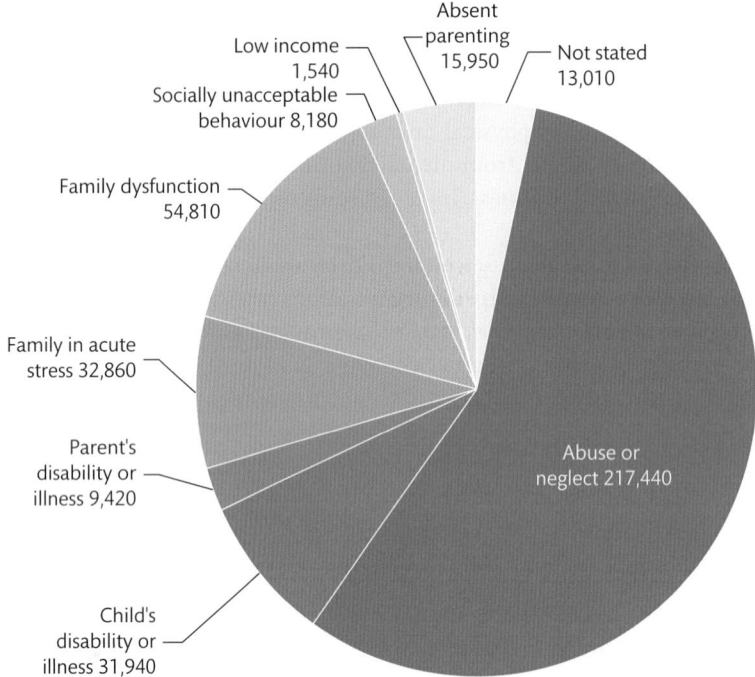

FIGURE 11.2 **Children in need at 31 March 2020 by primary need at assessment, England, 2020**

Source: Department for Education, *Characteristics of Children in Need: 2020 England* (2020).

---

[56] *Children Act 1989 Guidance and Regulations: Volume 2 Family Support, Day Care and Educational Provision for Young Children* (HMSO 1991).

[57] Department for Education, *Characteristics of Children in Need: 2018 to 2019 England* (2019).

11.4.2 How may a child come to the attention of children's services?

There are many different ways in which a child may come to the attention of the local authority's children's services team.

- In private law proceedings where there are child protection concerns, through a s37 direction. This says that in any family proceedings the court has the power to order the local authority to consider the child's circumstances and whether the authority should apply for a care or supervision order. This is discussed at 10.7.3.

- Through referrals and tip-offs from people concerned about the child, such as neighbours.

- Through a referral by the child's school. Referrals from education establishments have almost doubled in the last decade.[58]

- Because he or she is homeless.

- Because he or she is disabled, lacks mental capacity, or otherwise has specific needs. The local authority has duties towards a child because of his or her disability, whether or not there are any child protection concerns.

- Through a referral by a safeguarding lead at a hospital, or by another medical professional.

- Through a referral by the police, for example because they have been called out because of a domestic abuse incident in the home. The police are the single biggest category of referrers, accounting for about 28.6 per cent of referrals.[59]

- Self-referrals from a child, parent, or other family member.

- As someone who has committed a criminal offence. There can be an overlap with being a victim of a crime here: for example, children involved in 'county lines' drug selling are both committing a crime and also victims of grooming by criminal gangs. Children soliciting for prostitution are committing an offence, but these days we would properly refer to such children as victims of child sexual exploitation.

- As trafficked children or unaccompanied asylum seekers.

SCENARIO 2

Illustration 1: Maya

Fifteen-year-old Maya may have come to the local authority's attention for several reasons, such as her repeated running away, her involvement in minor crime, her being found by the police on drugs, and through intelligence about gang activity.

---

[58] Association of Directors of Children's Services *Research Report: Safeguarding Pressures Phase 6* (2018).
[59] Association of Directors of Children's Services *Research Report: Safeguarding Pressures Phase 6* (2018).

SCENARIO 1

Illustration 2: Andrzej and grandmother Lena

Andrzej's grandmother seeks advice from her GP about the difficulties that she is experiencing in caring for Andrzej's increasing needs as she gets older. She is, however, very worried about seeking help, in case he is removed from her care. Following the discussion with the GP, she contacts the local authority children's services department. As a result of this, a social worker undertakes an assessment of Andrzej's needs and Lena's ability to meet them, and whether Lena herself has any needs. The social worker explains that Andrzej is a child in need of services under s17 Children Act because he is disabled. Lena is assessed under 17ZC Children Act as a parent carer. Although not a parent, the definition of parent carer is a person aged 18 or over who provides or intends to provide care for a disabled child for whom the person has parental responsibility. That definition includes Lena, who has parental responsibility by virtue of the guardianship.

11.4.3 Services that the local authority may provide

If the local authority has assessed a child as being in need, then it should prepare a plan that sets out which services are to be provided to the child and his family, and who is to provide them.

These could include:

- advice, guidance and counselling (Schedule 2 para 8)
- occupational, social, cultural or recreational activities (para 8)
- home help, which may include laundry facilities (para 8)
- facilities for, or assistance with, travelling to and from home for the purpose of taking advantage of any other service provided under this Act or of any similar service (para 8)
- assistance to enable the child concerned and his family to have a holiday (para 8)
- daycare for a child aged under 5 who is not yet at school (s18)
- care or supervised activities for a child attending school (outside school hours or in holidays) (s18)
- accommodation (s17) (this is in addition to the power under s20)
- when the child is living apart from his family, services to enable him to live with his family or to promote contact between him and his family if necessary in order to safeguard or promote his welfare (para 10)
- family centres such as Sure Start[60] which provide advice to parents and a play space for children
- assistance in kind (such as furniture, food, clothing etc.) or in cash (s17)
- respite care or vouchers for respite care (para 6).

Services can be provided for the child or for any member of his family, as long as it is provided with a view to safeguarding or promoting the child's welfare: see s17(3). The 'family', in relation to such a child, includes any person who has parental responsibility for the child and any other person with whom he has been living.

---

[60] See House of Commons Library Briefing Paper 7257, *Sure Start (England)* (2017).

SCENARIO 1

Illustration 3: Andrzej and grandmother Lena

The social worker has advised Lena that Andrzej is a child in need of services under s17 Children Act. He meets the criteria under s17 by virtue of being disabled; it is not a requirement that he be neglected or mistreated. Nevertheless, when considering what needs he has, the local authority will consider Lena's capacity to care for him and her own needs. In this case, the local authority arranges for home help, comprising help with household chores and personal care for Andrzej, home adaptations such as equipment to help lift him from his wheelchair into bed, and respite care breaks outside the home. They refer Lena to a support group for carers and arrange for Andrzej to be collected each week and taken to a local art group for children with disabilities. The local authority arranges for someone to check whether Lena and Andrzej receive all the state benefits to which they are entitled, including disability living allowance and carers' allowance.

11.4.4 Limitations on the local authority's obligations

It is important to note that—aside from a duty to provide accommodation under s20 in some circumstances—the local authority does not owe an enforceable duty to provide services to any particular child in need, but only to the general category of children in need and their families. This is clear from Key Case *R (on the application of G) v Barnet London Borough Council.*

The local authority's duty extends only to maintaining a level and range of services sufficient to enable the authority to discharge its functions under the Part III of the Act and to assessing whether a child is in need. The Act does not require authorities to then meet those assessed needs of every child in need irrespective of the authority's resources.

There is an exception to this: the local authority may be obliged to provide support under s17 if necessary to prevent a breach of the family's human rights or European treaty rights.[61] This may be the case for some categories of migrants refused access to other public funds.

11.5 Provision of accommodation under Part III

We have previously seen (at 11.4.3) that local authorities have the power (but not duty) to accommodate children who are homeless under s17 as part of its general powers in relation to children in need. A further aspect of state support for children is contained in s20. This enables a local authority to offer accommodation to children and young adults in certain situations. Indeed, s20 sets out some situations in which the local authority has a legally enforceable duty to provide accommodation ('*shall* provide accommodation') to a particular child, as opposed to simply the power to do so. No court process is involved.

The key provisions are set out in Table 11.1.

---

[61] Nationality, Immigration and Asylum Act 2002 Sch 3. See NRPF Network, *Assessing and Supporting Children and Families Who Have No Recourse to Public Funds* (2018).

KEY CASE *R (on the application of G) v Barnet London Borough Council*
[2003] UKHL 57

This case comprises three conjoined appeals in which a parent argued that the local authorities concerned were under a duty to meet the assessed needs of their children for accommodation under s17 or s23, and that this included providing accommodation for the child and parent together, as distinct from the child alone. Note that s23 has since been repealed and replaced by ss22A-F.

Per Lord Nicholls:

> The financial resources of local authorities are finite. The scope for local authorities to increase the amount of their revenue is strictly limited. So, year by year, they must decide what priority to give to the multifarious competing demands on their limited resources. They have to decide which needs are the most urgent and pressing. The more money they allocate for one purpose the less they have to spend on another. In principle, this decision on priorities is entrusted to the local authorities themselves. In respect of decisions such as these, council members are accountable to the local electorate.[62]
>
> The ability of a local authority to decide how its limited resources are best spent in its area is displaced when the authority is discharging a statutory duty as distinct from exercising a power. A local authority is obliged to comply with a statutory duty regardless of whether, left to itself, it would prefer to spend its money on some other purpose. A power need not be exercised, but a duty must be discharged. That is the nature of a duty. That is the underlying purpose for which duties are imposed on local authorities. They leave the authority with no choice.[63]

By a majority (Lords Hope, Scott, and Millett) the Lords concluded that s17(1) imposed a 'general and overriding duty to maintain a level and range of services sufficient to enable the authority to discharge its functions under Part III of the Act' and did not impose a particular duty owed to a specific child.

The Lords all agreed that s23 also did not require the local authority to house homeless children with their parents because that particular section did not create a duty to house the child.

TABLE 11.1 Section 20 accommodation

Provision	Duty or Power	Age	Circumstances	Limitations
20(1)	Duty	Under 18	Child in need, where no one can care for him or no PR	Parental consent and ability to remove
20(2)	Duty	16 and 17	Where child's welfare would be seriously prejudiced without accommodation	Consent of young person
20(4)	Power	Under 18	Where accommodation would safeguard or promote the child's welfare	Parental consent and ability to remove, but only where child under 16
20(5)	Power	16 to 20 inclusive	Accommodation in community home to safeguard or promote welfare	Consent of young person

---

[62] At [11].
[63] At [12].

11.5.1 Interrelationship with s17

Where a child is in need, he may be accommodated under either s17 or s20. From the point of view of the child, accommodation under s20 is preferable. This is because those accommodated under s20 become looked after children, whereas those under s17 do not. (We consider looked after children at 11.4, but about 18 per cent of them are accommodated under s20.[64]) Looked after children are eligible for a wide range of services including into adulthood. It is therefore more costly to accommodate a child under s20 than s17. This is why in *R (G) v London Borough of Southwark* the local authority, Southwark, sought to accommodate the child under s17.[65] However, the House of Lords held that if the requirements of s20(1) or (2) were satisfied, the *duty* to accommodate G arose under s20, and the council could not side-step that duty by giving the accommodation a different label, such as s17 or saying that is a private arrangement between the child and those he lives with.[66]

SCENARIO 1

Illustration 4: Andrzej and grandmother Lena

One of the aspects of Andrzej's child in need plan is the provision of respite care to give Lena a break and to give Andrzej a change of scene. The local authority arranges for Andrzej to be accommodated in the home of foster carers. The legal basis could be s17(6), which gives local authorities the power to provide accommodation 'for any child within their area (even though a person who has parental responsibility for him is able to provide him with accommodation) if they consider that to do so would safeguard or promote the child's welfare', or it could be s20(4). There is now government guidance which explains how to determine which provision is most appropriate for the situation.[67] Both provisions require the consent of someone with parental responsibility, but the effect of him being accommodated under s20 would be that Andrzej became a looked after child, which is a status that carries with it certain entitlements. Lena may find looked after status to be reassuring, or she may feel that it implies that her care was inadequate.

11.5.2 What accommodation?

The accommodation provided by the local authority may take a number of different forms, reflecting the child's needs. As we see at 11.6.1, because children accommodated under s20 are looked after children, the local authority is under a duty to make arrangements for the child to live with a parent, a person who is not a parent but who has parental responsibility

---

[64] Department for Education, *Children Looked After in England (Including Adoption) year ending 31 March 2019* (2019).

[65] [2009] UKHL 26.

[66] Calling it a private arrangement is a way for the authority to avoid paying the child's carers an allowance and providing the child with the services it owes to looked after children. See *Southwark London Borough Council v D* [2007] EWCA Civ 182, *R (SA) v Kent County Council* [2011] EWCA Civ 1303, and *R (A) v Coventry City Council* [2009] EWHC 34.

[67] For how to determine which section should be applied, see the guidance in Department for Children, Schools, and Families, *Short Breaks: Statutory Guidance on How to Safeguard and Promote the Welfare of Disabled Children Using Short Breaks* (2010).

for the child, or a person who held a 'live with' order in respect of the child prior to the making of a care order, unless this is not consistent with the child's welfare or would not be reasonably practicable. If so, they must accommodate the child 'in the placement which is, in their opinion, the most appropriate placement available' (s22C).

11.5.3 The child's wishes and feelings

Under s.20(6), the local authority must ascertain the child's wishes and feelings regarding the provision of accommodation so 'far as is reasonably practicable and consistent with the child's welfare' and give 'due consideration (having regard to his age and understanding) to such wishes and feelings'. *Liverpool City Council v Hillingdon* tells us that a local authority should reach the conclusion that the child's wishes are decisive only as part of an overall judgment including an assessment of the child's welfare needs, and the type and location of accommodation that would meet those needs.[68] This may be with a relative or friend, with a local authority foster parent, or in a children's home or residential placement. Severely disabled children may be provided with long-term accommodation in specialist units. Some may be in supported or semi-independent housing such as that offered by the charity YMCA, or under a scheme such as Nightstop, which provides a few nights' emergency accommodation in host families until a more long-term solution can be reached.

11.5.4 The duty to accommodate children in need

Section 20(1) provides an enforceable duty on the local authority to accommodate a child (someone aged under 18) in the situations it lists: where there is no person with parental responsibility for a child or he is lost or abandoned (for example, because he is an unaccompanied asylum-seeker or trafficked child), or where a carer is prevented from looking after him. It may therefore be used if a parent is in hospital or prison or leaving an abusive

---

STATUTORY EXTRACT *s20 Children Act 1989*

Provision of accommodation for children: general

(1) Every local authority shall provide accommodation for any child in need within their area who appears to them to require accommodation as a result of—
  a) there being no person who has parental responsibility for him;
  b) his being lost or having been abandoned; or
  c) the person who has been caring for him being prevented (whether or not permanently, and for whatever reason) from providing him with suitable accommodation or care.

[(2) and (2A) omitted]

(3) Every local authority shall provide accommodation for any child in need within their area who has reached the age of sixteen and whose welfare the authority consider is likely to be seriously prejudiced if they do not provide him with accommodation.

---

[68] [2009] EWCA Civ 43 (Dyson LJ).

partner, or where the child has run away from or been kicked out of their home. There may be children accommodated under s20 whose parents have been classed as 'intentionally' homeless, a situation in which the local authority has a duty to house the children if they are in need, but not the adults.

The child must be a child in need. In *R (G) v Southwark London Borough Council*[69] Lady Hale suggested that there will be situations where a child will be homeless, but not in need. She gives the example of a child whose home has been damaged by fire or flood, but who can afford hotel accommodation. In that situation, the local authority has no obligation under s20.

If a child is in need, but does not fall within the circumstances set out in s20(1), then the local authority may still have a duty to house him under s20(3) if he is aged 16 or over and the authority considers that his welfare would otherwise be seriously prejudiced. Once the child reaches the age of 18, he will become a former child in need. He will not be accommodated under this section, but the local authority may offer him accommodation under s20(5) instead.

11.5.5 Discretionary powers to accommodate children and young people

Unlike the duty in s20(3), s20(4) provides a general power to 'provide accommodation for any child within their area (even though a person who has parental responsibility for him is able to provide him with accommodation) if they consider that to do so would safeguard or promote the child's welfare.' This section applies to any child aged under 18, but in relation to those aged under 16 some limitations apply including the requirement of parental consent which we discuss at 11.3.7. Note that s20(4) does not have an equivalent in the Social Services and Well-being (Wales Act) 2014.

Section 20(5) is a further power to house young people where doing so would safeguard or promote that person's welfare. This relates to those aged 16 to 20 but to accommodation in a community home, which would include supported or semi-independent housing for young people such as that offered by the YMCA. This section could be used for children who are 16 or 17 but in respect of whom s 20(3) does not apply because there is no serious prejudice.

STATUTORY EXTRACT *s20 Children Act 1989*

(4) A local authority may provide accommodation for any child within their area (even though a person who has parental responsibility for him is able to provide him with accommodation) if they consider that to do so would safeguard or promote the child's welfare.

(5) A local authority may provide accommodation for any person who has reached the age of sixteen but is under twenty-one in any community home which takes children who have reached the age of sixteen if they consider that to do so would safeguard or promote his welfare.

---

[69] [2009] UKHL 26.

Under both subsections, the local authority is exercising a discretionary power and is not under an enforceable duty to a particular child. This means that the availability of accommodation is likely to depend on the money available in the local authority budget.

11.5.6 The voluntary nature of s20 accommodation

The local authority's powers and duties under s20 should not be confused with care proceedings. In most cases, therefore, s20 is voluntary for the families involved. Parents of children in s20 accommodation do not lose their parental responsibility and the local authority does not acquire it. As such, there are no specific provisions around contact with an accommodated child (as there are under s34 in relation to a child in care) and so the level of contact may be determined by the parents, although they may not realise that.

If the local authority is concerned about the child's welfare, the involvement of the parents, or believe that the child may need to be accommodated long-term, then it would be appropriate, where the child is under 16, to make an application for a care order instead of continuing under s20. A care order would give the authority parental responsibility, the ability to curtail the parents' exercise of their parental responsibility (see 12.4.6) and involve the drawing up of a care plan for the child's future. Alternatively, the local authority could identify an appropriate guardian for the child under s5 Children Act 1989.

11.5.7 Limitations relating to children under 16

There are two important limitations which apply to those aged under 16:

1. Under subsection (7), a local authority may not provide accommodation under s20 for any child aged under 16 if there is an objection to this from any person who both (a) has parental responsibility for him; and (b) is willing and able to either provide accommodation for him or arrange for accommodation to be provided for him. A special guardian, a person with whom the child lives pursuant to a 'live with order', or an order under the inherent jurisdiction can, however, override the objection of others with parental responsibility.[70]

2. Even if a person with parental responsibility initially consented to accommodation under s20, under s20(8), he or she may, at any time, remove the child from that accommodation.

The requirement of consent

In practice, the ability of a person with parental responsibility to object to the child being accommodated has been treated as a requirement that the person actively consents, even though that is not mentioned in the statute. (Logically, if there was no requirement of consent, it would be easier to compulsorily remove a child from his family under s20 when there is no need for the care threshold to be met, than under s31 when the child is actually at risk of significant harm.[71]) If one parent consents and the other does not, it will

---

[70] Julie Stather, 'Is Time Running Out for s20 of the Children Act?' (*Family Law Week*, 17 April 2014) accessed 1 January 2020.
[71] *Northamptonshire County Council v AS and Others* [2015] EWHC 199 (Fam) at [29].

be necessary to consider whether the objecting party has parental responsibility. If they do and they can offer the child accommodation or arrange for accommodation, then their objection will prevent the local authority from accommodating the child. The requirement of consent therefore relates only to situations in which the parent both has PR and is willing and able to care for the child or arrange for a third party to do so.

In Key Case *Williams v London Borough of Hackney*, Lady Hale thought that it was confusing to talk of consent, because what is actually happening when a child is accommodated under s20 is that a parent is agreeing to delegate an aspect of their parental responsibility—the right to decide where the child lives—to the local authority, and the local authority has no power whatsoever to remove or retain the child without either that consent or a court order:

> ...a local authority cannot interfere with a person's exercise of their parental responsibility, against their will, unless they have first obtained a court order. Accordingly, no local authority have the right or the power to remove a child from a parent who is looking after the child and wants to go on doing so without a court order. Only the police can do that under section 46 of the 1989 Act.[72]

Where a parent does not have parental responsibility, as will be the case for some fathers who have not married the mother, it follows that their consent or objection is irrelevant. This may be a particular concern where the child is a newborn whose birth has not yet been registered, it being the naming of a father on the birth certificate that gives parental responsibility to unmarried fathers.

Despite Lady Hale's construction of s20 as involving the delegation of parental responsibility, the local authority does not acquire PR by virtue of the agreement. Ordinarily, parents are able to delegate aspects of their parental responsibility to any other adult by agreement, as we see at 8.6.1. Yet the Children Act does not provide any delegation to a local authority as a result of s20. Without full parental responsibility, the local authority's powers are limited to those contained in s3(5) Children Act 1989, which permits a person who does not have parental responsibility but who has care of the child to do whatever is reasonable in the circumstances to safeguard and promote the child's welfare (see 8.6.2). It is therefore extremely important that those with parental responsibility remain fully involved, although many parents report that this is not happening.[73]

There have been cases in which the local authority claims to have consent, but what they actually have is not true consent but the 'helpless acquiescence'[74] of a parent faced with a social worker implying that he or she has the power to remove or retain a child despite having no care order, as in *R (G) v Nottingham City Council*. In that case, the local authority was concerned about the mother's ability to care for the child, and decided to remove the newborn straight from the maternity ward even though it had not obtained any court order entitling it to do so. 'When the moment of separation arrived', the mother, who had given birth three hours before, 'did not actively resist' the removal of her newborn baby

[72] *Williams v London Borough of Hackney* [2018] UKSC 37 [38] (Lady Hale).
[73] C Lynch, *Cooperation or Coercion: A Good Practice Guide: Children Coming into the Care System under Voluntary Arrangements: Findings and Recommendations of the Your Family, Your Voice Knowledge Inquiry* (Family Rights Group 2015). See also a summary by the same author at [2018, February] *Family Law* 191.
[74] *R (G) v Nottingham City Council* [2008] EWHC 152 (Admin); [2008] EWHC 400 (Munby P).

but became very distressed at it. 'The idea that this mother in this situation—physically and emotionally weakened and distressed by events—can sensibly be said to have given consent to the removal of her baby verges, in my judgment, on the unreal', said Munby P, holding that acquiescence was not consent. (Contrast this with the position in relation to adoption, in which a mother is legally unable to consent to placement or adoption in the first six weeks following the child's birth.) Lady Hale, giving the court's decision in *Williams*, explicitly approves the approach taken in that case:

> . . . the decision in *R (G) v Nottingham City Council* was absolutely right. The mother had just given birth. She wanted to look after her baby. The local authority had no power to prevent her and neither did the hospital. Helpless submission to asserted power does not amount to a delegation of parental responsibility or its exercise.[75]

As Andrew Pack, a local authority social worker, has written:

> There are reasons why a parent might not come forward and object—most obviously that without access to a lawyer or it being explained they don't even know that they can, or they are afraid of rocking the boat, or they are having faith that the system will work and do the right thing, or that they are intimidated that if they object then the case will be rushed off to Court and that this will be bad for them.[76]

Parental right to child's return

The second important limitation is that a person with parental responsibility may, at any time, remove the child from that accommodation if they are willing to accommodate or arrange accommodation for the child. They do not need to give any notice to do that, and it would appear that they cannot be bound by any agreement to give notice.[77] This is the decision in Key Case *Williams v London Borough of Hackney*, in which Lady Hale gave the unanimous judgment of the Supreme Court.

KEY CASE *Williams v London Borough of Hackney* [2018] UKSC 37

Eight children were removed from their parents into police protection on the basis that their home was unfit for habitation and one of the children had complained of mistreatment. They were taken to stay with local authority foster carers. The parents were arrested and bailed not to have contact with the children.

The next day the parents signed a 'safeguarding agreement' drawn up by the local authority, in which they agreed that the children would remain with the foster carers. The agreement did not refer to s20 or state its legal basis. Shortly thereafter, the father, having sought legal advice, gave the local authority formal notice that he withdrew his consent to the accommodation. The local authority did not intend to bring care proceedings and agreed that the children should be returned, but were unwilling to do so because of the bail conditions. The police initially refused to amend the bail conditions but eventually did so, and the children returned home after about two months away.

75 *Williams v London Borough of Hackney* [2018] UKSC 37 [38] (Lady Hale).
76 'The Fast and the Furious – Tunbridge Wells Drift', Suesspicious Minds Blog 21 October 2015. Available at https://suesspiciousminds.com/2015/10/21/fast-and-the-furious-tunbridge-wells-drift/ accessed 1 January2020.
77 This was the view taken by Munby P in *Re N (Adoption: Jurisdiction)* [2015] EWCA Civ 1112 at [169].

The parents brought various proceedings against the local authority. All of their claims were dismissed apart from their claim to damages under s7(1) the Human Rights Act 1998. They asserted that the local authority breached their right to private and family life because there was no lawful basis to accommodate the children once the 72 hours of police protection had expired.

The Supreme Court upheld the local authority's appeal in part, holding that:

- Talking about consent is confusing and the statute does not mention it. What is actually happening under s20 is that a parent or other person with parental responsibility is delegating the exercise of their parental responsibility—the right to decide where their child lives—to the local authority, for the time being. 'Any such delegation must be real and voluntary. Otherwise the local authority has no power to interfere with parental responsibility by taking the child away' (without a court order under a different provision).[78]
- The 'best way' to ensure that consent is real and voluntary is 'to inform the parent fully of their rights under s20, but a delegation can be real and voluntary without being fully "informed"'.[79] Consent is not real and voluntary in the situations found in *Coventry City Council v C, B, CA and CH*[80] and 'nor should any impression be given that the parent has no choice in the matter, as happened in *Re W (Parental Agreement with Local Authority)*'.[81]
- No delegation is required where there is no-one with parental responsibility, the child is lost or abandoned, or the parent is not offering to look after the child. 'Thus, for example, a father who is separated from the mother and is not offering the child a home or offering to arrange an alternative cannot object to the local authority accommodating the child at the mother's request; or, for example, the mothers in *Re AS*[82] or in *Medway Council v M and T*[83] who were compulsorily detained in hospital could not object to the local authority accommodating the child unless they were able to arrange alternative accommodation. . . . The local authority have neither the power nor the duty to accommodate the child if a parent with parental responsibility proposes to accommodate the child herself or to arrange for someone else to do so. If the local authority consider the proposed arrangements not merely unsuitable but likely to cause the child significant harm they should apply for an emergency protection order.'[84]
- 'A parent with parental responsibility may remove the child from accommodation provided or arranged by a local authority at any time. There is no need to give notice, in writing or otherwise. The only caveat, as Munby J said in *R (G) v Nottingham City Council*, is the right of anyone to take necessary steps to protect a person, including a child, from being physically

[78] At [39].
[79] At [39].
[80] Also known as *Re CA* [2012] EWHC 2190. There was a question mark over the mother's capacity to consent: not only did she have learning difficulties but she consented to the accommodation of her newborn baby just a few hours after having life-saving surgery and while on morphine. Moreover, she was not told that refusal of consent would result in the child staying in hospital with her for another day or two.
[81] Mother placed children with paternal grandmother as a result of local authority concerns, and signed an agreement with the local authority which said that it was not a legal agreement but 'could be used in court as evidence if needed'. Munby P thought that this 'can only have been intended to have the effect of warning the mother that if she did not 'toe the line' the agreement would be used against her in some way in any proceedings that ensued.
[82] *Northamptonshire County Council v AS and Others* [2015] EWHC 199 (Fam). The mother was sectioned under the Mental Health Act 1983. The local authority removed the child from a neighbour's care and accommodated the child for a month. The mother did not consent or object but as she was sectioned she possibly lacked the mental capacity to do so. The court held that the local authority had breached the mother's rights under Articles 6 and 8 and awarded £3,000 in damages.
[83] [2015] EWFC B164. The mother had periods of serious mental illness. The child was in s20 accommodation for two years, without her mother's consent, and for some of that time the mother was unaware of this. She and the child were each awarded £20,000 damages.
[84] At [43].

harmed by another: for example, if a parent turned up drunk demanding to drive the child home.[85] In such circumstances the people caring for the child would have the power (under section 3(5) of the Children Act 1989) to do what is reasonable in all the circumstances for the purpose of safeguarding or promoting the child's welfare'.[86]

· There is 'nothing in section 20 to place a limit on the length of time for which a child may be accommodated. . . . although it is not a breach of section 20 to keep a child in accommodation for a long period without bringing care proceedings, it may well be a breach of other duties under the Act and Regulations or unreasonable in public law terms to do so. In some cases there may also be breaches of the child's or the parents' rights under article 8 of ECHR'.[87]

In this case, the father's objection was not an unequivocal request for the children to be returned. Instead, his solicitors had sensibly and collaboratively tried to give the parents time to allay the council's concerns by improving the state of the home, rather than request the children's immediate return and risk the council responding by issuing care proceedings. As the parents had not objected or unequivocally requested the children's immediate return, there was a lawful basis for their continued accommodation and the parents' Article 8 rights had not been breached.[88] The bail conditions were not an insurmountable reason to refuse to return the children.

As *Williams* makes clear, what is required is 'real and voluntary' consent given by someone with parental responsibility. Without this consent, accommodating the child under s20 will be unlawful *unless* the person with parental responsibility is unable to provide accommodation for him or arrange for accommodation to be provided for him. In that situation, accommodating the child would be lawful. If there is a concern about what would happen if someone with parental responsibility was to remove the child, or if a long-term plan is needed, then the local authority should consider a care application, or if the situation is urgent then they should consider police protection or an emergency protection order.[89]

In a number of the cases, there has been a question mark over the capacity of a parent to consent because of illness or disability. Capacity is situation-dependent, and a parent may be unable to make a decision about some aspect of his or her life while still having sufficient understanding to give consent under s20. The social worker who is seeking consent to accommodate the child must be satisfied that the person giving consent has capacity. Where they do not, then they cannot give valid consent and thus s20 should not be used.

If a local authority refuses to return a child, the parent has a number of remedies outlined in *Williams*. He or she could seek judicial review or lodge a writ of habeus corpus, an ancient remedy requiring a person unlawfully detained to be produced to a court. They could make a criminal complaint under the Child Abduction Act 1984 (see 10.10.1). They could simply take the child.

---

[85] This is in fact an example given by the Lord Chancellor when introducing this aspect of the Children Bill: he said that s3(5) allowed a foster carer to refuse to hand over a child to a parent who was drunk or incapable, or late at night when a child was asleep. See J Masson, 'Questioning the Use of s20' (*Family Law Week* 26 November 2015).

[86] At [44].

[87] At [49] and [52].

[88] At [62].

[89] See Lady Hale's judgment at [45].

There may be a situation where one parent consents to s20 accommodation but the other parent does not. If that other parent has parental responsibility and can house the child, they can prevent the local authority accommodating the child or remove him from accommodation. If the parents are at odds in this way, then it would be sensible to apply for a s8 order. A parent cannot remove a child from accommodation if a person with a 'live with' order consents to it.

SCENARIO 2

Illustration 2: Maya

Maya continues to run away from home. The local authority offers her accommodation under s20. Maya's mother consents to Maya being accommodated by the local authority. Maya's father, who has parental responsibility but is in prison, is opposed to this. However, he is unable to prevent her from being accommodated because he is unable to accommodate her himself or arrange for her to be accommodated. If Maya's mother chooses to remove Maya from local authority accommodation and the local authority is concerned about this, the authority will need to bring care proceedings. Indeed, accommodating Maya long-term under s20 is inappropriate: only if Maya has a real prospect of returning home in the short term would it be appropriate in her situation. If this is not likely, then the most appropriate mechanism is a care application.

11.5.8 The position of those over 16

Subsection (11) tells us that the limitations of parental consent and right to remove do not apply where a child who has reached the age of 16 agrees to being provided with accommodation. The child can choose to live in local authority accommodation even if a person with parental responsibility objects to that and is willing and able to accommodate them, and that person cannot remove them. This is the case even though someone who is 16 or 17 is still a minor. Where older children are concerned, the provided accommodation may well be semi-supported accommodation, so the young person may have much reduced supervision compared to that which their parents might provide.

Welbourne suggests that the ability of a young person to opt into local authority accommodation (resources permitting, where there is a power and not a duty to accommodate them) may well make it unnecessary for the local authority to bring care proceedings if it is concerned about the child.[90] If the authority can obtain the child's consent to accommodation then the parents cannot challenge that other than by asking a court to exercise its inherent jurisdiction: s20 does not enable any objection to the child's living arrangements where that child is over 16. Once a child reaches the age of 17 years, or 16 years and married, they cannot in any case be the subject of a care application.[91]

What if a child who is 16 or 17 wishes to refuse accommodation but all those with parental responsibility wish him to be accommodated? The local authority may nevertheless be under a duty to offer accommodation if it believes that his welfare would be seriously prejudiced without accommodation. It is extremely doubtful that a young person would be

---

[90] P Welbourne, 'Parents' and Children's Rights and Good Practice: Section 20' [2017, January] *Family Law* 80, 86.
[91] See 12.2.1.

forced into accommodation in this way, both because otherwise he may be homeless and because his wishes and feelings should lead the local authority towards a type of accommodation that he is happy with, whether that is with family or friends or in his own semi-supported flat. If the local authority is worried about the child leaving accommodation, then it will need to consider whether to invite a court to exercise the inherent jurisdiction.

11.5.9 Section 20 as a route to adoption

While s20 is voluntary, there is a potentially serious consequence of a child being accommodated under s20, which is that under s22 Adoption and Children Act 2002 the local authority *must* apply to court for an adoption placement order for the child if the following three conditions are met:

1. they are accommodating the child (as they are under s20); and

2. the child has no parent or guardian or the authority consider that the conditions in section 31(2) of the 1989 Act are met (the care threshold criteria); and

3. they are satisfied that the child ought to be placed for adoption.

Of course, in the same situation the local authority could apply for a care order and in those proceedings seek a plan for adoption. However, s22 of the 2002 Act is an alternative route to adoption, enabling the local authority to directly apply for a placement order, as in *LB v London Borough of Merton*.[92]

Local authorities in England (but not Wales) also have a statutory duty under s22C(9A) Children Act 1989 to consider 'fostering for adoption' arrangements.[93] As discussed at 12.5.6 this means that if a local authority has taken the view that 'the long term permanence plan for a named child is likely to be adoption'[94] it should consider placing the child with foster carers who are also approved as potential adopters. Given that parents are not entitled to non-means tested legal aid under s20 but only if court proceedings are contemplated, it is possible that a child may be placed with foster carers who seek to adopt her when the parents are not entitled to free independent legal advice or (at that point) any court oversight. The Family Rights Group found that

> 83 local authorities reported that 163 voluntarily accommodated children were placed in foster for adoption placements initiated since 25 July 2014. Whilst this averaged 2 per authority, it masks huge variation in practice, with 40 of the 83 reporting that they had not used foster for adoption arrangements for any voluntarily accommodated child; 84 local authorities reported the age breakdown of 144 voluntarily accommodated children in foster for adoption arrangements instigated since 25 July 2014. 127 (88%) were babies aged under 6 months including 111 (77%) new borns aged under 6 weeks old.[95]

---

[92] [2013] EWCA Civ 476.

[93] This requirement was inserted into the Children Act 1989 by the Children and Families Act 2014.

[94] *Children Act 1989 Guidance and Regulations Volume 2: Care Planning, Placement and Case Review* (Department for Education 2015).

[95] C Lynch, *Cooperation or Coercion: A Good Practice Guide: Children Coming into the Care System under Voluntary Arrangements: Findings and Recommendations of the Your Family, Your Voice Knowledge Inquiry* (Family Rights Group 2015).

There is a wide divergence between local authorities, with some never using fostering for adoption for s20 children, and some having most of their fostering for adoption arrangements initially under s20. The removal of newborn babies is something that we discuss in Chapter 12. The number may indicate that parents are not fully aware of their right to refuse s20 accommodation and force the local authority to evidence its concerns by way of a care application.

FOCUS Think Critically

When is s20 appropriate?

The reality is that many children accommodated under s20 *are* children about whom the local authority has child protection concerns. Some of these concerns may be temporary: perhaps the parents are struggling or need a break and an offer of accommodation under s20 is combined with the provision of other support services designed to help the family. In this situation, s20 is being used as envisaged. In *Herefordshire Council v AB* Mr Justice Keehan identified a number of situations in which s20 would be appropriate:

1. Where the parents have requested that the local authority accommodate a young person who has behavioural problems, where the parents and social workers are cooperatively to resolve the issues and enable the young person's return home.

2. Where the parent or parents of a child or young person have suffered an unexpected domestic crisis and require support for a short period of time. [For example, because the parent is in hospital].

3. Where an unaccompanied asylum-seeking child requires accommodation in circumstances where there are no grounds to believe that the threshold criteria for a care order are met.

4. As respite care for a child or young person with a medical condition or disability.

5. As a shared care arrangement between the parents and the local authority, whereby the care threshold is not yet met but intensive support by the local authority is needed periodically.[96] (Cafcass guidance also states that s20 may be appropriate 'for a child with disabilities where her/his parent/s are not able to manage the level of need but can share parenting successfully, sometimes over a longer period of time.'[97])

The Fostering Network Wales found that weekend-only accommodation under s20 had been used with families at risk of breakdown for a range of reasons including parental-adolescent conflict, sibling conflict, child ADHD, parental mental health difficulties, epilepsy, overcrowding and violence, as part of a wider package of support.[98] Indeed, research by Packman et al. prior to the Children Act showed that voluntary accommodation by the local authority as part of a package of support designed to avert family breakdown led to more collaborative working with the family and better planning for the children than in those cases where the children were the subject of emergency compulsory interventions when things reached a crisis point.[99] Similarly, post-Children Act Roberts found that short-term accommodation under s20 was being used (appropriately) to support families in which the parents were recovering from substance dependency or health challenges.[100]

---

[96] [2018] EWFC 10 at [15]. For a discussion of this case, see J Pepper, 'Misuse of s20' at [2018, May] *Family Law* 610.

[97] Association of Directors of Children's Services, Cafcass, and Association of Directors of Social Services Cymru, *Practice Guidance for the Use of S20 Provision in the Children Act 1989 in England and the Equivalent S76 of the Social Services and Well-Being (Wales) Act 2014 in Wales* (2016).

[98] P Williams, *Support Care: The Preventative Face of Foster Care. A report to disseminate the findings of The Foster Network Wales Support Care Project 2005–2008* (The Fostering Network Wales 2008).

[99] J Packman, J Randall, and N and Jacques, *Who Needs Care? Social Work Decisions about Children* (Blackwell 1986).

[100] L Roberts 'Using Part-Time Fostering as a Family Support Services: Advantages, Challenges and Contractions' (2016) 26(7) *British Journal of Social Work* 2120.

For some children, attempts at avoiding compulsory proceedings are unsuccessful and a s20 arrangement leads to a care application. However, it is not an alternative to care proceedings, and it is wrong to use it:

1. Because the local authority does not think it has grounds to bring a care application ('It can never be permissible to seek agreement to do that which would not be authorised by order solely because it is known, believed or even suspected that no such authorisation would be given and in order to circumvent that position').[101]

2. As a holding position to buy extra time because a 26-week timetable starts whenever care proceedings are issued, although per Munby P in *Re N (Adoption: Jurisdiction)* it may be appropriate as a short-term measure.[102]

3. Because it is cheaper and less onerous to simply remove the child from home-related risks rather than to prepare a court case.

The utilisation of s20 as a long-term alternative to care has led in some cases to 'section 20 drift'; that is, children who are accommodated for a long period of time without the permanency planning that accompanies the making of a care order. Because s20 is voluntary and does not involve compulsory intervention by the state, the section does not provide the same safeguards for the child and the parties that court proceedings provide.[103] Social work resources tend to be committed to care cases rather than s20 cases because only the former involves strict deadlines overseen by a court, and accordingly 'being in voluntary accommodation may therefore mean not getting much social work service at all'.[104] While the local authority should hold regular review meetings attended by the Independent Reviewing Officer—in fact, as Masson points out, 'it must review the child's case just as regularly as it must review the care of children subject to care orders'[105]—the child does not have a litigation guardian because there is no litigation, and nor do the parents have access to legal aid, which is especially of concern given the relationship to adoption.

Andrew Pack, again:

> ultimately, section 20 drift cases are about an imbalance of power – the State is taking advantage of the fact that parents without access to a lawyer won't object or will agree to section 20. And so it becomes an alternative to going into Court proceedings. Court proceedings are expensive, and involve a lot of work (going to Court, writing statements and chronologies etc) and of course in Court social workers don't necessarily get things their own way and the Court can disagree with them. So there can be a temptation, if the parents aren't demanding the child back, to just keep going with the section 20 foster placement. And this of course is the drift element – these children can wait months or even longer, sat in limbo – nobody has decided whether the child can ever go home or whether the child's future lays elsewhere, the case just drifts. By the time the case finally gets to Court, that relationship between child and parent can be hard to put back together, and the problems the parent has may take time to address and it can be harder for them to get the child back.[106]

There have been several cases in which claims for damages under the Human Rights Act for the misuse of s20 have been successful. These include the cases mentioned in *Williams–Northampton-*

---

[101] *Coventry City Council v C, B, CA and CH* [2012] EWHC 2190 at [157].

[102] [2015] EWCA Civ 1112 at [157].

[103] P Welbourne, 'Parents' and Children's Rights and Good Practice: Section 20' [2017, January] *Family Law* 80, 85.

[104] J Masson, 'The State as Parent: The Reluctant Parent: The Problem of Parents of Last Resort?' (2008) 35(1) *Journal of Law and Society* 52.

[105] J Masson, 'Questioning the Use of s20' (*Family Law Week* 26 November 2015).

[106] 'The Fast and the Furious – Tunbridge Wells Drift', Suesspicious Minds Blog 21 October 2015. Available at https://suesspiciousminds.com/2015/10/21/fast-and-the-furious-tunbridge-wells-drift/ accessed 1 January 2020.

shire County Council v AS and Others, Medway Council v M and T (which contains a useful table of the damages awarded in different cases)[107]—and *Williams* itself. *In Herefordshire Council v AB*, two children were in s20 drift for an 'egregious' eight and nine years respectively before proceedings were commenced.[108] A high turnover of social workers amid heavy workloads can compound with misunderstanding of the law and result in a child who is physically safe, but legally insecure.[109] That said, s20 is a useful tool for social workers and families in those situations in which compulsory intervention is not merited, and properly used alongside other local authority support services may reduce or avoid the need for further intervention.

11.6 Duties to looked after children under Part III

Children who are accommodated by the local authority are known as looked after children. This includes:

- when the child is provided with accommodation under s20 Children Act 1989 for a period of more than 24 hours.
- where the child has been removed from home under a child assessment order
- when the local authority is accommodating the child pursuant to a request by a police officer who has taken the child into police protection (ss46(3)(f) and 21 Children Act 1989) or where the child is the subject of an emergency protection order.
- where the child is subject to a care order or interim care order (ss31 and 38 Children Act 1989) or an adoption placement order (even if they have not yet been placed) (s18 Adoption and Children Act 2002). Care and placement orders are discussed in Chapter 12.

Finally, although it is outside the scope of this book, a child who is remanded to local authority accommodation such as a secure children's home, having been charged with a crime, or who is subject to a youth rehabilitation order which requires them to reside in Local Authority accommodation (s21 Children Act 1989), is also a looked after child.

At 31 March 2020, there were 80,080 looked after children.[110]

As you can see, children may become looked after for a wide range of different reasons, and under a range of different legal provisions. They may also be living in a number of different types of accommodation such as foster care, children's homes, supported housing for young people, or in the homes of kinship carers. The local authority will have parental responsibility for some looked after children (such as those in care) but not for others (such as those accommodated under s20), or may be able to exercise parental responsibility only for certain purposes as is the case with emergency protection orders.

---

[107] It is unclear whether these cases would have been successful if decided post-*Williams*. While the mothers did not give consent, both objection and alternative accommodation are required and it is possible that they would have been unable to provide alternative accommodation. However, given the procedural defects and the lack of consideration of capacity to consent, there may still have been an actionable breach.

[108] [2018] EWFC 10; 'egregious' is the description of Mr Justice Keehan.

[109] See the explanation given by the assistant director of children's services in *Worcestershire County Council v AA* [2019] EWHC 1855 (Fam), another case involving eight-year drift.

[110] Department for Education, *Children Looked After in England (Including Adoption) year ending 31 March 2020* (2021).

> **STATUTORY EXTRACT** *s22 Children Act 1989*
>
> **General duty of local authority in relation to children looked after by them**
>
> (3) It shall be the duty of a local authority looking after any child—
>   (a) to safeguard and promote his welfare; and
>   (b) to make such use of services available for children cared for by their own parents as appears to the authority reasonable in his case.

11.6.1 What duties are owed?

Irrespective of the legal route by which the child came to be looked after, the local authority has certain obligations towards looked after children. Section 22(3) Children Act 1989 sets out the 'general duty'.

The obligation is to act as a 'corporate parent' and to offer everything that a good parent would offer including acting in the best interests of the child, encouraging the child's views, and promoting high aspirations.[111]

In addition to the general duty and all this involves, there are a number of specific duties the most important of which are set out below. Note that the local authority can act in a way that is inconsistent with these duties if this is necessary in order to protect members of the public from serious injury (s22(6)).

Accommodation and maintenance

Section 22A requires a local authority to provide accommodation for a child in their care, and s22B requires them to maintain a looked after child. Section 22C sets out the ways in which these things should happen.

As we have seen, an important principle underlying the Children Act 1989 is that children are usually best looked after by their families. Part III is designed to support that aim. Accordingly, s22C Children Act imposes a duty on the local authority to make arrangements for the child to live with a parent, a person who is not a parent but who has parental responsibility for the child, or a person who held a 'live with' order in respect of the child prior to the making of a care order.

If this is not consistent with the child's welfare or would not be reasonably practicable, the local authority should instead place the child in 'the placement which is, in their opinion, the most appropriate placement available', meaning one that they consider will best promote and safeguard the child's welfare.[112] This could be with a kinship or friend carers, a local authority foster carer, in a children's home or somewhere else. In deciding what is the most appropriate placement, the local authority must give preference to a placement with a kinship or friend carer and ensure that the placement enables the child to live near his home, does not disrupt his education or training, and if disabled is suitable to his needs. If the child has a sibling who is also looked after, then it should enable the

---

[111] The Children and Social Work Act 2017 identified seven core principles of corporate parenting. See Department for Education, *Applying Corporate Parenting Principles to Looked After Children and Care Leavers: Statutory Guidance for Local Authorities* (February 2018).
[112] Section 22C(5).

child and the sibling to live together.[113] Where reasonably practicable, the child should be accommodated in the local authority area. Clearly, this is not always easy and may well be impossible in many situations. There may be no local placements for the child. A foster carer who looks after one child may be unable to take their sibling.

Schedule 2 paragraph 21 Children Act 1989 requires a local authority to consider whether to seek contributions towards the accommodation of the child from 'any person liable to contribute' (note that this does not apply where the child is under a care order). They cannot do this if a parent is on state benefits and they cannot recover more than the actual cost of accommodating the child. As one commentator has pointed out, there are a number of difficulties inherent in this power, which perhaps explains why most local authorities do not seek to recover the costs of care in this way.[114]

Contact

Local authorities are under a statutory duty to endeavour to promote contact between the child and his parents, those with PR, any person who is not a parent of his but who has parental responsibility for him, and any relative, friend or other person connected with him (including siblings). The exception is where this is not reasonably practicable or consistent with his welfare.[115]

Contact for a child *in care* is governed by s34 and we discuss this at 12.4.6.

Education

As Table 11.2 shows, there is an emphasis on supporting young people in education, including continuation of education or training post-16. A number of amendments have been made to the Children Act by the Children Act 2004, the Children and Young Persons Act 2008, and the Children and Social Work Act 2017, to try to address the poor educational outcomes that looked after children experience for a range of reasons.[116] Under s22(3A), the local authority is under a particular duty 'to promote the child's educational achievement'. Local authorities must include a personal education plan (PEP) within their care plan for the child. This is 'an evolving record of what needs to happen for looked-after children to enable them to make at least expected progress and fulfil their potential'.[117] They must take efforts to minimise disruption to the child's education.[118] This is important when it comes to decide where a child should live and whether a child should be moved. Local authorities have to provide certain kinds of financial support to previously looked after children who wish to pursue education or training up to the age of 25 and must appoint officers whose role is to promote their educational achievement.

---

[113] Section 22C(7).

[114] See Suesspicious Minds, 'Hope Your Child Enjoyed Their Stay, Now If You Could Just Settle Your Bill, Please' available at https://suesspiciousminds.com/2013/08/14/hope-your-child-enjoyed-their-stay-now-if-you-could-just-settle-your-bill-please/ accessed 2 January 2020.

[115] Schedule 2 para 15 Children Act 1989.

[116] D Berridge, 'Theory and Explanation in Child Welfare: Education and Looked-After Children' (2007) 12 *Child and Family Social Work* 1.

[117] See Department for Education, *Promoting the Education of Looked After Children and Previously Looked After Children: Statutory Guidance for Local Authorities* (February 2018). The information that must be covered in the PEP are specified in Schedule 1 para 2 of the Care Planning, Placement and Case Review (England) Regulations 2010, SI 959/2010, as amended.

[118] Care Planning, Placement and Case Review Regulations 2010, SI 959/2010 at s10.

Consultation

Section 22(4) says that before making any decision with respect to a child whom they are looking after, or proposing to look after, a local authority shall, so far as is reasonably practicable, ascertain the wishes and feelings of:

(a) the child;

(b) his parents;

(c) any person who is not a parent of his but who has parental responsibility for him; and

(d) any other person whose wishes and feelings the authority consider to be relevant.

Where the child has a litigation guardian, he or she should also be consulted.[119]

Subsection (5) says that in making a decision about a looked after child, the local authority must give due consideration to the child's wishes and feelings, having regard to his age and understanding, and to the wishes and feelings of the other consultees. They must also give due consideration to the child's religious persuasion, racial origin and cultural and linguistic background. However, the section does not indicate any order of importance that each view should have relative to any other, nor does it require the local authority to do more than simply consider them.

Independent visitors

An independent visitor is an adult volunteer who visits, befriends, and advises the child, for example by taking them on social outings such as to the cinema. The local authority must appoint an Independent Visitor if the child falls within certain categories, or (and this was added by the Children and Young Persons Act 2008), it appears to them that it would be in the child's interests to do so. A *Gillick*-competent child can decide to reject the appointment of an Independent Visitor. The Visitor cannot be an officer of the local authority.[120] Some charities such as Action for Children, the National Youth Advocacy Service, and Coram offer an Independent Visiting Service.

11.6.2 The care plan

All looked after Children must have a care plan.[121] This sets out how the local authority intends to meet its duties to the child. The plan will identify the child's needs and how these are to be met. It will include a health plan, a personal education plan, a placement plan (where the child is to live), and a permanence plan for looking after the child long-term,[122] such as that they are to be adopted or live in long-term foster care. It will also include the arrangements for contact with the child's family and the wishes and feelings of those it has to consult.[123] Where there is a child protection plan, this will usually end when the child becomes looked after, and be replaced by the care plan.[124] The local authority must monitor the care plan, which it does with oversight from an Independent Reviewing Officer.

---

[119] *R v North Yorkshire County Council ex p M* [1989] 1 All ER 143.

[120] Section 16 of the 2008 Act inserts 23ZB into the Children Act 1989.

[121] Care Planning, Placement and Case Review Regulations 2010, SI 959/2010 at Reg 5.

[122] Care Planning, Placement and Case Review Regulations 2010, SI 959/2010 at Reg 5(a).

[123] Care Planning, Placement and Case Review Regulations 2010, SI 959/2010 at Reg 5(b)(v).

[124] *Children Act 1989 Guidance and Regulations Volume 2: Care Planning, Placement and Case Review* (Department for Education 2015) para 2.10.

Chapter 12 considers both care plans in the context of a child who is the subject of a care order under s31 Children Act 1989 and permanence planning in further detail.

FOCUS Know-How

The role of the Independent Reviewing Officer

Independent Reviewing Officers (IROs) were established by the Adoption and Children Act 2002. The relevant provisions can be found in the Children Act 1989.

Each local authority must appoint an IRO, whose role relates to the children looked after by that local authority. If a local authority is looking after a child they must have an IRO for that child's case. The IRO must:

- monitor the local authority's performance in relation to each child's case
- participate in any review of the child's case
- ensure that any ascertained wishes and feelings of the child concerning the case are given due consideration by the local authority
- perform any other function which is prescribed in regulations.[125]

The *Statutory Guidance for Independent Reviewing Officers and Local Authorities on Their Functions in Relation to Case Management and Review for Looked After Children* says that 'the primary task of the IRO is to ensure that the care plan for the child fully reflects the child's current needs and that the actions set out in the plan are consistent with the local authority's legal responsibilities towards the child.'[126] The IRO should chair each meeting that takes place to review the care plan for the child and should ensure that the child's voice is not lost. The local authority should not change the child's care plan without notifying them.[127] The officer also has an important role in preventing drift in a child's case. As we discuss in the focus box at 11.3.9 (Focus: Think Critically: When is s20 appropriate?) this is particularly a concern in relation to children accommodated under s20.

The IRO has a crucial role in holding the local authority to account. As Holman J said in *London Borough of Haringey v Musa*, 'the whole point and purpose of the system and machinery of independent reviewing officers is precisely to keep the local authority (who are no doubt extraordinarily busy and overworked) on their toes and to be asking awkward questions.'[128] This is particularly important given that courts have limited powers to monitor if and how local authorities meet their obligations in relation to children in care after a care plan has been made, which are by way of judicial review or a claim under the Human Rights Act 1998. (See 12.4.6). There have, however, been concerns that IROs are not truly independent or sufficiently robust in challenging local authority decision or poor practice. The IRO is usually a qualified social worker with management experience, and they are recruited and paid by the local authority. However, if they were further separated from local authorities so as to appear more independent, then 'important opportunities to influence change would most likely be lost'.[129] Nevertheless, s11 Children and Young Persons Act 2008 gave government the power to transfer IRO services to a national body outside local authority control if it becomes necessary.

---

[125] s25B(1) Children Act 1989.

[126] *Statutory Guidance for Independent Reviewing Officers and Local Authorities on Their Functions in Relation to Case Management and Review for Looked After Children* (Department for Children, Schools, and Families 2010) para 2.10.

[127] *Statutory Guidance for Independent Reviewing Officers and Local Authorities on Their Functions in Relation to Case Management and Review for Looked After Children* (Department for Children, Schools, and Families 2010) para 3.71.

[128] *London Borough of Haringey v Musa* [2014] EWHC 1341 (Fam) [15] (Holman J).

[129] J Dickens, G Schofield, C Beckett, G Philip, and J Young, *Care Planning and the Role of the Independent Reviewing Officer* (Centre for Research on Children and Families, University of East Anglia 2015).

11.6.3 Duties to former looked after children

The local authority's obligations do not end when the child ceases to be looked after at the age of 16. A different set of obligations must then be met. What these obligations are depends upon which of the following categories applies to the child:

1. *An eligible child.* This is a child aged 16 or 17 who is currently looked after and has been looked after for at least 13 weeks since the age of 14. The 13 weeks do not need to be continuous.

2. *A relevant child.* This is a child aged 16 or 17 who is *not* currently looked after, but who was looked after for at least 13 weeks since the age of 14 including a period of time after their 16th birthday. Again, the 13 weeks do not need to be continuous.

Note that the child will cease to be looked after and become a qualifying care leaver instead if he returns to live with his or her parents, someone with parental responsibility, or someone who had a 'live with' order before he became looked after, and lives there for more than six months. If that arrangement breaks down, the child may return to being looked after.

3. *A former relevant child.*[130] This is a young person aged 18 to 21, or, if they are in full-time education, 18 to 25. Note that if they are still being assisted by the local authority at the age of 21, then they remain a former relevant child until they turn 25.

4. *A qualifying care leaver.* This is a young person aged 16 to 21 who was looked after (but not necessarily under a care order) for *fewer than* 13 weeks since the age of 14 and who thus is not eligible or relevant, but who was looked after for at least a day after they turned 16. If they are in full-time education, they are eligible for support until the age of 25. This category also includes young people aged 16 to 20 who were looked after at one time, but who ceased to be looked after on the making of a special guardianship order that is in force or remained in force until they were 18.

A child who does not fall into any of these categories will not be eligible for services. Thus, for example, a young person who was looked after for fewer than 13 weeks since the age of 14 but who permanently ceased to be looked after before their 16th birthday would not be eligible. (As Masson points out, this creates an incentive for local authorities to discharge children before the age of 16.[131])

SCENARIO 1

Illustration 5: Andrzej and grandmother Lena

As we saw, if the local authority accommodated Andrzej under s20 then he would become a looked after child. The authority would therefore owe him a number of duties outlined above. However, this support does not necessarily end when he reaches adulthood. We will need to wait until he is older (he is currently only 9) to see what level of accommodation the local authority has provided over the subsequent years in order to determine which of the above categories, if any, he falls into. This will determine the local authority's future obligations to him.

---

[130] By definition, all former relevant children will also be former eligible children.
[131] Judith Masson, 'The State as Parent: The Reluctant Parent: The Problem of Parents of Last Resort?' (2008) 35(1) *Journal of Law and Society* 52.

SCENARIO 2

Illustration 3: Maya

If Maya is accommodated long-term under s20 (which, as we have seen, is inappropriate in this case) or is the subject of a care order following a local authority application to court (see Chapter 12), then she has become a looked after child. The local authority continues to have responsibilities towards her into adulthood. For example, if she was looked after for at least 13 weeks since the age of 14 including a period of time after her 16th birthday then she is a relevant child. The local authority is responsible for her accommodation and living costs. Once she reaches the age of 18, she is a former relevant child, and the local authority must continue to financially support her in education or training.

Table 11.2 sets out the local authority's duties and powers in relation to children and young adults in these four categories.

11.6.4 Pathway plans

A key resource for children and young people in the first three categories is the pathway plan. This is a document that is designed to help the transition from being looked after to becoming independent. They are usually started when the young person is around the age of 15. The plan will identify what services the local authority will provide to meet the needs of the young person.

11.6.5 Staying put arrangements

Part V of the Children and Families Act 2014 introduced staying put arrangements, which enable a young person who has reached the age of 18 to continue to live with their former foster carer if both agree. (Note that as the arrangements concern adults, they are not current foster care arrangements and thus are not governed by fostering regulations.) Under s23CZA Children Act 1989, a young person is eligible for a staying put arrangement if they are a former relevant child who was looked after as an eligible child immediately prior to their 18th birthday, although local authorities can choose to provide staying put arrangements to other groups. This is likely to depend on resources, as local authorities must provide some financial support to the former foster carers.

Whether or not they provide financial support, local authorities must provide advice, assistance and support to the young person and the former foster parent. The aim of the legislation was to help young people 'to enter adult life with the same opportunities and prospects as their peers' rather than having to leave their homes at the age of 18' and support them 'to develop life skills including in relation to self-esteem and resilience, relationships with others; finances and budgeting; cooking; managing a home; and applying for jobs'.[132]

---

[132] Department for Education, *Children Act 1989 Guidance and Regulations Volume 3: Planning Transition to Adulthood for Care Leavers* (2015). 'Staying put' is called 'When I am Ready' in Wales.

TABLE 11.2 Local authority help for previously looked after children

	Eligible Child	Relevant Child	Former Relevant Child	Qualifying Care Leaver
Keep in touch	Yes	Yes	Yes	Yes
Personal adviser until the age of 25	Yes	Yes	Yes	No
Assess needs and produce pathway plan	Yes	Yes	Yes	No
Accommodation	Provided by the local authority as the child is looked after.	Will arrange and pay for this, including all utility bills.	Will provide and pay for accommodation during college or university holidays if studying away from home. If under 21, is a priority for housing under homelessness legislation. If over 21, priority if vulnerable.	Will provide and pay for accommodation during college or university holidays if studying away from home. May be priority for housing under homelessness legislation if vulnerable.
Financial help	Will maintain the child, but the money will usually go to the child's carers directly.	Will meet the child's basic living costs plus those things in the pathway plan. Must have a policy on other things that it will pay for.	Must pay for expenses relating to education and training, and contribute to the costs of living near to the place of education or training. If in higher education, young person is eligible for local authority bursary plus normal student finance grants and loans. Must pay a setting up home allowance (e.g., to buy furniture).	May pay for expenses related to education and training and contribute to living expenses related to education and training. May buy items for young person directly or exceptionally give cash, to the extent that the young person's welfare and education requires it.

Can they claim benefits?	Cannot claim income support, income-based jobseekers' allowance, or housing benefit as their living costs are met by the local authority, which cannot provide them with less than benefits would provide. Their right to benefits was removed by the Children (Leaving Care) Act 2000.	Cannot claim income support, income-based jobseekers' allowance, or housing benefit as their living costs are met by the local authority, which cannot provide them with less than benefits would provide. Their right to benefits was removed by the Children (Leaving Care) Act 2000.	May buy items for young person directly or exceptionally give cash, to the extent that the young person's welfare and education requires it.	Yes although eligibility may vary depending on their age.
	Can claim universal credit if they have limited capacity to work or are not fit to work, or are responsible for a child.	They can claim universal credit if they have limited capacity to work or are not fit to work, or are responsible for a child.	Should continue to pay for other things set out in the pathway plan.	
	Disabled children are eligible for disability related benefits, and carers for carers' allowance.	Disabled children are eligible for disability related benefits, and carers for carers' allowance.	Yes.	

11.7 Child protection investigations under Part V

We have considered what brings a child to the attention of social services and the local authority's services designed to support children remaining with their families. In this section, we consider what happens if a local authority becomes concerned about a child's welfare, how social workers may assess the situation, and what steps they may take next.

Local authority children's services departments will receive a great many referrals of children. Given the demand on resources, it is crucial to filter these according to the seriousness of the situation. In some cases, the local authority will simply refer the family to another agency or give advice and guidance. In others, it may need to undertake a fuller assessment of the situation. This will give the local authority more information about the child and his or her family and situation, so that social workers can decide whether the child has unmet needs (which may make them a child in need under s17 Children Act 1989) or whether child protection steps must be taken.

11.7.1 Section 47 investigations

At 10.7.3 we saw that under s37 Children Act 1989 a court may direct a local authority to investigate the child's circumstances and consider whether they should make an application for a care or supervision order, provide services to the child or his family, or take any other action about the child.

The duty to investigate may also arise under s47 Children Act in three situations:

1. where the local authority has reasonable cause to suspect that a child may be suffering or likely to suffer significant harm, which is the threshold for making a care or supervision application. Note that the duty to investigate is triggered by the authority having 'reasonable cause' to suspect significant harm. The authority does not need to believe on the balance of probabilities that the child is suffering harm, or likely to do so. It is unlikely to have that information at this stage.

2. where the child has been taken into police protection, which we discuss at 11.8.1.

3. where the court has made an emergency protection order relating to the child. We discuss emergency protection orders at 11.8.2.

In each of these situations, the local authority must investigate the child's well-being. It has no discretion not to do so.

The purpose of a s47 investigation is fourfold:

1. It should enable a local authority to decide whether it should make any application to court, such as for a care or supervision order.

2. It should enable the local authority to determine whether to exercise any of their powers. If the investigation reveals that the child is a child in need, then the authority may offer support under s17.

3. Where the child has been in police protection, the enquiry will enable the local authority to decide whether it ought to make an application for an emergency protection order to come into force at the end of police protection.

> **STATUTORY EXTRACT** *s47 Children Act 1989*
>
> (1) Where a local authority
>   (a) are informed that a child who lives, or is found, in their area
>   (i) is the subject of an emergency protection order; or
>   (ii) is in police protection; or
>   (b) have reasonable cause to suspect that a child who lives, or is found, in their area is suffering, or is likely to suffer, significant harm,
>
> the authority shall make, or cause to be made, such enquiries as they consider necessary to enable them to decide whether they should take any action to safeguard or promote the child's welfare.

4.   Whether it would be in the best interests of a child who is the subject of police protection to be in local authority accommodation.

The child's wishes and feelings are a relevant part of the assessment of what action if any should be taken by the authority: s47(5A).

A s47 investigation is multidisciplinary, and s47(9) imposes a duty on certain other professionals to assist with an investigation, unless that would be unreasonable in all the circumstances of the case. The duty is imposed upon any local authority; any local housing authority; the NHS commissioning boards; and any local clinical commissioning group or NHS trust. The investigation will usually involve social workers speaking to the person who made the initial referral as well as to any professionals connected to the child (such as the school's safeguarding lead); the child's family and any other caregivers; any brothers and sisters of the child; and the child themselves. This is to check on the physical and emotional condition of the child, hear what the child has to say, and record the household conditions. (If a care application is made, this information also forms part of the local authority's case papers.) The statutory guidance *Working Together to Safeguard Children*[133] says that social workers should consider the family's circumstances and history, the nature of the child's needs, and what is likely to be the most effective type of intervention (if, indeed, intervention is needed). The aim is to determine what level and type of risk the child may face, and how best to address that.

A s47 investigation does not entitle a social worker to forcibly enter the family home, but only to do so where invited. This means that a certain degree of cooperation from the child's family will be required. Social workers are under an obligation to take 'such steps as are reasonably practicable to obtain access to the child . . . unless they are satisfied that they already have sufficient information with respect to him' (s47(4)). However, if they are refused access to the child or denied information about his whereabouts, subsection

---

[133] HM Government, *Working Together to Safeguard Children: A Guide to Inter-Agency Working to Safeguard and Promote the Welfare of Children* (2015, revised 2018).

(6) says that the local authority shall (i.e., must) apply for either an emergency protection order, a child assessment order, a care order, or a supervision order 'unless they are satisfied that his welfare can be satisfactorily safeguarded without their doing so'. Seeing the child is almost always essential: the deaths of three of the children we discussed at 11.2, Kimberly Carlile, Tyra Henry, and Jasmine Beckford, all occurred after social workers had not been able to gain access to them.

Social workers must be careful in how they interview the child so as to get the highest possible quality of reliable evidence for any subsequent proceedings (you may come across references in cases to 'achieving best evidence' or 'ABE' interviews).[134] They may speak to a child without parental permission if they think that asking permission would put the child at further risk.

FOCUS Think Critically

Predicting risk

Predicting risk is extremely difficult. Information about the child's situation may not be easily obtained or may be unreliable. There is some evidence that social workers struggle to interpret new information neutrally, but use it to support their pre-existing theory about the situation.[135] Families may obstruct social workers. As we have seen, inter-agency cooperation can be lacking. As Munro explains:

> Identifying child abuse and assessing risk are more akin to making up a jigsaw puzzle than to any simple process of observation. Social workers need to gather together the little bits of information known to relatives, neighbours and professionals. They then have to try to fit the pieces together to arrive at a picture of the family. The task is far more complex than a typical jigsaw puzzle game. Social workers do not know in advance what the underlying picture is; they do not know if they have got all the pieces; and they are not sure if a particular piece belongs to this picture. To add to the complexity, they cannot be certain of the shape and colour of each piece: these are not made up of 'hard facts' but of information of varying degrees of reliability.[136]

Decision-making is also value laden. Different social workers may have different judgments about adequate parenting, and this may be filtered through experience. Tanner and Turney suggest that social workers may become desensitised, particularly in relation to 'unremitting low-level care'.[137] When the child is safe, such as in local authority accommodation, it is easy to take one's eye off long-term planning for the child in favour of dealing with crises elsewhere; hence the issue of section 20 drift discussed at 11.39 in the focus box 'Think Critically: When is s20 appropriate?' Sudden incidents, even if not the most serious within that family, or breaches of agreements by parents[138]

---

[134] Ministry of Justice, *Achieving Best Evidence in Criminal Proceedings* (March 2011).

[135] C Taylor and S White, 'Knowledge and Reasoning in Social Work: Educating for Humane Judgement' (2006) 36 *British Journal of Social Work* 937.

[136] E Munro 'Avoidable and Unavoidable Mistakes in Child Protection Work' (1996) 26(6) *British Journal of Social Work* 793.

[137] K Tanner and D Turney, 'What Do We Know about Child Neglect? A Critical Review of the Literature and Its Application to Social Work Practice' (2003) 8(1) *Child and Family Social Work* 25.

[138] J Masson, 'Emergency Intervention to Protect Children: Using and Avoiding Legal Controls' (2005) 17(1) *Child and Family Law Quarterly* 75.

can then cause reactive interventions that are perhaps, with the benefit of hindsight, unnecessary or disproportionate, although hindsight may alternatively indicate that they should have happened earlier. To this, we can add regional variations. As Masson says, 'resources, practices and cultures vary and this leads to different responses by local authorities, and even by different teams, to similar incidents.'[139]

It is inevitable that social workers will in some cases wrongly assess risk. We saw that in our history of child protection laws with the deaths of children such as Kimberley Carlile, Victoria Climbié, Dennis O'Neill, and Maria Colwell. For Munro, 'some mistakes are inevitable because of the complexity of the work and our level of knowledge. Ideally, social workers should protect all children who are at risk of abuse while not disrupting any family providing adequate care. . . . These ideals however are impossible to achieve.'[140]

Partnership was, as we have seen, a key theme of the Children Act 1989. Unnecessary or disproportionately serious intervention can be a human rights violation and can disrupt the family, reducing the chance for the local authority to work in partnership with parents. As Lady Hale has warned, 'rushing unnecessarily into compulsory procedures when there is still scope for a partnership approach may escalate matters in a way which makes reuniting the family more rather than less difficult'.[141]

Yet for those children for whom adoption proves the best outcome, any delay reduces their changes of permanency placement. Delays caused by an attempt to avoid compulsory proceedings in the best interests of the family, including the child, can in retrospect become unwise. As Masson says, 'hindsight, and the detailed evidence produced for proceedings, can make failings on the part of parents and harm to the child appear more obvious than it once was'.[142] Ultimately, even with all the available information, and with even the best professional judgment, decisions may be made that are wrong, either at the time or with the benefit of perfect hindsight.

Once a s47 assessment is completed, the local authority should arrange a strategy meeting or discussion to consider where to go next. The outcome of an assessment could be:

- *that the concerns are not justified and no further action is needed.* In some cases, there may remain concerns about the child's safety and welfare but not enough to take current action, in which case they may make arrangements to monitor the situation. (It may be that the child *did* suffer significant harm but is not still suffering nor is likely to be at risk of harm in the future, perhaps because the family's circumstances have changed or the person responsible for the harm is no longer in contact with the child.)

- *that the child is 'in need' of support services under s17 Children Act*, in which case the level and type of services that should be provided to the child needs to be determined. The provision of such services may ameliorate the need for compulsory intervention in the future.

---

[139] J Masson, 'The State as Parent: The Reluctant Parent: The Problem of Parents of Last Resort?' (2008) 35(1) *Journal of Law and Society* 52.

[140] E Munro 'Avoidable and Unavoidable Mistakes in Child Protection Work' (1996) 26(6) *British Journal of Social Work* 793.

[141] Lady Hale in *Williams v London Borough of Hackney* [2018] UKSC 37 at [34].

[142] J Masson, 'The State as Parent: The Reluctant Parent: The Problem of Parents of Last Resort?' (2008) 35(1) *Journal of Law and Society* 52.

- *to refer the family to another agency or give advice and guidance.* This would be appropriate where the child is not classified as a child in need under s17 Children Act 1989.

- *to refer the matter to an initial child protection conference*, which will be held within 15 working days of the strategy discussion. This may or may not lead to a care application being made, as we shall see.

11.7.2 Child assessment orders

We saw at 11.7.1 that if social workers are refused access to a child who is the subject of a s47 investigation, they must apply for either an emergency protection order, a child assessment order, a care order, or a supervision order 'unless they are satisfied that his welfare can be satisfactorily safeguarded without their doing so'. In most cases, an emergency protection order will be most appropriate, as it enables the local authority to accommodate the child and thus to interview them. However, an alternative option is to apply for a child assessment order. This directs a medical or other assessment of the child, rather than being directed at their immediate protection, as it does not necessarily require the child's removal from home. For this reason, the order is most appropriate where harm to the child is long-term and cumulative rather than sudden and severe.[143]

The order, which is made under s43 Children Act 1989, authorises the local authority or any authorised person[144] to carry out an assessment of the child, in order to provide the authority with information needed to determine whether or not the child is suffering, or likely to suffer, significant harm. The order itself will specify what type of assessment is being authorised, whether medical, psychological/psychiatric, social work, or education. In addition to authorising the assessment(s), the order requires the child's carers to produce the child for that purpose and to comply with any directions set out in the order. A *Gillick*-competent child may refuse to submit to the assessment.[145] The child is only removed from home if the order provides for that on the grounds that it is necessary to do so for the purpose of the assessment.

The court will only make the order if it is satisfied that the criteria set out in s43 are met. The welfare principle and no order principle in s1 Children Act 1989 also apply.

Note that s43(1) requires that the applicant only have 'reasonable cause' to suspect significant harm. While a court making an interim care order under s38 Children Act 1989 (see 12.2.5) can also order a medical or psychiatric examination of the child, an interim care order can only be made where the court is satisfied that there are reasonable grounds for believing that the care threshold in s 31(2) is met. That is not a necessary prerequisite to making an order under s43, which requires only that the local authority 'has reasonable cause to suspect' suffering. This is because child assessment orders are usually made before proceedings are issued, when it is uncertain whether they will need to be brought at all and the evidence to do so is not in place.

---

[143] Department of Health, *Emergency Protection of Children: Guidance* (Consultation Paper No.13, 1990) para 9A, and Department for Education, *Children Act Guidance Vol 1: Court Orders and Pre-Proceedings for Local Authorities* (2014) 36.

[144] The only 'authorised person' is the NSPCC.

[145] S43(8). For *Gillick* competency see 9.5.2.

> **STATUTORY EXTRACT:** *s43 Children Act 1989*
>
> **Child assessment orders**
>
> (1) On the application of a local authority or authorised person for an order to be made under this section with respect to a child, the court may make the order if, but only if, it is satisfied that—
>   (a) the applicant has reasonable cause to suspect that the child is suffering, or is likely to suffer, significant harm;
>   (b) an assessment of the state of the child's health or development, or of the way in which he has been treated, is required to enable the applicant to determine whether or not the child is suffering, or is likely to suffer, significant harm; and
>   (c) it is unlikely that such an assessment will be made, or be satisfactory, in the absence of an order under this section.

Subsection 11 specifies people who should be notified of the application: his parents and others with parental responsibility, anyone with whom the child spends time under a child arrangements order or who cares for the child, and anyone with whom the child spends time under a s34 order (contact with a child in care: see 12.4.6).[146] Any of these people can apply for the order to be varied or discharged or can appeal the order (or any refusal to make the order), as can the local authority. The orders lasts a maximum of 7 consecutive days, starting on a date set by the court, which means that it can be 'post-dated'.[147] Sections 43(9) and (10) enable the court to direct that the child is not returned home during some or all of this period, and if it does make such an order, it must also direct what contact the child should have with his or her family during this period.

Applications are rarely made, for a number of reasons. First, if the parents or a *Gillick*-competent child consent to assessment then it is not necessary to seek an order, and a *Gillick*-competent child is entitled to refuse to be examined. Most parents can be persuaded to cooperate because of the risks of the child being removed if they do not do so.[148] Second, the duration of the order—seven days—is generally too short a period for a full examination of the child. But nor is the order an emergency remedy. Indeed, the court may not make the order if there are grounds for an emergency protection order, and should treat the application for the assessment order as an application for an EPO instead: ss43(3) and (4). Finally, making an application may obstruct any prospects of cooperation with the family.

11.7.3 Forced marriage protection orders

Forced marriage protection orders and the separate criminal offence of forcing someone to marry are discussed in Chapter 2 when we look at consent to marriage. Local authorities

---

[146] As Mitchell points out, the mention of s34 'is curious, because s34 orders for contact only concern children committed to care. This must mean that a CAO may be obtained in relation to a child in care' even though the order is designed for an earlier pre-proceedings stage. G Mitchell, 'The Child Assessment Order: A Breach of Principle?' (1991) 13(1) *Liverpool Law Review* 53.

[147] Section 43(5).

[148] J Dickens, 'Assessment and the Control of Social Work: An Analysis of Reasons for the Non-Use of the Child Assessment Order' (1993) 15(2) *Journal of Social Welfare and Family Law* 88.

FOCUS Think Critically

Child assessment orders: Over-intervention versus under-intervention

Child assessment orders did not appear in the Children Act white paper but resulted from lobbying before and during the bill's passing.[149] As such, and in contrast to the rest of the Children Act, s43 was 'not the result of detailed reflection and review of the existing law'.[150] Opinion was split on the need for a type of order for use in 'circumstances where removing the child would be too drastic a step, but where there is nevertheless serious, although not urgent, concern about the health and well-being of the child'.[151]

The report into the death of Kimberley Carlile mooted the idea of an order that would 'require that the parent bring the child, within a very short period of time, to a clinic or general practitioner', something which would have helped to save Kimberley, who died from beatings and starvation.[152] The National Association for the Prevention of Cruelty to Children argued in favour of a separate child assessment order power, identifying four advantages over an emergency protection order:

- that parents would be able to retain parental responsibility
- that the child would be seen by a family doctor in a familiar environment
- that the parents were more likely to cooperate with this less intrusive order
- that it offered a way of protecting the child in non-emergency situations.[153]

The British Association of Social Workers, and Parents Against Injustice agreed with this stance. In contrast, the Cleveland Report[154] of the same year rejected it on the basis that an emergency protection order would be more appropriate, as did the Association of Directors of Social Services.[155] This is perhaps unsurprising given that the focus of the Cleveland Report was on the unnecessary removal of children from their homes on the basis of spurious medical evidence.

The child assessment order discussions therefore illustrate concerns about the dangers of both under-intervention (as in Kimberley's case) and of over-intervention (as in Cleveland). As Ruth Lavery explains, the order 'involves intrusion into family life and the life of the child at a time when there is no proof that this is justified', yet 'may also represent the best chance of preventing damage, or further damage to a child either from failure to act or by inappropriate intervention.'[156] This tension manifested in Parliament: the final enacted version of s43 bore little resemblance to the idea that some professional groups had initially supported and instead 'bore the hallmarks of confusion'.[157] The seven-day time limit renders it of limited use for conducting full-scale assessments of the child;

[149] J Dickens, 'Assessment and the Control of Social Work: An Analysis of Reasons for the Non-Use of the Child Assessment Order' (1993) 15(2) *Journal of Social Welfare and Family Law* 88.

[150] R Lavery, 'The Child Assessment Order – A Reassessment' [1996] *Child and Family Law Quarterly* 47.

[151] L Blom-Cooper, *A Child in Mind: Protection of Children in a Responsible Society: The Report of the Commission of Inquiry into the Circumstances surrounding the death of Kimberley Carlile* (London Borough of Greenwich and Greenwich Health Authority 1987), Chapter 25.

[152] L Blom-Cooper, *A Child in Mind: Protection of Children in a Responsible Society: The Report of the Commission of Inquiry into the Circumstances surrounding the death of Kimberley Carlile* (London Borough of Greenwich and Greenwich Health Authority 1987), Chapter 25.

[153] J Harding, 'A Child Assessment Order: To Be or Not to Be?' [1989, April] *Community Care* 6. Cited by J Dickens, 'Assessment and the Control of Social Work: An Analysis of Reasons for the Non-Use of the Child Assessment Order' (1993) 15(2) *Journal of Social Welfare and Family Law* 88.

[154] *Report of the Inquiry into Child Abuse in Cleveland 1987* (Cm 412, 1988).

[155] G Mitchell, 'The Child Assessment Order: A Breach of Principle?' (1991) 13(1) *Liverpool Law Review* 53.

[156] R Lavery, 'The Child Assessment Order – A Reassessment' [1996] *Child and Family Law Quarterly* 47, 47.

[157] J Dickens, 'Assessment and the Control of Social Work: An Analysis of Reasons for the Non-Use of the Child Assessment Order' (1993) 15(2) *Journal of Social Welfare and Family Law* 88, 91.

> but it is not an emergency remedy either. The order is a significant intrusion, but no court has determined that significant harm has actually happened or is likely to happen—all that is required is reasonable cause to consider that such harm may happen. Accordingly, s43 has been referred to as a 'rogue provision' that 'ill accords with the principle of judicial non-interference which informs the Act from beginning to end,'[158] and in any event that state intervention should only occur where a court has been satisfied that there is or is likely to be significant harm.[159]

comprise more than half of all applicants for this type of order, both as part of their responsibilities to vulnerable adults and as part of their child protection remit.

11.7.4 Female genital mutilation protection orders

Female genital mutilation (FGM) protection orders and the separate criminal offence are discussed at 7.5.10 when we look at domestic abuse.

Female genital mutilation is a form of violence against women and girls, and a matter of concern to those involved in child protection work. Local authorities may include FGM as part of their wider strategies and social work may involve the protection of children from FGM.[160] Social workers are required by law to report allegations by a girl who has been subjected to FGM to the police. Where a girl is believed to be at immediate risk of FGM, she may be taken into police protection, or made the subject of an emergency protection order. As we see in Chapter 12, female genital mutilation is always a form of significant harm to a child justifying the bringing of care proceedings. It therefore also acts as a trigger for a s47 investigation.

Local authorities are common applicants for FGM protection orders. As we discuss at 7.5.10, in 2019, there were 107 applications for an order, of which 105 were in relation to someone aged under 17. Of these applications, 65 were made by local authorities, none by the girl to be protected, and the rest by other agencies (such as the Official Solicitor) or the voluntary sector.[161]

11.7.5 Child protection conferences and plans

A child protection conference is designed to consider all the information obtained under the Section 47 enquiry and to determine the best course of action to safeguard and promote the welfare of the child, including the child being made the subject of a child protection plan. The conference is multi-disciplinary in accordance with the ethos of *Working Together to Safeguard Children*, and involves:

- the child (if of appropriate age and understanding)
- the parents and those with parental responsibility (who can bring a support person or lawyer with them)[162]

---

[158] G Mitchell, 'The Child Assessment Order: A Breach of Principle?' (1991) 13(1) *Liverpool Law Review* 53.
[159] Family Rights Group, *Children Bill Briefing, Child Assessment Oder: Government Proposal for a New Clause* (Family Rights Group 1989).
[160] See HM Government, *Multi-Agency Statutory Guidance on Female Genital Mutilation* (July 2020).
[161] Ministry of Justice, *Family Court Statistics Quarterly* (Underlying Dataset) (2020).
[162] People can be excluded if necessary (such as a violent person).

- members of the wider family
- those professionals most closely involved in the case (such as a health visitor, school nurse, paediatrician, GP, designated lead for child protection in schools)
- the investigating social worker, foster or residential carers
- a police representative.

Depending on the situation, there may also be professionals with expertise in the particular type of harm suffered by the child or the child's particular medical condition or disability; a midwife if the conference concerns an unborn child; probation or youth justice services; domestic abuse advisors; adult mental health workers who have worked with the family; a representative of the armed services where there is a service connection; or substance abuse advisers. The conference is often chaired by an Independent Reviewing Officer. The role of Independent Reviewing Officers is discussed in a focus box at 11.6.2.

The conference will discuss the family situation and decide whether the child should be the subject of a child protection plan by asking 'Is the child at risk of suffering significant harm?' Specifically:

- Can the child be shown to have suffered ill-treatment or impairment of health or development as a result of physical, emotional or sexual abuse or neglect, and is the conference's professional judgment that further ill-treatment or impairment is likely?

or

- Does professional judgment, substantiated by the findings of enquiries in this individual case or by research evidence, predict that the child is likely to suffer maltreatment or the impairment of health and development as a result of physical, emotional or sexual abuse or neglect?

If the answer to the question is *no*, then the child may still be a child in need within the meaning of s17 and the conference may make recommendations about how those needs should be met. However, there will be no need for a child protection plan.

If the answer to either of these questions is *yes*, however, then the conference should decide which category of abuse or neglect the child has suffered or is at risk of suffering before drawing up a child protection plan. The conference does not have the power start care proceedings themselves but can recommend that the local authority considers doing so.

The categories are:

1. *Neglect*, defined in *Working Together to Safeguard Children* as 'the persistent failure to meet a child's basic physical and/or psychological needs, likely to result in the serious impairment of the child's health or development'.[163] It can involve the parent or carer in failing to provide adequate food, clothing, shelter, or medical care, or failing to protect the child from other harms.

2. *Physical abuse*, which may involve 'hitting, shaking, throwing, poisoning, burning or scalding, drowning, suffocating, or otherwise causing physical harm to a child.

---

[163] HM Government, *Working Together to Safeguard Children: A Guide to Inter-Agency Working to Safeguard and Promote the Welfare of Children* (July 2018) Appendix A.

Physical harm may also be caused when a parent or carer fabricates the symptoms of, or deliberately induces illness in a child'.

3. *Sexual abuse*, which involves 'forcing or enticing a child or young person to take part in sexual activities, not necessarily involving a high level of violence, whether or not the child is aware of what is happening. The activities may involve physical contact . . . or non-contact activities, such as involving children in looking at, or in the production of, sexual images, watching sexual activities, encouraging children to behave in sexually inappropriate ways, or grooming a child in preparation for abuse'.

4. *Emotional abuse*, which is 'the persistent emotional maltreatment of a child such as to cause severe and persistent adverse effects on the child's emotional development. It may involve conveying to children that they are worthless or unloved, inadequate, or valued only insofar as they meet the needs of another person. It may include not giving the child opportunities to express their views, deliberately silencing them or "making fun" of what they say or how they communicate. It may feature age or developmentally inappropriate expectations being imposed on children. . . . It may involve seeing or hearing the ill-treatment of another. . . .'[164]

FOCUS Think Critically

The controversy around emotional harm

In recent years, there has been a substantial increase in the number of child protection plans generally, but there is a much more significant increase in the number of plans grounded on emotional harm than on other kinds of harm. In the nine years between 2008 and 2017, Bilson found that emotional harm categorisations had increased 164 per cent as against a 94 per cent increase generally.[165]

Of course, emotional harm may arise as a consequence of other types of harm. For example, when a child is physically or sexually abused or neglected, this will cause them emotional as well as physical harm. But the categorisation of emotional harm as the main harm has led to concern that emotional harm is seen as providing sufficient justification for child protection interventions by itself, when there is no accompanying physical or sexual harm or neglect. Part of this concern relates to the fact that a concept emotional harm seems vaguer than the other categories: just what does significant emotional harm look like? What one person may characterise as a form of abuse could be seen by another as poor-but-not-terrible parenting; a third person may simply characterise it as strict or 'old fashioned' parenting or attribute it to cultural differences as in the Victoria Climbié case.

A second concern relates to differences across local authorities: some use emotional abuse a great deal more than others. Does that reflect the reality of life in those authority areas, or could it reflect differing interpretations of emotional harm or when the significant harm threshold has been met? Bilson investigated this, finding that the suddenness of the increase meant that it was unlikely to be an increase in the actual occurrence of significant harm in children. After allowing for population, deprivation, and local authority performance, he concluded that the most likely explanation was that local authorities were increasingly seeing their role as about child rescue rather than about supporting the child in his family.

---

[164] HM Government, *Working Together to Safeguard Children: A Guide to Inter-Agency Working to Safeguard and Promote the Welfare of Children* (July 2018) Appendix A.

[165] A Bilson, 'Future Risk of Emotional Harm – Justified Grounds to Remove Children?' Paper delivered at the Transparency Project child protection conference, London, 15 September 2018.

The category of harm chosen should reflect the conference's primary concern at that time. More than one category should be indicated only if a second category also reaches the significant harm threshold and needs to be flagged in order to prevent a second risk being underestimated. If the conference cannot decide on the appropriate category, the final decision is made by the chair.

Once the harm has been appropriately categorised, a child protection plan will be drawn up. This will outline the child's needs and what services are required to meet these needs, and then identify the roles and responsibilities of family members, the local authority, and other agencies and professionals in meeting those needs. It will name a lead social worker for the child and how often they will see the child. A core group of those at the conference will monitor progress after three months and thereafter at least every six months.

The plan should identify specific outcomes and how these are to be achieved, and by what date. It should also describe how the family's progress will be reviewed and judged, including what should happen if circumstances change, such as if parents do not cooperate, another adult who poses a risk to children joins the household, another child is born, or there are new concerns or allegations. This may include recommending that the local authority seek a care order.

The plan will remain in place until the child is no longer considered at risk, moves out of the local authority area (in which case the receiving authority should take over), or reaches the age of 18. If the plan is discontinued because the child is no longer deemed to be at risk, the local authority may still need to provide them with services as a child in need. Sometimes, however, the risk to the child increases, and the local authority may need to apply for a care or supervision order, or an emergency situation arises which requires the child to be immediately taken into protection.

SCENARIO 2

Illustration 4: Maya

The local authority has undertaken a s47 investigation. They call a multidisciplinary child protection conference to which Maya (given her age and level of understanding) and her mother are invited (her father, in prison, is also consulted). The conference decides that Maya should be the subject of a child protection plan because she is at risk of suffering significant harm. The conference members record neglect as their primary concern, because they are concerned that Maya's mother is not protecting her from harm, but they also discuss whether the risk of sexual or exploitation by the gang justifies a secondary concern being recorded.

A core group of people from the child protection conference meet again a few days later to draw up the plan in detail. The local authority allocates a social worker who will visit Maya once per week. Maya's mother agrees to Maya remaining living at home. The child protection plan includes counselling for Maya and her mother, and a referral to an organisation that helps young women at risk of sexual exploitation. Maya and her mother agree that Maya should remain at home after 7pm each evening. Maya and her mother commit to Maya going to school every day and social workers arrange for a taxi to take her to school in order to help make this happen. The group agrees to meet again in three months to review progress.

11.7.6 How many children are involved with children's services?

Bilson and Martin looked at children born between 2009 and 2010 who had reached the age of 5.[166] They found that, in a statistically average class of 30 5-year-old children:

- seven had been referred to the local authority children's services department. Of the seven, four of those children were classed as children in need, one because of family dysfunction, and two because of suspected abuse or neglect.

- One or two children in the class of 30 (an average of 1.6) would be the subject of a formal investigation and on average one child would be on a child protection plan.

- One child in every two classes of 30 will be or have been in care.

This is illustrated in Figure 11.3, which shows the proportion of children reaching different stages of the child protection system if the results of Bilson and Martin's freedom of information request were seen in an average class of 30 children.

These are average figures: some local authorities will have greater numbers, some fewer. In the 10 per cent most deprived communities it is estimated that 45 per cent of children born in 2009–10 were referred to children's social care before their fifth birthday. Blackpool, an economically deprived area, has the highest number of child protection investigations: on average one out of every six children will be the subject not merely of a referral but of a child protection investigation.[167]

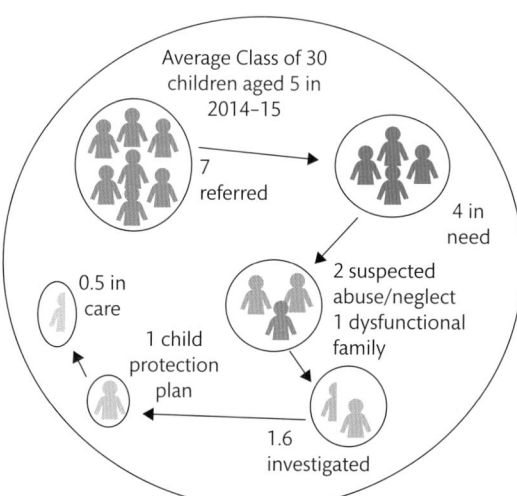

→ **Seven children:** referred to children's services

→ **Four referred children:** required services to achieve or maintain a reasonable standard of health or development (i.e. they were 'in need')

→ **Three children in need:** suspected of being abused or neglected (2 abuse or neglect and 1 dysfunctional family)

→ **1.6 children:** (1 or 2 in each class) formally investigated for suspected abuse

→ **One child:** suffering, or likely to suffer, significant harm (i.e., on a child protection plan)

→ **½ Child:** (one child in every other class) would have been in care.

FIGURE 11.3 Referrals and investigations into an 'average' class of 30 5-year-olds

Source: From A Bilson and KEC Martin, 'Referrals and Child Protection in England: One in Five Children Referred to Children's Services and One in Nineteen Investigated before the Age of Five' (2017) 47(3) *British Journal of Social Work* 793.

---

[166] A Bilson and KEC Martin, 'Referrals and Child Protection in England: One in Five Children Referred to Children's Services and One in Nineteen Investigated before the Age of Five' (2017) 47(3) *British Journal of Social Work* 793.

[167] A Bilson, B Featherstone, and K Martin, 'How Child Protection's "Investigative Turn" Impacts on Poor and Deprived Communities' (2017) 47 *Family Law* 316.

These figures show astonishingly high levels of social work involvement. But numbers have increased further since then. The Department for Education estimates that in the year ending 31 March 2020, in England, there were:

- 642,980 referrals to children's social care (compared to 615,000 in 2010/11)
- 201,000 section 47 enquiries
- 389,260 children in need, of which 51,510 children were on child protection plans (49,000 in 2010/11)[168]
- 80,080 looked after children.[169]

The number of initial contacts made with children's services departments increased by 37 per cent between 2009/10 and 2017/18, and the number of referrals to children's social care has risen by 9 per cent in the same period.[170] This creates considerable financial pressure on local authorities.[171] The Institute of Government (a 'think tank') notes that 'local authorities have persistently overspent on these services but, even so, the increase in spending has not kept pace with demand.'[172] In September 2016, the then-President of the Family Division, Sir James Munby, referred to the 'seemingly relentless rise in the number of new care cases', calling it a crisis and noting that 'the fact is that we are approaching a crisis for which we are ill-prepared and where there is no clear strategy to manage the crisis. What is to be done?'[173]

FOCUS Think Critically

What's behind the increasing numbers?

There are several potential reasons for increasing numbers of children involved with children's services. We know that the population of children has grown, although by itself this does not account for the increase. There has also been a rise in specific types of demand: there has been an increase in the number of children classed as disabled, who are one of the categories of children in need, from 6 per cent in 2005/06 to 8 per cent in 2016/17.[174] There has been an increase in the number of unaccompanied asylum-seeking children. There is increasing awareness of the risks to children from female genital mutilation, child sexual exploitation (for example following the Rotherham child sexual abuse scandal), forced marriage,[175] and radicalisation, which may have led to social workers and others professionals who work with children becoming more proactive or simply receiving more

---

[168] Department for Education, *Characteristics of Children in Need* (2020).

[169] Department for Education, *Children Looked After in England including Adoption: 2019 to 2020* (2021).

[170] Association of Directors of Children's Services *Research Report: Safeguarding Pressures Phase 6* (2018).

[171] A Turner, 'Councils Issue Stark Warnings as Children's Services Overspends Continue to Strain Most Budgets' (*Community Care* 4 October 2019). Available at https://www.communitycare.co.uk/2019/10/04/councils-warnings-childrens-services-overspends/ accessed 11 January 20.

[172] Institute for Government, *Performance Tracker 2019: Children's Social Care* (2019). Available at https://www.instituteforgovernment.org.uk/publication/performance-tracker-2019/children-social-care accessed 9 January 2020.

[173] 15th View from the President's Chambers. Available at https://www.judiciary.uk/publications/view-from-presidents-chambers/ accessed 21 January 20.

[174] Office for Budget Responsibility, *Welfare Trends Report* (The Stationery Office 2019).

[175] Forced marriage is discussed in Chapter 2.

referrals.[176] Indeed, local authorities are a frequent applicant for forced marriage protection orders see 11.7.3) and female genital mutilation protection orders (discussed at 11.5.4).

Another reason for the increasing numbers could be the wider economic context. There has been a period of economic austerity and there is a correlation between poverty and child protection interventions,[177] which we discuss further in the focus box 'child protection, risk, and poverty' in Chapter 12. Financial pressures have resulted in a reduction of those services that are designed to provide early intervention in families. Lack of early help for struggling families means that opportunities to avoid situations worsening have been more limited. The All Parliamentary Group for Children reported in 2017 that

> Early intervention, and other work with families where abuse or neglect is not taking place, appears to be bearing the brunt of this apparent mismatch between funding and demand. The Inquiry heard from a wide range of sources that resources are increasingly focused on children who have already suffered harm and those at the greatest risk. There is evidence that this is leading to unmet need elsewhere in the system and a rise in costly late intervention.[178]

It has also been suggested that cuts to early intervention may lead to more children being at risk from mental illness, substance abuse, and domestic violence.[179] The Association of Directors of Children's Services attributes part of the increase to demands caused by changes to other services, and financial pressures on those services:

> There is evidence of a clear ripple effect felt by local authority children's services stemming from changes to universal provision, such as schools and other partner agencies, who are also experiencing significant pressures. School academisation, together with severe reductions in funding and subsequent cuts in services provided by other agencies have resulted in increased demand for local authority children's services. Authorities reported that national Special Educational Needs and Disability (SEND) reforms, and schools 'off rolling' pupils[180] add to pressures in children's services and are an increasing concern.[181]

This suggests that children's services are absorbing work previously done by other agencies.

Of course, we could simply be better at assessing risk.[182] Bilson, Featherstone, and Martin looked at the period 2009 to 2015/16 and found that found that while there had been a 6.4 per cent increase in the number of referrals, there was a 93 per cent increase in the number of s47 investigations in the same period, meaning that social workers are using s47 investigations much more than before. However, they concluded that this probably does not reflect either better detection of abuse or neglect or a rise in abuse and neglect, because they have not led to a proportional increase in the number of child protection plans, which is what would happen if the child was believed to be at risk.[183]

---

[176] All Parliamentary Group for Children, *No Good Options: Report of the Inquiry into Children's Social Care in England* (2017).

[177] A Bilson, B Featherstone, and K Martin, 'How Child Protection's "Investigative Turn" Impacts on Poor and Deprived Communities' (2017) 47 *Family Law* 316.

[178] All Parliamentary Group for Children, *No Good Options: Report of the Inquiry into Children's Social Care in England* (2017) 13.

[179] All Parliamentary Group for Children, *No Good Options: Report of the Inquiry into Children's Social Care in England* (2017).

[180] The schools regulator Ofsted defines 'off-rolling' as 'the practice of removing a pupil from the school roll without using a permanent exclusion, when the removal is primarily in the best interests of the school, rather than the best interests of the pupil. This includes pressuring a parent to remove their child from the school roll.'

[181] Association of Directors of Children's Services *Research Report: Safeguarding Pressures Phase 6* (2018).

[182] All Parliamentary Group for Children, *No Good Options: Report of the Inquiry into Children's Social Care in England* (2017).

[183] A Bilson, B Featherstone, and K Martin, 'How Child Protection's "Investigative Turn" Impacts on Poor and Deprived Communities' (2017) 47 *Family Law* 316.

The Baby P effect

In the period studied by Bilson et al., one reason for the rise is very likely to be the impact of the death of 17-month-old Peter Connelly in 2007. This led to a serious backlash against the social work profession. More commonly known by the alias Baby P, Peter was killed, after a terrible catalogue of mistreatment, by his mother, her boyfriend, and the latter's brother. There had been 56 other child deaths in the same year, but it was his death that galvanised the media in a campaign to hold those responsible to account. This included not merely the perpetrators, but also social work and health professionals who had seen him more than 60 times in an eight-month period. As Eileen Munro has written

> Society's horror and outrage at some well-publicized cases where children endured terrible abuse before being killed has fuelled a public expectation that social workers should be able to protect children and, if a child dies from abuse, social workers have done something wrong.[184]

A petition in the *Sun* newspaper seeking the firing of the social workers concerned gained more than 1.4 million signatures. The government responded with the (then) Secretary of State for Children, Schools and Families, Ed Balls, firing the head of Haringey children's services live on television. To Nigel Parton, 'the depth of anger evident in the media at the death of Baby P seemed much stronger and more prolonged than anything seen before, including reaction to the deaths of Maria Colwell and Victoria Climbié.'[185]

It is difficult to overestimate the effect that Peter's death, and the resulting media whirlwind, had on social work practice. The 'Baby P effect' resulted in an increase in referrals to local authorities, increased numbers of s47 child protection investigations, and more child protection plans. One social worker recalls 'referrals flooding in' from other agencies terrified of missing another Baby P:

> Health, education, you name it, were piling it all into us. The police were very risk averse too, so we were going out on joint visits all over the place for things that should not have needed the police and a child protection social worker turning up at your door. Social workers became defensive in their practice, focused on following procedures rather than what would most make a difference to children.[186]

The trial of those responsible for Peter Connelly's death started in September 2008; in the subsequent six months there was a 50 per cent increase in care applications.[187] Most local authorities did not believe that Baby P had caused them to lower what Cafcass termed the 'threshold of concern at which applications are made' but, nonetheless, 'a substantial proportion of the increase can be attributed to Local Authorities re-evaluating their involvement with families where they [were] already providing a service'.[188] Thus, after a high-profile child death, or one in their locality, social workers may be more likely to turn to compulsory intervention instead of offering services. It may also be that people are more likely to make a report about a child for whom they are concerned.[189] The Care Crisis Review (2017) observed a 'culture of blame, shame and fear' in the system, affecting those

---

[184] E Munro 'Avoidable and Unavoidable Mistakes in Child Protection Work' (1996) 26(6) *British Journal of Social Work* 793.

[185] N Parton, *The Politics of Child Protection* (Palgrave 2014) 69.

[186] A McNicoll, 'Ten Years on from Baby P: Social Work's Story' (*Community Care* 3 August 2017).

[187] The number of care applications rose by 50 per cent October 2008 to March 2009, cf to April 2008 to September 2008.

[188] E Hall and J Guy, *The Baby Peter Effect and the Increase in s31 Care Order Applications* (Cafcass 2009). See also S Macleod, R Hart, J Jeffes, and A Wilkin, *The Impact of the Baby Peter Case on Applications for Care Orders* (National Foundation for Educational Research 2010).

[189] E Hall and J Guy, *The Baby Peter Effect and the Increase in s31 Care Order Applications* (Cafcass 2009). See also S Macleod, R Hart, J Jeffes, and A Wilkin, *The Impact of the Baby Peter Case on Applications for Care Orders* (National Foundation for Educational Research 2010).

working in it as well as children and families. This, it was suggested, has created an environment that is 'increasingly mistrusting and risk averse and prompts individuals to seek refuge in procedural responses'.[190] Adopting Fox Harding's categorisation of ideological perspectives on childcare laws (see 11.1.2), this would reflect a move away from defence of the birth family, with its ethos of positive support for families, into the realm of state paternalism and child protection.

11.8 Emergency protection of children under Part IV

Prior to the Children Act 1989, the state had considerable powers to remove a child from his or her home. Masson traces these powers as far back as the nineteenth century.[191] However, the Children Act sharply curtailed the use of the state's powers to remove children without a court order, in part because of the Cleveland scandal. It is therefore the case that social workers have no powers whatsoever to remove a child from his or her home without a court order such as a child assessment order, interim care order or final care order.

In an emergency situation, where there is a risk of significant harm to the child, there are two powers within the Children Act to remove a child to safety. Under s44 a court may make an emergency protection order authorising the child's removal for up to eight days, renewable once for a further seven. Under s46, the police can remove a child without a court order for up to 72 hours.

11.8.1 Police protection powers

Under s46 Children Act 1989 the police have short-term powers to protect children, and this does not require a court order.

This power enables a police officer to either remove the child to a place that is safe, or if she is already somewhere safe, to retain her there for up to 72 hours only (s46(6)). For example, if a child is hospitalised with injuries that doctors suspect may be non-accidental, then provided that the police officer has reasonable cause to believe that she would otherwise be likely to suffer significant harm, he may use these powers to require her to remain in hospital because that is a safe place. Alternatively, if she is not already safe the police officer can remove the child to a place of safety such as an emergency local authority foster placement or refuge. Police powers may also be used when a child is found on the streets, has run away from home, or where the parents are temporarily unfit, for example through drink. As such, the power is more commonly used by officers on general policing duty rather than as a planned response by specialist child protection investigators.[192] This means that those using the power may have little training and experience in child protection[193] and may be unable to make judgments about whether the risk of significant harm was sufficient to justify removal.[194]

[190] *Care Crisis Review: Options for Change* (Family Rights Group 2018).

[191] J Masson, 'Police Protection – Protecting Whom?' (2002) 24(2) *Journal of Social Welfare and Family Law* 157, 158.

[192] J Masson, 'Police Protection – Protecting Whom?' (2002) 24(2) *Journal of Social Welfare and Family Law* 157, 157.

[193] J Masson, 'Emergency Intervention to Protect Children: Using and Avoiding Legal Controls' (2005) 17(1) *Child and Family Law Quarterly* 75, 79.

[194] J Masson, 'Police Protection – Protecting Whom?' (2002) 24(2) *Journal of Social Welfare and Family Law* 157, 165.

> **STATUTORY EXTRACT** *s46 Children Act 1989*
>
> **Removal and accommodation of children by police in cases of emergency**
>
> (1) Where a constable has reasonable cause to believe that a child would otherwise be likely to suffer significant harm, he may
>   (a) remove the child to suitable accommodation and keep him there; or
>   (b) take such steps as are reasonable to ensure that the child's removal from any hospital, or other place, in which he is then being accommodated is prevented.
> (2) For the purposes of this Act, a child with respect to whom a constable has exercised his powers under this section is referred to as having been taken into police protection.

While the power lasts for a maximum of 72 hours, the average use is only 6 hours, and many children are initially taken to a police station for want of somewhere more appropriate, before being returned home.[195] If it is not safe for them to return home, then it would be appropriate for the local authority to make an application for an emergency protection order. Police protection may be used as an overnight measure pending the local authority making an application once the courts are open. The local authority may alternatively seek the parents' permission to accommodate the child under s20.[196] Masson found that where the police were contacted by family members, this was usually as a result of a child missing from home, but a significant proportion related to violent altercations or threats from the child of self-harm.[197]

For the interrelationship of police protection with emergency protection orders, see 11.6.2.

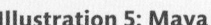

SCENARIO 2

Illustration 5: Maya

At the start of this chapter, we were told that the police found Maya on the streets under the influence of drugs. Police protection would have been the mechanism for the police to take Maya home or, if they thought that this was not a safe place, they may have taken Maya back to the police station and called the local authority to provide her with overnight accommodation. The local authority might then apply for an emergency protection order.

11.8.2 Emergency protection orders

An emergency protection orders (EPO) under s44 is a court order 'to enable the child in a genuine emergency to be removed from where he is or be kept where he is, if and only if this is necessary to provide immediate short-term protection'.[198] In practice, EPOs are often made where police protection has been used but is about to expire.

---

[195] J Masson, 'Police Protection – Protecting Whom?' (2002) 24(2) *Journal of Social Welfare and Family Law* 157, 163.
[196] Although note that for truly urgent situations such as abduction or disputes over life-saving medical treatment, a high court judge is available by telephone at all times. The Family Court Practice ('the red book') contains contact information.
[197] J Masson, 'Police Protection – Protecting Whom?' (2002) 24(2) *Journal of Social Welfare and Family Law* 157, 163.
[198] *Children Act 1989 Guidance and Regulations* Volume 1 (HMSO 1991) 51.

TABLE 11.3 Grounds for applying for an emergency protection order

Applicant for the EPO	Grounds for applying for the EPO: s44

The general ground which can be used by any person	**S44(1)**
	
	(a) There is reasonable cause to believe that the child is likely to suffer significant harm if
	
	  (i) he is not removed to accommodation provided by or on behalf of the applicant; or
	
	  (ii) he does not remain in the place in which he is then being accommodated

In addition to the general ground, the local authority could use this ground	**S44(b)** (i) Enquiries are being made with respect to the child under section 47(1)(b); and (ii) those enquiries are being frustrated by access to the child being *unreasonably* refused and the applicant has reasonable cause to believe that access to the child is required as a matter of urgency.
In addition to the general ground, an authorised person could use this ground (the only authorised person is the NSPCC)	**S44(c):** (i) The applicant has reasonable cause to suspect that a child is suffering, or is likely to suffer, significant harm; and (ii) the applicant is making enquiries with respect to the child's welfare; and (iii) those enquiries are being frustrated by access to the child being unreasonably refused to a person authorised to seek access; and applicant has reasonable cause to believe that access to the child is required as a matter of urgency.

As shown in Table 11.3, the grounds for applying for an emergency protection order differ according to who is applying. While anyone can apply for an emergency protection order, the most common applicant is a local authority.

The court can only make an order if satisfied that the ground has been made out.

Although the application can be made *ex parte* (without notice to those with parental responsibility for the child), this is not considered best practice and one day's notice should usually be given. If the application is made on notice, then notice must be given to:

- all those with parental responsibility, and if there is a care order all those who had parental responsibility immediately before the care order;
- the child's parents (the father may not have parental responsibility and thus not fall into the above category);
- anyone caring for the child or with whom the child is living, including a local authority if they are providing accommodation to the child, or a person providing a refuge if that is where the child is living; and
- the child, if *Gillick* competent.

Note that the welfare principle makes the child's welfare the court's paramount consideration, and the no (unnecessary) delay and no order principles apply, so that the court must be satisfied that the making of the order will be better for the child than making no order. The welfare checklist does not apply.

The effect of an emergency protection order

The order authorises the applicant to remove the child to a safe place, or retain her in a safe place if she is already there: s44(4). It may include the power to enter premises to search for the child, and the order may specify that social workers seeking to remove a child from her home may be accompanied by a registered medical practitioner, nurse, or midwife: s45(12). It is a criminal offence to obstruct an applicant who is exercising their powers under the order: s45(15). A police warrant may also be issued alongside the order: s44(9). The order may also require any person who knows of the child's whereabouts to disclose that information: s48(1).

The successful applicant obtains parental responsibility, but only to the extent that is reasonably required to safeguard or promote the welfare of the child.[199] The applicant may authorise, as an exercise of this parental responsibility, a medical or psychiatric assessment of the child: s44(6) A *Gillick*-competent child may refuse such an assessment, in which case a court order under the inherent jurisdiction would be needed to overrule refusal.[200]

In *Re X (Emergency Protection Orders)*[201] McFarlane J held that the following situations would rarely justify an EPO because they are not genuine emergencies:

- Mere lack of information or a need for assessment
- Cases of emotional abuse
- Cases of sexual abuse where the allegations are inchoate and non-specific, and where there is no evidence of immediate risk of harm to the child
- Cases of fabricated or induced illness, where there is no medical evidence of immediate risk of direct physical harm to the child

Where there is a need for assessment, the proper approach is to apply for a child assessment order or seek an assessment under s38(6) within care proceedings. In relation to the other concerns, McFarlane suggested that justices 'should actively consider refusing the EP application on the basis that the local authority should then issue an application for an interim care order'.[202] For social workers in Masson's study, '"having enough for an EPO" appeared to mean being able to point to an incident which justified immediate intervention', but even so in 45 per cent of cases neglect or abandonment precipitated the EPO.[203] A failure by the family to abide by agreements reached with social services (or, in some cases, imposed by them) could trigger emergency steps even when there was no immediate risk to the child. In this way, Masson writes, 'cases which were initially considered not to require compulsory action could be precipitated into courts'.[204]

---

[199] Section 44(5) Children Act 1989.

[200] Section 44(7).

[201] [2006] EWHC 510 (Fam).

[202] [2006] EWHC 510 (Fam).

[203] J Masson, 'Emergency Intervention to Protect Children: Using and Avoiding Legal Controls' (2005) 17(1) *Child and Family Law Quarterly* 75, 87.

[204] J Masson, 'Emergency Intervention to Protect Children: Using and Avoiding Legal Controls' (2005) 17(1) *Child and Family Law Quarterly* 75, 94.

The order can last for up to eight days and is renewable once only, for a further seven days, if the court has reasonable cause to believe that a child is likely to suffer significant harm if the order is not extended. If the child was in police protection immediately prior to the EPO this period counts towards the eight days.

Even if it has obtained an EPO, the local authority does not *have* to exercise its powers to remove the child and should consider less drastic alternatives. The applicant must keep the situation under review and return the child if 'it appears to them that it is safe for the child to be returned': s44(10). If the applicant has returned the child or allowed her to be removed from a place of safety, he can again exercise his powers with respect to the child (at any time while the emergency protection order remains in force) if it appears to him that a change in the circumstances of the case makes it necessary for him to do so: s44(12).

During the period of the order the applicant must allow the child 'reasonable contact' with certain members of her family although the EPO may cover this specifically. In Key Case *X Council v B (Emergency Protection Order)* Munby J said such arrangements for contact 'must be driven by the needs of the family, not stunted by lack of resources'.

Exclusion orders

Under s44A Children Act, an exclusion order can be attached to an EPO. This is a requirement that a specified person leave the dwelling house (i.e., a home rather than commercial premises), in which they live with the child, prevents them from going to the house where the child lives, and/or excludes that person from a defined area in which the dwelling house is situated, such as the road or street that it is on. This is similar to the power under a Family Law Act 1996 occupation order, and indeed the exclusion order provisions were inserted into the Children Act 1989 by that Act. The court may attach a power of arrest.

The court may only make an exclusion order if:

- there is reasonable cause to believe that with the order in place the child will not be likely to suffer significant harm; or that enquiries into the child's circumstance would stop being frustrated (i.e., the grounds set out in Table 11.3); and

- another person living in the house—whether or not a parent—is able and willing to give to the child the care which it would be reasonable to expect a parent to give him, and consents to the inclusion of the exclusion requirement.

By removing a person who poses a risk to the child, an exclusion requirement may therefore obviate the need for the child to be removed to a safe place.

Interrelationship with police protection

We have noted that an EPO may be preceded by police protection, with the latter being used while waiting for social workers to obtain the court order. Judith Masson's studies of the use of police protection and emergency protection orders found that some local authorities relied on police protection because the local courts were not equipped to deal with out-of-hours applications notwithstanding the fact that matters were better dealt with by social services, or simply because taking the child into police protection was considered easier as a short-term measure. Conversely, some social workers saw the police as overly ready to remove children, and too likely to respond to calls that were not true crises but rather an attempt by frustrated family members to get immediate assistance for longstanding parenting difficulties.[205] Nevertheless, Masson found that in approximately 10 in 86 cases of police protection, the local authority immediately initiated care proceedings, and mostly on the basis of chronic neglect. This raises the possibility that in at least some cases the evidence already existed and the decision not to intervene beforehand was, in hindsight, wrong.[206]

In *Langley v Liverpool City Council and the Chief Constable of Merseyside Police*, however, the issue was whether a police officer was correct to take a child into police protection when he was already subject to an emergency protection order, albeit one that had not yet been properly served by the applicant local authority. Using both literal and purposive interpretations of the relevant sections of the Children Act 1989 the Court of Appeal held that s44 emergency protection orders had primacy.[207] This was because Parliament intended that, if practicable, the removal of a child from where he or she is living should be authorised by a court order, a valuable safeguard given that removal of children is a very serious matter.[208] As the court points out, this is also preferable from the point of view of the children concerned, because the social workers may already be known to the family whereas 'uniformed police officers . . . will almost certainly be strangers'. In fact, as Masson has shown, over 90 per cent of EPO cases involved families already known to social services.[209]

KEY CASE *Langley v Liverpool City Council and the Chief Constable of Merseyside Police* [2005] EWCA 1173

The Langley family had four children. The father, Mr Langley, was legally blind, having tunnel vision and night blindness, and was also deaf. The three oldest children were on what was then known as the child protection register (we would now call this being subject to child protection plans). A number of child protection conferences had been held and recorded social workers' concerns that Mr Langley kept driving a car with the children as passengers, despite the assurances that he would not do so and without him having a valid driving licence. The local authority had decided to bring care proceedings.

The local authority then learned that Mr Langley had driven three of the children, and Mrs Langley, from Liverpool to Derby (a distance of about 92 miles) for a few days and that further journeys were planned imminently. The authority obtained an emergency protection order but had not been able to locate the parents to serve this, so sought police assistance. A police constable located one of the children, Callum, at home. Social workers told the police constable by telephone that they wanted Callum to be taken into care. The police officer then made his own independent judgment as to whether to remove Callum under s46 police protection, and did so. An interim care order was subsequently made.

The issue was whether the removal of Callum was lawful, or whether the council and/or the Chief Constable were liable for assault and false imprisonment.

---

[205] J Masson, 'Police Protection – Protecting Whom?' (2002) 24(2) *Journal of Social Welfare and Family Law* 157, 167.
[206] Masson et al., *Protecting Powers: Emergency Intervention for Children's Protection* (Wiley 2007). See also E Munro 'Avoidable and Unavoidable Mistakes in Child Protection Work' (1996) 26(6) *British Journal of Social Work* 793.
[207] See comment by R Bailey-Harris, 'Emergency Protection: *Langley v Liverpool City Council and the Chief Constable of Merseyside Police* [2005] EWCA 1173' [2006] *Family Law* 94.
[208] *Langley v Liverpool City Council and the Chief Constable of Merseyside Police* [2005] EWCA 1173 [36] (Dyson LJ).
[209] J Masson et al., *Protecting Powers: Emergency Intervention for Children's Protection* (Wiley 2007).

The Court of Appeal held that:

1. The police officer could not execute the emergency protection order because he was not the applicant for it and he was not working on behalf of the council. They could not lawfully delegate that task to the police: this is the effect of s45(12) and s48(9) of the Children Act 1989 read together. The council should have asked the police officer to find the children and then wait for social workers to come to the family home to execute the EPO.

2. Section 46 police protection can be invoked when an emergency protection order is in force, because otherwise it would be unlawful for a police officer to protect a child whom he has reasonable cause to believe is likely to suffer significant harm if not removed and where the officer is in ignorance of the existence of an EPO.

3. However, where the officer is aware of the EPO he or she should not remove the child to suitable accommodation under s46 without compelling reasons even if the statutory criteria for s46 are met (i.e., the constable has reasonable cause to believe that, unless the child is removed, he or she is likely to suffer significant harm). Dyson LJ gives as an example an EPO being obtained by one local authority, for example Liverpool, but the police officer coming across the child in Cornwall. Here, even if the officer was aware of the EPO his removal under s46 could be lawful if he considers the child in real danger and in urgent need of accommodation; he does not have to wait so that he can try to coordinate and contact social services to execute the EPO.

4. In this case, the police officer should have asked himself whether there were compelling reasons why he should invoke section 46 rather than leave it to the council to execute the EPO, such as if the council were unable to serve it for some time and whether it was practicable for him in the meantime to prevent Mr Langley from removing Callum from the house. Accordingly, both the council (because of their encouragement) and the police were responsible for the unlawful removal of Callum by the police officer.

Ending an emergency protection order

There is no appeal against the making of, or refusal of, an EPO, or against any direction that is part of an EPO. Nor is there any appeal against extending it. But there are four alternative ways of challenging the order:

1. Seek an order varying the terms of the EPO.

2. Bring judicial review proceedings. Although technically possible, this is obviously not particularly suitable for emergency situations.

3. Seek an injunction under s7 Human Rights Act 1998 for an actual or anticipated breach of human rights. Given the short duration of an order and the multiple proportionality protections offered by the guidance in Key Case *X Council v B*, this may not be successful.

4. Seek to discharge the EPO. An application to discharge the EPO can be made by either the child, any parent of hers (with or without parental responsibility), anyone with parental responsibility, or anyone with whom the child was living immediately before the making of the order *unless* they had at least one day's notice of the application and were present at the hearing. No application for the discharge of an EPO can be heard until 72 hours after the EPO was made: s45(9).

There are significant human rights implications in the use of EPOs. After all, they can involve police, social workers, and medical professionals coming to a person's home and taking their child. Guidance on their use was given in *X Council v B (Emergency Protection Order)*. The key messages are that an EPO is serious and must be a proportionate step with consideration given to the alternatives and to the length; that applications require full evidence, which is all the more important when the application is made *ex parte* (i.e., without prior notice to the respondent); and that the applicant must keep the case under constant review to ensure that parent and child are separated for no longer than is necessary to secure the child's safety. This guidance was praised and expanded upon by McFarlane J in a similarly named case, *Re X (Emergency Protection Orders)*.[210] In that case, McFarlane J said that the guidance provided by Munby J in *X Council v B* should be given to the justices hearing an EPO on each and every occasion such an application is made, and what happened at the *ex parte* hearing should be recorded or carefully noted.

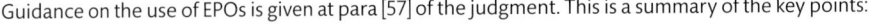

KEY CASE *X Council v B (Emergency Protection Order)* [2004] EWHC 2015

Guidance on the use of EPOs is given at para [57] of the judgment. This is a summary of the key points:

- An EPO should not be made unless the court is satisfied that it is both necessary and proportionate and that no other less radical form of order will achieve the essential end of promoting the welfare of the child. Separation is only to be contemplated if immediate separation is essential to secure the child's safety: 'imminent danger' must be 'actually established'.
- Any order must provide for the least interventionist solution consistent with the preservation of the child's immediate safety. No EPO should be made for any longer than is absolutely necessary to protect the child.
- The evidence in support of the application for an EPO must be full, detailed, precise and compelling. Unparticularised generalities will not suffice. The sources of hearsay evidence must be identified. Expressions of opinion must be supported by detailed evidence and properly articulated reasoning.
- Save in wholly exceptional cases, parents must be given adequate prior notice of the date, time and place of any application by a local authority for an EPO. They must also be given proper notice of the evidence the local authority is relying upon. The local authority must 'make out a compelling case for applying without first giving the parents notice': a genuine emergency or where there are compelling reasons to believe that the child's welfare will be compromised if the parents are alerted in advance to what is going on.
- The evidential burden on the local authority is even heavier if the application is made ex parte. Parents against whom an EPO is made ex parte are entitled to be given, if they ask, proper information as to what happened at the hearing and to be told, if they ask: (i) exactly what documents, bundles or other evidential materials were lodged with the court either before or during the course of the hearing; and (ii) what legal authorities were cited to the court.
- The local authority, even after it has obtained an EPO, is under an obligation to consider less drastic alternatives to emergency removal.
- Consistently with the local authority's positive obligation under Art 8 to take appropriate action to reunite parent and child, s44(10)(a) and s44(11)(a) impose on the local authority a mandatory obligation to return a child if it appears to [the local authority] that it is safe for the child to be returned'. This imposes on the local authority a continuing duty to keep the case under review and exercise exceptional diligence.
- A child who is subject to an EPO must have 'reasonable contact' with his parents. Arrangements for contact must be driven by the needs of the family, not stunted by lack of resources.

---

[210] [2006] EWHC 510 (Fam).

11.9 Conclusion

In this chapter, we considered the legal framework for supporting children in their families and protecting them when they face unacceptable risks. We looked first at the history of child protection and the inherent tension in protecting children while aspiring to support their life with their families, before considering local authorities' powers and duties, the scarcity of resources, and the ever-increasing numbers of children involved with social services, whether as children in need, looked after children, or as the subject of child protection investigations or applications. Social work as a profession, and social workers on an individual level, are torn between different aims. When is it right to intervene? How much support should be given to families? When should a child be removed from his or her home? How far should the state go to protect children from harm; to promote their physical, emotional and intellectual development; or to meet the needs of other family members such as parents and carers?[211] The answer to these questions are more than theoretical: they dictate social work practice up and down the country and thus the quality of children's lives and the safety and security of their families.

 KEY POINTS

- Over different eras, state intervention in families has had different aims. For Lorraine Fox Harding, the Children Act 1989 reflects four different ideological perspectives: (1) *laissez-faire* and patriarchy; (2) state paternalism and child protection; (3) defence of the birth family and parents' rights; and (4) children's rights and child liberation.

- Section 17(1) Children Act 1989 imposes a general duty on local authorities to 'safeguard and promote the welfare of children within their area who are in need' and, 'so far as is consistent with that duty, to promote the upbringing of such children by their families, by providing a range and level of services appropriate to those children's needs'. The Act does not require authorities to meet the assessed needs of every child in need irrespective of the authority's resources: *R (on the application of G) v Barnet London Borough Council* [2003] UKHL 57.

- Section 20 Children Act 1989 enables a local authority to offer accommodation to children and young adults in certain situations. There are important limitations in respect of children aged under 16. The utilisation of s20 as a long-term alternative to care has led in some cases to 'section 20 drift'; that is, children who are accommodated for a long period of time without the permanency planning that accompanies the making of a care order.

- A looked after child is one that is accommodated and/or cared for by the local authority, including under s20 or a care order. Children may become looked after for a wide range of different reasons, and under a range of different legal provisions. All looked after children must have a care plan setting out how the local authority intends to meet its duties to the child. Local authorities must consult before they make decisions. The local authority's obligations do not end when the child ceases to be looked after at the age of 16. A different set of obligations must then be met. What these obligations are depends upon whether the child is classed as (1) an eligible child; (2) a relevant child; (3) a former relevant child; or (4) a qualifying care leaver.

---

[211] E Farmer, 'Protection and Child Welfare: Striking the Balance?', Chapter 9 in N Parton (Ed.), *Child Protection and Family Support: Tensions, Contradictions and Possibilities* (Routledge 1997).

- Social workers may investigate a child protection concern under s47 Children Act, perhaps with the assistance of a child assessment order, although these are little used. As a result of this, the local authority may identify the child as being in need of services or call a child protection conference and draw up a child protection plan. The conference may recommend that the local authority commence care proceedings.

- The number of children subject to local authority investigations or interventions is increasing significantly. There are several potential reasons for this, including population increases, increasing numbers of disabled children and within certain vulnerability categories, increasing awareness, the effect of economic austerity including cuts to early intervention, different assessments of risk or attitudes to risk, especially following the death of baby Peter Connelly, and defensive social work practice.

- Under s46 the police have short-term powers to protect children, and this does not require a court order. An emergency protection order under s44 authorises the applicant to remove the child to a safe place, or retain her in a safe place if she is already there.

FURTHER READING: SOME STARTING POINTS

- There are a number of excellent discussions of the role of social workers, the values underlying the Children Act, and its aims, such as B Hoggett, 'The Children Bill: The Aim' [1989] *Family Law* 217, which is an overview of the bill by one of its key architects; and J Packman and B Jordan, 'The Children Act: Looking Forward, Looking Back' (1991) 21(4) *British Journal of Social Work* 315 (Packman's work has been very influential). On the tension between family support and child protection, see B Featherstone, K Morris, and S White, 'A Marriage Made in Hell: Early Intervention Meets Child Protection' (2014) 44(7) *British Journal of Social Work* 1735. A three-part BBC2 series called *Protecting Our Children* (2012) follows social workers in Bristol and highlights the same tension: this is available on Box of Broadcasts, to which your university may subscribe, and on other sites.

- We strongly recommend Lorraine Fox Harding's works 'The Children Act 1989 in Context: Four Perspectives in Child Care Law and Policy' Part I: (1991) 13(3) *Journal of Social Welfare and Family Law* 179 and Part II: (1991) 13(4) *Journal of Social Welfare and Family Law* 285. She developed these ideas in *Perspectives in Child Care Policy* (Longman 1995). A number of subsequent works discuss these perspectives, such as Roger Smith, 'Reconsidering Value Perspectives in Child Welfare' (2018) 48 *British Journal of Social Work* 616; Judith Masson, 'The State as Parent: The Reluctant Parent: The Problem of Parents of Last Resort?' (2008) 35(1) *Journal of Law and Society* 52; and Martin C Calder, 'Child Protection: Balancing Paternalism and Partnership' (1995) 25 *British Journal of Social Work* 749.

- E Munro 'Avoidable and Unavoidable Mistakes in Child Protection Work' (1996) 26(6) *British Journal of Social Work* 79 is a thought-provoking article on social work decision-making and confirmation bias. Nigel Parton's work highlights the political aspect of child protection law: 'Social Work, Child Protection and Politics: Some Critical and Constructive Reflections' (2014) 44 *British Journal of Social Work* 2042; and *The Politics of Child Protection* (Palgrave 2014).

- Good sources of statistics on children involved with local authorities can be found at Department for Education, *Characteristics of Children in Need* at https://explore-education-statistics.service.gov.uk/find-statistics/characteristics-of-children-in-need/2020; and for analysis see A Bilson, B Featherstone, and K Martin, 'How Child Protection's "Investigative Turn" Impacts on Poor and Deprived Communities' (2017) 47 *Family Law* 316 and A Bilson and KEC Martin, 'Referrals and Child Protection in England: One in Five Children Referred to Children's Services and One in Nineteen Investigated before the Age of Five' (2017) 47(3) *British Journal of Social Work* 793.

- Judith Masson has undertaken a number of research studies on the use of emergency protection and police protection including 'Police Protection – Protecting Whom?' (2002) 24(2) *Journal of Social Welfare and Family Law* 157 and 'Emergency Intervention to Protect Children: Using and Avoiding Legal Controls' (2005) 17(1) *Child and Family Law Quarterly* 75. See also *Protecting Powers: Emergency Intervention for Children's Protection* (Wiley 2007).

- While distressing, reading the inquiry reports into child deaths footnoted in this chapter is a good way to understand the ways in which social work operates in practice and where law or practice has fallen short. Many of these are freely available online, but if not you should be able to obtain them easily through your library. We particularly recommend *The Victoria Climbie Inquiry: Report of an Inquiry by Lord Laming* (Cmd 5730, 2003). Many local safeguarding boards also release case reviews into children's deaths in their areas if you are interested in local or recent reports, but you may need to be persistent in obtaining them from the source.

- Current statutory guidance is available online, but ensure that you do have the most current versions.

- Most family law journals will contain comments on the Key Cases discussed in this chapter. Although these are no substitute for reading the cases themselves, they do help contextualise them. Our Key Cases are *R (on the application of G) v Barnet London Borough Council* [2003] UKHL 57; *X Council v B (Emergency Protection Order)* [2004] EWHC 2015; *Langley v Liverpool City Council and the Chief Constable of Merseyside Police* [2005] EWCA 1173 (see also R Bailey-Harris, 'Emergency Protection: Langley v Liverpool City Council and the Chief Constable of Merseyside Police [2005] EWCA 1173' [2006] *Family Law* 94) and *Williams v London Borough of Hackney* [2018] UKSC 37.

 Visit the **online resources** to watch a video of Polly Morgan discussing this chapter topic, and to check your understanding of this chapter with self-test questions and scenario questions.

12 Child Protection: Care, Supervision, and Adoption

LEARNING CHECKLIST

By the end of this chapter, you should be able to:

- *Identify* the different elements of the threshold test for the making of a care or supervision order and *explain* the meaning of each element by reference to statute and case law

- *Critically evaluate* the degree to which the threshold criteria adequately balance the need to protect children and protect the interests of the family and the state

- *Identify* the different options that may be available to courts at the welfare stage of proceedings, and *explain* the principal legal and practical features of each option

- *Explain* the adoption process, *identify* how parents can challenge a plan for adoption, and *critically evaluate* the degree to which they are able to successfully do so

- *Explain* the principles set out in *Re B* and its line of subsequent case law

- *Critically discuss* how what is meant by a global, holistic, evaluation of the different options at the welfare stage and what factors may be relevant to a judge's decision about what order to make.

SCENARIO 1

Kerrie and Mike live together in a two-bedroom flat in Ipswich with their daughter, Ella, who is 18 months old. They are not married. The family first came to attention of social services as a result of a serious domestic abuse incident witnessed by Ella in the home, in which Mike kicked and punched Kerrie. He was charged with assault, and bailed not to return to the home. In her statement to police, Kerrie alleged that there was a substantial history of domestic abuse over a number of years, triggered by Mike's drug use. However, before the trial Kerrie said she refused to testify, and charges were dropped. Kerrie has told social workers that she and Mike have split up and Mike no longer lives with them.

Since then, social workers have become increasingly concerned about the situation in the home that Kerrie and Ella live in. Each time that they visited they found that Ella's clothes were dirty and her nappy had not been recently changed. The house was very dirty with animal faeces on the floor and Ella had some flea bites. The social worker noticed that Kerrie did not seem to demonstrate any warm feelings towards Ella and that Kerrie seemed unresponsive when Ella sought her attention. The social worker wondered if Kerrie was depressed.

Following a strategy discussion, it undertook a s 47 investigation which concluded that Ella was at risk of significant harm.

Mike and Kerrie were invited to a child protection conference. At the conference, it was decided that Ella was at risk of physical neglect and Ella was made the subject of a Child Protection plan. It included regular unannounced visits by social workers, a referral for Mike to a programme for perpetrators of domestic abuse, and some practical support in keeping the home clean. Kerrie's GP referred her to counselling and she was placed on a waiting list.

The local authority has been monitoring compliance with the plan. However, they have learned that Mike has moved back into the property. Social workers visiting the home found evidence of drug use and damage to the house where Mike had apparently punched the wall.

The local authority decides to bring the child protection plan to an early end by making an application for a care order.

12.1 **Introduction**

In Chapter 11, we looked at the powers and duties imposed on local authorities to help avoid the need for compulsory state intervention in the family, and we saw how these powers and duties represent different philosophical approaches to the role of the state in family life. This chapter picks up from these discussions by looking at what happens when compulsory intervention in the form of care or supervision applications is needed. We consider the legal tests, the processes, and the practicalities involved in proceedings and decisions about what should happen next.

Section 31(1) Children Act 1989 describes what is meant by a care or supervision order. It says that:

(1) On the application of any local authority or authorised person, the court may make an order—
(a) placing the child with respect to whom the application is made in the care of a designated local authority; or
(b) putting him under the supervision of a designated local authority.

A care order is therefore an order placing the child 'in the care' of the local authority. As of 31 March 2020, there were 61,320 children who were being looked after pursuant to a care order.[1] The most common reason was abuse or neglect. Other reasons include family dysfunction, families in acute distress, and absent parenting.[2]

As part of this, the local authority obtains parental responsibility for the child, which they will share with the parents and anyone else who has parental responsibility. However, the local authority can exercise their parental responsibility to the exclusion of the other PR holders. (At 12.4.6 we discuss the consequences of this, duties to consult, and challenging the local authority.) The local authority will decide where the child is to live. Most children in care are in foster care, living with an approved foster carer at the carer's family home. Other children may live in a children's home, residential unit, secure unit, or with family friends or relations.[3] Some children in care remain with their parents but this is

---

[1] Department for Education, *Children Looked After in England Including Adoption 2019 to 2020* (2021). Available at https://explore-education-statistics.service.gov.uk/find-statistics/children-looked-after-in-england-including-adoptions/2020 accessed 28 March 2021.
[2] Department for Education, *Children Looked After in England Including Adoption 2019 to 2020* (2021).
[3] Department for Education, *Children Looked After in England Including Adoption 2019 to 2020* (2021).

not common. Because the effect of a care order is to enable the local authority to make decisions about the child, the authority is free to change its mind about where the child should live.

As Harwin et al. note, supervision orders originally involved a probation officer who was to 'visit, advise and befriend' a child who had committed a crime.[4] Under the Children Act 1989, supervision orders are not a criminal penalty, but do serve a similar function: a supervisor, usually the local authority, must 'advise, assist and befriend the child'. Schedule 3 sets out further requirements. The local authority can direct where the child lives, and that the child is to meet with social workers and participate in specified activities. Those with PR must take 'all reasonable steps' to ensure that the child complies with these directions.

A court will only make a care or supervision order if the child is suffering or likely to suffer *significant harm*. That harm must be attributable to either the care being given to the child, or the child being beyond parental control. Under s 31(2) Children Act 1989:

> A court may only make a care order or supervision order if it is satisfied—
>
> (a) that the child concerned is suffering, or is likely to suffer, significant harm; and
> (b) that the harm, or likelihood of harm, is attributable to—
>   (i) the care given to the child, or likely to be given to him if the order were not made, not being what it would be reasonable to expect a parent to give to him; or
>   (ii) the child's being beyond parental control.

This is known as the 'threshold test'.

It is important to understand that the fact that a child ends up in care or subject to a supervision order does not imply that they were being mistreated or that they were unwanted. Some children will have been, but it is possible to satisfy the threshold test in relation to loving parents because love does not equate to parenting ability, and some parents have significant disabilities which mean they cannot look after their children even though they want to do so. A high proportion of children in care are disabled or have complex needs that parents cannot meet, and some children simply do not have parents at all.

Each of these elements of the test are discussed in this chapter, and it is important to note that the precise meaning of some of these phrases has had to be decided by case law, rather than being obvious. If the legal test for making a care or supervision order is met, the court must then consider what type of order is best for the child. This could be something other than a care or supervision order. In our discussion of this welfare stage, we consider the function of each of these types of order and when one may be more appropriate than the other. Before we do so, we need to consider how proceedings start in the first place.

12.2 **Making an application**

In order for the court to make a care or supervision order, it must be satisfied that the test laid out in s 31(2) Children Act 1989 is met (the 'threshold stage') and that it is the child's best interests for the care or supervision order to be made (the 'welfare stage'). A judge

---

[4] J Harwin, B Alrouh, L Golding, T McQuarrie, K Broadhurst, and L Cusworth, *The Contribution of Supervision Orders and Special Guardianship to Children's Lives and Family Justice* (Lancaster University Centre for Child and Family Justice Research/Nuffield Foundation 2019).

may decline to make the order sought by the local authority because another order (or no order) is better for the child. This is discussed further at 12.4.

As we see in Chapter 11, the local authority has no power whatsoever to remove a child without a court order. Prior to the Children Act 1989, social workers relied heavily on the inherent jurisdiction of the High Court to protect children in circumstances when the court otherwise had to be satisfied that there was *existing* harm to a child, not merely *anticipated* harm. The Act changed this, requiring local authorities to prove that the s31 criteria were met before the court would intervene. It is for this reason that the section is known as the *threshold test*, for it marks the threshold for compulsory state intervention in family life and thereby works to 'delineate, limit, and provide structure' for the local authority and the courts.[5]

12.2.1 Who can be taken into care or supervised?

Before the threshold test is applied, it is important to understand who can be taken into care or supervised. A care or supervision order may only be made with respect to a child under the age of 17 (or 16 if the child is married or civilly partnered). However, care and supervision orders are often made in respect of very young children. Between 2007/08 and 2016/17, 27 per cent of children in care proceedings were less than 1 year old[6] and approximately 11 per cent were under 1 *week* old, but there is significant regional variation: local authorities in some areas make far more newborn and infant applications than other local authorities. A local authority can obtain an interim care order to permit the child to be removed from the mother at the hospital or maternity centre if the baby is at imminent risk of significant harm.[7]

In law, a foetus is not recognised as a person before birth, so an order cannot be made pre-birth. If, on learning of a woman's pregnancy, the local authority has serious concerns about how she will care for the baby once they are born, it is 'essential and best practice'[8] that a risk assessment should be completed during the pregnancy and an application for an interim care order made the same day that the mother has given birth. While many such removals are children of parents who have already had children taken into care, just over half of the children in Broadhurst et al.'s study of newborn removal were the first children born to the mother. Broadhurst et al. found this surprising, because it calls into question how the mothers are identified as presenting a risk of significant harm to their baby when they have not previously parented.[9]

---

[5] *Yates and Gard v Great Ormond Street Hospital* [2017] EWCA Civ 410, [107] (McFarlane LJ).

[6] K Broadhurst, B Alrouh, C Mason, H Ward, L Holmes, M Ryan, and S Bowyer, *Born into Care: Newborn Babies Subject to Care Proceedings in England* (Lancaster University Centre for Child and Family Justice Research/Nuffield Foundation 2018).

[7] You can read an account of newborn removal by Annie, a woman whose children were taken into care, here: http://survivingsafeguarding.co.uk/2015/06/24/newborn-removal/ accessed 27 September 2020.

[8] *Nottingham City Council v M* [2016] EWHC 11(Fam) [31] (Keehan J).

[9] K Broadhurst, B Alrouh, C Mason, H Ward, L Holmes, M Ryan, and S Bowyer, *Born into Care: Newborn Babies Subject to Care Proceedings in England* (Lancaster University Centre for Child and Family Justice Research/Nuffield Foundation 2018).

FOCUS Think Critically

Child protection, risk, and poverty

In Scenario 1, the local authority has had some prior involvement with the family before deciding to bring care proceedings. This is very common. A study by Masson et al. showed that an average of 45 per cent of care applications related to children who had been involved with social services for more than five years.[10] The local authority will have brought the care or supervision application at the point that it decides that the risks to the child are too great to continue without making an application. This is also affected by a number of other factors not necessarily related to that particular child but to do with local authority policy or practice, or fear of wrong decision-making and the potentially awful consequences. For example, public anger surrounding the death of Peter Connelly (known pseudonymously as 'Baby P'), led to a significant increase in the number of care applications. Numbers have continued to rise ever since, and this cannot all be accounted for by population increases.

The increase in the number of applications nationally disguises considerable variation in the number of applications made in different local authority areas, and in the number of Looked After Children or children subject to child protection plans. According to Bywaters, some of this variation can be explained by differing rates of poverty.[11] Poverty has a direct and indirect relationship with child abuse and neglect, and 'evidence of this association is found repeatedly across developed countries, types of abuse, definitions, measures and research approaches, and in different child protection systems . . . At a population level each incremental increase in family socio-economic disadvantage correlates with an increased chance of child abuse and neglect'.[12] Unemployment, insecure or poor quality housing, and food and fuel poverty can have 'a direct material impact on the capacity of families to offer children a good developmental experience or as stresses that affect parents' ability to function effectively. Detrimental consequences of stress, such as excessive alcohol or substance use, exposure to intimate partner violence or poor mental health, can be seen as secondary to fundamental causes.'[13] The effects of poverty can therefore help to explain why children living in Blackpool (one of the most deprived areas of the UK, with shorter than average life expectancies and high rates of child poverty)[14] are the subject of care applications at a rate of 36.5 per 10,000 children, the highest in England and Wales.

But poverty alone does not explain the disparity between local authorities. In fact, 'intervention rates vary widely between local authorities for neighbourhoods at the same level of deprivation'.[15] What seems to matter is the relative wealth of the local authority. 'More advantaged local authorities employ proportionately more, often substantially more, "heavy end" interventions than relatively disadvantaged local authorities for an equivalent level of deprivation.'[16] In other words, if you live in a relatively deprived neighbourhood in a wealthy local authority, the chances of local authority

---

[10] J Masson, J Pearce, and K Bader, with O Joyner, J Marsden, and D Westlake, *Care Profiling Study*, Ministry of Justice Research Series 04/08 (Ministry of Justice and Department of Children, Schools and Families 2008).

[11] P Bywaters, 'Inequalities in Child Welfare: Towards a New Policy, Research and Action Agenda' [2013] *British Journal of Social Work* 1.

[12] P Bywaters, L Bunting, G Davidson, J Hanratty, W Mason, C McCartan, and N Steils, *The Relationship between Poverty, Child Abuse and Neglect: An Evidence Review* (Joseph Rowntree Foundation 2016) 3, 25.

[13] P Bywaters, G Brady, T Sparks, E Bos, L Bunting, B Daniel, B Featherstone, K Morris, and J Scourfield, 'Exploring Inequities in Child Welfare and Child Protection Services: Explaining the "Inverse Intervention Law"' (2015) 57 *Children and Youth Services Review* 98.

[14] See Joint Strategic Needs Assessment, Blackpool Council. http://www.blackpooljsna.org.uk/Developing-Well/Children-and-young-peoples-wellbeing/Child-Poverty.aspx

[15] P Bywaters, G Brady, T Sparks, and E Bos, 'Child Welfare Inequalities: New Evidence, Further Questions' (2016) 21(3) *Child and Family Social Work* 369.

[16] P Bywaters, G Brady, T Sparks, and E Bos, 'Child Welfare Inequalities: New Evidence, Further Questions' (2016) 21(3) *Child and Family Social Work* 369, 378.

intervention are higher. There are a number of potential reasons for this, including that such families stand out more, or that the local authority has more funds to bring proceedings, or the local authorities take different views on the level of risk they are prepared to tolerate before intervening. What the data does not tell us is whether those interventions are justified. As Bywaters asks:

> If more advantaged [local authorities] are using child protection plans and looked after children interventions more frequently because they have relatively more resources, are they getting the right balance between protection and prevention? Are the most disadvantaged local authorities with low rates . . . intervening too little because of insufficient resources? If you are a child in one of the most deprived 10% of neighbourhoods, is it right that you should have an 11 times greater chance of being in care than a child living in a nearby affluent neighbourhood?[17]

12.2.2 Who can apply?

Section 31(1) states that 'any local authority or authorised person' can make an application to court for a care or supervision order. The only 'authorised person' at present is the National Society for the Prevention of Cruelty to Children (NSPCC): s31(9). In reality, the local authority for the area in which the child resides will make the application and the NSPCC will simply refer any concerns it has (for example those stemming from calls to its helpline) to the police or local authority. The NSPCC is, in any case, under an obligation to consult the local authority before making an application: s31(6).

Note that once proceedings are issued, the local authority cannot withdraw them without the court's leave. It is therefore possible for the local authority to change its mind about the application, but for the court to continue to determine the matter, just as it is possible for the court to make a different kind of order such as a residence order or supervision order on an application for a care order. In such decisions, including deciding whether to grant leave to withdraw, s1 Children Act 1989 applies, and the child's welfare is the court's paramount consideration.[18]

12.2.3 The parties

Once an application has been made, all those with parental responsibility for the child are parties to the proceedings, as is the child him or herself. Parental responsibility is a legal status discussed in Chapter 8.

Whereas the child's mother will always be a party to the proceedings as by law a mother always holds parental responsibility, a father who is or was not married to the mother and has not acquired parental responsibility for the child is not automatically party to the proceedings.[19] In accordance with paragraph 3.1 to Practice Direction 12C, a father without parental responsibility should still should be notified, and 'if [he] wishes to participate as a

---

[17] P Bywaters, G Brady, T Sparks, and E Bos, 'Child Welfare Inequalities: New Evidence, Further Questions' (2016) 21(3) *Child and Family Social Work* 369, 378.
[18] *London Borough of Southwark v B* [1993] 2 FLR 559 (CA).
[19] For a discussion of when a father has PR, see 8.5.3.

party in care proceedings, he should be permitted to do so unless there is some justifiable reason for not joining him as a party.[20]

It is normally in the interests of the child that their birth father should be able to participate in the proceedings, but the court can give the local authority permission to not notify the father in exceptional circumstances—although this decision can be reversed if it becomes necessary to look for future carers within the father's side of the family.[21] The court may also authorise the non-notification of a person with parental responsibility, although this is extremely rare.[22]

FOCUS Know-How

Notification of fathers

Failing to notify a father of care proceedings is a potential interference with his Article 8 ECHR right to private and family life. After all, the ultimate outcome of the proceedings may be that the child is adopted. If he does have an Article 8 right, then he also has a civil right or obligation that is capable of being protected by Article 6's right to a fair trial.[23] However, remember that the father may not have Article 8 rights at all: as we see in Chapter 10, Article 8 does not protect the relationship between unmarried father and child if there is no pre-existing relationship.[24] Even if Article 8 does apply, it is not an absolute right. Interference can be justified under Article 8(2) and in this context the father's rights will be weighed against any risk of harm to the mother or child as a result of the father's participation, such as a risk of them being exposed to domestic abuse.

The issue of the notification of fathers came to public attention in later 2018 through the case of Sammy Woodhouse, who became pregnant by a man later convicted of grooming children for child sexual exploitation, and was subjected to rape, assault, and other acts designed to terrorize her.[25] The local authority sought a care order in respect of the child born of that 'relationship' and in doing so notified the father, who was in prison. It could have, and probably should have, made an application for authorisation not to notify him, given the circumstances.

More recently still, in 2020, the case A, B, and C (Adoption: Notification of Fathers and Relatives) joined three separate cases in which mothers who did not want their children's fathers or other relatives to know of the children's births, and wanted to voluntarily relinquish the children for adoption.[26] There were different reasons for this, including allegations that one of the babies had been conceived by rape, fear of family reaction, and the father's poor mental health. Peter Jackson LJ gave the leading judgment for the Court of Appeal, setting out the previous case law and identifying principles to be followed. He identified that the welfare of the child was an important factor but not the paramount consideration in an application about notification, and the court's role was to strike a fair balance between the various interests involved. These included

- Whether the father's (or another person's) Article 8 rights are engaged
- The substance of the parental and family relationships concerned

[20] Re B (Care Proceedings: Notification of Father without Parental Responsibility) [1999] 2 FLR 408, 412 (Holman J).
[21] Re X (A Child) (Care Proceedings: Notice to Father without Parental Responsibility) [2017] EWFC 34.
[22] Local Authority v M [2009] EWHC 3172 (Fam).
[23] But only if his Art 8 rights are engaged. Otherwise, he has no civil rights and obligations that require protection under Art 6: Re M (Notification of Step-Parent Adoption) [2014] EWHC 1128 (Fam).
[24] Lebbink v Netherlands [2004] 3 FCR 59.
[25] For the background to this high profile case, see http://www.transparencyproject.org.uk/the-sammy-woodhouse-story-and-associated-campaigns-an-update/ accessed 22 October 2019.
[26] Relinquishment is outside the scope of this book.

- The physical, psychological, or social impact on the mother or others of notification
- Cultural and religious factors. These may elevate risks to the mother, if the community or family disapprove, but conversely if the child is from a particular ethnic minority background the maintenance of family ties may be important for the child
- The consequences of the child's existence becoming known to the family later on, and the ease with which relatives can be identified. If the mother refuses to identify the father, she cannot be coerced; she may also not know who the father is
- The impact of procedural delay caused by notification, with its impact on the mother and child, especially if it would lead to a suitable adoptive placement being lost
- The likelihood of anyone notified being a realistic alternative carer instead of the child being adopted.[27]

If the father has parental responsibility for the child, that gives him automatic status in any proceedings which may lead to adoption, so compelling reasons are required not to notify him. We return to notification of fathers at 12.4.6.

The child will be represented by a guardian who, in turn, instructs a solicitor. The guardian's role is to represent the interests of the child in the litigation. This is not the same as being a special guardian or a guardian appointed because (for example) the parents have died. Because of the risk of confusion, we will call this person a 'litigation guardian' whenever we refer to this role.

Where a *Gillick*-competent child (see Chapter 9) has views that differ from those of his or her litigation guardian, the court may give permission for them to instruct their own solicitor, in which case there is no further role for the litigation guardian.[28] This is not common. Moylan LJ noted in Re *B (Children)* (2018) that 'It is not unusual for a child's views to differ from that of a guardian, and in my experience, such difference rarely requires separate representation.'[29]

SCENARIO 1

Illustration 1

The parties in our example case will be

- The local authority, who is the applicant for the care or supervision order
- As respondents: Kerrie, as the mother with parental responsibility, and Mike, provided that he has parental responsibility. At 8.5.3, we saw the ways in which a father who was not married to the mother could obtain parental responsibility. The most common method, for children born after 1 December 2003, is for the father to be named on the birth certificate. Kerrie and Mike may be represented by the same legal team or by separate teams, depending on

---

[27] [2020] EWCA Civ 41.
[28] Gillick competence is discussed at 9.5.2; see also Key *Case Mabon* at 9.4.2 and 10.2.4.
[29] [2018] EWCA Civ 3049 [8]. Note that there are a number of cases called *Re B* on care and adoption and students should be careful not to get them muddled.

whether their case is that they are a couple or that they are separated, so as to avoid creating a conflict of interest. It is more common for parents to be separately represented. As we see in 12.2.4, they will each be entitled to non-mean-tested and non-merits-tested legal aid, as will Ella.

- Ella, the 18-month-old child who is the subject of the application. Her interests will be represented by a litigation guardian.

12.2.4 The public law outline

The public law outline (PLO) is found in Practice Direction 12A and sets out the procedure to be followed in care and supervision proceedings, from before an application is issued through to disposal. You can see the process set out in Figure 12.1.

In non-emergency situations, the local authority will undertake a number of pieces of work before it files an application for a care or supervision order. This should include writing a 'pre-proceedings' letter to the parents and anyone else who has parental responsibility. This letter explains the local authority's concerns and invites the parents to a pre-proceedings meeting, and is sometimes known as a 'public law outline meeting'. The pre-proceedings letter acts as the trigger for the award of legal aid, enabling parents (with or without parental responsibility) to obtain representation. Non means-tested and non merits-tested legal aid is available for both care proceedings and proceedings which are 'related to' them. This reflects the 'draconian nature of the order being claimed by the local authority', which is one empowering them, as an organ of the state, to interfere with the

FIGURE 12.1 Process under the public law outline in Practice Direction 12A

parents' autonomy to raise their child as they want, and potentially to remove him permanently from his home and raise him elsewhere.[30] If there was no legal aid available in care cases that may well breach Article 6 ECHR, the right to a fair trial.

The pre-proceedings meeting is an opportunity to try to 'divert a case along a route which avoids the need for proceedings'[31] by enabling the parents to address concerns about the child. If the local authority feels that compliance with these pre-proceedings steps will put the child at risk, then it can instead make an application straight away, or seek an emergency protection order.

If it has not been possible to resolve the local authority's concerns, then the local authority will need to gather its evidence and draw up a care plan, which is a plan for the child's future if a care order is made. Part of this will involve determining whether there is anyone in the wider family who might become a carer for child instead of the parents and, if so, assess their suitability. All of this is ideally done prior to issue of the application.[32] The preparation for a case is therefore front-loaded, which has resource implications for the local authority.

Once the application is issued, Cafcass will allocate a litigation guardian to represent the child's interests, and the litigation guardian will in turn be represented by their own solicitor. The court will timetable the case in accordance with the public law outline. Care and supervision proceedings must be concluded within 26 weeks (six months) of issue and this can only be extended if 'necessary to enable the court to resolve the proceedings justly'.[33]

As Figure 12.1 shows, there are three principal hearings under the public law outline: a case management hearing, an issues resolution hearing, and a final hearing. The practice direction allows for additional hearings, however, and Masson et al. found that the average number of hearings is between four and five, although local practices vary.[34]

The first step is for there to be an advocates' meeting, no fewer than two days prior to a case management hearing. The purpose of this meeting is to enable the lawyers to identify the parties' positions and what, if any, expert assessments of reports may be required. At the case management hearing, the judge will need to make a decision about what evidence is required for the case to be determined fairly. For example, she may need to order the disclosure of certain documents or decide whether there are factual disputes that need to be addressed. The parents may seek a parenting assessment or other reports/assessments about the quality of their parenting or their capacity to change. Expert reports can only be submitted with the permission of the judge, who will only allow reports if they are 'necessary' in order for the court to dispose of the case fairly.[35] Unlike other witnesses who can

---

[30] *Re D (Non-Availability of Legal Aid)* [2015] 1 FLR 531, 540 (Munby P).

[31] Sir James Munby P, 'View from the President's Chambers: The Process of Reform: the revised PLO and the Local Authority' 17 May 2013. Available at https://www.judiciary.uk/publication-jurisdiction/family-2/ accessed 13 September 2019.

[32] While the application is usually freestanding it is possible to make the application within other family proceedings: s31(4).

[33] Section 32(1)(a) and (5) Children Act 1989, inserted by the Children and Families Act 2014.

[34] Judith Masson, Jonathan Dickens, Kay Bader, Ludivine Garside, and Julie Young, 'How Is the PLO Working? What Is Its Impact on Court Process and Outcome? The Outcomes of Care Proceedings for Children before and after Care Proceedings Reform Study Interim Report', (*Family Law Week* 17 February 2017).

[35] S38(7A) Children Act 1989 and s13(6) Children and Families Act 2014, and FPR r25.1.

only testify to what they have seen or heard, expert witnesses can give an opinion using their expertise. The court will prefer to have joint experts (experts who are instructed by all parties together) rather than rival experts for each party.[36] The court can also make an order joining others to the proceedings, such as prospective kinship carers (relatives) although this is not common even when kinship carers are being proposed. Other parties can get legal aid subject to the means and merits test. In other words, the court sets out what needs to be done and when, in preparation for the next stage, which is an issues resolution hearing.

There will be a further advocates' meeting, this time no fewer than seven days before the issues resolution hearing. The purpose of this is to identify if there are any gaps in the evidence that needs to be obtained, or any factual disputes that need to be resolved. It may be that everything is ready and the issues resolution hearing can be used as a final hearing. If not, the court will once again give orders designed to prepare the case for a final hearing, and this may include hearing evidence in order to narrow the issues remaining for the trial.

At the final hearing, the court will hear evidence from witnesses including any experts, social workers, and the parent(s). It will then have to consider two things:

(1) Is the threshold for the making of a care or supervision order crossed, and

(2) if so, what outcome is in the child's best interests?

The court will make an order that should have 'within it, or have annexed to it, a clear statement of the basis upon which the s31 threshold criteria have been established', if, indeed, they have been established.[37]

12.2.5 Interim care orders

An interim care order is a temporary care order made in order to safeguard the child while the proceedings are going on. In *Re G (A Child) (Interim Care Order: Residential Assessment)* Lord Scott described an interim care order as 'a temporary order . . . until sufficient information can be obtained about the child, the child's family, the child's circumstances and the child's need to enable a final decision in the care proceedings to be made'.[38] The power to make an interim care order is found in s38 Children Act 1989. Courts have no power to extend the order past the child's 17th birthday, or 16th if the child is married.[39]

An interim care order can also be made where the court has ordered a report under s37 Children Act, which (as discussed in Chapter 11) is when the court has asked the local authority to consider whether it should apply for a care or supervision order or provide assistance to the children in accordance with their statutory obligations towards children in need.

---

[36] Practice Direction 25C.
[37] *Re S and H-S (Children)* [2018] EWCA Civ 1282.
[38] [2005] 3 FCR 621 [2].
[39] *Re Q (Child: Interim Care Order: Jurisdiction)* [2019] EWHC 512 (Fam).

Re K (Children)[40] is a case in which two boys, aged 14 and 12, had been the subject of ten years of child arrangements litigation between their parents a harmful situation which had potentially moved out of the private law sphere and become a child protection issue.[41] The court ordered a s37 report, and made an interim care order placing the older child with foster carers; the younger child went to live with his father pursuant to a child arrangements order. The Court of Appeal upheld the interim care order: its retention meant that the local authority obtained parental responsibility, which it shared with the parents, enabling the authority to step in if necessary. However, it placed both children back with their mother under the interim order because removing them was disproportionate at that stage. In the course of his judgment in the Court of Appeal, Ryder LJ identifies four requirements for the making of an interim care order: threshold, safety, welfare, and proportionality. Let us consider each of these in turn.

1. *The interim threshold requirement.* The court has to be satisfied that there are reasonable grounds for believing that the care threshold in s 31(2) is met. This threshold is discussed in detail at 12.3 of this chapter. The court's decision must be limited only to those issues that cannot await later determination and 'must not extend to issues that are being prepared for determination at that fixture'.[42] There is no need for the court to be satisfied that the threshold is definitely met—that will require the evidence that the proceedings have probably been adjourned to acquire—but merely that there are reasonable grounds for believing that the child is suffering or likely to suffer significant harm attributable to their care or them being beyond parental control. Bainham has commented that the interim threshold test sets the bar 'very low', as 'virtually anything significantly negative in a parent's history will satisfy a test based on reasonable grounds for believing, especially as it embraces not merely current harm but the risk of harm.'[43]

2. *The safety requirement.* If the local authority wishes to remove the child from his or her home, then the court has to be satisfied that *the child's safety demands immediate separation* from their existing carer, i.e. is necessary within the meaning of Article 8. 'Safety' includes both physical safety and emotional harm. However, per *Re L-A (Care: Chronic Neglect)*, it is not necessary to show that there is an imminent risk of really serious harm.[44]

3. *The welfare requirement.* The child's welfare is the court's paramount consideration under s1 Children Act 1989 and the welfare checklist applies. The court must be satisfied that removal is in the best interests of the child. This involves balancing the impact of the child of remaining where they are against the impact of being removed from their parents.

---

[40] Re K (Children) [2014] EWCA Civ 1195.
[41] See 10.7.3.
[42] Re K (Children) [2014] EWCA Civ 1195.
[43] A Bainham, 'Interim Care Orders: Is the Bar Set Too Low?' [2011, April] *Family Law* 374. For a different view, albeit one based on a superseded requirement that the harm be serious imminent harm, is Darren Howe, 'Removal of Children at Interim Hearings: Is the Test Now Set Too High? [2009, April] *Family Law* 321.
[44] [2010] 1 FLR 80 (CA).

4. *The requirement of proportionality.* In *Re C (A Child)* the Court of Appeal noted that the removal of a child under an interim care order is 'a particularly sharp' interference with Article 8.[45] The court must therefore undertake 'a comparative welfare analysis of the options'[46] (which could include no order or making a child arrangements order, for example to a relation), before it can determine that removal is a proportionate response to the risk of harm if the child returns home, and therefore a proportionate interference with the child's and his parents' Article 8 rights. The local authority must inform the court of all available resources that might remove the need for separation such as, in (a different) *Re C*, the availability of a place at a residential assessment unit where the mother's parenting would be closely supervised.[47]

In addition to Article 8, Article 6 (the right to a fair trial) may be engaged because the application may be made at short notice without much time for the parents to prepare. Indeed, the hearing may be so urgent that there is an interim care order made followed soon after by a full interim care order hearing once the parents have had more time to prepare, as in *London Borough of Croydon v LN and Ors*.[48]

Some parents take a neutral position on an interim care order, neither agreeing to it (because they do not want it) nor opposing it (because they do not want to be seen as un-cooperative or seeking to minimise the local authority's concerns in case that means they are seen as permanently unable to safely parent). Others may not contest interim threshold because they see no prospect of successfully doing so.

Bainham argues that 'a fundamental problem with the current characterisation of [interim care orders] as "neutral" or "holding" orders is that, despite the endorsement of the higher courts, this is simply not credible to anxious parents.'[49] While an interim care order is intended to be a holding position, the potential separation of parent and child can be hugely distressing to both and can make parents feel that the court is against them. Even where an interim order is made on the basis that the child remains in the family home, social workers will be regularly visiting and share parental responsibility with the parents.

Assessments under an interim care order

Although it is not possible to attach conditions to a (final) care order, s38(6) permits conditions relating to medical, psychological or other assessment *of the child* to be attached to an interim care or supervision order. An assessment could be of the child's attachment to their parents, the degree to which have they have bonded with the child, the parents' current parenting skills and their capacity to learn and develop, and any risks they present to the child and how those risks can be managed.[50]

---

[45] *Re C (A Child)* [2019] EWCA Civ 1998 at [2].
[46] *Re G (Interim Care Order)* [2011] 2 FLR 955.
[47] *Re C (A Child) (Interim Separation)* [2020] EWCA Civ 257.
[48] [2015] EWFC B160, on BAILII.
[49] A Bainham, 'Interim Care Orders: Is the Bar Set Too Low?' [2011, April] *Family Law* 374.
[50] *Re G (Interim Care Order)* [2005] UKHL 68.

In *Re Y (A Child) (s38(6) Assessment)*[51] Peter Jackson LJ said that in order to grant a request for an assessment, the court had to ask two questions in the affirmative:

1. Does the proposed assessment falls within s38?

   In *Re G (Interim Care Order)* the House of Lords made it clear that the focus of the assessment should be the child, and designed to obtain the information necessary to make a decision about her future, rather than being about improving the parents' parenting skills, even if such help would enable the court to decide whether to make a care. It had to bring something to the case which neither the local authority nor the guardian was able to bring.[52] However, it is not always easy to draw a clear line between an assessment focused on the child and that focused on the environment in which she lives. Indeed, Jones argues that courts have 'given a very wide interpretation' to s38 as part of the obligation to ensure an Article 6-compliant process: 'the assessment's main focus is upon the child and it appears that, provided the court is satisfied that this is the case, then the majority of assessments can be correctly said to fall within the general scope of the section'.[53] Thus in *Re L and H (Residential Assessment)* the Court of Appeal held that an assessment of how the parents went about the task of parenting, and how their relationship coped with the stress of it, fell within the scope of s38(6).[54]

2. Is the assessment necessary to resolve the case fairly?

   This evaluation will be expert evidence for the final hearing, and because of this it can be a useful mechanism for parents to seek to challenge what they perceive as an existing local authority assessment that is of low quality or otherwise lacking in some way. However, the court will only permit a report to be prepared if one is 'necessary' to resolve proceedings, not merely because one would potentially a party's case.[55] Section 38(7B) sets out a list of factors to be considered in deciding whether the assessment is indeed necessary.

Note that children who are *Gillick*-competent to consent to or refuse an assessment can do so, although there is at least one case in which the court has overruled refusal under the inherent jurisdiction.[56]

SCENARIO 1

Illustration 2

The court has reasonable grounds for believing that the care threshold is met in Ella's case. In the home, she appears to be suffering from emotional and physical neglect at a time when good quality care is essential to her development. But the main concern relates to the return of Mike to the family home, his violence, and drug use. These present a real possibility of physical harm to Ella; and even if

---

[51] [2018] EWCA Civ 992.
[52] *Re G (Interim Care Order)* [2005] UKHL 68 at [71] (Lady Hale).
[53] M Jones, 'To Assess or Not to Assess: Is that the Question? Section 38(6)' [2011, November] *Family Law* 1233.
[54] [2007] EWCA Civ 213.
[55] The necessity requirement is found in s38(7A) Children Act 1989.
[56] *South Glamorgan County Council v W and B* [1993] 1 FLR 574. For Gillick competency and the use of the inherent jurisdiction to overrule it, see Chapter 9.

she is not herself the victim of domestic abuse at the hands of Mike, harm is defined in the Children Act to include witnessing harm to others, such as Kerrie. It is highly likely that this harm passes the threshold of being 'significant'.

If the local authority wants to use the interim care order to remove Ella from her parents' care, such as by moving her to live with foster carers, then the court must consider whether her safety demands immediate separation. There may be an alternative, less interventionist way of mitigating the risks to her. For example, is there a grandparent that she could go and live with under s 20 agreement instead of an interim care order? Is there a way for her to be sufficiently safe in her mother's care if Mike was not there? If so, then under s38A Children Act 1989, an exclusion requirement can be attached to an interim care order. This could be used to exclude Mike from the property. Section 38 requires that there be reasonable cause to believe that if he is excluded then Ella will cease to suffer, or cease to be likely to suffer, significant harm; and that Kerrie consents to the exclusion and is willing and able to give Ella the care that it would be reasonable to expect a parent to give her. Here, there are concerns about Kerrie's ability to care for Ella, so it is unlikely that removing Mike will mean that Ella ceases to suffer significant harm.

Therefore, it is likely that the court would consider that in this case Ella's safety—emotional and physical—demands immediate separation, and that this is in her best interests.

Once Ella is in foster care, the local authority will have the opportunity to assess her development and progress away from her parents' care, and to undertake any assessments of her that are necessary for their case.

12.3 **The threshold stage**

In the introduction to this chapter, we introduced the threshold test for the making of a care or supervision order, so called because it marks the threshold for compulsory intervention in family life. In order to make a care or supervision order, the court must be satisfied that the threshold criteria, set out in s31(2) Children Act 1989, are satisfied:

STATUTORY EXTRACT *Section 31(2) Children Act 1989*

A court may only make a care order or supervision order if it is satisfied:

(a) that the child concerned is suffering, or is likely to suffer, significant harm; and
(b) that the harm, or likelihood of harm, is attributable to—

   (i) the care given to the child, or likely to be given to him if the order were not made, not being what it would be reasonable to expect a parent to give to him; or
   (ii) the child's being beyond parental control.

As you can see, this test has a number of elements to it. The child must be suffering or likely to suffer; the harm must be significant, and it must be attributable either to the care of the child not being reasonable, or the child being beyond parental control. In this next part of the chapter, we break down what each element means. The local authority, as applicant, has the burden of proving that the test has been met on the balance of probabilities.

12.3.1 The burden of proof and the evidence

In order to determine whether the child concerned in a case is suffering, or is likely to suffer significant harm according to s31(2)(a) Children Act 1989, the local authority will draw up a list (the threshold statement), which sets out why the social workers believe that the child is suffering or likely to suffer significant harm. The local authority must therefore gather together the evidence it wants to use to support its case.

If one of the local authority's threshold allegations is that the children have been exposed to domestic abuse between their parents, for example, the authority will need to prove firstly that there was in fact domestic abuse, and secondly that the children were exposed to it, such as by being present when it took place or witnessing the after-effects. The authority will need to provide evidence, such as police reports, interviews with the parties themselves or other family members, or medical records. Different kinds of harms will require different evidence. The evidence needed to show that a child has suffered significant harm through neglect or inadequate parenting will be different to the evidence in cases involving the deliberate infliction of injury.

Writing his *View from the President's Chambers* Munby P gave an example of a threshold allegation of chronic neglect and the evidence that could be presented:

The parents have neglected the children. They have:

- Not fed them properly.
- Dressed them in torn and dirty clothes.
- Not supervised them properly.
- Not got them to school or to the doctor or hospital when needed.
- Not played with them or talked to them enough.
- Not listened to the advice of social workers, health visitors and others about how to make things better: and now will not let the social worker visit the children in the home. . . .

. . . Voluminous statements will usually not be required. . . . No more than four or five pages (if that) from each of the school teacher, the health visitor and the family's GP will surely suffice to establish much of the factual basis for the local authority's case, supported by similarly succinct and focused statements from the social workers who can speak of their own personal knowledge of conditions in the home and the attitude of the parents.[57]

SCENARIO 1

Illustration 3

As in the example given by Munby P, our scenario involves the neglect of 18-month-old Ella. The evidence that the local authority might present in our case could include:

- Medical records for Ella—is she meeting her developmental milestones? How does this compare with her progress in foster care?
- Records from the health visitor who will have visited the family home for up to the first year of Ella's life

---

[57] Sir James Munby, P. 'View from the President's Chambers: The process of reform: The revised PLO and the local authority' (2013) 43(6) *Family Law* 680.

- Social workers' records about the state of the home and Ella being dirty with a full nappy
- Police records about the domestic violence incidents
- Records from their GPs.

The evidence that Kerrie and Mike could present will depend upon what they are saying about what has happened, and their proposals for the future. Kerrie's strategy might be that Ella should be returned to her and that she will separate from Mike permanently. If that is her case, then she will want to persuade the court that she has really separated from him, that she is capable of giving good enough care to Ella, with local authority support, and why that has not happened to date. The court may be concerned as to whether Kerrie is capable of protecting Ella from witnessing Mike's violence, and whether their separation is permanent, or whether either she is misleading the court about that or will drift back into a relationship with him. She may ask the court for permission to undergo a parenting assessment—literally an assessment of her ability to parent—and she may engage with any counselling or therapy or parenting classes arranged by the local authority. Remember that the court will only order an expert report if 'necessary' to resolve the case fairly, and that her access to therapeutic services will depend upon their availability.

If she and Mike are presenting a united front, the situation will be different, and strategically much more risky.

The local authority will need to use the evidence it has gathered to prove that its allegations are true 'on the balance of probabilities'. This means a greater than 50 per cent likelihood of the allegation being true, or (to put it another way), it is 'more likely than not' to be true. An allegation which does not meet this standard is unproven—it's not a fact, it's just an allegation. In *Re H and Others (Minors) (Sexual Abuse: Standard of Proof)* the House of Lords made it clear that 'unproved allegations of maltreatment cannot form the basis of a finding by the court that either limb of s31(2)(a) is established . . . a conclusion that the child is suffering or is likely to suffer harm must be based on facts, not just suspicion.'[58]

The judge does not have to be sure beyond reasonable doubt, as in a criminal case. In *Re H*, Lord Nicholls seemed to suggest that more serious allegations would need more cogent (convincing) evidence.[59] But the consequence of that would be that it would be more difficult to protect children in the most serious cases, because the stronger evidence you needed might not be available. In *Re B*, the Lords took the opportunity to confirm that the standard of proof is the balance of probabilities irrespective of the seriousness of the allegation or the seriousness of the consequences for the people involved.

KEY CASE *Re B (Care Proceedings: Standard of Proof)* [2009] 1 AC 11

The wife was the mother of four children: two older children from a previous relationship, and two younger children with her husband. Following the parties' separation, one of the older children alleged that the husband had sexually abused her, which the husband denied. The judge at first

---

[58] *Re H and Others (Minors) (Sexual Abuse: Standard of Proof)* [1996] AC 563, 591G, 592H (Lord Nicholls).
[59] *Re H and Others (Minors) (Sexual Abuse: Standard of Proof)* [1996] AC 563, 586F-G (Lord Nicholls).

instance was unable to determine whether the child or the husband was telling the truth. He therefore held that the burden on the local authority to prove the allegation had not been discharged, and that the allegation was therefore untrue. The House of Lords upheld this decision:

- Per Lady Hale: 'The standard of proof in finding the facts necessary to establish the threshold under section 31(2) or the welfare considerations in section 1 of the 1989 Act is the simple balance of probabilities, neither more nor less. Neither the seriousness of the allegation nor the seriousness of the consequences should make any difference to the standard of proof to be applied in determining the facts.'[60]
- Per Lord Hoffman: 'There is no room for a finding that it might have happened. The law operates a binary system in which the only values are zero and one. The fact either happened or it did not. If the tribunal is left in doubt, the doubt is resolved by a rule that one party or the other carries the burden of proof. If the party who bears the burden of proof fails to discharge it, a value of zero is returned and the fact is treated as not having happened. If he does discharge it, a value of one is returned and the fact is treated as having happened.'[61]
- Per Lady Hale: In determining whether an allegation is true, courts can, however, take into account the inherent probabilities as well as the context:

'There is no logical or necessary connection between seriousness and probability. Some seriously harmful behaviour, such as murder, is sufficiently rare to be inherently improbable in most circumstances. Even then there are circumstances, such as a body with its throat cut and no weapon to hand, where it is not at all improbable. Other seriously harmful behaviour, such as alcohol or drug abuse, is regrettably all too common and not at all improbable. Nor are serious allegations made in a vacuum. Consider the famous example of the animal seen in Regent's Park. If it is seen outside the zoo on a stretch of greensward regularly used for walking dogs, then of course it is more likely to be a dog than a lion. If it is seen in the zoo next to the lions' enclosure when the door is open, then it may well be more likely to be a lion than a dog.'[62]

Thus 'findings of fact must be based on evidence, including inferences that can properly be drawn from the evidence and not on suspicion or speculation'.[63] This evidence may come in many forms. It can be live, written, direct, hearsay, electronic, photographic, circumstantial, factual, or by way of expert opinion. It can concern major topics and small details, things that are important and things that are trivial.[64] Sometimes, people will say 'you can't prove it', meaning that there is no 'smoking gun' or other compelling forensic evidence. But the standard of proof is only the balance of probabilities, and witness testimony itself is evidence. If a social worker testifies as to the condition of the family home, or a doctor testifies as to injuries they have seen on the child, that testimony itself is evidence that a judge can use to support a finding that the case against the parents is proven.

Of course, really complex cases can involve really complex evidence. This is particularly the case for alleged non-accidental injuries, where medical experts are needed. One notorious case of recent years is that of the toddler Poppi Worthington, who suffered fatal injuries

[60] *Re B (Care Proceedings: Standard of Proof)* [2009] 1 AC 11, 35 (Lady Hale).
[61] *Re B (Care Proceedings: Standard of Proof)* [2009] 1 AC 11, 17 (Lord Hoffman).
[62] *Re B (Care Proceedings: Standard of Proof)* [2009] 1 AC 11, 36 (Lady Hale).
[63] *Re A (A Child) (No 2)* [2011] EWCA Civ 12.
[64] *Re BR (Proof of Facts)* [2015] EWFC 41 [5].

in the care of her parents. As a result of this, care proceedings were brought in respect of Poppi's siblings. The court heard, over eight days, about the events surrounding Poppi's death and potential causes from several experts, including: a consultant pathologist, a consultant paediatric histopathologist, a consultant forensic paediatrician, and a consultant paediatric radiologist, a paramedic and ambulance driver called to the scene of Poppi's death, hospital staff including a locum consultant paediatrician, an associate accident and emergency specialist, a specialist anaesthetist, as well as four nurses, six police officers, a forensic scientist, and the two parents.[65] The purpose of these experts was to help the judge to establish the cause of Poppi's death, and which (if either) parent was responsible for it, so as to determine whether her siblings were likely to suffer future significant harm.

The judge, having heard all this testimony and read all these reports, must determine what is true—i.e., what is proven on the balance of probabilities—and what effect those facts have on the case. As Peter Jackson LJ put it in *Re BR (Proof of Facts)*:

> Evidence is evidence and the approach to analysing it remains the same in every case... Whether a man was in a London street at a particular time might be of no great consequence if the issue is whether he was rightly issued with a parking ticket, but it might be of huge consequence if he has been charged with a murder that occurred that day in Paris. The evidential standard to which his presence in the street must be proved is nonetheless the same. The court takes account of any inherent probability or improbability of an event having occurred as part of a natural process of reasoning. But the fact that an event is a very common one does not lower the standard of probability to which it must be proved. As [the barristers] felicitously observe: 'Improbable events occur all the time. . . . Somebody wins the lottery most weeks; children are struck by lightning.'[66]

In undertaking a finding as to what is true, judges 'are guided by many things, including the inherent probabilities, any contemporaneous documentation or records, any circumstantial evidence tending to support one account rather than the other, and their overall impression of the characters and motivations of the witnesses'.[67] It may be that he or she believes some evidence and disbelieves other evidence, on the balance of probabilities. The judge may prefer certain experts over other experts, based on their expertise in the relevant field. Sometimes a judge may believe that an expert is wrong because other, non-expert, evidence contradicts it. These things happen. Evidence from the parents or other carers has been described as being 'of the utmost importance' so that the court can form a clear assessment of their credibility and reliability. This includes their demeanour on the witness stand and 'the initial impact of the testimony as it unfolds – did it appear frank, candid, spontaneous and persuasive or did it seem to be contrived, lacking in conviction or implausible?'[68] But judges are cautioned to tell themselves that even if a witness has lied about one thing that does not mean they have lied about everything or that there are guilty reasons for the lie. Some lies can be caused by shame, misplaced loyalty, panic, or fear.[69] This is known as a 'Lucas direction'.

---

[65] *Cumbria County Council v M and F* [2014] EWHC 4886 (Fam) and [2016] EWHC 14 (Fam).
[66] *Re BR (Proof of Facts)* [2015] EWFC 41 [7].
[67] Lady Hale in *Re B (Children) (Care Proceedings: Standard of Proof)* [2009] 1 AC 11, 24.
[68] *Re B (A Child) (Care Proceedings: Threshold Criteria)* [2013] UKSC [108] (Lord Kerr).
[69] A Lucas direction stems from the criminal case *R v Lucas* [1981] QB 720 per Lord Lane CJ at 723C.

As you can see, the characteristics and personalities involved are important and the judge's assessment of the witnesses is crucial—perhaps more so than in other areas of law. While hearsay evidence is admissible in family proceedings,[70] a parent is entitled to challenge that evidence and if the local authority cannot 'produce the witnesses who can speak of such matters first-hand, may find themselves in great, or indeed insuperable, difficulties if a parent not merely puts the matter in issue but goes into the witness box to deny it.'[71] It also means that appeal courts, who do not see witnesses, almost always defer to the first instance judge's findings of fact, if not their application of the law. As the House of Lords explained in *Biogen Inc v Medeva Ltd*:

> The need for appellate caution in reversing the judge's evaluation of the facts is based upon much more solid grounds than professional courtesy. It is because specific findings of fact, even by the most meticulous judge, are inherently an incomplete statement of the impression which was made upon him by the primary evidence. His expressed findings are always surrounded by a penumbra of imprecision as to emphasis, relative weight, minor qualification and nuance (as Renan said, *la vérité est dans une nuance*), of which time and language do not permit exact expression, but which may play an important part in the judge's overall evaluation.[72]

Yet it is the role of the judge to make findings, and judges have to do this however complex or conflicting the evidence. They cannot sit on the fence. 'And, as any judge who has had to conduct such fact-finding hearings will know all too well, wading through a mass of evidence, much of it usually uncorroborated and often coming from witnesses who, for whatever reasons, may be neither reliable nor even truthful, the difficulty of discerning where the truth actually lies, what findings he can properly make, is often one of almost excruciating difficulty.'[73] Each piece of evidence must be considered in the context of the whole. Only when the judge has considered the totality of the evidence can he or she come to a conclusion about whether or not the case put forward by the local authority has been made out to the appropriate standard of proof. That does not mean that the judge has to know everything. In the Poppi Worthington case, the judge held that on the balance of probabilities 13-month-old Poppi died after being penetrated by her father, but precisely how this medically caused her death is unknown. What is known was sufficient to establish a risk of significant harm to her surviving siblings.[74]

Sometimes a child presents with an injury that doctors believe can only have been caused deliberately because the type of injury would be difficult to cause accidentally. In such cases, it is tempting to say to the parents: 'Prove that it was caused accidentally.' But this is not allowed. It is a reversal of the burden of proof: the parents do not have to prove their innocence. It will undoubtedly help their case if they can explain a way in which the injury was caused accidentally rather than deliberately, but they are not required to disprove the local authority's case. In *Re M* (2012), an 8-week-old baby suffered a number of linear bruises to his arms and one leg. The local authority's case was that the injuries were non-accidental and had been caused by either the mother or the father, with the parent

---

[70] *Humberside County Council v R* [1977] 1 WLR 1251.
[71] *Re A (A Child)* [2016] 1 FLR 1 [9].
[72] [1996] UKHL 18 [54] (Lord Hoffman).
[73] *Re A (Fact-Finding: Disputed Findings)* [2011] 1 FLR 1817 [20] (Munby LJ).
[74] *Cumbria County Council v F and M* [2014] EWHC 4886 (Fam) and [2016] EWHC 14 (Fam).

who had not caused the injuries failing to protect the child. Such young babies are not yet mobile: they cannot move about by themselves to bang into things. Various innocent explanations were considered and dismissed, and the court made a care order on the basis that the lack of innocent explanation means that it must be a deliberate injury. Upholding the mother's appeal, Ward LJ held that the judge's approach that 'absent a parental explanation, there was no satisfactory benign explanation, ergo there must be a malevolent explanation' was wrong:

> it is that leap which troubles me. It does not seem to me that the conclusion necessarily follows unless, wrongly, the burden of proof has been reversed, and the parents are being required to satisfy the court that this is not a non-accidental injury. . . . the judge has not properly respected the burden which is on the local authority to demonstrate that these parents had deliberately gone about in some unknown way, with some unknown implement, to inflict these injuries on the baby'.[75]

If the local authority has not satisfied that judge of its evidence on the balance of probabilities then the case must fail.

It is very unusual for children to give live witness evidence in care proceedings. In most cases where the children's evidence is important and they are of an age to be able to provide some information about what has happened to them, they will be interviewed by social workers (and police, if the allegations are criminal). There are strict rules about the conduct of such interviews, known as *Achieving Best Evidence* (ABE). If the interviewer does not follow this guidance, and (for example) asks leading questions, the evidential value of the children's evidence may be significantly reduced, making it very hard for a court to decide where the truth lies.

KEY CASE *Re W (Children)* [2010] UKSC 12

A 14-year-old girl, Charlotte, told her school that he mother's partner had sexually abused her on a number of occasions. She had made allegations before, but had retracted these although they had been investigated. On this occasion, an ABE interview took place, as a result of which the man was arrested and charged with 13 criminal offences against her.

Charlotte's brothers and sisters were taken into foster care, but returned to their mother when her partner left the house. However, because the mother then allowed her partner contact with the children, care proceedings were brought. The issue was whether Charlotte would need to go to court to give live evidence, or whether the ABE interview would be sufficient. The judge at first instance followed what was then existing law, which gave a starting point that children should not be required to give evidence.

The Supreme Court held that the issue was whether justice could be done to all the parties without further questioning of Charlotte. There was no presumption that children should give evidence, and no presumption that they should not. Giving live evidence and being cross-examined would be hugely distressing and harm Charlotte's welfare, and the court should give great weight to that risk. However, cross-examination may be the best way to get to the truth. After all, the mother's partner was being accused of an incredibly serious offence and the result of the case might be that the children were never returned to their mother's care. The court would need to look at what other evidence it had, the quality of the ABE interview, and what arrangements it could make to minimise the harm to her, such as recording the cross-examination rather than having it happen live in court.

---

[75] [2012] EWCA Civ 1580 [17–18] (Ward LJ).

12.3.2 The need for a causal link

In addition to proving the facts on which they rely, the local authority must be able demonstrate why these 'justify the conclusion that the child has suffered or is at risk of suffering significant harm of the type asserted by the local authority'.[76] In other words, they need to explain why the facts they have proven are true mean that the child is at risk of significant harm. In Key Case *Re A*, the local authority could not demonstrate how the father's years-old police caution for sex with an underage girl (a proven fact) meant that his 1-year-old son was likely to suffer significant harm.

> **KEY CASE** *Re A (A Child)* [2016] 1 FLR 1
>
> In *Re A*, the father had a police caution dating from when he was 17 for sex with a girl aged 13. The local authority argued that this (and other facts) meant that there was a real possibility of future significant harm to the child, A, because the child would learn the father's 'immoral' behaviour. The judge, Munby P, was scathing in his response:
>
> > The justification for state intervention is harm to children, not parental immorality . . . Secondly, how does any of this translate through to an anticipation of harm to A? The social worker ruminates on the 'current risk [the father] poses' to 'vulnerable young women'? What has that got to do with care proceedings in relation to the father's 1-year-old son? It is not suggested that there is any risk of the father abusing A. The social worker's analysis is incoherent.[77]
>
> He continued:
>
> > Some 17-year-old men who have sexual intercourse with 13-year-old girls may have significantly distorted views about sex and children, and therefore pose a risk to their own children of whatever age or gender, but that is not automatically true of all such men. The local authority must prove that the facts as proved give rise to a risk of significant harm to this child A. It has failed to do so, proceeding on an assumption that is not supported by evidence.[78]

The case is a good example of the local authority drafting its threshold statement poorly and creating what Munby P called 'a tottering edifice built on inadequate foundations'. The barrister Lucy Reed has complained about 'an uncomfortably high proportion of rubbish thresholds, not-threshold-at-all-thresholds, and thresholds-mixed-with-general-commentary-and-anxious-handwringing . . . rambling narrative accounts of "why we think this parent is rubbish" or "ten ways in which this child is not doing well, which is probably down to the parents"—which may well be entirely accurate but IS. NOT. THRESHOLD'.[79]

---

[76] *N (Children: Adoption: Jurisdiction)* [2015] EWCA Civ 1112.
[77] *Re A (A Child)* [2016] 1 FLR 1 [60].
[78] *Re A (A Child)* [2016] 1 FLR 1 [62].
[79] 'Threshold Again' on the Pink Tape blog, 3 October 2015. Available at http://www.pinktape.co.uk/rants/threshold-again/ accessed 22 September 2019.

12.3.3 Significant harm: s31(2)(a)

Under the threshold test, the child must either be suffering or likely to suffer significant harm. Harm is defined in s31(9) Children Act 1989 as 'ill-treatment or the impairment of health or development'. The statute specifically notes that 'ill-treatment' includes sexual abuse and forms of ill-treatment which are not physical. It 'will generally involve some active conduct, whether physical or sexual abuse, bullying or other forms of active emotional abuse.'[80] 'Impairment of health or development' includes physical or mental health; and physical, intellectual, emotional, social or behavioural development. It 'may also be the result of active conduct towards the child, but it could also be the result of neglecting the child's needs, for food, for warmth, for shelter, for love, for education, for health care.'[81] Included within the definition is impairment suffered 'from seeing or hearing the ill-treatment of another'; this was added by the Adoption and Children Act 2002.[82] When assessing whether an impairment of health or development is significant, we can compare the health or development of the child who is the subject of the care application with the health or development that could reasonably be expected of a similar child: s31(10). The comparator for a child who is truanting is a child who is attending school[83] and the appropriate comparator for a child with a disability is likely to be a child with the same disability, rather than none.

Note that the wording of the section is 'ill-treatment *or* impairment of health', so there is no need to prove both. And, as Lord Wilson pointed out in *Re B* (2013), the concept of 'ill-treatment' is absolute, whereas impairment is relative.[84] This means that 'ill-treatment in itself will be proof of harm and there is no need to show that there were any consequences of this for the child's health or development.'[85]

As you can see, what constitutes harm is drawn widely in the Act. However, the statutory test narrows the effect of this by limiting compulsory intervention to those cases in which this harm is *significant*. The Children Act 1989 does not define what 'significant' means. In *Humberside County Council v B* the court adopted a dictionary definition for 'significant', as meaning 'considerable, noteworthy, or important', and 'harm which the court should take into account in considering a child's future'.[86] These definitions are capable of encompassing harms that are cumulative in nature (for example the effect of neglect on the child's development), or one-off, as well as harms which are not intrinsically physically serious but where the nature of the harm is of a worrying type, such as those indicative of deliberate cruelty. The government guidance *Working Together to Safeguard Children* had this to say:

> There are no absolute criteria on which to rely when judging what constitutes significant harm. Consideration of the severity of ill-treatment may include the degree and the extent

---

[80] *Re B (A Child) (Care Proceedings: Threshold Criteria)* [2013] UKSC 33 [192] (Lady Hale).

[81] *Re B (A Child) (Care Proceedings: Threshold Criteria)* [2013] UKSC 33 [192] (Lady Hale).

[82] Adoption and Children Act 2002 s120.

[83] *Re O (A Minor) (Care Order: Education Procedure)* [1992] 4 All ER 905.

[84] *Re B (A Child) (Care Proceedings: Threshold Criteria)* [2013] UKSC 33 [25] (Lord Wilson).

[85] Claire Fenton-Glynn, *Adoption without Consent* (Directorate General for Internal Policies, European Parliament) 11. Available at http://www.europarl.europa.eu/RegData/etudes/STUD/2016/556940/IPOL_STU(2016)556940_EN.pdf accessed 29 August 2019.

[86] [1993] 1 FLR 257, 263.

of physical harm, the duration and frequency of abuse and neglect, the extent of premed-itation, and the presence or degree of threat, coercion, sadism and bizarre or unusual el-ements. Each of these elements has been associated with more severe effects on the child, and/or relatively greater difficulty in helping the child overcome the adverse impact of the maltreatment. Sometimes, a single traumatic event may constitute significant harm, for example, a violent assault, suffocation or poisoning. More often, significant harm is a com-pilation of significant events, both acute and long-standing, which interrupt, change or damage the child's physical and psychological development. Some children live in family and social circumstances where their health and development are neglected. For them, it is the corrosiveness of long-term emotional, physical or sexual abuse that causes impairment to the extent of constituting significant harm.[87]

Various judgments have also sought to clarify what 'significant harm' means, despite the risk that in doing so 'the courts might find in due course that they had travelled far from the word itself'.[88] One much cited statement is that of Lord Templeman, who said in a case called *Re KD (A Minor Ward) (Termination of Access)* that

> The best person to bring up a child is the natural parent. It matters not whether the parent is wise or foolish, rich or poor, educated or illiterate, provided the child's moral and physi-cal health are not in danger. Public authorities cannot improve on nature.[89]

This dictum was cited by Hedley J in the case *Re L (Care: Threshold Criteria)*, another much-mentioned judgment, which concerned parents with learning difficulties:

> . . . it is the tradition of the UK, recognised in law, that children are best brought up within natural families. . . . It follows inexorably from that, that society must be willing to tolerate very diverse standards of parenting, including the eccentric, the barely adequate and the in-consistent. It follows too that children will inevitably have both very different experiences of parenting and very unequal consequences flowing from it. It means that some children will experience disadvantage and harm, while others flourish in atmospheres of loving security and emotional stability. These are the consequences of our fallible humanity and it is not the provenance of the state to spare children all the consequences of defective parenting. In any event, it simply could not be done. . . .
>
> It would be unwise to a degree to attempt an all embracing definition of significant harm. . . . Significant harm is fact specific and must retain the breadth of meaning that human fallibility may require of it. . . . However, it is clear that it must be something unusu-al; at least something more than the commonplace human failure or inadequacy.[90]

Whether or not a situation reaches the level of significant harm is an issue of professional judgment. Local authorities will consider whether and when to apply for a care order by looking at such factors as the extent, frequency, and severity of any abuse or neglect; the extent to which there is evidence of harm being premeditated, deliberate or sadistic; and the cumulative effect on the child's well-being and development (although, a single inci-dent can meet the threshold if it is considerable, noteworthy, or important). The number of high-profile child deaths discussed in Chapter 11 illustrate just how difficult it is to

---

[87] Department for Children, Schools, and Families, *Working Together to Safeguard Children* (2010 edition) para 1.28.
[88] *Re B (A Child) (Care Proceedings: Threshold Criteria)* [2013] UKSC 33 [26] (Lord Wilson).
[89] [1988] 1 AC 806, 812.
[90] [2007] 1 FLR 2050 at [50]–[51].

assess risk in practice. As we have noted, significant harm can be cumulative, and the effect only apparent some time later. Information received by social workers may be partial and incomplete, misleading, or just plain wrong. Social workers may also suffer from confirmation bias.[91] While an evaluation of what constitutes significant harm does not depend on the resources available to the local authority, we also noted in Chapter 11 that there is considerable regional variation in the number of applications made by different local authorities.

12.3.4 Suffering or likely to suffer: s31(2)(a)

In order for a care or supervision order to be made, the child must be 'suffering or likely to suffer' significant harm. However, this phrase requires some explanation.

At the time that the local authority makes a care application, it is certainly possible that the child is (on the balance of probabilities) suffering significant harm. However, it is equally possible that the child has already been removed from the allegedly harmful situation and is not, therefore, suffering harm. This was the situation in *Re M (Minor) (Care Order: Threshold Conditions)* in which the suffering was caused by the father having murdered the mother.[92] The police, who had arrived at the murder scene, took the children into their protection (see 11.8.1). Three of them went to live with their aunt; the fourth, a baby, went to foster care. The local authority wished to leave open the possibility of that child being adopted outside the family, and thus required a care order. The issue was whether by the time care proceedings were issued, the baby was suffering significant harm. The House of Lords held that what mattered was whether 'at the time the application is to be disposed of, there are in place arrangements for the protection of the child by the local authority on an interim basis'.[93] If so, the date on which the child 'is suffering' is the date on which the local authority first took protective steps, provided those steps have been continuously in place from that point until the disposal hearing. The Lords held that this was the situation here, so a care order could be made, although by this point the local authority had conceded that the child should stay with his aunt. The making of a care order was nevertheless in the child's best interests as it obliged the local authority to provide support to the aunt.

Re M tells us that the relevant date for the purpose of assessing whether the child 'is suffering' is the date on which the local authority first took protective steps that have subsequently been continuous. In some cases that may be the date of the care application, but where the children have entered the process through emergency protection or interim care, it will be the date of those orders.

In many cases, the child will indeed be presently suffering, and unless action is taken it is likely that they will suffer in the future, too. However, the threshold is that the child is suffering *or* likely to suffer, not that both are true, so a child can be the subject of a care or supervision order when they have suffered no significant harm to date, but where future significant harm is possible. It is not necessary to show that a child 'is suffering'

---

[91] See 11.7.1.
[92] [1994] 2 AC 424.
[93] [1994] 2 AC 424, 434 (Lord Mackay LC).

if the local authority can show that the child is likely to suffer significant harm in the future.

The usual meaning of 'likely to suffer' would be 'more likely than not', i.e., a greater than 50 per cent chance of significant harm happening: a probability. For example, the phrase 'It's likely to rain' would be understood as 'It's probably going to rain'. But consider the consequences of this interpretation being used in the threshold test. It would mean that a care order could only be made if the child was probably—more than 50 per cent likely to—suffer significant harm. This would exclude a child who was (say) 49 per cent likely to suffer significant harm. In *Re H and Others (Minors) (Sexual Abuse: Standard of Proof)*, the House of Lords held that:

> In this context, Parliament cannot have been using "likely" in the sense of more likely than not. If the word were given this meaning, it would have the effect of leaving outside the scope of care and supervision orders cases where the court is satisfied that there is a real possibility of harm but that possibility falls short of being more likely than not. . ..When exposed to this risk a child may need protection just as much as when the risk is considered to be less than 50-50 as when the risk is of a higher order.'[94]

The interpretation of 'likely to suffer' cannot therefore mean 'more likely than not' if we are to protect children from harms that we consider to be socially unacceptable. What, then, does it mean? In *Re H*, the House of Lords held that 'It is enough that there is a real possibility, a possibility that cannot sensibly be ignored having regard to the nature and gravity of the feared harm in the particular case'.[95]

What this all means is that, in relation to this part of the threshold test—'likely to suffer'—the test is not that the significant harm is on the balance of probabilities going to happen, but a much lower standard, that there is a real possibility of it happening. Courts therefore have to evaluate the chance of this future significant harm happening[96] by looking at what we know so far. It is 'a prediction from existing facts, often from a multitude of such facts, about what has happened in the past, about the characters and personalities of the people involved, about the things which they have said and done, and so on.'[97] This real possibility has to be sufficient to justify the care or supervision order being made and what level of possibility is sufficient 'will depend upon the nature and gravity of the harm: a lesser degree of likelihood that the child will be killed will justify immediate preventive action than the degree of likelihood that the child will not be sent to school.'[98] As the 1987 white paper setting out the government's intentions for the forthcoming Children Act put it, 'It is intended that "likely harm" should cover all cases of unacceptable risk in which it may be necessary to balance the chance of the harm occurring against the magnitude of that harm if it does occur'.[99] 'Unacceptable risk' refers to the level of risk that society is unwilling to tolerate.

Prior to the Children Act 1989, it was not possible to make a care or supervision order solely based on a risk that the child might suffer harm in the future. This meant that local

---

[94] *Re H and Others (Minors) (Sexual Abuse: Standard of Proof)* [1996] AC 563, 585B-D (Lord Nicholls).
[95] *Re H and Others (Minors) (Sexual Abuse: Standard of Proof)* [1996] AC 563, 585F (Lord Nicholls).
[96] *Newham London Borough Council v A-G* [1993] 1 FLR 281.
[97] *Re B (Care Proceedings: Standard of Proof)* [2009] 1 AC 11 [22] (Baroness Hale).
[98] *Re S-B (Children)* [2009] UKSC 17 [9] (Lady Hale). See also Lady Hale in *Re B* (2013).
[99] *The Law on Child Care and Family Services* (Cm 62, 1987) para 60.

authorities could not take pre-emptive steps to prevent the harm from occurring.[100] Local authorities therefore used wardship and the inherent jurisdiction proceedings to fill the statutory gap.[101] However, as we have seen, it is now possible to make a care or supervision order on the basis that there is a real possibility of future significant harm despite the fact that there has been no harm so far, based merely on an 'indeterminate and probabilistic'[102] assessment of the chance of harm happening. This is understandably controversial, but it is important to remember that the assessment of future risk has to be based on thing we know—facts proven on the balance of probabilities. The other elements of the threshold test must also be fulfilled, and at the welfare stage a judge has to find that it is in the child's best interests to make such an order.

SCENARIO 1

Illustration 4

The local authority is concerned about existing harm to Ella and about the risk of future harm. It therefore bases its case on both 'is suffering' and 'likely to suffer' (although it is not in fact necessary to use both as only one is sufficient to pass the threshold). On the 'is suffering', the local authority will need to prove that Ella was, on the balance of probabilities, suffering significant harm at the point when it first took continuous protective action, which in this case is the point at which it made a care application. To prove that she is 'likely to suffer', the local authority only needs to show that there is a real possibility that she will suffer significant harm in the future, but will use facts proven on the balance of probabilities to show this. For example, the court's findings of fact might include the history of domestic abuse, any developmental delay that Ella is experiencing (this must be attributable to her care), drug use in the home, and the state of the home and Ella. Based on expert assessments, it may find that Kerrie and Ella have weak attachments to one another or even that one or both parents has a mental health condition affecting their ability to care for Ella.

It will then need to ensure that these are causally linked to the actual or risk of significant harm to Ella.

12.3.5 Summary so far

- If the local authority's case is based on the 'is suffering' phrase, the court must be satisfied on the balance of probabilities that the child was actually significantly harmed.

- If the case is based on 'likely to suffer' the court must be satisfied that there is a real possibility of future significant harm, *not* that such harm is likely on the balance of probabilities.

---

[100] Claire Fenton-Glynn, *Adoption without Consent* (Directorate General for Internal Policies, European Parliament) 11. Available at http://www.europarl.europa.eu/RegData/etudes/STUD/2016/556940/IPOL_STU(2016)556940_EN.pdf accessed 29 August 2019.

[101] Lord Mackay of Clashfern LC at the second reading of the Children Bill: *Hansard*, HL vol 502, col 492 (December 6, 1988).

[102] Claire Fenton-Glynn, *Adoption without Consent* (Directorate General for Internal Policies, European Parliament) 12. Available at http://www.europarl.europa.eu/RegData/etudes/STUD/2016/556940/IPOL_STU(2016)556940_EN.pdf accessed 29 August 2019.

- Some cases will be based on both existing harm and a real possibility of future harm, but only one of these is necessary to satisfy this element of the threshold.

- The assessment of whether there has been harm or whether there is a real possibility of harm must be based on facts proved on the balance of probabilities, not on suspicion or speculation.

- In deciding whether an allegation is true, the court can take into account the inherent probability of the allegation.

- These proven facts must be causally connected to existing significant harm or the risk of future significant harm to the child, i.e., that they have caused significant harm or there is a real possibility that they may do so.

12.3.6 Attributability and reasonable parental care: s31(2)(b)

We have explored what is required to meet s31(2)(a) Children Act 1989. We will now discuss s31(2)(b), which is the attributability element of the threshold test. Let us remind ourselves of what that is.

STATUTORY EXTRACT *Section 31(2)(b) Children Act 1989*

(b) that the harm, or likelihood of harm, is attributable to—

    (i) the care given to the child, or likely to be given to him if the order were not made, not being what it would be reasonable to expect a parent to give to him; or

    (ii) the child's being beyond parental control.

Three different situations may arise:

1. That the harm is attributable to the care that was/is being given to the child, and is not what it is reasonable to expect a parent to give to him;

2. That there is a real possibility of future harm that would be attributable to the care that is likely to be given to the child if the order were not made, being a level below what it would be reasonable to expect a parent to give to him; or

3. That the child is beyond parental control.

'Not what it would be reasonable to expect a parent to give him'

Let us look at the first two types of situation first. In these cases, the harm that is being considered has to be attributable to a lack, or likely lack, of reasonable parental care. The Children Act Guidance 2008 notes that 'parental care' is not defined. However, it is generally interpreted as including making proper provision for the child's health and welfare (including promoting his physical, intellectual, emotional, social and behavioural development), and not just meeting basic survival needs.'[103] What is 'reasonable care' will depend on the child. For example, the needs of a physically disabled child may well be

---

[103] *Children Act Guidance and Regulations* Volume 1 (The Stationery Office 2008) para 3.40.

different to those of an able-bodied child, and the care of a young child will differ from the care of an older child. It is not simply about the 'the characters and personalities of both the child and her parents. . . . [T]he court should identify the respects in which parental care is falling, or is likely to fall, short of what it would be reasonable to expect.'[104]

It is important to note that the attributability requirement is not that the parents have directly caused the harm to the child, although that may be what has happened. It also covers those situations in which the parents' lack of reasonable care enabled the child to come to harm from something else. 'The object is to limit intervention to certain kinds of harm – harm which should not happen if a child is being looked after properly.'[105]

The threshold test assesses whether the harm to the child is attributable to a lack of reasonable care, judged by an objective standard, that of the hypothetical reasonable parent. Key Case *Re B and G* illustrates this.

KEY CASE *Re B and G (Children)* [2015] EWFC 3

This case was a care application in respect of siblings, the young boy and girl of the case name. The local authority alleged that the girl had been subjected to female genital mutilation. There are four main types of FGM, the most serious of which (Type I) is the partial or total removal of the clitoris and at the least serious (Type IV) 'pricking, piercing, incising, scraping and cauterizing the genital area'.[106] The local authority was unable to prove, on the balance of probabilities, that a possible scar adjacent to the left clitoral hood indicated Type IV FGM as opposed to being natural variation to the look of the vulva. Accordingly, the application for a care order was dismissed.

In his judgment, Munby P held that all forms of FGM constitute significant harm. Yet Type IV FGM is less severe than male circumcision. Did that mean that male circumcision constituted significant harm—and, if so, why were male children not being taken into care on that basis? The answer lay in the part of the threshold test relating to the care of the child 'not being what it is reasonable to expect a parent to give to him': it 'can never be reasonable parenting to inflict any form of FGM on a child' but 'society and the law, including family law, are prepared to tolerate non-therapeutic male circumcision performed for religious or even for purely cultural or conventional reasons, while no longer being willing to tolerate FGM in any of its forms. . . . FGM in any form will suffice to establish "threshold" in accordance with section 31 of the Children Act 1989; male circumcision without more will not.'[107]

Key Case *Re B and G* brings home an important aspect of the care threshold: what society now considers so harmful to a child that it justifies state intervention and potentially permanent removal from the family may be have been acceptable at a previous point in history. For example, we no longer send children up chimneys or allow small children to crawl under factory machinery to repair it, as was common in the 1800s. It is no longer permissible to use a baby cage (a metal cage that one attaches outside a window, dangling in the air, and into which one puts the baby so he gets fresh air), which was used in the UK in the 1930s. It is no longer permissible in our society to cane a child, which was banned

---

[104] *Re B (A Child) (Care Proceedings: Threshold Criteria)* [2013] UKSC 33 [193] (Lady Hale).
[105] *Re S-B (Children)* [2009] UKSC 17 [20] (Lady Hale).
[106] These are the categories used by the World Health Organization.
[107] *Re B and G (Children)* [2015] EWFC 3 [72–3] (Munby P).

in all UK schools in 1996. Yet these were once common, accepted practices. Social norms change.

In most cases, the attributability element of the threshold test is not a contentious part of the care litigation process. If a child is being neglected or abused, that is easily causally linked to the quality of the caregiving, and it is usually fairly easy to demonstrate that this care is not reasonable care.

More difficult are those situations in which the caregiving in question is not being done by the parents.[108] The attributability criterion may still be satisfied in two ways:

1. *The parent should have prevented the harm*

The harm may have been caused to the child in circumstances in which reasonable parental care have prevented that harm. If a neglectful parent leaves a young child home alone any harm the child comes to is attributable to her. If the harm has been caused by a stranger or family friend, then it will only be attributable to parental care if it would have been reasonable to expect the parent to have prevented it. 'For instance, if a parent entrusts a child to a third party without taking the precautionary steps a reasonable parent would take to check the suitability of the third party, and subsequently the third party injures or sexually abuses the child, the harm suffered by the child may be regarded as attributable to the inadequate care of the parent as well as the third party.'[109] The connection to the harm does not need to be the sole or dominant cause, or even the direct cause, as long as it is a contributory cause.

2. *Under the principle in Lancashire County Council v B*

The threshold test refers to the level of care 'not being what it is reasonable to expect a parent to give to him', meaning that we judge the level of care experienced by the child by the standard of a reasonable parent. It does not explicitly say that the care has to be *by a parent*. As Lord Clyde says in our next Key Case, *Lancashire County Council v B* (sometimes known as *Lancashire County Council v A*) the phrase 'simply defines the standard or level of care'; it does not define who is delivering that care. As a result, it is possible for the threshold to be passed where the care is by a non-parent and the parents are not negligent.

KEY CASE *Lancashire County Council v B* [2000] UKHL 16

A 7-month-old baby was seriously and permanently injured as a result of having been shaken on more than one occasion. At the relevant times, the child had been cared for by the mother, the father, or the childminder; these three people were therefore the possible perpetrators. The local authority brought care proceedings in respect of the baby and in respect of the childminder's own child, on the basis that there was a real possibility of significant harm to her if (but only if) the childminder was the abuser. The judge was unable to determine which of the three adults had caused the baby harm, leading to a terrible dilemma:

> If the criteria are met and orders are made I am exposing one child to the possibility of removal from parents who are no risk and have done no wrong. . . . If the applications are dismissed then I will undoubtedly be causing one child to be returned to a parent or parents, one or both of whom are an obvious and serious unassessed risk.

---

[108] *Re S-B (Children)* [2009] UKSC 17 [40] (Lady Hale).
[109] *Lancashire County Council v B* [2000] 2 AC 147, 162 (Lord Nicholls).

Unable to decide, he held that the threshold was not crossed in relation to either child. The local authority appealed. The Court of Appeal held that the threshold was crossed in relation to the baby, but not the childminder's own child. The House of Lords refused permission to appeal in relation to the childminder's child, but considered whether the attributability criterion was met in relation to the baby. Could the harm be attributed to the care being given to the child not being what it is reasonable to expect a parent to give to him, if it was not a parent providing the care?

The Lords held that:

- It was not necessary for the purpose of s 31(2)(b) to make a finding that an individual parent was responsible for the harm suffered. It was enough that the harm was attributable to the care given to the child not being what it ought to have been.
- The phrase 'care given to the child' refers 'primarily to the care given to the child by a parent or parents or other primary carers', but where, as here, the care of the child was shared, it could also embrace those who shared that care. The injury to the child was attributable to the care falling short of a reasonable standard; thus the attributability requirement was met.
- Per Lord Clyde: That the harm must be attributable 'to the care given to the child' requires that the harm must be attributable to the acts or omissions of someone who has the care of the child and the acts or omissions must occur in the course of the exercise of that care. To have the care of a child comprises more than being in a position where a duty of care towards the child may exist [such as at school or in hospital]. It involves the undertaking of the task of looking after the child. However, no formal step is necessarily involved in taking on that task. The question of whether a person is giving care to a child is a question of fact.
- Per Lord Clyde: Harm which is not attributable to the care given to the child, for example, harm which has come about through some unforeseeable event against which no one could have taken any precaution, will not fall within the scope of the section. On the other hand the care which a parent would reasonably be expected to give to a child may include the need to confirm that a child may safely be entrusted to the care of some other person, before handing over the child into the care of that other person.
- Per Lord Nicholls: the attributability element would not usually be met where 'there is a one-off temporary entrustment of the child to a person reasonably believed by the parents to be suitable'.

The consequence of *Lancashire* is that the attributability condition can be satisfied by the acts of a non-parent carer who has assumed the task of caring for the child, whether short-term or long-term. However, Lord Nicholls suggests it probably won't be satisfied in circumstances in which there was 'a one-off entrustment' unless the parent should have taken steps to check that person's suitability. But between one-off entrustment and sharing care there may be a wide range of situations. This leaves a high degree of uncertainty as to whether the threshold will be passed in a given situation involving a non-parent carer.

For Herring, 'the real problem at the heart of the . . . decision is that it does not consider the purpose of the attributability condition' which, for him, is a form of protection of parental rights: that 'your child will only be removed if you do not treat your child as a reasonable parent would'.[110] Why should a child be taken into care if the parents have not been proven to have been at fault in any way? The barristers acting for the parents in *Lancashire* argued that 'Parliament cannot have intended that a child should be at risk of

---

[110] J Herring, 'The Suffering Children of Blameless Parents' (2000) 116(October) *Law Quarterly Review* 545.

being removed from his family, and the parents at risk of losing their child, because of an unforeseeable failure of care by a third party to whom the parents, wholly unexceptionably, had temporarily entrusted the child'.[111] The Lords considered the purpose of the provision to be to protect children from harm. That is why they endeavoured to capture a wide category of potential carers. Lord Nicholls explicitly states that he recognises that 'this interpretation of the attributable condition means that parents who may be wholly innocent, and whose care may not have fallen below that of a reasonable parent, will face the possibility of losing their child, with all the pain and distress this involves.' But he considered this subsidiary to the 'prospect that an unidentified, and unidentifiable, carer may inflict further injury on a child he or she has already severely damaged' if s31 could not be applied. He considered that this factor outweighed all others.

The Lords were at pains to emphasise that the fact that the s31 threshold could be met did not mean that a care order was an inevitable outcome. When the court decides what order to make, whether or not the parent was at fault will be relevant to their prospects of continuing to care for their child. But in making it easier to pass the threshold test, they presented judges with a problem at the welfare stage. If it is not necessary to determine which carer caused the harm, then how can you decide what option is best for the child? We will pick this up at 12.3.6, after we consider the other limb of the attributability criterion.

'Beyond parental control'

We have now seen that a care order can be made where the significant harm is attributable to the care not being what it would be reasonable for a parent to provide. However, s31(2)(b)(ii) also enables the threshold test to be satisfied where the child is 'beyond parental control'. In *M v Birmingham City Council*, the court held that this phrase was 'capable of describing a state of affairs in the past, in the present or in the future according to the context in which it falls to be applied'.[112] When the court is dealing with cases where the child is beyond parental control, the child does not have to be suffering at the time that the local authority takes action within the meaning of *Re M* (discussed at 12.3.4).

Cases that rely on this part of the threshold test are relatively rare. Local authority lawyer Andrew Pack was written that in eighteen years of working on child protection cases he has invoked it only twice, and in each case this was in relation to children who had been adopted, but were the subject of an application to take them from their adoptive parents. A child in care may still be beyond the control of even the very best carers if they are seriously disabled or still suffering the effects of pre-care harms, as in *Re K (Post-Adoption Placement Breakdown)*, where the behaviour of the young woman in question was a result of pre-care abuse and neglect.[113]

There is conflicting case law on whether there needs to be causal link between the harm or risk of harm to the child and the quality of parental care—i.e., whether the child has to be beyond parental control because the parents are lacking in ability. We suggest that the correct position is that stated in *WBC v A*: the child being beyond parental control does not have to be the fault of the parents or carers.[114] The fact that 'beyond parental

---

[111] Counsel for the parents in *Lancashire County Council v B*, quoted by Lord Nicholls.
[112] [1994] 2 FLR 141.
[113] [2013] 1 FLR 1 (HC).
[114] [2016] EWFC B70.

control' (s31(2)(b)(ii)) is a separate limb of the test to the 'attributable to the parents' phrase (s32(2((b)(i)) lends support to this interpretation. This also tallies with the interpretation in the *Children Act Guidance* itself:

> If the child is determined by the court as being beyond parental control, this means that, whatever the standard of care provided by the parents, the child is suffering or is likely to suffer significant harm because of lack of parental control. This requires the court to determine whether as a matter of fact, the child is beyond control: it is immaterial who, if anyone, is to blame. In such cases, the local authority will need to demonstrate how the child's situation will improve if the court makes an order—how his behaviour can be brought under control, and why an order is necessary to achieve this.[115]

Indeed, the provision is capable of encompassing children who are beyond parental control as a result of mental illness or learning disability, as well as behaviours within their control. The reason is 'immaterial'[116] to the threshold stage, although it may be relevant what arrangement is best for the child going forwards (the welfare stage discussed at 12.4).

12.3.7 Identifying the perpetrator

We have now come to the end of our analysis of the elements of the threshold test. As we have seen, the test can be satisfied even when the perpetrator is unknown, as in *Lancashire*, where the perpetrator could have been the childminder or a parent. In this section, we discuss how the court approaches situations in which the perpetrator could be any of several people, and what implications that has for the child's future.

Consider a situation in which the child only came into contact with their parents during the window in which an injury, found to be deliberate, was caused to the child. One of the parents caused the injury. But which parent? The court will carefully consider the circumstances surrounding the injury in order to decide who is responsible on the balance of probabilities. If the judge can identify a perpetrator, this will give certainty to social workers and others involved with the family, and may 'help the child in due course to understand and come to terms with what had happened and why he might have been removed from his family'.[117] It will be clear which parent presents no risk (although in some cases, the perpetrator of the harm may be one parent, but the other parent has failed to protect the child). But, as we see in *Lancashire*, in some cases it is simply not possible to tell to the requisite standard of proof, on the balance of probabilities, which parent is responsible. The court and the local authority may have their suspicions as to which parent is responsible, but suspicion is not enough. But, *Lancashire* also shows us that if we know that the child was harmed, we do not necessarily need to know who did the harm in order to pass the threshold and proceed to the welfare stage.[118] As Lord Nicholls said in *Re O*:

> Quite simply, it would be grotesque if such a case had to proceed at the welfare stage on the footing that, because neither parent, considered individually, has been proved to be

---

[115] *Children Act Guidance and Regulations* Volume 1 (The Stationery Office 2008) para 3.41.
[116] *A Local Authority v M and Another* [2018] All ER 28.
[117] *Re S-B* [2010] 1 All ER 705, [2010] 1 AC 678 [38].
[118] *Re S-B (Children)* [2009] UKSC 17 [35] (Lady Hale).

the perpetrator, therefore the child is not at risk from either of them. This would be grotesque because it would mean the court would proceed on the footing that neither parent represents a risk even though one or other of them was the perpetrator of the harm in question.[119]

At the welfare stage, which we discuss at 12.4, the court must consider what the future arrangements for the child should be. If both parents are going to be responsible for the future care of the child, and they are the only potential abusers, then there will be a real possibility of future harm because both potential abusers will have contact with the child.

Sometimes, the parents have separated, perhaps as a result of the proceedings. In this situation, one household is unsafe and the other safe—unless the parent who was not the perpetrator is also a risk to the child for other reasons, such as that they covered up harm to the child, or were negligent in failing to notice harm, or are (as is sometimes the case) still involved with one another while claiming to be separated. Local authorities often run cases on the basis that while only one parent has harmed the child, the other failed to protect the child from that harm, and therefore the child will not be safe with either parent.

If that is not the case, and one person has harmed the child but it is not known who that is, 'the court cannot shut its eyes to the undoubted harm which has been suffered simply because it does not know who was responsible.'[120] It has to do something to protect the child. Where there is a 'real possibility'—that phrase again, in a different context—that a person caused the injury, but not sufficient evidence to find on the balance of probabilities that they did so, they will be placed into a pool of possible perpetrators alongside others for whom there is also a 'real possibility'.[121] The court can then proceed to protect the child against all of them.

By definition, a person's presence in the pool of possible perpetrators does not equate to a finding that they did harm a child. If we could prove on the balance of probabilities that they had harmed a child they would not be in a pool of possible perpetrators: they would be *the* perpetrator. This brings us to the thorny issue in Key Case *Re J*, in which the Supreme Court had to decide whether the mother's presence in the pool of perpetrators relating to her child of a former relationship—meaning no more than that there was a real possibility that she had harmed that child, not that it was likely that she had—meant that her child from a new relationship was likely to suffer significant harm at her hands.

KEY CASE *Re J (Children) (Non-Accidental Injury: Past Possible Perpetrator in New Family)* [2013] UKSC 9

A 3-week-old baby, T-L, died by asphyxiation, with a number of rib fractures and bruises. The local authority brought care proceedings for T-L's surviving siblings, and in those proceedings the parents denied causing the injuries to T-L. The judge disagreed, finding that the injuries to T-L had been deliberately inflicted, but was unable to determine which parent was the perpetrator on the balance of

---

[119] *Re O and another (Minors)(Care: Preliminary Hearing)* [2003] UKHL 18, [27] (Lord Nicholls). For a discussion of *Re O* and Key Case *Lancashire*, see M Hayes, '*Re O and N; Re B* - Uncertain Evidence and Risk Taking in Child Protection Cases' (2004) 16 *Child and Family Law Quarterly* 63.
[120] *Re B (Care Proceedings: Standard of Proof)* [2009] 1 AC 11 [61].
[121] *North Yorkshire CC v SA* [2003] EWCA Civ 839.

probabilities, although one of them was—they were in a pool of possible perpetrators that consisted of just the two of them. The mother, JJ, subsequently formed a new relationship and had further children with that new partner. The issue was whether the children of that relationship were at risk of significant harm. This depended on whether JJ had been the person to cause the fatal injuries to T-L, or had failed to protect her.

The Supreme Court reiterated that an assessment of future harm has to be based on facts proven on the balance of probabilities. Thus 'a real possibility that a person has harmed a child in the past is not, *by itself*,[122] sufficient to establish the likelihood that she will cause harm to another child in the future'. It is not a proven fact.

However, the Court held that the fact that a previous child had been injured or killed in the same household as a parent 'normally comes associated with innumerable other facts which may be relevant to the prediction of future harm to another child'. Five of the seven judges who heard the case would allow a person's consignment to the pool of perpetrators to be considered alongside these proven facts, so that cumulatively the court could find that there was a real possibility of future harm.

In this case, such an approach was not possible. This was because, unusually, the local authority had run its case solely on the basis that the mother's presence in the pool of perpetrators in respect of T-L gave rise to a real possibility of future harm in relation to her other children, and did not rely on facts such as that the parents had colluded to cover up the injuries and not sought prompt medical care (these were findings that the first instance judge had made, proven on the balance of probabilities). In most cases, the Court emphasised, there will be 'a multitude of established facts' from which a real possibility can be established'. Had the local authority relied on these, they could have been used to establish a real possibility of future significant harm in JJ's current household, whether or not she had been the perpetrator of the fatal injuries.

The remaining two of the seven judges would not allow unproven allegations to be combined with facts to create a real possibility, but would consider them irrelevant: JJ's 'consignment to a pool has a value of zero on its own, it can, for this purpose, have no greater value in company'.[123] But as this was the minority view, the principle that we take from this case is that we can take proven facts and use them in combination with the fact that someone is in a pool in respect of another child, and by combining them demonstrate that it is likely that (that there is a real possibility that) their new child will be significantly harmed.

Re J has been the subject of both critical and supportive commentary by highly respected academics. Stephen Gilmore has asked why proven past harm to a child at the hands of one of two possible perpetrators should not be sufficient *by itself* to suggest a future risk to another child. He draws an analogy with that of an electrician who finds that a circuit is faulty, but cannot determine which of two light switches is the dangerous one. In that situation, the only safe thing to do is not to use either switch. The risk of electrocution through selecting the faulty switch is too great: it cannot sensibly be ignored.[124] Similarly, Mary Hayes has referred to *Re J* as 'an error of judgment' and 'a perilous risk' to children.[125]

---

[122] Emphasis added.
[123] *Re J (Children) (Non-Accidental Injury: Past Possible Perpetrator in New Family)* [2013] UKSC 9 [80] (Lord Wilson).
[124] Stephen Gilmore, '*Re J* : Bulwarks and Logic – the Blood Which Runs through the Veins of Law – But How Much Will Be Spilled in Future?' [2013] *Child and Family Law Quarterly* 215.
[125] Mary Hayes, 'The Supreme Court's Failure to Protect Vulnerable Children: *Re J (Children)*' [2013, August] *Family Law* 1015.

Andrew Bainham has written that 'the suggestion that a court, when considering the multitude of relevant facts which surface in every case, can or should ignore the previous death or serious injury of a child in one parent's household is simply not to live in the real world.'[126] But he finds it equally 'unacceptable in a democratic society that children should be removed in the longer term, as opposed to the interim, on the basis only of suspicion rather than proof. Otherwise, no parents under previous suspicion would ever feel able to have another child or rebuild their family lives without the spectre of local authority involvement hanging over them and their partners.' For him, the approach in *Re J* strikes the necessary balance between intrusion in family life and child protection.

12.3.8 Summary so far

- The harm or likelihood of harm must be attributable to the care that was/is being given to the child, or is likely to be given to him, not being what it is reasonable to expect a parent to give to him; or the child being beyond parental control.
- The phrase 'not being what it would be reasonable to expect a parent to give to him' encompasses the care of the parents as well as others who share the care of the child. It is not wholly clear which situations may fall into this category.
- The link to reasonableness enables the courts to consider current social norms.
- Courts should try to identify the perpetrator of harm on the balance of probabilities. If the court cannot identify the individual perpetrator of harm on the balance of probabilities, all people in respect of which there is a real possibility of harm to the child will be placed in a pool of possible perpetrators.
- A person's presence in a pool of possible perpetrators is not sufficient to show that they harmed a child on the balance of probabilities—if there was evidence to show that, they would be *the* perpetrator and a pool would not be needed. Accordingly, a person's presence in a pool cannot be used *by itself* to show that they present a risk to another child. However, it can be combined with facts proven on the balance of probabilities to cumulatively mean that the child is likely to suffer (meaning that there is a real possibility of them suffering) significant harm in the future.

12.4 The welfare stage

Once the threshold is met, the court still has to decide what to do with the child: what order, if any, must it make? The local authority will have a view, but the court is not bound to make the order for which the local authority has applied, even if the care threshold is met. Instead, it must consider the possible ways forward, and come it its own decision. The local authority, the guardian, and the parent(s) will each be arguing for their preferred outcome.

This decision about the outcome is known as the welfare stage, because the court must

1. Do what is best for the child.
2. Reach an outcome that is proportionate and human-rights compliant.

[126] Andrew Bainham, 'Suspicious Minds: Protecting Children in the Face of Uncertainty' (2013) 72(2) *Cambridge Law Journal* 266, 268.

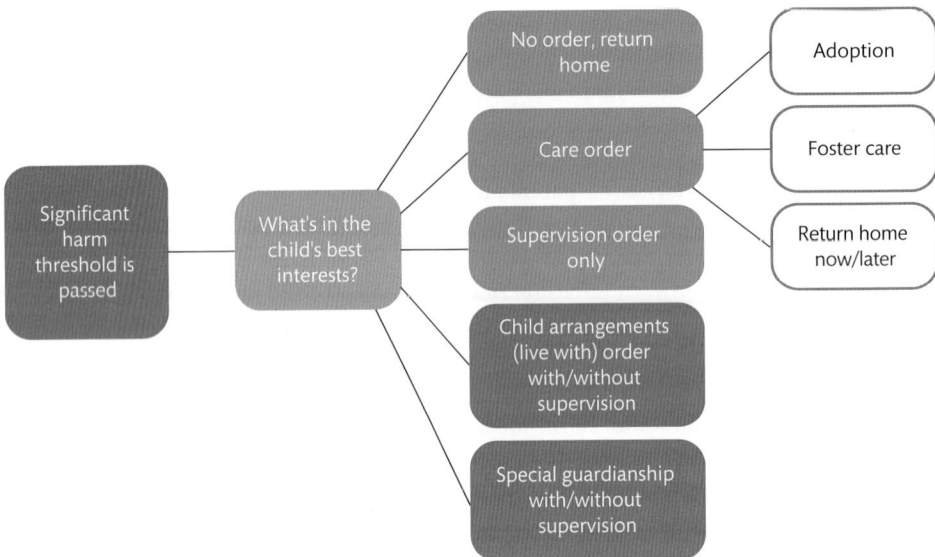

FIGURE 12.2 Potential outcomes of a care or supervision application

There are a number of potential outcomes of a case, as shown in Figure 12.2.

1. One or both parents may be seeking to have the child remain with them (or be returned to them). This is likely to involve a short transition period assuming they are not currently living with their parent(s). Return to parents may be under a number of different legal statuses. The court may make a care order where the children remain at home (which is unusual)[127] or make a supervision order under which the child's welfare is monitored by the local authority. If separated parents are in dispute between themselves as to which parent the child should live with, the court may resolve this with a child arrangements order under s8 Children Act 1989. The court may make no order at all, although again this is unusual.

2. A member of the extended family of the child, or a family friend, may be prepared to have the child live with them, subject to them being deemed suitable. This is called *kinship care*. This could be under the auspices of a child arrangements order or a special guardianship order (discussed at 12.4.7). Either order may be coupled with a supervision order. Some kinship carers may be approved foster carers, but this is unusual.

3. The child may be in (non-kinship) foster care under a care order, either long-term or pending either adoption or a return to the birth family. (The local authority may see foster care as a short-term measure while they work with the child's family to enable a safe return home for the child.) Some children in care will live in children's homes, residential schools, or secure accommodation rather than with foster families.

---

[127] It is unusual for a child under a care order to be placed with his parents, and begs the question of whether the care order should be discharged. See the Care Planning, Placement and Case Review (England) Regulations 2010 (SI 2010/959) Part IV.

4.   The local authority may want the child to be adopted. If the local authority is seeking an adoption order, it may ask the court to make a placement order at the final care hearing.

5.   An existing foster carer may put themselves forward to continue to look after the child under special guardianship order or child arrangements order instead of pursuant to a care order.

Note that not all of these options will be available in all cases. For example, there may be no one in the wider family who can assume care of the child (kinship care) under a child arrangements order or a special guardianship order in the event that the court decides that the parents are not able to care for the child any more. That may leave the court with a choice of a care or supervision order (one of which will be sought by the local authority) or no order at all (which may be sought by the parents).

In reaching a decision, the judge must consider what is in the child's best interests. In fact, there are two welfare principles to be considered:

1.   Care, supervision, special guardianship, and child arrangements orders are all orders to which the welfare principle in section 1 Children Act 1989 applies, as does the s1(5) 'no order' principle and the welfare checklist. We discuss this welfare principle at length in Chapter 9.

2.   If the court is 'coming to a decision relating to the adoption of a child', the welfare principle in s1 Adoption and Children Act 2002 applies. This includes situations in which the local authority is asking the court to approve a care plan for adoption and perhaps to make a placement order then and there at the final care hearing, as well as the later stages of making an adoption order, or giving leave to oppose an adoption.[128] A modified welfare checklist can be found at s1(4).

Table 12.1 sets out the two welfare checklists in full. The 2002 welfare principle is a modified version of the 1989 principle, and makes the court's paramount consideration the child's welfare 'throughout his life'. Although the Children Act welfare principle can also consider lifetime well-being, it does not actually say this. The effect of this variation in the 2002 Act is to render explicit the need to consider long-term benefits over short-term difficulties.

The Adoption and Children Act 2002 variation also specifically requires the court and adoption agency to consider the likely effect on the child (throughout his life) of having ceased to be a member of the original family and become an adopted person; the child's relationships with others; and the child's religious, racial, cultural, and linguistic heritage.

12.4.1 Considering the options

The public law outline requires that all *realistic options* for the future care of the child should be considered. During or before the proceedings the local authority may come

---

[128] See s1(7) Adoption and Children Act 2002, which defines what 'coming to a decision relating to the adoption of a child' includes.

TABLE 12.1 Comparison of the welfare checklists in the 1989 and 2002 Acts

Children Act 1989	Adoption and Children Act 2002
(a) the ascertainable wishes and feelings of the child concerned (considered in the light of his age and understanding);	(a) the child's ascertainable wishes and feelings regarding the decision (considered in the light of the child's age and understanding),
(b) his physical, emotional and educational needs;	(b) the child's particular needs,
(c) the likely effect on him of any change in his circumstances;	(c) the likely effect on the child (throughout his life) of having ceased to be a member of the original family and become an adopted person,
(d) his age, sex, background and any characteristics of his which the court considers relevant;	(d) the child's age, sex, background and any of the child's characteristics which the court or agency considers relevant,
(e) any harm which he has suffered or is at risk of suffering;	(e) any harm (within the meaning of the Children Act 1989) which the child has suffered or is at risk of suffering,
(f) how capable each of his parents, and any other person in relation to whom the court considers the question to be relevant, is of meeting his needs;	(f) the relationship which the child has with relatives, with any person who is a prospective adopter with whom the child is placed, and with any other person in relation to whom the court or agency considers the relationship to be relevant, including—
	(i) the likelihood of any such relationship continuing and the value to the child of its doing so,
	(ii) the ability and willingness of any of the child's relatives, or of any such person, to provide the child with a secure environment in which the child can develop, and otherwise to meet the child's needs,
	(iii) the wishes and feelings of any of the child's relatives, or of any such person, regarding the child.
	(5) In placing a child for adoption, an adoption agency in Wales must give due consideration to the child's religious persuasion, racial origin and cultural and linguistic background.
	(NB This requirement was removed from English law by the Children and Families Act 2014.)
(g) the range of powers available to the court under this Act in the proceedings in question. (5) Where a court is considering whether or not to make one or more orders under this Act with respect to a child, it shall not make the order or any of the orders unless it considers that doing so would be better for the child than making no order at all.	(6) In coming to a decision relating to the adoption of a child, a court or adoption agency must always consider the whole range of powers available to it in the child's case (whether under this Act or the Children Act 1989); and the court must not make any order under this Act unless it considers that making the order would be better for the child than not doing so.

to identify an alternative home for the child that would avoid the need for the child to be taken into care. In particular, the local authority must look for potential carers in the wider family and friends circle (kinship care). Rather than continue to seek a care order, the local authority may support one of the other applications, such as a special guardianship application by a kinship carer.

Under Practice Direction 12A, the parents will also be invited to set out their proposals for the future of the child. Some will accept that they cannot care for their child and may help to identify suitable kinship carers because keeping the child in the family is preferable to stranger adoption or long-term fostering. (There is a risk that kinship carers are pressured to put themselves forward, as discussed in the news article 'Take in your grandchildren or you won't see them again'.)[129] On other occasions, the birth parents may be strongly opposed to any carers other than themselves. Only in exceptional circumstances will the court release the local authority from their obligation to contact potential family carers (see 12.2.3). This work at identifying potential options for the child must be dealt with expeditiously and early in order to keep to the 26 week timetable for proceedings (see 12.2.4 and Figure 12.1).

If the authority identifies a potential kinship carer, social workers will need to undertake a viability assessment of whether that person can assume care of the child, bearing in mind the child's needs. This will involve looking at the carer's experience of child-raising, their financial and working position, their accommodation, age, health, and motivation for being willing to raise the child, as well as their understanding of why the local authority is concerned about the child.[130] If the outcome is positive, then the court will give directions for a full assessment to be carried out: s14A(8). If that, too, is positive then the local authority may encourage that person to apply for a special guardianship order or a child arrangements order. (Most kinship carers are not trained and registered foster carers so the legal structure for them to assume care is not usually a foster care arrangement.) If the outcome is negative, the potential carer should be informed so that they can challenge that if they wish to do so.

12.4.2 The care plan

The local authority will draw up a plan for the future care of the child, known as a *s31A care plan*. The authority must prepare a plan whenever there is an application on which a care order could be made, and must keep it under review so it can be revised if the local authority deem that desirable. The plan outlines the child's needs, the authority's proposals for the child's future, and the support they and other agencies should offer.

It will set out:

- The impact on the child of any harm that he or she has suffered; the child's needs (including those that arise out of that harm) and including educational and health, religious, linguistic, racial or cultural needs; and a plan for how the local authority will meet those needs.

- Where it is intended the child will live (the permanence provisions) and what orders it is inviting the court to make. The local authority will have a preferred option, which it is asking the court to order (such as a care order leading to adoption) as well as other options that it has considered but thinks are less desirable. The authority will need to

---

[129] Luke Jones, 'Take in your grandchildren or you won't see them again' (*BBC News website* 29 October 2019). Available at https://www.bbc.co.uk/news/education-50214031 accessed 29 October 2019.
[130] Family Rights Group, *Initial Family and Friends Care Assessment: A Good Practice Guide* (Family Rights Group 2017).

discuss what other realistic options the local authority has considered (such as those put forward by the family) and why it thinks these are not in the best interests of the child. Sometimes the local authority will have both a preferred plan (such as adoption) and a back-up plan (such as long-term fostering if no adoptive family can be found in the next six or so months). The local authority may have started the application believing that a care order needed to be made but then decided to support another application, such as a kinship carer's application for a special guardianship order.

- How the local authority will support these arrangements, such as the services it intends to provide.

- How the local authority will involve those with parental responsibility in decision-making.

- Any plans for the child to have contact with his or her birth family.

A court cannot make a care order until the court has considered those parts of the plan that govern where the child will live and under what legal structure (the permanence provisions) and proposals in relation to contact with the birth family.[131] In *Re W (Adoption Application: Reunification with Family of Origin)*, the High Court noted that the requirement to look at these aspects of the plan did not prevent the court from also considering other aspects.[132] This means that 'despite all the inevitable uncertainties, when deciding whether to make a care order the court should normally have before it a care plan which is sufficiently firm and particularised for all concerned to have a reasonably clear picture of the likely way ahead.'[133] For example, the court will want to know where the child is going to live. If this is with a family member or friend, the court will want to know who that is. If it is with a long-term foster carer the court will want the care plan to describe what the foster carers can offer.[134] This is important because once a care order is made, the responsibility for the child lies with the local authority and the court has no further role in what happens unless an application comes before for adoption or the termination of the care order.[135]

It is common for care plans to change as proceedings progress and further information or expert assessments are received. However, the court cannot tell the local authority what its care plan should be 'any more than it can dictate to any other party what their case should be'.[136] In *Nottinghamshire County Council v L*[137] the court cautioned against micro-managing the contents of a care plan, saying this risked it becoming 'a straitjacket rather than a tool for efficient social work'. If the judge is unhappy with the care plan because it does not represent what he or she thinks is in the child's best interests, or his or her findings of fact, the court can ask the local authority to return with a revised plan; refuse

---

[131] See s31(3A) and (3B). For a discussion of post-adoption contact, see 12.7.3.
[132] *Re W (Adoption application: Reunification with Family of Origin)* [2015] EWHC 2039 (Fam).
[133] *Re S (Minors)(Care Order: Implementation of Care Plan)* [2002] UKHL 10 [99] (Lord Nicholls).
[134] *Re W (Adoption application: Reunification with Family of Origin)* [2015] EWHC 2039 (Fam).
[135] *Re S (Minors)(Care Order: Implementation of Care Plan)* [2002] UKHL 10. See 12.4.6 on challenging local authority decisions.
[136] *Re S and D (Children: Powers of Court)* [1995] 2 FLR 456, 634G–635C; *Re T (A Child) (Placement Order)* [2018] 2 FLR 926 (CA).
[137] [2020] EWFC B58; on BAILII.

to make the order sought and make a different order or an interim care order; or simply adjourn the case.

Rarely, there may be a stand-off between the local authority and the court that has not been resolved. In this situation, there are two potential ways forward. Despite the care plan's undesirability, the court may reluctantly make the order sought by the local authority on the basis that it may yet remain the best option for the child—'the lesser of two evils', as Balcombe LJ phrased it in *Re S and D (Children: Powers of Court)*. Alternatively, the child's guardian could bring proceedings for judicial review against the local authority on the grounds of unreasonableness.[138] As the court said in *Re T*, 'What the court can . . . expect from a local authority is a high level of respect for its assessments or risk and welfare, leading in almost every case to those assessments being put into effect.'[139] It would almost certainly be *Wednesbury* unreasonable of the local authority to insist upon a plan that did not meet the court's findings as to any risks, or to refuse to provide support necessary to ensure that the order preferred by the court will work.[140]

SCENARIO 1

Illustration 5

The local authority in our case will have considered whether there are any viable family or friends (kinship) carers that could assume care of Ella. If there are potential alternative carers, the local authority should assess their suitability in meeting Ella's needs. It may come to support an application by a kinship carer for a child arrangements order or a special guardianship order. Alternatively, the local authority may believe that only adoption will meet Ella's needs throughout her life, and submit a care plan that provides for contact with Kerrie and Mike to gradually reduce and placement of Ella with potential adopters. Indeed, Ella may already be being fostered by potential adopters albeit under an interim care order rather than a placement order (see 12.4.8 on fostering for adoption and placement).

Kerrie may be seeking to have Ella returned to her perhaps with a supervision order to allay the local authority's concerns. It may be that Mike accepts that the relationship is over (if indeed it is) and that he cannot care for Ella, and thus supports Kerrie's application, but seeks contact with Ella.

The court's role is to consider which of these options is best for Ella. But, as we shall see, if the court is considering adoption it must ensure that this option is a necessary and proportionate way of meeting Ella's needs throughout her life.

We will now turn to considering what options the court may have before it, before considering how the court should approach the task of deciding between them. These are given in order from the least intervention in family life, to the greatest intervention: adoption. Do not forget that some of these can be coupled with one another.

---

[138] *W (A Child) v Neath Port Talbot County Borough Council* [2013] EWCA Civ 1227.
[139] *Re T (A Child) (Placement Order)* [2018] 2 FLR 926 (CA).
[140] *Re CH (Care or Interim Care Order)* [1998] 1 FLR 402, [81]–[83]. For a discussion of all of these cases, see *Re T-S (Children)* [2019] EWCA Civ 742. Wednesbury unreasonableness comes from *Associated Provincial Picture Houses Ltd v Wednesbury Corporation* [1948] 1 KB 223, HL.

12.4.3 **Reunification with the birth parent(s)**

In order for a child to be returned to their birth parent, the parent does not have to become perfect, but merely able to offer 'good enough' parenting. What is 'good enough' for a particular child depends upon the needs of that child. There is no formal definition, but it broadly encompasses putting the child's needs first, providing safe and consistent levels of care, and meeting his health and developmental needs. This means that children may be returned to homes where the care they receive will be to a lesser standard than if the child was with foster carers or adoptive parents. But a return to that home has still been adjudged to be best for the child, bearing in mind the comments discussed at 12.3.3 of this chapter that 'it is not the provenance of the state to spare children all the consequences of defective parenting.'[141]

When determining whether a child should be rehabilitated to his family, the court may have before it some assessments about the quality of parenting. These are necessarily subjective evaluations about the family, but there are various models or frameworks used by social workers and psychologists to undertake this task.[142] In *Re BR (Proof of Facts)* the local authority drew up a useful list of risk factors and protective factors which they had drawn from material produced by the NSPCC, the Common Assessment Framework and the Patient UK *Guidance for Health Professionals*. You will find this at Table 12.2. Risk factors are those that impede or prevent 'good enough parenting' and protective factors are those that help the parents to offer it. However, as the judge cautioned, 'In itself, the presence or absence of a particular factor proves nothing. Children can of course be well cared for in disadvantaged homes and abused in otherwise fortunate ones. . . . [E]ach case turns on its facts'.[143]

Some parents will concede that the threshold has been met. This does not avoid the need for the court to find that the threshold has been met on the evidence: the court cannot just accept this as read because the other parties agree it. There are tactical reasons why a parent may concede threshold: a parent who denies an obvious threshold or seeks to minimise legitimate concerns is likely to be considered a greater risk of harm to the child. Accepting the threshold and arguing that the parent has now become capable of offering good enough parenting is an easier argument to present than one that denies there was a problem in the first place.

Part of the care proceedings involves assessing the parents' capacity to effect long-term, meaningful change such that they become able to offer good enough care. This is partly dependent on their willingness and inherent ability to overcome risk factors such as those set out in Table 12.2, but it also depends on what assistance is available to them and how long that will take. Some parents will not, despite their love for their child, ever be able to offer the level of care required. Others could do so, but will need time to develop the necessary skills. Some are resistant to change: Ward, Brown, and Hyde-Dryden note that

> Apparent resistance may be the result of fear, stigma, shame, ambivalence, or a parent's lack of confidence in their ability to change. Parents may be resistant to the involvement of

---

[141] *Re L (Care: Threshold Criteria)* [2007] 1 FLR 2050 [51] (Hedley J).

[142] P Harnett, 'A Procedure for Assessing Parents Capacity for Change in Child Protection Cases' (2007) 29(9) *Children and Youth Services Review* 1179.

[143] [2015] EWFC 41.

TABLE 12.2 Risk and protective factors in parenting

Risk factors	Protective factors
1. Physical or mental disability in children that may increase caregiver burden	1. Supportive family environment
2. Social isolation of families	2. Nurturing parenting skills
3. Parents' lack of understanding of children's needs and child development	3. Stable family relationships
4. Parents' history of domestic abuse	4. Household rules and monitoring of the child
5. History of physical or sexual abuse (as a child)	5. Adequate parental finances
6. Past physical or sexual abuse of a child	6. Adequate housing
7. Poverty and other socioeconomic disadvantage	7. Access to health care and social services
8. Family disorganisation, dissolution, and violence, including intimate partner violence	8. Caring adults who can serve as role models or mentors
9. Lack of family cohesion	9. Community support
10. Substance abuse in family	
11. Parental immaturity	
12. Single or non-biological parents	
13. Poor parent–child relationships and negative interactions	
14. Parental thoughts and emotions supporting maltreatment behaviours	
15. Parental stress and distress, including depression or other mental health conditions	
16. Community violence	

Source: [2015] EWFC 41.

social workers rather than resistant to change in itself, particularly where they feel social workers are exercising power over them instead of with them in a supportive manner. . . . It is also clear that parental problems do not occur in isolation: they are influenced by stressors within the wider environment and family, such as poor housing, poverty and unemployment that magnify the challenges to parenting and increase the likelihood that problems will arise.[144]

As you can see from Table 12.2 there are a number of external factors that increase risk, and these may be outside the parents' control.

Even if a parent is capable of sustained change, one key issue is how long it will take them to achieve that. Child professionals often refer to 'the timescales of the child', by which they mean the parents' ability to change within an acceptable period of time, given the age of their child, and his or her needs and developmental milestones. It may well not be in a child's best interests to be in foster care waiting to return to a parent that is undergoing a lengthy period of therapy, or a course on domestic abuse, or confidence building, or a substance abuse treatment programme (for example). Ward et al. found that parents were

---

[144] H Ward, R Brown, and G Hyde-Dryden, *Assessing Parental Capacity to Change when Children are on the Edge of Care: An Overview of Current Research Evidence* (Centre for Child and Family Research Loughborough University 2014) 14–15.

unlikely to make sufficient changes to protect children from harm within an appropriate timeframe in families where the following factors are present: extreme domestic abuse where the perpetrator shows a pervasive pattern of disregard for and violation of the rights of others; there is both substance misuse and domestic abuse and violence in the home; children are not protected from perpetrators of sexual abuse; and/or where parents consciously and systematically cover up deliberate maltreatment.[145]

Even when parents are willing to engage with services to support their change, these may not be available (or there may be a waiting list) and there may still be a lengthy period before such work can be done, as well as a risk of relapse. 'Relapse is an integral part of the process of change, and it may take many years for the risk to diminish—five years to achieve stable recovery from alcohol; eight to ten years if the problem is misuse of heroin.'[146] If she becomes pregnant again, the mother may not be able to demonstrate change in sufficient time to prevent that further child from also being removed. As we discuss in the Focus box, a significant number of mothers in care proceedings have been in care proceedings before in relation to previous children they have had and, quite often, as the subject of proceedings when they were themselves children. Children who themselves received poor care growing up are more likely to have difficulties parenting their own children. These are, however, just the odds—some parents will beat these and be able to learn to offer 'good enough' care.

FOCUS Think Critically

Mothers in repeat care proceedings

Approximately a quarter of mothers in care proceedings have been in previous proceedings in the last seven years.[147] The younger the mother, the more likely this is.[148] Research by Broadhurst et al. found that there is, on average, only 17 months 'between the first time a mother appears in court with an infant and the second time she appears in court with another infant, suggesting a very short interval between pregnancies, which gives mums very little time to engage in their own rehabilitation.'[149] Their children are more likely to be younger than other children who are subject to proceedings because the local authority already has recorded concerns about the ability of the parents to look after previous children. Sometimes the child is intended to help assuage their grief

[145] H Ward, R Brown, and G Hyde-Dryden, *Assessing Parental Capacity to Change when Children are on the Edge of Care: An Overview of Current Research Evidence* (Centre for Child and Family Research Loughborough University 2014) 146.

[146] H Ward, R Brown, and G Hyde-Dryden, *Assessing Parental Capacity to Change when Children are on the Edge of Care: An Overview of Current Research Evidence* (Centre for Child and Family Research Loughborough University 2014) 146.

[147] K Broadhurst, C Mason, S Bedston, B Alrouh, L Morriss, T McQuarrie, M Palmer, M Shaw, J Harwin, and S Kershaw, *Vulnerable Birth Mothers and Recurrent Care Proceedings* (Lancaster University Centre for Child and Family Justice Research/Nuffield Foundation 2017).

[148] K Broadhurst, C Mason, S Bedston, B Alrouh, L Morriss, T McQuarrie, M Palmer, M Shaw, J Harwin, and S Kershaw, *Vulnerable Birth Mothers and Recurrent Care Proceedings* (Lancaster University Centre for Child and Family Justice Research/Nuffield Foundation 2017).

[149] Berg, 'Thousands of Mothers Have Multiple Babies Removed' (quoting Karen Broadhurst) (*BBC News* 23 June 2014). Available at https://www.bbc.co.uk/news/education-27943591 accessed 28 September 2019.

at the loss of previous children to care, but it can also be because the mothers lead chaotic lives and the pregnancy is unintended.[150]

Because of the frequency of mothers being involved in recurrent care proceedings and facing successive losses of their children, some programmes such as Pause have been developed to specifically help the mothers who have already had children taken into care address the underlying reasons for the proceedings and thereby minimise the risk of proceedings in relation to any further children.[151] Many mothers in care proceedings were themselves in care as children and may therefore be feeling the consequences of unstable childhoods, intergenerational poor parenting, or abuse and neglect.[152] Their work may therefore address issues such as abusive relationships, substance abuse, and homelessness. For some women, repeat child removal caused a long-term further deterioration in their well-being, impeding their ability to parent further children, whereas others were able to change their situations. There is some controversy about whether such women should be encouraged to start long-term contraceptive use and how far such encouragement should go.[153] However, some mothers in recurrent proceedings suffer from serious mental health difficulties or permanent intellectual disabilities which mean they are unable to parent safely.[154] Remember that although some parents whose children are taken into care will be abusive, many will simply be unable to offer 'good enough' parenting through no fault of their own.

There is therefore a real problem for parents wishing to have their children returned to them. Even if they are assessed as having the ability to change, many simply cannot do so within the timescales of the child. This means that when a court considers the advantages and disadvantages of different options for the child, there are significant disadvantages to any plan which involves the child living in a temporary situation while their parent works towards becoming 'good enough' to meet their needs.

You may well be wondering what responsibility the local authority has to address some of these issues. For example, can the local authority rely on poor housing as a risk factor when the parent may be stuck on a long waiting list for better quality council housing? It would be a humane and proportionate expense for the local authority or health authorities to pay for a parent to access intensive therapy in order to avoid a future child removal, rather than the far greater financial and social cost of taking a further child into care. The Court of Appeal made it clear in Key Case *Re B-S (Children) (Adoption: Leave to Oppose)* that the local authority cannot 'press for a more drastic form of order, least of all press for

---

[150] K Broadhurst, C Mason, S Bedston, B Alrouh, L Morriss, T McQuarrie, M Palmer, M Shaw, J Harwin, and S Kershaw, *Vulnerable Birth Mothers and Recurrent Care Proceedings* (Lancaster University Centre for Child and Family Justice Research/Nuffield Foundation 2017). See also M Jones, 'The continuing problem of care proceedings relating to children of parents who have already had previous children removed from their care: what is to be done?' (*Family Law Week*, 6 December 2018).

[151] https://www.pause.org.uk/ accessed 12 September 2019.

[152] See K Broadhurst, C Mason, S Bedston, B Alrouh, L Morriss, T McQuarrie, M Palmer, M Shaw, J Harwin, and S Kershaw, *Vulnerable Birth Mothers and Recurrent Care Proceedings* (Lancaster University Centre for Child and Family Justice Research/Nuffield Foundation 2017) esp. sections 2 and 3.

[153] K Broadhurst, M Shaw, S Kershaw, J Harwin, B Alrouh, C Mason, and M Pilling, 'Vulnerable Birth Mothers and Repeat Losses of Infants to Public Care: Is Targeted Reproductive Health Care Ethically Defensible?' (2015) 37(1) *Journal of Social Welfare and Family Law* 84.

[154] K Broadhurst, C Mason, S Bedston, B Alrouh, L Morriss, T McQuarrie, M Palmer, M Shaw, J Harwin, and S Kershaw, *Vulnerable Birth Mothers and Recurrent Care Proceedings* (Lancaster University Centre for Child and Family Justice Research/Nuffield Foundation 2017).

adoption, because it is unable or unwilling to support a less interventionist form of order. Judges must be alert to the point and must be rigorous in exploring and probing local authority thinking in cases where there is any reason to suspect that resource issues may be affecting the local authority's thinking.'[155] But the reality is that there are huge difficulties with sourcing and funding the kind of work that some birth parents require either during proceedings or between recurrent proceedings. In *Gloucester County Council v M, F, A, and MGA*, Judge Wildblood used a degree of pressure to encourage the local authority to arrange much-needed therapy, noting that the parents:

> . . . remain young and desperate to parent their children. Therefore, it has to be wholly foreseeable that they will consider having further children. Once again this case has seen combinations of professional people writing lengthy and expensive reports in which they recommend that therapy should be provided for parents. I have never heard a psychologist give evidence in a public law case without recommending that someone needs therapy and, almost invariably afterwards, there is the remark that the benefit of therapy is outwith the timescales of the child. . . .[156]

The unfortunate reality is that a significant proportion of abused or neglected children rehabilitated to their birth families will be re-abused or neglected once they returned home, and this finding has been repeated across a number of studies. In one study of particularly young children, over three quarters of those who returned 'suffered an adverse outcome, including re-abuse, failure to thrive, abnormal physical or neurological development or symptoms of persistent emotional disturbance. The authors concluded that either the decision to return them home was wrong or the follow-up interventions were inadequate.'[157]

12.4.4 A child arrangements order

A child arrangements order will be familiar to you as one of the private law orders discussed in Chapter 10. Section 8 Children Act 1989 allows the court to make an order that the child lives with or otherwise spends time with a named person or persons. Unless there is a dispute between those with PR, it will not be necessary for a child arrangements order to be made in favour of a parent in public law proceedings but this may be the legal structure used in order for the child to live with a kinship carer or family friend. Kinship care is the term used when the child lives with members of the birth family other than the parents. This is often a grandparent. A child arrangements order involves limited state intrusion: once the order is made, the local authority has no further role as it is incompatible with a care order. As with all child arrangements orders, the parents can at any time apply to amend or end it. (Even if there is a s91(14) order in force, this just requires them to get leave first). There is therefore a risk of instability if a parent is opposed to the child living with someone else. For this reason, courts may prefer a special guardianship order, which contains protections

---

[155] *Re B-S (Children) (Adoption: Leave to Oppose)* [2013] EWCA Civ 1146 [29] (Munby P).
[156] [2015] EWFC B177.
[157] N Biehal, Reuniting Children with their Families: Reconsidering the Evidence on Timing, Contact and Outcomes' (2007) 37 *British Journal of Social Work* 807. Biehal discusses the various studies; the study mentioned above is D Hensey, J Williams, and L Rosenbloom, 'Intervention in Child Abuse: Experience in Liverpool' (1983) 25 *Departmental Medicine and Child Neurology* 606.

against interference. Indeed, the rate of breakdown of child arrangements orders (known as the 'disruption rate') is high compared to adoption and special guardianship. Selwyn and Masson found that 25 per cent of child arrangements orders were disrupted within six years, and most disruptions occurred in the first two years of the order.[158]

12.4.5 A supervision order

A supervision order is an order under s31(1) (b) Children Act 1989 that puts a child under the supervision of a designated local authority. This requires the local authority to 'advise, assist and befriend the supervised child'. Under Schedule 3 para 2 Children Act, the supervisor has the power to give directions about where the child lives and for what period; when, where, and to whom the child is to present himself; and any activities in which he is to participate. The parents retain their parental status and their parental responsibility, and (unlike a care order) the local authority does not acquire parental responsibility for a supervised child. This means that a supervision order may more easily meet the requirement of being a proportional interference with family life under Article 8 in circumstances in which adoption, for example, is not a proportional response. (The need for proportionality of outcome is discussed further when we look at adoption.)

The court is free to make a supervision order on an application for a care order, or vice versa (see s31(5)). Although they can be freestanding, supervision orders are often coupled with another order, most commonly special guardianship, but it could be a child arrangements order.[159] As Harwin et al. point out, the obligation to advise, assist, and support means that they 'potentially play an important role in family reunification and supporting placements with relatives or friends'.[160] Conditions cannot be attached to a supervision order.[161] Had conditions been permitted, they could have been used to (for example) make the reunification of mother and child dependent on the mother leaving an abusive relationship. As it is, the Family Justice Review cautioned against reforming the law to permit conditional supervision orders, in case it promoted courts to return children to their parents in situations in which the arrangement was likely to break down and cause the child further distress.[162]

Supervision orders only last for one year, although they can be extended.[163] If the local authority has more serious concerns, it will need to go back to court asking for a care order.

---

[158] J Selwyn and J Masson, 'Adoption, Special Guardianship and Residence Orders: A Comparison of Disruption Rates', [2014, December] *Family Law* 1709.

[159] The child arrangements order rather than the supervisor will direct with whom the child should live.

[160] J Harwin, B Alrouh, L Golding, T McQuarrie, K Broadhurst, and L Cusworth, *The Contribution of Supervision Orders and Special Guardianship to Children's Lives and Family Justice* (Lancaster University Centre for Child and Family Justice Research/Nuffield Foundation 2019) para 1.2.3. See also J Harwin, B Alrouh, M Palmer, K Broadhurst, and S Swift, 'Spotlight on Supervision Orders: What Do We Know and What Do We Need to Know?' [2016, March] *Family Law* 365.

[161] *Re V (A Minor) (Care or Supervision Order)* [1996] 1 FLR 776 (CA), on appeal from *Re V (Declaration against Parents)* [1995] 2 FLR 1003 (Fam).

[162] David Norgrove, *Family Justice Review Final Report (Ministry of Justice 2011)* paras 3.94–3.95.

[163] *Wakefield Metropolitan District Council v T* [2008] EWCA Civ 199. On an application to extend a supervision order, the court has no power to make a care order: *Re A (Supervision Order: Extension)* [1995] 1 FLR 335.

12.4.6 Fostering under a care order

When a care order is made, it is the duty of the local authority designated by the order to receive the child into its care (s31) and to keep him in its care while the order remains in force. The local authority must provide the child with accommodation (s22G) and maintain him (for example, by paying an allowance to foster carers), although it can recoup any financial maintenance from the birth parents in certain circumstances. It is under a duty to safeguard and promote the child's welfare (s22(3)).

If the child is placed under a care order with a person who is not a parent or a person with parental responsibility, that person is known as a foster carer (s23(3)). This status requires them to have been trained, assessed, and pre-approved by the local authority or an independent fostering agency.[164] Kinship carers are not considered foster carers unless they have been through this process, although in an emergency, they can be temporarily approved as foster carers for up to 16 weeks, which can be extended by a further eight weeks.[165] As such, most foster carers will be strangers to the child, and most kinship carers will care for the child under the authority of a special guardianship order or child arrangements order instead.

There were approximately 55,000 children fostered as at 31 March 2019.[166] About three quarters of these are living with a foster family.[167] Some foster carers will only offer emergency care, for example when a child has been removed from a household under police protection, or respite care. Some children will be in interim care pending a final care hearing and a more long-term solution, and some will be in foster care with a plan to be rehabilitated to the birth family. Some will be accommodated with foster carers with the consent of their family. This is known as s20 accommodation and is discussed at 11.5.4. Some will be with foster carers who intend to adopt them: so-called 'fostering to adopt' situations (see 12.5.6).

For some children, though, fostering is a long-term option rather than a stop on the way back home or elsewhere. It may be particularly suitable for children whose parents or other kindship carers are not able to look after them but for whom adoption is not appropriate. It can, for example, be difficult to find adoptive placements for children who are older (prospects of adoption fall sharply once the child turns 4 and reduces by 20 per cent for every year of delay),[168] and older children may reject adoption because of their years with their birth family. Long-term foster care can also be the fall-back position for those children for whom adoption is the plan, but for whom an adoptive family cannot be found. Some children may drift into long-term foster care for lack of a long-term plan, although this should not happen.[169]

---

[164] See Fostering Services (England) Regulations 2011 (SI 2011/581) and the *Fostering Services National Minimum Standards* (Department for Education 2011).

[165] Care Planning, Placement and Case Review (England) Regulations 2010 (SI 2010/959) paras 24 and 25.

[166] Ofsted, *Fostering in England 2018 to 2019: Main Findings* (2020).

[167] Ofsted, *Fostering in England 2018 to 2019: Main Findings* (2020).

[168] J Selwyn, W Sturgess, D Quinton, and C Baxter, *Costs and Outcomes of Non-Infant Adoptions* (British Association for Adoption and Fostering 2006).

[169] J Selwyn and D Quinton, 'Stability, Permanence, Outcomes and Support: Foster Care and Adoption Compared' (2004) 28(4) *Adoption and Fostering* 6, 7.

Unlike post-adoption, where contact with the birth family will probably cease, foster care involves the continuation of contact with the birth family and the retention of their status as family. For some children, this is of crucial importance. Children in foster care are more likely to live close to their birth family home than children in other placement types.[170] But foster care can be marked by frequent changes or carer, school, and social worker, hindering the child's ability to settle and to feel a sense of belonging. The commitment of long-term foster carers may mitigate this when compared to short-term foster care, but placements may still end for a variety of reasons both within and outside the control of the foster parent(s) and the child, and including challenges by the birth family. In *Re LRP (Care Proceedings: Placement Order)* Pauffley J said that

> Long term foster care is an extraordinarily precarious legal framework for any child, particularly one a young as LRP. Foster placements, long or short term, do not provide legal security. They can and often do come to an end. Children in long term care may find themselves moved from one home to another sometimes for seemingly inexplicable reasons. Long term foster parents are not expected to be fully committed to a child in the same way as adoptive parents. Most importantly of all in the current context, a long term foster child does not have the same and enduring sense of belonging within a family as does a child who has been adopted. There is no way in which a long term foster child can count on the permanency, predictability and enduring quality of his placement as can a child who has been adopted.[171]

For many children, there is indeed a difference in 'feel' between being someone's foster child and being their adopted child, although research by Schofield shows that this is far from being a universal experience.[172]

Making decisions about a child in care

On the making of a care order, the local authority obtains parental responsibility for the child. As Munby J said in *Re A (A Child) (Residential Assessment)*, 'It is a cardinal principle of the Children Act 1989 that once a care order has been made, whether interim or final, it is for the local authority, and not the court, to decide how to meet its parental responsibilities for the child.'[173] This includes deciding where the child should live. The parental responsibility of others such as the birth parents is not extinguished, but co-exists with that of the local authority. The exception is that any person who has parental responsibility only by virtue of a s8 order (i.e., not by automatic operation of law or under s4), will lose that parental responsibility because section 8 orders fall on the making of a care order.[174] Importantly, though, the local authority has the power to limit the exercise of parental responsibility by others, provided that it is 'satisfied that it is necessary to do so in order to safeguard or promote the child's welfare'. In *Cornwell v Newham LBC*, Charles J referred to this as giving the local authority 'predominant parental responsibility'.[175] There are

---

[170] M Narey and M Owens, *Foster Care in England: A Review for the Department for Education* (2018).

[171] [2013] EWHC 3974 (Fam) at [39].

[172] See, e.g., Gillian Schofield, 'The Significance of a Secure Base: A Psycho-Social Model of Long-Term Foster Care' (2002) 7(4) *Child and Family Social Work* 259.

[173] [2009] EWHC 865 (Fam) at [1].

[174] See Chapter 8 for parental responsibility.

[175] [2000] 1 FLR 595 at 603.

limitations: the local authority cannot 'cause the child to be brought up in any religious persuasion other than that in which he would have been brought up if the order had not been made'; the child's surname cannot be changed by anyone (s33); and the child cannot be removed from the United Kingdom except by the authority without either the written consent of all those with parental responsibility for the child or the leave of the court.

Before exercising its predominant parental responsibility, the local authority must ascertain and consider the wishes and feelings of the child and others with parental responsibility (s22(4)).

The local authority must regularly review its plans for the child, so as to avoid the child 'drifting' in care without a route to permanence. The care plan must also be reviewed periodically by an Independent Reviewing Officer, a person outside the local authority social work team. The IRO is not involved in managing social workers, but holds them accountable (both generally and on a case-by-case basis) for poor practice and ensures that the local authority meets its responsibilities towards the child. The role of the IRO is outlined at 11.6.1. In particular, the IRO will scrutinise the local authority's plans for the child, chair care plan review meetings, and make sure that the child's wishes and feelings are given full consideration (and those wishes and feelings may change over time). The *IRO Handbook: Statutory Guidance for Independent Reviewing Officers and Local Authorities on Their Functions in Relation to Case Management and Review for Looked After Children* says that 'The primary task of the IRO is to ensure that the care plan for the child fully reflects the child's current needs and that the actions set out in the plan are consistent with the local authority's legal responsibilities towards the child. As corporate parents each local authority should act for the children they look after as a responsible and conscientious parent would act.'[176]

The reality, however, is that a care order provides the local authority with considerable scope to make sometimes hugely significant decisions. In *Re D (Non-Availability of Legal Aid)* this included deciding that the child should be moved from living with his parents under a care order to living in foster care and being placed for adoption.[177] (The care plan approved by the court had anticipated that if the arrangement broke down, the child would be placed in foster care pending a viability assessment of the grandparents, but in the event there were no suitable kinship carers). The parents cross-applied to convert the care order into a supervision order under s39. Legal aid is available to parents in care proceedings and related proceedings, but the legal aid rules excluded this type of case from legal aid. This meant that the parents, one of whom had a learning disability, had to try to challenge the local authority's exercise of the care order and make their own application without being able to pay a lawyer, even though the application they were facing was the permanent loss of their child.

There are nevertheless several potential routes to challenging some decisions made by the local authority:

1. Use the authority's internal complaints procedure. If that procedure has been exhausted or if it would be unreasonable to use it, it is possible to apply to the Local Government and Social Care Ombudsman. The ombudsman cannot consider court

---

[176] At para 2.10.
[177] [2014] EWFC 39.

decisions (the route to challenge a court decision is an appeal) or a decision to place a child on a child protection plan. The usual remedy is an award of modest damages: the ombudsman has no ability to force the local authority to act in a certain way although the authority may agree to do so, but can ask the authority to improve its procedures to prevent similar issues arising.[178]

2. As the local authority is a public body, it is possible to apply for judicial review of the local authority's actions, which will involve proving that the decision made by the local authority was irrational (*Wednesbury* unreasonable),[179] unlawful, or involved an unfair process. Proportionality is generally considered to be an aspect of irrationality. Applications for judicial review are expensive.

3. Under s7 Human Rights Act, an individual can apply for 'such relief or remedy as is appropriate', which can include an injunction against anticipated infringement of a person's human rights, or damages. A number of applications based on misuse of s20 Children Act 1989 have been successful. This is discussed in Chapter 11. In the care context, the potential adopter in *RCW v A Local Authority* lost her sight while caring for a child under a placement order, and successfully sought an injunction to prevent the child from being removed.[180] Her Article 6 and 8 rights had been infringed.

4. Apply to discharge the care order under s39 Children Act 1989 or for a private law order that is inconsistent with a care order, such as a s8 'live with' order. If this application is successful, it will bring the care order to an end. Section 39 also enables a supervision order to be made as a replacement to a care order. These options are discussed in more detail in the section 'Leaving Care'.

5. Apply for an order under the inherent jurisdiction. In *Re SL (Permission to Vaccinate)* the court used the inherent jurisdiction to authorise the local authority to get a baby in interim care vaccinated against his mother's wishes.[181] Vaccination is one of the exercises of parental responsibility that would usually require the consent of all those with parental responsibility (in this case the local authority and the mother), or an order under s8 (specific issues).[182] As a local authority cannot utilise s8 Children Act 1989, the inherent jurisdiction was used.

6. Bring a claim in tort law. There are several tort law claims that can be made such as misfeasance in public office (which requires targeted malice) or negligence. Such cases are extremely complex and depend on the precise scope of the duties of the individual concerned, as well as wider public policy issues.[183]

As many parents and children within the care process are particularly vulnerable, you may wish to consider whether these options are truly accessible to them, or whether they are too complex, too expensive, and/or unlikely to yield the remedy sought.

---

[178] For a case in which the local authority housed a homeless teenager in a tent, see the Ombudsman's report at https://www.lgo.org.uk/information-centre/news/2018/oct/cornwall-council-leaves-homeless-teenager-in-a-tent accessed 3 November 2019.

[179] *Associated Provincial Picture Houses Ltd v Wednesbury Corporation* [1948] 1 KB 223, HL.

[180] [2013] EWHC 235 (Fam).

[181] [2017] EWHC 125 (Fam).

[182] See 8.6.3.

[183] For an unsuccessful example, see *Poole Borough Council (Respondent) v GN* [2019] UKSC 25.

Contact with a child in care

Once a child is in care, whether under an interim or 'final' order, contact is regulated not by s8 Children Act but by s34.[184] Remember that a s8 'spend time with' order cannot be made in respect of a child in care and that under s92(2) any existing order is automatically discharged by the making of a care order.

Section 34 imposes a statutory duty on the local authority to 'allow' the child to have 'a reasonable amount of contact' with his parents; any guardian or special guardian; any step-parent with parental responsibility; anyone who held a 'live with' order or with immediately prior to the care order; and anyone who had care of the child as a result of wardship. In reality, such contact is very likely to require facilitation by a social worker or the person with whom the child is living under the care order.

As the court must consider contact arrangements before making a care order (see 12.4.2), the local authority's contact proposals will form part of its care plan. If one of the individuals specified in s34 is unhappy with the level or nature of contact, then he or she may apply to court. Section 34 enables the court to 'make such order as it considers appropriate' which would include determining what contact would be reasonable in a particular case and imposing conditions where necessary. Any other person who wishes to make an application (grandparents, for example) will need prior leave.

As a result of amendments to s34 made by the Children and Families Act 2014, the court can also make an order specifically authorising the local authority to refuse contact. The local authority itself can only refuse contact for up to seven days before requiring a court order, and only where 'necessary to do so in order to safeguard or promote the child's welfare', where refusal must be decided as a matter of urgency.

Even where the plan is for adoption, contact can play an important role in help the child to come to terms with the loss of their usual carer and be reassured about that person's own well-being. This is discussed in more detail in 12.7.3. Where the local authority is considering rehabilitating the child to the birth family, contact is both important for the continuation of that relationship and for the birth parents to demonstrate their attachment to the child, and caring abilities.

Leaving care

Under s39 Children Act, the child, the local authority, or any person who has parental responsibility for the child can apply for the discharge of a care order. The applicant must demonstrate that there has been a significant change in circumstances since the care order was made. If this application is successful, it brings the care order to an end. In the first six months following the making of the care order, no application can be made without the court's leave, except by the child.[185]

The same individuals may also apply to substitute a supervision order for an existing care order. As the threshold is already met, the court does not have to re-hear the threshold (s39(5)), but will need to do so if the situation is reversed and the local authority is seeking a care order to replace a supervision order.

---

[184] Unless the application is by a child in care for contact with another child, in which case s8 applies but the applicant child will need prior leave.
[185] *Re A (Care: Discharge Application by Child)* [1995] 1 FLR 599.

An alternative method of achieving the same end is to apply for a private law 'live with' order under s8 Children Act. As this is incompatible with a care order, a successful order that the child lives with you would bring the care order to an end. If the child is adopted, the care order would also come to an end. This route would need to be used by a person who does not fall into the three categories described above. However, they may need leave to bring the application.[186]

If the order is not brought to an end prematurely then it lasts until the child turns 18 (s91(12)). Once the child reaches the age of 16, the local authority should begin to prepare the child to leave care upon him reaching 18. When he does leave care, the local authority has an obligation to 'advise, assist and befriend him with a view to promoting his welfare when they have ceased to look after him'.[187] These obligations can include practical and financial support as well as help planning the future. The precise nature of the local authority's obligations depends upon whether the child is 'an eligible child', a 'relevant child', a 'former relevant child' or a 'qualifying care leaver', categories which are discussed in more detail at 11.4.3 but which broadly relate to the length of time the child has been looked after by the local authority and whether they are still being looked after. Some support will last until the child reaches the age of 25.

Concern about the prospects facing children leaving care at 18 led to the introduction in the Children and Families Act 2014 of 'staying put' arrangements, under which the young people can continue to live with their foster carers after their 18th birthday (with the carers' permission) until they turn 21. About half of young people take advantage of this.[188] As adults, they are not, however, still subject to a care order and so are not classed as foster children. Staying put arrangements are discussed at 11.6.5.

12.4.7 A special guardianship order

A special guardianship application can be made either as a freestanding application or, more commonly, in care proceedings as an alternative to the child being subject to a care order.

Special guardianship was introduced by the Adoption and Children Act 2002 and the relevant provisions inserted as ss14A-F Children Act 1989. The preceding White Paper, *Adoption: A New Approach* had identified a category of children who needed stability and long-term care away from the birth parents, but for whom adoption was not in their best interests:

> Some older children do not wish to be legally separated from their birth families. Adoption may not be best for some children being cared for on a permanent basis by members of their wider birth family. Some minority ethnic communities have religious and cultural difficulties with adoption as it is set out in law.[189] Unaccompanied asylum-seeking children may also need secure, permanent homes, but have strong attachments to their families

---

[186] See sections 9 and 10 Children Act 1989.

[187] Children (Leaving Care) Act 2000 s1, amending Schedule 2 Part II para 19 of the Children Act 1989.

[188] Ofsted, *Fostering in England 2017 to 2018: Main Findings* (2019). 'Staying put' is called 'When I am Ready' in Wales.

[189] For example, in Islam, Kafala is Quaran-sanctioned a way to provide long-term care for children but without replacing the birth family. Adoption in the sense of the termination of parental status and transplant to another family is not recognised in Islam.

abroad. All these children deserve the same chance as any other to enjoy the benefits of a legally secure, stable permanent placement that promotes a supportive, lifelong relationship with their carers, where the court decides that is in their best interests.[190]

Special guardianship therefore aims 'to provide permanence short of the legal separation involved in adoption'. It can be thought of as falling somewhere between adoption and a child arrangements order. It gives more security than a child arrangements order, in that interference by third parties is restricted, and is similarly a form of private law order, but unlike adoption it does not does not involve the permanent termination of legal parenthood.

The effect of a special guardianship order

Under a special guardianship order, the child lives with the special guardianship and any existing care order or child arrangements order is terminated.[191] The special guardian acquires parental responsibility for the child, and, although the parents' PR is retained, s14C Children Act 1989 authorises the guardian to exercise their own parental responsibility to the exclusion of any other person with parental responsibility (save for a jointly appointed special guardian). The parental responsibility of the birth parents is thus 'effectively and largely neutered'.[192] 'In this respect, it is substantially different from a [live with] order which . . . does not confer on any person who holds the order the exclusivity in the exercise of parental responsibility which accompanies a special guardianship order.'[193] There are limitations to this, which are set out in s14C: the guardian cannot do anything contrary to any enactment or rule of law that requires the consent of all those with PR; cannot change the child's surname, remove him or her from the UK for more than three months, or consent to his adoption, and cannot consent to serious medical treatment. In each of these situations, either the consent of the court or of every person who has parental responsibility is needed, just as would be the case if there was no special guardianship order.

Despite these limitations, there is much less scope for interference by others in the child's life. Usually, parents can apply under as of right for a s8 order, even if the father has not acquired parental responsibility. However, where there is a special guardianship order, they cannot make an application for a 'live with' order, or to end the special guardianship, without the prior leave of the court: s10(7A) and 10(7B) Children Act 1989. Where prior leave is required, this is dealt with in the normal way and if the court thought that the parents were abusing this route, it could make a s91(14) order (see 10.7.4). Curiously, there is no leave requirement in respect of any other kind of s8 order, so if a parent was opposed to the actions of a special guardian exercising their parental responsibility on an issue that would be covered by a specific issues or prohibited steps application, the parent could apply to court without needing permission.

---

[190] Cm 5017, 2000. In *Re S (Adoption Order or Special Guardianship Order)* [2007] EWCA Civ 54, the Court of Appeal said, when referring to the examples given in the white paper, that 'It is important to emphasise that these are only illustrations. There can be no routine solutions.'
[191] *Re S (Adoption Order or Special Guardianship Order)* [2007] EWCA Civ 54.
[192] *Re S (Adoption Order or Special Guardianship Order)* [2007] EWCA Civ 54.
[193] *Birmingham City Council v LR and Others* [2006] EWCA Civ 1748.

Who can become a special guardian?

Any person over the age of 18 can apply to be a special guardian as long as they are not the parent of the child in question: s14A(2). Some people require prior leave to make the application and this would be dealt with in the same way as any other leave application in children proceedings. Those who do not require leave are:

- any foster carer or relative with whom the child has lived for the last year

- any guardian of the child or any person named in a child arrangements order as a person with whom the child is to live;

- any person listed in s10(5)(b) or (c) Children Act 1989: Any person with whom the child has lived for at least three of the last five years; if there is a 'live with' order already, any person who has the consent of the persons named in that order as the person(s) with whom the child lives; where there is a care order, any person who has the consent of the local authority; in any other case, anyone who has the consent of all of those who have parental responsibility.

Special guardianship orders can be made in favour of two people jointly, such as two grandparents, or aunt and uncle together.

Importantly, the court cannot make a special guardianship order unless:

1. There is an application for an order and the applicant has given three months' notice to the local authority of their intention to apply for that order as required by s14(7); or (if the parties agree that an application should be dispensed with[194]) the court considers that a special guardianship order should be made despite there being no application: s14(6)(b). (It follows that either there is no application at all, or there is three months' notice and then an application; it does not appear that a court can make an order on two months' notice in reliance on s14(6)(b)). The application should be made by the prospective special guardian(s) or the local authority on their behalf.

2. The court has before it a report on the suitability of the applicant to be a special guardian and any other matters prescribed by the relevant Secretary or State or considered relevant by the local authority. The court will usually direct that this report be prepared by the local authority. See ss14(9)-(11). There is no power to make the order without this report, although sometimes a prior report prepared for a previous purpose will satisfy this requirement.

These requirements mean that if there is a possibility of a special guardianship order being made, the court and local authority will need to identify this early in the proceedings.[195] This means that the local authority will need to identify prospective special guardians, assess them under pressure of time, and then propose them in the proceedings. The prospective guardians will not be eligible for legal aid, something that would help them advocate for their position and obtain a package of support from the local authority.

---

[194] *Re H (A Child) (Analysis of Realistic Options and SGOs)* [2015] EWCA Civ 406 per Ryder LJ at [26]: 'It is only where the parties agree that an application for a SGO should be dispensed with that the s14A(6)(b) Children Act 1989 power can be exercised without good reason. In any other case, the use by the court of this power must be reasoned.'

[195] See 12.4.1. Note a recent ruling that a special guardianship order can exist alongside a care order: *Re F and G (Discharge of Special Guardianship Order)* [2021] EWCA Civ 622.

The most frequent special guardians are people who had previously cared for the child as local authority foster carers (and who have the support of the local authority, although this is not required), followed by kinship carers such as the child's grandparents, aunts or uncles.

Because it does not involve the alteration of the legal relationships within a family, special guardianship is often preferred over adoption when the carers are related to the child, as familial ties remain intact and the child's sense of identity is preserved. *Re T (A Child: Refusal of Adoption Order)* is an unusual case in which the court preferred grandparent adoption over special guardianship, but the decision was tipped towards adoption by two things: the fact that the mother had been imprisoned for threats towards the grandmother, and there was therefore a real risk of future instability even with a special guardianship order, and the fact that the family's Black South African culture did not assign titles such as 'aunt' or 'grandmother' based on biology but on relationship function. This meant that the adoption would not alter the roles and titles that the child was used to.[196]

In this case, as in many others, the making of a special guardianship order involved the rejection of a placement with either parent (assuming they are alive and can be found). This can place kinship guardians in a very difficult position. Some special guardians may be relatives that have not been close to the child's family unit and therefore have little if any knowledge of the child.[197] Grandparents may have expected a more relaxed retirement with occasional visits to grandchildren rather than the work of everyday parenting, only to find themselves raising a child in later life. The wider family may have strong views about whether the special guardian should have placed themselves into a role which, in some cases, involves actively protecting the child against the birth parents.

When making a special guardianship order, the courts are required by s14B(1) to consider whether or not to make a child arrangements order addressing contact between the child and others, such as the birth parents, or whether to vary or end any existing s8 order. A very significant proportion of special guardians experience issues when facilitating contact between the child and the birth parents, including the birth parents' unreliability at attending contact, attempts by the birth parents to destabilise the arrangement, and the influence of drugs and alcohol.[198] As the Family Rights Group has said,

> Kinship carers will need to be able to manage any personal feelings of disapproval or anger about the child's parents, and protect the child from this. . . . the potential carer will need to be able to respect the child's relationship with their parent(s), allow them to enjoy a positive but realistic view of their parent(s) and avoid the child developing divided loyalties. At the same time, the carer will need to prioritise the safety of the child and comply with any safeguarding requirements that are formally stipulated by the local authority or the courts.[199]

[196] [2020] EWCA Civ 797.
[197] Public Law Working Group, *Recommendations to Achieve Best practice in the Child Protection and Family Justice Systems: Special guardianship Orders* (Family Justice Council 2020).
[198] J Harwin, B Alrouh, L Golding, T McQuarrie, K Broadhurst, and L Cusworth, *The Contribution of Supervision Orders and Special Guardianship to Children's Lives and Family Justice* (Lancaster University Centre for Child and Family Justice Research/Nuffield Foundation 2019) para 7.4.8.
[199] Family Rights Group, *Initial Family and Friends Care Assessment: A Good Practice Guide* (Family Rights Group 2017).

This complexity helps to explain why special guardianship orders are often coupled with supervision orders, because the latter enables the local authority to monitor the situation. Nevertheless, this coupling has been described by the Public Law Working Group chaired by Keenan J as 'a red flag. . . likely to signify a lack of confidence in the making of an SGO at that time'.[200] The risk of harmful parental interference is something for the court to consider at the welfare stage. If severe, the court may need to consider adoption instead.[201]

Ending a special guardianship

The circumstances in which a special guardianship order can be brought to an end are limited. The order will end naturally when the child reaches the age of 18 (unlike a residence order, which usually ends at 16), but otherwise it can only be terminated (a) if the child is made subject to a care order, (b) by the court of its own volition, which would normally happen in the course of other proceedings, or (c) if an application is made to end the special guardianship: s91(13). The court may vary or discharge a special guardianship order on the application of the special guardian (or any of them, if there are more than one); any parent or guardian of the child concerned; any one in whose favour there is a child arrangements 'live with' order; anyone who has parental responsibility for the child, or had it immediately before the making of the special guardianship order; the child him- or herself; the local authority if a care order is made; or the court of its own volition.[202]

The only person who can apply to end the special guardianship without prior leave is the guardian him or herself. Others, such as the parents, can apply with leave but they must demonstrate that there has been a significant change in circumstances since the special guardianship order was made[203] and that they have 'some realistic possibility of success'.[204] Although s24(3) refers to *significant* changes, Wilson LJ in *Re G* (2010)[205] held that the test was the same as for the revocation of a placement order (see 12.5.7) which does not require change to be significant. In *Re M* (2021) Peter Jackson LJ disagreed, holding that in this context significant (considerable, noteworthy, or important) change was essential. Even the child themselves will need prior permission from the court, which must grant leave if the child has sufficient understanding to participate as a party.[206] These restrictions help explain why special guardianship is associated with low rates of disruption (breakdown).

Local authority obligations towards special guardians

The local authority has a legal duty to provide support to special guardians, which it does not have in relation to private law s8 orders. Section 14F Children Act and the Special Guardianship Regulations 2005[207] require local authorities to provide 'special guardianship

---

[200] Public Law Working Group, *Recommendations to Achieve Best practice in the Child Protection and Family Justice Systems: Special guardianship Orders* (Family Justice Council 2020).

[201] *Re S (Adoption Order or Special Guardianship Order)* [2007] EWCA Civ 54.

[202] Section 14D. Note that it is not automatically ended by a care order: see *Re F and G (Discharge of Special Guardianship Order)* [2021] EWCA Civ 622.

[203] Section 14(d)(5).

[204] *Re F and R (Section 8 Order: Grandparents' Application)* [1995] 1 FLR 524.

[205] *Re G (A Child)* [2010] EWCA Civ 300; *Re M (Special Guardianship Order: Leave To Apply To Discharge)* [2021] EWCA Civ 442.

[206] Section 14D(4); see also 10.2.4.

[207] SI 2005/1109.

support services' under a special guardianship support plan. Services may include mediation, practical assistance, and therapy. Special guardians also receive an allowance from the authority, just as foster carers do, where the authority considers this necessary.[208] Amounts vary across different areas, but local authorities usually start with fostering rates and then vary downwards.[209] Children who were looked after immediately before the special guardianship order are also entitled to additional support from the Adoption Support Fund as part of local authorities' obligations towards former Looked After Children. All other things being equal, this can encourage potential carers to put themselves forward as potential special guardians in preference to a child arrangements order.

There is a postcode lottery of support. Guardians interviewed by Harwin et al. had a wide range of experiences of their local authority, from negative through to positive.[210] Some kinship carers are under terrible financial strain as a result of looking after multiple children in overcrowded accommodation.[211] Speaking to the World at One radio programme, former President of the Family Division Sir James Munby warned of the 'serious inadequacy of financial, professional and other support' for kinship carers 'in stark comparison to the support available to foster carers and adoptive parents'.[212] Generally, outcomes for children in kinship care are better than outcomes for children in local authority care, but less good than children in the general population, with higher reported rates of anxiety and depression, lower educational attainment and an increased chance of being in neither education or employment.[213] Masson found relatives can be 'reluctant to seek the support they need for fear of giving the impression that they lack commitment to the child' and encourage the local authority to prefer unrelated foster carers'.[214]

FOCUS Think Critically

Which option offers more stability?

You might come across the phrase 'permanence planning', which refers to finding an option for the child that provides them with 'a sense of security, continuity, commitment and identity . . . a secure, stable and loving family to support them through childhood and beyond'.[215]

In the 1960s, the psychologist John Bowlby developed 'attachment theory', the idea that young children have a strong biological imperative to bond to someone, usually their mother, so that that

---

[208] See Special Guardianship Regulations 2005, SI 2005/1109 at Reg 6.

[209] *R (TT) v London Borough of Merton* [2012] EWHC 2055 (Admin).

[210] J Harwin, B Alrouh, L Golding, T McQuarrie, K Broadhurst, and L Cusworth, *The Contribution of Supervision Orders and Special Guardianship to Children's Lives and Family Justice* (Lancaster University Centre for Child and Family Justice Research/Nuffield Foundation 2019) para 7.4.2.

[211] S Wellard, S Meakings, E Farmer, and J Hunt, *Growing Up in Kinship Care: Experiences as Adolescents and Outcomes in Young Adulthood* (Grandparents Plus/Paul Hamlyn Foundation 2017).

[212] Luke Jones, 'Take in your grandchildren or you won't see them again' (*BBC News* website 29 October 2019). Available at https://www.bbc.co.uk/news/education-50214031 accessed 29 October 2019.

[213] S Wellard, S Meakings, E Farmer, and J Hunt, *Growing Up in Kinship Care: Experiences as Adolescents and Outcomes in Young Adulthood* (Grandparents Plus/Paul Hamlyn Foundation 2017).

[214] J Masson, 'The State as Parent: The Reluctant Parent: The Problem of Parents of Last Resort?' (2008) 35(1) *Journal of Law and Society* 52.

[215] Department for Children, Schools and Families, *Children Act 1989 Guidance and Regulation* Volume 2 (The Stationery Office 2010).

person keeps them safe and meets their needs.[216] A child uses their attachment to a person as a safe base from which to explore their world. While there are various different theories surrounding attachment and in particular if and when a child can attach securely to more than one person, attachment theorists believe that this early attachment is key to the child's ability to build future relationships. When a child loses their primary caretaker, or if that person is incapable of meeting the child's needs, the child may experience long-term harm to their cognitive, social, and emotional development. This is the situation for some children entering care. Most foster children in Schofield and Beek's study, for example, had early lives that

> had been pervaded by experiences of loss and inadequate caregiving which had left them feeling unloved and unlovable. Care and interest shown by previous birth family caregivers had been sporadic, unpredictable, or conditional on particular behaviour or responses from the child. Family life had been frightening at times, and the tendency of young children to see themselves as having a magical responsibility for negative events had led some children to experience themselves as dangerous, bad, and worthy only of punishment.[217]

Going forward, children who have insecurely attached may develop defensive mechanisms that hinder the building of a relationship with alternative carers such as foster carers. Repeated changes of placement exacerbate such problems which, in turn, cause further placement breakdowns (including those triggered by the child forcing breakdown), creating a vicious circle. Dance and Rushton found that even children who are ultimately adopted experience, on average, 3.5 years in care before permanent placement and about half of these children had four or more moves.[218]

Stable placements—whatever legal structure the child is under—are important to enabling children to develop relationships with others. Children who experience many changes of placement—moving for example from a family home into foster care, and then multiple changes of foster care, and/or arrangements that break down—experience repeated loss and mistrust. McCarthy has identified three main consequences of frequent moves within care. These are:

1. 'Children are deprived of the opportunity to establish secure and enduring relationships with caregivers. Children coming into the care system often already have a very negative view of both close relationships and themselves, and frequent moves are further likely to reinforce these negative models of self and others.
2. When children move placement they often have to deal with a whole set of related events and issues. These include changing schools, losing contact with friends and acquaintances, moving to a new geographical area, moving home and making new relationships with carers. . . . many of these changes are often associated with increased levels of distress . . . For vulnerable children, many of whom lack supportive relationships, the impact of the events and experiences caused by moving placement are likely to be particularly difficult to deal with.
3. The impact on the emotional functioning of these children is likely to be severe, leading to an increasing sense of confusion, alienation, withdrawal and anger.'[219]

Biehal et al. found that high levels of placement instability correlates to later difficulties in employment, money management, housing, and social relationships.[220] Perhaps also due to instability, in

[216] J Bowlby, *Attachment and Loss* (Basic Books 1969).
[217] G Schofield and M Beek, 'Providing a Secure Base: Parenting Children in Long-Term Foster Family Care' (2005) 7(1) *Attachment & Human Development*, 3, 15.
[218] C Dance and A Rushton, 'Joining a New Family: The Views and Experiences of Young People Placed with Permanent Families during Middle Childhood' (2005) 29(1) *Adoption and Fostering* 18.
[219] Gerard McCarthy, 'The Developmental Histories of Children Who Experience High Levels of Placement Instability in the Care System' (2004) 28(4) *Adoption and Fostering* 60, 60.
[220] N Biehal, J Clayden, M Stein, and J Wade, *Moving On: Young People and Leaving Care Schemes* (HMSO 1995). See also ER Munro and A Hardy, *Placement Stability—A Review of the Literature* (Loughborough University 2007).

2014, only 12 per cent of Looked After Children achieved five or more GCSEs at grades A* to C (equivalent to 4-9 under the numeric grading system), compared with 52 per cent of children not looked after, although a higher than average proportion of children such have specific learning difficulties.[221] Children in care are four times more likely to suffer ill health even decades later compared to those growing up with their parents.[222] The Howard League for Penal Reform found that 'despite accounting for less than 1 per cent of the total population, a 2012/13 survey of 15- to 18-year-olds in young offender institutions found that a third of boys and 61 per cent of the girls surveyed reported being in local authority care at some point'.[223] However, this is not solely because of placement instability or the effect of the pre-proceedings home life. While challenging behaviours are relatively common in children in care, the Howard League points out that 'police were frequently being called to deal with incidents where children's homes could not cope with a child's disruptive behaviour and that they sought to use the police as a way to discipline children.' This results in children being criminalised for behaviour that, had the child lived at home, would be dealt with within the family.

The stability of a particular placement is thus relevant to the judge's consideration of which option will meet the child's welfare needs throughout his or her life, which is of course the welfare principle contained in the Adoption and Children Act 2002.

The court's decision as to the best option to achieve permanence for the child does not end the risks associated with placement moves, however. Selywn and Masson compared disruption rates for adoption, special guardianship orders and 'live with' orders. They found that in a 12-year period, 3.2 per cent of children returned to be looked after by the local authority after an adoption order was made. In comparison, the rate for special guardianship was 5.6 per cent over five years and child arrangements orders were 25 per cent over six years.[224] There was significant age variation: the most risky age for adoptive children was the teenage years and, given the average age of adoption was 4 years old, means that disruptions tend to happen some significant time after the adoption has happened. For the other two orders the riskier time was the first two years and the children tended to be aged under 11. Children placed with relatives or family friends were less likely to experience placement breakdown.

Harwin and Alrouh found that 20 per cent of cases in which a supervision order was made will return to court in the next five years because of concerns about significant harm, compared to 4 per cent for special guardianship orders and 7 per cent for special guardianship orders with an attached supervision order. While they note that 'It is unclear whether this reflects new events that occurred within the follow up period that could not be anticipated or whether the supervision order was overoptimistic or was poorly implemented post-proceedings,' that is a very high rate.[225] It implies that the order is not effective in helping to establish long-term good enough care. A different study found that when children remained with their parents under a supervision order, 22 per cent were the subject of further court proceedings in the next two years.[226]

[221] Department for Education, *Children Looked After in England Including Adoption: 2017 to 2018* (2018). See also J Sebba, D Berridge, N Luke, J Fletcher, K Bell, S Strand, S Thomas, I Sinclair and A O'Higgins, *The Educational Progress of Looked After Children in England: Linking Care and Educational Data* (Nuffield Foundation 2015).

[222] ET Murray, R Lacey, B Maughan, A Sacker, 'Non-Parental Care in Childhood and Health up to 30 Years Later: ONS Longitudinal Study 1971–2011' (2020) 30(6) *European Journal of Public Health* 1121.

[223] Howard League for Penal Reform, *Criminal Care: Children's Homes and Criminalising Children* (2016).

[224] J Selwyn and J Masson, 'Adoption, Special Guardianship and Residence Orders: A Comparison of Disruption Rates' [2014, December] *Family Law* 1709.

[225] J Harwin and B Alrouh, 'Supervision Orders and Special Guardianship: How Risky Are They? Findings from a National Study of Supervision Orders and Special Guardianship' [2017, May] *Family Law* 513.

[226] The figure was 31% over six years for children when the order was made 2009/10 and 22% over two years for children placed 2014/15. The Children and Families Act came into existence in the interim. See J Dickens, J Masson, L Garside, K Bader, and J Young, *Reforming Care Proceedings 2: Children's Outcomes* (University of East Anglia 2018).

12.4.8 Summary so far

- At the welfare stage, the court must determine what is the best way forward for the child, guided by the welfare principles and checklists in s1 Children Act 1989 and s1 Adoption and Children Act 2002.

- Potential options are that the child is returned to their birth family under a child arrangements order, supervision order, or no order; that the child is placed with friends and family (kinship) carers under a child arrangements order or special guardianship, often coupled with a supervision order; or that the child is adopted (see Figure 12.2).

- Each option is associated with different levels of stability and has different advantages and disadvantages. Each option also represents a different level of interference in family life.

12.4.9 An adoption order

The final option open to the courts is to make an adoption order. This is the most interventionist of them all, because it brings existing family life to an end and reconstitutes the child in a new family. In the next sections of this chapter, we deviate into a description of what adoption is, how the process of adoption works, and cases in which the parents' consent to adoption is not required. We will discuss how courts have attempted to reconcile child protection with the human rights of families.

We then resume our consideration of the welfare stage at which the court decides which of the options is best for the child in light of this discussion.

12.5 Adoption in depth

Section 41(6) Adoption and Children Act 2002 defines adoption as 'an order made by the court on an application under section 50 or 51 giving parental responsibility for a child to the adopters or adopter'. This definition, however, does not fully encapsulate the enormity of adoption, which involves the permanent severance of the legal ties between the child and his or her birth parents so that they are no longer parents and child, and the transplanting of the child into a new family. Under s67 of the 2002 Act, the adopted child is treated in law as being born to the adopters and no one else. 'It transfers a child from membership of one family into membership of another family, another dynasty, another future. There is no more important or deep form of order that can be made.'[227] It is not, therefore, simply a transference of parental responsibility: it is a transference of parenthood itself. It is a profound interference by the state in family life and as such has significant human rights implications. As Harris-Short says, 'through adoption the state is thus uniquely involved in the process of creating and destroying family life'.[228] As Theis J said in *ZH v HS & Ors (Application to Revoke Adoption Order)*, 'an adoption order is transformative for a child; it recasts in a lifelong way that child's status with his or her birth parents and the person(s)

---

[227] *Re K* [2015] EWHC 3921 Fam.
[228] S Harris-Short, 'Making and Breaking Family Life: Adoption, the State, and Human Rights' (2008) 35(1) *Journal of Law and Society* 28, 28.

that apply for such an order.'[229]

While we have so far discussed adoption as an outcome of care proceedings, that is not always the case. Intra-family adoptions, step-parent adoptions, and voluntary relinquishment of a baby all exist. However, most of these are outside the scope of this edition of the book, and we are going to primarily assume that the child is being considered for adoption as an outcome in care proceedings.

We will start our discussion of adoption by outlining who can be adopted.

12.5.1 Who can be adopted?

Only a child can be adopted, that is someone who is aged under 18 on the date of the adoption application. A child may be adopted as an adult if the application was made before their 18th birthday.[230] However, an adoption order cannot be made once the child turns 19, or if the child is or has been married or civilly partnered.

A child who has been adopted once can be adopted again: as a result of s67, the adoptive parents are in the place of the birth parents for the purposes of the care and adoption process. Thus if the local authority believes the child to be suffering or at risk of suffering significant harm in her adoptive family, it can bring care proceedings against the adoptive parents, and the potential outcomes of an application are exactly the same as if the child had been entering care for the first time.

12.5.2 Who can adopt?

The adopter (or both of them, if a couple) must be aged 21 or over. At least one of them must be domiciled in the British Islands and both must have been habitually resident for at least one year.[231] However, where one of the couple is the legal mother or father of a child to be adopted, they can adopt at 18 provided that their partner is at least 21.[232] If a person is adopting as an individual rather than as part of a couple, they cannot adopt if they are married, unless their spouse cannot be found, they are separated permanently, their spouse is incapable of making an application (as a result of ill health), or they are the partner of a birth parent.[233]

Prior to the 2002 Act, only a married couple could adopt a child. A person in an unmarried relationship would need to adopt the child by themselves and then delegate the exercise of their parental responsibility to their partner. Giving their partner parental responsibility addressed most of the practicalities of day-to-day parenting but was very different to being a legal adoptive parent, both legally and in terms of the way it may have felt to the parties. However, the 2002 Act widened the pool of adopters to encompass civil partners, single adopters, and unmarried couples (different-sex or same-sex) living

---

[229] [2019] EWHC 2190 (Fam).

[230] *FAS v Bradford MDC & the Secretary of State for the Home Office* [2015] EWHC 622 (Fam). See also s49(5) Adoption and Children Act 2002.

[231] Section 49 Adoption and Children Act 2002.

[232] Section 50

[233] Section 51.

as partners in an enduring family relationship. This was one of several measures designed to increase the number of adoptions.

The 2002 Act also changed the position of step-parents. It had been the case that in order for a step-parent to acquire parental responsibility for the child, they had to adopt the child, thereby ending the parent status of the existing parents. As adoption was then only available to married couples, the step-parent and whichever of the birth parents he was now married to would have to co-adopt the child. That would make the latter an adoptive parent even though they were a birth parent, and the other birth parent would no longer be a parent at all. The 2002 Act sensibly enabled step-parents to acquire parental responsibility without needing to adopt the child.[234]

12.5.3 Adoption agencies and the local authority

The Adoption and Children Act refers to adoption agencies. Adoption agencies work before, during, and after the adoption process. They find, evaluate, and approve prospective adopters. They assess the child's needs and then match him or her with suitable prospective adopters and provide support and guidance during the placement period. Once an adoption is made, they may provide ongoing support. Adoption agencies also provide support to parents who have lost their children to adoption, and can facilitate post-adoption contact.

Section 3 of the Adoption and Children Act 2002 requires all local authorities to have an adoption service. A case may segue from care proceedings to adoption, with the same body acting first as a local authority with child protection obligations, and second, as an adoption agency charged with finding permanent homes for children. There are also independent voluntary adoption agencies, registered and regulated by Ofsted, the Office for Standards in Education, Children's Services and Skills. Voluntary adoption agencies do not care for children directly, and often undertake work on behalf of local authorities. In the past there were a number of religious adoption agencies. Some of these closed when the number of people able to adopt was increased to encompass same-sex couples and single people, because of the requirement that they not discriminate.[235] Some have since become so-called adoption support agencies, helping those who were adopted and want to trace their birth parents, rather than undertaking statutory adoption tasks.

12.5.4 The adoption process

The adoption process involves several stages, which can be seen in Figure 12.3. First, the local authority must have persuaded the court to approve a care plan for adoption. Then, with its adoption agency hat on, it needs to match the child with prospective adopters, and then place the child with them. Finally, assuming the placement has been successful, it needs to obtain an adoption order. At each stage, it may face opposition from the birth

---

[234] It did this by inserting a new s4A into the Children Act 1989.

[235] See, e.g., Martin Beckford, 'Last Catholic Adoption Agency Faces Closure after Charity Commission Ruling: The last remaining Roman Catholic adoption agency to resist Labour's equality laws is facing closure, after the charity watchdog ruled that it could not avoid considering same-sex couples as potential parents' (*The Telegraph*, 19 August 2010).

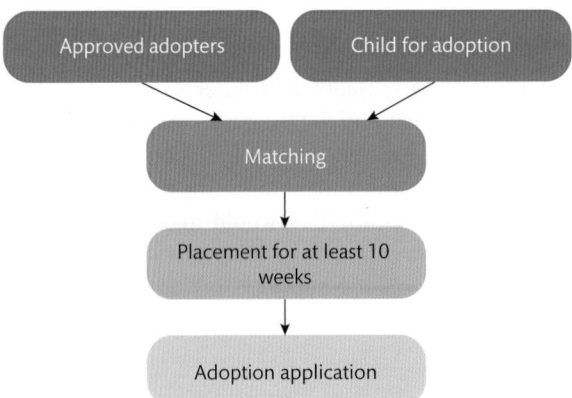

FIGURE 12.3 The adoption process

parents although, as we shall see, the law provides them with limited opportunities to reverse the process towards adoption.

It is common for the court to make a final care order, approve a plan for adoption, and make a placement order at the same hearing. That does not necessarily mean that the agency has matched the child with specific adopters already. The placement order enables them to place the child with any prospective adopters they select, and they may not have decided yet.

12.5.5 Matching

The process of being approved as a potential adopter is relatively rigorous and involves a detailed months-long assessment by the adoption agency, which will draw up a prospective adopter report. The report will be considered by an adoption panel. This is a quasi-independent group that makes recommendations to the adoption agency's decision-maker (sometimes known as the 'ADM'), about whether a child should be placed for adoption, the suitability of a particular person or couple to adopt a child, and the matching of a child to a prospective adopter. The ADM makes the ultimate decision.[236]

Once a person or couple are approved by the ADM as adopters, the next stage is to match them with a child or children. The agency will know the needs of each child: the issue is which approved adopters can meet those needs. It therefore involves 'fitting parents' strengths to the needs of children awaiting placement'.[237] The agency will identify suitable children in its area or may search a wider area. Some adopters are approved only for particular age groups, and some for sibling groups rather than individual children. In many local areas, the adoption agency arm of the local authority will be alerted to any care proceedings that are issued and become involved at an early stage in planning for the

---

[236] For more on the role of the ADM, see *London Borough of Bexley v Mr and Mrs B and Child A* [2020] EWFC B2.
[237] M Ward, 'Family Paradigms and Older-Child Adoption: A Proposal for Matching Parents' Strengths to Children's Needs' (1997) 46 *Family Relations* 257.

child.[238] Nevertheless, in the period 2017–2019, there was on average 171 days between the court authorising placement and the child being matched.[239]

It was previously the case—and still is the case in Wales—that adoption agencies 'must give due consideration to the child's religious persuasion, racial origin and cultural and linguistic background' when trying to find a placement. In 2014, the coalition government, via the Children and Families Act, abolished this requirement for England.[240] This was the result of concern at the lower rates of adoption for Black and mixed ethnicity children, who are already disproportionately represented in the number of Looked After Children, and the fact that such children take on average a year longer to be adopted. Lower adoption rates may be partly attributable to the fact that such children are more likely to be older on entering care than non-Black and mixed ethnicity children, and age significantly affects adoption prospects.[241] It may also be the case that social workers are holding out for adopters who perfectly match the child's heritage:

> the belief persists that ensuring a perfect or near perfect match based on the child's ethnicity is necessarily in the child's best interests, and automatically outweighs other considerations, such as the need to find long-term stability for the child quickly. In Professor Elaine Farmer's study for the Adoption Research Initiative, attempts to find families of similar ethnicity were a cause of delay for 70% of the black and minority ethnic children who experienced delay. Ethnicity encompasses not only race, but also cultural, religious and linguistic background. A study by Dr Julie Selwyn found that children's profiles often included the specific requirement for the prospective adoptive parents to match the child's ethnicity, with "same-race" placements dominating the Child Permanence Report over and above other needs. This study also found that some social workers were so pessimistic about finding ethnically matched adopters that there was little family finding activity. Consequently many minority ethnic children had their plan changed away from adoption.[242]

In an attempt to increase the number of adoptions, some local authorities have held adoption parties or activity days. The aim of these types of social event is to enable a number of approved prospective adopters to meet a number of children who are waiting to be placed, to see if any connections are made. The reality is that older children and children with disabilities are much harder to place. For such children, there may need to be an alternative plan of long-term fostering if an adoptive match cannot be found. However, some local authorities will compromise in order to pursue a less than ideal adoptive match. Farmer and Dance found that while 73 per cent of the matches they studied were good matches ('of course this was much easier to achieve for very young children without additional needs'), 14 per cent involved 'some compromise which was outweighed by other positive factors, whilst 13 per cent involved serious compromise on either the matching requirements or

---

[238] Coram BAAF, *Adoption Matching Practice Guide* (Coram 2016).

[239] Department for Education, *Children Looked After in England Including Adoption: 2017 to 2018* (2018).

[240] Section 3 of the 2014 Act amends s1(5) Adoption and Children Act 2002.

[241] C Owen and J Statham, *Disproportionality in Child Welfare: The Prevalence of Black and Minority Ethnic Children within 'Looked After' and 'Children in Need' Populations and on Child Protection Registers in England*. Research Report DCSF-RR124 (Department for Children, Schools and Families 2009).

[242] Department for Education, *An Action Plan for Adoption: Tackling Delay in England and Wales* (2012), citing E Farmer at al., *An Investigation of Family Finding and Matching in Adoption*, research report DfE-RBX-10-05 (Department for Education 2010), and J Selwyn et al., *Pathways to Permanence for Black, Asian and Mixed Ethnicity Children* (British Association for Adoption and Fostering 2010).

on adopters' preferences. . . . The more complex the children's needs, the greater the likelihood that some compromise would be needed.'[243]

12.5.6 Fostering for adoption

Some local authorities operate 'fostering for adoption' arrangements in which a (usually very young) child is fostered by people who are approved foster carers and intend to adopt him. Fostering for adoption was introduced by the Children and Families Act 2014 as a way of mitigating the effect of the child becoming settled with foster carers only to have the disruption of moving to different prospective adopters.[244] As Kotilaine has written, it prioritises placement with fostering for adopters over non-adoptive foster carers, trumping 'other considerations that would otherwise apply . . . such as proximity to the child's home, disruption of the child's education or training, placement with siblings, disability needs (if any).'[245] A placement that is designed to assure stability therefore comes at a price, which may be a change of school, leaving friends and potentially siblings, and limited contact with the birth family for reasons of distance.[246] Once the child is with the prospective adopters, they will stay there through the various changes in status from foster care, to placement, to adopted child. As you can imagine, it is also extremely problematic if the court does not then approve a plan for adoption because strong attachments will have formed on the assumption that adoption would occur.

SCENARIO 1

Illustration 6

In Ella's case, the court has found that the local authority has proven its case and that the threshold has been reached for the making of a care and supervision order. The court has turned to the welfare stage at which it considers the options.

Ella is only 18 months old. Long-term fostering is not likely to meet a child's needs for the reasons given by Pauffley J in *Re LRP (Care Proceedings: Placement Order)*, discussed in 12.4.4. No kinship carers have been assessed as suitable; if there had been, then a child arrangements order or special guardianship order could have been made in their favour. The court is faced with a choice:

1. Return Kerrie to her mother, perhaps with a supervision order to support that. As Mike supports Kerrie's position that Ella should live with her, there is no need to make a special guardianship order or a child arrangements 'live with' order in Kerrie's favour, (although a 'spend time with' order may be needed to regulate Mike's contact with Ella, which might need to be supervised). The issue with returning Ella to Kerrie is whether she can learn to offer good enough care, and do so within the timescales of the child (see 12.4.2).

---

[243] Elaine Farmer and Cherilyn Dance, 'Family Finding and Matching in Adoption: What Helps to Make a Good Match?' (2016) 46(4) *British Journal of Social Work* 974.

[244] The Welsh scheme is called 'Foster to adopt' and falls under the Social Services and Well-Being (Wales) Act 2014.

[245] Jennifer Kotilaine, 'Children and Families Act 2014 – A Guide for Public Children Lawyers' (*Family Law Week* 17 April 2014).

[246] Jennifer Kotilaine, 'Children and Families Act 2014 – A Guide for Public Children Lawyers' (*Family Law Week* 17 April 2014).

2. Approve the local authority's plan for adoption. If Ella is in a 'fostering for adoption' situation then the intention will be for her to be adopted by the people currently caring for her under a care order. It is highly likely that at the same hearing at which the court decides the threshold is met, the local authority will ask the court to approve its plan for adoption and immediately make a placement order.

12.5.7 Placement

Placement is when the adoption agency places the child in the home of someone it has assessed as suitable to eventually adopt the child. In *Re S-H (A Child)*, the Court of Appeal noted that 'The necessary foundation for a placement order is that, broadly speaking, the child is presently in a condition to be adopted and is ready to be adopted'.[247] If the child is not ready to be adopted, perhaps because they need some therapeutic work first, then placement should wait.

Placement can occur either:

- with the consent of all those with parental responsibility (s19); or
- because the court has made a placement order (s21).

In some circumstances, set out in s22, the local authority is legally required to apply to court for a placement order.

Because placement has specific consequences, it is important to note when placement starts. It is not on the giving of consent or the making of the order, but when the child moves to live with the prospective adopters in their capacity as prospective adopters.[248] In a fostering-for-adoption arrangement, the child will already be living with people who hope to adopt him, but this will be in their capacity as foster carers. The placement will start once the agency recognises the child as staying with them by virtue of them being the child's prospective adopters.[249]

Placement by parental consent under s19

Those parents (or guardians[250]) with parental responsibility may consent to placement. Such consent must be unconditional. The consent may relate either to specified adopters or to any prospective adopters chosen by the agency in the future. A parent can withdraw their consent up to the point at which an application for an adoption order is made. If they do this, the local authority will need to seek a placement order within 14 days or must return the child.[251] Once an adoption application is made, it is too late to withdraw consent.

---

[247] *Re S-H (A Child) sub nom NS-H v Kingston upon Hull City Council and MC* [2008] 2 FLR 918 (CA).
[248] *Coventry City Council v O (Adoption)* [2011] 2 FLR 936.
[249] *Coventry City Council v O (Adoption)* [2011] 2 FLR 936.
[250] The term 'guardian' is defined in s 144 Adoption and Children Act 2002 as having the same meaning as in the Children Act 1989, in which s105(1) defines 'guardian of a child' as meaning a guardian appointed under s5. It includes a special guardian. From this point on, we will just refer to parents, but note that guardians have PR and are in the same position: their consent is needed.
[251] Sections 30–33 Adoption and Children Act 2002.

At the same time that they consent to placement, a parent may consent to the future making of an adoption order. This means that it will not be necessary to contact the birth parents at the time that an adoption order is being applied for; indeed the birth parents can elect not to be further involved. Although under s18 a child under the age of 6 weeks can be *placed* with written parental consent, under s52(3) the birth mother cannot provide consent to the *adoption* itself until the child reaches 6 weeks of age. Once the child is 6 weeks old, she should be then asked to sign a new consent under s19.

Consent to placement becomes relevant to one of the tests for making an adoption order—the first condition in s47 (see 12.5.9). Note that consent to placement given fewer than six weeks post-birth cannot be used for that purpose.[252]

Who is a parent for the purpose of consent?

Note that s52(6) defines 'parent' only as a parent with parental responsibility. The consent of a parent without parental responsibility—such as a father not married to the child's mother—is not needed. Some couples will give the father status in the proceedings by entering into a parental responsibility agreement.[253] However, s52(9) and (10) state that if the child has been placed with the consent of the mother and the father later acquires parental responsibility, he is treated as having consented at the same time as the mother and in the same terms. This means that any refusal by him to consent to the placement and adoption is ineffective.

Placement by order under s21

If not all of the parents or guardians with parental responsibility consent, the local authority must obtain a placement order. This is a court order that authorises the local authority to place a child for adoption with any prospective adopters of the authority's choice.

Under s21 Adoption and Children Act 2002, the court cannot make a placement order unless three elements are satisfied:

1. the child must be either under a care order, or the court must be satisfied that the care threshold is passed, or the child has no parent or guardian; and

2. there must be consent from those with parental responsibility (or they did consent and have not withdrawn it), or the court has chosen to dispense with that consent; and

3. it must be in the child's best interests to make the order. The relevant welfare principle is that found in the Adoption and Children Act 2002, i.e., the child's welfare 'throughout his life'.

Thus the court can choose to dispense with the requirement of parental consent to the placement. Under s52, the court can dispense with the parents' consent to placement *only if* the parent or guardian cannot be found or lacks capacity to give consent; or the welfare of the child requires the consent to be dispensed with. The meaning of this latter phrase, 'the welfare of the child requires the consent to be dispensed with', is crucially important and discussed in a number of Key Cases. These are considered in section 12.5.10, on

---

[252] *Re C (A Child) (Adoption: Parental Consent)* [2009] Fam. 83.
[253] As in *Re X (Children) (Care Proceedings: Parental Responsibility)* [2000] Fam 156.

dispensing with parental consent to adoption. This is because the phrase has the same meaning at both placement and adoption stages.

SCENARIO 1

Illustration 7

Given that Kerrie and Mike do not want Ella to be adopted, the chances are that they are not prepared to consent to placement, and the local authority will then have to apply for a placement order. (As both have parental responsibility, both will need to consent.) If Ella is living with potential adopters under a fostering for adoption arrangement, once a placement order is made the status changes from one of fostering to one of placement. Alternatively, she may be living with short-term foster carers and the local authority may begin (or may have already begun) a search for suitable adopters with whom they can place her pursuant to a placement order.

In order to make a placement order, there are three elements that must be passed. In this case, Ella is under a care order and there is no parental consent, so the court will need to dispense with that consent and be satisfied that it is in Ella's best interests to make the placement order.

The court can only dispense with parental consent to placement where the welfare of the child throughout her life *requires it*. The welfare of the child requires parental consent to be dispensed with only when adoption is necessary—when, in the words of the Supreme Court in *Re B* (2013) 'nothing else will do'. This is discussed further in section 12.5.10.

The effect of a placement order

The placement order gives the prospective adopters parental responsibility for the child, but they will share this with the local authority and the birth parents. As a consequence, a placement order is incompatible with certain types of order. While a care order still exists, it has no effect during the period in which a placement order is in force. Any existing supervision order or s8 order ceases to have effect and the court cannot make a prohibited steps or specific issues order, supervision order, or child assessment order. An applicant will need leave to apply for a 'live with' (residence) order or a special guardianship order. The effect of making a 'live with' order or special guardianship order in respect of a placed child would be to bring that placement to an end. While the court can make a 'spend time with' order (for example, to replace any s8 or s34 order that has ceased to have effect), this would be pursuant to s26 Adoption and Children Act 2002.

The adoption agency can bring the placement to an end on seven days' notice to the prospective adopters, and must notify the birth parents that the placement has been unsuccessful.[254] This situation is known as 'adoption disruption'. However, if there is an outstanding adoption, special guardianship or live with order application, or an application for leave to apply, then the prospective adopter is not required to return the child unless a court orders them to do so. In *RY v Southend Borough Council*, the prospective adopter, RY, applied for an adoption order in respect of a child placed with her. The adoption agency, Southend Borough Council, then served notice to end the placement on the basis that the prospective adopter was not meeting the child's medical needs and obstructing her medical

---

[254] Section 35(2) Adoption and Children Act 2002.

care. The court held that the placement should only be brought to an end if the child was thought to be suffering harm, as this reflected the Article 8 family life that existed between prospective adopter and child.[255] Similarly, in *RCW v A Local Authority*, a placement order was made in favour of a young woman who, during the placement, went blind as a consequence of surgery for a brain tumour.[256] The local authority terminated the placement after meeting with her on the day she left hospital. Cobb J granted an urgent injunction under s7 Human Rights Act 1998,[257] holding that 'a decision to remove a child who has been placed with prospective adopters is a momentous one. It has to be a solidly welfare-based decision, and it must be reached fairly.' In this case, it had not been reached fairly.

Apart from this, once a placement order is made, it remains in force until either the child turns 18, marries or enters into a civil partnership, is adopted, or the placement order is revoked under s24. An application for an adoption order can be made once the placement has lasted for at least ten weeks.

Challenging a placement order

There are two routes to challenging the making of a placement order. First, it is possible to appeal the making of the order. There are strict time limits, as is the case with all appeals, and it will be necessary to show that the judge was 'wrong' to make the placement order. This is discussed further at 12.7.1.

Second, any person can apply under s24 Adoption and Children Act 2002 for the placement order to be revoked, as long as the child has not yet been placed. Once the child is placed, the next opportunity to challenge the process is to seek to oppose the adoption order at the later point at which the prospective adopters make their adoption application. This means that any application for revocation has to be made between making of a placement order and the actual placement, which may be a very narrow window if the prospective adopters are already identified and even more so if the child is already living with them under a 'fostering for adoption' arrangement. A child cannot be placed once a revocation application has been made but not yet determined, so the effect is to halt the placement process while the revocation application is heard.

To make a revocation application, an applicant other than the child or the adoption agency will need to first obtain leave from the court. The most likely applicant is, of course, a birth parent or parents who do not want their child to be adopted. The court cannot give permission to make the application unless they can show on the balance of probabilities that there has been a change in their own or the child's circumstances[258] since the placement order was made (s24(3)). If there has not, the application for revocation fails. The change in circumstances does not have to be 'significant', but must 'be of a nature and degree sufficient, on the facts of the particular case, to open the door to the exercise of the judicial discretion' as to whether leave to apply should be given'.[259] The Court of

---

[255] On the facts, the judge addressed significant harm even though he thought that significant was not required and that in this context was illusory: see [2015] EWHC 2509.

[256] [2013] EWHC 235 (Fam).

[257] This is injunctive relief against a public authority seeking to act unlawfully in breaching someone's human rights.

[258] Re G (A Child) [2015] EWCA Civ 119.

[259] *Re P (A Child) (Adoption Order: Leave to Oppose Making of Adoption Order)* [2007] EWCA Civ 616 [30] (Wall LJ).

Appeal cautioned in Key Case *Re P (A Child) (Adoption Order: Leave to Oppose Making of Adoption Order)* that the test 'should not be set too high, because parents should not be discouraged from bettering themselves or from seeking to prevent the adoption of their child by the imposition of a test that is unachievable'.[260]

If there has been a change in circumstances, the court must then go on, as a second stage, to consider whether 'in all the circumstances, including the [parents'] prospect of success in securing revocation of the placement order and [the child's] interests, leave should be given'.[261] Note that the prospects of success relate to the application to revoke the placement order, not the decision that the child should be adopted: a successful application does not mean the child automatically returns to live with their birth parents.[262] Leave may still be granted even if there is no prospect of the parents being able to resume care.[263]

In *M v Warwickshire County Council*, Wilson LJ said:

> In relation to an application for leave under s.24(3) of the Act I therefore hold that, on establishment of a change in circumstances, a discretion arises in which the welfare of the child and the prospect of success should both be weighed. My view is that the requisite analysis of the prospect of success will almost always include the requisite analysis of the welfare of the child. For, were there to be a real prospect that an applicant would persuade the court that a child's welfare would best be served by revocation of the placement order, it would surely almost always serve the child's welfare for the applicant to be given leave to seek to do so. Conversely, were there not to be any such real prospect, it is hard to conceive that it would serve the welfare of the child for the application for leave to be granted.[264]

Note that at this second stage the child's welfare is relevant as Wilson LJ says, but rather unusually it is not the court's paramount consideration.[265] Compare this to an application for leave to oppose an adoption order (discussed at 12.5.11 of this chapter), where the Adoption and Children Act's welfare principle *does apply* to render the child's welfare the paramount consideration.[266]

12.5.8 Applying for an adoption order

Under s42 Adoption and Children Act 2002, the child must live with the prospective adopters under a placement order for a prescribed period of time before the prospective adopters can apply for an adoption order. The periods are set out in Table 12.3.

During this period, the adoption agency will need to ensure that it has had sufficient opportunities to see the child with the applicants in their home, because the court cannot make an adoption order unless it is satisfied that this has happened (s42). The agency will

---

[260] *Re P (A Child) (Adoption Order: Leave to Oppose Making of Adoption Order)* [2007] EWCA Civ 616 [32] (Wall LJ).
[261] *Re S-H (A Child) sub nom NS-H v Kingston upon Hull City Council and MC* [2008] 2 FLR 918 (CA) [27], cited with approval by the Court of Appeal in *Re B-S*.
[262] *Re G (A Child)* [2010] EWCA Civ 300.
[263] *Re S-H (A Child) sub nom NS-H v Kingston upon Hull City Council and MC* [2008] 2 FLR 918 (CA).
[264] [2007] EWCA Civ 1084 [29] (Wilson LJ).
[265] *M v Warwickshire County Council* [2007] EWCA Civ 1084.
[266] 'It is as clear that s.1 of the Act does not apply to an application for leave to apply to revoke a placement order under s.24(2) as it is that it does apply to an application for leave to oppose the making of an adoption order under s.47(5)': *M v Warwickshire County Council* [2007] EWCA Civ 1084 [22] (Wilson LJ).

TABLE 12.3 Periods of living with prospective adopters before adoption application can be made

Status of adopters	Child must have had his home with the applicant (or one of them if a couple) at all times for . . .
Child placed by an adoption agency or under a court order	10 weeks preceding the application
Applicant for adoption (or one of them) is a parent of the child	10 weeks preceding the application
Applicant for adoption (or one of them) is the partner of one of the child's birth parents	6 months preceding the application
Local authority foster parents	1 year preceding the application, but the court can shorten this
Everyone else	3 out of the last 5 years (whether continuous or not), and court can shorten

also need to submit a report to the court that addresses the suitability of the applicants to adopt the child by reference to the welfare checklist in the Adoption and Children Act 2002.

In the case of a non-agency adoption, s44 requires that the prospective adopters must give notice of their intention to adopt to the local authority not more than two years or less than three months before the application is made for the adoption order. This is to enable the local authority to prepare a similar report. Where a person needs leave to apply for an adoption order because the child has not lived with them for the requisite period, they cannot give notice of intention to adopt before they obtain that leave.

12.5.9 Making an adoption order

An adoption order may not be made if the child has a parent or guardian unless *one* of the conditions set out in s47(1) Adoption and Children Act 2002 is met.

STATUTORY EXTRACT *s47 Adoption and Children Act 2002*

(2) The first condition is that, in the case of each parent or guardian of the child, the court is satisfied—

   (a) that the parent or guardian consents to the making of the adoption order, [or]

   (b) that the parent or guardian has consented under section 2020[267] [advance consent to adoption given at the same time as consent to placement] (and has not withdrawn the consent) and does not oppose the making of the adoption order, or

   (c) that the parent's or guardian's consent should be dispensed with. . . .

---

[267] Adoption and Children Act 2002, not to be confused with voluntary accommodation under s20 Children Act 1989. Section 20 of the 2002 Act involves a parent giving advance consent to adoption at the same time that they give consent to placement.

(4) The second condition is that—

    (a) the child has been placed for adoption by an adoption agency with the prospective adopters in whose favour the order is proposed to be made, [and]

    (b) either—

        (i) the child was placed for adoption with the consent of each parent or guardian and the consent of the mother was given when the child was at least six weeks old,[268] or

        (ii) the child was placed for adoption under a placement order, and

    (c) no parent or guardian opposes the making of the adoption order.

Remember that only one of these conditions needs to be met.

Consider:

- Does the parent/guardian actually consent to the making of an adoption order? If so, the first condition is satisfied and an adoption order can be made.

- Even if the parents/guardian do not consent to the adoption now, did they give their consent to the adoption at the same time they gave consent to placement? If so, then:

  - Did they withdraw that consent to adoption *before* the application for an adoption order was made? Withdrawal of consent after an adoption application is made is ineffective: s52(4). If they did withdraw that consent, the court will need to consider limb (c), dispensing with the requirement of parental consent.

  - If they did not withdraw that consent (at all, or in time), the court can still make an adoption order *as long as they do not oppose the adoption*. As we see below, a parent will be treated as not opposing the order unless they obtain the court's permission to oppose the order.

- Where they have never consented to adoption and still do not consent, then under the first condition adoption can only take place if the court is prepared to dispense with the requirement that they consent.

- Under the second condition, the court can make an adoption order if there was a placement order and the parent does not have leave to oppose the adoption order. However, remember that the court will only have made a placement order in the face of a parent's refusal to consent if it has decided that the parents' consent can be dispensed with.

We therefore come to three concepts that need further explanations: Whose consent is needed? What does it mean to oppose an adoption application? and What does it mean to dispense with parental consent to adoption?

12.5.10 Consenting to adoption

Section 52(5) defines consent as 'consent given unconditionally and with full understanding of what is involved; but a person may consent to adoption without knowing the identity of the persons in whose favour the order will be made.'

As with consent to placement, the consent that we need is from those with parental responsibility. This includes a mother who is herself a minor, provided that she has sufficient

---

[268] If the mother's only consent was given when the child was less than 6 weeks old, this does not count as consent for these purposes.

understanding of the decision she is making; in other words where she is 'Gillick-competent' (see Chapter 9). In the context of adoption, this includes understanding that she will cease to be the child's parent, that adoption is irreversible, and that she will have no right to see the child again.[269] Where she is unable to consent, the court will need to dispense with the requirement that she consent.

The consent of a parent without parental responsibility, such as some fathers not married to the mothers who are not named on the child's birth certificate, is not required. Section 52 states that if the child was placed with the consent of the mother, and the father later acquires parental responsibility, he is treated as having consented to that placement at the same time as the mother did. There are cases where the court has given leave to dispense with service of the proceedings on the father so that he has no knowledge of them at all, whether or not he has PR.[270] In *A & B v P Council* Theis J held that the court had power under its inherent jurisdiction to grant exception from the FPR 2010 requirements to notify the father, and consequently could give notice of an adoption application to a father who did not hold parental responsibility and equally decide not to give such notice to a father who did hold parental responsibility. We have discussed non-notification of care proceedings at 12.2.3 in the box *Focus: Know-How: Notification of fathers*, and the same approach applies for adoption.

12.5.11 Opposing the adoption application

A parent or guardian may be against the adoption with every fibre of their being, but s47(3) and (5) (governing the first and second conditions respectively) states that they will be treated as not opposing it unless they have the court's permission (leave) to oppose it. To get leave they must show that there has been a change in circumstances since the consent of the parent or guardian was given or the placement order was made.

If a parent successfully gets leave to oppose, the effect is that the court will need to apply the first condition to be able to make an adoption order. (The second condition is only available in circumstances in which no parent or guardian opposes the adoption order.)

You may remember that the first condition has three limbs, two of which relate to parental consent. The third limb is the only one now available. The court can only proceed if the consent of the parents or guardians can be dispensed with. It can only dispense with their consent if the child's welfare requires that they do so. This is shown in Figure 12.4.

FIGURE 12.4 Obtaining leave to oppose an adoption order

[269] *Re S (Child as Parent: Adoption: Consent)* [2017] EWHC 2729 (Fam).
[270] For example, *A & B v P Council* sub nom *Re M (Notification of Step-Parent Adoption)* [2014] EWHC 1128 (Fam).

In Key Case *Re B-S*, Munby P described the 'crucial' effect of a parent being given leave to oppose an adoption application under 47(5):

> not merely is the parent able to oppose the making of an adoption order, but the parent, notwithstanding the making of the earlier placement order, is entitled to have the question of whether parental consent should be dispensed with considered afresh and, crucially, considered in the light of current circumstances (which may, as in the present case, be astonishingly different from those when the placement order was made).[271]

Thus the final adoption hearing will be contested, and the parents/guardian will be able to make arguments as to why the adoption order should not be made. It is about the opportunity to oppose, not about ultimate success: the court may still make the adoption order by dispensing with the requirement that the parents consent, after hearing from all parties.

What change in circumstances is sufficient to obtain leave?

The court takes the same approach to a change in circumstances at this stage as it would take on an application to revoke a placement order, so that the court considers first whether there has been a change in circumstances. This is likely to be 'an unexpected change in the basic facts and expectations on which the court relied when it made the placement order'.[272]

Second, if there has been a change in circumstances, the court then considers whether it should grant leave, with this stage involving consideration of the child's welfare and the parents' prospect of success if they argue the case at the final hearing. There is therefore a two-stage process:

1.   Has there been a change in circumstances? If not, no leave can be granted.

2.   If yes, should leave to oppose be given?

In answering the second question, the welfare of the child needs to be considered, However, there is one crucial difference between considering a change of circumstances when hearing an application to revoke a placement order, and considering a change of circumstances one step further on, when the court is considering whether to make an adoption order. In this latter stage, unlike placement, the child's welfare throughout his life is the court's paramount consideration, and the court will need to consider the welfare checklist found in s1 Adoption and Children Act 2002.

The Key Case is *Re P (A Child) (Adoption Order: Leave to Oppose Making of Adoption Order)*.

KEY CASE *Re P (A Child) (Adoption Order: Leave to Oppose Making of Adoption Order)* [2007] EWCA Civ 616

The parents had a highly volatile relationship that included drug use and violence. The child, P, was made the subject of a care order with a plan for adoption and placed with prospective adopters. The parents had another baby and a residential assessment of their capacity to look after that baby

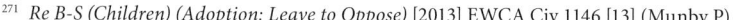

[271] *Re B-S (Children) (Adoption: Leave to Oppose)* [2013] EWCA Civ 1146 [13] (Munby P).
[272] *Re SSM (A Child)* [2015] EWHC 327 [16] (Fam) Mostyn J.

had been positive. The father had also successfully resumed contact with his two children from a previous relationship. They applied for leave to oppose P's adoption on the basis that the change in circumstances was that they had addressed all of the social workers' concerns. Wall LJ refused the appeal and gave the judgment of the court.

- '[T]he judicial decision whether or not to give leave to a parent to defend adoption proceedings under section 47(5) is 'a decision relating to the adoption of a child' and that, accordingly, it is governed by section 1 of the 2002 Act. . . .
- First of all, the court has to be satisfied, on the facts of the case, that there has been a change in circumstances within section 47(7). If there has been no change in circumstances, that is the end of the matter, and the application fails. If, however, there has been a change in circumstances within section 47(7) then the door to the exercise of a judicial discretion to permit the parents to defend the adoption proceedings is opened, and the decision whether or not to grant leave is governed by section 1 of the 2002 Act. In other words, 'the paramount consideration of the court must be the child's welfare, throughout his life'.
- . . . a change in circumstances can embrace a wide range of different factual situations. Section 47(7) does not relate the change to the circumstances of the parents. The only limiting factor is that it must be a change in circumstances 'since the placement order was made'. . . .
- the test should not be set too high, because . . . parents . . . should not be discouraged either from bettering themselves or from seeking to prevent the adoption of their child by the imposition of a test which is unachievable. We therefore take the view that whether or not there has been a relevant change in circumstances must be a matter of fact to be decided by the good sense and sound judgment of the tribunal hearing the application.'

In considering the child's best interests, the Adoption and Children Act checklist requires the court to consider factors such as:

- the likely effect on the child (throughout his life) of having ceased to be a member of the original family and become an adopted person;
- the relationship which the child has with relatives, with any person who is a prospective adopter with whom the child is placed, and with any other person in relation to whom the court or agency considers the relationship to be relevant;
- the likelihood of any such relationship continuing and the value to the child of its doing so; and
- the ability and willingness of any of the child's relatives, or of any such person, to provide the child with a secure environment in which the child can develop, and otherwise to meet the child's needs.

(Note that there is a comparison between this checklist and that of the Children Act at Table 12.1.)

In *Re W (A Child: Leave to Oppose Adoption)*, Peter Jackson LJ described the purpose of the leave requirement as being to prevent courts being asked to revisit issues that were determined when the placement order was made with its accordant delay to the child's life and the potential instability that may cause.[273] Although *Re P* tells us that the hurdle as to whether there has been a change in circumstances should not be set too high, the reality is

---

[273] [2020] EWCA Civ 16.

that by this point in time, the child may have lived with potential adopters for some time and thus what the parents are requesting is to 'reverse the direction in which the child's life has travelled since the inception of the original public law care proceedings.'[274]

The paramountcy of the child's welfare therefore means that the parent may fail to obtain leave to oppose despite being able to demonstrate a change in circumstances. As Munby P said in *Re B-S*, 'one can well see why the parent's prospects must be more than just fanciful and must be solid—for how otherwise can it be consistent with the child's welfare to allow matters to be reopened?'[275] As Coleridge J expressed it in another case called *Re W*:

> No one can have anything but the profoundest sympathy for this mother who seems to have turned her life round in the course of the last two years and to have conquered her addiction to hard drugs. If the court was in the business of rewarding parents for effort in these circumstances no doubt, she would succeed . . . However, whilst she has been sorting out her life, her child's life has inevitably moved on in her absence. He has not seen her for three years and is now completely embedded in his new family. To unravel the whole process through which the child and the adopters have passed since the child's original removal and placement is quite simply a horrendous prospect both from the point of view of the adopters but more importantly the child himself. It seems to me that it is 'entirely improbable' . . . that the mother would in the end succeed in overturning the adoption order much less the overall plan for adoption so that the child would return to live with her. Even to embark on the process cannot be in his best interests, let alone actually to remove the child from his current home. I doubt it is really in the mother's interest either, merely having the effect of raising false hope for it to be dashed later.[276]

This 'stringent' approach meant that a parent would only get permission in 'exceptionally rare circumstances'.[277] However, this changed with Key Case of *Re B-S*, in which the Court of Appeal, in light of the human rights discussion in Key Case *Re B (A Child) (Care Proceedings: Threshold Criteria)* (2013), held that:

> Both phrases ['stringent' and 'exceptionally rare'] are apt to mislead, with potentially serious adverse consequences. In the light of *In re B* they convey quite the wrong message. Neither, in our judgment, any longer has any place in this context. Their use in relation to section 47(5) should cease. . . . Section 47(5) is intended to afford a parent in an appropriate case a meaningful remedy—and a remedy, we stress, that may endure for the benefit not merely of the parent but also of the child. . . . Unthinking reliance on the concept of the 'exceptionally rare' runs the risk—a very real and wholly unacceptable risk—of rendering section 47(5) nugatory and its protections illusory. Except in the fairly unusual case where section 47(4)(b)(i) applies,[278] a parent applying under section 47(5) will always, by definition, be faced with the twin realities that the court has made both a care order and a placement order and that the child is now living with the prospective adopter. But, unless section 47(5) is to be robbed of all practical efficacy, none of those facts, even in combination, can of themselves justify the refusal of leave.[279]

---

[274] *Re W (Adoption Order: Set Aside and Leave to Oppose)* [2011] 1 FLR 2153 [13] ('Thorpe LJ).
[275] *Re B-S* [2013] EWCA Civ 813 [59] (Munby P).
[276] *Re W* [2011] 1 FLR 2153 [30].
[277] Both phrases used by Thorpe LJ in *Re W (Adoption Order: Set Aside and Leave to Oppose)* [2011] 1 FLR 2153.
[278] Adoption under the second condition where placement was by parental consent.
[279] *Re B-S* [2013] EWCA Civ 813 [68] (Munby P).

Munby P continued:

> In relation to the second question—If there has been a change in circumstances, should leave to oppose be given . . . the court will in particular have to consider two inter-related questions: one, the parent's ultimate prospect of success if given leave to oppose; the other, the impact on the child if the parent is, or is not, given leave to oppose, always remembering, of course, that at this stage the child's welfare is paramount. . . . As a general proposition, the greater the change in circumstances (assuming, of course, that the change is positive) and the more solid the parent's grounds for seeking leave to oppose, the more cogent and compelling the arguments based on the child's welfare must be if leave to oppose is to be refused. The mere fact that the child has been placed with prospective adopters cannot be determinative, nor can the mere passage of time. On the other hand, the older the child and the longer the child has been placed the greater the adverse impacts of disturbing the arrangements are likely to be.[280]

The current position, therefore, is that leave to oppose must be attainable in some cases, and does not require the change of circumstances to be exceptional. However, as Munby P says, the fact that the child's welfare is paramount may mean that leave is refused on the basis that the child is now settled elsewhere.

Note that the section refers to parents or guardians opposing an adoption application. The statutory provision does not give that ability to any other person. A grandparent, for example, would need to achieve similar ends through a different statutory route, such as applying for a child arrangements 'live with' order, which they would require leave to do under s24(b). While an applicant under s24(b) is not required to show a change in circumstances, this is still likely to be 'of great relevance to the prospects of success for the proposed residence application and when considering the welfare of the child', both aspects the court must consider in deciding whether to grant leave.[281]

Dispensing with parental consent to placement or adoption

When we considered placement, we noted that the court can make a s21 placement order without the consent of the parents/guardian if the welfare of the child 'requires' that their consent be dispensed with. When we considered the conditions for the making of adoption orders, we noted, similarly, that under the first condition for the making of an adoption order, s47, the court can dispense with the consent of the parents or guardian if the welfare of the child 'requires' it. In this section we look at what this phrase means.

In *Re P (Children) (Adoption: Parental Consent)* the court held that the word 'requires'

> was plainly chosen as best conveying . . . the essence of the Strasbourg jurisprudence. And viewed from that perspective 'requires' does indeed have the connotation of the imperative, what is demanded rather than what is merely optional or reasonable or desirable.[282]

The Strasbourg jurisprudence mentioned here is the case law of the European Court of Human Rights. As we have seen, there are significant human rights implications to the care and adoption processes. Article 6, the right to a fair trial, is engaged. This has implications for the fairness and transparency of the legal process, including whether the parents

---

[280] *Re B-S* [2013] EWCA Civ 813 [74] (Munby P).
[281] *Re G (A Child)* [2014] EWCA Civ 432.
[282] [2008] EWCA Civ 535.

have a fair opportunity to respond to the case against them, the degree to which there is unnecessary delay, and their access to legal aid. Depending on the seriousness of the harm to the child, Articles 2 (the right to life) or 3 (the right not to be subjected to inhuman or degrading treatment) may be engaged. The latter two articles are absolute. Article 8, the right to private and family life is also engaged. While there is a tendency to think about adoption as being a breach of the birth parents' Article 8 rights, it is also of course an interference with the child's rights to family life with his or her birth parents. However, for the child there is an inherent conflict between that right and his right to be free from harm. The adoptive parents, too, may acquire family life within the meaning of Article 8.

Let us remind ourselves of Article 8:

> **STATUTORY EXTRACT** *Article 8 ECHR*
>
> 3. Everyone has the right to respect for his private and family life, his home and his correspondence.
> 4. There shall be no interference by a public authority with the exercise of this right except such as is in accordance with the law and is necessary in a democratic society in the interests of national security, public safety or the economic well-being of the country, for the prevention of disorder or crime, for the protection of health or morals, or for the protection of the rights and freedoms of others.

The European Court of Human Rights has repeatedly confirmed that interference in the family must, in order to be Article 8 compliant, be necessary within the meaning of Article 8(2); that is, it must be necessary because it pursues a legitimate aim (such as protecting the rights of the child) and be a proportionate means of achieving that aim.

The Court has repeatedly held that taking a child into care should be regarded as a temporary measure with the ultimate aim of reuniting the family (*Haase v Germany*),[283] unless this would harm the child's health and development. In *K v Finland* it held that the 'guiding principle' was that

> a care order should in principle be regarded as a temporary measure, to be discontinued as soon as circumstances permit, and that any measures implementing temporary care should be consistent with the ultimate aim of reuniting the natural parents and the child . . . The positive duty to take measures to facilitate family reunification as soon as reasonably feasible will begin to weigh on the responsible authorities with progressively increasing force as from the commencement of the period of care, subject always to its being balanced against the duty to consider the best interests of the child.[284]

The circumstances in which ties are severed permanently, as is the case with adoption, should therefore be considered exceptional (*YC v United Kingdom*)[285] and can 'only be justified if they were motivated by an overriding requirement pertaining to the child's best interests' (*Johansen v Norway*).[286]

---

[283] App No. 11057/02, reported at [2004] 2 FLR 39 [93].
[284] [2001] 2 FCR 673 [178].
[285] (2012) 55 EHRR 967 [134].
[286] (1996) 23 EHRR 33.

In Key Case *Re B (A Child) (Care Proceedings: Threshold Criteria)*, the Supreme Court used these phrases from the European Court of Human Rights to interpret the phrase 'if the welfare of the child requires it' in a way that was compatible with Article 8.

KEY CASE *Re B (A Child) (Care Proceedings: Threshold Criteria)* [2013] UKSC 33

Re B involved the making of a care order in respect of a little girl, aged nearly 3, dubbed Amelia by the court. Amelia was removed from her parents' care as soon as she was born, so there was no evidence that she had suffered significant harm, and the case was based on the second limb of the threshold test—that she was 'likely to suffer' (i.e., had a real possibility of suffering) significant harm in the future. Prior to the child's birth the mother had had a long-term abusive sexual relationship with her stepfather, whose malign influence led her to commit dishonesty-based criminal offences, for which she was sent to prison. She suffered from a chronic psychiatric somatisation disorder, which 'drives the sufferer to misuse physical symptoms in order to elicit care from others or for other purposes'. She also had a factitious disorder which caused her 'repeatedly to exaggerate symptoms or altogether to fabricate them and to offer false histories'. The child's father had convictions for 52 offences mainly of dishonesty but some for drugs and violence, and had spent about 15 years of his adult life in prison. Evidence showed he used cannabis but there was no evidence of continued use of any harder drugs.

The local authority sought a care order with a plan for adoption. At first instance, the judge made a care order based on the risk of future significant emotional harm that would be attributable to the mother's illnesses, concerns about the parents' personality traits, the mother's lying, the father's 'active, but less chronic, tendency to dishonesty and vulnerability to the misuse of drugs', and physical harm to Amelia such as through over treatment or inappropriate treatment by doctors as a result of the mother's somatisation disorder. The judge considered whether anything short of adoption could reduce the risk of harm, but concluded that the parents were unable to honestly cooperate with professionals, not least because the mother had made 23 complaints about professionals seeking to work with her.

However, the parents had received supervised contact with Amelia for at least three days per week since she was removed from them at birth, and had been assiduous in attending. The first instance judge had found that they were devoted to Amelia and 'had given her child-centred love and affection "in spades"'.

On the requirements of Article 8

All five judges agreed that while a finding that the care threshold is crossed is not itself an interference with the Article 8 ECHR right to private and family life, Article 8 is relevant at the welfare stage. This means that an outcome that interferes with Amelia's and her parents' private and family life, as adoption does, will only be lawful if it falls within Art 8(2) i.e., the interference must be 'in accordance with the law' and 'necessary in a democratic society'. Lord Wilson noted that in *Johansen v Norway*[287] the European Court of Human Rights said that 'the notion of necessity implies that the interference corresponds to a pressing social need and, in particular, that it is proportional to the legitimate aim pursued', which in this case was to keep Amelia safe. It is not enough that it would be better for a child to be adopted than to live with her natural family.

The judges emphasised that *when the court is asked to make any order with a view to adoption, such as a care order with a plan for an adoption order, a placement order, or an adoption order,*

---

[287] (1996) 23 EHRR 33 [83].

including dispensing with parental consent, the order must be a proportionate response to the risk the child faces. While the Adoption and Children Act itself makes no mention of proportionality, once the ECHR became part of our domestic law with the Human Rights Act 1998, 'not only the local authority, but also the courts as public authorities, came under a duty to act compatibly with the Convention rights'.[288]

An order that severs the relationship between parent and child is, in the words of Lord Neuberger:

> a very extreme thing, a last resort, . . . because the interests of a child would self-evidently require her relationship with her natural parents to be maintained unless no other course was possible in her interests. That is reinforced by the requirement in section 1(3)(g) that the court must consider all options, which carries with it the clear implication that the most extreme option should only be adopted if others would not be in her interests. As to article 8, the Strasbourg court decisions . . . make it clear that such an order can only be made in 'exceptional circumstances', and that it could only be justified by 'overriding requirements pertaining to the child's welfare' or, putting the same point in slightly different words, 'by the overriding necessity of the interests of the child'.

Other judges used similar wording.

Lord Wilson said that Article 8 required 'a high degree of justification' before an order was made. Lord Clarke said:

> A care order cannot be made unless it is necessary in the best interests of the child. Nothing less than necessity will do, either under our domestic law or under the European Convention on Human Rights. Only in a case of necessity will an adoption order removing a child from his or her parents be proportionate.

Lady Hale noted that:

> The test for severing the relationship between parent and child is very strict: only in exceptional circumstances and where motivated by overriding requirements pertaining to the child's welfare, in short, where nothing else will do. In many cases and particularly where the feared harm has not yet materialised and may never do so, it will be necessary to explore and attempt alternative solutions.

The outcome

The judges held that in this case the judge at first instance had not been 'wrong' in his decision and that therefore an appeal could not succeed.

Lady Hale dissented. While she agreed that an adoption order could only be made where 'nothing else would do', she thought that on the facts it could not be said that the adoption of Amelia was necessary. To her, the order was not, therefore, a proportionate response to the harm which was feared.

Following the Supreme Court judgment, the case was remitted to a High Court judge who, in fact order a new assessment to see if anything had changed. A placement order was ultimately made on the basis that there were no realistic alternative options other than adoption.[289]

Re B tells us that the welfare of the child requires parental consent to be dispensed with only when adoption is necessary—when, in the words of the Supreme Court, 'nothing else will do'. This reflects the requirement in Article 8(2) that the right to private and family life be breached only if necessary, and that such a breach be a proportionate response to a

---

[288] Lord Clarke at [194].
[289] H Markham, '*Re B* and What Followed — The End of the Story' (*Local Government Lawyer*, 26 March 2014).

legitimate aim, child protection. *Re B* therefore mashes together the welfare principle with Article 8. While our judges have on several occasions expressed the view that there is no inherent incompatibility between the two approaches, at 9.6 we looked at why this view has been challenged by a number of lawyers and academics.

Soares de Melo v Portugal is a European Court of Human Rights case in which adoption was held *not* to be a proportionate response and thus a violation of Article 8.[290] Ms Soares de Melo was the mother of ten children, seven of whom were taken into care with a view to them being adopted. The basis of state intervention was neglect caused by poverty (they lived on a monthly income of 339 euros), the absence of the children's father, and the mother's refusal to undergo sterilisation. There was no evidence that the children were being abused and there were strong emotional ties within the family. The mother could not be said to be particularly unfit. The Court held that the family had not received adequate help and support such that would meet the state's positive obligations to try to keep the family together, and therefore the placement of the children for adoption in several different homes had not been 'necessary'. The Portuguese authorities should have considered less restrictive measures with a view to reuniting the family.

Soon after *Re B*, the Court of Appeal delivered its judgment in the case of *Re B-S*, and used the opportunity to reinforce *Re B*'s message and the implications for practitioners.

KEY CASE *Re B-S (Children) (Adoption: Leave to Oppose)* [2013] EWCA Civ 1146

This was an appeal by a mother against a refusal to give her leave to oppose the making of an adoption order in relation to her two children. When dismissing her appeal, Munby P, with whom Lord Dyson MR and Black LJ agreed, used the opportunity to set out some important guidance on the conduct of adoption cases in light of the Supreme Court's very recent decision in *Re B*.

Interpreting *Re B*

Munby P identified three principles arising from the judgments in *Re B*:

1. 'Although the child's interests in an adoption case are paramount, the court must never lose sight of the fact that those interests include being brought up by the natural family . . . unless the overriding requirements of the child's welfare make that not possible.'
2. 'The court "must" consider all the options before coming to a decision. The court should adopt the least interventionist approach. This should be considered to be in the better interests of the children . . . unless there are cogent reasons to the contrary.'
3. The court's assessment of whether the parents can provide 'good enough' care for the child 'must take into account the assistance and support which the authorities would offer' so that when making an adoption order 'the court must be satisfied that there is no practical way of the authorities (or others) providing the requisite assistance and support.' The local authority 'cannot press for a more drastic form of order because it is unable or unwilling to support a less interventionist form or order'.

He notes that:

the consent of a parent with capacity can be dispensed with only if the welfare of the child 'requires' this. 'Require' here has the Strasbourg meaning of necessary, 'the connotation of

---

[290] Application no. 72850/14 (2016).

the imperative, what is demanded rather than what is merely optional or reasonable or desirable': *Re P (Placement Orders: Parental Consent)* [2008] EWCA Civ 535, paras 120, 125. This is a stringent and demanding test. . . .

The language used in *In re B* is striking. Different words and phrases are used, but the message is clear. Orders contemplating non-consensual adoption—care orders with a plan for adoption, placement orders and adoption orders—are 'a very extreme thing, a last resort . . . Behind all this there lies the well-established principle . . . that the court should adopt the "least interventionist" approach'. As Hale J said in *In re O (Care or Supervision Order)* [1996] 2 FLR 755, 760: 'the court should begin with a preference for the less interventionist rather than the more interventionist approach. This should be considered to be in the better interests of the children . . . unless there are cogent reasons to the contrary.'

On the evidence and the judge's role

Munby P goes on to note that he and his fellow judges 'have real concerns . . . about the recurrent inadequacy of the analysis and reasoning put forward in support of the case for adoption, both in the materials put before the court by local authorities and guardians and also in too many judgments.' He continues:

Two things are essential . . . both when the court is being asked to approve a care plan for adoption and when it is being asked to make a non-consensual placement order or adoption order. . . .

1. First, there must be proper evidence both from the local authority and from the guardian. The evidence must address all the options which are realistically possible and must contain an analysis of the arguments for and against each option. . . . We draw attention in particular to the need for 'analysis of the pros and cons' and a 'fully reasoned recommendation'. These are essential if the exacting test set out in [*Re B*] and the requirements of Articles 6 and 8 of the Convention are to be met.
2. The second thing that is essential, and again we emphasise that word, is an adequately reasoned judgment by the judge. . . . The judicial task is to evaluate all the options, undertaking a global, holistic and . . . multi-faceted evaluation of the child's welfare which takes into account all the negatives and the positives, all the pros and cons, of each option.

Re B-S had an instant and considerable effect on courts' and social workers' practice which came to be known as 'the *Re B-S* effect'. The number of placement and adoption orders fell sharply, with courts turning to less interventionist alternatives to adoption, particularly those which involved kinship care arrangements and thereby preserved family ties. The number of special guardianship orders almost doubled in the subsequent year, leading to concern that orders were being made in situations in which adoption orders should have been made. In a number of subsequent cases, judges attempted to address this. A clearly frustrated Munby P, the author of the judgment in *Re B-S*, said in *Re R (A Child)* that

There appears to be an impression in some quarters that an adoption application now has to surmount 'a much higher hurdle' or even that 'adoption is over', that 'adoption is a thing of the past'. There is a feeling that 'adoption is a last resort' and 'where nothing else will do' have become slogans too often taken to extremeness, so that this is now a 'shying away from permanency if at all possible' and a 'bending over backwards' to keep the child in the family if at all possible. . . . I wish to emphasize, with as much force as possible, that *Re B-S* was not intended to change and has not changed the law. Where adoption is in the child's best interests, local authorities must not shy away from seeking, nor courts from making, care orders with a plan for adoption, placement orders and adoption orders. The fact is that there are occasions when nothing but adoption will do, and it is essential in such cases that a child's welfare should not be compromised by keeping them within their family at all costs.[291]

Given this confusion, we now turn to ask what the current approach to dispensing with parental consent to adoption is.

12.5.12 Where are we now?

In 12.3.3 of this chapter, we noted the well-known statement by Hedley J in *Re L* that 'society must be willing to tolerate very diverse standard of parenting' and that it is 'not the province of the state to spare children all the consequences of defective parenting'.[292] Indeed, the care threshold does not do so: it permits removal of a child only once the threshold is passed and only if that is in the best interests of the child. Yet removal of a child to another home is a significant human rights violation. The making of an adoption order is the most profound interference with family life known to the state: the removal of the very status of family. In order to interfere with a family's Article 8 rights, the interference has to be necessary within the meaning of Article 8(2). This means, to use Lady Hale's phrase, 'where nothing else will do' apart from adoption.

While 'where nothing else will do' is oft-repeated, and is a phrase with which Lords Neuberger and Kerr associated themselves, it can be misleading. Clearly, if an adoptive family cannot be found for the child to be placed with, something other than adoption will have to do, but that does not mean that a placement order should never have been made. Often, local authorities will take a dual planning approach: look for an adoptive family, but revert to long-term foster care if adopters cannot not be found in a specified period of time (often six months), so that the child is not left in limbo. In *Re P (Placement Orders: Parental Consent) (Children)* the Court of Appeal held that 'a local authority can be "satisfied that the child ought to be placed for adoption" within the meaning of section 22(1)(d) of the 2002 Act even though it recognises the reality that a search for adoptive parents may be unsuccessful and that, if it is, the alternative plan will have to be for long-term fostering'.[293] Post-*Re B*, the parents in *CM v Blackburn with Darwen Borough Council* argued that adoption could not be seen as necessary if the local authority was taking a dual planning approach. The Court of Appeal rejected that, holding that such contingency plans are desirable and does not mean that adoption is not a proportionate response.[294]

---

[291] [2014] EWCA Civ 1625 [41/44].
[292] *Re L (Care: Threshold Criteria)* [2007] 1 FLR 2050 [51] (Hedley J).
[293] [2008] EWCA Civ 535 [137] (Wall LJ).
[294] [2014] EWCA Civ 1479.

KEY CASE *Re W (A Child)* [2016] EWCA Civ 793

The child, A, was born in May 2014 and in October 2014 was made the subject of a care order with a plan for adoption and a placement order was made. Thus, by the age of 8 months old, A was living with her prospective adopters, Mr and Mrs X. The birth parents had refused to provide the local authority with information about other family members so that the court was not able to consider kinship care. In June 2015, A's birth parents had another child and during proceedings in relation to that child, the paternal grandparents learned of A's existence. They were assessed as viable carers for the new baby, and wanted to also care for A. The issue was whether, in light of *Re B*, adoption could be said to be necessary given that there were viable kinship carers available.

The Court of Appeal held that:

- There is no right or presumption that a child should be raised by his or her birth family. The existence of family rights under Article 8 is a question of fact. The relationship that existed between Mr and Mrs X and A was sufficient to establish family life. The paternal grandparents did not have any Article 8 family life rights as they had never met A, so the only relationships which fall to be afforded respect in the context of Article 8's 'family life' were those between Mr and Mrs X and A. A may have some 'private life' rights with respect to her birth family.
- Under the 2002 Act welfare checklist, the court has to consider 'the relationship which the child has with relatives, with any person who is a prospective adopter with whom the child is placed, and with any other person in relation to whom the court or agency considers the relationship to be relevant': s1(4)(f).[295]
- The best interests of the child may be different when a child has been in an adoptive placement for some time and has secure, stable and robust attachment to the prospective adopters compared to when placement has not yet happened. This is because the welfare consideration must now accommodate the weight to be given to the child's place within the adoptive family. The court will need to consider what harm the child may suffer if that relationship is now broken.

- The phrase 'where nothing else will do':

    is meaningless and potentially dangerous, if it is applied as some freestanding, shortcut test divorced from, or even in place of, an overall evaluation of the child's welfare. Used properly, as Baroness Hale explained, the phrase 'nothing else will do' is no more, nor no less, than a useful distillation of the proportionality and necessity test as embodied in the ECHR and reflected in the need to afford paramount consideration to the welfare of the child throughout her lifetime (s1 Adoption and Children Act 2002). The phrase 'where nothing else will do' is not some sort of hyperlink providing a direct route to the outcome of a case so as to bypass the need to undertake a full, comprehensive welfare evaluation of all the relevant pros and cons.[296]

- Only once courts have undertaken a full analysis of the child's interests does the overall proportionality/necessity/'where nothing else will do' of a plan for adoption come to be considered.
- The existence of a viable placement with the grandparents made that option 'a runner' but not automatically 'a winner' without full consideration of any other factor relevant to her welfare.

[295] In *Re M'P-P (Children)* [2015] EWCA Civ 584, the Court of Appeal held that a local authority foster carer who intended to put herself forward in due course as a prospective adopter is not a prospective adopter with whom the child is placed but falls within 'any other person'.
[296] [2016] EWCA Civ 793.

The Court of Appeal remitted the case to be heard again by another judge, but cautioned that 'In later life A will probably read these judgments on the Internet. She will decide whether the positions adopted by the Xs and by the grandparents were reasonable. She will also make up her own mind about whether we were right or wrong to allow the present appeal.'

In a later case, *Uddin v The Secretary of State for the Home Department*, the Court of Appeal held that 'the test for family life within the foster care context is no different to that of birth families'. The fact that the arrangement involved the foster carers being paid to look after the child did not determine the outcome; what mattered was the relationship they had formed.[297]

You may find that the phrase 'where nothing else will do' does not fully capture the nuance of the test or the meaning Lady Hale intended for it.[298] There are several ways of referring to the same test, including the form of words used in *Re B* by Lord Neuberger that no other course was possible in the child's interests. We suggest that you consider the words of Black LJ in *Re M (A Child: Long-Term Foster Care)*: 'whether there is another course which is both possible *and* in the child's interests. This will inevitably be a much more sophisticated question and entirely dependent on the facts of the particular case. Certain options will be readily discarded as not realistically possible, others may be just about possible but not in the child's interests . . .'[299]

In addition to adoption, the available options could include no order at all; rehabilitation to the birth family perhaps with a supervision order; kinship care under a 'live with' order or a special guardianship order; or a foster placement under a care order. Some children with serious medical needs may require a placement in a specialist institution. If one of these options is both possible *and* in the child's interests then it follows that adoption is not necessary and thus not proportionate, and the less interventionist option should be taken. In Key Case *Re W*, notwithstanding a viable kinship carer, adoption was the only option that was both possible and, given the length of time she had been with the prospective adopters, in her welfare interests. It was accordingly true to say that nothing else would do and that adoption was necessary and proportionate.

FOCUS Know-How

What about the child's views?

One of the Court of Appeal's criticisms in *Re W* was the way in which—notwithstanding her very young age—the child's personality, attributes, and achievements which 'should have been centre stage' in a welfare analysis 'did not shine out' from any reading of the court papers or from the judgment. Similarly, in our discussions in the chapter so far the child may have seemed the passive recipient of others' decisions about the course of her life.

---

[297] [2020] EWCA Civ 338.

[298] If the case law has you tearing your hair out, you should read 'Adoption Law Illustrated by Way of Passive-Aggressive Post-It Notes on a Student Fridge', which takes the metaphor of cheese in a student fridge to describe the various cases and is both funny and helpful and used in judicial training. Available at https://suesspiciousminds.com/2016/12/10/adoption-law-illustrated-by-way-of-passive-aggressive-post-it-notes-on-a-student-fridge/ accessed 29 October 2019.

[299] *Re M (A Child)* [2014] EWCA Civ 226 [32].

To some extent this is true. Children are represented in care and adoption proceedings but unless they are competent to instruct their own solicitors[300] are not directly involved. Research by Minnis and Walker found that 'whilst children had reported that the decisions to take them into care were the right ones, many reported there was little choice about where they would live. They wanted more choice in the final decisions made around where and with whom they should live.'[301] That they felt disenfranchised in this way is concerning given the centrality of children views as reinforced in the Care Planning Regulations, the *Independent Reviewing Officer Handbook*, Fostering Services National Minimum Standards and the Adoption National Minimum Standards. The local authority has a duty to consult them and give their views due consideration, and there are a number of applications that the child can bring himself including applications for contact, applications to discharge a care order. The child's wishes and feelings in light of their age and understanding is a factor in both the Children Act and Adoption and Children Act welfare checklists.

12.6 How does the court decide which option is in the child's interests?

In his or her judgment about which option is both possible *and* in the child's interests, the judge 'must address all the options which are realistically possible and must contain an analysis of the arguments for and against each option' by reference to the welfare checklist factors. Where the court is considering a care plan for adoption, both the welfare principle and checklist in the Children Act 1989 and those in the Adoption and Children Act 2002 apply.[302] In *Re C (A Child) (Care and Placement Order: Special Guardianship Order)* McFarlane LJ said that

> Any judge, who is aware that (either at the current hearing or at a hearing shortly thereafter) he or she is going to be considering whether or not to make a placement for adoption order, would be wise only to approve a care plan for adoption where such a plan seems likely to meet the welfare requirements of ACA 2002, s1 [the child's welfare 'throughout his life'] and s52 [dispensing with parental consent to adoption].[303]

There is no point in making a care order with a plan for adoption in the first place if the court is unlikely to hold that adoption is proportionate and necessary, and thus the court should bear in mind the requirements of *Re B* (2013) at the welfare stage and through any subsequent steps towards adoption.[304] Indeed, it is common for a court to be dealing with a placement application at the final care hearing. Later, when the court is considering the adoption order, only the 2002 Act principle and checklist will apply.

Not every option will need to be explored, but before the local authority argues for adoption, it must explore 'realistic, sensible and practical' alternatives[305] and what the local authority could offer by way of support if the child was rehabilitated to the birth family

---

[300] See 12.2.3.

[301] M Minnis and F Walker, *The Experiences of Fostering and Adoption Processes—the Views of Children and Young People: Literature Review and Gap Analysis* (National Foundation for Educational Research 2012).

[302] *Re R (A Child)* [2014] EWCA Civ 1625.

[303] [2013] EWCA Civ 1257 [29] (McFarlane LJ).

[304] *Re B (A Child) (Care Proceedings: Threshold Criteria)* [2013] UKSC 33 [34] (Lord Wilson).

[305] *Re R (A Child)* [2014] EWCA Civ 1625.

or placed with a kinship carer. It is only with this information that a court can conclude whether adoption is necessary. It is not open to a local authority to decline to identify these services or refuse to help identify the best solution to the problem.[306] *Re B-S* emphasises that what is required of local authorities is a considered analysis of the pros and cons of each option that they have considered, based on the particular circumstances of the child in question, so that they can demonstrate to the court that adoption is necessary and proportionate. In *London Borough of Bexley v Mr and Mrs B and Child A* Her Honour Judge Lazarus was scathing about a report that justified the local authority's adoption plan with the words 'given A's age the only permanency option viable for A is adoption', calling it 'shockingly poor and in breach of the relevant law and guidance'.[307]

12.6.1 The need for a holistic evaluation

One potential problem facing judges and local authorities when they consider the pros and cons of each option is the risk that they will discount each option in turn until they are left only with only one way forward that may on balance have greater flaws than one of those already discarded. *Re B-S* cautioned against linear judgments in which this happened, and required judges and local authorities to undertake a holistic, global, examination of the options to find what is best for the child. This is a value judgment. In *Re W*, Ryder LJ noted that

> Setting out the positives and negatives or if you prefer the benefits and detriments of each placement option by reference to the welfare checklist factors is an illuminating and essential intellectual and forensic exercise that will highlight the evidential conclusions and their implications and how they are to be weighted in the evaluative balance that is the value judgment of the court.[308]

It can be hard to envisage what a holistic, global examination might look like. *Northamptonshire County Council v AB & CD* is a good example. Another excellent example is that of Her Honour Judge Troy in *Re R (A Child)*.[309]

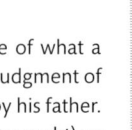

KEY CASE *Northamptonshire County Council v AB & CD* [2019] EWHC 1807 (Fam)

This case does not establish any new principle of law, but is provided as an example of what a global, holistic evaluation of the options looks like. Below is an edited extract from the judgment of Mr Justice Keehan about a 4-year-old boy, CD, whose brother, EF, had been murdered by his father. The court had to decide between returning the child to his mother (which the mother sought) or making a care order and approving the local authority care plan which was for adoption with a back-up plan for long-term fostering if an adoptive family could not be found in six months.

The judge said:

> I have no doubt that the mother loved EF and that she deeply loves CD . . . I accept that she, as I have mentioned, is a vulnerable young woman and that her own chaotic and damaging childhood did nothing to prepare her to become a parent, but she is a parent.

---

[306] [2016] EWCA Civ 793 [81] (Ryder LJ).
[307] [2020] EWFC B2.
[308] [2016] EWCA Civ 793 [78] (Ryder LJ).
[309] Not to be confused with the other *Re R* discussed in this chapter. This is a lower court decision at [2016] EWFC B3, and can be found on BAILII.

I accept, without hesitation, the evidence . . . that the mother does not have the skills to afford any child, let alone CD, with safety and security. She did not know that [the father] would ultimately kill EF but she had numerous opportunities to take steps to protect him and keep him safe and she did not. Her inconsistency in her attendance with contact with CD . . . further demonstrated her self-centred approach to life. . . . Her behaviour in the approach to this hearing of abandoning GH and staying away from him in a hotel while she undertook binge drinking with friends, underlines, if it needs to be underlined, the selfish approach that this young mother has adopted. . . .

As matters stand with this mother, I am satisfied that any child in her care would be in danger of suffering serious harm. Positive and sustained change is a very long way off and the mother, to date, has exhibited no willingness or ability to change. . . . I am entirely satisfied that rehabilitation, now or in the future, of CD to his mother's care is not a realistic option because he would be at risk of serious harm. Little CD needs unconditional love and unconditional commitment so that he may be cared for in a safe, secure and stable home. I am entirely satisfied the mother is not capable of undertaking that task. Accordingly, CD cannot be placed in his mother's care now or in the foreseeable future. . . .

I completely understand [the foster carers'] decision, given their respective ages, and other family commitments, not to seek to adopt CD nor to seek to be assessed as special guardians for him. . . . Making CD the subject of placement order and being placed for adoption has the advantage that he will have his forever family, a family where he feels entirely secure and where they are wholly committed to him. It has the very great considerable disadvantage of severing all legal ties between CD and not only his mother, but also his half-sibling, GH. . . . up until the age of 3, CD had been cared for by his mother and lived with his wider family and he had suffered the tragedy of the loss of his brother EF.

Long-term foster care has the advantage of keeping alive those familial links and of enabling ongoing contact to take place between CD and his mother and/or GH, but carries with it the significant disadvantage that a social worker and the local authority will be involved in CD's life throughout his minority and there will be the need for regular looked after children reviews, visits by social workers and permission sought if CD wished to stay overnight at a friend's home, for example.

Those being the only realistic options for CD, I have to balance one against the other. I may only determine the balance falls in favour of adoption if I am satisfied that it is justified, it is proportionate to the circumstances of the case and that no other step will meet CD's welfare needs throughout the whole of his life. The local authority propose that a search is made for an adoptive placement for CD for a period of 6 months, failing which the plan would revert to one of long-term foster care. The social worker, Ms Z, and the children's [litigation] guardian, are clear that this is the plan which best meets and promotes the welfare best interests of CD. It gives him the chance, that they say he deserves, for a forever family.

SCENARIO 1

Illustration 8

A placement order having been made, Ella has now lived with her prospective adopters for more than ten weeks and the local authority has visited and is happy with how the relationship is progressing. Accordingly, the prospective adopters apply for an adoption order.

As Kerrie and Mike did not consent to placement, it is highly unlikely that they will consent to the adoption order. This means that under the first condition adoption can only take place if the court is prepared to dispense with the requirement that they consent. Under the second condition, the court can make an adoption order if there was a placement order and the parent does not have leave to oppose the adoption order. There is a placement order, and in making it the parents' consent was dispensed with. Ultimately, therefore, it comes down to whether the child's welfare *requires* the parents' consent to be dispensed with, and this has the meaning ascribed to it in *Re B* (2013). The court has to be satisfied that nothing other than adoption will do before it can hold that the welfare of the child requires the parents' consent to be dispensed with, or, to put it another way, it has to consider whether there is an alternative to adoption which is both possible and in the child's interests. Here, the only alternatives are long-term foster care, which we have already identified as unsuitable for a very young child, or a return to Kerrie. The issue with returning Ella to Kerrie is whether she can learn to offer good enough care, and do so within the timescales of the child. These are possible—but are they in Ella's interests?

In deciding whether adoption is necessary, i.e., whether it is the only option that is both possible and in her interests, the court must consider and weigh up each of the possible options in a global, holistic evaluation. The judge must consider the welfare principle and the welfare checklist in the Adoption and Children Act 2002.

Ella is too young to have ascertainable wishes and feelings but she has a need to be safe and if she could express an opinion it would be to have stability and love. If adopted, she may feel a sense of loss and seek information about her birth family. The severance of family ties is a last resort. But adoption can give her stability and a sense of belonging. She is very young and has already been living with the prospective adopters and has adjusted well and is settled. The adoptive parents are committed to her. She not only has a relationship with her birth family, but also one that she has built with the prospective adopters, and with whom she may have—pursuant to *Re W*—family life under Article 8. If she returns to her mother there is a real possibility of further harm which may be significant. Although the local authority will offer a package of support, that may not be sufficient to reduce the risks to her. Kerrie has not been able to become a good enough parent during the court process, and Ellie cannot wait in foster care for her mother to be ready, which may never happen, as such delay is harmful to her welfare. What she needs now, at a developmentally significant age, is stability. Adoption therefore is the only option that is in her interests and accordingly making an adoption order is necessary and thus proportionate.

12.7 After the order

In this section, we consider the effects of the order made on the lives of the parties with a particular focus on adoption. That is because adoption is unique in having broken apart and reformed a family or families. One option is to appeal the order that is made, but as we shall see, that is difficult in light of the discretionary exercise undertaken at the welfare stage. We consider a line of cases in which those who were adopted as children or their birth relatives have sought to undo the adoption years afterwards, and the effect this may have on people seeking to become adopters, and we consider what role post-adoption contact with the birth family may play in enabling all involved to come to terms with what has happened.

12.7.1 Appealing an order

There are considerable difficulties in successfully appealing a court order. These relate to time, cost, and prospects of success. A judge's decision (on threshold, disposal or any subsequent stage) can be appealed within 21 days (it is seven days for case management and interim care order decisions). Permission to appeal is required, and this permission will only be granted (by the trial judge or by applying to the appellate court) if the appeal has a real prospect of success. That means a realistic, as opposed to fanciful, prospect.[310] It is not necessary to show that the appeal is probably going to succeed.[311]

Once you have obtained permission, then you proceed to the appeal, where you must demonstrate that the lower court was 'wrong'. This does not generally involve any reconsideration of the facts found by the first instance judge. In *Re B* (2013) the Supreme Court gave the following rationale for this:

> [T]his is traditionally and rightly explained by reference to good sense, namely that the trial judge has the benefit of assessing the witnesses and actually hearing and considering their evidence as it emerges. Consequently, where a trial judge has reached a conclusion on the primary facts, it is only in a rare case, such as where that conclusion was one (i) which there was no evidence to support, (ii) which was based on a misunderstanding of the evidence, or (iii) which no reasonable judge could have reached, that an appellate tribunal will interfere with it. This can also be justified on grounds of policy (parties should put forward their best case on the facts at trial and not regard the potential to appeal as a second chance), cost (appeals on fact can be expensive), delay (appeals on fact often take a long time to get on), and practicality (in many cases, it is very hard to ascertain the facts with confidence, so a second, different, opinion is no more likely to be right than the first).[312]

Thus, as we see in 12.3.1, the deference to judges of first instance means that 'Although it is possible to appeal against a finding of fact, it is notoriously difficult to succeed in so doing'.[313]

Once the judge has made a finding of fact, he or she then has to proceed to the welfare stage and make whatever order is best for the child (or no order at all). Where the order is one leading to adoption, this involves considering whether that outcome was necessary and proportionate within the meaning in *Re B*. Lady Hale and Lord Kerr both argued in that case that appeal courts, as public authorities, had to be satisfied for themselves that the order made by the lower court was necessary and proportionate in order to comply with the appeal court's own obligations under the Human Rights Act. For the majority of the judges, however, this was not necessary, so appeal courts have a limited role in reviewing necessity and proportionality. For Lord Neuberger, with whom Lord Clarke expressly agreed, the treatment of the trial judge's conclusion on proportionality should be as set out in Table 12.4. Only if the trial judge was wrong in their assessment of proportionality will the appeal succeed, and because this is a discretionary evaluation of the evidence in the case, it will not be easy to show that the judge was wrong. (This is an issue throughout family law, which involves judicial discretion in many areas.).

---

[310] *Swain v Hillman and Another* [2001] 1 All ER 91 (CA); confirmed *Tanfern v Cameron-MacDonald (Practice Note)* [2001] 1 WLR 1311 (CA).
[311] *Re R (A Child: Possible Perpetrator)* [2019] EWCA Civ 895 [31] (Peter Jackson LJ).
[312] *Re B (A Child) (Care Proceedings: Threshold Criteria)* [2013] UKSC 33 [53] (Lord Neuberger).
[313] *Re S (Abduction: Custody Rights)* [2002] EWCA Civ 908 [25] (Ward LJ).

TABLE 12.4 How an appeal court will treat a trial judge's conclusion on proportionality

An appellate judge may conclude that the trial judge's conclusion on proportionality was:	Outcome of appeal
(i) the only possible view	The appeal will be dismissed.
(ii) a view which she considers was right	
(iii) a view on which she has doubts, but on balance considers was right	
(iv) a view which she cannot say was right or wrong	Appeal will be dismissed. 'There will be a number of cases where an appellate court may think that there is no right answer, in the sense that reasonable judges could differ in their conclusions.' This category is most likely to apply where the trial judge's decision was based on his assessment of the witnesses' reliability or likely future conduct.
(v) a view on which she has doubts, but on balance considers was wrong	'The appellate judge should think very carefully about the benefit the trial judge had in seeing the witnesses and hearing the evidence, which are factors whose significance depends on the particular case. However, if, after such anxious consideration, an appellate judge adheres to her view that the trial judge's decision was wrong, then I think that she should allow the appeal'.[314]
(vi) a view which she considers was wrong	The appeal must be allowed.
(vii) a view which is unsupportable	

Source: [2013] UKSC 33, [93–4].

Rarely, adoptions orders are appealed significantly out of time—the record being 51 years—or set aside because of defects in the procedure. These cases are discussed at 12.7.2 below.

12.7.2 Can an adoption be undone?

As we have seen, the transplant model of adoption in our jurisdiction means that adoption has what has been referred to as a 'peculiar finality'.[315] It is designed to provide the child with the permanence that can only come from being a member of a new family for all purposes. Adoption does not, therefore end on the child attaining adulthood.

If the relationship between the adoptive parents and the child breaks down, the situation is no different to that involving a child born to the adoptive parents: the state can only intervene compulsorily if the child is suffering significant harm. If so, then the child will be the subject of further care proceedings in which the adoptive parents will be in

---

[314] *Re B (A Child) (Care Proceedings: Threshold Criteria)* [2013] UKSC 33 [93–94] (Lord Neuberger).
[315] *Re B (Adoption: Jurisdiction to Set Aside)* [1995] Fam 239, 249 (Swinton Thomas LJ).

the place of the birth parents, and all of the potential outcomes discussed in this chapter, including a further adoption, are once more on the table.

Adoption orders can also be appealed, as discussed at 12.7.1, within tight time frames and where the judge was wrong to make an adoption order. A more contentious issue involves whether adoptions can be undone perhaps years later. Sometimes this is referred to as 'revoking' an adoption, but it is technically either an appeal of the adoption order substantially out of time or an exercise of the inherent jurisdiction, both of which require leave.[316]

The consequence of a successful appeal is a return to the situation that existed before the adoption order, namely that the birth parents' status both as parents and as persons with parental responsibility is reinstated. Their view on the application is therefore relevant.[317] This does not mean that such children are automatically returned to their birth families: successful applications may, assuming the child is still a minor, result in a return to court for further consideration of the way forward, which may include staying with the adopters under a different legal framework.

There are a number of situations in which adoptions have been undone, albeit that the number of successful applications are very few indeed. There have been several cases in which the procedure was so seriously flawed as to constitute a breach of natural justice. These include cases in which proceedings were not properly served, such as *Re F (An Infant)*[318] and *Re W (A Child)*,[319] but service defects can often be remedied allowing the adoption order to be remade subsequently. Sometimes an order will not be made again, if the initial order was made under a false premise. In *Re K (Adoption and Wardship)*, the adoption of a foreign national was in breach of assurances given to a foreign government.[320] *Re J* was another successful application in light of a significant procedural flaw, namely that the mother and stepfather had falsely claimed not to know the father's identity.[321] In *ZH v HS & Ors (Application to Revoke Adoption Order)* the lack of notice to the birth family and their consequent lack of consent went 'to the very root of the adoption process'.[322] As we have written elsewhere, 'procedural irregularity is therefore a well-established basis for court intervention albeit that not all such flaws will be sufficient'.[323] Similarly, mistakes as to the law provide a valid ground of appeal. In *Case O* an adoption order has been made in favour of the child's legal mother and her civil partner when the fertility clinic they had used lost the consent paperwork that was essential to give the civil

---

[316] *Re W (Inherent Jurisdiction: Permission Application: Revocation and Adoption Order)* [2013] EWHC 1957 (Fam), *PK v Mr and Mrs K* [2015] EWHC 2316 (Fam), and *ZH v HS & Ors (Application to Revoke Adoption Order)* [2019] EWHC 2190 (Fam) are examples of the use of the inherent jurisdiction rather than an appeal out of time. An appeal is more appropriate where the case is based on procedural irregularity. As to the term 'revocation', where a father adopts the child and then marries the mother, the adoption can be undone under s55 Adoption and Children Act 2002; this is properly called revocation.

[317] See comments by Thorpe LJ in *Re W (A Child)* [2010] EWCA Civ 1535.

[318] *Re F (R) (An Infant)* [1970] 1 QB 385; *Re RA (Minors)* [1974] 4 Fam Law 182.

[319] [2010] EWCA Civ 1535.

[320] [1997] 2 FLR 221.

[321] [2018] EWFC 8.

[322] [2019] EWHC 2190 (Fam).

[323] P Morgan, '*ZH v HS & Ors (Application to Revoke Adoption Order)*: Three Groups of Revocation Cases' (2020) 42(2) *Journal of Social Welfare and Family Law* 246.

partner the status of parent.[324] Munby P held that the adoption was unnecessary as a matter of law, and declared the women to be the child's parents.

In contrast, other kinds of mistakes have not led courts to overturn an adoption. In *Webster v Norfolk County Council*, three children were taken into care because of a number of fractures to one of them, found to be non-accidental.[325] They had lived with their adoptive families for several years when the Websters sought permission to appeal out of time on the basis that new evidence suggested the injuries may have been the result of scurvy, a severe vitamin C deficiency, and so a care order should not have been made, and therefore no subsequent adoption order should have been made. Even though it was possible, if not probable, that the judge's conclusions had been wrong with the benefit of some years' hindsight, the process was fair. This meant that the adoption had been validly obtained and would not be disturbed after several years. As Herring has argued,

> the reasoning is not such that would convince the person in the street. . . .What sense is there in being willing to overturn an adoption order based on failure to serve the correct papers, but not based on a fundamental failure of expert evidence? . . .Adoptive parents should feel protected from having their adoption orders set aside due to an injustice, but should parents be entitled not to have their parenthood set aside based on false evidence?[326]

Adoptions that turn out badly have also not been held to be sufficient to revoke or set aside the adoption. This is because allowing 'ill-starred'[327] adoptions to be reversed in this way sends a damaging message. Adoption is 'sold' to adoptive parents and adoptees as permanent; it is this which encourages adoptive parents to come forward and provides the children with the stability that they require. If the public perceived that adoptions could be undone, then the number of people willing to adopt may fall, and the children who are adopted may continue to be insecurely attached to their new family. This is a public policy argument, and we see it in cases such as *Re B (Adoption: Jurisdiction to Set Aside)*,[328] in which the now-adult child argued that his adoption was the result of mistake as to his ethnic heritage, and *Re PW*, in which the applicant held the adoption to have devastated her life over the subsequent 50 years.[329]

Although there are a handful of cases not cited here, this section has discussed almost all of the cases in which someone has sought to appeal an adoption out of time, rather than immediately after an order was made. You can see, therefore, how rare it is for such applications to be successful.

12.7.3 Contact with the birth family

The 'spend time with' provisions in s8 Children Act 1989 do not apply to a child in care or after adoption. As we see in section 12.4.6, when the child is in care the local authority has an obligation to provide reasonable contact under s34 Children Act 1989 and the court has

---

[324] *Case O (Human Fertilisation and Embryology Act 2008)* [2016] EWHC 2273 (Fam)).
[325] [2009] EWCA Civ 59.
[326] J Herring, 'Revoking Adoptions' (2009) 159(7360) *New Law Journal* 377.
[327] The phrase used by Simon Brown LJ in describing the situation in *Re B*.
[328] [1995] Fam 239.
[329] [2013] 1 FLR 96.

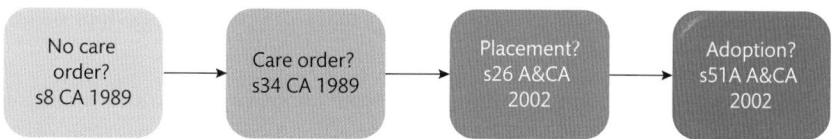

FIGURE 12.5 Contact provisions in care and adoption process

the power to intervene to regulate that if difficulties arise. Once the child is placed, contact is regulated under s26 Adoption and Children Act 2002 instead. The court should consider the issue of contact when making a placement order. It is likely that the local authority will want to reduce the frequency of contact with a view to there being a final session of 'goodbye contact' before the making of the adoption order. The court has a duty to consider contact arrangements when dealing with an adoption application (s46(6) Adoption and Children Act 2002) and there is a statutory power to order post-adoption contact. Once an adoption order is made, any order under s26 ceases to have effect and contact become regulated by s51A Adoption and Children Act 2002.

The transfer from one legal provision regulating contact to another as the child's legal status changes is set out in Figure 12.5.

Under s51A Adoption and Children Act 2002, the court may, when making an adoption order or afterwards, make a contact order requiring the person in whose favour the adoption order is or has been made to allow the child to visit or stay with a named person, or for that person and the child to otherwise to have contact with each other. The only persons who can be named are:

- those who, but for the child's adoption, would be related to the child by blood (including half-blood), marriage or civil partnership; this includes siblings who may have been adopted by different family or not taken into care;

- any former guardian of the child;

- any person who had parental responsibility for the child immediately before the making of the adoption order;

- any person who was entitled to make an application for an order under section 26;

- any person with whom the child has lived for a period of at least one year. This does not need to be continuous but must not have begun more than five years before the making of the application.

However, while the child, local authority, and adoptive parents do not require leave to make a contact application, others, including those named above, do need the prior leave of the court under s51A(4)(c). In deciding whether to grant leave, the court must consider both the applicant's connection with the child and any risk there might be of the proposed application disrupting the child's life to such an extent that he or she would be harmed by it, as well as the views of the child and the adopters. These considerations are likely to provide some reassurance to adoptive families opposed to post-adoption contact. Section 51A also enables the court to make a 'no contact' order, an order prohibiting a person named in the order from having contact with the child. In practical terms, this can be extremely difficult and in some cases desperate birth parents have resorted to social media to locate and contact their adopted children.

There are three main reasons why courts rarely make orders for post-adoption contact. These are:

1. Once adopted, the child becomes part of the adoptive family and it is up to the adoptive parents to decide what contact their child should have with others. In *Re G (Adoption: Contact)* Ward LJ said 'It must, I think, be kept in mind that by adopting these children the prospective adopters become their parents. This is an obvious truism, but important. They exclusively will have PR for the children and their position (on post-adoption contact) must, inevitably, be given substantial weight.'[330] Remember that once the child is adopted they cease in law to be recognised as the child of the birth parents. This also means that the birth parents' and child's right to family life under Article 8 ceases: there is no family life with the birth family left for Article 8 to protect. Accordingly, there is no human right to post-adoption contact.[331] 'The legal consequences of adoption militate against judicial interference with the autonomy of adoptive families . . . adopters become arbiters of their children's well-being and birth families are rendered (legally) invisible'.[332]

2. Courts are fearful of destabilising the adoptive family by imposing contact on them against their wishes: as Butler-Sloss P said in *Re T (Adoption: Contact)*, 'the prevalence and finality of adoption and the importance of letting the new family find its own feet ought not to be threatened in any way by an order in this case'.[333] Accordingly, the views of the adoptive parents have been treated as 'virtually determinative of the question' of whether there should be contact. This view has been re-iterated in a number of cases since. In fact, there is no empirical evidence to suggest that post-adoption contact is destabilising to the adoptive family.[334] It may, however, be that the prospect of post-adoption contact may be of concern to those considering whether to adopt.

3. The 'no order' principle, that the court should not make an order unless it considers that doing so would be better for the child than making no order at all, means that if the adoptive parents agree to contact, the court may well decide that making an order is not necessary, and leave the issue in the hands of the adoptive parents.

The judicial approach to post-adoption contact reflects both the transplant conception of adoption and the fact that in the past adoption was often seen a service to childless couples rather than a service to children. Over the years, however, social work practice has developed to promote the idea that there may be post-adoption contact in some circumstances. Neil's research shows that a key factor in whether there will be post-adoption contact is whether the adoption agency are pro-contact and have prepared the potential

[330] [2004] EWCA Civ 1187.
[331] *Seddon v Oldham Metropolitan Borough Council (Adoption: Human Rights)* [2015] EWHC 2609 (Fam).
[332] C Smith, 'Trust v Law: Promoting and Safeguarding Post-Adoption Contact' (2005) 27(3) *Journal of Social Welfare and Family Law* 315.
[333] [1995] 2 FLR 251.
[334] C Smith, 'Trust v Law: Promoting and Safeguarding Post-Adoption Contact' (2005) 27(3) *Journal of Social Welfare and Family Law* 315.

adopters for that.[335] In *Re B (A Child) (Post-Adoption Contact)*, however, the Court of Appeal noted that new research may influence 'advice and counselling to prospective adopters' but 'the law remains. . . that it will only be in an extremely unusual case that a court will make an order stipulating contact arrangement to which the adopters do not agree.'[336] The likelihood, therefore, is that where contact occurs post-adoption, it is usually the result of an agreement between the birth parents and the adopters, not the result of a court order.

Even if an order is made or agreement reached, it is extremely rare for contact to take place at the frequency common between separated parents in private law proceedings, or the reasonable contact required where the child is in care. The most common type of post-adoption contact is an annual or bi-annual exchange of letters although some children have face-to-face contact a few times per year. When making a contact order, the court can also include directions or conditions, such as that the letters are to be sent first to the local authority for screening, to be forwarded onto the adopters, or to the birth parents who may not know the child's location or name.

There are of course situations in which post-adoption contact would never be in the child's best interests. It may simply be prolonging a bad or abusive relationship. It can also be very difficult to sustain indirect contact such as letter contact. Neil et al. found that direct contact arrangements are more likely to last than indirect ones.[337]

However, remember that most children are taken into care as a result of neglect, not abuse. For many such children, post-adoption contact may have a number of benefits. It may help them understand their identity and the family history that resulted in their adoption. This is not the same as wanting to build an ongoing relationship: Neil et al. found that some children did not want further contact once their questions had been answered.[338] The child may, depending on their age on entering care, have strong memories of their birth family and strong emotional ties. Contact here enables the children to be reassured that their birth parents are alright, and maintain those emotionally important relationships.

Contact may also have benefits for the birth parents. Emotions around contact may run high, but the contact can serve to help them to feel reassured about their children's happiness and that they still have a positive role to play. In that sense, it may help them to come to terms with grief and loss surrounding adoption. While the courts have been concerned with the effect on adoptive parents, the research also suggests that getting to know the birth family can help the adopters to see the birth parents as 'real' people rather than stereotypes, and feel less threatened them.

---

[335] E Neil et al., *Contact after Adoption: A Longitudinal Study of Adoptive and Birth Families* (Centre for Research on Children and Families, University of East Anglia 1996-) Available at http://www.uea.ac.uk/contact-after-adoption/home accessed 3 November 2019.

[336] [2019] EWCA Civ 29 [59] (McFarlane P).

[337] E Neil et al., *Contact after Adoption: A Longitudinal Study of Adoptive and Birth Families* (Centre for Research on Children and Families, University of East Anglia 1996-) Available at http://www.uea.ac.uk/contact-after-adoption/home accessed 3 November 2019.

[338] E Neil et al., *Contact after Adoption: A Longitudinal Study of Adoptive and Birth Families* (Centre for Research on Children and Families, University of East Anglia 1996-) Available at http://www.uea.ac.uk/contact-after-adoption/home accessed 3 November 2019.

12.8 **Conclusion**

In Chapter 11, we considered the powers and duties that local authorities have to offer services that reduce or avoid the need for the state to intervene in the family on a compulsory basis. In this chapter, we considered what happens when the local authority comes to feel that compulsory intervention, in the form of care or supervision proceedings, is now necessary. We saw that the local authority must satisfy the court that the child is suffering or likely to suffer (meaning a real possibility of suffering) significant harm attributable to their care or to them being beyond parental control. The significant harm threshold identifies the level of harm to which we as a society are willing to expose children before the state intervenes. If we were to change any element of the threshold test, such as the standard of proof, the definition of likely to suffer, or the attributability criterion, we would change the number of children who could be subject to a care or supervision order. You may feel that the test is too high, so that it is difficult to protect a child, or too low, so that children are taken into care when they should be left with their families. The delicate balance of the different elements of the threshold test reflect the different interests at stake and the various philosophical perspectives about the role of the state that we discussed in Chapter 11.

Once the threshold is passed, the court then has to decide what to do with the child. At this stage, the best interests of the child are paramount, and the court must consider all realistic options for the child's future. The tests that have to be satisfied in order to make a care or adoption order (or any of the other orders described in this chapter) are set down in statute, but important key cases have interpreted and expanded upon them. In particular, the courts have had to reconcile the need to do what is best for the child with the requirements of Article 8 ECHR that respect be given to the family life of the child, their birth family, and in some cases, the prospective adopters. This has not been easy, and the tension between child protection and family autonomy are apparent. Society is not static, and our views on child-raising and the respective roles of family and state have changed over the years. As time marches on, our views on when and how states should protect children may change too, and the careful balance of the threshold test give way to a different viewpoint on child protection.

 KEY POINTS

- A care order is an order under s31 Children Act 1989 placing the child 'in the care' of the local authority. A supervision order is an order, also under s31, requiring a local authority to advise, assist, and befriend a named child. A court will only make a care or supervision order if the test set out in s31(2) Children Act 1989 is met (the threshold test) and if it is in the best interests of the child.

- The application is brought by the local authority. They will need to gather evidence to prove that the child is suffering (meaning suffering when they first took continuous protective action) or likely to suffer (meaning a real possibility of suffering) significant harm. The assessment of whether there has been harm or whether there is a real possibility of harm must be based on facts proved on the balance of probabilities, not on suspicion or speculation.

- The significant harm must be attributable to the care that was or would be given to the child not being what it would be reasonable of a parent to provide. Alternatively, the harm has to be attributable to the fact that the child is beyond parental control. Once the threshold is met, the court still has to decide what order to make. This is called the welfare stage, because it is based on what option is best for the child. The court is under a duty to consider all realistic options for the future care of the child.

- If the local authority's permanence plan for the child involves adoption, the child will need to be matched with the prospective adopters and then placed with them either with the permission of all those with parental responsibility or under a placement order.

- An adoption order may not be made if the child has a parent or guardian unless one of the two conditions set out in section 47(1) Adoption and Children Act 2002 is met. These conditions require either parental consent or that the consent of the parent or guardian is dispensed with on the basis that the welfare of the child requires it. The consent of a person without parental responsibility (e.g., some unmarried fathers) is not required.

- When considering whether the welfare of the child requires that the consent of the parents or guardians be dispensed with, the word 'requires' means that adoption has to be necessary and a proportionate response to the harm, in accordance with Article 8 ECHR. The court must undertake a holistic evaluation of all realistic options open to it.

- It is extremely difficult to appeal a court order. There are very limited timescales for doing so and it will be necessary to show that the judge was wrong, which is very difficult when a holistic evaluation is an exercise of judicial discretion. In some cases, courts have been prepared to revoke adoptions many years after the event, but this is very rare.

- Post adoption contact with the birth family is not often ordered by courts, who defer to the wishes of the child's adoptive parents. However, an informal agreement for contact may be reached with the adoptive parents and may help the child and the birth family to come to terms with the adoption.

FURTHER READING: SOME STARTING POINTS

- This is an area of law in which reading the cases is even more important than usual. The selection below are the Key Cases discussed in this chapter, plus a few extra ones also mentioned either for their influence or because they are excellent illustrations of the law.

- On the threshold criteria, read *Re H and Others (Minors) (Sexual Abuse: Standard of Proof)* [1996] AC 563; *Lancashire County Council v B* [2000] 2 AC 147; and *Re S-B (Children)* [2009] UKSC 17; *Re B (Care Proceedings: Standard of Proof)* [2009] 1 AC 11; *Re J (Children) (Non-Accidental Injury: Past Possible Perpetrator in New Family)* [2013] UKSC 9 and *Re A (A Child)* [2016] 1 FLR 1. There are a number of very good articles on the difficulties of balancing child protection against the risks of over intervention and the risks of being wrong, for example Andrew Bainham, 'Suspicious Minds: Protecting Children in the Face of Uncertainty' (2013) 72(2) *Cambridge Law Journal* 266; Stephen Gilmore, '*Re J*: Bulwarks and Logic – the Blood Which Runs through the Veins of Law – But How Much Will Be Spilled in Future?' [2013] *Child and Family Law Quarterly* 215; Mary Hayes, 'The Supreme Court's Failure to Protect Vulnerable Children: *Re J (Children)*' [2013, August] *Family Law* 1015; and Mary Hayes, '*Re O and N; Re B* - Uncertain Evidence and Risk Taking in Child Protection Cases' (2004) 16 *Child and Family Law Quarterly* 63.

- On the welfare stage, read *Re S (Adoption Order or Special Guardianship Order)* [2007] EWCA Civ 54; *Re B (A Child) (Care Proceedings: Threshold Criteria)* [2013] UKSC 33; *Re B-S (Children) (Adoption: Leave to Oppose)* [2013] EWCA Civ 1146; and *Re W (A Child)* [2016] EWCA Civ 793. *London Borough of Bexley v Mr and Mrs B and Child A* [2020] EWFC B2 is a wide-ranging judgment taking in the post-*Re B* case law and the welfare analysis. Two cases that are good illustrations of a holistic evaluation in practice are *Northamptonshire County Council v AB & CD* [2019] EWHC 1807 (Fam) and *Re R (A Child)* [2016] EWFC

B3. If you are finding the *Re B* 'where nothing else will do' idea difficult, then you may well like Suesspicious Minds, 'Adoption Law Illustrated by Way of Passive-Aggressive Post-It Notes on a Student Fridge' at https://suesspiciousminds.com/2016/12/10/adoption-law-illustrated-by-way-of-passive-aggressive-post-it-notes-on-a-student-fridge/. This is a very funny blog post by a local authority lawyer that is now used in judges' training because it goes through all the case law using cheese in a student fridge as a metaphor for adoption.

- For parents seeking to challenge the making of an adoption order, Claire Fenton-Glynn's *Adoption without Consent* (Directorate General for Internal Policies, European Parliament) is a clear summary of the law on adoption. It is available at http://www.europarl.europa.eu/RegData/etudes/STUD/2016/556940/IPOL_STU(2016)556940_EN.pdf For the human rights implications of adoption (albeit not covering more recent case law), see Sonia Harris-Short, 'Making and Breaking Family Life: Adoption, the State, and Human Rights' (2008) 35(1) *Journal of Law and Society* 28.

- Practice Directions 12A (the public law outline) and 25C (on experts in children proceedings) set out the procedural steps and requirements for a care case.

- There are a number of important pieces of research on different aspects of the care system. We particularly recommend Harwin et al.'s *The Contribution of Supervision Orders and Special Guardianship to Children's Lives and Family Justice* (Lancaster University Centre for Child and Family Justice Research/Nuffield Foundation 2019) and Broadhurst et al.'s *Born into Care: Newborn Babies Subject to Care Proceedings in England* (Lancaster University Centre for Child and Family Justice Research/Nuffield Foundation 2018). Eileen Munro is a widely respected expert on child protection law and ER Munro and A Hardy, *Placement Stability—A Review of the Literature* (Loughborough University 2007) is a good summary of the evidence on permanency.

 Visit the **online resources** to watch a video of Polly Morgan discussing this chapter topic, and to check your understanding of this chapter with self-test questions and scenario questions.

Additional Chapter:
Elderly Care

To broaden your learning, go to the online resources to read an additional chapter on elderly care (available November 2021).
www.oup.com/he/morgan1e

INDEX

n. = footnote. *f.* = figure/diagram. *t.* = table. *b.* = box.

welfarism 708
Wellard, S. 828
Welstead, Mary 141
Wenar, L. 552
Westaway, J. 208
Westlake, D. 774
Weston, R. 619
wheelchair users 705, 721; *see also* disabilities
Whippman, Michael 353
Whitcombe, S. 671, 672
widower's pension 76, 164
Wikeley, Nick 351–7, 372, 393
Wildblood, H.J., QC (n212) 212, 816
Wilkinson, Sue 76, 85–7, 91, 96
William, Marquess of Northampton 99
Williams, C. 310, 510–11
Williams, D., QC 693
Williams, Justice 27, 29, 30, 32, 185, 816
Williams, P. 733
Wills 126, 183, 279, 280, 303, 305, 309, 315, 324, 325, 328; *see also* death; inheritance

cohabitants 348
divorce, effect of 314
dying with 306–7
executors 303, 305–7, 314
making 303
marriage, effect of 314
out-of-date 304
testators 303–7, 316, 326, 348
video-conferencing, use of 303
Wilson, John, QC 271, 290
Wilson, Lord 118, 167, 199, 205, 211–12, 215, 219, 225, 233, 326, 571, 654, 792–3, 804, 827, 841, 850–1, 857
Wilson, Mary Ellen 706
Winn, Lord Justice 679
Wlasny, M. (402n) 402, 453
Wolfers, J. 144
Wolfram, S. 100, 102, 190
Women's Convention *see* United Nations Convention on the Elimination of all Forms of Discrimination Against Women

Woodhouse, Barbara Bennett 546
Woodhouse, Sammy 776
Woods, Clare 421
Woodward, H. 4, 164–6, 168, 175, 176, 218, 255, 301, 330, 331, 349, 650, 655, 656, 677, 704
workhouses 352, 707
Wormwood, A. 684n.
Wrangham, Justice 112, 134
Wright, J.D. 140–1
Wright, Lord 327
Wright, M. 693
writs
    habeus corpus 730
    ne exeat regno 370
wrongdoing 31, 102, 104, 352
wrongness, defined 241
YBA Wife campaigns (1970s) 14
YMCA (Young Men's Christian Association) 724, 725
Young, Baroness 142
Zhu, Y. 355
Zorca, J. 660